Economics
Principles and Policy

Economics
Principles and Policy

William J. Baumol

New York University
and
Princeton University

Alan S. Blinder

Princeton University

Harcourt Brace Jovanovich, Inc.

New York   San Diego   Chicago   San Francisco   Atlanta

To my three children, Ellen, Daniel, and now Sabrina
W. J. B.

To Scott, age six, a pensive second baseman,
and William, age two, who loves to laugh
A. S. B.

Requests for permission to make copies of any part of the work should be
mailed to: Permissions, Harcourt Brace Jovanovich, Inc., 757 Third Avenue,
New York, NY 10017.

Illustrations by Carol Schwartzbach.
Credits and acknowledgments appear on page 848.

Printed in the United States of America
Library of Congress Catalog Card Number: 78–71569
ISBN: 0–15–518805–4

Preface

For decades, the "principles of economics" book has been expected to codify the entire discipline of economics, to blanket the field, to be encyclopedic. In recent years, this has become at once more imperative and more difficult. On the one hand, the explosion of economic knowledge during the last several decades has made it impossible to put all of economics, even at an introductory level, between two covers. On the other hand, it seems that more and more public policy issues either are basically economic in nature or involve important economic considerations. Intelligent citizens can no longer afford to be innocent of economics.

This dilemma has guided us in the preparation of this book. We have studiously avoided the encyclopedic approach and abandoned the fiction, so popular among textbook writers, that literally everything is of the utmost importance. Since students are, in any event, sufficiently intelligent to see through this ruse, we have tried to highlight those important ideas that are likely to be of lasting significance—principles that you will want to remember long after the course is over because they offer insights that are far from obvious, because they are of practical importance, and because they are widely misunderstood by intelligent laymen. A dozen of the most important of these ideas have been selected as "12 Ideas for Beyond the Final Exam," and are called to your attention when they occur through the use of the book's logo.

All modern economics textbooks abound with "real world" examples, but we have tried to go beyond this, to elevate the examples to preeminence. For in our view, the policy issue or everyday economic problem ought to lead the student naturally to the economic principle, not the other way around. For this reason, many of the chapters start with a real policy issue or practical problem that may seem puzzling or paradoxical to noneconomists, and then proceed to describe the economic analysis required to remove the mystery. In doing this, we have tried to utilize technical jargon and diagrams only where there is a clear need, never for their own sake.

Still, economics is a somewhat technical subject and, except for a few rather light chapters, this is a book for the desk, not for the bed. We have, however, made strenuous efforts to simplify the technical level of the discussion as much as we could without sacrificing content. Fortunately, almost every important idea in economics can be explained in plain English, and this, in general, is how we have tried to explain them. Yet, even while reducing the technical difficulty of the book, we have incorporated some elements of economic analysis that have traditionally been left out of introductory books but that are really too important to omit. Foremost among these is our extensive treatment of prices and inflation in Parts Two and Three. Introductory (and even intermediate) texts typically devote many chapters to a hypothetical economy in which prices never rise. Here, from the very beginning, we analyze the world as it really is, with prices all too easily driven upward.

We have so far emphasized the distinguishing features of this book, but we should point out that in terms of subject matter and organization we have by and large tried to avoid novelty. The main outline of the book follows the paths that experience has shown to be desirable and that have therefore become traditional. Though our purely introductory materials (Part One) are deliberately kept briefer than usual, we follow tradition in beginning with a discussion of the elementary principles of supply and demand, choice, and opportunity cost. Courses may then head in one of two directions. The chapters have been organized so that macroeconomic theory and policy (Parts Two and Three) come first, though some instructors may prefer to take up microeconomics (Parts Four through Seven) before macroeconomics. The remaining parts deal with economic growth and the quality of life (Part Eight), international economics (Part Nine), and alternative economic systems (Part Ten).

Whatever the order of your course, we would like to offer one suggestion. Unlike some of the other courses you may be taking, principles of economics is cumulative—each week's lesson builds on what you have learned before. You will save yourself a lot of frustration (and also a lot of work) if you keep up on a week to week basis. To help you do this, there is a chapter summary, a list of important terms and concepts, and a selection of discussion questions to help you review at the end of each chapter. In addition to these aids, many students will find the *Study Guide*, designed specifically to accompany this text by Professor Craig Swan, helpful as a self-testing and diagnostic device. When you encounter difficulties in the *Study Guide*, you will know which sections of the text you need to review.

Finally, and with great pleasure, we turn to the customary acknowledgments of indebtedness. Routine expressions of gratitude are appropriate only for small debts, while ours are large. In these days of specialization, not even a pair of authors can master every subject that an introductory text must cover. Our friends and colleagues William Branson, Lester Chandler, Stephen Goldfeld, Claudia Goldin, Peter Kenen, Arthur Lewis, Burton Malkiel, Edwin Mills, Harvey Rosen, and Laura Tyson have all given generously of their knowledge in particular areas. We have learned much from them, and only wish we had learned more.

Several economists at other colleges and universities, including Paul Barkley of Cornell University, Michael Lovell of Wesleyan University, Deborah Parsons of Ohio State University, Bernard Saffran of Swarthmore College, Craig Swan of the University of Minnesota, and James Wetzel of Virginia Commonwealth University, read parts of the manuscript at different stages and offered their advice. Of these, Professor Barkley must be singled out as one of the most thorough and conscientious readers that any authors could ever hope for. While the writing of the book was ours, almost every other aspect of its production was handled by the pleasant and capable people at Harcourt Brace Jovanovich: Gary Burke, the executive editor; Barbara Rose, the manuscript editor; Karen Bierstedt, the copy editor; Geri Davis, the designer; Fran Wager, the production manager.

Preface

The gestation period of human life is only nine months, but this book took three years from conception to birth. Through it all, our wives, Hilda Baumol and Madeline Blinder, were models of forbearance and astute critics of the more elliptical portions of the text. In addition, Hilda Baumol displayed her usual incredible skill in tracking down inaccessible information, much of which we had been assured did not even exist. Our sanity and survival were assured by the intelligence, ability, and pleasantness of our secretaries, Sue Anne Blackman, Phyllis Durepos, Judah Gesmundo, and Carolyn Riportella, who did so many things and did them all well.

And finally, academic etiquette normally requires authors to assume full responsibility for any errors in their work. Co-authorship gives each writer someone else to blame, but both of us hereby undertake to resist that temptation.

William J. Baumol
Alan S. Blinder

I must insist on a personal note in memory of Robert Syron, who as editor at Harcourt Brace Jovanovich first arranged for the writing of this book. He was able, gentle, and understanding. More than that, he was a friend.

William Baumol

Contents

Contents

Contents

Contents

Contents

Contents

Contents

Contents

Contents

Contents

one

What Is
Economics
All About?

1

What Is Economics?

Why does public discussion of economic policy so often show the
abysmal ignorance of the participants? Why do I so often want to cry
at what public figures, the press, and television commentators say
about economic affairs?

Robert M. Solow, *Challenge*,
(March–April 1978), page 39

Economics is a broad-ranging discipline, both in the questions it asks and the methods it uses to seek answers. So many alternative definitions of economics have been proposed that we prefer to avoid any attempt to define the discipline in a single sentence or paragraph. Instead, in this chapter we will introduce you to economics by letting the subject matter speak for itself.

The first part of this chapter is intended to give you some idea of the types of problems that can be approached through economic analysis and the kinds of solutions that economic principles suggest. By the time you finish this course, we can promise that you will have a better understanding of some of the nation's and the world's most pressing problems and some greater insights into how solutions to these problems may be found. These are the real payoffs of studying economics.

The second part briefly examines the methods of economic inquiry, introducing you to the tools that economists use in their search for answers. You will also find these tools useful in your life as a citizen, consumer, and worker after the course is over.

Ideas for Beyond the Final Exam

We are college professors. As such we realize that it is inevitable that you will forget much of what you learn in this course—perhaps with a sense of relief—very soon after the final exam has been graded. There is not much point bemoaning this fact; elephants may never forget, but people do.

Nevertheless, we believe there are a number of economic ideas that are important enough for you to remember well beyond the final exam. You will want to remember them because they offer meaningful insights into the workings of the economy, because their significance is enduring, and because you will have shortchanged your own education if you forget them as soon as the course is over.

To help you pick out a few of these crucial ideas, we have selected 12 of them from among the many contained in this book. Some bear on important policy issues that often appear in the newspapers and that may have relevance to your own future decisions. Others point out common misunderstandings that occur among even the most thoughtful lay observers. As the opening quotation of this chapter indicates, many learned judges, politicians, business people, and university administrators who failed to grasp these economic principles could have made far wiser decisions than they did.

Each of the 12 Ideas for Beyond the Final Exam will be discussed in depth as it occurs in the course of the book's narrative. But we believe it will be useful here to discuss two of them as illustrations and then briefly describe the others—although at this point we can only hint at their underlying analyses.

IDEA 1:
The Illusion of High Interest Rates

In 1961, banks were happy to lend young families money to build houses at a rate of less than 6 percent annual interest. In 1974, the interest rate had reached 9 percent and more; yet even at these apparently high prices, mortgage money dried up in many parts of the country and housing construction came to a grinding halt. Was this because the banks had grown greedy in the intervening years? Not at all.

Any conclusion based on a direct comparison of the two interest rates is an illusion. In a real sense the 1974 interest rate of 9 percent, despite its appearance, was much *lower* than the 1961 interest rate of 6 percent! Why? In 1961, there was virtually no inflation; prices typically were rising by less than 1 percent a year. But by 1974 inflation was rampant; prices rose by more than 12 percent in a single year.

What does inflation have to do with interest rates? Consider the position of a person who lends $100 for one year at a rate of 9 percent interest a year when the inflation rate is 12 percent. At the end of the year the lender gets back his $100, plus $9 in interest. But over that same year, because of inflation, his $100 has lost $12 in purchasing power. Thus *he is left $3 poorer in terms of what his money can now buy!* No wonder bankers were reluctant to lend money in 1974.

Now consider someone who lends $100 at 6 percent interest when prices are rising only 1 percent a year. This lender gets back the original $100, plus $6 in interest, and loses only $1 in purchasing power—for a net gain of $5.

In the early 1970s, policymakers in many states failed to understand this simple principle and so stood steadfastly behind laws and regulations that prohibited interest charges higher than $8\frac{1}{2}$ percent a year because they considered such high rates to be evidence of heartless profiteering by the lenders. Yet the ceiling on interest rates condemned lenders to lose purchasing power as a reward for their willingness to lend money. As a result, the home-building industry languished for lack of funds. As is so often the case, a lack of basic understanding of economic principles led policymakers, despite their good intentions, to make decisions that had serious and unwanted consequences.[1]

IDEA 2:
Economic Principles to Protect the Environment

Free-market economies have produced a vast abundance of consumer goods—an achievement that is not inconsequential. But they have been far less successful in their efforts to protect the cleanliness of waterways and streets and the purity of the air. Why is it that our economy serves us so well in providing jeans but so poorly in providing a clean environment?

Economists believe that they know what the trouble is, and they feel that economic analysis can help remedy it. A simple example will illustrate the principle.

When a manufacturer makes jeans he pays all the costs himself—he pays for labor, equipment, raw materials, and energy. These are all expensive resources, so it will pay him to do everything in his power to avoid wasting them. But when a paper mill pours chemical wastes into a nearby river, its owners pay nothing to correct the resulting damage to the environment. Yet someone must pay, because those wastes cause the water to lose its capacity to support life.

The paper mill uses oxygen to dilute its chemical wastes just as it uses a trucking company to haul away its solid wastes. But there is one important difference—the owners of the mill pay for the trucking services, but they get the oxygen for nothing. Since the oxygen is free, the firm does not lose anything by using it wastefully. It can pour wastes into the river as if the resulting damage did not matter to anyone.

The basic source of the problem, then, is that the cost of producing jeans is borne inter-

nally, and so it pays the firm to avoid waste in the manufacturing process. But the cost of waste disposal—the oxygen that is destroyed—is borne by the general public, not by the paper mill. Consequently, the mill has no incentive to be careful in its use of the waterway, a public resource.

Economists believe there is a straightforward remedy for this problem: Make the paper mill pay for the damage it causes. Specifically, as we shall see in Chapter 34, they recommend that a *tax* be levied on every gallon of chemical waste that the firm spills into the river. In this way, they argue, the firm will be given an incentive to reduce its pollution just as it has an incentive to limit its other costs.

IDEA 3:
Inflation and Unemployment

Ever since the U.S. economy struck the bottom of the Great Recession in 1975, there has been a highly partisan debate over whether the government should do more to speed the pace of recovery. The more liberal politicians, business people, and economists have argued for more government action to increase spending. The more conservative debators have opposed these plans, insisting that such actions would worsen the problem of inflation and not help reduce unemployment.

The public is often confused by such claims and counterclaims, and justifiably so. After all, the years of highest unemployment in recent history (1974–1976) followed (and even partly coincided with) the years of highest inflation (1973–1975). Apparently, in our modern economy high unemployment and high inflation go hand in hand. So how can anyone claim that by *lowering* unemployment the government runs the risk of *raising* inflation? Don't the facts speak for themselves?

The facts most assuredly do not speak for themselves. Despite the undeniable coexistence of high unemployment and high inflation in the

---

[1] We will explore this issue in more detail in Chapter 6.

mid-1970s, government policymakers face a *fundamental trade-off between inflation and unemployment:* most of the things they can do to alleviate one problem serve to make the other more serious. We will discuss reasons for this in Part Three, especially Chapter 15, where we will also consider some conceivable ways out of the dilemma.

IDEA 4:
Increasing Equality May Require Sacrificing Output

Many people feel that the distribution of income in the world today is unjust, that it is inequitable for the superrich to sail yachts, keep staffs of servants, and give expensive parties, while there are people who live in slums, do not have enough to eat, and are unable to maintain their health.

Most economists agree that greater equality is a sensible goal. But they emphasize that it is not sensible to think that this goal can be achieved without cost. There is good reason to believe that if we force the proverbial pie to be divided more equally, the economy will end up with a considerably smaller pie to divide. Policies that promote equality tend to discourage production.[2]

Simply put, there is a costly *trade-off* between the size of a nation's production and the degree of equality with which the products are divided among the nation's families. The more equal we force incomes to be, the smaller the production of the economy will become. It does not follow, however, that measures to increase equality are foolish. What *does* follow is that policymakers should always be conscious of what such measures do to output. More equal shares of a much smaller pie may actually make the poor poorer, and that may be contrary to what policymakers want to achieve.

[2]The reasons for this will be examined in Chapter 29.

IDEA 5:
The Crisis in Urban Services

There is a distressing phenomenon occurring in cities throughout the industrialized world. Many urban services have apparently been growing poorer—fewer police officers on the beat, larger classes in public schools, less reliable garbage pickups—while the public is paying more and more for them. Indeed, the costs have risen substantially and consistently faster than has the rate of inflation. A natural response is to attribute the problem to political corruption and government inefficiency. But this is certainly not the whole story.

As we shall see in Chapter 35, one of the major causes of the problem is economic. And it has nothing to do with corruption or inefficiency of public employees; rather, it has to do with the dazzling growth in efficiency of private manufacturing industries! Because technological improvements make workers more productive in manufacturing, wages rise. And they rise not only for the manufacturing workers but also for police officers, teachers, and other public employees. But since it still takes two officers to staff a police cruiser, and one teacher to teach a class, the cost of these city services is forced to rise.

This is important to understand not because it excuses the financial record of our cities, but because an understanding of the problem suggests what we should expect the future to bring and, perhaps, indicates what policies should be advocated to correct it.

IDEA 6:
Interferences with the "Laws" of Supply and Demand

In a free market, no one is very surprised if the price of a commodity is relatively high when demand for it is abundant and supply is low. Similarly, we expect the price to be relatively low when supply is abundant and demand scarce.

But simply because we expect these price fluctuations does not mean we are happy about them.

Politicians from the dawn of history have believed they know what to do to stabilize prices. They pass a law declaring the unpopular price illegal. A ceiling (maximum) may be placed over the price of natural gas or rents, or a floor (minimum) may be placed under the price of wheat or wages. But the passage of laws does not always make the politicians' wish come true. History shows that price floors and ceilings usually either fail to achieve their aims or, where they do succeed, create other problems that are often more serious than those they were designed to cure.

For example, when the Spaniards surrounded Antwerp in 1584, hoping to starve the city into surrender, profiteers found ways to smuggle food into the city at relatively high prices. To end the "exploitation," the city fathers placed price ceilings on food. They succeeded so well that the smugglers were driven out of business—but they also helped the Spaniards achieve their goal. Analogously, the floors that President Franklin Roosevelt placed under the prices of agricultural products during the Great Depression forced the government to organize the destruction of millions of pigs and to prevent crop growing on millions of acres of farmland—all this while millions of Americans went hungry.

As we shall learn in Chapter 4, and indeed throughout this book, such results are no accident. They follow *inescapably* from the nature of price regulations.

IDEA 7:
A New Way to Measure Costs

Economists do not measure costs in the same way that accountants and other people do. Rather than looking only at the monetary costs of purchasing an item, economists ask, *What did you have to give up to acquire this item?*

The costs of a college education provide a vivid example—and one that is probably close to the hearts of all students reading this book. How much do you think it *costs* to go to college? Most likely you would answer this question by adding together your expenditures on tuition, room and board, books, and the like, and then deducting any scholarship funds you may receive. Economists would not. They would first want to know how much you could be earning if you were not attending college. You may think this is an irrelevant question, but because you *give up* these earnings by attending college, they must be added to your tuition bill as a cost of your education. Nor would economists accept the university's bill for room and board as a measure of your living costs. They would want to know by how much this exceeds what it would have cost you to live at home, and only this extra cost would be counted as an expense. On balance, a college education probably costs more than you think.

These costs that economists measure are called opportunity costs, a concept we will return to again and again in this volume.

IDEA 8:
The Surprising Principle of Comparative Advantage

In the period since World War II, the Japanese economy has expanded explosively. Spectacular improvements in the efficiency of its production and in the quality of its products have prompted Americans to buy cars, TV sets, cameras, and other products from Japan in huge quantities. American TV manufacturers, steel producers, auto makers, and electronics firms have complained about the competition and demanded protection against the flood of imports that, in their view, threatens American standards of living. Is this view justified?

The most common argument made in support of protective legislation is entirely fallacious. It runs as follows: What if a combination of higher productivity and lower wages were to permit Japan to produce *everything* more cheaply than we could? Would it not then be true that Americans would have no work and that our nation would be impoverished?

A remarkable result, called the law of comparative advantage, shows that even in this extreme event it would still pay the two nations to trade and that both would gain as a result! We will explain this principle fully in Chapter 36, where we will also note some potentially valid arguments in favor of protection, but for now a simple parable will make the reason clear.

Suppose Sam grows up on a farm and is a whiz at plowing, but he is also a successful country singer and gets paid $2000 a performance at hotels and nightclubs. Does it pay Sam to refuse some singing engagements to leave time for plowing? Of course not. Rather, it pays him to hire Alfie, a much less efficient farmer, to plow for him. Sam is the better farmer, but he earns so much more by specializing in singing that it pays him to leave the farming to Alfie. Alfie, though a poorer farmer than Sam, is an even worse singer. Thus Alfie earns a living by specializing in the job at which he at least has a *comparative* advantage (his farming is not quite as bad as his singing), and both Alfie and Sam gain. The same is true of two countries, even when one of them is more efficient at everything. Both countries come out ahead if they each produce the things they do best *comparatively*.

IDEA 9:
The Importance of Marginal Analysis

Many pages in this book will be spent explaining, and extolling the virtues of, a type of decision-making process called marginal analysis. Here we can best illustrate this process by an example.

Suppose that a U.S. airline company is told by its accountants that the full cost of transporting one passenger from Los Angeles to New York is $250. Can the airline profit by offering a reduced rate of $150 to students who fly on a standby basis? The surprising answer is: probably yes. The reason is that most of the $250 cost per passenger must be paid whether the plane carries 20 passengers or 120 passengers. Marginal analysis says that full costs— which include costs of maintenance, landing rights, ground crews, and so on—are irrelevant to the decision at hand. The only costs that are relevant in deciding whether to carry standby passengers for reduced rates are the extra costs of writing and processing additional tickets, the food and beverages these passengers consume, handling their baggage, and so on. These costs are called marginal costs, and they are probably quite small in this instance. Any passenger who pays the airline more than its marginal cost will add something to the company's profit, so it probably is more profitable to let the students ride for the reduced fare than to fly the plane with some empty seats.

There are many real cases in which decision makers, not understanding marginal analysis, have rejected advantageous possibilities like the reduced fare in our hypothetical example. These people were misled by calculating in terms of *average* rather than *marginal* cost figures—an error that can be quite costly.

IDEA 10:
Stabilizing the Economy
Without "Big Government"

Nowadays there is wide agreement that one proper function of government is to regulate the pace of economic activity—restraining the economy when it would otherwise race ahead too quickly, and nudging it forward when it would otherwise show signs of sluggishness. Parts Two and Three are largely devoted to explaining why the government may have to take on this responsibility, and how it tries to do the job.

Yet some people worry that frequent

government actions to stabilize the economy will lead inevitably to a larger and larger public sector. The slogan "creeping socialism" is sometimes used to describe this alleged phenomenon—with evident disapproval.

Economists argue that this worry arises from confusing two issues that ought to be kept separate. The first issue is how tenacious the government should be in its efforts to promote economic stability. The second issue is how large a government the country should have. As we shall learn in this book, there is plenty of room for disagreement over both issues.

But we shall also see that it is a serious logical error to intertwine the two. Why? Because there are alternative policies that can promote economic stability with either a growing, an unchanged, or even a *shrinking* public sector. For example, as we will see in Chapter 10, when it is advisable to speed up economic activity, the size of the public sector can be *expanded* by increasing government spending or *contracted* by reducing taxes. Thus, differences among individuals over how much the government should intervene to promote economic stability ought not to be based on their ideas about how large a government we should have.

IDEA 11:
The Consequences of Budget Deficits

Most American presidents, including many under whom the national debt has grown very rapidly, have vehemently opposed government budget deficits. President Carter is only the latest in a long line of chief executives to adopt a balanced budget as a major goal.

Economists recognize that government deficits often have undesirable effects. But they emphasize that whether or not a deficit is appropriate depends mainly on the state of the economy. To summarize briefly an argument that will be made at great length in Part Three, most economists believe that deficits are quite desir-

able when there is high unemployment but quite undesirable when there is high inflation.[3]

They also argue that the fears many people express that the large national debt, which results from budget deficits, will bankrupt the nation or place an intolerable burden upon future generations are entirely without foundation. (The reasons why these fears are groundless will be discussed in Chapter 16.) In sum, economists view the national debt with much less alarm than does the general public.

IDEA 12:
Why Speculation Can Be a Good Thing

When the price of a scarce commodity skyrockets, or when stock market prices collapse, or when the value of a nation's money plunges, much of the blame is invariably assigned to evil "speculators." But *how* they cause these things to happen is never quite explained.

Perhaps the widespread aversion to speculators stems from a puritanical objection to gambling, for it is true that speculators deliberately deal in risks. But economists believe that speculators fulfill a useful role in society. Once again, an example will illustrate.

Suppose a bakery signs a contract to deliver bread to the armed forces for a whole year at a prearranged price. Whether that contract will bring profit or loss to the bakery depends on the weather, which will determine the size and price of the wheat crop. No one can eliminate that risk. But a professional speculator may offer to relieve the baker of the risk by assuming it herself.

For example, she may be willing to sign a contract with the bakery guaranteeing to deliver the flour when it is needed, and to do so at some specified mutually agreeable price. Of course, this price will include some fee to the speculator for taking over the risk. If, later on, the market price of flour falls, the speculator will

[3]The issue is far less clear when there is both high unemployment and high inflation. We will examine this question in later chapters.

make a tidy profit, for she will buy the flour cheaply and deliver it to the bakery at the price set in their contract. But if the market price of flour rises, it is the speculator, not the baker, who will take the financial beating. She will have to pay the high market price and will receive from the baker only the amount specified in the contract.

In other words, speculators sell an important service—they take over other people's risks (and their worries). In effect, they provide insurance policies to those who engage in unavoidably risky activities. Furthermore, as we shall learn in Chapter 24, there is good reason to believe that, contrary to popular misconceptions, the activities of professional speculators usually make price fluctuations *smaller* than they would otherwise have been.

EPILOGUE

These, then, are the dozen fundamental concepts that we hope you will retain beyond the final exam. Do not try to learn them perfectly right now, for you will hear much more about each as the book progresses. Instead, keep them in mind as you read—we will point them out to you as they occur by the use of the book's logo ▨ —and look back over this list at the end of the course. You may be amazed to see how natural, or even obvious, they will seem then.

Inside the Economist's Tool Kit

Now that you have some idea of the kinds of policy issues economists deal with every day, you should know something about how they grapple with these problems.

As a discipline of study, economics has something of a split personality. Clearly the most rigorous of the social sciences, it nevertheless looks decidedly more "social" than "scientific" when compared with physics. Economists strive to be humanists and scientists simultaneously, thus bridging C. P. Snow's celebrated "two cultures."

Economists borrow modes of investigation from numerous fields, adjusting each to fit the particular problems posed by economic events. Usefulness, not methodological purity, is the criterion for including a technique in the economist's tool kit.

WHAT ECONOMISTS DO

An economist is, by necessity, a jack of several trades and master of none. Mathematical reasoning is used extensively in economics, but so is historical study. And neither looks quite the same as when practiced by a mathematician or a historian. Statistical inference too is among the most important methods used in economic inquiry, but economists have had to modify the standard procedures of statistics to fit the kinds of data they deal with. Philosophy, political science, and sociology also play a role. In 1926, John Maynard Keynes, the great British economist, summed up the many faces of economic inquiry in a statement that still rings true today:

> The master-economist . . . must understand symbols and speak in words. He must contemplate the particular in terms of the general, and touch abstract and concrete in the same flight of thought. He must study the present in the light of the past for the purposes of the future. No part of man's nature or his institutions must lie entirely outside his regard. He must be purposeful and disinterested in a simultaneous mood; as aloof and incorruptible as an artist, yet sometimes as near the earth as a politician.[4]

[4]As quoted by Robert Heilbroner in *The Worldly Philosophers*, revised edition (New York: Simon and Schuster, 1972), page 250.

Clearly, economics is more easily distinguished by the types of problems it addresses than by the investigative techniques it employs to study them. An introductory course in economics will not make you an economist, but it *will* help you approach urgent social problems from a pragmatic and dispassionate point of view. You will not find the solutions to all these problems in this book, but you will learn how to pose the right *questions*—questions that will help produce answers that are both useful and illuminating.

THE ROLE OF ABSTRACTION

Some students find economics unduly abstract and "unrealistic." The stylized world envisioned by economic theory seems only a distant cousin to the world they see around them. There is an old joke about three people—a chemist, a physicist, and an economist—stranded on an isolated island with an ample supply of canned foods but no implements to open the cans. In debating what they should do, the chemist suggested that they light a fire under the cans, expanding their contents, hoping to cause the cans to burst. The physicist doubted that this would work. He advocated building a catapult with which they could smash the cans against some nearby boulders. Then they turned to the economist for his suggestion. He thought for a moment and announced his solution: "Let's assume we have a can opener."

Economists do make unrealistic assumptions, and you will encounter many of them in the pages that follow. But this propensity to abstract from reality results from the incredible complexity of the real world, not from any fondness economists have for sounding absurd.

Compare the chemist's task of explaining the interactions of compounds in a chemical reaction with the economist's task of explaining the interactions of people in an economy. Are molecules ever motivated by greed or altruism, by envy or ambition? Do they ever emulate other molecules? Do forecasts about them ever influence their behavior? People, of course, do all these things, and many, many more. It is therefore immeasurably more difficult to predict human behavior than it is to predict chemical reactions. If economists tried to keep track of every aspect of human behavior, they could surely never hope to understand the nature of the economy.

Abstraction from unimportant details is necessary to understand the functioning of anything as complex as the economy.

SOME ILLUSTRATIONS OF THE NEED FOR ABSTRACTION

To appreciate why the economist abstracts from details, put yourself in the following hypothetical situation. You have just arrived, for the first time in your life, in Los Angeles. You are now at the Los Angeles Convention Center. This is the point marked *A* in Figures 1–1 and 1–2, which are alternative maps of part of Los Angeles. You want to drive to the famous La Brea tar pits, marked *B* on each map. Which map would you find more useful? You will notice that Map 1 (Figure 1–1) has the full details of the Los Angeles road system. Consequently, it requires a major effort to read it. In contrast, Map 2 (Figure 1–2) omits many minor roads so that the freeways and major arteries stand out more clearly.

Most strangers to the city would prefer Map 2. With its guidance they are likely to find the tar pits in a reasonable amount of time, even though a slightly shorter route might have been found by careful calculation and planning using Map 1. Map 2 seems to abstract successfully from a lot of confusing details while retaining the essential aspects of the city's geography. Economic theories strive to do the same thing.

FIGURE 1–1

Map 1 gives complete details of the road system of Los Angeles. If you are like most people, you will find it hard to read and not very useful for figuring out how to get from the Convention Center (point *A*) to the La Brea tar pits (point *B*). For this purpose, the map carries far too much detail, though for some other purposes (for example, locating some very small street in Hollywood) it may be the best map available.

FIGURE 1–2

Map 2 shows a very different perspective of Los Angeles. Minor roads are eliminated—we might say, *assumed away*—in order to present a clearer picture of where the major arteries and freeways go. As a result of this simplification, several ways of getting from the Convention Center (point *A*) to the La Brea tar pits (point *B*) stand out clearly. For example, we can take the Harbor Freeway north to Wilshire Boulevard, and then follow Wilshire west to the tar pits. While we might find a shorter route by poring over the details of Map 1, most of us will feel more comfortable with Map 2.

12

FIGURE 1–3

Map 3 strips away still more details of the Los Angeles road system. In fact, only major trunk roads and freeways remain. This map may be useful for passing through the city or getting around it, but it will not help the tourist who wants to see the sights of Los Angeles. For this purpose, too many details are missing.

Map 3 (Figure 1–3), which shows little more than the major interstate routes that pass through the greater Los Angeles area, illustrates a danger of which all theorists must beware. Armed only with the information provided on this map, you might never find the La Brea tar pits. Instead of a useful idealization of the L.A. road network, the map makers have produced a map that is oversimplified for our purpose. Too much has been assumed away.

Of course, this map was never intended to be used as a guide to the La Brea tar pits, which brings us to a very important point:

There is no such thing as one "right" degree of abstraction for all analytic purposes. The optimal degree of abstraction depends on the objective of the analysis. A model that is a gross oversimplification for one purpose may be needlessly complicated for another.

Economists are constantly treading the thin line between Map 2 and Map 3, between useful generalizations about complex issues and gross distortions of the pertinent facts. How can they tell when they have abstracted from reality just enough? There is no objective answer to this question, and here the science of economic analysis becomes the art of applied economics. One of the factors distinguishing good economics from bad economics is the degree to which analysts are able to find the factors that constitute the equivalent of Map 2 (rather than Maps 1 or 3) for the problem at hand. It is not always easy to do, as the following examples illustrate.

The Distribution of Income

Suppose you are interested in learning why different people have different incomes, why some are fabulously rich while others are pathetically poor. People differ in many ways, too many to enumerate, much less to study. The economist ignores most of those details in order to focus on a few important facts. The color of a person's hair or eyes probably is not important to the problem at hand, but the color of his skin certainly is. Height and weight may not matter, but his parents' bank balance may. Proceeding in this way, we pare Map 1 down to the manageable dimensions of Map 2. But there is a danger of going too far. To make it easy to analyze a problem we can end up stripping away some of its most crucial features.

The Determination of National Income

Now suppose we want to know what factors determine the size of the output of the whole economy. Since the volume of goods and services turned out by the whole economy is affected by literally millions of decisions by investors, business managers, employees, government officials, and others, a complete enumeration of all the factors determining the nation's output clearly makes analysis unworkable (Map 1). Abstraction is necessary. We must prune the list to manageable size. Parts Two and Three of this book are devoted to explaining how economists have done this; that is, how they have drawn up a Map 2 of the nation's output.

Several shortcuts to this process have been proposed, but in the opinion of their critics, they have proved on inspection to be like Map 3. For instance, one of the determinants of national output that we will discuss in Part Three is the supply of money, and it is certainly a very important one. For a number of years, a small group of economists thought they could explain the nation's total production almost exclusively from the behavior of the money supply. The critics argued that this would be like making a map of Los Angeles that marked only the Hollywood Freeway.

THE ROLE OF ECONOMIC THEORY

A person "can stare stupidly at phenomena; but in the absence of imagination they will not connect themselves together in any rational way." These words of the renowned American philosopher–scientist C. S. Peirce succinctly express the crucial role of theory in scientific inquiry and help explain why economists are so enamored of it. To the economist or the physical scientist, the word theory does not mean what it does in common speech. In scientific usage, a theory is *not* an untested assertion of alleged fact. The statement that the presence of the chemical PCB in drinking water causes cancer is not a theory; it is a *hypothesis,* which will either prove to be true or false after the right sorts of experiments have been completed.

DEFINITION
In the language of scientific method, a *theory* is a deliberate simplification (abstraction) of factual relationships that attempts to explain how those relationships work. In other words, it is an explanation of the mechanism behind observed phenomena.

Astronomers' data describe the paths of the planets, and gravity forms the basis of theories that are intended to explain the movement of these bodies. Similarly, economists have data suggesting that government policies can affect the degree of a country's prosperity. Keynesian theory (which will be discussed in Part Three) seeks to describe and explain these relationships. To economists, theorizing is not a luxury; it is a necessity. Economic theory provides a logical structure for organizing and analyzing economic data. Without theory, economists could only "stare stupidly" at the world. With theory, they can attempt to understand it.

People who have never studied economics often draw a false distinction between *theory* and *practical policy.* Politicians are particularly guilty of this, scoffing at abstract economic theory as something that is best ignored by "practical" policymakers. The irony of these statements is that:

It is precisely the concern for policy that makes economic theory so necessary and important.

If there were no possibility of changing the economy through public policy, economics might be a historical and descriptive discipline, asking, for example, What happened in the United States during the Great Depression of the 1930s? or How is it that industrial pollution got to be so serious in the 1960s and 1970s?

But deep concern about public policy forces economists to go beyond such historical and descriptive questions. To formulate rational policy, they are *forced* to deal with possibilities that have not actually occurred. For example, to learn how to prevent depressions, they must investigate whether the Great Depression could have been avoided by more astute management of the nation's money supply. Or another example: To determine what environmental programs will be most effective, they must examine what might happen to industrial and automotive pollution in the 1980s if government places taxes on industrial waste discharges and automobile emissions.

As Peirce pointed out, not even a lifetime of ogling at real-world data will answer such questions. Because most issues like these hinge on some question of *cause and effect,* only a combination of theoretical reasoning and data analysis can hope to provide solutions. We must understand *how,* if at all, a greater money supply will lead to a lower unemployment rate or *how* a tax on emissions will reduce pollution.

WHAT IS AN ECONOMIC "MODEL"?

Economists generally express such cause-and-effect relationships in terms of economic models. The notion of a "model" is familiar enough to children, and economists (in common with other scientists) use the term in much the same way that children do.

A child's model automobile or airplane looks and operates much like the real thing, but it is much smaller and much simpler, and so it is much easier to manipulate and understand. Engineers for General Motors and Boeing also build models of cars and planes. While their models are far bigger and much more elaborate than a child's toy, they use them for much the same purposes: to observe the workings of these vehicles "up close," to experiment with them in order to see how they might behave under different circumstances ("What happens if I do this?"). From these experiments, they make educated guesses as to how the real-life version will perform. Often these guesses prove uncannily accurate, as exemplified by the success of the Boeing 747. But sometimes they are wide of the mark: The chronic mechanical problems of General Motors' Corvair prompted Ralph Nader's acclaimed book *Unsafe at Any Speed,* which helped launch the consumer movement.

Economists use models for similar purposes and with similarly mixed results. A. W. Phillips, the famous engineer-turned-economist who discovered the "Phillips curve" (discussed in Chapter 15), was talented enough to construct a working model of the determination

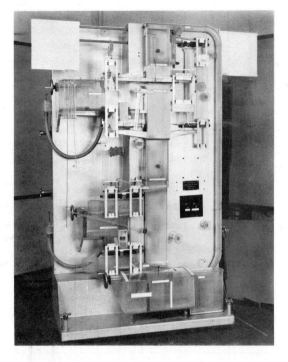

FIGURE 1–4

THE PHILLIPS MACHINE

The late Professor A. W. Phillips, while teaching at the London School of Economics in the early 1950s, built this machine to illustrate Keynesian theory. This is the same theory that we will explain with words and diagrams later in the book; but Phillips's background as an engineer enabled him to depict the theory with the help of tubes, valves, and pumps. Because economists are not very good plumbers, few of them try to build models of this sort; most rely on paper and pencil instead. But the two sorts of models fulfill precisely the same role. They simplify reality in order to make it understandable.

of national income in a simple economy, using colored water flowing through pipes. For years this contraption, depicted in Figure 1–4, graced the basement of the London School of Economics. However, most economists lack Phillips's manual dexterity, so economic models are generally built with paper and pencil rather than with hammer and nails.

Many of the models we'll be using in this book are depicted in diagrams. Hence, in the next chapter we explain the construction and use of various types of graphs. But sometimes economic models are expressed only in words. The statement "Business people produce the level of output that maximizes their profits," is the basis for a behavioral model whose consequences are explored in some detail in Parts Four and Six.

Don't be put off by seemingly abstract models. Think of them as useful road maps, and remember how hard it would be to find your way around Los Angeles without one.

THE CONCEPT OF "RATIONAL" BEHAVIOR

Many economic models rest on a fundamental assumption: namely, that the decision maker—be it a consumer or a business firm—behaves "rationally." What do we mean by rational behavior?

First, we do not use the phrase as a term of approval. It is not necessarily "better" to be rational than to be irrational. Some people usually behave rationally and some do not. This is simply a fact, and we are not concerned with judging the virtues of either behavior.

Second, and perhaps more important, we use the term "rationality" to characterize *means* rather than *ends*. It is neither more nor less rational to want a pistachio ice-cream cone than to want a mushroom pizza. But once the consumer decides that he wants either the ice cream or the pizza, it is irrational for him to go to the shoe repair shop for it. In sum:

DEFINITION

Rationality is defined in economics as characterizing those decisions that are most effective in helping the decision maker achieve his own objectives, whatever they may be. The objectives themselves (unless they are self-contradictory) are never considered either rational or irrational.

REASONS FOR DISAGREEMENTS: IMPERFECT INFORMATION AND VALUE JUDGMENTS

"If all the earth's economists were laid end to end, they could not reach an agreement," or so the saying goes. If economics is a scientific discipline, why do economists seem to quarrel so much? Politicians and reporters are fond of pointing out that economists generally argue both sides of every issue of public policy. Physicists, on the other hand, do not debate whether the earth revolves around the sun or vice versa.

The question reflects a misunderstanding of the nature of science. First of all, the apparently extreme disagreement is attributable in part to the greater visibility of economic discussions. As a matter of fact, physicists formerly did argue over whether the earth revolves around the sun, often with rather grim results for themselves. (Economists, fortunately, are not often burned at the stake!) Nowadays, physicists argue about "black holes," the existence of certain subatomic particles, and other esoteric phenomena. These arguments often go unnoticed by the public because most of us do not understand what they are talking about. In contrast, everyone is eager to join economic debates over inflation, unemployment, pollution, and almost everything else. Because economics is a *social* science, its disputes are aired in public, and almost everyone is personally concerned with the subject matter. Anyone who has ever bought or sold anything, it seems, fancies himself an amateur economist.

Second, there is a much greater area of agreement among economists than most people think. Virtually all economists, regardless of their politics, agree that taxing polluters is one of the best ways to protect the environment (see Chapters 31 and 34), that a negative income tax is superior to most alternative antipoverty programs (see Chapter 29), that free trade among nations is preferable to the erection of barriers through tariffs and quotas (see Chapter 36). The list could go on and on. It is probably true that the issues about which economists agree *far* exceed the subjects on which they disagree.

Third, it is unreasonable to expect scientific inquiry to be free of disputes. Once a relationship is so firmly established that there are no longer any grounds for disagreement, scientists lose interest and go on to a newer problem. Vocal debate is the norm, not the exception, at the forefront of any science—particularly in a social science, where debate often centers around controversial issues of public policy. Should the federal government reduce business taxes? Should IBM be broken up into a number of smaller companies?

While economic science can contribute something to the resolution of such controversies, it can never be the final arbiter.

Economists can contribute the best theoretical and factual knowledge there is on a particular issue, but the final decision on policy questions typically rests either on information that is not currently available, or on tastes and ethical opinions about which people differ (the things we call ''value judgments''), or on both.

To illustrate what we mean, consider the following problems.

Taxing Industrial Wastes

As you will learn in Chapter 34, the proper tax to levy on industrial wastes depends on quantitative estimates both of the harm done by the pollutant and the costs of pollution abatement. For most waste products, these numbers are not yet known, although knowledge is accumulating rapidly. So a lack of complete information has made it difficult to reach a decision.

Inflation and Unemployment

Government policies that succeed in shortening a recession are virtually certain to cause higher inflation for a while. Using tools that we will describe in Part Three, many economists

believe they can even measure how much more inflation the economy will suffer as the price of fighting a recession. Is it worth it? An economist cannot answer this any more than a nuclear physicist could have determined whether dropping the atomic bomb on Hiroshima was a good idea. The decision rests on value judgments about the moral trade-off between inflation and unemployment, judgments that can be made only by the citizenry through its elected officials.

These examples underscore what we said earlier in this chapter about economics being unable to provide all the answers but being able to teach you to ask the right questions. By the time you finish studying this book, you should have a good understanding of when the right course of action turns on disputed facts, when on value judgments, and when on some combination of the two.

THE ECONOMIST'S ODD VOCABULARY

George Bernard Shaw once remarked that America and England are two nations separated by a common language. Much the same might be said of economists and the rest of the population, for economists often assign peculiar meanings to commonly used words. Here are two examples; you will find many others later on.

Cost

We have already mentioned that when economists speak of ''costs'' they are normally referring to opportunity costs.

DEFINITION
To measure the *opportunity cost* of doing anything, you must compare your present activity with the next-best alternative (for example, working instead of going to school).

Accountants, on the other hand, almost always measure costs as the direct monetary expenses involved in any activity. Thus, in calculating the costs of the same activity, the accountant and the economist may arrive at two very different results, as the example of the costs of going to college illustrates. Accountants and economists are indeed divided by a common language.

Money

Most people work for money, or so they think. Again, the economist disagrees. He will insist that people work to earn *income,* which often happens to be paid—for reasons of convenience—in the form of *money.* What is the difference? To the economist, money refers to the amount of cash and bank-account balances you own at any particular moment. Your holdings of money change frequently, often several times in a single day. But income refers to the rate at which you earn money over time. A worker would answer the question "What is your income?" by saying "$10,000 a year," or "$200 a week," or something like that. Income probably changes much less frequently than holdings of money, perhaps only once a year. The distinction between money and income is important, and it will occupy our attention in Part Three.

The economist, it would appear, is much like Humpty Dumpty in *Alice in Wonderland* who said imperiously, "When I use a word it means just what I choose it to mean—neither more nor less." Why such obstinacy? Because economists need a *scientific jargon,* just as other scientists do. Any dictionary will testify to the fact that most words in any language have a multiplicity of meanings. Scientists must be more precise than that. And, rather than conjure up entirely new words, as natural scientists frequently do, economists take ordinary words and give them slightly special meanings. One wag pointed out that Canada has a radical group called *separatists* whose members steadfastly refuse to speak English, and that America also has such a group—but calls them *economists.* Who, though, would prefer that we say "phlogiston" instead of "cost" or "nutches" instead of "money"?

SUMMARY

1. To help you get the most out of your first course in economics, we have devised a list of 12 important ideas that you will want to remember *Beyond the Final Exam.* Very briefly, they are:
   (1) Interest rates that appear very high may actually be very low if they are accompanied by rapid inflation.
   (2) The environment can be protected by tax devices that make polluters pay for the cost of their pollution.
   (3) Government policies that reduce unemployment are likely to intensify the inflation problem, and vice versa.
   (4) Most policies that equalize income will exact a cost by reducing the nation's output.
   (5) The operation of free markets is likely to lead to rising prices for urban services.
   (6) Lawmakers who try to repeal the "law" of supply and demand are liable to open a Pandora's box of troubles they never expected.
   (7) To make a rational decision, the *opportunity cost* of an action must be measured, because only this calculation will tell the decision maker what he has given up.

(8) Two nations can gain from international trade, even if one is more efficient at making everything.

(9) Rational decisions often require the use of *marginal analysis* to isolate the costs and benefits of that particular decision.

(10) Active government policy to stabilize the economy need not imply a large public sector.

(11) Budget deficits are not nearly so bad as the public thinks, and in some circumstances they are quite advisable.

(12) Speculation serves a useful social function and may even reduce price fluctuations.

2. Economics is a discipline that uses a variety of approaches, some of them scientific and others humanistic, to address important social questions.

3. Because of the great complexity of human behavior, the economist is forced to abstract from many details, make generalizations that he knows are not quite true, and organize what knowledge he has according to some theoretical structure.

4. Economists use simplified models to understand the real world and predict its behavior, much as a child uses a model railroad to learn how trains work.

5. While these models, if skillfully constructed, can illuminate important economic problems, they rarely can answer the questions that policy-makers are confronted with. For this purpose, value judgments must be supplied, and the economist is no better equipped to do this than is anyone else.

6. A course in economics seeks to teach the student how to formulate the right questions, questions that point to the value judgments or unknown pieces of data that must be obtained in order to make an intelligent deci-sion. It does not try to provide all the answers.

CONCEPTS FOR REVIEW

Abstraction and generalization
Theory
Model
Comparative advantage
Speculation

Rationality
Opportunity cost
Marginal analysis
Marginal costs

QUESTIONS FOR DISCUSSION

1. Think about how you would construct a "model" of how your college is governed. Which officers and administrators would you include and exclude from your model if the objective were
   a. to explain how decisions on tuition payments are made?
   b. to explain the quality of the football team?
   Relate this to the map example in the chapter.

2. Relate the process of "abstraction" to the way you take notes in a lecture. Why do you not try to transcribe every word the lecturer utters? Why do you not just write down the title of the lecture and stop there? How do you decide, roughly speaking, on the correct amount of detail?

3. Explain why a government policymaker cannot afford to ignore economic theory.

2

The Use and Misuse of Graphs

Everything should be made as simple as possible,
but not more so.

Albert Einstein

In the preceding chapter we pointed out that economic models frequently appear as diagrams. And if you flip through the pages of this book you will see that indeed they are used quite often. Because many of you may not be familiar with diagrams, this chapter explains how some of the simple graphs used by economists are constructed and how they are to be interpreted.

Most readers of this book eventually will encounter graphs quite frequently in everyday life. If you become a doctor, you will see graphs depicting trends in costs of medical care as well as graphs recording the behavior of patients' vital

functions. If you are concerned about social problems, you will have to read graphs depicting changes in ethnic composition of the population of a city or those detailing frequency of conviction for a felony and its relation to family income. If you work for a large corporation, you will encounter graphs of sales, profits, and the like. Graphs appear almost daily in the financial pages of the newspaper.

Graphs are invaluable because of the large quantity of data they can display and because of the way they facilitate the interpretation and analysis of the data. They enable the eye to take in at a glance important statistical relationships that would be far less apparent from lengthy prose descriptions or long lists of numbers. It is therefore worth the effort needed to learn how data can be portrayed in graphs, for graphs may prove useful to you in the future. At the very least, you will want to avoid the serious errors into which one can easily be led by graphs that are misleading or distorted.

In this chapter we show, first, how to read a graph that depicts a relationship between two variables. Second, we define the term slope and describe how it is measured and interpreted. Third, we explain how the behavior of three variables can be shown on a two-dimensional graph. Fourth, we discuss how misinterpretation is avoided by adjusting many economic graphs to accommodate changes in the purchasing power of the dollar, in the population of the nation, and in other pertinent developments. And finally, we examine several other common ways in which graphs can be misleading if not drawn and interpreted with care.

Graphs Used in Economic Analysis*

TWO-VARIABLE DIAGRAMS

Much of the economic analysis to be found in this and other books requires that we keep track of two variables simultaneously. For example, in studying the operation of markets, we will want to keep one eye on the price of a commodity and the other on the quantity that is bought and sold.

For this reason, economists frequently find it useful to display real or imaginary figures in a two-dimensional graph, which simultaneously represents the behavior of two economic variables. The numerical value of one variable is measured along the bottom of the graph (called the horizontal axis) and the numerical value of the other is measured along the side of the graph (called the vertical axis).

DEFINITION

The lower left-hand corner of a graph where the two axes meet, is called the *origin*. Both variables are equal to zero at the origin.

*Students who have a nodding acquaintance with geometry and feel quite comfortable with graphs can safely skim over the first sections of this chapter and proceed directly to the second part, which begins on page 27.

Figure 2–1 is a typical graph used in economic analysis; it depicts a "demand curve,"

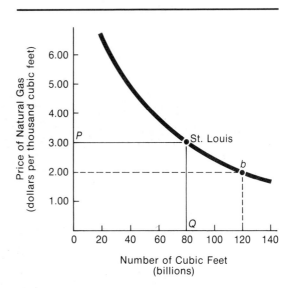

FIGURE 2–1

A DEMAND CURVE

This demand curve shows the relationship between the price of natural gas and the quantity of it that will be demanded. For example, the point labeled "St. Louis" indicates that at a price of $3.00 per thousand cubic feet (point P), the quantity demanded in that city will be 80 billion cubic feet (point Q).

represented by the heavy red line. The diagram shows the price of natural gas on the vertical axis and the quantity of gas that people want to buy on the horizontal axis. (Demand curves will be studied in detail in Chapter 4.)

Economic diagrams are generally read as one reads latitudes and longitudes on a map. On the demand curve in Figure 2–1, the point marked "St. Louis" represents the hypothetical position of St. Louis; that is, it represents price and quantity demanded at that geographic location. By drawing a horizontal line leftward from that point to the vertical axis, we learn that the average price for gas in St. Louis is $3.00 per thousand cubic feet. By dropping a line straight down to the horizontal axis, we find that 80 billion cubic feet are wanted by consumers at this price. The other points on the graph give similar information. For example, point b indicates that if natural gas in St. Louis cost only $2 per thousand cubic feet, demand would be higher—up to 120 billion cubic feet.

Notice that information about price and quantity is *all* we can learn from the diagram. The demand curve will not tell us what kinds of people live in St. Louis, how large their homes are, or the condition of their furnaces. It tells us the price and the quantity demanded at that price; no more, no less.

A diagram abstracts from many details, some of which may be quite interesting, in order to focus on the two variables of primary interest—in this case, the price of natural gas and the amount of gas that is demanded at each price. All the diagrams used in this book share this basic feature. They cannot tell the reader the "whole story" any more than a map's latitude and longitude figures for a particular city can make someone an authority on that city.

THE DEFINITION AND MEASUREMENT OF SLOPE

One of the most important features of the diagrams used by economists is the rapidity with which the line, or curve, being sketched runs uphill or downhill as we move to the right. The demand curve in Figure 2–1 clearly slopes downhill (the price falls) as we follow it to the right (as more gas is demanded). In such instances we say that *the curve has a negative slope, or is negatively sloped, because one variable falls as the other one rises.*

The four panels of Figure 2–2 show all the possible slopes for a straight-line relationship between two unnamed variables called Y (measured along the vertical axis) and X (measured along the horizontal axis). Figure 2–2(a) shows a negative slope, much like our demand curve. Figure 2–2(b) shows a positive slope, because variable Y rises (we go uphill) as variable X rises (we move to the right). Figure 2–2(c) shows a zero slope, where the value of Y is the same irrespective of the value of X. Figure 2–2(d) shows an infinite slope, meaning that the value of X is the same, irrespective of the value of Y.

Slope is a numerical concept, not just a qualitative one. It is easy to provide a formal definition of the slope of a straight line:

DEFINITION
The *slope of a straight line* is the ratio of the vertical change to the corresponding horizontal change as we move along the line, or, as it is often said, the ratio of the "rise" over the "run."

The two panels of Figure 2–3 show two positively sloped straight lines with different slopes. The line in Figure 2–3(b) is clearly steeper. But by how much? The labels should help you compute the answer. In Figure 2–3(a) a horizontal movement, *AB,* of 10 units (13 − 3) corresponds to a vertical movement, *BC,* of 1 unit (9 − 8). So the slope is *BC / AB* = 1/10. In Figure 2–3(b), the same horizontal movement of 10 units corresponds to a vertical movement of 3 units (11 − 8). So the slope is 3/10, which is larger.

The slope of any particular *straight* line is the same no matter where on that line we choose to measure it. That is why we can pick

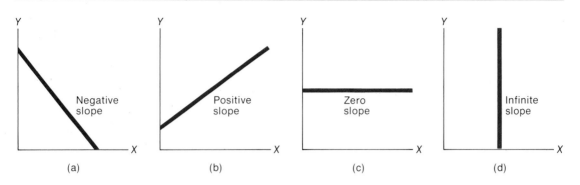

FIGURE 2–2

DIFFERENT TYPES OF SLOPE OF A STRAIGHT-LINE GRAPH

In Figure 2–2(a), the curve goes downward as we read from left to right, so we say it has a negative slope. The slopes in the other figures can be interpreted similarly.

any horizontal distance, *AB,* and the corresponding slope triangle, *ABC,* to measure slope. But this is not true of lines that are curved.

Curved lines also have slopes, but the numerical value of the slope is different at every point.

The four panels of Figure 2–4 provide some examples. The curve in Figure 2–4(a) has a negative slope everywhere, while the curve in Figure 2–4(b) has a positive slope everywhere. But these are not the only possibilities. In Figure 2–4(c) we encounter a curve

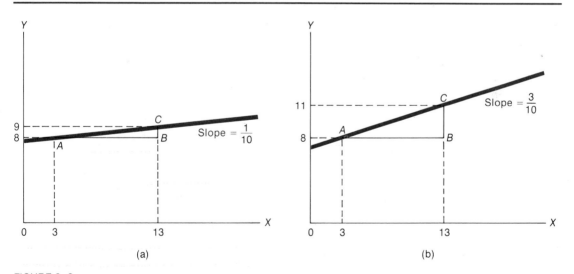

FIGURE 2–3

HOW TO MEASURE SLOPE

Slope indicates how much the graph rises per unit move from left to right. Thus, in Figure 2–3(b), as we go from point *A* to point *B,* we go $13 - 3 = 10$ units to the right. But in that interval, the graph rises from the height of point *B* to the height of point *C,* that is, it rises 3 units. Consequently, the slope of the line is $BC/AB = 3/10$.

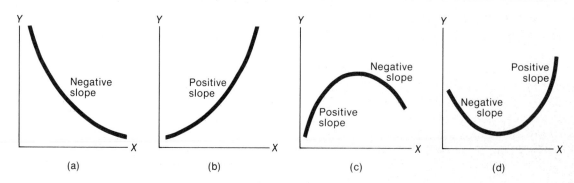

FIGURE 2–4

BEHAVIOR OF SLOPES IN CURVED GRAPHS
As Figures 2–4(c) and 2–4(d) indicate, where a graph is not a straight line it may have a slope that starts off as positive but that turns out negative, or vice versa.

that has a positive slope at first but a negative slope later on. Figure 2–4(d) shows the opposite case: a negative slope followed by a positive slope.

It is possible, however, to measure the slope of a smooth curved line numerically *at any particular point*. This is done by drawing a *straight* line that *touches,* but does not *cut,* the curve at the point in question. Such a line is called a tangent to the curve.

DEFINITION
The *slope of a curved line* at a particular point is the slope of the straight line that is tangent to the curve at that point.

In Figure 2–5 we have constructed tangents to a curve at two points. Line *tt* is tangent at point C, and line *TT* is tangent at point F. We can measure the slope of the curve at these two points by applying the above definition. The calculation for point C, then, is the following:

$$\text{Slope at point } C = \text{Slope of line } tt$$
$$= \frac{\text{Distance } BC}{\text{Distance } AB} =$$
$$= \frac{6 - 2}{10 - 0} = \frac{4}{10} = +0.4$$

A parallel calculation yields the slope of the curve at point F, which as we can see from Figure 2–5, must be smaller:

$$\text{Slope at point } F = \text{Slope of line } TT$$
$$= \frac{14 - 9}{50 - 0} = \frac{5}{50} = +0.1$$

EXERCISE
Show that the slope of the curve at point D is between $+0.1$ and $+0.4$.

What would happen if we tried to apply this graphical technique to the high point in Figure 2–4(c) or to the low point in Figure 2–4(d)? Take a ruler and try it. The tangents that you construct should be horizontal, meaning that they should have a slope of exactly zero. It is always true that where the slope of a smooth curve changes from positive to negative, or vice versa, there will be at least a single point with a zero slope.

Curves that have the shape of a hill, such as Figure 2–4(c), have a zero slope at their *highest* point. Curves that have the shape of a valley, such as Figure 2–4(d), have a zero slope at their *lowest* point.

RAYS THROUGH THE ORIGIN AND 45° LINES

The point at which a straight line cuts the vertical (Y) axis is called the Y-intercept. For example, the Y-intercept of line *tt* in Figure 2–5 is 2, while the Y-intercept of line *TT* is 9. Lines whose Y-intercept is zero have so many special uses that they have been given a special name.

DEFINITION

A straight line emanating from the origin is called a *ray through the origin* or, sometimes, just a *ray*.

Figure 2–6 contains three rays through the origin, and the slope of each is indicated in the diagram. The ray in the center—whose slope is 1—is particularly useful in many economic applications because it marks off points where X and Y are equal (as long as X and Y are measured in the same units). For example, at point A we have X = 3 and Y = 3, at point B, X = 4 and Y = 4, and a similar relation holds at any other point on that ray. How do we know that this is always true for a ray whose slope is 1? If we start from the origin (where both X and Y are

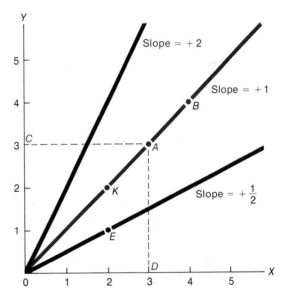

FIGURE 2–6

RAYS THROUGH THE ORIGIN

Rays are straight lines drawn through the zero point on the graph (*the origin*). Three rays with different slopes are shown. The middle ray, the one with slope = +1 has two properties that make it particularly useful in economics: (1) it makes a 45° angle with either axis, and (2) any point on that ray (for example, point A) is exactly equal in distance from the horizontal and vertical axes (length DA = length CA). So if the items measured on the two axes are in equal units, then at any point on that ray, such as A, the number on the X-axis (the abscissa) will be the same as the number on the Y-axis (the ordinate).

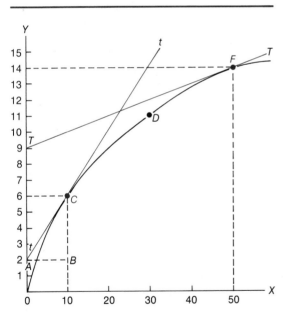

FIGURE 2–5

HOW TO MEASURE SLOPE AT A POINT ON A CURVED GRAPH

To find the slope at point F, draw the line TT, which is tangent to the curve at point F; then measure the slope of the straight-line tangent TT as in Figure 2–3. The slope of the tangent is the same as the slope of the curve at point F.

zero) and the slope of the ray is 1, we know from the definition of slope that:

$$\text{Slope} = \frac{\text{Vertical change}}{\text{Horizontal change}} = 1$$

This implies that the vertical change and the horizontal change are always equal, so the two variables must always remain equal.

Rays through the origin with a slope of 1 are called 45° lines because they form an angle of 45° with the horizontal axis.

DEFINITION
A *45° line* is a ray through the origin with a slope of +1. It marks off points where the variables measured on each axis have equal values.[1]

If a point representing some data is above the 45° line, we know that the value of Y exceeds

[1]The definition assumes that both variables are measured in the same units.

the value of X. Conversely, whenever we find a point below the 45° line, we know that X is larger than Y.

SQUEEZING THREE DIMENSIONS INTO TWO: CONTOUR MAPS

Sometimes, because a problem involves more than two variables, two dimensions just are not enough, which is unfortunate since paper is only two dimensional. When we study the decision-making process of a business firm, for example, we may want to keep track simultaneously of three variables: how much labor it employs, how much machinery it uses, and how much output it creates.

Luckily, there is a well-known device for collapsing three dimensions into two, namely, a contour map. Figure 2–7 is a contour map of Mount Rainier, the highest peak in the state of Washington. On several of the irregularly shaped "rings" we find a number indicating the

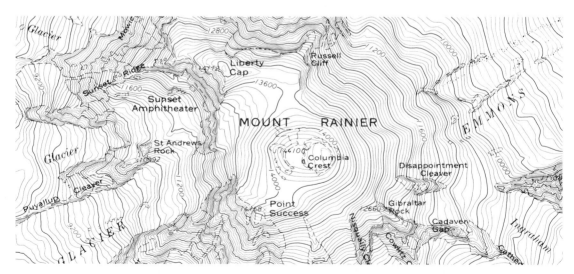

FIGURE 2–7

A GEOGRAPHIC CONTOUR MAP
All points on any particular contour line represent geographic locations that are at the same height above sea level.

height above sea level at that particular spot on the mountain. Thus, unlike the more usual sort of map, which gives only latitudes and longitudes, this contour map exhibits three pieces of information about each point: latitude, longitude, and altitude.

Figure 2–8 looks more like the contour maps one encounters in economics. It shows how some third variable, called Z (think of it as a firm's output, for example), varies as we change either variable X (think of it as a firm's employment) or variable Y (think of it as the use of a firm's machines). Just like the map of Mount Rainier, any point on the diagram conveys three pieces of data. At point A, we can read off the values of X and Y in the conventional way (X is 30 and Y is 40), and we can also note the value of Z by checking to see on which contour line point A falls. (It is on the $Z = 20$ contour.) So point A is able to tell us that 30 hours of labor and 40 hours of machine time produce 20 units of output.

While most of the analyses presented in this book will be based on the simpler two-variable diagrams, contour maps will find their applications, especially in the appendixes to Chapters 19 and 21.

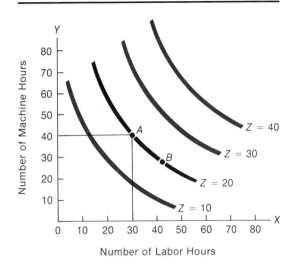

FIGURE 2–8

A PRODUCTION CONTOUR MAP
In this contour map, all points on a given contour line represent different combinations of labor and capital capable of producing a given output. For example, all points on the curve $Z = 20$ represent input combinations that can produce 20 units of output. Point A on that line means that the quantity of output can be produced using 30 labor hours and 40 machine hours. Economists call such maps *production indifference maps*.

Perils in the Interpretation of Graphs

The preceding materials contain just about all you will need in order to understand the simple graphics used in economic models. We turn now to the second objective of this chapter: to learn how statistical data are portrayed on graphs and some of the pitfalls to watch out for.

THE INTERPRETATION OF GROWTH TRENDS

Probably the most common form of graph in empirical economics is a year-by-year (or per-

haps a month-by-month) depiction of the behavior of some economic variable—the profits of a particular corporation, or its annual sales, or the number of persons unemployed in the U.S. economy, or some measure of consumer prices. For example, Figure 2–9 is this sort of time series graph showing the month-by-month unemployment rate in the United States from 1965 to 1978. It shows that the percentage of the labor force that was jobless was low during the prosperous period 1965–1969 but then rose sharply at the beginning of the 1970s, particularly at the peak of the recession in 1975. Time series graphs are a type of two-

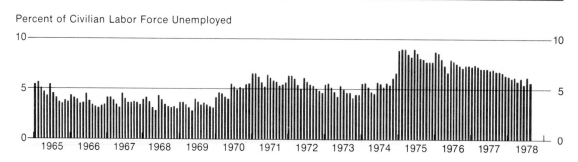

Percent of Civilian Labor Force Unemployed

FIGURE 2–9

TIME SERIES GRAPH

This graph shows the percentage of the labor force that was unemployed in each of the months indicated, from January 1965 through August 1978.

variable diagram in which time is always the variable measured along the horizontal axis.

Such graphs can be quite illuminating, offering an instant visual grasp of the course of the relevant events. *However, if misused, such graphs are very dangerous.* They can easily mislead persons who are not experienced in dealing with them.[2] Perhaps even more dangerous are the lies perpetrated accidentally and unintentionally by people who draw graphs without sufficient care and who may innocently mislead themselves as well as others.

A fine example of this latter occurrence is illustrated by Figure 2–10. Many people felt that there was a "cultural boom" under way in the 1960s that led to an explosion in the demand for tickets to all sorts of artistic performances. This boom, it was thought, accounted for the rapidly rising prices of theater tickets. Figure 2–10 shows the time series graph that formed the basis for this allegation. The growth in spending for theater tickets certainly looks impressive; expenditures rose about 240 percent from 1929 to 1963.

[2]An interesting and informative book on the subject is called *How to Lie with Statistics,* by Darrell Huff and Irving Geis.

But there is less to this graph than meets the eye—much less. Most of the spectacular growth in spending on theater admissions was a reflection of three rather banal facts. First, there were many more Americans alive in 1963 than in 1929, so spending *per person* rose by much less than Figure 2–10 suggests. Second, the price of almost everything, not just theater tickets, was higher in 1963 than in 1929. In fact, average prices were nearly double their 1929 levels. Third, the average American was richer in 1963 than in 1929, and consequently was more inclined to spend money on everything— not just on cultural activities.

All three of these factors can be accounted for by expressing spending on theater admissions as a *fraction* of total consumer income. The results of this "correction" are shown in Figure 2–11. The explosive growth suggested by the uncorrected data really amounts to a decline in the share of income that the average American spent on theater tickets—from about 15 cents out of each $100 in 1929 to only 11 cents in 1963! How misleading it can be to simply "look at the facts."

There is a general lesson to be learned from this example.

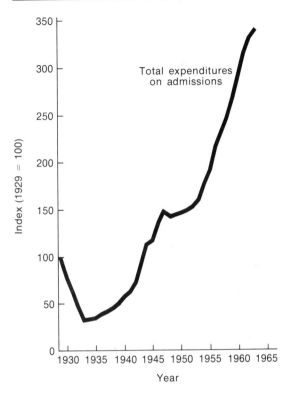

FIGURE 2–10

INDEX OF EXPENDITURES ON ADMISSIONS
TO ARTISTIC PERFORMANCES
This graph, showing expenditures on admissions to
artistic performances, seems to indicate that since
about 1932 Americans have become much more
interested in attending the performing arts.

The facts, as portrayed in a time series graph,
most assuredly do not "speak for themselves."
Because almost everything grows in a growing
economy, one must use judgment in interpreting growth trends. Depending on what kind of
data are being analyzed, it may be essential to
correct for population growth, for rising prices,
for rising incomes, or for all three.[3]

[3]For a full discussion of how to use a "price index" to
correct for rising prices, see the appendix to Chapter 6.

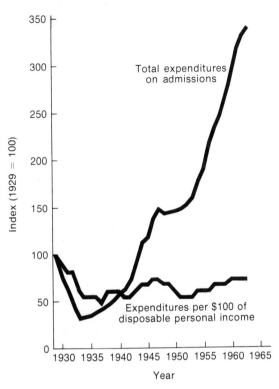

FIGURE 2–11

APPEARANCE AND REALITY IN ARTS
EXPENDITURE
The upper graph shows correctly that the number of
dollars spent on the arts by Americans rose
dramatically since 1932. But because of inflation, a
dollar in 1965 was worth much less than in 1929, and
there were many more Americans in the latter year,
who were also wealthier on the average. After
correction for inflation, population changes, and so on,
the upper line is transformed into the lower line,
showing that in 1963 an average American actually
spent less of his purchasing power on the arts than
in 1929.

DISTORTING TRENDS BY CHOICE
OF THE TIME PERIOD

In addition to possible misinterpretations of
growth trends, users of statistical data must be
on guard for distortions of trends caused by

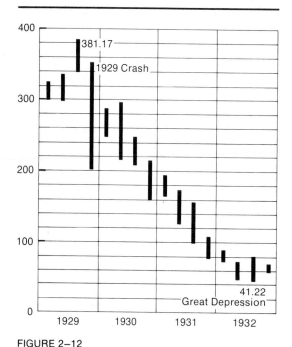

FIGURE 2–12

STOCK PRICES 1929–1932

This graph seems to show that stock market prices generally go down.

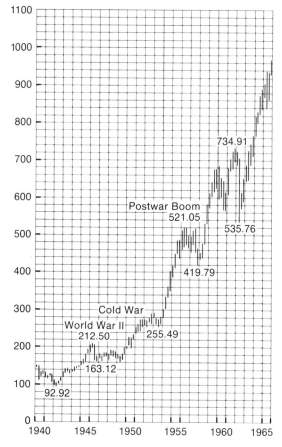

FIGURE 2–14

STOCK PRICES FROM 1940 TO 1965

This graph seems to show that the value of stocks is on a never-ending climb.

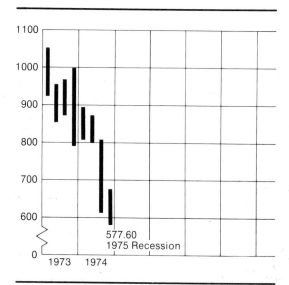

FIGURE 2–13

STOCK PRICES 1973 TO 1974

This figure also seems to show that stock prices generally fall.

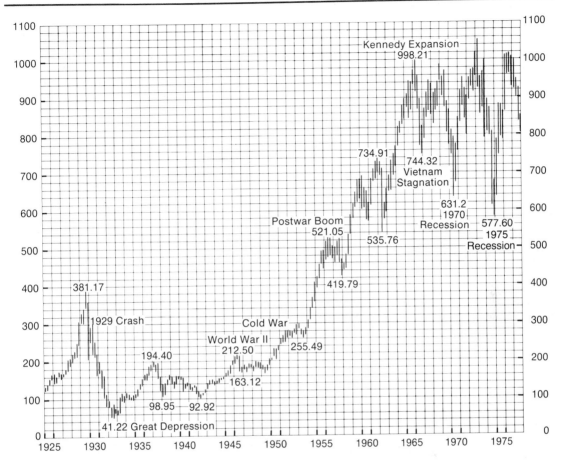

FIGURE 2–15

THE FULL HISTORY OF STOCK PRICES, 1925–1977

Here we see that stock prices have lots of ups and downs, though they have risen quite a bit on the average.

unskillfully chosen first and last periods for the graph. This is best explained by an example.

Figures 2–12 and 2–13 show the behavior of average stock market prices over the periods 1929–1932 and 1973–1974. They both display a clear downhill movement and would suggest to anyone who does not have other information that stocks are a terrible investment.

However, an unscrupulous seller of stocks could use the same set of stock market statistics to tell exactly the opposite story by carefully selecting another group of years. Figure 2–14 shows the behavior of average stock prices from 1940 through 1965. The persistence and size of the increase is quite dramatic. Stocks now look like a rather good investment.

An even longer and less biased period gives a less distorted picture (Figure 2–15). It indicates that investments in stocks are sometimes profitable and other times unprofitable.

The deliberate or inadvertent distortion resulting from an unfortunate or unscrupulous choice of time period for a graph must constantly be watched for.

There are no rules that can give absolute protection from this difficulty, but several precautions can be helpful.

1. Make sure the first date shown on the graph is not an exceptionally high or low point. In comparison with 1929, a year of unusually high stock market prices, the years immediately following are bound to give the impression of a downward trend.
2. For the same reason, make sure the graph does not end in a year that is extraordinarily high or low (although this may be unavoidable if the graph simply ends with figures that are as up-to-date as possible).
3. Make sure that (in the absence of some special justification) the graph does not depict only a very brief period, which can easily be atypical.

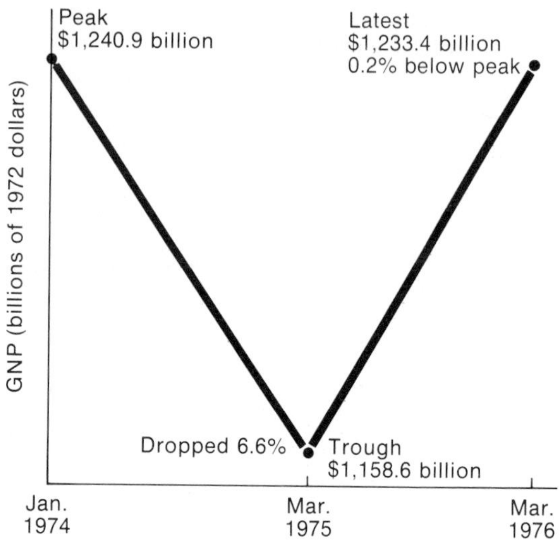

FIGURE 2–16

A GRAPH SHOWING OMISSION OF THE ORIGIN
A hasty glance at this figure seems to show that, from 1974 to 1975, gross national product fell from about $1200 billion almost to zero, and then shot up again about as fast.

DANGERS OF OMITTING THE ORIGIN

Frequently, an economic variable described on a graph will be characterized by very high numbers. For example, this is true of graphs showing gross national product (GNP)—one of the standard measures of the economy's total production, which will be defined and discussed in Chapter 5. In our "two-trillion dollar economy," the GNP figure never gets remotely close to zero. It is then tempting to omit all the "wasted space" between the origin and the levels of GNP actually encountered in the period considered. The graph in Figure 2–16, adapted from The New York Times, is an example of such an omission—its lowest point (though that is nowhere stated explicitly) is about 1.1 trillion dollars.

What is wrong with the drawing? The an-swer is that it vastly exaggerates the size of the drop and the rise in GNP that are depicted. It makes the recession of 1975 look like a catastrophic depression in which the bottom dropped out of the economy. The more meaningful graph, which includes the origin as well as the "wasted space" in between is shown in Figure 2–17. Note how this alternative presentation puts matters into perspective. It shows that in 1975 the economy did indeed experience a drop in GNP, but that it was nowhere nearly as severe as the graph in The New York Times would have suggested to the unwary reader.

Omitting the origin in a graph is dangerous because it always exaggerates the magnitudes of the changes that have taken place.

Sometimes, it is true, the inclusion of the origin would waste so much space that it is un-

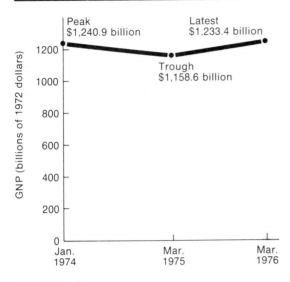

FIGURE 2–17

GNP FIGURES INCLUDING POINT OF ORIGIN
Adding the point of zero GNP to the previous graph
shows that the fall and rise in GNP from 1974 to 1976
was in fact not so enormous as the earlier graph
suggests.

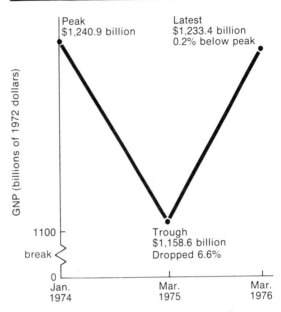

FIGURE 2–18

A BREAK IN A GRAPH
An alternative way of warning the reader that the
zero point has been left out is to put a break in the
graph, as illustrated here.

desirable to include it. In that case, a good
practice is to put a very clear warning on the
graph to remind the reader that this has been
done. Figure 2–18 shows one way of doing so.

UNRELIABILITY OF STEEPNESS AND CHOICE OF UNITS

The last problem we will consider has consequences very similar to the one we have just
discussed. The problem is that we can never
trust the impression we get from the steepness
of an economic graph. A graph of stock market
prices that moves uphill sharply (has a large
positive slope) appears to suggest that prices
are rising rapidly, while another graph in which
the rate of climb is much slower seems to imply
that prices are going up sluggishly. Yet the fact
is, depending on how one draws the graph, that

exactly the same statistics can produce a graph
that is rising very quickly or one that is rising
very slowly.

The reason for this possibility is that in economics there are no fixed units of measurement.
Coal production can be measured in hundredweight (hundreds of pounds) or in tons. Prices
can be measured in cents or in dollars or in
millions of dollars. Time can be measured in
days or in months or in years. Any of these
choices is perfectly legitimate, but it makes all
the difference to the rapidity with which a graph
using the resulting figures rises or falls.

An example will bring out the point. Suppose that we have the following (imaginary)
figures on daily coal production from a mine,
which we measure both in hundredweight and
in tons (remembering that 1 ton = 20 hundredweight):

YEAR	PRODUCTION IN TONS	PRODUCTION IN HUNDREDWEIGHT
1965	5000	100,000
1970	5050	101,000
1975	5090	101,800

Look at Figures 2–19(a) and 2–19(b), one graph showing the figures in tons and the other showing the figures in hundredweight. A change in unit of measurement stretches or compresses the axis on which the information is represented, which automatically changes the slope of the graph.

Unfortunately, we cannot solve the problem by agreeing always to stick to the same measurement units. Pounds may be the right unit for measuring demand for beef, but they will not do in measuring demand for cloth or for coal. A penny may be the right monetary unit for postage stamps, but it is not a very convenient unit for the cost of airplanes or automobiles.

We must never place much faith in the apparent implications of the slope of an ordinary graph in economics.

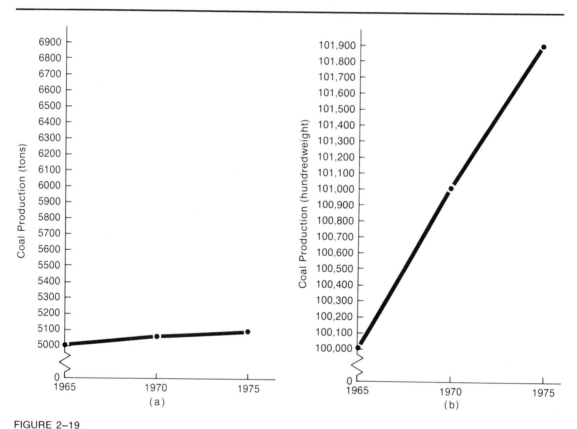

FIGURE 2–19

SLOPE DEPENDS ON UNITS OF MEASUREMENT

(a) Coal production is measured in tons, and production seems to be rising very slowly. (b) Production is measured in hundredweight (hundred-pound units), so the same facts now seem to say that production is rising spectacularly.

Later, in Chapter 18 on demand analysis, we will encounter a useful approach economists have adopted to deal with this problem. Instead of calculating changes in "absolute" terms—like millions of tons of coal or millions of barrels of oil—they use as their common unit the *percentage* increase. We will see that by using percentages rather than absolute figures the problem can be avoided. The reason is simple. If we look at our hypothetical figures on coal production again, we see that no matter whether we measure the increase in output from 1965 to 1970 in tons (from 5000 to 5050) or in hundredweight (from 100,000 to 101,000), the *percentage* increase has been the same. Fifty is 1 percent of 5000, and 1000 is 1 percent of 100,000. Since a change in units affects both the numbers *proportionately,* the result is a washout—it does not do anything to the answer of the percentage calculation.

SUMMARY

1. Because graphs are used so often to portray economic models, it is important for students to gain some understanding of their construction and use. Fortunately, the graphics used in economics are not very complex.
2. Most economic models are depicted in two-variable diagrams. We read data from these diagrams just as we read the latitude and longitude on a map. Thus, each point represents the values of two variables at the same time.
3. In a few instances, three variables must be shown at once. In these cases, economists use contour maps, which, as the name suggests, show "latitude," "longitude," and "altitude" all at the same time.
4. Often, the most important property of a line or curve drawn on a diagram will be its slope, which is defined as the ratio of the "rise" over the "run," or the vertical change divided by the horizontal change. Curves that go uphill as we move to the right have positive slopes, while curves that go downhill have negatives slopes.
5. By definition, a straight line has the same slope wherever we choose to measure it. The slope of a curved line changes, but the slope at any point on the curve can be calculated by measuring the slope of a straight line tangent to the curve at that point.
6. A time series graph is a particular type of two-variable diagram that is useful in depicting statistical data. Time is measured along the horizontal axis, and some variable of interest is measured along the vertical axis.
7. While time series graphs are invaluable in helping us condense a great deal of information in a single picture, they can be quite misleading if they are not drawn and interpreted with care. For example, growth trends can be exaggerated by inappropriate choice of units of measurement or by failure to correct for some obvious source of growth (such as rising population). Omitting the origin can make the ups and downs in a time series appear much more extreme than they actually are. Or, by a clever choice of the starting and ending points for the graphs, the same data can be made to tell very different stories. Readers of such graphs—and this includes anyone who ever reads a newspaper—must be on guard for problems like these or they may find themselves misled by "the facts."

CONCEPTS FOR REVIEW

Two-variable diagram
Origin of a graph
Tangent to a curve
Y-intercept
Ray through the origin
45° line

Contour maps
Time series graph
Horizontal and vertical axes
Slope of a straight line or a curved line
Negative, positive, zero, and infinite slope

QUESTIONS FOR DISCUSSION

1. Look for a graph in your local newspaper, on the financial page or elsewhere. What does the graph try to show? Is someone trying to convince you of something with this graph? Check to see if the graph is distorted in any of the ways mentioned in this chapter.
2. Portray the following hypothetical data on a two-variable diagram:

ENROLLMENT DATA: UNIVERSITY OF NOWHERE

ACADEMIC YEAR	TOTAL ENROLLMENT	ENROLLMENT IN ECONOMICS COURSES
1974–1975	3000	300
1975–1976	3100	325
1976–1977	3200	350
1977–1978	3300	375
1978–1979	3400	400

Measure the slope of the resulting line, and explain what this number means.
3. From Figure 2–5, calculate the slope of the curve at point D.
4. From Figure 2–6, determine the values of X and Y at point K and at point E. What do you conclude?
5. From Figure 2–8, interpret the economic meaning of points A and B. What do the two points have in common? What is the difference in their economic interpretation?
6. Suppose that between 1969 and 1979 expenditures on dog food rose from $35 million to $70 million and that the price of dog food doubled. What do these facts imply about the popularity of dog food?
7. Suppose that between 1965 and 1975 U.S. population went up 10 percent and that the number of people attending professional wrestling matches rose from 3,000,000 to 3,100,000. What do these facts imply about the growth in popularity of professional wrestling?

3

Scarcity and Choice: *The* Economic Problem

Our necessities are few but our wants are endless.

(Inscription found in a fortune cookie.)

In this chapter we examine the subject that many economists consider to be *the* fundamental issue of economic analysis: the fact that virtually no resources are available in limitless supply and the consequent need for people to live within their means. A materialist may dream of a world in which everyone has a yacht, a private airplane, and five automobiles, but the earth almost certainly does not have natural resources sufficient to make that dream possible.

In this chapter we will look at new ways to describe the choices available to decision makers in terms of the resources at their command. The same sort of analysis will be shown to apply to the decisions of the consumer, of the business firm, and of the government agency. Perhaps more important, it will be shown to apply to the range of options available to society as a whole. We will also describe the sort of cost calculation that is fundamental for rational decision making in the presence of scarce resources. Finally, we will apply this analysis to such concepts as inefficiency in the use of scarce resources and to economic growth. All the material in this chapter, therefore, serves as a necessary introduction to the analysis of the decisions of the consumer, the firm, and the government—topics that are discussed throughout the remainder of this book.

THE "INDISPENSABLE NECESSITY" SYNDROME

The first half of the 1970s brought with it an unaccustomed tightening of finances in a number of areas. The financial problems of the nation's cities and its colleges and universities were among those most widely publicized. New York City's financial woes received the most attention. But New York's problems were not unique. Even such formerly well-financed city governments as Chicago, Seattle, New Orleans, St. Louis, Kansas City, and Raleigh, North Carolina, and such formerly affluent universities as Stanford and Yale found themselves in financial difficulties and were forced to undergo an unpleasant belt-tightening.

When the politicians and the university administrators could no longer postpone the harsh decisions—which services or courses or departments to cut out, which to cut back and by how much—they found that their constituents were unprepared to accept *any* reductions. A proposal by a city administration to close a clinic or a firehouse or a library invariably brought out a group of marchers carrying signs that labeled the proposed cutback a "false economy," and that described the affected service as an "indispensable necessity" for the city's future. College and university administrators from one end of the country to the other were distraught to find that department heads were unwilling to set priorities upon the different parts of their budgets. Suggestions that one might reduce library reading hours, or eliminate remedial programs for students with difficulties, or cut out poorly attended courses, or limit the use of the Xerox machines all too frequently were met with the cry that each of these was *absolutely* essential, with the implication that none was less essential than the others.

Yet cities did once operate with fewer firehouses, and colleges were once able to educate students without the aid of Xerox machines. It is, of course, painful and regrettable to have to give up any of these good things; yet reduced budgets mean that *something* will have to go.

If everyone meets the issue by declaring *everything* to be essential, if every department head argues that library hours and teaching staff and student services must *never* be cut but suggests nothing else that can be cut instead, the decision maker, deprived of rational guidance, is likely to end up making cuts that are

---

Scarcity and Choice in a City's School System

In Toledo, where schools have been closed since October 28, voters approved an emergency tax increase after turning down four such proposals in the last two years. Said one protax campaigner: "For the first time, the people faced up to the fact that the schools were bankrupt."

At the same time, Ohio voters rejected tax hikes for schools in Canton, Cincinnati, Dayton, Columbus, and Parma.

Reprinted from *U.S. News & World Report*, November 21, 1977, page 104. Copyright 1977 U.S. News & World Report, Inc.

bad for everyone. When the budget is reduced, the decision maker must cut back somewhere. The issue is not whether reductions can be avoided altogether, but what cuts are likely to prove *least damaging* to the people affected.

It is nonsense to assign top priority to everything. No one can afford everything. An optimal decision is one that chooses the most desirable *among the possibilities that the available resources permit.*

SCARCITY, CHOICE, AND OPPORTUNITY COST

One of the basic themes that runs through most of economics is the fact that the resources of decision makers, no matter how large they may be, are always limited, and that, as a result, everyone has some hard decisions to make. Even Philip II, of Spanish Armada fame and one of the most richly endowed kings of history, frequently had to cope with rebellion on the part of his troops, whom he was often unable to pay or to supply with even the most basic provisions.

It is not only shortages of money that force hard decisions upon us. Physical resource limitations also constrain the things our community and our society can do. The supply of fuel has never been unlimited, and if fuel does really become scarce, some choices will have to be revised. We may be forced to keep our homes cooler, we may have to live closer to our jobs, we may have to give up such fuel-using conveniences as dishwashers, or we may have to do several or even all of these things.

The main lesson to be learned here is that virtually *no* resource is unlimited in supply. We all know about the scarcity of oil. But the same problem affects all the earth's mineral deposits. Iron, copper, aluminum, uranium, and every other such resource is finite in supply.

At any given time in history, the labor supply, too, is limited by the size of the population

and by its age structure. This becomes particularly clear in wartime, when the demands for military personnel and for persons to run the factories that produce the airplanes and the guns place a heavy strain on the civilian sector—the portion of the economy that turns out food, clothing, and other goods for the non-military population.

Even goods that can be produced are always in limited supply because their production requires fuel, labor, and other limited resources. Wheat and rice can be grown, yet nations have suffered famines because the land, the labor, the fertilizer, and the water needed to grow these crops were unavailable. We can increase our output of cars, but the required labor, steel, and fuel means that if we increase car production, something else, perhaps the production of refrigerators, must be cut back.

☑ This all adds up to the following fundamental principle of economics; one we will encounter again and again in this text.

Virtually all resources are scarce, meaning that humanity has less of them than it would like. So choices must be made among a *limited* set of possibilities, in full recognition of the inescapable fact that a decision to have more of one thing means we must give up some of another thing.

Economics examines the options left open to households, business firms, governments, and other groups by the limited resources at their command; and it studies the logic of the choices they make among the available possibilities.

This logic is grounded in a concept fundamental for decision making in the presence of scarce resources: the concept of *opportunity cost* that was introduced in Chapter 1 as one of the 12 Ideas for Beyond the Final Exam. The economist's fundamental principle of cost calculation for rational decision making is based on opportunity cost:

The relevant cost of any decision is its opportunity cost. ☑

To illustrate opportunity cost, we can continue the example in which we spoke of additions to the production of cars requiring society to reduce its production of refrigerators (or some other goods) because the steel, labor, and fuel used in making the additional cars become unavailable for use elsewhere. While the production of a car may cost $3000 per vehicle, or some other money amount, its real cost to the community consists of the number of refrigerators it must forgo to get an additional car. If the labor, steel, and fuel needed to make a car are also sufficient to make five refrigerators, we say that the opportunity cost of a car is five refrigerators. This principle is of such general applicability that we will devote nearly this entire chapter to an elaboration of the opportunity cost concept.

SCARCITY AND CHOICE FOR THE HOUSEHOLD

The nature of opportunity cost is perhaps most clearly illustrated by a household that must decide how to divide up its income among the goods and services that compete for the family's trade. Unless at some time the decision maker carries out an explicit comparison of the available choices, weighing the desirability of each in turn against the others, he or she is obviously likely to end up with decisions that do not serve the preferences of the family very efficiently. The family that, without thinking, contracts to buy a very expensive car on credit may regret this decision later when it is forced to cut other purchases sharply to pay back the debt. This example is not intended to preach the virtues of economy and saving or any other special pattern of budgeting. It is meant only to indicate how useful it is for the decision maker to recognize not only that money is scarce, but also what range of choices the available funds leave open. Only when we recognize opportunity costs explicitly—that the purchase of more

butter leaves less money for buns; that to buy a new car the family must economize on movies and put off buying a new color TV set—can we begin to set priorities intelligently and to make choices effectively.

Rational decision making therefore requires us to examine what choices the available resources *do* permit. By looking at and comparing all the possibilities we can begin to decide which of them best serves the objectives of the decision maker. We turn therefore to a geometric device, the *budget line,* that enables us to examine the available choices in a systematic manner.

GEOMETRY OF THE AVAILABLE CHOICES: THE BUDGET LINE

Suppose, for simplicity, that there are only two commodities on which consumers spend their money—hamburgers and movie tickets. Any household must then decide how to divide its income between these two goods. If the household has a given income and prices of hamburgers and movies are outside its control, what combinations of the two items can it afford to buy?

Table 3–1 helps to supply the answer. Suppose hamburger meat sells for $2 per pound, that a movie admission costs $3, and that the consumer has $24 to spend on the two items. The consumer can buy anything from zero movie tickets (spending the entire $24 on 12 pounds of hamburger meat) to (at the other extreme) 8 movie tickets with nothing left over for hamburgers. These extreme cases are represented, respectively, in the first and last rows of the table.

For economic analysis it is convenient to display this menu of choices in a graph (Figure 3–1). On the axes we show number of movie admissions and quantity of hamburger, so that any point in the diagram represents a *bundle* of commodities. For example, point *A* represents 4 movie admissions and 10 pounds of hamburger.

Geometry of the Available Choices: The Budget Line

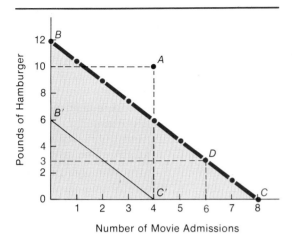

Number of Movie Admissions

FIGURE 3–1

THE OPPORTUNITY OR BUDGET SET FOR A HOUSEHOLD

The set is shown by the shaded area. It shows all combinations of the two goods that the family can afford to buy with the fixed amount of money it has available. Points below the line *BC* use less than the available amount of money. Points on line *BC* represent combinations of the two goods that cost every penny of the available household money. Line *BC* is the *budget line*. The shaded area is the *opportunity set*.

First, observe that if every penny of the consumer's $24 were spent on movie tickets, the buyer would end up at point *C,* going to the movies 8 times, but with no food, since with movie tickets costing $3 each, the $24 would just cover the cost of 8 admissions. Similarly, if *all* the money were spent on meat, the buyer would end up at point *B*—with 12 pounds of hamburger and no movies.

Next, connect points *B* and *C* by a straight line. The points on this line show the available choices when the shopper has $24 to divide between the two goods. For example, point *D* tells us that if the household buys 6 movie admissions, it will have only enough money left over to purchase 3 pounds of hamburger. The reader can verify that the dots on the budget line *BC* in Figure 3–1 correspond to the numbers in columns 1 and 4 in Table 3–1. Each dot refers to a single pair of numbers, and vice versa. Thus the table and the graph give exactly the same information.

Line *BC* in Figure 3–1 is called the budget line, which may be located by calculating all the combinations of both outputs that the

TABLE 3–1

ALTERNATIVE ALLOCATIONS OF A $24 BUDGET BETWEEN MOVIE ADMISSIONS (AT $3 EACH) AND HAMBURGERS (AT $2 A POUND)*

(1) NUMBER OF MOVIE ADMISSIONS	(2) TOTAL COST OF ADMISSIONS (price per admission times number of admissions)	(3) REMAINING CASH (total budget minus total cost of admissions)	(4) POUNDS OF HAMBURGER CONSUMER CAN AFFORD (remaining cash divided by price of hamburger)
0	$0	$24	12
1	3	21	$10\tfrac{1}{2}$
2	6	18	9
3	9	15	$7\tfrac{1}{2}$
4	12	12	6
5	15	9	$4\tfrac{1}{2}$
6	18	6	3
7	21	3	$1\tfrac{1}{2}$
8	24	0	0

*These calculations are all derived from the formula: Price of admissions × Number of admissions + Price of hamburgers × Quantity of hamburgers = Total budget.

available money will buy. Note that the amount of money (the resources) available to the household determines the location of the budget line. For example, suppose our household had only $12 to spend instead of $24 as in our previous illustration. Then the household could buy only half as much as before; that is, only 4 movie tickets (rather than 8) if it bought no hamburger, or only 6 pounds of meat (rather than 12) if it went to no movies. Thus with a $12 budget, the budget line becomes *B'C'*. In other words, it is halfway toward the zero point on the diagram (the origin) from the budget line *BC,* which applies when the family has $24 to spend on movies and hamburgers.

DEFINITION
The *budget line* for a household represents graphically all the possible combinations of two commodities that it can purchase, given some fixed amount of money at its disposal. All points in the shaded area on *or below* that line represent choices open to the household given the resources it has available. This shaded area is called the household's *opportunity set.*

In Chapter 19 we will go on to examine further how the consumer can make rational decisions among the choices available in the budget line and the opportunity set.

SCARCITY AND CHOICE FOR THE FIRM

Firms also have to stick to their opportunity sets, but for the firm this is a bit more complex than for the household. Like the household, the firm is a purchaser of goods. Only instead of buying consumer goods, like movie tickets and hamburgers, the firm usually buys inputs—fuel, raw materials, and labor time. Even here, as we will soon see, the opportunity set for the firm is somewhat different in character from the household's. But the firm also has another type of

activity—production—that does not usually take place inside the household. And, in production, decisions must also be made within an opportunity set. It simply is impossible to produce everything one wants to; one can produce only what the available resources will allow.

A farmer with a given amount of land and a given amount of capital can divide up his land between, say, the production of wheat and soybeans. The more land used for one crop, the less there is available for the other. But some lands are better suited for growing the one crop and some better for the other. This means that as the farmer puts more and more land into wheat production, the opportunity cost (in terms of soybeans that are forgone) is likely to increase because he must use more and more land that is suitable for soybeans for the cultivation of wheat. As a result, the farmer's production possibilities will not usually be given by a straight line like the household's budget line. Rather, as shown in Figure 3–2, it will curve away from the origin (curve *RS*). This curve is called the production opportunity frontier.

DEFINITION
The *production opportunity frontier* shows the different combinations of various goods that a producer can turn out by reallocating the available resources among different products.

Let us examine the curvature of the production opportunity frontier a little more carefully. Suppose our farmer has been producing 30,000 bushels of soybeans and 40,000 bushels of wheat (point *C*). Then the price of wheat rises and he decides to change his production plans. If the opportunity frontier at point *C* had been a straight line, *TU,* he could have expanded his wheat production to 60,000 bushels and still have been able to turn out 20,000 bushels of soybeans (point *B*). In other words, a 20,000-bushel gain in wheat production would have had only a 10,000-bushel cost in soybean output forgone if the opportunity frontier had been a straight line. However, the curvature of

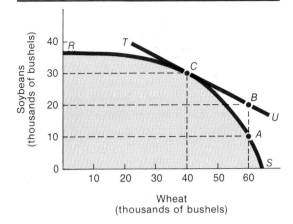

FIGURE 3–2

PRODUCTION OPPORTUNITY FRONTIER AND OPPORTUNITY SET FOR PRODUCTION BY A FIRM
With a given set of inputs, the firm can only produce an output combination given by a point in the shaded area. The production opportunity frontier, *RS*, is not a straight line but one that curves more and more as it nears the axes. That is, when the firm specializes in only one product, those inputs that are especially adapted to the production of the other good lose at least part of their productivity.

the actual opportunity frontier indicates that once the farmer is devoting so high a proportion of his land to wheat, further increases in wheat output must use land that is better suited to soybean production, and the additional 20,000 bushels of wheat will therefore have a higher opportunity cost. Soybean output will fall from 30,000 bushels (point *C*) to 10,000 bushels (point *A*). More generally:

The *production opportunity frontier* for a single firm is not generally a straight line. But whatever its shape, it will always mark off an area, the production opportunity set (shaded area in Figure 3–2), that indicates all output combinations that are possible with the given quantity of resources. In making its production plans, the firm must choose among those available possibilities.

SCARCITY AND CHOICE FOR THE GOVERNMENT

Even a rich and powerful government like the United States or the Soviet Union must cope with an opportunity set imposed by scarce resources. Much of the battle between Congress and the Ford administration was over the choice between military expenditure and programs to finance jobs for the unemployed, day care centers for the children of working mothers, and other programs intended to promote the public welfare.

Governments buy some goods and services and produce others themselves. For the things it buys, a government has to deal with a budget line just like that shown in Figure 3–1 for the household. For example, with a given budget, if a tank costs twice as much as a day care center, the administration's budget line for tanks and day care centers might look like that in Figure 3–3. The figure indicates that with the available budget, the administration can afford

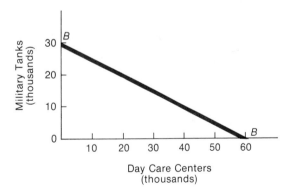

FIGURE 3–3

A GOVERNMENT BUDGET LINE: MILITARY TANKS VERSUS DAY CARE CENTERS
The more money the government spends on tanks, the less it has available for day care centers. In the extreme case, if it buys 30,000 tanks, nothing is left for any day care centers.

30,000 tanks and zero day care centers, or 60,000 day care centers and zero tanks, or any of the various intermediate combinations represented by points along the budget line *BB*.

But governments also engage in the production of services—education, police protection, operation of libraries, and so on. Here, the opportunity frontier is likely to be curved, like the private producer's in Figure 3–2, and for exactly the same reasons.

SCARCITY AND CHOICE IN OTHER PARTS OF THE ECONOMY

Constraints are not limited to households, firms, and governments. Some sort of restricted opportunity set is imposed on the decisions of all economic entities, including, for example, charitable foundations.

The case of foundations is clearly analogous to that of households. They cannot give away more than they have available. When the Ford Foundation, with its capital in the neighborhood of $4 billion, decided a few years ago to spend more of its money on the problems of cities and minorities, less was left for other purposes. As a result, the support that the Foundation had formerly provided to the arts, to education, and to other sections of society had to be reconsidered and, in some cases, cut back.

Then, in 1973, this very wealthy foundation suddenly ran into financial problems, and it was decided that its spending would have to be reduced sharply. One consequence of the cutback was that many members of the staff were fired or not replaced as they retired or left for other reasons.

The "philanthropoids" were forced to make difficult choices about the distribution of their support money as their opportunity set shrank. Grants were cut back sharply, and many groups that had depended on Ford and other foundations as a continuing source of support sud-

denly found that their easier days had come to an end.

For example, Table 3–2 shows how some Ford Foundation grants changed over a 5-year period. Note that the cutbacks were not perfectly uniform. Public broadcasting was particularly hard hit, dropping by as much as 92.1 percent, while support to public education was cut back only 24.3 percent. This suggests that there was a process of explicit choice—not a uniform cutback, but a considered response to the reduction in the Foundation's resources.

At the same time, other nonprofit groups—hospitals, colleges, theaters, and orchestras—have seen their budgets grow tighter. Their funds have typically been rising but not as quickly as their expenditures, and the necessity of hard decisions, often accompanied by strikes and turmoil, was the inescapable result. Yet even in their most affluent days, in the decade of the 1960s, life was never easy for the nonprofit organizations. In some parts of the theater, for example, wages of $50 a week (during the periods when there was work for the actor) were considered extremely lush. Wages of

TABLE 3–2

PERCENTAGE CHANGE IN GRANTS FOR SELECTED CATEGORIES, FORD FOUNDATION, 1970 TO 1975

CATEGORIES OF GRANTS	PERCENT CHANGE
1. National affairs, resources and environment	−40.1
2. Public education	−24.3
3. Higher education and research, humanities and arts	−49.3
4. Public broadcasting	−92.1
5. International division	−36.4
Total grants including other categories not shown	−19.2

Source: Ford Foundation annual reports.

dancers were frequently even lower. Many small theaters had to operate with inadequate lighting, virtually no dressing facilities for the cast, and uncomfortable seating for the audiences. Even when grants were relatively liberal, hard choices were unavoidable.

SCARCITY AND CHOICE FOR THE WHOLE ECONOMY

Like the individual firm, the economy as a whole is constrained by an opportunity set. Also like the firm, the limitations for the economy are determined, not by a budget and prices, but by available technology, personnel, and physical resources. Thus we would not expect the economy's opportunity set to be bounded by a straight budget line as is the household's. Instead, we would expect the economy's production opportunity frontier to have a curved boundary, just like the opportunity set of the firm.

The economy's choices are much like the firm's, for it must allocate resources among its products. For example, consider the production of cheese and phonograph records. The economy will have a production opportunity frontier for cheese and records such as curve BC in Figure 3–4. If most of the workers are employed on dairy farms, the production of cheese can be large but the output of records will then be relatively low. If resources are transferred from the farms to the factories, this output combination can be changed toward increased output of phonograph records at some sacrifice in cheese production (the move from D to E). However, something is likely to be lost in the transfer process—the hay that helped produce the dairy output will not help in record production. Unlike money, which is perfectly transferable from one commodity to another, physical resources tend to be specialized. So, as we move to the right in our diagram, representing increases in the economy's output of records, the opportunity

frontier may well curve downward toward the axis. We may even reach a point where the only resources left are items that are not very useful outside a dairy farm. In that case even an additional sacrifice of dairy output, which is very large, will enable the economy to produce very few more records. That is the meaning of the steep segment, FC, of the boundary of our opportunity set. At point C there is very little more output of records than at F, even though at C cheese output has been given up altogether.

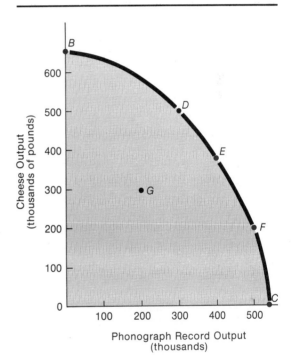

FIGURE 3–4

THE OPPORTUNITY SET FOR PRODUCTION BY THE ENTIRE ECONOMY

This opportunity set also has a curved boundary because resources are not perfectly transferable from cheese production to record production. The limits on available resources place a ceiling, C, on the output of one product and a different ceiling, B, on the output of the other product.

The position and shape of the opportunity set that constrains the choices of the economy are determined by the economy's physical resources, its skills, its willingness to work, and its investment in factories, research, and innovation.

OPPORTUNITY COST ONCE MORE

The central lesson of Figure 3-4 is that if the economy wants more phonograph records, it will have to give up something else. At least, this is true as long as all resources are fully employed. If we want more space exploration or a larger army, we will have to give up some school or hospital construction or something else.

The true cost of a dishwasher is not the price of the electricity, or the steel used to make it, but the other useful things that the steel or electricity could have made. Thus, the opportunity cost is the true sacrifice the economy must incur in order to get the dishwasher.

You may well wonder whether the opportunity cost of the dishwasher in our example has any relation to its money cost. The answer is that the two are often very closely tied because of the way the economy sets the price of the steel or the electricity that goes into the production of dishwashers. Steel is valuable because it can be used to make other things. If those things that steel can make are themselves valuable, the price of steel will be high. But if the other things steel can make have very little value, the price of steel will be low. In sum, if a dishwasher has a high opportunity cost, that means the resources that are needed to produce the dishwasher will have high prices. The steel and the electricity will cost a good deal of money, and so the dishwasher will also have a high money cost. In sum:

Goods that have a high opportunity cost will tend to have a high money cost, and goods whose opportunity cost is low will tend to have a low money cost.

Yet it is dangerous to treat the two costs as the same thing. A simple example will show why this is so, and will also illustrate how we use the concept of opportunity cost. Recall from our example in Chapter 1 that if you go to college instead of working at a weekly salary of, say, $150, then school attendance has an opportunity cost to you of $150 per week, for that is the money that you forgo by attending college. Similarly, if you draw $1000 out of your bank account, which pays 6 percent interest, and use it to buy a used car, the car has an opportunity cost of $60 per year (6 percent of $1000).

Suppose now that Sherlock Bones is offered the opportunity to buy a detective agency that will bring in an annual income of $32,000. The agency will cost him $200,000, which he now has invested in bonds that are paying 7 percent a year. He also will have to give up his current job at which he earns $20,000 a year. Is this a good deal for Sherlock?

Considered in terms of money costs and revenues, it sounds like a very good deal—an annual profit of $32,000. But look at the opportunity cost—$20,000 in wages given up and $14,000 (7 percent of $200,000) in interest payments given up. The total opportunity cost of $34,000 is more than the return. Sherlock gives up $2000 more on the deal than he gets from it. And he might even get shot for his trouble! He may still want to buy the agency, but he should surely not do it as a good *financial* investment.

APPLICATION: UNEMPLOYMENT AND OTHER WASTES OF RESOURCES

When the economy is using its resources *efficiently,* it will always end up at some point on the production opportunity frontier. But if it ends up at some point in the opportunity set that is *below* the frontier, it is said to be operating *inefficiently*. Why?

Figure 3–4 tells the story. Suppose point G represents the economy's output combination—the production of 200,000 records and 300,000 pounds of cheese. But any other point in the opportunity set is just as available to the economy, given the quantity of resources it has at its disposal. For example, instead of point G, it could have produced point D and obtained 300,000 records and 500,000 pounds of cheese. Thus, with the same resources, point D offers the economy more of *every* product than it obtains at point G. No wonder G is considered inefficient. It involves a wasteful use of the economy's resources, because if instead it had used them in such a way as to get the economy to point D, society would have obtained a greater abundance of all goods.

There are a number of ways in which such a waste of resources occurs in real-life situations. The most important of them, unemployment, is an issue that will take up a substantial part of this book (Chapters 5–16). When many workers are unemployed, the economy finds itself at a point like G, inside the opportunity set. Why? Turning back to our example, we can see that by putting the unemployed to work in both the cheese and the record industries the economy can produce more records and cheese. The economy will then move from point G to the right (more records) and upward (more cheese), toward a point like D on the production opportunity frontier. Only when there is no "avoidable" unemployment is it possible to be at a point on the frontier like D or E, where no resources are wasted by unemployment or misuse.

Notice that analogous problems can occur in the firm or in the household. If the firm uses electricity wastefully, or if the family wastes money, it will end up at a point *inside* its opportunity set rather than somewhere on its northeastern boundary (the production opportunity frontier in the case of the firm, and the budget line in the case of the household).

APPLICATION: ECONOMIC GROWTH

Economies can grow in a number of ways—by the discovery of new resources, by the construction of new factories, or by successful innovation. Roughly speaking, economic growth means that the average inhabitant will be better off in terms of consumer goods or income than she was before. For the economy as a whole, this can be represented by an *outward shift* of its production opportunity frontier as shown in Figure 3–5(a) and (b). In each case growth is represented by a shift in the frontier from black curve FF to red curve GG, constituting an increase in the opportunity set. As a result of this growth, consumers can have both more records and more cheese than they could have obtained before. For example, in Figure 3–5(a), after growth the economy may choose to produce 300,000 records and 500,000 pounds of cheese (point B), whereas before growth about the nearest it could have come to this output combination is point A, which yields only 200,000 records and 400,000 pounds of cheese.

Figure 3–5(b) represents an economy that is growing much more quickly than the one shown in Figure 3–5(a), assuming that the shift in the diagrams takes the same amount of time in both cases. For in Figure 3–5(b), the increase in possible output combinations is far greater than in part (a). That is, the production opportunity frontier in the former has moved outward far more than it has in the latter. (Economic growth will be studied in detail in Chapter 33, and again in Chapter 38 on less developed countries.)

Note that there can be an outward shift in the boundary of the household's or the firm's opportunity set that is analogous to that produced by economic growth for the economy as a whole. If the consumer's income increases, her budget line will shift upward, as we have seen. And a firm that borrows money to acquire more land, labor, and equipment will find that its production opportunity frontier will have

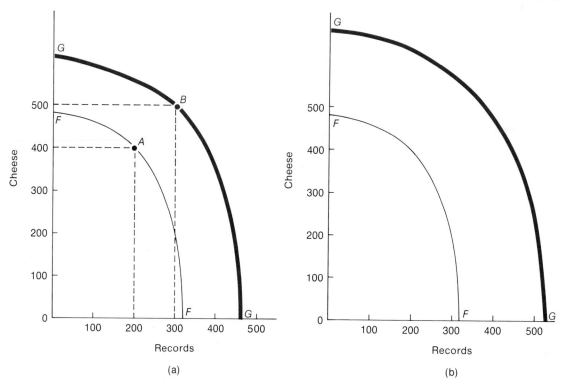

FIGURE 3–5

GROWTH IN TWO ECONOMIES

Growth shifts the production opportunity frontier *FF* outward to the red frontier *GG,* meaning that the economy can produce more of both goods than it could before. If the shift in both economies occurs in the same period of time, then the economy in part (b) is growing faster than the one in part (a). That is because the outward shift in part (b) is much greater than the one in part (a).

shifted outward because of the increase in its resources.

We will meet the concepts of opportunity set and (even more frequently) opportunity cost

many times throughout this book. There are few economic issues for which it is not relevant, for almost all of economics deals with choice when options (opportunities) are limited.

SUMMARY

1. Supplies of resources are limited. This is clearly true of fuels and minerals and of labor time in a population of a given size. It is also true of manufactured items, such as cloth or chemicals, because these need labor, fuel, and other scarce inputs to produce them.
2. When resources are scarce, rational decisions require a choice among the options that are possible with the remaining resources.

3. It is irrational to assign highest priority to everything. No one can afford everything, and so hard choices must be made.
4. With limited resources, if we decide to obtain more of one item, we must give up some of another item. What we give up is called the *opportunity cost* of what we get.
5. The true cost of any decision is its opportunity cost. This is one of the 12 Ideas for Beyond the Final Exam.
6. The budget line of a household shows the quantities of commodities a household can afford when it has a given income to spend. It is a straight line that shifts upward if the household's income rises.
7. The firm's production opportunity frontier shows the combinations of commodities a firm can produce with a given quantity of resources. It usually is not a straight line. It shifts upward if the firm obtains larger quantities of resources.
8. The economy as a whole has a production opportunity frontier like that of a firm.
9. If a firm or an economy ends up at a point below its production opportunity frontier, it is using its resources inefficiently or wastefully. This is what happens, for example, when there is unemployment.
10. Economic growth means there is an upward shift in the economy's production opportunity frontier. The faster the growth, the faster this shift will occur.

CONCEPTS FOR REVIEW

Budget line
Production opportunity frontier
Scarcity
Choice

Opportunity cost
Opportunity set
Inefficiency
Economic growth

QUESTIONS FOR DISCUSSION

1. Discuss the resource limitations that affect the following:
   a. the poorest person on earth
   b. the richest person on earth
   c. a firm in Switzerland
   d. a government agency in China
   e. the population of the world.
2. If you were president of your college, what would you change if your budget were cut by 5 percent? by 20 percent? by 50 percent?
3. If you were to drop out of college, what things would change in your life? What, then, is the opportunity cost of your education?
4. Draw a budget line for shoes and hats for a consumer who has $120 to spend on these items. A pair of shoes costs $30 while a hat costs $12.
5. Draw the budget line for the consumer in the previous example if the consumer's budget falls to $90.
6. A person rents a house for which he pays the landlord $3000 a year and keeps money in a bank account that pays 6 percent a year. The house is offered for sale at $70,000. Is this a good deal for the potential buyer? Where does opportunity cost enter the issue?

4

Supply and Demand:
An Initial Look

In this chapter we introduce the important economic "laws" of supply and demand. We will begin by defining the demand curve and the supply curve, showing that the former describes the relationship between the price of a good and the quantity of the good that people want to buy, and that the latter describes the relationship between the price of a good and the quantity of the good that firms wish to provide. We go on to explain how these two curves determine the price and the quantity that will be sold in a free market, and then show how these tools (the curves) can be used to analyze the effects of such events as tax changes upon both price and quantity sold. Finally, we will examine the typical consequences of attempts by government to force changes in prices by interfering with the operations of free markets. We will see that in many cases such government interventions will produce unintended and undesirable side effects.

Our supply—demand analysis makes heavy use of the sorts of graphs you were introduced to in Chapter 2. As you read this chapter, keep in mind that the analysis described here will play a fundamental role in the discussions presented throughout the book. It will be used to help analyze topics as diverse and important as unemployment and inflation, competition and monopoly, and the problems of the cities.

APPLICATIONS: ATTEMPTS TO CONTROL THE PRICE MECHANISM

One does not have to be an economist to talk about supply and demand. Legislators and other lay people, for instance, often attack certain proposals on the grounds that they conflict with the "law of supply and demand"; and we will see that such popular evaluations often have a solid basis in fact. Indeed, the problem is that the public's understanding and appreciation of the strength of market forces often do not go far enough.

As a result, public opinion frequently does unwittingly encourage legislative attempts "to repeal the law of supply and demand" by *controlling prices*. The consequences usually are quite unfortunate, exacting heavy costs from the general public and often aggravating the problem the legislation was intended to cure. This is another of the 12 Ideas for Beyond the Final Exam, and it will occupy our attention throughout this chapter.

There are countless instances in which the public's sense of justice has been outraged by the prices charged on the open market, particularly when the sellers of the expensive items belong to a group that does not enjoy great popularity—landlords, moneylenders, oil companies, or supermarket chains. Attempts to control interest rates (which may be thought of as the price of borrowing money) go back hundreds of years before the birth of Christ, at least to the code of laws compiled under Hammurabi in Babylonia about 1800 B.C. Our

historical legacy includes a rather long list of price ceilings on foods and other products imposed in the reign of Diocletian, emperor of the declining Roman Empire. Modern legislators, too, continually seek to keep down rents on apartments, interest rates on mortgages, prices of fuels and groceries, brokerage charges on the sale of theater tickets, and a host of other items.

In the period since World War II, Americans have been offered the "protection" of a variety of price controls. Ceilings have been placed on various prices to protect consumers, while floors have been placed under other prices, such as those for farm products, to protect the earnings of the suppliers. In New York City, rents continue to be regulated, long after every other major city has dropped such wartime controls. Theater ticket brokers are still subjected to a ceiling on the price of their services, which has remained unchanged through a long inflationary period despite the fact that many other prices have been permitted to rise freely and substantially.

Many if not most of these measures were adopted in response to popular opinion, and there is a great outcry whenever it is proposed that any one of them be weakened or eliminated. Yet, somehow, everything such regulation touches seems to end up in even greater trouble than those things that are left alone. Despite controls, rents in New York City have about doubled in the last ten years.[1] Theater tickets for popular shows sell at tremendous premiums—seats to one popular musical, whose designated price was $15, were recently reported to be selling regularly at $37.50. People wanting to build dwellings sometimes find that mortgage money simply is not available at the legal interest rate. And when natural gas shortages reached a crisis point in 1977, customers in the eastern United States were not

[1] Lawrence N. Bloomberg, *The Rental Housing Situation in New York City 1975*. The City of New York, Housing and Development Administration, January 1976, page 198.

only denied requests for increases in the amount of fuel they needed to meet their requirements, but were actually forced to cut back. The result was that some plants and offices closed down, and families shivered in their inadequately heated homes.

Still, legislators continue to turn to controls whenever the economy does not work to their satisfaction. Recent years have seen a return to rent controls in many American cities, a brief experiment with overall price controls by a Republican administration that had vowed never to turn to them, and determined resistance to abolition of ceilings on interest rates on mortgages. In addition, the debate over whether (and how) to let energy prices rise has been unceasing since 1974.

To see what is likely to go wrong whenever controls are adopted, and why it is so difficult to back out of an attempt to set prices by government directive once it has been started, we must first study the machinery of supply and demand. Then, later in the chapter, we will turn to the control of taxicab fares as an example of an attempt to interfere with the market, and to see what proponents of such measures have overlooked.

THE DEMAND CURVE

References in nonprofessional discussions to the "law of supply and demand" imply that it is some sort of vaguely defined but powerful influence affecting the course of economic affairs by raising prices when goods are scarce and lowering prices when goods are abundant. To economists, the supply—demand mechanism is something far more concrete. It is a manifestation of market forces that shows just how prices interact with quantities supplied and demanded. Its relationships are spelled out rather precisely, and the way in which they determine prices and the quantities of goods and services bought and sold is explained in the analysis. The basic tools used for this purpose are the supply and de-

mand curves. We begin our analysis with a discussion of demand curves.

Noneconomists are apt to think of consumer demands as fixed amounts. Studies for business firms and for government agencies dedicate themselves to finding such figures, sometimes referring to them as "market potential" or "quantities needed." Trends in consumption of fuel are studied to determine just how much will be "required" in succeeding years. When the production of a new type of machine tool is proposed, management asks, "What is its market potential? How many will we be able to sell?" When the government undertakes a program for the training of engineers, it appoints a committee to determine "how many engineers will be needed."

Economists respond that there is no answer to these questions—that there is no *single* number that describes the information required. Rather, they say, the quantity of natural gas or the number of machine tools, or the number of engineers that will be demanded, *depends upon the price that will be charged for each.* The quantity demanded also depends upon a number of other variables, such as consumer incomes, the weather, and the prices of other, substitute goods—for example natural gas demand will depend on coal and electricity prices. For the purposes of our discussion, we will concentrate on one of these—the effect of the price of gas on the quantity of gas demanded.

If gas is offered at a very high price, its "market potential" is likely to be zero because buyers are apt to find it less expensive to use some other fuel instead. If the price charged is fairly high, but not prohibitive, perhaps it will attract a few customers for whom the gas is much more convenient than oil or other substitute fuels. If the price is lower still, even more of this fuel is likely to be demanded. Thus:

There is no *one* demand figure for natural gas, for machine tools, or for engineers, but rather a series of alternative demand quantities, each corresponding to a different price.

This information is most easily summarized by means of a graph, the demand curve, *DD'*, illustrated in Figure 4–1.

DEFINITION

A *demand curve* is a graph showing the quantities of some commodity that will be demanded during a specified time period at each of the possible prices for that period.

The demand curve in Figure 4–1 simply describes in detail the story we have just summarized. At a very high price for natural gas, say $7 per thousand cubic feet, demand for it will be zero (point *D* in the figure). At the lower price, say $6, a relatively small market (10 billion cubic feet per year) will emerge (point *B*). At a com-

TABLE 4–1

QUANTITIES OF NATURAL GAS DEMANDED AND SUPPLIED AT VARIOUS PRICES

PRICE (per thousand cubic feet)	QUANTITY DEMANDED (billion cubic feet)	QUANTITY SUPPLIED (billion cubic feet)
$1	82	5
2	70	22
3	55	36
3.50	50	50
4	40	55
5	23	66
6	10	78
7	0	90

paratively low price, say $2 (point *C*), the market will be considerably larger, with 70 billion cubic feet being demanded. The curve enables us to determine, in just the same way, how much will be demanded at any other price that may be set. The same information as is given by the demand curve is also summarized in the first two columns of Table 4–1.[2]

THE SUPPLY CURVE

Price not only influences quantity demanded, it also affects the *amounts* that will be *supplied* either by a single firm or by an entire industry.

A very low price cannot cover the supplier's cost at any output level, and so at prices that are below a profitable level, none of the good will be produced. At a higher price it will pay to undertake some production, the quantity produced depending on the price the commodity

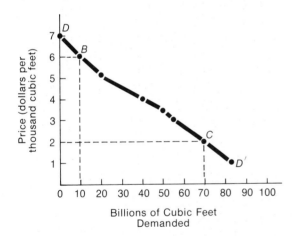

FIGURE 4–1

DEMAND CURVE FOR NATURAL GAS
This curve shows the relation between price and quantity demanded. To sell 70 billion cubic feet of gas, the price must be only $2. If, instead, price is $6, only 10 billion cubic feet will be demanded, and at a $7 price, demand will be zero. To sell more gas, the price must be reduced. That is what the negative slope of the demand curve means.

[2]QUESTION: What would the demand curve look like if the demand for gas were a fixed number that does not change when gas price changes? ANSWER: A vertical line at the fixed number of cubic feet.

will fetch. And at even higher prices, it may be expected that more firms will produce the commodity and thus increase the output of the entire industry. Thus to economists, supply, like demand, cannot be considered a single fixed quantity. Rather, a relationship between the quantity supplied and the price at which the good is offered can conveniently be described by a supply curve (Figure 4–2), which is perfectly analogous to the demand curve shown in Figure 4–1. The corresponding numerical data are given in the first and third columns of Table 4–1.

DEFINITION

A *supply curve* for a firm or for an industry is a graph showing what quantities of some commodity will be offered for sale during a specified time period at each of the prices that may prevail during that period.

EXERCISE

How might a shortage of natural gas affect the supply curve of gas? What influences other than price may affect quantity supplied?

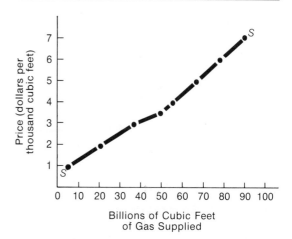

FIGURE 4–2

SUPPLY CURVE FOR NATURAL GAS
This curve shows the relation between price and quantity supplied. To stimulate a larger supply, price must be increased. That is the meaning of the positive slope of the supply curve.

DEMAND, SUPPLY, AND PRICE

In analyzing the determination of price in a market, it is convenient to utilize a graphic apparatus called the supply–demand diagram in which the supply curve and the demand curve are *both* drawn on the same graph. This graph shows, for any particular good, not only how quantity demanded and quantity supplied are affected by price *but also how, in turn, price responds to the influences of supply and demand.* In a later chapter it will be shown that this supply–demand diagram can be utilized legitimately only in certain circumstances. However, the conclusions derived with its aid, if taken as approximations, are widely applicable.

Figure 4–3 shows the supply and demand curves for our illustrative natural gas market,

with *DD* the total demand curve of all consumers in the area (reproduced from Figure 4–1) and *SS* the supply curve of natural gas by the entire industry (reproduced from Figure 4–2). We notice first that, as the curves are drawn, *DD* has a negative slope while *SS* is taken to have a positive slope.[3] Most supply–demand diagrams are drawn with these slopes.

This pattern of slopes has a straightforward interpretation: The negative slope of a demand curve, such as *DD,* asserts that price must be decreased if one wishes to induce an increase in purchases. For example, to increase the number of cubic feet of gas demanded from 23 billion to 70 billion cubic feet per year, price must be reduced from $5 to $2 per thousand cubic feet. Similarly, the positive slope of the supply curve in this case asserts that price

[3]*Slope* was defined in Chapter 2; see especially pages 22–24. A curve is said to have a *positive slope* if, as we go from left to right, the curve moves *upward.* It is said to have a *negative* slope if, as we go from left to right, the curve moves downward.

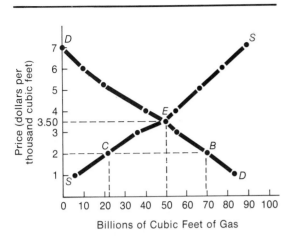

Billions of Cubic Feet of Gas

FIGURE 4–3

SUPPLY–DEMAND EQUILIBRIUM

In a competitive industry, price and quantity sold are determined by the supply curve and the demand curve. The equilibrium price ($3.50) and quantity (50 billion cubic feet) are given by point E, where the two curves intersect. Any other price is inconsistent with equilibrium. For example, at a price of $2, demand is 70 (point B) while supply is only 22 (point C), so that price will be driven up by the unsatisfied demand.

must be increased if one wishes to induce suppliers to bring more of the good to market.

More important for our analysis is the distinction between equilibrium and nonequilibrium prices, and the corresponding distinction between equilibrium and nonequilibrium quantities. In Figure 4–3, the (one and only) equilibrium price is $3.50 per thousand cubic feet, meaning that the quantity of gas supplied (50 billion cubic feet) will be exactly equal to the quantity of gas demanded. At any other price, these two quantities will be unequal and market pressures will force prices to change.

For example, at a price of $2, only 22 billion cubic feet of gas will be supplied (point C) whereas 70 billion cubic feet will be demanded (point B). In such circumstances, we can well imagine that in an unregulated market, competition among potential buyers would promptly bid up the price. Price, in a free market,

cannot remain at $2. In the same way, if the price happens to be $5 per thousand cubic feet, which is higher than the equilibrium value of $3.50, the reader should be able to show with the help of the diagram that quantity supplied will be greater than quantity demanded. Such an oversupply can be expected to force the price downward toward its equilibrium level. Similarly, at any other point in the diagram except that corresponding to a price of $3.50, either quantity demanded will exceed quantity supplied or vice versa.

DEFINITION

An *equilibrium* in economics refers to a situation in which there are no inherent forces that will produce any change. Changes from an equilibrium will occur only as a result of "outside events" that disturb the status quo. Thus, an equilibrium combination of price, supply, and demand refers to a price at which quantity supplied and quantity demanded are equal so that there need not be any frustrated buyers who will bid prices up nor any frustrated sellers who will cut prices to stimulate sales.[4]

In sum, for the example given in Figure 4–3, the price of $3.50 per thousand cubic feet is the only price, and the quantity 50 billion cubic feet is the only quantity, that will not be changed by the market forces of supply and demand. We will see soon what happens when one attempts to legislate some price that does not correspond to the intersection of the supply and demand curves.

The supply–demand diagram is helpful in showing how vague generalizations about the "forces of supply and demand" can be translated into a concrete equilibrium price—the price that equates quantities supplied and de-

---

[4]However, such occurrences as a change in consumer tastes or a new invention that makes production cheaper are outside events that will affect a price, even if it was previously in equilibrium. This will happen because a change in taste will move the position of the demand curve, while a new invention will change the position of the supply curve.

manded, and a corresponding equilibrium quantity—the amount that both buyers and sellers are willing to exchange at the equilibrium price. In the circumstances depicted in Figure 4–3, the equilibrium price will be $3.50, as indicated by point E, the point of intersection between the supply and demand curves. At that price the quantity exchanged will be 50 billion cubic feet. That is, the analysis shows that market forces do not simply constitute a vague, amorphous set of general influences on price and quantity.

In principle, in a free market, the forces of supply and demand are capable of selecting a unique price toward which we may expect price to converge in practice, and a unique quantity, which the amount exchanged will tend to approximate.

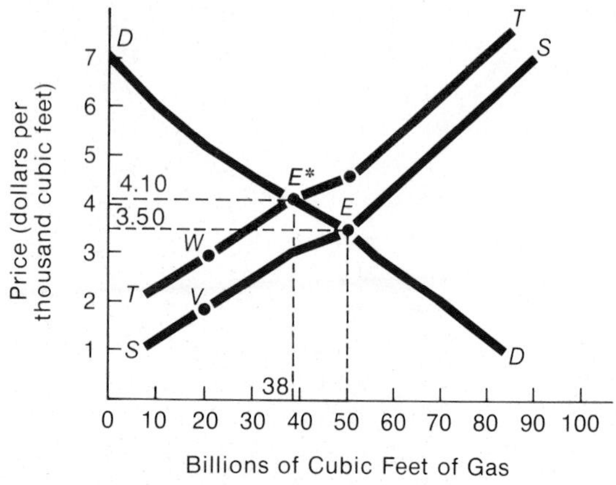

FIGURE 4–4

EFFECT OF A SALES TAX ON NATURAL GAS
A tax of $1 per thousand cubic feet of gas raises the supply curve from SS to TT. Curve TT is exactly $1 higher than SS. The equilibrium point changes from E to E*, and price rises from $3.50 to $4.10, leaving 40 cents of the tax to be paid by suppliers.

APPLICATION: WHO REALLY PAYS A SALES TAX?

The real power of the diagram is its ability to describe the effects on price and quantity exchanged of some prescribed *change* of circumstances. That is, it helps us to determine *how these two crucial quantities respond to a change in any of the conditions that influence them*. For example, let us examine the effect of the imposition of a sales tax, say a tax of $1 per thousand cubic feet, on the price of natural gas. Some may expect sellers simply to raise their price by $1 per thousand cubic feet (or perhaps even more) and pass on the whole of the tax to consumers. Whether sellers are people of good will or soulless gougers does not matter in the case considered. Regardless of their intentions, sellers will be able to pass on *some but not all* of the tax to the consumer.

Figure 4–4 reproduces Figure 4–3 but adds one more supply curve, which takes account of the presence of the tax. This curve, TT, represents the price after tax at which sellers are will-

ing to supply a given quantity of product—that is, the price including the amount the seller must pass on to the government to pay the tax. Suppose, for example, that in the absence of a tax, sellers were willing to supply 22 billion cubic feet of gas at a price of $2 per thousand cubic feet. Then after the tax of $1 per thousand cubic feet, it will take a price of $3 to get suppliers to provide the same amount. Why? Because now, out of every $3 paid by consumers, the supplier receives only $2. We will see next that curve TT must lie exactly $1 above the old supply curve SS at every level of output—it takes exactly $1 more than before to elicit a given quantity of output. For this reason, for example, point V on SS is exactly $1 below point W on the after-tax supply curve TT. Point W tells us that sellers are willing to supply 22 billion cubic feet of gas if they receive a price of $3 per thousand cubic feet including $1 for taxes. This means (point V) that they are willing to supply this amount for a price of $2 *net of taxes*. This is, of course, the price that is relevant to the seller.

The same information is also shown in Table 4–2, which gives the data from which Figure 4–4 is drawn. Table 4–2 is obtained from the information in Table 4–1, giving the supply and demand information for the case where there is no tax. The first thing we notice in Table 4–2 is that the tax creates a difference between the price paid by the buyer and the price received by the seller (first two columns of the table). The price received by the seller (column 2) is always exactly $1 less than that paid by the buyer (column 1). As a result, the supply curve must shift relative to its position where there are no taxes. Thus supply and demand are no longer equal at the $3.50 price that produces equilibrium when the tax is zero. Instead, supply and demand are now equal at a higher price, $4.10, at which 38 billion cubic feet are sold (red entries in the table).

The equilibrium point *after* the tax is imposed must lie at point *E**, the intersection of demand curve *DD* with supply curve *TT*, the *after-tax* supply curve.

TABLE 4–2

EFFECT OF A $1 TAX PER THOUSAND CUBIC FEET ON PRICE OF GAS AND QUANTITY SOLD

(1) PRICE INCLUDING TAX (price to buyers)	(2) PRICE NET OF TAX (price to sellers)	(3) QUANTITY DEMANDED (billion cubic feet)	(4) QUANTITY SUPPLIED (billion cubic feet)
1	0	82	0
2	1	70	5
3	2	55	22
3.50	2.50	50	30
4	3	40	36
4.10	3.10	38	38
5	4	23	55
6	5	10	66
7	6	0	78

To determine the effect of the tax we must compare price and quantity exchanged at the new equilibrium point, *E**, with the price and quantity exchanged that one would encounter if there were no tax (point *E*—the intersection point between the demand curve and the original supply curve, *SS*). We note first that the quantity exchanged will (as might be expected) fall as a result of the sales tax, in this case from 50 down to 38 billion cubic feet.

More interesting for our purposes is what happens to price. We see that, at this quantity, the total price including tax will have risen from $3.50 to $4.10, which means that the price net of tax will have fallen to $3.10. The $1 tax will have been passed on to consumers only in part—price including taxes will have risen 60 cents, from the $3.50 that was charged before to the $4.10 equilibrium price that prevails after the tax. But the remaining part of the tax (40 cents) must be paid by the supplier, not as an altruistic gesture but because the forces of supply and demand give him no alternative. He may try to pass on the entire tax to the consumer; but if he does, consumers will decrease their demand and so automatically *force* him to take back part of the price increase. This will be true as long as the demand curve has a negative slope, because a rise in price encounters consumer resistance in the form of reduced willingness to purchase.

Thus we see that the forces of supply and demand can limit the amount of a tax that suppliers can shift to consumers. The burden of a tax will normally be shared by suppliers and consumers. This fact—that businesses normally cannot avoid paying some of a tax on their products out of their own pockets—may help explain the opposition of industry to proposals to increase taxes.

This conclusion is not to be interpreted as necessarily desirable or undesirable. We might have preferred more or less of the tax to be paid by the supplier. The diagram merely tells us what distribution of the tax burden will be dictated by market forces; it does not tell us whether or not we should be happy about the outcome. It does indicate, for example, that if, as President Carter proposed in 1977, the tax on gasoline is increased in an attempt to conserve fuel, part of it will be paid by consumers, and that may indeed deter them from buying as much gas as before. But part of the tax will be paid by suppliers, and that may perhaps discourage exploration for petroleum in the United States, which may, in turn, decrease its production. The reader can judge whether, on balance, the proposed tax increase was a good idea.

SHIFTS IN DEMAND AND SUPPLY CURVES

Most of our diagrams so far seem to suggest that price is the *only* influence that determines the quantity of a commodity that will be demanded or supplied. The move from one point on a demand curve to another (for example, the move from B to C in Figure 4–1) does, of course, represent the response in the quantity of a commodity demanded to a change in its price. However, quantity demand clearly is influenced by a number of other variables as well.

Some of these variables are controlled by the supplier. For example, the supplier decides how much to spend on advertising, how much to devote to packaging of the product or to increasing its durability. These factors are called decision variables, and they can obviously be used to stimulate demand, though the cost of doing so may not always be worthwhile to the supplier. For example, if doubling the firm's advertising budget brings a 3 percent increase in sales, demand will have been stimulated, but very likely by not enough to make the expenditure worthwhile.

Demand also can be affected heavily by influences that are beyond the control of anyone

in the industry. For example, an increase in consumer incomes that results from general prosperity in the economy will induce higher demands for automobiles and restaurant meals. An increase in rainfall will increase the demand for umbrellas and raincoats. Such factors as consumer incomes and rainfall, which are beyond the control of anyone involved in the analysis, are called exogenous variables— variables whose magnitudes are determined "from outside."

Quantities supplied are also affected by exogenous variables. Discovery of a cheaper fertilizer or a better treatment for plant diseases or an increase in rainfall can all increase the size of crops.

A change in any demand-affecting variable other than price will produce a shift in the demand curve—that is, it will change the position of the curve. This is true whether the variable is a decision variable or an exogenous variable. Such a shift is illustrated in Figure 4–5, which shows how a rise in consumer incomes may affect the demand for natural gas. Suppose that a rise in income leads many families to build larger houses, a substantial proportion of which may be heated by natural gas. (Assume, for simplicity, that this is the only way in which consumer incomes affect the demand for gas.)

Then we see that at a price of $5 per thousand cubic feet, instead of demanding 23 billion cubic feet per year (the amount consumers wanted at their previous, lower incomes, point A), they will now want 43 billion cubic feet (point B). Similarly, at a price of $3 per thousand cubic feet, demand will increase from 55 billion cubic feet (point K) to 82 billion cubic feet (point L). Thus, as a result of the rise in income, at each price the quantity demanded will be larger than it was before. We say that *the demand curve has shifted to the right,* from DD to HH. More generally:

A change in the value of any variable (other than price) that influences demand will produce a *shift* in the demand curve, meaning that *at any*

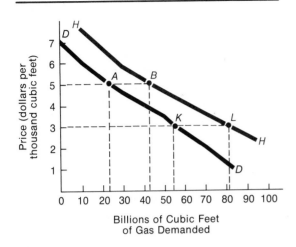

FIGURE 4–5

A SHIFT OF THE DEMAND CURVE

A rise in consumers' incomes shifts the demand curve to the right, from DD to HH. This means that at any given price, more gas will be demanded because consumers can afford more than before. For example, at a price of $5, demand for gas rises from 23 billion cubic feet (point A on DD) to 43 billion cubic feet (point B on HH).

given price consumers will want to buy a different quantity than they wanted before. Similarly, a change in any variable (other than price) that affects quantity supplied will produce a *shift* in the supply curve.

The idea of a shift in a supply or a demand curve is very important for the analysis of policy as we will see in much of the rest of this chapter.

It is also a notion that politicians, journalists, and others sometimes confuse with the effects of a price change on quantity supplied or demanded, and the result is likely to be a badly garbled piece of logic that yields badly garbled conclusions.

As a particularly clear example, consider the following excerpt from a speech by the late Senator John H. Bankhead in which he was arguing in favor of an increase in agricultural price supports. He claimed, among the other virtues he attributed to such supports, that they would help reduce inflation.

> Floors under prices [can] bring about adequate production. . . . The best way to hold down prices of any commodities, and especially of agricultural commodities, is to produce in ample quantities, and the ample supply will in itself automatically bring about fair and reasonable prices.[5]

It is not difficult to track down the fallacy in this argument once one understands the difference between an *increase in supply* that results from a *shift in the supply curve* and an increase in *quantity supplied* resulting from a change in price—that is, from a *move from one point to another on a given supply curve.* Of course, the senator was right in arguing that prices are held down by increasing the abundance of supply—meaning an *outward shift* in the supply curve. In Figure 4–6(a) it can be seen that if an improvement in weather conditions or in agricultural techniques shifts the supply curve from SS to WW, the equilibrium price will drop from P to R. For at the old price, P, the quantity supplied, B, will now be greater than the quantity demanded, A, and price will be forced downward.

But a price support program only forces price up above its equilibrium level, from P to U in Figure 4–6(b), and produces *no shift* in the supply curve. In that case, the best that can be hoped for, from the point of view of inflation, is that the pressures of the resulting excess of supply over demand, N minus M, will force price back to its old, equilibrium level, P, in which case nothing is lost aside from the cost of running the abortive price support program. On the other hand, if the price supports *do* work and the government does succeed in keeping prices raised to U, how then does "the ample supply . . . bring about fair and reasonable prices"? The answer is simple: It does not.

[5]Congressional Record—Senate, April 6, 1943, page 2961.

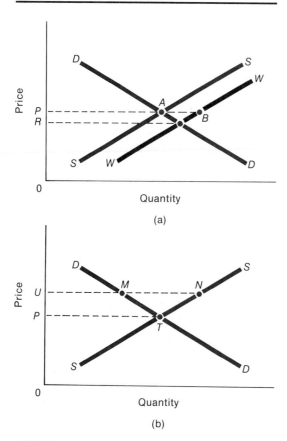

FIGURE 4–6

TWO MEANINGS OF AN "INCREASE IN SUPPLY"

An "increase in supply" can mean either of two things: (a) a rightward shift in the supply curve, meaning that more will be supplied at any given price, or (b) a move along the supply curve, from *T* to *N*. A shift in the supply curve will reduce price (from *P* to *R*), because supplies are more abundant at any given price. But a movement along the supply curve from *T* to *N* in (b) will not make goods cheaper, because by definition it results from a price rise from *P* to *U*.

ATTEMPTS TO RESTRAIN THE MARKET MECHANISM

Whether one likes the price system or not, it has in fact proved to be a powerful piece of machinery that strongly resists attempts to circumvent it.

As we have already noted, there have been many cases where those in authority have been dissatisfied with the decisions produced by the market mechanism. Sometimes, rather than trying to make adjustments in its workings, governments have tried to attack the mechanism directly. When they have been dissatisfied by price levels arrived at by an uncontrolled economy, they have often sought by law either to raise or to lower the prices of specific commodities. In more recent times, fairly comprehensive price controls have been imposed in many economies during the two World Wars and again during the inflationary period at the beginning of the 1970s. Today, governments seek in a variety of ways to keep agricultural prices from falling too low and rents, natural gas prices, and interest rates from rising too high. Regulators determine prices of taxicab rides, electricity, airline tickets, and telephone calls; and when steel companies or auto producers raise their prices, they are likely to find themselves under strong government pressure to rescind or at least to reduce these increases. In short, interference by government in the workings of the market mechanism is a pervasive phenomenon in our economy.

In many of these cases, the feeling of those in authority was that the prices set by the market mechanism were, in some sense, immorally low or immorally high. Penalties were therefore imposed on anyone offering the commodities in question at prices lower or higher than those determined by the regulators.

In each case where such penalties were imposed, virtually the same set of consequences ensued:

1. A persistent shortage of the items whose prices were controlled. Queuing, direct rationing, or any of a variety of other devices, usually inefficient and unpleasant, had to be substituted for the distribution process provided by the price mechanism.

2. An illegal, or "black" market almost invariably arose to supply the commodity at illegal prices. There are, apparently, always some individuals who are willing to take the risks involved in meeting unsatisfied demands illegally, if legal means will not do the job.

3. The prices charged by the black market were almost certainly higher than those that would prevail in an uncontrolled market. After all, black marketeers do expect compensation for the risk of being caught and punished.

4. In each case, a substantial portion of the price, instead of going to those who produced the good or who performed the service, fell into the hands of the black market supplier. For example, a constant complaint in the series of hearings that have marked the history of theater ticket price controls has been that the "ice" (the illegal excess charge) falls into the hands of "ticket scalpers" rather than going to those who invested in the play, or to its producer, or to the playwright, or to the actors.

In many cases attempts to enforce price controls by increased penalties and more active enforcement measures succeeded only in raising the prices charged on the black market, in response to the greater risks to which black marketeers were consequently exposed.

It may be useful to examine a little more closely one of the more recent attempts to circumvent the market mechanism. The next section of this chapter describes a fairly typical example of the regulation of taxi services.

REGULATION OF TAXICABS IN CHICAGO[6]

The market for taxis in Chicago is subject to a dual set of regulations. Fares are controlled by

[6]Much of the information that appears in this section is from Edmund W. Kitch, Marc Isaacson, and Daniel Kasper, "The Regulation of Taxicabs in Chicago," *Journal of Law and Economics,* vol. XIV (October 1971), pages 285–350.

government, but so is the supply of licensed taxicabs. In effect, the law not only prevents prices from rising to their equilibrium level, but it also restricts the supply of taxi services, thereby effectively preventing any fall in the equilibrium price.

Legislation to limit the number of taxicabs in Chicago goes back to 1934. Today, under the Chicago municipal code, 4600 licenses are authorized. This means that some 700 fewer cabs are now authorized than in 1929.

The limited supply of transferable licenses coupled with ever-increasing demand drove up the price of a license on the open market. The price of a license for a single cab has been estimated to be as high as $18,000, with $15,000 probably the typical figure.

Perhaps because regulated fares prevent the payment of competitive wages, there seems to be an unsatisfied demand for taxi drivers by the two large firms that hold 80 percent of the licenses. This is reported by the companies and substantiated by their constant advertising in Chicago's daily and college newspapers. Either as a result or because of deliberate company policy, the two largest firms have been estimated to operate only some 55 percent of the taxicabs for which they have licenses.

Although we will find in Chapters 22 and 23 that the presence of two large firms is not quite consistent with the market conditions that underlie our supply–demand analysis, the situation can nevertheless usefully be characterized with the aid of a supply–demand diagram. In Figure 4–7, as before, SS represents the supply–price relationship that would hold in the absence of controls. However, with the number of licenses limited by law to 4600, the supply of taxi services cannot rise beyond 4600 (point M), no matter what the price. Thus, the effective supply curve cannot lie anywhere to the right of vertical line MU. The effective supply curve, in fact, is now given by the red line STU, which includes the vertical portion TU. That means if price were high enough, say at R, the supply of taxi service would be at

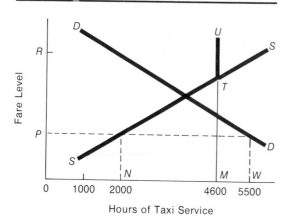

FIGURE 4–7

THE MARKET FOR TAXI SERVICE IN CHICAGO
The number of taxicab hours is not permitted to go higher than *M* so that instead of *SS* the supply curve becomes *STU*. If there is a price ceiling that forces price down to *P*, quantity demanded (*W*) will be above the supply ceiling (*M*) as well as above the actual quantity supplied (*N*). Thus there will be two reasons for the shortage in supply.

the maximum level, *M,* permitted by regulation. However, when price controls are effective, taxi rates may be forced down so far (say to *P*) that the quantity supplied (*N* = 2000) is well below the ceiling. Yet at that price, *P,* the total quantity demanded (that is, *W* = 5500) is considerably greater than *M* = 4600, the maximum supply permitted by law, let alone the amount, *N* = 2000, that is actually supplied. The resulting shortage is typical of what happens whenever price ceilings are put into effect.

Ceilings that reduce prices below their equilibrium level are normally accompanied by shortages. At the equilibrium price, supply and demand are equal. A lower price, which stimulates demand and reduces supply, must therefore make demand greater than supply—it must produce a shortage.

It is not surprising, in these circumstances, that a "gray market" has developed to fill the gap. As in other cities with similar regulations, Chicago is served by a substantial number of illegal taxis. These operate predominantly in the city's poorer black neighborhoods. Many are radio dispatched, usually ordered by telephone. And apparently, very little is done by the police to prevent their operation.

Many observers have concluded that the entire regulatory arrangement leaves much to be desired. The operations of the large taxi firms seem to be on the margin of profitability despite the legal ban on entry of new competitors. Meanwhile, riders complain periodically that taxis are in short supply, and it has been estimated that if a free market in taxi services were permitted in Chicago, the total service supplied would increase somewhere between 42 and 54 percent.

Even if it were generally agreed that the current method of taxicab regulation is undesirable, its elimination would be very difficult. If, for example, it were decided to allow freedom of entry into the taxi business, permitting anyone who wished to do so to operate a cab after, say, passing a strict driving test and a test of knowledge of the streets, the old taxi licenses would clearly become worthless, and current owners of licenses could complain with some justice (and considerable political effect!) that they had arbitrarily been robbed of an investment worth many thousands of dollars, an investment they had made in good faith. This illustrates a very basic point:

Price controls, once adopted, are very difficult to abolish. The reason is that those who are in a position to benefit from those controls, for example, holders of taxi medallions, usually have to pay for the item that entitles them to the privilege, and they will suffer a considerable loss if the controls are eliminated. Such a group typically forms a powerful lobby for retention of the controls.

DISADVANTAGES OF INTERFERENCE WITH THE MARKET MECHANISM

The interests of the general public are the prime concern of economists predisposed against interferences with the market mechanism. In addition to the problems we have already discussed, there are several other unfortunate consequences of interference with the market mechanism. It is appropriate to end the chapter with a brief discussion of some of these.

Unenforceability

Whenever an industry is characterized by a large number of suppliers so that the regulating government agency must monitor the behavior of many independent sellers, attempts to control prices are almost certain to fail. Either black or gray markets will emerge, which charge illegal prices, or some ways will be found in the legitimate sector of the market to evade the law. For example, people who want a scarce rent-controlled apartment will be charged an illegal amount (called "key money") by the landlord or his agent or by the previous tenant, or they may be required to buy some old furniture that goes with the apartment at a high price. The effect is that something akin to the free-market price will generally manage to reemerge, but with this difference: Since the evasion mechanism, whatever its form, will have some operating costs, those costs must be borne by someone. Of course, that someone will be the consumer.

Auxiliary Restrictions

The danger of breakdown of a system of price controls invariably leads to a series of secondary regulations designed to shore up the shaky edifice. Consumers are told when and from whom they are permitted to buy. Attempts are made to prevent the entry of new types of suppliers, sometimes making full use of the powers of the police and the courts. Occasionally, an intricate system of market subdivision is imposed, giving each firm or group of firms its protected category of operations in which others are not permitted to compete. An example is provided by regulation of banking in the United States, where, as part of the process of controlling interest rates, banks are classified into different categories—investment banks, commercial banks, savings banks, and savings and loan associations—each being assigned a set of permissible interest rates and a set of activities at least partly protected by regulation from incursion by others. For example, to keep down interest rates, consumers are "protected" by law from receiving interest on checking accounts issued by commercial banks. To prevent these banks from suffering "undue" competition by savings banks, which can pay interest, it was therefore necessary to prevent savings banks from issuing checks.

Discounts That Take Unwanted Forms

Where prices are controlled, regulation prohibits firms from competing for customers via inducements the customers want most: direct financial benefits. (If these were not what the customers preferred, the regulations would presumably be unnecessary in the first place.) Hence, there is frequent recourse to second-best sorts of inducements. Banks give away cameras and power tools rather than offering higher interest rates. Airlines offer attractive costumes displayed by stewardesses instead of lower fares. But how many dollars is the display of that Italian designer's outfit really worth to the passenger?

Limitation of Volume of Transactions

To the extent that the control mechanism does succeed in affecting price, it can be expected to lead to a corresponding reduction in the volume of transactions. Curiously, this is true whether the regulated price is above or below the free market's equilibrium price. If it is above the price that would equate supply and demand, we can expect demand to be restricted by its imposition. On the other hand, if the imposed price is below the free-market level, supply will be cut down. Since sales volume cannot exceed either the quantity supplied or the quantity demanded, a reduction in the volume of a product that is actually exchanged is likely to result. An important example is provided by agricultural supports, which frequently lead to the production of supplies far greater than consumers are willing to buy at the regulated prices and consequently cause embarrassing surpluses that must be destroyed, given away, or stored at high cost.

Encouragement of Inefficiency

A price that is above the equilibrium level permits the survival of less efficient firms whose high operating costs would prevent them from competing in an unrestricted market. This invitation to continued inefficiency becomes still more serious when entry of new suppliers is prevented as part of the program of enforcement of price regulations. Moreover, with the penalties for inefficiency severely restricted, the motiva-

tion for continued economy of operation by *any* firm is reduced.

Misallocation of Resources

Economists emphasize that departures from free-market prices are likely to produce misuse of the economy's resources—its fuel, raw materials, and labor supply. For by breaking the connection between production costs and prices, consumers are induced to switch demand from commodities and services that can satisfy their desires at a low cost in real resources to other items that are more costly to the economy. Thus, shippers use trucks or barges over routes where the resource cost of rail transportation is lower because artificial restrictions impose floors on railroad rates.

In addition, the regulations are likely to lead directly to significant waste in the use of resources. Just as more complex locks lead to more sophisticated burglary tools, more complex regulations lead to the use of increased resources for their avoidance and evasion. New jobs are created for executives, lawyers, and economists. It may well be conjectured that at least some of the expensive services of these professionals could otherwise have been used more productively elsewhere.

SUMMARY

1. The demand for a product cannot be expressed by a fixed number. Rather, there will generally be a different quantity demanded at each price at which the product is offered.
2. For most products, the higher the price, the lower the quantity demanded. This is what causes the demand curve to have its characteristic negative slope.
3. Price also affects the quantity of a commodity that will be supplied.
4. A positively sloping curve for a given product means that it takes an increase in price to induce suppliers to offer a larger quantity of that good.
5. The price at which quantity supplied equals quantity demanded is shown by that point on a graph where the supply and the demand curves intersect. This point also indicates the quantity that will be sold.
6. A tax on a good sold in a market controlled by supply and demand will raise the price, but usually by an amount equal to only *part* of the tax. Thus the seller, as well as the buyer, will have to pay part of the tax. This

is so because the rise in price will tend to reduce demand, thus keeping a downward pressure on price.

7. Changes in consumer incomes, advertising, prices of competing products, and many other influences, will affect demand and supply. These variables will cause a shift in the demand or supply curves and will produce a change in price and quantity sold, which can be determined from the supply–demand diagram.

8. An attempt by government to force prices above or below their equilibrium levels is likely to lead to shortages or oversupplies, black markets in which goods are sold at illegal prices, and to a variety of other problems. This is one of the 12 Ideas for Beyond the Final Exam.

CONCEPTS FOR REVIEW

Demand curve
Supply curve
Equilibrium price
Equilibrium quantity
Decision variables

Exogenous variables
Shift in supply or demand curve
Black or gray markets
Price ceilings

QUESTIONS FOR DISCUSSION

1. How often do you go to the movies? Would you go less often if a ticket cost twice as much? Distinguish between your demand curve for movie tickets and your "quantity demanded" at the current price.
2. What would you expect to be the shape of a demand curve
   a. for a type of medicine that means life or death for the patient?
   b. for the gasoline sold by Sam's Gas Station, which is surrounded by many other gas stations?
3. Show on a supply–demand diagram what will happen to the quantity of wheat demanded and supplied if a government decree places a minimum on the price of wheat that is above the equilibrium price. What are the likely results? What would happen if the minimum price is set below the equilibrium price?
4. Consider a medicine that is a matter of life and death for a patient, and suppose its price is determined by supply and demand. If a tax of $1 is charged on each bottle of the medicine, how much do you think its price will rise? Why is this result different from the case of a tax on natural gas considered in the text?
5. Show how the following demand curves are likely to shift in response to the indicated changes:
   a. the effect on the demand curve for umbrellas when rainfall increases
   b. the effect on the demand curve for tea when coffee prices rise
   c. the effect on the demand curve for tea when sugar prices rise
6. Discuss the likely effects of
   a. rent ceilings on the supply of apartments
   b. minimum wages on the demand for teen-age workers
7. Use supply–demand diagrams to show what may happen in each of the two cases considered in Question 6 above.
8. Drinking water is costly to supply. Draw a supply–demand diagram showing how much water would be bought if water were supplied by a private industry controlled by supply and demand. In the same diagram show how much will be consumed if water is supplied by a city government at zero charge. What do you conclude from these results about areas of the country in which water is in short supply?

two

Introduction
to Macroeconomics:
Basic Concepts

5

Macroeconomics
and Microeconomics

Economics has traditionally been divided into two fields: microeconomics and macroeconomics. These rather inelegant words are derived from the Greek—"micro" means something small and "macro" means something large. Although they were not specifically described as such, some of the basic notions and subject matter of microeconomics were introduced in Chapters 3 and 4. This chapter does the same for macroeconomics.

We begin the chapter by investigating the dividing line between microeconomics and macroeconomics. How do the two parts of the discipline differ and why? Next, we stress that

while the *questions* studied by macroeconomists differ from those addressed by microeconomists, the underlying *tools* each group uses are almost the same. Supply and demand provide the basic organizing framework for constructing macroeconomic models, just as they do for microeconomic models. Third, we define some important macroeconomic concepts, like recession, inflation, and gross national product. Fourth, we look briefly at the broad sweep of American economic history to obtain some evaluation of the prevalence and seriousness of the macroeconomic problems of recession and inflation. And, finally, we preview what is to come in Part Three by introducing the notion of government management of the economy.

DRAWING A LINE BETWEEN MACROECONOMICS AND MICROECONOMICS

In microeconomics *we study the behavior of individual decision-making units.* The fleet owners, taxi drivers, and passengers of Chapter 4 are all individual decision-making units; so are the homeowners and firms who purchase natural gas. How do they decide what courses of action are in their own best interests? How are these millions of decisions coordinated by the market mechanism, and with what consequences? Questions like these are the substance of microeconomics and are taken up in Parts Four through Seven.

Although Plato and Aristotle might wince at the abuse of language, microeconomics includes the decisions of some astonishingly large units. General Motors Corporation and the American Telephone and Telegraph Company, for instance, have annual sales that exceed the total production of many of the smaller nations of the world. Yet someone who studies the pricing policies of AT&T is a microeconomist, whereas someone who studies inflation in Trinidad–Tobago is a macroeconomist. So the micro versus macro distinction in economics is certainly not predicated solely on size.

What, then, is the basis for this time-honored distinction? Whereas microeconomics focuses on the decisions of individual units (no matter how large), *macroeconomics concentrates on the behavior of entire economies* (no matter how small). Rather than looking at the price and output decisions of a single company, macroeconomists study the overall price level, unemployment rate, and other things that we call economic aggregates.

AGGREGATION AND MACROECONOMICS

What is an "economic aggregate"? Nothing but an *abstraction* that people find convenient in describing some salient feature of economic life. For example, while we observe the prices of butter, telephone calls, and movie tickets every day, we can never observe "the price level." Yet many people (not only economists) find it both natural and convenient to speak of "the cost of living"—so convenient in fact, that the Bureau of Labor Statistics' monthly attempts at measuring it are widely publicized by the news media.

Among the most important of these abstract notions that are used in macroeconomics is the concept of national output. The process by which real objects like hairpins, baseballs, cigarettes, and theater tickets get combined into an abstraction called national output is called aggregation, and it is one of the foundations of macroeconomics. We can illustrate it by a simple example.

Imagine a nation called Agraria, whose economy is far simpler than the U.S. economy: Business firms in Agraria produce nothing but foodstuffs to sell to consumers. Rather than deal separately with all the markets for pizzas, candy bars, hamburgers, milk, and so on, macroeconomists group them all into a single abstract "market for output." Thus, when macroeconomists in Agraria announce that "firms in Agraria produced 10 percent more output this year than they did last year," are they referring to more potatoes or hot dogs, more soybeans or green peppers? The answer is: They do not care! Gertrude Stein once said "rose is a rose is a rose." In the aggregate measures of macroeconomics, output is output, no matter what form it takes.

Amalgamating the many markets into one means that distinctions among the different products are ignored. Can we really believe that no one cares whether the national output of Agraria consists of $800,000 worth of pickles and $200,000 worth of ravioli rather than $500,000 each of lettuce and tomatoes? Surely this is too much to swallow! Macroeconomists clearly do not believe that no one cares; instead, they rest the case for aggregation on two foundations.

First: While the *composition* of demand and supply in the various markets may be terribly interesting and important for *some* purposes (such as how income is distributed and what kinds of diets the citizens enjoy or endure), it may be of little consequence for the economy-wide issues of inflation and unemployment—the issues that concern macroeconomists.

Second: During economic fluctuations, markets tend to move in unison.

When demand in the economy rises, there is more demand for potatoes *and* tomatoes, more demand for artichokes *and* pickles, more demand for ravioli *and* hot dogs.

There are, of course, exceptions to both these principles, but they seem serviceable enough as approximations. In fact, if they were not, there would be no discipline called macroeconomics, and this book would be only half as long as it is. (Lest this cause you a twinge of regret, bear in mind that such things as unemployment and inflation would be far more difficult to control without macroeconomics, and that would be even more regrettable.)

THE LINE OF DEMARCATION REVISITED

These two principles—that markets normally move together and that the composition of demand and supply may be unimportant for some purposes—enable us to draw a different kind of dividing line between the territories of microeconomics and macroeconomics.

In macroeconomics, we typically assume that most details of resource allocation and income distribution are of secondary importance to the overall rates of inflation and unemployment.

In microeconomics, we typically ignore inflation and unemployment and focus instead on how individual markets allocate resources and distribute income.

To use a well-worn metaphor, the macroeconomist analyzes the determination of the size of the economic "pie," paying scant attention to what is inside it or to how it gets divided among the dinner guests. A microeconomist, on the other hand, assumes that we have a pie of the right size and frets over its ingredients and its division. If you have ever baked or eaten a pie, you will realize that either approach alone is a trifle myopic.

Microeconomists worry, for example, about whether or not society would be better off if 1000 workers left peanut farming and started drilling for oil instead. But who, after all, would really care about such allocation problems if the economy were constantly beset by ruinous depressions and disruptive inflations? If millions of potential workers were neither farming nor drilling nor doing any other productive work, it would be of secondary importance whether society could benefit by shifting 1000 workers from one job to another. So:

Only successful macroeconomic policy will create the conditions under which the questions addressed by microeconomics are important.

By the same token, who would really be interested in expanding the size of the economy if the market mechanism stubbornly turned out goods and services that consumers did not want or that even did them harm? Thus:

Without a properly functioning microeconomic mechanism for allocating resources, the importance of many macroeconomic issues would be rather minor.

In some chapters of this book (especially in Part Three), macroeconomic issues are discussed as if they could be divorced from questions of resource allocation and income distribution. In other chapters (especially those in Parts Four through Seven), microeconomic problems are investigated with scarcely a word about overall inflation and unemployment. Only much later in the book (especially in Parts Eight through Ten) are the two modes of analysis brought to bear simultaneously on the same social problems. This grouping arrangement is just a pedagogical device. The crucial interconnection between macroeconomics and microeconomics is with us all the time in the real world. There is, after all, only one economy.

SUPPLY AND DEMAND IN MACROECONOMICS

Some students reading this book will be taking a course that concentrates on macroeconomics while others will be studying microeconomics. Yet Chapter 4's discussion of supply and demand will serve as an invaluable introduction to both fields. Why? Because the basic apparatus of supply and demand is just as applicable in macroeconomics as it is in microeconomics.

Figure 5–1 shows two diagrams that should look familiar from Chapter 4. In Figure 5–1(a), there is a downward-sloping demand curve, labeled *DD,* and an upward-sloping supply

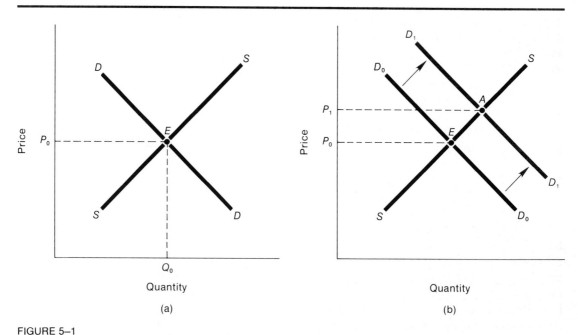

FIGURE 5–1

TWO INTERPRETATIONS OF AN INCREASE IN DEMAND

Part (a) shows an equilibrium at point *E,* where demand curve *DD* intersects supply curve *SS.* Part (b) shows how this equilibrium moves from point *E* to point *A* if the demand curve moves outward. If this graph represents the market for natural gas, as it did in the previous chapter, then it shows an increase in the price of gas. But if the graph represents the aggregate market for "national output," then it shows inflation—a rise in the general price level.

curve, labeled SS. The axes labeled "Price" and "Quantity" do not specify what commodity they refer to because this is a multipurpose diagram. To start on familiar terrain, first imagine that this is a picture of the market for natural gas, so the price axis measures the price of gas while the quantity axis measures the amount of gas demanded and supplied. As we know, if there are no interferences, equilibrium will be at point E, with the price of gas at P_0 and the quantity of output at Q_0.

Next, suppose that something happens to shift the demand curve outward. For example, we learned in Chapter 4 that an increase in consumer incomes might do this. Figure 5–1(b) shows this shift as a rightward movement of the demand curve from D_0D_0 to D_1D_1. Equilibrium has shifted from E to A, so both price and output have risen.

Now let us reinterpret Figure 5–1 as representing an abstract market for "national output." This is one of those abstractions—an economic aggregate—that we described earlier. No one has ever seen, touched, smelled, or eaten a "unit of national output," but these are the kinds of abstractions upon which macroeconomic analysis is built. To continue the interpretation, think of the price measured on the vertical axis as being another abstraction— the overall price index, or "cost of living." Then DD in Figure 5–1(a) is called an aggregate demand curve, and SS is called an aggregate supply curve.

With this reinterpretation, Figure 5–1(b) can be used to view the macroeconomic problem of inflation, that is, of rising prices. We see from the figure that the increase in aggregate demand, whatever its cause, has pushed up the price level from P_0 to P_1. If demand kept shifting out month after month, we would say that the economy was suffering from inflation.

DEFINITION
Inflation refers to a sustained increase in the price level.

Deflation refers to a sustained decrease in the price level.

The other principal problems of macroeconomics, recession and unemployment, also can be illustrated on a supply–demand diagram, this time by shifting the demand curve in the other direction. Figure 5–2 repeats the supply and demand curves of Figure 5–1(a) and in addition depicts a *decrease* in aggregate demand, which shifts the demand curve from D_0D_0 to D_2D_2. Equilibrium now moves from point E to point B so that national output declines from Q_0 to Q_2. This is what we normally mean by a recession.

DEFINITION
A *recession* is a period of time during which the total output of the economy declines.

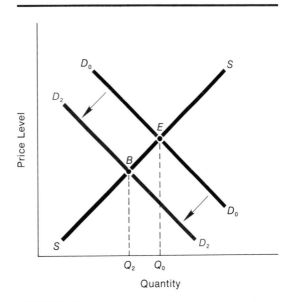

FIGURE 5–2

AN ECONOMY SLIPPING INTO A RECESSION
In this aggregate supply–demand diagram, there is an initial equilibrium at point E, where demand curve D_0D_0 intersects supply curve SS. When demand falls from D_0D_0 to D_2D_2, equilibrium moves to point B, and output falls from Q_0 to Q_2.

THE GROSS NATIONAL PRODUCT

While there are several ways to measure total output of the economy, the most popular choice undoubtedly is the gross national product, a term you have probably encountered in the news media. The gross national product, or "GNP" for short, is the most comprehensive measure of the output of all the factories, offices, and shops in the U.S. economy. In Chapter 17 we spend several pages defining the GNP in much more detail and explaining how government statisticians measure it. For now, we can settle for a less complete definition.

DEFINITION
Gross national product is the total value of all the final goods and services produced by the economy during a specified period of time, usually one year.[1]

The word *value* in the definition raises the question of what prices are used in evaluating the different outputs. The official data offer two choices. First, we can value each good and service at the price at which it was actually sold during the year. If we do this, the resulting measure is called *nominal GNP,* or *money GNP,* or *GNP in current dollars.* This seems like a perfectly sensible choice. But as a measure of output, it has one serious drawback: nominal GNP rises when prices rise, even if there is no increase in actual production. For example, if hamburgers cost 75 cents this year but cost only 60 cents last year, then 100 hamburgers will contribute $75 to this year's nominal GNP, but only $60 to last year's. But 100 hamburgers are still 100 hamburgers—output has not grown.

---

[1]The word *final* means that we only count goods and services that are produced for their ultimate users. "Intermediate" goods, those that will subsequently be used to produce other goods, are not counted. For a full discussion of this, see Chapter 17, pages 315–316.

For this reason, government statisticians have devised an alternative measure that corrects for inflation by evaluating all goods and services at some fixed set of prices. (Currently, the prices of 1972 are used.) For example, if the hamburgers were valued at 60 cents each in both years, $60 worth of hamburger output would be included in GNP in each year. When we treat every output in this way, we obtain the *real GNP,* or *GNP in constant dollars.* The news media often refer to it as "GNP corrected for inflation." Throughout most of this book, and certainly when we are discussing the nation's output, it is the real GNP that we shall be concerned with.

DEFINITION
Nominal GNP is calculated by valuing all outputs at current market prices.

Real GNP is calculated by valuing all outputs at the prices that prevailed in some agreed-upon year (currently 1972). Therefore, real GNP is a far better measure of changes in national production.

These specific definitions lead us to a working definition of a recession as a period in which real GNP declines.

THE ECONOMY ON A ROLLER COASTER

With these concepts in mind, Figures 5–3 and 5–4 provide a capsule summary of American economic history since the Civil War. Figure 5–3 charts the behavior of real GNP over a period of approximately 100 years. The pronounced upward slope of the line indicates that the main feature has been economic growth. But the figure also shows that recessions—periods during which the real GNP decreased—have been a persistent feature of America's economic performance.

The history of the price level (Figure 5–4) displays a broadly similar pattern, but one that differs in some important respects. Prices also have been generally rising—that is, inflation has been much more common than deflation—but there have been several periods of marked price stability, such as 1922–1929. And there have also been periods, generally in serious recessions or depressions, in which prices have fallen, such as 1929–1933.

The following exercise may be enlightening. Cover the portions of Figures 5–3 and 5–4 that deal with the period beginning in 1941, the portions to the right of the shaded area in each figure. The picture that emerges for the 1867–1940 period is of an economy on a roller coaster. In Figure 5–3, the ups and downs around the underlying growth trend are frequent and sometimes quite pronounced. In Figure 5–4 we see periods of both inflation and deflation, with hardly any upward trend at all. Indeed, prices at the eve of World War II were not much higher than they were at the close of the Civil War.

Now do the reverse. Cover the data prior to 1946 and look only at the postwar period. There is, indeed, a difference. The upward trend in real GNP predominates more, and the periodic recessions are much less severe. While perfection has not been achieved, things do look much better. When we turn to the price level, however, things look rather worse. Gone are the periods of falling prices that occurred before World War II; even the periods of price stability are rather rare.

This quick inspection of the data suggests that something has happened. The U.S. economy behaved differently in 1946–1977 than it did in 1867–1940. Many economists attribute this shift in the economy's behavior to lessons the government has learned about managing the economy—lessons that we will be learning in Part Three. When you look at the pre-1941 data, you are looking at an unmanaged economy that went through booms and recessions for "natural" economic reasons. The government did little about either. When you examine the post-1945 data, on the other hand, you are looking at an economy that has been increasingly managed by government policy—sometimes successfully and sometimes unsuccessfully. The booms are less exuberant and the recessions less severe. But a cost seems to have been exacted: the economy appears to be more inflation-prone than it was in the more distant past.

THE GREAT DEPRESSION OF THE 1930s

As you look at these graphs, the Great Depression of the 1930s is bound to catch your eye. The decline in economic activity from 1929 to 1933 (see Figure 5–3) was the most severe in our nation's history, and the rapid deflation (see Figure 5–4) was most unusual. The Depression is but a dim memory now, but those who lived through it (your grandparents?) will never forget it.

While statistics usually conceal the true drama of economic events, this is not so of the Great Depression—they stand here as a bitter testimony to its severity. From its 1929 high to its 1933 low, the production of goods and services dropped 31 percent and the price level fell 22 percent. Business investment almost ceased entirely, and stock market values slumped to less than one-sixth their 1929 level. The unemployment rate rose ominously from about 3 percent in 1929 to 25 percent in 1933— one person in four was jobless. From the data alone, one can virtually conjure up pictures of soup lines, beggars on street corners, closed factories, and homeless families. (See the boxed insert on page 78.) And, unlike many earlier and later recessions that plagued the U.S. economy, the Great Depression was a worldwide event. No country was spared its ravages. This traumatic episode literally changed the history of many nations. In Germany, it facilitated the ascendancy of the Nazi party. In the United States, it enabled Franklin Roosevelt's Democratic party to engineer one of the most dramatic political realignments in history and to push through a host of political and economic reforms.

The worldwide depression also caused a much-needed revolution in the thinking of economists. Up until the 1930s, the prevailing economic theory held that a capitalist economy, while it occasionally misbehaved, had a "natural" tendency to cure recessions or inflations by itself. The roller coaster bounced around but did not normally run off the tracks.

Nor was this optimistic view confined to academia. It characterized the views of most politicians (certainly including President Herbert

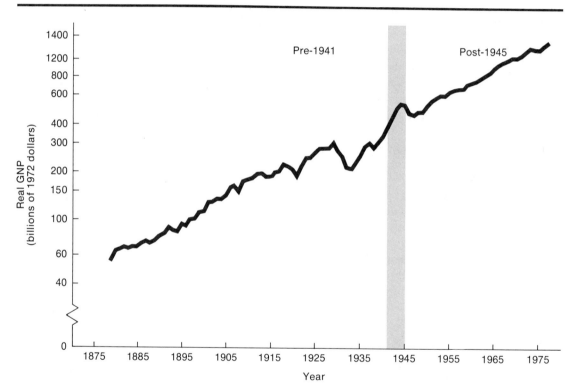

FIGURE 5–3

REAL GROSS NATIONAL PRODUCT OF THE UNITED STATES, 1879–1977
This time series chart displays the behavior of real gross national product in the United States from 1879 to 1977. (Real GNP is measured in 1972 prices.) The Great Depression (1929–1933) stands out vividly. The years during World War II are shaded. Does the line look smoother to the right of this shaded area? Notice that the vertical axis is calibrated by what is called a "ratio scale." This means, for example, that the distance between 1000 and 100 is the same as the distance between 100 and 10.

Source: Constructed by the authors from data for 1889–1977 in *Historical Statistics of the United States* and *Survey of Current Business,* and for 1879–1888 kindly furnished by Professor Benjamin Klein.

The Great Depression of the 1930s

Hoover) and business leaders as well. As the great American humorist Will Rogers remarked with characteristic sarcasm:

It's almost been worth this depression to find out how little our big men knew. Mayby [sic] this depression is just "normalcy" and we don't know it. It's made a dumb guy as smart as a smart one. . . . Depression used to be a state of mind. Now it's a state of coma, now it's permanent. Last year we said, "Things can't go on like this," and they didn't, they got worse.[2]

[2]From *Sanity Is Where You Find It* by Will Rogers, edited by Donald Day; copyright © 1955 by Rogers Company; reprinted by permission of Houghton Mifflin Company; pages 120–21.

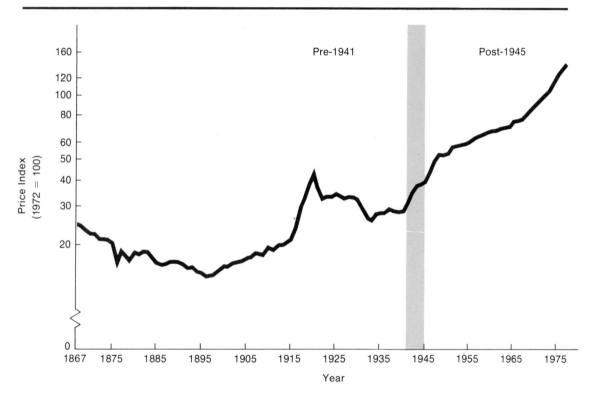

FIGURE 5–4

THE PRICE LEVEL IN THE UNITED STATES, 1867–1977

This time series chart portrays the behavior of the U.S. price level from 1867 to 1977. (The specific price index used is called the *GNP deflator,* and it is defined as the ratio of nominal GNP divided by real GNP.) Once again, the vertical axis has a ratio scale, and the World War II years are shaded. The difference between the 1867–1940 period and the 1946–1977 period is quite pronounced.

Source: Constructed by the authors from data for 1889–1977 in *Historical Statistics of the United States* and *Survey of Current Business,* and for 1867–1888 kindly furnished by Professor Benjamin Klein.

The stubbornness of the Great Depression shook almost everyone's faith in the ability of the economy to right itself. In Cambridge, England, this questioning attitude led John Maynard Keynes, one of the world's most respected economists, to write *The General Theory of Employment, Interest, and Money* (1936). Probably the most important book in economics of the twentieth century, it carried a rather revolutionary message. Keynes discarded the notion that the economy always gravitated toward high levels of employment, replacing it with the assertion that—if a pessimistic outlook led business firms and consumers to curtail

Life in "Hooverville"

During the worst years of the Great Depression, unemployed workers often congregated in shantytowns on the outskirts of many major cities. Conditions in these slums were deplorable. With a heavy dose of irony, these communities were known as "Hoovervilles," in honor of the president of the United States who preached rugged individualism. A contemporary observer described a Hooverville in New York City as follows:

> It was a fairly popular "development" made up of a hundred or so dwellings, each the size of a dog house or chickencoop, often constructed with much ingenuity out of wooden boxes, metal cans, strips of cardboard or old tar paper. Here human beings lived on the margin of civilization by foraging for garbage, junk, and waste lumber. I found some splitting or sawing wood with dull tools to make fires; others were picking through heaps of rubbish they had gathered before their doorways or cooking over open fires or battered oilstoves. Still others spent their days improving their rent-free homes, making them sometimes fairly solid and weatherproof. . . . Most of them, according to the police, lived by begging or trading in junk; when all else failed they ate at the soup kitchens or public canteens. They were of all sorts, young and old, some of them rough-looking and suspicious of strangers.

They lived in fear of being forcibly removed by the authorities, though the neighborhood people in many cases helped them and the police tolerated them for the time being.

A Hooverville in New York City.

Source: Mathew Josephson, *Infidel in the Temple* (Alfred A. Knopf, New York, 1967), pages 82–83.

their spending plans—the economy might be condemned to stagnation for years and years.

While this doleful prognosis sounded all too realistic at the time, Keynes closed his book on a hopeful note. For he showed how government actions might shove the economy out of its depressed state. The lessons he taught the world then are the lessons we shall be learning in Part Three. They show how governments can manage their economies so that recessions will not turn into depressions and depressions will not last as long as the Great Depression. While Keynes was working on *The General Theory,* he wrote his friend George Bernard Shaw that, "I believe myself to be writing a book on economic theory which will largely revolutionize . . . the way the world thinks about economic problems." In many ways, he was right.

THE AMERICAN ECONOMY SINCE WORLD WAR II

The Great Depression finally ended with mobilization for war in the early 1940s. With total spending at extraordinarily high levels during the war, mostly because of government expenditures, the economy boomed and the unemployment rate fell as low as 1.2 percent.

Wartime spending of this magnitude usually leads to inflation, but much of the potential inflation during World War II was contained by legal limitations on prices. With prices held below the levels at which quantity supplied equaled quantity demanded, many goods had to be rationed, and shortages of consumer goods were quite common. All of this ended with the lifting of controls after the war. The shortages, rationing, and black markets were replaced by a burst of inflation.

The period from the end of the war until the early 1960s showed a considerable resemblance to the earlier period of growth with recessions prior to 1929. The main difference was that the four recessions between 1948 and

1961 were noticeably shorter and less severe than their prewar counterparts. Moderate but persistent inflation also became a fact of life.

When the economy emerged from recession in 1961, it entered what proved to be the longest uninterrupted period of expansion in our nation's history. GNP grew smartly and unemployment declined steadily, while the price level, though continuing to rise, showed no tendency to accelerate.

The 1962–1966 boom was credited widely to the success of what came to be called "The New Economics," a term the media created for the policy of economic management prescribed by Keynes in the 1930s. For a while it looked as if we could avoid both unemployment and inflation. But the optimistic verdicts were premature in both cases.

Inflation was the first problem to crop up, beginning in about 1966. Its major cause, as it had been so many times in the past, was high levels of wartime spending—this time for the Vietnam War. Federal defense expenditures skyrocketed from $49 billion in 1965 to $77 billion in 1968. Most economists agree that the inflation that still plagues us had its origins in that episode, though much has happened since.

Unemployment was the next problem to arise. The economic expansion ground to a halt in 1969, and a short and mild recession ensued. Despite this, inflation continued at rates that were very high by the standards of that time—5 to 6 percent a year.

In the face of the persistent inflation, and with the economy beginning to pick up steam once again, President Richard Nixon instituted his "New Economic Policy" in a dramatic radio and television address to the nation in August 1971. This sweeping change in policy included America's first experiment with wage and price controls in peacetime. The controls program, which will be discussed in Chapter 16, held the inflation rate in check for a time as the economic expansion of 1971–1973 progressed. But inflation worsened dramatically in 1973, mainly because of the explosion in food prices caused by poor harvests around the world in 1972 and 1973.

THE GREAT RECESSION AND ITS AFTERMATH

Then, in October 1973, things began to get much worse, not only for the United States, but for all the oil-importing nations of the world. The war between Israel and the Arab nations led to an embargo on oil shipments to several Western countries and then to a quadrupling of the price of oil by the Organization of Petroleum Exporting Countries (OPEC). The rate of inflation skyrocketed in 1974 to levels not seen in this country since 1947.

While staggering price increases for oil and other energy resources were a principal component of this rapid inflation, they were not the only ones. Continued poor harvests in 1974 in many parts of the globe kept world food prices rising rapidly. Prices of other raw materials also skyrocketed. Naturally, these higher costs of fuel and other materials soon were reflected in the prices of manufactured goods.

By unhappy coincidence, these events coincided with the lifting of wage and price controls. The decontrol process began gradually in the closing months of 1973 and was complete by April 1974. Just as had happened after World War II, the elimination of controls led to an acceleration of inflation as prices that had been held artificially below equilibrium levels were allowed to rise.

For all these reasons, the inflation rate in the United States soared to above 12 percent during 1974. Most other nations suffered a similar inflationary surge—many much worse than ours.

Meanwhile, real GNP, which had stagnated but not declined during 1973, began to slide in 1974. In late 1974 and early 1975, this slide turned into a rout as the U.S. economy plummeted into its longest and most severe reces-

sion since the 1930s. In total, real GNP fell by about 6 percent between late 1973 and early 1975. The unemployment rate rose from less than 5 percent to nearly 9 percent over this same period. Thus, both of the twin evils of macroeconomics—inflation and unemployment—were unusually virulent in 1974 and 1975. Indeed, a new term—stagflation—was coined to refer to the simultaneous occurrence of economic *stag*nation and rapid in*flation*.

Thanks partly to government actions, but mostly to natural economic forces, the economic collapse ended in the spring of 1975, and a sustained, if unspectacular, recovery began—a recovery that, at this writing, is still proceeding. However, since it started from such a low ebb—an unemployment rate of 9 percent in early 1975—and proceeded at such a moderate pace, the recovery period was 3 years old before the unemployment rate was down to $6\frac{1}{4}$ percent, a rate that would have been considered intolerably high in the 1960s.

On the price front, three major forces contributed to a remarkably fast diminution of inflation beginning in mid-1975. First, the explosion in food and fuel prices was not repeated. These prices settled down at *levels* far higher than in the early 1970s, but ceased being engines of *inflation*. Second, the adjustment to the end of price controls ended in late 1974, and price behavior returned to normalcy. Third, just as had happened in the past, the severity of the recession put a brake on inflation. The inflation rate tumbled from over 12 percent a year in 1974 to around 5 percent in 1976, and, except for an acceleration in early 1978, has generally remained in the 5 to 7 percent range since then.

THE PROBLEM OF MACROECONOMIC STABILIZATION

This brief look at the historical record shows that our economy has not generally produced a steady pattern of growth without inflation. Rather, it has been buffeted by periodic bouts of unemployment or inflation, and sometimes has been plagued by both. There was also a hint, in the discussion, that government policies may have had something to do with the fact that macroeconomic performance during the years 1946 to 1973 was so greatly superior to what it had been prior to World War II. Let us now expand upon this hint a little bit.

DEFINITION

Stabilization policy is the name given to government economic programs designed to prevent or shorten recessions and to counteract inflation (that is, to *stabilize* prices).

We can provide a preliminary analysis of stabilization policy by using the basic tools of aggregate supply and aggregate demand analysis that were introduced early in this chapter. To facilitate this, we have reproduced as Figures 5–5 and 5–6 two of the diagrams found earlier in this chapter [Figures 5–1(b) and 5–2], but we now give them slightly different interpretations.

Figure 5–5 gives a simplified view of government policy to fight unemployment. We suppose that, in the absence of government intervention, the economy would have reached an equilibrium at point *E,* where demand curve D_0D_0 crosses supply curve *SS.* Now if the

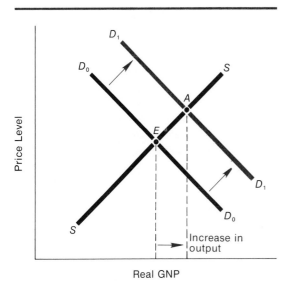

FIGURE 5–5

STABILIZATION POLICY TO FIGHT UNEMPLOYMENT

This diagram duplicates Figure 5–1(b), but here we assume that point *E*—the intersection of demand curve D_0D_0 and supply curve *SS*—corresponds to high unemployment. With the kind of policy tools that we will study in Part Three, the government can shift the aggregate demand curve upward to D_1D_1. This would raise output and lower unemployment.

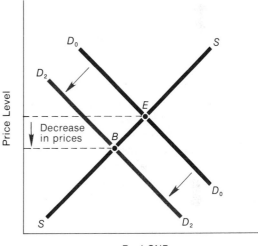

FIGURE 5–6

STABILIZATION POLICY TO FIGHT INFLATION

This diagram duplicates Figure 5–2, but here we assume that point *E*—the equilibrium the economy would attain without government intervention— represents high inflation (that is, the price level corresponding to point *E* is far above last year's price level). By using its policy instruments to shift the aggregate demand curve down to D_2D_2, the government can keep this year's price level lower than it would otherwise have been; in other words, the government can reduce inflation.

output corresponding to point E is so low that many workers are unemployed, *the government can reduce unemployment by increasing aggregate demand.* In the diagram, this action shifts the demand curve to D_1D_1, causing equilibrium to move to point A. In general:

Recessions and unemployment are often caused by insufficient aggregate demand. When this is so, government polices that augment demand—such as increases in government spending—can be an effective way to increase output and reduce unemployment.

The opposite type of demand management is called for when inflation is the main macroeconomic problem. Figure 5–6 illustrates this case. Here again, point E, the intersection of demand curve D_0D_0 and supply curve SS, is the equilibrium that would be reached in the absence of government policy. But now we suppose that the price level corresponding to point E is considered "too high." This means that the *change* in the price level from the previous period to this one would be too rapid if the economy moved to point E. Inflation would be too high. A government program that reduces demand from D_0D_0 to D_2D_2 (for

example, a reduction in government spending) can keep prices down and thereby reduce inflation. Thus:

Inflation is frequently caused by aggregate demand racing ahead too fast. When this is the case, government policies that reduce aggregate demand can be effective anti-inflationary devices.

This, in brief, summarizes the job of stabilization policy. The government can limit both recessions and inflations by managing aggregate demand; pushing it ahead when it would otherwise lag, and restraining it when it would otherwise grow too quickly. The specific methods by which the task of demand management is accomplished will occupy our attention in several subsequent chapters. While studying these materials, it is important not to lose sight of the basic aim of stabilization policy: to keep the growth of aggregate demand in balance with that of aggregate supply. It is also important to remember that economists still have much to learn about the problem, and that demand management does not always work out in the way we would like!

SUMMARY

1. Microeconomics studies the decisions of individuals and firms, how these decisions interact, and how they influence the allocation of society's resources and the distribution of income. Macroeconomics looks at the behavior of entire economies and studies the pressing social problems of inflation and unemployment.
2. While their respective subject matters differ greatly, the basic tools of microeconomics and macroeconomics are virtually identical. Both rely heavily on the supply and demand analysis introduced in Chapter 4.
3. Macroeconomic models use abstract concepts like "the price level" and "national output" that are derived by amalgamating many different markets into one. This process is known as aggregation, and should not be taken literally but should be viewed as a useful approximation.
4. The best specific measure of the abstract concept "national output" is the gross national product (GNP), which is obtained by adding up the values of all final goods and services. These outputs can be evaluated at

current market prices (to get nominal GNP) or the prices of some previous year (to get real GNP).

5. America's economic history is one of growth punctuated by periodic recessions, that is, periods in which real GNP declined. While the distant past included some periods of falling prices (deflations), more recent history shows only rising prices (inflation).

6. The Great Depression of the 1930s was the worst in our country's history. It had profound effects both on our nation and on countries throughout the world and led also to a revolution in economic thinking, thanks to the work of John Maynard Keynes.

7. From World War II to the early 1970s, the American economy exhibited much steadier growth than it had in the past. Many observers attribute this to the implementation of the economic policies that Keynes suggested. At the same time, however, the price level seems only to rise, never to fall, in the modern economy. The economy seems to have become more "inflation prone."

8. In the mid-1970s, the U.S. economy suffered its worst recession since the Great Depression. At the same time, inflation was unusually virulent. This unhappy combination of economic stagnation with rapid inflation was nicknamed "stagflation."

9. One major cause of inflation is that aggregate demand may grow more quickly than aggregate supply. In such a case, a government policy that reduces aggregate demand may be able to check the inflation. We will study this and other policies in Part Three.

10. Similarly, recessions often occur because aggregate demand grows too slowly. In this case, a government policy that stimulates demand may be an effective way to fight the recession.

CONCEPTS FOR REVIEW

Macroeconomics	Recession
Microeconomics	Gross national product (GNP)
National output	Nominal versus real GNP
Aggregation	"Stagflation"
Aggregate supply and	Stabilization policy
aggregate demand	Managing aggregate demand
Inflation	

QUESTIONS FOR DISCUSSION

1. Which of the following problems are likely to be studied by a micro-economist and which by a macroeconomist?
   a. The allocation of a university's limited budget
   b. Why the Great Depression lasted so long
   c. Why Japan's economy grows faster than the United States's economy, while Britain's grows slower
   d. Why General Motors sells more cars than Ford Motor Company

2. You probably use "aggregates" quite frequently in everyday discussion. Try to think of some examples. (Here is one: Have you ever said, "The student body at this college generally . . ."? What, precisely, did you mean?)

3. Explain why macroeconomic questions would be much less important if the microeconomic mechanism were continually malfunctioning, and why microeconomics would be much less important if there were always a lot of unemployment.
4. Use an aggregate supply and demand diagram to study what would happen to an economy in which the aggregate supply curve never moved while the aggregate demand curve continually shifted outward year after year.
5. Try asking a friend who has not studied economics in which year he or she thinks prices were higher: 1870 or 1900? 1920 or 1940? (You can find the correct answers by referring to Figure 5–4.) Most people your age think that prices have always risen. Why do you think they have this opinion?
6. When were the two worst recessions (or depressions) of the past 60 years?

6

Unemployment and Inflation: The Twin Evils of Macroeconomics

Among the many trials faced by Ulysses, the hero of Homer's *Odyssey,* one of the most difficult was to steer his fragile boat through a narrow strait. On one side lay the rock Scylla, which threatened to break his craft into pieces, and on the other was the menacing whirlpool Charybdis. The makers of national economic policy face a similarly difficult task in trying to chart a middle course between the Scylla of unemployment and the Charybdis of inflation. If they steer the economy far from the rocks of unemployment, they run the risk of being swept up in the swift currents of inflation. But if they maintain a safe distance from inflation, they may run aground on the shoals of unemployment.

In Part Three we will explain how these economic planners attempt to strike a balance between high employment and low inflation, why these goals cannot be attained with machinelike precision, and why improvement on one front generally spells deterioration on the other. A great deal of attention will be paid to the *causes* of inflation and unemployment in

Part Three. But before getting involved in such important issues of theory and policy, we will, in this chapter, take a rather close look at the twin evils themselves. Why is it that a rise in the unemployment rate is generally considered bad news? Why is inflation so loudly deplored? Can we measure the costs of unemployment and inflation? The answers to some of these questions may at first seem obvious, but we will see that there is more to them than meets the eye.

The chapter is divided into two parts. In the first part we deal with unemployment. We begin with a detailed discussion of both the human and the economic costs of high unemployment, quantifying these costs wherever possible. We turn next to our country's system of unemployment insurance, noting the extent to which the system succeeds in reducing or eliminating these costs. Then we learn how government statisticians measure unemployment; and, finally, we conclude by considering the difficulties in defining the concept of "full employment."

In the second part of this chapter we turn to inflation, and begin by exploding some of the persistent myths about inflation, myths that help explain why inflation is so universally deplored. But the costs of inflation are not all mythical. The first real cost we consider is how and why inflation redistributes income and wealth from one group of people to another. Next, we learn how certain laws cause inflation to have very heavy economic costs that could be avoided if the laws were written differently. This leads us to one of our 12 Ideas for Beyond the Final Exam mentioned in Chapter 1. We shall see that it is the failure to understand the effect of inflation on interest rates that explains the existence of some of these laws and accounts for other costs of inflation as well. Finally, we define and analyze the difference between creeping and galloping inflation and explode a final myth about inflation: the myth that creeping inflation always leads to galloping inflation. In an appendix to the chapter, we explain how inflation is measured.

The Social Costs of Unemployment

The human costs of unemployment are probably sufficiently obvious, although they are much less severe now than they were during the dark days of the Great Depression. In the 1930s, loss of a job meant not only enforced idleness and a catastrophic drop in income, it often led to hunger, cold, ill health, and even death. This is the way one unemployed worker in late 1931 described his family's plight in a mournful letter to the governor of Pennsylvania:

> I have six little children to take care of. I have been out of work for over a year and a half. Am back almost thirteen months and the landlord says if I don't pay up before the 1 of 1932 out I must go, and where am I to go in the cold winter with my children? If you can help me please for

God's sake and the children's sakes and like please do what you can and send me some help, will you, I cannot find any work. I am willing to take any kind of work if I could get it now. Thanksgiving dinner was black coffee and bread and was very glad to get it. My wife is in the hospital now. We have no shoes to were [sic]; no clothes hardly. Oh what will I do I sure will thank you.[1]

Nowadays, unemployment does not have such dire consequences for most families, although it still holds these terrors for some. Part of the sting has been taken out of temporary unemployment by our system of unemploy-

From *The Great Depression 1929–1933,* by Milton Meltzer, page 103. Copyright © 1969 by Milton Meltzer. Reprinted by permission of Alfred A. Knopf, Inc.

ment insurance (discussed just below), and there are other social welfare programs to support the incomes of the poor (see Chapter 29). Yet many families still suffer a painful loss of income when their breadwinner becomes unemployed. During the Great Recession of 1974–1975 the rolls of the poverty population swelled by about $2\frac{1}{2}$ million families.

Even families that are protected by unemployment compensation from falling below the poverty line suffer when joblessness strikes. Ours is a work-oriented society. A man's "place" has always been in the office or factory or shop, and lately this has become increasingly true of women as well. A worker forced into idleness by a recession endures a psychological cost that is no less real for our inability to measure it. Enforced joblessness is a demoralizing mental burden on the unemployed worker. High unemployment leads to a higher incidence of psychological disorders, divorces, suicides, and the like. (See the boxed insert on page 88.)

Nor are the costs only psychological. The accumulation of work experience is a valuable asset. When forced into idleness, workers not only cease accumulating this experience, but lengthy periods of unemployment make them "rusty," and thus less productive when they are reemployed. Short periods of unemployment exact different kinds of costs. A record of steady employment is important in applying for a new job. And a worker who has frequently been laid off will lack this record of reliability.

It is important to realize that these costs, whether large or small in total, are distributed most unevenly across the population. At the bottom of the most recent recession, in May 1975, the unemployment rate among all workers reached 9 percent, a shockingly high figure. But in that same month, almost 13 percent of blue-collar workers were unemployed, as were more than 14 percent of nonwhite workers. For teen-agers the situation was worse still, with unemployment above 20 percent, and that of nonwhite teen-agers above 37 percent. Married men had the lowest rate—5.7 percent. Although these rates are all unusually high, the relations among them are quite typical.

In good times and bad, married men suffer the least unemployment and teen-agers suffer the most; nonwhites are unemployed much more often than whites; women endure moderately more unemployment than men; and blue-collar workers have above-average rates of unemployment.

UNEMPLOYMENT INSURANCE: THE INVALUABLE CUSHION

One of the most valuable pieces of legislation to emerge from the trauma of the Great Depression was the Social Security Act of 1935. Among other things, it established a system of unemployment insurance, which is now administered by each of the 50 states under federal guidelines. Thanks to this system, many—but, as we shall see, not all—American workers need never experience the complete loss of income that so many suffered during the 1930s.

While the precise amounts vary substantially, the average weekly benefit check to unemployed workers in 1977 was about $75. This amounted to about 40 percent of average earnings. Though a 60 percent drop in earnings still poses serious problems, the importance of this 40 percent income cushion can scarcely be overestimated, especially since it is tax free and may be supplemented by funds from other welfare programs. Families covered by unemployment insurance simply do not go hungry when they lose their jobs, and they are only rarely dispossessed from their homes.

Who is eligible to receive these benefits? Precise qualifications vary from state to state, but some stipulations apply quite generally.

Health, Crime, and Unemployment

The social costs of unemployment are by no means limited to narrow economic losses such as reduced incomes and output. It is widely believed, for example, that high unemployment breeds crime, mental anxiety, and ill health. In a 1976 study prepared for the Joint Economic Committee of Congress, a researcher at Johns Hopkins University documented the strong association between unemployment and various measures of mental and physical health and criminal aggression that has prevailed over the 1940–1973 period.

Using these statistical relationships, it is possible to estimate how many more cases of various maladies the United States would have had in 1979 if the unemployment rate over the 1975–1979 period had been one percentage point higher than it actually was. The results are summarized in the accompanying bar chart. For example, such a rise in unemployment would be expected to lead to about 21,750 more deaths from heart disease (about 2 percent of the actual mortality from such diseases). The other figures in the chart have similar interpretations.

In looking at these numbers, it should be kept in mind that the study found a high correlation between unemployment and the various maladies, which does not necessarily imply that unemployment was the *cause* of these ills. Still, the figures were dramatic enough to lead the late Senator Hubert Humphrey to remark that, "The human tragedy . . . of unemployment revealed by this study is shocking."

Source: Harvey Brenner, *Estimating the Social Costs of National Economic Policy: Implications for Mental and Physical Health, and Criminal Aggression,* A study for the Joint Economic Committee, 94th Congress, 2nd Session, U.S. Government Printing Office, 1976. Data adapted to 1979 population by the authors.

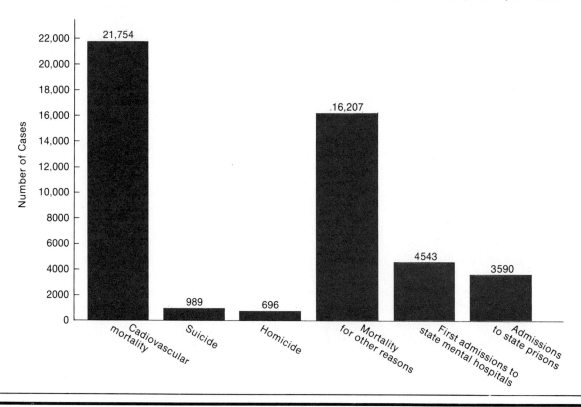

1. Only experienced workers qualify. The amount of experience necessary to establish eligibility varies state by state; but persons just joining the labor force (for instance, new graduates of high schools or colleges) or reentering after a protracted absence (such as women resuming work after many years of child rearing) are never eligible.

2. Only workers in "covered" employment qualify. Historically, unemployment insurance has not covered all experienced workers. However, legislation in 1976 expanded coverage greatly so that 97 percent of U.S. workers are now covered.

3. You must be looking for work to qualify. People unwilling or unable to work cannot receive unemployment benefits, and a recipient of benefits cannot reject a "suitable" job.

4. Benefits end after six months of unemployment. This time limit typically is extended by Congress when there is a recession, but there is always some limit.

Because of all these limitations, only a little more than half the roughly $6\frac{1}{2}$ million persons who were unemployed during 1977 actually received benefits.

The importance of unemployment insurance to those who are or who have been unemployed is obvious. But there are also significant benefits to citizens who never become unemployed. During recession years many billions of dollars are paid out in unemployment benefits, and since recipients probably spend almost all of their benefits, unemployment insurance limits the severity of recessions by providing additional purchasing power when and where it is most needed.

The unemployment insurance system is one of several "cushions" that have been built into our economy since 1933 to prevent the possibility of another Great Depression. By giving money to those who become unemployed, the system helps prop up aggregate demand during recessions.

While the U.S. economy is now probably "depression proof," this should not be a cause for too much rejoicing, for the severe recession of 1974–1975 amply demonstrated that we are far from being "recession proof."

THE ECONOMIC COSTS OF HIGH UNEMPLOYMENT

The fact that unemployment insurance and other social welfare programs replace a significant fraction of lost income has led some skeptics to claim that unemployment is no longer a serious problem. But the fact is that:

Unemployment insurance is no more than its name says—an *insurance* program. And insurance can never prevent a catastrophe from occurring, it can only *spread the costs* of a catastrophe among many people instead of letting them all fall on the shoulders of those few unfortunate souls whom it directly affects.

Fire insurance is an example. If you are covered by fire insurance and your house burns down, you will probably suffer only a small financial loss because the insurance company will pay most of the expenses. Where does it get the money? It cannot create it out of thin air. Rather, it must have collected the funds from the many other families who purchased insurance but did not suffer any fire damages. Thus, one family's loss of perhaps $50,000 is covered by the insurance payments of 500 families each paying $100 a year. In this way, the costs of the catastrophe are spread among hundreds of families, and in the process, made much more bearable.

But despite the insurance, the family whose house is destroyed by fire still suffers anguish and inconvenience. No insurance policy can eliminate this. Furthermore, society loses a valuable resource—a house. It will take a great deal of wood, cement, nails, paint, and labor to replace the burnt-out home. *An insurance policy cannot insure society against losses of real resources.*

The case is precisely the same with insurance against unemployment. All workers and employers pay for the insurance policy by a tax that the government levies on wages and salaries. With the funds so collected, the government compensates the victims of unemployment. Thus, instead of letting the costs of unemployment fall entirely on the minority of workers who are out of work, the system of payroll taxes and unemployment benefits *spreads* the costs over the entire population. But it does not eliminate the basic economic cost.

When the economy does not generate enough jobs to employ all those who are willing to work, a valuable resource is lost. Potential goods and services that might have been enjoyed by consumers are lost forever. This is the real economic cost of high unemployment, and no insurance plan can eliminate it.

And these costs are by no means negligible. Table 6–1 summarizes the idleness of workers and machines, and the resulting loss of national output, for some of the years of lowest economic activity since World War II. The first column lists the unemployment rate, and thus measures the unused labor resources. The second lists the fraction of industrial capacity that U.S. manufacturers were actually using, and thus indicates the extent of unused plant and equipment. And the third column shows how much more output (real GNP) could have been produced if these labor and capital resources had been fully employed.

Notice how the year 1975 stands out. With 8.5 percent of the labor force unemployed, and only about 74 percent of industrial capacity in use, our economy produced $115 billion *less* output than it could have produced if it had utilized the available labor and capital resources.

In fact, the inability to utilize all of the nation's available resources has been a persistent problem in our economy in recent decades. The red line in Figure 6–1 shows the actual real GNP in the United States from 1952 to 1977, while the black line shows the real GNP we *could have* produced if "full employment" had

TABLE 6–1

THE ECONOMIC COSTS OF HIGH UNEMPLOYMENT

YEAR	UNEMPLOYMENT RATE (percent)	CAPACITY UTILIZATION RATE (percent)	REAL GNP LOST DUE TO IDLE RESOURCES (billions of 1972 dollars)
1949	5.9	74.2	N.A.
1954	5.5	80.1	16
1958	6.8	75.0	42
1961	6.7	77.3	43
1971	5.9	78.0	38
1975	8.5	73.6	115

N.A. = not available.
Sources: Bureau of Labor Statistics, Federal Reserve System, and Council of Economic Advisers.

been maintained.[2] This last statement represents a concept called potential GNP.

DEFINITION

Potential gross national product is the real GNP the economy would produce if the labor force were fully employed.

[2]The concept of full employment is considered later in this chapter, pages 93–95.

As the diagram shows, more often than not our actual GNP has fallen short of potential GNP. When added up, the total shortfall of actual GNP below potential GNP during the past 25 years provides some startling information.

The cumulative gap between actual and potential GNP over the years 1952–1977 (all evaluated in 1972 prices)—which is shown by the

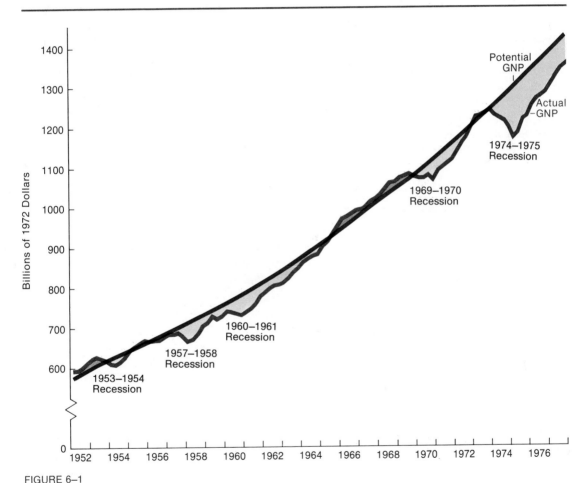

FIGURE 6–1

ACTUAL AND POTENTIAL GNP IN THE UNITED STATES, 1952–1977
This chart compares the growth of actual GNP (red line) with that of potential GNP (black line). There have been three lengthy periods during which real GNP remained below its potential (1957–1964, 1969–1972, and 1974 to the present), but only one lengthy period during which GNP remained above potential (1965–1968).

shaded area in Figure 6–1—is an astounding $568 billion. At 1978 levels of output, this loss in output as a result of unemployment would be about 5 months' worth of production. And there is no way to redeem these losses. The wasted labor in 1976 and 1977 cannot be utilized in 1980.

Those who argue that unemployment is nothing to worry about today because of unemployment insurance, or because unemployment is concentrated among certain kinds of workers (such as teen-agers), or because most unemployed workers become reemployed within a few weeks, should ponder Figure 6–1. Is the loss of this much output really no cause for worry? Would these optimists react the same way if the government collected a fraction of the output of every factory in America and dumped it into the sea? Waste is waste no matter who ultimately pays the cost.

COUNTING THE UNEMPLOYED: THE OFFICIAL STATISTICS

The Bureau of Labor Statistics (BLS) of the Department of Labor is responsible for measuring unemployment. How do they do it? How accurate are their measurements? Does the official unemployment rate overstate or understate the true amount of unemployment, as critics on both sides have claimed?

The BLS's basic method for counting the unemployed is quite direct: it asks people. Specifically, a survey of over 50,000 households is conducted each month. The census-taker asks several questions about the employment status of each member of the household. On the basis of these answers, each person is categorized as being *employed, unemployed,* or *not in the labor force.*

The first category is simplest to define. It includes everybody who is currently working at a job, including part-time workers. Although

some part-time workers work less than a full week because they choose to, others do so only because they cannot find a suitable full-time job. Nevertheless, these workers are not considered "unemployed," though many would consider them "underemployed."

The second category is a bit trickier. For those not currently working, the BLS first determines whether they are temporarily laid off from a job to which they will return. If so, they are counted as unemployed. The remaining workers are asked whether they actively sought work during the previous week. If they did, they are also counted as unemployed. But if they did not, they are classified as not in the labor force; that is, since they failed to look for a job they are not considered unemployed.

This seems a reasonable way to draw the distinction—after all, we would not want to count all college students who work during the summer months as unemployed between September and May. Yet, there is a problem: research has shown that many unemployed workers give up looking for jobs after a time. These so-called *discouraged workers* are victims of poor job prospects, just like the officially unemployed. Ironically, when they give up hope, the official unemployment statistics decline! Some critics have therefore argued that an estimate should be made of the number of discouraged workers, and that these people should be added to the roles of the unemployed. In 1977, the BLS estimated that about 1 million workers fell in this category.

Involuntary part-time work, loss of overtime or shortened work hours, and discouraged workers are all examples of "hidden" or "disguised" unemployment. And those who are concerned about these phenomena argue that we should include them in the official unemployment rate because, if we do not, the magnitude of the problem will be *underestimated.*

There is, however, an opposing school of thought that argues that the official unemployment rate really *overestimates* the unemployment problem. First, they argue, the unemployment rate of 1978 is not directly comparable to the unemployment rate of, say, 1956 because the composition of the labor force has changed dramatically over these years. Specifically, a much higher fraction of all workers are young and female today than was the case 20 years ago. These groups have always had higher rates of unemployment than adult males. Therefore, even if adult men, adult women, and teen-agers each had the *same* unemployment rates in 1978 that they had in 1956 (when overall unemployment was about 4 percent), the unemployment rate for the entire population in 1978 would have been around 5 percent.[3] Second, they argue, to count as unemployed, a person need only *say* that he is looking for work, even if he is not really interested in finding a job. No one knows to what extent the unemployment problem is overstated on account of this, but some think that it may be considerable.

HOW MUCH EMPLOYMENT IS "FULL EMPLOYMENT"?

Full employment is often cited as the principal goal of macroeconomic policy. How are we to define this goal? One clearly *incorrect* answer would be "a zero measured unemployment rate." Ours is a dynamic and highly mobile economy. Households move from one state to another. Individuals quit jobs to look for better positions or to "retool" for more attractive occupations. Old jobs disappear and new ones spring up as patterns of demand and cost shift. All of these phenomena, and many more, produce some irreducible minimum amount of unemployment—people who literally are

[3]If you do not understand why, consider the following analogy. Suppose your college class contains a mixture of "smart" and "dumb" students. If, between your freshman year and your senior year, more "dumb" students enter the class as transfers from other colleges, your class's overall grade point average will decline even if *every student earns the same grades as a senior that he or she did as a freshman.*

between jobs. Economists call this the level of frictional unemployment.

DEFINITION
Frictional unemployment is the amount of unemployment that is due to the normal workings of the labor market. It includes people who are temporarily between jobs because they are moving or changing occupations, or because their old firm went out of business, or the like.

People tend to think of frictional unemployment as irreducible, but that is not the case. During World War II, for example, unemployment in this country fell substantially below the frictional level. Frictional unemployment is "irreducible" only in the sense that—under normal circumstances—it is socially undesirable to reduce it.

Geographical and occupational mobility play important roles in our market economy—enabling the "right people" to find the "right jobs." Similarly, waste is avoided by allowing the inefficient firms, or firms producing items no longer desired by consumers, to be replaced by new firms. Inhibition of either of these phenomena must hamper the workings of the market economy. But, when these adjustment mechanisms are allowed to operate, there must be some temporarily unemployed workers looking for jobs just as there must be some firms with unfilled positions looking for workers. This is the genesis of frictional unemployment. And, because the U.S. labor market is more fluid than in most other countries, frictional unemployment is higher here than elsewhere.

A second type of unemployment is often difficult to distinguish from frictional unemployment, but has very different implications. This is called structural unemployment.

DEFINITION
Structural unemployment refers to workers who have lost their jobs because they have been displaced by automation, because their skills are no longer in demand, or for other similar reasons.

Frictionally unemployed workers may also lose their jobs for these reasons. The crucial difference is that, unlike a frictionally unemployed worker, a structurally unemployed worker cannot be considered "between jobs" in any meaningful sense. Instead, he may find his skills and experience unwanted in the changing economy in which he lives. He is thus faced with either a prolonged period of unemployment or the necessity of making a major change in his occupation. For older workers, in particular, this may be very difficult.

Which of these types of unemployment is allowed in a "full employment" economy? The Employment Act of 1946, the landmark piece of legislation in which the U.S. government first explicitly stated its commitment to maintain "conditions under which there will be afforded useful employment opportunities . . . for those able, willing and seeking to work," did not make this entirely clear. However, a common interpretation was that the act called upon the government to hold unemployment around the frictional level. How much was that? During the prosperous years of the late 1940s and early 1950s, unemployment rates were consistently below 4 percent, dropping as low as 2.9 percent in 1953 during the Korean War. This led President John F. Kennedy, in 1961, to select a 4 percent unemployment rate as an "interim target." The federal government was, for the first time, committed to a numerical goal.

Starting from the high 6.7 percent rate of 1961, unemployment was eroded, more or less steadily, to 3.8 percent in 1966. The interim target was exceeded, but inflation was starting to rear its ugly head. Then the additional military spending for the Vietnam War pushed unemployment down still further. The overall rate reached 3.5 percent in 1969, the lowest rate for a full year since 1953.

During the Nixon and Ford administrations, the 4 percent goal posted by President Kennedy's New Frontier was rejected as being outmoded, although no new numerical target was put in its place. There were several reasons for this rejection of 4 percent.

First, economists of the Nixon–Ford administration argued that the 4 percent target set during the Kennedy administration had to be adjusted upward for the early and middle 1970s because of the changed composition of the labor force. As already mentioned, this alone could raise "full employment" to about 5 percent. Second, they suggested, the increased generosity of unemployment compensation was lessening any individual's incentive to get himself off the unemployment rolls. Why work if unemployment benefits and other programs provide an income nearly as large as the salary one could earn on the job? This lack of work incentives made 4 percent unemployment much harder to achieve. Finally, these economists claimed, substantial increases in the federal minimum wage during the 1970s made it harder to employ teen-agers and other workers whose productivity was low. If, for example, their productivity was exceeded by the legal minimum wage, who would hire them?[4]

Today there is no agreement as to the numerical definition of "full employment." Nor is there agreement as to what unemployment rate is the most desirable, given the distressing fact that pushing the unemployment rate down generally causes the inflation rate to go up.

Ever since 1975, the *Full Employment and Balanced Growth Bill*—commonly known as the Humphrey–Hawkins Bill because of its principal congressional sponsors—has occupied a prominent place on the political agenda. As a candidate in the 1976 election, Jimmy Carter gave the bill—which proposed a 3 percent target rate of unemployment for adults—only lukewarm support at best. He worried that the 3 percent adult target was unrealistically low, and he had other reservations as well. Incumbent Gerald Ford unequivocally opposed the bill. But

---

[4]For a full discussion of minimum wage laws, including their effect on unemployment, see Chapter 27.

the bill was rewritten in 1977, weakening it, and once again installing 4 percent as the nation's "full employment" target. In late 1977, President Carter endorsed the bill, and in late 1978 Congress passed it into law. However, many people continue to be skeptical of the government's ability to achieve 4 percent unemployment.

The Social Costs of Inflation

Both the human and the economic costs of inflation are less obvious than the costs of unemployment. But this does not necessarily make them any less real; if one thing is crystal clear about inflation, it is that people do not like it.

Public opinion polls consistently show that inflation ranks high on people's list of major national problems, generally behind unemployment but occasionally ahead of it. Surveys also find that inflation, like unemployment, causes a deterioration in consumers' sense of well-being —it makes people unhappy. Finally, studies of voting behavior have shown that during congressional elections voters penalize the party that occupies the White House when inflation is high.

The fact is beyond dispute: People view inflation as something bad. Why?

INFLATION: THE MYTH AND THE REALITY

At first, the question may seem ridiculous. During times of inflation, people must keep paying higher prices for the same quantities of goods and services they had before. So more and more income is needed just to maintain the same standard of living. Is it not obvious that this erosion of purchasing power—that is, the decline in what money will buy—makes everyone worse off?

This would indeed be the case were it not for one very significant fact. The wages people earn are also prices—prices for labor services. During a period of inflation, wages also rise and, in fact, the average wage rises more or less in tune with prices. Thus, contrary to the popular myth, workers as a group are not usually victimized by inflation.

The purchasing power of wages is not systematically eroded by inflation. Sometimes wages rise faster than prices. And sometimes prices rise faster than wages. The fact is that in the long run wages tend to outstrip prices as new capital equipment and innovation increase output per worker.

Figure 6–2 illustrates this simple fact. The red line shows the annual rate of increase of consumer prices in the United States for each year since 1948, while the black line shows the annual rate of wage increases. Generally, wages rise faster than prices, reflecting the steady advance of technology and of labor productivity. So the black line is usually above the red line. The recession year 1974 stands out as the only year in which wages did not rise faster than prices.

The feature of Figure 6–2 that virtually jumps off the page is the way the two lines seem to dance together. Wages rise rapidly when prices rise rapidly, and they rise slowly when prices rise slowly. But you should not draw any hasty conclusions from this association. We cannot, for example, learn from this figure whether rising prices cause rising wages or whether rising wages cause rising prices. Remember the warnings given in Chapter 1 about trying to infer causation just by looking at data. But analyzing cause and effect is not our purpose right now. We merely want to explode

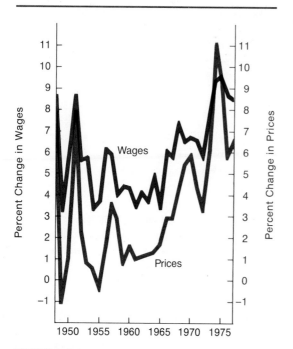

FIGURE 6–2

RATES OF CHANGE OF WAGES AND PRICES
IN THE UNITED STATES, 1948–1977
This chart compares the rate of price inflation (red
line) with the rate of growth of nominal wages in the
postwar period. The patterns are clearly quite similar,
with wages and prices normally accelerating or
decelerating together. Notice that the traditional gap
between wage increases and price increases did not
prevail in the mid-1970s.

the myth that inflation inevitably robs workers of
their wages.

Why is this myth so widespread? Imagine a
world without inflation in which wages are rising
3 percent a year because of the increasing
productivity of labor. Now imagine that, all of a
sudden, inflation sets in and prices start rising 5
percent a year but that nothing else changes.
Figure 6–2 suggests that, with perhaps a small
delay, wage increases will accelerate to 3
percent plus 5 percent, or 8 percent a year.

Will workers view this change with equa-
nimity? Probably not. To each worker, the 8
percent wage increase will be seen as something he earned by the sweat of his brow. In his
view, he *deserves* every penny of his 8 percent
raise. And, in a sense, he is right because "the
sweat of his brow" earned him a 3 percent
increment in purchasing power that, when the
inflation rate rises to 5 percent, can only be
achieved by increasing his wages by a total of 8
percent. An economist would divide the wage
increase in the following way:

REASON FOR WAGE INCREASE	AMOUNT
Higher productivity	3%
Compensation for higher prices	5%
Total	8%

But the worker will probably keep score
differently. Feeling that he earned the entire 8
percent by his own merits, he will view inflation
as having "robbed" him of 5 percent of his just
deserts. The higher the rate of inflation, the
more of his raise the worker will feel robbed of.

Of course, nothing could be further from
the truth. Basically, the economic system is
rewarding the worker with *the same 3 percent
increment for higher productivity regardless of
the rate of inflation*. The "evils of inflation" are
often exaggerated because of a failure to understand this mechanism.

A second reason for misunderstanding the
effects of inflation is due to what economists
call money illusion. For example, if an inflation
doubles both prices and wage rates, the worker
labors exactly the same amount of time as
before to earn the price of a loaf of bread. But
because he is now paying $1 a loaf instead of
50 cents, he has the illusion that the price of
bread is scandalously high. In fact, nothing has
changed; but he remains stuck with his idea of
what bread *should* cost.

A third misperception results from failure to
distinguish between a *rise in the general price*

TABLE 6–2

ITEM	LAST YEAR'S PRICE	THIS YEAR'S PRICE	PERCENTAGE INCREASE
Candy bar	$ 0.20	$ 0.22	10
Movie ticket	3.00	3.30	10
Automobile	6000	6600	10

TABLE 6–3

ITEM	LAST YEAR'S PRICE	THIS YEAR'S PRICE	PERCENTAGE INCREASE
Candy bar	$ 0.20	$ 0.20	0
Movie ticket	3.00	4.00	33.3
Automobile	6000	6400	6.7

level and a change in relative prices, that is, a rise in the price of one commodity relative to that of another. To see the distinction most clearly, imagine first a *pure inflation* in which *every* price rises by 10 percent during the year, so that relative prices do not change. Table 6–2 gives an example in which movie tickets go up from $3 to $3.30, candy bars from 20 cents to 22 cents, and automobiles from $6000 to $6600. After the inflation, just as before, it will still take 15 candy bars to buy a movie ticket, 2000 movie tickets to buy a car, and so on. A person who manufactures candy bars in order to purchase movie tickets will be neither helped nor harmed by the inflation. Neither will a theater owner who likes cars.

But real inflations are not like this. When there is 10 percent general inflation—meaning that the "average price" rises by 10 percent[5]— some prices may jump 20 percent or more while others actually fall. Suppose that, instead of the price raises shown in Table 6–2, prices rise as shown in Table 6–3. Movie prices go up by $33\frac{1}{3}$ percent, but candy prices do not change. Surely, candy manufacturers who love movies will be disgruntled because it now costs 20 candy bars instead of 15 to get into the theater. They will blame inflation for raising the price of movie tickets, even though their real problem stems from the *increase in the price of movies relative to candy.* (They would have been hurt just as much if movie admissions had remained

[5]The way statisticians figure out "average" price increases is discussed in the appendix to this chapter.

at $3 while the price of a candy bar fell to 15 cents.)

Since car prices have risen by less than 7 percent, theater owners in need of new cars will be delighted by the fact that an auto now costs only 1600 movie admissions (just as they would have cheered if car prices had fallen to $4800 while movie tickets remained at $3.) However, they are unlikely to attribute their good fortune to inflation—as indeed they should not. What has actually happened is that *cars became cheaper relative to movies.*

Because real-world inflation proceeds at *uneven* rates, relative prices are constantly changing. There will be gainers and losers, just as some would gain and others lose if relative prices changed without any general inflation. Inflation, however, gets a bad name because losers are likely to blame inflation for their misfortune while gainers are unlikely to credit inflation for their good luck. Alas, nobody loves inflation.

These three kinds of misconceptions may go a long way toward explaining why respondents to public opinion polls consistently list inflation as a major national issue, why higher inflation rates depress consumers, and why voters express their ire at the polls when inflation is high.

Inflation does not systematically erode the purchasing power of wages. Nor does it lead to "unfair" prices. Nor is it usually to blame when some goods become more expensive relative to others.

But not all of the costs of inflation are mythical. Let us now turn to some of its real costs.

INFLATION AS A REDISTRIBUTOR OF INCOME AND WEALTH

We have just seen that the *average* person is neither helped nor harmed by inflation. But almost no one is exactly average! Some persons gain from inflation and others lose. It is hard to say anything more systematic than this about the effects of inflation on particular prices and wages.

But inflation does have systematic effects on the distribution of income and wealth. Senior citizens trying to scrape by on pensions or other fixed incomes suffer badly from inflation. Since they earn no wages, it is little solace to them that wages are keeping pace with prices. Their pension incomes are not.[6]

This example actually illustrates a much more general problem. We can think of pensioners as people who "lend" money to an organization (the pension fund) when they are young in order to be "paid back" with interest when they are old. Because of the rise in the price level during the intervening years, the unfortunate pensioners get paid back in less valuable dollars than those they originally loaned. In general:

Those who lend money are victimized by inflation.

While lenders lose heavily, borrowers do quite well. For example, homeowners who borrowed money from banks in the form of

mortgages back in the 1950s, when interest rates were 3 or 4 percent, have gained enormously from the surprisingly virulent inflation of the late 1960s and 1970s. They have paid back dollars of much lower value than those that they borrowed. And the same is true of other borrowers.

Borrowers gain from inflation.

Since the redistribution caused by inflation generally benefits borrowers at the expense of lenders, and since both lenders and borrowers can be found at every income level, we must conclude that:

Inflation does not always steal from the rich to aid the poor, nor does it always do the reverse.

Why, then, is the redistribution caused by inflation so widely condemned? Because its victims are selected capriciously. Nobody legislates this redistribution. Nobody enters into it voluntarily. The gainers do not earn their spoils, and the losers do not deserve their fate. Moreover there have been particular classes of people whom inflation has systematically robbed of purchasing power year after year—old-age pensioners, people who have saved money and "loaned" it to banks, and workers on long-term contracts or those whose wages and salaries do not adjust easily for some other reason. Even if people "on the average" suffer no damage from inflation, that offers little consolation to those who are hurt by it persistently and systematically. This is the fundamental indictment of inflation.

Inflation redistributes income in an arbitrary way that distorts society's distribution of income. The actual income distribution should reflect the interplay of the operation of free markets and the deliberate efforts of government to alter the distribution. Inflation interferes with and distorts this process.

---

[6]This is not, however, true of recipients of social security. Social security benefits are financed out of tax revenues rather than directly through accumulated savings, and Congress has generally raised benefit levels to compensate recipients for changes in the price level. Since 1975 these cost-of-living adjustments have been automatic. For further discussion of the social security system, see Chapter 32.

REAL VERSUS NOMINAL INTEREST RATES

But wait. Must inflation always rob lenders to bestow gifts upon borrowers? If both parties see the inflation coming, why don't the lenders demand that the borrowers pay a higher interest rate as compensation for the coming inflation? Often they do. For this reason, economists draw a conceptual distinction between inflation that is *expected* and inflation that comes as a surprise.

What happens when inflation is fully expected by both parties? Suppose Diamond Jim wants to borrow $1000 from Scrooge, and both agree that, in the absence of inflation, which erodes the value of money, a fair rate of interest would be 4 percent on a one-year loan. This means that Diamond Jim would pay back $1040 at the end of the year for the privilege of having $1000 now.

If both expect prices to increase by 6 percent, Scrooge may reason as follows, "If Diamond Jim pays me back $1040 a year from today, that money will buy less than what $1000 buys today. Thus I'll really be *paying him* to borrow from me! I'm no philanthropist. Why don't I charge him 10 percent instead? Then he'll pay back $1100 at the end of the year. With prices 6 percent higher, this will buy roughly what $1040 is worth today. So I'll get the same 4 percent increase in purchasing power that we would have agreed on in the absence of inflation, and won't be any worse off. That's the least I'll accept."

Diamond Jim may follow a similar chain of logic. "With no inflation, I was willing to pay $1040 a year from now for the privilege of having $1000 today, and Scrooge was willing to lend it. He'd be crazy to do the same with a 6 percent inflation. He'll want to charge me more. How much should I pay? If I offer him $1100 a year from now, that will have roughly the same purchasing power as $1040 today, so I won't be any worse off. That's the most I'll pay."

This kind of thinking will lead Scrooge and Diamond Jim to write a contract with a 10 percent interest rate—4 percent as the increase in purchasing power that Diamond Jim pays to Scrooge and 6 percent as compensation for the expected inflation. Then, if the expected 6 percent inflation actually occurs, neither party will be made better or worse off than was expected at the time the contract was signed.

This example illustrates a very general principle. The 4 percent increase in purchasing power that Diamond Jim agrees to hand over to Scrooge is called the real rate of interest.

DEFINITION
The *real rate of interest* is the percentage increase in purchasing power that the borrower pays to the lender for the privilege of borrowing. It indicates the increased ability to purchase goods and services that the lender earns.

The 10 percent contractual interest charge that Diamond Jim and Scrooge write into the loan agreement is called the nominal rate of interest.

DEFINITION
The *nominal rate of interest* is the percentage by which the money the borrower pays back exceeds the money that he borrowed, making no adjustment for any fall in the purchasing power of this money that results from inflation.

The nominal rate of interest is arrived at by adding the expected rate of inflation to the real rate of interest. The expected inflation is added to compensate the lender for the loss in purchasing power that he is expected to suffer as a result of inflation. Because of this:

Inflation that is accurately predicted need not redistribute income between borrowers and lenders. Instead, the expected rate of inflation will be added to the real interest rate. If expectations prove correct, no one gains and no one loses. However, to the extent that expectations prove incorrect, inflation will still redistribute income.[7]

It need hardly be pointed out that errors in predicting the rate of inflation are the norm, not the exception. Published forecasts bear witness to the fact that economists have great difficulty in predicting the rate of inflation. The task is no easier for businesses, consumers, and banks. This is one reason why inflation is so widely condemned as unfair and undesirable. It sets up a guessing game that no one likes.

USURY LAWS, INTEREST RATE CEILINGS, AND OTHER LEGAL IMPEDIMENTS

One major source of the costs of inflation stems from the fact that no one can foresee what the future rate of inflation will be. But there are other costs, perhaps even more serious, that arise from high inflation rates, even when the rates are predicted with perfect accuracy. These costs are consequences of laws that make it *illegal* for borrowers and lenders to add the expected rate of inflation to their desired real interest rate.

The most obvious example of such legislation is usury laws.

DEFINITION
A *usury law* sets down a maximum permissible interest rate for a particular type of loan. Loans at rates above the usury ceiling are illegal.

Usury laws date back to biblical days and command rather widespread popular support. The problem is that they place limits on *nominal* interest rates, rather than on *real* interest rates,

[7]EXERCISE: Who gains and who loses if the inflation turns out to be only 4 percent instead of the 6 percent that Scrooge and Diamond Jim expected? What if the inflation rate is 8 percent?

and thus can have rather perverse effects in an inflationary environment.

Let us recall our previous example in which Scrooge and Diamond Jim both correctly foresee a 6 percent rate of inflation. But now suppose that a usury law sets a maximum rate of 8 percent on consumer loans. Diamond Jim is willing to pay a 10 percent nominal interest rate (4 percent real interest plus 6 percent for expected inflation) in order to get his hands on some money a year earlier, and Scrooge is willing to lend at this rate. But the law intervenes. "Thou shalt not charge usurious interest." The deal cannot be completed, and both Diamond Jim and Scrooge go away disappointed.

Usury laws produce such undesirable consequences because they were not formulated with inflation in mind. They were framed in periods of fairly steady prices, when there was no great difference between nominal and real interest rates. If, for example, the usury law had set the legal maximum at a 4 percent *real* rate of interest, it would not have prevented Scrooge from lending to Diamond Jim. As it is, however, a loan carrying a 4 percent real interest rate is perfectly legal at zero inflation but illegal at 6 percent inflation!

This phenomenon helps explain why rapid inflation often has disastrous consequences for homebuilding. Usury laws fix maximum interest rates on home mortgages in most states. If the usury ceiling is, for example, 9 percent interest, mortgage loans will look like a very bad investment in an inflationary environment when banks can buy bonds of large corporations paying 10 percent interest and more. As a result, banks will stop making mortgage loans, and the housing market will come to a screeching halt. This is precisely what happened in the United States in 1974, and it took several years for the construction industry to recover from the debacle.

Usury laws are just one example of a general phenomenon:

Many of the laws that govern our financial system may be useful in an inflation-free world but become counterproductive in an inflationary environment, causing problems that were never intended by the legislators.

And it is important to note that *these are major costs of inflation that are not purely redistributive*. Society as a whole is the loser when mutually beneficial transactions are prohibited by law, when houses go unbuilt, when loans are not provided to those who need them, and when other useful acts are prevented by obsolete legislation.

MONEY ILLUSION AND INTEREST RATES

Why, then, are our laws still being framed this way? It seems that we must attribute this phenomenon to a general lack of understanding of the difference between real and nominal interest rates. People seem not to understand that it is the *real* rate of interest that matters in an economic transaction because only that rate reveals how much borrowers pay (and lenders receive) *in terms of the goods and services which that money can buy*. They consider high nominal interest rates to be unjustifiable, even if these rates correspond to very low real interest rates. The example of usury ceilings on nominal interest rates has already been given. Here are some others that may help you appreciate how widespread and important this particular type of money illusion is.

Regulation of Public Utilities

During the period 1959 to 1965, when the rate of inflation averaged about $1\frac{1}{4}$ percent a year, interest rates on high-grade corporate bonds hovered just below $4\frac{1}{2}$ percent, yielding a real rate of interest of just over 3 percent. There were few public complaints suggesting that there was anything scandalous about such earnings rates.

Yet during 1974, when the rate of inflation rose above 10 percent and corporate interest rates rose to perhaps 9 percent (a *negative* real rate of interest!), there was a public uproar. Regulated utilities, which asked the regulatory agencies to permit them a rate of return closer to 10 percent so that they could afford to borrow the money needed to serve expanding public demand, found that their requests were considered exorbitant by the commissions and by the general public. As a result, they failed to increase their capacities sufficiently.

Investment and Profits

Amazingly, even business managers were subject to the same form of money illusion. Often they were taken aback by the notion that their investors actually lost out (earned a negative *real* rate of return) when the company was earning a 9 percent profit. The managers noted that 9 percent was the company's highest earnings rate in recent history; but with inflation at 10 percent, it turned out that in real terms it was in fact the firm's lowest.

Interest Rate Regulations

The same illusion is also partly responsible for the regulations that impose ceilings around 5 percent on interest paid on savings accounts. Thus, *by government decree* the small saver is robbed of 4 or 5 percent of his purchasing power or more every year during a period of rapid inflation.

Thus, money illusion has been known to impoverish savers during a period of inflation. It has devastated the housing construction industry. It has sometimes made it impossible for electric companies and other public utilities to raise the capital they need to serve rising consumer demands; and power shortages and failures have been a predictable result.

▨ The difference between real and nominal interest (and profit) rates, and the fact that it is the real rate that matters in terms of economic effects but the nominal rate that is politically significant, are matters that are of the utmost importance and yet are understood by very few people, including many persons who make public policy decisions in these areas.

This concept is one of the 12 Ideas for Beyond the Final Exam, and if you remember it 10 years from now you will truly have gotten a great deal out of studying economics. ▨

OTHER COSTS OF INFLATION

Another cost of inflation is that rapidly changing prices make it difficult to enter into long-term contracts. In an extremely severe inflation, the "long term" may be only a few days. But even moderate inflations can have remarkable effects on long-term loans. Suppose a corporation wants to borrow $1 million to finance the purchase of some new equipment and needs the loan for 20 years. If the inflation rate averages 8 percent over this period, the $1 million it repays at the end of 20 years will be worth only $214,548 in today's purchasing power. If inflation averages 4 percent instead, it will be worth $456,387. If there is no inflation, it will be worth $1 million. Lending or borrowing for this long a period is obviously a big gamble. With the stakes this high, the outcome may be that neither lenders nor borrowers want to get involved in long-term contracts. But without long-term loans, business investment becomes impossible. The economy stagnates.

Inflation also makes life difficult for the shopper. You probably have a group of stores that you habitually patronize because you know they generally carry the items you want to buy at (roughly) the prices you want to pay. This knowledge saves you a great deal of time and energy. But when prices are changing rapidly, your list becomes obsolete very quickly. You return to your favorite clothing store only to find that the price of jeans has risen drastically. Should you buy? Should you shop around at other stores? Will they have also raised their prices? And business firms have precisely the same problem with their suppliers. Rising prices force them to shop around more than they are accustomed to, which imposes costs on the firms and, more generally, reduces the efficiency of the whole economy.

CREEPING VERSUS GALLOPING INFLATION

The preceding litany of costs of inflation alerts us to one very important fact: *predictable inflation is far less burdensome than is unpredictable inflation.* When will an inflation be most predictable? When it proceeds year after year at more or less the same rate. Thus the *variability of the inflation rate* is a crucial factor. Inflation of 6 percent a year for three consecutive years will exact far lower social costs than inflation that is 8 percent in the first year, zero in the second, and 10 percent in the third. In general:

Steady inflation is much more predictable than variable inflation and therefore has much smaller social and economic costs.

But the *average level of the inflation rate* is also important. Partly because of the legal impediments mentioned above and partly because of the more rapid breakdown in normal customer relationships that we have just mentioned, a steady inflation of 10 percent a year is more damaging than a steady inflation of 5 percent a year.

Creeping Versus Galloping Inflation

Economists distinguish between creeping inflations and galloping inflations partly on their average level and partly on their variability.

DEFINITION

Creeping inflation refers to an inflation that proceeds for a long time at a moderate and fairly steady pace.

Modern Sweden provides a good example. During the 13-year period from 1954 to 1967, prices climbed a total of 64 percent (compared with only 24 percent in the United States), for an average annual inflation rate of 3.9 percent. And the pace of inflation was remarkably steady, rarely dropping below $2\frac{1}{2}$ percent or rising above 5 percent.

DEFINITION

Galloping inflation refers to an inflation that proceeds at an exceptionally high rate, perhaps only for a relatively brief period. Galloping inflations are generally characterized by accelerating rates of inflation so that the rate of inflation is higher this month than it was last month.

Germany after World War I suffered through one of the more severe inflations in history. Wholesale prices increased about 80 percent during 1920, over 140 percent in 1921, and a colossal 4100 percent during 1922. At this point, what had been a very impressive galloping inflation simply got out of control. Between December 1922 and November 1923, when a hard-nosed reform finally broke the inflationary spiral, wholesale prices in Germany increased by almost 100 million percent! But even this experience was dwarfed by the great Hungarian inflation of 1945–1946, the greatest inflation of them all. For a period of one year, the rate of inflation averaged about 20,000 percent *per month*. And in the final month (July 1946), the price level skyrocketed 42 quadrillion percent!

While the distinction between creeping and galloping inflation is a quantitative one, we refrained from putting any specific numbers into the definitions. This is because different societies at different points in time have very different conceptions about what rate constitutes creeping inflation and what rate constitutes galloping inflation. For example, in the United States today, annual rates of inflation in the 5 to 7 percent range are generally considered to be "creeping," while rates in the 20 to 25 percent range would surely be construed as "galloping." In most Latin American countries, however, inflation consistently in the 20 to 25 percent range would surely be viewed as

In Weimar Germany, children built their castles with cash, worth no more than the sand or sticks used by children elsewhere.

"creeping." And in the United States of the 1950s and early 1960s, a 7 percent annual inflation would probably have been branded "galloping."

THE COSTS OF CREEPING VERSUS GALLOPING INFLATION

If you review the costs of inflation that have been enumerated in this chapter, you will see why the distinction between creeping and galloping inflation is so fundamental. Many economists now feel that we can live very nicely, indeed can prosper, in an environment of creeping inflation. No one feels we can survive very well under galloping inflation.

Under creeping inflation, the rate at which prices will rise is relatively easy to predict and to take into account in setting interest rates (as long as the law allows this). Under galloping inflation, where prices are rising at ever-increasing rates, this will be very difficult, and perhaps impossible, to accomplish. The potential redistributions become monumental, and as a result, lending and borrowing may cease entirely.

Any inflation makes it difficult to write long-term contracts. With creeping inflation, the "long term" may be 20 years, or 10 years, or 5. But with galloping inflation, the "long term" may be measured in weeks or even hours. Restaurant prices may change before you finish your dessert. Railroad fares may go up while you are in the middle of your journey. When it is impossible to enter into contracts of any duration longer than a few minutes, economic activity becomes paralyzed. We conclude that:

The horrors of galloping inflation either are absent in creeping inflation or they are present in such muted forms that they can scarcely be considered horrors.

CREEPING INFLATION DOES NOT NECESSARILY LEAD TO GALLOPING INFLATION

We noted earlier that inflation is surrounded by a mythology that bears precious little relation to reality. It seems appropriate to conclude this chapter by disposing of one particularly persistent myth: that creeping inflation invariably leads to galloping inflation.

There is neither statistical evidence nor theoretical support for the myth that creeping inflation leads to galloping inflation. To be sure, creeping inflations sometimes accelerate. But at other times they slow down.

While creeping inflations have many causes, galloping inflations have occurred only when the government has printed incredible amounts of money, usually to finance wartime expenditures.

In the German inflation of 1923, the government finally found that its printing presses could not produce enough paper money to keep pace with the exploding prices. Not that it did not try. By the end of the inflation, the *daily* output of currency was over 400 quadrillion marks! The Hungarian authorities in 1945–1946 tried even harder. The average growth rate of the money supply was more than 12,000 percent *per month*. Needless to say, these are not the kind of inflation problems that are likely to face the United States in the foreseeable future.

But this should not be interpreted to imply that there is nothing wrong with creeping inflation. Much of this chapter has been spent analyzing the very real costs of any inflation, no matter how slow. A case against even moderate inflation can indeed be built, but it does not help this case to shout foolish slogans like "Creeping inflation always leads to galloping inflation." Fortunately, it is simply not true.

SUMMARY

1. Unemployment exacts heavy financial and psychological costs upon those who are its victims, and these costs are borne quite unevenly by different groups in the population.

2. Unemployment insurance replaces nearly one-half the lost income for unemployed persons who are insured. But only about half the unemployed are covered by insurance, and no insurance program can bring back the lost output that could have been produced had these people been working.

3. In recent decades, the U.S. economy typically has produced less output than it could have were it operating at full employment. This shortfall has been particularly large since the mid-1970s.

4. Unemployment is measured by means of a government survey. Some critics claim that the survey methods understate the unemployment problem while others contend that the methods overstate the problem.

5. Frictional unemployment arises when people are between jobs for normal reasons. Thus, most frictional unemployment is desirable.

6. Structural unemployment is due to shifts in the pattern of demand or to technological change that results in certain skills becoming more or less obsolete.

7. While the Employment Act of 1946 was not terribly specific on this point, it was widely interpreted as committing the government to limiting unemployment to the frictional variety. However, it set no numerical goals.

8. President Kennedy first enunciated the goal of 4 percent unemployment in 1961. Although this goal will be much harder to achieve in the 1980s than it was in the 1960s, the Full Employment and Balanced Growth Act of 1978 once again seeks to set 4 percent as an official target.

9. Many of the reasons why people dislike inflation are the results of simple misconceptions. For example, many people believe that inflation systematically erodes the purchasing power of wages, are appalled by rising prices even when wages are rising just as fast, and blame inflation for any unfavorable changes in relative prices. All of these are myths.

10. Other costs of inflation are very real indeed. For example, inflation often redistributes income from lenders to borrowers.

11. This redistribution can be eliminated by adding the expected rate of inflation to the interest rate, but (a) legal limitations sometimes prevent this, and (b) expectations often prove to be quite inaccurate.

12. The real rate of interest is the nominal rate of interest minus the expected rate of inflation. Since the real rate of interest indicates the command over real resources that the borrower surrenders to the lender, it is of primary economic importance.

13. Yet public attention often is riveted to nominal rates of interest, and this confusion can lead to costly policy mistakes when high inflation converts high nominal interest rates into very low real interest rates. This is one of the 12 Ideas for Beyond the Final Exam.

14. Creeping inflation, which proceeds at moderate and fairly predictable rates year after year, carries far lower social costs than galloping inflation, which proceeds at high and variable rates.

15. The notion that creeping inflation inevitably leads to galloping inflation is a myth with no foundation in economic theory and no basis in historical fact.

CONCEPTS FOR REVIEW

Unemployment insurance
Potential GNP
Frictional unemployment
Structural unemployment
Employment Act of 1946
Full employment
Purchasing power
Money illusion

Relative prices
Redistribution by inflation
Real rate of interest
Nominal rate of interest
Expected rate of inflation
Usury laws
Creeping inflation
Galloping inflation

QUESTIONS FOR DISCUSSION

1. Why is it not so terrible to become unemployed nowadays as it was during the Great Depression? Explain.
2. "Since unemployed workers receive unemployment benefits and other benefits that make up for almost 100 percent of their lost wages, unemployment is no longer a social problem." Comment.
3. Using what you learned about aggregate demand and aggregate supply in Chapter 5, try to explain why the U.S. economy has failed so frequently to produce up to its potential. (You will be learning much more about this question in chapters to come, so don't worry if you find the question difficult at this stage.)
4. Do you think that the Bureau of Labor Statistics overestimates or underestimates the number of people that are unemployed? Why?
5. Why is it so difficult to define "full employment"? What unemployment rate should the government be shooting for today?
6. Show why each of the following complaints is based on a misunderstanding about inflation:
   a. "Inflation must be stopped because it robs workers of their purchasing power."
   b. "Inflation is a terrible social disease. It leads to unconscionably high prices for basic necessities."
   c. "Inflation makes it impossible for working people to afford many of the things they were hoping to buy."
   d. "Inflation must be stopped today, for if we do not stop it, it will surely accelerate to ruinously high rates and lead to disaster."
7. What is the real interest rate paid on a loan bearing 12 percent nominal interest per year, if the rate of inflation is
   a. zero
   b. 2 percent
   c. 7 percent
   d. 12 percent
   e. 14 percent
8. Suppose you agree to lend money to your friend on the day you both enter college, at what you both expect to be a *zero real* rate of interest. Payment is to be made at graduation, with interest at a *fixed nominal* rate. If inflation proves to be *lower* during your four years in college than what you both had expected, who will gain and who will lose?
9. Explain how usury laws have harmed the housing market during periods of high inflation. How could these laws have been rewritten to avoid this harm? Why were they not rewritten in this way?
10. You have lived with inflation all your life. Think about the costs that inflation has imposed on *you* personally. How do these costs relate to the material in this chapter?

Appendix
How Statisticians Measure Inflation

INDEX NUMBERS FOR INFLATION

Inflation is generally measured by the change in some index of the general price level. For example, between 1970 and 1977, the Consumer Price Index (CPI), which stood at 100 in 1967, rose from 116.3 to 181.5, an increase of 56.1 percent. The meaning of the *change* is clear enough. But what is the meaning of the 116.3 figure for 1970 and the 181.5 figure for 1977?

These numbers are index numbers; each expresses the cost of a market basket of goods *relative to its cost in some "base" period.* Since the CPI uses 1967 as its base period, the CPI of 181.5 for 1977 means that it cost $181.50 to purchase the same basket of goods and services that cost $100 in 1967.

Now, the particular basket of consumer goods and services under scrutiny really did not cost $100 in 1967. When constructing index numbers, it is conventional to set the index at 100 in the base year. How is this conventional figure used in obtaining index numbers for other years? Very simply. Suppose the budget needed to buy the roughly 400 items included in the CPI was $500 per month in 1967 and $581.50 per month in 1970. Then the index is defined by the following rule:

$$\frac{\text{CPI in 1970}}{\text{CPI in 1967}} =$$
$$\frac{\text{Cost of the 400-item market basket in 1970}}{\text{Cost of the 400-item market basket in 1967}}$$

Since the CPI in 1967 is set at 100:

$$\frac{\text{CPI in 1970}}{100} = \frac{\$581.50}{\$500} = 1.163$$

or

$$\text{CPI in 1970} = 116.3$$

Exactly the same sort of equation enables us to calculate the CPI in any other year. We have the rule:

CPI in given year =
$$\left(\frac{\text{Cost of market basket in given year}}{\text{Cost of market basket in base year}}\right)^{[8]}$$

Of course, not every combination of consumer goods that cost $500 in 1967 rose to $581.50 by 1970. For example, a color TV set that cost $500 in 1967 might have sold for $450 in 1970, but a $500 hospital bill in 1967 might have ballooned to $625. Since no two families buy precisely the same bundle of goods and services, no two families suffer precisely the same increase in their cost of living unless all prices rise at the same rate. Economists refer to this phenomenon as the index number problem.

When relative prices are changing, there is no such thing as a "perfect price index" that is correct for every consumer. Any statistical index will understate the increase in the cost of living for some families and overstate it for others. At best, the index can represent the situation of an "average" family.

[8] This and other cost-of-living formulas must then be multiplied by 100 to convert numbers like 1.163 to numbers like 116.3.

TABLE 6–4

RESULTS OF HYPOTHETICAL STUDENT EXPENDITURE SURVEY, 1972

ITEM	AVERAGE PRICE	AVERAGE QUANTITY PURCHASED PER MONTH	AVERAGE EXPENDITURE PER MONTH
Hamburger	$ 0.40	70	$28.00
Jeans	12.00	1	12.00
Movie tickets	2.50	4	10.00
		Total	$50.00

THE CONSUMER PRICE INDEX

The most closely watched price index is surely the Consumer Price Index, which is calculated and announced each month by the Bureau of Labor Statistics (BLS). When you read in the newspaper or see on television that the "cost of living" rose by 0.5 percent last month, chances are the reporter is referring to the CPI.

The CPI is measured by pricing the items on a list representative of a typical urban household budget. To know what items to include and in what amounts, the BLS conducts an extensive survey of spending habits roughly once every decade (the last one was in 1972). This means that the *same* bundle of goods and services gets priced for about 10 years, whether or not spending habits change.[9]

A simplified example will help us understand how the CPI is constructed. Imagine that college students purchase only three items—hamburgers, jeans, and movie tickets—and that we want to devise a cost-of-living index (call it SPI, for "student price index") for them. First we would conduct a survey of spending habits in the base year (suppose it is 1972). Table 6–4 represents the hypothetical results. You will note that the frugal students of that day spent

[9]Economists call this a *base-period weight index,* because the relative importance it attaches to each price depends on how much money consumers actually choose to spend on it during the base period.

only $50 per month: $28 on hamburgers, $12 on jeans, and $10 on movies.

Table 6–5 presents hypothetical prices of these same three items in 1979. Each price has risen by a different amount, ranging from 25 percent for jeans to 60 percent for movies. By how much has the SPI risen? Pricing the 1972 student budget at 1979 prices, we find that what once cost $50 now costs $73.

COST OF 1972 STUDENT BUDGET IN 1979 PRICES

70 hamburgers at $0.60.	$42.00
1 pair of jeans at $15	15.00
4 movie tickets at $4.	16.00
Total	$73.00

Thus, the SPI, based on 1972 = 100, is

$$SPI = \frac{Cost\ of\ budget\ in\ 1979}{Cost\ of\ budget\ in\ 1972} = \frac{\$73}{\$50} = 1.46$$

TABLE 6–5

HYPOTHETICAL PRICES IN 1979

ITEM	PRICE	PERCENTAGE INCREASE OVER 1972
Hamburger	$ 0.60	50
Jeans	15.00	25
Movie tickets	4.00	60

So the SPI in 1979 stands at 146, meaning that students' cost of living has increased 46 percent over the 7 years.

HOW TO USE A PRICE INDEX TO "DEFLATE" MONETARY FIGURES

One of the most common uses of price indexes is in the comparison of monetary figures relating to two different points in time. The problem is that, if there has been inflation, the dollar is not a good measuring rod because it is worth less now than it was in the past.

Here is a simple example. Suppose that the average student spent $50 per month in 1972, and that this monthly spending figure had grown to $70 per month by 1979. If there was an outcry that students had become spendthrifts, how would you answer the charge?

The obvious answer is that a dollar in 1979 does not buy what it did in 1972. Specifically, our SPI shows us that it takes $1.46 in 1979 to purchase what $1 would purchase in 1972. To compare the spending habits of students in the two years, we must divide the 1979 spending figure by 1.46. Specifically, *real* spending per student in 1979 (where "real" is defined by 1972 dollars) is:

Real spending in 1979 =
$$\frac{\text{Nominal spending in 1979}}{\text{Price index of 1979}}$$

Thus,

$$\text{Real spending in 1979} = \frac{\$70}{1.46} = \$47.95$$

In sum, this calculation shows that, despite appearances to the contrary, the change in nominal spending from $50 to $70 actually represented a *decrease* in real spending.

This calculation procedure is called deflating by a price index, and it serves to translate noncomparable monetary figures into more directly comparable real figures. In general:

To find the real value of some monetary magnitude, we must divide by some appropriate price index. This process is called *deflating*.

THE GNP DEFLATOR

In macroeconomics, one of the most important of the monetary magnitudes that we have to deflate is the nominal gross national product (GNP). The price index used to do this is called the GNP deflator. Our general principle for deflating a nominal magnitude tells us just how to go from nominal GNP to real GNP:

$$\text{Real GNP} = \frac{\text{Nominal GNP}}{\text{GNP deflator}}$$

Economists often consider the GNP deflator to be a better measure of overall inflation in the economy than the Consumer Price Index. The main reason for this is that the two price indexes are based on different market baskets. As already mentioned, the CPI is based on the budget of a typical urban family. But the GNP deflator is constructed from a market basket that includes *every* item that is included in the GNP—that is, every final good and service produced by the economy. Thus, in addition to prices of consumer goods, the GNP deflator includes the prices of airplanes, lathes, and other goods purchased by business. It also includes government services. For this reason, the measures of inflation that these two indexes give are rarely the same. Fortunately, however, their disagreements usually are minor.

SUMMARY

1. Inflation is measured by the percentage increase in an index number of prices, which shows how the cost of some basket of goods has changed over a period of time.
2. Since relative prices are changing all the time, and since all families purchase different items, no price index can represent precisely the change in the cost of living for any particular family.
3. The Consumer Price Index (CPI) tries to measure the cost of living for an "average" urban household by pricing a "typical" market basket every month.
4. Price indexes like the CPI can be used to *deflate* monetary figures to make them more comparable. This amounts to dividing the monetary magnitude by the appropriate price index.
5. The GNP deflator is a better measure of economy-wide inflation than is the CPI because it includes the prices of every good and service in the economy.

CONCEPTS FOR REVIEW

Index number
Index number problem
Consumer Price Index

Deflating monetary figures by
a price index
GNP deflator

QUESTIONS FOR DISCUSSION

1. Just below you will find the amounts (in billions of dollars) that American consumers spent on various items in 1967 and in 1977. The Consumer Price Index in 1977 (on a base of 1967 = 100) was 181.5. Use this to deflate all the 1977 figures and to compare them with the 1967 figures. Which type of spending has grown most rapidly?

		ITEM	
YEAR	FOOD	GASOLINE AND OIL	HOUSING
		(billions of dollars)	
1967	109.6	17.0	74.1
1977	245.2	46.5	184.6

2. Just below you will find nominal GNP and the GNP deflator for 1957, 1967, and 1977.
   a. Compute real GNP for each year.
   b. Compute the percentage change in nominal and real GNP from 1957 to 1967, and from 1967 to 1977.
   c. Compute the percentage change in the GNP deflator over these two periods.

GNP STATISTICS
(billions of dollars)

	1957	1967	1977
Nominal GNP	$442.8	$796.3	$1887.2
GNP deflator	65.0	79.0	141.6

3. (More difficult) The example in the appendix showed that the Student Price Index (SPI) rose by 46 percent from 1972 to 1979. You can understand the meaning of this better if you:

    a. Use Table 6–4 to compute the fraction of total spending accounted for by each of the three items in 1972. Call these the "expenditure weights."

    b. Compute the weighted average of the percentage increases of the three prices shown in Table 6–5, using the expenditure weights you have just computed.

    c. You should get 46 percent as your answer. This shows that "inflation," as measured by the SPI, is a weighted average of the percentage price increases of all the items that are included in the index.

7

Aggregate Demand and the Powerful Consumer

In Chapter 5 we saw how the strength of aggregate demand influences the performance of the economy. When aggregate demand is growing briskly, the economy is likely to be booming, though it may also be having trouble with inflation. Similarly, when aggregate demand stagnates, a recession is likely to follow.

This chapter begins our detailed study of the *determination* of aggregate demand, a study that will lead to an understanding of how the government can *manage* aggregate demand.

Since consumer spending accounts for the lion's share of total demand, it is natural to begin with the consumer. In the next three chapters we will also bring investment spending and government spending into the picture.

We start the chapter with some definitions of alternative concepts of economic activity— distinguishing carefully between total *spending* (aggregate demand), total *output*, and total *income* in the economy. Second, we turn to the interaction between these three concepts, using a convenient pictorial device that shows how they are all interrelated in a market economy. Third, we note that government attempts to influence consumer spending have sometimes succeeded and sometimes failed, and we pose the question: Why? The bulk of the chapter is devoted to answering this question. To accomplish this, we first describe the important relationship between consumer income and consumer spending, and we use this relationship to show *how* government policies have worked *when* they have been successful. Then we discuss some complications that arise from the fact that consumer income, while crucially important, is not the only factor governing consumer spending. One of these complications enables us to understand why the aggregate demand curves of Chapter 5 were drawn with a negative slope. Another holds the clue to why government policies have sometimes failed to influence consumer spending as expected.

AGGREGATE DEMAND, NATIONAL PRODUCT, AND NATIONAL INCOME[1]

We begin with some definitions. Aggregate demand is a concept that we have been using already, but it is now time for a formal definition.

DEFINITION
Aggregate demand is the total amount that all consumers, business firms, and government agencies are willing to spend on goods and services.

As we noted in Chapter 5, aggregate demand is a schedule, just like any demand curve: The precise quantity demanded depends on the price level. One of the reasons why this demand schedule slopes downward will be explained later in this chapter.

[1]We will explore these and other concepts in much more detail in Chapter 17.

It will be convenient to have separate names for the three components of aggregate demand. Consumer expenditure ("consumption" for short) is simply the total demand for all consumer goods and services. This is the focus of the current chapter, and we shall abbreviate it by the letter C.

Investment spending, which we abbreviate by the letter I, is the amount that firms spend on factories, machinery, and the like, plus the amount that families spend on new houses. Notice that this is a very different usage of the word "investment" from that which is found in common parlance. Most people speak of "investing" in the stock market or in a bank account. This kind of "investment" merely swaps one form of financial asset (such as money) for another form (such as a share of stock). When economists speak of "investment," they mean instead the purchase of some *new physical* asset, like a drill press or an oil rig or a home. It is only this kind of investment that adds to the total demand for goods in the economy.

Finally, the last major component of aggregate demand is government purchases of goods and services; that is, things like paper, typewriters, airplanes, ships, and labor that all levels of government—federal, state, and local—buy. We use the shorthand symbol G to denote this variable. Given all these abbreviations, we have the following shorthand definition of aggregate demand.

Aggregate demand is the sum of $C + I + G$.

For the most part, what is demanded gets produced in a market economy. This fact leads to our next important concept.

DEFINITION
National product is the total output of the economy, including all the final goods and services produced by the nation's factories, offices, and shops.

This is what government statisticians measure when they compute the gross national product, and we shall use the GNP as our measure of national product.

Last we have the concept of the total *income* of all the individuals in the economy. There are two versions of this: one for before-tax incomes and for after-tax incomes.

DEFINITION

National income is the sum of the incomes of all the individuals in the economy from wages, interest, rents, and profits, *before* deductions for taxes.

Disposable income is the sum of the incomes of all the individuals in the economy after all taxes have been deducted.

The term "disposable income" is meant to be descriptive: It tells us how many dollars consumers actually have available to spend or to save. Because it plays such a prominent role in this chapter, we shall need an abbreviation for it as well; we call it *DI*.

THE CIRCULAR FLOW OF SPENDING, PRODUCTION, AND INCOME

How do these three concepts interact in a market economy? We can answer this best with a rather elaborate diagram (Figure 7–1), which the balance of this section seeks to explain. For obvious reasons, Figure 7–1 is called a circular flow diagram. It depicts a large circular tube in which a fluid is circulating in a clockwise direction. There are several breaks in the tube where either some of the fluid leaks out or additional fluid is injected in.

Let us examine this system beginning on the far left. Here, at point 1 on the circle, we find consumers. Disposable income (*DI*) is flowing into them, and two things are flowing out: consumption (*C*), which stays in the circular flow, and saving (*S*), which "leaks" out of the

flow. This just says that consumers normally spend less than they earn and save the balance.

The upper loop of the circular flow represents expenditures, and as we move clockwise to point 2, we encounter the first "injection" into the flow: investment spending (*I*). The diagram shows this as coming from "investors"—a group that includes both business firms and consumers who buy new homes.[2] As the circular flow moves beyond point 2, it is bigger than it was before. Total spending has increased from *C* to *C* + *I*.

At point 3 there is yet another injection. The government adds its demand for goods and services (*G*) to those of consumers and investors (*C* + *I*). Thus, by the time we have passed point 3, we have accumulated the full amount of aggregate demand, *C* + *I* + *G*.

The circular flow diagram shows this aggregate demand for goods and services arriving at the business firms, which are located at point 4 on the extreme right of the diagram. Responding to this demand, firms produce the national product. As the circular flow emerges from the firms, however, we have renamed it *national income*. Why? The reason is that, except for some complications that need not detain us here:[3]

National income and national product must be equal.

Why is this the case? Because when a firm produces and sells $100 worth of output, it must pay a good deal of the proceeds to its workers, to people who have lent it money, and to the landlord who owns the property on which it is located. All of these payments become *income* to some individuals. Suppose, for example, that the wages, interest, and rent that the firm pays add up to $90, while its output is $100. What happens to the remaining $10? The answer is that the owners of the firm receive it as *profits*.

---

[2]You are reminded of the specific definition of investment on page 113.

[3]For a fuller explanation, see Chapter 17, pages 321–322.

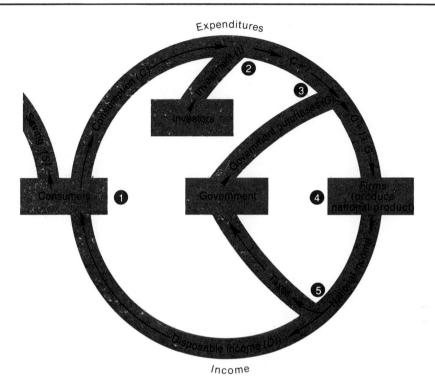

FIGURE 7–1

THE CIRCULAR FLOW OF EXPENDITURE AND INCOME

The upper half of this circular flow diagram depicts the flow of expenditures on goods and services, which comes from consumers (point 1), investors (point 2), and government (point 3), and goes to the firms that produce the output (point 4). The lower half of the diagram indicates how the income paid out by firms (point 4) flows to consumers (point 1), after some is siphoned off by the government in the form of taxes (point 5).

But these owners are also citizens of the country, so their incomes count in national income, too. Thus, when we add up all the wages, interest, rents, *and* profits in the economy to obtain the national income, we must arrive at the value of the national output.

The lower loop of the circular flow diagram traces the flow of income by showing the national income leaving the firms and heading for consumers. But there is a detour along the way. At point 5, the government siphons off a portion of the national income in the form of taxes. Once it has passed point 5, the remaining

income—now called disposable income—flows unimpeded to consumers at point 1, and the cycle repeats.

This diagram raises several complicated questions. Although we pose them here, we will not try to answer them fully at this early stage. The answers will be made clear in subsequent chapters.

1. Is the output that the firms produce at point 4 (the GNP) equal to aggregate demand? If so, what makes these two quantities equal? If not, what happens?

2. Is the flow of spending and income growing larger or smaller as we move clockwise around the circle, and why?

Chapter 8 provides the answers to questions 1 and 2.

3. Are the government's accounts in balance, so that what flows in at point 5 (taxes) is equal to what flows out at point 3 (government purchases)? What happens if they are not?

This important question is first addressed in Chapter 10 and then recurs many times.

The reason we cannot discuss these issues profitably now is that first we need to acquire an understanding of what goes on at point 1 (where consumers make decisions) and point 2 (where investors make decisions). We turn next, therefore, to the determinants of consumer spending.

DEMAND MANAGEMENT AND THE POWERFUL CONSUMER

As we learned in Chapter 5, the government often wants to shift the aggregate demand curve. And there are a number of ways in which it can try to do so. One direct approach is to alter its own spending (*G*), becoming extravagant when private demand is weak and miserly when private demand is strong. But the government can also take a more indirect route by using taxes and other policy tools to influence *private* spending decisions. A government desiring to change private spending can choose to concentrate its energies either on consumer spending (*C*) or on investment spending (*I*). At various times in our history, the U.S. government has elected to pursue one or the other of these courses of action; sometimes it has endeavored to do both. Since consumer expenditures constitute more than 70 percent of gross

national product, *C* presents the most tempting target. For this reason, demand management is often consumption oriented.

While there are many things it can do to alter consumer spending, the government's principal weapon is the personal income tax. Many of you already have encountered Form 1040, the unwelcome New Year's greeting that every taxpayer receives from the federal government each January. Many more of you probably have been on a payroll and seen a share of your wages deducted and sent to the Internal Revenue Service. It should be no mystery, then, how changes in the income tax affect consumer spending. Any reduction in income taxes leaves consumers with more disposable income to spend. Any increase in taxes leaves less. The linkage from taxes to disposable income to consumer spending seems direct and unmistakable, and, in a certain sense, it is. But a look at the recent history of tax changes aimed at altering *C* is sobering. The varying degrees of success both of the measures themselves and of the predictions of their effects explain why economic research into the relationship between taxes and consumption continues.

CASE 1:
The 1964 Tax Reduction

The year 1964 was a good one for the economy but an even better one for economists. For years economists had been proclaiming that a cut in personal taxes would be an excellent way to stimulate a stagnating economy. But the plea fell on deaf ears until President John F. Kennedy was persuaded of the basic logic of the argument. Under his successor, Lyndon B. Johnson, the Congress reduced personal taxes by about $9 billion per year, almost 18 percent of the total personal taxes then being collected. The legislation was designed to spur consumer spending, and it succeeded admirably. Consumers reacted just about as the textbooks of the day predicted, the economic situation improved rapidly and markedly, and economists smiled knowingly.

CASE 2:
The 1968 Tax Increase

The euphoria of 1964 and 1965 was both un-warranted and short-lived. In 1968–1969 we learned—the hard way—that economists did not have all the answers. Largely because of the massive defense spending associated with the Vietnam War, the macroeconomic problem of 1966–1968 was precisely the opposite from 1964: too much demand rather than too little. It appeared logical, then, to prescribe the oppo-site medicine; and economists were quick to suggest an increase in personal income taxes to force consumers to spend less.

After a considerable delay, President Johnson recommended a temporary tax increase and Congress enacted a 10 percent rise in personal tax payments (calling it a "surcharge"). However, this attempt to cut aggregate demand by reducing C enjoyed only modest success. While consumer spending probably was below what it would have been in the absence of the surcharge, it was substan-tially above what the 1964 experience had led economists to predict. The economic textbooks of 1968 obviously needed to be revised.

CASE 3:
The 1975 Tax Reduction

The next major change in tax laws for stabi-lization purposes also met with only partial success. In the spring of 1975, as the economy neared the bottom of its worst postwar reces-sion, President Gerald R. Ford and Congress agreed on a double-edged tax cut amounting to over $20 billion. First, they returned to each taxpayer part of the taxes paid in 1974. Second, they reduced income tax rates for the balance of 1975. (This was subsequently extended.)

What happened? Not as much as had been hoped. Consumers confounded the wishes of the president and Congress by saving a good deal of their rebates rather than spending them.

What went wrong in 1968 and 1975 that had not gone wrong in 1964? Although economic research on this important question is not yet complete, this chapter will attempt to provide some answers. We begin by exploring the important relationship between consumer income and consumer spending, more or less retracing the chain of logic that led government economists to the right conclusion in 1964. Once this is accomplished, we turn to some of the complications that made things go awry in 1968 and 1975.

CONSUMER SPENDING AND INCOME: THE IMPORTANT RELATIONSHIP

An economist interested in predicting how consumer spending will respond to a change in personal income tax payments must first ask how C is related to income, for an increase in taxes is just a way to lower after-tax disposable income (refer to Figure 7–1) and a reduction in taxes is just a way to raise after-tax income. This section, therefore, will examine what we know about the response of consumer spending to a change in disposable income.

Figure 7–2 depicts the historical paths of C and DI for the United States since 1929. The association is obviously rather close and certainly suggests that consumption will rise whenever disposable income does, and fall whenever income falls. The difference between the two lines is personal saving. Notice how little saving consumers did during the Great Depression of the 1930s, where the two lines are very close together, and how much they did during World War II, when many consumer goods were either unavailable or rationed so that there was little on which to spend money.

117

Of course, knowing that consumer expenditures, *C*, will move in the same direction as disposable income, *DI*, is not enough for the policy planner. He needs to know *how much* one will go up when the other rises a given amount. Figure 7–3 presents the same data that we saw in Figure 7–2 but in a way designed to help answer the "how much" question. Econ-

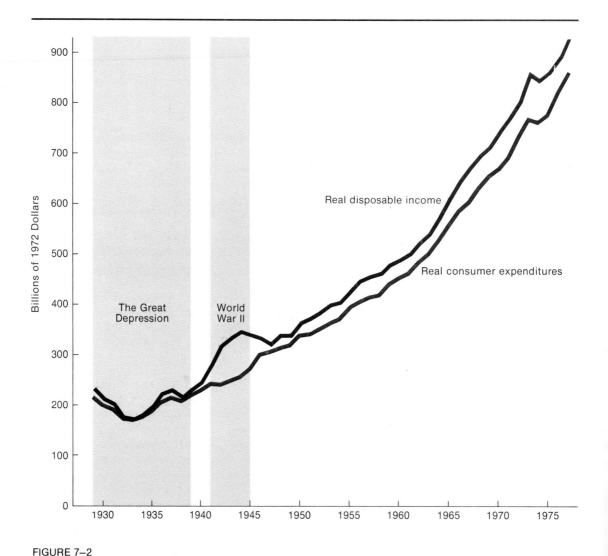

FIGURE 7–2

CONSUMER SPENDING AND DISPOSABLE INCOME IN THE UNITED STATES SINCE 1929
This time series chart shows the behavior of consumer spending and disposable income in the United States since 1929. Except for the World War II years, the correspondence between the two variables is remarkably close. The distance between the two lines represents consumer saving, which was obviously quite small during the Great Depression of the 1930s and quite large during World War II.

Source: U.S. Department of Commerce.

omists call such pictures *scatter diagrams,* and they are very useful in predicting how one economic variable (in this case, consumer spending) will change in response to a change in another economic variable (in this case, disposable income). Each dot in the diagram represents the data on C and DI corresponding to a particular year. For example, the point

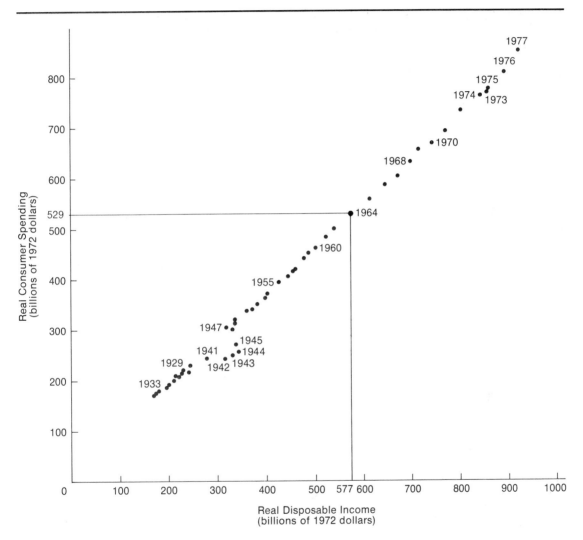

FIGURE 7–3

SCATTER DIAGRAM OF CONSUMER SPENDING AND DISPOSABLE INCOME IN THE UNITED STATES, 1929–1977

This diagram shows the same data as depicted in Figure 7–2 but in a different manner. Each point on the diagram represents the data for both consumer spending and disposable income during a particular year. For example, the point labeled "1964" indicates that in that year consumer spending was $529 billion while disposable income was $577 billion. Diagrams like this one are called "scatter diagrams."

labeled "1964" shows us that real consumer expenditures in 1964 were $529 billion (which we read off the vertical axis), while real disposable incomes amounted to $577 billion (which we read off the horizontal axis). Similarly, each year from 1929 to 1977 is represented by its own dot in Figure 7–3.

How can such a diagram assist the fiscal policy planner? Imagine that this is 1963 and you must decide whether to recommend to Congress a tax cut of $5 billion, $10 billion, or $15 billion. (It has already been decided that a cut smaller than $5 billion is not worth the legislative effort and that a cut of more than $15 billion is politically infeasible). You have forecasts of what consumer expenditures are expected to be if taxes are not reduced. This, plus other forecasts of investment and government spending, has led you to conclude that aggregate demand in 1964 will be insufficient if taxes are not reduced.

To assist your imagination, another scatter diagram is given in Figure 7–4. This one removes the points for 1964 through 1977, which appeared in Figure 7–3; after all, these would not have been known in 1963. Years prior to 1947 have also been removed because both the Great Depression and wartime rationing seriously disturbed the normal relationship between DI and C. With no more training in economics than you have right now, what would you do?

One rough-and-ready approach is to get a ruler, set it down on Figure 7–4 and sketch a straight line that comes as close as possible to hitting all the points. Try that now. If your ruler is straight, you will not be able to hit each point exactly, but you will find that you can come remarkably close. The line you have just drawn summarizes, in a very rough way, the consumption–income relationship that is the focus of this chapter. We see at once that it confirms something we might have guessed—that a rise in income is associated with a rise in consumer spending. The slope of the line is certainly positive.

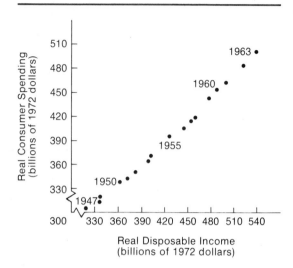

FIGURE 7–4

SCATTER DIAGRAM OF CONSUMER SPENDING AND DISPOSABLE INCOME IN THE UNITED STATES, 1947–1963
This scatter diagram omits some of the data found in Figure 7–3 and indicates the information that policy planners might have used in deciding upon the size of the 1964 income tax cut.

The slope of your line is very important.[4] It provides the answer to such questions as, If DI rises by $100 billion, by how much will C rise? We can use the line through the dots to answer this question. That line has been drawn into Figure 7–5, and we note that the horizontal move from point A to point B represents a rise of $100 billion in disposable income, from $420 billion to $520 billion. Corresponding to it there is a rise in consumption represented by the vertical move from point D to point E, a rise of about $90 billion. The slope of the line is:

$$\text{Slope} = \frac{\text{Vertical distance}}{\text{Horizontal distance}}$$
$$= \frac{\$90 \text{ billion}}{\$100 \text{ billion}} = 0.90$$

[4]To review the concept of *slope*, turn back to page 22.

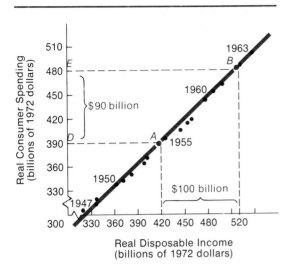

FIGURE 7–5

SCATTER DIAGRAM OF CONSUMER
SPENDING AND DISPOSABLE INCOME
IN THE UNITED STATES, 1947–1963
This diagram is the same as Figure 7–4 except for the
addition of a straight line that comes about as close as
possible to fitting all the data points.

In terms of the policy issue of 1964, this
line can help to provide answers to the question: How much more consumer spending will
be induced by tax cuts of $5 billion, $10 billion,
or $15 billion if the effects are similar to those
observed in the past described by the graph?
To answer this question, we need only multiply
each prospective tax cut by the observed slope
(0.90) to get $4.5 billion, $9.0 billion, and $13.5
billion, respectively. Similar questions
addressed by economists in 1964 led to a decision to cut taxes by about $9 billion.

SUMMARY
From a graph relating consumption to disposable income, we can estimate how large a tax
cut is necessary to induce any desired change
in consumption. To do so, we draw in the

vertical line representing the desired change in
spending and read off the corresponding horizontal distance to obtain the required change in
taxes.

Later in this and other chapters, we will
encounter several reasons why this procedure,
while basically valid, must be used with great
caution.

THE CONSUMPTION FUNCTION
AND THE MARGINAL PROPENSITY
TO CONSUME

It has been said that economics is just systema-
tized common sense. Let us, then, try to organize and generalize what has been a completely
intuitive discussion thus far.

One thing we have learned is that there
is a close and apparently reliable relationship
between consumer spending, C, and disposable
income, DI. Economists call this relationship the
consumption function.

DEFINITION
The consumption function is the relationship
between total consumer expenditure and total
disposable income in the economy. It is
described by a graph like Figure 7–5.

A second fact we have picked up from
these figures is that the slope of the consumption function is fairly constant. We infer this
from the fact that our straight line in Figure 7–4
came so close to touching every point. If the
slope of the consumption function had changed
a lot, we would not have been able to do so well
with a single straight line. Because of its importance in such applications as the tax-cut
example, economists have given a special name
to this slope—the marginal propensity to
consume.

DEFINITION

The *marginal propensity to consume* (or MPC for short) tells us how many more dollars consumers will spend if disposable income rises by $1 billion. On a graph, it appears as the slope of the consumption function. Its formula is

$$\text{MPC} = \frac{\text{Change in consumption}}{\begin{array}{c}\text{Change in income that produces the}\\\text{change in consumption}\end{array}}$$

This concept is best illustrated by an example, and for this purpose we turn away from U.S. data for a moment and look at the consumption and income data of a hypothetical country called Macroland (see Table 7–1). The data for Macroland resemble those for the United States, except that C and DI figures happen to be nice round numbers in Macroland, which facilitates computation.

Columns 1 and 2 of Table 7–1 show annual consumer expenditure from 1974 to 1978 and disposable income from 1974 to 1979. These two columns constitute Macroland's consumption function and are plotted in Figure 7–6. Column 3 shows the marginal propensity to consume (MPC), which is the slope of the line in Figure 7–6; it is derived from the first two columns. Ignore column 4 for now; we will come back to it later. We can see that between

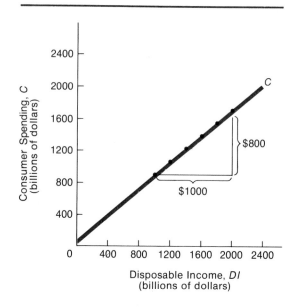

FIGURE 7–6

THE CONSUMPTION FUNCTION OF MACROLAND

This diagram is similar to Figure 7–4, except that it applies to a hypothetical (and blissfully simple!) economy called Macroland. As can be seen, a straight-line consumption function passes through every point exactly. The slope of this line is 0.8, which is the marginal propensity to consume in Macroland.

TABLE 7–1

CONSUMPTION AND INCOME IN MACROLAND

YEAR	(1) CONSUMPTION, C (billions of dollars)	(2) DISPOSABLE INCOME, DI (billions of dollars)	(3) MARGINAL PROPENSITY TO CONSUME, MPC	(4) AVERAGE PROPENSITY TO CONSUME, APC
1974	900	1000		0.900
1975	1060	1200	0.8	0.883
1976	1220	1400	0.8	0.871
1977	1380	1600	0.8	0.863
1978	1540	1800	0.8	0.856
1979	—	2000	0.8	—

1974 and 1975, *DI* rose by $200 billion (from $1000 to $1200) while *C* rose by $160 billion (from $900 to $1060). Thus the MPC was:

$$\frac{\text{Change in consumption}}{\text{Change in disposable income}} = \frac{\$160}{\$200} = 0.80$$

As you can easily verify, the MPC between any other pair of years was also 0.80. This explains why the slope of the line in Figure 7–5 was so crucial in estimating the effect of a tax cut. This slope, which we found to be 0.90, is nothing but the MPC. And it is the MPC that tells us how much *additional* spending will be induced by each dollar *change* in income. For each $1 of tax cut, economists expect consumption to rise by $1 times the marginal propensity to consume. Thus:

To estimate the initial effect of a tax cut on consumer spending, economists must first estimate the MPC and then multiply the amount of the tax cut by the estimated MPC. But since they never know the true MPC with certainty, this prediction is always subject to some margin of error.[5]

In 1963, for example, economists multiplied the anticipated $9 billion tax cut by the estimated MPC of 0.90 and concluded that consumer spending would initially rise by about $8 billion. This calculation seems to have been remarkably accurate.

MOVEMENTS ALONG VERSUS SHIFTS OF THE CONSUMPTION FUNCTION

Unfortunately, this sort of calculation does not always yield such precise results. Among the most important reasons for this is that the

consumption function does not always stand still; sometimes it shifts.

You will recall from Chapter 4 the important distinction between a *movement along* a demand (or supply) curve and a *shift of* the curve.[6] A similar distinction is vital to understanding real-world consumption functions. Any change in disposable income (caused, for example, by a change in the income tax) leads to a movement along the consumption function. This is the sort of phenomenon we have been considering in the last two sections. But consumption also has other determinants. And since the consumption schedule relates *C* to *DI*, any change in one of these "other determinants" of consumer spending (which we will consider in the following sections) will shift the entire consumption function. It is these unexpected shifts that account for many of the errors in forecasting consumption. To summarize:

Any change in disposable income moves us along a given consumption function. But a change in any of the other variables that influence consumption results in a shift in the entire consumption schedule.

Let us now see what some of these "other variables" are.

Other Determinants of Consumer Spending

One factor is simple *inertia,* the fact that households normally take some time to adjust to changed economic circumstances. If income rises at an extraordinary pace—as in an economic boom—consumer spending probably will not surge ahead as fast as income. You can see this by a close-to-home example. Unless you continue on to graduate study, your income will register a very sharp increase when you graduate from college and get a job. See how

---

[5]The word "initial" in the first sentence is an important one. Later chapters explain why the effects discussed in this chapter are only the beginning of the story.

[6]If you need review, consult pages 58–60.

long it takes until your spending habits have caught up. The same process works in reverse. At the onset of a recession, consumers normally try to maintain their customary spending levels despite losses of income.

A second factor is consumers' *wealth,* which is a source of demand in addition to income. Consider two consumers, both earning $20,000 this year. One of them has $100,000 in the bank, while the other has no assets at all. Who do you think will spend more this year? Presumably the one with the big bank account. The general point is that current income is not the only source of funds that households have; they can also finance spending by withdrawals from their bank accounts or by cashing in other forms of wealth. A stock market boom may therefore raise the consumption function, while a collapse of stock prices may lower it.

The Price Level and Consumer Spending

The next determinant of consumer spending— *the price level*—is very important for the construction of our aggregate demand curve.

We know from our discussion of inflation in Chapter 6 that a rise in prices, unless it has been fully expected, will impose a loss upon lenders (who get back dollars of lower purchasing power than those they lent) and bestow a gift upon borrowers. In the U.S. economy, consumers as a group are the biggest lenders, generally lending much more than they borrow. They lend money to banks when they deposit money in their checking and saving accounts; they lend to corporations when they buy corporate bonds; and they lend to the government when they buy government bonds. For this reason:

Consumers' purchasing power normally is eroded by higher prices, and this leads consumers to demand fewer goods and services.

On the other hand, should prices fall, consumers would enjoy a windfall gain because the banks, corporations, and governments that had borrowed money would have to pay consumers back in dearer dollars. Thus:

Consumers' purchasing power is enhanced by lower prices, and this leads consumers to spend more.

Thus we see that the price level is another variable that can shift the consumption function. Consumers lose purchasing power when prices rise because of reductions in the value of the money they have lent to banks, corporations, and government; and this deters spending. Since there is less spending at any given income level, rising prices pull the consumption function down. Similarly, falling prices push the consumption function up.

This is one reason why we drew our aggregate demand schedules in Chapter 5 with negative slopes, indicating that total demand is lower when prices are higher. Higher prices, we now see, lead to lower consumer spending, *C.* And since *C* is a component of aggregate demand (the sum of $C + I + G$), higher prices lead to lower aggregate demand. Other reasons for the downward slope of the aggregate demand schedule will be encountered in subsequent chapters.

ARE ALL CONSUMERS ALIKE?

One aspect of the consumption function often bothers students. When we draw up a consumption function, we assume that *total* consumer spending depends on *total* disposable income, not on how it is distributed among the individual consumers. This is just the usual process of *aggregation,* which we discussed in Chapter 5.

However, this is one instance in which students often find the aggregation assumption totally unbelievable. "Do you really expect us to believe," they ask, "that total spending will not change if David Rockefeller gives $1000 to each one of us?" Clearly, we do not. The aggregation assumption cannot be literally true. It does seem clear that this hypothetical transfer of money would lead to an increase in consumption, even though it does not change total money income in the community. So the way income is distributed apparently does affect total consumption. Yet despite this, the macroeconomic consumption function still works.

One reason for its apparent success is that people's marginal propensities to consume are much closer together than is commonly supposed. In thinking intuitively about the notion that the rich spend less of their income than the poor, most people naturally gravitate not toward the MPC but toward a different concept, which we can now profitably define.

DEFINITION

The *average propensity to consume* (or APC for short) is the ratio of consumption to disposable income. It tells us what fraction of disposable income is spent.

Look back at Table 7–1 on page 122. In column 4 you will find the average propensity to consume in Macroland for each year from 1974 to 1978. For example, since 90 cents of every dollar of income was spent in 1974, the APC was 0.900. Similarly, in 1975 consumers in Macroland spent $1060 billion out of $1200 billion, so the APC was $1060/$1200 = 0.883.

To check your understanding of the distinction between the MPC and the APC, fill in the blank spaces in Table 7–1. If the MPC remains 0.8 in 1979, how much will consumers spend? (Answer: $1700 billion). Given this spending total, what is the APC? (Answer: $1700/$2000 = 0.85).

This distinction helps us understand why a redistribution of income from David Rockefeller to you might not change total consumer spending as much as is commonly supposed.

To see why, imagine that the years 1974–1979 in Table 7–1 represent different *people* instead of different *points in time*. The poor man with an income of $1000 consumes 90 percent of what he earns, while the rich man with an income of $2000 consumes only 85 percent. Rich people *do* have lower APCs than poor people, just as is commonly believed. But, at least in this example, *every* person has the same MPC, and it is the MPCs that matter. Suppose, for instance, that Smith loses $100 to Jones. Then Smith's spending will fall by $80 (since the MPC for everyone is 0.8), while Jones's spending will rise by the same amount. With equal MPCs for all, then, there is no change in total spending whether Smith is richer than Jones or the other way around. How the total income of society is distributed has no bearing on total consumption.

The explanation of a consumption function with equal MPCs for all but lower APCs for the rich is pretty simple. A poor person has to make certain expenditures on necessities whether he has the income or not; if he does not, he must borrow and fall into debt. That is why he has a large APC. It will generally be close to 1. But if he then gets *another* $1, he may use 20 cents of it to help pay back some debt, and 80 cents to help pay for more food. Thus his MPC is only 0.8, despite the fact that his APC is about 1. Rockefeller, for his part, might put 20 cents of an additional $1 into the bank and devote 80 cents to the purchase of caviar. These behavior patterns are clearly quite different. Yet both the pauper and Rockefeller have reacted to the receipt of an additional $1 by spending 80 cents and saving 20 cents. The general lesson is that:

Marginal propensities to consume among people in different income classes are much closer together than *average* propensities to consume. Since it is the MPCs that govern how total consumer spending varies when income gets redistributed, most changes in the distribution of income have little effect on total spending.

There is a second reason why the distribution of income has only a minor effect on the consumption function. Income changes in the real world tend to be much less extreme than the example of transferring money from David Rockefeller to you. Between 1976 and 1977, for example, disposable income in America rose by $119 billion, and virtually every household participated in this change. While a few did suffer a reduction in income, most households gained. On the average, the increases in income were distributed among households in approximately the same way as were initial 1977 incomes, so the distribution of income hardly changed.[7] Little wonder, then, that the distribution of income did not influence total spending very much.

In comparing any two years of American history, the differences in the distribution of income are likely to be quite small. Thus, even if MPCs for individual consumers varied widely, society's MPC would probably not fluctuate much from year to year.

WHY TAX POLICY FAILED IN 1968 AND 1975

Let us now return to a question raised early in the chapter: What went wrong when the U.S. government tried to influence consumption by raising taxes in 1968 and by cutting taxes in 1975? To explain these episodes, we must consider income in years other than the years in which those changes occurred. As is often the case, people's feelings about the future probably hold the key.

[7]Statisticians call this the "law of large numbers"; the man in the street calls it the "law of averages." The simplest illustration of the law of large numbers is in flipping a coin. If you flip a coin once and try to guess whether it will land heads or tails, you will err about half the time. But if you flip a fair coin 10,000 times and predict that between 4900 and 5100 heads will appear, you will almost always be right. These are the kinds of predictions macroeconomists make. The law of large numbers is what makes macroeconomics work.

To understand how expectations of future incomes affect current consumer expenditures, consider the abbreviated life histories of three consumers given in Table 7–2. The reason for giving our three imaginary individuals such odd names will be apparent shortly.

The consumer named "No Cut" earned $100 in each of the 4 years considered in the table. The consumer named "Temporary Cut" earned $100 in 3 of the 4 years, but had a bad year in 1968. The consumer named "Permanent Cut" suffered a permanent drop in income in 1968 and was clearly the poorest.

Now let us use our common sense to figure out how much each of these consumers might have spent in 1968. "Temporary Cut" and "Permanent Cut" had the same income. Do you think they spent the same amount? Not if they had some ability to foresee their future incomes, because "Temporary Cut" was richer in the long run.

Now compare "No Cut" and "Temporary Cut." No Cut had 25 percent higher income in 1968 ($100 versus $80) but only about 5 percent more over the entire 4-year period ($400 versus $380). Do you think her spending was closer to 25 percent above Temporary Cut's or closer to 5 percent above? Most people guess the latter.

The central point of this example is that it is reasonable for consumers to decide on their *current* consumption spending by looking at their *long-run* income prospects. This should not be a shocking idea to most college students. How many of you are spending only

TABLE 7–2

INCOMES OF THREE CONSUMERS

CONSUMER	INCOMES IN EACH YEAR				TOTAL INCOME
	1967	1968	1969	1970	
No Cut	100	100	100	100	400
Temporary Cut	100	80	100	100	380
Permanent Cut	100	80	80	80	340

what you earn this year? Probably not very many. And this is not because you are all foolish spendthrifts. On the contrary, you are rational planners. Knowing that your college education gives you a reasonable expectation of future income prospects much greater than those you now have, you are no doubt spending with that in mind.

Now let us see what all this has to do with the failure of the 1968 income tax surcharge. For this purpose, imagine that the three rows in Table 7–2 stand for the whole economy under three different government policies. Recall that 1968 was the year of the surtax. The first row ("No Cut") shows the unchanged path of disposable income if no tax hike was enacted. The second ("Temporary Cut") shows a drop in disposable income attributable to a tax increase *for one year only.* Finally, the bottom row ("Permanent Cut") shows a policy of reducing *DI* in *every future year* by raising taxes permanently in 1968. Which of the two lower rows do you imagine would have generated the least consumer spending in 1968? The bottom row ("Permanent Cut"), of course. What we have concluded, then, is this:

Permanent increases in income taxes cause greater reductions in consumer spending than do temporary increases of equal magnitude.

The application of this analysis to 1968 is immediate. The president and Congress stated very clearly that the surcharge was to be in force for only one year (although they subsequently reneged on this pledge). The typical consumer thus suffered an income loss that was like "Temporary Cut," not like "Permanent Cut." By contrast, the tax cuts of 1964 and 1965 were "permanent"; indeed, these alterations in the tax code are still on the books. Little wonder, then, that the 1968 tax increase failed to work as well as the 1964 tax cut.

The tax cuts of 1975 were originally announced to be even more temporary in nature than the tax increases of 1968, although they too were subsequently extended. About half of them came in the form of lower tax rates for 1975; in this respect, they were like a repeat performance of 1968 but in the opposite direction. The remaining portion of the 1975 cuts were accomplished by returning some of the 1974 taxes that households had already paid. *No future income was affected.* Thus, it was a pure windfall gain to 1974 taxpayers and, as might have been expected, their expenditures responded in muted fashion. The fiscal authorities had apparently not learned the following lesson:

A permanent decrease in income taxes provides a greater stimulus to consumer spending than does a temporary decrease of equal magnitude.

We have, then, what appears to be a general principle, backed up both by historical evidence and common sense. Permanent changes in income taxes have a more significant impact on consumer spending decisions than do temporary changes. Though it may now seem obvious, this is not a lesson you would have learned from the introductory textbooks of 1968; it is one that we learned the hard way, through bitter experience. The tax surcharge of 1968 was meant to stop, or at least slow down, inflation. Yet consumer prices rose faster in 1968 than they had in 1967, and faster in 1969 than in 1968. The tax reductions of 1975 were meant to halt a precipitous downswing in economic activity. It was subsequently learned that the recession had bottomed out, of its own accord, before the cuts became effective, and the recovery in consumer spending was not all that spectacular.

THE PREDICTABILITY OF CONSUMER BEHAVIOR

We have now learned enough to see why the economist's problem in predicting how consumers will react to an increase or decrease in taxes is not quite as simple as suggested earlier in this chapter.

The principal problem seems to be anticipating how taxpayers will view any changes in the income tax law. If the government *says* that a tax cut is permanent, will consumers *believe* them and increase their spending accordingly? Perhaps not, if the government has a history of raising taxes after promising to keep them low. Similarly, when (as in 1968) the government specifically announces that a tax hike is temporary, will consumers always believe this? Or might they greet such an announcement with a hefty dose of skepticism? This is quite possible if there is a long history of "temporary" tax increases that stayed on the books indefinitely. Thus the effectiveness of any *future* tax policy move may well depend on the government's *past* track record. A government that repeatedly uses a succession of so-called "permanent" tax cuts and tax increases for short-run stabilization purposes may find consumers beginning to ignore the tax changes entirely. The story of the boy who cried wolf is not yet required reading for fiscal policy planners; but some day it may be.

Nor is this the only problem. Economists may underestimate or overestimate the degree of inertia in consumer behavior. Their predictions may fail to account adequately for large and rapid accumulations of wealth (as happened immediately after World War II, when consumption forecasts were notoriously low) or for sizable losses of wealth (such as the drastic decline in the stock market in 1973–1975, when consumption forecasts were too high). Poor forecasts of future prices may lead consumption forecasts astray. Sudden changes in the income distribution may (but normally do not) foul up predictions. And there are further hazards that we have not even mentioned here. Economic predictions are inexact, and the lesson of predictions based on the consumption function illustrates this well.

There is much more that could be said about the determinants of consumption, but it is best to leave the rest to more advanced courses in macroeconomics. For we are now ready to apply our knowledge of the consumption function to the construction of the first model of the whole economy. While it is true that income determines consumption, the consumption function also helps determine the level of income. If that sounds like circular reasoning, read the next chapter!

SUMMARY

1. Aggregate demand is the total amount of goods and services that consumers, businesses, and government units are willing to purchase. It can be expressed as the sum $C + I + G$, where C is consumer spending, I is investment spending, and G is government spending.
2. Economists reserve the term "investment" to refer to purchases of newly produced factories, machinery, and houses.
3. National product is the total output of final goods and services of the economy. It is most commonly measured by the gross national product.
4. National income is the sum of the before-tax wages, interest, rents, and profits received by all individuals in the economy. By necessity, it must be equal to national product.
5. Disposable income is the sum of the after-tax incomes of all individuals in the economy, and is the chief determinant of consumer expenditures.
6. All of these concepts, and others, can be depicted in a circular flow diagram that shows expenditures on all three sources flowing into business firms and national income flowing out.

7. The government often has tried to manipulate aggregate demand by influencing private consumption decisions, usually through the personal income tax. Although this policy seemed to work very well in 1964, it did not work very well in 1968 and 1975.

8. The close relationship between consumer spending (*C*) and disposable income (*DI*) is called the consumption function. Its slope, which is used to predict the change in consumption that will be caused by a change in income taxes, is called the marginal propensity to consume (MPC).

9. Changes in disposable income move us along a given consumption function. Changes in any of the other variables that affect *C* will shift the entire consumption function. Among the most important of these other variables are total consumer wealth, the price level, and expected future incomes.

10. Because consumers typically lend much more than they borrow, they lose out when prices rise, which leads them to reduce their spending. This decline in consumer demand when prices rise helps explain why the aggregate demand curve slopes downward.

11. Future income prospects help explain why tax policy did not affect consumption as much as was hoped in 1968 and 1975. This is because the 1968 tax increase and the 1975 tax cut were both temporary, and therefore left future incomes unaffected. By contrast, the 1964 tax cut was "permanent," and affected future as well as current incomes. It is no surprise, then, that the 1964 actions had stronger effects on spending than did the 1968 or 1975 actions.

12. The income distribution does not affect the consumption function as much as many people think. One reason is that marginal propensities to consume among rich and poor people are much closer together than are average propensities to consume. Another is that year-to-year fluctuations in national income usually do not change the distribution of income very much.

CONCEPTS FOR REVIEW

Aggregate demand
$C + I + G$
National product
National income
Disposable income
Circular flow diagram
Consumption function
Marginal propensity to consume

Movements along versus shifts of the consumption function
Average propensity to consume
Temporary versus permanent tax changes
Downward slope of the aggregate demand curve

QUESTIONS FOR DISCUSSION

1. What are the three components of aggregate demand? Which of these is the largest?

2. Suppose investment spending were always $100, government spending were always $50, and consumer spending depended on the price level in the following way:

PRICE LEVEL	CONSUMER SPENDING
80	370
90	360
100	350
110	340
120	330

On a piece of graph paper, use these data to construct an aggregate demand curve of the type we used in Chapter 5. Why do we suppose that consumption is lower at higher price levels in this example?

3. What is the difference between "investment" as the term is used by most people and "investment" as defined by an economist? Which of the following acts constitute "investment" according to the economist's definition?
   a. General Motors constructs a new assembly line
   b. You buy 100 shares of General Motors stock
   c. A small steel company goes bankrupt, and U.S. Steel purchases its factory and equipment
   d. Your family buys a newly constructed home from a developer
   e. Your family buys an older home from another family (*Hint:* Are any *new* products demanded by this action?)

4. What would the circular flow diagram (Figure 7–1, page 115) look like in an economy with no government? Draw one for yourself.

5. The marginal propensity to consume (MPC) for the nation as a whole is roughly 0.90. Explain in words what this means. What is your personal MPC?

6. The average propensity to consume (APC) for the nation as a whole is roughly 0.94. Explain in words what this means. What is your personal APC? Does it differ from your personal MPC?

7. Look at the scatter diagram in Figure 7–3 (page 119). What does it tell you about what was going on in this country in the years 1942–1945?

8. What is a "consumption function," and why is it a useful device for government economists planning a tax cut?

9. On a piece of graph paper, construct the consumption function for Simpleland from the data given below:

YEAR	CONSUMER SPENDING	DISPOSABLE INCOME
1981	1100	1000
1982	1550	1500
1983	2000	2000
1984	2450	2500
1985	2900	3000

What is the MPC? What is the APC for each year?

10. Explain why permanent tax cuts are likely to lead to bigger increases in consumer spending than are temporary tax cuts.

Appendix
The Saving Function and the Marginal Propensity to Save

There is an alternative way of looking at the relationships we have discussed in this chapter that will prove useful later. Disposable income that is not spent for consumption must be saved. Therefore we can examine the effect of income on *saving* as well as its effect on consumer *spending*.

To see how saving appears on the consumption function diagram, we have repeated the consumption function of Macroland (see Figure 7–6) in Figure 7–7 and added a 45° line. You will recall that a 45° line marks those points where the distances along the horizontal and vertical axes are equal. (If you wish to review, see page 26.) In this case, the 45° line shows where consumer spending equals disposable income; that is, where saving is exactly zero. As can be seen in the diagram, only one point on the consumption function satisfies this requirement—point *D*, where consumption and disposable income are both $500 billion. When income is above $500 billion, the consumption schedule is below the 45° line. This means that consumer spending is less than income, so some is being saved. Conversely, when income is below $500 billion, the consumption schedule is above the 45° line, so consumer spending exceeds income. Is this impossible? Normally, not. Consumers usually have bank accounts and other sources from which they can obtain funds when their income is low.

To find the amount of saving at each level of income, we need only read the vertical distance (positive or negative) from the consumption function to the 45° line. For example, when income is $2000 billion, saving is the distance *AB,* or $300 billion. When income

is $500 billion, saving must be zero, since the consumption function and the 45° line intersect.

There is also a more direct way to find saving. Table 7–3 repeats the consumption and

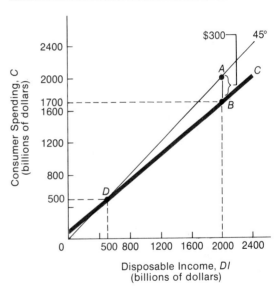

FIGURE 7–7

THE CONSUMPTION FUNCTION
OF MACROLAND
The consumption function of Macroland, which we encountered in Figure 7–6 (page 122), is repeated here, and a 45° line is added for convenience. Since consumption and saving must always add up to disposable income, the vertical distance between the two lines represents saving. For example, points *A* and *B* indicate that when disposable income is $2000 billion, saving is $300 billion. The two lines cross at point *D* (income level $500 billion). Since consumption equals disposable income at this point, there is exactly zero saving.

TABLE 7–3

SAVING IN MACROLAND

YEAR	(1) CONSUMPTION, C	(2) DISPOSABLE INCOME, DI	(3) SAVING, S	(4) MARGINAL PROPENSITY TO SAVE, MPS	(5) AVERAGE PROPENSITY TO SAVE, APS
1974	900	1000	100		0.10
1975	1060	1200	140	0.2	0.117
1976	1220	1400	180	0.2	0.129
1977	1380	1600	220	0.2	0.138
1978	1540	1800	260	0.2	0.144
1979	1700	2000	300	0.2	0.150

disposable income data for Macroland from Table 7–1 (which appeared on page 122). Then, in column 3, saving is computed as the difference between income and consumption.

DEFINITION

Aggregate saving is the difference between disposable income and consumer expenditure. In symbols,

$$S = DI - C$$

This subtraction is, of course, exactly what we showed graphically in Figure 7–7. Columns 2 and 3 of Table 7–3 constitute what economists call the *saving function*.

DEFINITION

The *saving function* is the schedule relating total consumer saving to total disposable income in the economy.

These data are portrayed in Figure 7–8, which is constructed from the numbers in Table 7–3. It could equally well have been constructed as the difference between the 45° line and the C line in Figure 7–7. (Because saving is so much less than consumption, we have stretched the scale of the vertical axis considerably.) Points A, B, and D correspond to the same points in Figure 7–7. The horizontal axis in Figure 7–8 shows all the places where saving is exactly zero, just as the 45° line did in

Figure 7–7. When the consumption function is a straight line, and thus has a constant slope, the same will be true of the saving function. In Figure 7–8, we show this slope as the ratio of distance AB to distance DA, or $300/$1500 = 0.2. Economists call this slope the marginal propensity to save.

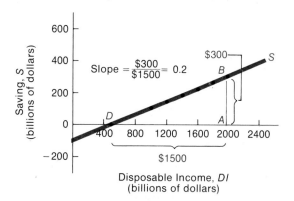

FIGURE 7–8

THE SAVING FUNCTION OF MACROLAND

The saving function of Macroland, depicted here, can be constructed either from the data in Table 7–3 or from Figure 7–7. This is because when we plot saving against income (as we do here), we are also plotting the difference between consumption and income (the vertical distance between line C and the 45° line in Figure 7–7) against income.

DEFINITION

The *marginal propensity to save* (or MPS) is the slope of the saving function. It tells us how much more consumers will save if disposable income rises by $1 billion.

You may have noticed that the MPS is 0.2 while the MPC for Macroland was 0.8. They add up to 1, and not by accident. Since each additional dollar of disposable income must be divided between spending and saving, the MPC

and the MPS always add up to 1. It is a simple fact of accounting.

The MPC and the MPS always add up to 1, meaning that an additional dollar of income must be divided between consumption and saving. In symbols,

$$MPC + MPS = 1$$

This enables us to compute either one of them from the other.

SUMMARY

1. Instead of studying the consumption function, it is possible to study the same data by looking at the saving function, which is defined as the relationship between disposable income and consumer saving.
2. Since consumer saving is merely the difference between disposable income and consumer expenditures, everything we have learned about the consumption function applies to the saving function.
3. The amount of additional saving caused by a growth of $1 in disposable income is called the marginal propensity to save, or MPS.
4. Since each additional $1 of disposable income is either spent or saved, the MPC and the MPS must always add up to 1. Thus, knowledge of one implies knowledge of the other.

CONCEPTS FOR REVIEW

Aggregate saving
Saving function
Marginal propensity to save

QUESTIONS FOR DISCUSSION

1. Look at the circular flow diagram in Figure 7–1 (page 115). Where does the saving function enter the picture?
2. If the MPC in the U.S. economy is about 0.90, how large is the MPS?
3. Take the data from Simpleland in Question 9 on page 130 and use them to construct a saving function for Simpleland on a piece of graph paper.
4. (More difficult) If taxes are cut *temporarily* and consumer spending does not increase much, what must happen to consumer saving? Ask your instructor what happened to consumer saving immediately after the 1975 tax cuts.

three

The National Economy: Income Determination and Stabilization Policy

8

Income Determination: Unemployment, Inflation, or Both?

I n this chapter, we begin a lengthy investigation, spanning six chapters, of the modern economic theory of *income determination*—the theory that explains why the economy sometimes stagnates and sometimes prospers. A simple model of income determination, in which both government and the financial system are mostly ignored, is constructed in this chapter and the next. Simple as it is, this model can teach us much about the causes of unemployment and inflation. Then, in Chapter 10, we bring the government into the analysis and get a somewhat more complicated picture of how the economy operates. After we acquire some

understanding of the financial system and how it works in Chapters 11 and 12, we will be ready to construct and utilize our most complete and realistic model of income determination in Chapter 13.

We learned in Chapter 5 that the strength of aggregate demand largely determines whether the economy will boom or stagnate and whether America's resources of labor and capital will be fully employed or unemployed. In this chapter we begin to study how this important process works. In the last chapter we examined the largest component of aggregate demand, which is consumer expenditure (*C*); here, we turn our attention first to the most volatile component, investment (*I*), and discuss its determinants and the reasons why investment spending is so variable and so difficult to predict.[1] Then, rather than waiting for a full discussion of the third component of aggregate demand, government purchases (*G*), we construct an abbreviated model of the determination of national income based only on the *C* and *I* components. We use this model to provide a preliminary description of how the state of aggregate demand determines (1) the level of the gross national product (GNP), (2) whether or not the economy will operate at full employment, and (3) whether or not there will be inflation. We also use the model to consider a question of great importance to policymakers: Can the economy be expected to achieve full employment of its resources if the government does not intervene?

THE EXTREME VARIABILITY OF INVESTMENT

The first thing to be said about investment spending is that it is extraordinarily variable.

Unlike consumer spending, which follows movements in disposable income with great (though not perfect) reliability, investment spending swings from high to low levels with annoying rapidity. As John R. Hicks, a British Nobel Prize winner and leading interpreter of Keynes put it, "Investment . . . is a flighty bird, which needs to be controlled."[2]

During recessions, for example, the decline in investment is almost always quite a substantial fraction of the total drop in real GNP— roughly 50 to 80 percent in a typical U.S. recession—despite the fact that investment is only a small portion of GNP—about 10 percent in the postwar United States.

What accounts for these movements of investment demand? While many factors influence business people's desires to invest, Keynes himself laid great stress on the *state of business confidence,* which in turn depends on *expectations about the future.*

While tricky to measure, it does seem obvious that businesses will be more prone to build factories and purchase new machines when their expectations are optimistic. Conversely, their investment plans will be very cautious if the economic outlook appears bleak. Keynes pointed out that psychological perceptions like these are subject to abrupt shifts, so that fluctuations in investment can be a major cause of instability in aggregate demand. Thus, we see the logic in Hicks's analogy to a "flighty bird."

Unfortunately, neither economists nor, for that matter, psychologists have any very good ideas about how to *measure* or how to *control* business expectations and confidence. Therefore, economists usually focus on several more objective determinants of investment—determinants that are easy to quantify and that are more easily influenced by government policy.

The Rate of Interest

A good deal of business investment is financed by borrowing, and the interest rate indicates how much firms must pay for that privilege. The higher the interest rate, the more costly it is to borrow. Some investment projects that look profitable at an interest rate of 7 percent will look disastrous if the firm has to pay 12 percent.

[1]We repeat the warning given in the previous chapter about the meaning of the word *investment.* It *includes* spending by businesses and individuals on *newly produced* factories, machinery, and houses. But it *excludes* sales of *used* industrial plants, equipment, and homes, and it *also excludes* purely financial transactions, such as the purchase of stocks and bonds.

[2]From *The Crisis in Keynesian Economics,* by Sir John Hicks, page 10, © 1974 by Sir John Hicks, Basic Books, Inc., Publishers, New York.

Thus:

The amount that businesses will want to invest depends on the interest rate they have to pay on their borrowings. The lower the rate of interest, the more investment spending there will be.

In Chapter 12 we will study in some detail how the government can exercise control over the rate of interest. Since interest rates influence investment, policymakers have a handle on aggregate demand—a handle they do not hesitate to use. The point is that, unlike business confidence, interest rates are visible and manipulable. Therefore, even if investment responds much more dramatically to changes in confidence than to changes in interest rates, interest rates are nonetheless a more important instrument of government policy.

The Level of Capacity Utilization

There will be a strong incentive to invest when firms find that demand is pressing against their capacity, that is, when existing plant and equipment are straining to produce the amount of goods that consumers wish to buy. Under these circumstances, firms are very likely to feel that any addition to capacity can be employed profitably. By contrast, if there is a great deal of spare capacity (unused machinery, empty factories, and so on), business managers will not find investment attractive even at very low interest rates.

The Growth Rate of Demand

Since it takes a substantial amount of time to order machinery or to build a factory, investment plans are made with an eye toward the future. Even when pressures on current capacity are not particularly severe, a firm experiencing rapid growth in sales is likely to

start investing *now* so that it will have the needed capacity available in the future. In addition, briskly growing sales are likely to make business people more optimistic. Conversely, slow growth of output will discourage investment.

We can summarize these last two points by saying that:

High levels of sales and rapid economic growth create an atmosphere favorable to investment. On the other hand, low levels of sales and slow growth are likely to discourage investment.

Government stabilization policy thus has another handle on investment spending, for by stimulating aggregate demand it can probably persuade business firms to invest more, though the precise amount may be hard to predict.

Tax Provisions

The government has still another important way to influence investment spending—by altering various provisions of the tax law. There is, for example, a federal *tax on corporate profits,* and the government has sometimes reduced it when it wanted firms to invest more and raised it when it wanted firms to invest less. Another incentive is the *investment tax credit,* a device invented by President Kennedy's economists in 1961 and used many times since then. The investment tax credit is, in effect, a bribe to do more investing. The government currently offers to reduce a firm's tax bill by 10 cents for every $1 the firm invests in new industrial equipment. And there are still other tax incentives, which are best left to more advanced courses. To summarize:

The tax law gives the government several ways to influence business spending on investment goods. But its control is quite imperfect. Investment remains a ''flighty bird.''

A SIMPLIFIED CIRCULAR FLOW

Let us now put together the aggregate demand components of consumption and investment and see how they interact, using as our organizing framework the circular flow diagram that we introduced in the last chapter. For this purpose, we simplify the circular flow somewhat by leaving out the government. There are two reasons for doing this. The first is pedagogical: The workings of the model will be much clearer if we strip away some of its complications. But

there is a much more important reason. One of the crucial questions surrounding government attempts to stabilize the economy is whether the economy would *automatically* gravitate toward full employment if the government simply left it alone. We can study this issue best by imagining an economy that has no government, so that all the aggregate demand comes from the private sector. This is just what we do in this chapter.

Look now at Figure 8–1, which is the same as Figure 7–1 of the last chapter except that the government has been omitted. The first thing

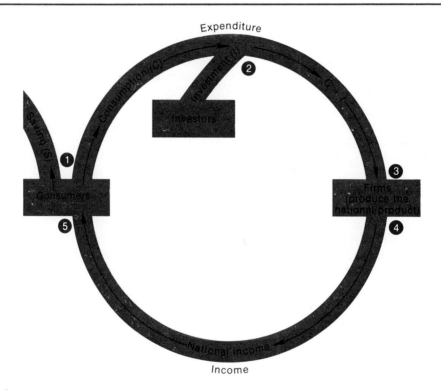

FIGURE 8–1

A SIMPLIFIED CIRCULAR FLOW

Here we show a simplified version of the circular flow of income and expenditures that we introduced in Chapter 7. The simplification amounts to shutting off the pipes leading into and out of the government. Thus, this circular flow represents an economy with no government. Notice that aggregate demand now has only two components (consumer spending and investment spending) and that the entire national income flows to consumers without taxation.

you may notice is that, with the government out of the picture, there is no leakage out of the national income for taxes. So there is no important difference between national income and disposable income. Second, there is no government component of total spending; instead, spending is the sum of $C + I$.

THE MEANING OF EQUILIBRIUM INCOME

We can use Figure 8–1 to begin the construction of a simple model of the determination of national income. A first step is to understand what we mean by "equilibrium income."

As was explained in the last chapter, national *product* and national *income* must of necessity be equal. But the same cannot automatically be said of total spending. Look again at Figure 8–1 and imagine that, for some reason, the total expenditures $(C + I)$ that are being made at point 3 are greater than the output that is being produced by the business firms.

Two things may happen in such a situation. Since consumers and firms together are buying (in the forms of C and I) more than firms are producing, business firms are being forced to take goods out of their warehouses to meet customer demands. Thus, inventory stocks must be falling. These inventory reductions are a signal to retailers of a need to increase their orders, and to manufacturers of a need to step up their production. Thus, production is likely to rise. At some later date, if there is evidence that the high level of aggregate demand is not just a temporary aberration, either manufacturers or retailers (or both) may also respond to the buoyant sales performances by raising their prices. Economists, therefore, say that neither output nor the price level is in equilibrium when aggregate demand exceeds the current rate of production.

DEFINITION
Equilibrium refers to a situation in which consumers and firms have no incentive to change their behavior. They are content to continue with things as they are.

It is clear from the definition that the economy cannot be in equilibrium when aggregate demand exceeds production, for the falling inventories demonstrate to firms that their production and pricing decisions were not quite appropriate. Thus, since we normally use GNP to measure output:

The *equilibrium level of GNP* cannot be one at which aggregate demand exceeds output because firms will notice that inventory stocks are being depleted. They may first decide to increase production sufficiently to meet the higher demand. Later they may decide to raise prices as well.

Now let us imagine the other case, in which the flow of aggregate demand reaching firms falls short of current production. Some output remains unsold, and these unwanted goods wind up as additions to the inventories of some firms. The inventory pile-up acts as a signal to firms that at least one of their decisions was wrong. Once again, they will probably react first by cutting back on production, causing the GNP to fall. If the imbalance persists, they may also lower prices in order to stimulate sales. But they are certainly not likely to be happy with things as they are. Thus:

The equilibrium level of GNP cannot be one at which aggregate demand is less than output because firms will not allow inventories to continue to pile up. They may decide to decrease production, or they may decide to cut prices in order to stimulate demand. Normally, firms are reluctant to cut prices until they are quite certain that the low level of demand is not a temporary phenomenon. So they rely more heavily on reducing their output.

INCOME DETERMINATION: THE EQUILIBRIUM LEVEL OF GNP

You may have noticed that we have now determined, through a process of elimination, the equilibrium level of national income and product. We have reasoned that whenever GNP is below aggregate demand (C + I) the GNP will rise; and that whenever GNP is above C + I, the GNP will fall. Equilibrium can only occur, then, when there is just enough aggregate demand to absorb the existing level of production (GNP). Under such circumstances, producers conclude that their price and output decisions were correct, and they have no incentive to change them. We conclude that:

The *equilibrium level of national income* is the one at which aggregate demand equals production. In such a situation firms find their inventories remaining at desirable levels, and so there is no incentive to change output or prices.

Notice that it is normal market forces that drive the economy toward its equilibrium level. When aggregate quantity demanded (C + I) exceeds aggregate quantity supplied (the GNP), output rises; and when aggregate quantity supplied exceeds aggregate quantity demanded, output falls.

The simple circular flow diagram, then, has given us an understanding of what the concept of the *equilibrium level of national income* is and of how the economy is driven toward it. It leaves unanswered, however, the most important questions that concern us in this chapter:

1. How large is the equilibrium level of GNP?
2. Will the economy suffer from unemployment, inflation, or both?

To approach these specific questions we shall need a more specific apparatus.

CONSTRUCTING THE EXPENDITURE SCHEDULE

Our objective now is to determine precisely the equilibrium level of GNP and to see what factors it depends upon. To make the analysis more concrete, we turn to a numerical example. Specifically, we examine the relationship between aggregate demand and GNP in Macroland, the hypothetical economy that was introduced in the last chapter.

Columns 1 and 2 of Table 8–1 repeat the consumption function of Macroland that we first encountered in Table 7–1. They show how consumer spending, C, depends on national income, which we now begin to symbolize by the letter Y.[3] Column 3 provides the other component of aggregate demand, I, through the simplifying assumption that investment spending is $300 billion in Macroland, regardless of the level of GNP.

By adding together the second and third columns, we calculate C + I, or aggregate demand, which is displayed in column 4. Columns 1 and 4, shaded in red, show how aggregate demand depends on income in Macroland. We call this the expenditure schedule.

Figure 8–2 shows the construction of the expenditure schedule graphically. The line labeled C is the consumption function of Macroland and simply duplicates Figure 7–6 of the last chapter. It plots on a graph the numbers given in columns 1 and 2 of Table 8–1. The line labeled C + I in the diagram depicts the total expenditure schedule that we have just derived by plotting the data in columns 1 and 4 of the table. That is, at each level of income (or GNP) measured along the horizontal axis, the

---

[3]Perceptive students may notice that the consumption function in Chapter 7 related C to *disposable* income, not to national income. However, with the government ignored in this chapter, there is no difference between the two income concepts.

Constructing the Expenditure Schedule

TABLE 8–1

AGGREGATE DEMAND IN MACROLAND (billions of dollars)

(1) INCOME (Y)	(2) CONSUMPTION (C)	(3) INVESTMENT (I)	(4) AGGREGATE DEMAND (C + I)
1000	900	300	1200
1200	1060	300	1360
1400	1220	300	1520
1600	1380	300	1680
1800	1540	300	1840
2000	1700	300	2000
2200	1860	300	2160
2400	2020	300	2320
2600	2180	300	2480
2800	2340	300	2640
3000	2500	300	2800

This table illustrates the derivation of the expenditure schedule, which is shaded in red. It is derived from the consumption schedule, columns 1 and 2, and from the investment schedule, columns 1 and 3, by simple addition. This is because aggregate demand is the sum C + I.

FIGURE 8–2
CONSTRUCTION OF THE
EXPENDITURE SCHEDULE
This figure shows in a diagram what Table 8–1 showed numerically—the construction of a total expenditure schedule from its components. Line C is the consumption function that we first encountered in Figure 7–6. Line C + I is the expenditure schedule and is obtained by adding investment (assumed always to be $300 billion in this example) to the consumption function.

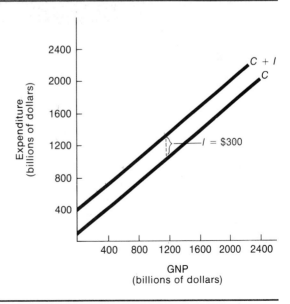

143

height of the C + I line indicates the sum of consumption plus investment.

The difference between the two lines, therefore, is investment. In the diagram, the lines are parallel; that is, the distance between them is always the same. This distance is $300 billion — the volume of investment assumed in the example. If investment were not always $300 billion, the two lines would either come closer together (at income levels at which investment was below $300 billion) or grow farther apart (at income levels at which investment was above $300 billion). For example, our list of determinants of investment spending suggested that I might be larger at higher levels of GNP. Because of this added investment—which is called induced investment—the resulting C + I schedule would have a steeper slope than the C schedule.

THE MECHANICS OF INCOME DETERMINATION

We are now in a position to determine the equilibrium level of GNP in Macroland. Look first at Table 8–2, which presents the logic of our circular flow argument in tabular form. The first two columns of this table reproduce the expenditure schedule that was constructed in Table 8–1. The other columns explain the process by which equilibrium is approached. Let us see why a GNP of $2000 billion must be the equilibrium level.

Consider first any output level below $2000 billion. For example, at output level $Y = $1400 billion, total expenditure is $1520 billion (column 2), which is $120 billion more than production. With sales greater than output

TABLE 8–2

THE DETERMINATION OF EQUILIBRIUM OUTPUT

(1) OUTPUT (Y) (billions of dollars)	(2) TOTAL SPENDING (C + I) (billions of dollars)	(3) BALANCE OF SPENDING AND OUTPUT	(4) INVENTORIES ARE:	(5) PRODUCERS WILL RESPOND BY:
1000	1200	Spending exceeds output	Falling	Producing more
1200	1360	Spending exceeds output	Falling	Producing more
1400	1520	Spending exceeds output	Falling	Producing more
1600	1680	Spending exceeds output	Falling	Producing more
1800	1840	Spending exceeds output	Falling	Producing more
2000	2000	Spending = output	Constant	Not changing production
2200	2160	Output exceeds spending	Rising	Producing less
2400	2320	Output exceeds spending	Rising	Producing less
2600	2480	Output exceeds spending	Rising	Producing less
2800	2640	Output exceeds spending	Rising	Producing less
3000	2800	Output exceeds spending	Rising	Producing less

Columns 1 and 2 are the expenditure schedule that was derived in the previous table. The remaining columns explain how the equilibrium level of national income can be derived from these data. For example, reading across the first row we see that when GNP is $1000 billion, total spending is $1200 billion. Thus spending exceeds production (by $200 billion), so that inventories must be falling. Producers are likely to respond to this drop in inventory stocks by raising their rate of production. The other rows are read similarly, and together they show that only $2000 billion can be the equilibrium level of GNP. This is the only output level that firms will not want to change.

(column 3), inventories will be disappearing (column 4). As the table suggests, this will be a signal to producers to raise their output (column 5). Clearly, then, no output level below $Y = \$2000$ billion can be an equilibrium. Output is too low.

A similar line of reasoning can eliminate any output level above $2000 billion. Consider, for example, $Y = \$2400$ billion. The table shows that total spending would be $2320 billion if national income were $2400 billion. So $80 billion of the GNP would go unsold. This would raise producers' inventory stocks and signal them that their rate of production is too high. If current output is too high, GNP will have to fall.

Just as we concluded from our circular flow diagram, then, equilibrium will be achieved only when aggregate demand $(C + I)$ is equal to GNP (Y). In symbols, our condition for equilibrium GNP is:

$$C + I = Y$$

The table shows that this occurs only at a GNP of $2000 billion. This, then, must be the equilibrium level of GNP.

Figure 8–3 shows this same conclusion graphically, by adding a 45° line to Figure 8–2. Why a 45° line? Recall that a 45° line marks off all points on a graph at which the value of the variable measured on the horizontal axis is equal to the value of the variable measured on the vertical axis. In this convenient graph of the expenditure schedule, gross national product (Y) is measured on the horizontal axis and aggregate demand $(C + I)$ is measured on the vertical axis. So the 45° line shows all the points at which output and spending are equal; that is, where $Y = C + I$. The 45° line therefore displays all the points at which the economy *can possibly* attain equilibrium.

Now we must compare these potential equilibrium points with the actual combinations of spending and output that the economy can attain, given the behavior of consumers and investors. That behavior, as we have seen, is

described by the $C + I$ line in Figure 8–3, which shows how total expenditures vary as income changes. Thus, the economy will *always* be on the $C + I$ line; no point in the diagram that is off that $C + I$ line can ever be observed. Similarly, if the economy is in equilibrium, it must be on the 45° line. As Figure 8–3 shows, these two requirements together imply that the only viable equilibrium is at point E, where the $C + I$ line intersects the 45° line. Only this point is consistent both with equilibrium and with the actual propensities to consume and invest.

Notice that to the left of the equilibrium point, E, the $C + I$ line lies above the 45° line. This means that aggregate demand exceeds

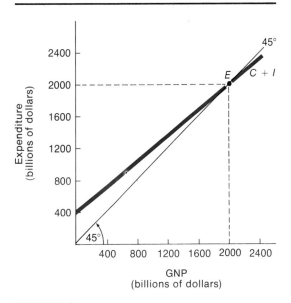

FIGURE 8–3

INCOME–EXPENDITURE DIAGRAM
This figure adds a 45° line—which marks off points where expenditure and output are equal—to Figure 8–2. Since the condition for equilibrium GNP is that expenditure and output must be equal, this line can be used to determine the equilibrium level of GNP. In this example, equilibrium is at point E, where GNP is $2000 billion—precisely as we found in Table 8–2.

output, as we have already noted in words and with numbers. The opposite is true to the right of equilibrium point E; here, aggregate demand falls short of output.

Diagrams like this one will recur so frequently in this and the next several chapters that it will be convenient to have a name for them. Let us, therefore, call them income—expenditure diagrams since they show how expenditures vary with income. Sometimes we shall also refer to them simply as $45°$ line diagrams.

EQUILIBRIUM INCOME AND THE PRICE LEVEL

We have not yet brought the price level into our simple model of the national economy, and it is now time to remedy this omission. For only by including this factor will we be able to address important questions relating to inflation and deflation.

Fortunately, no further mechanical apparatus is required. The price level can be brought into our income—expenditure analysis by recalling something we learned in the last chapter: At any given level of income, higher prices lead to lower real consumer spending. That is, at a higher price level, any rise in the number of dollars the consumers spend will not be enough to make up for the fall in the purchasing power of each dollar. Recall that this is due to the fact that consumers are more often lenders than borrowers, and hence lose purchasing power when prices rise.

In terms of our $45°$ line diagram, then, a rise in the price level will lower the consumption function and, hence, lower the total expenditure schedule. Conversely, a fall in the price level will raise both the C and $C + I$ schedules in the diagram. Figure 8–4 illustrates both these sorts of shifts.

What, then, do changes in the price level do to real aggregate demand and, hence, to the

equilibrium level of real GNP? The answers can be found in the two parts of Figure 8–5. Part (a) shows that a rise in the price level, by shifting the expenditure schedule downward from $C_0 + I$ to $C_1 + I$ leads to a reduction in the equilibrium level of real income from Y_0 to Y_1. Similarly, Figure 8–5(b) shows that a fall in the price level, by shifting the expenditure schedule upward from $C_0 + I$ to $C_2 + I$, leads to a rise in equilibrium real income from Y_0 to Y_2. To summarize:

A rise in the price level leads to a lower equilibrium level of real aggregate demand and output, whereas a fall in the price level leads to higher equilibrium real output. This relationship between the price level and equilibrium GNP is depicted in Figure 8–6 and is precisely what we called the *aggregate demand curve* in earlier chapters.

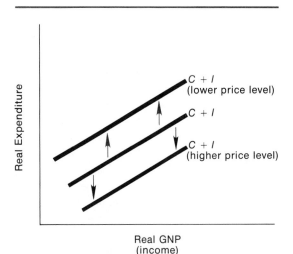

FIGURE 8–4

THE EFFECT OF THE PRICE LEVEL ON THE EXPENDITURE SCHEDULE
A higher price level will cause the $C + I$ schedule to shift downward, as shown by the black arrows. A lower price level will cause the $C + I$ schedule to shift upward, as shown by the red arrows.

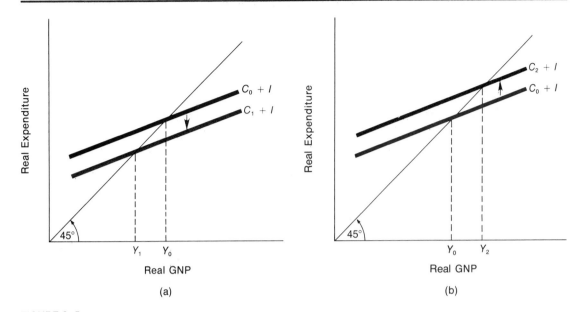

FIGURE 8–5

THE EFFECT OF THE PRICE LEVEL ON EQUILIBRIUM INCOME

Because a change in the price level causes the expenditure schedule to shift, it will also change the equilibrium level of GNP. Part (a) shows what happens when the price level rises, causing the expenditure schedule to shift downward from $C_0 + I$ to $C_1 + I$. Equilibrium output falls from Y_0 to Y_1. Part (b) shows what happens when the price level falls, causing the expenditure schedule to shift upward from $C_0 + I$ to $C_2 + I$. Equilibrium output rises from Y_0 to Y_2.

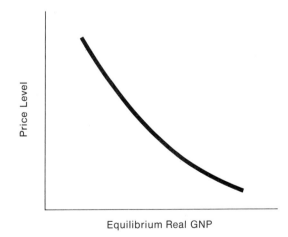

FIGURE 8–6

THE AGGREGATE DEMAND CURVE

The graphical analysis in Figure 8–5 showed that higher prices lead to lower equilibrium income. This relationship is called the aggregate demand curve and is shown in this figure.

What we have learned so far about the effects of the price level is precisely how the aggregate demand curve is derived and why it slopes downward. We have also been warned that:

An income–expenditure diagram can only be drawn up for a specific price level. At different price levels, the $C + I$ schedule will be different and, hence, the equilibrium level of GNP will be different.

As we shall now see, this finding is crucial to understanding the genesis of unemployment and inflation.

EQUILIBRIUM INCOME AND FULL EMPLOYMENT

The discussion of prices allows us to provide a partial answer to the second major question of this chapter: Will the economy achieve an equilibrium at full employment without inflation, or will there be unemployment, inflation, or both?

In the income–expenditure diagrams used so far, equilibrium income has been shown as the intersection of the expenditure schedule and the 45° line, regardless of whatever level of GNP might correspond to full employment. Equilibrium, apparently, can fall either above or below full employment. However, as we will see now, when equilibrium income falls above full employment, the economy probably will be plagued by inflation. And when equilibrium falls below full employment, there will be unemployment and recession.

This remarkable fact was one of the principal messages of Keynes's *General Theory of Employment, Interest, and Money*. Writing during the Great Depression, it was natural for him to stress the case in which equilibrium national income falls short of full employment so that there are unemployed resources. Figure 8–7 shows this possibility. A vertical line has been

erected at the full-employment level of GNP (called "potential GNP"), which is assumed to be $2200 billion in the example. We see that the $C + I$ curve cuts the 45° line at point E, which corresponds to a GNP ($Y = 2000 billion) below potential GNP. Thus unemployment must occur because not enough output will be produced to keep the entire labor force busy. The distance between the equilibrium level of output and the full-employment level of output (that is, potential GNP) is called the recessionary gap—and is shown by the horizontal distance from E to B.

DEFINITION
The *recessionary gap* is the amount by which the equilibrium level of GNP falls short of potential GNP.

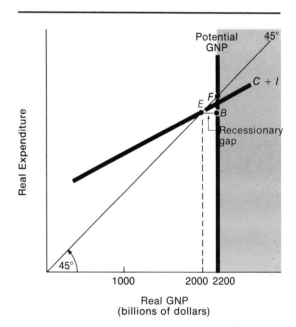

FIGURE 8–7

A RECESSIONARY GAP
Sometimes equilibrium GNP may fall below potential GNP, so that some workers are unemployed. This diagram illustrates such a case. The horizontal distance EB between equilibrium GNP and potential GNP is called the recessionary gap.

It is clear from Figure 8–7 that full employment can be reached only by raising the total spending schedule to eliminate the recessionary gap. Specifically, the $C + I$ schedule must move upward until it cuts the 45° line at point F. Can this happen without government intervention? We shall return to this question shortly, but first let us consider the other case: in which equilibrium GNP exceeds full employment.

Figure 8–8 illustrates this possibility. The expenditure schedule intersects the 45° line at point E, where GNP is $2400 billion. But this exceeds the full-employment level, $Y = \$2200$ billion. To reach an equilibrium at full employ-

ment, prices would now have to *rise* enough to drive the $C + I$ schedule *down* until it passes through point F. The horizontal distance BE—which indicates the amount by which actual GNP exceeds potential GNP—is called an inflationary gap.

DEFINITION
The *inflationary gap* is the amount by which equilibrium GNP exceeds the full-employment level of GNP. If there is an inflationary gap, a higher price level or some other means of reducing aggregate demand is necessary to reach an equilibrium at full employment.

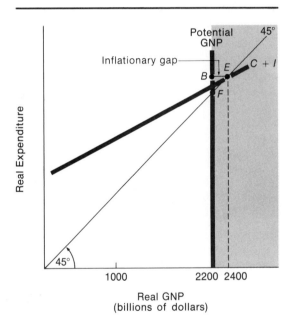

FIGURE 8–8
AN INFLATIONARY GAP
Sometimes equilibrium GNP may lie above potential GNP, meaning that there are more jobs than required for full employment. This diagram illustrates such a case. The horizontal distance BE between potential GNP and equilibrium GNP is called the inflationary gap. It is gradually eliminated by rising prices, which pull the $C + I$ schedule down until it passes through point F.

ADJUSTING TO AN INFLATIONARY GAP: INFLATION

Precisely how can higher prices eliminate an excess of equilibrium income over full-employment income? Let us consider what happens to an economy that finds itself with an inflationary gap, like the one depicted in Figure 8–8. We will see that the gap produces forces that eventually tend to eliminate it—it self-destructs, although the process of doing so may be slow and painful.

When equilibrium GNP is above potential, jobs are plentiful and labor is in great demand. Although some workers still may be unemployed, this minimal unemployment is less than the frictional level—that is, less than the number we usually expect to be jobless because they are moving, changing occupations, and so on. Many firms, on the other hand, are having trouble finding workers. They may even be having trouble hanging on to their current employees, as other firms try to lure them away with higher wages.

Such a situation is bound to lead to rising wages, and rising wages add to business costs. Firms will no longer find it profitable to produce $2400 billion worth of output at the old price level as they did at point *E* in Figure 8–8. They will produce this volume of output only at a *higher* price, which means that:

An inflationary gap soon leads to rising prices—that is, to inflation.

We have just learned that rising prices do precisely what is necessary to eliminate the inflationary gap between equilibrium GNP and potential GNP: They push the expenditure schedule that is shown in Figure 8–8 downward. As consumers lose purchasing power they spend less, so the *C + I* curve falls until it passes through point *F*, where full employment is restored at a higher price level.

How does this self-curing process work? There is a straightforward way of looking at what happens. The trouble arises in the first place because consumers and investors demand more output than the economy is able to produce—"too much demand chasing too few goods." Naturally, prices rise. Rising prices then eat away at consumers' purchasing power and force them to cut their demands back to the available supply. That, in essence, is how the problem is able to cure itself, though perhaps not in a way that leaves any of us very satisfied.

DEMAND INFLATION AND STAGFLATION

Simple as it is, this adjustment model teaches us a number of important lessons about inflation in the real world. First of all, Figure 8–8 reminds us that the real culprit in this particular inflation is the excessive level of aggregate demand. The expenditure schedule is so high that it cuts the 45° line at an income level higher than the full-employment level. While this is not the only possible cause of inflation in the real world, it certainly is the cause in our example. However, business managers and journalists are very likely to blame rising wages for the inflation.

In a superficial sense, of course, they are correct, because the higher wages do indeed lead firms to raise their prices. But in a deeper sense they are wrong. Both rising wages and rising prices are only symptoms of an underlying malady: too much aggregate demand. Blaming labor for inflation in such a case is a bit like blaming high doctor bills for making you ill.

Second, we know that output falls while prices rise as the economy adjusts from point *E* to point *F* in Figure 8–8. This is because the *C + I* line in the figure shifts downward as prices rise and consumer purchasing power falls. This process provides one explanation—though not the only one—of the phenomenon of *stagflation*, which, as we learned in Chapter 5, means simultaneous business *stag*nation and price in*flation*. So we see that:

A period of stagflation is part of the normal aftermath of a period of excessive aggregate demand.

It is easy enough to understand why stagflation occurs. When aggregate demand is excessive, the economy will (temporarily) produce beyond its normal capacity. Labor markets become very tight and wages rise. Machinery and raw materials may also become scarce and so start rising in price. Faced by higher costs, the natural reaction of business firms is both to produce less and to charge a higher price. This is stagflation.

Journalistic accounts are often misleading on this point. Newspaper readers may get the impression that stagflation is a complete mystery to economists. Not so. The mystery comes in trying to figure out ways to *avoid* it, not in understanding how it arises in the first place.

It may be useful to summarize what we have learned about inflationary gaps thus far.

If aggregate demand is exceptionally high, the economy may reach a short-run equilibrium above full employment. When this occurs, the tight situation in the labor market soon forces wages to rise. Since wages are business costs, prices rise and there is inflation. With cuts in consumer purchasing power, the inflationary gap begins to close. As the inflationary gap is closing, output falls while prices continue to rise, so the economy experiences stagflation until the inflationary gap is eliminated. At this point, a long-run equilibrium is established with a higher price level and with GNP equal to potential GNP.

AN EXAMPLE FROM RECENT HISTORY: THE UNITED STATES FROM 1966 TO 1970

Because the years since 1974 have seen continuously high unemployment, and have been special in other respects as well, one has to go back to the late 1960s to find a "textbook" example of an inflationary gap.

During 1966–1968, the U.S. economy was booming, unemployment was continually below 4 percent, and jobs were plentiful. According to official estimates, real GNP (measured in 1972 prices) exceeded its potential by an average of $17 billion during those three years. There was an inflationary gap.

Our analysis suggests that wages should have been accelerating, and indeed they were. The bright red bars in Figure 8–9 illustrate this acceleration. The rate of change of wages rose from less than 3 percent in 1963 and 1964 to more than 6 percent in 1968 before stabilizing. The diagram also shows that, except for a minor dip in 1967, the rate of inflation followed the rate of increase of wages—rising from $1\frac{1}{2}$ percent a

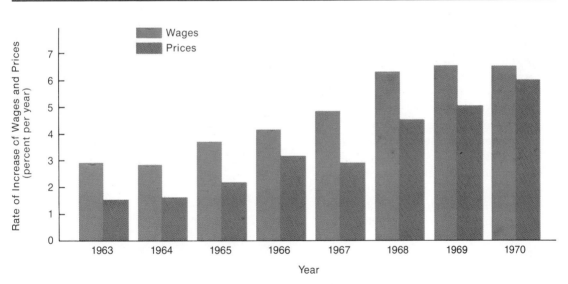

FIGURE 8–9

GROWTH RATES OF WAGES AND PRICES IN THE UNITED STATES, 1963–1970

These data illustrate what happened when an inflationary gap arose in the United States during the years 1966–1968. Notice the acceleration of both wages and prices beginning in about 1965. By 1969, the gap was eliminated, and wage increases leveled off. There was a minor recession in 1969–1970, but inflation continued.

Source: *Economic Report of the President,* 1978.

year to over 5 percent. This is, again, in line with what our model predicts.

The upsurge in inflation naturally ate away the inflationary gap, which was gone by the end of 1969. Yet inflation continued unabated through a mild recession in 1969–1970. The U.S. economy was in the stagflation phase. Despite outcries of "excessive" wage demands that "caused" inflation, it is clear that the ultimate cause of the acceleration in both wages and prices was the excessive aggregate demand of the Vietnam War episode. The economy was behaving just as our simple model suggests it should.

ADJUSTING TO A RECESSIONARY GAP: DEFLATION OR UNEMPLOYMENT?

Let us now consider what can happen when the economy is in a short-run equilibrium *below* full employment—that is, when there is a recessionary gap. This might be caused either by inadequate consumer spending or by anemic investment spending.

Figure 8–7 on page 148 illustrates such a case and gives an impression of the economic situation inherited by President Carter when he assumed office in 1977. The unemployment rate, which had been below 5 percent in early 1974, averaged 8.5 percent for 1975 and 7.7 percent for 1976. As is to be expected, the inflation rate dropped from its 1974 high of 12 percent to 7 percent in 1975 and to only 5 percent in 1976.

You might expect that we could just run our previous analysis in reverse: High unemployment leads to falling wages; falling wages reduce business costs, so firms cut prices; the lower price level eliminates the recessionary gap by pushing the $C + I$ schedule up; and full employment is restored. Very simple. And very irrelevant to our modern economy!

Why is it irrelevant? In Chapter 5, our brief review of the historical record showed that, while the economy may have operated like that long ago, it certainly does not work that way now. The history of the United States shows many examples of falling wages and prices before World War II but none since then. Not even the Great Recession of 1974–1975, during which unemployment climbed as high as 9 percent, was able to force prices and wages down.

Exactly *why* wages and prices are rigid in the downward direction is not really known, though the question is being actively investigated by economists right now. For our purposes, we had best just accept it as a fact without trying to explain it. In our modern economy, prices and wages will rise when

"With this depression on, Maria, I s'pose we ought to go out tonight and consume something."

demand is strong, but they generally will not fall when demand is weak.

The implications of this rigidity are quite serious. For a recessionary gap cannot cure itself without some deflation. And if wages and prices will not fall, deflation cannot occur. This means that *the economy gets stuck at an equilibrium below full employment.* Keynes was the first economist to point out the possibility of equilibrium below full employment and to distinguish it from the full-employment equilibrium that we have just been considering.

When aggregate demand is low, the economy may get stuck in an *unemployment equilibrium.* There is a recessionary gap, but wages and prices refuse to fall. So the $C + I$ schedule does not shift upward, and the gap persists. The economy endures a prolonged period of production below potential GNP.

DOES THE ECONOMY HAVE A SELF-CORRECTING MECHANISM?

Now a situation like this would, presumably, not last forever. As the recession lengthened, and perhaps deepened, more and more workers would be unable to obtain jobs at the prevailing high wages. Eventually their resistance to wage cuts would be worn down by their need to be employed. Firms, too, would become increasingly willing to cut prices as the period of weak demand lasted longer and longer and managers became convinced that the slump was not merely a temporary aberration. Prices and wages did, in fact, fall during the Great Depression of the 1930s. And they might fall again if a sufficiently drastic depression were allowed to occur.

It was reasoning of precisely this sort that led the Hoover administration, in the dark days of the early 1930s, to adopt a hands-off attitude toward the deteriorating economy. The reasoning was that if government only showed patience and refrained from tampering with the private economy, wages and prices would fall far enough to restore consumer demand and to re-employ the work force. Americans now consider themselves fortunate that the political activists of the Roosevelt administration did not have such monumental patience!

The same issue arose again during the three recessions of the Eisenhower administration. Rather than take positive actions to end any of these recessions, the Eisenhower economists preferred to wait for the private economy to right itself by wage and price deflation, despite warnings from then Vice-President Richard Nixon that it might cost them the election in 1960. Later, President Kennedy's New Frontiersmen, like the New Dealers, were unwilling to stand by while the economy cured itself of its recessionary illness.

Today a healthy bipartisan attitude prevails. At least since President Nixon said "I am now a Keynesian" in 1970, politicians of both parties believe it is folly to wait for falling wages and prices to eliminate a recessionary gap. But while they agree that *some* government action is both necessary and appropriate under recessionary conditions, there is still vocal—and highly partisan!—debate over *how much* and *what kind* of intervention is warranted. We will discuss these issues in subsequent chapters.

THE COORDINATION OF SAVING AND INVESTMENT

The discussion so far certainly points to price rigidity—the refusal of wages and prices to fall despite weak demand—as the basic cause of lingering unemployment. And, in a sense, it is. However, more interesting questions from the practical point of view are: What made aggregate demand so low in the first place? and Why don't demanders want to buy all the output that suppliers want to sell?

We can understand what goes wrong with

the economy in a recession, and at the same time see why business fluctuations are hardly a problem at all in planned economies like that of the U.S.S.R., by restating our equilibrium condition in a slightly different way.

To do this, let us look back at our simplified circular flow diagram (Figure 8–1 on page 140) and ask: How can the full-employment level of GNP fail to be an equilibrium? Suppose that firms produce the full-employment level of GNP,

Biographical Note: John Maynard Keynes (1883–1946)

It may be one of history's great ironies that the death of Karl Marx, the prophet of capitalism's doom, and the birth of John Maynard Keynes, who many consider capitalism's savior, both occurred in the same year—1883. The son of a

prominent upper-class British economist, Keynes was something of a child prodigy. After an outstanding scholastic career at Eton and Cambridge, Keynes took the civil service examination. But his second-place score was not good enough to land him the position he wanted and should have had (in the Treasury), so in 1907 he found himself in the India Office. Some years later, reflecting on the fact that his lowest score on the exam was in the economics section, he suggested with characteristic immodesty that, "The examiners presumably knew less than I did."* He was probably right.

While Keynes disliked his sojourn in India, his time there was not wasted. It was during that period that he wrote his *Treatise on Probability* (1909), which drew the admiration of Bertrand Russell and won Keynes election as a lifetime Fellow of Cambridge's King's College.

During World War I, Keynes was called to the Treasury to assist in planning various financial aspects of the war. There his "unique combination of the guts of a burglar and the intellect of a first-class economist"‡ established him as a dominant figure. And at the war's end, though only 36, Keynes represented the British Treasury at the peace conference in Versailles.

The conference was a turning point in Keynes's life, though it was one of his few failures.

*Quoted in E. A. G. Robinson, "John Maynard Keynes," in R. Lekachman, ed., *Keynes' General Theory: Reports of Three Decades* (New York: St Martin's Press, Inc., 1964), page 25.

‡Robert Lekachman, *The Age of Keynes* (New York: Random House, 1966), page 27. This book contains a marvelous biography of Keynes, as does Robert Heilbroner's *The Worldly Philosophers,* 4th edition (New York: Simon and Schuster, 1972).

and this becomes the national income that emerges at point 4 in the diagram. This full-employment level of income then flows to consumers at point 5, who save some of it and spend the rest. The saving, you will note, "leaks out" of the circular flow at point 1. So, once we pass this point, consumption is less than full-employment GNP. But then at point 2, an additional source of spending enters: investment. Recalling that the condition for equilibrium is

---

He sought unsuccessfully to persuade the Allies to take a less punitive attitude toward the vanquished Germans, and then left the conference in protest in June 1919, telling David Lloyd George, the English Prime Minister, "I am slipping way from this scene of nightmare."§ Keynes immediately went to work on his *Economic Consequences of the Peace,* which created a furor when it was published in 1919. In addition to stinging personal portraits of Lloyd George, Georges Clemenceau, and Woodrow Wilson ("the blind and deaf Don Quixote"), Keynes demonstrated with exquisite logic that the Germans could never meet the harsh economic terms of the treaty and that its very viciousness posed the threat of continued instability and perhaps another war in Europe. Sadly, his visions were remarkably accurate.

No longer welcome in government, Keynes returned to Cambridge and to his distinguished circle of literary and artistic friends in London's Bloomsbury district—a group that included Virginia Woolf, Lytton Strachey, and E. M. Forster. In 1925 he married the beautiful ballerina Lydia Lopokova, who gave up her stage career for him (though she later acted in a theater that Keynes himself established).

Between the wars, Keynes devoted himself to making money (both for himself and for King's College), to economic theory, and to political economy. Spending about one-half hour each morning with newspapers and financial reports (apparently while still in bed!), Keynes managed to make himself a rich man and increase his college's unrestricted fund from £30,000 to £380,000 by speculating in international currencies and commodities. As a scholar, he wrote the *Tract on Monetary Reform* (1923), a stunning denunciation of the gold standard, which was published two years before Churchill once again tied the pound to gold and, in the view of contemporary observers, sealed Britain's economic doom. In 1936, he published his masterpiece, *The General Theory of Employment, Interest, and Money,* upon which modern macroeconomics is based. Finally, as a tireless political activist and polemicist, he used newspaper and magazine articles, and visits to Whitehall and Washington, to urge governments to lift their economies out of the Depression (which began for Britain in the 1920s) through policies that we would now call "Keynesian."

A heart attack in 1937 reduced Keynes's activities somewhat, though he maintained careers as both an academic economist and a businessman. He returned to the Treasury during World War II and conducted several delicate financial negotiations with the Americans. Then, as the capstone to a truly remarkable career, he represented the United Kingdom—and by all accounts dominated the proceedings—at the conference in Bretton Woods, New Hampshire, in 1944 that established an international financial system that served the Western world for 27 years. (See Chapter 37.)

He died of a heart attack at his home on Easter Sunday of 1946 as Lord Keynes, Baron of Tilton, a man who had achieved almost everything that he sought, and who had only one regret: He wished he had drunk more champagne.

§Quoted in R. F. Harrod, *The Life of John Maynard Keynes* (New York: Macmillan, 1951), page 253.

that the sum $C + I$ equals the GNP, we have the following conclusion:

The economy will reach an equilibrium at potential GNP only if the amount that consumers wish to save out of full-employment incomes is precisely equal to the amount that investors want to invest. If these two magnitudes happen to be unequal, then full employment will not be an equilibrium for the economy.

Specifically, we can see from the circular flow diagram that if saving exceeds investment at full employment, then the total demand arriving at the firms (point 3) will fall short of total output because the added investment spending is not enough to replace the leakage to saving. With demand inadequate to support production at full employment, we know that the GNP must fall below potential. There will be a recessionary gap. Conversely, if investment exceeds saving when the economy is at full employment, then total demand ($C + I$) will exceed potential GNP and production will rise above the full-employment level. There will be an inflationary gap.

Now this discussion does nothing but restate what we already know in different words.[4] But these words hold the key to understanding why the economy can find itself stuck below full employment (or above it, for that matter), for *the people who do the investing are not the same people who do the saving.* In a modern capitalist economy, most investing is done by corporations, while most saving is done by consumers. It is easy to imagine that their plans may not be well coordinated. If they are not, we have just seen how either unemployment or inflation can arise.

Notice that these problems would never arise if the acts of saving and investing were not separated. Imagine a primitive capitalist economy of farmers, each of whom invests only in his own farm. There is no borrowing or lending, and no financial system. In this world, any farmer who wanted to buy a new plow or tractor (that is, wanted to *invest*) would have to refrain from consuming part of his income (that is, would have to *save*). Therefore, the amount that all farmers together planned to save out of full-employment income would of necessity be equal to the amount of planned investment. Total spending and production would always have to be equal at full employment.

Almost the same sequence holds true in a centrally planned economy like that of Soviet Russia. There, the state decides how much will be invested and has a great deal of leverage over how much saving people do. If the planners do their calculations correctly, they can force saving to be equal to investment at full employment.

Keynes observed that modern market economies differ from either primitive societies or centrally planned societies in this fundamental way, and that this flaw in the market mechanism is what leaves them vulnerable to recessions. However, one should not conclude that in order to avoid unemployment and recession the U.S. economy should revert to either a primitive form of capitalism or to rigid central planning. These "remedies" may be far worse than the disease. Fortunately, there are policies the government can follow in an advanced capitalist economy to ease the pain of unemployment and recession— policies that we shall be studying in the following chapters.

---

[4]In symbols, our previous equilibrium condition was $C + I = Y$. If we note that Y is also the sum of consumption plus saving, $Y = C + S$, it follows that $C + I = C + S$, or $I = S$, is a restatement of the equilibrium condition. The saving = investment approach is described in the appendix to this chapter.

SUMMARY

1. Investment is the most volatile component of aggregate demand, largely because it is tied so closely to the state of business confidence and to expectations about the future performance of the economy.

2. Government policy cannot influence business confidence in any reliable way, so policies designed to alter investment spending are aimed at more objective, though possibly less important, determinants of investment. Among these are interest rates, the overall state of aggregate demand, and tax incentives.

3. The equilibrium level of national income and product is the level of income at which aggregate demand just equals production (GNP). In this chapter we ignore government demand, so aggregate demand is the sum of consumption plus investment. Thus, in symbols, the condition for equilibrium is $Y = C + I$.

4. Income levels below equilibrium are bound to rise because, when aggregate demand exceeds output, firms will see their inventory stocks depleted and will react by stepping up production.

5. Income levels above equilibrium are bound to fall because, when aggregate demand is insufficient to absorb total output, inventories will pile up and firms will react by curtailing production.

6. The determination of the equilibrium level of GNP can be portrayed on a convenient "income–expenditure diagram" as the point at which the expenditure schedule—defined as the sum of the consumption and investment schedules—crosses the 45° line. The 45° line is significant because it marks off points at which spending and output are equal (that is, at which $C + I = Y$), and this is the basic condition for equilibrium.

7. An income–expenditure diagram can only be drawn up for a specific price level. Thus the equilibrium GNP so determined must depend on the price level.

8. Because higher prices reduce the purchasing power of consumers, and hence reduce their spending, equilibrium GNP is lower when prices are higher. This downward-sloping relationship is known as the aggregate demand curve.

9. The equilibrium GNP can be above or below potential GNP, which is defined as the GNP that would be produced if the labor force were fully employed.

10. The reason the equilibrium GNP can be above or below potential GNP is that the saving that consumers want to do at full-employment income levels may differ from the investing that investors want to do. This problem is not likely to arise in a planned economy or in a primitive economy.

11. If equilibrium GNP exceeds potential GNP, the difference is called an "inflationary gap." Inflationary gaps are so named because they normally lead to inflation. Inflation eats away at the inflationary excess demand until a final equilibrium is reached at full employment.

12. During the process by which an inflationary gap self-destructs, the economy experiences both rising prices and falling output. That is, it experiences stagflation.

13. If equilibrium GNP falls short of potential GNP, the resulting difference is called a "recessionary gap." Unlike inflationary gaps, recessionary gaps will not cure themselves, at least not for a long time. This is because the

cure requires deflation of the price level, something that simply does not happen in the modern economy.

14. This failure of the economy's self-correcting mechanism means that there may be prolonged periods of high unemployment if the government does not intervene.

CONCEPTS FOR REVIEW

Equilibrium income
Expenditure schedule
Induced investment
$C + I = Y$
Income–expenditure (or 45° line) diagram
Full-employment level of income

Recessionary gap
Inflationary gap
Wage and price rigidity
Unemployment equilibrium
Coordination of saving and investment

QUESTIONS FOR DISCUSSION

1. Why would someone interested in stabilization policy want to study a model of an economy in which there is no government?

2. Since 1974 there have been constant warnings that the rate of business investment in the United States is too low. Does this chapter give you any ideas about what is meant by the phrase "too low?" What factors do you think account for the low level of investment spending? (You may want to discuss this last issue with your instructor.)

3. Why is not any arbitrary level of GNP an equilibrium for the economy? (Do not give a mechanical answer to this question, but explain the economic mechanism involved.)

4. From the following data, construct an expenditure schedule on a piece of graph paper. Then use the income–expenditure (45° line) diagram to determine the equilibrium level of GNP.

INCOME	CONSUMPTION	INVESTMENT
100	80	30
150	125	30
200	170	30
250	215	30
300	260	30

5. From the following data, construct an expenditure schedule on a piece of graph paper. Then use the income–expenditure (45° line) diagram to determine the equilibrium level of GNP.

INCOME	CONSUMPTION	INVESTMENT
100	110	0
150	140	15
200	170	30
250	200	45
300	230	60

Compare your answer with your answer to Question 4.

6. Explain how rising prices help eliminate an inflationary gap. Do this both in plain English and in terms of the 45° line diagram.
7. Explain why, far from coming as a surprise, a period of stagflation can be expected to follow a period during which aggregate demand is excessively high.
8. Does the economy this year seem to have an inflationary gap or a recessionary gap? (If you do not know the answer from reading the newspaper, ask your instructor.)
9. Why are there no recessions in the Soviet Union?
10. (More difficult) Consider an economy in which the consumption function takes the following simple algebraic form:

$$C = 100 + 0.8Y$$

and in which investment (I) is always 300. Find the equilibrium level of GNP from the requirement that $C + I = Y$. Compare your answer to Table 8–2 and Figure 8–3.

Appendix
The Saving and Investment Approach

As we mentioned earlier in the chapter, there is another way of looking at the determination of the equilibrium level of GNP. Instead of studying the condition that aggregate demand ($C + I$) is equal to production (Y), we can study the condition that saving (S) is equal to investment (I). This is what we will do in this appendix.

It must be emphasized at the outset that there is nothing *new* in this approach. It is merely another way of looking at precisely the same phenomenon. The reason is that income (Y) must be either spent on consumer goods (C) or saved (S). Since $Y = C + S$ *always*, and since $Y = C + I$ *when Y is at its equilibrium value,* we can describe equilibrium by the condition that $C + S = C + I$, or simply:

$$S = I$$

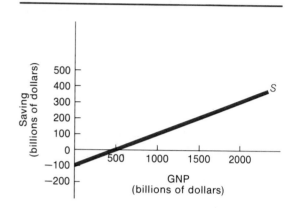

FIGURE 8–10
THE SAVING SCHEDULE
This diagram shows the relationship between saving and income in Macroland and duplicates Figure 7–8 (page 132).

GRAPHICAL ANALYSIS

This way of looking at equilibrium has a different graphical representation: It does not use the 45° line diagram, but it contains precisely the same information. Recall that in the appendix to Chapter 7 we constructed the saving schedule, which we repeat here as Figure 8–10. Since the equilibrium condition now under scrutiny is $S = I$, we can complete the story by providing an investment schedule. In the example used in the text, investment was taken to be a fixed number irrespective of income. We again do this here, so the investment schedule is as shown in Figure 8–11.

To find the point at which saving and investment are equal, we need only put both

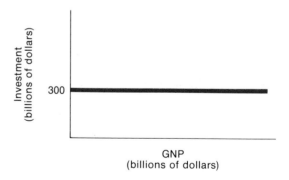

FIGURE 8–11
THE INVESTMENT SCHEDULE
In this simple example, investment spending is a fixed number—$300 billion—regardless of the level of GNP. Therefore, the investment schedule is a horizontal line at $300 billion.

Induced Investment

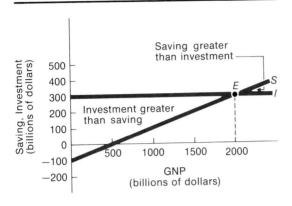

FIGURE 8–12
DETERMINATION OF EQUILIBRIUM GNP
BY SAVING = INVESTMENT
This diagram, which combines Figures 8–10 and 8–11, depicts the equilibrium of the economy at point E, where the saving and investment schedules intersect. The equilibrium is at a real GNP of $2000 billion, which, as must be the case, is the same conclusion that we reached with the aid of the 45° line diagram (Figure 8–3 on page 145).

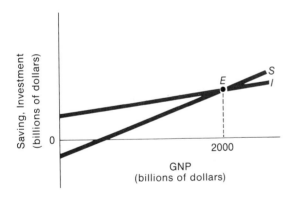

FIGURE 8–13
INCOME DETERMINATION
WITH INDUCED INVESTMENT
When investment rises with GNP ("induced investment"), the investment schedule acquires a positive slope. Apart from this, the determination of equilibrium output is precisely as it was before. Point E, where the S and I schedules cross, is the equilibrium.

these curves on the same diagram, which we have done in Figure 8–12. Point E shows the equilibrium level of GNP, which is at an income level of $2000 billion. As must be the case, this is the same answer we obtained with the 45° line diagram.

You will notice that at income levels below $2000 billion, investment exceeds saving, just as C + I exceeded output in the 45° line diagram. Similarly, at income levels above $2000 billion, S exceeds I. (In the 45° line diagram, Y exceeded C + I in this range.) The economic analysis behind the two graphs is precisely the same.

INDUCED INVESTMENT

Earlier in the chapter we mentioned the possibility of induced investment, that is, of an investment schedule that rises as GNP rises, but we did not examine this possibility in our graphs. (However, this case did arise in Discussion Question 5.) The reason is that what matters in the 45° line diagram is the slope of the combined C + I schedule, not the individual slopes of the C and I schedules. So an upward-sloping investment schedule does not make much difference to the analysis.

When using the saving and investment approach, however, the slope of the investment schedule becomes more apparent, if not more important. So Figure 8–13 illustrates the case of induced investment. In this diagram, the investment schedule is upward sloping. Equilibrium, however, is still at point E—where the S and I schedules cross. Thus, allowance for induced investment does not change our analysis in any significant way.[5]

[5]Some students may wonder what happens if the slope of the investment schedule exceeds that of the saving schedule. This is a difficult question and one that is best reserved for more advanced courses. Suffice it to say here that the simple model of income determination constructed in this chapter will not work in such a case.

SUMMARY

1. The condition for equilibrium GNP—which we gave earlier in the chapter as the equation of aggregate demand with output ($C + I = Y$)—can be stated alternatively as the equation of saving and investment ($S = I$). This does not change anything but simply says the same thing in different words.
2. These different words lead to a different graphical presentation, in which we look for equilibrium at the point where the saving schedule crosses the investment schedule.
3. Induced investment—that is, investment that rises as the GNP rises— leads to an upward-sloping investment schedule, but requires no other change in the analysis.

CONCEPTS FOR REVIEW

$S = I$ Investment schedule
Saving schedule   Induced investment

QUESTIONS FOR DISCUSSION

1. From the data in Discussion Question 4 at the end of the chapter, construct the saving schedule and the investment schedule on a piece of graph paper. (In doing this, remember that any income that is not consumed must have been saved.) Use these constructions to find the equilibrium level of GNP.
2. Do the same thing with the data in Discussion Question 5. (*Hint:* you will find *negative* saving at income level 100. There is nothing wrong with this. You do negative saving any time you draw down your bank account balance.)

9

Multiplier Analysis: Changes in Output and Prices

In the last chapter we described in some detail the notion of equilibrium income and its determination. In this chapter we will study how that equilibrium can *change*—in particular, how and why it shifts if either consumers or investors decide to increase their spending.

The central topic of this chapter is the multiplier—the idea that an increase in spending will bring about an *even larger* increase in equilibrium GNP. Just how much larger the increase is, and how this effect works, is the first topic we will discuss. We approach the subject from

three different perspectives, each of which provides the reader with a different basis for understanding the nature of the process used in determining the nation's output. First, the idea is illustrated graphically using the income–expenditure diagram from the last chapter. Next, we reach the same conclusion through the use of a numerical example; and finally, we offer an algebraic statement. Each of these is an expression of the remarkable multiplier result.

Once this concept is fully understood, we bring inflation back into the picture. First, we study how an increase in spending raises the equilibrium price level; that is, how it causes inflation. To do this we must supplement our investigation of aggregate demand by adding the aggregate supply curve, which was introduced in Chapter 5. Then, with the aid of aggregate supply and demand analysis, we see how inflation affects the multiplier process.

To review what we have learned, we close the chapter by considering how the multiplier process runs in reverse, that is, how *decreases* in spending lead to decreases in both output and prices.

THE MAGIC OF THE MULTIPLIER

Because it is subject to such abrupt swings, investment spending is often the cause of business fluctuations in the United States and elsewhere. Let us, therefore, ask what would happen to equilibrium income in our fictitious country, Macroland, if firms there suddenly

decided to spend more on investment goods. As we shall see, such a decision would have a *multiplied* effect on GNP in Macroland. The same would be true in the U.S. economy.

To begin, refer to Table 9–1, which looks very much like Table 8–1 of the last chapter (page 143). The only difference is that we assume here that, for some reason, firms in Macroland now want to invest $80 billion more than they previously did—for a total of $380 billion. The multiplier principle says that Macroland's GNP will rise by *more* than the $80 billion increased investment.

DEFINITION

The *multiplier* is the ratio of the change in equilibrium GNP (*Y*) divided by the original change in spending that causes the change in GNP. In shorthand, when we deal with the multiplier for investment (*I*), the formula is:

$$\text{Multiplier} = \frac{\text{Change in } Y}{\text{Change in } I}$$

TABLE 9–1

AGGREGATE DEMAND AFTER THE RISE IN INVESTMENT SPENDING
(billions of dollars)

(1) INCOME (Y)	(2) CONSUMPTION (C)	(3) INVESTMENT (I)	(4) AGGREGATE DEMAND (C + I)
1000	900	380	1280
1200	1060	380	1440
1400	1220	380	1600
1600	1380	380	1760
1800	1540	380	1920
2000	1700	380	2080
2200	1860	380	2240
2400	2020	380	2400
2600	2180	380	2560
2800	2340	380	2720
3000	2500	380	2880

This table shows the construction of a total expenditure schedule for Macroland after investment has risen to $380 billion. As indicated by the numbers shaded in red, only income level Y = $2400 billion is an equilibrium for the economy because only at this level is aggregate demand (C + I) equal to production (Y).

Let us now verify that the multiplier is indeed greater than 1.

Table 9–1 shows how to derive a new expenditure schedule by adding up C and I at each level of Y, just as we did in the previous chapter. If you compare the last column of Table 9–1 to that of Table 8–1, you will see that the new expenditure schedule lies uniformly above the old one by $80 billion. Figure 9–1 illustrates this diagrammatically. The schedule marked $C + I_0$ is derived from the last column of Table 8–1, while the higher schedule marked $C + I_1$ is derived from the last column of Table 9–1. The two $C + I$ lines are parallel and $80 billion apart.

So far no act of magic has occurred — things look just as you might expect. But one more step will bring the multiplier rabbit out of the hat. Let us see what the upward shift of the $C + I$ line does to equilibrium income. We see in Figure 9–1 that equilibrium moves outward from point E_0 to point E_1, that is, from $2000 billion to $2400 billion. The difference — $2400 billion minus $2000 billion — is an increase in national income of $400 billion. All this from an $80 billion stimulus to investment? That is the magic of the multiplier.

Because the change in I is $80 billion and the change in equlibrium Y is $400 billion, by applying our definiton, the multiplier is:

$$\text{Multiplier} = \frac{\text{Change in } Y}{\text{Change in } I} = \frac{\$400}{\$80} = 5$$

This tells us that, in our example, every additional dollar of investment demand will add $5 to the equilibrium GNP!

This does indeed seem mysterious. Can something be created from nothing? Let us, therefore, check to be sure that the graph has not deceived us. Once we have verified this, we turn to the logic of the multiplier. We shall see that the multiplier loses its mystery once we remember the circular flow of income and expenditure, and the simple fact that one person's spending is another person's income.

The first and last columns of Table 9–1

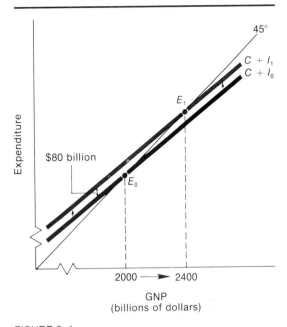

FIGURE 9–1

ILLUSTRATION OF THE MULTIPLIER

This figure depicts the multiplier effect of a rise in investment spending of $80 billion. The expenditure schedule shifts upward from $C + I_0$ to $C + I_1$, thus moving equilibrium from point E_0 to point E_1. The rise in income is $400 billion, so the multiplier is $400/$80 = 5.

show in numbers what Figure 9–1 shows in a picture. Notice that, at any income level below $2400, spending ($C + I$) exceeds output ($Y$). As we learned in the last chapter, this cannot be an equilibrium situation, because inventories would be disappearing. On the other hand, at any income level above $2400, inventories would be piling up, since $C + I$ is less than Y. Only at $Y = $2400 billion are spending and production in balance, as Table 9–1 shows. This is $400 billion higher than the $2000 billion equilibrium GNP obtained in the discussion of Table 8–1, where investment was only $300 billion. Thus an $80 billion rise in investment leads to a $400 billion rise in equlibrium GNP, which goes up from an initial value of $2000 billion to $2400 billion. The multiplier really is 5.

DEMYSTIFYING THE MULTIPLIER: HOW IT WORKS

We can obtain an understanding of how the multiplier works, and see why it is exactly 5 in our model economy, by looking more closely at what actually happens in the economy if businesses decide to spend an additional $1 million on investment goods.

For the sake of concreteness, suppose that Generous Motors—a major corporation in Macroland—decides to spend $1 million to retool a factory to manufacture pollution-free electronically powered automobiles. Its $1 million expenditure goes to construction workers and owners of construction companies as wages and profits. That is, it becomes their *income.*

But the owners and workers of the construction firms will not simply keep their $1 million in the bank. They will spend some of it. If they are "typical" consumers, their spending will, by definition, be $1 million times the marginal propensity to consume (MPC). In our example, the MPC is 0.8. So let us assume that they spend $800,000 and save the rest. *This $800,000 expenditure is a net addition to the nation's demand for goods and services exactly as GM's original $1 million expenditure was.* So, at this stage, the $1 million investment has already pushed GNP up some $1.8 million.

But the process by no means stops here. Shopkeepers receive the $800,000 spent by construction workers, and these shopkeepers in turn also spend 80 percent of their new income. This accounts for $640,000 (80 percent of $800,000) in additional consumer spending in the "third round." Next follows a fourth round in which the recipients of the $640,000, in their turn, spend 80 percent of this amount, or $512,000, and so on. At each stage in the spending chain, people spend 80 percent of the additional income they receive, and the process continues.

Where does it all end? Does it all end? The answer is that it does, indeed, eventually end—with GNP a total of $5 million higher than it was before Generous Motors spent the original $1 million. The multiplier, as stated, is 5.

Table 9–2 displays this conclusion. In the table, "round 1" represents GM's initial investment, which creates $1 million in income for construction people; "round 2" represents the construction workers' spending, which creates $800,000 in income for shopkeepers. The rest of the table proceeds accordingly. Each entry in column 2 is 80 percent of the previous entry, and column 3 tabulates the running sum of column 2. We see that after 10 rounds of spending the initial $1 million investment has mushroomed to nearly $4.5 million, and the sum is still growing. After 20 rounds, the total increase in GNP is over $4.9 million—quite near its eventual value of $5 million. While it takes quite a few rounds of spending before the multiplier chain is near 5, we see from the table that it gets up to around 4 rather quickly. If each income recipient in the chain waits, say, 2 months before spending his new income, the multiplier will reach 4 in only about 14 months.

Figure 9–2 on page 168 provides a graphical presentation of the numbers in the last column of Table 9–2. Notice how the multiplier builds up rapidly at first, and then tapers off to approach its ultimate value (5 in this example) gradually.

ALGEBRAIC STATEMENT OF THE MULTIPLIER

Figure 9–2 and Table 9–2 probably make a persuasive case for the fact that the multiplier eventually reaches 5. But for the remaining skeptics we offer a simple algebraic proof.[1] Most of you learned about an "infinite geometric progression" in high school. This is

---

[1]Students who blanch at the sight of algebra should not be put off. Anyone who can balance a checkbook (even many who cannot!) will be able to follow the argument.

TABLE 9–2

THE MULTIPLIER SPENDING CHAIN

(1) ROUND NUMBER	(2) SPENDING IN THIS ROUND	(3) CUMULATIVE TOTAL
1	$1,000,000	$1,000,000
2	800,000	1,800,000
3	640,000	2,440,000
4	512,000	2,952,000
5	409,600	3,361,600
6	327,680	3,689,280
7	262,144	3,951,424
8	209,715.20	4,161,139.20
9	167,772.16	4,328,911.36
10	134,217.73	4,463,129.09
.	.	.
.	.	.
20	14,411.52	4,942,353.93
.	.	.
50	17.84	4,999,928.64
.	.	.
.	.	.
"Infinity"	0	5,000,000

This table shows how the multiplier unfolds through time. Round 1 is GM's initial spending, which leads to $1 million in additional income to construction workers. Round 2 shows the construction workers spending 80 percent of this amount, since the marginal propensity to consume is 0.8. The other rounds proceed accordingly, with spending in each successive round equal to 80 percent of that in the previous round. Technically, the full multiplier of 5 is reached only after an "infinite" number of rounds. But, as can be seen, we are quite close to the full amount after 20 rounds.

simply an infinite series of numbers, each one of which is a fixed fraction of the previous one. This fraction is called the "common ratio." A geometric progession beginning with 1 and having a common ratio equal to 0.8 would look like this:

$$1 + 0.8 + (0.8)^2 + (0.8)^3 + \ldots$$

More generally, a geometric progression beginning with 1 and having a common ratio R would be:

$$1 + R + R^2 + R^3 + \ldots$$

A simple formula enables us to sum such a progression as long as R is less than 1.[2] The formula is:[3]

$$\text{Sum of infinite geometric progression} = \frac{1}{1 - R}$$

[2] If R exceeds 1, nobody can possibly sum it—not even with the aid of a modern computer!

[3] The proof is simple. Let the symbol S stand for the (unknown) sum of the series:

$$S = 1 + R + R^2 + R^3 + \ldots$$

Then, multiplying by R,

$$RS = R + R^2 + R^3 + \ldots$$

By subtracting RS from S, we obtain:

$$S - RS = 1$$

or

$$S = \frac{1}{1 - R}$$

167

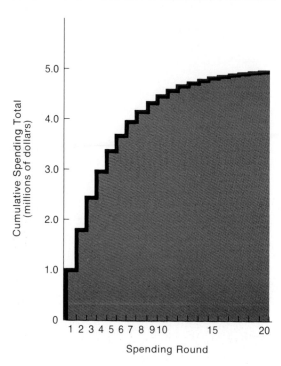

FIGURE 9–2

HOW THE MULTIPLIER BUILDS
This diagram portrays the numbers from Table 9–2 and shows how the multiplier builds through time. Notice how the effect grows quickly at first and how the full effect is almost reached after 15 to 20 rounds.

Now we can recognize that the multiplier chain in Table 9–2 is just an infinite geometric progression with 0.8 as its common ratio. That is, each $1 spent by GM leads to a (0.8) × $1 expenditure by construction workers, which in turn leads to a (0.8) × (0.8 × $1) = (0.8)² × $1 expenditure by the shopkeepers, and so on. Thus, for each initial dollar of investment spending, the progression is:

$$1 + 0.8 + (0.8)^2 + (0.8)^3 + (0.8)^4 + \ldots$$

Applying the formula for the sum of such a series, we find that:

$$\text{Multiplier} = \frac{1}{1 - 0.8} = \frac{1}{0.2} = 5$$

Notice how this result can be generalized. If we did not have a specific numerical value for the marginal propensity to consume, but simply called it "MPC," the geometric progression in Table 9–2 would have been

$$1 + \text{MPC} + (\text{MPC})^2 + (\text{MPC})^3 + \ldots$$

which has the MPC as its common ratio. Applying the same formula for summing a geometric progression to this more general case gives us the following general result:

Oversimplified Formula for the Multiplier

$$\text{Multiplier} = \frac{1}{1 - \text{MPC}}$$

We call this formula "oversimplified" because it ignores many factors that are important in the real world. One of them is *inflation*, a complication that will occupy our attention in this chapter. A second is *income taxation*, a point we will elaborate in the next chapter. A third factor arises from the *financial system* and, after we discuss money and banking in Chapters 11 and 12, we will explain it in Chapter 13. As it turns out, each of these factors *reduces* the size of the multiplier. Thus:

While the multiplier is larger than 1 in the real world, it cannot be calculated with any degree of accuracy from the oversimplified formula. The actual multiplier is *lower* than the formula suggests, though no economist knows its exact value.

THE MULTIPLIER EFFECT OF CONSUMER SPENDING

Business firms that invest are not the only ones that can work the magic of the multiplier; so can consumers. Before we investigate the complications, let us see how the multiplier works when the process is initiated by an upsurge in consumer spending.

First, we need to distinguish between two types of change in consumer spending. When C rises because income rises—that is, when consumers move outward *along* the consumption function—we call the increase in C an *induced* increase in consumption. However, if instead C rises because the entire consumption function *shifts* up, we call this an autonomous increase in consumption. The name indicates that consumption changes independently of income, and Chapter 7's discussion pointed out that a number of events, such as a change in

the price level or in the stock market, could initiate such a shift.

Let us suppose that, for some reason, consumer spending rises autonomously by $80 billion. In this case, our table of aggregate demand would have to be revised to look like Table 9–3. Comparing this to Table 9–1 on page 164, we note that each entry in column 2 is $80 billion *higher* than the corresponding entry in Table 9–1 (because consumption is higher) and each entry in column 3 is $80 billion *lower* (because investment is lower).

The equilibrium level of income is clearly Y = $2400 billion once again. Indeed, the entire expenditure schedule is the same as it was in Table 9–1. The initial rise of $80 billion in spending leads to an ultimate rise of $400 billion in GNP, just as occurred in the case of higher investment spending. In fact, Figure 9–1 applies to this case without any changes. The multiplier for autonomous changes in consumer spending, then, is also 5 ($400/$80). The

TABLE 9–3

AGGREGATE DEMAND AFTER CONSUMERS DECIDE TO SPEND $80 BILLION MORE
(billions of dollars)

(1) INCOME (Y)	(2) CONSUMPTION (C)	(3) INVESTMENT (I)	(4) AGGREGATE DEMAND (C + I)
1000	980	300	1280
1200	1140	300	1440
1400	1300	300	1600
1600	1460	300	1760
1800	1620	300	1920
2000	1780	300	2080
2200	1940	300	2240
2400	2100	300	2400
2600	2260	300	2560
2800	2420	300	2720
3000	2580	300	2880

This table shows the construction of the total expenditure schedule for Macroland following an autonomous increase of $80 billion in consumption rather than in investment. Notice that columns 2 and 3 differ from the corresponding columns in Table 9–1, but column 4 is the same in both tables. Thus the expenditure schedule in the 45° line diagram is the same as in the earlier example.

reason is straightforward. It does not matter who injects an additional dollar of spending into the economy, whether it is the business investors or the consumers. Wherever it comes from, 80 percent of it will be respent if the MPC is 0.8, and the recipients of this second round will in turn spend 80 percent of their additional income, and so on and on. And that is what constitutes the multiplier process.

In the next chapter we will learn, not surprisingly, that this same multiplier applies equally well to the third component of aggregate demand—government purchases of goods and services.

AGGREGATE SUPPLY AND PRICES: A DIGRESSION

Now that we understand the workings of the basic multiplier process, let us turn to the first of the reasons why the multiplier formula is oversimplified—inflation.

This first complication turns out to be nothing more than a restatement of one of the central ideas of economics: that prices are determined both by demand and supply. In this case, our story about the multiplier—whether told in words, with numbers, or in an algebraic formula—dealt only with the aggregate demand side. As we stressed in Chapter 8, the $C + I$ schedule in an income–expenditure diagram is drawn up for a given price level. It therefore cannot tell us what the price level will be nor whether prices will change. Let us now ask what is likely to be happening on the supply side of the economy as the multiplier process unfolds. Will this additional demand be taken care of by firms without raising prices?

Often, the answer is no; it will only be provided at higher prices. Thus, as the multiplier chain progresses, raising income and employment, prices will also be rising. And this, as we know from Chapter 7, will dampen consumer spending because rising prices reduce

consumers' purchasing power. So the multiplier chain will not proceed as far as it would have in the absence of inflation. How much inflation results from the rise in demand? How much of the multiplier chain is cut off by inflation? The answers depend on the economy's aggregate supply curve.

DEFINITION
The *aggregate supply curve* tells us, at each possible price level, what quantity of goods and services all the nation's businesses are willing to produce.

This curve, and the aggregate supply and demand analysis that goes with it, were introduced in Chapter 5. There we portrayed the equilibrium output and price level of the economy as the point where the aggregate demand and supply curves cross. Figure 9–3 repeats one of these diagrams for your convenience; point E marks the equilibrium.

The aggregate supply curve, SS, is drawn sloping upward from left to right. This means that, *other things held equal,* businesses will have to receive higher prices if they are to supply more output.[4] The slope of the aggregate supply curve, then, gives us just the information we need to see how much inflation will be caused by the multiplier chain of expanding demand—it tells us by how much prices must rise if output is to expand by a given amount. Let us now see how we can use this information to learn how inflation reduces the multiplier.

INFLATION AND THE MULTIPLIER

For a concrete example of the analysis, let us return to the $80 billion increase in investment spending with which we began this chapter. As

[4]A full analysis of business price and output decisions can be found in Chapter 20.

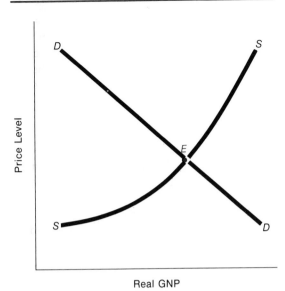

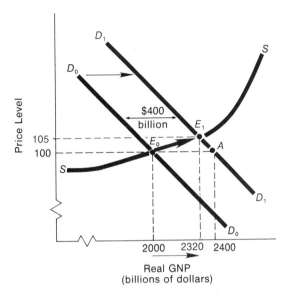

FIGURE 9–3

AGGREGATE SUPPLY AND DEMAND ANALYSIS

This figure reviews the aggregate supply and demand analysis that was introduced in Chapter 5. *DD* is the aggregate demand curve; its downward slope was explained in Chapters 7 and 8. *SS* is the aggregate supply curve, and its upward slope is explained in this chapter. Equilibrium is at point *E*, where the two curves cross.

FIGURE 9–4

INFLATION AND THE MULTIPLIER

This figure illustrates the complete analysis of the multiplier, including the effect of inflation. The simple multiplier analysis, which ignores changes in the price level, appears here as a *horizontal* shift of $400 billion in the aggregate demand curve, meaning that the multiplier would be $400/$80 = 5 if prices did not rise. However, when aggregate demand shifts from $D_0 D_0$ to $D_1 D_1$, prices rise. In the diagram, the price level increases from 100 to 105, or by 5 percent. Consequently, equilibrium real income increases from $2000 billion to only $2320—for a rise of $320 billion, or a multiplier of $320/$80 = 4.

we learned from our 45° line diagram, this leads—through the multiplier process—to an ultimate increase of $400 billion in the *aggregate quantity demanded at the initial price level.* But to know the actual quantity that will ultimately be produced, and the actual price level, we must bring the aggregate supply curve into the picture.

Figure 9–4 does this. Here we show a *horizontal shift* of the aggregate demand curve, from $D_0 D_0$ to $D_1 D_1$, equal to the $400 billion we calculated from the oversimplified multiplier formula (which ignored rising prices). The aggregate supply curve, *SS*, then tells us how this expansion of demand is apportioned

between higher output and higher prices. We see that as the economy's equilibrium moves from point E_0 to point E_1, real GNP does not rise by $400 billion. Instead, prices rise, which, as we know, tends to discourage part of the rise in quantity demanded by consumers. So output increases only from $2000 billion to $2320 billion—an increase of $320 billion. So in our example, inflation has reduced the multiplier from $400/$80 = 5 to $320/$80 = 4. In general:

As long as the aggregate supply curve is upward sloping, any increase in aggregate demand will push up the price level. This will, in turn, drain off some of the higher real demand by eroding consumers' purchasing power. Thus, inflation reduces the multiplier below that suggested by the oversimplified formula.

Notice also that the price level in this example has been pushed up (from 100 to 105, or 5 percent) by the rise in investment demand. This, too, is a general result:

As long as the aggregate supply curve is upward sloping, any upward shift in the aggregate demand curve will cause some rise in prices in the economy.

The economic behavior behind these results certainly cannot be considered surprising. Firms faced with a large increase in the aggregate quantity demanded at their original prices respond to these changed circumstances in two natural ways: They raise production (so GNP rises) and they raise prices (so the price level rises). But this rise in the price level reduces the purchasing power of the bank accounts and bonds held by consumers, and they also react in the natural way: They cut down on their spending. Such a reaction amounts to a movement *along* aggregate demand curve $D_1 D_1$ in Figure 9–4 from point A to point E_1. Higher prices thus play their usual dual role in a market economy: They encourage suppliers to produce more and, at the same time, encourage demanders to consume less. In this way, equilibrium is reestablished at higher levels of output and higher prices through the process of inflation.

THE MULTIPLIER IN REVERSE

A good way to check your understanding of the entire multiplier process is to run it in reverse:

What happens if, for example, consumers autonomously decide to spend less?

Before trying to trace through the mechanics, it may be useful to sum up the steps of the analysis that we have just completed.

STEPS IN CALCULATING THE MULTIPLIER
1. Shift the expenditure schedule in the 45° line diagram vertically by the amount of the autonomous shift in spending.
2. Use the 45° line diagram, or the oversimplified multiplier formula, to calculate the multiplier effect on GNP that *would* occur if the price level did not change.
3. Now move from the 45° line diagram to the supply and demand diagram to see how the price level will react. Enter the multiplier effect calculated in step 2 as a horizontal shift of the aggregate demand curve in the supply–demand diagram.
4. The supply–demand diagram will now show the actual effect on real output as well as the resulting inflation or deflation.

Let's follow these steps to see what would happen to our hypothetical economy if the consumption function shifted downward. We begin by assuming that a wave of thriftiness comes over the people of Macroland so that, no matter what their total income, they now want to save $100 billion more than they did previously.

Step 1 tells us to consider first what happens to the expenditure schedule in our 45° line diagram. Now a decision to save $100 billion more out of any given level of income is, by necessity, a decision to consume $100 billion less. Therefore, consumer spending—and thus the total expenditure schedule—falls by $100 billion. This is shown in Figure 9–5 as a downward shift of the $C + I$ schedule from $C_0 + I$ to $C_1 + I$. The horizontal distance between these two parallel lines is the $100 billion drop in spending.

Step 2 calls for us to calculate the simple multiplier effect, ignoring any changes in prices. There are two ways of doing this. First, our

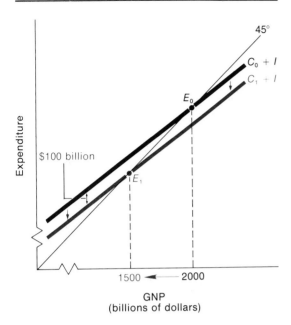

FIGURE 9–5

THE MULTIPLIER IN REVERSE

This diagram shows the first steps in analyzing the multiplier effect of an autonomous decline in consumer spending of $100 billion. The decline appears as a downward shift of $100 billion in the expenditure schedule, which falls from $C + I_0$ to $C + I_1$. Equilibrium, which is always at the intersection of the expenditure schedule and the 45° line, moves from point E_0 to point E_1, and income falls from $2000 billion to $1500 billion.

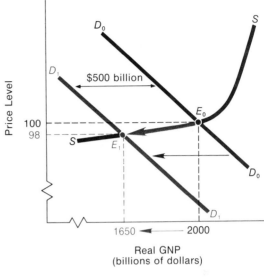

FIGURE 9–6

THE MULTIPLIER IN AGGREGATE SUPPLY AND DEMAND ANALYSIS

This figure takes the finding from Figure 9–5—that income would fall by $500 billion if the price level did not change—and transfers it to an aggregate supply and demand diagram. We see that the $500 billion leftward shift of the aggregate demand schedule from D_0D_0 to D_1D_1 leads to a decline in income from $2000 billion to $1650 billion and to a decline in the price level from 100 to 98. The final multiplier, then, is $350/$100 = 3.5.

oversimplified multiplier formula tells us that the multiplier is

$$\frac{1}{1 - MPC} = \frac{1}{1 - 0.8} = \frac{1}{0.2} = 5$$

So a $100 billion drop in demand would lead to a full multiplier effect of $500 billion *if* the price level did not change. Alternatively, we can read this conclusion from Figure 9–5. Here the economy's equilibrium point moves down the 45° line from point E_0 to E_1; income drops

from $2000 billion to $1500 billion—a decline of $500 billion.

This completes step 2 and, *if the price level does not fall*, the analysis ends here. We noted in the last chapter that the price level often stubbornly resists falling, so this may be a real possibility. However, to make the analysis complete, let us suppose that prices do fall, at least a little bit.

If this happens, we must proceed to step 3 to see how the decline in demand gets divided up between lower output and lower prices. Figure 9–6 is the aggregate supply and demand

173

diagram on which we can portray this division. It shows the initial equilibrium at point E_0, where demand curve D_0D_0 cuts supply curve SS. Our finding from step 2 is transferred to this diagram by shifting the aggregate demand curve *horizontally* by $500 billion—from D_0D_0 to D_1D_1. That is all there is to step 3.

In step 4 we need only read the results of the analysis from Figure 9–6. We see that equilibrium has moved from point E_0 to point E_1, meaning that output has fallen from $2000 billion to $1650 billion. The decline in GNP is, therefore, $350 billion, which is smaller than the initial decline in aggregate demand of $500 billion. The multiplier, then, is $350/$100 = 3.5.

What has happened to reconcile the two results? We see from the figure that the price level has fallen by 2 percent—from 100 to 98. Deflation has augmented the purchasing power of the money and bonds held by consumers, thus persuading them to cut their spending by less than $500 billion.

Now let us compare the analysis of a decline in aggregate demand that is summarized in Figures 9–5 and 9–6 with our previous analysis of an increase in aggregate demand, as shown in Figures 9–1 and 9–4 on pages 165 and 172, respectively. You will see that everything is simply turned in the opposite direction. There is only one minor quantitative difference. Since prices tend to be much more rigid in the downward direction than in the upward direction, the *de*flation caused by a

decrease in aggregate demand will be less than the *in*flation caused by an equal increase in aggregate demand. It may even be zero.

This important fact of real-world economic life is reflected in the way we have drawn our aggregate supply curves in this chapter: They get steeper as we move to the right, meaning that supply gets less responsive to price changes as the economy gets closer to its full capacity.

THE PARADOX OF THRIFT

This last example of multiplier analysis teaches us an important lesson: It shows that an increase in the desire to save will lead to a cumulative fall in national income. And this drop in income will pull saving (and consumption) down. So while saving may pave the road to riches *for an individual,* if *the nation as a whole* decides to save more, the result may be poverty for all! This remarkable result is called the paradox of thrift. It is important because it is contrary to most people's thinking and it means that greater saving may be a mixed blessing if it is not accompanied by equally greater invest-ment. We shall have occasion to return to this lesson in the chapter on economic growth (Chapter 33), where it is discussed in greater detail.

SUMMARY

1. Any autonomous increase in expenditure has a multiplier effect on GNP; that is, it increases GNP by more than the original increase in spending.
2. The reason for this multiplier effect is that one person's additional expen-diture constitutes a new source of income for another person, and this additional income leads to still more spending, and so on.
3. The multiplier also works in reverse: an autonomous decrease in any component of aggregate demand leads to a multiplied decrease in national income.
4. A simple formula for the multiplier says that its numerical value is $1/(1 - \text{MPC})$. While too simple to give accurate results, this formula is nonetheless a useful first approximation.

Questions for Discussion

5. Among the reasons why the oversimplified multiplier formula is wrong is the fact that it ignores any inflation that may be caused by an increase in aggregate demand. Such inflation would lower the multiplier by reducing consumer spending, because we know that consumers as a group suffer a loss of purchasing power when prices rise.

6. The economy's aggregate supply schedule tells us how much the price level must rise (or fall) in order to induce firms to produce any desired increase (or decrease) in GNP.

7. Shifts in aggregate demand can be apportioned between higher output and higher prices by using an aggregate supply and demand diagram.

8. If the nation as a whole decides to save more, that is, to consume less, the resulting decline in national income may serve to make everyone poorer. This possibility that thriftiness, while a virtue for the individual, may be disastrous for an entire nation, is called the paradox of thrift.

CONCEPTS FOR REVIEW

The multiplier
Autonomous increase in
   consumption

Aggregate supply curve
Paradox of thrift

QUESTIONS FOR DISCUSSION

1. Try to remember where you last spent a dollar. Explain how this dollar will lead to a multiplier chain of increased income and spending. (Who received the dollar? What will he or she do with it?)

2. Ignoring the complications caused by changes in the price level, use both numerical and graphical methods to find the multiplier effect of the following shift in the consumption function in an economy in which investment is always $100.

INCOME	CONSUMPTION BEFORE SHIFT	CONSUMPTION AFTER SHIFT
$510	$440	$470
540	460	490
570	480	510
600	500	530
630	520	550
660	540	570
690	560	590
720	580	610

(*Hint:* What is the marginal propensity to consume?)

3. Turn back to Discussion Question 4 in Chapter 8 (page 158). Suppose investment spending rises to $40, but the price level is fixed. By how much will the equilibrium GNP increase? Derive the answer both numerically and graphically.

4. Now add the following aggregate supply and demand schedules to the data in Question 3 to see how inflation affects the multiplier.

(1) PRICE LEVEL	(2) AGGREGATE DEMAND (when investment is $30)	(3) AGGREGATE DEMAND (when investment is $40)	(4) AGGREGATE SUPPLY
90	$210	$310	$110
95	205	305	155
100	200	300	200
105	195	295	245
110	190	290	290
115	185	285	335

Draw these schedules on a piece of graph paper. Then:
a. Notice that the difference between columns 2 and 3 (the aggregate demand schedule at two different levels of investment) is always $100. Discuss how this relates to your answer in the previous problem.
b. Find the equilibrium GNP and the equilibrium price level both before and after the increase in investment. What is the value of the multiplier?
5. Explain in words why rising prices reduce the multiplier effect of an autonomous increase in aggregate demand.
6. Use an aggregate supply and demand diagram to show that multiplier effects are smaller when the aggregate supply curve is steeper. Which case gives rise to more inflation—the steep aggregate supply curve or the flat one?
7. What is the meaning of an aggregate supply curve that is very flat at low levels of output and very steep at high levels of output? Does this strike you as a reasonable characterization of the way American industry might behave? Why or why not?
8. Explain the paradox of thrift. Why do you think it is called a paradox?

10

Managing Aggregate Demand
Through Fiscal Policy

In the last two chapters, we constructed and analyzed a model of an economy in which there is neither government spending nor taxes. But in our modern economy, purchases by government at all levels (federal, state, and local) account for more than 20 percent of gross national product. So to make our model fit the U.S. economy, our task in this chapter is to put the government back into the picture.

We begin by expanding the basic model to allow, first, for government purchases of goods and services as a third component of aggregate demand, and second, for an income tax that makes disposable income less than national income. As we shall see, neither of these complications requires any fundamental change in the way we analyze the determination of national income and the price level, although taxes do reduce the multiplier. But, while the *model* does not have to change much when the government is introduced, the *policy implications* of the analysis must be drastically altered. In fact, the main topic of this chapter is how the government can use its spending and taxing programs to manage the level of aggregate demand.

Once we have mastered some mechanics, we will see why there are always a variety of budgets capable of producing more or less the same effect upon aggregate demand. How, then, does the government decide on the preferred mix of taxing and spending each year? This question will be addressed toward the end of the chapter. In addition, we will consider some further complications that simple economic models ignore but that policy planners cannot afford to overlook.

HOW BUDGET DECISIONS ARE MADE

In January of each year, the president of the United States sends to Congress two economic messages that often touch off a vigorous debate—his Budget Message and his Economic Report. The reason for the heated response to these messages is that they outline the administration's proposed fiscal policy, a highly volatile issue.

DEFINITION

The government's *fiscal policy* is its plan for spending and taxation. It is designed to steer aggregate demand in some desired direction.

In these statements, the president outlines his taxing and spending proposals, explains the effects that government economists expect these proposals to have on aggregate demand, and offers an explanation indicating why this is the right policy at that time. Congress then follows a set procedure for either agreeing or disagreeing with the president's proposals.

During the spring, after it has had about three months to consider the president's suggestions, Congress passes its First Concurrent Resolution on the Budget, stating its own notions of how much spending and taxing the government should do. When Congress and the White House are in the hands of different political parties, as was the case when the fiscal year 1977 budget was introduced, these two notions may be quite far apart.[1]

A process of either reconciliation or legislative–executive warfare then ensues, during which time Congress may pass bills inconsistent with the president's proposed budget, and the president may veto legislation voted by Congress. Then, in the fall, Congress passes its Second Concurrent Resolution on the Budget. Under normal circumstances, this will represent the federal government's budget policy for the fiscal year about to begin.[2]

This chapter is concerned with the way in which these important budget decisions are, or should be, made. If you were a legislator, how would you decide whether to vote for or against one of the concurrent resolutions? How much spending is the right amount? How much taxation is appropriate? Perhaps more to the point, how can you as a voter decide whether your elected representatives have made sound decisions?

GOVERNMENT PURCHASES AND EQUILIBRIUM INCOME

Before attempting to answer questions like these, we must integrate the government into our model of the determination of national income and the price level. We do this in stages, starting first with government purchases of goods and services (G), and then adding taxes. Thus, in considering once again the circular flow of income and expenditure (see Figure 10–1), we ignore for the moment the flow of tax revenues to the government at point 5 (and also the partially offsetting flow of "transfer

[1]The fiscal year for the United States government runs from October of one calendar year through September of the following calendar year. Thus, for example, fiscal year 1980 begins in October 1979 and ends in September 1980.

[2]Should the need arise, the law allows for a Third Concurrent Resolution, or even more.

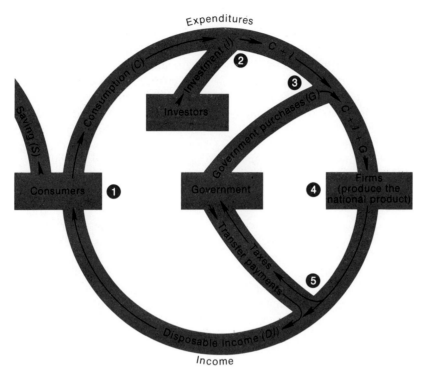

FIGURE 10–1

THE CIRCULAR FLOW OF EXPENDITURE AND INCOME

payments'' that will be explained later in this chapter). How would the equilibrium level of GNP be determined in an economy in which the government spent money but did not levy any taxes?

The circular flow diagram shows us the answer, just as it did in an economy with no government (Chapter 8). If the size of the circular flow of income and expenditure is to be maintained, then the total amount of new goods and services that firms produce at point 4 (Y) must be equal to the sum of the demands of consumers at point 1 (C), investors at point 2 (I), and government at point 3 (G). We thus obtain the following restatement of the condition for equilibrium GNP:

Equilibrium GNP occurs when the sum of consumption demand, investment demand, and government demand for goods and services just equals the GNP. In symbols:

$$Y = C + I + G$$

The reasoning behind this equilibrium condition is precisely the same as it was in Chapter 8. At income levels below equilibrium, the sum $C + I + G$ would exceed Y; and so inventories would be disappearing, signaling firms that they should raise their production. Conversely, at income levels above equilibrium, $C + I + G$ would be less than Y, so that unwanted inventories would be accumulating, and firms would have incentives to cut back production.

179

Table 10–1, which may usefully be compared to Table 8–1 in Chapter 8 (page 143), illustrates this process. The first three columns give the same consumption and investment schedules that we worked with there. The fourth column reflects the assumption that government purchases will be $400 billion, irrespective of the level of GNP. Summing these three components gives us our new total expenditure schedule in columns 1 and 5.

What, then, is the equilibrium level of GNP? As the table indicates, only a GNP of $4000 billion can be an equilibrium, for only at this level is aggregate demand in balance with production.

Figure 10–2 shows the same conclusion graphically. The line labeled C is the same consumption function we used in previous chapters. The line labeled C + I adds the fixed $300 billion in investment to this; again, this amount is taken from previous chapters. Finally, the line labeled C + I + G adds an additional $400 billion in government spending to the C + I line, which gives us our new total expenditure schedule.

Just as in previous chapters, the equilibrium of the economy is at point E, where the total expenditure schedule crosses the 45° line. This is because the 45° line includes all the points at which C + I + G add up to Y. The diagram shows that equilibrium is at a GNP of $4000 billion, which consists of $3300 billion in consumption, $300 billion in investment, and $400 billion in government purchases. This agrees precisely with Table 10–1, as must be the case. If all this seems familiar from previous chapters, it should; for the analysis is precisely the same.

In Chapter 9 we stated that when government spending is introduced the multiplier for G

TABLE 10–1

DERIVATION OF AN AGGREGATE DEMAND SCHEDULE WITH GOVERNMENT PURCHASES

(1) NATIONAL INCOME (Y)	(2) CONSUMPTION (C)	(3) INVESTMENT (I)	(4) GOVERNMENT PURCHASES (G)	(5) AGGREGATE DEMAND (C+I+G)
$1800	$1540	$300	$400	$2240
2000	1700	300	400	2400
2200	1860	300	400	2560
2400	2020	300	400	2720
2600	2180	300	400	2880
2800	2340	300	400	3040
3000	2500	300	400	3200
3200	2660	300	400	3360
3400	2820	300	400	3520
3600	2980	300	400	3680
3800	3140	300	400	3840
4000	3300	300	400	4000
4200	3460	300	400	4160

This table adds government purchases of $400 billion to our model economy. Notice that the equilibrium level of GNP grows to $4000 billion, for this is the level at which output is equal to aggregate demand (the sum of C + I + G).

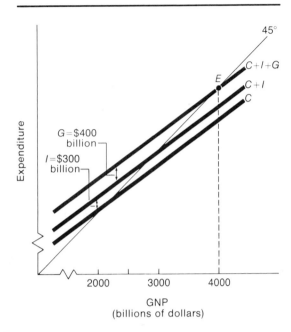

FIGURE 10–2

INCOME DETERMINATION WITH
GOVERNMENT SPENDING

This diagram adds government purchases of goods
and services (G) to the income–expenditure diagrams
that we have been using. The C + I + G curve is the
total expenditure schedule, and the point where it
crosses the 45° line (point E) marks the equilibrium
level of GNP. The C + I + G line is parallel to the
C + I line because of the assumption that whatever the
level of GNP, government spending remains at $400
billion.

is the same as the multiplier for autonomous
changes in C and I. We can now demonstrate
this conclusion.

If you flip back to page 144, you will see
that the equilibrium reached there was at a level
of output Y = $2000 billion. Now, in an
economy that is identical with the one in
Chapter 8 except for the $400 billion in govern-
ment spending, we see that the equilibrium is at
Y = $4000 billion. Thus a $400 billion increment
in G (from zero to $400 billion) has pushed up

GNP by $2000 billion. In this example, then, the
multiplier for government spending is
$2000/$400 = 5, which, you will recall, was also
the value of the multiplier for autonomous
increases in investment or consumption.

The two multipliers are identical because
the logic behind them is identical. In the last
chapter we studied an example of a multiplier
spending chain set in motion when Generous
Motors spent $1 million to build a factory. This
process could equally well have been kicked off
by the federal government buying $1 million
worth of new cars from GM. Thereafter, each
recipient of additional income would spend 80
percent of it (the assumed marginal propensity
to consume), until $5 million in new income had
eventually been created.

And the qualification that we placed on the
oversimplified multiplier formula in Chapter 9
also applies here: Government spending
normally leads to some inflation, which pulls
down consumer spending and thus reduces the
value of the multiplier below our illustrative
figure of 5.

INCOME TAXES AND THE CONSUMPTION SCHEDULE

You can see, then, that it takes little effort to
bring government purchases into our model of
income determination. Let us turn our attention
next to taxes and, in particular, to the personal
income tax.

For our purposes, the most important
aspect of taxes is that they create a discrepancy
between gross national product (GNP) and
disposable income (DI). If you look again at the
circular flow diagram (Figure 10–1), you will
notice that two things intervene between GNP
and DI at point 5: Tax revenues flow out of the
circular flow and into the hands of the government, while transfer payments made by the
government enter the circular flow.

DEFINITION
Government transfer payments are sums of money that certain individuals receive as outright *grants* from the government rather than as payments for *services* rendered to employers.

These transfer payments include unemployment compensation, social security benefits, and other types of payments. As we can see from the circular flow, the following accounting identity relates GNP and *DI*:[3]

$DI = GNP - \text{Taxes} + \text{Transfer payments}$

The effects of transfer payments on our income determination analysis will be considered presently. For now, let us concentrate on taxes.

We learned in Chapter 7 that there is a close and reliable relationship between consumer spending and *disposable* income. Therefore, if we want to construct a relationship between consumer spending and GNP, we first have to allow for the fact that taxes are deducted from GNP before *DI* is arrived at. The importance of this piece of accounting is that when taxes are increased, disposable income falls—and hence so does consumption—*even if GNP is unchanged.* In other words:

An increase in personal income taxes shifts the consumption schedule in our 45° line diagram downward. Similarly, a reduction in taxes shifts the consumption schedule upward.

The specific manner in which the consumption schedule shifts depends on the nature of the tax change. One way to reduce taxes is to introduce a flat, per person tax credit, such as the $30 per person tax credit of 1975. The increase in disposable income from this legislation is the *same* regardless of the level of GNP; hence the increase in consumer spending is the same. In a word, the *C* schedule shifts upward in a parallel manner, as shown in Figure 10–3(a).

[3]As pointed out in Chapter 17, this equation ignores a few minor items, which are not important here.

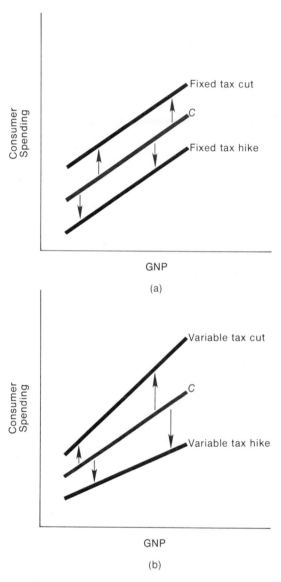

(a)

(b)

FIGURE 10–3

HOW TAX POLICY SHIFTS THE CONSUMPTION SCHEDULE

Because consumption depends on disposable income, not GNP, any change in taxes will shift the consumption schedule. Part (a) shows how the curve shifts for changes in taxes of fixed amounts. Part (b) shows how the *C* curve shifts if the tax cut (or tax rise) is larger at high incomes than at low incomes.

But often tax policy is designed to make the change in disposable income depend on the level of income, normally being larger at high income levels than at low ones. This is true, for example, when Congress alters the bracket rates in the personal income tax code, as it did in 1964 and again in 1978. Since this sort of tax policy accounts for a greater change in disposable income when GNP is higher, the downward shift in the C schedule is sharper at high income levels than at low ones. Figure 10–3(b) illustrates how this type of tax policy shifts the consumption schedule.

TAX POLICY AND EQUILIBRIUM INCOME

We are now in a position to put taxes into our model of income determination. To do this, we must first adjust the consumption schedule we have been using to allow for an income tax. Table 10–2 does this on the assumption that taxes are 25 percent of GNP. Column 1 shows alternative values of GNP ranging from $1.6 trillion to $2.6 trillion, and column 2 indicates that taxes are always one-quarter of this amount. Column 3 subtracts column 2 from column 1 to arrive at disposable income (DI). Column 4 then shows the amount of consumer spending corresponding to each level of DI. Note that columns 3 and 4 just repeat the consumption function that we studied in Chapter 7. The consumption schedule that we need for our 45° line diagram relates C to Y and is therefore found in columns 1 and 4.

To derive the new expenditure schedule for an economy with taxes, we need only replace the old consumption schedule with this new one—that is, we must replace column 2 of Table 10–1 with column 4 of Table 10–2. This is done numerically in Table 10–3, and the results are shown diagrammatically in Figure 10–4. In particular, the expenditure schedule contained in columns 1 and 5 of Table 10–3 is shown as the $C + I + G$ line in Figure 10–4. Naturally, the inclusion of taxes has lowered the expenditure schedule.

Since the 45° line is given in the diagram, we can immediately locate the equilibrium level of GNP at point E. Here, gross national product is $2000 billion, consumption is $1300 billion, investment is $300 billion, and government purchases are $400 billion. As we know, full employment may occur above or below $Y = $2000 billion. If below, there is an inflationary gap. Prices probably will start to rise,

TABLE 10–2

DERIVATION OF A CONSUMPTION SCHEDULE WITH INCOME TAXATION

(1) GROSS NATIONAL PRODUCT	(2) TAXES	(3) DISPOSABLE INCOME (GNP minus taxes)	(4) CONSUMPTION
$1600	$400	$1200	$1060
1800	450	1350	1180
2000	500	1500	1300
2200	550	1650	1420
2400	600	1800	1540
2600	650	1950	1660

Because taxes (column 2) must be subtracted from gross national product (column 1) to get disposable income (column 3), this table shows how an income tax lowers the consumption schedule (column 4) in a concrete example. (Compare column 4 with the consumption schedule in Table 10–1 to see that the C schedule has indeed fallen.)

TABLE 10–3

THE AGGREGATE DEMAND SCHEDULE WITH TAXES AND GOVERNMENT PURCHASES

(1) GROSS NATIONAL PRODUCT (Y)	(2) CONSUMPTION (C)	(3) INVESTMENT (I)	(4) GOVERNMENT PURCHASES (G)	(5) AGGREGATE DEMAND ($C + I + G$)
$1000	$ 700	$300	$400	$1400
1200	820	300	400	1520
1400	940	300	400	1640
1600	1060	300	400	1760
1800	1180	300	400	1880
2000	1300	300	400	2000
2200	1420	300	400	2120
2400	1540	300	400	2240
2600	1660	300	400	2360
2800	1780	300	400	2480
3000	1900	300	400	2600

This table replaces the previous consumption schedule with a new one that adjusts for the income tax (as shown in Table 10–2) and shows that the equilibrium level of income is $2000 billion.

FIGURE 10–4

INCOME DETERMINATION WITH GOVERNMENT SPENDING AND TAXATION

This diagram adds a 25 percent income tax to the model economy portrayed in Figure 10–2. Because of this, the C schedule is shifted down (and hence the $C + I$ and $C + I + G$ schedules are also shifted down). Equilibrium is at point E, where the $C + I + G$ schedule crosses the 45° line. Thus equilibrium GNP is $2000 billion, the same as it was in the economy with no government. This, however, is certainly not a general result; government actions can either raise or lower GNP.

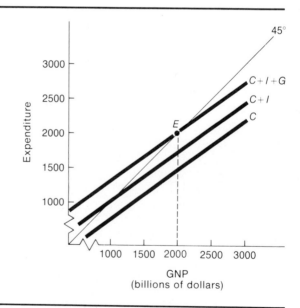

pulling the expenditure schedule down and reducing equilibrium GNP. If above, there is a recessionary gap, and history suggests that prices will not fall. Instead, there will be persistent unemployment.

In a word, once we adjust the expenditure schedule to include the effects of taxes, the determination of national income proceeds exactly as before. The effects of government spending and taxation, therefore, are fairly straightforward, and can be summarized as follows:

Government purchases of goods and services *add to* aggregate demand directly through the G component of $C + I + G$. Taxes indirectly *reduce* aggregate demand by lowering disposable income, and thus reduce the C component of $C + I + G$. On balance, then, the government's actions may raise or lower the equilibrium level of GNP. It all depends on how much spending and taxing it does.

MULTIPLIERS FOR TAX POLICY

We saw earlier that government purchases (G) have a multiplier effect on GNP. So do changes in tax policy. But because they work indirectly via consumption, the multipliers for tax changes must be worked out in two steps.

Step 1. Before turning to the 45° line diagram, we must figure out what any proposed change in the tax law is likely to do to the consumption schedule.

Step 2. We can then enter this effect as a shift of the $C + I + G$ schedule in the 45° line diagram, and work out the multiplier.

A reduction in income taxes provides a convenient example of this two-step analysis, because we have already done Step 1 in an

earlier chapter. Specifically, in Chapter 7 we studied how consumer spending would respond to a cut in income taxes. We concluded that if the tax reduction were viewed as permanent, consumers would increase their spending by an amount equal to the tax cut times the marginal propensity to consume. (If you need review, turn back to pages 117–123.)

This is the shift that must be entered in the 45° line diagram to complete Step 2, and Figure 10–5 displays such a shift. The tax cut raises the expenditure schedule from $C_0 + I + G$ to $C_1 + I + G$ by raising its C component. The diagram then shows the multiplier effect on GNP, which rises from Y_0 to Y_1.

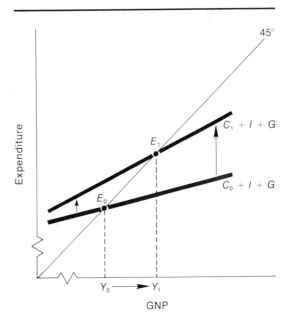

FIGURE 10–5

THE MULTIPLIER FOR A REDUCTION IN INCOME TAXES

The $C + I + G$ schedule is shifted upward, from $C_0 + I + G$ to $C_1 + I + G$, by a tax cut in this example. Equilibrium GNP therefore increases from Y_0 to Y_1.

GOVERNMENT TRANSFER PAYMENTS AND FISCAL POLICY

We now come to the last major tool of fiscal policy: government transfer payments. How are transfers treated in our models of income determination—like purchases of goods and services (G) or like taxes?

The answer follows readily from the accounting identity on page 182, for the important thing to understand about transfer payments is that they intervene between gross national product (Y) and disposable income (DI) in precisely the *opposite* way from income taxes. Specifically, starting with the wages, interest, rents, and profits that constitute the national income, we *subtract* income taxes to calculate disposable income. We do so because these taxes represent the portion of incomes that are *earned* but never *received* by consumers. But then we *add* transfer payments because they represent sources of income that are *received* though they were not *earned* in the process of production. Thus, transfer payments are basically *negative taxes*. Giving a consumer $1 in the form of a transfer payment is equivalent to reducing her taxes by $1.

This answers our question. In terms of the 45° line diagram, *increases in transfer payments can be treated simply as decreases in taxes.*

So Figure 10–5, which we devised to illustrate a tax cut, can also be used to illustrate a rise in unemployment benefits, or in social security benefits, or in any other such transfer payment. Similarly, the analysis of a decrease in transfer payments would proceed exactly like the analysis of an increase in taxes.

THE MULTIPLIER REVISITED

We now have acquired all the tools we need to understand how fiscal policy decisions are made. But, before senators or congressmen

vote on one of the concurrent resolutions on the budget, they should have an idea of the magnitude of the multiplier. Our figure of 5 is too high, and we can now see how the income tax works to lower its value.

Before getting involved in the mechanics, let us understand the basic reason. As we learned in Chapter 9, the multiplier works through a chain of spending and responding, as one person's expenditure becomes another's income. But through taxation some of the additional income leaks out of the circular flow at each stage. Specifically, if the income tax rate is 25 percent, when Generous Motors spends $1 million on salaries, workers actually receive only $750,000 in *after-tax* (or disposable) income. If workers spend 80 percent of this amount (based on a marginal propensity to consume of 0.8), spending in the next round will be only $600,000. Notice that this is only *60 percent* of the original expenditure, not *80 percent* as in our earlier example. Thus the multiplier chain for each original dollar of spending shrinks from

$$1 + 0.8 + (0.8)^2 + (0.8)^3 + \cdots = \frac{1}{1 - 0.8}$$
$$= \frac{1}{0.2} = 5$$

to

$$1 + 0.6 + (0.6)^2 + (0.6)^3 + \cdots = \frac{1}{1 - 0.6}$$
$$= \frac{1}{0.4} = 2\tfrac{1}{2}$$

This is clearly a very large reduction in the multiplier. We thus have a second reason why our oversimplified multiplier formula of the previous chapter gives an exaggerated impression of the size of the multiplier:

REASONS WHY THE OVERSIMPLIFIED MULTIPLIER FORMULA IS WRONG

1. It ignores price-level changes, which serve to reduce the size of the multiplier.
2. It ignores income taxes, which serve to reduce the size of the multiplier.

Of the two reasons, the second is much more important in reality. In later chapters, we shall encounter still more reasons.

This conclusion about the multiplier is shown graphically in Figure 10–6, where we have drawn our $C + I + G$ schedules with a slope of 0.6, to reflect an MPC of 0.8 and a tax rate of 25 percent, rather than the 0.8 slope that we used previously. The figure depicts the effect of an increase in government purchases of goods and services of $100 billion, which shifts the $C + I + G$ schedule from $C + I + G_0$ to

$C + I + G_1$. Equilibrium moves from point E_0 to point E_1—a growth in GNP from $Y = \$2000$ billion to $Y = \$2250$ billion. Thus, if we ignore for the moment any increases in the price level (which reduce the multiplier shown in Figure 10–6), a $100 billion increment in government spending leads to a $250 billion increment in GNP. So when taxes are included in our model, the multiplier is only $\$250/\$100 = 2\frac{1}{2}$, just as we concluded before.[4]

AUTOMATIC STABILIZERS

So higher rates of income taxation reduce the size of the multiplier. Is this helpful or harmful to the economy?

From the perspective of a fiscal policy planner, it might be considered unfortunate because it means that any desired change in GNP can be achieved only by a stronger dose of fiscal policy. But that would be an unduly myopic view. For, as Keynes stressed, the economy is continually buffeted by unexpected shifts in the C and I schedules—events that, we now know, have multiplier effects on GNP. Income taxes reduce the sensitivity of the economy to these shocks, thus increasing the degree of stability. For this reason, the income tax is considered our major automatic stabilizer.

The ability of the income tax to act as a shock absorber derives from the fact that it makes disposable income, and thus consumer spending, less sensitive to fluctuations in GNP. When GNP rises, disposable income (DI) rises also, but by less than the rise in GNP because part of the income is siphoned off by the U.S. Treasury. This helps limit the upward fluctuation in consumption spending. And when GNP falls, DI falls less sharply because part of the loss is absorbed by the Treasury rather than by

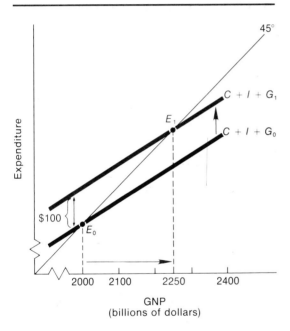

FIGURE 10–6

THE MULTIPLIER IN THE PRESENCE OF AN INCOME TAX
This diagram illustrates that an economy with an income tax (in this case a 25 percent income tax) has a lower multiplier than an economy without one. Specifically, the $C + I + G$ curve is shifted upward by a $100 billion increase in G, and the diagram shows that equilibrium GNP rises by $250 billion—from $2000 billion to $2250 billion. The multiplier is, therefore, $\$250/\$100 = 2\frac{1}{2}$, whereas without an income tax it is 5.

[4]For those interested in a general formula, the multiplier in the presence of an income tax is:

$$\frac{1}{1 - [MPC \times (1 - \text{Tax rate})]}$$

consumers. So consumption does not drop as much as it otherwise might. Thus, although everybody likes to grumble about it, the personal income tax—which affected very few families in 1929, but affects almost everyone now—is one of the many modern institutions that help ensure us against a repeat performance of the Great Depression.

There are many other automatic stabilizers in our economy. For example, in Chapter 6 we studied the U.S. system of unemployment insurance. This serves as an automatic stabilizer in a similar way. When GNP begins to fall and people lose their jobs, unemployment benefits prevent the disposable incomes of the jobless from falling as much as their earnings. As a result, unemployed workers can maintain their spending, and consumption need not fluctuate as dramatically as employment.

The corporate profits tax is another example. Because corporate profits fluctuate violently as GNP rises and falls, receipts from corporation income taxes rise steeply in economic expansions (thus curbing purchasing power) and fall just as steeply in contractions (thus propping up purchasing power). And the list could continue. The basic principle is the same: Each of these automatic stabilizers, in one way or another, serves as a shock absorber by reducing the size of the multiplier.

DEFINITION

An *automatic stabilizer* is any institution that serves to support aggregate demand when it would otherwise sag and hold down aggregate demand when it would otherwise surge ahead. In this way, an automatic stabilizer reduces the sensitivity of the economy to shifts in demand.

PLANNING EXPANSIVE FISCAL POLICY

Now, at last, you are ready to pretend that you are a congressman or congresswoman deciding

on how to respond to the president's proposed budget. Suppose that the economy would have a GNP of $2000 billion if last year's budget were simply repeated. Suppose further that your goal is to achieve a fully employed labor force and that staff economists tell you that your goal can be achieved with a GNP of approximately $2250 billion. What budget should you vote for?

The question is far from hypothetical. During every year since 1974, there has been a sizable gap between actual and potential GNP, often in excess of $100 billion, and legislators in Washington have had to make decisions very much like the one you are facing. Whether and how the economy should be stimulated through fiscal policy was a major topic on the political agenda in 1976 and 1977, and finally led to the tax reduction of 1978. What were the options open to Congress?

If we ignore for the moment the fact that inflation was also high on the list of the nation's economic woes and concentrate on policies designed to cure unemployment, this chapter has taught us just what those options were. Congress could have raised government purchases, reduced taxes, or increased transfer payments by enough to close the recessionary gap between actual and potential GNP.

Figure 10–7 illustrates the problem, and its cure through higher government spending, on our 45° line diagram. Figure 10–7(a) shows the equilibrium of the economy if no changes are made in the budget. Except for the full-employment line at $Y = \$2250$ and the corresponding recessionary gap, it looks just like Figure 10–4. With an expenditure multiplier of $2\frac{1}{2}$, you can figure out that an additional $100 billion of government spending will be needed to push the GNP up $250 billion and eliminate this gap ($250 \div 2\frac{1}{2} = \$100$).

So you might vote to raise G from $400 billion to $500 billion, hoping to move the $C + I + G$ curve in Figure 10–7(a) out to the position indicated in Figure 10–7(b), thereby achieving full employment. Of course you might prefer to achieve this fiscal stimulus by lowering income

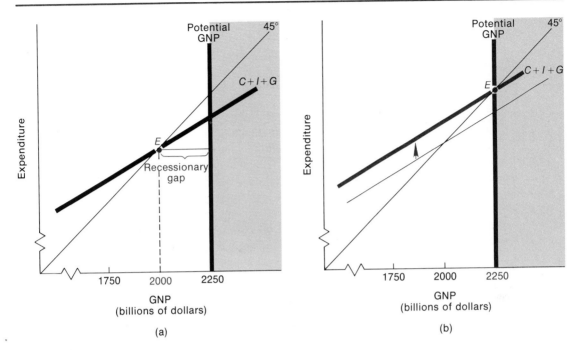

FIGURE 10–7
FISCAL POLICY TO ELIMINATE A RECESSIONARY GAP
This diagram shows, with more precision than can actually be achieved in practice, how fiscal policy can eliminate a recessionary gap. Part (a) shows the gap: Equilibrium GNP ($2000 billion) falls short of potential GNP ($2250 billion). Part (b) shows how fiscal policy—by moving the $C + I + G$ curve up just enough—can wipe out this gap and restore full employment. With a multiplier of $2\frac{1}{2}$, a rise in G of $100 billion or a cut in taxes large enough to shift C up by $100 billion would do the trick.

taxes rather than increasing expenditures. Or you might prefer to rely on more generous transfer payments. The point is that there are a variety of budgets capable of pushing the economy up to full employment by increasing GNP by $250 billion. Figure 10–7 applies equally well to any of them.

PLANNING RESTRICTIVE FISCAL POLICY

The preceding example assumed that the basic problem of fiscal policy is to overcome a defi-

ciency of aggregate demand, as has been the case during much of the Carter administration. Often this is so. But at other times—such as during the last half of the Johnson administration—the problem was that demand was excessive relative to the economy's capacity to produce. In this case, fiscal policy should assume a restrictive stance in order to reduce inflation.

It does not take much imagination to run our previous analysis in reverse. If, under a continuation of current budget policies, there were to be an inflationary gap, there are fiscal policy tools that can eliminate it. Either by cutting spending programs out of the budget, or by raising taxes, or by some combination of these policies, the government can pull the $C + I + G$ schedule down to a noninflationary position and achieve an equilibrium at full employment.

Notice the difference between this way of eliminating an inflationary gap and the natural self-correcting mechanism of the economy that we discussed in Chapter 8. There we observed that if the economy were left to its own devices, a cumulative but self-limiting process of inflation eventually would eliminate the inflationary gap and return the economy to full employment. Here we see that it is not necessary to put the economy through the inflationary wringer. Instead, a restrictive fiscal policy can limit aggregate demand to the level that the economy can produce at full employment.

THE CHOICE BETWEEN SPENDING POLICY AND TAX POLICY

In principle, fiscal policy can nudge the economy in the desired direction equally well by changing government spending (G) or by changing taxes. What, then, are some of the practical considerations that favor one type of policy over the other?

It used to be thought that changes in tax legislation inevitably languished in Congress for such a long time that their usefulness for short-run stabilization policy was dubious. This "fact" was used to argue that the government should rely on increases in G to stimulate demand and decreases in G to restrict demand. However, the legislative record in the case of the Tax Reduction Act of 1975 largely dispelled these doubts. President Gerald Ford recommended a tax cut in January; the Congress, though it changed the president's recommendation substantially, still managed to pass the bill in March. Thus the entire legislative process was compressed into less than three months. (By contrast, 18 months elapsed between President Johnson's request

for a tax increase in 1967 and its eventual enactment in 1968.) Clearly, Congress *can* act quickly. Whether or not it actually *will* do so is a question not so easily answered, since it invariably depends more on politics than on economics.

The argument that G is the more flexible instrument is also muddied by the fact that, for both technical and political reasons, it may be hard to start or stop government spending projects on short notice. Public works, for example, may need a long lead time for preparation; and then stopping them when aggregate demand revives may be both wasteful and politically unpopular. Imagine, if you will, trying to explain to people in a community that construction of their local school had to be halted because something as abstract as "aggregate demand" was too high!

Finally, and perhaps most important, each citizen and legislator should ask: How large a public sector should America have?

One point of view, expressed most eloquently in the writings of John Kenneth Galbraith, is that there is something amiss when a country as well endowed with private wealth as the United States has such an impoverished public sector. In Galbraith's view, America's most pressing needs are not for more stereo tape decks, sports cars, and CB radios, but rather for better schools, more efficient public transportation systems, and cleaner and safer city streets. Those who agree with him believe that we should *increase G* when the economy needs stimulus, and pay for these improved public services by *increasing taxes* when the economy needs to be reined in.

An opposing opinion, whose best-known advocate is Milton Friedman, is that the government sector is already too large; that we are foolish to rely on government to do things that private individuals and businesses could do better on their own; and that the growth of government interferes too much in our everyday lives, and in so doing, circumscribes our freedom. Those who hold this view argue for *tax cuts* when macroeconomic considerations call for expansionary fiscal policy, and for *reductions in public spending* when restrictive policy is required.[5]

☑ This is such an important point, and one on which so many people are confused, that it is one of the 12 fundamental principles that we hope you will remember well Beyond the Final Exam. Too often the active use of fiscal policy for economic stabilization is erroneously associated with a large and growing public sector— that is, with "big government." This need not be the case. Individuals favoring a smaller public sector can advocate an active fiscal policy just as well as those who favor a larger public sector. The dissension between the two groups should arise over the particular *tactics* to employ, not over the basic stabilization *strategy*. Advocates of big government budgets should seek to expand demand (when appropriate) through higher government spending and contract demand (when appropriate) through tax rises. By contrast, advocates of small public budgets should seek to expand demand by cutting taxes and reduce demand by cutting expenditures. ☑

SHOULD THE BUDGET BE BALANCED?

There is a belief that runs deep in the American character that there is something inherently wrong with government budget deficits. Using the analogy of an individual who spends more than he earns, the doomsayers argue that calamitous consequences will result if government spending exceeds tax receipts. Should the government balance its budget?

The principles of fiscal policy that we have just been expounding certainly do not lead to

[5]We will take a much more detailed look at the economics of John Kenneth Galbraith and Milton Friedman in Chapter 41.

this conclusion. Instead, they point to the desirability of budget *deficits* when private demand $(C + I)$ is too weak and budget *surpluses* when private demand is too strong. The budget should be balanced, according to these principles, only when $C + I + G$ under a balanced-budget policy approximately equals full-employment levels of output. This may sometimes occur, but it will not necessarily be the norm.

There are a number of fallacies, and a germ of truth, in the argument against deficit spending; and we will consider the subject more fully in Chapter 16. However, the central point is already clear from our present discussion of stabilization policy.

Consider the fiscal policy that would be followed by an administration that believed in balanced budgets and had the votes in Congress to turn its beliefs into reality. If private spending sagged for some reason, the multiplier would pull down national income. Since personal and corporate income taxes—the two most important sources of federal government revenues—are sensitive to national income, the budget would inevitably swing into the red. To a true budget-balancer, this would be a signal either to reduce spending or raise taxes— exactly the opposite of the appropriate policy response.

Thus budget balancing—as was practiced, say, by President Hoover during the Great Depression—will prolong and deepen recessions.

Economists and politicians of both political parties today realize the truth of this judgment. Therefore, actions are rarely taken to eliminate budget deficits during periods of substantial unemployment. President Carter, for example, has stated time and again that he wishes to balance the budget; yet his important fiscal policy decisions have more often than not led to greater rather than smaller deficits.

Budget balancing can also lead to inappropriate fiscal policy when an economic boom begins. If rising tax receipts induce a budget-balancing government to spend more or cut taxes, fiscal policy will "boom the boom"—with disastrous inflationary consequences. Fortunately, believers in budget balancing usually are not alarmed by surpluses.

THE INFLATIONARY EFFECTS OF BUDGET DEFICITS

One indictment of the use of fiscal policy to fight recessions that certainly *does* have validity under most circumstances is the charge that it may lead to inflation. Why? Because when government policy pushes aggregate demand up, firms may find themselves unwilling or unable to produce the higher quantities that are being demanded at the going prices. Prices will therefore have to rise, and this will induce two types of responses. First, firms will find it profitable to supply a greater quantity of output; and second, consumers will demand a smaller quantity because of their reduced purchasing power.

Figure 10–8 is an aggregate supply and demand diagram that shows this analysis graphically. Initially, equilibrium is at point E_0—where demand curve D_0D_0 and supply curve SS intersect. Output is $2000 billion, and the price index is at 100. The diagram indicates that the economy is operating below full employment; there is a recessionary gap. If the government does nothing to reduce the resulting unemployment, we know from Chapter 8 that this recessionary gap will linger for a long time. The economy will suffer through a prolonged period of unemployment.

Rather than permit such a long recession, we have shown in this chapter how the government can raise its spending or cut its taxes enough to shift the aggregate demand schedule upward from D_0D_0 to D_1D_1. Such a policy can wipe out the recessionary gap and the associated unemployment—but not without an inflationary cost. The diagram shows that the new

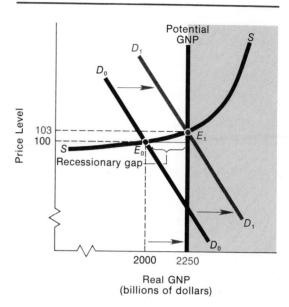

FIGURE 10–8

THE INFLATIONARY EFFECTS OF EXPANSIONARY FISCAL POLICY

This diagram uses the aggregate supply and demand analysis, rather than the 45° line diagram, to show how fiscal policy can be used to eliminate a recessionary gap. The advantage of this is that we also can see the additional inflation that such a policy is likely to cause. In the diagram, expansionary fiscal policy pushes the aggregate demand curve out from D_0D_0 to D_1D_1, causing equilibrium to move from E_0 (where there is unemployment) to E_1 (where there is full employment). But because aggregate supply curve SS slopes upward, the price level is pushed up from 100 to 103. That is, there is a 3 percent inflation.

equilibrium price level is at 103—3 percent higher than before the government acted. This, then, is the trade-off that policymakers face:

Expansionary fiscal policy can shorten recessions and make them less severe. The cost, however, is that for a period of time the price level normally will rise faster than it otherwise would. That is, because of the expansionary policy, there will be more inflation.

SOME HARSH REALITIES

The mechanics outlined in this chapter may make the fiscal policy planner's job look rather simple. These elementary diagrams suggest, rather misleadingly, that the authorities can drive GNP to any level they please simply by manipulating their spending and tax programs. It seems as though they should be able to hit the full-employment bull's eye every time. But, in fact, a better analogy is that they are shooting through a dense fog at an erratically moving target with a gun of uncertain accuracy. The target is moving because, in the real world, the investment schedule (and, to a lesser extent, the consumption schedule) is constantly shifting about due to changes in expectations, new technological breakthroughs, changes in consumers' tastes, and the like. This means that the policies decided upon today, which are to take effect at some future date, may no longer be appropriate by the time that future date rolls around. Policy must be based, to some extent, on *forecasting,* and no one has yet discovered a foolproof method of economic forecasting.[6] Since our forecasting ability is so modest, and because fiscal policy decisions may sometimes take a long time to be implemented, the government may occasionally find itself fighting the last recession just when the new inflation gets under way.

A second misleading aspect of these diagrams is that the multipliers are not known with as much precision as our numerical examples may suggest. Thus while the "best guess" might be that a $10 billion cut in government purchases will reduce GNP by $25 billion, the actual outcome might be as little as $16 billion or as much as $32 billion. It is therefore impos-

sible to "fine tune" every wrinkle out of the economy's growth path through fiscal policy; economic analysis is simply not that precise. The point is even more cogent with respect to tax policy, for here we get involved in trying to guess whether consumers will view tax changes as permanent or temporary.

A third complication is that our target—full-employment GNP—may be only dimly visible, as if through a fog. Especially when the economy's last experience with full employment is very far in the past, economists may have difficulty estimating the GNP level that represents full employment. In fact, as was mentioned in Chapter 6, there is today a great deal of controversy over how much unemployment constitutes "full employment."

Finally, in trying to decide whether to push the economy out of a position of unemployment—as was illustrated by Figures 10–7 and 10–8—legislators would like to know what the inflationary costs will be. This crucial *trade-off between unemployment and inflation* is an area of great controversy nowadays. Indeed, it is so important that we will devote an entire chapter to it later (Chapter 15). For the moment, suffice it to say that our knowledge of the trade-off is less than perfect.

As you read this book, government economists in Washington are losing sleep over just these issues. Where will the economy be six months or a year from now? What kinds of policies will be appropriate then? If one of the fiscal policy levers is pushed today, what will be the short- and long-run effects on the economy? How close or far are we from a normal "full employment" level of gross national product? If we stimulate demand to raise GNP, how much inflation will we have to endure? Unfortunately for the policymakers, precise answers to these questions cannot be found in this or any other textbook on economics.

[6]Some problems and techniques of economic forecasting are considered in Chapter 14.

SUMMARY

1. The government's fiscal policy is its plan for managing aggregate demand through its spending and taxing programs. It is made jointly by the president and Congress.

2. Government purchases of goods and services (G) are a direct component of aggregate demand. Therefore, they have the same multiplier as do autonomous changes in consumption or investment.

3. When income taxes are introduced, there is a difference between GNP and disposable income. Since consumer spending (C) depends on disposable income, any change in taxes will shift the consumption schedule on a 45° line diagram.

4. Shifts in the consumption function caused by tax policy are subject to the same multiplier as autonomous shifts in the consumption schedule.

5. Government transfer payments are treated like negative taxes, not like government purchases of goods and services, because they influence aggregate demand only indirectly.

6. The net effect of the government on aggregate demand—and hence on equilibrium output and prices—depends on whether the expansionary effects of its spending are greater or smaller than the contractionary effects of its taxes.

7. Because it reduces the multiplier and thus makes the economy less sensitive to shifts in the C and I schedules, the income tax is called an automatic stabilizer. There are many other automatic stabilizers in the modern economy, including unemployment insurance and the corporate profits tax.

8. If the multiplier were known precisely, it would be possible to plan any of a variety of fiscal policies to eliminate either a recessionary or an inflationary gap. Recessionary gaps (inadequate demand) can be cured by raising G, cutting taxes, or increasing transfers. Inflationary gaps can be cured by cutting G, raising taxes, or reducing transfers.

9. Active stabilization policy can be carried out either by means that tend to expand the size of government (by raising either G or taxes when appropriate) or by means that hold back the size of government (by reducing either G or taxes when appropriate). This is one of the 12 Ideas for Beyond the Final Exam.

10. Rigid adherence to budget balancing would make the economy less stable by reducing aggregate demand (via tax rises and reductions in G) when private spending is low, and raising aggregate demand when private spending is high.

11. Expansionary fiscal policy can cure recessions, but it normally exacts a cost in terms of higher inflation. This makes it all the more difficult to decide whether or not to stimulate the economy and by how much.

CONCEPTS FOR REVIEW

Fiscal policy
Concurrent resolutions
Government purchases of goods and services
Transfer payments
Trade-off between unemployment and inflation

Effect of income taxes on the multiplier
Automatic stabilizer
Budget balancing
Inflationary effects of budget deficits

QUESTIONS FOR DISCUSSION

1. Where in its annual budget cycle is the federal government right now? (Bring yourself up to date by reading the financial page of your local newspaper.)

2. Consider an economy in which tax collections are always $200 and in which the three components of aggregate demand are as follows:

GNP	TAXES	DI	C	I	G
$480	$200	$280	$210	$100	$200
540	200	340	255	100	200
600	200	400	300	100	200
660	200	460	345	100	200
720	200	520	390	100	200

Find the equilibrium of this economy graphically. What is the marginal propensity to consume? What is the multiplier? What would happen to equilibrium GNP if government purchases were raised by $15 and the price level were unchanged?

3. Now consider a related economy in which investment is also $100, government purchases are also $200, and the price level is also fixed. But taxes now vary with income, and as a result the consumption schedule looks like the following:

GNP	TAXES	DI	C
$480	$160	$320	$240
540	180	360	270
600	200	400	300
660	220	440	330
720	240	480	360

Find the equilibrium graphically. What is the marginal propensity to consume? What is the tax rate? Use your diagram to show the effect of an increase of $15 in government purchases. What is the multiplier? Compare this answer with your answer to Question 2 above. What do you conclude?

4. Explain why G has the same multiplier as autonomous shifts in C or I, while taxes have a different multiplier.

5. Return to the hypothetical economy given in Question 2 and suppose that *both* taxes and government purchases are increased by $60. Find the new equilibrium under the assumption that consumer spending continues to be exactly three-quarters of disposable income (as it is in Question 2).

6. If the government today decides that aggregate demand is excessive and is causing inflation, what options are open to it? What if it decides that aggregate demand is too weak instead?

7. Discuss the difference between a government purchase of a good or service and a government transfer payment.

8. What is an "automatic stabilizer"? List as many as you can of the automatic stabilizers that we now have but did not have in 1929. (Your instructor may be able to help you add to your list.)

9. Suppose that you are in charge of the fiscal policy of the economy given in Question 2. There is an inflationary gap with income at $600, and you want to reduce income to $540. What specific actions can you take to achieve this goal?

10. Now put yourself in charge of the economy in Question 3, and suppose that full employment comes at a GNP of $720. How can you push income up to that level?

11

Banking
and the Creation of Money

Throughout the last several chapters we have constructed a model of the determination of national income and the price level, and used this model to show how fiscal policy can manage the level of aggregate demand. There is, however, another way to manage demand that is equally important and useful: *monetary policy*. Up to now, we have not been able to discuss monetary policy because we have not yet brought money and the financial system into our model. The next three chapters are devoted to this task.

The present chapter has three major objectives. It first seeks to explain the nature of money: what it is, what purposes it serves, and how it is measured. Once this is done, we turn our attention to the banking system, explaining its historical origins, the nature of banking as a business, and why this industry is so heavily regulated. Finally, in the last parts of the chapter, we learn how banks create money—a subject that is of great importance because it is simply impossible to understand monetary policy without knowing how money is created.

At the end of the chapter, we will see why government authorities *must* control the supply of money in a modern economy, and this leads naturally into the discussion in Chapter 12 of *central banking,* that is, the techniques by which monetary policy is implemented. Then, in Chapter 13 we integrate what we will by then have learned about money and monetary policy into our model of income determination, and culminate our study of macroeconomic theory that began with Chapter 8.

POLICY ISSUE: WHY REGULATE THE BANKS?

Banking is one of the most strictly regulated industries in America. Yet banking is not heavily monopolized. While there are financial giants such as Bank of America (California) and Citibank (New York), the industry is populated by literally thousands of small banks distributed in cities and towns throughout the country. There are more than 14,000 banks nationwide. So why the extensive structure of government regulations?

A first reason is that the major "output" of the banking industry—the nation's supply of money—is of vital importance to the health of the economy. Bank managers presumably do what is best for their stockholders. That, at any rate, is their job. But as we shall see, what is best for bank stockholders may not be best for the whole economy. For this reason, the government does not allow bankers to determine the level of the nation's money supply by profit considerations alone.

A second reason for the extensive regulation of banks is concern for the safety of depositors. In a free-enterprise system, new businesses are born and die every day; and no one save those people immediately involved takes much notice of these goings-on. When a firm goes bankrupt, stockholders lose money and employees may lose their jobs. (The latter

may not even happen if new management takes over the assets of the bankrupt firm.) But, except for the case of very large firms, that is about it.

But banking is different. If banks were treated like other firms, depositors would lose money whenever one went bankrupt. That is bad enough by itself, but the real danger comes in the case of runs on a bank. When depositors get jittery about the security of their money, they may all rush in at once to cash in their accounts. For reasons we will learn in this chapter, most banks could not survive a "run" like this and would be forced into insolvency. Worse yet, this disease is highly contagious. If Jones hears that her neighbor has just lost his life savings because the Main Street National Bank went broke, she is quite likely to rush to her own bank to make a hefty withdrawal.

Without modern forms of bank regulation, therefore, one bank failure might lead to another; and indeed, bank failures were quite common throughout most of America's history (see Figure 11–1). But the failure of a major bank nowadays is an event rare enough to be newsworthy. The reason is that government has taken steps to ensure that such an infectious disease, if it occurs, will not spread. It has done this in several ways that will be mentioned later in this chapter.

BARTER VERSUS MONETARY EXCHANGE

Money is so much a part of our day-to-day existence that we are likely to take it for granted, failing to appreciate all that it accomplishes. But it is important to realize that money is very much a social contrivance. Like the wheel, it had to be invented. The most obvious way to trade commodities is not by using money, but by barter—a system in which people exchange one good directly for another. And the best way to appreciate what monetary exchange accom-

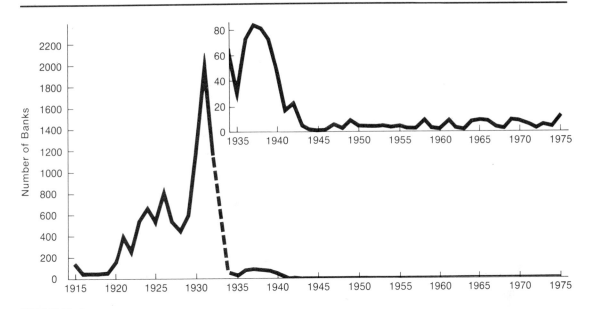

FIGURE 11–1

BANK FAILURES IN THE UNITED STATES, 1915–1975

This chart shows the number of banks that failed each year from 1915 until 1975. Notice the sharp drop in the number of failures from 1932 (nearly 1200) to 1934 (about 60). Failures clearly are much less common in the postwar period than they were in earlier years.

Source: Federal Deposit Insurance Corporation.

plishes is to imagine a world without it.

Under a system of direct barter, if Farmer Jones grows corn and has a craving for peanuts, he has to find a peanut farmer with a taste for corn. If he finds such a person (this was called the double coincidence of wants by the classical economists), they make the trade. If this sounds easy, try to imagine how busy Farmer Jones would be if he had to repeat the sequence for every commodity he consumed in a week. For the most part, the desired double coincidences of wants are more likely to turn out to be double wants of coincidence. Jones gets no peanuts and the peanut farmer gets no corn. Worse yet, with so much time spent in looking for trading partners, Jones would have far less time to grow corn.

Money greases the wheels of exchange, and thus makes the whole economy more productive.

Under a monetary system, the corn farmer gives up his corn for money. He does so, not because he wants the money per se, but because of what that money can buy. Money makes Farmer Jones's shopping tasks much easier, for he only need locate a peanut farmer who wants money. And what peanut farmer does not?

For these reasons, monetary exchange replaced barter at a very early stage of human civilization, and only extreme circumstances, like destructive wars and runaway inflations, have been able to bring barter (temporarily) back.

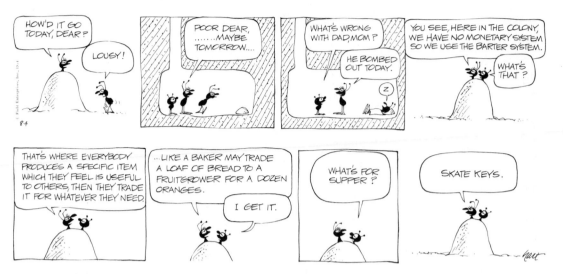

A CARTOONIST LOOKS AT BARTER

Cartoonist Johnny Hart illustrates that exchange may not be very efficient under a barter system.

THE CONCEPTUAL DEFINITION OF MONEY

Viewing monetary exchange as the alternative to direct barter makes the following a natural definition of money.

DEFINITION

Money is the standard object used in exchanging goods and services. In short, money is the *medium of exchange.* In a system of monetary exchange, people trade money for goods when they purchase something and trade goods for money when they sell something, but they do not trade goods directly for other goods.

This definition describes money's principal role. But once it has come into use as the medium of exchange, whatever object is serving as money is bound to take on other functions as well.

For one, it will inevitably become the *unit of account,* that is, the standard unit for quoting prices. How foolish it would be, after all, for

inhabitants of an idyllic tropical island to use coconuts as money but quote prices in terms of sea shells!

For another, it may also become used as a store of value. If Farmer Jones temporarily produces and sells corn of more value than he wants to consume right away, he may find it convenient to store the difference in the form of money until he wants to use it. This is because he knows that money can be "sold" easily for goods and services at a later date, whereas land, gold, and other stores of value might not be. Of course, if money pays no interest and inflation is substantial, he may decide to forgo the convenience of money and store his wealth in some other form, rather than see its purchasing power rapidly eroded. So this role of money is far from inevitable.

Since money may not always serve as a store of value, and since there are many stores of value other than money, it is best not to include the store-of-value function as part of our conceptual definition of money. Instead, we simply label as "money" whatever serves as the medium of exchange.

WHAT SERVES AS MONEY?

Anthropologists and historians will testify that a bewildering variety of things have served as money in different times and places. Cattle, stones, wampum, cigarettes, woodpecker scalps, porpoise teeth, and candy bars are only a few of the more colorful examples.

In primitive or less organized societies, the commodities that served as money generally had value in themselves. If not used as money, cattle could be slaughtered for food, cigarettes could be smoked, and so on. But such commodity moneys generally run into several severe difficulties. To be useful as a medium of exchange, the commodity must be divisible. This makes cattle a very poor choice. It must also be of uniform, or at least readily identifiable, quality so that inferior substitutes are easy to recognize. This may be why woodpecker scalps never achieved great popularity. The medium of exchange must also be storable and durable, which presents a serious problem for candy-bar money. Finally, because commodity moneys need to be carried and stored, it is helpful if the item is compact, that is, has high value per unit of volume and weight.

All of these traits make it natural that gold and silver have circulated as money in so many times and places. Since they have high value in nonmonetary uses, a lot of purchasing power can be carried without too much weight. Pieces of gold are also storable, divisible (with a little trouble), and of identifiable quality (with a little more trouble).

The same characteristics suggest that paper would make an ideal money. Since we can print any number on it that we want, we can make paper money as divisible as we please and also make it possible to carry a large value in a lightweight and compact form. Paper is easy to store and, with a little cleverness, we can make conterfeiting very hard (though never impossible). Paper cannot, however, serve as a commodity money because its value per square inch in alternative uses is so small. A paper currency that is repudiated by its issuer can, perhaps, be used as wallpaper or to wrap fish, but these uses will surely represent only a small fraction of the paper's value as money. Contrary to the popular expression, such a currency literally *is* worth the paper it is printed on, which is to say that it is not worth very much.[1] Thus paper money is always fiat money.

DEFINITION
Fiat money is money that is decreed as such by the government. It is of little value as a commodity, but it maintains its value as a medium of exchange because people have faith that the issuer will stand behind the pieces of printed paper and limit their production.

Money in the contemporary United States is almost entirely fiat money. Look at a dollar bill. It states, next to George Washington's picture, that "this note is legal tender for all debts, public and private." Nowhere on the certificate is there a promise, stated or implied, that the U.S. government will exchange it for anything else. A dollar bill is convertible into 4 quarters, 10

COMMODITY MONEY
Years ago "money" consisted of commodities that were useful wholly apart from their use as a medium of exchange.

[1]The first paper money issued by the federal government, the Continental dollar, was essentially repudiated. (Actually, the new government of the United States redeemed the Continentals for 1 cent on the dollar in the 1790s.) This gave rise to the derisive expression, "It's not worth a Continental."

dimes, 20 nickels, or any other similar combination, but not into gold, chocolate, or any other commodity.

Why do people hold these pieces of paper? Only because they know that others are willing to accept them for things of intrinsic value—food, rent, shoes, and so on. If this confidence ever evaporated, these dollar bills would cease serving as a medium of exchange and, given that they make ugly wallpaper, would become virtually worthless.

But don't panic. This is not likely to occur. Our current monetary system has evolved over hundreds of years during which commodity money was first replaced by "full-bodied" paper money—paper certificates that were backed by gold or silver of equal value held in the issuer's vaults. Then the full-bodied paper money was replaced by certificates that were only partially backed by gold and silver. Finally, we arrived at our present system, in which paper money has no "backing" whatsoever. Like a hesitant swimmer who first dips her toes, then her legs, then her whole body into a cold swimming pool, we have "tested the water" at each step of the way—and found it to our liking. It is unlikely that we will ever take a step back in the other direction.[2]

HOW THE QUANTITY OF MONEY IS MEASURED

As we will learn in coming chapters, the amount of money circulating in the economy is of profound importance for the determination of national income and the price level. Thus it becomes important for the government to know how much money there is at any given time.

Our conceptual definition of money describes it as the medium of exchange. But this raises questions about just what items should

be included and what items excluded when we count up the money supply. Some items are easy. All of our coins, the small change of our economic system, clearly should count as money. So should paper money, which accounts for a far greater volume of transactions. But the lion's share of our nation's monetary payments are made neither in metal nor in paper, but by check.

Checking deposits, which account for roughly three-quarters of America's money supply, are merely bookkeeping entries in bank ledgers. Many people think of checks simply as a convenient way to give coins or dollar bills to someone else. But, in fact, checks are something quite different, which is why the country can have more money in the form of checking deposits than it has in the form of currency. For example, if you pay the grocer $50 by check, no dollar bills or coins normally will change hands. Instead, that check will travel back to your bank, where $50 will be deducted from the bookkeeping entry that records your account and added to the bookkeeping entry for your grocer's account. (If you and the grocer hold accounts at different banks, more books get involved; but still no coins or bills are likely to be moved.) Since so many transactions are made by check, it seems imperative that checking deposits be included in any specific definition of the money supply.

At this point, many economists draw the line on the grounds that these three things—coins, paper, and checking accounts—and no others, should be considered as the medium of exchange.

DEFINITION
The narrowly defined money supply, usually abbreviated M_1, is the sum of all coins and paper money in circulation, plus all checking account balances held at commercial banks.[3]

---

[2]Indeed, the international monetary system is now in the midst of a similar process of "demonetizing" gold, as we shall see in Chapter 37.

[3]Commercial banks are banks that issue checking accounts.

The top portion of Figure 11–2 shows this narrowly defined money supply and its composition in September 1978.

But other economists object to having the line drawn so soon. What is the real difference, they ask, between funds held in a checking account and funds held in a savings account? Probably not much, especially if both accounts are held at the same bank. These economists prefer a broader definition of money, which includes some categories of savings accounts.

DEFINITION
The broadly defined money supply, usually abbreviated M_2, is the sum of all coins and paper money in circulation plus all checking deposits and most savings deposits held at commercial banks.

M_2 is shown in the bottom portion of Figure 11–2. It can be seen that savings deposits are substantially bigger than checking deposits.

Other economists prefer still broader definitions of the money supply (called M_3, M_4, and so on), which include more and more varieties of savings deposits. They do not do this because they view savings accounts as a medium of exchange. It is clear that savings balances are rarely used to make payments directly;[4] instead, we generally convert our savings balances into checking balances or cash when we want to purchase something. However, it sometimes takes as little as a telephone call to transfer funds from a savings account to a checking account. Besides, these economists reason, our real concern with the money supply derives from its influence on aggregate demand. And it may be that M_2, or even a broader measure, is more relevant to aggregate demand

---

[4]Recently there have been exceptions to this in some states. Savings banks are now allowed to offer consumers the privilege of writing checks on their savings account balances. At present, the amount of money involved is small. But if this practice grows, the official definitions of the money supply may have to be revised.

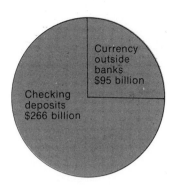

$M_1 = \$361$ billion

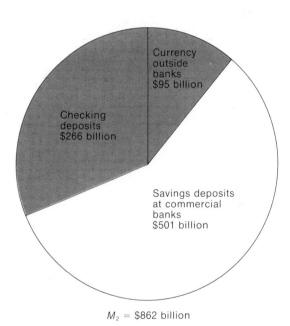

$M_2 = \$862$ billion

FIGURE 11–2
TWO DEFINITIONS OF THE MONEY SUPPLY
(September 1978)
Source: Federal Reserve Bank of St. Louis.

than is M_1, because consumers will spend more when they have more funds in their savings accounts.

The trouble with this approach is that there is no obvious line of demarcation between those assets that are "money" and those that are not. If we define an asset's liquidity as the ease with which it can be converted into cash, there is a range of assets of varying degrees of liquidity. M_1 is completely "liquid," passbook savings accounts a bit less so, and so on, until we encounter such things as short-term government bonds, which, while still quite liquid, would be unlikely to be included in the money supply by anyone's definition. Any number of different "M's" can be defined—and have been—by drawing the line in different places.

In this book, we adhere to the convention that only M_1 is "money," because it is the medium of exchange. But we hasten to point out that this is an arbitrary definition and that some other liquid assets may be as important as money in the determination of aggregate demand. Fortunately, no very important matters of principle hinge on the particular definition of money that is chosen.

HOW BANKING BEGAN

When Adam and Eve left the Garden of Eden, they did not encounter a branch of the Bank of America. Banking had to be invented, and it took some time before banking came to be practiced as it is today. With a little imagination, we can see how the first banks must have begun.

When money was a full-bodied commodity money, such as gold, it was most inconvenient for consumers and merchants to carry it around and to have to weigh and assay it for purity every time a transaction was made. So it is not surprising that the practice developed of leaving one's gold in the care of a goldsmith, who had rather safe storage facilities, and carrying in

its place a receipt from the goldsmith stating that John Doe did indeed own 5 ounces of gold of a certain purity. The goldsmiths, of course, charged a fee for this service. When people began trading goods and services for the goldsmiths' receipts, rather than for the gold itself, the receipt became an early form of paper fiat money.

At this stage, the paper money was fully backed by gold. But gradually the goldsmiths began to notice that the amount of gold they were actually required to pay out in a day was but a small fraction of the total gold they had stored in their warehouses. Then one day some enterprising goldsmith hit upon a momentous idea that must have made him rich.

His thinking probably ran something like this. "I have 2000 ounces of gold stored away in my vault, for which I collect storage fees from my customers. If I get much more, I'll need an expensive new vault. But in the last year, there has not been a single day on which I was called upon to pay out more than 100 ounces. What harm could it do if I lent out, say, half the gold I now have? I'll still have more than enough to pay off any depositors that come in for a withdrawal, so no one will ever know the difference. And I could earn 30 additional ounces of gold each year in interest on the loans I make (at 3 percent interest on 1000 ounces). With this profit, I could lower my service charges to depositors and so attract still more deposits. I think I'll do it."

With this resolution, the modern system of fractional reserve banking was born.

DEFINITION
Fractional reserve banking is a system under which bankers keep in their vaults as reserves only a fraction of the funds they hold on deposit.

This system has three important features— features that are centrally important to this chapter.

1. Bank profitability. By getting deposits at zero interest and lending some of them out at positive interest rates, goldsmiths made a profit. The history of banking as a profit-making industry was begun and has continued to this date. *Banks, like other businesses, are in business to earn profits.*

2. Bank discretion over the money supply. When goldsmiths decided that they could get along by keeping only a fraction of their total deposits on reserve in their vaults, and lending out the balance, they acquired the ability to *create money*. As long as they kept 100 percent reserves, each ounce of gold was represented by one gold certificate that circulated as money. So whether people decided to carry their gold or leave it with their goldsmith did not affect the money supply, which was set by the volume of gold.

With the advent of fractional reserve banking, however, new paper certificates were added whenever goldsmiths lent out some of the gold they held on deposit. The loans, in effect, created new money. In this way, the total amount of money came to depend on the amount of gold that each goldsmith felt compelled to maintain as reserves in his vault. The lower these reserves, the more paper certificates, and therefore the more money there would be. While we no longer use gold to back our money, this principle remains true today. *Bankers' business decisions influence the supply of money.*

3. Exposure to runs. A goldsmith who kept 100 percent reserves never had to worry about a run on his vault. Even if all his depositors showed up at the door at once, he always had enough gold to return their deposits. But as soon as the first goldsmith decided to get by with only fractional reserves, the possibility of a run on the vault became a real concern. If that first goldsmith who lent out half his gold had found 51 percent of his customers at his door one unlucky day, he would have had a lot of

explaining to do. Similar problems have worried bankers for centuries. *The danger of a run on the bank has induced bankers to keep prudent reserves and to lend out money carefully.*

PRINCIPLES OF BANK MANAGEMENT: PROFITS VERSUS SAFETY

Bankers have a reputation, probably deserved, for conservatism both in politics and in business affairs. From what has been said so far, the economic rationale for this conservatism should be clear. Checking deposits are pure fiat money. Years ago, these deposits were ''backed'' by nothing more than the bank's promise to convert them into currency on demand. If people lost trust in a bank, the bank was doomed. Thus, it has always been imperative for bankers to acquire a reputation for prudence. They did this (and continue to do it) in two principal ways. First, they had to maintain a sufficiently generous level of reserves to minimize their vulnerability to runs. Second, they had to be somewhat cautious in making loans and investments, since any large losses on their loans could undermine the confidence of depositors.

It is important to realize that banking under a system of fractional reserves is an inherently risky business that is rendered relatively safe only by cautious and prudent management. America's history of bank failures bears sober testimony to the fact that many bankers were neither cautious nor prudent. Why? Because this is not a recipe for high profits. Bank profits are maximized by keeping reserves as low as possible, by making at least some risky investments, and by giving loans to borrowers of questionable credit standing (because these borrowers will pay the highest interest rates). The art of bank management is to strike the appropriate balance between the lure of profits and the need for safety. When a banker errs by being too stodgy, his bank will earn inadequate profits. When he errs by taking unwarranted risks, his bank may not survive at all.

BANK REGULATION

The public authorities, however, apparently have decided that the balance struck by profit-minded bankers often would not be at the place where society would like it struck. So government has thrown up a web of regulations designed to insure the safety of depositors and to control the supply of money.

The principal innovation guaranteeing the safety of bank deposits is deposit insurance. Today most bank depositors are insured against losses by the Federal Deposit Insurance Corporation (FDIC)—an agency of the United States government established in 1933. If your bank belongs to the FDIC (and most do), your checking account is insured for up to $40,000 regardless of what happens to the bank. Thus, while bank failures may spell disaster for the bank's stockholders, they do not give many depositors cause for concern. In fact, when the Franklin National Bank of New York, the nation's 20th largest, failed in 1974, not a single cent was lost by any depositor. Deposit insurance eliminates the motive for customers to rush to their bank just because they hear some bad news about the bank's finances. Many observers give this innovation much of the credit for the pronounced decline in bank failures since 1933 (refer to Figure 11–1 on page 199).

In addition to insuring depositors against loss, the government takes steps to see that banks do not get into financial trouble. For one thing, various regulatory authorities conduct periodic *bank examinations and audits* in order to keep tabs on the financial condition and business practices of the banks under their purview. For another, laws and regulations *limit the kinds and quantities of assets in which banks may*

invest. For example, most banks are prohibited from purchasing common stock. Both these forms of regulation are clearly aimed at maintaining bank safety.

A final type of regulation also has some bearing on safety but is motivated primarily by the government's desire to control the money supply. We have seen that the amount of money any bank will issue depends on the amount of reserves it elects to keep. For this reason, most banks are subject by law to minimum required reserves. While banks may (and sometimes do) keep reserves in excess of these legal minimums, they may not keep less. It is this regulation that places an upper limit on the money supply. The rest of this chapter is concerned with the details of this mechanism.

HOW BANKERS KEEP BOOKS

Before we can fully understand the mechanics of modern banking and the process by which money is ''created,'' we must acquire at least a nodding acquaintance with the way in which bankers keep their books.

DEFINITION
An *asset* of a bank is something that the bank *owns*. This ''thing'' may be a physical object, such as the bank building, a typewriter, or a vault, or it may be just a piece of paper, such as an IOU of a customer to whom the bank has made loans.

A *liability* of a bank is something that the bank *owes*. Most bank liabilities are in the form of bookkeeping entries. For example, if you have a checking account in the Main Street Bank, your bank balance there is a liability of the bank. (It is, of course, an asset to you.)

There is an easy test to see whether some piece of paper or bookkeeping entry is an asset or a liability. Ask yourself: If this paper were converted into cash, would the bank receive the cash (an asset) or have to pay it out (a liability)? This test makes it clear that loans to customers are bank assets, while customers' deposits are bank liabilities.

When accountants draw up a complete list of all the bank's assets and liabilities, the resulting document is called the bank's balance sheet. Typically, the value of all the bank's assets exceeds the value of all its liabilities. (On the rare occasions when this is not the case, the bank is in serious trouble.) In what sense, then, do balance sheets "balance"?

They balance because accountants have invented the concept of *net worth* to balance the books. Specifically, they have defined the net worth of a bank to be the difference between the value of all its assets and the value of all its liabilities. Thus, by definition, when accountants add net worth to liabilities, the sum they get must be the same as the value of the bank's assets. In short:

$$\text{Assets} = \text{Liabilities} + \text{Net Worth}$$

Table 11–1 illustrates this with the balance sheet of a fictitious bank, Bank-a-mythica, whose finances are extremely simple. On December 31, 1978, it had only two kinds of assets (listed on the left-hand side of the balance sheet)—$1 million in cash, which it held as reserves in its vault, and $4,500,000 in outstanding loans to its customers, that is, in customers' IOUs. And it had only one type of liability (listed on the right-hand side)—$5 million in checking deposits. The difference between total assets ($5.5 million) and total liabilities ($5 million) was the bank's net worth ($500,000) and is shown on the right-hand side of the balance sheet.

THE LIMITS TO MONEY CREATION BY A SINGLE BANK

Let us now turn to the process of deposit creation. Many bankers will deny that they have any ability to "create" money. (The very phrase has a suspiciously hocus-pocus sound to it.) But they are not quite right. For although any individual bank's ability to create money is severely limited in a system with many banks, the banking system as a whole can achieve much more than the sum of its parts. Through the modern alchemy of deposit creation, it can turn one dollar into many dollars. But to understand this important process, we had better proceed in steps, beginning with the case of a single bank, our hypothetical Bank-a-mythica.

According to the balance sheet in Table 11–1, Bank-a-mythica is holding cash reserves in its vault that are equal to 20 percent of its deposits. ($1 million in cash is equal to 20

TABLE 11–1

BALANCE SHEET OF BANK-A-MYTHICA
DECEMBER 31, 1978

ASSETS		LIABILITIES AND NET WORTH	
Cash in vault	$1,000,000	**Liabilities**	
Loans outstanding	4,500,000	Checking deposits	$5,000,000
Total assets	$5,500,000		
		Net Worth	
		Stockholders' equity	500,000
		Total liabilities and net worth	$5,500,000

percent of the $5 million in deposits.) Let us assume that this is the minimum reserve ratio prescribed by law and that the bank strives to keep its reserves down to the legal minimum.

Now let us suppose that a week goes by, and in this week Bank-a-mythica (a) receives $100,000 in new currency deposits, (b) sets aside the required $20,000 in additional reserves in its vault, and (c) lends out the remaining $80,000. Table 11–2 shows only the *changes* in the balance sheet during the week January 1–7, 1979. It is tables such as this— rather than the balance sheets themselves—that will help us to follow the money-creation process.

If we look at this table, keeping in mind our specific definition of money, it appears at first that the chairman of Bank-a-mythica is right when he claims not to have engaged in the nefarious practice of "money creation." All that happened was that in exchange for the $100,000 in cash it received, the bank issued its depositors checking accounts amounting to $100,000. This does not change M_1; it merely converts one form of money into another.

But wait. What happened to the $100,000 in cash? The table shows that $20,000 was retained by Bank-a-mythica in its vault. Since this currency is no longer held by the public, it no longer counts in the official money supply. (Notice that Figure 11–2 included only "currency outside banks.") But the other $80,000, which the bank lent out, is still in circulation and probably will be redeposited in some other bank. But even before the $80,000 is moved, the original $100,000 in cash has supported a rise in the money supply: There is now $100,000 in checking accounts and $80,000 in cash available for circulation, making a total of $180,000. The money-creation process has begun.

MULTIPLE MONEY CREATION BY A SERIES OF BANKS

Let us now trace this $80,000 in cash and see how the process of money creation gathers momentum. Suppose that Bank-a-mythica's $80,000 loan goes (in cash) to the Hard-Pressed Construction Company, which banks across town at the First National Bank. Hard-Pressed presumably deposits these funds into its bank account. If the management of First National Bank behaves like that of Bank-a-mythica, the arrival of $80,000 in new cash will induce it to lend out an additional $64,000 to Al's Auto Shop, keeping only the required $16,000 in reserves. Table 11–3 shows the effects of these events on First National Bank's balance sheet. At this stage in the chain, the original $100,000 in cash has led to $180,000 in deposits— $100,000 at Bank-a-mythica and $80,000 at First National Bank—and $64,000 in cash is still in circulation (in the hands of Al's Auto Shop). Thus a total of $244,000 in money supply ($180,000 in checking deposits plus $64,000 in cash) has been derived from the original $100,000.

But, to coin a phrase, the bucks do not stop here. Al's Auto Shop will presumably deposit

TABLE 11–2

CHANGES IN BANK-A-MYTHICA'S BALANCE SHEET

ASSETS		LIABILITIES	
Cash in vault	+ $20,000	Checking deposits	+ $100,000
Loans outstanding	+ 80,000		

When it receives $100,000 in cash deposits, Bank-a-mythica keeps the required $20,000 in reserves and lends out the remaining $80,000 to Hard-Pressed Construction Company.

TABLE 11–3

CHANGES IN FIRST NATIONAL BANK'S BALANCE SHEET

ASSETS		LIABILITIES	
Cash in vault	+$16,000	Checking deposits	+$80,000
Loans outstanding	+ 64,000		

Hard-Pressed deposits its $80,000 in First National Bank, which sets aside the required $16,000 in reserves and lends $64,000 to Al's Auto Shop.

the proceeds from its loan into its own account at Second National Bank, leading to the balance sheet adjustments shown in Table 11–4 when Second National makes an additional loan. You can see how the money-creation process continues.

Table 11–5 *adds up* the balance-sheet changes of the first five banks, beginning with Bank-a-mythica and proceeding through the Fourth National Bank, assuming that each bank holds exactly 20 percent reserves and that each loan recipient redeposits the proceeds in his own bank. At this stage, $336,160 in bank deposits have been created, and there is still $32,768 in cash circulating (the original $100,000 less $67,232 in cash in bank vaults), for a total money supply of $368,928. And the chain does not end there. For the Main Street Movie Theater, which received the $32,768 loan from the Fourth National Bank, then deposits these funds into the Fifth National, and so on.

What are the final effects on the money supply? If you look carefully at the three sections of Table 11–5, you will see that each column of numbers forms a *geometric progression*;

specifically, each entry is equal to exactly 80 percent of the entry that preceded it. Recall from the discussion of the multiplier in Chapter 9 that we learned how to sum an infinite geometric progression, which is just what each of these chains eventually will be. In particular, if the common ratio is R, the sum of an infinite geometric progression is

$$1 + R + R^2 + R^3 + \cdots = \frac{1}{1 - R}$$

By applying this formula to the chain of checking deposits on the right-hand side of Table 11–5, we get:

$$
\begin{aligned}
&\$100,000 + \$80,000 + \$64,000 \\
&\qquad\qquad\qquad + \$51,200 + \cdots \\
&= \$100,000 \times (1 + 0.8 + 0.64 + 0.512 + \cdots) \\
&= \$100,000 \times (1 + 0.8 + 0.8^2 + 0.8^3 + \cdots) \\
&= \$100,000 \times \frac{1}{1 - 0.8} = \frac{\$100,000}{0.2} = \$500,000
\end{aligned}
$$

So eventually the original $100,000 in cash will support $500,000 in new checking deposits—a

TABLE 11–4

CHANGES IN SECOND NATIONAL BANK'S BALANCE SHEET

ASSETS		LIABILITIES	
Cash in vault	+$12,800	Checking deposits	+$64,000
Loans outstanding	+ 51,200		

When Al deposits his $64,000 in Second National Bank, that bank retains $12,800 in cash and lends out the remaining $51,200.

TABLE 11–5

CHANGES IN THE COMBINED BALANCE SHEETS OF THE FIRST FIVE BANKS

ASSETS		LIABILITIES	
Cash in Vault		**Checking Deposits**	
Bank-a-mythica	+ $20,000	Bank-a-mythica	+ $100,000
First National Bank	+ 16,000	First National Bank	+ 80,000
Second National Bank	+ 12,800	Second National Bank	+ 64,000
Third National Bank	+ 10,240	Third National Bank	+ 51,200
Fourth National Bank	+ 8,192	Fourth National Bank	+ 40,960
Total	+ $67,232	Total	+ $336,160
Loans Outstanding			
Bank-a-mythica	+ $80,000		
First National Bank	+ 64,000		
Second National Bank	+ 51,200		
Third National Bank	+ 40,960		
Fourth National Bank	+ 32,768		
Total	+ $268,928		
Total change in assets	+ $336,160		

After five banks have participated, the chain of deposit creation looks like this.

multiple expansion of $5 for every one original dollar.[5]

Notice that 5 is the reciprocal of 20 percent (that is, $5 = 1/0.2$). The general formula for multiple deposit creation when the required reserve ratio may be some number other than 20 percent should not be surprising:

OVERSIMPLIFIED FORMULA FOR MULTIPLE DEPOSIT CREATION

If the minimum required reserve ratio is some fraction, m, an injection of $1 of reserves into the banking system can lead to the creation of $1/m$ in new deposits.

Table 11–6 shows the ultimate effect of the entire chain of deposit creation on the balance sheet of the banking system as a whole. The banks have converted $100,000 in cash into $500,000 in checking deposits—for a net increase in the money supply of $400,000.

While we have derived this result in a rather mechanical fashion, there is a simple piece of logic behind it. If banks want to hold only the legal minimum in cash reserves, then an injection of $1 in *actual* reserves into the banking system must induce them to expand their loans until the reserves *required* as a result of the expansion of deposits have risen by $1. Only then will all *excess* reserves have been eliminated.[6]

[5]EXERCISE: Use the formula for the sum of a geometric progression to show that the total addition to bank reserves will ultimately be $100,000 in this example, while the total amount of new loans outstanding will be $400,000.
ANSWER: The progression of bank reserves can be written:
$$\$20,000 \times (1 + 0.8 + 0.8^2 + 0.8^3 \ldots)$$
$$= \$20,000 \times (1/0.2)$$
$$= \$100,000$$
The progression of new loans can be written:
$$\$80,000 \times (1 + 0.8 + 0.8^2 + 0.8^3 \ldots)$$
$$= \$80,000 \times (1/0.2)$$
$$= \$400,000$$

[6]Excess reserves are simply any reserves held in *excess* of legal requirements.

TABLE 11–6

CHANGES IN COMBINED BALANCE SHEET OF THE ENTIRE BANKING SYSTEM

ASSETS		LIABILITIES	
Cash in vault	+$100,000	Checking deposits	+$500,000
Loans outstanding	+ 400,000		
		Addendum: Change in Money Supply	
		Demand deposits	+$500,000
		Currency outside banks	− 100,000
		Net change	+$400,000

By the end of the chain of deposit creation, the entire $100,000 of cash has found its way into bank vaults, where it can support $500,000 in deposits. The money supply has expanded by $400,000.

But if each dollar of deposits requires only a fraction m (1/5 in our example) of a dollar in reserves, then we must have:

$m \times$ The expansion in deposits
$= \$1$ Addition to reserves

or, dividing both sides of this equation by the fraction m,

Expansion in deposits
$= \$1/m \times$ Addition to reserves

That is, deposits must grow by $\$1/m$ ($5 in our example) to "use up" the $1 in reserves. This is the common sense behind the deposit-creation formula.

THE PROCESS IN REVERSE: MULTIPLE CONTRACTIONS OF THE MONEY SUPPLY

Let us now briefly consider how this deposit-creation mechanism operates in reverse—as a system of deposit destruction. In particular, suppose that some eccentric customer of Bank-a-mythica decides to withdraw $100,000 from his checking account and stash the money in his mattress. Bank-a-mythica's *required* reserves

fall by $20,000 as a result of this transaction (20 percent of $100,000), but its *actual* reserves fall by $100,000. The bank is $80,000 short, as indicated in Table 11–7(a).

How does it react to this discrepancy? As some of its outstanding loans are routinely paid off, the bank will cease granting new ones until it has accumulated the necessary $80,000 in required reserves. The data for Bank-a-mythica's contraction are shown in Table 11–7(b), assuming that borrowers pay off their loans in cash.[7] But where did the borrowers get this money? Probably by making a withdrawal from another bank. In this case the other bank, say, First National Bank, loses an $80,000 deposit and $80,000 in reserves. It finds itself short some $64,000 in reserves [see Table 11–8(a)] and therefore must reduce its loan commitments by $64,000 [see Table 11–8(b)]. This, of course, causes some other bank to suffer a loss of reserves and deposits of $64,000, and the whole process repeats just as it did in the case of deposit expansion. After five banks had become involved, the picture would be just as shown in Table 11–5, except that all the *plus* signs would be *minus* signs. And the final results are just the mirror image of Table

[7]In reality, they would probably pay with a check drawn on another bank. Bank-a-mythica would then cash these checks to acquire the reserves.

TABLE 11–7

CHANGES IN THE BALANCE SHEET OF BANK-A-MYTHICA

(a) ASSETS	(a) LIABILITIES	(b) ASSETS	(b) LIABILITIES
Cash in vault − $100,000	Checking deposits − $100,000	Cash in vault + $ 80,000 Loans outstanding − 80,000	
Addendum: **Bank reserves**			
Required reserves − 20,000 Excess reserves − 80,000			

When Bank-a-mythica loses a $100,000 deposit, it must reduce its loans by $80,000 to replenish its reserves.

11–6: Deposits shrink by $500,000, loans fall by $400,000, and bank reserves are reduced by $100,000.

During the height of the radical student movement of the late 1960s, a circular appeared in Cambridge, Massachusetts, urging citizens to withdraw all funds from their checking accounts on a prescribed date, hold them in cash for one week, and then redeposit them. This act, the circular argued, would surely wreak havoc upon the capitalist system. Obviously, some of these radicals were well-schooled in modern money

TABLE 11–8

CHANGES IN THE BALANCE SHEET OF FIRST NATIONAL BANK

(a) ASSETS	(a) LIABILITIES	(b) ASSETS	(b) LIABILITIES
Cash in vault − $80,000	Checking deposits − $80,000	Cash in vault + $64,000 Loans outstanding − 64,000	
Addendum: **Bank Reserves**			
Required reserves − 16,000 Excess reserves − 64,000			

First National Bank's loss of an $80,000 deposit forces it to cut back its loans by $64,000.

mechanics, for the argument was basically correct. The tremendous multiple contraction of the banking system and consequent multiple expansion that a successful campaign of this sort could have caused might have disrupted the local financial system quite seriously. But history records that the appeal met with little success. Checking-account withdrawals are not the stuff of which revolutions are made.

WHY THE MONEY CREATION FORMULA IS OVERSIMPLIFIED

Just as we did in the case of the expenditure multiplier, we must stress that the oversimplified formula for money creation is accurate only under very particular circumstances. These circumstances require that:

1. Every recipient of a bank loan must redeposit the proceeds of that loan into another bank.
2. Every bank must hold reserves no larger than the legal minimum.

Let us see what happens to the chain of deposit creation when either of these assumptions is violated.

Suppose first that the business firms and individuals who receive bank loans decide not to redeposit all of the proceeds into their bank accounts. For example, Hard-Pressed Construction Company and all the other borrowers might decide to hold half of their loan proceeds in cash and deposit only the remaining half. Then First National Bank would receive only a $40,000 deposit, and could, therefore, make only a $32,000 loan. Second National Bank would then receive only $16,000 (half of $32,000), and so on. The whole chain of deposit creation would be reduced drastically. Thus:

If individuals and business firms decide to hold more cash, the multiple expansion of the money supply will be curtailed because fewer dollars of cash will be available in bank vaults to be used as reserves to support new checking deposits. Consequently, the money supply will be smaller.

Normally, people's demands for cash fluctuate between narrow boundaries and are easily predictable. For instance, people always want more cash during the Christmas shopping season. But during the banking panics that occurred periodically in the days before universal deposit insurance, the public's propensity to hold cash would almost invariably rise dramatically. We now understand how this could cause a violent contraction of the money supply.

Next, suppose that Bank-a-mythica's management becomes very conservative, or that the outlook for loan repayments worsens because of a recession. The bank might then decide to keep more reserves than the legal requirement (say, $33\frac{1}{3}$ percent) and lend out less than the $80,000 assumed in Table 11–2 (say, $66,667). If this happens, then First National Bank will receive a smaller injection of cash reserves than that shown in Table 11–3. And if First National's management is as jittery as Bank-a-mythica's, it too will hold more in reserves and lend out less. Thus:

If banks wish to keep cash reserves above the legal minimums, the multiple expansion of the money supply will be restricted. A given amount of cash will support a smaller supply of money than would be the case if banks held no excess reserves.

If we pursue this point a bit further, we will see why government regulation of the money supply is so important for economic stability. We have already suggested that banks will wish to keep excess reserves when they do not foresee profitable and secure opportunities to make loans. This is likely to happen during the downswing and around the trough of a business contraction. If it occurs, the propensity of banks to hold excess reserves will turn the money-creation process into one of money destruction.

During a recession, profit-oriented banks would be prone to reduce the money supply by increasing their excess reserves if the monetary authorities did not intervene. As we will learn in subsequent chapters, such a contraction of the money supply would exacerbate the severity, and probably also the length, of the recession.

On the other hand, banks will want to squeeze the maximum possible money supply out of any given amount of cash reserves by keeping their reserves at the bare minimum when the demand for bank loans is buoyant, profits are high, and many investments suddenly start to look profitable. This reduced incentive

to hold excess reserves in prosperous times means that:

During an economic boom, the behavior of profit-oriented banks is likely to make the money supply expand, adding undesirable momentum to the booming economy and paving the way for a burst of inflation. The authorities must intervene to prevent this.

Regulation of the money supply, then, is necessary because bankers, in the pursuit of profit, might otherwise provide the economy with a wildly gyrating money supply that dances to the tune of the business cycle. Precisely how the authorities can keep the money supply under control will be the subject of the next chapter.

SUMMARY

1. It is much more efficient to exchange goods and services by using money as a medium of exchange than by direct barter.
2. In addition to being the medium of exchange, whatever serves as money is likely to become the standard unit of account and a popular store of value.
3. Throughout history, all sorts of things have served as money. Commodity moneys gave way to full-bodied paper money (certificates backed 100 percent by some commodity, like gold), which in turn gave way to partially backed paper money. Nowadays our paper money has no commodity backing whatsoever: that is, it is pure fiat money.
4. The most widely used definition of the U.S. money supply is M_1, which includes coins, paper money, and checking deposits. However, many economists prefer to work with data based on an M_2 definition, which adds to M_1 most savings deposits held at commercial banks.
5. Under our modern system of fractional reserve banking, banks keep cash reserves equal to only a fraction of their total deposit liabilities. This is the key to their profitability, since their remaining funds can be loaned out at interest. But it also leaves them potentially vulnerable to runs.
6. Because of this vulnerability, bank managers are generally very conservative in their investment strategy, and they also like to keep a prudent level of reserves. Even so, the government keeps a watchful eye over banking practices.
7. Before 1933, bank failures were quite common; but they are rare events today. Many observers attribute this development to deposit insurance.
8. Because it holds only fractional reserves, even a single bank can create money. But its ability to do so is severely limited because the funds it lends out probably will be deposited in another bank.

9. As a whole, the banking system can create several dollars of deposits for each dollar of cash reserves it receives. Under certain assumptions, the ratio of new deposits to new reserves will be $1/m$, where m is the required reserve ratio.
10. The same process works in reverse, as a system of money destruction, when cash is withdrawn from the banking system.
11. Because both banks and their customers may want to hold more cash when the economic climate is shaky, the money supply would probably contract under such circumstances if the monetary authorities did not intervene. Similarly, the money supply would probably expand rapidly in boom times if it were unregulated.

CONCEPTS FOR REVIEW

Run on a bank
Barter
Double coincidence
    of wants
Medium of exchange
Store of value
Commodity money
Fiat money
M_1 versus M_2
Liquidity

Fractional reserve
    banking
Deposit insurance
Federal Deposit
    Insurance Corporation
Reserve requirements
Asset
Liability
Balance sheet
Excess reserves
Deposit creation

QUESTIONS FOR DISCUSSION

1. If ours were a barter economy, how would you pay your tuition bill? What if your college did not want the goods or services you offered in payment?
2. How is "money" defined, both conceptually and in practice? Does the U.S. money supply consist of commodity money, full-bodied paper money, or fiat money?
3. What is fractional reserve banking, and why is it the key to bank profits? (*Hint:* What opportunities to make profits would banks have if reserve requirements were 100 percent?) Why does fractional reserve banking give bankers discretion over how large the money supply will be? Why does it make banks potentially vulnerable to runs?
4. Do you hold a checking account in a bank? If so, what will happen to your account if the bank goes bankrupt?
5. Suppose that no banks keep excess reserves and no individuals or firms hold on to cash. If someone suddenly discovers $1 million in buried treasure, explain what will happen to the money supply if the required reserve ratio is one-sixth (16.67 percent).
6. How would your answer to Question 5 differ if the reserve ratio were 25 percent? If the reserve ratio were 100 percent?
7. Each year during the Christmas shopping season, consumers and stores wish to increase their holdings of cash. Explain how this could lead to a multiple contraction of the money supply. (As a matter of fact, the author-

ities prevent this contraction from occurring by methods explained in the next chapter.)

8. Excess reserves make a bank less vulnerable to runs. Why, then, don't bankers like to hold excess reserves? What circumstances might persuade them that it would be advisable to hold excess reserves?

12

Central Banking
and Monetary Policy

From what we learned in Chapter 11 about normal, profit-oriented banking practices, we might expect the money supply to expand rapidly during prosperous times and to grow sluggishly, or not at all, during recessions. Fortunately, the historical record for the postwar United States does not exhibit this pattern. Why not? The reason is that America's central bank, the Federal Reserve System, has prevented it from happening.

The "Fed," as it is often called, is a bank, but a very special kind of bank. Though it turns out to be quite an effective profit maker, its actions are not guided by the profit motive. Instead, the Fed acts in what it perceives to be the national interest. While its actions are certainly not free from error, and while many people do not share its view about what constitutes the national interest, the Fed's actions have by and large caused the money supply to be a stabilizing influence on the U.S. economy. Just how the Fed regulates the money supply, and why its performance has fallen short of perfection, are the main subjects of this chapter.

THE FEDERAL RESERVE SYSTEM: ORIGINS AND STRUCTURE

When the Federal Reserve System was established in 1914, the United States joined the company of most of the other advanced industrial nations. Up until then, the United States was almost the only modern economic power without a central bank; the Bank of England, for example, dates from 1694.

The impetus for the establishment of a central bank in the United States came not from the logic of economic theory but from some painful experiences with economic reality. Four severe banking panics between 1873 and 1907 convinced legislators and bankers alike that a central bank that would regulate credit conditions was not a luxury but a necessity. After the 1907 crisis, the National Monetary Commission was established to find out just what was wrong with America's banking system. Its report in early 1912 led directly to the establishment of the Federal Reserve System.

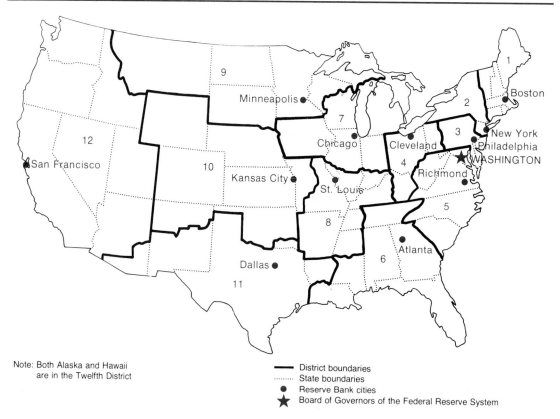

Note: Both Alaska and Hawaii are in the Twelfth District

— District boundaries
...... State boundaries
● Reserve Bank cities
★ Board of Governors of the Federal Reserve System

FIGURE 12–1

THE TWELVE FEDERAL RESERVE DISTRICTS

This map shows the boundaries of the 12 Federal Reserve districts and the locations of the 12 Federal Reserve banks. In which Federal Reserve district do you live?

Although the basic idea of central banking was imported from Europe, some changes in the system were necessary to accommodate it to the needs of this country. Thus the Federal Reserve System became a uniquely American institution. Owing to the vastness of our country, the extraordinarily large number of commercial banks (in Europe, banking is a far more concentrated industry), and our tradition of dual state—federal regulations, it was decided that the United States should have not one central bank but 12! The boundaries of the 12 Federal Reserve districts and the location of each of the 12 district banks are shown in Figure 12–1.

Technically, each of the Federal Reserve banks is a joint stock company; its stockholders are the banks that belong to it. But your bank, if it is a member of the System, does not enjoy the privileges normally accorded to stockholders: It receives only a token share of the Federal Reserve's immense profits (the bulk is donated to the U.S. Treasury), and it has no control over the decisions of the corporation.

Who, then, controls the Fed? Most of the power resides in the seven-member Board of Governors of the Federal Reserve System, headquartered in Washington, and especially in its chairman, who is now G. William Miller, a former business executive. Members of the board are appointed by the president of the United States, with the advice and consent of the Senate, for 14-year terms. The president also designates one of the members to serve a 4-year term as chairman of the board, and thus to be the most powerful central banker in the world; for the United States differs from many other countries in that the Federal Reserve Board, once appointed by the president, is *independent* of the rest of the government as long as it stays within the statutory authority delineated by Congress. It alone has responsibility for determining the nation's monetary policy.

Closely allied with the board of governors is the powerful Federal Open Market Committee (FOMC), which meets monthly in Washington (more frequently when necessary). For reasons that will be explained in this chapter, the decisions of the FOMC largely determine the size of the U.S. money supply. The 12-member committee consists of the 7 governors of the Federal Reserve System and either the president or vice-president of five of the district banks.

THE INDEPENDENCE OF THE FED

The institutional independence of the Federal Reserve System is looked upon as a source of pride by some and as an antidemocratic embarrassment by others. The proponents of Federal Reserve independence argue that it enables monetary policy decisions to be made on objective, technical criteria and keeps monetary control out of the "political thicket." Without this independence, it is argued, there would be a tendency for politicians to force the Fed to expand the money supply too rapidly, thereby contributing to chronic inflation and undermining faith in America's financial system.

Opponents of this view counter that there is something profoundly undemocratic about having a group of unelected bankers and economists make decisions that affect the well-being of 220 million Americans. Monetary policy, they argue, ought to be formulated by the elected representatives of the people, just like fiscal policy. Those who argue for executive or congressional control over the Fed can point to historical instances in which monetary and fiscal policy have been at loggerheads—with the Fed undoing or even overwhelming the economic impact of fiscal policy decisions.

There is plenty of middle ground between the two extremes. One less drastic proposal, advocated by candidate Jimmy Carter during the 1976 presidential election, would simply shift the term of the chairman of the Federal Reserve Board to make it coincide with that of the president. As things stand today, a newly elected president must retain the chairman that his predecessor appointed whether or not he agrees with his policies.

Another suggested reform would require the Fed to announce its ultimate targets for unemployment and inflation and explain how it expected its monetary policy actions to further these goals. An extreme version of this proposal would require that the Fed adhere to the goals of the administration or of Congress. But a softer version simply would require that the Fed announce its own goals and subject them to public scrutiny.

A small step in this direction was taken during 1975 when the Fed, in response to congressional wishes, began announcing "ranges of tolerance" both for growth rates of the money supply (by four different definitions!) and for interest rates. That is, the chairman of the Federal Reserve Board now periodically tells Congress *in advance* what the maximum and minimum permissible growth rates for the money stock are in the coming months, and how high or low it will allow interest rates to go. A problem with this procedure, however, is that the Fed is often unable to keep *both* the money supply *and* the interest rate within its own target ranges. Indeed, sometimes it misses on both targets! Some reasons for the Fed's difficulties will be explained later in this chapter.

How people view these and other reform proposals that revolve round the issue of the Fed's independence depends on how they perceive the office. Are governors of the Federal Reserve System akin to judges, and therefore, at least in principle, best thought of as nonpartisan and independent technocrats? The 14-year terms of office certainly suggest an analogy to the judicial system, but the board's role is most assuredly one that involves policy making, not just "impartial" interpretation of the law. Or are the governors more like members of the Cabinet, that is, policy-making officials who should properly serve only at the pleasure of the president? Since neither analogy fits precisely, the issue is a vexing one.

CONTROLLING THE MONEY SUPPLY: RESERVE REQUIREMENTS

Chapter 11 taught us one important way in which the monetary authorities influence and, with a little luck, control the nation's money supply: that is, by varying the minimum required reserve ratio. To see how this works, consider the balance sheet of a hypothetical bank shown in Table 12–1. If the minimum required reserve ratio is 20 percent, and the bank wishes to hold only the legal minimum in reserves, Middle American Bank is in equilibrium on October 14, 1979. Its $1 million in checking deposits mean that its required reserves amount to $200,000, which just matches its actual reserves. Excess

TABLE 12–1

BALANCE SHEET OF MIDDLE AMERICAN BANK, October 14, 1979

ASSETS		LIABILITIES AND NET WORTH	
Reserves	$ 200,000	Checking deposits	$1,000,000
Loans outstanding	1,000,000	Net worth	200,000
Total assets	$1,200,000	Total liabilities plus net worth	$1,200,000

If the required reserve ratio is 20 percent, Middle American Bank holds exactly its required reserves on October 14, 1979—no more and no less. However, if the reserve ratio falls to 15 percent, its required reserves will fall to only $150,000 (15 percent of $1 million), and it will have $50,000 in excess reserves.

TABLE 12–2

BALANCE SHEET OF MIDDLE AMERICAN BANK, October 15, 1979

ASSETS		LIABILITIES AND NET WORTH	
Reserves	$ 150,000	Checking deposits	$1,000,000
Loans outstanding	1,050,000	Net worth	200,000
Total assets	$1,200,000	Total liabilities plus net worth	$1,200,000

If Middle American Bank does not wish to hold excess reserves, its balance sheet will look like this after it loans out the extra $50,000 in excess reserves. At this point, it once again has no excess reserves.

reserves, which are the difference between actual and required reserves, are zero.

Now suppose that the Federal Reserve Board decides that the money supply needs to be increased. One action it could take would be to lower the required reserve ratio. To take an exaggerated example, suppose it reduces reserve requirements to 15 percent of deposits. Middle American Bank's balance sheet is unaffected by this action, but the bank's managers are sure to react to it. For now required reserves are only $150,000 (15 percent of $1 million), so the bank is holding $50,000 in excess reserves —funds that are earning no interest for the bank. The effect is the same as if a new depositor had brought in cash: The bank now has more money to lend. When it lends out this $50,000, its balance sheet will be as shown in Table 12–2; it now holds $50,000 less in reserves and $50,000 more in loans.

Although no new deposits are created by this transaction, we know from the previous chapter that the wheels of a multiple expansion of the banking system have been set in motion. For the recipient of the loan will deposit the proceeds in his own bank, giving that bank excess reserves and, therefore, the ability to grant more loans, and so on.

Table 12–3 shows the actual legal reserve ratios in effect on July 31, 1978. These were last changed in December 1976 when ratios were reduced by from one-half to one-quarter of a percentage point.

TABLE 12–3

RESERVE REQUIREMENTS OF THE FEDERAL RESERVE SYSTEM FOR CHECKING DEPOSITS (as of July 31, 1978)

First $2 million	7 %
$2–10 million	$9\frac{1}{2}$%
$10–100 million	$11\frac{3}{4}$%
$100–400 million	$12\frac{3}{4}$%
$400 million and above	$16\frac{1}{4}$%

Source: Federal Reserve Bulletin, August 1978.

SOME DIFFICULTIES WITH THE RESERVE RATIO

It is not hard for the Fed to estimate the expansion of the money supply that a change in the reserve ratio will cause.[1] But *estimating* the ultimate monetary expansion is a far cry from *knowing it* with certainty. As we know from Chapter 11, the simple deposit-creation formula is predicated on the assumptions that people will want to hold no more cash and that banks

[1] We know from the last chapter that each dollar of bank reserves can support $1/m$ dollars of checking deposits if the fraction m is the required reserve ratio. When m is lowered from 20 percent to 15 percent, this number rises from $1/0.20 = 5$ to $1/0.15 = 6.67$. So the demand-deposit component of the money supply should increase by about one-third (6.67 is one-third larger than 5).

will want to hold no more excess reserves as the monetary expansion proceeds. In practice, these assumptions are unlikely to be literally true. So, if the Fed is to predict the eventual effect of its action on the money supply correctly, it must first estimate (a) how much firms and individuals will want to add to their currency holdings, and (b) how much banks will want to add to (or subtract from) their excess reserves. Neither of these can be estimated with great precision.

By lowering required reserve ratios, the central bank can increase the money supply. But, because of fluctuations in people's desires to hold cash and banks' desires to hold excess reserves, it cannot predict the consequences of these actions with perfect accuracy. Thus, over short periods, control over the money supply must of necessity be imperfect.

It does not take much imagination to see what the Fed must do to reserve requirements when it wants to engineer a *contraction* of the supply of money. If banks are not holding excess reserves, an increase in the required reserve ratio will force them to contract their loans and deposits until their reserve deficiencies are corrected. Of course, if banks do have sufficient excess reserves, they can flout the Fed's wishes. But the Fed normally will be trying to rein in the money supply when the economy is booming, and these are precisely the times when banks will not want to hold more idle reserves than they have to.

CONTROLLING THE MONEY SUPPLY: OPEN MARKET OPERATIONS

While a change in reserve requirements is the most obvious way to force the money supply to expand or contract, it is not the way the Fed normally chooses to do it. Partly for historical

reasons, most manipulations of the money supply are accomplished through what are called open market operations. Whereas changes in reserve ratios leave the banks with either excess or deficient reserves by changing the legal requirements, open market operations have the effect of giving the banks more cash or taking cash away from them.

How does this work? Suppose the Federal Open Market Committee decides that the money supply is too low. It can issue instructions that the money supply should be expanded through operations in the open market. Specifically, this means that the Federal Reserve System must *purchase* U.S. government securities (generally short-term securities called "Treasury bills") from any individual or bank that wishes to sell.[2]

Suppose the order is to purchase $100 million worth of securities, and that commercial banks are the sellers. *The Fed makes payment by giving the banks $100 million in new reserves.* So, if they held only the required amount of reserves initially, the banks now have $100 million in excess reserves, as shown in Table 12–4. This will induce a multiple expansion of the banking system in the usual way.

Where does the Fed get the money that it gives to the banks in return for the securities? It could pay in cash, but normally does not. Instead, it manufactures the funds out of thin air, or, more literally, out of pen and ink. Specifically, the Fed pays the banks for the securities by adding the appropriate sums to the accounts that the banks maintain at the Fed. The balances in their accounts constitute bank reserves, just like cash in bank vaults. While this process of creating bookkeeping entries at the Federal Reserve is commonly referred to as "printing money," the Fed does not literally

[2]In fact, the Fed almost always deals with one of a small group of dealers who "make a market" in government securities. However, this is an institutional detail that has no effect on the basic principles. The dealers are simply intermediaries, intervening between the ultimate buyer (the Fed) and the ultimate seller.

TABLE 12–4

EFFECTS OF AN OPEN MARKET PURCHASE OF SECURITIES ON THE BALANCE SHEETS OF BANKS AND THE FED

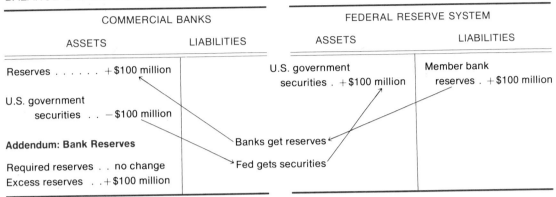

When the Fed buys $100 million worth of securities from the banks, it adds this amount to the bookkeeping entries that represent the banks' accounts at the Fed (called "member bank reserves"). Since deposits have not increased at all, required reserves are unchanged by this transaction. But actual reserves are increased by $100 million, so there are $100 million in excess reserves. This will trigger a multiple expansion of the banking system.

run the printing presses. Instead, it simply exchanges its IOUs for an existing asset (a government security). But, unlike your IOUs, the Fed's IOUs constitute legal bank reserves, and thus are the equivalent of cash in their ability to support a multiple expansion of the money supply. The banks, not the Fed, actually increase the money supply; but the Fed's actions give the banks the wherewithal to do it.

To summarize briefly:

When the Federal Reserve System wants to increase the money supply, it purchases U.S. government securities in the open market. It pays for these securities by creating new bank reserves, and these additional reserves lead to a multiple expansion of the money supply.

The procedures followed when the FOMC wants to *contract* the money supply are just the opposite of those we have just explained. In brief, it orders a *sale* of government securities in the open market. This takes reserves *away* from banks, since banks pay for the securities by

drawing down their deposits at the Fed. A multiple *contraction* of the banking system ensues. The principles are exactly the same as when the process operates in reverse.

In discussing reserve requirements, we emphasized that the Fed cannot know for sure how great an expansion of the money supply will be caused by a given change in legal reserve ratios. The same is true of changes in the Fed's holdings of government securities accomplished through operations in the open market—and for the same reasons. On the basis of its past experience, the System can *estimate* the ultimate effects of open market purchases and sales on the money supply; and, in normal times, these estimates are quite accurate. (That, presumably, is the definition of "normal times.") But at other times banks may surprise the Fed by holding larger (or smaller) excess reserves than anticipated, or businesses and consumers may surprise it by holding more (or less) currency. In such cases, the Fed will not get the money supply it was shooting for, and will have to readjust its policies.

CONTROLLING THE MONEY SUPPLY: LENDING TO BANKS

When the Federal Reserve System was first established, its founders did not intend it to pursue an active monetary policy to stabilize the economy. Indeed, the basic ideas of any economic stabilization policy were foreign at the time, dating only from Keynes's *General Theory of Employment, Interest, and Money* in 1936. Instead, the Fed's founders viewed it as a means of preventing the supplies of money and credit from drying up during economic contractions, as had happened so often in the pre-1914 period. One of the principal ways in which the Fed was to provide such insurance against financial panics was to act as a "lender of last resort." That is, when risky business prospects made commercial banks hesitant to extend new loans, the Fed would step in by lending money to the banks, thus inducing the banks to lend more money to their customers.

Loans from the Federal Reserve banks to individual commercial banks have existed from the very first days of the System. When the Fed extends borrowing privileges to a bank in need

of reserves, that bank receives a credit in its deposit account at the Fed (see Table 12–5). This addition to bank reserves may lead to an expansion of the money supply; or it may eliminate a reserve deficiency, and thereby prevent a multiple contraction of the banking system. In either case, the Fed makes monetary conditions more expansive by making borrowing easier.

Federal Reserve officials regulate the volume of member bank borrowing in two ways. One is by setting the *rate of interest charged on these loans*. (For historical reasons, this is called the "discount rate.") If it wants to give banks more reserves, it can reduce the interest rate that it charges, thereby tempting more banks to borrow. Alternatively, it can soak up reserves by raising its rate and persuading the banks to reduce their borrowings.

While this type of *active* manipulation of the discount rate is practiced widely in foreign countries, where the rate is often the center-piece of monetary policy, it is much less common in the United States, where the Fed usually relies on open market operations in conducting its monetary policy. More often the Fed adjusts its discount rate *passively* to keep it in line with market interest rates.

TABLE 12–5

BALANCE SHEET CHANGES FOR BORROWING FROM THE FED

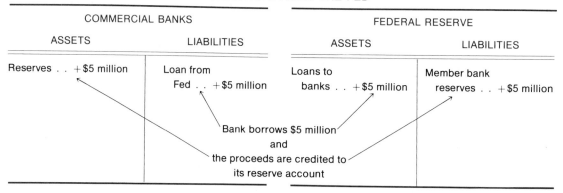

COMMERCIAL BANKS		FEDERAL RESERVE	
ASSETS	LIABILITIES	ASSETS	LIABILITIES
Reserves . . +$5 million	Loan from Fed . . +$5 million	Loans to banks . . +$5 million	Member bank reserves . . +$5 million

Bank borrows $5 million and the proceeds are credited to its reserve account

When the Fed lends $5 million to a bank, it simply adds this amount to the bookkeeping entry that represents that bank's account at the Fed. Once again, actual reserves increase while required reserves do not change (because commercial bank deposits have not changed). Hence this loan would be expected to initiate a multiple expansion of the banking system.

As in the case of changes in reserve requirements and open market operations, the Fed cannot predict with certainty how banks will react to changes in its lending rate. Sometimes they may respond vigorously to a cut in the rate, borrowing a great deal from the Fed and lending a correspondingly large amount to their customers. Other times they may essentially ignore the Fed's actions. The link between the lending rate and the money supply is, at times, a very loose one.

Often, though, the Fed tries to tighten this link by using its second way of controlling the volume of bank borrowing—moral suasion. This phrase refers to some not-so-subtle methods that the Fed has for letting banks know when it thinks they are borrowing too much. Since banks are anxious to maintain the good will of the Fed, they often respond to warnings that they have overused their borrowing privileges— especially when such warnings are accompanied by a veiled threat that these privileges might be suspended if the offending bank does not mend its ways. As the Fed often reminds the banks, borrowing is "a privilege, not a right."

TIGHTENING MONETARY CONTROL: SOME SUGGESTED REFORMS

The fact that each of the Federal Reserve's principal instruments of monetary control is somewhat imperfect has led to a number of suggested reforms designed to improve the System's ability to regulate the supply of money.

Because banks' discretion over the amount of reserves they hold (subject only to the legal minimums) makes the link between changes in Federal Reserve policy and changes in the money supply rather slippery, some economists would like to see a return to a system of 100 percent reserve requirements. Under such a rule, no bank could add to or subtract from its excess reserves because there would never be any excess reserves. Each dollar of bank reserves would support exactly one dollar of deposits, no more and no less; so there would be no such thing as a multiple expansion or contraction of the banking system. The Fed can now control bank reserves with great precision; and under a system of 100 percent reserve requirements its control over the money supply would be equally precise.

While such a change in banking regulations undoubtedly would make the Fed's job easier, it also would change the face of banking in dramatic and possibly unpredictable ways. It will be recalled from Chapter 11 that banking as we know it today evolved from that first goldsmith's momentous discovery that he could get along with only fractional reserves. This discovery has been the mainspring of bank profits ever since. Abolishing fractional reserve banking should therefore be viewed as a major overhaul of the financial system. This does not necessarily mean that it is a bad idea, only that it should be approached with some caution.

A less dramatic reform aimed at tightening the link between bank reserves and the money supply is to require all commercial banks to belong to the Federal Reserve System or, what amounts to the same thing, to keep the same required reserves as member banks. As things stand today, membership in the Fed is voluntary, and any bank chartered by a state government can opt out if it so pleases.[3] Because the System generally imposes stiffer reserve requirements than do the state banking authorities, state banks pay a financial penalty for the privilege of belonging to the Fed—they have to hold more reserves. While they gain certain privileges, such as the ability to borrow from the Fed, more and more banks have decided that membership in the Fed is just too expensive. The trend in Fed membership is unmistakably downward. For example, almost 7000 banks belonged to the Federal Reserve System at the end of 1947, and these banks accounted for

[3]Banks chartered by the national government have no choice. They are required to belong to the Federal Reserve System.

about 85 percent of demand deposits. By the middle of 1978, less than 5700 banks belonged to the System, and they accounted for only 73 percent of demand deposits. This trend is a cause of some concern to Fed officials, who feel that it may imperil their control of the money supply. Recently, there has been some discussion of the Fed paying interest on reserves as a way of encouraging banks to remain members of the System.

Finally, some observers have suggested that lending to member banks, far from aiding the Fed's monetary control, actually undermines it, and therefore the Fed should stop lending except in emergency cases. Their reasoning goes as follows. When the Fed is trying to force a contraction of the banking system, some banks may resist this desire by borrowing the reserves they need. Similarly, some banks may relinquish reserves to pay back loans just when the Fed wants the money supply to expand. No doubt this occasionally happens. But there are also occasions when Federal Reserve lending is a valuable supplement to open market policy. Since it is by no means clear that monetary control would be tighter without lending, the Fed is understandably reluctant to give up one of its major traditional weapons.

THE MONEY SUPPLY MECHANISM: A SUMMARY

For purposes of integrating money into the basic macroeconomic model of Chapters 8, 9, and 10, the analysis of the last chapter and the present one can be summed up in the following statement:

As interest rates rise, banks normally find it more profitable to expand their volume of loans and deposits, thus increasing the supply of money. This poses the danger that the money supply would expand rapidly during a period of inflation and economic boom and advance slowly, or even contract, during a period of recession—just the opposite from what stabilization policy requires. However, the Fed can shift the relationship between the money supply and interest rates by employing any of its principal weapons of monetary control: open market operations, changes in reserve requirements, or changes in lending policy to banks.

These ideas are depicted graphically in Figure 12–2. Figure 12–2(a) shows a typical money supply schedule labeled *MS*, illustrating the fact that bank behavior makes the money stock an increasing function of interest rates. Notice that the sensitivity of the money supply to interest rates is rather weak in the diagram—a large rise in the rate of interest (from 4 percent to 6 percent) induces only a small increase in the supply of money (from $290 billion to $300 billion). The drawing is deliberately constructed that way because that is what the statistical evidence shows.

The curve in Figure 12–2(a) shows the money supply schedule corresponding to some specific monetary policy. Figure 12–2(b) portrays how the money supply schedule responds to an *expansionary change in monetary policy.* This could mean an open market purchase of government bonds, a reduction in reserve requirements, or a drop in the Fed's lending rate. The money supply schedule shifts outward from $M_0 S_0$ to $M_1 S_1$, as indicated by the arrows. After banks have adjusted to the change, there is more money at any given interest rate. Figure 12–2(c) shows what happens in the reverse case—*contractionary monetary policy* accomplished through open market sales of securities, increased reserve requirements, or a rise in the lending rate. The money supply schedule shifts inward from $M_0 S_0$ to $M_2 S_2$.

As we have stressed, the diagrams make things look rather more precise than they actually are. Since the Fed's control over the money supply schedule is imperfect in the short run, the actual *MS* schedule is obscured by a bit

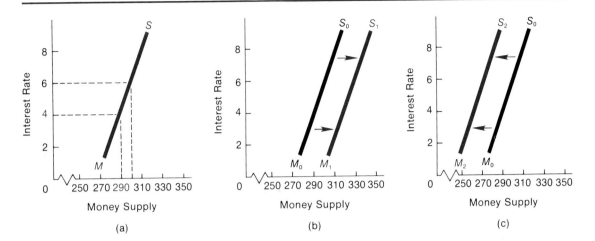

FIGURE 12–2

THE SUPPLY SCHEDULE FOR MONEY

(a) A typical supply schedule for money. It is rising as we move toward the right, meaning that banks will supply more money when interest rates are higher. (b) What happens to the money supply schedule if the Fed purchases securities in the open market, or lowers required reserves, or provides banks with more loans? The supply schedule shifts outward. (c) The effect of using these same policy instruments in the opposite (contractionary) direction. The supply schedule shifts inward.

of fog. In what follows, we portray all the graphs as clean straight lines only for pedagogical simplicity. The Fed wishes things were as simple in the real world!

THE DEMAND FOR MONEY

Just as we must know something about both the supply of and the demand for wheat before we can predict how much will be sold and at what price, it is necessary to know something about the demand for money if we are to understand the amount of money actually in existence, and the prevailing interest rate.

The definition of money given in Chapter 11 suggests the most important reason why people hold money balances: The medium of exchange is needed to carry out purchases and sales of goods and services. Since the nominal gross national product (GNP) is considered to be the best measure of the total money value of all goods and services traded in the economy, it seems safe to say that the higher the nominal GNP, the higher will be the demand for money. And, indeed, an impressive amount of statistical evidence supports this supposition. Notice that nominal GNP, and hence the demand for money, rises if *either* real output *or* the price level rises—a fact that will assume some importance in the next chapter.

But income is not the only factor affecting the demand for money; interest rates matter, too. At first, that may seem surprising because money balances, which consist either of currency or of checking deposits, pay no interest. Why, then, are interest rates relevant? They are relevant because money is only one of a variety of forms in which individuals can hold their wealth. Holders of money *give up* the opportunity to hold one of these other assets, such as savings deposits or government bonds, in order to gain the convenience of money. In so doing, they *give up* the interest that they could have earned on one of these alternative assets.

This is an example of the concept of *opportunity cost* in action.[4] On the surface, it seems virtually costless to hold money. But, *compared with the next best alternative,* this action is not costless at all. For example, if the next best alternative to holding $100 in cash is to put those funds into a savings account that pays 6 percent interest, then the opportunity cost of holding that money is $6 per year (6 percent of $100).

How, then, should the rate of interest influence the quantity of money that people demand? It is natural to assume that when interest rates are high people will make strenuous efforts to economize on their holdings of money balances, efforts that would not be worthwhile at lower interest rates. In a word, rational behavior of consumers and business firms should make the demand to hold money *decline* as the interest rate *rises*. And, once again, careful analysis of the data shows this to be true. To summarize:

People and business firms hold money primarily to finance their transactions. Therefore, the demand for money increases as real output rises or as prices rise. However, the quantity of money that is demanded decreases as the rate of interest rises because the rate of interest is the opportunity cost of holding money balances.

EQUILIBRIUM IN THE MONEY MARKET

It is possible to portray the demand for money by a graphical device, as shown in Figure 12–3. There we show a demand schedule for money (the curve labeled *MD*) that decreases as the rate of interest rises. To do this, we must hold

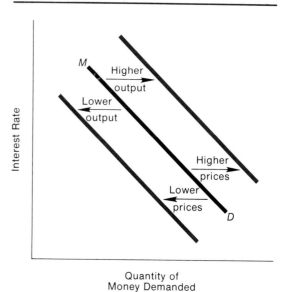

Quantity of
Money Demanded

FIGURE 12–3

THE DEMAND SCHEDULE FOR MONEY
The downward-sloping line *MD* is a typical demand schedule for money. It slopes down because money is a less-attractive asset when interest rates on alternative assets are higher. The entire curve is shifted if either the number of transactions (which is often measured by real GNP) or the average price of a transaction (which is measured by the price level) changes.

both real output and the price level constant. Shifts in either of these variables will move the *MD* curve in the manner indicated in the diagram because at higher levels of nominal GNP, demand for money is higher; and at lower levels of nominal GNP, it is lower.

Figure 12–4 combines the money supply schedule of Figure 12–2(a) (labeled *MS*) with the money demand schedule of Figure 12–3 (labeled *MD*). Point *E* is the equilibrium of the money market. The diagram thus shows that *given* real output and the price level (which locates the *MD* curve) and *given* the Federal Reserve's monetary policy (which locates the *MS* curve), the money market is in equilibrium at an interest rate of 6 percent and a money

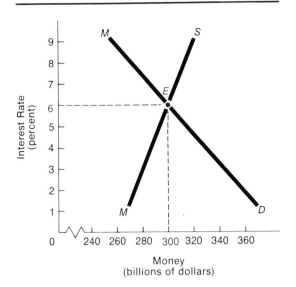

FIGURE 12–4

EQUILIBRIUM IN THE MONEY MARKET

Equilibrium in the market for money is determined by the intersection of demand curve *MD* and supply curve *MS*. At point *E*, the interest rate is 6 percent, and the money supply is $300 billion. At no other interest rate would the demand for and the supply of money be in balance. (See Discussion Question 8 at the end of the chapter.)

stock of $300 billion. Since the Fed's actions can shift the *MS* curve, the Fed can alter this equilibrium.

MONETARY POLICY AND INTEREST RATES

DEFINITION

Monetary policy refers to actions that the Federal Reserve System takes in order to change the equilibrium of the money market, that is, to alter the money supply, move interest rates, or both.

Expansionary monetary policy actions include purchasing government securities in the open market, reducing reserve requirements, and encouraging banks to borrow. Any of these actions will provide additional excess reserves to the banking system, thus encouraging banks to increase their loans and deposits. As money becomes more plentiful, interest rates drop. Our supply–demand analysis of the money market shows this in Figure 12–5(a). By shifting the money supply schedule outward from $M_0 S_0$ to $M_1 S_1$, the Fed moves the market equilibrium from point *E* to point *A*—thus forcing the interest rate down.

Contractionary monetary policy actions, such as selling securities in the open market, raising reserve requirements, and discouraging borrowing, have the opposite effect. They push interest rates up, as Figure 12–5(b) shows. Thus:

Monetary policies that expand the money supply normally lower interest rates. Monetary policies that reduce the money supply normally raise interest rates.

CONTROLLING THE MONEY SUPPLY VERSUS CONTROLLING INTEREST RATES: THE POLICY DILEMMA

This graphical apparatus enables us to understand one of the important policy issues facing the Fed: Should the Federal Reserve use its policy tools to control the money stock (*M*) or to control the rate of interest (*r*)? As we shall see, there is no agreement among economists on this question. But one thing is sure: *The Fed does not have enough instruments to control both M and r.*

To see why, suppose that the demand schedule for money suddenly rises. This might happen because incomes rise or simply because people decide to hold more money. If the Fed is content with a money supply of $300 billion and an interest rate of 6 percent (point *E* in Figure 12–4), what can it do?

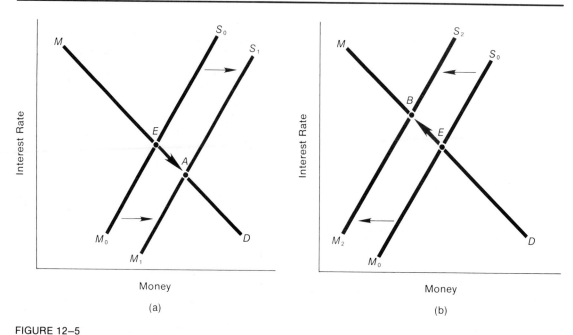

FIGURE 12–5

THE EFFECTS OF MONETARY POLICY ON THE MONEY MARKET
The two parts of this figure show the effects of monetary policy on the money supply (M) and the rate of interest (r). (a) Expansionary monetary policies that shift the supply schedule from M_0S_0 to M_1S_1 push the equilibrium from point E to point A. M rises while r falls. (b) Contractionary policies pull the supply schedule in from M_0S_0 to M_2S_2, causing equilibrium to move up from point E to point B. M falls as r rises.

If the Fed takes no action, the upward shift in the demand curve will push up both the quantity of money (M) and the rate of interest (r). Figure 12–6 shows this graphically. The demand schedule for money shifts outward from M_0D_0 to M_1D_1 and, if there is no change in monetary policy (so that supply schedule MS does not move), equilibrium moves from point E to point A. The money stock rises to $310 billion and the interest rate rises to 8 percent.

But if the economy is already operating near full employment, the Fed might be unwilling to let M rise. In that case, it can use any of its contractionary weapons to prevent M from rising. If it does this, it will push r up even higher because, with no increase in the money supply, it will require an even higher interest

rate to prevent demand from exceeding supply. This is also shown in Figure 12–6. After the demand curve for money shifts, point E is simply unattainable. The Fed must choose from among the points on M_1D_1, and point X is the point on this curve that keeps the money supply at $300 billion. At point X, however, the interest rate has skyrocketed to 10 percent.

Alternatively, if the economy is operating at low levels of resource utilization, the Fed might decide that a rise in M is just what is needed, but that a rise in r is to be avoided. Why? Because, as we learned in the discussion in Chapter 8 of the determinants of investment, investment spending normally declines when interest rates rise. In this case, the Fed would be forced to engage in expansionary monetary

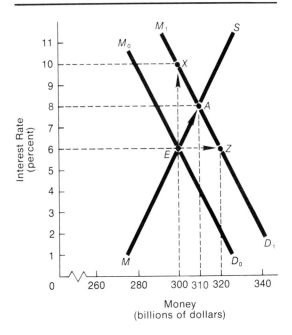

FIGURE 12–6
THE FEDERAL RESERVE'S POLICY DILEMMA
This diagram illustrates the dilemma facing the Fed
when the demand schedule for money shifts. In this
case, we suppose that it increases from M_0D_0 to M_1D_1.
If the equilibrium at point E satisfied its goals both for
the money supply ($300 billion) and for the rate of
interest (6 percent), either one or both of these goals
will have to be abandoned after the demand schedule
shifts. Points X, A, and Z illustrate three of the many
choices. At X, the Fed is keeping the money supply
at $300 billion through contractionary policies, but at
a cost of skyrocketing interest rates. At Z, the Fed is
holding interest rates at 6 percent, but the required
expansionary monetary policies raise the money
supply to $320 billion. At A, the Fed is not adjusting
its policy, and is accepting an increase in both the
money supply and the rate of interest.

policy to prevent the rise in the demand for
money from pushing up r. The reason is that
only by providing additional money can the Fed
equate supply to the higher demand without a
rise in interest rates. In terms of Figure 12–6,
the interest rate can be held at 6 percent by
picking point Z. But to get there, the Fed will

have to push the money supply up to $320
billion. To summarize this discussion:

When the demand for money increases, the Fed
must tolerate either a rise in interest rates, a rise
in the money stock, or both. It simply does not
have the weapons to control *both* the supply of
money *and* the interest rate. If it tries to keep M
steady, then r will rise sharply. Conversely, if it
tries to stabilize r, then M will shoot up.

This explains why the Fed often finds it
impossible to meet its targets for both the
money supply and the rate of interest. A shift in
the demand schedule for money simply may
make previously selected targets for M and r
unattainable.

WHAT SHOULD THE FED DO?

Given the need to sacrifice one goal or the
other, it is not surprising that a debate has
raged for years over which goal the Fed should
stick to. Should it adhere rigidly to its target
growth path for the money supply, irrespective
of the consequences for interest rates? Should
it hold interest rates steady even if that causes
wild gyrations in the money stock? Or is some
middle ground more appropriate?

In the early part of the postwar period, the
predominant view held that the interest rate
target was much the more important of the two.
The rationale for this view is that gyrating
interest rates will cause abrupt and unsettling
changes in investment spending, and this will in
turn make the whole economy fluctuate. In this
view, stabilization of interest rates is the best
way to stabilize GNP. If fluctuations in the
money supply are required to keep interest rates
on a steady course, that is nothing to worry
about.

In the 1960s, this prevailing view came
under increasing attack. Leading the assault
was Professor Milton Friedman and a group of

economists called *monetarists.*[5] They argued that the Fed's obsession with stabilization of interest rates actually *destabilized* the economy because it led to undue fluctuations in the money supply. The monetarist prescription was simple. The Fed should stop worrying about minor fluctuations in interest rates, and make the money supply grow at a constant rate from month to month and year to year.

Monetarism made some important inroads at the Fed in the early 1970s, but never gained the ascendancy. While the Fed now keeps much closer tabs on the money stock than it used to, it still polices movements in interest rates. Many economists believe that this dual approach is the most appropriate, though it naturally invites attack from both sides.

The problem with a rigid growth rule for the *supply* of money is that the *demand* for money does not cooperate by growing at a steady rate from month to month; instead it dances about quite a bit in the short run. This confronts the fixed-money-growth-rate rule with two problems.

1. It is almost impossible to achieve. Since the volume of money in existence depends on *both* the demand *and* the supply schedules, it would require exceptional dexterity on the part of the Fed to keep *M* growing at 4 percent a year in the face of significant fluctuations in the rate of growth of demand.
2. For reasons that were just explained, rigid adherence to a money-growth rule might lead to undue fluctuations in interest rates, which could create an unsettled atmosphere for business decisions.

By the same token, powerful objections can be raised against exclusive concentration on interest rate movements—objections that the monetarists have enunciated quite persua-

[5]Monetarism is considered fully in the next two chapters.

sively. Since increases in national income shift the demand schedule for money upward (as in Figure 12–6), a central bank determined to keep interest rates from rising would have to expand the money supply in response. Conversely, when income sagged, it would have to contract the money supply to keep rates from falling. Thus interest rate pegging would make the money supply expand in boom times and contract in recessions—with potentially grave consequences for the stability of the economy. It is ironic that this sort of monetary behavior is precisely what the Federal Reserve System was designed to prevent.

Nowadays most economists believe that the Fed is correct in pursuing a middle way, trying to limit interest rate fluctuations while at the same time stabilizing the growth path of the money stock. Nevertheless, this procedure leaves the Fed in a rather awkward position, not unlike the political "moderate" who is constantly being harangued by the left for being too conservative and vilified by the right for being too liberal. Whenever the data show a jump in either the growth rate of the money supply or the rate of interest, the Fed knows it will be upbraided by one group of critics or another.

CONCLUSION AND PREVIEW

We have now gained an understanding of how the Fed is organized, what tools it has available for regulating the money supply, why these tools give it only imperfect control over the money stock, and why it is often not clear what the right level for the money supply is anyway. As if this does not leave things muddled enough, the next chapter explores yet another area of great controversy and disagreement— how the Federal Reserve's monetary decisions affect the overall state of the economy.

SUMMARY

1. The Federal Reserve System is America's central bank. There are 12 Federal Reserve banks, but most of the power is held by the Board of Governors in Washington and by the Federal Open Market Committee.

2. The Federal Reserve is independent of the rest of the government. There is controversy over whether this independence is a good idea, and a number of reforms have been suggested in recent years that would make the Fed more accountable to the president or to the Congress.

3. The Fed has three major weapons for controlling the money supply: open market operations, reserve requirements, and its lending policy to the banks.

4. By lowering or raising reserve requirements, the Fed makes it possible for each dollar of reserves to support more or fewer dollars of deposits. Thus lowering or raising the reserve ratio is one way to increase or decrease the money supply.

5. But the Fed does not do this very often. More typically, it raises the money supply by purchasing government securities in the open market. The Fed's payments to the banks for such purchases provide banks with new reserves and, hence, lead to a larger money supply. Conversely, open market sales of securities take reserves from the banks and lead to a smaller money supply.

6. The Fed can also increase the money supply by allowing banks to borrow more reserves, pehaps by reducing the interest rate it charges on such loans. Alternatively, by discouraging borrowing, it can make the money supply contract.

7. None of these weapons, however, gives the Fed perfect control over the money supply in the short run, because it cannot predict perfectly how far the process of deposit creation or destruction will go.

8. The money supply schedule shows that more money is supplied at higher interest rates because, as interest rates rise, banks find it more profitable to expand their loans and deposits. This schedule can be shifted by Federal Reserve policy.

9. The money demand schedule shows that less money is demanded at higher interest rates because interest is the opportunity cost of holding money. This schedule shifts when output or the price level changes.

10. The equilibrium money stock (M) and the equilibrium rate of interest (r) are determined by the intersection of the money supply and money demand schedules.

11. Federal Reserve policy can shift this equilibrium. Expansionary monetary policies cause M to rise and r to fall. Contractionary policies reduce M and increase r.

12. Because it cannot control the demand curve for money, the Fed cannot control *both M and r*. If the demand for money changes, the Fed must decide whether it wants to hold M steady or hold r steady. There are arguments for and against each policy stance.

13. In practice, the Fed does not adhere rigidly to a policy of keeping M on target. Nor does it always try to fix r. It has adopted a mixed strategy of watching both variables.

CONCEPTS FOR REVIEW

Central bank
Federal Reserve System
Federal Open Market Committee
Independence of the Fed
Reserve requirements
Open market operations
Contraction and expansion of the
   money supply

Federal Reserve lending to banks
Moral suasion
Supply of money
Demand for money
Equilibrium in the money market
Monetary policy
Controlling M versus controlling r

QUESTIONS FOR DISCUSSION

1. Why does a modern industrial economy need a central bank?
2. Do you think it is a good idea to have an independent central bank? Explain your reasons.
3. Suppose there is $50 billion cash in existence, and that all of it is held in bank vaults as *required* reserves (that is, banks hold no *excess* reserves). How large will the money supply be if the required reserve ratio is $16\frac{2}{3}$ percent? 20 percent? 25 percent?
4. Show the balance sheet changes that would take place if the Federal Reserve Bank of San Francisco purchased an office building from the Bank of America for a price of $100 million. Compare this to the effect of an open market purchase of securities shown in Table 12–4. What do you conclude?
5. Suppose that the Fed purchases $10 million worth of government bonds from David Rockefeller, who banks at the Chase Manhattan Bank of New York. Show the effects on the balance sheets of the Fed, the Chase Manhattan Bank, and David Rockefeller. (*Hint*: What will Rockefeller do with the $10 million check he receives from the Fed in payment?) Does it make any difference if the Fed buys bonds from a bank or from an individual?
6. Why would the Fed's control over the money supply be tighter under a system of 100 percent reserves?
7. Explain why the supply of money normally is higher and the demand for money normally is lower at higher interest rates.
8. Referring to Figure 12–4, explain why no interest rate other than 6 percent can be an equilibrium interest rate. What steps can the Fed take if it wants to drive this equilibrium interest rate down to 5 percent?
9. Use supply and demand diagrams to show the choices open to the Fed following an unexpected decline in the demand for money.

13

Money and the
National Economy

In this chapter we bring together our analysis of income determination and the price level from Chapters 7 through 10 and our analysis of money and monetary policy from Chapters 11 and 12. In doing so, we complete the construction of our model of the entire macroeconomy. We will then use this model to understand how and why the Federal Reserve's ability to manage the money supply also enables it to manage the level of aggregate demand—and hence to influence the rates of unemployment and inflation.

Because it *synthesizes* so many aspects of the macroeconomic theory we have constructed in past chapters, this chapter requires that you keep many things in mind at the same time. As such, it merits careful study. Fortunately, however, it does not require any new technical apparatus. Literally everything we need can be borrowed from earlier chapters. Following is a list of the things we will be referring to in the pages to come, with an indication of where you should look if you need to review any of them:

How aggregate supply and aggregate demand interact to determine the price level (from Chapters 5 and 9)

- How the circular flow of income and expenditure determines equilibrium output (from Chapter 8)
- The analysis of the multiplier (from Chapters 9 and 10)
- The workings of fiscal policy (from Chapter 10)
- How the supply of and the demand for money interact to determine the quantity of money and the interest rate, and how the Fed can influence this equilibrium (from Chapter 12)

We begin the chapter by studying a very old, and very simple, macroeconomic model: the *quantity theory of money,* and its modern reincarnation, *monetarism.* Each of these models links money to aggregate demand in a very obvious and direct way. Since, on the surface, this approach seems to allow no role for fiscal policy (which contrasts sharply with the Keynesian $C + I + G$ model of Chapters 8 through 10), we follow by bringing money into the Keynesian model and showing how monetary policy—just like fiscal policy—can influence aggregate demand.

Although monetarist and Keynesian theory seem to be two contradictory views of how monetary and fiscal policy work, we will see that the conflict is more apparent than real. In fact, the disagreement is akin to hearing a Briton say, "Yes," and a French person say, "Oui." The uninitiated hear two different languages, but knowledgeable listeners understand that they mean the same thing. However, while a major objective of this chapter is to show that the differences between the two theories are greatly exaggerated, there *are* significant differences between the two schools of thought—not outright contradictions but differences in emphasis—differences that we will take up in the following chapter.

We conclude the chapter with a discussion of a policy issue that is very controversial today: Does deficit spending by government "crowd out" private spending and therefore fail in its goal of reducing unemployment?

MONEY AND INCOME: THE CONCEPT OF VELOCITY

Throughout this chapter we take the liberty of ignoring some of the important lessons of the last chapter and pretend that the Fed can control the money supply, M, or the rate of interest, r, with perfect accuracy. We know that this is not really possible, but we adopt the fiction to focus attention on the linkages between monetary policy and the state of the economy, without clouding the picture with repetitive discussions of the problems that intervene between Federal Reserve actions and changes in M. You should understand, however, that this latter set of difficulties is always present, lurking in the background. With this warning, let us proceed to a simple accounting identity that will serve as the first building block in linking M to economic activity.

We learned in Chapter 11 that because barter is so cumbersome virtually all economic transactions in advanced economies are conducted by the use of money. This means that if there are, say, $2000 billion worth of transactions in the economy during a particular year, and there is an average money stock of $400 billion during that year, then each dollar of money must get used an average of 5 times during the year (since $5 \times \$400$ billion $= \$2000$ billion). The number 5 in this example is called the velocity of circulation, or just velocity for short, because it indicates the speed at which money circulates. For example, a particular dollar bill might be paid by the U.S. government to a soldier in January; the soldier might use it to buy a sweater in March; the storekeeper might then use it to pay his electric bill in May; the electric company could pay it out to a stockholder in October; and the stockholder might spend it on a Christmas present in December. This would mean that the dollar was used 5 times during the year. If it were used only 4 times during the year, its velocity would be only

4, and so on. Similarly, a $20 bill circulating with a velocity of 4 would be the monetary instrument used to finance $80 worth of transactions in that year.

As we noted in Chapter 12, the gross national product in current prices (nominal GNP) is the most widely used measure of the economy's total transactions (the number of dollars changing hands in a year). This measure leads to the following specific definition of velocity:

DEFINITION
Velocity indicates the number of times each year that an "average dollar" changes hands. It is the ratio of the number of dollars changing hands in a year, as measured by the nominal GNP, to the number of dollars in the money stock. That is:

$$\text{Velocity} = \frac{\text{Nominal GNP}}{\text{Money stock}}$$

or in symbols:

$$V = \frac{\text{Nominal GNP}}{M}$$

THE QUANTITY THEORY OF MONEY

By multiplying both sides of this definition by M, we arrive at an accounting relationship that relates the money supply and GNP. It is called the equation of exchange.

DEFINITION
The equation of exchange states that the money value of GNP transactions must be equal to the product of the average stock of money times velocity. That is:

$$\text{Money supply} \times \text{Velocity} = \text{Nominal GNP}$$

or in symbols:

$$M \times V = \text{Nominal GNP}$$

In the equation of exchange, we have quite an obvious link between the stock of money, M, and the nominal value of the nation's output. But this is only a matter of arithmetic, not of economics. For example, it does not imply that the Fed can raise GNP by increasing M. Why not? Because V might simultaneously fall by enough to prevent $M \times V$ from rising. That is, if there were more dollar bills in circulation than before, but each bill changed hands more slowly, total spending would not necessarily rise.

The *quantity theory of money* transforms the equation of exchange from an accounting identity into an economic model by assuming that changes in velocity are so minor that, for practical purposes, velocity can be taken to be a constant.

You can see that if V never changed, then it would be useful to turn the equation of exchange around to read,

$$\text{Nominal GNP} = V \times M$$

which would be a very simple economic model of income determination. It would say, for example, that if the Federal Reserve wanted to increase nominal GNP by 12.7 percent, it need only raise the money supply by 12.7 percent. In such a simple world, economists could use the equation of exchange to *predict* GNP simply by predicting the quantity of money. And policymakers could *control* GNP simply by controlling the money supply.

In the real world things are not so simple, because velocity is not a fixed number. But this does not necessarily vitiate the usefulness of the quantity theory. We explained in Chapter 1 why all economic models make assumptions that are at least mildly unrealistic—for without such assumptions they would not be models at all, just tedious descriptions of reality. The question is really whether the assumption of constant velocity is a useful abstraction from annoying detail or a gross distortion of facts.

Figure 13–1 sheds some light on this question by showing the behavior of velocity since 1929. You will undoubtedly notice a downward trend in the graph from 1929 until 1946, and an upward trend thereafter. Quite clearly, *velocity is not constant over long periods of time*.

Upon closer examination of monthly or quarterly data, some rather substantial fluctuations of velocity about its trend become apparent. Consider, for example, Figure 13–2, which shows the quarterly behavior of velocity since 1973. Such fluctuations have led most economists to the conclusion that *velocity is not constant in the short run either.* Nor have predictions of nominal GNP based on the

product of *V* times *M* fared very well. It seems, then, that the strict quantity theory of money must be abandoned as a model of aggregate demand and, for the most part, it has been.

THE DETERMINANTS OF VELOCITY

Since, it is abundantly clear that velocity is a variable, not a constant, what, then, are the determinants of velocity? What factors decide whether *V* will be 4 or 5 or 6, that is, whether the money supply will, on the average, change hands four or five or six times a year?

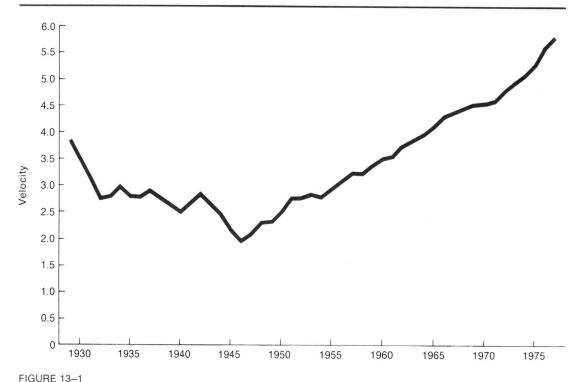

FIGURE 13–1

VELOCITY OF CIRCULATION, 1929–1977

Over a period of American history of almost 50 years, velocity fell from nearly 4 in 1929 to about 2 in 1946, and since then has risen to nearly 6. Quite clearly velocity is not constant over long periods of time.

Source: Constructed by the authors from data in *Historical Statistics of the United States, Federal Reserve Bulletin,* and *Survey of Current Business.*

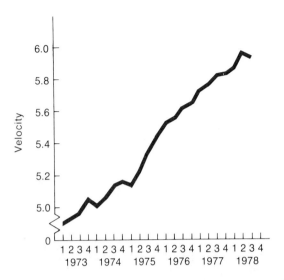

FIGURE 13–2

VELOCITY OF CIRCULATION, 1973–1978

This diagram shows quarterly data on velocity since 1973 and reveals that velocity is not constant over short periods of time either. It has risen from under 5 in early 1973 to nearly 6 by the middle of 1978. Growth of velocity was unusually rapid in 1975, and economists are still not sure why.

Source: Constructed by the authors from data in *Survey of Current Business* and *Monetary Trends* (prepared by the Federal Reserve Bank of St. Louis).

Perhaps the principal factor, though it evolves so slowly over time that it is easy to predict, is the *frequency with which paychecks are received.* This can best be explained through a numerical example, such as a worker who earns $12,000 a year, paid to her in 12 monthly paychecks of $1000 each. Suppose that she spends the whole $1000 over the course of each month and maintains a minimum balance in her checking account of $500. Then each payday her bank balance will shoot up to $1500 and then be gradually whittled down as she makes withdrawals to purchase goods and services. Finally, on the day before her next paycheck arrives, her checking balance will be just $500. Over the course of a typical month, then, her average checking account balance will be $1000 (halfway between $1500 and $500).

Now suppose her employer switches to a twice-a-month payroll. Her paychecks come twice as often, but are reduced to $500 each. There is no reason for her rate of spending to change, but her *cash balances* will change. For now her checking balance will shoot up to only $1000 on payday (the $500 minimum balance plus the $500 paycheck), and it will still be drawn down gradually to $500. Her average cash balance will therefore decline to $750 (halfway between $1000 and $500). Why is this so? Because, with the next paycheck coming sooner than before, it is not necessary to keep as much cash in the bank in order to carry out a given quantity of transactions.

What does this have to do with velocity? Notice that when she was on a monthly payroll, this worker's personal velocity was:

$$V = \frac{\text{Annual income}}{\text{Average cash balance}} = \frac{\$12,000}{\$1000} = 12$$

When she switched to a semimonthly payroll, velocity rose to:

$$V = \frac{\text{Annual income}}{\text{Average cash balance}} = \frac{\$12,000}{\$750} = 16$$

The general lesson to be learned is that more frequent wage payments mean that people can conduct their transactions with lower average cash balances. Since they will want to hold less cash, money will circulate faster. In other words, velocity will rise.

A second factor influencing velocity is the *efficiency of the payments mechanism,* including how quickly checks clear through banks, the use of credit cards, and other methods of transferring funds. It is easy to see how this works. The example in the previous paragraph assumed that our worker holds her entire paycheck in the form of money—meaning either in currency or in her checking account—until she uses it to make a purchase. But, given that money pays no interest, this method may not be the most rational behavior. If it is possible to convert interest-bearing assets into money on short notice and at low cost, a rational individual might use her paycheck to purchase such assets and then use credit cards for most purchases, making periodic transfers to her checking account as necessary. For the same amount of total transactions, then, she would require lower money balances. This means that money would circulate faster: Velocity would rise.

The incentive to limit cash holdings depends on the ease and speed with which it is possible to exchange money for other assets. This is what we mean by the "efficiency of the payments mechanism." If computerization speeds up the bookkeeping procedures of banks, if financial innovations make it possible (as it now is) to make rapid transfers between checking accounts and other assets, if credit cards are used instead of cash, then the need to hold money balances declines. By definition then, velocity rises. Such innovations account for some of the upward trend in velocity since World War II. Fortunately, like the length of the pay period, such basic changes in the payments mechanism usually take place only gradually, and thus often are easy to predict. But this is not always so. For example, a host of financial innovations instituted during the middle 1970s gave analysts fits in predicting velocity.

A third determinant of velocity, is the rate of interest. The basic motive for economizing on money holdings is that money (at least M_1) pays no interest, while many alternative stores of value do. The higher these alternative rates of interest, the greater the incentive to economize on holding money. Therefore, as interest rates rise, people want to hold less money. So the existing stock of money circulates faster, and velocity rises.

It is this factor that most directly undercuts the usefulness of the quantity theory of money as a guide for monetary policy. For in the last chapter we learned that expansionary monetary policy, which increases M, normally also decreases the interest rate. Now we see that these reductions in interest rates will reduce V. Thus, *when the Fed raises the money supply* (M), *the product* $M \times V$ *goes up by a smaller percentage than does* M *itself.*

One component of the interest rate is worth singling out for special attention: *the expected rate of inflation.* We explained in Chapter 6 why an "inflation premium" equal to the expected inflation rate often gets built in to market interest rates.[1] Thus, in many instances, high inflation is the principal cause of high nominal interest rates. High rates of inflation, which erode the purchasing power of money, therefore lead both individuals and businesses to hold as little money as they can get by on—actions that increase velocity.

To summarize this discussion of the determinants of velocity:

Velocity is not a strict constant but depends on such things as the frequency of payments, the efficiency of the financial system, the rate of interest, and the rate of inflation. Only by studying these determinants of velocity can we hope to predict the level of nominal GNP from knowledge of the money supply.

MONETARISM: THE QUANTITY THEORY MODERNIZED

But this does not mean that the equation of exchange cannot be a useful framework within which to organize macroeconomic analysis. It can be. And during the past 25 years a group of

[1] If you need review, turn back to pages 99–100.

economists called *monetarists* has convincingly demonstrated that this is so.

Monetarists recognize that velocity is not a constant. But they stress that it is fairly *predictable*—certainly in the long run and probably also in the short run. This leads them to the conclusion that the best way to study economic activity is to start with the equation of exchange: $M \times V$ = nominal GNP. From here, careful study of the determinants of M (which we provided in the previous two chapters) and of V (which we just completed) can be used to *predict* the behavior of GNP. Similarly, given an understanding of movements in V, control over the money supply gives the Federal Reserve *control* over GNP. These are the central tenets of monetarism.

DEFINITION

Monetarism is a mode of analysis that uses the equation of exchange to organize macroeconomic data. When something happens in the economy, monetarists ask:

1. What does this event do to the stock of money?
2. What does this event do to velocity?

From the answers, they assert that they can predict the path of nominal GNP.

By comparing the monetarist approach with the Keynesian approach that we described in Chapters 8 through 10, we can put both doctrines into perspective and gain an appreciation of the limitations of each. As we mentioned earlier, they differ more in style than in substance.

Monetarism leads analysts to organize their knowledge into two neat compartments— labeled "M" and "V"—and then use a simple accounting identity that says $M \times V$ = *nominal* GNP to bring this knowledge to bear in predicting aggregate demand. Keynesians, as we learned in Chapters 8, 9, and 10, divide economic knowledge into three boxes—marked

"C," "I," and "G"—and unite them all with the equilibrium condition that $C + I + G$ = *real* GNP.

The bit of arithmetic that multiplies M and V to get nominal GNP is neither more nor less profound than the one that adds up C and I and G to get real GNP. And certainly both approaches are correct. The only substantive difference is that the monetarist equation leads to a prediction of *nominal* aggregate demand, whereas the Keynesian equation leads to a prediction of *real* aggregate demand.

Why, then, do we not simply mesh the two theories—using the monetarist approach to study nominal GNP and the Keynesian approach to study real GNP? It seems that by doing so we could use the separate analyses of real and nominal GNP to obtain a prediction of the future behavior of the price level, which, of course, is the source of any difference in behavior of real and nominal GNP.

The reason that this appealing procedure will not work helps point out the major limitation of each theory. Taken by itself, either theory is incomplete. It gives us a picture of the *demand* side of the economy without saying anything about the *supply* side. To try to predict both the price level and real output solely from these demand-oriented models would be like trying to predict the price of peanuts by studying only the behavior of consumers and ignoring that of farmers. It just will not work. In terms of our earlier aggregate supply and demand analysis, which is depicted in a diagram like Figure 13–3:

Both the monetarist and Keynesian analyses are ways of studying the *aggregate demand curve*. In neither case is it possible to learn anything about both output and the price level without also studying the *aggregate supply curve*.

Economists thus are forced to choose between two alternative ways of predicting aggregate demand. If the monetarist route is chosen, the economist will use velocity and

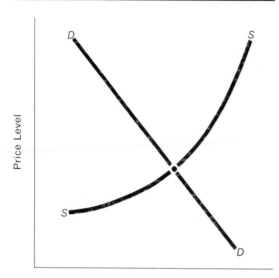

Real GNP

FIGURE 13–3

DETERMINATION OF REAL OUTPUT
AND THE PRICE LEVEL BY AGGREGATE
SUPPLY AND DEMAND
As we have learned in earlier chapters, it takes both
aggregate demand and aggregate supply to determine
the equilibrium levels of real output and the price level.

the money supply to study the demand for
nominal GNP, that is, the demand for goods and
services measured in money terms, and then
have to consider the supply side in order to estimate how any predicted change in nominal
income gets apportioned between changes in
production and changes in prices. On the other
hand, an economist working with the Keynesian
$C + I + G$ approach will start by predicting
movements in the demand for *real* GNP, that is,
the demand for goods and services measured in
dollars of constant purchasing power, and then
turn to the aggregate supply curve to try to estimate the inflationary consequences of this real
demand. It is therefore not surprising that some
economists opt for one approach while others
favor the alternative.

MONEY AND AGGREGATE DEMAND
IN THE KEYNESIAN MODEL

Monetarism, then, provides one way of studying
how monetary policy affects aggregate demand.
Its distinguishing feature is that it starts with
total demand—the nominal GNP—and only
later, if ever, worries about breaking demand
down into its constituent parts. The effect of
money on spending can also be studied,
however, in the more conventional Keynesian
framework that we used in earlier chapters. The
hallmark of this approach is to consider how
monetary conditions affect each of the components of aggregate demand, $C + I + G$, and
then add all these separate effects together to
get the full effect on real GNP.

Which component of aggregate demand is
most sensitive to monetary policy? Most economists agree that it is investment, including both
business investment and investment in new
houses.

Business investment in new factories and
machinery is sensitive to interest rates for
reasons that have been explained in earlier
chapters.[2] Since the rate of interest that must
be paid on borrowings is one element of the
cost of making an investment, business executives will find investment prospects less attractive as interest rates rise. Therefore, they will
spend less.

Many potential home buyers may be
deterred by high interest rates for similar
reasons. Since the interest costs of a home
mortgage are a major component of the total
cost of owning a home—probably more than
half—fewer families will want to buy a new home
when interest rates are high than when interest
rates are low. Besides this, high interest rates
are bad for home building for a reason that was
mentioned in our discussion of the costs of
inflation in Chapter 6.[3] We observed there that

[2]See, for example, Chapter 8, pages 138–139.
[3]See, in particular, pages 100–102.

usury ceilings on the rates that can be charged on home mortgages, as well as other types of interest-rate ceilings, often have the effect of making mortgages impossible to obtain when interest rates are very high. Without mortgages, there is little home building. We conclude that:

Higher interest rates lead to lower investment spending. But investment (*I*) is a component of aggregate demand (*C* + *I* + *G*). Therefore, when interest rates rise, total spending falls. In terms of the 45° line diagram of previous chapters, a higher interest rate leads to a lower *C* + *I* + *G* schedule. Conversely, a lower interest rate leads to a higher *C* + *I* + *G* schedule.

Figure 13–4 depicts this conclusion graphically.

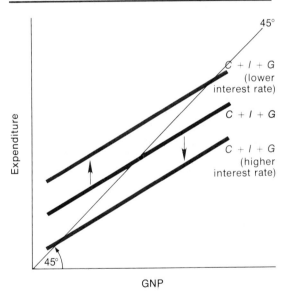

FIGURE 13–4
THE EFFECT OF INTEREST RATES
ON AGGREGATE DEMAND
Because interest rates are an important determinant of investment spending, *I*, the *C* + *I* + *G* schedule shifts whenever the rate of interest changes. Specifically, as shown above, lower interest rates shift the curve upward and higher interest rates shift it downward.

MONETARY POLICY IN THE KEYNESIAN MODEL

The effect that interest rates have on spending provides the mechanism by which monetary policy affects aggregate demand in the Keynesian model. We know from our analysis of the money market in Chapter 12 that monetary policy can have a profound effect on interest rates. Let us, therefore, outline the effect of monetary policy in the Keynesian model.

Suppose the Federal Reserve, seeing the economy stuck with unemployment and a recessionary gap, raises the money supply. We learned in Chapter 12 that this normally would be done by purchasing government securities in the open market, but the specific weapon that the Fed uses is not terribly important for present purposes. What matters is that the money supply (*M*) expands.

With the demand schedule for money (temporarily) fixed, such an increase in the supply of money has the effect that an increase in supply always has in a free market—it lowers the price. In this case, the price is the rate of interest, *r*, so *r* falls.

Next, for reasons we have just outlined, investment spending (*I*) rises in response to the lower interest rates. But, as we learned in Chapter 9, such an autonomous rise in investment kicks off a multiplier chain of increases in output and employment.

Thus, finally, we have completed all the links from the money supply to the level of GNP. In brief, monetary policy works as follows:

A higher money supply leads to lower interest rates, and these lower interest rates encourage investment, which has multiplier effects on GNP.

The process operates equally well in reverse. By contracting the money supply, the Fed can force interest rates up, causing investment spending to fall and pulling down GNP via the multiplier mechanism.

This, in outline form, is how monetary policy operates in the Keynesian analysis. Since the chain of causation is fairly long, the following schematic diagram may help clarify it.

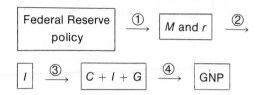

In this causal chain, link 1 indicates that the actions of the Federal Reserve cause money and interest rates to change. Link 2 stands for the effect of interest rates on investment. Link 3 simply notes that investment is one component of aggregate demand. And link 4 is the multiplier, relating an autonomous change in any component of aggregate demand to an ultimate change in GNP. Let us next review what we have learned about each of these links in previous chapters, and, in the process, see what Keynesians must study if they are to estimate the effect of monetary policy. (We already know that monetarists must study velocity.)

Link 1 was the subject of the last chapter, and Figure 13–5 reviews the analysis. Given the initial level of real GNP and prices, the demand schedule for money is shown by curve *MD*. The Fed's expansionary action shifts the supply schedule out from M_0S_0 to M_1S_1, resulting in an increase in the money stock from \$300 billion to \$320 billion in this example and a decline in the interest rate from 6 percent to 5 percent. Thus the first thing a Keynesian economist must know is how sensitive interest rates are to changes in the supply of money.

Link 2 translates the drop in the interest rate into an increase in investment spending (*I*), which we take to be \$50 billion in this example. To estimate this effect in practice, a Keynesian economist must study the sensitivity of investment demand to interest rates.

Link 3 instructs us to enter this \$50 billion rise in *I* as an autonomous shift in the $C + I + G$

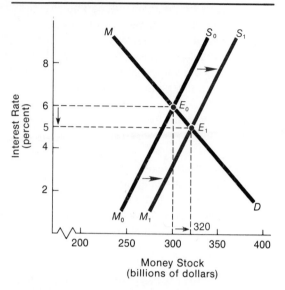

FIGURE 13–5

THE EFFECT OF EXPANSIONARY MONETARY POLICY ON THE MONEY SUPPLY AND RATE OF INTEREST
An expansionary monetary policy pushes the money supply schedule outward from M_0S_0 to M_1S_1, causing equilibrium in the money market to shift from point E_0 to point E_1. The money supply rises from \$300 billion to \$320 billion, while the interest rate falls from 6 percent to 5 percent.

schedule of a 45° line diagram. Figure 13–6 carries out this step. The expenditure schedule rises from $C + I_0 + G$ to $C + I_1 + G$.

Finally, link 4 applies multiplier analysis to this vertical shift in the expenditure schedule in order to predict the eventual increase in GNP. In our examples, we have been using a multiplier of 2.5. Multiplying \$50 billion by 2.5 gives the final effect on GNP—a rise of \$125 billion. This is shown in Figure 13–6 as a shift in equilibrium from E_0 (where GNP is \$2000 billion) to E_1 (where GNP is \$2125 billion). Of course, the size of this multiplier itself must also be estimated. To summarize:

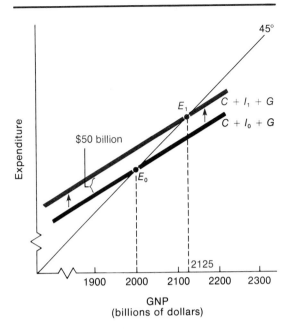

FIGURE 13–6

THE EFFECT OF EXPANSIONARY MONETARY
POLICY ON AGGREGATE DEMAND
Expansionary monetary polices, which lower the rate
of interest, will cause the $C + I + G$ schedule to shift
upward from $C + I_0 + G$ to $C + I_1 + G$, as shown
here. In this example, since the multiplier is 2.5, a $50
billion rise in investment leads, via the multiplier
process, to a $125 billion rise in GNP.

The effect of monetary policy on aggregate
demand depends on the sensitivity of interest
rates to the money supply, on the responsiveness of investment spending to the rate of
interest, and on the size of the multiplier.

MONEY AND THE PRICE LEVEL: THE COMPLETE KEYNESIAN MODEL

One need only recall the inflation of the 1970s
to realize that we have forgotten something.
What happens to the price level? To answer

this, we must simply remember a basic principle
of economics—that prices are determined
jointly by supply and demand. In this case, the
relevant supply is *aggregate supply*, the relevant
demand is *aggregate demand*, and the relevant
price is the overall *price level*.

The analysis of monetary policy that we
have completed so far has shown us how an
increase in the money supply raises the aggregate demand curve, that is, raises the quantity
of output that is demanded *at any given price
level*. But to learn what happens to the price
level and to real output, we must bring aggregate supply into the picture as well.

Specifically, when we considered shifts in
aggregate demand caused by *fiscal* policy in
Chapter 10, we noted that an upsurge in total
spending normally induces firms to increase
output somewhat *and* to raise prices somewhat.
This is just what an aggregate supply curve
shows. Whether prices or real output exhibit the
greater response depends mainly on the degree
of capacity utilization. An economy operating at
full employment has only a limited ability to
increase production; it therefore responds to
greater demand mainly by raising prices. On the
other hand, an economy with a substantial
amount of unemployed labor and unused
capital is able to increase output a great deal
without raising prices.

Now this analysis of output and price
responses applies equally well to monetary
policy or, for that matter, to any other event that
raises aggregate demand. We conclude, then,
that:

Expansionary monetary policy causes some
inflation under normal circumstances. But how
much inflation it causes depends on what state
the economy is in. If the money supply is
expanded when unemployment is high and
there is much unused industrial capacity, then
the result may be little or no inflation. If,
however, increases in the money supply occur
when the economy is fully employed, then the
main result is likely to be inflation.

The effect of a rise in the money supply on the price level is depicted graphically in Figure 13–7, which is one of our aggregate supply and demand diagrams. The curved shape of aggregate supply curve SS reflects the assumptions that output rises with little inflation when the economy is depressed, while prices rise with little gain in output when the economy is near full employment.

In the example we have been using, the Fed's actions raise the money supply by $20 billion, and this increases aggregate demand (through the multiplier) by $125 billion. We enter this in Figure 13–7 as a horizontal shift of $125 billion in the aggregate demand curve, from D_0D_0 to D_1D_1. The diagram shows that this

expansionary monetary policy raises the economy's equilibrium from point E to point B— the price level therefore rises from 100 to 103, or 3 percent. The diagram also shows that real GNP rises by only $100 billion, which is less than the $125 billion stimulus to aggregate demand. The reason, as we know from earlier chapters, is that the rising prices stifle demand.

By including the effect of an increase in the money supply on the price level, we have completed our story about the role of monetary policy in the Keynesian model. We can thus expand our schematic diagram of monetary policy as follows:

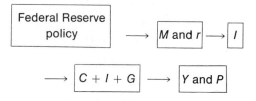

The last link now recognizes that *both* output *and* prices normally are affected by changes in the money supply.

FIGURE 13–7
THE INFLATIONARY EFFECTS OF EXPANSIONARY MONETARY POLICY
Raising the money supply normally causes inflation. When expansionary monetary policy causes the aggregate demand curve to shift outward from D_0D_0 to D_1D_1, the economy's equilibrium shifts from point E to point B. Real output expands (in this case by $100 billion), but prices also rise (in this case by 3 percent).

WHY THE AGGREGATE DEMAND CURVE SLOPES DOWNWARD

Having studied the effect of money on the price level, we are now in a much better position to understand why higher prices reduce aggregate demand, that is, why the aggregate demand curve slopes downward. In earlier chapters, we explained this phenomenon by observing that rising prices reduce the purchasing power of certain assets held by consumers, especially money and government bonds, and that this in turn retards consumption spending. While these observations are true, higher prices have a much more important effect on aggregate demand through a channel that we are now in a position to explain.

Money is demanded primarily to conduct transactions, and we saw in Chapter 12 that a rise in the *average money cost* of each transaction—as a result of a rise in the price level—will increase the demand for money. It simply takes more cash to buy a given quantity of goods at higher prices. This means that when expansionary policy of any kind pushes the price level up, more money will be demanded at any given interest rate. But, if the supply of money is *not* increased, these increases in the quantity of money demanded at any given interest rate must force the cost of borrowing money—the rate of interest—to rise. As we know, such increases in interest rates reduce investment and, hence, reduce aggregate demand. This, then, is the main reason why the economy's aggregate demand curve has a negative slope, meaning that aggregate quantity demanded is lower when prices are higher.

At higher price levels, there is a greater demand for money. Given the money supply, therefore, a higher price level must lead to a higher interest rate. Since high interest rates discourage investment, aggregate demand is lower when the price level is higher. That is, the aggregate demand curve slopes downward to the right.

FISCAL POLICY AND INTEREST RATES

These observations about how the demand for money behaves when aggregate demand changes lead us to an important discovery: They show us that monetary policy is not the only type of policy that affects interest rates.

Fiscal policy also affects interest rates. Specifically, increases in government spending or tax cuts normally push interest rates higher, whereas restrictive fiscal policies normally pull interest rates down.

It is not hard to understand why. Let's see what happens to real output and the price level following, say, a rise in government purchases of goods and services. We learned in Chapter 10 that both real GNP (Y) and the price level (P) rise. But Chapter 12's analysis of the demand for money taught us that rising Y and P pull up the demand for money. With greater demand for money, and no change in supply, the rate of interest must rise. So expansionary fiscal policy raises interest rates.

If the government uses its spending and taxing weapons in the opposite direction, the same process operates in reverse. Falling output and (possibly) falling prices reduce the demand for money. With a given supply of money, equilibrium in the money market leads to a lower interest rate.

The way fiscal policy affects interest rates may not seem to be a very interesting subject; but, in fact, this connection has important implications. In the balance of this chapter we will show that a recognition of the effect of fiscal policy on interest rates (1) opens the way to a complete reconciliation of the Keynesian and monetarist theories of stabilization policy and (2) enables us to understand the so-called "crowding-out" controversy.

RECONCILING THE KEYNESIAN AND MONETARIST VIEWS

We have already come quite a long way toward reconciling the Keynesian and monetarist views of how the economy operates. While Keynesian analysis lends itself naturally to the study of fiscal policy, since G is a part of $C + I + G$, we have just seen that it also provides a powerful and important role for monetary policy. For we know now that an increase in the money supply reduces interest rates, which, in turn, stimulate the demand for investment. Thus, the Keynesian approach provides a role for monetary policy as well as for fiscal policy.

Can the monetarist approach also handle fiscal policy? The fact that fiscal policy affects interest rates shows that it can, even though the equation of exchange, $M \times V$ = nominal GNP, seems to take no account of any role for government spending and taxation. But that role is there. The way it works is that a rise in government spending, for example, can push up the rate of interest. And rising interest rates push up velocity because people want to hold less money when the interest they can earn on alternative assets increases. So it is through the V term in $M \times V$ that fiscal policy does its work in the monetarist framework.

Any of the government policies that a Keynesian would call expansionary—higher spending, lower taxes, and so on—forces interest rates higher, thus increasing V. The equation of exchange, $M \times V$ = nominal GNP, then implies that nominal GNP must rise when government spending increases, even if M is fixed. The given supply of money can finance more transactions when velocity is higher. Conversely, restrictive fiscal policies, like tax rises and expenditure cuts, reduce the demand for money and lower interest rates. The consequent drop in velocity lowers income through the equation of exchange, because the money supply circulates more slowly.

The translation, then, seems to be complete. The Keynesian story about how fiscal policy works can be phrased in the monetarist dialect. And the monetarist tale about monetary policy can be told with a Keynesian accent. Furthermore, both modes of analysis help only to explain the mysteries of aggregate *demand*, and must be supplemented by an analysis of aggregate *supply* to be complete. We must conclude, then, that:

The differences between Keynesians and monetarists have been grossly exaggerated by the news media. Indeed, when it comes to matters of basic economic theory, there are hardly any differences at all.

But this does not mean that Keynesians and monetarists must agree on everything any more than the fact that English prose can be translated into French implies that the English and the French always see eye to eye. There are important differences of emphasis and policy that we will take up in the following chapter.

THE CROWDING-OUT CONTROVERSY

We turn now to the other important consequence of the fact that higher levels of government spending generally lead to higher interest rates. Recall, first, that higher interest rates deter private investment spending. What this means is that when the government raises the G component of $C + I + G$, one of the side effects of its action will be to reduce the I component (by raising interest rates). Consequently, the sum $C + I + G$ will not rise as much as the simple multiplier analysis might suggest. In a word, the surge in government demand (G) discourages some private demand (I).

This phenomenon provides another reason why the oversimplified multiplier formula, $1/(1 - MPC)$, exaggerates the size of the multiplier. Because any rise in G (or, for that matter, any autonomous rise in C or I) pushes interest rates higher, and hence deters some investment spending, the increase in the sum $C + I + G$ is smaller than what the oversimplified multiplier formula predicts.

There is another way of looking at this fact—a way that explains why it is often called the crowding-out effect. Consider what happens in financial markets when the government engages in deficit spending. When it spends more than it takes in through tax revenues, the government must borrow the balance from private citizens. It does this by issuing bonds, and these bonds compete with corporate bonds and other financial instruments for the available supply of funds. When some private savers are persuaded to buy government bonds, there must be fewer funds remaining to invest in private bonds. Thus some private borrowers will get "crowded out" of the financial markets as the government claims an increasing share of the economy's total pool of saving.

Some critics of fiscal policy who have taken this lesson to its illogical extreme argue that each $1 of deficit spending by government crowds out exactly $1 of private spending, so that fiscal policy has no net effect on total demand. In their view, when G rises, I falls by the same amount, so that $C + I + G$ is unchanged. Under normal circumstances, this would not be expected to occur. First, moderate budget deficits will push up interest rates only moderately. Second, the sensitivity of private spending to interest rates is not that great. Even at the higher interest rates that government deficits cause, most corporations will continue to borrow to finance their investments.

Furthermore, there is a counterforce that might be called the crowding-in effect. Deficit spending in time of economic slack presumably quickens the pace of economic activity; that, at least, is its purpose. As the economy expands, businesses will begin to find it both necessary and profitable to add to their capacity in order to meet the greater demands of consumers. Because of this *induced investment,* as we called it in earlier chapters, any increase in G tends to *increase* investment, rather than *decrease* it as predicted by the crowding-out hypothesis. The strength of this crowding-in effect depends on how much additional GNP is stimulated by the government spending (that is, on the size of the multiplier) and on how sensitive investment spending is to the improved profit opportunities that accompany rapid growth in GNP. It is even conceivable that the crowding-in effect could dominate the crowding-out effect, so that investment would rise on balance.

But how can this be true in view of the crowding-out argument? Certainly, if government is borrowing more *and the total pool of saving is fixed,* then private industry must be borrowing less. While this little bit of arithmetic is correct, the fallacy in the strict crowding-out argument comes in supposing that the economy's pool of saving is really fixed. If government deficits succeed in their goal of raising production, there will be more income and therefore more saving. That way *both* government *and* industry can borrow more.

Which effect dominates, crowding out or crowding in? The crowding-out hypothesis stems from the increases in interest rates that deficit spending causes; this is certainly bad for investment. But the crowding-in hypothesis stems from the increases in production and profitability, which are good for investment. Under different sets of circumstances, one or the other force may prove to be stronger.

For example, a report issued by the Congressional Budget Office near the bottom of the Great Recession in June 1975 argued that "on balance . . . it appears likely that more investments would be 'crowded in' by a stimulative fiscal policy than would be 'crowded out,' given the present state of the economy."[4] The report explained that, with so much slack in the economy, a surge in G would very likely lead to a considerable increase in real output because the more buoyant demand would not cause much inflation and, consequently, the multiplier would be large. In terms of our graphical apparatus, the aggregate supply curve would be rather flat when the economy is in the range indicated by Region I in Figure 13–8.

But the same report hastened to add, "The opposite conclusion might well be drawn if resources were more fully employed." This is because the economy would then be operating in the steep portion of Region III of the aggre-

[4]Congressional Budget Office, *Inflation and Unemployment: A Report on the Economy* (Washington, D.C.: U.S. Government Printing Office, June 30, 1975), page 58.

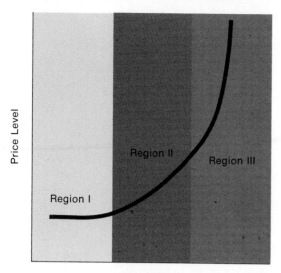

FIGURE 13–8

A TYPICAL AGGREGATE SUPPLY CURVE
The aggregate supply curve depicted here has three
regions. In Region I, output can increase with almost
no change in prices, because there is a great deal of
unused labor and spare industrial capacity; thus the
supply curve is virtually horizontal. In Region III,
resources are more-or-less fully employed, so even
rather small increases in output necessitate substantial
price increases; the supply curve is very steep. Region
II is intermediate between these two extremes.

gate supply curve shown in Figure 13–8, so that
demand stimulation would lead to only limited
gains in real output.[5] If real GNP growth is
minor, then so must be the amount of induced

[5]EXERCISE: Show that any given horizontal shift in the
aggregate demand curve has a smaller effect on real GNP in
Region III than it does in Region I.

investment. The crowding-in effect therefore
would be weak. Instead, government spending
would push up the price level, raise the demand
for cash balances, and crowd out private
borrowers.

Let us summarize what we have learned
about the crowding-out controversy.

SUMMARY

1. The basic argument of the crowding-out
   hypothesis is sound: *Unless there is enough
   additional saving,* more government
   borrowing will force out some private
   borrowers who are discouraged by the high
   interest rates. This will reduce investment
   spending and cancel out some of the expansionary effects of higher government
   spending.
2. This force is very rarely strong enough to
   cancel out the *entire* expansionary thrust of
   government spending, however. Some net
   stimulus to the economy remains.
3. If the deficit spending induces substantial
   growth in GNP, then there will be more
   saving. There might even be so much more
   that private industry could borrow *more* than
   before, despite the greater government
   borrowing.
4. The crowding-out effect is likely to dominate
   when the economy is operating near full
   employment. The crowding-in effect is likely
   to dominate when there is a great deal of
   slack.

We shall have reason to return to this topic in
Chapter 16 when we discuss the so-called
"burden" of the national debt. There we will
learn that whether the national debt is indeed a
burden depends in large measure on the
strength of the crowding-out effect.

SUMMARY

1. Velocity (V) is the ratio of nominal GNP to the stock of money. It indicates how quickly money circulates, that is, how many times money changes hands in a year.
2. If velocity were constant, it would be possible to predict and control nominal GNP by predicting and controlling the supply of money. However, V is not constant.
3. Among the determinants of velocity is the rate of interest (r). At higher interest rates, people find it less attractive to hold money because it pays no interest. Thus, when r rises, money circulates faster, and V rises.
4. Monetarism is a type of national income analysis that focuses attention on velocity and on the money supply (M). Though monetarists realize that V is not constant, they believe that it is predictable enough to make it a useful tool for policy analysis and forecasting.
5. Monetarist and Keynesian analyses are two different ways of studying the determination of aggregate demand. Neither is a complete theory of the behavior of the economy until aggregate supply is brought into the picture.
6. Investment spending (I), including business investment and investment in new homes, is sensitive to interest rates. Specifically, I is lower when r is higher.
7. This fact explains how monetary policy works in the Keynesian model. Raising M leads to lower r; the lower interest rates stimulate more investment spending; and this investment stimulus, via the multiplier, then raises GNP.
8. However, while output rises, prices are also likely to rise. The amount of inflation caused by increasing the money supply depends on the levels of unemployment and of capacity utilization. There will be much inflation when the economy is near full employment, but little inflation when there is a great deal of slack.
9. The main reason why the aggregate demand curve slopes downward is that higher prices increase the demand to hold money in order to finance transactions. Given the money supply, this pushes interest rates up; and this, in turn, discourages investment.
10. Because it raises output and prices, and hence increases the demand for money, expansionary fiscal policy pushes interest rates higher.
11. This is how a monetarist explains the effect of fiscal policy. Because higher r leads to higher velocity, it leads to a higher product $M \times V$ even if M is unchanged.
12. Since government deficit spending forces interest rates higher, it discourages private investment spending. This is called the *crowding-out* effect, and is another reason why the real-world multiplier is less than the oversimplified multiplier formula suggests.
13. But there is also a *crowding-in* effect from higher government spending (G): If expansionary fiscal policy succeeds in raising real output, there will be some induced investment caused by the higher Y.
14. Which effect is stronger, crowding out or crowding in, depends mainly on the state of the economy. When unemployment is high, crowding in probably dominates, so higher G does not cause lower I. But when the

economy is near full employment, the proponents of the crowding-out hypothesis are probably right: High government spending just displaces private investment.

CONCEPTS FOR REVIEW

Velocity
Equation of exchange
Quantity theory of money
Effect of interest rate on velocity
Monetarism
Effect of interest rate on investment

Inflationary effects of monetary policy
Why the aggregate demand curve slopes downward
Effect of fiscal policy on interest rates
Crowding-out effect
Crowding-in effect

QUESTIONS FOR DISCUSSION

1. How much money (including cash and checking account balances) do you typically have at any particular moment? Divide this into your total income over the past 12 months to obtain your own personal velocity. Are you typical of the nation as a whole?

2. Just below you will find data on nominal gross national product and the money supply (M_1 definition) for selected years. Compute velocity in each year. Can you see any trend?

YEAR	NOMINAL GNP (billions of dollars)	MONEY SUPPLY (billions of dollars) (end of year)
1947	233	113
1957	443	136
1967	796	187
1977	1887	337

3. Use the concept of opportunity cost to explain why velocity is higher at higher interest rates.

4. Explain the difference between the "equation of exchange" and "the quantity theory of money." Why is one a theory while the other is not?

5. How does monetarism differ from the quantity theory of money? How does it differ from Keynesian analysis?

6. Explain why both business investments and purchases of new homes are expected to decline when interest rates rise.

7. Explain what a $30 billion increase in the money supply will do to real GNP under the following assumptions:
   a. Each $10 billion increase in the money supply reduces the rate of interest by 1 percentage point.
   b. Each 1 percentage point decline in interest rates stimulates $25 billion of new investment spending.
   c. The expenditure multiplier is 2.
   d. There is so much unemployment that prices do not rise noticeably when demand increases.

8. Explain how your answer to Question 7 would differ if each of the assumptions were changed. Specifically, what sorts of changes in the assumptions would make monetary policy very weak?
9. Explain why the aggregate demand curve has a negative slope.

14

The Keynesian–Monetarist
Debate over Stabilization Policy

Part Three of this text so far has been devoted to constructing a model of the economy that will enable us to understand how stabilization policy works; that is, how government spending, taxation, and the supply of money affect the amount of unemployment and the rate of inflation. Beginning with Chapter 8, and proceeding in steps through Chapter 13, we have developed a fairly comprehensive view of this process.

Our discussion, however, has been almost entirely objective and technical. Because we have sought to understand *how* the national economy works and *how* government policies affect the economy, we have paid little attention to what the government *actually does* or to what it *should do*. We have, in a word, not considered the intense economic and political controversies that surround the conduct of stabilization policy. Chapters 14 through 16 are about precisely these issues. In this chapter, we will explore several of these controversies. The chapter title is derived from the fact that the opponents in these debates typically are groups of economists that the news media have dubbed *Keynesians* and *monetarists*.

We begin the chapter by considering whether it is best to rely on fiscal or monetary policy to stabilize the economy. While one would guess from reading the newspapers that this is the most important bone of contention between Keynesians and monetarists today, we shall see that in fact it is the *least* important. It is unimportant because debating it is futile—the job of stabilizing the economy is so difficult that it is foolish to argue over which of our hands we should tie behind our backs!

Instead, a much more important question will occupy our attention for most of the chapter: Should the government conduct any stabilization policy at all? Everything we have said in earlier chapters seems to indicate that it should. But, as we shall see, there are several important factors that point in the opposite direction—factors that we have not yet considered. These factors lead a number of economists, many of them monetarists, to conclude that it is unwise to try to stabilize the economy through monetary and fiscal policy. One reason for this conclusion is that economists' abilities to forecast the future are rather limited. So our discussion then turns to the techniques and accuracy of economic forecasting.

Finally, we close the chapter by discussing a third major controversy between Keynesians and monetarists: When the authorities stimulate aggregate demand by fiscal or monetary policy, is the main result more likely to be a drop in unemployment or an acceleration of inflation? We shall see that Keynesians take the former position, monetarists take the latter, and that either can be right under the appropriate circumstances.

media: Should the government rely mainly on fiscal or on monetary policy?

As we stressed in the last chapter, the Keynesian and monetarist approaches can be thought of as two different languages. And each language provides a role for *both* fiscal *and* monetary policy. Nonetheless, as is clear by comparing the English with the French, the language that people speak can influence their attitudes about many issues.

Adopting the Keynesian language biases things subtly toward thinking that fiscal policy is very powerful, simply because it acts so directly; that is, because G is a piece of $C + I + G$. By contrast, we have seen that the channels through which fiscal policy affects aggregate demand are quite indirect in the monetarist approach. It is no surprise then that:

Keynesians have historically given primary emphasis to government spending and taxation as the centerpieces of stabilization policy, whereas monetarists have been skeptical.

The roles are reversed in the analysis of monetary policy. To monetarists, the effect of the money supply (M) on aggregate demand is too obvious to be missed—it follows directly from velocity (V) through the equation of exchange: $M \times V$ = nominal GNP. While monetary policy also affects demand in the Keynesian model, the mechanisms are rather complex, and there is obviously room for a slip-up. On these grounds, then:

Some Keynesians have their doubts when monetarists attribute great stabilizing powers to monetary policy.

KEYNESIANS VERSUS MONETARISTS: FISCAL VERSUS MONETARY POLICY

Let us start with the aspect of the Keynesian—monetarist debate over stabilization policy that has received the most attention in the news

LAGS IN FISCAL AND MONETARY POLICY

More important than the issue of which type of policy is more *powerful* is the related question:

Which type of medicine—fiscal or monetary— cures the patient more *quickly?*

In our discussions of fiscal and monetary policy so far, we have ignored such subtle questions of timing and proceeded as if the authorities instantly noticed the need for stabilization policy, decided upon a course of action, and administered the appropriate medicine. In reality, each of these steps is time consuming. First, delays in data collection and processing mean that the latest macroeconomic data always refer to the economy as it was a few months ago. Second, one of the prices of democracy is that the government often takes a good deal of time to decide what should be done, to muster the necessary political support, and to put its decisions into effect. Finally, our $2 trillion economy is a bit like a sleeping elephant—it reacts rather sluggishly to moderate fiscal and monetary prods. As it turns out, these lags in stabilization policy, as they are called, play a pivotal role in the choice between fiscal and monetary policy. It is not hard to see why.

The main policy tool for manipulating consumer spending (C) is the personal income tax, and Chapter 7 documented why the fiscal policy planner can feel fairly secure that each $1 of tax reduction will lead to about 90 to 95 cents of additional spending *eventually.* But not all of this will happen at once. First consumers must learn about the tax change. Then more time may elapse before many consumers are convinced that the change is permanent. Finally, there is the simple force of habit: Households need time to adjust their spending habits when circumstances change. For all these reasons, consumers may increase their spending by only 30 to 50 cents for each $1 of additional income within the first few months after a tax cut. Only gradually, over a period of perhaps several years, will they raise their spending until they are finally consuming 90 to 95 cents of each additional dollar of income.

Lags are much longer for investment (I), which, while it also can be influenced by fiscal policy (tax incentives), provides the main vehicle by which monetary policy affects aggregate demand. Planning for capacity expansion in a large corporation is a long drawn-out process. Ideas must be submitted and approved. Plans must be drawn up, funding acquired, orders for machinery or contracts for new construction placed. And most of this occurs *before* any appreciable amount of money is spent. Economists have found that most of the response of investment to changes in interest rates or tax provisions is delayed for several years.

This last fact—that C responds more quickly than I—has important implications for the multiplier effects of alternative stabilization policies. The reason is that the most common varieties of fiscal policy affect aggregate demand either directly (G is a component of C + I + G) or work through consumption with a relatively short lag, while monetary policy has its major effects on investment. Therefore:

Conventional types of fiscal policy actions, such as changes in G or in income taxes, probably affect aggregate demand much more promptly than does monetary policy.

Notice that the statement says nothing about which instrument is more *powerful.* It simply asserts that the fiscal weapon, whether it is stronger or weaker, acts more *quickly.*

This important fact has been used to build a case that fiscal policy should bear the major burden of economic stabilization. But before you jump to such a conclusion, you should realize that the sorts of lags we have been discussing are not the only ones affecting the timing of stabilization policy.

Apart from these lags in expenditure, which are beyond the control of the policymakers, there are further lags that are due to the behavior of the policymakers themselves! We are referring here to the delays that occur while the policymakers are studying the state of the economy, contemplating what steps they should take, and putting their decisions into effect. And here most observers believe that monetary policy has an important edge; that is:

Policy lags are normally shorter for monetary policy than for fiscal policy.

The reasons for this are fairly apparent. The Federal Open Market Committee (FOMC) meets routinely once each month and can be called together more frequently than this when circumstances warrant it. Thus monetary policy decisions are made every month and, once the FOMC decides on a course of action, it normally can be executed within a few days by buying or selling bonds on the open market.

Contrast this with fiscal policy. Federal budgeting procedures operate on a one-year budget cycle. Except in rare circumstances, then, *major* fiscal policy initiatives that affect spending can only occur at the time of the annual budget.[1] Tax laws can be changed at any time, but the wheels of Congress grind slowly and it may take many months before Congress acts on a presidential request to change taxes. In sum, one has to be very optimistic to suppose that important fiscal policy actions can be taken on short notice.[2]

Where does the combined effect of expenditure lags and policy lags leave us? With nothing conclusive, we are afraid. As one economist put it, the debate over whether the nation should rely only on monetary policy or only on fiscal policy is a bit like arguing whether a safe car is one with good headlights or one with good brakes. It is not very wise to venture out unless you have both.

[1]Some minor budget changes, like speeding up or slowing down the rate at which previously appropriated funds are spent, can be accomplished by executive order.

[2]In a near-crisis atmosphere just before the bottom of the 1974–1975 downswing, Congress modified President Ford's request and enacted a tax cut in little more than 2 months. It thus showed that it *can* act quickly when the need is apparent. The question is whether it *will* act quickly. In 1967–1968, for example, President Johnson's request for a tax rise was bottled up for 1½ years in Congress.

KEYNESIANS VERSUS MONETARISTS: SHOULD THE GOVERNMENT INTERVENE?

During the 1960s and early 1970s the choice between fiscal and monetary policy dominated the debate between the more partisan Keynesians and monetarists. Extreme monetarists claimed that fiscal policy was futile, while extreme Keynesians countered that monetary policy was useless. But during the 1970s accumulating evidence made each extreme view seem less and less tenable. More and more monetarists had to admit that fiscal policy did affect output and prices, and at least *could* be put into action promptly. More and more Keynesians had to concede the same to monetary policy. By 1976, two economists surveying the debate could write that "the shift has been so great that we wonder whether anything more than machismo and habit propels the controversy today." While echoes of this battle are occasionally heard today, they sound more like quaint relics of the past than like live issues.

But the Keynesian–monetarist battles did not end there. As the proponents of the views that either fiscal policy or monetary policy did not matter gave up the fight, the two schools of thought regrouped along new, and more productive, battle lines. One major controversy nowadays is about whether the government should conduct *any* stabilization policy at all, be it a monetary or a fiscal stabilization policy.

This argument is not surprising given the political differences between these adversaries. As it happens, monetarists tend to be conservative politically and Keynesians tend to be liberal, which explains why the two schools differ markedly in the degree to which they think the government should try to manage the economy.

Monetarists point to the uncertainties that surround the operation of both fiscal and monetary policies—uncertainties that we have stressed repeatedly in earlier chapters. Will the

257

Fed's actions have the desired effects on the money supply? What will these actions do to interest rates? How will they affect spending, and how long will it take before the effects will appear? Can fiscal policy actions be taken promptly? Will consumers view tax changes as temporary or permanent? How large is the expenditure multiplier? The list could go on and on.

Monetarists look at this formidable catalogue of difficulties, add a dash of skepticism about our ability to forecast the future state of the economy,[3] and conclude that stabilization policy is likely to do more harm than good. They advise both the fiscal and monetary authorities to pursue a passive policy rather than an active one—adhering to *fixed rules* that, while they will not iron out all the bumps in the economy's growth path, will at least keep it roughly on track in the long run.

Keynesians, though they admit that perfection is unattainable, are much *more optimistic* about the possibility of achieving a successful stabilization policy. And they are much *less optimistic* than the monetarists about how smoothly the economy would function in the absence of demand management. They therefore advocate discretionary increases in government spending (or decreases in taxes) and more rapid growth of the money supply when the economy has a recessionary gap, and less of each when it has an inflationary gap. By this policy mix, they believe, government can keep the economy closer to its full-employment growth path.

Naturally, each side can point to evidence that buttresses its own view. Keynesians like to look back with pride at the tax cut of 1964 and the sustained period of economic growth that it helped usher in. They also point to the tax cut of 1975, which was enacted just about at the trough of our worst postwar recession. Monetarists remind us of the government's refusal to curb what was obviously a situation of runaway demand during the 1966–1968 Vietnam buildup,

[3]Economic forecasting is discussed later in this chapter.

and of the failure of the 1968 tax increase to do the job even after it was enacted. They also find many historical instances when the Fed's actions seem to have been destabilizing. If it demonstrates anything, the record of history shows that there have been many instances where appropriate stabilization policy *could have been* helpful but instead the authorities either took inappropriate steps or did nothing at all.

Let us, therefore, look more closely at the question of whether the government should adopt passive rules or attempt an activist stabilization policy. As we shall see, the lags we have just been discussing play a pivotal role in the debate.

LAGS AND THE RULES-VERSUS-DISCRETION DEBATE

The reason that lags lead to a fundamental difficulty for stabilization policy—a difficulty so formidable that it has led many economists to conclude that attempts to stabilize economic activity are likely to do more harm than good—can be explained best by reference to Figure 14–1. Here we plot the behavior of both actual and potential GNP over the course of a business cycle in a hypothetical economy in which no stabilization policy is attempted. At point *A*, the economy begins to slip into a recession and does not recover to full employment until point *D*. Then, between points *D* and *E*, it overshoots and is in an inflationary boom.

The usual case for stabilization policy runs like this. The recession is recognized to be a serious problem at point *B*, and appropriate actions are taken. These have their major effects around point *C* and thus curb both the depth and length of the recession.

But suppose the lags are really much longer than this. Suppose, for example, that policy lags delay policy actions until point *C* (roughly, the

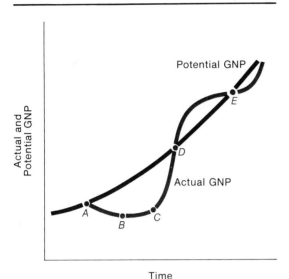

FIGURE 14–1

A TYPICAL BUSINESS CYCLE

This is a stylized representation of the relationship between actual and potential GNP during a typical business cycle. The imaginary economy slips into a recession at point *A*, bottoms out at point *C*, and is in a recovery period until point *D*. After point *D*, it enters an inflationary boom that lasts until point *E*.

bottom of the recession) and that expenditure lags are so long that the major effects of stimulative policies are not felt until after point *D*. Then policy will be of little help during the recession, and will be actually harmful during the ensuing boom.

In the presence of long lags, attempts at stabilizing the economy can actually succeed in destabilizing it.

Because of this, some economists—most notably Milton Friedman—have argued that we are better off letting the economy alone and relying on automatic stabilizers and the economy's natural self-corrective mechanism to cure recessions and inflations. Instead of embarking on periodic programs of monetary

and fiscal stimulus or restraint, they advise policymakers to stick to *fixed rules,* that is, to rigid formulas that ignore current economic events.

The rule most emphasized by monetarists—that the Fed keep the money supply growing at a fixed rate—was discussed in Chapter 12. The corresponding rule for fiscal policy—that the government keep the so-called full-employment budget in balance—needs some explanation.

DEFINITION

The *full-employment budget* is the hypothetical budget we *would have* if the economy were operating at full employment.

When the economy is below full employment, actual tax receipts will be lower than those counted in the full-employment budget because people have lower incomes. At the same time, expenditures on unemployment compensation and other transfer programs will be higher. Thus, if the full-employment budget is balanced, the actual budget will show more spending than receipts—a budget deficit.

When the economy is operating above full employment, the reverse is true. A balanced full-employment budget will mean that there is a surplus in the actual budget.

According to this rule, the federal government should decide how much to spend on goods and services and then set tax and transfer laws so that the budget *would be* balanced any time the full-employment level of national income was reached. These policy settings should then be adhered to regardless of the behavior of the economy, except in emergencies. If GNP falls below full employment, falling tax receipts and rising transfer payments provide an automatic cushion for disposable income. And if income booms beyond full employment, the corresponding budget surplus automatically siphons off some of the aggregate demand.

Thus, advocates of this rule *do* recommend deficit spending during recessions, but only the limited kinds of deficits that arise *automatically* from falling tax receipts and rising transfer payments. They *do not* recommend deliberate *discretionary* increases in the deficit through tax cuts or increases in federal spending. But neither do they recommend old-fashioned budget balancing.

A quick glance at the postwar record of budget policy shows that the government has certainly *not* adhered to anything like such a rule in practice. Figure 14–2 traces the behavior of both the full-employment budget and the actual budget since 1955. You will notice that the full-employment budget was typically in

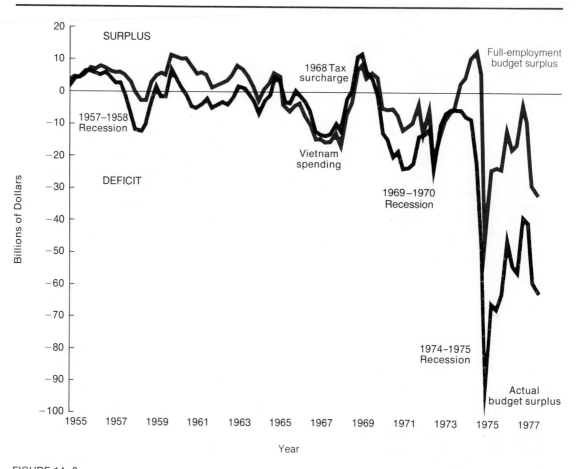

FIGURE 14–2

FULL-EMPLOYMENT AND ACTUAL BUDGET SURPLUSES, 1955–1977

The black line charts the behavior of the surplus (positive numbers) or deficit (negative numbers) in the federal government budget. The red line charts the behavior of the full-employment surplus, which, instead of subtracting actual government spending from actual tax collections, subtracts full-employment spending from full-employment tax receipts. Both budget concepts frequently have shown deficits, though this is much more true of the actual budget than it is of the full-employment budget.

Source: Council of Economic Advisers.

surplus during the decade from 1955 to 1965, although the actual budget often exhibited a deficit. Then the full-employment budget swung into deficit under pressure from heavy spending on the Vietnam War, only to return (briefly) to a surplus position after the income tax surcharge of 1968. Since 1970, the actual budget has been continually in deficit. The full-employment budget has also typically shown a deficit (though a much smaller one), but in 1974 and early 1975 there was a full-employment surplus.

STABILIZATION POLICY: DISCRETIONARY MEASURES OR FIXED RULES?

Would it have been better to rely on rules and automatic stabilizers? As usual, the answer depends on many factors.

How Fast Does the Economy's Self-Correcting Mechanism Work?

We stressed in Chapter 8 that the economy does have a self-correcting mechanism. If the economy could cure recessions and inflations very quickly by itself, then the case for intervention is weak. For if such problems typically last only a short time, then lags in discretionary stabilization policy mean that the medicine will often have its major effects only after the disease is over. (In terms of Figure 14–1, this would be a case where point D comes very close to point A.) While the more extreme advocates of rules argue that this is what indeed happens, most economists agree that the economy's self-correcting mechanism is slow and not terribly reliable, even when supplemented by the automatic stabilizers. On this count, then, a point is scored for discretionary policy.

How Long Are the Lags in Stabilization Policy?

As we explained, long lags before stabilization measures are adopted or can take effect make it unlikely that policy can do much good, while short lags point in the other direction. Thus, advocates of fixed rules emphasize the length of lags while proponents of discretion discount them. Who is really right depends on the circumstances. In the most optimistic scenario, fiscal policy actions are taken promptly, and the economy feels much of the stimulus from expansionary policy in less than a year after slipping into a recession. While far from an instant cure, these actions certainly are felt soon enough to do a lot of good. But, as we have seen, more pessimistic scenarios raise the possibility that policy may actually be destabilizing. No general conclusion can be drawn.

How Accurate Are Economic Forecasts?

One way to cut down the policy-making lag enormously is to have good economic forecasts. If we could see a recession coming a full year ahead of time (which we certainly *cannot* do), even a rather slow-acting policy response would still be timely. (In terms of Figure 14–1, this would be a case where the coming recession is predicted well before point A arrives.) Techniques of economic forecasting are considered later in this chapter. It is sufficient to say here that forecasts leave a lot of room for improvement. On balance, the record of economic forecasters probably shows a point scored for the advocates of fixed rules.

In trying to strike a balance among all of these factors, one's basic view of the economy is very important. Some economists believe that the economy, if left unmanaged, would generate a series of ups and downs that are hard to predict, but that it would correct each of them by itself in a relatively short period of time. They conclude that, because of long lags and poor forecasts, our ability to anticipate whether the economy will be heading up or down by the time policy actions have their effects is quite limited. And so they are led to advocate fixed rules.

By contrast, other economists liken the economy to a giant glacier with a great deal of inertia. This means that if we observe an inflationary or recessionary gap today, it is likely still to be there a year or two from now because the self-correcting mechanism is so slow. In such a world, accurate forecasting is not imperative, even if policy lags are long. If we base policy on a forecast of a $100 billion gap between actual and potential GNP a year from now, and the gap turns out to be only $50 billion, then we still will have done the right thing despite the horrible forecast. Holders of this view of the economy, then, are likely to advocate the use of discretionary policy.

While there is no consensus on this issue either among economists or among politicians, a prudent view might be that:

The case for active discretionary policy is very strong when the economy has a serious deficiency or excess of aggregate demand. However, advocates of fixed rules are right that it would be foolish to try to iron out every little wiggle in the growth path of GNP.

OTHER DIMENSIONS OF THE RULES-VERSUS-DISCRETION DEBATE

While lags and forecasting play major roles in the debate between advocates of rules and advocates of discretionary policy, these are not the only battlegrounds.

One bogus argument that is nonetheless quite often heard is that an activist fiscal policy must inevitably lead to a growing public sector. Since proponents of fixed rules tend also to be opponents of big government, they view this as

undesirable. Of course, others think that a large public sector is just what society needs. This argument is, however, completely beside the point, as we pointed out first in the list of Ideas for Beyond the Final Exam in Chapter 1 and then in Chapter 10 (page 191).

One's opinion about the proper size of government should have nothing to do with one's view on stabilization policy.

When recessions occur, advocates of big government can call for greater spending while advocates of small government can insist on tax cuts. Similarly, if there is a demand-induced inflation, we can make the public sector smaller by cutting expenditures or bigger by raising taxes. While such choices may be quite momentous from other points of view, they simply do not bear on the question of whether we should fight the recession or the inflation.

Advocates of rules are on stronger ground when they argue that frequent changes in tax laws, government spending programs, or monetary conditions will make it difficult for firms and consumers to formulate and carry out rational plans. They argue that by adhering to fixed rules, which are known to businesses and consumers, the authorities can provide a more stable environment for the private sector.

While no one disputes that a stable environment is good for private planning, supporters of discretionary policy point out the difference between stability in the government budget (or in Federal Reserve operations) and stability in the economy. The goal of discretionary policy is to help *prevent* gyrations in the pace of economic activity by *causing* timely gyrations in the government budget (or in monetary policy). Which atmosphere is better for business, they ask, one in which fiscal and monetary rules keep things peaceful on Capitol Hill and at the Federal Reserve System while recessions and inflations rack the economy, or one in which policy instruments are changed abruptly on occasion but the economy grows more steadily? They think that the answer is self-evident.

A final argument used by advocates of rules is of a political rather than an economic nature. Fiscal policy, they note, is decided upon by elected politicians: the president and members of Congress. At least when elections are on the horizon (and for members of the House of Representatives they *always* are), these men and women are likely to be at least as concerned with keeping their offices as with doing what is right for the economy. This leaves fiscal policy subject to all sorts of "political manipulations," meaning that inappropriate actions may be taken to attain short-run political goals. In a system of purely automatic stabilization, its proponents argue, a rule of law would replace the rule of men, and this peril would be eliminated.

There is certainly a *possibility* that politicians could deliberately *cause* economic instability to help their own reelection—a possibility we will examine in Chapter 16. And some observers of these "political business cycles" have claimed that several American presidents have taken full advantage of the opportunity. Furthermore, even if there is no pernicious intent, politicians may take the wrong actions for perfectly honorable reasons; decisions in the political arena are never clear-cut. It certainly is easy to find examples of grievous errors in the history of U.S. fiscal policy. So, taken as a whole, the political argument against discretionary policy seems to have a great deal of merit.

But what are we to do about it? Because policy actions that help on the employment front normally do harm on the inflation front, and vice versa, the "correct" policy action is almost always an inherently political matter. It is foolhardy to believe that such decisions could or should be made by a group of objective and nonpartisan technicians. Steering the economy is not like steering a rocket to the moon. In a political democracy, if we take decisions on economic policy out of the hands of elected officials, there are no other hands into which we can put them.

This harsh fact may seem worrisome in view of the possibilities for political chicanery, but it should not bother us any more (or any less) than similar maneuvering in other areas of policy making. After all, the same thing applies to international relations, issues of national defense, formulation and enforcement of the law, and so on. Politicians make all these decisions for us, subject to only sporadic accountability at election times. Why should economic decisions be any different? To summarize:

The question of whether the government should take an active hand in managing the economy, which is one of the main bones of contention between Keynesians and monetarists today, is as much a matter of ideology as of economics. Liberals have always looked to government activism to solve social problems, while conservatives have consistently pointed out that many efforts of government fail despite the best of intentions.

Because of its political nature, we suspect that this disagreement will continue for some time, and that this is one area where consensus in the Keynesian—monetarist debate is a long way off.

ECONOMIC FORECASTING: THE USE OF ECONOMETRIC MODELS

Because a successful stabilization policy requires at least a modicum of forecasting accuracy, economists in universities, government agencies, and private businesses have, over the course of many years, developed a variety of techniques—none of them foolproof—to assist them in predicting the future economic situation.

Among the most widely publicized forecasts are those generated by the use of an econometric model of the economy. Put simply, an econometric model is merely a mathematical version of the models of macroeconomic activity that we have been describing throughout Part Three. The difference is that the basic notions are cast in the form of mathematical equations rather than in diagrams. For example, our consumption function could have been expressed by the standard formula:

$$C = a + b\,DI$$

where C is consumer spending and DI is disposable income, instead of by a graph.[4]

The builder of an econometric model takes equations like these and uses actual data to estimate the sizes of a and b. For example, statistical analysis may lead a forecaster to the conclusion that the correct magnitude of a in the previous formula is approximately 100 and that the most reasonable value of b is 0.8. Then the consumption function formula is

$$C = 100 + 0.8\,DI$$

This says that consumer spending is $100 (billion) plus 80 percent of disposable income. The economist can complete his model by adding a definition of disposable income as GNP minus tax receipts:

$$DI = Y - T$$

and appending the fact that GNP is the sum of C, I, and G:

$$Y = C + I + G$$

In this simple model, then, we have a total of three equations. If we hypothesize that government purchases, tax receipts, and investment are all unaffected by the relationships in the model, these three equations are just enough to

[4]This is nothing but the formula for a straight line with a slope of b and an intercept of a.

determine the values of the three remaining variables: C, DI, and Y. These last three variables are called the model's *endogenous variables,* meaning that their values are determined *inside* the model. The remaining variables—G, T, and I—are called the model's *exogenous variables* because they must be provided from outside the model.

With this nomenclature, it is easy to describe how the user of an econometric model forecasts the state of the economy.

An econometric forecaster uses a model to transform forecasts of the exogenous variables into corresponding forecasts of the endogenous variables.

Models actually used for forecasting the U.S. economy have hundreds of variables and equations. Because of their complexity, the only practical way to solve them for forecasts of all the endogenous variables is to use a high-speed computer. But you can understand what is going on inside these baffling machines if you can follow the illustrative example that is worked out in the boxed insert on the opposite page. The mechanics are that simple.

But making the forecast accurate is not simple because of the "garbage in, garbage out" problem: If you feed junk into the computer, that's exactly what will come out at the end. In the forecasting context, this "junk" could be either a bad set of predictions of the exogenous variables or an inaccurate set of equations. This is why model builders are constantly seeking to improve their equations. But they have yet to achieve anything like perfection. And, even if they did, their forecasts would still not be infallible because there is a certain amount of unavoidable randomness in macroeconomic behavior. After all, we are dealing with literally millions of individuals and business firms. So the forecasts of the exogenous variables are bound to be wide of the mark at times.

Forecasting with an Econometric Model

Modern econometric models of the whole economy are giants that defy description. But their basic logic is simple enough that we can illustrate their use through our example of a model with only three equations:

$$C = 100 + 0.8\,DI \qquad (1)$$
$$DI = Y - T \qquad (2)$$
$$Y = C + I + G \qquad (3)$$

To obtain a forecast for the GNP, Y, we must first solve the equations for Y. It may seem at first that the last equation already gives us what we want. However, since the first two equations tell us that C also depends on Y, we actually have a situation in which Y appears on both sides of the equation. We therefore must collect terms to bring all the Ys together.

If we substitute the first two equations into equation (3), we get:

$$Y = \quad C \quad\quad + I + G$$

$$= 100 + 0.8DI \quad + I + G \qquad \text{[from equation (1)]}$$

$$= 100 + 0.8(Y - T) + I + G \qquad \text{[from equation (2)]}$$

$$= 100 + 0.8Y - 0.8T + I + G$$

Subtracting $0.8Y$ from both sides gives:

$$0.2Y = 100 - 0.8T + I + G,$$

and dividing by 0.2 gives:

$$Y = \frac{100 + I + G - 0.8T}{0.2}$$

The solution for Y can then be written as:

$$\boxed{Y = 500 + 5I + 5G - 4T}$$

This last equation, which we have set off in a box, is our desired result. Given forecasts of I, G, and T, it enables us to forecast GNP. For example, if we expect I to be \$300 billion, G to be \$400 billion, and T to be \$500 billion, then our GNP forecast is:

$$Y = 500 + (5 \times 300) + (5 \times 400) - (4 \times 500)$$
$$= 500 + 1500 + 2000 - 2000$$
$$= \$2000 \text{ billion}$$

OTHER TECHNIQUES OF ECONOMIC FORECASTING[5]

Leading Indicators

A second forecasting method, pioneered at the National Bureau of Economic Research, exploits observed historical timing relationships through the use of leading indicators.

DEFINITION
A *leading indicator* is a variable that, experience has shown, normally turns down before recessions start and turns up before expansions get started. Leading indicators give advance warning of future economic events.

For example, the stock market is often considered to be a leading indicator because stock market downturns normally begin several months before downturns in industrial production. *Why* is this happening? Is it the decline in the stock market that causes economic downturns by reducing consumer spending? Or are both the stock market and industrial production just reacting to some other influence, with the stock market's reaction coming sooner? Certainly these are fascinating questions. But, the answers may not be crucial to a forecaster *if* the stock market continues to be as good a leading indicator for industrial production in the future as it has been in the past. In that event, we will be able to make use of the observed relationship between stock prices and industrial production for forecasting even if we do not entirely understand its origins.

As it turns out, however, excessive reliance on any single leading indicator produces a very unimpressive forecasting record. An obvious solution is to look at many indicators; but once we start to do this, we will often receive conflicting signals. If one indicator is rising

[5]This section is adapted from Alan S. Blinder, *Fiscal Policy in Theory and Practice* (Morristown, N.J.: General Learning Press, 1973).

rapidly while another is falling, what are we to do? One way to resolve this conflict is to form an average of several leading indicators. For example, the Commerce Department publishes a composite index that is a weighted average of 12 of their leading indicators. Figure 14–3 compares the behavior of this index with movements in real GNP. As you can see, the agreement is usually quite good. The leading indicators occasionally call for a recession that never comes (as in 1956), and occasionally they give clear early warning signals of a downturn (as in 1969 and 1973). But normally the leading indicators follow movements in real gross national product so closely that the leads are too short to be of much use to policymakers.

Survey Data

A third source of information that is used by many forecasters is periodic surveys of the intentions of business and consumers. The Bureau of Economic Analysis of the Commerce Department and the Securities and Exchange Commission regularly ask firms how much money they plan to invest in factories and machinery over the next 3 to 12 months. These data are published in the financial press and are widely used by economists in industry, government, and academia. The Survey Research Center of the University of Michigan regularly conducts a survey of how consumers feel about both their personal finances and the general state of the economy. Some economists have found that this information on consumer sentiment helps improve forecasts of consumer spending.

Judgmental Forecasters

This term is used to describe those desperate (and probably prudent!) forecasters who refuse to rely on any one method, but look instead at every scrap of evidence they can get their hands on. They study the outputs of the econometric models; they watch the leading indicators; and they scrutinize the findings of surveys. At times, it seems, they even gaze at the stars! In any case, judgmental forecasters distill all this information in their heads and somehow arrive at a forecast of GNP and other key variables. How do they go about it? An outside observer can never really tell, since the very nature of judgmental forecasting precludes the existence of a formula that can be written down or described.

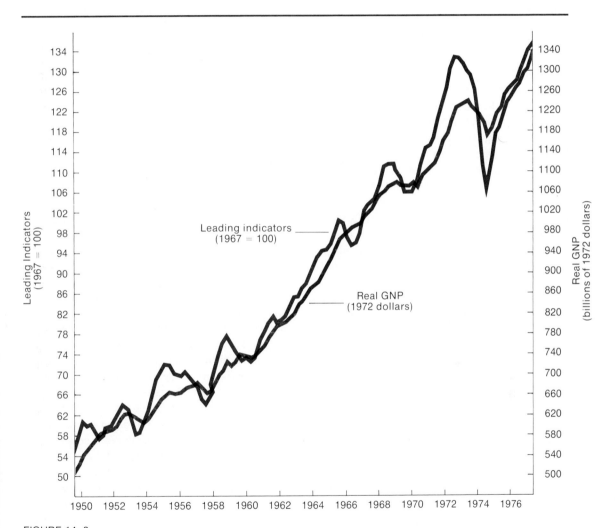

FIGURE 14–3

REAL GNP AND THE LEADING INDICATORS, 1950–1977

This diagram compares the path of the leading indicators (in red) with that of real GNP (in black). The scales have been adjusted to make the two series comparable. It can be seen that the leading indicators sometimes give advance warning of a turning point in economic activity (for example, in 1973) but often give false signals of turning points that never occur (for example, 1956).

Source: *Business Conditions Digest* and *Survey of Current Business*.

THE ACCURACY OF ECONOMIC FORECASTS

Which method wins the prize for the most accurate forecasts? First, no technique is clearly superior all the time. If it were, no one would do it any other way. Second, because econometric forecasters use surveys, lead-lag patterns, and judgment in forming their predictions of exogenous variables, and since judgmental forecasters watch the models, a clean comparison is impossible. In recent years, however, it seems that the most accurate forecasts have been derived by judgmental adjustment of forecasts from econometric models.

How accurate are economic forecasts? That depends both on the variable being forecast (consumption is easier than investment) and on the time period (the first half of the 1970s were tough years for forecasters; the last half has been much easier). To give a rough idea of magnitudes, forecasts of the annual inflation rate for a particular year made late in the preceding year typically erred by 2 to 4 percentage points during the turbulent years 1973 and 1974. This, however, was probably the worst period for forecasters. In more recent years, most inflation forecasts have come within a single percentage point of being correct. Forecasts of real GNP for the coming year made during the 1970s typically erred by between $\frac{1}{2}$ and 1 percent.[6]

Is this record good enough? That depends on what the forecasts are used for. It is certainly not good enough to support so-called "fine tuning," that is, attempts to keep the economy always within a hair's breadth of full employment. But it probably is good enough if our interest in using discretionary stabilization policy is to close persistent and sizable gaps between actual and potential GNP.

[6]Stephen K. McNees, "An Assessment of the Council of Economic Advisers' Forecast of 1977," *New England Economic Review*, March–April 1977, pages 3–7.

KEYNESIANS VERSUS MONETARISTS: THE AGGREGATE SUPPLY CURVE

A third, and final, major battleground of the Keynesian–monetarist controversy today is over the shape of the economy's aggregate supply schedule. We pointed out in the last chapter that aggregate supply is not an integral part of either the Keynesian or the monetarist approach. Nonetheless, most Keynesians tend to think of the aggregate supply curve as fairly flat in the short run, as in Figure 14–4(a), so that large increases in output can be achieved with rather little inflation. Monetarists, in contrast, picture the supply curve as quite steep, as in Figure 14–4(b), so that prices are very responsive to changes in output. The differences for public policy, as we shall see, are substantial.

In the Keynesian view, expansionary fiscal or monetary policy that raises the aggregate demand schedule can buy large gains in real GNP at little cost in terms of inflation. This is shown in Figure 14–5(a), where a stimulation of demand leads to a substantial rise in output with only a pinch of inflation. Conversely, a restrictive stabilization policy will not be an effective way to cure inflation; instead, it will serve mainly to reduce real output, as Figure 14–5(b) shows.

The monetarists see things differently. To them, the aggregate supply curve is so steep that expansionary fiscal or monetary policies are likely to cause a good deal of inflation without adding much to the real GNP [see Figure 14–6(a)]. Similarly, contractionary policies are effective ways of bringing down the price level, without much of a sacrifice of real output [see Figure 14–6(b)].

The resolution of this debate is of fundamental importance for the proper conduct of stabilization policy. If the Keynesian view is right, stabilization policy is much more effective at combating recession than inflation. If the

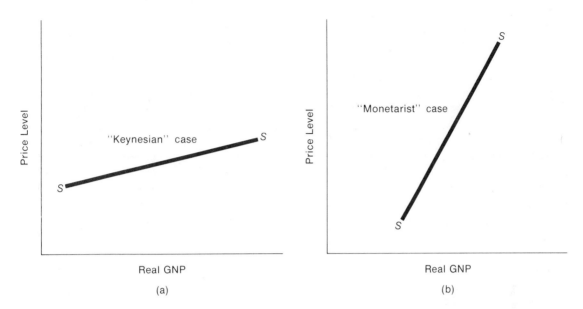

FIGURE 14–4

ALTERNATIVE VIEWS OF THE AGGREGATE SUPPLY CURVE

Keynesians tend to think of the economy's aggregate supply schedule as very flat, as in part (a), whereas monetarists tend to think of it as rather steep, as in part (b).

monetarist view is correct, the reverse is true.
While the debate over aggregate supply is even
less settled than that over aggregate demand,
the dim outline of a consensus view seems to be
emerging. This view stresses that the steepness
of the aggregate supply schedule depends on
the degree of slack in the economy.

If industry has a great deal of spare
capacity, then increases in demand will not call
forth large price increases. Similarly, when
many workers are unemployed, employment can
rise without causing much acceleration in the
rate at which wages are growing. In a word, the
aggregate supply curve is quite flat.

On the other hand, when businesses are
producing near capacity and unemployment is
near the frictional level, greater demand for

goods will induce firms to raise prices; and
greater demand for labor will push wages up
faster. In brief, the aggregate supply schedule
will be steep.

Figure 14–7 shows a version of the aggregate supply curve that embodies these ideas. It
has the same general shape as most of the
supply curves that we have used in this book. At
low levels of GNP, like Y_1, it is nearly horizontal;
then its slope starts to rise gradually until at very
high levels of GNP, like Y_2, it becomes almost
vertical. The implication is that any change in
aggregate demand will have most of its effect on
output when economic activity is slack (the
Keynesian case) but on *prices* when the
economy is operating near full employment (the
monetarist case). In summary:

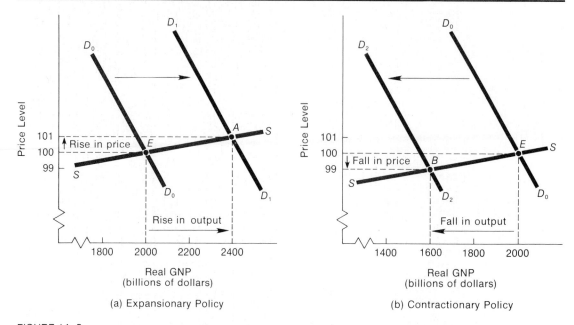

(a) Expansionary Policy

(b) Contractionary Policy

FIGURE 14–5

STABILIZATION POLICY WITH A FLAT AGGREGATE SUPPLY CURVE: THE KEYNESIAN CASE
These two diagrams show that stabilization policy is much more effective as an antirecession policy than as an anti-inflation policy when the aggregate supply curve is very flat. In part (a), monetary or fiscal policies push the aggregate demand curve outward from D_0D_0 to D_1D_1, causing equilibrium to shift from point E to point A. It can be seen that output rises substantially (from $2000 billion to $2400 billion), while prices rise only slightly (from 100 to 101, or 1 percent). So the policy is quite successful. In part (b), contractionary policies are used to combat inflation by pushing the aggregate demand curve inward from D_0D_0 to D_2D_2. Prices do fall slightly (from 100 to 99) as equilibrium shifts from point E to point B, but real output falls much more dramatically (from $2000 billion to $1600 billion); so the policy has had little success. Keynesians tend to believe in this case.

Keynesians believe that the aggregate supply curve is rather *flat* in many circumstances, especially when the economy is operating at low levels of resource utilization. They therefore stress the effects of demand management on output, and belittle the effects on prices.

Monetarists believe that the aggregate supply curve is rather *steep* in many circumstances, especially when the economy has little slack. They therefore emphasize the effects of demand management on prices, and belittle the effects on real output.

A middle-of-the-road view would hold that the Keynesian case is quite strong when there is

a great deal of unemployment, while the monetarist case is stronger when the economy is near full employment.[7]

Thus the nature of the trade-off between output gains (which reduce unemployment) and inflation, as embodied in the slope of the aggregate supply schedule, plays a fundamental role in the design of an appropriate stabilization policy. We explore this trade-off in the following chapter.

[7]Recall from the last chapter that the shape of the aggregate supply schedule also plays a pivotal role in the crowding-out controversy. Keynesians tend to be critical of the crowding-out argument, while monetarists tend to support it.

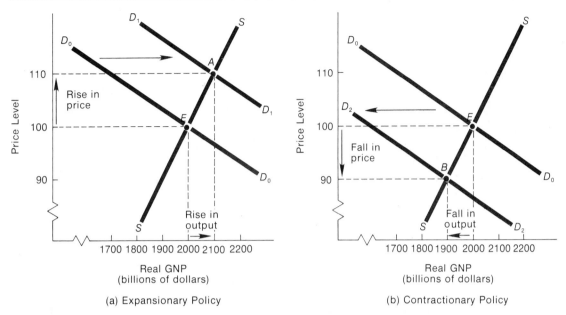

(a) Expansionary Policy   (b) Contractionary Policy

FIGURE 14–6

STABILIZATION POLICY WITH A STEEP AGGREGATE SUPPLY CURVE: THE MONETARIST CASE

These two diagrams show that stabilization policy is much more effective at fighting inflation than at fighting recession when the aggregate supply curve is very steep. In part (a), expansionary policies that push aggregate demand outward from D_0D_0 to D_1D_1 raise output by only $100 billion but push up prices by 10 percent, as equilibrium moves from point E to point A. So demand management is not a good way to end a recession. In part (b), contractionary policies that pull aggregate demand inward to D_2D_2 are successful in that they lower prices quite markedly (from 100 to 90, or about 10 percent) but reduce output only slightly (from $2000 billion to $1900 billion). Monetarists tend to believe in this case.

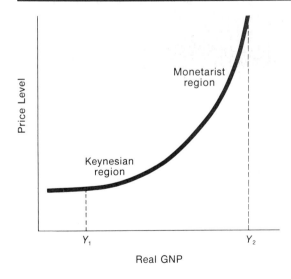

FIGURE 14–7

AN AGGREGATE SUPPLY CURVE WITH BOTH STEEP AND FLAT REGIONS

As this diagram suggests, either the Keynesians or the monetarists may be right under the appropriate circumstances. The Keynesian view of a flat supply curve is likely to be most accurate when there is much unemployment and unused capacity. The monetarist view of a steep supply curve is likely to be more accurate when there is full employment and high capacity utilization.

SUMMARY

1. While Keynesian and monetarist theory both provide for an effect of fiscal *and* monetary policy on aggregate demand, Keynesians tend to believe more in the effectiveness of fiscal policy while monetarists tend to believe more in the effectiveness of monetary policy.

2. Because fiscal policy actions affect aggregate demand either directly through G or indirectly through C, the expenditure lags between fiscal actions and their effects on aggregate demand are probably fairly short. By contrast, monetary policy operates mainly on investment, I, which responds very slowly to lower interest rates.

3. However, the policy-making lag normally is much longer for fiscal policy than for monetary policy. Hence, when the two lags are combined, it is not clear which type of policy acts more quickly.

4. Many monetarists believe that our imperfect knowledge of the channels through which stabilization policy works, and the long lags involved, make it unlikely that a successful discretionary stabilization policy can be achieved.

5. When there are long lags in the operation of fiscal and monetary policy, it becomes possible that attempts to stabilize economic activity might actually succeed in destabilizing it.

6. Keynesians recognize these difficulties but do not believe they are as serious as monetarists think. On the other hand, Keynesians place much less faith in the economy's ability to cure recessions and inflations on its own. They therefore think that discretionary policy is not only advisable, but essential.

7. The full-employment budget, instead of counting actual spending and tax receipts, counts the spending the government would be doing, and the taxes it would be collecting, if the economy were operating at full employment.

8. Like other liberals, Keynesians believe that government should try to solve society's problems—in this case the problems of inflation and unemployment—as best it can. Like other conservatives, monetarists are skeptical of the government's ability to do what it sets out to do, and are worried that its attempts to do good may turn out to be harmful.

9. Economic forecasts are made by econometric models, by exploiting leading indicators, and by judgment. Each method seems to play a role in arriving at good forecasts; but no method is foolproof, and economic forecasts are not as accurate as many people would like them to be.

10. Keynesians believe that the aggregate supply curve is rather flat in the short run. This means that increases in aggregate demand will add much to the nation's real output and add little to the price level. Stabilization policy thus has much to recommend it as an antirecession device, but it has little power to combat inflation.

11. Monetarists believe that the aggregate supply curve is very steep. This means that increases in aggregate demand increase real output rather little and succeed mostly in pushing up prices. Consequently, while stabilization policy can do much to fight inflation, it is not a very effective way to cure unemployment.

12. The Keynesian view probably is most applicable to an economy with much unemployment, while the monetarist view applies best to an economy producing near capacity levels.

CONCEPTS FOR REVIEW

Lags in stabilization policy
Rules-versus-discretionary policy
Full-employment budget
Econometric models

Leading indicators
Judgmental forecasts
Shape of the aggregate supply curve

QUESTIONS FOR DISCUSSION

1. Distinguish between the expenditure lag and the policy lag in stabilization policy. Does monetary or fiscal policy have the shorter expenditure lag? What about the policy lag?

2. Explain why lags make it possible for policy actions aimed at stabilizing the economy actually to succeed in destabilizing it.

3. "The full-employment budget is a useless concept when the economy is operating far below its full-employment potential." Comment.

4. Which of the following events would strengthen the argument for the use of discretionary policy, and which would strengthen the argument for rules?

   a. Structural changes make the economy's self-correcting mechanism faster and more reliable than before.

   b. New statistical methods are found that improve the accuracy of economic forecasts.

   c. A Republican president is elected when there is an overwhelmingly Democratic Congress. The Congress and the president differ sharply on what should be done about the national economy.

5. Explain why their contrasting views on the shape of the aggregate supply curve lead Keynesians to argue much more strongly for stabilization policy to fight unemployment while monetarists argue much more strongly for stabilization policies to fight inflation.

6. (More difficult) Use the following hypothetical econometric model of the U.S. economy to obtain a forecast of the GNP in 1984:

$$C = 9 + 0.9\, DI$$
$$DI = Y - T$$
$$T = 10 + \tfrac{1}{3} Y$$
$$Y = C + I + G$$

   I and G are exogenous variables, and their forecasted values for 1984 are $I = 360$, $G = 600$.

7. Suppose the forecasts turn out to be correct. What will the actual budget surplus be in 1984? If full employment for this economy comes at a GNP of 2700, what will be the full-employment surplus?

15

The Trade-Off Between
Inflation and Unemployment

During the 1976 presidential campaign between incumbent Gerald Ford and challenger Jimmy Carter, the proper conduct of macroeconomic policy was a major issue. Indeed, according to many journalists and political pundits, it was the single most important issue of the campaign.

With inflation apparently stabilized in the 5 to 6 percent range, and unemployment hovering just below 8 percent, President Ford defended his policy of moderation. Strong stimulation of the economy through monetary and fiscal policy, he argued, posed a serious danger of rekindling the kind of rapid inflation the economy had experienced in 1974. Carter disagreed. He saw an 8 percent rate of unemployment as unconscionably high, and argued that it should be brought down promptly by stimulative policies.

The implicit position of both candidates was that gains on one front could be bought only at the expense of losses on the other. But an alternative view was also popular about the same time—mainly among politicians and journalists, but also among some economists (of both political persuasions). According to this alternative, the trade-off between inflation and unemployment was a thing of the past. The liberal version of this theory held that we could reduce unemployment without aggravating the inflation problem. The conservative variant held that inflation could be fought without causing increased unemployment. Ironically, both camps used the "evidence" from the 1973–1975 experience to support their case.

Who was right? Was it Ford, arguing that we should not seek to reduce unemployment rapidly because of the inflationary risk? Was it Carter, who advocated raising employment rapidly? Or was it the optimists who claimed that both goals could be pursued at once?

In this chapter we will learn why the optimists who claimed that the trade-off was a relic of an earlier age were wrong. And we will see that, *even though the economy may sometimes experience both rising inflation and rising unemployment, the trade-off does indeed exist for policymakers.* Anything they do to lower unemployment is likely to increase inflation, and vice versa. This trade-off, you may recall, is one of the 12 Ideas for Beyond the Final Exam that we listed in Chapter 1.

The importance of the trade-off between inflation and unemployment can hardly be overestimated. Nowadays, it is probably the one area of macroeconomics where confusion is most widespread. And because this confusion can have disastrous consequences for the conduct of stabilization policy, the trade-off merits the comprehensive examination that we give it in this chapter. Without a thorough understanding of the dimensions of this trade-off, it is impossible for a citizen to make an informed judgment about macroeconomic policy.

The chapter, however, will not tell you whether Ford or Carter was correct in 1976. Apparently, the voters sided with Carter. What this chapter will show is that voting is as good a way as any to settle the issue, for once economists have done their job—a job explored in this chapter—the choice of the "right" policy turns largely on value judgments.

DEMAND INFLATION: A REVIEW

Let us begin our investigation of the trade-off by reviewing some of what we have learned about inflation in earlier chapters.

One major cause of inflation, though not the only one, is *excessive aggregate demand.* What happens if, for some reason, either consumers or investors decide to increase their spending? We know, first of all, that such an autonomous increase in spending will have a multiplier effect on aggregate demand; that is, each additional $1 of C or I will lead to perhaps $2 to $2.50 of additional demand. Second, we know that such a stimulus to aggregate demand will normally pull up *both* real output *and* prices. The reason, to review our earlier findings, is that firms normally will be able to supply the additional output only at higher costs; and these higher costs lead to higher prices.

The slope of the aggregate supply curve measures the amount of inflation that accompanies any specified rise in output, and therefore embodies the most important aspects of the trade-off between unemployment and inflation. We concluded in the last chapter that this trade-off will be very favorable when the economy is operating at low levels of capacity utilization and high levels of unemployment. Under such circumstances, firms can expand their operations substantially without running into higher costs. On the other hand, if a demand stimulus occurs in a fully employed economy, firms will find it quite difficult to raise output, and so will respond mostly by raising prices. Thus, the trade-off is very unfavorable when unemployment is low.

OBSERVING THE TRADE-OFF: THE QUESTION OF TIMING

This is all old hat. Let us now add one new element to the story—the question of timing.

Greater demand induces firms to raise both production and prices. But which variable responds first—output or prices? Research has shown that prices in our economy—and in other advanced economies—do not react promptly to higher demand but move rather sluggishly. This means that when aggregate demand rises, the economy will initially enjoy a burst of higher output without accompanying inflation. Only later will prices begin to rise and eat away at the excessive aggregate demand via the two mechanisms that we have studied:

1. Rising prices erode the purchasing power of bank accounts and bonds owned by consumers, and therefore depress consumer spending.
2. Rising prices increase the demand for money, because more dollar bills are required to conduct the same number of transactions. This increase in the demand for money, given a fixed money supply, pushes up interest rates; and rising interest rates depress investment spending.

Because of the different timing of the responses of output and prices, the trade-off between inflation and unemployment may be difficult to observe in the real world. Our graphical analysis will help us understand why.

Figure 15–1 depicts an economy that is initially in equilibrium at point E where aggregate demand curve D_0D_0 intersects aggregate supply curve SS. Real GNP is $2000 billion, and the price index is 100. Now suppose that consumers decide to spend more, or that firms decide to invest more. The aggregate demand curve shifts outward from D_0D_0 to D_1D_1, as indicated in the figure. The new equilibrium is at point A, where both output and prices are

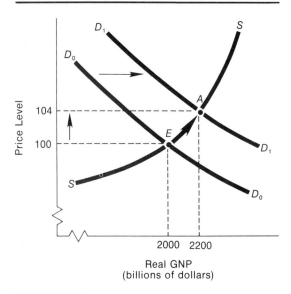

FIGURE 15–1

DEMAND INFLATION

If aggregate demand increases from D_0D_0 to D_1D_1, the equilibrium of the economy shifts upward and to the right from point E to point A. In this example, prices rise by 4 percent (from 100 to 104). This is the process of *demand inflation*.

higher than they were at point E. Since there must be a period of *inflation* (that is, rising prices) as the *price level* rises from 100 to 104, Figure 15–1 illustrates the process of demand inflation. Notice that the amount of inflation that accompanies the rise in real output from $2000 billion to $2200 billion depends on the slope of the aggregate supply schedule.

Now let us bring timing into the picture. Since prices react more slowly than production, the position of the economy does not jump abruptly from point E to point A. Instead, it follows a path something like the red path in Figure 15–2. Here the supply and demand curves are identical to those in Figure 15–1, but we try to give some indication of how the economy moves from point E to point A. At first,

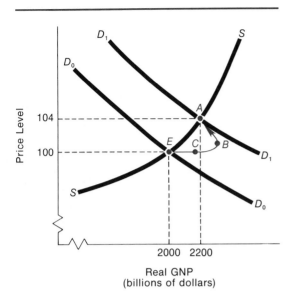

FIGURE 15–2

THE TIMING OF A DEMAND INFLATION

When aggregate demand increases (from D_0D_0 to D_1D_1 in the figure), the economy does not actually move straight up supply curve SS from point E to point A. Instead, prices are steady for a while as output expands (the economy moves rightward toward point C). Then, prices start to rise as production continues to grow (the movement from point C to point B in the diagram). Finally, there is a stagflation phase where output is falling despite rising prices (the movement from B to A).

Phase 1. Output rises with no increase in the price level (the segment of the path from point E to point C). To a casual observer, there would be no apparent trade-off between inflation and unemployment.

Phase 2. Prices start to rise as the increase in output continues. This is happening between points C and B, and only here is the trade-off directly visible.

Phase 3. Prices continue rising while output falls. This is shown by the path from B to A, which indicates what is commonly known as stagflation—the simultaneous occurrence of rising prices and falling production. As we learned in Chapter 8 and repeat here for emphasis:

A period of stagflation often follows a rapid expansion in aggregate demand. This happens because adjustments of prices occur much more sluggishly than adjustments of real output. As both prices and output adjust to equilibrium, stagflation occurs.

The point we are stressing now is that the existence of phases 1 and 3 do *not* cancel the trade-off between higher output and higher prices. Compare point E, the initial equilibrium, with point A, the final equilibrium. It is clear that the $200 billion increase in real GNP has been "bought" at the cost of a 4 percent increase in the price level. So there *is* a trade-off. The general point is:

The trade-off between higher output and higher prices cannot be observed simply by watching the behavior of output and prices over a short period of time.

output rises strongly and prices do not budge; so the economy starts to move horizontally from point E to point C. But, with demand exceeding supply in many markets, prices gradually adjust upward and the economy travels from point C to point B. Eventually, some of the original increase in output is canceled out by the adverse effects of inflation on aggregate demand that we have just mentioned, and output falls as the economy adjusts from point B to point A. Thus, Figure 15–2 depicts the three characteristic phases of an inflation fueled by a rise in aggregate demand:

THE ECONOMY'S SELF-CORRECTING MECHANISM: MORE REVIEW

There is one other bit of analysis that is crucial to understanding the trade-off that policymakers face. We learned in Chapter 8 that the economy has a self-correcting mechanism that will cure both inflations and recessions *eventually* even if the government does nothing. Why is this relevant? Because it tells us that we cannot observe the true effects of policy actions on output and prices simply by watching how the economy behaves after a policy action is taken. We also have to ask: What would the economy have done in the absence of the policy action? In other words, if the government adopts a program to deal with a particular economic problem and things *do* subsequently get better, how do we know whether the problem was cured as a result of the government program or as a consequence of the self-correcting mechanism?

To answer this question, let us review how the self-correcting mechanism works. If there is an inflationary gap—that is, if equilibrium output exceeds potential GNP—we know that a cumulative process of inflation will begin. With production exceeding normal capacity levels, firms will be prone to raise prices. And with employment exceeding "full employment," wages will be rising rapidly. The resulting inflation will destroy the inflationary gap by reducing aggregate demand. Specifically, higher prices will deter consumer spending by lowering the purchasing power of consumer wealth. And higher prices will deter investment spending by forcing up interest rates. The inflationary gap will self-destruct. But, in the process, *prices will rise while output is falling.*

Figure 15–3 shows this conclusion diagrammatically. When the aggregate demand curve is DD and the aggregate supply curve is S_0S_0, the economy reaches a short-run equilibrium at point E, which is beyond full employment. There is an inflationary gap, measured by the distance EB, and both prices and wages begin to rise. The higher wages represent increases in production costs, so the aggregate supply curve begins to shift upward toward higher prices. The process comes to an end only when the supply curve has reached the

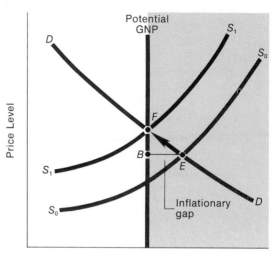

FIGURE 15–3

THE ELIMINATION OF AN INFLATIONARY GAP
When the aggregate supply curve is S_0S_0 and the aggregate demand curve is DD, the economy will reach equilibrium (point E) with an inflationary gap. The resulting inflation of wages will push the supply curve upward toward higher prices until it has shifted to the position indicated by curve S_1S_1. Here, with equilibrium at point F, the economy is at normal full employment. But, during the adjustment period from E to F, there will have been inflation.

position indicated by S_1S_1. Here the inflationary gap is closed, the economy is at a full employment equilibrium at point F, and the inflation ceases.

As we learned in Chapter 8, however, recessionary gaps do not cure themselves so smoothly. It seems to be a fact of modern economic life that average wages and the price level do not fall, even when equilibrium GNP is well below potential GNP and many workers are unemployed. Consequently, the economy gets stuck with a recessionary gap and unemployment for a long time. However, it is likely that if this gap lasts long enough the resistance of

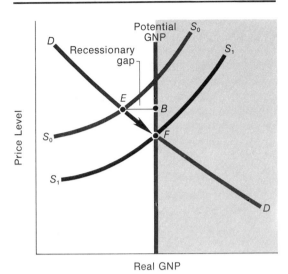

(y-axis: Price Level; x-axis: Real GNP)

FIGURE 15–4

THE ELIMINATION OF A RECESSIONARY GAP
This figure shows how a recessionary gap would *eventually* be eliminated by falling wages and prices. When equilibrium is at point *E*, there is a recessionary gap and substantial unemployment. If wages fall as a result, the supply curve will move downward toward the position indicated by curve S_1S_1. At this point (point *F*) equilibrium at full employment is established.

workers to wage reductions and the resistance of firms to price reductions will be broken. Then a process of deflation will close the recessionary gap, just as a process of inflation closes an inflationary gap.

Figure 15–4 illustrates the process. Initially, equilibrium is at point *E*, where demand curve *DD* intersects supply curve S_0S_0. This intersection is below full employment, so there is a recessionary gap measured by the distance *EB*. The economy may linger around point *E* for a long time if no government actions are taken. But, eventually, deflation will set in, driving the aggregate supply curve downward toward lower prices, that is, toward S_1S_1. At this point, the price at which a given output is supplied will be

lower than it was before the prices of inputs fell. The lower prices, in turn, will stimulate consumer demand. Consequently, *prices will fall and output will rise as* full employment is established. The adjustment is quite analogous to that portrayed in Figure 15–3. The most significant difference is something that the diagrams do not show:

The economy's self-correcting mechanism is much more efficient at eliminating inflationary gaps than it is at eliminating recessionary gaps.

FIGHTING RECESSIONS THROUGH FISCAL AND MONETARY POLICY

Let us now apply this analysis to the question debated by President Ford and candidate Carter in the 1976 campaign: If fiscal and monetary policies are used to reduce unemployment, how much inflation will they cause?

When the economy has a recessionary gap and is suffering from unemployment, we know from previous chapters what types of actions can cure this problem. If the money supply is increased, aggregate demand will be spurred by higher investment spending. If taxes are cut, the spurt will be concentrated on consumer spending. Or the government might simply buy more goods and services itself. For present purposes, the source of the stimulus is immaterial. What matters is that expansionary fiscal or monetary policy can raise aggregate demand and eliminate a recessionary gap.

Such a stimulus to aggregate demand, we know, will cause both output and prices to rise. But this is not quite enough information to permit us to appraise the policy because, as we have just seen, *output eventually would have recovered to full employment anyway*. Thus, the increase in production that policy achieves is not quite as much as it might seem at first. Similarly, the rise in prices that follows expansionary policy may underestimate the inflation that

279

policy causes because, *in the absence of stimulative policy, prices eventually would have fallen.*

Figure 15–5 makes the comparison graphically. Owing to the depressed state of demand, there is a recessionary gap with equilibrium at point E. Real GNP is $2000 billion and the price level is 100. If no policy actions are taken to shift the demand curve upward, falling wages eventually cause the supply curve, SS, to slide down the stationary aggregate demand curve D_0D_0 until full employment is reached at point F. But the road from E to F is rocky and slow. By contrast, an expansionary fiscal or monetary policy can raise the aggregate demand curve from D_0D_0 to D_1D_1, causing equilibrium to rise from point E to point A.

Like point F, point A is a full-employment equilibrium. But what a difference! The path from E to F is slow and agonizing, with unemployment persisting for a long time. The path from E to A is rather quick, and almost painless. Why "almost"? Because there is an inflationary price tag to be paid. Comparing points F and A, we see that the price level winds up about 6 percent higher (104 versus 98) as a result of the expansionary policy. To get to this higher *level* of prices, the *speed at which prices rise*—which is just what we mean by the *inflation rate*—must be higher for a period of time. To summarize:

When there is unemployment and a recessionary gap, it is not necessary to wait until "normal" economic forces restore full employment. These normal self-correcting forces work only through deflation, and that may take years and years. Instead, the government can stimulate demand by monetary or fiscal policy. This will significantly speed the recovery to full employment, but it will also create some inflation.

There are two important aspects of the effects of this policy: *both* the employment gains *and* the inflation losses are *temporary.*

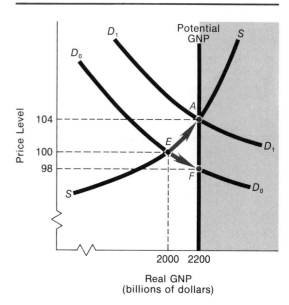

FIGURE 15–5

TWO PATHS TO FULL EMPLOYMENT
The economy depicted here starts out with aggregate demand curve D_0D_0, aggregate supply curve SS, and equilibrium with a recessionary gap at point E. It has two principal alternatives. If aggregate demand is unchanged, the supply curve *eventually* will be shifted down by falling wages until full employment equilibrium is reached at point F. But this may take many, many years. Alternatively, fiscal or monetary policy can be used to shift the demand curve to D_1D_1, eliminating the recessionary gap rather quickly.

The private economy would eventually have eradicated unemployment on its own; policy simply gets the job done faster. By the same token, the inflation that policy causes does not last forever. It too is temporary. But the fact that the effects of policy on inflation and unemployment are *temporary* does not mean that they are unimportant. These "temporary" effects may be quite long-lived and serious. Loosely speaking, the state of the economy in 1990 will hardly be affected by the policy actions taken in 1980. But the economic situation in 1981, 1982, and 1983 will be very much affected.

Figure 15–6 is intended to give you the flavor of what difference expansionary policy might make for the path of unemployment over time. We suppose that 5 percent unemployment corresponds to full employment and that the economy indicated by point *E* of Figure 15–5 has 7 percent unemployment in 1979. This is the year in which stimulative policy actions are assumed to be taken, if they are taken at all. The red line in Figure 15–6 then shows how the unemployment rate might react: dropping quickly from 7 percent in 1979 to 5 percent in 1981, and then remaining near full employment. The black line shows instead how the unemployment rate might behave without any policy actions: It falls slowly, reaching full employment

only by 1985. The shaded area, then, shows the temporary gains that can be achieved by stimulative fiscal or monetary policy actions.

But these benefits are not achieved without cost. As we have explained, with no policy stimulus there eventually would have been a slow and gradual *de*flation as the recession pushed prices and wages down. This is indicated by the black "no-policy" path in Figure 15–7, which charts the hypothetical behavior of the *inflation rate* (or, the rate of change of prices) over time. With expansionary policy, there is a burst of *in*flation instead, as shown by the red "policy" path. The shaded area between the two lines shows the inflationary price tag of fighting the recession.

In a very real sense, the shaded areas in Figures 15–6 and 15–7 represent the fundamental trade-off faced by the policymakers.

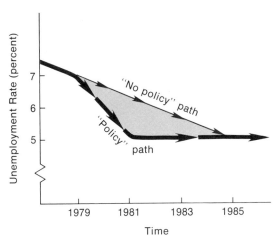

FIGURE 15–6

ANOTHER VIEW OF THE TWO PATHS TO FULL EMPLOYMENT

This figure portrays the behavior of the unemployment rate under the two alternative policies considered in Figure 15–5. With a "hands-off" policy, the economy's self-correcting mechanism gradually erodes unemployment, as indicated by the black line. With expansionary policies, full employment is reached much more quickly, as indicated by the red line. The shaded area measures the payoff to antirecession policy.

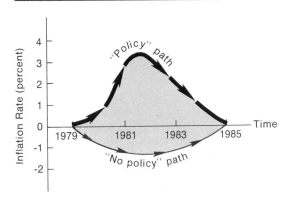

FIGURE 15–7

THE INFLATIONARY COST OF FIGHTING A RECESSION

Shortening a recession normally entails inflationary costs. The black line indicates how the inflation rate might behave in our hypothetical economy under a "hands-off" policy, while the red line shows how it might react to expansionary demand management policies. The shaded area measures the extra inflation that must be endured in order to abbreviate the recession.

They can create a *temporary* improvement in the employment picture (the shaded area in Figure 15–6) if they are willing to endure a *temporary* acceleration of inflation (the shaded area in Figure 15–7), leading to a *permanently* higher price level. This acceleration of inflation caused by expansionary policy actions may be highly visible if it comes at a time when the economy is already suffering from substantial inflation, or it might be invisible if it merely prevents a mild deflation from occurring. But it is almost always present.

FORD VERSUS CARTER: WHO WAS RIGHT?

Should the government pay the inflationary costs of recession-fighting in order to reap its benefits? Was Ford right in arguing for a "hands-off" policy in 1976? Or was Carter right in calling for more fiscal intervention?

While each of you will have to answer this question for yourself, the preceding analysis has highlighted three major issues upon which your answer should rest.

The Position of the Economy

It is clear from the analysis that the sacrifice in terms of the price level depends on the shape of the economy's aggregate supply schedule. If it is very flat, the final price level will not be much different with or without stimulative policy. (Look back at Figure 15–5 and imagine that the supply curve is nearly horizontal.) By implication, then, the inflation during the adjustment period cannot be very large. But if the supply curve is steep, the inflationary price tag will be high. This puts the matter rather mechanically, but there is a simple intuition behind the shape of the aggregate supply curve. As we learned in earlier chapters, the shape of this curve is governed in part by the degree of slack in the

economy. When there is high unemployment and much unutilized capacity in industry, output can expand without higher prices, So the supply curve will be flat, and the trade-off will be rather favorable. On the other hand, when the economy is closer to capacity, firms can raise production only if they charge higher prices. In this case, the curve is steep and the trade-off is unfavorable.

The Efficiency of the Economy's Self-Correcting Mechanism

We have stressed that natural economic processes will *eventually* cure a deflationary gap and end a recession, even if the government takes no action. The question here is: How long do we want to wait? Obviously, policy action looks like a better idea if this self-correcting mechanism is slow and unreliable, but it becomes much more questionable if the self-correcting mechanism acts promptly and surely.

Costs of Unemployment and Inflation

As Chapter 6 pointed out, social costs are attached more to *rising* prices than to *high* prices. So, in appraising the costs of recession-fighting, we are probably concerned more with the temporary bulge in the *inflation rate* than with the permanent rise in the *price level*. But how do we balance the improvement in unemployment shown in Figure 15–6 against the deterioration in inflation shown in Figure 15–7?

Each of the twin evils causes social problems—problems that we explored in depth in Chapter 6, and it finally comes down to a matter of judgment in deciding which problems are the more serious. Obviously, those who are most concerned about unemployment will look more favorably upon recession-fighting than will those who worry most about inflation.

These three considerations explain very well the policy differences between Gerald Ford and Jimmy Carter in 1976. Carter argued that the aggregate supply curve was very flat because of the high unemployment rates that prevailed throughout the presidential campaign. Ford believed that Carter exaggerated the favorable nature of the trade-off. For his part, Ford argued that the economy's self-correcting mechanism was working well, and would continue to do so if left alone. Carter denied this, claiming that Ford's policies would lead to years of high unemployment. On these two issues, then, both the challenger and incumbent were acting like economists arguing over how to interpret the facts. And, indeed, there were economists who backed each position, for the pertinent facts are certainly open to various interpretations.

But their real positions probably were decided by the third issue: Which is the bigger social problem, unemployment or inflation? And here they certainly both acted like politicians. Ford bet that more voters were afraid of renewed inflation than of becoming unemployed, while Carter gambled on the importance of unemployment. These positions reflect the traditional views of the Republican and Democratic parties, and history records that the Democrats prevailed this time.

FIGHTING DEMAND INFLATION THROUGH FISCAL AND MONETARY POLICY

The same annoying trade-off arises when the principal problem facing the economy is inflation, for the usual methods of bringing down inflation are almost certain to cause unemployment. Given what has been said so far, this cannot be a very surprising conclusion. But let us see just what stabilization policy can do for an economy that finds itself with an inflationary gap.

As we know, if aggregate demand is so strong that equilibrium is (temporarily) above full employment, there will be strong upward pressures on wages and prices. With workers in great demand, wages will be rising rapidly. Faced with rising costs, and with strong demand for their products, firms will find it a propitious time to raise prices. This wage–price spiral will cause a cumulative inflation that eventually will reduce aggregate demand by enough to eliminate the inflationary gap.

Contractionary stabilization policy can change all this by removing the basic cause of the inflation—too much aggregate demand. By reducing its own spending, or by raising taxes, or by contracting the money supply, the government can cut aggregate demand down to size, reduce the inflationary gap, and consequently reduce the amount of inflation that is necessary to restore "normal" full employment.

Figure 15–8 shows this conclusion graphically. With aggregate demand at D_0D_0 and aggregate supply at SS, the economy's equilibrium is at point E, with an inflationary gap equal to distance AE. If nothing is done to shift demand downward, the self-correcting mechanism will eliminate this gap through an inflation that drives the supply schedule upward toward higher prices until it passes through point F. Prices in this example will wind up 3 percent higher.

But appropriate stabilization policy, by pulling the aggregate demand curve down to a position like D_1D_1, can moderate the inflation. In this example, contractionary policies reduce the inflationary gap to ae, which is smaller than AE. The supply curve must still rise (because wages will rise), but now only until it passes through point A. Thus the adjustment does not require price inflation. Wages rise by enough to eliminate the extraordinary demand for labor. But prices nonetheless remain stable because the drop in demand counters the inflationary tendencies from the supply side.[1]

[1] EXERCISE: Sketch in the final equilibrium supply schedules for the two cases shown in Figure 15–8, and convince yourself that the shift in the supply curve needed to reach point A is less than the shift needed to reach point F.

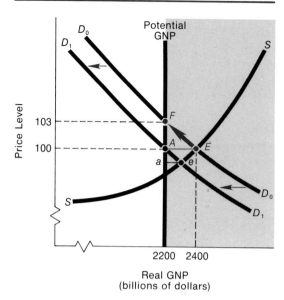

FIGURE 15–8

TWO WAYS TO ELIMINATE AN INFLATIONARY GAP

The economy depicted here starts out with aggregate demand curve D_0D_0, aggregate supply curve SS, and an inflationary gap at point E. If the government takes no action, rising wages will push the aggregate supply curve upward until it intersects the aggregate demand curve at point F. At this point, inflation will stop. Alternatively, contractionary monetary and fiscal policies can eliminate the bout of inflation by pulling the aggregate demand curve down to D_1D_1. Then only a much smaller rise in the aggregate supply curve is needed to establish equilibrium at point A. Comparing points E and A, we see that the price level does not have to rise.

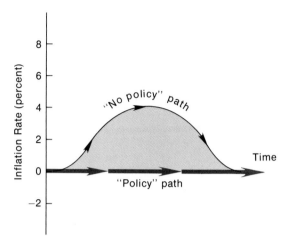

FIGURE 15–9

THE PAYOFF TO ANTI-INFLATION POLICY
If a successful anti-inflation policy is pursued, the inflation rate may remain at zero, as indicated by the red line. By comparing this with the path of inflation under a "hands-off" policy (the black line), we can see the payoff to anti-inflation policy (the shaded area).

This does indeed seem to be a happy outcome, although the trade-off remains. If we compare the inflation performance implied by the two cases considered in Figure 15–8, a picture something like Figure 15–9 emerges. With no policy actions, the price level gradually drifts up, so there is a period of inflation as the inflationary gap is eliminated. This is shown by the black line in Figure 15–9. With the proper policy action, the price level is roughly stable,

as shown by the red line. The shaded area indicates the payoff to anti-inflation policy.

But now consider the implications for production. In Figure 15–8, with no policy intervention, output falls gradually from its abnormally high level of $2400 billion to the sustainable full-employment level of $2200 billion. The implications for unemployment are shown by the black "no policy" path in Figure 15–10. The unemployment rate also rises if a dose of contractionary policy is applied; but it rises more quickly, as indicated by the red "policy" line in Figure 15–10. The shaded area in this diagram represents the cost in terms of higher unemployment.

Thus the trade-off remains as it was in the case of antirecession policy: Inflation is held down only by reducing output and employment. The difference is that one may legitimately question whether the reduction in employment repre-

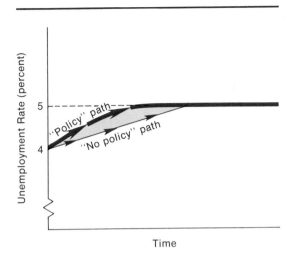

FIGURE 15–10

THE COST OF ANTI-INFLATION POLICY
Anti-inflation policy that reduces aggregate demand
will also reduce real output and employment. The
black line indicates the economy's unemployment rate
if no policy actions are taken; it gradually rises to the
normal full-employment level. With contractionary
policy, the unemployment rate also rises to full
employment, but rises more swiftly. The shaded area
shows the extra unemployment caused by fighting the
inflation.

sented by the shaded area in Figure 15–10 is
really a social problem.

In either case, unemployment is below the
"frictional" level for a time. But, when jobs are
so plentiful, a reduction in the demand for labor
may reasonably be considered a small price to
pay for the easing of inflationary pressure.
Indeed, the stabilization policy is simply a way to
do more quickly what the economy would do on
its own anyway: It matches the demand for labor
to the available supply. Thus, although the
quicker elimination of the inflationary gap
undeniably results in some loss of output, it is
arguable that the economy has reaped gains on
both fronts. It has reduced inflation, and at the
same time achieved a balance of supply and
demand in the labor market more quickly.

When inflation is caused by excessive
aggregate demand, fiscal and monetary policies
that reduce demand can have big payoffs in
terms of reduced inflation rates at very little
social cost. While output must fall, it is at least
arguable that the economy is better off with the
lower volume of production.

A RECAPITULATION

What we have learned so far is that expansionary monetary and fiscal policies can reduce
the severity and length of recessions, but only
by giving the economy more inflation than it
otherwise would have had. Similarly, contractionary demand-management policies designed
to fight inflation have their desired effects only
by reducing output and employment for a time.

We have couched our discussion in terms
of speeding the economy's recovery to full
employment. But this is not necessary. The
same *qualitative* trade-off holds no matter when
a dose of stabilization policy is applied. For
example, even in the high-unemployment
economy of the mid-1970s, there were those
who argued against stimulating the economy on
the grounds that it would cause an acceleration
of inflation.

The difference between a fully employed
economy and an economy with a lot of slack
comes in the *quantitative* dimensions of the
trade-off. As we have stressed repeatedly,
expansionary policy carries a lower inflationary
cost when the economy is very depressed
(because the aggregate supply curve is flat),
and contractionary policy reduces inflation with
only a small drop in employment when there is
full employment (because the aggregate supply
schedule is steep).

Finally, let us note that the same trade-off
applies to any event that changes aggregate
demand. There is nothing special in this regard
about stabilization policy. (Except, of course, for
the fact that government can control it!) Thus:

Fluctuations in aggregate demand, whatever their cause, can be expected to produce an inverse relationship between inflation and unemployment. That is, one of the two will go down whenever the other goes up.

Our analysis has taught us that the trade-off is basically a reflection of the fact that the aggregate supply curve slopes upward: More output will be produced only if it can be marketed at a higher price.

THE PHILLIPS CURVE

More than 20 years ago, economist A. W. Phillips plotted data on unemployment and on the rate of change of *wages* (not prices) for several extended periods of British history on a series of scatter diagrams, one of which is reproduced as Figure 15–11. He then sketched in a curve that seemed to "fit" the data. This type of curve, which is now called a Phillips curve, shows that wage inflation normally is high when unemployment is low and is low when unemployment is high.

Phillips curves have also been constructed for *price* inflation, and one of these for the postwar United States is shown in Figure 15–12. The curve appears to fit the data moderately well, though far from perfectly. Notice the characteristic shape of the Phillips curve: It is steep when the unemployment rate is low and it flattens as the unemployment rate increases. This confirms our theoretical expectation that the slope of the aggregate supply curve will increase at higher levels of output. When unemployment is already low, reducing it further causes a considerable amount of inflation.

During the 1960s and early 1970s, economists often used a Phillips curve like that shown in Figure 15–12 to portray the "menu" of choices available to policymakers. They could opt for low unemployment and high inflation—

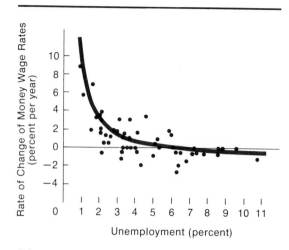

FIGURE 15–11

THE ORIGINAL PHILLIPS CURVE
This scatter diagram, reproduced from the original article by A. W. Phillips, shows the rate of change of money wages and the rate of unemployment in the United Kingdom between 1861 and 1913. Each year is represented by a point in the diagram.

Source: A. W. Phillips, "The Relation Between Unemployment and the Rate of Change of Money Wages in the United Kingdom, 1861–1957," *Economica,* New Series, vol. 25, November 1958.

as was done in 1951 and 1969. Or they might prefer higher unemployment coupled with lower inflation—as, for example, in 1954 and 1961. The Phillips curve, it was said, described the *quantitative* trade-off between inflation and unemployment. And, for a number of years, it worked rather well.

Then something happened. The behavior of the economy in 1973–1977 was far worse than what would have been expected from the Phillips curve depicted in Figure 15–12. In particular, given the unemployment rates in each of those years, inflation was astonishingly high by historical standards. This is shown in Figure 15–13, which simply adds to Figure 15–12 the points for 1973–1977. Clearly some-

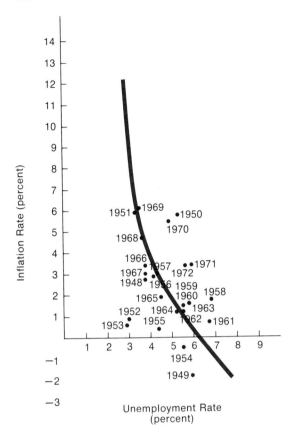

FIGURE 15–12

A PHILLIPS CURVE FOR THE UNITED STATES
This Phillips curve relates *price* inflation (rather than
wage inflation) to the unemployment rate in the United
States for the years 1948–1972. Though it misses
badly in a few instances (for example, 1972), it
generally "fits" the data moderately well.

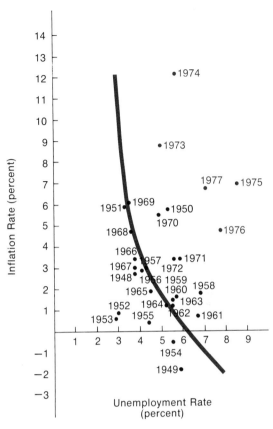

FIGURE 15–13

A PHILLIPS CURVE FOR THE UNITED
STATES?
This scatter diagram adds the points for 1973–1977 to
the scatter diagram shown in Figure 15–12. It is clear
that inflation in each of those years was much higher
than the Phillips curve would have led us to predict.

thing had gone wrong. In fact, if you go back
and look carefully at Figure 15–12 you might
see a hint of the things that were to come, for
the points for the years 1970, 1971, and 1972
are all substantially above the Phillips curve.

The sorry performance of the economy
during these years led to the cry that the Phillips
curve was dead—which may or may not have

been true—and that therefore the trade-off
between inflation and unemployment no longer
existed—which certainly was *not* true. It is clear
enough from Figure 15–13 that the simple
Phillips curve cannot explain the state of the
economy in the mid-1970s; no one disputes this.
But the inference that therefore the trade-off no
longer exists was, and still is, unwarranted.

What we have learned here is that:

Inflations caused by fluctuations in aggregate demand can be expected to lead to a Phillips-curve relation in the data.

And the 1948–1972 experience bears this out. But demand fluctuations are not the only cause of inflation, and, in particular, they have played a rather minor role in the inflation we have been experiencing since 1973. This inflation, the worst in our postwar history, was a new kind of inflation—caused by restrictions in aggregate supply.

SUPPLY INFLATION

What was going on during 1973–1975 that caused so much more inflation than was expected, given the state of aggregate demand at that time? Just what were the causes of this new type of inflation? Several things.

First, the nations constituting the Organization of Petroleum Exporting Countries (OPEC) got together on a collusive agreement to limit production and force up the price of oil. The cartel was so successful during and after the 1973 Arab—Israeli War that it managed to quadruple the price of crude oil in only a few months. To American consumers, this showed up as a substantial increase in the prices of gasoline and home heating fuels. To American businesses, this action meant that one of the important inputs into the production process—energy—rose drastically in price, thus increasing the cost of doing business. If John Q. Manufacturer could produce 500,000 door-knobs at a price of $2.50 per knob when energy was cheap, he might discover that he needed to charge $2.60 each to produce this many door-knobs profitably when energy became expensive. When all businesses experience this cost increase, as they did in 1974, the economy's aggregate supply curve shifts upward as shown

in Figure 15–14. Such an upward shift is just a way of expressing the fact that any given level of GNP can be produced only at a higher price level than was the case before the OPEC increase. For example, in the diagram, a real GNP of $2000 billion would have been produced at a price level of 100 before the oil price rise but only at a price level of 104 after OPEC's action.

Second, energy products were not the only things that suddenly became scarcer. While the formation of a cartel caused a *contrived scarcity* of oil, nature caused a very *real scarcity* of food. Crop failures in many parts of the world during 1972–1974 sent agricultural prices soaring.

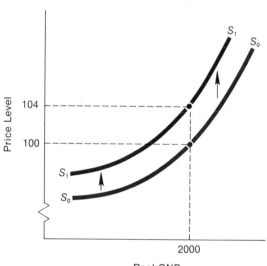

FIGURE 15–14

A DECREASE IN AGGREGATE SUPPLY
Any factor that restricts supply (such as a crop failure) or autonomously pushes up prices (such as OPEC's decisions in 1973–1974) will cause the aggregate supply curve to shift upward. This means that any particular level of output (such as $2000 billion) can now be produced only at a higher price level than previously (104 versus 100).

Because food prices are an important component of the cost of living (about 25 percent), this shortage played a direct role in creating the inflation. And it also contributed to the supply inflation in two more indirect ways. First, since some agricultural products are used as inputs into manufacturing processes, the higher agricultural prices led to higher industrial prices. Second, the accelerating consumer prices encouraged labor to strive for more generous wage increases. All of these factors served to push the supply curve upward, as shown in Figure 15–14.

Finally, the U.S. experiment with mandatory wage and price controls—an episode that we will discuss in the next chapter—came to an end in the spring of 1974. Price and wage increases that had been suppressed by controls suddenly came to the surface in an inflationary bulge as businesses that had been compelled by regulations to keep prices down were all at once released from these constraints. Starting in the spring of 1974, they were free to charge the higher prices dictated by the law of supply and demand.

These were some of the *causes* of the reduction of aggregate supply in 1973–1974. What were the *effects*? We expect in such a case that production will be reduced. And in order to reduce demand to the available supply, prices have to rise. The result is the worst of both worlds: falling production and rising prices. This is shown in Figure 15–15, which superimposes an aggregate demand curve, *DD*, upon the two aggregate supply curves of Figure 15–14. The economy's equilibrium shifts upward to the left from point *E* to point *A*; thus, output falls while prices rise. *Stagflation is the typical result of supply inflation.*

The numbers used in Figure 15–15 are roughly indicative of what happened in the United States between 1973 (represented by supply curve S_0S_0 and point *E*) and 1975 (represented by supply curve S_1S_1 and point *A*). Real GNP, in 1972 prices, fell by about $35 billion, while the price level rose about 20 percent.

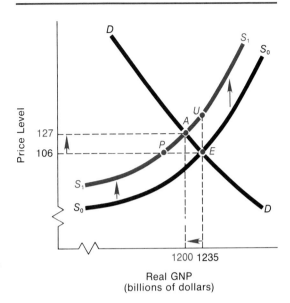

FIGURE 15–15

THE POLICY DILEMMA OF SUPPLY INFLATION

If the aggregate supply curve shifts upward from S_0S_0 to S_1S_1, and policymakers do not shift the aggregate demand curve *DD*, equilibrium will move from point *E* to point *A*. Output will fall while prices rise. If the policymakers are unhappy about the drop in output, they can push the aggregate demand curve outward until it intersects S_1S_1 at point *U*. This would prevent output from falling but would push prices even higher. Alternatively, by pulling the demand curve downward so that it intersects the supply curve at point *P*, policymakers can prevent the price level from rising, but only by depressing output even further.

The typical result of supply inflation is for falling output to accompany accelerating inflation. This is one reason why the world economy was plagued by stagflation in the mid-1970s. And it can happen again if another series of supply-reducing events takes place.

Thus, there is a big difference between macroeconomic fluctuations that are initiated on the *demand* side and those that have their origins on the *supply* side. We saw earlier that unemployment normally falls in a demand inflation, and we now see that unemployment normally rises in a supply inflation. Once this fundamental distinction is understood, we can understand why:

The fact that the Phillips curve cannot explain the inflation of the 1970s does not mean that policymakers need no longer worry about the trade-off between inflation and unemployment. Because fiscal and monetary policy generally affect only *aggregate demand,* not *aggregate supply,* the trade-off for policymakers remains. If they use monetary and fiscal measures to combat the unemployment that results from a reduction in aggregate supply, they will only stimulate demand and thereby aggravate the inflation. If they try to limit the inflation, they will make the employment picture still worse.

THE POLICYMAKERS' RESPONSE TO SUPPLY INFLATION

Let us briefly explore the choices open to policymakers when the economy is victimized by an inflationary shock from the supply side. For the sake of concreteness, we will talk about a rise in the price of oil, but the same principles apply to any such shock.

We shall see that when the economy's problems come from the supply side, rather than from the demand side, there is much less that policymakers can do to set things right. In fact, we shall see that the economy is condemned to suffer either more inflation or more unemployment or some combination of the two. Policymakers can decide which of the twin evils of macroeconomics they want to concentrate their efforts on. But they simply do not have enough tools to counteract both problems.

The policymakers' choices can be portrayed explicitly in terms of our supply and demand diagram. Specifically, what can the government do when the aggregate supply curve contracts, as from S_0S_0 to S_1S_1 in Figure 15–15?

One alternative—which is roughly what the administration and the Federal Reserve chose to do in 1974—is not to respond at all. Under such a policy, the economy is pushed rapidly from point E toward point A by the supply shock. In other words, there is a sudden surge of both inflation and unemployment, just as occurred in 1974–1975.

The public will undoubtedly find this an unsatisfactory state of affairs. And, indeed, the policies followed in the mid-1970s were criticized from both the left and the right. Liberals found the resulting high unemployment to be intolerable, while conservatives were displeased with the lack of a vigorous response to the high inflation rates.

Let us first consider what could have been done by a government unwilling to permit OPEC to cause unemployment. In Figure 15–15 there is a point marked U that has the same real output as point E but a price level even higher than at point A. A sufficiently large dose of demand stimulation can push the economy's aggregate demand curve outward to achieve point U. The recession would be prevented, and the oil shortage would not cause increased unemployment. But the cost, as always, would be even higher inflation than would have occurred otherwise, and a permanently higher price level.

On the other hand, a government determined to resist inflation at all costs could react by cutting back aggregate demand. A sufficiently large reduction in demand, in fact, could keep the overall price level constant despite the inflationary push from OPEC. Specifically, if the aggregate demand curve were pulled back so that it passed through point P, prices would not have to rise at all. But the costs in terms of unemployment would be quite severe.

The range of choices that we have just outlined is not likely to bring joy to the hearts of politicians. It certainly gave President Ford little cause for rejoicing when he assumed office in 1974.

Unlike the case of demand inflation, where a properly conceived and executed policy of demand management can stop inflation at little social cost, there is no "right" policy to follow after an inflationary shock from the supply side. The economy's performance is going to be bad no matter what the fiscal and monetary authorities do. Their only choice is whether to pay the price mainly through unemployment or mainly through inflation.

It is this experience with stagflation caused by reductions in aggregate supply since 1973 that has given rise to much of the confusion over the trade-off between inflation and unemployment. Seeing that high inflation and high unemployment went hand in hand in the middle and late 1970s, many people erroneously concluded that the trade-off was obsolete. They clamored for government policies that promised improvement on both fronts at once. And, naturally, there were politicians only too willing to promise the impossible. (Fortunately, neither President Ford nor President Carter was among these.)

But our analysis of supply inflation has taught us two lessons, which bring us back to one of our 12 Ideas for Beyond the Final Exam.

First, when aggregate supply contracts, there is nothing the government can do to aggregate demand that will restore the previous combination of output and prices (point *E* in Figure 15–15). The old situation is unattainable *unless* there is some way of moving the aggregate supply curve back to its original position. Unfortunately, when the drop in supply is caused by OPEC or by nature, there is little the government can do to accomplish this.

Second, despite the fact that adverse shifts in the supply schedule cause both inflation and unemployment to rise together, anything the government does with its stabilization policy can only make unemployment and inflation move in opposite directions. It can raise demand to cut down on unemployment, but this will make inflation worse. Or it can fight inflation by restricting demand, but this will make unemployment worse. The reason the government's ability is so circumscribed, of course, is that we have learned only how to control the aggregate *demand* curve, not how to shift the aggregate *supply* curve.

This unhappy state of affairs naturally has led to a vigorous search for a way out of the dilemma. Both economists and public officials have sought a policy that offers some improvement on both fronts simultaneously, or that eases the pain of either inflation or unemployment. The next chapter considers several of these approaches.

SUMMARY

1. An excess of aggregate demand over the economy's normal capacity to produce is one major cause of inflation. The amount of inflation it causes depends on the shape of the aggregate supply schedule.
2. In a demand inflation, output normally responds much more quickly than prices. Later, when prices start to rise, the harmful effects of higher prices on aggregate demand cause output to fall.
3. Thus we often will fail to see the inverse relationship between changes in output and changes in prices when we look at data for short periods of time. Nonetheless, the trade-off is there.

4. The economy has a self-correcting mechanism whereby inflationary gaps are cured by a cumulative, but self-limiting, process of inflation that reduces aggregate demand back to a level that the economy can produce.

5. There is a similar self-correcting mechanism to end recessionary gaps, but it is much less reliable. Wages and prices must fall in order to increase demand and end the recession.

6. If stimulative monetary or fiscal policies are used to fight recessions, this self-correcting mechanism will not operate. Instead, the expansionary stabilization policy may cause inflation instead of deflation.

7. Because recessions do not normally last forever, both the reduction in unemployment and the increase in inflation that expansionary policies cause will be "temporary." However, this certainly does not make them unimportant, because in this instance "temporary" may mean a very long period of time.

8. Whether the government should use active stabilization policy to limit recessions depends on the level of capacity utilization, the speed with which the economy's self-correcting mechanism works, and the relative costs of inflation and unemployment.

9. Reducing aggregate demand is an effective way to fight inflation, but it causes a temporary loss of output and jobs. Once again, the gains and losses are both temporary, because the economy's self-correcting mechanism would have brought the inflation under control in any case.

10. When gyrations in the economy are primarily caused by fluctuations in aggregate demand, a Phillips curve will be shown by the data. That is, there will be an inverse relationship between the rate of inflation and the rate of unemployment.

11. The Phillips-curve relation seemed to work well in the United States from about 1948 until about 1972. Then it started to fall apart because the main source of economic instability in the mid-1970s came from the supply side.

12. Unlike inflation caused by excess demand, supply inflation normally is accompanied by falling output. The contrived scarcity of oil and the genuine scarcity of food in 1973–1974, therefore, were major causes of the worldwide stagflation.

13. Supply inflation, however, does not repeal the trade-off between inflation and unemployment *for policymakers*. Since stabilization policy consists largely of manipulation of aggregate demand, any policy action that reduces unemployment is likely to exacerbate inflation, and any policy action that moderates inflation is likely to make unemployment more severe. This is the fundamental trade-off that was listed among our 12 Ideas for Beyond the Final Exam.

CONCEPTS FOR REVIEW

Trade-off between inflation and unemployment	Self-correcting mechanism
Demand inflation	Phillips curve
Stagflation	Supply inflation
	Policy response to supply inflation

QUESTIONS FOR DISCUSSION

1. Why did some observers in the mid-1970s think that there was no longer a trade-off between inflation and unemployment? Were they right?

2. "There is no sense in trying to shorten recessions through fiscal and monetary policy because the effects of these policies on the unemployment rate are sure to be temporary." Comment on both the truth of this statement and its relevance for policy formulation.

3. When aggregate demand rises, which macroeconomic variable usually responds more quickly: real output or the price level? Why do you think this is so? (You may want to discuss this last point with your instructor.)

4. Why is the economy's self-correcting mechanism more efficient at eliminating inflationary gaps than it is at eliminating recessionary gaps?

5. Distinguish between a permanent increase in the *price level* and an increase in the *rate of inflation*. Which of these is likely to exact the greater social costs?

6. Why is it said that decisions on fiscal and monetary policy are, at least in part, political decisions that cannot be made by "objective" economists?

7. Does the economy have a recessionary gap or an inflationary gap today? What should be done about this? What facts would you want to know in preparing an answer to this question?

8. What is a "Phillips curve"? Why did it seem to work so much better in the 1948–1972 period than it has since the mid-1970s?

9. Explain the dilemma that policymakers face when there is an episode of supply inflation. What do you think should have been done in 1974? What would you recommend if there were a severe bout with supply inflation today?

16

Further Controversies over Stabilization Policy

We have pointed out that stabilization policy decisions are inherently political and, as a consequence, they are almost always immersed in controversy. Several of these controversies were examined in the last two chapters, and we turn our attention now to some of the others.

In the first part of the chapter we will look into a variety of methods for improving, or even eliminating, the trade-off between unemployment and inflation. Some of these plans have actually been tried; others are still untested

ideas. They range from governmental exhortations to hold down wage and price increases to outright prohibition of wage or price rises. They include efforts to improve the functioning of labor markets, plans to enlist the tax system in the battle against inflation, and institutional changes designed to rob inflation of its social costs. Although each of these ideas is worth being considered, we must emphasize in advance that none is a panacea.

In the second part of the chapter we consider the fascinating possibility that business cycles may be politically induced, that is, that economic fluctuations may be caused by election-minded government officials. Might the president and Congress use fiscal policy to *cause* business fluctuations rather than to prevent them? How could they gain by doing such a thing? Is there evidence that political business cycles actually have occurred, either in the United States or elsewhere? Recent research has produced tentative answers to each of these questions.

Finally, in the third part of the chapter we examine the arguments that government budget deficits—whether accumulated for stabilization purposes, to finance wars, or for other reasons—place an unfair *burden on future generations*. After exploding a number of myths about the national debt, we shall see that there is one reason why the debt might indeed place a burden on future generations. As it turns out, whether or not the national debt is a burden depends on *why* the debt was accumulated.

Can We Improve the Trade-Off Between Unemployment and Inflation?

The analysis of the last chapter made it clear that the trade-off between inflation and unemployment often puts policymakers in an unenviable position. Since anything they do to fight unemployment is likely to aggravate inflation, and anything they do to counteract inflation is likely to cause unemployment, policymakers are in an awkward position when the nation suffers from both problems at the same time. This dilemma naturally has led economists and government officials to search for a way out. The search has not as yet turned up any simple solutions, but it is still in progress today—and with a sense of considerable urgency.

INCOMES POLICY

Incomes policy is a generic term used to describe a wide variety of measures aimed at curbing inflation *without* reducing aggregate demand.

As practiced in the United States during the last 20 years, incomes policy has run the gamut from verbal admonitions all the way to President Nixon's outright prohibition of wage and price increases in 1971. And in some foreign countries that rely upon incomes policy far more

heavily than we do, a still more bewildering variety of alternative measures has emerged. Indeed, there may be only one common thread linking these disparate policies: No hard evidence exists that any of them has succeeded in *permanently* improving the trade-off between unemployment and inflation. Note that the emphasis here is on the word "permanently," for many attempts at incomes policy—including some in this country—have enjoyed temporary success.

Jawboning

The mildest form of incomes policy is commonly referred to as jawboning. The term is descriptive. It is meant to conjure up in your mind an image of the president of the United States calling some corporate executive on the carpet for announcing a price increase deemed to be contrary to the national interest. The objective is to persuade him to change his mind. And since corporate executives are likely to feel surrounded, and perhaps even threatened, under these circumstances, jawboning has occasionally enjoyed spectacular success.

Perhaps the best-known instance was President Kennedy's confrontation with the steel industry in 1962. All sorts of informal pressures were brought to bear on the big steel companies—ranging from a tongue-lashing by the president to a cancellation of steel orders by the Defense Department—until the industry caved in and rescinded a previously announced price increase. Years later, U.S. Steel's Roger M. Blough wrote that "never before in the nation's history have so many forces of the federal government been marshalled against a single American industry. . ."[1] Jawboning can have teeth.

But, while this episode received the most notoriety, President Johnson probably jawboned more than anyone else, and it was President Nixon who first established an official agency to monitor price increases and "blow the whistle" on those that were unwarranted. After a temporary hiatus under President Ford, this so-called "open mouth policy" was reinstated by President Carter in early 1978. Under his "deceleration strategy," the president urged both labor and business to increase their wages and prices at a slower rate in 1978 than they had in 1976 and 1977. And he assigned his counselor Robert Strauss and the director of the Council on Wage and Price Stability, Barry Bosworth, to do most of the jawboning for him.

The main argument in favor of jawboning is that it is a relatively painless way to try to improve the trade-off between inflation and unemployment. Large corporations, it is argued, have the market power to raise prices even when price rises are not justified by cost increases. But, since these corporate giants are also very conscious of their public-relations images, proponents of jawboning argue, why not use the prestige of the federal government to dissuade them from exercising their market power?

Opponents of jawboning respond that market power, which undoubtedly exists, can explain *high* prices. But why, they ask, would a firm with market power wait until this month to

raise prices when it could have done so last month, or the month before? They answer that large corporations raise prices only when changes in demand or cost considerations make it profitable to do so, not because they have a residue of unused market power. Furthermore, there is an inevitable element of inequity in jawboning. By its very nature it must be discriminatory, picking on some firms while letting others go scot-free.

On balance, a fair assessment of jawboning would probably conclude that it does little good and little harm.

Wage–Price Guideposts

The next step up from jawboning is the establishment of an official standard for "permissible" rates of increase in wages and prices. These so-called wage–price guideposts were initiated by the Kennedy administration in early 1962 but used most notably by the Johnson administration. Lacking an enforcement mechanism, they collapsed amid the inflationary pressures of 1967. In late 1978 they were resurrected by President Carter, who was convinced that jawboning was not enough. Economist Alfred Kahn was appointed to administer the new guideposts.

The logic behind guideposts is both simple and compelling. In an ideally functioning economy, if worker productivity (measured by output per hour) rises by 2 percent a year, then wages can rise by 2 percent a year with no increase in costs or prices. Alternatively, wages can increase at a 4 percent annual rate while prices rise at 2 percent a year, and so on. In general, price inflation proceeds at a rate roughly 2 percentage points below wage inflation.

A set of wage–price guideposts is obtained by picking a target rate of inflation, say 5 percent a year, and adding 2 percent to get a consistent target for wage increases—7 percent in this example. The government then announces that (a) wage increases that exceed this standard will be deemed "inflationary," (b)

[1]Roger M. Blough, *The Washington Embrace of Business* (New York: Columbia University Press, 1975), page 94.

firms enjoying productivity increases faster than the national average are expected to raise their prices more slowly than 5 percent a year while, (c) firms obtaining sub-par productivity improvements are allowed to have higher-than-average price increases so that, (d) the overall price level can increase at a rate of 5 percent a year.

As noted, guideposts are quite logical. The problem comes in deciding what to do if some union or corporation violates them. Experience shows that voluntarism goes only so far when economic self-interest is threatened.

If the government responds by jawboning—as frequently happened in the 1960s—we are back to the first type of incomes policy, but with an important difference. The uniformity of the guideposts means that the firms or unions singled out for public scrutiny earned that status. Official guideposts remove much of the element of capriciousness from an *ad hoc* jawboning policy.

An alternative approach, adopted by President Carter in 1978, is for the government to buy goods and services only from firms that comply with the guideposts. A still stronger response would be to give the guideposts the force of law, which brings us to the next variety of incomes policy.

Wage–Price Controls

Once the government is given the legal authority to *force* labor and industry to adhere to a set of guideposts, we have moved to a system of mandatory wage–price controls. While the United States used such a policy with great success during World War II and again during the Korean War, the Nixon administration's efforts to apply wage–price controls in peacetime is generally considered to have been a failure. This experience has soured many people on the idea of ever using them again.

Before considering some pros and cons of controls, let us stop for a moment to be clear about what economists mean when they say that 1971–1974 price controls "failed." They surely do *not* mean that inflation was not reduced by controls; most students of this period have found that in fact it *was* reduced. Instead, they mean that by middle-to-late 1975 the price level was no lower than it would have been without controls. The implication is that the *lower* inflation rates that prevailed while controls were in effect were counterbalanced by *higher* inflation rates during the year or so after controls were lifted.

This is a fairly typical instance of an incomes policy that was effective in the short run but not in the long run. Instead of improving the trade-off, the controls managed to increase the variability of inflation—making it lower in 1972–1973 and higher in 1974–1975 than it would otherwise have been. In Chapter 6 we pointed out that the *variability* of inflation often exacts more serious social costs than the *average level*. In this sense, then, the controls program was counterproductive, and this is why many economists say that they "failed."

A major justification for controls, to which spokesmen for the Nixon administration and others who supported controls appealed, is that inflation gathers a substantial momentum once workers, consumers, and business managers begin to expect that it will continue. These inflationary expectations encourage workers to demand higher wage increases. Firms, in turn, are willing to grant the workers' demands because they believe they will be able to pass the cost increases on to consumers in a general inflationary environment. Consumers contribute their part to the shell game by purchasing durable goods ahead of their needs in anticipation of higher prices in the future; an action that increases demand and helps fuel the inflation engine. Thus, to a great extent, *inflation occurs because people expect it to occur.*

This analysis provides the best intellectual case for controls. A tough and thorough program of wage and price controls, it is argued, can break the vicious cycle of inflationary expectations. By announcing a controls program, the government serves notice on workers that they do not need anticipatory wage rises to preserve their purchasing power. Firms are warned that they may not be able to pass on higher costs to consumers. And consumers may conclude that buying now to beat future price rises is a poor strategy. By breaking inflationary expectations, supporters argue, a controls program can reduce the rate of inflation.

In practice, it is not clear that this reasoning is valid. For example, it may be that astute workers, business executives, and consumers realize that no controls program can remain in force forever—at least not in a free-market economy like ours. They may then view the temporary dip in the inflation rate caused by controls as an aberration soon to be corrected, and therefore not as a major event that warrants changing their long-term expectations.

Why cannot wage–price controls be a permanent feature of the U.S. economy? We learned the answer to this back in Chapter 4. When price ceilings are effective, they force the price to be below the equilibrium price, so that demand exceeds supply. This is shown by Figure 16–1, in which the equilibrium price of hamburgers is assumed to be 75 cents. If controls do not allow the price of hamburgers to rise above 60 cents, demand will exceed supply by 1 million hamburgers.

With price no longer serving as the rationing device, some other method of rationing is necessary. One possibility is long lines of eager eaters waiting their turn for hamburgers. Scenes like this are quite typical in the Soviet Union, and were witnessed in this country at gasoline stations during the early months of 1974 when gasoline was in short supply. Another is government ration coupons, giving the owner the right to buy a hamburger—a device used successfully during World War II. Neither of these is likely to be popular with the electorate in peacetime. And both are likely to spawn a black market, which erodes respect for law and order at the same time that it abrogates the effects of controls. As critics of controls have pointed out, controls give perfectly law-abiding citizens an incentive to become crimi-

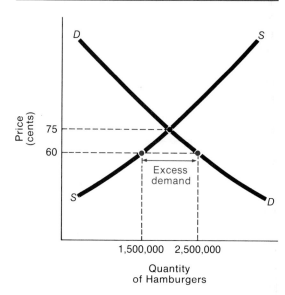

FIGURE 16–1

THE EFFECTS OF PRICE CONTROLS
This diagram portrays the market for hamburgers under an effective price control system. Since the equilibrium price is 75 cents per hamburger, a regulation that holds the price at 60 cents makes the quantity of hamburgers demanded (2,500,000 per year) exceed the quantity supplied (1,500,000 per year). There is a shortage of 1,000,000 hamburgers per year, and some sort of rationing scheme probably will be necessary.

nals by participating in illicit black-market activities.

Wage–Price Freezes

An extreme case of mandatory controls is a "freeze" on wages and prices—a statute making it illegal to increase wages or prices above their levels on some specified date. President Nixon ushered in his controls program with a three-month freeze beginning in mid-August 1971. And there was an even shorter freeze on prices (but not wages) in June–August 1973.

Such an action cannot be considered a constructive incomes policy; it is meant to be a shock treatment—a dramatic action intended to break inflationary expectations. A wage–price freeze also gives an administration contemplating controls some breathing space to plan a rational program. Nothing could be worse than letting people know today that a controls program is on the way. Every firm in America would jack up prices violently. Even news reports that a controls program may begin can have this effect. Former Secretary of the Treasury George P. Shultz explained that the epidemic of rumors of impending controls forced President Nixon to freeze wages and prices in August 1971.

OTHER POLICIES DESIGNED TO SHIFT THE TRADE-OFF

Over the years, a variety of other policies have been designed with the intention of shifting the trade-off between unemployment and inflation in a favorable direction—that is, of reducing the path for the inflation rate that corresponds to any chosen path for the unemployment rate. In terms of our model, these programs can be thought of as efforts at shifting the aggregate supply curve downward.

Vocational training and retraining programs are one example. When successful, they help unemployed workers with obsolete skills to acquire the abilities that are currently in demand. In so doing, they help alleviate upward pressures on wage rates in jobs where qualified workers are in short supply. If an unemployed aerospace engineer can be taught the techniques of pollution control, then progress against both inflation *and* unemployment may be possible. One engineer leaves the ranks of the unemployed, while the addition of one anti-pollution expert helps alleviate the shortage in that profession.

Although the idea sounds appealing and still has many adherents, practical successes with training programs have been rather limited in scope. Too often, people are trained for jobs that do not exist by the time they finish their training—if indeed they ever existed. Even when successful, these programs are quite expensive, which curtails the number of workers that can be accommodated.

The United States Employment Service, and similar agencies at the state and local levels, also try to improve the match of workers to jobs, but not by retraining workers. Instead, they seek to funnel information from prospective employers to prospective employees. Firms are encouraged to list their job vacancies with the Employment Service, and also to inspect the Service's list of people looking for work. Unemployed workers, or people wanting to change jobs, are encouraged to register with the Employment Service and to study its list of openings. In this way, it is hoped, the simultaneous occurrence of unemployed workers with unfilled jobs will be reduced. Most observers agree that the idea is sound and that the U.S. Employment Service has been a constructive force. But, again, it has operated on a scale that is simply too small to make a serious dent in the trade-off. Apparently, many workers do not know about the Employment Service or are reluctant to use it.

Recently, the many government regulations that serve to keep prices artificially high—ranging from agricultural price supports to elimination of price competition among airlines to regulations that require trucks to return empty after delivering their loads—have come under increasing public scrutiny. Each of these, no doubt, serves to prop up specific prices, and thereby to make it more and more unlikely that the general price level will fall. During the Ford administration, which began in the middle of our worst inflation, many of these government interferences with free-market processes came under vigorous verbal assault. And the Carter administration is scrutinizing them once again. While there has been some progress along these lines (for example, in airplane fares), concrete reforms have been minimal to date. It may be that the decade of the 1980s will see substantial price reductions due to regulatory reforms; if so, that would be one factor serving to keep the 1980s less inflationary than the 1970s.[2]

TAX-BASED INCOMES POLICY

A relatively new type of incomes policy has been receiving increasing attention in recent years. Advocated originally by Professor Sidney Weintraub of the University of Pennsylvania, Governor Henry Wallich of the Federal Reserve System, and Arthur Okun of the Brookings Institution, tax-based incomes policy (TIP) seeks to use the tax system to fight inflation. The idea behind TIP is a simple one, though its implementation might be quite complex in practice. TIP would give employers and employees a financial stake in fighting inflation by lowering taxes for firms or workers who abided by national guideposts for wage–price behavior, or by raising taxes for those who violated them.

While there are many TIP plans, one particular example will bring out the flavor of all of them. Suppose the government wants to limit wage increases to 7 percent a year. It could pass legislation granting a 2 percent *decrease* in payroll taxes to all employees of firms in which average wages increased by no more than 7 percent. Then, for example, workers who settled for a (noninflationary) $6\frac{1}{2}$ percent raise would actually wind up with *more* after-tax income than those who settled for an (inflationary) 8 percent raise. They would get $6\frac{1}{2}$ percent more from their employers, plus 2 percent more from the government in the form of lower taxes, for a total gain of $8\frac{1}{2}$ percent. This incentive, it is hoped, would lead labor and management to settle for slower wage

increases; and these slower wage increases, in turn, would lead to slower price increases.

Other TIP plans focus on corporation taxes rather than on payroll taxes, or utilize the "stick" rather than the "carrot" by penalizing the violaters of the wage–price guideposts rather than rewarding those who obey. But the basic principle is always the same: to make noninflationary behavior profitable for either firms or workers, or both.

Is TIP workable? We really have no way of knowing because it never has been tried. However, in late 1978 President Carter asked Congress to enact a modified version of TIP, which he called "real wage insurance."

INDEXING

A very different, but almost as untested, approach to the inflation–unemployment trade-off is indexing.

Indexing refers to provisions in a law or a contract whereby monetary payments are *automatically* adjusted whenever a specified price index changes. Wage rates, pensions, interest payments on bonds, income taxes, and many other things can be indexed in this way, and have been. Sometimes such contractual provisions are called *escalator clauses*.

The mechanics of indexing can be explained best through an example. In the United States the most common form of indexed contract is an escalator clause in a wage agreement. An escalator clause provides for an automatic increase in money wages—without the need for new contract negotiations—any time the price level rises by more than a specified amount. Suppose that with the Consumer Price Index (CPI) sitting at 190, a union and a firm agree on a three-year contract setting wages at $5.50 per hour this year, $5.75 next year, and

---

[2]While these policies would have permanent effects only on the *price level*, not on the *rate of inflation*, their "temporary" effects on inflation might last several years.

$6.00 in the third year. They might then add an escalator clause stating that wages will be increased above these stipulated amounts by 3 cents per hour for each point by which the CPI exceeds 200 in any future year of the contract. Then, if the CPI in year 3 of the contract reaches 210, workers will receive an additional 30 cents per hour (3 cents for each of the 10 points by which 210 exceeds 200), for a total wage of $6.30 per hour. In this way, workers are partly protected from inflation.

Nowadays, about half of all workers employed by large unionized firms in the United States are covered by some sort of escalator clause. However, very few nonunion workers or employees of small firms enjoy such protection.

Interest payments on bonds or savings accounts can also be indexed, although this is not currently done in the United States.[3] The mechanics here are quite simple. If you had an indexed savings account, your bank might guarantee you a 2 percent *real interest rate* on your savings by automatically increasing your balance by the amount of inflation. For example, suppose you deposited $1000 on January 1 and withdrew it on December 31. An ordinary savings account, paying 5 percent interest, would pay you $1050 at the end of the year— your original $1000 plus 5 percent interest. But if this were an indexed bank account paying 2 percent, and prices rose by 4 percent during the year, your balance at year-end would be $1060—your original $1000 plus 2 percent real interest ($20) plus 4 percent ($40) to compensate you for your loss of purchasing power. The *nominal interest rate* would thus be 6 percent. (Real versus nominal interest rates, one of our 12 Ideas for Beyond the Final Exam, was discussed in detail in Chapter 6.)

In general, the nominal rate would be 2 percent *plus* the rate of inflation. Thus if inflation turned out to be less than 3 percent that year, you would receive less than $1050.

[3]Some other countries, with much higher inflation than ours, do extensive indexing of interest rates. Brazil and Israel are notable examples.

Indexing is not designed to keep interest rates *high*, but to make real interest payments independent of inflation—to cut down the chances that the purchasing power of savings will be eroded by inflation.

With a conventional 5 percent savings account you get a real interest rate of 5 percent if there is zero inflation, 3 percent if there is 2 percent inflation, 1 percent if there is 4 percent inflation, and so on. With an imaginary 2 percent indexed account, you would receive 2 percent real interest no matter what the inflation rate. Indexing thus enables the saver to avoid gambling on inflation. For this reason, many economists have advocated that the U.S. government issue an indexed savings bond that small savers could use to protect themselves against inflation.

The most extensive indexing to be found in the United States today is in government transfer payments. Social security benefits, for instance, are fully indexed so that retirees are not victimized by inflation. A variety of government income maintenance and social insurance programs also pay benefits that are tied directly to prices.

INDEXING AND THE SOCIAL COSTS OF INFLATION

Some economists believe that the United States should follow the example of several foreign countries and adopt a much more widespread system of indexing. Why? Because, they argue, it would take most of the sting out of inflation. To see how indexing would accomplish this, let us review some of the social costs of inflation that we enumerated in Chapter 6.

One important cost was the capricious redistribution of income caused by unexpected inflation or deflation. We saw that borrowers and lenders normally incorporate an *inflation premium* equal to the *expected rate of inflation* into the interest rate. Then, if inflation turns out to be higher than expected, the borrower enjoys a windfall gain while the lender suffers a windfall loss. By contrast, if inflation turns out to be lower than expected, the lender wins and the borrower loses.

But if interest rates on loans were indexed, none of this would occur. Borrowers and lenders would agree on a fixed *real* rate of interest, and then the borrower would compensate the lender for whatever *actual inflation* occurred. No one would have to guess what the inflation rate would be.

A second social cost we mentioned in Chapter 6 stemmed from the fact that certain legal restrictions and regulations on interest and profit rates that may or may not be sensible in a noninflationary world can have incredibly perverse effects in an inflationary environment. For example, we cited the case of usury ceilings on home mortgages, which, while intended to protect home buyers, have the effect of making it almost impossible to build a home when inflation rates are high. If these regulations were

stated in terms of *real* interest and profit rates, none of these strange—and unintended—distortions would arise.

A final problem noted in Chapter 6 was that uncertainty over future price levels makes it difficult to enter into long-term contracts—rental agreements, construction agreements, and so on. One way out of this problem is to write indexed contracts, which specify all future payments in real terms.

In the face of all these benefits, and others we have not mentioned here, why do many economists oppose indexing? Probably the major reason is the fear that indexing will lead to an acceleration of inflation. With the costs of inflation reduced so markedly, they argue, what will stop governments from inflating more and more? They fear that there is a very simple answer to this question: Nothing. Voters who stand to lose nothing from inflation are unlikely to pressure their legislators into stopping it. Opponents of indexing worry that a mild inflationary disease could turn into a ravaging epidemic in a highly indexed economy.

Are There Politically Induced Business Cycles?

Much of Part Three of this text has been devoted to explaining how monetary and fiscal policy can be used to *smooth out* business fluctuations that are caused by gyrations of private demand. But can it be that the government sometimes uses its influence over aggregate demand to *cause* business cycles rather than to eliminate them? Many economists and political scientists believe that this sometimes happens—not only in the United States, but also in other democratic nations.

LAGS IN ECONOMIC BEHAVIOR

To understand how and why political business cycles can work, we must review what we have

learned about some of the lags involved in macroeconomic behavior and add several new pieces of information.

The first new aspect is that increases or decreases in employment systematically lag behind increases or decreases in production. Suppose, for example, that the government raises taxes or reduces the growth of the money supply. After a while, income and sales begin to fall. But, in the early stages of the contractionary process, firms typically respond to the lower demands without decreasing their payrolls very much. They try to reduce production without firing many workers. Why? Because they are not sure how long the period of reduced demand will last, and so hesitate to lay off trained workers whom they may not be able to get back when sales perk up again. Of course, if the downswing persists, layoffs will surely follow.

The second new piece of information is that the unemployment rate—the most closely watched barometer of the state of the labor market—moves even more slowly than employment. Indeed, unemployment may not budge an inch for many months after a fiscal policy action, and then it may decline precipitously (in the case of a tax cut) or rise dramatically (in the case of a tax rise).

The main reason why unemployment lags behind employment is that the size of the labor force is sensitive to employment prospects. When the outlook for jobs brightens, many so-called "secondary workers"—teen-agers, older men, and some women—are attracted into the labor force to look for work. Some of them find jobs, but others join the ranks of the unemployed. The outcome may be that the number of *unemployed* people stays roughly constant (or even increases) while the number of *employed* people rises. Similarly, when business conditions deteriorate, many of these secondary workers become discouraged and give up looking for work. At this point they drop out of the official labor-force statistics and are no longer counted as "unemployed." So unemployment does not rise as quickly as employment falls.

Eventually, however, the response of the labor force is played out. There are, after all, only a certain number of workers who can be discouraged. Breadwinners, for example, simply have to keep looking for jobs. At this point, the unemployment rate may skyrocket. The 1974–1975 downswing provides a stunning example. The unemployment rate drifted up from 5 percent to $5\frac{1}{2}$ percent during the first 8 months of 1974, and then leaped from $5\frac{1}{2}$ percent to $8\frac{1}{2}$ percent in only 7 months.

When we combine these two lags with some aspects of the behavior of the economy with which we are already familiar, a scenario something like the following emerges. Suppose the government takes any of a variety of actions

FIGURE 16–2
THE MACROECONOMIC BATTING ORDER

GOVERNMENT SPENDING OR
THE MONEY SUPPLY RISES
↓
GROSS NATIONAL PRODUCT RISES
↓
EMPLOYMENT RISES
↓
UNEMPLOYMENT FALLS
↓
WAGE INFLATION ACCELERATES
↓
PRICE INFLATION ACCELERATES

that stimulate aggregate demand. The first variable to show much reaction probably will be the real GNP. Lagging somewhat behind the rise in real GNP will come an increase in employment and, with yet another delay, unemployment will fall. The Phillips curve, which was introduced in the previous chapter (see pages 286–288), shows that a reduction in unemployment will lead next to an acceleration in wages. And we have mentioned many times that rising wages lead to rising prices, with yet another lag. Figure 16–2 summarizes the macroeconomic "batting order" that we have just outlined. With all these intervening steps, the total lag between government actions that stimulate aggregate demand and any appreciable acceleration of inflation can easily be 2 years or more.

THE POLITICAL BUSINESS CYCLE: THEORY

As we shall see now, the batting order that we have just summarized gives politicians the raw materials with which to engineer what have been called political business cycles, that is, business fluctuations caused not by fluctuations

303

in private demand nor by fluctuations in aggregate supply, but by the deliberate manipulation of fiscal and monetary policy for political ends.

But to make the medicine work, politicians must have the cooperation of the electorate. Political scientists and economists who have studied the way voters react to macroeconomic events have concluded tentatively that while many other influences (such as personality) are important:

1. Voters do indeed react to economic conditions, penalizing incumbents in bad times and rewarding them in good times.
2. Of all the economic variables, voters apparently care most about their real disposable incomes. To a lesser extent they want to see low unemployment and low inflation.
3. People have short memories when it is time to vote. The evidence is that the most important economic variable to voters is *the growth rate of real income during the year prior to the election*. Incredible as this may sound, the implication of this finding is that three years of stagnation followed by a single year of exuberant growth provides an ideal economic platform on which to run!

Finally, it is abundantly clear that politicians of both parties are aware both of the voting patterns just enumerated and of the relevant lags in economic behavior. Indeed, these voting patterns and economic lags are not unique to the United States. More or less the same patterns seem to hold for other political democracies as well.

The stage now is set to play out the political business cycle. The script reads like this. Some time between one and two years before the election, an incumbent president (with the help of an election-minded Congress) opens up the fiscal policy throttles. New spending programs, high transfer payments, tax cuts, and the like set in motion a vigorous economic expansion. If he can, the president also persuades the

Federal Reserve to join the cast by increasing the rate of expansion of the money stock.

Real income responds most quickly to such stimuli, with unemployment next and inflation last. Thus, when election day arrives GNP is expanding smartly. Depending on how skillful the timing is, the unemployment rate may be either high but falling rapidly, moderate and still falling, or stable and low. And the incipient inflation has yet to show its face. All in all, these are very pleasant circumstances under which to stand for reelection.

At some point after the election, the president and Congress will come under pressure to "do something about the inflation." They can then engineer a "made-in-Washington" recession, which the voters will have conveniently forgotten by the next presidential election.

We would not wish to exaggerate the ease with which such an operation can be pulled off. Economic lags are variable and hard to predict with great precision. Successful orchestration of a political business cycle like the one just described requires both consummate skill and remarkable luck. But, of course, so does a successful campaign for the White House.

THE POLITICAL BUSINESS CYCLE: EVIDENCE

Has a political business cycle ever happened in the United States? Many observers feel that it has, and that the first Nixon administration is perhaps the best example. Upon assuming office in 1969 as the inheritor of President Johnson's Vietnam inflation, President Nixon took an appropriately hard line on government spending. With the Fed also clamping down on money and credit, the mild recession of 1969–1970 ensued, although the incipient gains on the inflation front were barely visible when wage and price controls were instituted in August

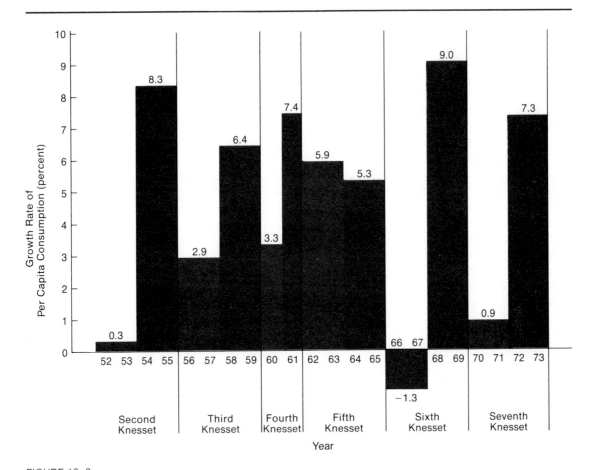

FIGURE 16–3

THE POLITICAL BUSINESS CYCLE IN ISRAEL

This diagram shows the growth rate of consumption per capita in Israel from 1952 to 1973. Election times are indicated by the vertical lines. In all cases but one, the growth of consumption was much higher in the preelection period (the dark red bars) than in the postelection period (the light red bars). This seems to be evidence for a political business cycle.

Source: Yoram Ben-Porath, "The Years of Plenty and the Years of Famine—A Political Business Cycle?" *Kyklos,* vol. 28, 1975, Fasc. 2, page 401.

1971. Astute politicians are, after all, no more patient than voters.

These contractionary monetary and fiscal policies were abruptly reversed in the election year of 1972, as the federal pocketbook was proffered to all sorts of petitioners suddenly deemed "worthy." The result was predictable:

1972 was a boom year. Mr. Nixon's landslide reelection took place with income growing briskly, unemployment falling, and the inflation rate continuing to recede.

While this may have been the most extreme episode, the election year stimulation of the economy in 1972 was by no means unique. In an examination of U.S. data from 1947 to 1976, Yale political scientist Edward Tufte found that, when the Eisenhower years are excluded, the growth in real disposable income per capita sped up in 8 of 11 election years and slowed down in 8 of 10 odd-numbered years.[4] A coincidence? Perhaps. But try duplicating this pattern by tossing a coin. (The chances are 1 in 284!)

The Nixon example should not be misconstrued as suggesting that political business cycles are a Republican game. Far from it. We have just noted that President Eisenhower was a conspicuous exception to the usual pattern. And many people have wondered whether President Ford's reluctance to stimulate the economy in 1976 did not cost him the election.

Nor is the political business cycle restricted to the United States. When Tufte compiled data on 27 democracies over the period 1961–1972 (a total of 295 country-years and 90 elections), he discovered "evidence for an electoral-economic cycle . . . in 19 of the 27 countries; in those 19, short-run accelerations in real disposable income per capita were more likely to occur in election years than in years without elections. . . . Real disposable income accelerated in 77 percent of election years compared with 46 percent of years without elections."[5]

The case of Israel is particularly fascinating. Figure 16–3 (page 305) is a diagram reproduced from an article by the Israeli economist Yoram Ben-Porath. Time is measured along the horizontal axis, which is subdivided according to when elections were held in Israel. The vertical lines indicate the election dates. (The "Knesset" is the Israeli parliament.) The annual growth rate of per capita consumption is measured on the vertical axis. To quote Ben-Porath: "The systematic difference between the rate of growth in the post- and pre-election period is glaring and probably nothing more need be said."[6]

It appears, then, that if there is no such thing as a political business cycle, then there are a lot of stunning coincidences to be explained in a lot of countries.

Is the National Debt a Burden?

Few subjects have been debated for so many years with so much heat and so little light as the national debt. Doomsayers have argued, year after year, that the next increase in debt would mark our downfall as a nation. Exactly how or why this was supposed to happen was always a bit mysterious, but the fact that it has never happened has not stopped the outcries against "ruinous" budget deficits.

Shortly, we will review some of the bogus arguments that claim to show that the national debt is a "burden on future generations." And we will also learn that there is one major valid argument. But before doing so, it is worthwhile to get the facts straight. How large a public debt do we have? How did we get it? Who owns it? Is it really growing rapidly?

SOME FACTS ABOUT THE NATIONAL DEBT

To begin with the simplest question, the public debt is enormous: At the beginning of 1978, it amounted to about $730 billion, roughly $3300

---

[4]Edward R. Tufte, *Political Control of the Economy* (Princeton: Princeton University Press, 1978), page 15. According to Tufte, Eisenhower's administration seemed to care more about balancing the budget in election years than about stimulating the economy.

[5]Tufte, *Political Control of the Economy*, page 11.
[6]Yoram Ben-Porath, "The Years of Plenty and the Years of Famine—A Political Business Cycle?" *Kyklos*, vol. 28, 1975, page 400.

for every man, woman, and child in America. But nearly 35 percent of this outstanding debt is owned by agencies of the U.S. government—in other words, one branch of the government owes it to another. If we deduct this portion, the net national debt is only about $475 billon, or around $2100 per person. Furthermore, when we compare the debt with the gross national product—the volume of goods and services our economy produces in a year—it does not seem so large after all. With a GNP of almost $2000 billon in early 1978, the net debt was less than one-quarter of a year's income. By contrast, many families who own homes owe *several years'* worth of income to the bank that granted them a mortgage. Many U.S. corporations also owe their bondholders much more than one-quarter of a year's sales.

But before these analogies make you feel too comfortable, we should point out that simple analogies between public and private debt are almost always misleading. A family with a large mortgage debt also owns a home with a value that presumably exceeds the mortgage. A solvent business firm has assets (factories, machinery, inventories, and so forth) that far exceed its outstanding bonds in value. Is the same thing true of the U.S. government?

"Oh, it's great here, all right, but I sort of feel uncomfortable in a place with no budget at *all*."

Nobody knows. How much is the White House worth? Or the national parks? And what about military bases, both here and abroad? Simply because these government assets are *not* sold on markets, no one can tell whether the federal government's assets exceed its debt or not. But, fortunately, the answer to this question is not momentous. For, while a family or a firm whose debts exceed its assets is in deep trouble, the same is not true of the U.S government.

Figure 16–4 charts the irregular increase in the national debt from 1915 to 1978. You will notice that most of the debt was acquired during wars, especially World War II. Other than wars, recessions loom as the biggest reason why the U.S. government has accumulated such a debt, especially the latest recession. When economic activity falls, tax receipts of the federal government fall because of the heavy reliance on income taxes. As we shall see later, the *cause* of the debt is quite germane to the question of whether or not the debt is a burden. So it is important to remember that:

Most of the U.S. national debt has been accumulated in financing wars and through the losses of tax revenues that accompany recessions.

Figure 16–5 takes the next step and divides the national debt, year by year, by the gross national product as a measure of the size of the debt relative to our income. Thus, the height of the graph indicates the fraction of a year's output that the national debt represents. Here, in contrast to Figure 16–4, we see an unmistakable downward trend since the dizzying heights of World War II, interrupted only by the huge deficits (the largest ever in peacetime) of the Great Recession of 1974–1975. In 1945, for example, the national debt was the equivalent of 13 months' national income. By 1974 this figure had been whittled down to 2 months. If we use this as a crude indicator of the nation's ability to "pay off" its debt, then the burden of the debt has clearly been easing since 1945.

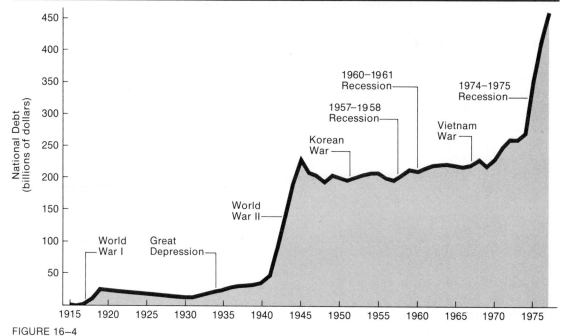

FIGURE 16–4

THE U.S. NATIONAL DEBT, 1915–1978

This graph charts the behavior of the public debt in the United States, after subtracting out the portion of the debt that is held by government agencies. It is clear that just about all the increases can be accounted for by wars and recessions. Few people realize that the public debt was about the same in 1972 as it was in 1945.

Source: Constructed by the authors from data in *Historical Statistics of the United States* and *Economic Report of the President.*

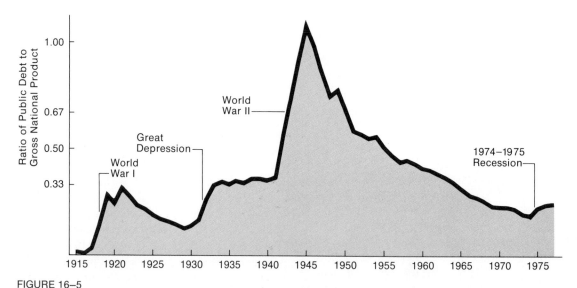

FIGURE 16–5

RATIO OF PUBLIC DEBT TO GROSS NATIONAL PRODUCT

This graph takes the data in Figure 16–4 and divides each year's debt by the gross national product of that year. We can see that the debt grew relative to GNP during the two world wars, during the Great Depression, and during the Great Recession. Other than that, the debt generally has fallen relative to GNP.

BOGUS ARGUMENTS ABOUT THE BURDEN OF THE DEBT

Having gained some perspective on the facts, let us now turn to some of the arguments advanced by those who claim that by accumulating such a debt we have placed an intolerable burden on future generations.

Argument 1: Our children and grandchildren will be burdened by heavy interest payments. To meet these payments there will have to be higher taxes.

Answer: It is certainly true that a higher debt will necessitate higher interest payments and, other things being equal, this will lead to higher taxes paid by our children and grandchildren. But think who will receive the higher interest payments as income: our children and grandchildren! Thus one group of future Americans will, essentially, be making interest payments to another group of future Americans. We conclude that:

As long as the national debt is owned by domestic citizens, as the great bulk of the U.S. debt is, the future interest payments merely amount to shuffling money from one group of Americans to another, and this can hardly constitute a burden to the nation as a whole.

However, this argument *is* valid to the extent that foreigners hold our debt. To pay the interest on this portion of the debt will be a burden on future generations of Americans. Another possibly valid element of the argument is that the higher taxes and interest payments amount to a *redistribution of income* that may be deplored by some (though applauded by others).

Argument 2: It will ruin the nation when we have to pay the enormous debt back.

Answer: A first answer to this merely rephrases the answer to the previous argument: Only the part owned by foreigners involves any burden; the rest is paid by one group of Americans to another. But there is a much more fundamental point. *Unlike a private family, the nation need never pay off its debt.* Instead, each time the principal is due, the U.S. Treasury can simply "roll it over" by floating more debt. Indeed, this is precisely what the Treasury does.

Is this a bit of chicanery? How can the U.S. government get away with making loans that it never intends to pay back? The answer is found by recognizing the fallacy of comparing the U.S. government to a family or individual. People cannot be extended credit in perpetuity because they will not live that long. Sensible lenders will not extend long-term credit to very old people because their heirs cannot be forced to pay up. But the U.S. government will never "die"; at least, we hope not! So this factor does not arise. In this respect, the government is in much the same position as a large corporation. The American Telephone and Telegraph Company never worries about paying off its debt. It too rolls it over by floating new debt all the time. We can contrast this with shaky governments in unstable countries. Because investors have legitimate fears that these governments might "die," these nations often find it difficult to secure credit.

Argument 3: It will bankrupt the nation. Like any family or any business firm, a nation has a limited capacity to borrow. If it exceeds this limit, it is in danger of being unable to pay its creditors. It may go bankrupt with calamitous consequences for everyone.

Answer: This is another example of a false analogy. What is claimed about private debtors is certainly true. But the U.S. government need never fear defaulting on its debt. Why? First, because it has enormous power to raise revenues by taxation. Imagine if you had such power; you would never have to fear bankruptcy either.

But there is a still more fundamental point— one that distinguishes the U.S. debt from that of many foreign nations. *The American national debt is an obligation to pay U.S. dollars:* Each debt certificate obligates the Treasury to pay the holder so many U.S. dollars on a prescribed date. But the U.S. government is the source of these dollars; it prints them up! *No nation need ever fear defaulting on debts that call for repayment in its own currency.* At the very worst, it can always print whatever money it needs to pay off its creditors.

Two qualifications should be placed on this conclusion. First, it does not follow that acquiring debt through budget deficits is therefore always a good idea. Sometimes it is clearly a very bad idea. Printing money to pay the debt will expand demand and cause inflation, and this often will be undesirable. The point is not that budget deficits are either good or bad—we already know that they can be either under the appropriate circumstances. Rather, the point is that worrying about a possible default on the national debt is unnecessary and even foolish.

Second, many foreign governments, especially those of the less developed countries, are not in such a fortunate position. Because of uncertainties about the value of their currency, most debts incurred by these nations call for repayment in some other currency, usually U.S. dollars. Since no foreign government has the ability to manufacture U.S. dollars, these countries must earn their dollars by exporting goods. They therefore do have a limited capacity to borrow (just as the United States has a limited capacity to borrow German marks) and can conceivably default on their debts.

THE REAL BURDEN OF THE NATIONAL DEBT

Having cleared the air of these fallacious arguments, we are now in a position to explore the one potential burden of the debt that is real.

Valid Burden-of-the-Debt Argument: Because of the large national debt, we may bequeath less physical capital to future generations. If they inherit less plant and equipment, these generations will be burdened by a lower productive capacity—a lower potential GNP.

The logic of this argument is simple and quite compelling. When it runs a deficit and has to borrow funds, the U.S. Treasury drives up the rate of interest. (This is what always happens to a price in a market when the demand schedule is increased and the supply schedule is fixed.) But higher interest rates discourage investment. Future generations will therefore have less capital to work with.

If this argument sounds familiar to you, it should. We are just repeating the "crowding-out" hypothesis that we discussed at the end of Chapter 13. The idea is simply that federal government borrowing reduces investment by crowding out private borrowers. In Chapter 13, where we learned the essential truth in this argument, we also saw that there could be a strong "crowding-in" effect if there are unemployed resources. That is, the government spending or tax cuts that cause the deficit have multiplier effects on real GNP, and this GNP growth stimulates more investment spending and saving. Thus:

When government budget deficits take place in a high-employment economy, the crowding-out effect will probably dominate, so the deficits will exact a burden by leaving a smaller capital stock to future generations. However, deficits in a slack economy may well lead to more investment rather than less. In this case, where the crowding-in effect dominates, the debt is a blessing rather than a burden.

Let us now go back to the historical facts and recall how we have accumulated such a large national debt. The first cause was the financing of wars, especially World War II. This debt was contracted in a fully employed economy, and thus undoubtedly constituted a burden in the formal sense. It left future generations with less capital because some of our nation's resources were diverted from private investment into government production. The bombs, ships, and planes that it financed were used up in the war, not bequeathed as capital to future generations. Yet what were the alternatives? We could have tried to finance the entire war by taxation, and thus placed the burden on consumption rather than on investment. But that would truly have been ruinous, and probably even impossible, given the colossal wartime expenditures. Or we could have printed money, but that would have unleashed an inflation that nobody wanted. Or we could have just done much less government spending and perhaps not have won the war. So, in retrospect, the generations alive today and in the future may not feel unduly burdened by the decisions of the people in power in the 1940s. Imagine how much of a different kind of burden they would have inherited had the United States not won the war.

The second major contributor to the national debt has been the series of recessions, especially the latest one. But these are precisely the circumstances under which increasing the debt might prove to be a blessing rather than a burden.

So, if we look for the classic type of deficits to which the valid burden-of-the-debt argument applies—deficits acquired in a fully employed peacetime economy—we have a hard time finding them in the U.S. record.

Let us now summarize our evaluation of the burden of the national debt, and thereby restate one of the 12 Ideas for Beyond the Final Exam introduced in Chapter 1. First, the arguments that a large national debt may lead the nation into bankruptcy, or unduly burden future generations who have to make onerous payments of interest and principal, are mostly bogus. Second, the national debt *will* be a burden if it is contracted in a fully employed peacetime economy, because in that case it will reduce the nation's capital stock. Third, there are circumstances in which budget deficits are quite appropriate for stabilization reasons. Fourth, and finally, the actual public debt of the United States government was contracted as a result of wars and recessions—precisely the circumstances under which the valid burden-of-the-debt argument does not apply. We are thus led to the conclusion that the current national debt cannot reasonably be considered a serious burden.

SUMMARY

1. Many varieties of incomes policies have been used in this and other countries in an effort to improve the trade-off between inflation and unemployment. While some have led to temporary improvements, none has had any lasting effects.
2. The weakest varieties of incomes policies simply set up standards for permissible wage and price increases (wage–price guideposts) and apply verbal admonitions against violators (jawboning). Stronger variants may actually set legal limits on wage and price increases or even ban them outright (a wage–price freeze).
3. One argument in favor of short-term wage–price controls is that they can reduce inflationary expectations and thereby rob inflation of some of its momentum.
4. Policies that improve the functioning of the labor market—including retraining programs and various types of employment services—can also improve the trade-off between inflation and unemployment. However, the

U.S. government has had only modest success with these measures to date.

5. A new and different approach to incomes policy would use tax incentives to encourage more moderate wage and price increases. This so-called "tax-based incomes policy" has yet to be tried.

6. Indexing is another way to approach the trade-off problem. Instead of trying to improve the trade-off, it concentrates on reducing the social costs of inflation—perhaps eliminating them altogether. Opponents of indexing worry, however, that the economy's resistance to inflation may be lowered by indexing.

7. Politically induced business cycles are a theoretical possibility because, following a dose of expansionary fiscal or monetary policy, real income is the first variable to respond, followed by unemployment, with inflation bringing up the rear. These lags give politicians the opportunity to expand the economy just before elections, causing output to rise but deferring the inflationary price tag until after the election. Since voters seem to be very myopic, this strategy can conceivably pay off at the polls.

8. There seem to be examples of political business cycles in the United States and in foreign countries as well.

9. The public has many misconceptions about the national debt. For example, while the national debt is very large, it generally has grown much less rapidly than has national income in the postwar period.

10. Fallacious arguments that the public debt will burden future generations because they will have to make huge payments of interest and principal are based on false analogies. In fact, most of these payments of interest and principal are simply transfers from some Americans to other Americans. Besides, the Treasury can, and normally does, "roll over" its debt rather than pay it off. In doing this, it is following the practice of most large private corporations.

11. The bogus argument that a large national debt can bankrupt a country like the United States ignores the fact that our national debt consists of obligations to pay U.S. dollars—a currency the government can raise by taxation or create by printing money.

12. There is, however, one potentially real burden of the debt. Because government borrowing pushes up interest rates, some private investors may be "crowded out" of the financial markets so that the volume of private investment may be reduced. If this happens, future generations will inherit a smaller capital stock and hence a smaller productive capacity.

13. The validity of this argument depends on how and why the government ran these deficits in the first place. One example is deficits contracted to fight recessions. It is possible that more investment was "crowded in" by the increases in income that these deficits made possible than was "crowded out" by the increases in interest rates. Or another example: Even though deficits contracted to carry on wars certainly impair the future capital stock, they may not be considered a burden for noneconomic reasons. Since these two examples account for most of America's public debt, our national debt cannot reasonably be considered a serious burden. This is one of the 12 Ideas for Beyond the Final Exam.

CONCEPTS FOR REVIEW

Incomes policy
Jawboning
Wage–price guideposts
Wage–price controls
Inflationary expectations
Wage–price freezes

Tax-based incomes policy (TIP)
Indexing (escalator clauses)
Real versus nominal interest rates
Political business cycle
National debt

QUESTIONS FOR DISCUSSION

1. Do you think it is proper for the president of the United States to "jawbone" some corporations into reducing their price increases?
2. Explain some of the differences between wage–price guideposts and wage–price controls.
3. Suppose that a program of wage–price controls is under consideration by the government. What are the possible benefits to the nation from such a program? What are the possible costs? How would you go about balancing the benefits against the costs?
4. Explain the basic idea behind "TIP" (tax-based incomes policy). Try to devise a TIP plan of your own. Can you foresee some practical difficulties with your plan?
5. Ordinary savings accounts now pay approximately $5\frac{1}{2}$ percent *nominal* interest. Would you prefer to trade yours in for an indexed bank account that paid a zero *real* rate of interest? What if the real interest rate offered were 1 percent? What if it were –1 percent? What do your answers to these questions reveal about your personal attitudes toward inflation?
6. Suppose government transfer payments increase by $10 billion. Put the following series of events into their proper order (which comes first, which second, and so on?):
   a. The unemployment rate drops by 0.3 percent
   b. Real GNP increases by $20 billion
   c. Disposable income increases by $10 billion
   d. Wages rise by 1 percent
   e. Prices rise by 1 percent
   f. Employment increases by 600,000 persons
7. Explain why the political business cycle might not work if either:
   a. voters realized that stimulation of the economy would subsequently lead to more inflation, and they disliked inflation
   b. voters based their decision on the growth of real disposable income during the previous *four* years
8. Comment on the following: "Deficit spending paves the road to ruination. If we keep it up, the whole nation will go bankrupt. Even if things do not go this far, what right have we to burden our children and grandchildren with these debts while we live high on the hog?"
9. Explain how the United States government has managed to accumulate a debt of more than $700 billion. To whom does it owe this debt? Can this debt be considered a burden on future generations?

17

Measurement in Macroeconomics

The focus of Part Three has been on why the economy may often need to be steered by stabilization policy, how these policies work, and why they do not always succeed. But before policymakers can try to *control* the economy, they must be able to *measure* its performance. We cannot know where we are going if we do not know where we are.

Some instructors prefer to treat the materials in this chapter before the materials in Chapters 8–16. To this end, the chapter has been written to be understood by students who have not yet read Chapters 8–16. Only the last two sections need be omitted by students learning the materials in this order.

The first objective of this chapter, therefore, is to gain some understanding of how government economists and statisticians take the pulse of the economy. Since the gross national product (GNP) is the primary indicator of the pace of economic activity, we begin with a much more precise and detailed definition of the GNP than we have used in earlier chapters. We then study how the GNP is measured and note that there are several ways to go about this task.

We turn next to a consideration of what the GNP is *not*. This is important because the press and the public often treat the GNP as a measure of the nation's well-being. But as we shall see, it is not a measure of well-being and was never intended to be.

Finally, by looking at some of the details of our national accounting system, we will begin to understand some of the ways in which the actual economy is far more complicated than the models we have constructed suggest. We will then see how this complexity explains the unwieldy size of the giant computer models that many economists use to study macroeconomic behavior. However, we will also see that in their fundamental relationships, when all inessential details have been cleared away, these complex models are really based on just the kind of analysis we have been presenting in Part Three. Thus, while the picture we have painted in earlier chapters is certainly simplified, it does help us understand the real world, much as Map 2 of Los Angeles in Chapter 1 (page 12) helps explain the geography of that city even though it leaves out most of the rich detail provided in Map 1.

NATIONAL INCOME ACCOUNTING

The type of macroeconomic analysis presented in this book dates from the publication of John Maynard Keynes's *The General Theory of Employment, Interest, and Money* in 1936. But at that time there was really no way to test Keynes's theories against actual data because the necessary data did not exist. It took some years for the theoretical notions used by Keynes to find concrete expression in real-world data. The system of measurement devised for this purpose is called national income accounting.

The development of this system of accounts ranks as a great achievement in applied economics, perhaps as important in its own right as Keynes's theoretical work. For, without it, the practical value of Keynesian analysis would be severely limited. Many men and women spent long hours wrestling with the numerous difficult conceptual questions that arose in translating the theory into numbers, but they had one acknowledged leader: Professor Simon Kuznets of Harvard University, who, in 1971, was awarded the Nobel Prize in Economics for his contributions to economic measurement techniques. Along the way some more-or-less arbitrary decisions and conventions had to be made. You may not agree with all of them, but the accounting framework that was devised is eminently serviceable, though, inevitably, it has some limitations that must be understood.

THE GROSS NATIONAL PRODUCT: DEFINITION

Our first task is to define the gross national product. Just *which* goods and services should be counted in the GNP and which ones should be excluded? National income accountants have decided to define the GNP as follows:

DEFINITION
Gross National Product (GNP) is the sum of the money values of all final goods and services that are produced during a specified period of time, usually one year.

Several aspects of this definition need to be underscored, and then we shall note some exceptions. First, you will notice that:

We add up the *money values* of things.

The GNP consists of a bewildering variety of goods and services: mousetraps and computers, bologna and caviar, ballet performances and hula hoops, tanks and textbooks. How are we to combine all of these into a single number? To an economist, the natural way to do this is first to convert every good and service into *money* terms. If we want to add 10 apples and 20 oranges, we first ask: How much *money* does each cost? If apples cost 20 cents and oranges cost 25 cents, then the apples count for $2 and the oranges for $5, so the sum is $7 worth of "output." The market *price* of each good or service is used as an indicator of its *value* to society simply because *someone* is willing to pay that much money for it.

This already suggests one problem with using the GNP as a measure of the nation's well-being. Each of you probably can think of some things that are not, in your own opinion, "worth" what they cost. Indeed, you no doubt can think of things you would not want even if they were offered to you free. Yet someone values these things, or else they could not be sold at a positive price. Similarly, there are other things that you no doubt consider a bargain; to you, they are "worth" more than they cost. This means that if each individual were to value all the items that society produces according to his or her own preferences, then each person would come up with a different figure for the GNP. As this certainly will not do, market prices are used as a kind of common denominator, reflecting the value that a "typical" consumer places on each item. But this means that some activities that increase the GNP may be of no value *in your opinion*. In fact, they might even have negative value. If you are a nonsmoker, for example, an increase in the output of the cigarette industry is not only useless to you, but may make you genuinely unhappy if someone blows smoke in your face. But the new cigarettes count in the GNP nevertheless, since someone else prizes them.

The next important aspect of the definition is that:

The GNP for a particular year includes only those goods and services that are produced during that year. In other words, sales of items that were produced in previous years are explicitly excluded.

For example, suppose you buy a perfectly beautiful 1968 Pontiac next week and are overjoyed by your purchase. The national income statistician will not share your glee because she already counted your car in the GNP in 1968 when it was first produced and sold; the car will never be counted again. The same holds true of houses. An old house (unlike an old car) often will sell for more than its purchaser originally paid; yet the resale value of the house does not count in the GNP since it was already counted in the year it was built. For the same reason, transactions on the stock market and other exchanges of existing assets are not included in the GNP.

Third, you will notice we have used the adjective "final."

DEFINITION
Final goods and services are those that are purchased by their ultimate users.

For example, when the gas company buys gas from an interstate pipeline company, the transaction is not included in the GNP because the gas company does not want the gas for itself. It buys gas only for resale to homeowners. Only when the gas is sold to homeowners is it considered a final product. When the gas company buys it, economists consider it an intermediate good.

DEFINITION
An *intermediate good* is a good purchased for resale or for use in producing another good. The GNP does not include sales of intermediate goods or services.

To exemplify this idea better, let us consider the data in Table 17–1. Our illustration begins when a farmer who grows soybeans sells them to a mill for $3 a bushel. This transaction does *not* count in the GNP, because the miller does not purchase them for his own use. The miller then grinds up the soybeans, and sells the resulting bag of soy meal to a factory that

TABLE 17–1

AN ILLUSTRATION OF FINAL AND INTERMEDIATE GOODS

ITEM	SELLER	BUYER	PRICE
Bushel of soybeans	Farmer	Miller	$ 3
Bag of soy meal	Miller	Factory	4
Gallon of soy sauce	Factory	Restaurant	8
Gallon of soy sauce used as seasoning	Restaurant	Consumers	10
		Total:	$25
		Addendum: Contribution to GNP:	$10

produces soy sauce. The miller receives $4, but GNP still has not increased because the ground beans are also an intermediate product. Next, the factory turns the beans into soy sauce, which it sells to your favorite Chinese restaurant for $8. Still no effect on GNP. But then the big moment arrives: The restaurant sells the sauce to you and other customers as a part of your meals, and you eat it. At this point, the $10 worth of soy sauce becomes a final product and is included in the GNP.

What is the logic of this procedure? After all, transactions in intermediate goods also have value. Why do we not count these along with transactions in final goods? The reason is that we are interested in measuring the economy's new output, and if we counted all the intermediate goods, we would be double or triple counting, and would get an exaggerated impression of the amount of economic activity that is actually going on.

Look again at Table 17–1, which summarizes the four transactions in the life of the soybeans. As we have just noted, only the last transaction counts in the GNP. So all of this activity raises GNP by $10. If we had also counted the three intermediate transactions (farmer to miller, miller to factory, factory to restaurant), we would have come up with $25— two and one-half times too much.

Why is it too much? The reason is straightforward. Neither the miller nor the factory owner

nor the restauranteur value the product we have been considering *for its own sake*. Only the customers who eat the final product (the soy sauce) have had an increase in their material well-being. So only this last transaction counts in the GNP. However, as we shall learn later in this chapter, there is another way to come up with the right answer ($10), which involves counting only *part* of each transaction.

Finally, although the definition does not state this explicitly:

Only goods and services that pass through organized markets count in the GNP.

This, of course, deliberately excludes many economic activities. In some cases, the exclusion is a matter of principle. For example, even if they could hope to measure them, national income accountants do not want to include illegal activities in the GNP. Thus gambling services in Chicago are not in the GNP, but gambling services in Las Vegas are. But, aside from illegal goods and services, the definition mainly reflects the statisticians' confession that they could not hope to measure the value of many of the economy's most important activities, such as housework, do-it-yourself repairs, and leisure time. While these are certainly economic activities that result in currently produced goods or services, they all lack that important measuring rod—a price.

This omission results in certain oddities. For example, suppose that each of two neighbors hires his neighbor's wife to clean house, generously paying her $1000 a week for her services. Each homeowner can easily afford such generosity since his own wife collects an identical salary from his neighbor. Nothing real would have changed, but the GNP would go up by $100,000 a year. If this arrangement seems foolish, consider the effect that the women's liberation movement could have on the GNP. Presumably, more and more housework will be done by hired men and women (and thus channeled through the market) and less and less will be done by unpaid housewives. Thus more housework will count in the GNP, and billions of dollars may be added to the GNP in this way.

EXCEPTIONS TO THE RULES

Now for the exceptions. First, the treatment of government output involves a minor departure from the principle of using market prices. Outputs of private industries are sold on markets, and their prices are measured when this occurs. But "outputs" of government offices are not sold; indeed, it is sometimes even difficult to define what those outputs are. Lacking prices for outputs, national income accountants fall back on the only prices they have: prices for the inputs from which the outputs are produced. Thus:

Government outputs are valued at the cost of the inputs needed to produce them.

This means, for example, that if a clerk at the Department of Motor Vehicles earns $7 an hour and spends one-half hour torturing you with explanations of why you cannot get a driver's license, that particular government "service" is considered as being worth $3.50, and will increase GNP by that amount.

Second, some goods that are not actually sold on markets during the year are nevertheless counted in that year's GNP. These are goods that are produced during the year but not sold; that is, goods that firms stockpile as *inventories*. Goods that are added to inventories are part of the GNP even though they do not pass through markets.

National income statisticians treat inventories as if they were "bought" by the firms that produced them, even though this "purchase" never takes place.

Finally, the treatment of investment goods runs slightly counter to the rule that only final goods are to be counted. In a broad sense, factories, generators, machine tools, and the like might be considered as intermediate goods. After all, their owners want them only for use in producing other goods, not for any innate value that they possess. But this would present a real problem, for factories and machines normally are never sold to consumers. So when would we count them in GNP? National income statisticians avoid this problem by defining investment goods as final products demanded by the firms that buy them.

Now that we have an elaborate definition of just what the GNP is, let us turn to the problem of actually measuring it. National income accountants have devised three ways to perform this task, and we consider each of them in turn.

GNP AS THE SUM OF FINAL GOODS AND SERVICES

The first way to measure GNP seems to be the most natural, since it follows directly from the definition. It also turns out to be the most useful definition from the point of view of macroeconomics. We simply add up the final demands of all consumers, business firms, and the government. Using the symbol C (for consumption) to denote the final goods and services demanded by *consumers*, the symbol *I* (for investment) to denote the final goods demanded by business firms and other *investors*, and the symbol *G* (for government purchases) to denote the final goods and services demanded by all levels of *government*, we have:

$$GNP = C + I + G$$

The *I* that appears in the actual U.S. national accounts is called gross private domestic investment. The word "gross" will be explained presently. "Private" indicates that government investment is considered part of *G*, and "domestic" just means that machinery sold by American firms to foreign companies is not included. Gross private domestic investment in the United States has three components: business investment in plant and equipment, residential construction (home building),[1] and inventory investment. This is perhaps a good place to note that *only* these three things are investment in national income accounting terminology. In common parlance, all sorts of activities that are not part of the GNP are often called "investment." People are said to "invest" in the stock market when they purchase shares. Or wealthy individuals "invest" in works of art. But since transactions like these merely exchange one type of asset (money) for another (stock or art works), they are not included in the GNP.

DEFINITION
As defined in the national income accounts, *investment* includes only newly produced goods, such as machinery, factories, and new homes. It does not include exchanges of existing assets.

As we stated earlier, the symbol *G*, for government purchases, represents the *volume of current goods and services purchased by all*

[1]Thus purchases of new homes are considered part of *I* rather than part of *C*.

levels of government. Thus, anything the government pays to its employees is counted in *G*, as are its purchases of paper, pencils, airplanes, bombs, typewriters, and so forth.

Very few citizens realize that *most of what the federal government spends its money on is not for purchases of goods and services*. Instead, it is on what economists call transfer payments—literally, giving away money—to either individuals or to other levels of government. Figure 17–1 illustrates this in a pie

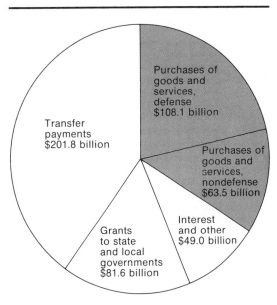

FIGURE 17–1
THE FEDERAL BUDGET FOR
FISCAL YEAR 1979
This pie diagram indicates the composition of the budget for fiscal year 1979 (October 1978 through September 1979) that President Carter proposed to the Congress in early 1978. Few people realize that federal spending consists largely of shuffling money from some people to others. Transfer payments to individuals and grants to state and local governments account for more than half the budget. Direct purchases of goods and services, other than those for the national defense, account for a minor share of federal spending (the shaded portion of the pie).

Source: *Survey of Current Business*, February 1978.

diagram. The full circle illustrates President Carter's proposed budget for fiscal year 1979, which he sent to Congress in January 1978. Of the more than $500 billion in total spending, only about $170 billion—or 34 percent—was to buy goods and services. And most of this was accounted for by the defense budget. Transfer payments to individuals—social security benefits, unemployment compensation, food stamps, public assistance, and the like—amounted to a full 40 percent of the proposed budget, while grants to state and local governments added another 16 percent. The remainder was made up of interest on the national debt and a few other miscellaneous categories.

The importance of the conceptual distinction lies in the fact that G represents the part of the national product that government uses up for its own purposes—to pay for armies, bureaucrats, paper, and ink—whereas transfer payments merely represent shuffling of purchasing power from one group of citizens to another group. Except for the administrators needed to run the programs, real economic resources are not used up in this process. Thus in adding up the nation's total output as the sum of C + I + G, we are summing the shares of GNP that are used up by consumers, investors, and government, respectively. Since transfer payments merely give someone the capability to spend on C, it is logical to exclude them from our definition of G. If we included them, the same spending would get counted twice: once in G and again in C. Table 17–2 shows the GNP for 1977 computed as the sum of C + I + G.

You will notice that there is an additional item in Table 17–2 beyond the usual C + I + G. It is called net exports, and is simply defined as our exports *minus* our imports. Why must this be included? GNP is meant to measure *the production of the U.S. economy*. But any of you who have enjoyed French wine or German beer know that part of C is not produced in the United States but is *imported* from

TABLE 17–2

GROSS NATIONAL PRODUCT IN 1977
AS THE SUM OF FINAL DEMANDS

ITEM	AMOUNT (billions of dollars)	
Personal consumption expenditures	$1206.5	
Gross private domestic investment	297.8	
Government purchases of goods and services	394.0	
Net exports	−11.1	
Exports		175.5
Imports		186.6
Gross national product	$1887.2	

Source: U.S. Department of Commerce.

other countries. Similarly, part of I is also imported. Thus, to arrive at a figure for production in the United States, we must *subtract* all imported items. Conversely, part of America's production is not purchased by Americans, but is *exported* to foreigners. These goods are missed when we add up C + I + G, and thus must be added back at the end. This is why we *add* exports. On balance, net exports have little effect on the GNP of the United States: Although exports and imports were both very large numbers in 1977, their difference was only about $11 billion—less than 1 percent of GNP.

GNP AS THE SUM OF ALL FACTOR PAYMENTS

There is another way to count up the GNP—*by adding up all the incomes in the economy.* Let's take a particular example. General Electric sells a generator to General Motors for a price of $1 million. In the first method of adding up GNP, the $1 million is counted as part of I. In the second method we ask: What incomes resulted from the production of this generator? The answer might be something like this:

Wages of G.E. employees	$400,000
Interest to bondholders	50,000
Rentals of buildings	50,000
Profits of G.E. stockholders	100,000

The total is $600,000. The remaining $400,000 is accounted for by inputs that G.E. purchased from other companies: steel, circuitry, tubing, rubber, and so on. But if we traced this $400,000 back further, we would find that it is accounted for by the wages, interest, and rentals paid by these other companies, *plus* their profits, *plus* their purchases from other firms. In fact, for *every* firm in the economy, there is an accounting identity that says:

Revenues from sales = Wages paid +
Interest paid +
Rentals paid +
Profits earned +
Purchases from
other firms

Why must this always be true? Because profits are the balancing item; they are what is *left over* after the firm has made all its other payments. In fact, this accounting identity is really just the definition of profits: sales revenue less all costs of production.

Now, when we consider this accounting identity for *all the firms in the economy*, we obtain the following:

Total sales = Total wages +
Total interest +
Total rents +
Total profits +
Total purchases from
other firms

But the total purchases from other firms are precisely what we have called *intermediate goods*. What, then, do we get if we subtract these intermediate transactions from both sides

of the equation? On the right-hand side, we have the sum of all factor incomes: payments to labor, land, and capital. On the left-hand side, we have: total sales minus sales of intermediate goods. This means that we have only sales of *final* goods, which is precisely our definition of GNP. Thus, the accounting identity for the entire economy can be rewritten as:

GNP = Wages + Interest + Rents + Profits

and this gives national income accountants another way to measure the GNP.

Table 17–3 shows 1977's GNP measured by the sum of all incomes. Once again, a few details have been omitted in our discussion. The sum of wages, interest, rents, and profits actually adds up to only $1515 billion (whereas GNP

TABLE 17–3

GROSS NATIONAL PRODUCT IN 1977
AS THE SUM OF INCOMES

ITEM		AMOUNT (billions of dollars)
Compensation of employees (wages)		$1153.4
plus		
Net interest		95.4
plus		
Rental income		22.5
plus		
Profits		244.0
Corporate profits	144.2	
Proprietors' income	99.8	
equals		
National income		1515.3
plus		
Indirect business taxes and miscellaneous items		176.7
equals		
Net national product		$1692.0
plus		
Depreciation		195.2
equals		
Gross national product		1887.2

Source: U.S. Department of Commerce.

was $1887 billion). We call this sum the national income because it is the sum of all factor payments. But the actual selling prices of goods include another category of income that we have ignored so far: sales taxes, excise taxes, and the like. National income statisticians call these *indirect business taxes,* and when we add these to national income we obtain the net national product (NNP).

Now we are almost at the GNP. The only difference between GNP and NNP is depreciation of the nation's capital stock: GNP includes depreciation while NNP does not.

DEFINITION
Depreciation is the value of the portion of the nation's capital equipment that is used up within the year. It tells us how much output is needed just to keep the economy's capital stock intact.

Thus, when we add depreciation to the NNP, we obtain the GNP. The difference between "gross" and "net" simply refers to whether depreciation is included or excluded.

From a conceptual point of view, most economists feel that NNP is a more meaningful indicator of the economy's output than GNP. After all, the depreciation that we add to get GNP represents the output that is needed just to repair and replace worn out factories and machines; it is not available for anybody to *use.* So NNP seems to be a better measure of well-being than GNP. But, alas, GNP is much easier to measure because depreciation is a particularly tricky item. What fraction of a tractor does Farmer Jones "use up" this year? How much did the Empire State Building depreciate during 1978? If you ask yourself these difficult questions, you will understand why most economists feel that GNP is measured more accurately than is NNP. For this reason, most economic models are based on GNP.

In Table 17–3 you can hardly help noticing the preponderant share of employee compensation in total national income—more than 75 percent. Labor is by far the most important

factor of production. The return on land is truly minute—less than 2 percent; and interest accounts for less than 7 percent. Profits account for the remaining 16 percent, though the size of corporate profits (less than 8 percent of GNP) is much less than the public thinks. If, by some magic stroke, we could eliminate all corporate profits without upsetting the performance of the economy, the average worker would get a raise of about 10.5 percent!

GNP AS THE SUM OF VALUES ADDED

We come now to the third, and final, way to measure the GNP. But before we explain this method, we must introduce a new concept, called value added.

DEFINITION
The *value added* by a firm is its revenue from selling a product minus the amounts paid for goods and services purchased from other firms.

The intuitive sense of the concept is clear: If a firm buys some inputs from other firms, does something to them, and sells the resulting product for a price higher than it paid for the inputs, we say that the firm has "added value" to the product. If we sum up the values added in this way by all the firms in the economy, we must get the total value of all final products. Thus:

GNP can be measured as the sum of the values added by all firms.

To verify that this is so, look back at the accounting identity on page 321. If we subtract purchases from other firms from both sides, we have:

$$\left.\begin{array}{c}\text{Revenues from sales} \\ \text{minus} \\ \text{Purchases from} \\ \text{other firms}\end{array}\right\} = \left\{\begin{array}{l}\text{Wages paid +} \\ \text{Interest paid +} \\ \text{Rentals paid +} \\ \text{Profits earned}\end{array}\right.$$

The left-hand side of this equation is just what we mean by the firm's value added. Thus:

$$\text{Value added} = \text{Wages} + \text{Interest} + \text{Rents} + \text{Profits}$$

Since the second method we gave for measuring GNP is to add up wages, interest, rents, and profits, we see that the value-added approach must also yield the same answer.

The value-added concept is particularly useful in avoiding double counting. Often it is hard to distinguish intermediate goods from final goods. Paint bought by a painter, for example, is an intermediate good. But paint bought by a do-it-yourselfer is a final good. What happens, then, if the professional painter has some paint left over and uses it to refurbish his own garage? The intermediate good becomes a final good. You can see that the line between intermediate goods and final goods is a fuzzy one in practice.

If we measure GNP by the sum of values added, however, it is not necessary to make such subtle distinctions. In this method, *every* purchase of a new good or service counts, but we do not count the entire selling price, only the part that represents value added.

To illustrate the procedure, let us return to our soybean example. (Refer back to Table 17–1 on page 317.) Ignoring the minor items (such as fertilizer) that the farmer purchases from others, the entire $3 selling price of the bushel of soybeans is value added. The miller then grinds the beans and sells them for $4. He has added $4 − $3 = $1 in value. When the factory turns this soy meal into soy sauce and sells it for $8, it has added $8 − $4 = $4 more in value. And finally, when the restaurant sells it to hungry customers for $10, a further $2 of value added is created.

Table 17–4 shows this chain of creation of value added by adding an additional column to Table 17–1. We see that the total value added by all four firms is $10, exactly the same as the restaurant's selling price. This is as it must be, for only the restaurant sells the soybean as a final product. We can also see why we would have erred if we simply added up all the transactions. The $3 value added by the farmer would have been counted four times (giving $12); the $1 value added by the miller would have been counted three times (giving $3); the $4 value added by the factory would have been counted twice (giving $8). Only the $2 value added by the restaurant would have been

TABLE 17–4

AN ILLUSTRATION OF VALUE ADDED

ITEM	SELLER	BUYER	PRICE	VALUE ADDED
Bushel of soybeans	Farmer	Miller	$ 3	$ 3
Bag of soy meal	Miller	Factory	4	1
Gallon of soy sauce	Factory	Restaurant	8	4
Gallon of soy sauce used as seasoning	Restaurant	Consumers	$10	2
		Totals:	$25	$10

Addendum: Contribution to GNP
Final Products...................... $10
Sum of values added............ $10

correctly counted only once. If we had added $12 + $3 + $8 + $2, we would have ended up with the inflated total of $25 in total transactions.

ALTERNATIVE MEASURES OF THE INCOME OF THE NATION

Economists use the term *national income* in two different ways. The most common usage is as a general term indicating the size of the income of the nation as a whole, without being very specific as to exactly how this income is to be measured. This is the sense in which the term "national income" is used in this book. The second, and much more precise, use of the term refers to a very specific concept in national income accounting, which we encountered earlier in the chapter in Table 17–3 on page 322: that is, the sum of wages, interest, rents, and profits.

Aside from this formal definition of national income, what other accounting concept might we use to measure the total income of the nation? The first and most obvious candidate is the GNP itself. GNP, however, is intended to be a measure of *production*, and so has several drawbacks as a measure of *income*. First, it includes some output that represents income to no one—output that simply replaces worn out machinery and buildings (depreciation). When we deduct this depreciation, we obtain the net national product (NNP), as shown in Figure 17–2. Second, because of sales taxes and related items (indirect business taxes), part of the price paid for each good and service does not represent the income of any individual. When we deduct these indirect business taxes from NNP, we arrive at the formal definition of national income (refer again to Figure 17–2). Both these accounting concepts have already been described.

There are, however, two other alternative measures of income. Personal income is intended to be superior to national income as a measure of the income that actually accrues to individuals. It is obtained from national income by *subtracting* corporate profits taxes, retained earnings, and payroll taxes (because these items are never received by individuals), and then *adding in* transfer payments (because these sources of income are not part of the wages, interest, rents, or profits that constitute the national income). As Figure 17–2 suggests, this adding and subtracting normally results in a number that is rather close to national income. Finally, if we subtract personal income taxes from personal income, we obtain disposable income.

Among all the concepts of the nation's income depicted in Figure 17–2, only two are used frequently in the construction of models of the economy: gross national product (GNP) and disposable income (*DI*). Therefore, these are the two measures of national income that we have utilized in Chapters 5 through 16. Apart from depreciation and retained earnings (which we ignore in the theoretical models of this book), GNP and *DI* differ only by taxes and transfers.

LIMITATIONS OF THE GNP: WHAT GNP IS NOT

Having seen in some detail what the GNP *is*, it is worth pausing to expand upon what it *is not*. In particular:

Gross national product is not a measure of the nation's economic well-being.

The GNP is not intended to measure economic well-being, and does not do so for several reasons.

1. Only market activity is included. Work done by housewives and do-it-yourselfers certainly contributes to the nation's well-being, but it is

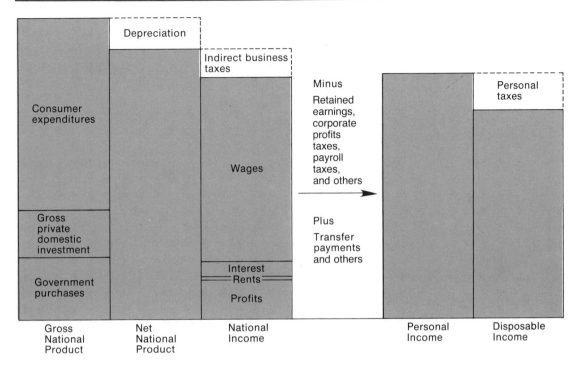

FIGURE 17–2

ALTERNATIVE MEASURES OF THE INCOME OF THE NATION

This bar chart indicates the relationships among the five alternative measures of the total income of the nation, starting with the largest and most comprehensive measure (GNP) and ranging down to the measure that most closely approximates the spendable income of consumers (disposable income).

Source: U.S. Department of Commerce.

not measured in the GNP because it has no price tag.

An important implication of this exclusion is seen when we try to compare the GNPs of developed and less developed countries. Americans are always incredulous to learn that the per capita GNP of the poorest African countries is less than $200 a year. Surely, no one could survive in America on $4 a week. How can Africans do it? One part of the answer, of course, is that these people are incredibly poor. We shall study their plight in Chapter 38. But another part of the answer is that:

International GNP comparisons are vastly misleading when the two countries differ greatly in the fraction of economic activity that each conducts in organized markets.

This fraction is relatively large in the United States and relatively small in the less developed countries, so when we compare their respective measured GNPs we are not comparing the same economic activities at all. Many things that get counted in the U.S. GNP are not counted in the GNPs of less developed nations. So it is ludicrous to think that these people, poor as they are, survive on what to Americans would amount to $4 a week.

2. No value is placed on leisure. As a country gets richer, one of the things that happen is that its citizens take more and more leisure time. The steady decrease in the length of the typical workweek in the United States is sufficient evidence for this. What this means, however, is that the gap is steadily widening between official GNP and some truer measure of national well-being that would include the value of leisure time. For this reason, growth in GNP systematically *understates* the growth in national well-being. But there are also reasons why the GNP *overstates* how well off we are; we consider these next.

3. "Bads" as well as "goods" get counted in GNP. Suppose there is a natural disaster—say, the melting of a heavy snowfall that causes the Susquehanna River to overflow its banks. (Those of you who live in the area will realize that this is not a hypothetical example.) Surely the well-being of the nation is *diminished* by this event: Many homes and businesses are destroyed or damaged; some people may be killed. Yet the disaster will cause the GNP to *rise*. Consumer spending to replace lost possessions will add to *C*. Rebuilding and repairing the damaged homes, stores, and factories will add to *I*. Extra government spending for disaster relief will add to *G*. Yet no one would think that the nation is better off for its higher GNP.

Wars represent an extreme example of this. Mobilization for outright war always causes a country's GNP to rise rapidly. But men called into the army could be producing civilian output. Factories needed to produce armaments could instead be making cars, washing machines, and televisions. A country at war is surely worse off than a country at peace, but this fact will not be reflected in its GNP accounts.

4. Ecological costs are not netted out of the GNP. Many of the activities in a modern industrial economy that produce goods and services also have undesirable side effects on the environment. Automobiles provide enjoyment and a means of transportation, but they also despoil the atmosphere. Factories pollute rivers and lakes while manufacturing valuable commodities. Almost everything seems to produce garbage, which creates the problem of what to do with it. None of these ecological costs are deducted from the GNP in an effort to give us a truer measure of the *net* increase in economic welfare that our economy produces. Is this foolishness? Not if we remember the job that national income statisticians are trying to do: They are measuring the economic activity conducted through organized markets, not national welfare.

FROM LITTLE ACORNS, BIG OAK TREES GROW[2]

The models we developed in Part Three used only a few of the many concepts of national income accounting: GNP, consumption, investment, government purchases, and disposable income were about all we needed. Similarly, these models had only a few "equations."[3] One equation described consumers' demand for goods and services; another described firms' demand for factories and machines. Two other equations described the supply of money by banks and the demand for money by households and firms. Finally, there were equations that said that prices and wages rise (fall) when-

---

[2]The remainder of this chapter assumes knowledge of the earlier chapters of Part Three.

[3]We did not actually write out the equations in mathematical form, as that was not necessary. Instead, we discussed them in words and portrayed them in diagrams. Yet behind each verbal or graphical explanation was an equation. You can find these equations written out explicitly in many intermediate and advanced texts.

ever production is beyond (below) the full-employment level.

The actual economic models that are used for forecasting and policy analysis use much more of the national income accounts and have hundreds of equations. Why? There are two principal reasons for this complexity: the need to break down the components of aggregate demand into finer categories, and the necessity of coping with certain annoying details one finds in real life.

Let us take the breakdown of aggregate demand first. We spoke of a single "consumption function." But economists who have studied consumer behavior in the United States have found that they can explain and predict C better by using *several* equations, each explaining a different part of total consumer spending. For example, one equation might predict the purchases of new cars, another might predict spending on other types of durable goods, and a third might handle the nondurable goods and services. The same is true for investment. Models generally include separate equations for business investment in plant and equipment, house building, and inventory investment. And so on throughout the entire model. Many of these subsidiary equations lead to still more equations. For example, an equation to explain purchases of new homes will probably have to include the interest rate to be paid on home mortgages. But then the model must provide an answer to the question: What determines the interest rate on mortgages? In this way, answering one question raises another, and to solve the pyramiding set of questions the model must grow bigger and bigger.

Some economists believe that model-builders have taken the process too far. By adding more and more detail, they argue, model-builders have lost sight of the basic objective: to predict the GNP. Whether these critics are right or not is a matter of professional debate right now. But one thing is clear: The

models have become so large and so complicated that few people besides the model-builders themselves can take the time to truly understand them.

The second reason for "big models" is that they must account for many annoying details that need not concern us in an introductory course. One example will serve to illustrate this. Economists need to predict disposable income because of the crucial role it plays in the consumption function. But how do they get this variable? As we have seen in this chapter, the national income accounts give the answer in stages:

1. From the *GNP*, deduct depreciation to get the *NNP*.
2. From the *NNP*, deduct indirect business taxes (and a few other miscellaneous items) to get *national income*. To execute this step, the model-builder will need equations to predict the level of indirect business taxes—taxes that are levied by all three levels of government: federal, state, and local.
3. From *national income*, deduct certain items that never find their way into the hands of consumers (for example, the retained earnings of corporations), and then add certain items that consumers receive that are not factor payments (for example, social security and unemployment benefits). This gives us *personal income*; but these additions and deletions require more equations.
4. Finally, using still more equations, subtract personal income-tax payments from *personal income* to get *disposable income*.

While no great economic issues are involved in this process, you can easily see how it leads to rather large models of the economy. The "Map 2" that we have tried to provide in this book starts to look alarmingly like "Map 1." But, at their heart, these mammoth computer monsters—which may include 300 to 400 equations and 500 to 600 variables—are little different from the simple models that we have constructed in previous chapters.

ECONOMETRIC MODELS

To use any of these models as a tool for actual forecasting or policy analysis, it is necessary to have numerical estimates of the various coefficients in the equations. The statistical procedures used to arrive at these estimates are called econometrics, and, not surprisingly, the models that result are called econometric models.

Econometric models have their origin in the work that the Dutch economist Jan Tinbergen did for the League of Nations in the 1930s. This and other achievements earned him a share of the first Nobel Prize in Economics in 1969. The chief American pioneer of econometric models has been Lawrence Klein of the University of Pennsylvania, who served as Jimmy Carter's principal economic adviser during the 1976 presidential campaign. (This is not meant to suggest that giant econometric models help woo voters!) So it is no surprise that the oldest working econometric model of the United States is the Wharton model (named for the University of Pennsylvania's famous business school), whose predictions and policy analyses are sold to business firms and government agencies all over the country and throughout the world.

Another major model of the U.S. economy was constructed under the auspices of the Federal Reserve System by a team of government and academic experts headed by Franco Modigliani of M.I.T. and Albert Ando of the University of Pennsylvania. This Fed-M.I.T.-Penn model is today an important tool used in the formulation of monetary policy.

Although Wharton Econometric Forecasting is a nonprofit corporation headed by Professor Klein, and the Fed-M.I.T.-Penn model is a joint government–academic venture, other econometric models have been constructed and sold for a profit on the private market—much like soapsuds and cigarettes. The two most prominent of these are models built by Data Resources, Inc., of Lexington, Massachusetts (whose president, Otto Eckstein of Harvard, served on President Lyndon Johnson's Council of Economic Advisers), and by Chase Econometrics of Philadelphia, an offshoot of the giant Chase Manhattan Bank (headed by Michael Evans, who learned his trade working on the Wharton model). The fact that these and other firms can sell their products for a handsome profit is testimony to the fact that econometric models have passed the ultimate test of economic usefulness: Someone is willing to pay for them. The services of econometric models also count in the GNP!

SUMMARY

1. The national income accounts provide the data that are used in the actual construction of models of the U.S. economy.
2. Gross national product (GNP) is the sum of the money values of all final goods and services produced during a year and sold on organized markets. There are, however, certain exceptions to this definition.
3. One way to measure the GNP is to add up the final demands of consumers, investors, and the government: $GNP = C + I + G$.
4. A second way to measure the GNP is to start with all the factor payments—wages, interest, rents, and profits—that constitute the national income, and then add indirect business taxes and depreciation.
5. A third way to measure the GNP is to sum up the values added by every firm in the economy (and then once again add indirect business taxes and depreciation).

6. Except for possible bookkeeping and statistical errors, all three methods must give the same answer.
7. The GNP is meant to be a measure of the *production* of the economy, not of the increase in its *well-being*. For example, the GNP places no value on housework and other do-it-yourself activities, nor on leisure time. On the other hand, even commodities that might be considered as "bads" rather than "goods" are counted in the GNP (for example, activities that harm the environment).
8. The actual econometric models used to forecast the state of the U.S. economy and to prescribe policy changes are much more complicated than the simple models used in this book. But their conceptual basis is quite similar.

CONCEPTS FOR REVIEW

National income accounting
Gross national product (GNP)
Final goods
Intermediate goods
Inventories
Investment
Government purchases
Transfer payments
Net exports

National income
Net national product (NNP)
Depreciation
Value added
Personal income
Disposable income
Econometrics
Econometric models

QUESTIONS FOR DISCUSSION

1. Which of the following transactions are included in the gross national product, and by how much does each raise GNP?
   a. Smith pays a carpenter $4000 to build a garage for his house.
   b. Smith purchases $1000 worth of lumber and materials and builds himself a garage, which is worth $4000.
   c. Smith goes to the woods, cuts down a tree, and uses the wood to build himself a garage that is worth $4000.
   d. An unemployed worker receives a government check for $100 in unemployment compensation.
   e. The Jones family sells its old house to the Reynolds family for $50,000. The Joneses then buy a newly constructed house from a builder for $80,000.
   f. Mr. Black and Mr. Blue, each out for a Sunday drive, have a collision in which their cars are destroyed. Black and Blue each hire a lawyer to sue the other, paying the lawyers $1000 each for services rendered. The judge throws the case out of court.
   g. IBM builds a $10 million factory to make computers.
   h. Your university purchases a used computer from another university, paying $500,000.
   i. Your university purchases a new computer from IBM, paying $1 million.
   j. You lose $100 in a Las Vegas casino.
   k. You lose $100 in the stock market.

2. Explain the difference between final goods and intermediate goods. Why is it sometimes difficult to apply this distinction in practice? In this regard, why is the concept of value added useful?

3. Explain the difference between government spending and government purchases of goods and services (*G*). Which is larger?

4. Explain why national income and gross national product would be exactly equal if there were no depreciation and no indirect business taxes.

5. Give some reasons why the gross national product is not a suitable measure of the well-being of the nation. (Have you noticed newspaper accounts in which journalists seem to use GNP for this purpose?)

four

Consumers, Firms, and Markets: Introduction to Microeconomics

18

The Nature
of Consumer Demand

Economists who work for business firms are frequently assigned the task of studying consumer demand for the products their companies produce. Business managers count the results of such studies among the most important of all the information they get—but they also know it is among the most difficult to obtain. Government agencies, too, are very interested in demand information, which they use for making estimates about such widely diverse matters as general business conditions in the economy and expected receipts from sales taxes.

In this chapter, which is the first of two chapters devoted to the nature of consumer demand and the role demand information plays in rational choice, we will examine the reasons why demand information is so important and why, also, it is so difficult to obtain.

We begin, first, by explaining how demand varies when there are changes in advertising expenditures, prices, and other pertinent influences. Second, we describe the "law" of demand, which states that higher prices generally reduce the quantity demanded. Third, we explain the importance of the time period to which a demand curve refers. Fourth, we show how demand curves for products of an entire industry are determined by the demand curves of individual consumers of the industry's product. Fifth, we define and discuss the concept of *elasticity of demand,* which is designed to measure the responsiveness of the demand for a product to a change in its price. And, finally, we examine some problems that occur in making a statistical analysis of demand curves.

With an understanding of these concepts established, Chapter 19 looks behind the demand curves to see how they are formulated through the interaction of prices, consumer incomes, and consumer preferences.

A REAL APPLICATION OF DEMAND ANALYSIS

One of the nation's largest producers of packaged foods conducted a statistical study to determine the effectiveness of its advertising expenditures, which amounted to nearly $100 million a year, in stimulating demand. A company statistician collected year-by-year figures on company sales and advertising outlays. He then constructed a statistical relationship between the two and, to his delight, discovered they showed a remarkably close relationship. The trouble was that the relationship seemed just too perfect. In economics, data on demand and any one of the elements that influence it almost never make a neat, simple pattern. Human tastes and other pertinent influences are just too variable to permit such neat behavior.

Suspicious company executives asked an economist to examine the analysis. The economist was able to explain the too-neat relationship between observed sales and advertising outlay quite easily. More important, he was able to show that the statistical relationship was *not* what the company's management was looking for and that it was in fact dangerous and mis-

leading for the purposes of decision making. No deep dark methods of economic analysis were needed to reach this conclusion. By the end of this chapter, you will understand how the economist reached his conclusions and be able to avoid similar pitfalls yourself.

DEMAND DEPENDS ON MANY VARIABLES

When a firm's managers consider the introduction of a new product on the market, they frequently will hire one of the many companies that specialize in market surveys to undertake a study of the prospective demand for the new item. The market research organization typically will use any of a variety of interview techniques and, on the basis of the responses of prospective customers, arrive at a figure sometimes called the product's *market potential.* What market potential means is that if the quality of the product proves to be satisfactory, and a reasonably effective advertising campaign and other appropriate marketing measures are undertaken, then an average of, say, 1,750,000 units of the new item will be sold per year over the next 5 years. The important point to notice about this definition is that demand is represented by a single number: market potential.

Economists are very unhappy with this approach. They maintain that the market potential number is undefined and unknowable under the vague conditions specified and, more important, that any such number simply does not give the decision maker the needed information. In economic analysis, prospective demand is not considered a fixed number but something that is determined by the values of *several* pertinent variables. It is the relationship between these variables and the quantity demanded that can tell the decision maker whether his product will be successful.

Specifically, it is not enough to speak about a "reasonably effective" advertising campaign.

Normally, the quantity sold will depend on the number of dollars the company spends advertising the product. And within reasonable limits (if its advertising program is not too repugnant), the more dollars spent on advertising, the more a company will sell—up to a point. Yet, even the most enthusiastic advertising agency will admit, reluctantly, that it is possible to spend too much on advertising.

To decide rationally how much to spend on this part of its marketing effort, management obviously should know just how quantity demanded is affected by advertising expenditure—how much more it will be able to sell per additional dollar of advertising, and when additional advertising dollars cease being effective. It needs to have, not a fixed number representing potential demand, but a graph or a statistical equation describing the relationship between sales and advertising. Such a relationship may look something like the one depicted in Figure 18–1. Notice that in our illustration most of the curve goes uphill as we move to the right (it has a positive slope).[1] This means that additional advertising will continue to bring in business until (at a budget of x million dollars) people become so saturated by the message that it begins to repel them and turn them away from the product.

Even in cases in which the saturation level cannot be reached within the range of outlays the firm can afford, the curve is likely to level off, becoming flatter and flatter as the amount spent on advertising gets larger and larger, and saturation is approached. The point at which the curve begins to flatten is the point at which returns from advertising begin to diminish. When the total advertising budget is small, even a \$1 addition to the campaign may bring in as much as \$10 in new sales and so be very much worthwhile to the firm. But when the market approaches saturation, each additional dollar may contribute only 30 cents in new sales, and that is not sound business.

[1]For the definition of *slope* see Chapter 2, pages 22–24.

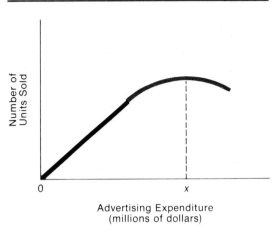

FIGURE 18–1

ADVERTISING EXPENDITURE BY A FIRM AND NUMBER OF UNITS OF OUTPUT IT IS ABLE TO SELL

Sales may rise in proportion to the amount of money spent on advertising until a point at which returns begin to diminish. There may even be an amount (x dollars) beyond which further advertising actually repels consumers and reduces sales.

Prospective demand does not depend on advertising alone, however. It will also be affected by the price the firm will decide to charge for the product. Here again, that price should not be set arbitrarily. Rational decision making requires that the firm consider how large its volume will be at alternative prices.

Once the firm has decided on its advertising budget, a standard demand curve can be drawn that will tell managers what quantities will be demanded at each of several alternative prices. This sort of demand curve has already been discussed in Chapter 4, where we considered the supply and demand mechanism. Figure 18–2 represents a demand curve such as those presented in Chapter 4.

By now one might (correctly) assume that even an analysis that considers the effects of both advertising *and* price on demand would be an oversimplification. Other company decisions,

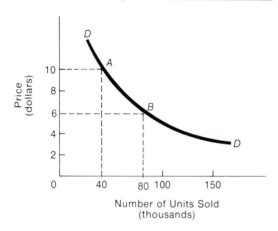

FIGURE 18–2

A STANDARD DEMAND CURVE (*DD*)

The points on this curve show what quantities of the product will be demanded at each alternative price. For example, it shows (point *A*) that if the price is $10, then 40,000 units of the product will be demanded. The negative slope of the curve means that a reduction in price increases the quantity demanded. Thus, comparing points *A* and *B* we see that a fall in price from $10 to $6 increases quantity demanded from 40,000 to 80,000.

for example, how large the sales force is to be, will also affect sales volume. And variables that are beyond the control of management, such as the pricing and advertising decisions of competitors and the gross national product (GNP), which represents the general state of the economy, must also be dealt with. It is neither possible nor particularly important for us to try to present an exhaustive list of variables here. What is essential is that the student understand that:

Prospective demand is not a fixed quantity. It depends on the values of a number of variables, some of them under the control of a firm's management and some of them not. Rational decision making requires that managers have information about the relationships between those variables, for example, that they understand the connection between their decisions and the prospective demand for their products.

THE DEMAND CURVE

Among all the variables affecting quantity demanded, economists have focused the bulk of their attention on the *price* of a commodity. Although we, too, will be primarily concerned with the price variable, the same analysis can be applied to any of the other variables affecting quantity demanded.

To represent the relationship between quantity demanded and price, it is customary to employ a demand curve of the sort we have just shown in Figure 18–2. The demand curve is generally assumed to have a negative slope— that is, it goes downhill as one moves toward the right, as shown in the figure. What the negative slope means in this case is that quantity demanded increases as price decreases. This assertion, of course, makes good sense. But there are exceptions to this relationship, some of which may be significant to decision making.

One common exception occurs when quality is judged on the basis of a price—the more expensive the better. Some years ago the U.S. Department of Agriculture released a statement indicating that, as far as its tests could determine, milk labeled "grade A" came from the same spigot as the significantly less expensive milk labeled "grade B." Nevertheless, despite the wide publicity the press gave the announcement, the former continued to outsell the latter by a substantial amount.

Another factor that could create a positively rather than a negatively sloping demand curve is snob appeal. If a good part of the reason for purchasing a Rolls Royce is to advertise one's wealth, a decrease in the car's price may actually reduce sales.

Other types of exceptions have also been noted by economists; but for most commodities it seems quite reasonable to assume that demand curves have a negative slope, an assumption that is supported by the data. Later we will discuss in more detail why this sort of behavior, called the "law" of demand, is to be expected.

DEFINITION
The *"law" of demand* states that a higher price generally reduces the amount of a commodity people are willing to buy. So, for most goods, demand curves have a negative slope.

Note, incidentally, that we have put the word *law* in quotation marks to remind the reader that it is not without exceptions.

In public or business discussions one sometimes hears references to a "change in demand." By itself, this expression does not really mean anything. Remember from our discussion in Chapter 4 that it is vital to distinguish between a response to a price change (*a movement along the demand curve*) and a change in the relationship between price and quantity demanded (*a shift in the demand curve*). When price falls, the quantity demanded generally responds by rising. This is a movement *along* the demand curve. On the other hand, an effective advertising campaign may mean that more will be bought *at any given price*. This would be a rightward *shift* in the demand curve. In fact, such a shift can be caused by a change in the value of any of the variables affecting quantity demanded other than price. While the distinction between a shift in a demand curve and a movement along it may seem trivial on paper, it is a significant difference in practice and one that can cause problems if it is confused or ignored.

THE TIME DIMENSION
OF THE DEMAND CURVE
AND DECISION MAKING

There is one more characteristic of the demand curve, which is not observable from the graph,

that is of fundamental importance. This feature—the *time* dimension—imparts a peculiar character to the demand curve as economists define it and makes statistical estimates more difficult than we have so far indicated. Yet the way time is taken into account is dictated inescapably by the logic of decision making and so must be examined with some care.

When management undertakes to find the best price for one of its products for, say, the next 6 months, it must consider the range of alternative prices available to it for that 6-month period, and the consequences of each possible choice. For example, if management is reasonably certain that the best price lies somewhere between $3.50 and $5.00, it should perhaps consider each of the four possibilities, $3.50, $4.00, $4.50, and $5.00, and estimate how much it can expect to sell at each of these potential prices during the 6-month period in question. The result of these estimates may appear in a format similar to that shown in the table below.

Potential price	$3.50	$4.00	$4.50	$5.00
Expected quantity demanded	75,000	73,000	70,000	60,000

This information, which supplies management with what it needs to know to make a pricing decision, contains the same data the economist uses to draw a demand curve.

The demand curve describes a set of hypothetical responses to a set of potential prices, of which only one can actually be charged. All of the data represented by points on the demand curve refer to alternative possibilities for the *same* period of time—the period for which the decision is to be made.

Thus the demand curve as just described is no abstract notion that is useful primarily for academic discussion. Rather it offers precisely the information that one needs for rational decision making. If the choice of next year's price or advertising budget is to be one that serves the company best, management must estimate the sales that will result from each of the various candidate prices and budgets *for that one period of time.*

The fixed time period for all entries in the table, which we will later interpret as points on the demand curve, also applies to other relationships that economists use, including the supply curve and many of the other concepts that appear in this book. That is, every point on any such curve refers to the same time period. The reason is that the logic of rational choice means that the consequences of all possible decisions must be compared before one can know which is the most desirable.

AGGREGATION OF DEMAND CURVES

The demand curve for a product may refer to the potential purchases of one individual (an individual demand curve), or it may describe the price responses of all the customers of a given firm (a firm's demand curve), or it may be an *aggregate demand curve* for the entire market (a market demand curve) representing the potential purchases of the product by all consumers from all producers.

If we assume that each individual, when making a purchase decision, pays no attention to other people's purchase decisions, we may easily determine an aggregate demand curve from the customers' individual demand curves. We simply add the (negatively sloping) individual demand curves *horizontally* as shown in Figure 18–3. There we see the individual demand curves DD and SS for two people, Daniel and Sabrina, and the total (market) demand curve MM.

Specifically, this market demand curve is constructed as follows: *Step 1:* Pick any relevant price, say $10. *Step 2:* At that price, determine Daniel's demand (9 units) from Daniel's demand curve in Figure 18–3(a) and Sabrina's demand (6 units) from Sabrina's demand curve in Figure 18–3(b). Note that these quantities are indicated by length AA for Daniel and length BB for Sabrina. *Step 3:* Add Sabrina's and Daniel's demand at the $10 price (length AA + length BB = 9 + 6) to yield the total market demand for that price [length CC, with total demand equal to 15 units in Figure 18–3(c)]. Now repeat the process for all the alternative prices to obtain other points on the market demand curve until the shape of the entire curve MM is indicated. When there are no interactions among the demand curves, that is all there is to the aggregation process.

When there are interactions, however, as when the quantity demanded by one individual affects the quantities that others will be willing to purchase, this process is not so easy. In such cases it is not possible simply to add the individual demand curves together. For example, an increased use of vests by a fashion leader (involving only a move *along her own* demand curve) may cause a shift in the demand curves of other customers.

RESPONSIVENESS TO PRICE CHANGES: ELASTICITY OF DEMAND

Two demand curves may differ considerably in the degree of responsiveness to price changes they represent. For several reasons it is convenient to have an index of the degree of that responsiveness, and for these purposes a standard measure is used that is called the price elasticity of demand, or simply, the elasticity of demand. An elasticity measure of responsiveness is used for all sorts of pairs of variables in economics. For instance, the income elasticity of a nation's total imports is of some significance in international trade theory. The following definition therefore can be applied considerably beyond basic demand theory by making suitable changes in the variables specified:

DEFINITION

The *price elasticity of demand* is (the absolute value of) the ratio of the percentage change in quantity demanded to the percentage change in price that brings about the change in demand.

Several characteristics of this definition require explanation. First, we use the absolute value (that is, eliminate the minus sign) in this ratio because, with demand curves negatively sloped, the ratio would otherwise normally be a negative number. If, say, quantity demanded fell 10 percent (demand change = −10 percent) when price went up 5 percent, the ratio between the two percentages would be −2. By eliminating the minus sign and calling the price elasticity of demand 2, we simply facilitate the use of the measure.

The second aspect of the definition that needs clarifying is its formulation in terms of *percentage* changes in price and in quantity. The purpose here is to standardize units, which in economics is often very difficult. Thus, if we want to compare the price responsiveness of the demand for cider with that of the demand for silk cloth, there is no ready device for translating quarts of one into yards of the other. Can we say that a 200-quart increase in the demand for cider is greater or smaller than a 50-yard increase in the demand for silk? As we saw in Chapter 2, the slopes of the demand curves will not do as the measure of responsiveness we are seeking because units in economics cannot be fixed and made comparable for all commodities. A change in the unit we use to measure quantity or price will change the slope of the graph, even though that change in unit of measurement has no economic significance.

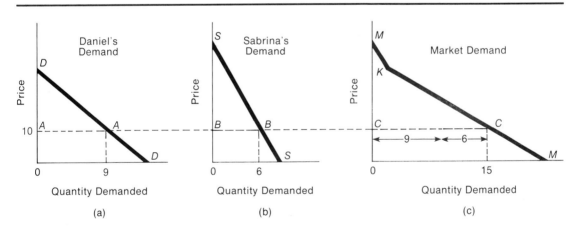

FIGURE 18–3

THE RELATIONSHIP BETWEEN TOTAL MARKET DEMAND AND THE DEMANDS OF INDIVIDUAL CONSUMERS WITHIN THAT MARKET

If Daniel and Sabrina are the customers for a product, and at a price of $10 Daniel demands 9 units [*AA* in (a)] and Sabrina demands 6 units [*BB* in (b)], then total market demand at that price is 9 + 6 = 15 [*CC* in (c)]. In other words, we obtain the market demand curve by horizontal addition of all points of each consumer's demand curve at each given price. Thus, at a $10 price we have length *CC* on the market demand curve equal to *AA* + *BB* on the individual demand curves. The sharp angle at point *K* on the market curve occurs because it corresponds to the price at which Daniel enters the market. At any price higher than this, only Sabrina is willing to buy anything.

To avoid these difficulties, we make the comparison in terms of *percentage* variations in demand—saying that the demand for silk is the more responsive of the two if it increases by a greater percentage in response to a 1 percent fall in price. Note that price changes are also measured in percentage terms because, even though the dollar is a standardized unit for all commodities, the economic significance of a dollar is not. A $1 change in the price of an ordinary ball-point pen presumably has a much greater significance than a $1 change in the price of a diamond tiara. Once again, the percentage change seems to capture the variation in which we are interested.

Elasticities are not readily recognizable from a demand diagram, but some generalizations are possible. In Figure 18–4 we show four different types of demand curves. In Figure 18–4(a) we have depicted a demand curve that is simply a vertical straight line. This curve is *zero elastic* throughout, which means that no matter what the price, the quantity demanded will remain the same (percentage change in quantity equals zero). Such a demand pattern may perhaps be expected only where the relevant price range considered already involves very low prices from the point of view of the consumer (will anyone use more toilet tissue if its price is lowered?), or if the item is considered vital by the consumer (medicines), although even here the demand will remain zero elastic only as long as price does not go beyond what the consumer can afford.

In Figure 18–4(b) we have a demand curve that represents the opposite extreme in responsiveness to price changes. It is said to be *perfectly elastic* (or "infinitely" elastic). If there is the slightest rise in price, demand will drop to zero. This may be expected to occur where a rival product that is just as good in the consumers' view is available at the going price ($5 in our diagram). In cases where no one will pay more than the going price, if the seller raises his

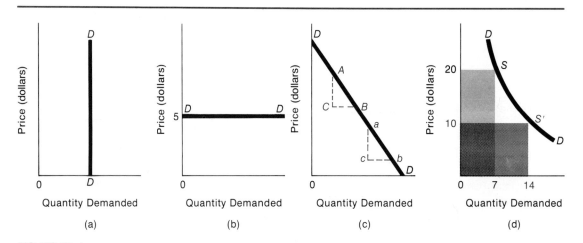

FIGURE 18–4

DEMAND CURVES WITH DIFFERENT ELASTICITIES
(a) The vertical demand curve is *perfectly inelastic* (elasticity = 0)—no change in price affects quantity demanded. (b) The horizontal demand curve is *perfectly elastic*—at any price above $5, quantity demanded falls to zero. (c) A *straight-line demand curve*—its *slope* is constant, but its elasticity is not. (d) A demand curve with constant unit elasticity throughout (a *unit-elastic* demand curve). A change in price does not affect total expenditure. When price equals $20, total expenditure is price times quantity, $20 × 7 = $140; and when price equals $10, expenditure equals $10 × 14 = $140.

price even one penny higher he will lose all his customers.

Other things being equal, the *flatter* the demand curve, the *greater* its elasticity. This is true because flat demand curves mean that small changes in price call forth large changes in demand. However, one should not jump to the conclusion that there is a simple relationship between slope and elasticity. On the contrary, because the latter is expressed in terms of *percentage* changes, the relationship between the two is not obvious. In Figure 18–4(c) we have a straight-line demand curve whose slope is therefore constant throughout its length. However, it is easy to show that its elasticity varies all along the line. If we move from A to B the price decrease is the same as when we move from a to b. But in the former the *percentage* price decrease is considerably smaller since we start off from a higher initial price. Similarly, the percentage quantity increase from A to B is much greater than that from a to b. Thus, between A and B the elasticity of the demand curve in Figure 18–4(c) is different from that between a and b (it is, in fact, higher).

If a straight-line demand curve is not a curve of constant elasticity, what is the appearance of a demand curve with the same elasticity of demand throughout its length? For reasons stated in the next section, it looks like the curve in Figure 18–4(d), which represents a curve with elasticity equal to 1 throughout (a *unit-elastic* demand curve). Its formula is:

Price times quantity demanded is equal to some fixed number (a constant)

Using symbols: $P \times q = $ a constant

ELASTICITY, PRICE CHANGES, AND REVENUES

It is conventional to speak of a curve whose elasticity is greater than 1 as an *elastic* demand curve, and of one whose elasticity is less than 1 as an *inelastic* curve. This terminology is convenient for discussing the last property of the elasticity measure with which we will concern ourselves.

The elasticity formula turns out to have a simple and useful relationship with the effect of a price change on the buyer's total expenditure (or the seller's total revenue). In particular, it can be shown that:

If demand is elastic, a rise in price will decrease total expenditure. If demand is unit elastic, a change in price will leave total expenditure unaffected. If demand is inelastic, a rise in price will raise total expenditure.

These relationships hold because total expenditure equals price times quantity bought, $p \times q$, and a rise in price will have two partially offsetting effects on $p \times q$. It will, by definition, increase p and (if the demand curve is negatively sloped) decrease q. The net outcome depends on the elasticity. If price goes up 10 percent and quantity declines 10 percent (a case of unit elasticity), the two will cancel out: $p \times q$ will remain constant. On the other hand, if price goes up 10 percent and quantity declines 15 percent (a case where elasticity exceeds 1), $p \times q$ will naturally decrease. Finally, if a 10 percent price rise leads to a 5 percent decline in quantity (an inelastic case), $p \times q$ clearly will rise.

This is the logic of the proposition, and it shows, incidentally, why a demand curve with unit elasticity satisfies the equation $p \times q = $ constant, whose graph is depicted in Figure 18–4(d).

The connection between elasticity and total expenditure is easily depicted graphically. For example, Figure 18–5 shows an elastic portion of a demand curve, *DD*. At a price of $6 the quantity sold will be 4 units, and so total expenditure, $4 \times \$6 = \$24$, will be represented by the shaded rectangular area. When price falls to $5, the percentage increase in quantity will be com-

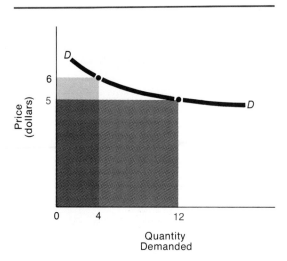

FIGURE 18–5

AN ELASTIC DEMAND CURVE
When price falls, quantity demanded rises by a greater
percentage, increasing the total expenditure. Thus,
when price falls from $6 to $5, quantity demanded rises
from 4 to 12, and total expenditure rises from $6 × 4
= $24 to $5 × 12 = $60.

paratively large because the curve is elastic. We
assume, for the example, that 12 units are
bought. Consequently, the new expenditure
($60 = $5 × 12), now measured by the red
rectangle, will be larger than the old. Similarly,
by going back to Figure 18–4(d), the unit-elastic
demand curve, one can see how expenditure,
$p × q,$ can remain constant even though selling
price changes. Total spending is $140, whether
the price is $20 (and 7 units are sold) or the
price is $10 (and 14 units are sold).

The preceding result warns us of the
dangers in the notion that a rise in price or a
rise in volume must always increase a company's sales revenue. A price rise will increase
sales revenue only if demand is *inelastic,* while
an increase in quantity sold, which is induced
by a price reduction, will increase total revenue
only if demand is *elastic.*

One application of the elasticity concept
may be stated as an affirmative result: If the

firm's objective is to maximize its profit and *if its
demand is inelastic* (or even unit elastic) it can
always do better for itself by raising its price.
For by doing so it will earn at least as much as
before while delivering a smaller quantity of
goods to its customers—a pretty good deal! A
slight restatement of this result may prove helpful later. If the firm wishes to maximize profits
but has chosen a product price (and, consequently, an output level) at which its demand
is inelastic (or unit elastic), then management
must have made a mistake. The prices and
outputs upon which it has decided are not those
that *maximize* company profits, since with unit-
elastic or inelastic demand a rise in price must
be capable of increasing profits further.

SUBSTITUTES AND COMPLEMENTS

Although we have been focusing on the demand for *individual* commodities, studying one
good at a time, this approach can be misleading
for two reasons. First, the money the family
spends on various goods comes out of a single
source—the family income. With a limited income, the more the family spends on one good,
the less it has available for others. This fact
creates an interdependence among demands
for different commodities. The next chapter examines some consequences of this relationship.

Second, the uses of some goods are so interrelated that the desirability of one depends
on the amount one possesses of the other.
Certain goods make one another more desirable. Cream and sugar can increase the
desirability of coffee, and vice versa. The
same is true of mustard or ketchup and hamburgers. In some extreme cases, neither of two
products has any use without the other—an
automobile and tires, a pair of shoes and shoe-
laces, and so on. Such goods, each of which
makes the other more valuable, are called
complements.

At the other extreme, there are goods that

make one another less valuable. These are called substitutes. A person who has just consumed several cups of coffee is not likely to want tea. Ownership of a motorcycle may decrease the desire for a bicycle. If your pantry is stocked with cans of tuna fish, you are less likely to rush out and buy cans of salmon.

The demand curves of complements and substitutes are interrelated. A rise in the price of coffee is likely to affect the demand for sugar. How? When coffee prices rise, less coffee will be drunk and therefore less sugar will be demanded. The opposite will be true of a fall in coffee prices. A similar relationship holds for other complementary goods.

When the price of a good rises, the demand for *complementary* goods generally falls. The opposite will occur when the price of a good falls.

As one might suspect, things work out the opposite way with substitute goods: When the price of new houses rises, people demand fewer new houses, so the demand for old houses goes up. When the price of coffee goes up, people drink less coffee, so they demand more tea or tomato juice. More generally:

When the price of a good goes up, we can expect the demand for *substitute goods* to go up. The opposite occurs when the price goes down.

A measure that is useful for determining whether two products are substitutes or complements is their cross elasticity of demand. This measure is defined much like the ordinary price elasticity of demand, only instead of measuring the responsiveness of the demand for, say, coffee to a change in the price of that commodity, cross elasticity of demand measures the responsiveness of the demand for coffee to a change in the price of, say, sugar.

DEFINITION
The *cross elasticity of demand* for product x to a change in the price of another product y is the ratio of the percentage change in quantity demanded of product x to the percentage change in the price of product y that brings about the change in quantity demanded.

For example, if a 20 percent rise in the price of sugar reduces coffee demand by 5 percent (a change of *minus* 5 percent in demand) then their cross elasticity of demand will be

$$\frac{\% \text{ change in quantity of coffee demanded}}{\% \text{ change in sugar price}}$$

$$= \frac{-5\%}{20\%} = -\frac{1}{4}$$

Using the cross elasticity of demand measure, we come to the following rule about complements and substitutes:

If two goods are substitutes, their cross elasticity of demand will normally be positive. If two goods are complements, their cross elasticities will normally be negative.

This result is really a matter of common sense. If the price of a good goes up and there is a substitute available, people will tend to switch to the substitute. If the price of Coke goes up (and the price of Pepsi does not), at least some people will switch to Pepsi. Thus, a *rise* in the price of Coke causes a *rise* in the demand for Pepsi. Both percentage changes are positive numbers and so their ratio, the cross elasticity of demand, will also be positive.

On the other hand, if two goods are complements, a rise in the price of one will discourage its own use and it will also discourage use of the complement good. Automobiles and car radios are obviously complements. A large increase in the price of cars will depress the sale of cars, and this is also likely to reduce the sale of car radios. Thus, a positive percentage change in price leads to a negative percentage change in demand for car radios. The ratio of these numbers, the cross elasticity of demand for cars and radios, will therefore be negative.

STATISTICAL ANALYSIS OF DEMAND RELATIONSHIPS

It turns out to be very difficult to obtain information about demand curves or other demand relationships from statistical data. It can be done, but the task is full of booby traps and can usually be carried out successfully only by using advanced and sophisticated statistical methods.

There are at least two reasons for these difficulties. First, demand *is not* affected by just one variable, such as price, but as we mentioned earlier in this chapter, it is simultaneously affected by advertising, GNP, and many other variables. The demand for umbrellas also depends on rainfall, the demand for tea depends on the price of coffee, and so on.

Second, as we learned, all of the points on the demand curve that one needs for decision making must refer to the same period of time. Managers who are trying to determine a price for 1980 must consider and compare a number of alternative prices for the same year and decide what each of these *potential prices* will mean for demand in that year.

Let us see why these two facts cause problems. The most obvious (but incorrect) way to go about estimating a demand curve statistically is to collect a set of figures on prices and quan-

The Use of Cross Elasticity in Practice: The Supreme Court's Decision in the DuPont Antitrust Case

In 1956 the Supreme Court decided a historic antitrust case. The Department of Justice had sued DuPont, charging that it "monopolized trade in cellophane." DuPont sold about 75 percent of the cellophane used in the United States, so it was clear that it produced a dominant share of the product. But the Supreme Court also considered whether substitute products provided enough competition to prevent DuPont from acting like a monopolist. It used cross elasticity of demand as an important piece of evidence on the matter, and on that basis concluded that DuPont was not guilty—that it did not "monopolize." Here is an excerpt from its decision:

Sec. 2-B   DuPont & Co. (Cellophane) 247

An element for consideration as to cross elasticity of demand between products is the responsiveness of the sales of one product to price changes of the other. If a slight decrease in the price of cellophane causes a considerable number of customers of other flexible wrappings to switch to cellophane, it would be an indication that a high cross elasticity of demand exists between them; that the products compete in the same market. The court below held that the "[g]reat sensitivity of customers in the flexible packaging markets to price or quality changes" prevented DuPont from possessing monopoly control over price. The record sustains these findings. . . .

We conclude that cellophane's interchangeability with the other materials mentioned suffices to make it a part of this flexible packaging material market.

Source: *U.S. Reports,* vol. 351 (Washington, D.C., 1956), page 400.

TABLE 18–1

	JAN.	FEB.	MARCH	APRIL	MAY
Price	$7.20	$7.83	$7.20	$8.00	$8.20
Quantity sold	95,000	93,000	97,000	90,000	91,000

tities sold, like those given in Table 18–1. These points can then be plotted on a diagram with prices and quantities on the axes, as shown in Figure 18–6. One can then proceed to draw in a line (the broken line *TT*) that connects these points reasonably well and that appears to be the demand curve.

Unfortunately, *TT,* which we refer to as the historical demand curve, may bear no relationship to the demand curve we are after, which we call the analytical demand curve. You may notice at once that the prices and quantities on the historical demand curve refer to different points in time, and that they all have been *actual,* not *hypothetical,* prices and quantities at some time. The distinction is not insignificant. Over the period covered by the historical demand curve, the analytical demand curve, which we really want, may well have shifted. The true picture of what has happened may be as shown in Figure 18–7. Here we see that in January the analytical demand curve had the shape given by *JJ,* but by February the curve had shifted to *FF,* by April to *AA,* and so on.

Note that the slope of the historical demand curve can be very different from the slopes of the analytical demand curves, as is true of the

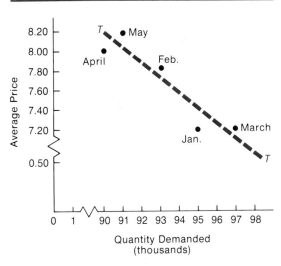

FIGURE 18–6

USE OF STATISTICAL DATA TO CONSTRUCT A HISTORICAL DEMAND CURVE
The dots labeled Jan., Feb., and so on, represent actual prices and quantities sold in the months indicated. The red historical demand curve is drawn to approximate the dots as closely as possible.

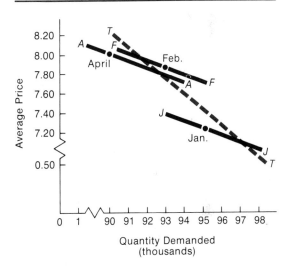

FIGURE 18–7

THE HISTORICAL DEMAND CURVE *TT* FROM FIGURE 18–6 AND THE ANALYTICAL DEMAND CURVES FOR JANUARY, FEBRUARY, AND APRIL
An analytical demand curve shows how demand in a particular month is affected by the different prices considered during that month. In the case shown, the analytical curves are much flatter (more elastic) than is the historical demand curve. This means that a cut in price will induce a far greater increase in quantity demanded than the historical demand curve indicates.

case shown in Figure 18–7. This means that the decision maker can be seriously misled if he selects his price on the basis of the historical demand curve. He may, for example, think that demand is quite insensitive to changes in price (as the historical demand curve, *TT,* in the diagram seems to indicate), and so he may reject the possibility of a price reduction when in fact (as the analytical curves show), a given price reduction will increase demand substantially. It can be estimated from the graph that if in February he were to charge a price of $7.80 rather than $8, the historical demand curve would promise him an increase in quantity demanded of only 1000 (92,500 − 91,500) units per year, whereas in fact the actual increment would be much larger; it would actually be 2500 units (94,000 − 91,500).

A historical demand curve may even be so extreme in its misrepresentation of the slope of the analytical demand curve that it reverses the sign of the slope. To see how this can occur, suppose that, over the period in question, the demand curve happens to be shifting substantially while the supply curve remains fixed. We may get a situation such as that depicted in Figure 18–8. In January the price and quantity sold will be given by point *A,* the intersection of the supply and demand curves that prevailed in that month. Similarly, *B* and *C* represent the February and March prices and quantities, respectively, and the historical "demand" curve that fits these points (line *TT*) will then have a positive slope. Indeed, the historical "demand" curve is really the supply curve in this case.[2]

It should now be clear why it is simply incorrect and totally misleading to the decision maker to present him with a historical demand curve, obtained by plotting actual quantities sold against actual prices. This information will not tell him what difference in his volume will result from the alternative decisions available to

[2]You should be cautioned that this queer result is not generally true. If the supply curve also shifts from month to month, the historical demand curve will be neither the analytical demand curve nor the supply curve.

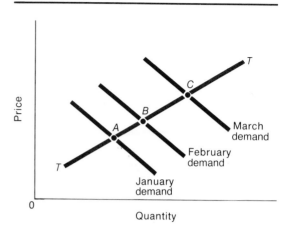

FIGURE 18–8

A HISTORICAL "DEMAND" CURVE WITH A POSITIVE SLOPE
Shifting analytical demand curves can even produce an upward-sloping historical demand curve. Suppose the supply curve has a positive slope and does not shift. Then if the demand curve shifts, as shown in the figure, the equilibrium points *A, B,* and *C* (the intersection points of the supply and demand curves) will go uphill toward the right. Consequently, the historical demand curve through points *A, B,* and *C* must have a positive slope.

him in setting his price. Indeed, since the historical demand curve often provides misinformation that has the appearance of being relevant, it may be much worse than offering him no data at all. These are the reasons that economists have designed special statistical techniques capable, at least in principle, of telling us when curves are shifting and of getting at the analytical rather than the historical demand curve.[3]

[3]The material you have just read is an introductory discussion of what is called the *indentification problem,* that is, the problem of using statistics to separate an analytical economic relationship such as a demand curve from the other economic relationships (such as the supply curve), which also affect observed phenomena such as price and quantity sold. This problem is studied in the branch of economics called *econometrics,* which uses the special statistical methods needed to analyze economic issues. The identification problem is analyzed in every standard textbook of econometrics.

In light of this discussion it is astonishing how often in practice one encounters demand studies that use apparently sophisticated statistical techniques to arrive at no more than a historical demand curve. One must not allow oneself to be misled by the amount of computer time used or the apparent complexity of the equations employed to fit a curve to historical data. If these merely plot historical quantities against historical prices, only the historical demand curve will be found.

OUR REAL ILLUSTRATION: THE ADVERTISING—DEMAND RELATIONSHIP

A disregard for the principles just presented explains the suspiciously close statistical relationships found between sales and advertising expenditure described at the beginning of this chapter—a relationship the food-processing company had hoped to use in determining its advertising outlays. The investigator had in fact constructed a historical demand curve relating company sales and its advertising expenditure. The statistician was quite pleased to find that the data exhibited a regular pattern showing a close and stable relationship between advertising expenditure and sales, and indicating that every increase in advertising expenditure brought with it a proportionate increase in sales volume.

However, a little deliberation showed that matters were not what they seemed. The stability of the relationship arose from the fact that, in the past, the company had based its advertising outlays on its sales, automatically allocating a fixed percentage of its sales revenues for the purpose. As in Figure 18—8, where our historical "demand" curve in fact traces out the stationary supply curve, the historical advertising—demand relationship described only the company's budgeting practices. If management had used this curve in planning its advertising campaigns, it might have made some regrettable decisions.

SUMMARY

1. Demand is not a single fixed number. Rather, it should be described by a relationship showing how quantity demanded is affected by price, advertising expenditure, and other pertinent influences.
2. The "law" of demand tells us that demand curves normally have a negative slope, meaning that a rise in price will reduce quantity demanded.
3. If a demand curve is to be helpful in choosing among alternative price decisions, all points on the demand curve must refer to the *same* time period—the time during which the price decided upon will be in effect.
4. To measure the responsiveness of quantity demanded to a change in price we use the elasticity of demand, which is defined as (minus) the percentage change in quantity demanded divided by the percentage change in price.
5. If elasticity is greater than 1, a rise in price will reduce the seller's total revenue. If elasticity is equal to 1, a rise in price will not change total revenue. If elasticity is less than 1, a rise in price will increase total revenue.
6. Goods that make each other more desirable (hot dogs and mustard or wrist watches and watch straps) are called *complements*. Goods such that if we have more of one we usually want less of another (steaks and hamburgers or Coke and Pepsi) are called *substitutes*.
7. Two substitute products will normally have a positive cross elasticity of demand. Two complementary products will normally have a negative

cross elasticity of demand. Cross elasticity is a measure of the percentage change in the demand for one good divided by the percentage change in the price of the good that causes the change in demand.

8. Simply comparing statistics of sales with prices over a period of time does not give us the analytical demand curve since demand curves are likely to shift from period to period.

CONCEPTS FOR REVIEW

Shift in a demand curve
Price elasticity of demand
"Law" of demand
Complement

Substitute
Cross elasticity of demand
Analytical demand curve
Historical demand curve

QUESTIONS FOR DISCUSSION

1. What factors besides price and advertising budget are likely to affect the quantity of a product that is demanded?
2. Which of the following goods may conceivably have positively sloping demand curves? Why?
   a. diamonds
   b. steel
   c. aspirin
   d. glue
3. Suppose a government agency is trying to set a price for rail freight transportation for 1981. It is considering whether to charge $70, $75, or $80 per ton along a particular route for a given product. What numbers should the agency consider?
4. If a rise in price from $10 to $20 reduces quantity demanded from 60 thousand to 40 thousand units, how would you calculate the price elasticity of demand?
5. Which of the following product pairs do you consider substitutes and which do you consider complements?
   a. trousers and belts
   b. gasoline and big cars
   c. bread and crackers
   d. butter and margarine
6. For each of the previous product pairs, what would you guess about their cross elasticity of demand:
   a. Do you expect it to be positive or negative?
   b. Do you expect it to be a large or a small number? Why?

19

The Common Sense of Consumer Choice

In the last chapter we discussed the analysis of demand, using demand curves and the elasticity measure that describes their shape. In this chapter we will probe into the influences that lie behind that shape and explore the reasons why the demand curve has a negative slope.

To some extent this discussion must rely on consumer psychology. But since economists claim no qualifications for making deep pronouncements about consumer psychology, our exploration will not go very far below the surface. It will, however, describe some powerful tools used in the analysis of pertinent consumer attitudes and attempt to cast some light on a number of interesting issues tangentially related to the negative slope of the demand curve.

One such issue is the diamond–water paradox, called to our attention by Adam Smith just about two hundred years ago. Smith suggested that the price people are willing to pay for a commodity has little to do with its usefulness. He cited as an example the fact that we are willing to pay little or nothing for a gallon of water, even though water is essential to life; yet we will pay hundreds, even thousands of dollars for a diamond, which has very limited uses. We will see later how this paradox is easily resolved through a concept called marginal utility, and, in the process, we will also examine the reasons for the shape of the demand curve.

A PUZZLE: RISING WAGES AND FALLING SUPPLY OF LABOR

To illustrate the type of issues that the analysis we will offer in this chapter can help us understand, we turn first to the behavior of the supply curve of labor.

By now you will be quite at home with the negative slope of the demand curve—the common-sense notion that the lower the price of a commodity, the more of it consumers will be induced to buy.

An equally common-sense view of the matter suggests that the quantity supplied of a commodity can be increased by a rise in its price.

Yet this is not always, or even usually, the way things work out. The labor market is a noteworthy example. Throughout the twentieth century, with only brief exceptions, wages have been rising year after year, both in number of dollars paid per hour and in the quantity of goods those dollars can buy, as is clearly shown by the data depicted in Figure 19–1. Yet labor has asked for and received *reductions* in the length of the workday and the workweek. At the beginning of the century a workweek of 5½ days and a workday of 10 or more hours was standard, making a workweek of 50 to 60 hours. Since then, labor hours have generally gone down. Today the standard workweek is down to 35 to 40 hours, with some firms even considering a four-day workweek.

Where has the common-sense view of the matter gone wrong? Why, as hourly wages have risen, have workers not tried to force employers to purchase more of the hours they have available instead of pressing for a shorter and shorter workweek? As usual, the answer has many elements. One of these elements is a concept called marginal utility.

FIGURE 19–1

TRENDS IN REAL WAGES AND HOURS WORKED
This graph shows how real wages (measured in dollars of 1967 purchasing power) have been rising throughout the twentieth century in the United States, while hours worked per week have been declining, despite the higher rewards for each hour of work. Data on both weekly hours and hourly earnings pertain to the entire economy for the 1947–1977 period, but only to the manufacturing sector for earlier years due to the unavailability of economy-wide data. The sharp drop in hours during the 1930s reflects the high unemployment of the Great Depression.

Source: Compiled by the authors from data in *Historical Statistics of the United States* and *Economic Report of the President*.

MARGINAL UTILITY

To make the concept of utility tangible, let us measure the utility of a particular good to a consumer by the *maximum* amount of money that the person is willing to pay for it. If the person is considering the purchase of 6 pounds of bananas and is willing to give up no more than

$1.11 for them, then $1.11 can be used as a measure of the total utility to the consumer of the 6 pounds. The total utility of his purchases is what really matters to a consumer. The greater the total utility he derives, the better off he is. That is true by definition, since total utility is defined simply as a measure of the benefit that the consumer enjoys.

Suppose now that 7 pounds of bananas are worth a total of $1.14 to the consumer. We note then that, in his view, the 7th pound of bananas is worth only 3 cents ($1.14 − $1.11). This additional outlay is referred to as his marginal utility, measured in money terms.[1]

DEFINITION
The *marginal utility* of a commodity (measured in money terms) is the maximum amount of money an individual is willing to pay *for one more unit* of that commodity.

The marginal utility of a consumer's purchases is really of no direct interest to the consumer. It is merely an instrument of calculation that helps an observer analyze and determine which purchases best serve the consumer's interests. It is like the pressure gauge on an oil-storage tank. Pressure is not the objective of the operation of the tank. Yet one must pay attention to the pressure gauge or the results may be quite unsatisfactory, to say the least. In the same way, it is important to understand the behavior of marginal utility, not because marginal utility is any sort of goal in itself, but because it is a means toward the analysis of what it takes

TABLE 19–1

TOTAL AND MARGINAL UTILITY OF BANANAS (MEASURED IN MONEY TERMS)

NUMBER OF POUNDS	TOTAL UTILITY	MARGINAL UTILITY
0	$ 0	
		$0.30
1	0.30	
		0.28
2	0.58	
		0.22
3	0.80	
		0.18
4	0.98	
		0.09
5	1.07	
		0.04
6	1.11	
		0.03
7	1.14	

to achieve the relevant goal—maximization of total utility.

The calculation of marginal utility from total utility can be seen with the aid of the numerical illustration in Table 19–1. The table shows the amount of money that different quantities of bananas are worth to the consumer—a single pound is worth (no more than) 30 cents, 2 pounds are worth 58 cents, and so on. These are the *total* utility figures for different quantities of bananas. The *marginal* utility is the *difference* between two successive total utility figures. In other words, if the consumer already has 3 pounds (worth 80 cents to him) an additional pound brings his total utility up to 98 cents. His marginal utility is therefore the difference be-- tween the two, or 18 cents.

[1]In more technical discussions economists call this concept the *marginal rate of substitution* between money and the good whose utility is being evaluated. Rather than trying to "psych" the individual and look inside his head to judge the strength of his feelings about the worth of an additional amount of a commodity, we use the observable measure of how much money he is willing to spend (or the money he offers) for the good as a means of calculating its marginal value to him. The use of money as an indicator of marginal utility (marginal rate of substitution) is a more modern way of looking at consumer preferences. Earlier writers treated marginal utility as a number that could be measured in some sort of psychological unit rather than as some directly observable entity, such as money.

THE "LAW" OF DIMINISHING MARGINAL UTILITY

So far we have been dealing only with definitions—not even with "superficial" human psychology as we had promised. But with our definitions we can now propose a simple hypothesis about consumer tastes. This hypothesis asserts that the more of a good a consumer has, the less the *marginal* utility that an additional unit will bring.

In general, this is a plausible proposition. The argument usually given to support the idea is the assertion that for every human there is a hierarchy of uses to which he or she will put a particular commodity. All of these uses are valuable, but some are more valuable than others. Let's consider bananas again. Our consumer may use them to give to his family to eat raw, to feed a pet monkey, to make banana cream pie (which is a bit rich for his tastes), or to give to a brother-in-law, for whom he has no deep affection. If he has only 1 pound it will be used only for the family to eat raw. The 2nd, 3rd, and 4th pounds may be used to feed the monkey; and a 5th may go into the banana cream pie. But the only use he has for a 6th pound, alas, is to give it to his brother-in-law.

The point is obvious. Each pound of bananas contributes something to the satisfaction of the consumer's needs for the product; but each additional pound contributes less than its predecessor because the use to which it can be put has a lower priority. This is, in essence, the so-called law of diminishing marginal utility.

DEFINITION
The *"law" of diminishing marginal utility* asserts that successive additions of a given commodity to a person's total consumption will yield successively smaller contributions to his or her well-being. As the individual's holdings increase, the marginal utility of each additional unit declines.

The last column of Table 19–1 illustrates this relationship. The marginal utility of the 1st pound of bananas is 30 cents. That is, the consumer is willing to pay *up to* 30 cents per pound if he has 0 pounds to begin with. The 2nd pound offers a marginal utility of 28 cents; a 3rd only 22 cents; and so on until, after he has 5 pounds, the consumer is willing to pay only 4 cents per pound (the marginal utility of a 6th pound is 4 cents).

The assumption upon which this "law" is based is plausible for most consumers and for most commodities. But, like most laws, there are exceptions. For some people, the more they have of a particular good, the more they want. Consider the needs of addicts and collectors, for example. The stamp collector who has a few stamps may consider the acquisition of one more to be mildly amusing. The person who has a large and valuable collection may be prepared to go to the ends of the earth for another stamp. Similarly, the alcoholic who finds a dry martini quite pleasant when he first starts drinking may find one more to be absolutely irresistible once he has already consumed four or five. Economists, however, generally treat such cases of *increasing marginal utility* as abnormalities. In other words, for most goods and most people, marginal utility probably declines as consumption increases.

THE OPTIMAL AMOUNT FOR A CONSUMER TO BUY

The concept of marginal utility also permits us to formulate a fundamental rule that tells us what quantity of a commodity a consumer will buy if he or she is to gain as much as possible from the exchange. This rule for optimal purchases may be expressed as follows:

It always pays the consumer to buy any quantity of a commodity whose marginal utility (measured in money) is more than its price. But when possible, the consumer should buy the quantity at which price and marginal utility are *equal,* because only such a quantity will maximize the total *utility* he or she gains from the purchase.

Why is this so? Our table of marginal utilities of bananas indicates the answer. Suppose the supermarket is selling bananas at 12 cents per pound and our consumer considers buying only 2 pounds. We see that this is not a wise decision because with that sized purchase the marginal utility of bananas (28 cents) is greater than its 12-cent price. Now suppose the consumer increases his planned purchase to 3 pounds of bananas. The additional pound costs 12 cents, but it is worth 22 cents—thus the purchase of a 3rd pound brings him a clear net gain of 10 cents. Obviously, at the 12-cent price he is better off with 3 pounds of bananas than with 2.

Similarly, at this price, 6 pounds is not an optimal purchase because the 4-cent marginal utility of a 6th pound is less than its 12-cent price. Our consumer would be better off with only 5 pounds since that would save him 12 cents with only a 4-cent loss in utility—a net gain of 8 cents resulting from the decision to buy 1 pound less.

Our rule about the optimal purchase quantity tells us that our consumer should buy 4 pounds, since any purchase above this amount yields a marginal utility that is less than price. The reader can make some easy calculations and see that by switching from a 4-pound purchase to either a 3- or 5-pound purchase the consumer will suffer a loss of utility.

MARGINAL UTILITY AND DEMAND CURVES

The optimal-demand rule we have just considered will now permit us to deal rapidly with the two issues whose resolutions have been postponed so far—the generally negative slope of the demand curve and the diamond—water paradox.

We observe first that the shape of a demand curve is in fact determined by the rule that the consumer benefits most only if he buys the quantity of a commodity at which the marginal utility is (approximately) equal to its price. Let us assume that the consumer is "rational" in the sense of getting as much utility for his money as possible. Then, armed with our rule

and with information about the consumer's marginal utility, we can predict how much of a particular commodity he will buy at each possible price. That is precisely what his demand curve is designed to tell us. By definition, it gives us the amount he will want to buy at each of the alternative prices to be considered.

We illustrate the relationship between price and demand by considering several possible banana prices, say 18 cents and 20 cents per pound. From Table 19–1, the table of marginal utilities for our consumer, we find that a price of 8 cents per pound for bananas stimulates him to buy 5 pounds. And at a 20-cent price, the optimal purchase is only 3 pounds. We see, then, that the marginal utility information and the optimal purchase rule relating price and marginal utility give us all the information we need to determine the consumer's responses to various prices. That is, they determine the consumer's *demand curve.*

The individual consumer's demand curve is determined by the pattern of his marginal utility; that is, by the magnitude of the numbers in his marginal utility table, the speed with which they decline, and so on.

Why Demand Curves Slope Downward

To see why demand curves generally have a negative slope, that is, why less will be demanded as prices rise, we must bring into the picture our detour into amateur psychology— the "law" of diminishing marginal utility. First, simply viewing the matter mechanically, we note that if the quantity purchased must be such that price is approximately equal to marginal utility, then the law of diminishing marginal utility *requires* purchases to increase when prices fall. Suppose, for instance, the price of bananas starts at 20 cents. It pays the consumer to buy 3 pounds of bananas because his marginal utility of a 3rd banana is 22 cents, while that of a 4th banana is only 18 cents. Now suppose the price drops to 10 cents. What can he do to bring the marginal utility of bananas down into line with the new lower price? The law of diminishing marginal utility tells us there is only one way he can accomplish the act—buy more bananas. For only if he buys more will the marginal utility of bananas fall.

This discussion is useful because it shows us how economists are able to reason their way from assumptions to conclusions about human behavior. From two premises—the assumptions that the consumer behaves so as to maximize the utility he gains from his purchases and that the marginal utility of a good decreases when the quantity purchased goes up—we are able to *deduce* something about the usual shape of the demand curve.

While this discussion is a bit abstract and mechanical, it can easily be rephrased in common-sense terms. We have seen that the various uses to which an individual puts a commodity have different priorities. Bananas can be eaten by the family directly as they are, fed to a pet monkey, baked into a pie, or given to a brother-in-law. If their price is high it will pay the consumer to buy only enough for the high-priority uses—the uses that contribute a high marginal utility. When price declines, however, it pays to purchase some more of the good—enough for some lower-priority uses. This is really the essence of what makes the analysis work.

This line of reasoning explains why *individual demand curves* have a downward slope for many persons. However, *market demand curves* may still have this property even when individual demand curves do not. People differ in their fondness for bananas. True devotees may maintain their purchases of bananas even at an exorbitant price, while others would not eat a banana even if it were offered free of charge. As the price of bananas rises, the less enthusiastic banana eaters will drop out of the market entirely, leaving the expensive fruit to the more devoted consumers. Thus the quantity demanded declines as price rises—that is, the

demand curve for bananas has a negative slope—simply because higher prices induce more people to kick the banana habit. Indeed, for many commodities, this phenomenon (more *new* customers at lower prices) rather than negatively sloped *individual* demand curves, accounts for the law of demand. For example, if a bookstore reduces the price of a popular novel, it may draw many new customers, but few old customers will be induced to buy a second copy.

Scarcity, Declining Marginal Utility, and the Diamond–Water Paradox

Finally, we can use the marginal utility analysis to remove the mystery from Adam Smith's diamond–water paradox—his observation that the price of diamonds is so much higher than the price of water even though water seems to offer far more utility.

Since a *paradox* is usually defined as an apparent contradiction, to resolve a paradox one must explain why something that seems to involve an inconsistency really does not. The resolution of the diamond–water paradox is based on the distinction between marginal and total utility.

The *total* utility of water—its total life-giving benefit—is indeed much higher than that of diamonds, and it is this that Smith observed. But price, as we have seen, is not related directly to total utility. Rather, the optimal purchase rule tells us that price will tend to be close to *marginal* utility. And there is very good reason to expect the marginal utility of water to be low and that of diamonds to be high. Water is extremely plentiful in many parts of the world. If consumers use correspondingly large quantities of water, by the principle of diminishing marginal utility, its marginal utility to a typical household will be pushed down to a very low level. On the other hand, diamonds are naturally scarce (and the diamond suppliers try to ensure that they stay that way). As a result, the supply of diamonds will not expand to a point at which their marginal utility is driven far below its maximum level.

The scarcer the commodity, the higher its marginal utility and, consequently, the higher its market price.

Thus, like many paradoxes, the diamond–water price relationship has a straightforward explanation. In this case, all one has to remember is that scarcity raises *marginal* utility but not necessarily *total* utility, and that it is marginal not total utility that is directly related to price.

INCOME AND DEMAND: INFERIOR GOODS

So far we have been concerned primarily with the effects of price changes on the quantity of a good that will be demanded. But quantity demanded is also affected by other variables, such as advertising, prices of substitute goods, and consumer incomes. Let us consider briefly the effects of one of these—the income of the consumer.

Normally, we would expect a simple relationship between income and quantity demanded. The more money the consumer has to spend, the more she will be able to buy, and so the more we would expect her to buy. But this does not apply to all commodities. There is an important class of commodities, called inferior goods, for which the demand behaves in the direction opposite from what we would normally expect.

DEFINITION
Inferior goods are commodities whose consumption *decreases* when the purchaser's income rises.

As people become wealthier they generally reduce their purchases of such inferior goods

as reconditioned automobile tires, poor-quality clothing, and bus tickets. In each instance where this is true, they do so because a more desirable alternative is available. The upshot is that we cannot draw definite conclusions about the effects of a rise in the consumer's income. Probably the result will be an increase in demand for most commodities. But there will usually be a few commodities, the inferior goods, for which the demand will decline.

INCOME AND SUBSTITUTION EFFECTS OF A PRICE CHANGE

Either a decline in the price of a commodity or an increase in income will make the consumer better off by increasing his or her purchasing power. In either case, the consumer can end up with more goods and a higher level of utility. Of course, a rise in income alone does not change the *relative* cost of two commodities. If a pair of shoes costs twice as much as a pair of gloves (say $20 versus $10), a change in income will not alter this price ratio. But a 25 percent drop in the price of shoes, besides increasing the consumer's overall purchasing power, increases the purchasability of shoes relative to gloves.

Economists have provided a more precise interpretation of these two phenomena, calling them the income effect and the substitution effect of a price change.

DEFINITION
The *income effect* of a decrease in the price of a good means that the consumer is able to buy more of it or of other goods, and thus reach a higher level of utility, just as she could as the result of a rise in income

Conversely, an *increase* in a price has an income effect that is very much like a *drop* in income. The utility level that the consumer can reach is lower after the price rise than it was before.

DEFINITION

The *substitution effect* of a decrease in the price of a good refers to the fact that even if the consumer experienced the same level of utility, the good would still become more attractive in price relative to one that did not decrease in price.

Conversely, a price *increase* has a substitution effect that makes the particular commodity *less* attractive than competing goods.

These two concepts, which many beginning students in economics think were invented to torture them, are really quite useful. But before we demonstrate their usefulness it may help if we dispose of one frequent misunderstanding. Many students mistakenly close their books thinking that substitution effects are the effects of changes in prices, while income effects are the effects of changes in income. This is incorrect. *Any change in price sets in motion both a substitution effect and an income effect.*

With this caution in mind, let us see how economists use these concepts. Suppose the price of some commodity, say hamburgers, declines, while the price of cheese remains unchanged. The *substitution effect* clearly induces the consumer to buy more hamburgers in place of grilled cheese sandwiches because hamburgers are now comparatively cheaper. What of the *income effect?* Unless hamburger is an inferior good, it leads to the same decision. The fall in price makes the consumer "richer," which induces an increase in purchases of all but inferior goods. This example alerts us to two general points.

If a good is not inferior, it must have a downward-sloping demand curve, since income and substitution effects reinforce each other. However, an inferior good may violate the law of demand because the income effect of a decline in price leads consumers to buy less.

Will all inferior goods, then, have upward-sloping demand curves? Certainly not, for we have the substitution effect to reckon with, and the substitution effect always favors a downward-sloping demand curve. Thus we have a kind of tug-of-war in the case of an inferior good. If the income effect dominates, the demand curve will slope upward. If the substitution effect prevails, the demand curve will slope downward.

Economists have generally found that the substitution effect wins out; so while there are many examples of inferior goods, there are few examples of upward-sloping demand curves. When can the income effect prevail over the substitution effect? Certainly it will not prevail if the good in question (say, margarine) is a very small fraction of the consumer's budget, for then a fall in price will not make the consumer much "richer." But it may do so if the good makes up a very substantial portion of the consumer's budget. If the price of rice increases, this may so impoverish an Asian peasant that she will actually buy *less* fish and *more* rice.

Tables 19–2 and 19–3—one table for a rise in price, the other for a fall in price—summarize what we have just learned in compact form. They should prove useful for future reference.

TABLE 19–2

EFFECTS OF AN INCREASE IN THE PRICE OF A GOOD

TYPE OF EFFECT	DIRECTION OF EFFECT IF GOOD IS:	
	NOT INFERIOR	INFERIOR
Substitution effect	Consumption falls	Consumption falls
Income effect	Consumption falls	Consumption rises
Combined effects	Consumption falls	Unclear, probably consumption falls

TABLE 19–3

EFFECTS OF A DECREASE IN THE PRICE OF A GOOD

| TYPE OF EFFECT | DIRECTION OF EFFECT IF GOOD IS: | |
	NOT INFERIOR	INFERIOR
Substitution effect	Consumption rises	Consumption rises
Income effect	Consumption rises	Consumption falls
Combined effects	Consumption rises	Unclear, probably consumption rises

APPLICATION:
THE LABOR-SUPPLY PARADOX

Income and substitution effects find innumerable applications in economics. For example, they have been used to resolve the puzzle with which this chapter began. Looking back over long periods of American history we see that real wages have risen steadily while the number of hours people want to work has fallen. Why has the increase in remuneration failed to encourage people to work more?

Part of the answer becomes clear if one thinks of *leisure time* as a commodity. When wages rise, the opportunity cost of taking leisure also rises because workers must give up more money for the hours they do not spend working. Thus, if one were to view the question in terms of the substitution effect, it would seem that rising wages—and its corollary, rising cost of leisure—would indeed cause people to work harder because the high price of leisure makes it less attractive.

But this reasoning is misleading because we have not yet accounted for the income effect. As workers get richer they will buy more of *every* commodity that is not an inferior good. As long as leisure is not an inferior good, then, the income effect of increasing wages induces workers to "buy more leisure," that is, to work less hard. And leisure is surely not an inferior good. Vacations and other leisure-time activities are events almost everyone looks forward to and wants to spend money on. Therefore, it is the income effect of rising wages that makes labor supply respond in the "wrong" direction.

SUMMARY

1. Economists distinguish between the total and marginal utilities of a quantity of goods. Total utility is what the "rational" consumer seeks to make as great as possible. Marginal utility is merely a calculating instrument—a set of numbers designed to determine what set of purchases does in fact maximize total utility.
2. The money marginal utility of a commodity is the maximal amount of money a consumer is willing to pay for an additional unit of that commodity. For example, the marginal utility of the 11th unit of a product is equal to the total utility of 11 units minus the total utility of 10 units.
3. The "law" of diminishing marginal utility is a psychological hypothesis that states that as a consumer acquires more and more of a commodity, the marginal utility of additional units of the commodity will decrease even though the total utility will increase.

357

4. To maximize the utility obtained from spending money on a commodity, the consumer must purchase a quantity such that the price is equal to the commodity's money marginal utility.

5. If the consumer acts to maximize utility, and if his marginal utility of some good does decline when larger quantities are purchased, then his demand curve for the good must have a negative slope. The reason is that a reduction in price will induce the purchase of more units despite their lower marginal utility.

6. Abundant goods tend to have a low marginal utility regardless of whether their total utility is high or low. That is why water can have a low price despite its high total utility.

7. An inferior good, such as second-hand clothing, is a commodity consumers buy less of when they get richer.

8. A rise in the price of a commodity has two effects on the demand for it: (a) a substitution effect, which makes it less attractive because the commodity has become more expensive than it was previously, and (b) an income effect, which decreases the consumer's total utility because higher prices cut his purchasing power.

9. Any increase in the price of a good always has a *negative* substitution effect; that is, considering only the substitution effect, a rise in price must reduce the quantity demanded.

10. The income effect of a rise in price may, however, have a negative or positive effect. But it will be positive only if the commodity is an inferior good because the rise in price makes the person poorer, which forces him or her to buy more inferior goods.

CONCEPTS FOR REVIEW

Diamond–water paradox	Scarcity and marginal utility
Marginal utility	Inferior good
Total utility	Income effect of a price change
Diminishing marginal utility	Substitution effect of a price change
Optimal purchase of a good	Income–leisure choice

QUESTIONS FOR DISCUSSION

1. Describe some of the different things you do with water. Which would you give up if the price of water rose a little? If it rose by a fairly large amount? If it rose by a very large amount?

2. Which is greater: Your *total* utility from 10 gallons of water per day or from 20 gallons per day? Why?

3. Which is greater: Your *marginal* utility at 10 gallons per day or your marginal utility at 20 gallons per day? Why?

4. Some people who do not understand the optimal purchase analysis argue that if a consumer buys so much of a good that its price equals its marginal utility, she could not possibly be behaving optimally. Rather, they say, the person would be better off quitting when ahead, that is, buying such a quantity that marginal utility is much greater than price

because she would then experience a net benefit. What is wrong with this argument? (*Hint:* What opportunity does the consumer then miss? Is it maximization of marginal or total utility that serves the consumer's interests?)

5. What inferior goods do you purchase? Why do you buy them? Do you think you will continue to buy them when your income is higher?

6. Suppose that gasoline and safety pins each rise in price by 10 percent. Which will have the larger income effect upon the purchases of a typical consumer? Why?

7. Suppose that the price of shoes and the price of leisure both rise 10 percent. Which will have the larger income effect upon the purchases of a typical consumer? Why?

8. Using the concept of opportunity cost (see pages 39–40 in Chapter 3), explain what the economist means by saying that the wage rate is the price of a worker's leisure.

Appendix
Indifference Curve Analysis

The analysis of consumer demand presented in this chapter has one analytical shortcoming. By treating the consumer's decision about the purchase of each commodity as an isolated event, it conceals the necessity of choice imposed on the consumer by his limited budget. It does not indicate explicitly the hard choice behind a decision to buy—the sacrifice of some goods to obtain others. If you spend more money on rent, you have less to spend on entertainment. If you buy more clothing, you have less money for food. To represent the consumer's choice problem explicitly, economists have invented two geometric devices, the *budget line* and the *indifference curve,* which this appendix describes. The budget line has already been described in Chapter 3, "Scarcity and Choice," and this part of the discussion is simply review.

GEOMETRY OF THE AVAILABLE CHOICES: THE BUDGET LINE

Suppose, for simplicity of discussion, there were only two commodities produced in the world, say cheese and pop records. The decision problem of any household then would be to determine the allocation of its income between these two goods. Clearly, the more it spends on one the less it can have of the other. But just what is the trade-off? A simple but very useful calculation provides the answer.

In Figure 19–2, quantities of these two goods are represented on the axes. Any point in the diagram represents a *bundle* of commodities. For example, point *A* might represent the

combination of goods with which our purchaser emerges from the supermarket on the day we are considering. Point *A* tells us that he would be returning home with 5 pounds of cheese and 2 hit records.

Now, suppose that at this particular market, cheese is priced at $2 per pound while records sell at $3 each. Suppose also that our shopper

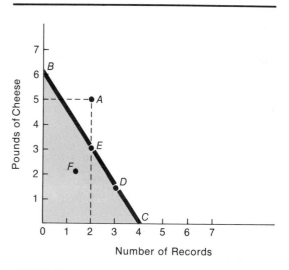

FIGURE 19–2

A BUDGET LINE
This budget line shows the different combinations of cheese and records the consumer can buy with $12 if cheese costs $2 per pound and records cost $3 each. At point *B* the consumer buys 6 pounds of cheese and has nothing left over for records. At point *C* the consumer spends the entire budget on records. At intermediate points (such as *E*) on the budget line, the consumer buys some of both goods (2 records and 3 pounds of cheese).

enters the store with $12 in purchasing power. We can now readily describe his available options. First, we note that if every available penny were spent on music, the consumer would end up at point C, bringing home 4 records and no food. Similarly, if he were to devote his resources exclusively to food, he would end up at point B—with 6 pounds of cheese and no records.

Next, if we connect points B and C by a straight line, the red line in the diagram, we trace out the available range of possibilities if the money is divided between the two goods. For example, point D tells us that if the consumer buys 3 records there will be only enough money left over to purchase $1\frac{1}{2}$ pounds of cheese. This is readily seen to be correct, for 3 records at $3 each and $1\frac{1}{2}$ pounds of cheese at $2 each do just add up to the available $12. Similarly, point E tells us that with a purchase of 2 records there will be enough money left to buy 3 pounds of cheese.

Line BC is thus called the budget line.

DEFINITION
The *budget line* for a household represents graphically all the possible combinations of two commodities that it can purchase, given the prices of the commodities and some fixed amount of money at the disposal of the household.

PROPERTIES OF THE BUDGET LINE

Let us now use r to represent the number of records purchased by our consumer and c to indicate the amount of cheese he acquires. Thus, at $2 per pound, he spends on cheese a total of $2c$ dollars $= 2 \times$ (number of pounds of cheese bought). Similarly, he spends $3r$ dollars on records, making a total of $2c + 3r = \$12$, if the entire $12 is spent on the two commodi-

ties. This is the equation of the budget line. And, as anyone who has studied elementary algebra should recognize, it is also the equation of a straight line as it has been drawn in the diagram.[2]

We note also that the budget line represents the maximal amounts of the commodities in question that the consumer can afford. Thus, for any given purchase of records, it tells us the greatest amount of cheese his money can buy. If our consumer wants to be thrifty, he can choose to end up at a point below the budget line, say at F. Clearly, then, the choices he has available include not only those points on the budget line BC, but also any point in the shaded triangle formed by the budget line BC and the two axes.

The position of the budget line is determined by two types of data: the prices of the commodities purchased and the income at the buyer's disposal. We can end our discussion of the graphics of the budget line by examining briefly how a change in either of these magnitudes affects its location.

Obviously, an increase in the income of the household will increase the range of options available to it. Specifically, *increases in income will produce parallel shifts in the budget line,* as shown in Figure 19–3. The reason simply is that a, say, 20 percent increase in available income will permit the family to purchase exactly 20 percent more of *either* commodity. Point B in Figure 19–2 will then shift upward by 20 percent of its distance from the origin, while point C will

[2]The reader may have noticed one problem that arises in this formulation. If every point on the budget line BC is to be a possible way for the consumer to spend his money, there must be some manner in which he can buy fractional records. Perhaps the purchase of $1\frac{1}{2}$ records can be interpreted to include a down payment of $1.50 on a record on his next shopping trip! Throughout this book it is convenient to assume that commodities are available in fractional quantities when drawing diagrams. This does not really affect the analysis and makes the graphs clearer.

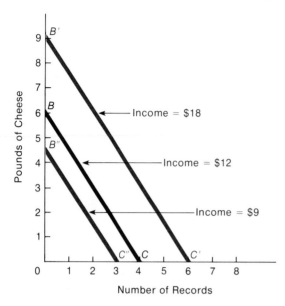

FIGURE 19–3

THE EFFECT OF INCOME CHANGES
ON THE BUDGET LINE
A change in the amount of money in the consumer's
budget causes a parallel shift in the budget line. A rise
in the budget from $12 to $18 raises the budget line
from BC to B'C'. A fall from $12 to $9 lowers the
budget line from BC to B''C''.

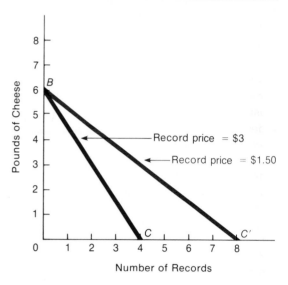

FIGURE 19–4

THE EFFECT OF PRICE CHANGES
ON THE BUDGET LINE
A fall in the price of records causes the end of the
budget line on the records axis to swing away from the
origin. A fall in record price from $3 to $1.50 swings
the price line from BC to red line BC'. This happens
because at the higher price, $12 buys only 4 records,
but at the lower price it can buy 8 records.

move to the right by 20 percent.[3] Figure 19–3
shows three such opportunity lines corresponding to incomes of $9, $12, and $18, respectively.

Finally, we can see what happens to the
opportunity line when there is a change in the
price of some commodity. In Figure 19–4 we
see that when the price of records *decreases,*
the opportunity line moves outward, but the

[3]An algebraic proof is simple. Let *M* (which is initially $12)
be the amount of money available to our household. The
equation of our opportunity line can be solved for *c,* obtaining

$$c = -(3/2)r + M/2.$$

This is the equation of a straight line with a slope of $-3/2$ and
with vertical intercept $M/2$. A change in *M*, the quantity of
money available, will not change the *slope* of the opportunity
line. It will therefore lead only to parallel shifts in that line.

move is no longer parallel because the point on
the cheese axis remains fixed. Once again, the
reason is fairly straightforward. A 50 percent
reduction in the price of records permits the
family's $12 to buy twice as many records as
before: Point *C* is moved rightward to point
C', at which 8 records are shown to be obtainable. However, since the price of cheese has
not changed, point *B*, the amount of cheese
purchasable for $12, is unaffected. Thus
we have the general result that a reduction in
the price of one of the two commodities swings
the opportunity line outward along the axis
representing the quantity of that item while
leaving the location of the other end of the line
unchanged.

WHAT THE CONSUMER PREFERS: THE INDIFFERENCE CURVE

We have used the budget line to tell us what choices are available to the consumer. We now must examine the consumer's *preferences* in order to determine which of the possibilities open to him he will want to choose.

After much investigation, economists have determined what they believe to be the minimum amount of information about the purchaser's psychology that is needed to analyze his purchase choices. This information consists of a *ranking* of the alternative bundles of commodities that are available. Suppose, for instance, the consumer is offered a choice between two bundles of goods, bundle *W* containing 3 phonograph records and $1\frac{1}{2}$ pounds of cheese and bundle *T* containing 2 records and 3 pounds of cheese. The economist wants to know for this purpose only whether the consumer prefers *W* to *T*, *T* to *W*, or whether he is *indifferent* about which one he gets. Note that the analysis requires no information about *degree* of preference—whether the consumer is wildly more enthusiastic about one of the bundles or just prefers it slightly.

Graphically, the preference information is provided by a family of curves called indifference curves (Figure 19–5). But before we examine these curves, let us see how such a curve is interpreted. A single point on an indifference curve tells us nothing by itself. For example, point *R* on curve I_a simply represents the bundle of goods composed of 4 records and 1 pound of cheese. It does *not* suggest that the consumer is indifferent between 1 pound of cheese and 4 records. For the curve to tell us anything, we must consider at least two of its points. For example, points *S* and *W*, since they represent two different combinations that are on the same indifference curve, are of equal desirability to our consumer.

DEFINITION

An *indifference curve* is simply a line connecting all possible combinations, or bundles, of the same commodities, each of which is equally desirable to the consumer.

PROPERTIES OF THE INDIFFERENCE CURVES

As yet, we still do not know which bundle our consumer prefers; we know only that a choice

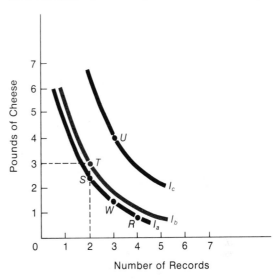

FIGURE 19–5

THREE INDIFFERENCE CURVES FOR CHEESE AND RECORDS

Any point in the diagram represents a combination of cheese and records (for example, *T* represents 2 records and 3 pounds of cheese). Any two points on the same indifference curve (for example, *S* and *W*) represent two different combinations of the goods such that the consumer likes both combinations equally. If two points, such as *T* and *W*, lie on different indifference curves, the one on the higher indifference curve represents the combination of goods preferred by the consumer.

363

between certain bundles will lead to indifference. So before we can use the indifference curves to investigate the consumer's choice, we must examine a few of their properties. Most important for us is the following:

If the consumer desires *more* of each of the commodities in the diagram, every commodity bundle represented by a point on a higher indifference curve will be preferred to every bundle on a lower indifference curve.

In other words, until satiation is reached, among indifference curves, higher is better. The reason is obvious. Given two indifference curves, say I_b and I_c in Figure 19–5, the higher curve will contain points lying above and to the right of some points on the lower curve. Thus, point U on curve I_c lies above and to the right of point T on curve I_b. This means that U represents larger quantities of *both* commodities than does T. At U the consumer gets more records *and* more cheese than at T. Assuming that he is not sated, our consumer must prefer U to T. Since every point on curve I_c is, by definition, equal in preference to point U, and the same relation holds for point T and all other points along curve I_b, any point on curve I_c will be preferred to *any* point on curve I_b

Another property that characterizes the indifference curves is their *negative slope.* Again, this holds only if the consumer wants more of both commodities. Consider two points, such as S and R, lying on the same indifference curve. If the consumer is indifferent between them, one cannot contain more of *both* commodities than the other. Since point S contains more cheese than R, R must offer more records than S, or the consumer could not be indifferent about which he gets. This means that as we move from one point to another along the curve, if, say, we move toward the one with the larger number of records, the quantity of cheese must decrease. The curve will always slope downhill toward the right, a negative slope.

A final property of indifference curves is the nature of their curvature—the way they round toward the axes. This shape, which is described as "convexity toward the origin," means that they flatten out (their slopes decrease in absolute value) as they extend from left to right. To understand why this is so we must first examine the economic interpretation of the slope of an indifference curve.

THE SLOPES OF AN INDIFFERENCE CURVE AND THE BUDGET LINE

In Figure 19–6 it can be seen that the slope of the curve between points M and N is represented by RM/RN. RM is the quantity of cheese the consumer gives up when he moves from M to N. Similarly, RN is the increased number of records he acquires through this move. Since the consumer is indifferent between bundles M and N, the gain of RN records must just suffice to compensate him for the loss of RM pounds of cheese. Thus the ratio RM/RN represents the terms on which the consumer is just willing—*according to his own preferences*—to trade one good for the other. If RM/RN equals 1.5, the consumer is willing to give up (no more than) $1\frac{1}{2}$ pounds of cheese for an additional record.

The slope of an indifference curve, referred to as *the marginal rate of substitution* between the commodities involved, represents the maximum amount of one commodity the consumer is willing to give up in exchange for one more unit of another commodity.

The slope of the budget line BB has an interpretation directly analogous to that of the indifference curve. The slope of BB is also a rate of exchange between cheese and records. But it no longer reflects the consumer's subjective willingness to trade. Rather, the slope represents the rate of exchange *the market* offers to the consumer when he gives up money in exchange for cheese and records. Recall that the budget line is defined as representing all commodity combinations a consumer can get by spending a fixed amount of money. The budget line is thus a curve of constant expenditure. At current prices, if the consumer reduces his planned purchase of cheese by amount *DE* in Figure 19–6, he will save just enough money to buy an additional amount, *EF,* of records, since at points *D* and *F* he is spending the same total number of dollars.

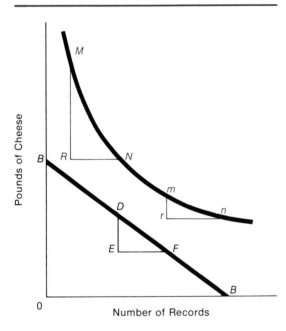

FIGURE 19–6

SLOPES OF A BUDGET LINE AND AN INDIFFERENCE CURVE

The slope of the budget line shows how many pounds of cheese, *ED,* can be exchanged for *EF* records. The slope of the indifference curve shows how many pounds of cheese, *RM,* the consumer is just willing to exchange for *RN* records. When the consumer has more records and less cheese (point *m* as compared with *M*), the slope of the indifference curve decreases, meaning that the consumer is willing only to give up *rm* pounds of cheese for *rn* records.

The slope of the budget line is the amount of one commodity the market requires an individual to give up in order to obtain one additional unit of another commodity without any change in the amount of money spent.

The slopes of the two types of curves, then, are perfectly analogous in their meaning. One tells us the terms on which the *consumer* is willing to trade one commodity for another, and the other reports the rate of exchange currently offered on the *market.*

It is useful to carry our interpretation of the slope of the budget line one step further. One would think that the market's rate of exchange between cheese and records would be related to their prices, p_c and p_r, and it is easy to show that this is so. Specifically, the slope of the budget line is equal to the ratio of the prices of the two commodities. The reason is straightforward. If one record exchanges for $1\frac{1}{2}$ pounds of cheese, it must mean that the price of one record, p_r, must be $1\frac{1}{2}$ times as high as the price of a pound of cheese, p_c.

p_r/p_c = the quantity of cheese that exchanges for one record = the slope of the budget line.

Before returning to our main subject, the study of consumer choice, we pause briefly and use our interpretation of the slope of the indifference curve to discuss the third of the properties of the indifference curve—its convexity to the origin (the zero point in the diagram), which we left unexplained. With indifference curves of that shape, the slope will decrease as we move from left to right. We have seen in Figure 19–6 that at point *m,* toward the right of the diagram, the consumer will be willing to give up far less cheese for one more phonograph record (quantity *rm*) than he is willing to trade at point *M,* toward the left. This is because at *M* he has a relatively large quantity of cheese to begin with, while at *m* his initial stock of cheese is low. In general terms, the curvature premise on which indifference curves are usually drawn asserts that consumers will be relatively eager to trade away a commodity of which they have a large amount, but that they will be more reluctant to trade goods of which they hold small quantities. This psychological premise, which need not be valid universally, is what is implied in the convexity of the indifference curves to the origin.

However, there *are* exceptions. As we noted earlier in the chapter, in the case of a passionate collector or an addict, the more of the good in question that he has, the more he is likely to want. As a stamp collector's holding of stamps expands he may well value each further addition to his collection more highly, and the same (up to a point) may be true of martinis for an alcoholic. In these cases, then, the relevant indifference curves would have the opposite curvature from that shown in the diagrams—the curves would be concave when viewed from the origin.

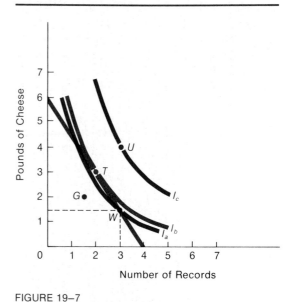

FIGURE 19–7

OPTIMAL CONSUMER CHOICE
Point *T* is the combination of records and cheese that gives the consumer the greatest benefit for his money. I_b is the highest indifference curve that can be reached from the budget line. *T* is the point of tangency between the budget line and I_b.

THE CONSUMER'S CHOICE

We can now deduce from our indifference curve apparatus how the consumer will choose among the combinations of commodities he can afford to buy, that is, the combinations of records and cheese shown by his budget line. Figure 19–7 brings together in the same diagram the budget line from Figure 19–2 and the indifference curves from Figure 19–5.

Since according to the first of the properties of indifference curves the consumer prefers higher to lower curves, he will go to the point on his budget line that lies on the highest indifference curve attainable. This will be point *T* on indifference curve I_b. He can afford no other point that he likes as well. For example, neither point *G* below the budget line nor point *W* on the budget line gets him on as high an indifference curve, and any point on an indifference curve above I_b, such as point *U*, is out of the

question because it lies beyond his financial means.

Where the indifference curves are smooth, as we have drawn them, we generally end up with a simple rule of consumer choice:

The consumer will select the most desired combination of goods obtainable for his money. The choice will be that point on the budget line at which the budget line is tangent to an indifference curve.

We can see why no point except the point of tangency, *T* (2 records and 3 pounds of cheese), will give the consumer the largest utility that his money can buy. Suppose the consumer were instead to consider buying 3 records and $1\frac{1}{2}$ pounds of cheese. This would put him at point *W* on the budget line and on indifference curve I_a. But then, by buying fewer records and more cheese (a move to the left on the budget line), he would get to an indifference curve that was higher and hence more desirable. It clearly does not pay him to end up at W. Only at the point of tangency, T, is there no move that would improve his choice.

At a point of tangency, where the consumer's benefits from his purchases of cheese and records are maximized, the slope of the budget line will equal the slope of the indifference curve. This is true by definition of a point of tangency.

We have just seen that the slope of the indifference curve is the marginal rate of substitution between cheese and records, and that the slope of the budget line is the ratio of the prices of records and cheese. We can therefore restate the requirement for the optimal division of the consumer's money between the two commodities as follows:

The consumer will get the most benefit from his or her money by choosing a combination of commodities whose marginal rate of substitution is equal to the ratio of their prices.

This conclusion is useful not because of what it states itself, but because of the logic that underlies it. It may be useful to reexamine why it would not be profitable for the consumer to choose any other point, say W. At W the slope of the budget line is -1.5 while that of the indifference curve is about -1. That is, at W the consumer is willing to trade cheese and records nearly one for one. But the price of a record is higher than a pound of cheese, so the market offers our consumer $1\frac{1}{2}$ pounds of cheese for every record he gives up. If the consumer fails to take advantage of the market's offer, he is not using his money wisely. Thus he would do well to give up one record and gain $1\frac{1}{2}$ pounds of cheese. In other words, it pays to move to the left and upward (fewer records, more cheese) along the budget line from W to T, just as the diagram indicates.

CONSEQUENCES OF PRICE CHANGES

Earlier in the chapter we discussed the effect of price changes on the quantity demanded. We have seen that a reduction in the price of records causes the budget line to swing outward along the horizontal axis while leaving unchanged the location of the end of the budget line on the vertical axis. The reason, to review it briefly, is that the end of the budget line on the horizontal axis represents the number of records the consumer can buy if he chooses to spend his money only on that commodity, and a similar interpretation holds for the other end of the budget line.

In Figure 19–8 we now depict the effect of a

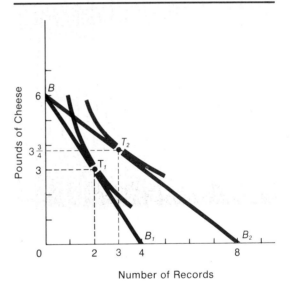

FIGURE 19–8

CONSEQUENCES OF PRICE CHANGES
A fall in record price swings the budget line outward from line BB_1 to BB_2. The consumer's equilibrium point (the point of tangency between the budget line and an indifference curve) moves from T_1 to T_2. The desired purchase of records increases from 2 to 3, and the desired purchase of cheese increases from 3 pounds to $3\frac{3}{4}$ pounds.

range of alternative prices on the demand for records. As the price of records falls, the budget line swings accordingly from BB_1 to BB_2. The tangency points, T_1 and T_2, also move in a corresponding direction, causing the quantity of records demanded to change from 2 to 3. The price of records has fallen, and the quantity demanded has risen: The demand curve for records is negatively sloped. This diagram brings out another important point that the demand curve analysis did not show. A change in the price of records also has consequences for the demand for cheese because it affects the amount of money left over for cheese purchases. In the example illustrated, the decrease in the price of records increases the demand for cheese from 3 to $3\frac{3}{4}$ pounds.

CONSEQUENCES OF INCOME CHANGES: INFERIOR GOODS

Finally, it is useful to examine what happens to the consumer's purchases when there is a rise in family income. We know that a rise in income produces a parallel outward shift in the budget line, such as the shift from BB to CC in Figure 19–9. This moves the consumer's equilibrium from tangency point T_1 to tangency point T_2 at a higher indifference curve. But a rise in income may or may not increase the demand for a commodity. In the case shown in Figure 19–9, the rise in income does lead the consumer to buy more goods *and* more records. But his indif-

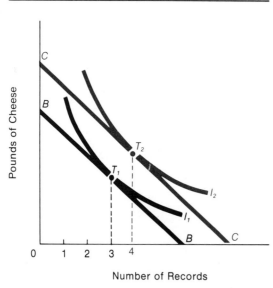

FIGURE 19–9

A RISE IN INCOME AND A CORRESPONDING RISE IN DEMAND FOR TWO GOODS, NEITHER OF WHICH IS INFERIOR

The rise in income causes a parallel shift in the budget line from *BB* to *CC*. The demand for records rises from 3 to 4, and the demand for cheese also increases.

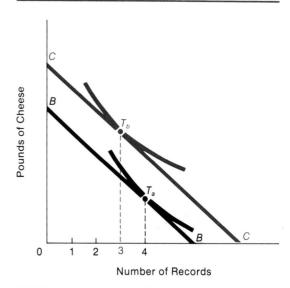

FIGURE 19–10

A RISE IN INCOME AND A CORRESPONDING DROP IN DEMAND FOR RECORDS FOR A CONSUMER TO WHOM RECORDS ARE AN INFERIOR GOOD

The upward shift in the budget line from *BB* to *CC* causes demand for records to fall from 4 (point T_a) to 3 (point T_b).

ference curves need not always be positioned in a way that yields this sort of result. In Figure 19–10 we see that as the consumer's budget line rises from *BB* to *CC,* the tangency point moves leftward from T_a to T_b, so that when his income rises he actually buys *fewer* records. In this case we infer that records are considered an *inferior good.*

SUMMARY

1. Indifference-curve analysis permits us to study the interrelationships of the demands for two (or more) commodities.
2. The basic tools of indifference-curve analysis are the consumer's budget line and his indifference curves.
3. A budget line shows all combinations of two commodities that the consumer can afford, given the prices of the commodities and the amount of money the consumer has available to spend.
4. The budget line is a straight line whose slope equals the ratio of the prices of the commodities. A change in price changes the slope of the budget line. A change in the consumer's income causes a parallel shift in the budget line.
5. Two points on an indifference curve represent two combinations of commodities such that the consumer does not prefer one of the combinations over the other.
6. Indifference curves normally have negative slopes and are convex to the origin. The slope of an indifference curve indicates how much of one commodity the consumer is willing to give up in order to get an additional unit of the other.
7. The consumer will choose the point on his budget line that gets him to his highest attainable indifference curve. Normally this will occur at the point of tangency between the two curves. This choice indicates the combination of commodity quantities that gives him the greatest benefits for the amount of money he has available to spend.

CONCEPTS FOR REVIEW

Budget line
Indifference curves
Marginal rate of substitution

Slope of a budget line
Slope of an indifference curve

QUESTIONS FOR DISCUSSION

1. John Q. Public spends all his income on gasoline and hot dogs. Draw his budget line when:
   a. His income is $60, and one gallon of gasoline and one hot dog each cost 60 cents.
   b. His income is $90, and the two prices are as in part a.
   c. His income is $60, hot dogs cost 60 cents each, and gasoline costs $1 per gallon.
2. Draw some hypothetical indifference curves for John Q. Public on a diagram identical to the one you constructed for part a of Question 1.
   a. Approximately how much gasoline and records will Public buy?
   b. How will these choices change if his income increases to $90, as in part b of Question 1? Is either good an inferior good?

   c. How will these choices change if, instead, gasoline prices rise to $1 per gallon, as in part c of Question 1.

3. Explain what information the *slope* of an indifference curve conveys about a consumer's preferences. Use this to explain the typical convexity of indifference curves.

20

The Common Sense
of Business Decisions:
Outputs and Prices

When General Motors makes plans for its new car models, it must decide the prices at which they will be offered and it must estimate the number of cars of each type it will have to produce to meet the resulting demand. These are clearly among the most crucial decisions the firm must make. They will have a vital influence on the company's purchases of raw materials, on its labor requirements, and on the reception given the product by consumers. This chapter describes the tools that can be used by firms like General Motors in seeking optimal decisions on outputs and prices, and which are also, as we will see in later chapters, the tools that government agencies or nonprofit organizations can use in making analogous decisions.

We begin this chapter by examining the relationship between the firm's price decisions and the quantity of product it sells. We then describe the basic tools of optimal decision making by the firm: total, average, and marginal revenue; and total, average, and marginal cost. Next we explain why firms do not necessarily try to make optimal decisions; and finally, we present a detailed analysis of the logic behind optimal output decisions.

TWO ILLUSTRATIVE CASES

Price and output decisions can run into complications that often perplex even the most experienced business people, as the following real-life illustrations show:

CASE 1:
A Beer-Pricing Problem

The managers of one of the largest producers of beer in the United States became concerned when a rival company introduced onto the market a cheaper substitute for one of their firm's products, a brew that was currently selling some 10 million six-packs annually.[1] Some members of the management group advocated a reduction in the price of a six-pack from $1.50 to $1.35. This stimulated a heated debate. It was agreed that the price should be cut if it was likely to cause no reduction in the company's profits. And although one segment of the group maintained that the cut made sense because of the demand it would stimulate, the opposing group held that the price cut would hurt the company by cutting profit per unit of output. The company, incidentally, had reliable information about costs but no statistical information on consumer responsiveness to price changes. At this point a group of consultants was called in to offer its suggestions. The resolution of the issue, as well as the tools of analysis this group used, are described in this chapter.

CASE 2:
An Output-Expansion Decision[2]

A supplier of a canned meat product was selling 10 million units per year at a wholesale price of $1.10 per unit. It found that rising wages and raw material prices had increased its costs to $1.30 per unit, which was clearly a losing proposition. (The annual loss amounted to 10 million × 20 cents, or $2 million.) Yet the availability of competing canned meats convinced managers of the firm that they could not get away with a price rise. At this point a purchasing agent for a foreign government approached the firm and offered to buy an additional 10 million units, but at a price of only 80 cents per unit. At first, management considered rejecting the offer as ludicrous, since the 80-cent price came nowhere near covering the unit cost of $1.30. But after some analysis, using reasoning like that which will be discussed in this chapter, management was able to show that the firm could actually clear up its financial problem by agreeing to the proposed sale even though it was "below cost!"

This case has important analogues that are encountered frequently throughout the economy. The canned meat supplier was offered the opportunity to deal with a new class of customers at a price that appeared not to cover costs but, as we will see, really did. The same sort of issue frequently faces a firm considering the introduction of a new product or the opening of a new branch, perhaps in another country. In each of these cases it is likely that the new operation may *appear* not to cover costs as measured by standard accounting conventions. Yet to follow the apparent implications of those cost figures would amount to throwing away a valuable opportunity to add to the net earnings of the firm and, perhaps, to contribute to the welfare of the economy. These remarks are

---

[1]As in many of the illustrations, the figures are "doctored" to help preserve the confidentiality of the information and to simplify the calculations.

[2]The details of the following illustration are hypothetical, but the situation is real—a composite of several cases.

offered as a way of suggesting the importance of the analytic tools we are about to study.

PRICE AND QUANTITY— ONE DECISION, NOT TWO

This chapter is about how firms like those in the preceding illustrative cases select a product *price* and *quantity* that best serve their financial interests. While it would seem that firms must choose two numbers, in fact they can pick only one. Once they have selected the price, the quantity they will sell is up to the consumers. Or firms may instead decide *how much* they want to sell, but then they must leave it to the market to determine what *price* such a quantity will require. Management gets its two numbers by making only one decision.

The firm's demand curve confirms that these decisions come in inseparable pairs, and it specifies the pairings explicitly. That is, given any output that the firm wishes to sell, the demand curve tells us what the corresponding price must be, or vice versa. For discussion purposes, let us examine a hypothetical firm, Rollatron, Inc., and let its product be ball-bearing units, that is, sets of ball bearings locked together in a turning device. Rollatron's demand curve, *DD,* in Figure 20–1 shows that if the company decides to charge the relatively high price of $15 per ball-bearing unit (point *A* on the curve), then it can sell only 1 million units of its product per year. On the other hand, if it wants to sell as many as 6 million units per year, it can do so only by offering its product at the low price of $5 (point *C*).

In summary, each point on the demand curve represents a price–quantity pair. The firm can pick any such pair. But to attain its goals, it can never pick the price corresponding to one point on the demand curve and the quantity corresponding to another point, since such an output would never be sold at the selected price.

Throughout this chapter, then, we will not discuss price and output decisions separately, for they are merely two different aspects of the same decision.

Of course, price is not the only way a firm can affect the quantity it sells. By advertising, or increasing its sales force, or improving its product design or its packaging, it can also stimulate business. Just the same sort of analysis that the firm uses for its pricing decision can also be applied to any of these other decisions.

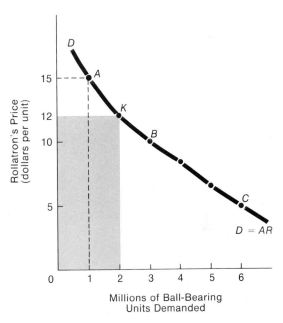

FIGURE 20–1

AVERAGE REVENUE (DEMAND) CURVE
This graph shows the quantity of product demanded at each relevant price. For example, the curve shows (point *K*) that at a price of $12, 2 million units of the commodity will be demanded. Such a demand curve is also a curve of average revenue. If at point *K, each* of the 2 million units of product is sold at a price of $12, then by definition the average revenue from that sale must be $12.

PROFIT MAXIMIZATION AS THE OBJECTIVE OF FIRMS

In economic theory it is usually assumed that management's exclusive goal is to earn as much profit as possible for the firm. This is an oversimplification. Since business people are like all other human beings, their motives are varied and complicated. If given the choice, many executives might prefer to control the largest and most powerful firm rather than the most profitable one. Some may be influenced by envy, others by a desire to "do good." Thus, any characterization of the objectives of management in terms of one number (profit) is bound to be an oversimplification. Nevertheless, for a wide range of situations the profit-maximization premise seems to fit the facts fairly well and we can learn a good deal with its aid. Therefore, throughout this chapter and much of the remainder of the book, we will use the standard assumption that *firms have a single objective—to maximize their profits.*

AVERAGE AND TOTAL REVENUE AS AFFECTED BY QUANTITY SUPPLIED

Profit is defined by the equation:

$$\text{Profit} = \text{Revenue} - \text{Cost}$$

In other words, profit is the difference between the money the firm takes in from its sales to consumers and the money it spends producing and selling its products. Both of these, the revenues and the costs, depend on the output–price combination the firm happens to select.

In this section, we will discuss the tools that are used to analyze the behavior of revenues when price (or output) changes, leaving the examination of costs to the next section. The behavior of the firm's revenues in relation to

its output can be determined directly from its demand curve. Indeed:

As long as the firm sells its product for the same price to all customers, the demand curve for its products can be used to show the firm's *average revenue* at each output level.

This is true because the demand curve shows, for every level of output, the price at which the firm can expect to sell its product, or what *revenue per unit* it will receive for each unit it sells. For instance, in Figure 20–1 we saw that if the firm wishes to sell an output of 3 million units per year, it must sell each unit at $10 (point *B*). This means, by definition, that at this output level the firm's revenue-per-unit sold will also be $10. Hence, the demand curve, *DD,* becomes, by this simple reinterpretation, an average revenue curve for the firm.

DEFINITION
The *average revenue* of the firm is the average amount of money it earns per unit of output sold. It is calculated by taking the total amount of money the firm earns from the sale of its output and dividing that *total revenue* figure by the total number of units it sells. Thus, both total revenue and average revenue depend on the number of units sold.

In Table 20–1 we see for our sample firm, Rollatron, Inc., how total revenue and average revenue are related to the number of ball-bearing units it produces and sells. The figures correspond to the demand curve in Figure 20–1.

We note, for example, that if Rollatron decides to place 2 million units on the market, then the market price will settle at $12 per unit. Since Rollatron will then receive $12 for each ball-bearing unit it sells, it will clearly receive $12 for an average unit. At that price–output combination its total revenue will be:

(Average revenue) × (Number of units sold)
= $12 × 2 million = $24 million

TABLE 20–1

TOTAL AND AVERAGE REVENUES FOR
ROLLATRON, INC.

(Data Corresponding to Figure 20–1)

NUMBER OF BALL-BEARING UNITS SUPPLIED (millions per year)	TOTAL REVENUE (millions of dollars)	AVERAGE REVENUE (dollars per unit)
0	0	—
1	15	15
2	24	12
3	30	10
4	34	8.5
5	33	6.6
6	30	5

In a diagram like Figure 20–1, this total revenue is always represented by a shaded rectangle like that next to point *K*. This is so because:

Total revenue = Average revenue × Number of units = 12 × 2 = Height of shaded rectangle × Length of its base = Area of shaded rectangle.

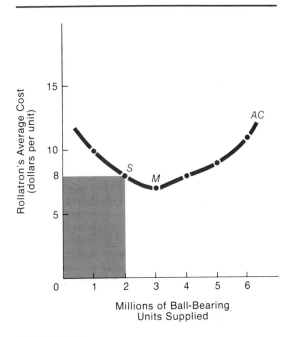

FIGURE 20–2

AVERAGE COST CURVE

The graph shows, for each level of output, the cost-per-unit incurred to produce that output. For example, at point *S*, if 2 million units of the good are produced, the average cost will be $8 per unit.

AVERAGE AND TOTAL COST

To determine Rollatron's profits, it is not enough to analyze the behavior of its revenues. We must also examine its costs. Table 20–2 and Figure 20–2 (showing average cost curve *AC*) give the average costs and total costs for Rollatron, just as Table 20–1 and Figure 20–1 reported its average and total revenues. For example, point *S* indicates that if the firm produces 2 million ball-bearing units per year, it will have to spend an average of $8 per unit or $16 million in total.

The shape of the average cost curve in Figure 20–2 is determined by the assumption that in this (ball-bearing) industry there is an opti-

TABLE 20–2

TOTAL AND AVERAGE COSTS FOR
ROLLATRON, INC.

NUMBER OF UNITS SUPPLIED (millions of units per year)	TOTAL COST (millions of dollars)	AVERAGE COST (dollars per unit)
0	0	—
1	10	10
2	16	8
3	21	7
4	32	8
5	45	9
6	66	11

mum size firm, so that if the firm is smaller or larger than the optimum its costs will be higher. That is why the average cost curve is drawn to be U-shaped. Its lowest point, *M,* drawn to occur where output is 3 million units, gives the level of output at which the firm operates at lowest average cost.

The total cost of supplying 2 million units of output per year is shown by the red rectangle in Figure 20–2. That this is true is shown by the following calculation:

Total cost = Average cost × Number of units supplied = 8 × 2 = Height of rectangle × Base of rectangle = Area of red rectangle.

TOTAL PROFIT: THE IMPORTANT DIFFERENCE

By bringing together into a single diagram (Figure 20–3) the demand, or average revenue, curve of Figure 20–1 and the average cost curve of Figure 20–2, we can determine the total profit for any particular level of output. For instance, at 2 million units per year, emphasized in the revenue and cost diagrams, we see that:

Total profit at an output of 2 million units per year is represented by the red rectangle *SKTU,* which is the difference between the total revenue rectangle (whose upper right-hand corner is *K*) and the total cost rectangle (whose upper right-hand corner is *S*). That is,
    Total profit = Total revenue − Total cost

Exactly the same procedure can be used to find the total profit at any other output level. And it follows, then, that the firm can affect this total profit figure by deciding to produce one output level rather than another. The question is, How can it decide which will be the *most profitable* of the many output levels among which it can choose? To answer this question it

is necessary to build upon the material just accumulated in order to obtain a more powerful analytic tool, called *marginal analysis*—which is the primary instrument used for optimal decision making.

But before we examine the ways to make optimal decisions, we first need to discuss what an optimal decision is.

DIGRESSION: DO FIRMS ALWAYS TRY TO MAKE OPTIMAL DECISIONS?

The term *optimality* implies that the consequences of a decision, either explicitly or implicitly, have been compared with the consequences of all available alternatives. This follows from the definition of *optimum,* which we take to mean ''the best'' in terms of whatever objective we have chosen. It represents the maximal level of achievement of a particular goal as measured by the appropriate variable: profit, GNP, human longevity, or whatever. Thus, if the objective of a fire department is to maximize the number of lives saved, an optimal decision by the fire chief would be one that contributes as much as possible toward the objective of saving lives.

The requirements for making an optimal decision are important just because they are met so infrequently. They are far more easily agreed to than adhered to. In deciding on how much to invest, on what price to set for a product, on how much to allocate to the advertising budget, the range of available alternatives is enormous. And information about each alternative is often expensive and difficult to acquire. As a result, when a firm's management decides on an $18 million construction budget it rarely compares the consequences of that decision in any detail with the consequences of the possible alternatives—such as budgets of $17 million or of $19 million. Rather, management normally studies with care only the likely effects of the proposed decision itself. What sort of plant will it obtain

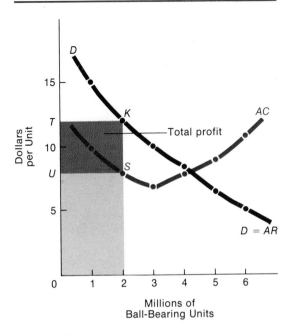

FIGURE 20–3
AVERAGE REVENUE, COST, AND PROFIT
The curve labeled AR is the average revenue curve
from Figure 20–1. The curve labeled AC is the average
cost curve from Figure 20–2. At any output, profit per
unit is the average revenue minus the average cost.
For example, at output 2 million, profit per unit is
$K - S$, or $12 - $8 = $4. Therefore, total profit equals
output times profit per unit, or 2 million × $4 = $8
million. This is represented by the area of the red
rectangle.

for the money? How costly will it be to operate
the plant? How much revenue is it likely to obtain from the sale of the plant's output? Such
information constitutes evidence indicating
*whether the decision will produce results that
satisfy the firm's standards of acceptability —*
whether its risks will not be unacceptably great,
whether its profits will not be unacceptably low,
and so on. But it does not provide any presump-
tion of optimality, because, though the decision
may be good, some of the alternatives that have
not been investigated may be better, perhaps
even far better.

Decision making that seeks only acceptable

solutions has been called *satisficing* to contrast
with *optimizing,* and some observers have concluded that decision making in industry and
government is characteristically of the satisficing variety.

Optimal decision making is more easily said
than done. It requires that the decision maker
compare the likely consequences of all possible
alternatives with one another before making a
selection. Without such a comparison the belief
that one is carrying out an optimization process
is a delusion.

MARGINAL PROFIT: GUIDE TO AN OPTIMUM

To determine an optimum, then, decision
makers need large amounts of information
about the proposed alternatives and their consequences. They also need calculation procedures that will permit them to organize the data
in such a way that the best possible choice is
effectively extracted. Economists use a variety
of such calculation techniques—among them,
linear and nonlinear programming and the differential calculus. The oldest and most widely
used technique is the latter, which in economics, is called marginal analysis.

To show how marginal analysis works let us
return to the basic problem of this chapter—the
output–price decision of Rollatron, Inc., a firm
that is attempting to maximize its *total* profits.
The marginal analysis provides a gauge by
which the firm can determine which level of
advertising outlay will yield maximal profit.
This gauge is called the marginal profit.

DEFINITION
The *marginal profit* from a change in output is
the *addition* to total company profit resulting
from the *addition of one unit* to its total output.
Marginal profit thus equals marginal revenue
less marginal cost.

Suppose, for example, Rollatron increases its output from 2 million to 3 million units per year. Going back to Table 20–1 we see that its total revenue will rise from $24 million to $30 million. That is:

When output starts out at 2 million units, the marginal revenue from a (million) unit(s) of additional output = (total revenue when output is 3 million) − (total revenue when output is 2 million) = $30 − $24 = $6 million.

Similarly, Table 20–2 tells us that:

When output starts out at 2 million units, the marginal cost from a (million) unit(s) of additional output = (total cost when output is 3 million) − (total cost when output is 2 million) = $21 − $16 = $5 million.

Finally, we may conclude that:

When output starts out at 2 million, marginal profit = marginal revenue − marginal cost = $6 − $5 = $1 million.

Clearly, the firm is not interested in concepts like marginal profit, marginal revenue, and marginal cost for their own sakes. Rather, it is interested in them because of what they imply about *total* profits. Marginal profit is like the needle on the pressure gauge of a boiler: the needle itself is of no concern to anyone, but if one fails to watch it the consequences may be quite dramatic.

The marginal profit is relevant because it is an indicator of the *opportunity of further gain that is sacrificed* by a particular decision. For example, Rollatron's marginal profit figure, which we just calculated, shows that a decision to produce only 2 million units of output is definitely not optimal, because at that output marginal profit ($1 million) is still positive. This means that an output of 2 million ball-bearing units wastes the opportunity to add $1 million to total company profits by the production of an additional (million) unit(s) of output.

To summarize, if any proposed decision involves a *positive* marginal profit, it cannot be an optimal decision.

By exactly parallel reasoning, we can show that:

An output decision will not be optimal if the marginal profit at that output level is *negative*.

For example, Rollatron's marginal profit yield from a further expansion of output to 4 million units per year would be minus $7 million. (The reader might want to verify this as an exercise.) This means that if it were producing 4 million units per year, the company could *increase* its profits by $7 million by *cutting its output* from 4 million to 3 million units.

Neither positive nor negative marginal profits, then, are compatible with an optimal decision. And so we arrive at the following rule, which is the basic theorem of marginal analysis of price—output decisions for a profit-maximizing firm:

RULE 1
An output decision will generally *not* be optimal unless it corresponds to a zero marginal profit, that is, unless marginal revenue is equal to marginal cost.

An easy way to think of this rule is as the requirement that there be zero wasted opportunity. Thus, a positive marginal profit means that the firm is wasting the opportunity to increase its profit by *adding to* its output. A negative marginal profit implies that the firm is wasting the opportunity to increase its profit by *reducing* its output. Only a zero marginal profit means that the firm has taken advantage of all its opportunities. The wasted opportunity is zero, and that is precisely what we mean by an optimum.

GEOMETRIC INTERPRETATION

Figure 20–4 helps bring out the logic of the foregoing analysis. The horizontal axis represents the output chosen by the firm, and the vertical axis represents the corresponding *total* profit for each output choice. For example, point Q on the total profit curve indicates that with an output of 1 million units per year the company obtains a net profit of $5 million.

The amount of *marginal* profit is also shown in the diagram. It is represented by the *slope* of the corresponding segment of the total profit curve. (Recall that the slope of a segment of a curve is the length of the vertical change involved, positive or negative, divided by the corresponding horizontal change.)

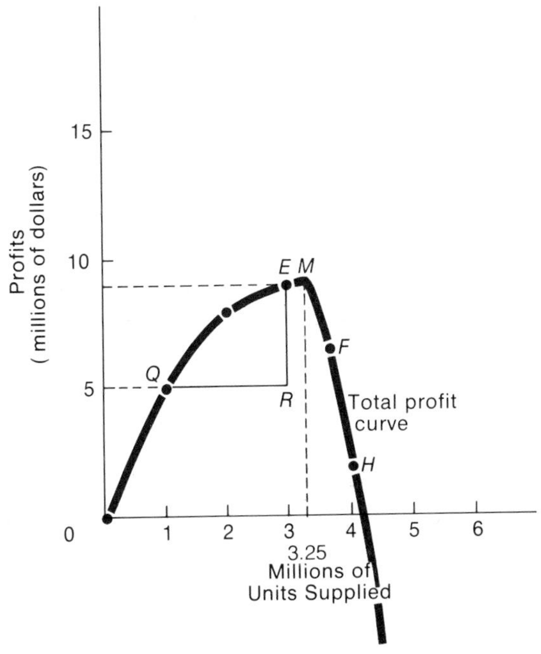

Consider the segment of the curve labeled QE. In moving from Q to E, we traverse, in effect, the horizontal distance QR, which in the diagram involves a 2-million-unit increase in output. And we also go vertically from R to E, a total increase in profit of $4 million. The slope is, by definition, $4 million/2 million units, or $2 per unit. In this case, the slope of the curve also indicates that profit will rise by $4 million (RE) for a 2 million rise in unit output (QR). That is, an additional unit of output brings in an incremental net profit of $2. This is, by definition, the marginal profit—the incremental profit per dollar of added expenditure. Thus in this case, slope and marginal profit are the same, and exactly the same sort of argument shows that this is always so.

The slope of the total profit curve is the marginal profit.

Having obtained this geometric interpretation of the concept of marginal profit, we can now show the logic of the basic rule: *An output decision cannot be optimal unless the corresponding marginal profit yield is zero,* that is, unless the corresponding marginal revenue and marginal cost are equal. We have seen that for an interval such as QE, over which the total profit curve is rising, the marginal profit is positive. Now, profits cannot be maximal anywhere along such an interval, because we can increase profits by moving farther to the right. In other words, if the firm had decided to stick to point Q (by producing only 1 million units of output), it would have wasted the opportunity to increase profits further (to point E, and beyond) by increasing its output further.

Similarly, the firm is not at an optimal point if it is anywhere in an interval, such as FH,

FIGURE 20–4
TOTAL PROFIT AND ITS MAXIMUM
The red curve shows how total profit is affected by the firm's choice of output level. Profit is highest at point M, which can be attained when output is 3.25 million units. At the point of maximum profits, M, the profit graph must be level, that is, neither rising nor falling.

where the slope of the curve is negative (its height declines as the firm's output moves to the right), because that means the marginal profit is negative. And at that portion of the curve, the firm can, by *reducing* output, raise its net profit to F dollars and beyond.

Only at a point such as *M,* where the total profit curve is neither rising nor falling, can the firm possibly be at the top of the profit hill rather than on one of the sides of the hill. And only at a point such as *M,* precisely because the curve is neither rising nor falling, will the slope—and hence the marginal profit—be zero.

SOME POSSIBLE MISINTERPRETATIONS

One of the most common misunderstandings that arises out of discussions of the marginal criterion of optimality is the idea that it seems foolish to go to a point where marginal profit is zero. "Isn't it better to earn a positive marginal profit?" Undoubtedly this notion springs from a confusion between the quantity one is seeking to maximize (*total* profit) and the gauge that indicates whether such a maximum has in fact been attained (*marginal* profit). Of course, it is better to have a positive *total* profit than zero total profit. But a zero value on our *marginal* gauge merely indicates that all is apparently well, that *total* yield may be at its maximum.

This misunderstanding reflects doubts about the validity of the basic rule of marginal analysis, and it is a characteristic assumption among people who are somewhat skeptical of it. But a second and perhaps even more significant error is made by people who have been over-sold on the power of the basic rule. These people interpret that rule as making the following (fallacious) assertion: If marginal profit has been shown to be zero, the decision maker can feel confident *without any further investigation* that he has achieved his optimum.

An examination of Figure 20–5 will show that, in general, this assumption simply is not valid. Not all profit curves take the form of the single hill shown in Figure 20–4. Thus, in Figure 20–5 we see a profit curve with three humps. The three points *A, C,* and *E* represent the tops of local hillocks. But only one of these, *C,* is the true optimum, the top of the highest hill. Yet at all three points the marginal profit (the slope of the profit curve) is zero. We find, then, that while marginal profit will indeed be zero at the true maximum, it may also be zero at a number of other points as well.

In fact, not all these other points with zero marginal profit need even be "local *maxima,*" like *A* and *E.* Clearly, the *minimum* points on the diagram (*B* and *D*) must also be points at which the profit curve is neither rising nor falling. That is, marginal profit yield will generally be zero at a minimum, just as it is at a maximum. We can conclude, therefore, that the basic formula offers no guarantee that any point that passes

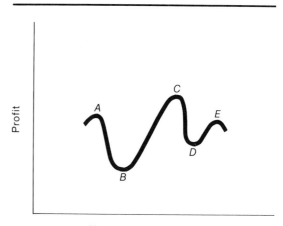

FIGURE 20–5

A TOTAL PROFIT CURVE WITH SEVERAL PEAKS AND VALLEYS
This curve proves that not all horizontal points on a total profit curve must be a maximum. Points *A, B, D,* and *E* are all horizontal, but only point *C* is the maximum.

the test—"marginal profit equals zero"—will automatically be the optimum. Indeed, that is why the basic proposition is best put in negative form: Any point at which the marginal profit is positive or negative *cannot* normally represent an optimum because such a point must lie on an uphill or downhill side of a total profit curve.

THE ARITHMETIC OF OPTIMAL OUTPUT—PRICE DECISIONS

For a final step in the calculation of the profit-maximizing price and output decisions, we return to the tables and graphs with which this chapter began to see how they can be completed to include the relevant elements of the marginal analysis. Our objective will be to find the output(s) at which marginal profit (marginal revenue minus marginal cost) is approximately zero. But to do so, we must first calculate the marginal revenue and marginal cost figures.

Table 20–3 reproduces the average and total revenue data previously given in Table 20–1, and it adds a final column for marginal revenue. This column does not require us to

gather any new information about the firm. All of its entries have been calculated from the column of total revenues with the aid of the basic definition of marginal revenue.

For example, we see that if output were 2 million units per year, total revenue would be $24 million, while if a 3-million-unit output were selected instead, total revenue would be $30 million. Consequently, the corresponding marginal revenue is $30 million − $24 million = $6 million. Thus, the number 6 is entered into the last column of Table 20–3 *between* the rows corresponding to 2 and 3 million units of output. Every other entry in the last column is calculated in the same way.

In Table 20–4, we calculate marginal *costs* in the same way we have just calculated marginal *revenues*, reproducing the total and average cost figures from Table 20–2. For example, the fourth entry in the last column is the marginal cost corresponding to a switch from an output of 3 to 4 million units per year. This figure is arrived at by the following calculation:

(Total cost of 4 million units) −
   (Total cost of 3 million units) = $32 − $21
                                = $11 million

TABLE 20–3

TOTAL, AVERAGE, AND MARGINAL REVENUES FOR ROLLATRON, INC.

NUMBER OF BALL-BEARING UNITS SUPPLIED (millions per year)	TOTAL REVENUE (millions of dollars)	AVERAGE REVENUE (dollars per unit)	MARGINAL REVENUE (dollars per unit)
0	0	—	
			15
1	15	15	
			9
2	24	12	
			6
3	30	10	
			4
4	34	8.5	
			−1
5	33	6.6	
			−3
6	30	5	

TABLE 20–4

TOTAL, AVERAGE, AND MARGINAL COSTS FOR ROLLATRON, INC.

NUMBER OF BALL-BEARING UNITS SUPPLIED (millions per year)	TOTAL COST (millions of dollars)	AVERAGE COST (dollars per unit)	MARGINAL COST (dollars per unit)
0	0	—	
			10
1	10	10	
			6
2	16	8	
			5
3	21	7	
			11
4	32	8	
			13
5	45	9	
			21
6	66	11	

To clarify the search process for the optimal output level, at which marginal cost equals marginal revenue, we have reproduced in Table 20–5 the marginal cost and marginal revenue figures from the two preceding tables. We see that for all outputs up to 3 million units, marginal revenue is greater than marginal cost (marginal profit, marginal revenue minus marginal cost, is positive). Consequently, at such output levels the firm has not yet chosen an output sufficiently large to capture all potential profits. These outputs are all too small to maximize the company's total profits.

Similarly, output levels at 4 million units and above are excessive for this purpose, for any such output involves a *negative* marginal profit. The marginal cost and marginal revenue figures from Table 20–5 are shown graphically in Figure 20–6, where the reader can confirm that at outputs below 3 million units, marginal cost is less than marginal revenue, and that the opposite is true when output is greater than 4 million units. We can infer that the profit-maximizing output level is somewhere between 3 and 4 million units per year.

There are two ways that this conclusion can

TABLE 20–5

MARGINAL REVENUES, COSTS, AND PROFIT FOR ROLLATRON, INC.

NUMBER OF BALL-BEARING UNITS SUPPLIED (millions)	MARGINAL REVENUE (dollars per unit)	MARGINAL COST (dollars per unit)	MARGINAL PROFIT (dollars per unit)
0			
1	15	10	5
2	9	6	3
3	6	5	1
4	4	11	−7
5	−1	13	−14
6	−3	21	−24

TABLE 20–6

TOTAL REVENUES, COSTS AND PROFIT FOR ROLLATRON, INC.

NUMBER OF BALL-BEARING UNITS SUPPLIED (millions)	TOTAL REVENUE	TOTAL COST	TOTAL PROFIT
		(millions of dollars)	
0	0	0	0
1	15	10	5
2	24	16	8
3	30	21	9
4	34	32	2
5	33	45	−12
6	30	66	−36

be confirmed. In Table 20–6, we actually calculate total profit levels for each output by reproducing from Tables 20–3 and 20–4 the total revenue and total cost figures and subtracting the cost from the revenue for each output. The last column of the table confirms that total profit is zero when output is zero, rises steadily as output increases until it reaches $9 million per year at an output of 3 million units, then begins to fall abruptly, and finally, at an output of 5 million units and above, turns into a resounding loss. Maximum total profits can indeed be obtained by producing something like 3 million units.

The second approach to confirming our conclusion is graphic. The most appropriate graph to use for the purpose is a curve of total profit, which is plotted with the aid of the data in the last column of Table 20–6. As a matter of fact, we have already seen that graph as Figure 20–4. There the hill-shaped profit curve is seen to reach its maximum at an annual output of 3.25 million units per year.

We can also get a clearer picture of what is going on by referring to Rollatron's marginal revenue and marginal cost curves in Figure 20–6. Once again the diagram shows

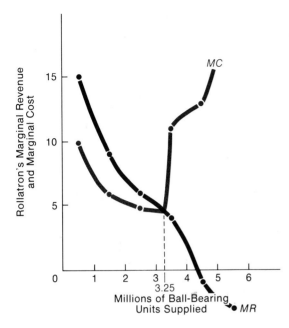

FIGURE 20–6

MARGINAL COST, MARGINAL REVENUE, AND PROFIT-MAXIMIZING OUTPUT
The curve *MR* shows marginal revenue at each output—it shows how much revenue the firm would gain from an added unit of output. The curve *MC* is a marginal cost curve—it shows how much the firm's total cost is increased by another unit of output. Profit is maximized at output 3.25 million, at which marginal cost equals marginal revenue, because any further increase in output will add at least as much to cost as it adds to revenue, so that no profit can be gained by a further output rise.

that when output is less than 3.25 million units per year, marginal revenue is greater than marginal cost. For larger outputs the opposite is true. But at the output level 3.25 million, marginal revenue equals marginal cost, so that the requirement of maximal total profits is satisfied. Thus, in this example the marginal indicator has done its work. It has told us the output level at which the firm obtains the largest total profit it can get.

FIXED AND VARIABLE COSTS

So far in our cost discussion we have assumed that all costs vary when the firm's output changes. The more steel produced by a steel plant, the more coal, iron, and labor it will have to use, which is why the costs of these three inputs are called *variable.* On the other hand, some costs are not affected by the amount of output. The cost of the land on which a railroad lays its tracks will not be affected by the number of trains that run over that land, so that cost is called *fixed.* Table 20–7 shows the total, average, and marginal land cost of the railroad. The first column shows that, by definition of a fixed cost, the total land cost will be the same ($100 million) whether one, two, three, or any other number of trains traverse this route. Whether 100 trains pass over it in a day or none, the total land cost is the same.

The second column shows that average fixed cost always gets smaller and smaller as the number of units of output over which the overhead is spread increases. If ten trains per day use the route, the land cost per train will obviously be only one-fifth as great as it would be if only two trains per day used the route.

TABLE 20–7

FIXED LAND COST FOR A RAILROAD

NUMBER OF TRAINS	TOTAL LAND COST	AVERAGE LAND COST PER TRAIN	MARGINAL LAND COST PER ADDITIONAL TRAIN
		(millions of dollars)	
0	100	—	
1	100	100	0
2	100	50	0
3	100	33.33	0
4	100	25	0

Finally, we note that marginal fixed cost is always zero. Why? Because, by definition, *additional output adds nothing to fixed costs*. Running four trains on this route instead of only three adds nothing to total fixed costs.

The distinction between fixed and variable cost is important in many industrial decisions. It is important in pricing decisions because it affects the relationship between price and marginal cost. Where fixed costs are important, price must generally be considerably higher than marginal cost or else the firm will lose money. Why is this so? Table 20–7 indicates the answer. We have seen that marginal fixed cost is always zero but average fixed cost can be far above this figure. Therefore, a price equal to marginal cost will include no contribution to fixed cost, and that is a very good way for the firm to go bankrupt rather quickly. For that reason, in industries with heavy fixed costs it is usually expected that price will be considerably higher than marginal cost, a point that is emphasized frequently in pricing decisions made by regulatory agencies such as the Civil Aeronautics Board (CAB) which regulates air fares, the Interstate Commerce Commission (ICC) which regulates railroad rates, and the Federal Communications Commission (FCC) which regulates the price of telephone service. More will be said on this subject in Chapter 26.

THE RELATIONSHIP BETWEEN TOTAL, AVERAGE, AND MARGINAL DATA

The reader may already have surmised that there is some connection between the average revenue and cost curves in Figures 20–1 and 20–2 and the marginal revenue and cost curves in Figure 20–6. After all, we deduced our total revenue figures from the average revenues and then calculated our marginal revenues from the total revenues; and a similar chain of deduction applied to costs. As a result, we can make the general conclusion that:

Marginal, average, and total figures are inextricably bound together: From any one of the three, the other two can be calculated.

This conclusion follows directly from the definitions of marginal, average, and total revenues (or costs). For example, given either average or total revenue, we can calculate the other by means of the following rules:

RULE 2a
Average revenue equals total revenue divided by number of units sold.

RULE 2b
Total revenue equals average revenue times number of units sold.

Similarly, given the firm's total revenue we can calculate its marginal revenue for any output from the *subtraction* process already illustrated. Thus we have:

RULE 3a
Marginal revenue of an increase in output from, say, 2 to 3 units of output equals total revenue from 3 units minus total revenue from 2 units.

We can also go in the opposite direction—from marginal revenue to total revenue by the reverse, *addition*, process.

RULE 3b
Total revenue from, say, 3 units of output equals marginal revenue from the 1st unit of output plus marginal revenue from the 2nd unit plus marginal revenue from the 3rd unit.

Rule 3b can be checked by referring back to Table 20–3, in which it can be seen that total revenue from 3 units of output is $30 million—indeed equal to $15 + $9 + $6 million, the sum of the preceding marginal revenues. A similar relation holds for any other total revenue figure in the table, as the reader should verify.

A second general conclusion about the nature of total, average, and marginal data is that:

Total, average, and marginal figures bear relationships to one another that hold for *any* variable, such as revenue, cost, or profit, that is affected by the number of units in question. That is, Rules 2 and 3 are equally valid for revenue or cost or profit calculations.

To illustrate and emphasize the wide applicability of marginal analysis, we switch our example from profits, revenues, and costs to a noneconomic variable, human body weights. We do so because calculation of weights is a more familiar concept to most people than is calculation of profits, revenues, or costs. And with the aid of the examples presented below we can then deduce several other fundamental relationships between average and marginal figures.

In Table 20–8, the first and last columns describe the general picture.[3] We begin with an empty room (total weight of occupants is equal to zero). A person weighing 100 pounds enters; marginal and average weight are both 100 pounds. If the first person is followed by a person weighing 140 pounds (marginal weight equals 140 pounds), the average weight rises to 120 pounds (240/2), and so on.

The way to calculate average weight from total weight should now be quite clear. The first entry in the average weight column is blank because there can be no average weight when there are no persons in the room. But when, for example, there are four persons in the room with a total weight of 500 pounds, the average weight must be 500/4 = 125 pounds, as shown in the corresponding entry of the third column.

Calculation of marginal weight figures from total weight figures is analogous to the calculation of marginal revenue or marginal cost. Thus, when the fourth person enters the room, *total*

[3]Note that in this illustration, persons in room is analogous to units of output; total weight to total revenue or cost; and so on.

TABLE 20–8

WEIGHTS OF PERSONS IN A ROOM

NUMBER OF PERSONS IN ROOM	TOTAL WEIGHT	AVERAGE WEIGHT (pounds)	MARGINAL WEIGHT
0	0	—	
			100
1	100	100	
			140
2	240	120	
			135
3	375	125	
			125
4	500	125	
			100
5	600	120	
			60
6	660	110	

weight rises from 375 to 500 pounds, and hence the corresponding marginal weight is 500 − 375 = 125 pounds, as is shown in the last column. Notice again that we can calculate average weight from just a single entry in the total weight column. But to calculate the marginal entry we need *two* successive totals—the "before" and the "after."

In addition to these simple arithmetic relationships, which we encountered previously, there are two other relationships that will subsequently prove useful. The first of these relationships may be stated as:

RULE 4
For the first unit (person), in the absence of fixed costs (weight), the marginal, average, and total figures must all be equal.

This rule holds because when there is only one person in the room, whose weight is *x* pounds, the average weight will obviously be *x*, the total weight must be *x*, and the marginal weight must also be *x* (since the total must have risen from 0 to *x* pounds). Put another way, when the marginal person is alone, he or she is obviously also the average person, and also represents the totality of all relevant persons.

Now for the second and very important relationship:

RULE 5

If the marginal figure is lower than the average figure, then the average figure must fall when output (number of persons) increases. If marginal exceeds the average, the average figure must rise when output (number of persons) increases; and if the marginal and the average are equal, the average figure must remain constant when output (number of persons) increases.

These three possibilities are all illustrated in Table 20–8. Notice, for example, that when the third person enters the room, the average weight rises from 120 to 125 pounds. That is because this person's (marginal) weight is 135 pounds, which is above the average, as Rule 5 requires. Similarly, when the sixth person—who is a 60-pound child—enters the room, the average falls from 120 to 110 pounds, because marginal weight, 60 pounds, is below the average weight.

The reason Rule 5 works is easily explained with the aid of our example. When the third person enters, we see that the average rises. At once we know that this person must be above average weight, for otherwise his arrival would not have pulled up the average. That is, average weight in the room can be raised only by a person who contributes a marginal weight above the average of the weights of the persons already there. Similarly, the average will be pulled down by the arrival of a person whose weight is below the average (marginal weight is less than average weight). And the arrival of a person of average weight (marginal equals average weight) will leave the old average figure unchanged. That is all there is to the matter.

We will see presently why this rule is important. But first it is essential to avoid a common misunderstanding of the rule: It does *not* state, for example, that if the average figure is falling the marginal figure must be falling. When the average falls, the marginal figure may fall, rise, or remain unchanged. The arrival of two persons both well below average will pull the average down in two successive steps even if the

second new arrival is slightly heavier than the first. We see such a case in Table 20–8, where the arithmetic shows that while the average rises successively from 100 to 120 to 125, the marginal value falls from 140 to 135 to 125.

GRAPHIC REPRESENTATION OF MARGINAL AND AVERAGE CURVES

We have shown how, from a curve of total profit (or total cost or total anything else), one can determine the corresponding marginal figure. We found in Figure 20–4 that the marginal value at any particular point is equal to the *slope* of the corresponding total curve at that point. But for some purposes it is convenient to use a graph that records marginal (and average) values directly rather than deriving them from the curve of totals.

We can obtain such a graph by plotting the data contained in a table of marginal figures, such as Table 20–8. The result looks like the graph shown in Figure 20–7. Here we have indicated the number of persons in the room on the horizontal axis and the corresponding average and marginal figures on the vertical axis. The solid dots represent average weights; the small circles represent marginal weights. Thus, for example, point A shows that when two persons are in the room, their average weight is 120 pounds, as was reported on the third line of Table 20–8. Similarly, point B on the graph represents information provided in the next column of the table, that is, that the marginal weight of the third person to enter the room is 135 pounds. For visual convenience these points have been connected into a marginal curve and an average curve, represented respectively by the solid and the broken curves in the diagram. This is the representation of marginal and average values that economists most frequently use.

Notice that Figure 20–7 illustrates two of our rules. Rule 4 leads us to expect that for the first unit the marginal and average values will be the same. And that is precisely why the two curves start out together at point *C*. When there is only one person in the room, marginal and average weight *must* be the same.

The graph also follows the requirements of Rule 5: Over the entire range between points *C* and *E*, where the average curve is *rising*, the marginal curve lies *above* the average. (Notice, however, that over part of the range the marginal curve *falls* even though the average curve is constantly rising—Rule 5 says nothing about the rise or fall of the marginal curve.) We see also that over range *EF*, where the average curve is falling, the marginal curve is below the average curve, again in accord with Rule 5. Finally, at point *E*, where the average curve is neither rising nor falling, the marginal curve meets the average curve: average and marginal weights are equal at that point.

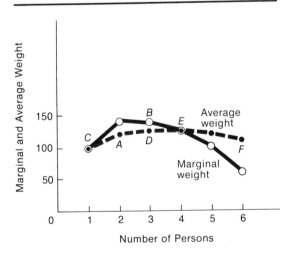

FIGURE 20–7

THE RELATIONSHIP BETWEEN MARGINAL AND AVERAGE CURVES

If the marginal curve is above the average curve, the average curve will be pulled upward. Thus, wherever the marginal is above the average the average must be going upward (red segment of curves). The opposite is true where the marginal curve is below the average curve.

MARGINAL ANALYSIS IN REAL DECISION PROBLEMS

The material in this chapter will serve us again and again later in this book. But we have already gone far enough to put the analysis to use. For one thing, we can use it to shed some light on the decision problems with which we began this chapter.

CASE 1:
The Beer-Pricing Problem

Recall that our first problem dealt with the choice between a price of $1.50 and $1.35 for a six-pack of beer. To make that decision optimally, the firm would have needed marginal revenue information, which it could determine only from its demand curve. However, the firm did not have the statistical data from which its demand curve could be calculated. As we indicated, the debate among the firm's managers finally reached a compromise on one point: The price cut would be instituted if no profit were likely to be lost as a result.

Fortunately, the data needed to judge the direction of the effect on profit *were* obtainable. It was known that initial annual sales volume was 10 million units, and the firm's engineers maintained emphatically that marginal costs were very close to constant at $1.20 per package over the output range in question. By using a straightforward bit of analysis, the consultants were able to shed light on the problem. Instead of trying to determine the actual increase in sales volume that would result from the price change, they decided to try to determine the *minimum necessary* increase in sales volume, or quantity demanded, required to avoid a decrease in profits. It was clear that the firm needed an increment in revenue (marginal revenue) at least as great as the marginal cost of supplying the added volume.

The consultants knew that total revenue at the initial price of $1.50 per six-pack was $15 million ($1.50 per unit times 10 million units), and that marginal costs were $1.20 per six-pack. Letting x represent the unknown number of six-packs necessary to prevent a decrease in profit at the proposed new price ($1.35 per six-pack), the economists compared added revenue with the added cost of serving this added demand, which was equal to the marginal cost of $1.20 for each of the x units above the initial 10 million sales volume. In mathematical terms, this came to

$$\text{Added cost} = \$1.20\,(x - 10)$$

This was to be compared with the added revenue. We can write the equation for added revenue as

$$
\begin{aligned}
\text{Added revenue} &= \text{New revenue} - \text{Old revenue}\\
&= \$1.35x - \$15 \text{ million}
\end{aligned}
$$

We can see that no loss will result from the price change if the added revenue is greater than or equal to the added cost. The minimum x necessary to avoid a loss will be that at which added revenue equals added cost, or

$$1.35x - \$15 \text{ million} = 1.2x - \$12 \text{ million}$$

or

$$\$0.15x = \$3 \text{ million}$$

This will be true if, and only if, x, the quantity sold at the lower price, is

$$x = 20 \text{ million units}$$

In other words, this calculation showed that in order for the firm to break even as a result of the 15-cent price reduction, the demand for its product would have had to rise at least 100 percent, from 10 to 20 million units. And since past experience indicated that such a rise in demand was hardly possible, the price reduction proposal was quickly abandoned. This case, besides showing how marginal analysis can help solve real-life problems, also illustrates two points. First, in application one must be prepared to modify the specifications of the theoretical structure. Second, when ideal data are not available one can sometimes get by with much less.

CASE 2:
The Output-Expansion Problem

You may remember that our second real-life example described a firm that was losing money because the price of its canned meat product was less than its average cost, and that was then offered the questionable opportunity to sell more of its product to a foreign buyer at a price that was lower still. The relevant information is summarized in Table 20–9.

Obviously, this firm was in a bad way financially. Its average cost was $13, and yet the price it was charging for its product was only $11 per unit. In such circumstances the company could not help but lose money on this product. Indeed, we see that it lost $20 million on the 10 million units of output it sold.

The management of this company might well have reasoned this way: It would be desir-

TABLE 20–9

INITIAL COSTS AND REVENUES OF THE CANNED MEAT PRODUCER

MILLIONS OF UNITS SOLD	TOTAL COST (millions of dollars)	AVERAGE COST	MARGINAL COST	PRICE (dollars)	TOTAL REVENUE	TOTAL COST	PROFIT OR LOSS
		(dollars)			(millions of dollars)		
10	130	13	3	11	110	130	−20

able to expand our volume, but we can't afford to do so. Instead, we must raise our price, even if it cuts down our sales. In fact, we must raise our price above our $13 average cost.

While the managers were pondering their dilemma, a foreign purchasing group offered to buy an additional 10 million units of the company's canned meat product, if the company would supply the units at a discount price of $8. On an average cost calculation this arrangement seemed disastrous. After all, average costs per unit were $13, and the company was already losing money at an $11 price. How could it possibly afford to take up further sales at an even lower price?

But was the proposition so ludicrous? With its marginal costs approximately constant at $3, by accepting the offer the company could change its situation from that shown in Table 20–9 to that shown in Table 20–10. We see that the total number of units sold will have doubled, from 10 to 20. Total costs will have risen from $130 million to $160 million. That is, they will have gone up $30 million (marginal cost $\times$ increase in quantity supplied $= \$3 \times 10$ million). The arithmetic shows that, as a consequence, average cost *must* have fallen from $13 = 130/10$ to $8 = 160/20$. The last three columns report the resulting "miracle." The apparently ridiculous proposition that 10 million additional units of canned meat be sold at a price below the old average cost in fact succeeded in eliminating the deficit and actually put the company into the black, to the tune of $30 million in net profits!

Just how was this "miracle" accomplished? The answer becomes clear when we apply the rules we have learned in this chapter. In Table 20–9, on which the original pricing analysis was based, it can be seen that the average cost figure was indeed $13. But the corresponding *marginal* cost figure was only $3. Therefore, every *additional* unit sold to the foreign buyer at a price of $8 must bring in a marginal profit of $8 − $3 = $5. On such terms the more one sells the better off one is.

CONCLUSION: THE FUNDAMENTAL ROLE OF MARGINAL ANALYSIS

An important conclusion can be drawn from the two examples we have just discussed:

In any decision about whether to expand an activity, it is always the *marginal* cost (and the *marginal* revenue) that is the relevant factor. A calculation based on *average* figures is likely to lead the decision maker to miss all sorts of opportunities, some of them critical.

This is an illustration of one of the 12 Ideas for Beyond the Final Exam.

In decision making, wherever possible, make use of *marginal* information—marginal cost, not just average cost; marginal revenue, not just price or average revenue—otherwise the decision is unlikely to be anywhere near optimal. Indeed, very likely, it will not even be rational.

TABLE 20–10

COST AND REVENUES OF THE SUPPLIER OF CANNED MEAT AFTER SALES "BELOW COST"

MILLIONS OF UNITS SOLD	TOTAL COST (millions of dollars)	AVERAGE COST (dollars)	MARGINAL COST	TOTAL REVENUE	TOTAL COST (millions of dollars)	PROFIT OR LOSS
20	160	8	3	190	160	+30

SUMMARY

1. In general, the firm can choose the quantity of its product it wants to sell or the price it wants to charge, but it cannot choose both, because price affects the quantity demanded.

2. The basic concepts of optimality analysis are (a) the firm's total revenue equals price times quantity sold, (b) average revenue equals total revenue divided by quantity sold, (c) marginal revenue equals the revenue added by the sale of an additional unit of output, (d) total cost, (e) average cost equals total cost divided by quantity sold, and (f) marginal cost equals the cost of producing an additional unit of output.

3. The firm's demand curve is normally its average revenue curve. The reason is that if the firm sells each unit of its product for a price of, say, $10.39, its average revenue will, by definition, be $10.39.

4. A fixed cost is defined as a cost that does not change when the firm increases its output. Marginal fixed cost is therefore always zero.

5. Optimal decision making requires careful comparison of the alternative choices available to the decision maker to determine which of them serves his purposes most effectively.

6. If the firm wants to choose the output combination that maximizes its *total* profit, it must find an output at which *marginal* profit equals zero, or (what amounts to the same thing) one at which marginal cost equals marginal revenue.

7. Marginal cost and revenue are not important for their own sake. They are merely the means we use to find the output that maximizes *total* profit.

8. Geometrically, the profit-maximizing output level occurs at the highest point of the "hill" formed by the curve representing total profit. There the slope of the total profit curve is zero, meaning that marginal profit is zero.

9. (a) If average revenue falls when output increases, marginal revenue is lower than average revenue; (b) if average revenue rises when output increases, marginal revenue is above average revenue; (c) if the average revenue curve is horizontal, marginal revenue must equal average revenue. Similar relationships apply to average and marginal cost.

10. It may pay a firm to expand its output if it is selling at a fixed price greater than marginal cost, even if that price happens to be below average cost.

11. Optimal decisions must be made on the basis of marginal cost and marginal revenue figures, not average cost and average revenue figures. This is one of the 12 Ideas for Beyond the Final Exam.

CONCEPTS FOR REVIEW

Profit maximization
Average revenue and cost
Total revenue and cost
Marginal revenue and cost
Satisficing
Marginal analysis

Total profit
Optimal decision
Marginal profit
Fixed costs
Variable costs

QUESTIONS FOR DISCUSSION

1. "It may be rational for a firm not to try to make optimal decisions." Discuss why this statement may make sense.
2. Suppose the firm's demand curve indicates that at a price of $5 per unit, customers will demand 2 million units of its product. Suppose management decides to pick *both* price and output, produces 3 million units of its product, and prices it at $7. What will happen?
3. Suppose a firm's management would be pleased to increase its share of the market, but if it expands its production the price of its product will fall and so its profits will decline somewhat. What choices are available to this firm? What would you do if you were president of this company?
4. Why does it make sense for a firm to seek maximum *total* profit, but not maximum *marginal* profit?
5. A firm's marginal revenue is $17 and its marginal cost is $9. What amount of profit does the firm fail to pick up by refusing to increase output by one unit?
6. A firm's total cost is $150 if it produces 1 unit, $250 if it produces 2 units, and $300 if it produces 3 units of output. Draw up a table of total, average, and marginal cost for this firm, similar to Table 20–4.
7. Draw an average and marginal cost curve for the firm in Question 6. Describe the relationship between the two curves.

21

The Common Sense
of Business Decisions:
Input Choices

In the last chapter we considered one of the most crucial decisions of the business firm — how much it should produce of any given commodity. In this chapter we take the next logical step and investigate the decisions the firm must make about techniques for producing its goods. Should it use a lot of expensive machinery and other labor-saving devices? Is it worthwhile to change the current method of production when output expands? These and similar questions are called input decisions, and studying them will teach us much about the nature of the firm's

costs. Toward the end of the chapter we can then usefully return for another look at the firm's cost curves.

THE CRUCIAL CONTRIBUTION OF MARGINAL ANALYSIS

The main conclusion that emerged from the last chapter has implications far beyond the immediate subject of that chapter:

If you want to make *optimal* decisions, use *marginal analysis* in your planning calculations.

This rule is true whether the objective is to make as much profit for a business firm as possible or to maximize per capita output in a less developed country. It applies as much to decisions on input proportions and advertising as to decisions about output levels and prices. Indeed, this is one of the 12 Ideas for Beyond the Final Exam.

In this chapter we will see how marginal analysis helps us to understand optimal input choice where the objective is to produce any given output of given quality as cheaply as possible. This objective is shared among many segments of society—for instance, by nationalized industries, profit-making firms, central planners, and such nonprofit organizations as private hospitals and universities.

A real-life example will help clarify the way in which marginal criteria can aid in making decisions outside the profit-making firm. For some years before it was decided to admit women to Princeton University (and to several other colleges), the cost of the proposed change was frequently cited as a major obstacle. Presumably on the basis of a calculation of average cost, some critics spoke of figures as high as $80 million. To economists it was clear, however, that the relevant figure was the *marginal* cost, or the incremental cost figure representing the addition to total cost that would result from the introduction of the additional students. The women students would, of course, bring to Princeton additional tuition fees. If these fees were just sufficient to cover the amount they would add to costs, the admission of the women would leave the university's financial picture unaffected.

A careful calculation showed that the admission of women would add far less to the university's financial problems than the *average cost* figures indicated. One reason was that women's course preferences are characteristi-

cally different from men's, and hence women frequently elect courses that are undersubscribed in exclusively male institutions. Therefore, the admission of one thousand women to a formerly all-male institution may require fewer additional courses than if one thousand more men had been admitted.[1]

More important, it was found that a number of classroom buildings were underutilized. The cost of operation of these buildings was largely fixed—their total utilization cost would not be changed materially by the influx of women. The corresponding incremental cost was therefore virtually zero and certainly well below the average cost (cost per student).[2]

For all these reasons, it turned out that the relevant marginal cost figure was much smaller than the figures that had been bandied about earlier. Indeed, this cost was something like a third of the earlier estimates. There is little doubt that this careful marginal calculation played a critical role in the admission of women to Princeton and to some other institutions that made use of the calculations in the Princeton analysis.

A PUZZLE: SIDE EFFECTS OF REGULATORY PROFIT CEILINGS

In the United States, the private firms in a number of industries, including electric utilities, aviation, and telecommunications, have their earnings regulated by government agencies. In order to prevent these large firms from earning monopoly profits, the regulatory agencies determine what they consider to be a "fair rate of

[1] See Gardner Patterson, "The Education of Women at Princeton," *Princeton Alumni Weekly*, Vol. LXIX, Sept. 24, 1968.

[2] One must not jump to the conclusion that this total cost is absolutely fixed so that marginal cost must be zero. Increased building use may add to the cost of electricity, janitorial services, and the like. In addition, expanded use may increase wear and tear. Moreover, if the student body had been growing already, the excess capacity might have been quite temporary; in such a case, the admission of women might speed up the need for new buildings, a very real financial cost.

return," which is intended as a ceiling on the profits that any regulated company is permitted to earn.

The purpose of such a ceiling is obvious, and few people argue against the desirability of some sort of restriction on the profits of the most powerful of the regulated firms. Yet any such regulatory restriction can be expected to have some unintended—and perhaps undesirable—side effects. For example, it has been argued before the Federal Communications Commission and other regulatory agencies that a ceiling on rate of return can provide an incentive to the regulated firm to use too much machinery relative to labor (see the boxed insert on the opposite page). This means, it is contended, that these firms will be induced to use a capital–labor ratio that is inefficient and therefore undesirable because it causes waste in the economy. What is the connection between a regulatory ceiling on company profits and the firm's decision on its capital–labor ratio? The relationship may seem remote, but it is not. And one of the purposes of this chapter is to enable the reader to understand such connections.

ANOTHER PUZZLE: EVIDENCE ON ECONOMIES OF SCALE

One of the most distinctive features that is popularly considered to characterize modern business is economies of large-scale production, or economies of scale. Later in the chapter we will be in a position to formulate a precise definition of this concept. Roughly, it means that when the firm expands all of its outputs, its cost per unit of output will go down. This is not true of every type of industry, but it seems to characterize many of them, at least up to some level of production. Automation, assembly lines, sophisticated machinery and equipment are all believed to help many large firms reduce their production costs. But because the equipment usually has such enormous capacity and represents so

large an investment, small companies cannot benefit very much from these products of modern technology. In other words, only large-scale production can offer the associated savings in costs.

This is a very important policy issue for many reasons, the most apparent being the desirability of having large rather than small business firms. If an industry is made up only of one or a few large firms, monopoly power can become a serious problem. Therefore, most economic analysts agree that some acceptable evidence that an industry has economies of scale is necessary to justify its being made up of one or a few large firms. The question is: What evidence is enough?

Sometimes, data such as those shown in Figure 21–1 are offered to the courts when they

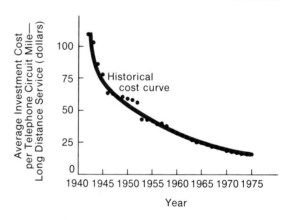

FIGURE 21–1

HISTORICAL COST CURVE FOR LONG DISTANCE TELEPHONE TRANSMISSION
By 1975, the dollar cost per circuit mile had fallen to less than 15 percent of what it was in 1942. Because prices have more than tripled in that period, the decline in *real* cost was even more sensational. In constant dollars, in 1975 the investment cost per circuit mile was about 5 percent of its 1942 level. Yet this historical cost curve is not legitimate evidence *one way or the other* about scale economies in telecommunications.
Source: AT&T.

Do Public Utilities Use Too Much Capital?

Public utilities that are regulated by a ceiling on profits normally are permitted to earn a "fair rate of return" on their invested capital. Items that are included in the eligible capital stock constitute the utility's "rate base." In 1974, the Federal Power Commission (FPC) proposed to add to the rate base any construction work currently in progress. Hearings on this proposal gave interested parties a chance to comment on the proposal and, indeed, to raise objections to the entire system of regulation through profit ceilings.

You will find below excerpts from a submission filed by the Municipal and Rural Electric Systems and Associations in March 1976, arguing that the regulatory system leads to overinvestment in capital. The tortured phrase "utility management would have every incentive to construct as much [sic] facilities as could be reasonably defended" is the lawyers' way of hinting that regulated firms will invest in capital whenever they can get away with it, even if it is inefficient. The article by Averch and Johnson that is cited in the submission was the first scholarly work to point out this potential problem of rate-of-return regulation. The article itself is tough sledding for beginning students, but the basic idea is explained later in this chapter.

United States of America before the Federal Power Commission

Amendments to Uniform Systems of Accounts for Public Utilities and Licensees and for Natural Gas Companies (Classes A, B, C, and D) and to Regulations Under the Federal Power Act and the Natural Gas Act, to Provide for Inclusion of Construction Work in Progress in Rate Base

Docket No. RM75-13

COMMENTS OF PUBLIC SYSTEMS ON
ISSUES LISTED FOR DISCUSSION AT ORAL ARGUMENT

These comments are filed on behalf of the municipal and rural electric cooperative electric systems, and associations thereof, listed in the appendix hereto. These Public Systems serve consumers in 16 states throughout the United States and purchase electric power and energy from 27 investor-owned public utility electric companies subject to this Commission's jurisdiction. Public Systems, and the millions of consumers served by them, are vitally concerned with the proposal to permit construction work in progress ("CWIP") to be included in rate base and strongly oppose the proposal.

The importance of this issue cannot be over-stated because the Commission does not currently possess the statutory authority to regulate the construction of new facilities by electric utilities and there is a clear and obvious financial incentive for electric utilities to construct new facilities under the proposed regulatory scheme. We believe this issue was placed in sharp focus by Messrs. Averch and Johnson in "Behavior of the Firm Under Regulatory Constraint," *American Economic Review*, December, 1972, pp. 1052–1069, and our initial comments addressed the issue in some depth (Section III, B, pp. 13–18). Accordingly, it is sufficient to note that utility management would have every incentive to construct as much facilities as could be reasonably defended since such expenditures would automatically earn a return and taxes. [Emphasis added.]

consider cases involving the issue of monopoly. These figures, provided by AT&T, indicate that since 1942, as the volume of messages rose, the capital cost of long distance communication by telephone dropped enormously. Note that the graph has no correction for inflation, so that in real terms (in dollars of constant purchasing power) the fall is even more sensational. Yet economists maintain that, while this graph may be valid evidence of efficiency, innovation, and perhaps other virtues of the telecommunications industry, it does *not* constitute legitimate evidence, one way or another, about the presence of scale economies. Specifically, this information, even though it shows that costs have fallen as the telephone company's volume of business has grown, does not show that a large firm is more efficient than a small one. Later in this chapter we will see precisely what is wrong with such evidence and what sort of evidence really is required.

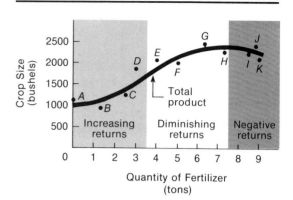

FIGURE 21–2

TOTAL PRODUCT WITH DIFFERENT QUANTITIES OF FERTILIZER
At first, additional fertilizer makes increasing marginal contributions to output, but then the marginal returns begin to diminish, and finally, when there is much too much fertilizer, output begins to fall.

INPUTS AND OUTPUTS: THE "LAW" OF DIMINISHING RETURNS

In deciding how much of an input to use, the firm must consider the relationship between its inputs and its outputs. But we can say much more than this about the input–output connection. Let us conduct, conceptually, a controlled experiment in which Farmer Phil Pfister, who grows corn, decides to see what happens when he changes the amount of fertilizer he uses but keeps all other input quantities unchanged. He divides his land, which is quite uniform in quality, into plots of equal size, treating each plot exactly as he treats every other, except for the amount of fertilizer he applies. At the end of the season he compares the crops that grew on the different pieces of land and obtains the results shown by the dots in Figure 21–2.

The dots confirm, as anyone might have guessed, that larger quantities of fertilizer do

permit more output. Even without any fertilizer something will grow (point *A*), but not very much. After that, more fertilizer yields more output (points *B*, *C*, and so on), with production up to a point growing rapidly as more fertilizer is used. But then, as the ground begins to be saturated with fertilizer, the growth in output slows down (points *E* to *H*). Finally, a level of fertilizer saturation is reached at which further additions actually damage the crop (points *H* to *K*).

The graph has been divided into three zones corresponding to these three cases. The shaded area (at the left) is the zone of *increasing returns* to more fertilizer. The middle area is the zone where additional fertilizer yields positive but *diminishing returns*. Finally, the zone on the right is characterized by *negative returns*.

Remembering that we are dealing with the results of Farmer Pfister's *controlled* experiment in which all other inputs have been held constant, we have just observed a pattern of the input–output relationship that has played a key role in economics for two centuries.

The "law" of diminishing returns asserts that when we increase the amount of any one input, holding the amounts of all others constant as in this hypothetical controlled experiment, the returns to the expanding input ultimately will begin to diminish.[3] The so-called law is in fact no more than an (alleged) empirical regularity based on some observation of the facts. It is not a theorem deduced analytically.

The diminishing returns relationship certainly holds widely if not universally. It applies not only to fertilizer, but to all of the inputs used by our mythical Farmer Pfister—seeds, labor time, equipment, and so on. It applies to the inputs used by real farmers and real manufacturers as well.

DIMINISHING RETURNS AND MARGINAL PHYSICAL PRODUCT

The law of diminishing returns, as we have described it so far, is vague in at least one important respect—we have not yet indicated precisely what it is that diminishes. After all, in Figure 21–2, a glance at the total product curve that has been drawn in to describe the general relationship shows that in the region labeled "diminishing returns," total output is still increased by additional fertilizer. If output is not being decreased, then what is diminishing?

To answer the question we must extend the marginal analysis to the relation between inputs and outputs. For this purpose we want to know what *addition* to total production is made possible by the use of an additional unit of fertilizer.

DEFINITION
The *marginal physical product* of an input is the increase in output that results from a one-unit

[3]The "law" is generally credited to Anne Robert Jacques Turgot (1727–1781), one of the last Comptrollers-General of France before the Revolution, whose liberal policies, it is said, represented the old regime's last chance to save itself. But, with characteristic foresight, the king fired him.

increase in the input while all other input quantities are held constant.

We know from the previous chapter that *marginal profit* is represented by the slope of the *total profit* curve, that *marginal revenue* is represented by the slope of the *total revenue* curve, and that *marginal cost* is represented by the slope of the *total cost* curve. For exactly the same reasons we gave in Chapter 20:

The *marginal physical product* of a given quantity of input is equal to the *slope* of the *total product curve* at that input quantity.

Figure 21–3 reproduces the total production curve for fertilizer from Figure 21–2. Suppose we want to see what happens when Farmer Pfister goes from a plot of land on which

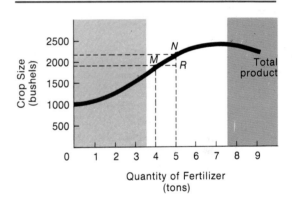

FIGURE 21–3

TOTAL PRODUCT CURVE
FOR FERTILIZER
The marginal product of an input is measured by the slope of the total product curve. For example, when the quantity of fertilizer used increases from 4 to 5 tons, we move along the total product curve from point M to point N. The marginal product is given by the increase in output divided by the increase in fertilizer use. Specifically, the slope of the total product curve along arc MN is the ratio of the distance RN divided by the distance MR; that is, 250 bushels / 1 ton, or 250 bushels per ton of fertilizer.

he uses 4 tons of fertilizer to one on which he uses 5 tons. We see this brings us from point *M* to point *N* on the total product curve, so that output increases by 250 bushels. That is, it rises from 1900 bushels where only 4 tons of fertilizer have been used, to 2150 bushels where fertilizer use is 5 tons. The difference, 250 = 2150 − 1900, is the marginal product of the 5th ton of fertilizer, and it is measured by the slope of the total production curve along the arc *MN*. (It corresponds to the rise in the curve resulting from a move to the right by one unit.)

Now we can see just what is diminishing in the middle zone of the diagram—it is the *marginal* product of fertilizer. In the left-hand (shaded) zone we see that the slope of the total product curve rises as we move to the right. That is, the marginal product of fertilizer actually rises when we use more of it. Then when we enter the second zone the slope begins to decrease (the total product curve flattens out), meaning that marginal product is decreasing. Finally, in the third (red) zone the slope of the total product curve actually becomes negative, meaning that any further use of fertilizer actually brings a reduction in total output—a negative marginal product.

This relationship may be confirmed by referring to Table 21–1. The second column gives the total outputs corresponding to different quantities of fertilizer—1000 bushels can be produced without any fertilizer, 1100 bushels with 1 ton of fertilizer, and so on. These numbers are represented by the dots in Figure 21–2. The next column in the table represents the marginal products given by the increase in total output obtainable from an additional ton of fertilizer. For example, it tells us that 1 ton of fertilizer has a marginal physical product of 100 bushels because it increases total output from 1000 to 1100 bushels. The marginal physical product column shows how that figure rises gradually from 100 to 400 bushels, then ultimately falls back to 30 bushels, and finally becomes negative.

DIMINISHING RETURNS AND THE POPULATION PROBLEM

The law of diminishing returns first became important to economists as a vital link in their argument about the perils of population growth. The dire predictions of Malthus and Ricardo, to which we will return in Chapter 33, were based on the observation that although the labor force increases when the population grows, the quantity of land available for agriculture remains more or less constant. Diminishing returns to labor therefore set in because the quantity of land remains constant. And this must mean that the amount of food and other agricultural products is unable to keep up with the growth of the population. The consequence is that standards of living have to fall, and outright famine may become a very real threat. Many people feel that this prognosis is already applicable to some of the less developed countries with high birth rates, and that even the more prosperous nations face the same threat in the somewhat more distant future.

MARGINAL PRODUCT AND THE OPTIMAL QUANTITY OF AN INPUT

The second reason for the importance of the law of diminishing returns lies at the heart of the analysis of this chapter—the determination of optimal input quantities for the firm. Just what do Farmer Pfister's experiments tell him about the quantity of fertilizer he should use? Suppose fertilizer cost $140 per ton and that the farmer's product is worth $2 per bushel. Suppose he is considering the use of 3 tons of fertilizer, while the marginal product of the 4th ton is 400 bushels (fourth entry in the marginal physical product column of Table 21–1). Is 3 tons of fertilizer optimal for him? The answer is no, because although a 4th ton of fertilizer would cost him

TABLE 21–1
MARGINAL PRODUCTS OF FARMER PFISTER'S FERTILIZER (applied to a 5-acre plot)

TONS OF FERTILIZER	TOTAL PRODUCTION (bushels)	MARGINAL PHYSICAL PRODUCT (bushels)	VALUE OF MARGINAL PRODUCT (at $2 per bushel)
0	1000		
1	1100	100	$200
2	1250	150	300
3	1500	250	500
4	1900	400	800
5	2150	250	500
6	2275	125	250
7	2350	75	150
8	2380	30	60
9	2330	−50	−100

$140 it would yield him an additional 400 bushels, which at the price of $2 would add $800 to his revenue. Thus he comes out $800 − $140 = $660 ahead if he adds that 4th ton.

DEFINITION
The *value of the marginal product* of an input is equal to the marginal physical product of the input multiplied by the price of the product. It is the additional amount of *money* the producer gets when his product sells at a fixed price and he uses an additional unit of the input.

The value of the marginal product of Farmer Pfister's fertilizer when he uses 4 tons per plot of land is $2 × 400 bushels = $800. Using this terminology, the preceding analysis leads us to conclude that:

When the value of the marginal product of an input is more than its price, it pays the producer to expand his use of that input. Similarly, when the value of the marginal product of the input is less than its price, it pays the producer to use less of that input.

From these two observations we deduce that an optimal quantity of an input requires the value of its marginal product to be neither higher nor lower than its price:

The optimal quantity of an input, from the point of view of the producer, is that at which the value of its marginal product is equal to its price.

DIMINISHING RETURNS ONCE MORE

At this point the law of diminishing returns reenters the story. How does the producer get to the level of input use that satisfies the optimality rule? In principle he can calculate his way there step by step. Having seen that 3 tons of fertilizer is not enough because the value of the marginal product of the 4th ton ($800) is greater than its price ($140), what does Farmer Pfister do now? He considers buying a 4th ton and then a 5th, each time comparing value of marginal product with price. Ultimately, he will find a stopping point because, as he expands his use of fertilizer, its marginal product will fall (diminishing returns), and finally it will go all the way down to the $140 price of fertilizer. At that point it will pay him to stop. Further increases in his input use will not bring him any further net gains.

The illustrative figures of Table 21–1 show this process more explicitly. We can see that the farmer should not stop his employment of fertilizer at 5 tons or even at 6 tons, since a 7th ton, even though it yields fewer returns than the 5th, still brings in more (value of marginal product = $150) than its $140 cost. But that is about where it pays him to stop. Certainly a full 8th ton is *not* a good idea since it will bring in a marginal product whose value is only $60, and so it will not repay the cost of purchasing it.

In sum, it always pays the producer to expand his input use until diminishing returns set in and reduce the value of the marginal product to the price of the input.

A common fallacy maintains that it never pays the producer to go beyond the point where returns begin to diminish. On the contrary, it *usually* pays him to do so! It is optimal for the profit-maximizing firm to expand its input use up to the point where diminishing returns bring the value of the marginal product down to the price of an additional unit of the input. It can also be shown that a fairly similar result holds for decision makers pursuing goals other than profits.

CHOICE OF INPUT PROPORTIONS: THE PRODUCTION FUNCTION

So far we have dealt with the choice of each input quantity as if it could be decided separately, with each decision made in isolation from the others. This is somewhat misleading, for the choices do and must depend upon one another. The amount of labor and machinery it will pay Farmer Pfister to use depends on the number of

acres he decides to rent and lease, and vice versa. The marginal physical products of labor and fertilizer depend on the amount of machinery he uses. It is therefore important to see how decisions about the quantities of different inputs depend upon one another.

For this purpose economists have invented a concept they call a production function. The production function is just a summary of the technical and engineering information about the relationships between input and output quantities in a given firm (or for a given industry). It indicates just how much output Farmer Pfister can produce if he has a given amount of land, labor, seed, fertilizer, and so on.

DEFINITION
The production function indicates the *maximum* amount of product that can be obtained from any specified combination of inputs, given the current state of knowledge. That is, it shows the *largest* quantity of goods that any particular collection of inputs is capable of producing.

Any given output usually can be produced in a number of different ways using different combinations of inputs. In a country where wages are high, we expect to find a great deal of expensive machinery used per worker in order to reduce the amount of labor needed in the production process, and we expect the reverse relationship to hold where hourly earnings are very low. This means that a producer has considerable flexibility in the choice of input combination utilized in producing a given amount of his product. He may produce an output of 50 student desks with the aid of highly automated processes using very little labor per unit of output, or at the other extreme, the furniture production may be carried out with the assistance of nothing more sophisticated than handsaws and hammers.

A table can be used to describe such a production function. Table 21–2 shows how total output varies when there are changes in either the amount of labor or the amount of land used

TABLE 21–2
A PRODUCTION FUNCTION

	Quantity of Labor (days)						
	0	10	20	30	40	50	60
0	0	—	—	—	—	—	—
10	—	—	—	—	—	—	—
20	—	—	—	—	—	—	5.0
30	0	3.6	4.1	4.5	4.8	5.0	5.1
40	—	—	—	5.0	—	—	—
50	—	—	—	—	—	—	—
60	—	—	5.0	—	8.5	—	—
70	—	—	—	—	—	—	—
90	—	—	—	—	—	—	16.0

Quantity of Land (acres) (row labels)

The figures (in thousands) show how output (in thousands of bushels) depends on quantities of land and labor inputs.

by the firm, or both. To make Table 21–2 easier to read, most of the numbers that normally would be entered (but that are not relevant to our purposes) deliberately have been omitted and replaced by dashes.

The table is read like a mileage chart. For example, to see how much can be produced with 20 days of labor applied to 30 acres, we look at the red 30 in the column of numbers on the left indicating quantity of land, and the red 20 in the row of numbers across the top representing quantity of labor. Then, in the spot horizontally to the right of the 30 and vertically below the 20 we find the red number 4.1, meaning that this input combination can produce 4.1 (thousand) bushels of output per year. Similarly, you should be able to verify that with 60 acres and 40 days of labor, 8.5 thousand bushels can be produced.

DIMINISHING RETURNS AND ECONOMIES OF SCALE

Earlier in this chapter we discussed economies of scale. Is there a relationship between economies of scale and the phenomenon of diminishing returns, which has played such a large role in our discussion? It may seem at first that the two are contradictory, or at least that one tends to offset the other. After all, if the producer gets diminishing returns from his inputs as he uses more of them, does this not prevent him from obtaining scale economies?

The answer is that it does not, for they deal with two fundamentally different issues:

1. How much can output expand if we increase the quantity of just *one* input by some specified amount, *holding all other input quantities unchanged?*
2. How much can output expand if *all* inputs are increased *simultaneously* by the same percentage?

The law of diminishing returns provides an answer to the first of these questions, while economies of scale are pertinent to the second question. (Note the analogy to a scale model, in which all components are changed in size *proportionately.*)

Referring again to Table 21–2, we can see that the production function that is represented satisfies the law of diminishing returns, but that it also offers economies of scale. To show that the table's production function satisfies the law of diminishing returns, we must hold the quantity of one input constant while letting the other vary. The numbers in the fourth row of the table do just that since they all involve 30 acres of land but different amounts of labor. (Of course, any other row of the table could have just as easily been used to test whether or not the law of diminishing returns is satisfied.) We see from the second entry in that row that the use of 10 days' labor with the 30 acres yields 3.6 thousand bushels of output. The next entry, involving the employment of another 10 days' labor, shows that this additional labor produces a *marginal* yield of 500 bushels (that is, the total of 4.1 thousand bushels produced by the 20 days of labor minus the 3.6 thousand bushels obtained from the first 10 days). Similarly, a third set of 10 days of labor brings in a smaller marginal product of 400 = 4500 − 4100 bushels, and so on. The law of diminishing returns is clearly satisfied.

Returns to scale, on the other hand, describe the production response to a proportionate increase in *all* inputs. If, for example, a 12 percent increase in *both* land *and* labor yields a 14 percent increase in output, we say that *increasing returns to scale* are present. If both inputs bring in only a 12 percent addition to output, we call the situation one of *constant returns to scale.* The remaining situation, that of a less than proportionate increment in output, is called *diminishing returns to scale.*

To test for returns to scale we no longer can keep the quantity of one input constant, because we are interested in what happens when *both* inputs increase simultaneously. We note from the table that with 20 days of labor and 30 acres of land we get 4.1 thousand bushels of output. If both inputs are doubled, to 40 days' labor and 60 acres, output *more than* doubles to 8.5 thousand bushels. Finally, if we treble both inputs from their initial levels, output nearly *quadruples,* going up to 16 thousand bushels. It is clear that returns to scale are increasing.

The special case in which, if we double all inputs, output also doubles—called the case of constant returns to scale—has played a very important role in economic analysis, and we will meet up with it again.

THE CHOICE OF INPUT COMBINATIONS

Now suppose that our hypothetical grower decides to produce some given output, say 5000 bushels. Table 21–2 shows us that there are various input combinations that can produce this same output. We see, for example, that 60 days of labor on 20 acres can do the job, mak-

ing up for the shortage of land by intensive care. But the same output can also be turned out by 30 days of labor on 40 acres, or by 50 days of labor on 30 acres. That is, it is possible to substitute one input for another, making up with increased acreage for a decrease in labor time devoted to careful tending of the crop. Similarly, in the real world, one can substitute capital for land and/or labor, using tractors to make up for scarcity of labor, and better seeds or more fertilizer to make up for scarcity of soil.

But the firm needs to know which of the input combinations capable of producing the 5000 bushel output will be the most profitable. A moment's consideration suggests that it depends on the relative prices of the different inputs. Common sense tells us that if the price of land is high but labor is cheap, the number of workers per acre will be large; and the opposite will be true if the cost of land is low and wages are high. In the United States, land is more abundant and wages are higher than in the United Kingdom. As a result, we are not surprised to find that a typical farm worker in the Great Plains covers a far larger area than his British counterpart.

All of this fits in with our theoretical analysis of the amount of each input that it pays a firm to use. We saw earlier in this chapter that it pays the firm to use the quantities of labor and land at which

Price of land

= Value of marginal product of land

and at which

Price of labor

= Value of marginal product of labor[4]

---

[4]Dividing one of these equations by the other, we obtain the basic rule for the optimal *proportions* of land and labor for any given quantity of output.

$$\frac{\text{Price of land}}{\text{Price of labor}} = \frac{\text{Value of marginal product of land}}{\text{Value of marginal product of labor}}$$

Of course, this same equation holds for any other two inputs.

We can use this basic rule to determine what will happen if, starting from an initial situation in which the preceding equations are satisfied, there is a change in relative input prices, say, a fall in the price of land. A fall in the price of land will mean that the price of land now is less than the value of its marginal product. It will pay the farmer to rent more land until the point at which diminishing returns to land bring its marginal product down to its new lower price. Obviously, the opposite would be true if the price of land rose.

To summarize and generalize:

If the price of input x falls and/or the price of input y rises, it normally will pay to produce any given output with more x and less y. Diminishing returns will reduce the marginal product of x and raise the marginal product of y until at the new prices, the equalities

Price of x = Value of marginal product of x

Price of y = Value of marginal product of y

are restored.

RATE OF RETURN REGULATION AND INPUT PROPORTIONS

In an illustrative problem stated at the beginning of the chapter, it was suggested that regulation of the profits of public utilities may have some effects on the input proportions used by these firms. We can now begin to see how such a connection can arise.

First, we must examine the form such profit ceilings usually take. The regulatory agency cannot just pick some arbitrary number of dollars and prohibit the public utility from earning more than that randomly chosen amount. For one thing, such a profit ceiling would eliminate any incentive to expand sales or cut costs. For another, no single and uniform ceiling on total profits can be put on all firms in an industry. An electric utility serving a large, densely inhabited region with lots of business and lots of investment cannot be expected to earn the same number of dollars as a much smaller electric company. As a result, regulators usually do not set a limit on *total* profits but instead determine what they call "a fair rate of return" on the company's investment. The utility may be permitted to earn, say, $9\frac{1}{2}$ percent *on its investment* but no more. Thus the large electric company will be permitted to earn $9\frac{1}{2}$ percent on its multibillion dollar investment, while the smaller firm is permitted to earn the $9\frac{1}{2}$ percent on its much smaller investment. The latter will end up earning far fewer dollars than the former.

This clearly solves the problem of providing a suitably flexible ceiling on earnings. But, as we will see now, such regulations can also affect input choice. The purchase of equipment and construction of plants are, by definition, additions to the firm's investment. If a company meets an upward shift in the demand curve by putting $25 million into a new plant, it is permitted to earn more dollars in profit; specifically, it is allowed to add $9\frac{1}{2}$ percent of $25 million to its profits. But if it simply tries to meet the higher demand by hiring more labor, that does not increase the firm's investment. Since the firm is permitted to earn profit only on the basis of its investment, it may not be permitted to earn any more profit when it spends more money on labor.

The result is that, unless the regulations are framed very carefully, the process of profit regulation may give the utility a stronger incentive to purchase equipment than to purchase labor. It is as if the use of capital by the firm were given a bonus or a subsidy that lowers its price relative to the price of labor. Thus, in effect, a given amount of the regulated firm's money buys relatively less labor and more capital than it would in an unregulated market. As we have seen, a fall in the price of one input relative to the other will induce the firm to use more of the input whose relative price has gone down and less of the input whose relative price has gone up. That is precisely what happens here—the firm can be induced by the regulatory ceiling to purchase more capital and less labor than it would have otherwise.

In other words, regulation of profits may have unintended side effects upon the input proportions used by the firm, distorting the firm's choice of production technique. As has already been noted, this hypothesis is a matter of concern to regulatory agencies and the courts, where it has been suggested that the process just described is a source of inefficiency introduced by regulation. Certainly it is a matter that bears watching by policymakers as they reexamine our regulatory institutions.

INPUT PRICES, PRODUCTION FUNCTIONS, AND COST CURVES

Because the preceding chapter was devoted to an analysis of the firm's output decisions, most of the discussion there relied on the concepts of the firm's total cost curve, its average cost curve, and its marginal cost curve. In that chapter we simply assumed that these cost curves were known, seemingly decreed by some mysterious authority. But, in fact, production costs depend on the firm's input choices. Since we have now analyzed how the firm makes its input choices, we can also show how its cost curves are determined.

The relationship is straightforward. We saw that the firm's production function determines the marginal products of each of the firm's inputs (refer to the discussion of the law of diminishing returns earlier in this chapter). Next we learned that the quantity of inputs x and y that it pays the firm to use *in producing some given quantity of output* is determined by the equations

Price of x = Value of marginal product of x

Price of y = Value of marginal product of y

Now, once the firm knows how much x and y to use, it merely needs to multiply each input by the corresponding price to compute its total costs; that is,

Total cost = Price of x × Quantity of x +
Price of y × Quantity of y

The firm's lowest total cost of producing a given output is obtained by finding out how much of each input it pays the firm to use to produce that output, multiplying each input quantity by its price, and then adding all the resulting figures together.

For example, suppose the firm decides to produce 500,000 bushels in a year, the wage of a farmhand is $12,000 per year, and the rent of an acre of land is $1000 per year. With a production function like that in Table 21–2, suppose we determine that it pays the firm to use 50 workers on 80 acres. The total cost of the 500,000 bushels will then be

Price of land × Quantity of land +
Price of labor × Quantity of labor
= $1000 × 80 + $12,000 × 50 = $680,000

In exactly the same way, we can calculate how much it would cost the firm to produce 300,000 bushels, or 400,000 bushels, or 600,000 bushels. Suppose, for instance, the figures are those given in Table 21–3. This table gives us just the numbers needed to plot four different points on the firm's *total cost curve* (lines 1 and

TABLE 21–3
DATA FOR THE FIRM'S COST CURVES

1. Output (thousands of bushels)	300	400	500	600
2. Total cost (thousands of dollars)	500	600	680	900
3. Average cost (dollars per bushel)	1.67	1.5	1.36	1.5

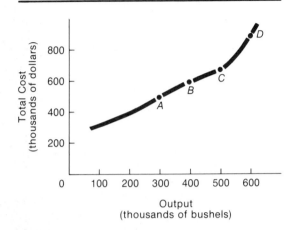

FIGURE 21–4

TOTAL COST CURVE, FROM COST AND
OUTPUT DATA IN TABLE 21–3
Point *A* shows that to produce 300,000 bushels, a total
of $500,000 in cost must be incurred, just as the table
indicates.

recur throughout the book as well as in eco-nomic writings more generally. Frequently we say that so and so will be true "in the short run." But what exactly do economists mean by the term short run?

It sometimes may pay a firm to operate tem-porarily at a loss, because it expects things to get better in the future and because it happens to be stuck with some plant or some contract that does not pay for itself. Such commitments are usually temporary commitments. Once they lapse, the firm is free to reexamine the situation and decide what new commitments, if any, it wishes to enter into. It may, for example, have an unfortunate contract with a raw material sup-plier of 1 year's duration or an uneconomically small (or large) plant whose economic life is 15 years. At the end of 1 year it can reopen negoti-ations with the supplier or turn to one of his competitors, and after 15 years it may even ask

2 of the table), which is the total cost curve shown in Figure 21–4. Point *A* shows the $500,000 total cost of 300,000 bushels of out-put, point *B* shows the $600,000 total cost of 400,000 bushels, and so on.

By dividing the total cost for each output by the quantity of the output, we obtain the corre-sponding average cost. For example, when out-put is 300,000 bushels, total cost is $500,000, so that average cost is $500,000/$300,000 = $1.67 (approximately). In the same way, the table gives us three other figures that can be used to plot the average cost curve shown in Figure 21–5. The same data can also be used to deter-mine the firm's marginal cost curve.

THE TIME ELEMENT: SHORT, INTERMEDIATE, AND LONG RUNS

Our discussion of cost curves provides us with the opportunity to deal with several issues that

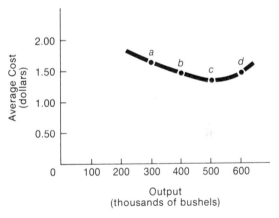

FIGURE 21–5

AVERAGE COST CURVE FOR THE FIRM,
FROM DATA IN TABLE 21–3
The points *a, b, c,* and *d* correspond, respectively, to
points *A, B, C,* and *D* in Figure 21–4. For example,
point *A* in Figure 21–4 and point *a* in Figure 21–5 both
correspond to an output of 300,000 bushels. And since
point *A* in Figure 21–4 indicates that the total cost of
this output is $500,000, its average cost is $500/$300
= $1.67, as shown by point *a* above.

an architect to design a more suitable plant. Economists have formalized these distinctions by speaking of the short run, the intermediate run, and the long run. These are not specific time periods equal in length for everyone, but vary in duration with the nature of the firm's commitments.

DEFINITION
The *short run* is a period so brief that *none* of the decision maker's fixed commitments comes to an end.

In the example just given, if the two commitments represent all of the firm's obligations, then the short run is any period less than 1 year. Similarly:

DEFINITION
The *long run* is a period sufficiently extensive for *all* of the decision maker's commitments to lapse.

In our example, the long run is anything over 15 years. And any time interval that falls between the two periods is an intermediate run.

These distinctions arise in many parts of economic analysis and we will encounter them again. At the moment they interest us because of their effect on the shape of cost curves, for the shape of the curves will vary with the length of the time period being considered.

We can be more specific about the relationship between the long run and short run average cost curves. Consider a firm, say the publisher of a small newspaper, that has a choice between two sizes of printing press, both of whose economic lives are 10 years. If it purchases the smaller press, its unit cost will be that given by curve *SS* in Figure 21–6. That means, if management is pleasantly surprised and its circulation grows to 50,000 copies per day, its cost will be 12 cents per paper (point *V*). It may then wish it had purchased the bigger press (whose average cost curve is shown as *BB*), which

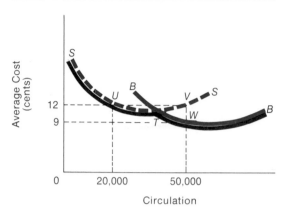

FIGURE 21–6

SHORT- AND LONG-RUN AVERAGE COST CURVES FOR A NEWSPAPER PUBLISHER
The publisher has a choice of two printing plants, a small one with average cost curve *SS,* and a big one with average cost curve *BB.* These are the short-run curves that apply as long as the publisher is stuck with his chosen plant. But in the long run, when he has his choice of plant size he can pick any point on the colored lower boundary of these curves. This lower boundary, *STB,* is the long-run average cost curve.

would have enabled the firm to cut unit cost to 9 cents (point *W*). However, in the short run nothing can be done, and its average cost curve remains *SS.* Similarly, if it had chosen to buy the larger press, its short-run cost curve would have been *BB,* and it would have been committed to this cost curve for 10 years—even if business were to decline sharply.

In the long run, however, after the 10 years have passed and the machine must be replaced, management has its choice once again. If it expects a circulation of 50,000 copies, it will now purchase the larger press and its cost will be 9 cents per copy. Similarly, if it expects sales of only 20,000 copies, it will arrange for the smaller press and for unit cost at 12 cents (point *U*). In sum, in the long run, for any given output level, the firm will select that plant size (that short-run cost curve) that is most economical for that output level. The long-run cost curve then consists of all the lower segments of the short-run cost curves. In Figure 21–6 this composite curve is the thick curve *STB*.

Similarly, the firm's supply curve is also dependent on cost. Obviously, the price at which a competitive firm offers a given quantity will depend on the cost of producing that quantity. Thus, we may also expect the long-run and the short-run supply curves to differ from each other. Logically, we would expect supply to be far less responsive to price changes in the short run than in the long run. In the short run, even if price rises, the firm can do very little to expand its supply. It may only be able to bring more of its goods out of storage. Then, given enough time, management may be able to arrange for more materials to be shipped in and for employees to work overtime. Given still more time, new staff can be trained and, finally, even the plant can be expanded. Thus, there is good reason to assume as a general rule that "the longer the run" the more *elastic* the supply curve will be, that is, the greater will be the output response to any rise in price.

HISTORICAL VERSUS ANALYTICAL COST CURVES

There is another important issue involving the role of time and the interpretation of a cost curve:

All points on a cost curve used in economic analysis refer to *the same period of time.* One point on the cost curve of an auto manufacturer will tell us how much it would cost it to produce 1.5 million cars during 1980, while another point on the curve will tell us what will happen to the firm's costs if, *instead,* it produces 2 million cars in 1980. Such a cost curve is called an *analytical* cost curve to distinguish it from a *historical* cost curve, which shows how costs vary from year to year.

The different points on the cost curve represent *alternative possibilities.* In 1980 the car manufacturer will produce either 1.5 or 2 million cars (or some other amount) but certainly not both. Thus, at most, only one point on this cost curve will ever be observable. The company may, indeed, produce 1.5 million in 1980 and 2 million in 1981, but the latter is not relevant to the 1980 cost curve. By the time 1981 comes around the cost curve may well have shifted, so the 1981 cost figure will not apply to the 1980 cost curve.

We can, of course, draw a different sort of cost curve that indicates, year by year, how costs and outputs have varied. Such a curve, which gathers together the statistics for a number of different periods, may be called a *historical cost curve* to distinguish it from the *analytical cost curves,* which are the ones used by economists. An example of a historical cost curve was given at the beginning of the chapter: Recall that Figure 21–1 showed how actual telecommunications costs varied from year to year from 1942 to 1975.

But why do economists rarely use historical cost curves and instead deal primarily with analytical cost curves, which are much more difficult to explain and to obtain statistically? The answer is that analysis of real policy problems—such as the desirability of having a single (monopoly) supplier of telephone services—leaves no choice in the matter. That is, if economists are to be helpful in making rational decisions from alternative choices, they *must* use analytical cost curves. Let us see why.

Since the 1940s there has been a great deal of technological progress in the telephone industry. From ordinary open wire, the industry has gone to microwave systems (which are, essentially, radio transmissions), to coaxial cables of enormous capacity, and new techniques using laser beams are on the horizon. Innovations in switching techniques and in the use of computers to send messages along uncrowded routes are equally impressive—for example, a long distance call is now likely to switch routes automatically and unobtrusively in midconversation as the degree of crowding varies along different segments of the path.

All of this means that the *entire* analytical cost curve of telecommunications must have shifted downward quite dramatically from year to year. Innovation must have reduced not only the costs of large-scale operation *but also the cost of smaller-scale operations.*

Now if we are to determine whether in 1980 a single supplier can provide telephone service more cheaply than can a number of smaller competing firms, we must compare the costs of *both* large- and small-scale production *in 1980*. It does no good to compare the cost of a large supplier in 1980 with his own costs as a smaller firm back in 1942, because that cannot possibly give us the information we need. It is true that costs of small suppliers were higher in 1942, but that is irrelevant for today's decision between large and small suppliers. No small firm today would use the obsolete high-cost techniques of 1942. Until we can compare the costs of the large and small supplier *today* we cannot make a rational choice between single- and multi-firm production. It is the analytical cost curve, all of whose points refer to the same period, that by definition supplies this information.

Figures 21–7 and 21–8 show two extreme hypothetical cases, one in which economies of scale are present and one in which they are not. Yet both of them show the same historical average cost curve (in black) with its very sharply declining cost pattern. (This curve is reproduced from Figure 21–1.) It also shows (in red) two possible analytical cost curves, one for 1942 and one for 1980. In Figure 21–7 the analytical cost curve (in red) has shifted downward very sharply from 1942 to 1980, as technological change reduced all costs. Moreover, both of the analytical cost curves slope downward to the right—in either year, the larger the firm the more cheaply it could produce. Thus the situation shown in Figure 21–7 really does represent a case in which there are economies to large-

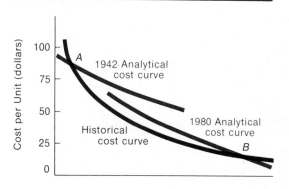

FIGURE 21–7

DECLINING HISTORICAL COST CURVE WITH THE ANALYTICAL AVERAGE COST CURVE ALSO DECLINING IN EACH YEAR
The two analytical cost curves shown indicate how the corresponding points (A and B) on the historical cost curve are generated by that year's analytical cost curve. Because the analytical cost curves are declining, we know that there are scale economies in the production activity whose costs are shown.

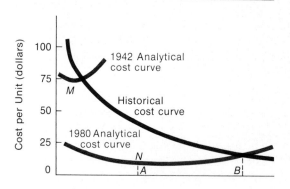

FIGURE 21–8

DECLINING HISTORICAL COST CURVE WITH U-SHAPED ANALYTICAL COST CURVES IN EACH YEAR
Here the behavior of the average cost does not show scale economies.

scale production so that one firm can supply more cheaply than can many.

But now look at Figure 21–8, which shows exactly the same historical cost curve as Figure 21–7. Here both analytical cost curves are U-shaped. In particular we note that the 1980 analytical curve has its minimum point at *N*. This corresponds to an output level, *A*, that is less than one-half the current output, *B*, of the monopoly supplier. This means that, in the situation shown in Figure 21–8, despite the sharp downward slope of the historical cost curve, a smaller company can supply more cheaply than

can a large one. In this case, one cannot justify a monopoly on the ground that its costs are lower. In sum, the shape of the historical cost curve tells us nothing about the cost advantages or disadvantages of single-firm production. More generally:

Because the historical cost curve does not permit the decision maker to compare the costs of the alternative choices at the dates when they will actually apply, it will not help in the selection of the best of the available decisions. Only the analytical cost curve fills this role.

SUMMARY

1. Marginal analysis is an indispensible tool for optimal *input* decisions just as it is for optimal *output* decisions.
2. The marginal physical product of any input is the increase in total output resulting from a unit increase in the use of that input, holding the quantities of all other inputs constant.
3. The law of diminishing returns states that if we increase the amount of one input (holding all other input quantities constant), the marginal physical product of the expanding input will eventually begin to decline.
4. The profit-maximizing firm, which buys inputs at a fixed price per unit, will hire inputs such as labor up to the point at which the price of the input is equal to the value of its marginal product.
5. A production function indicates the maximal quantity of output that a firm can produce from any given combination of input quantities.
6. If a doubling of all the firm's inputs just permits it to double its output, the firm has constant returns to scale. If with doubled inputs it can more than double its output, it has increasing returns to scale. If a doubling of inputs does not permit even a doubling of output, it has decreasing returns to scale.
7. The firm's cost curves can be obtained by determining, for each level of output, the optimal quantities of each input and multiplying each optimal input quantity by its price.
8. The long run is a period sufficiently long to enable the firm to change the capacity of its plant and for any other constraining commitments to end. The short run is a period so short that none of the firm's fixed commitments comes to an end.

CONCEPTS FOR REVIEW

"Law" of diminishing returns
Marginal physical product
Value of the marginal product
Economies of scale
Production function

Increasing, constant, and diminishing returns to scale
Short run
Long run
Analytical and historical cost curves

QUESTIONS FOR DISCUSSION

1. If the value of the marginal product of a kilowatt hour of electric power is 8 cents and the cost of a kilowatt hour is 12 cents, what can the firm do to increase its profits?

2. Industry A has economies of scale while industry B does not. In which is a monopoly easier to justify? Why?

3. A firm hires 2 workers and rents 15 acres of land for a season and produces 100,000 bushels of its crop. If it had doubled its land and labor, production would have been 300,000 bushels. Does it have constant, diminishing, or increasing returns to scale?

4. Suppose wages are $10,000 per season and land rent per acre is $3000. Calculate the average cost of 100,000 bushels and the average cost of 300,000 bushels, using the figures in Question 3 above. Note that average costs diminish when output increases. What is the connection with the firm's returns to scale?

5. Farmer Pfister has bought a great deal of fertilizer. Suppose he now buys more *land,* but not more fertilizer, and spreads the fertilizer evenly over all his land. What will happen to the marginal physical product of fertilizer? What, therefore, is the role of input proportions in the determination of marginal physical product?

6. Labor costs $10 per hour. Nine workers produce $180 of product per hour. Ten workers produce $196 of product; 11 workers produce $208; and 12 workers produce $215. Draw up a table of total and marginal products of 9, 10, 11, and 12 workers. How many does it pay the firm to hire?

7. (More difficult) A firm finds there is a sudden increase in the demand for its product. In the short run, it must operate longer hours and pay higher overtime wage rates. In the long run, however, it will pay the firm to install more machines and not operate them for longer hours. Which do you think will be lower, the short-run or the long-run cost of the increased output? How is your answer affected by the fact that the long-run cost includes the new machines the firm buys, while the short-run cost includes no machine purchases?

Appendix:
Production Indifference Curves

To describe a production function—that is, the relationship between input combinations and size of total output—we can use a graphic device called the production indifference curve instead of the sort of numerical information described in Table 21–2.

DEFINITION
A *production indifference curve* is a curve in a graph showing quantities of *inputs* on its axes. The indifference curve indicates all combinations of input quantities capable of producing some specified quantity of output. For each quantity of output, there is a separate indifference curve.

If you read the appendix on indifference curves in Chapter 19 on consumer choice, you will recognize a close analogy in logic (and in geometric shape) between consumers' and producers' indifference curves. Figure 21–9 represents different quantities of labor and capital capable of producing given amounts of furniture. The indifference curve labeled 100,000 indicates that an output of 100,000 pieces of furniture can be obtained with the aid of *any one* of the combinations of inputs represented by points on that curve. For example, it can be produced by 6000 hours of labor and $2 million of capital (point *A*) or, instead, it can be produced by the labor–capital combination shown by point *B* on the same curve. Because it lies considerably below and to the right of point *B*, point *A* represents a more labor-intensive process—it involves a labor–capital ratio, OL/OC, that is much higher than that at point *B*.

Points *A* and *B* can be considered *technically indifferent* because each represents a

bundle of inputs capable of yielding the same quantity of finished goods. However, "indifference" in this sense does not mean that the producer will be unable to make up his mind between input combinations *A* and *B*. Input prices will permit him to arrive at that decision. The two input choices are not economically indifferent.

The production indifference curves in a diagram such as Figure 21–9 constitute a complete

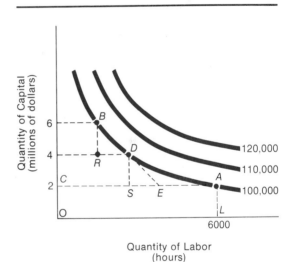

Quantity of Labor
(hours)

FIGURE 21–9

A PRODUCTION INDIFFERENCE MAP
The figure shows three indifference curves, one for the production of 100,000 pieces of furniture, one for 110,000 pieces, and one for 120,000 pieces. For example, the lowest curve shows all combinations of capital and labor capable of producing 100,000 pieces of furniture. Point *A* on that curve shows that 6000 hours of labor and $2 million of capital are enough to do the job.

description of the production function. For each combination of inputs, they show what quantity of output can be produced. As it is drawn, in two dimensions, the diagram can deal only with a situation in which two inputs are involved. In more realistic situations, there may be many more than two inputs, and an algebraic analysis must be used. But all the principles we need to analyze such a situation can be derived from the two-variable case.

CHARACTERISTICS OF THE PRODUCTION INDIFFERENCE CURVES

Before discussing input pricing and quantity decisions we should examine what can reasonably be said about the shapes of the indifference curves and the interpretation of those shapes.

The main characteristics of production indifference curves themselves are straightforward and entirely analogous to the properties of normal consumer indifference curves discussed in the appendix to Chapter 19.

Characteristic 1

Higher curves correspond to larger outputs. Since corresponding parts of the higher indifference curve represent larger quantities of *both* inputs, larger outputs can be produced.

Characteristic 2

The indifference curve will generally have a negative slope—it goes downhill as we move toward the right. All this means is that if we reduce the quantity of one input used, and we do not want to cut production, we must use more of another input. If we want to use less labor to produce 100,000 pieces of furniture, we will have to use more machinery to make up for the reduced labor input.

Characteristic 3

The curves are typically assumed to curve inward toward the origin near their "middle." This is a reflection of the law of diminishing returns—diminishing returns to too large an amount of either input compared to the other. For example, in Figure 21–9, points B, D, and A represent three different input combinations, all capable of producing the same quantity of output. At point B a lot of capital and relatively little labor is used, while the opposite is true at A. At the intermediate point D, there is also an intermediate use of both inputs. Indeed, point D is chosen so that its use of capital is exactly halfway between the amounts of capital used at A and at B.

Now consider the choice among these input combinations. As management, in its planning process, considers first the input proportion at B, then the one at D, and finally the one at A, it is considering the use of less and less capital, making up for it by the use of more and more labor so that it can continue to produce the same output. But the trade-off does not proceed at a constant rate because of diminishing returns in the substitution of labor for capital. When the firm considers moving from B to D it gives up BR units ($2 million) of capital and instead hires RD additional units of labor. Similarly, the move from D to A involves giving up another $2 million of capital since DS = BR. But this time, hiring an additional SE = RD units of labor will no longer do the job of making up for the reduced use of capital. Diminishing returns to labor as we hire more and more labor to replace more and·more capital means that now a much larger quantity of additional labor, SA rather than SE, will be needed to make up for the reduction (DS = BR) in the use of capital. Notice that if there had been no such diminishing returns, the indifference curve would have been a straight line, DE. The curvature of the indifference curve through points D and A shows the diminishing returns to substitution of inputs.

THE CHOICE OF INPUT COMBINATIONS

A production indifference curve only describes what input combinations *can* produce a given output; that is, it only indicates the technological possibilities. Management cannot decide which of the possible input combinations suits its purposes best without the corresponding cost information: the relative prices of the inputs. As we saw in Chapter 3, for any purchaser of goods with given prices, this information is shown by the *opportunity*, or *budget*, line, a line indicating all input combinations that can be bought for some specific amount of money.

If farmhands are paid $9000 per year and land rents for $1000 per acre per year, then a farmer who has $360,000 budgeted for the purpose can hire 40 farmhands but rent no land (point *K* in Figure 21–10), or he can rent 360 acres but have no money left over for farmhands (point *J*). But it is undoubtedly more sensible for the farmer to pick some intermediate point on his budget line *JK*, at which he divides his $360,000 between the two inputs.

But just where on the budget line does it pay him to end up? We expect that if the farmer is going to spend $360,000, he would like to get as much output for his money as possible. That is, he will want to get on the highest indifference curve his money permits.

Figure 21–10 shows three production indifference curves as well as the $360,000 budget line *JK*. The highest of these indifference curves yields a crop of 300.000 bushels. But the farmer cannot get there with the amount he plans to spend. No point on the budget line crosses the indifference curve labeled "300," meaning that $360,000 is not enough to buy him any input combination that can produce 300,000 bushels. Next, consider the lowest indifference curve (100,000 bushels). The farmer *can* get there for

$360,000—there are two points, *S* and *U,* on the budget line that can get him to that indifference curve. But he can do better than that. By moving to point *T,* between *S* and *U* on the budget line, he gets to the highest indifference curve his budget permits. There the indifference curve for 240,000 bushels is tangent to the budget line, and so any move along the budget line must force him down to a lower indifference curve.

The most productive input combination for any given expenditure is indicated by the point of tangency between a production indifference curve and the firm's budget line for the given expenditure level.

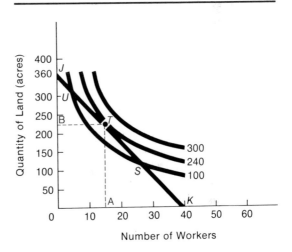

FIGURE 21–10

A PRODUCTION INDIFFERENCE MAP SHOWING OPTIMAL INPUT COMBINATION
The budget line *JK* and the production indifference curves together determine the optimal input combination. The highest indifference curve that can be reached with budget line *JK* is the one to which it is tangent at point *T*. That is, with that particular budget, the largest possible output is 240,000 bushels. But to get to point *T* the producer must use 16 workers (point *A*) and 230 acres (point *B*). This is the optimal input combination when the budget line is *JK*.

EFFECTS OF CHANGES IN INPUT PRICES

Suppose now that the annual rental of land rises from $1000 per acre to $1500 per acre. This means that the $360,000 will be able to rent fewer acres than before. We see by comparing Figure 21–11(a) with (b) that the left end of the budget line will fall from point J (360 acres) to point W (240 acres). Similarly, if the price of labor falls, the $360,000 will be able to hire more labor than before, so the right-hand end of the budget line will shift farther from the original, say from K to V.

A rise in the price of the input on the vertical axis will lower the left-hand end of the price line because the budget will buy less of that input than before. A fall in that input price will raise that end of the price line. Similarly, a rise

in the price of the input on the horizontal axis will move the right-hand end of the budget line toward the origin, and a fall in the price of that input will do the opposite.

In Figure 21–11(a) we see that budget line JK represents a case in which rents are fairly low compared to wages (the firm's money buys a large amount of land but a relatively small amount of labor). In this case, point T represents the best combination of the two inputs that the company can get for its money. Similarly, line WV in (b) represents a budget line for which rents are comparatively high, and point E is then the optimal input combination. Finally, by combining the two in one diagram (Figure 21–12), we can see that point E lies below and to the right of T, meaning that, in this case at least, as wages decrease and rents increase the firm will tend to hire more labor and rent less land. Thus, with higher rents, it pays the firm to use more

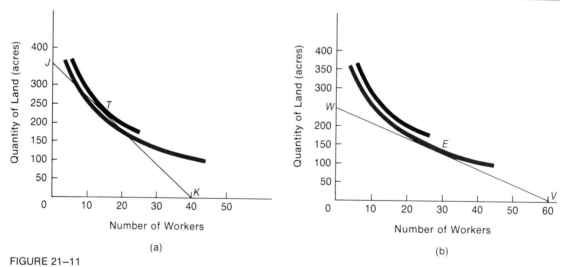

(a)   (b)

FIGURE 21–11

OPTIMAL INPUT CHOICE AT TWO SETS OF INPUT PRICES

When the price of land rises and the price of labor falls, the budget line for land and labor becomes less steep because the amount of money available can buy less land than before—240 acres in part (b) instead of the 360 acres in part (a)—and it can also buy more labor than before. As a result, the equilibrium point shifts from T in part (a) to E in part (b). It will now pay to substitute labor for land in the production process because labor has become cheaper relative to land.

labor-intensive processes. As common sense suggests, when the price of one input rises in comparison with that of others, it will pay the firm to hire less of this input and more of other inputs to make up for its reduced use of the more expensive input.

FIGURE 21–12

HOW CHANGES IN INPUT PRICES AFFECT INPUT PROPORTIONS

A fall in wages permits the amount of labor that the budget will buy to increase from K to V. A rise in the rent of land reduces the amount of land that the budget can buy from J to W. Then the optimal input combination changes from T to E. It will now pay to hire more labor and rent less land than before because point E lies to the right of and below point T.

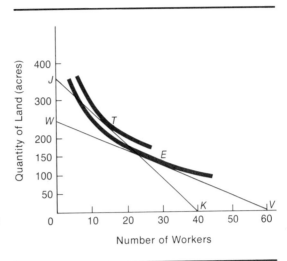

SUMMARY

1. A production function can be fully described by a family of production indifference curves, each of which shows all the input combinations capable of producing a specified amount of output.
2. As long as each input has a positive marginal product, production indifference curves have a negative slope, and higher curves indicate larger amounts of output. Because of diminishing returns, these curves characteristically curve toward the origin near their middle.
3. The optimal input proportions for any given level of expenditure are indicated by the point of tangency between a production indifference curve and the appropriate budget line.
4. When input prices change, firms will normally use more of the input that becomes relatively less expensive and less of the input that becomes relatively more expensive.

CONCEPTS FOR REVIEW

Production indifference curve
Optimal input choice

QUESTIONS FOR DISCUSSION

1. Typical Manufacturing Corporation (TMC) produces gadgets with the aid of two inputs: labor and glue. If labor costs $5 per hour and glue costs $5 per gallon, draw TMC's budget line for a total expenditure of $100,000.

In this same diagram, sketch in a production indifference curve indicating that TMC can produce no more than 1000 gadgets with this expenditure.

2. Now suppose that wages rise to $10 per hour and glue prices rise to $6 per gallon. How are TMC's optimal input proportions likely to change? (Use a diagram to explain your answer.)

22

The Firm
in the Marketplace

Industries have many forms of economic organization. The two most extreme forms are pure competition and pure monopoly. It is useful to analyze these two ends of the spectrum and to employ them as reference points, but in reality few absolutely pure examples of either can be found. Rather, the economy is made up mostly of industries having intermediate forms of organization. For example, the bulk of U.S. manufactured goods is produced by industries called oligopolies—industries comprising a fairly small number of firms, some of which are enor-

mous in size. These firms do often compete actively with one another; but they also have a good deal of power over developments in the market—over price changes, product design, and the like—power of the sort we usually associate with monopolies.

The material in this and the following chapter deals with some of the forms that monopoly power can take and some of the resulting policy problems. This chapter focuses on the individual firm and its behavior under pure competition and under two alternative market forms. In the following chapter, our attention is directed to the entire industry under monopoly and pure competition.

Specifically, this chapter will begin by defining pure competition and showing its implications for the demand curve of the individual firm. Next, we will examine a competitive firm's pricing, output, and advertising decisions, showing that in a state of equilibrium it must provide goods to consumers at the minimum cost at which the firm can continue to operate. Third, we contrast the implications of pure competition with those of monopolistic competition, in which *small* firms each provide products with special brands or other unique features over which the supplying firm has a monopoly. We will show that the unit cost of the firm's product under monopolistic competition tends to be higher and its output smaller than those of a comparable firm operating under pure competition. Finally, we will turn to oligopoly, in which the industry has a few large firms, and we will see that in this form of organization the rivalry of firms is likely to be more vigorous and direct than it is under pure competition.

APPLICATION: ADVERTISING UNDER COMPETITION

To illustrate the explanatory power of our analysis, we begin with a puzzling phenomenon—the relatively low level of advertising in industries that economists consider to be highly competitive. One tends to think of advertising as a competitive activity. Rival car manufacturers, or rival producers of breakfast cereals or of different brands of cigarettes, spend many millions of dollars every year on advertising. Most economists, though, would classify agriculture as a much more competitive industry than automobile manufacturing or the production of breakfast cereals or cigarettes. Yet one never hears of individual farmers spending much on advertising. In fact, many farm products are virtually

unadvertised. How does one explain this phenomenon? This chapter will provide the reader with the tools necessary to answer this and other issues relating to industrial behavior.

PURE COMPETITION

In any discussion of the concept of pure competition, it is helpful to define what is meant by the word *market.* In this context market is *not* used to denote only an organized exchange operating in a well-defined physical location. The more general and more abstract notion of a market, as utilized here, refers to a set of sellers (firms) and buyers (consumers) whose activities affect the price at which a *particular commodity* is sold. For example, the sale of two lots of General Motors stock at different ends of the country may be considered to take place on the same market, while the sale of two unrelated commodities in neighboring stalls of a market square may, in our sense, occur on totally different markets.

DEFINITION
A market is said to operate under *pure competition* when the following four conditions are satisfied:

1. *Numerous participants:* Each seller and purchaser in the market constitutes so small a proportion of the total market that his output or purchase decisions have no effect on the price. This requirement, by definition, rules out trade associations or other collusive arrangements strong enough to affect price.
2. *Homogeneity of product:* As far as any buyer is concerned, the product offered by any one seller is identical to that supplied by every other seller. As a result the buyer does not care from whom he buys.
3. *Freedom of entry and exit:* New firms desiring to enter the market can do so on terms as good as those available to firms already

there. Similarly, if production and sale of the good proves to be insufficiently profitable, there are no special impediments preventing firms from leaving the market.

4. *Perfect information:* Each firm and each customer is well informed about the available products and their prices.

The first and second of these requirements of pure competition are intended to ensure that none of the firms within the market has any trace of monopoly power. The third and fourth conditions prevent any firm from earning monopoly profits. We will see presently just how these conditions produce those effects.

There are no industries that satisfy perfectly the requirements of pure competition, but some do come close. Two common examples are standardized farm products sold on the national and international market (for example, certain varieties of wheat or cotton) and the stock market, in which all shares of any particular company, such as IBM, are identical (homogeneous) and most individual buyers or sellers have little or no control over the behavior of the market. But the case of pure competition is important for another reason—it is a reference point whose analysis will tell us a great deal about the economy as a whole.

THE COMPETITIVE FIRM AND THE COMPETITIVE INDUSTRY

To discover what happens in a market in which pure competition prevails, we must deal with two separate but related issues, the behavior of the *firm* and the behavior of the *industry*. It is important to know what factors determine how much a typical competitive firm will produce, what price it will charge for its product, and what it will do about advertising. The same information is needed about an entire industry— and we will discuss that in depth in the following chapter.

One of the basic differences between the firm and the industry under competition relates to pricing. Under pure competition, the firm has no control over the price it can charge. The presence of a vast number of competitors, each offering identical products, forces each firm to meet but not exceed the price charged by the competition. Like the farmer selling a few truckloads of wheat, or the stockholder selling 100 shares of General Electric, the firm simply finds out what price is now being offered on the market and has no choice but to accept that price as its own.

But while the individual firm has no influence over price under pure competition, the industry does. This influence is not conscious or planned—it happens spontaneously through the impersonal forces of supply and demand, as we have already observed in Chapter 4.

THE COMPETITIVE FIRM AND ITS DEMAND CURVE

So far, we have assumed that the slope of a demand curve is always negative; that is, if a firm wishes to sell more (without increasing its advertising or changing its product specification), it must reduce the price of its product. The competitive firm is an exception to this general principle.

The demand curve of a perfectly competitive firm is always horizontal. That is, it can double or triple its sales without any reduction in the price of its product.

How is this possible? The answer is that the competitive seller has absolutely no influence over price. The farmer who sells his soybeans through an exchange in Chicago must accept the current quotation his broker reports to him. Whether that farmer decides to ship one or two or three truckloads, no ripple will be felt on the market, which deals in the shipments of many

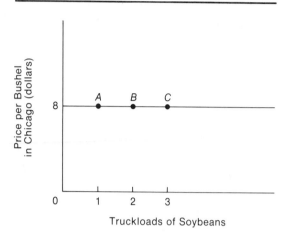

FIGURE 22–1

DEMAND CURVE FOR A FIRM UNDER
PURE COMPETITION
Under pure competition the size of the output of a firm
is always so small a portion of the total industry supply
that it cannot affect the market price of the product.
Even if the firm's output increases many times, market
price remains $8.

thousands of farmers. The Chicago price per
bushel will not budge just because Farmer
Jones decides he doesn't like the price and
holds back a truckload for storage. Thus we get
the demand curve for Farmer Jones's soybeans
shown in Figure 22–1; the price he is paid in
Chicago will be $8 per bushel whether he sells
one truckload (point A) or two (point B) or three
(point C).

SHORT-RUN EQUILIBRIUM
OF THE COMPETITIVE FIRM

We now have sufficient background to analyze
how the competitive firm determines the amount
it will produce.

To begin, we refer back to the basic analysis of the equilibrium of the firm (Chapter 20)
and its apparatus—the average cost and average revenue curves. In addition, we must consider the firm's equilibrium condition, which
requires it to pick a price and output level that
make its *marginal cost equal to its marginal
revenue.*

Figure 22–2 shows the short-run equilibrium of the competitive firm, utilizing these relationships. The only feature that distinguishes
the equilibrium of the competitive firm from that
of any other type of firm is the fact that its demand curve is horizontal.

To analyze the implications of the horizontal
demand curve we must show that:

The competitive firm's average and marginal
revenue curves must always be horizontal
straight lines, and both of them must coincide
with the demand curve.

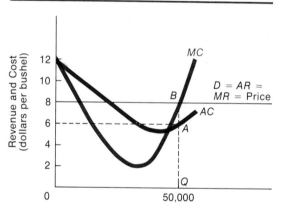

FIGURE 22–2

SHORT-RUN EQUILIBRIUM
OF THE COMPETITIVE FIRM
The profit-maximizing firm will select output Q at which
marginal cost equals marginal revenue (point B). The
demand curve, D, is horizontal because the firm's
output is too small to affect market price; thus it is also
a curve of marginal revenue. In the short run, demand
may be either high or low in relation to cost. Therefore
each unit it sells may return a profit (AB) or a loss.

Why must the average revenue curve be horizontal? Because, by definition, the demand curve and the average revenue curve must always be the same thing. An example will make this clear. If the firm is selling 5000 bushels of soybeans at $8 per bushel, *each* bushel it sells brings in a revenue of $8. Thus, since the revenue of each unit is equal to its price, the *average* of those equal revenues must also equal the price. Therefore, the demand curve, which shows the *price* the seller gets for whatever quantity he sells, by definition also shows his average revenue.

Under pure competition, this demand-equals-average-revenue curve is also the firm's marginal revenue curve because, as shown in Chapter 20:

If an average revenue curve is neither rising nor falling (it is horizontal), the marginal revenue curve cannot lie either above it or below it. For if marginal revenue were above the $8 average revenue, it would pull up the average (the average revenue curve would have to slope uphill). By the same token, if marginal revenue were below average revenue, the average revenue curve would have to slope downhill. Thus, since the average revenue curve of the competitive firm is indeed horizontal, the marginal revenue curve must coincide with it everywhere.

Now that we know the position of our firm's marginal revenue curve, we can use this and the position of the marginal cost curve shown in Figure 22–2 to determine the equilibrium output, price, and profit. As usual, the profit-maximizing output is that at which marginal cost equals marginal revenue. This competitive firm's profit-maximizing output is 50,000 bushels (point Q), which corresponds to the output at which marginal cost and marginal revenue (equals average revenue equals price) are equal at $8 (point B). As the graph indicates, the firm will be able to earn large profits. This is so because at output level 50,000 the $8 price, which

is equal to the height of point B on the demand curve, lies well above point A, which represents the average cost ($6). In other words, on *each* of the 50,000 units of output the firm sells, it will earn a profit of AB, or $2, making a total profit of $2 × 50,000 = $100,000.

Notice that the competitive firm's equilibrium is at the place where price is equal to marginal cost (point B in Figure 22–2). This is generally true.

Equilibrium for a profit-maximizing firm under pure competition is at the level of output at which price is equal to marginal cost.

Such profits (or losses, for that matter) *are* possible for the competitive firm. But they can only be temporary. The freedom of new firms to enter the industry or of old firms to leave it will, in the long run, eliminate these profits.

LONG-RUN EQUILIBRIUM OF THE COMPETITIVE FIRM

If very high profits accrue to firms in the industry, new companies will find it profitable to enter the business. Expanded production will force the market price to fall from its initial level, $8 per bushel, as we will explain later. The firm's horizontal demand curve, therefore, will shift downward by the amount of the fall in market price. And at the same time, as the industry's production increases, its usage of inputs will expand. It is therefore plausible that input prices will be forced upward so that the firm's cost curve will tend to shift up. Together, these two developments will wipe out the firm's short-run profits. With its demand curve (its selling price) being pushed downward and its cost curve upward, the profits with which it began will soon be wiped out.

This process can be clarified with the aid of Figure 22–3. In Figure 22–3(a) the demand

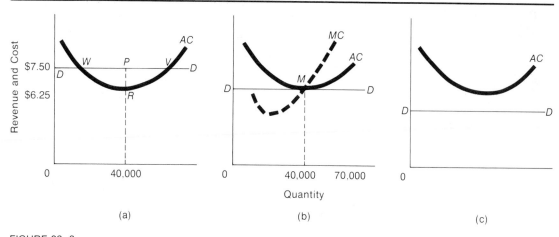

FIGURE 22–3

LONG-RUN EQUILIBRIUM OF THE COMPETITIVE FIRM

Long-run equilibrium of the firm under pure competition can only occur when the demand and average cost curves are tangent so the firm can just cover its costs [point *M* in part (b)]. If the average cost and demand curves intersect, the firm can earn a profit [*RP* in part (a)]. If the two curves do not meet, average cost will exceed price at any output and the firm must lose money [part (c)].

curve has shifted downward and the average cost curve upward from their positions in Figure 22–2. But the two curves still cross. This means that while profits have been squeezed, they have not been wiped out altogether. At any output level between intersection points *W* and *V*, say at an output of 40,000 bushels, price, *P* = $7.50, will still exceed *R* = $6.25, the average cost. New enterprises will, therefore, still find it profitable to enter into competition with our firm.

Under these circumstances, the shift in the demand and the cost curves will continue. Where will it stop? Figure 22–3(c) represents a situation in which matters have gone too far. The demand curve now lies below the average cost at every output level. There is no output level that enables the firm to earn enough to cover its costs, including the price it must pay to lenders (investors) for its capital. When this happens, the capital flow reverses itself; firms and investors want to transfer *out* of the industry.

In Figure 22–3(b) we see the only position compatible with long-run competitive equilibrium. It is the case intermediate between those in Figures 22–3(a) and (c), at which the demand and average cost curves have achieved tangency. The output level of 40,000 bushels corresponding to the point of tangency, *M,* just enables the firm to break even.

In long-run equilibrium under pure competition the firm must earn *zero economic profit.*

At this point, the price exactly covers the unit cost of *all* the firm's inputs, *including the cost of its capital.* At any other output level, say 70,000 bushels—see Figure 22–3(b), the returns of the firm will be insufficient to cover its costs. Therefore management will be forced to produce 40,000 bushels because zero profit is the most it can hope to get, and at any other output it will do even worse—it will end up with losses.

ZERO ECONOMIC PROFIT: THE OPPORTUNITY COST OF CAPITAL

Something is obviously strange about the preceding conclusion that all competitive firms will end up earning zero profits. One might legitimately ask why anyone bothers to go into business. The answer is that the zero profit concept as used in economic writings does not mean the same thing that it does in ordinary usage.

To see what is involved, we must note again that the elimination of the firm's profits must be ascribed to the third of the characteristics of pure competition listed in our definition earlier in the chapter: freedom of entry and exit. Freedom of entry in our competitive industry guarantees that those who invest in that industry will receive a rate of return on their capital no greater than the return that capital can earn elsewhere in the economy. Since money always flows from industries whose return is low to industries whose return is high, the rate of return on capital in all competitive industries will be driven toward the same level; this is called the opportunity cost of the capital.[1]

DEFINITION

The *opportunity cost* of a given investment is the highest return that money can earn in any other market. It is the potential earnings that investors forfeit by tying up their money in the industry in which they choose to invest.

Freedom of entry permits capital to be attracted into any industry in which unusually high profits are (temporarily) being realized. The new capital will increase output in that industry, which will then drive down prices and profits until the point at which the rate of return on capital has been reduced to the level of its op-

portunity cost—the return that capital can earn elsewhere.

Similarly, freedom of exit of capital guarantees that in the long run, once capital has had a chance to move, no industry will provide a rate of return lower than the opportunity cost of capital. For if returns in one industry are particularly low, resources will flow out of it. Plant and equipment simply will not be replaced as they wear out. As a result, output will fall, and prices and profits will ultimately rise to their opportunity level.

Economists prefer to consider this opportunity cost rate of return on capital as the *cost of the firm's capital.* In these terms, this rate represents the amount management will have to pay for capital if it utilizes other people's money rather than its own. The logic here is that no one will provide such resources to a firm unless he receives in return as much as he can get for his money elsewhere. If such a rate of return is not possible, funds simply will not be made available to this industry. The price of a company's capital is a cost of hiring an input just as clearly as is the wage of labor. It is true that management itself may provide capital or labor to the firm, but these choices also incur an opportunity cost because each input could have been earning money elsewhere. To capital and labor supplied by management, we therefore also assign a cost figure—equal to the level of its opportunity cost.

Economic profit equals net earnings, in the ordinary sense, minus the firm's opportunity cost of capital.

So in the economist's language, in order to break even (earn zero profit), a firm must earn enough not only to cover the cost of labor, fuel, and raw materials, but also the cost of its funds, including the opportunity cost of any funds supplied by the owners of the firm. To illustrate the difference between this definition and the term *profit* in its ordinary sense, suppose U.S. gov-

---

[1]The fundamental concept of opportunity cost—one of our 12 Ideas for Beyond the Final Exam—was defined in Chapter 3.

ernment bonds are paying 7 percent, and the owner of a small shop is receiving a 3 percent return on her business investment. The shopkeeper might say she is earning a 3 percent profit, but the economist would point out that she is *losing* 4 percent on every dollar she has tied up in her business. The reasoning is that by keeping the money tied up in the firm, she gives up the chance to buy government bonds and receive a 7 percent return. Furthermore, she can earn this money without having to put forth any effort.

A further example of this concept is that "the fair rate of return" that regulatory agencies permit public utilities to earn is usually intended to approximate the opportunity cost of capital. This amount is what the company could expect to earn if it were operating in a competitive industry, and provides no "excess profit" on top of the latter amount.

With this explanation of the meaning of economists' zero profit condition, we can now summarize the results of the preceding section:

Long-run equilibrium of the purely competitive firm requires its returns to equal the opportunity cost of its capital (zero economic profit). There must be tangency between the firm's demand curve and its average cost curve. Its profit-maximizing output level will then correspond to the point of tangency.

This completes our discussion of the competitive firm. In the next chapter we will return to pure competition to discuss the competitive industry. But first, because the comparison is so direct, it is convenient to turn to the firm under monopolistic competition.

EQUILIBRIUM OF THE FIRM UNDER MONOPOLISTIC COMPETITION

Monopolistic competition is a concept associated with the work of the late Professor Ed-

ward Chamberlain of Harvard University and that of Joan Robinson of Cambridge University conducted in the early 1930s.

DEFINITION
A market is said to operate under conditions of *monopolistic competition* if it satisfies four conditions:

1. *Numerous participants:* Many buyers and sellers, all of whom are small.
2. *Freedom of exit and entry.*
3. *Perfect information.*
4. *Heterogeneity of products:* As far as the buyer is concerned, each seller's product is at least somewhat different from every other's product.

Monopolistic competition differs from pure competition in only one respect: the distinctiveness of each seller's product. That is, while under pure competition all sellers' products are identical, under monopolistic competition they differ from seller to seller—in quality, in price, in packaging, or in supplementary services offered (for example, length of the guarantee, car window washing by a gas station, and so on). The relevant product differences are only those that are perceived as such by the purchaser. Two products may perform quite differently in quality tests, but if the consumer knows nothing about this difference, it is irrelevant. On the other hand, differences in packaging or in associated services can and do distinguish a product, even though it is no different qualitatively from its competing products. Thus, if one seller's salespersons are more efficient and polite than another's, their products may be differentiated quite effectively. The term *monopolistic competition* suggests that sellers under this form of organization do have a monopoly (they are the *only* sellers) of their own product variants, but that they are subject to substantial competitive pressures from sellers of substitute products.

Monopolistic competition is the first of the

market forms on our list that we encounter frequently in our economy. It is particularly characteristic of retailing, where the small shopkeeper still plays a significant role, and of many of the economy's services, such as medical and legal, which are provided under similar conditions. Gas stations are another common example.

Since the defining characteristic of monopolistic competition is that competing products are not identical, there is no reason to expect them to sell at the same price, nor any reason to expect the price of any one product to remain unchanged when the quantity supplied varies. Each seller, in effect, deals in a market slightly separated from the others. He caters to a set of customers who vary in their "loyalty" to his product. If he raises his price somewhat, he may expect to drive some but not all of his customers into the arms of his competitors. If he lowers his price, he may expect to attract some trade from his rivals. But since his product is not a perfect substitute for theirs, if he undercuts them slightly he will not attract away *all* their business as he would in the competitive case. In sum, we may expect his demand curve to be negatively sloped; by cutting his price a little, he can expand his sales a little. This is quite different from pure competition, in which the demand curve is always horizontal.

Given that he has his little monopoly, a product distinguished from all others, can we expect the monopolistic competitor to earn more than the pure competitor? In the short run, perhaps. The short-run equilibrium of the monopolistically competitive firm is exactly like that of other firms. As described in Chapter 20, the firm operates at a price and an output level at which marginal cost equals marginal revenue, and the firm may, temporarily, earn a profit; or if luck is bad, it may suffer a loss.

But in the long run under monopolistic competition extraordinary profits will also attract new entrants—not entrants with products *identical* to our firm's as under pure competition, but with outputs sufficiently substitutable to hurt. If one gas station's location enables it to do a thriving business, it can confidently expect another, selling a *different* brand, to open across the street. When one seller adopts a new, attractive packaging, he can be sure that his rivals will soon follow suit, with a slightly different design and color of their own. Thus, in the long run, under monopolistic competition the firm will earn no more on its capital than it could earn elsewhere. Just as under pure competition, price will be driven to the level of average cost including the opportunity cost of capital.

Diagrammatically, this once again requires tangency between the firm's demand curve and its average cost curve. For if the two curves intersect, there must be some output levels at which average revenue exceeds average costs, which means that extraordinary profits can be earned and there will be an additional influx of new substitute products. Similarly, if the average cost curve fails to touch the demand curve altogether, the firm will be unable to obtain returns equal to those that its capital can get elsewhere. Hence, long-run equilibrium calls for a relationship such as that depicted in Figure 22–4 on the next page. The equilibrium output, 1000 units in the example, corresponds to the point of tangency, *T*, between the two curves.

This seems quite similar to the competitive solution, and in terms of the profits earned by the firm, it is. Moreover, this equilibrium corresponds fairly well to what we gather from casual observation. Filling station operators whose market, roughly speaking, has the characteristics of monopolistic competition, do not earn notably higher profits than do wheat farmers who operate under conditions closer to those of pure competition.

EXCESS CAPACITY AND MONOPOLISTIC COMPETITION

There is one difference between pure and monopolistic competition that many economists consider very important. Look at Figure 22–4

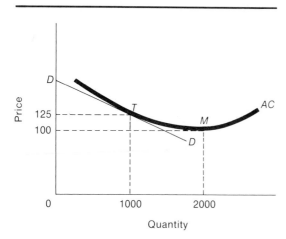

FIGURE 22–4

EXCESS CAPACITY UNDER MONOPOLISTIC COMPETITION

The firm produces output 1000, at which the demand and average cost curves are tangent. Because the demand curve slopes downward, however, output will be less than the quantity (2000) at which average cost is at a minimum. That is also the output that would be produced by a purely competitive firm.

again. Under monopolistic competition, the tangency point between the average cost and the demand curves, *T,* must occur along the negatively sloping portion of the average cost curve, since at that point it must have the same slope as the demand curve. If the average cost curve is U-shaped, the tangency point must lie above and to the left of *M,* the minimum point on the average cost curve.

On the other hand, under pure competition, since the firm's demand curve is horizontal, tangency must take place at that minimum point on the average cost curve, as is easily confirmed by referring back to Figure 22–3(b). This observation leads to the following conclusion:

Under monopolistic competition, the firm will in the long run tend to produce an output lower than that which minimizes its unit costs, and hence unit costs of the monopolistic competitor

will be "unnecessarily high." This has been called the *excess capacity theorem of monopolistic competition.*

It follows that if every firm under monopolistic competition were to expand its output, cost per unit of output would be reduced. But we must be careful about jumping to policy conclusions from that observation. It does *not* follow that it would be a good thing for *every* monopolistically competitive firm to produce more. Remember, such an overall increase in industry output means that a smaller portion of the economy's resources will be available for other uses; and from the information at hand we have no way of knowing whether that leaves us ahead or behind in terms of social benefits. It is even possible, in an extreme case, that no one will want any more of the output produced by the monopolistically competitive firm, so that even at its lower cost such a purchase will turn out to be a poor bargain. Like shoe horns that sell for 50 cents, or two for 85 cents, we may be better off on balance with the smaller output despite its higher *unit* cost.

Yet the situation represented in Figure 22–4 can still be interpreted to represent a substantial inefficiency. While it is not clear that society would gain if *every* firm were to achieve lower costs by expanding its production, a net gain *can* be obtained if firms combine into a smaller number of larger companies but among them still produce the same total "industry" output. That is, if the initial output is produced by fewer firms, each supplying a larger volume than before, there must be a clear net saving. For example, suppose in the situation shown in Figure 22–4 there were initially ten monopolistically competitive firms each producing 1000 units of output. The total cost of this output, according to the figures given in the diagram, would be

(Number of firms) × (Output per firm) ×

(Cost per unit) = 10 × 1000 × $125

= $1,250,000

If, instead, the number of companies were cut in half, to five, and each produced 2000 units, that is, twice its original output, total "industry" production would be unchanged. But now, since the average cost of the firm declines when output increases, total costs will have fallen to $5 \times 2000 \times \$100 = \$1,000,000$, a clear net saving of $250,000 *for the same total output quantity.*

This result is not dependent on the particular numbers used in our illustration. It follows directly from the observation that, if total production is unchanged, a lower cost per unit must always yield a net saving. The standard example in the literature is the traffic circle with four filling stations where two could serve the available customers with little increase in delays, and achieve a saving in costs via a decrease in idle time of employees and equipment.

Yet even this conclusion must be accepted with at least one important reservation. Even if a smaller number of larger firms can reduce costs, society may not benefit from the change because it necessarily means that a smaller range of choice is available to the consumer. Since under monopolistic competition all products are at least slightly different, a reduction by half in the number of firms means that the number of different products will have fallen as well. We will have achieved greater efficiency at the cost of greater standardization. In many cases consumers may agree that there has been a clear net gain, particularly where the variety of products available was initially so great that it only served to confuse them. But for many products, most consumers would probably agree that a diversity of choice is worth more than the saving they might realize from greater standardization.

OLIGOPOLY

In terms of the proportion of dollar value of all manufactured goods produced in our economy, there seems little doubt that first place must be assigned to the third of our market forms—oligopoly.

DEFINITION

An *oligopoly* is a market on which all products sold are identical or are close substitutes, and the outputs are supplied by only a few firms, at least several of which are relatively large.

We consider a firm to be relatively large if changes in its output decisions within its normal range of operation can significantly affect market prices.

In highly developed economies, it is not monopoly, but oligopoly, that is virtually synonymous with "big business." The management of almost every large firm is concerned about its giant rivals. In this form of economic organization, rival products may be identical, as are the outputs of most steel manufacturers, or differentiated by such things as advertising, packaging, or physical specification, as is true in the case of automobiles, liquor, gasoline, and tobacco products. In each of these industries the market contains a group of huge firms, each keeping a watchful eye on the actions of the others.

Under oligopoly, rivalry among firms takes its most direct and active form. It is here that one encounters such moves and countermoves as the frequent introduction of new products, free samples, and highly competitive, if not nasty, advertising campaigns. One firm's price decision or selling campaign is likely to elicit a cry of pain from its rivals, and competition is often a continuing battle in which strategies are planned day by day and each major decision can be expected to induce a direct countermove.

The manager of a large oligopolistic firm who has occasion to study some economics is usually somewhat taken aback by the notion of pure competition, because it is devoid of all harsh competitive activity as he knows it. Remember that under pure competition the managers of firms make no price decisions—they simply accept the price dictated by market forces and adjust their output accordingly. The competitive firm does not advertise, it adopts no sales gimmicks, and it does not even know who most of its rivals are. But since oligopolists are not as dependent on market forces, they do not enjoy such luxuries. They must worry about prices, spend fortunes on advertising, and try to understand their competitors' behavior patterns and psychology.

The relative freedom of choice in pricing of at least the largest firms in an oligopolistic industry, and the necessity for them to take direct account of their rivals' responses, are troublesome from the point of view of economic analysis. Once producers are able to influence market price, they will find it expedient to adjust the quantities of their inputs or their outputs as a means of securing more favorable buying and selling prices. This activity is likely to be at the expense of the consumer and detrimental to the economy's efficient use of resources.

WHY OLIGOPOLISTIC BEHAVIOR IS SO HARD TO ANALYZE

A second reason economists are somewhat disturbed by the nature of oligopolistic competition concerns a problem that is created for them rather than for society. The problem is simply that oligopolistic behavior is much more difficult to analyze than the other forms of economic organization, and in fact, there exists no well-defined and coherent body of theory describing the pricing and output decisions of the firm under oligopoly. The difficulty arises out of the interdependent nature of oligopolistic decisions. For example, Ford's management knows that its actions may well lead to countermoves by General Motors, which in turn may require a readjustment in Ford's plans, thereby producing a

modification in GM's response, and so on. Where such a sequence of moves and countermoves may lead is difficult enough to ascertain. But the fact that Ford executives know all this in advance, and may try to take it into account in making their initial decision, makes even that first step difficult, if not impossible, to analyze and predict.

The truth is that almost anything can happen under oligopoly, and sometimes it does. The early railroad kings were known to go so far as to employ gangs of hoodlums who engaged in pitched battles to try to prevent the operation of a rival line. At the other extreme, overt or more subtle forms of collusion have been employed to avoid rivalry altogether—to transform an oligopolistic industry, at least temporarily, into a monopolistic one. Many kinds of in-between arrangements have also been utilized, many of them designed to make it possible for the firms to live and let live: price leadership arrangements under which one company in the industry, in effect, is delegated the task of making pricing decisions that others are informally committed to follow; implicit or explicit agreements allocating geographic areas among the different firms; and so on.

Because of this rich variety of behavior patterns it is not surprising that economists have been unable to construct one or even a few models that encompass all oligopolistic activity. Yet this should not be taken to imply that oligopoly theory is virtually nonexistent. On the contrary, it contains many remarkable pieces of analysis. The first really sophisticated work of mathematical economics, written by A. A. Cournot, in France in 1838, contained a highly illuminating model of oligopoly, which still occupies a significant place in the literature. Outstanding mathematicians, notably the great John von Neumann, have since occupied themselves with the subject. Their highly instructive results have helped us understand the behavior of some oligopolists. But they have not closed the books on the theory of oligopoly.

THE KINKED DEMAND CURVE MODEL

To exemplify the many standard models of oligopoly, we start by describing one that is designed to account for stickiness in oligopolistic pricing, meaning that prices in an oligopolistic market change far less frequently than do prices in a competitive market.[2] The model makes use of two different demand curves representing two different but relevant conditions. One curve

[2]Variants of this model were constructed by Hall and Hitch in England and by Sweezy in the United States. See R. L. Hall and C. J. Hitch, "Price Theory and Business Behavior," *Oxford Economic Papers,* No. 2, May 1939, and P. M. Sweezy, "Demand Under Conditions of Oligopoly," *Journal of Political Economy*, vol. 47, August 1939.

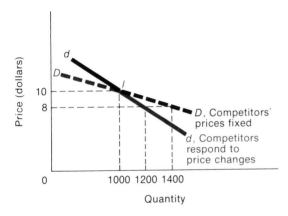

FIGURE 22–5

OLIGOPOLY AND STICKY PRICES

It has been suggested that oligopolists are deterred from changing prices frequently because they fear the reactions of their rivals. If they raise prices, they will lose many customers to competitors because the competitors will not match the price increase. (Elastic demand curve DD therefore applies to price increases.) But if they cut prices, competitors will be forced to match the price cut, so that price cut will not bring many new customers. (The inelastic demand curve dd applies to price cuts.) Thus, the demand curve facing the firm is the kinked, red curve Dld, which discourages price changes in either direction.

represents the quantities a given oligopolistic firm can sell at different prices *if competitors match its price moves,* and the other demand curve represents what happens when competitors stubbornly *stick to their initial price levels.*

Point *I* in Figure 22–5 represents the initial price and output of our firm; that is, 1000 units at $10 each. Through that point pass two demand curves: *DD,* which represents our company's demand if competitors keep their prices fixed, and *dd,* the curve indicating what happens when competitors match our firm's price cuts or price increases. The *DD* curve is the more elastic (flatter) of the two, and a moment's thought indicates why this should be so. If our firm cuts its price from its initial level of $10 to, say, $8, and if competitors do not match this cut, we would expect our firm to get a larger number of customers away from its rivals (its demand will jump to 1400) than it would if its competitors responded by also reducing their prices (its demand will rise to only 1200). Conversely, when it raises its price, our firm may expect a larger loss of sales if its rivals fail to match its increase, which the reader may readily verify by observing the relative steepness (inelasticity) of the curve *dd* in Figure 22–5.

How does this relate to sticky oligopolistic prices? Here our firm's fears and expectations must be brought into the matter. The hypothesis of those who designed this model was that a typical oligopolistic firm has good reason to fear the worst, whether it raises or lowers its prices. If it lowers its prices and its rivals do not, its sales will seriously cut into its competitors' volume, and so the rivals will *have* to match the price cut in order to protect themselves. The inelastic demand curve, *dd,* will therefore apply if our firm decides on a price reduction (points below and to the right of point *I*). On the other hand, if our company chooses to *increase* its price, management will fear that its rivals will continue to sit at their old price levels, calmly collecting the customers that have been driven to them. Thus, if our company assumes that when it raises its price there will be no competitive price response, the relevant demand curve for price increases will be *DD*. In sum, our firm will figure that it will face a segment of the elastic demand curve *DD* if it raises its price and a segment of the inelastic demand curve *dd* if it decreases its price. Its true demand curve will then be given by the heavy red line. For obvious reasons, this is called a kinked demand curve.

In these circumstances, it will pay management to vary its price only under extreme provocation, that is, only if there is an enormous change in its costs. For the kinked demand curve represents a "heads you lose, tails you lose" proposition in terms of any potential price change. If it raises its price, the firm will lose many customers (demand is elastic), if it lowers its price, the increase in volume will be comparatively small (demand is inelastic).

If this is in fact the way oligopolists feel about their competitors' behavior, it is easy to see why they may be reluctant to make frequent price changes. We can also understand why they may be willing to delegate the position of price leadership to some one firm in their industry, for the price leader can, in times of inflation for instance, raise prices when it thinks it appropriate, confident that it will not be left out on a limb (a kink?) by others' unwillingness to follow.

There may well be other reasons for price stickiness under oligopoly. For example, management undoubtedly realizes that interdependence means that the consequences of its actions are unforeseeable. If a firm's managers feel they can live with their current prices, they may prefer to leave matters calm rather than to stir up their rivals and initiate a sequence of events whose outcome they cannot predict.

THE GAME-THEORY APPROACH

Game theory, contributed in 1944 by mathematician John von Neumann (1903–1957) and economist Oskar Morgenstern (1902–1977), adopts a more abstract and a more imaginative approach than any other analysis of oligopoly. It attacks the issue of interdependence directly by assuming that rather than trying to outguess the strategies and reactions of competitors, each firm's managers proceed on the assumption that their rivals are extremely ingenious decision makers. Accordingly, managers determine their firms' optimal defensive counterstrategy since they believe their opponents will always adopt the most profitable moves and countermoves.

The term game theory is used to imply that the analysis is relevant to many types of rivalry—in business, in war, in the playing of games, and even in politics. Each oligopolist is seen as a competing player in a business game. In fact, much of the game-theoretic analysis has focused on an oligopoly of two firms—a *duopoly*.

Two fundamental concepts of game theory are the strategy and the payoff matrix. A strategy represents an operational plan for one of the participants. In simplest form it may refer to just one of a participant's possible decisions, for example, "I will add to my product line a car with a TV set that the driver can also watch," or "I will cut the price of my car to $3500."

A payoff matrix is illustrated in Table 22–1 for a two-person game. This matrix, read like a mileage chart, reports the payoffs that our firm will receive for each possible pair of its own and its rival's strategies. For example, if our firm selects strategy B (cut price to $3500) and its rival chooses W (offer diesel engine), we can see that our company will end up with 70 percent of the market (third column, second row).

The special case of pure rivalry, in which every addition to the payoff obtained by our firm means *exactly* an equal loss for its competitor, and vice versa, is referred to as a *constant sum game*. In these circumstances, our firm's returns as well as our competitor's must always add up to the same fixed total. In the constant sum case, the payoff matrix has the convenient property of telling us just about all we need to know about our competitor's payoff matrix as

TABLE 22–1

A PAYOFF MATRIX

		Rival's Strategy	
	U	V	W
			Offer
	Set Price	Set Price	Diesel
	at $4000	at $3000	Engine
A: Install TV set	80	35	30
B: Cut price to $3500	28	45	70
C: Offer three-year loan	60	50	90

Our Strategy (row label)

The entries represent the share of market our firm will receive under any combination of strategies offered by itself and its competitor.

well as the payoffs of our own firm. For it lets us know how our rival's payoff must vary from strategy combination to strategy combination. Given the market share of one firm, we can immediately deduce the competitor's payoff by subtraction. For example, if the matrix tells us that our firm's market share will be 70 percent of the total, we know that the competitor's market share must be 30 percent.

We can now begin to discuss optimal strategy choices for the two firms. Since our firm is in direct conflict with the other firm, we know that our rival will try to keep our profits as low as possible, and vice versa. Thus, in evaluating its strategies, the management of our firm may reason as follows: If I select strategy A, the worst that can happen to me is that my competitor will select counterstrategy W, which would cut our market to its minimum level, 30 percent, the red number in the first row of the payoff matrix. Similarly, if I utilize strategy B, the outcome we must be prepared for is 28 percent, which is the (red) minimum payoff to that strategy. Finally, if I use strategy C, my competitor can damage me most by using strategy V, which gives me 50 percent.

What, if anything, can management do to maximize its chances for success, given the inevitable consequences of its choices? Game theory suggests that it can select the strategy (in this case, strategy C) whose minimum payoff is higher than the minimum payoff for any other strategy. This is called the *maximin* criterion— one seeks the *maximum* of the *minimum* payoffs to the various strategies, the highest of the red entries. In this case, the maximin payoff is 50 percent and leads, as just noted, to the choice of strategy C by our firm.

There is, of course, a great deal more to game theory than we have been able to suggest in the preceding paragraphs. We have only sought to suggest a little of its flavor. Game theory also provides, for example, an illuminating analysis of coalitions, indicating, for cases involving more than two firms, which firms would do well to align themselves together against which others.

The theory of games has also proved to be a useful way of looking at a variety of complicated problems outside the realm of oligopoly theory. It has been employed in management training programs and has entered into the discussions that take place in a number of private and government agencies. It is used in political science and in formulating military strategy. In terms of its applicability, it has been helpful primarily as a new way of looking at intractable problems rather than as a method for finding solutions. It has been presented here to offer the reader a glance at the type of work that is taking place on the frontiers of economic analysis and to suggest how economists think about complex analytical problems.

ADVERTISING, OLIGOPOLY, AND PURE COMPETITION

Early in the chapter we noted that although advertising seems obviously to be an instrument of competition between firms, the competitive agricultural industry spends far less on this activity than does the oligopolistic (and therefore "less competitive") automobile industry. From the analysis in this chapter we can now explain this apparent contradiction rather easily. The explanation depends on an understanding of the horizontal demand curve of the firm under pure competition and the direct interdependence of the decisions of oligopolistic firms.

Remember that the pure competitor's horizontal demand curve means that the individual firm in a competitive industry is so insignificant a part of the total that it can sell as much or as little as it wants (two truckloads or three or four) without reducing the price or running out of customers. Given this fact, there is absolutely no reason why the firm should spend money advertising.

Now let's compare this with what happens in an oligopolistic industry. A big rise in General Motors' advertising is likely to hurt Ford, and certainly will not go unnoticed by Ford's management. Ford is almost certain to respond. Much of advertising expenditure represents the strategy of one giant oligopolistic firm against another, with each adopting behavior calculated to protect itself most effectively against the strategic options of the other. Because the prosperity of one oligopolistic firm depends on the behavior of the other, and because they are engaged in a very earnest competitive game, each must advertise to protect itself against what the other can do to it.

This brings out an important difference between the sort of rivalry that characterizes an industry under pure competition and the sort that one finds under oligopoly:

Oligopolistic competition is an active process of rival moves and countermoves, in which one firm's victory is likely to be at the expense of another. Oligopolistic competition can be intense and aggressive.

Under pure competition, on the other hand, rivalry is entirely passive. Each firm is so small and insignificant that no one of them cares what another does. Yet this passive competition is quite effective. The sheer weight of numbers ties the hands of any management of a purely competitive firm and deprives it of any opportunity to ''exploit'' consumers.

SUMMARY

1. An industry is said to operate under pure competition if it contains many small firms selling identical products and if firms can enter or leave the industry without impediment, whenever it pays them to do so.
2. The competitive firm has a horizontal demand curve because its output is so small a proportion of the total industry's output that a change in its output cannot affect industry price.
3. Profit maximization by competitive firms requires that price and marginal cost be equal.
4. In long-run equilibrium under pure competition, the firm will not advertise, it will produce the output at which average cost is lowest, and it will earn zero economic profit, that is, no more than the opportunity cost of its capital.
5. Under monopolistic competition, each firm's products differ from every other firm's products in brand name, quality, packaging, and so on; that is, each firm has a partial ''monopoly'' of some product characteristics.
6. The demand curve of the firm under monopolistic competition will normally have a negative slope, and in long-run equilibrium its output will be less than it will at the point where average cost is lowest. Thus, such a firm is said to have ''excess capacity'' and to have an average cost that is ''unnecessarily high.''

7. An oligopolistic industry is composed of a few large firms all selling identical or similar products.
8. Under oligopoly each firm carefully watches the major decisions of its rivals and will often plan counterstrategies. As a result, rivalry under oligopoly is much more vigorous and direct than it is under pure competition—and the outcome is difficult to predict.

CONCEPTS FOR REVIEW

Industry
Firm
Pure competition
Zero economic profit
Opportunity cost of capital
Monopolistic competition

Oligopoly
Sticky price
Kinked demand curve
Game theory
Strategy
Payoff matrix

QUESTIONS FOR DISCUSSION

1. How many real industries can you name that are oligopolistic? How many that operate under monopolistic competition? Pure competition? Which of these is hardest to find in reality? Why do you think this is so?
2. Consider some of the products that are widely advertised on TV. By what kind of firm is each produced—a perfectly competitive firm, an oligopolistic firm, or what? How many major products can you think of that are *not* advertised on TV? Why are some "indispensable" products, such as coal and electricity, rarely—if ever—advertised?
3. In what ways may the small retail sellers of the following products differentiate their goods from those of their rivals to make themselves monopolistic competitors: hamburgers, gasoline, aspirin, facial tissues?
4. Pricing of securities on the stock market is said to be done under conditions in many respects similar to pure competition. The auto industry is an oligopoly. How often do you think the price of a share of Ford Motor Company's common stock changes? How about the price of a Ford Pinto? How would you explain the difference?
5. Suppose General Motors hires a popular movie star to advertise its compact automobiles. The campaign is very successful and the company increases its share of the compact-car market substantially. What is Ford likely to do?
6. Using game-theory rationale, set up a payoff matrix similar to one Ford's management might employ in the above problem.
7. By working much harder, Farmer Jones manages to double his production and sales of corn. What is Farmer Bones likely to do?

23

The Industry under Pure Competition and Monopoly

In the preceding chapter we considered *the individual firms* that exist within an industry, examining in particular how the degree of competition or monopoly power in the industry affects a firm's prices and output levels. In this chapter we will examine the net results *for the industry* of the firm's behavior.

First, though, a qualification must be expressed about the apparently neat distinction between a firm and an industry.

DEFINITION
An *industry* is a collection of *all* the firms that supply a given set of identical or very similar goods in some market.

By definition, then, a monopolistic firm and a monopolistic industry are one and the same thing. In other words, the discussion of pure monopoly would have been just as appropriate in the last chapter as it is in this chapter. It is included here because, as we will see, the most useful insights about the effects of monopoly are obtained by comparing it with the competitive *industry,* not the competitive firm. For example, it is often alleged that a monopoly tends to restrict its output. But that does not mean that a giant monopolist's output will be smaller than that of a tiny competitive firm. Rather, it means that the monopolist's output can be expected to be smaller than that *of a comparable competitive industry.* Thus, to test this proposition we must compare industry with industry, not firm with firm.

The material presented in this chapter proceeds as follows. First, we will review the supply—demand equilibrium of a competitive industry. Second, we will show how cost determines the supply curve of a competitive industry. Third, we will investigate the forces that drive the price and output of a competitive industry toward their equilibrium levels. Fourth, we will examine the equilibrium of a monopoly industry, showing that where costs and demands are similar to those of a competitive industry, unregulated monopoly will tend to produce less and charge more than the competitive industry. And finally, we will show that even a monopoly cannot generally pass *all* of a tax on to its customers by raising the price of its product by an amount equal to the tax.

APPLICATION: TAX SHIFTING AND POLLUTION CONTROL

We begin by examining a real-life problem, which is only one of many possible examples that could illustrate how the analysis in this chapter can be helpful in understanding everyday economic problems.

As will be pointed out in Chapter 34 on environmental protection, most economists maintain that one effective way to control pollution is to charge the polluter heavily, making him pay increasing amounts to the pollution-control agency the more pollution he emits. By making it sufficiently expensive for firms to pollute, it is said, they will be induced to find ways to reduce their emissions.

A frequent response to this proposal is that it simply will not work when the polluting firm has a lot of monopoly power. "The monopolist can just raise the price of his product, pass the pollution charge on to his customers, and go on polluting as before, with total impunity." After

all, if a firm is a monopoly, what is to stop it from raising its price when it is hit by a pollution charge?

Yet observation of the behavior of firms faced with pollution charges suggests that there is something wrong with this objection. If the polluter could escape the penalty completely unscathed, we would expect him to acquiesce or to put up only token opposition to it. Yet wherever a law has been proposed imposing a charge on the emission of pollutants (or any other financial incentive against environmental damage), the outcry of the potentially affected firms has been enormous, no matter how large these companies are. The lobbyists are dispatched at once to do their best to stop the legislation. In fact, rather than agree to being charged for their emissions, the firms usually indicate a preference for direct controls that will *force* them to adopt specified processes that are less polluting than the ones they are now using. For some reason, even if they have monopoly power, the firms act as if they cannot pass the charges entirely to their customers.

The tools of this chapter will enable us to understand the true relationships between pollution charges and prices, and thus to see whether the monopolist is justified in his apparent fear that such fees cannot be passed on.

INDUSTRY DEMAND AND SUPPLY UNDER PERFECT COMPETITION

In order to get to a systematic analysis of the industry as such, it is necessary to return to the case of pure competition. Under this market form, as we know from Chapter 4, price is determined by the supply of and demand for the products of the industry. We must therefore return to the supply—demand analysis. We begin with the demand curve for the industry. We learned in the preceding chapter that no firm in a competitive industry has any power to influence price. In our grain-market example, for instance, we saw that a decision by Farmer Jones to treble his day's deliveries or to withhold them altogether is not even noticed in the market's price quotations. But let there be a 20 percent rise in *total* deliveries to the market by all farmers together and we *can* expect substantial price consequences, even under pure competition. For this reason, unlike the horizontal demand curve for the individual *firm* under pure competition, the slope of the *industry* demand curve is negative, because a substantial increase in the industry's output *can* usually be expected to affect the price that consumers are willing to pay for the product. In Figure 23–1, line *DD* represents the negatively sloping demand curve for the output of the entire industry.

We turn next to the supply curve of the competitive industry. We will show that:

It follows from the zero-profit feature of competitive equilibrium that, in the long run, the supply curve of the competitive industry is a curve of the industry's average cost (including its cost of capital).

Suppose it were otherwise; for example, that at output 130,000 units, as shown in Figure 23–1, the long-run average cost was $8.50 (point *U*), and thus fell below the corresponding point on the supply curve (point *W*). That would mean that the industry was prepared to supply an output of 130,000 units only at a price ($10) that exceeds its unit cost at that output ($8.50), including the cost of capital. Under pure competition, such a situation could not persist in the long run. The reason is that the industry would expect, at that output level, a profit that exceeds the cost of capital by $1.50 per unit ($10 − $8.50). And the entry of new firms would soon eliminate these supplementary profits, driving the price at which 130,000 units of output is supplied down to the level of average costs. Note that the entry of new firms (or the exit of old ones) in response to profits or losses in the industry is the key influence that drives down the competitive industry's supply curve to its av-

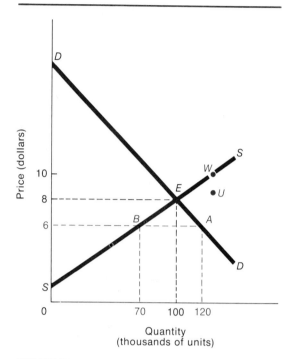

FIGURE 23–1

SUPPLY–DEMAND EQUILIBRIUM OF A COMPETITIVE INDUSTRY
The only equilibrium combination of price and quantity is a price of $8 and the quantity of 100,000 units, at which the supply curve *SS* and the demand curve *DD* intersect (point *E*). At a lower price, such as $6, quantity demanded—120,000 units (as shown by point *A* on the demand curve) will be higher than the 70,000 unit supply (point *B*). Thus the price will be driven back up toward the $8 equilibrium. The opposite will happen at a price such as $10, which is above equilibrium.

erage cost in the long run. In the short run, when the number of firms has not had time to change, the industry supply curve is simply given by the sum of the supply curves of the individual firms in the industry, and these firms may obtain either profits or losses. But in the long run that cannot happen, because the number of firms will change in response to profit opportunities in that industry and elsewhere.

Normally, we expect the competitive industry's long-run supply curve to be upward sloping, because of increasing average costs (diminishing returns) as the size of its output expands. But it is also possible for the supply curve of a competitive industry to have a *negative slope.* A negative slope will occur when the average cost of supplying output decreases as the volume of *industry* output expands (economies of scale for the industry). Chapter 20 discussed the way that large-scale equipment and other technological advantages can reduce the costs of the firm when it produces a larger volume of output. The same may be true of an entire industry. For example, if there is an increase in coal mining activity by all the mines in an area, it may become profitable to build a railroad line to serve them more economically than can be done by trucks. No one mine by itself may be big enough to make the construction of the rail line profitable, but when all the mines expand simultaneously, each firm will find that its transportation bill will become smaller.

In a competitive industry, the pressure of competition will force suppliers to pass the resulting saving back to consumers, so that the price charged by suppliers will fall when output expands. That is, the supply curve must have a negative slope when the industry benefits from economies of scale such as were just described. To see why the saving must be passed on to consumers under pure competition, we must briefly summarize the entire process whereby output expands in such an industry. Suppose that the coal industry is competitive and is initially in equilibrium, with price just covering cost. Then there is an increase in demand for coal. Initially, this will cause a (temporary) price rise, which will induce each mine operator to expand production. That, in time, will induce the construction of the new rail line, and thereby reduce costs. With higher prices and lower costs than before, the mines will now bring in large profits. But as we know, under pure competition such profits will attract more firms into the industry. New mines will be opened, and as

their product flows into the market, prices will be forced downward until they once again only cover costs, thus passing the cost saving to the consuming public.

SUPPLY–DEMAND EQUILIBRIUM OF THE COMPETITIVE INDUSTRY

DEFINITION
The *supply–demand equilibrium* is the point at which the supply and demand curves intersect.

Point *E* on Figure 23–1 is the equilibrium point for the competitive industry because it is only at that combination of price, $8, and quantity, 100,000 units, that neither purchasers nor sellers will be motivated to upset matters. For at a price of $8, the amount sellers are willing to offer will be exactly equal to the amount consumers would like to purchase.

Is there any reason to expect that price will actually reach or at least approximate this equilibrium level? The answer is yes. To see why this is so, we must contrast the case of equilibrium with the situation in which price is not at its equilibrium level; say, it takes a lower value, such as $6. At that price, our diagram tells us that the quantity supplied, 70,000 units, will be lower than the equilibrium value. But at that lower price the quantity demanded, 120,000 units, will exceed its equilibrium level. Thus, quantity demanded will be greater than the quantity offered for sale on the market, and we cannot expect price to remain at the nonequilibrium level of $6.

In the situation shown in Figure 23–1, prices and quantities can, in fact, be expected to move toward their equilibrium levels. For where price is below its equilibrium level, say at $6, because of the position of the supply and demand curves, quantity demanded (120,000 units) must *exceed* quantity supplied (70,000 units). We may anticipate that unsatisfied buyers will offer to pay higher prices. So the market price will be forced *upward,* in the direction of its equilibrium value, $8. Similarly, if we begin with a price such as $10, which is higher than equilibrium, we may readily verify that quantity supplied will exceed quantity demanded. Under these circumstances, frustrated sellers are likely to reduce their prices, so price will be forced downward. In the circumstances depicted in Figure 23–1, then, there is in effect a magnet at the equilibrium price of $8 that will pull the actual price in its direction if for some reason the actual price starts out at some other level.

In practice, there are few, if any, cases in which competitive markets, over a very long period of time, seem not to have moved toward equilibrium prices. Thus, in the long run, matters seem to work out as depicted in Figure 23–1. But there have been periods, sometimes of distressingly long duration, when the "bottom has dropped out" of some nearly competitive markets—the stock exchanges and the markets for standardized farm products. During such market "crashes," it certainly seemed as if prices were not moving toward an equilibrium.

Yet, as we have just seen, there are powerful forces that do move prices toward equilibrium—toward the level at which supply and demand curves intersect. This is of fundamental importance for economic analysis, for if there were no such forces, prices in the real world would usually bear little relationship to equilibrium prices. We would have little reason to study supply–demand analysis. Fortunately, as we have seen, the required equilibrating forces do exist.

WHY WE CANNOT ANALYZE THE INDUSTRY UNDER MONOPOLISTIC COMPETITION

In the last chapter we compared the behavior of the *firm* under pure competition with that of the *firm* under monopolistic competition. Later in

this chapter we will compare the behavior of the *industry* under pure competition with that of the *industry* under pure monopoly. But economic analysis contains very little, if any, analysis of the *industry* under monopolistic competition. The reason is simply that economists are not sure how to define an industry in this case. By definition, under monopolistic competition products differ. Starting with a given product, say Ivory soap, we can envision a long chain of substitutes for it, perhaps starting with other soaps that are slightly more scented, some that are still more highly scented, and so on until we get to pure perfume itself, which someone constitutionally "allergic" to baths may prefer to use as a substitute for soap. Just where in this chain can we locate the borderline between the soap industry and the scent industry? Does it even make sense to say that a firm producing industrial laundry soap is in the same industry as one producing an expensive toilet soap, while a perfume manufacturer is not? Because there are no definitive answers to questions like these, this book (like other texts) contains no explicit analysis of the monopolistically competitive industry. Yet we must not go overboard in our reservations about our ability to recognize what constitutes an industry in practice. Many industries *are* quite distinct and easy to recognize, even under monopolistic competition. Gasoline stations and fast-food shops are two clear examples.

THE PURE MONOPOLY

Pure monopoly constitutes the other end of the spectrum from perfect competition. There are, in fact, quite a few monopolies in reality: for example, the telephone company, local utility suppliers, railroads, and the postal service. Each of these is a firm that also constitutes the entire industry in markets in which they operate. Each of them is "the only supplier in town." But in practice, one does not often encounter industries (firms) that behave like the pure monopolist of economic theory. The reason is that any such firm would no doubt soon be subjected to extensive regulation or, in some countries, might simply be nationalized. Yet the monopolistic model must be studied if we are to understand just what it is the regulations may be intended to prevent.

DEFINITION

A *pure monopoly* is defined as a firm that is also an industry. It is the only supplier of some particular commodity for which there exist no close substitutes.

Only one of the phrases in the definition requires any comment. The producer of a particular brand of beer may, with a loose interpretation of the term, be said to hold a monopoly. But certainly that company does not possess much monopoly power, however one may wish to interpret the expression. It cannot, for example raise its price much above the level of other beers that consumers consider about as good. Most commodities are affected to some extent by the competition of substitutes. Fish prices may have to respond to a reduction in the selling price of poultry. The sale of steel is affected by conditions in the aluminum market, and so on. Without attempting to be precise, we therefore say that a firm is a *pure* monopoly (it constitutes the entire industry) only if there are no *close* substitutes for its product. An example is the supplier of telephone service to a particular city. But note that this is not quite true of the firm that supplies electricity to that same city, for in the heating market that firm must compete with the suppliers of fuel oil and other fuels. That is, the electricity supplier does not constitute the *entire* fuel industry.

Only a few additional steps are required to go from the supply–demand model of the competitive industry to a model of monopoly output and price setting. Suppose that, somehow, our competitive industry, with its multitude of small suppliers, is suddenly taken over by a single firm whose objective is maximization of profits.

From our competitive demand analysis, we can infer the market demand that the monopolist will face. In a similar manner, the competitive long-run supply curve, which is the industry's long-term average cost curve, as we saw on pages 436–437, tells us about the cost conditions imposed by the industry's technology.

More specifically, in Figure 23–2 we have reproduced the supply and demand curves of the original competitive industry from Figure 23–1. The demand curve for the competitive industry, *DD*, remains the demand curve facing

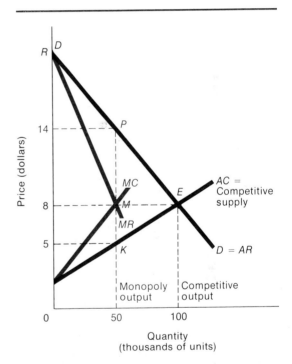

FIGURE 23–2
EQUILIBRIA OF COMPETITIVE
AND MONOPOLISTIC INDUSTRIES
Competitive equilibrium, *E,* occurs at price $8 and quantity 100,000 units, which is where the supply and demand curves intersect. The smaller monopoly output (50,000 units) occurs where the marginal cost and revenue curves meet (point *M*). The monopoly price, $14, is given by point *P* on the demand curve at the monopoly output.

the monopolist—at any given price it indicates what quantity of his product the public is willing to buy. As usual, this demand curve for the monopoly firm is also its curve of average revenue. That is, if at 100,000 units of output the product can be sold at a price of $8 per unit, then $8 is obviously the per unit revenue the monopolist receives at that output level. But now there is also a *marginal* revenue curve that we must take into consideration in examining the monopolist's profit-maximizing output decision. In Chapter 20 we saw that the firm maximizes its profit by choosing an output level at which marginal cost equals marginal revenue. That is why we now have to determine the monopoly's marginal revenue curve from its demand curve, as we did in Chapter 20. For the present we need recall only that since the average revenue (demand) curve is downward sloping, the marginal revenue curve, *MR,* will lie *below* it except at the vertical axis, as shown in the diagram.[1] In a moment, we will see how this affects the monopoly equilibrium.

The cost side of the picture is quite similar. As we have seen, if the supply curve is a *long-run* relationship for the competitive industry, it must also be a curve of long-run average cost for that industry. If technology and input costs do not change when the monopolist takes over, the industry's average costs will be unaffected by its reorganization into a monopoly. Thus the competitive long-run supply curve will simply represent for the monopoly its long-run average cost curve, now consequently labeled *AC* in the diagram.

To find the profit-maximizing output level at which marginal revenue equals marginal cost, we must derive the marginal cost curve from the average cost, as we have just done for the revenue curves. This is done in accord with the procedures described in Chapter 20. The curve *MC* in Figure 23–2 represents the marginal cost curve obtained from our curve of average costs.

Since in the diagram (as in the usual supply–demand analysis), average cost is rising when output increases, we know from the rules of Chapter 20 that the marginal cost curve must be above the average cost curve.

The *MC* and the *MR* curves intersect at point *M,* corresponding to an output level of 50,000. Consequently, an output of 50,000 is that which our monopolist will find most profitable. In order to be able to sell that amount, we see from his demand curve that he must set his price at $14 per unit, which is, therefore, the monopolist's profit-maximizing price. At that price and output, his average cost is $5 (point *K* in Figure 23–2). Therefore he will earn a profit per unit sold equal to price minus average cost, $14 − $5 = $9. He will earn a total profit over and above the cost of capital equal to his unit profit times his output, $9 × 50,000 = $450,000. This amount is *pure monopoly profit.* It is entirely above and beyond the normal return on the firm's capital and is attributable only to its monopoly power in the market.

That completes our discussion of the monopolist's price–output decision, taken by itself. But in order to draw some useful conclusions from the analysis, we must have a reference point against which the resulting price and output levels can be compared. Such a reference point is provided by the competitive equilibrium that was described earlier. Under pure competition, price and quantity are given by the intersection point, *E,* between the competitive supply and demand curves; that is, competitive output will be 100,000 and competitive price will be $8, given by the height of the point on the demand curve corresponding to that output level.

The comparison between the competitive and the monopolistic price and output levels is now immediate, at least for the case depicted in the graph. The monopolistic output level (50,000 units) is significantly lower than the competitive level of supply (100,000 units). Similarly, the monopolist's price, $14, is considerably higher than the competitive industry's $8. The analysis apparently confirms all the popular

---

[1]For a full explanation of the reasons, with detailed numerical examples, see Chapter 20, pages 384–387.

notions about the workings of a monopoly—that the monopolist will deliberately keep his output small in order to force up its market price.

It is essential to determine whether this result necessarily follows from the analysis, or whether, if the curves had been drawn somewhat differently, matters might have been reversed. For this purpose we recall again the relationship between marginal and average curves discussed in Chapter 20. We learned there (pages 386–387) that when an *average* curve has a *negative* slope, the *marginal* curve must lie *below* the average curve, just as the *MR* curve in Figure 23–2 lies below the *AR* curve. Similarly, the same proposition tells us that when an average curve has a *positive* slope, as does the *AC* curve in Figure 23–2, the corresponding marginal curve must lie *above* the average curve.[2]

Since the marginal revenue curve lies below the average revenue curve and the marginal cost curve lies above the average cost curve, the intersection point *M* between the two marginal curves must necessarily lie to the left of point *E,* the intersection point of the average curves. It follows that:

If the demand curve has a negative slope and the average cost curve has a positive slope, the monopolist's output must always be smaller, and therefore his price must be higher, than those of a competitive industry.

have just seen, sometimes also slope downhill toward the right. It is at least conceivable that if average costs decline with sufficient rapidity, the monopolistic output will be greater than that of the competitive industry. The reason, simply, is that in this case the economies that the monopolist can achieve by expanding his production (the rate of decline in his average cost curve) more than offset the effect on his profits of a reduction in price resulting from the larger output flow. In such a case policymakers may well judge that monopoly is the more effective way to serve the public interest, and it is customary to refer to such a situation as one involving natural monopoly.

DEFINITION
A *natural monopoly* is an industry in which economies of scale and other related forms of saving make it cheaper to produce when there is one firm rather than several.

Many of the public utilities are permitted to operate as monopoly suppliers for the sort of reason just described. It is believed that their technology enables them to achieve substantial economies when they produce large quantities of output. It is therefore often considered desirable to permit these firms to obtain the cost reductions they achieve by having the entire market to themselves, and to subject them to regulatory supervision rather than breaking them up into a number of competing firms. This issue will be examined in detail in Chapter 26.

SCALE ECONOMIES AND NATURAL MONOPOLY

Now, while we generally assume that the demand (average revenue) curve will have a negative slope, the average cost curve may, as we

SOME FURTHER COMPARISONS BETWEEN MONOPOLY AND COMPETITION

Despite the exception just noted, the diagrammatic analysis of the preceding section seems to indicate that there is good reason for the common view that an unregulated monopoly

[2]For extensive numerical examples and a detailed discussion of these results, you may wish to review Chapter 20, pages 384–385.

tends to produce smaller outputs and higher prices than would prevail under competition. But there is more to the matter. So far, our analysis rests on a direct transition from a competitive to a monopolistic demand curve, and from the competitive supply curve to the monopolistic average cost curve. In Figure 23–2, we have assumed that the demand curve of the monopolist will simply be the same as that of the competitive industry. But is this necessarily so? The two curves will be the same if the monopolist does nothing about his demand, but that hardly seems likely.

We have seen that under pure competition purchasers consider the products of all suppliers to be identical, and so no supplier has any reason to undertake any advertising expenditure. The farmer who sells wheat through one of the major markets has absolutely no motivation to spend money on advertising because his product will simply take its place anonymously in some miller's inventory. And since the farmer can sell all the wheat he wants to at the going price, advertising will in no way facilitate this selling process.

When the monopolist takes over, however, it may very well pay him to advertise. If he believes that the touch of Madison Avenue can make consumers' hearts beat faster as they rush to the market to purchase the wheat product whose virtues have been extolled on television, the monopolist will do as any large firm usually does and allocate a substantial sum of money to accomplish this feat. This will increase his costs and shift his cost curves upward. But his advertising outlays should also shift his demand curve outward. After all, that is the purpose of these expenditures. The monopolist's demand and cost curves and those of the competitive industry will then no longer be the same. The higher demand curve for the monopolist's product will perhaps induce him to expand his volume of production and to reduce the difference between the competitive and the monopo-

listic output levels indicated in Figure 23–2. It will also, however, induce him to charge even higher prices.

Similarly, the advent of a monopoly may produce other shifts in the average cost curve. On the one hand, the sheer size of the monopolist's organization may lead to higher costs through bureaucratic inefficiencies, coordination problems, and the like. On the other hand, the monopolist may have greater bargaining power in his dealings with input suppliers and so he may be able to get labor, raw materials, and other inputs at prices lower than those paid by the competitive industry. He may also be able to eliminate certain types of duplication that are unavoidable for a number of small independent firms: one purchasing agent may do the job where many buyers were needed before, and a few large machines may replace many small items of equipment in the hands of the competitive firms. If the unification achieved by monopoly does succeed in producing a downward shift in the average cost curve, monopoly output will thereby also tend to move closer to the competitive level, and the monopoly price will tend to be moved down closer to the competitive price.

MONOPOLY AND THE ALLOCATION OF RESOURCES

Suppose, however, that we encounter a situation that corresponds relatively closely to the one depicted in Figure 23–2. The monopolist's output is lower and his price higher than that of the competitor. Let's see why the economist is disquieted by these differences.

First, there is the issue of the wealth the monopolist is able to accumulate. Economists may well be disturbed if the monopolist's higher price enables him to grow rich at the consumer's expense. This is perhaps one of the main reasons for the strength of public reaction against monopoly. Regulation of the natural monopolies invariably involves some sort of ceiling on the earnings of the company for precisely this reason.

In addition, we may well suspect that the monopolist's "artificial" restriction of output is likely to lead to a misallocation of resources. The output of the monopolist's product may be too small from the viewpoint of the consumers' best interests. This is matched by the artificially high prices set by the monopolist. These high prices distort consumer demand. Consumers are induced by the high prices of the monopolist's goods to buy larger quantities of competitively produced goods and smaller quantities of the monopolist's products than they would if the relative prices in the two types of industries simply reflected comparative production costs, undistorted by monopolistic pressures toward artificially high prices for the monopoly products. (This is a topic to which we will return in Chapters 25 and 31.)

MONOPOLY AND THE SHIFTING OF POLLUTION CHARGES

We can now return to the practical application of this chapter's analytic tools—the effectiveness of pollution charges as a means to reduce emissions by polluting firms. Recall that the issue is whether the monopoly can raise its prices enough to make up for any pollution tax, thus shifting these charges entirely to its customers and evading them altogether, thereby preventing the program from working.

The answer is that to some extent any firm or industry can, usually, shift *part* of a tax to its customers. We saw in Chapter 4 that this is true under the supply–demand mechanism that determines the prices of the competitive industry. Economists argue that this shifting is a

proper part of a pollution control program, whose aim is to induce consumers to alter their demand from goods that are highly polluting to goods that are not. Surely, a significant increase in taxes on leaded gasoline with, perhaps, a simultaneous decrease in the taxes on unleaded gasoline will send more motorists to the unleaded-gas pumps, and that will reduce dangerous lead emissions into the atmosphere.

But more important for our discussion here is the other side of the matter. While some part of a pollution charge is usually shifted to the consumer, even under pure competition, *the seller will usually be stuck with some part of the charge, even if he is a monopolist.* Why? Because of the negative slope of his demand curve. If he raises his price he will lose customers, and that will eat into his profits. He will then always lose less by absorbing some of the charge himself than he will if he tries to pass all of it on to his customers. This is illustrated in Figures 23–3(a) and (b) on the following page.

In the first of these diagrams we show the monopolist's demand, marginal revenue, and marginal cost curves. As in Figure 23–2, equilibrium output is again 50,000 units—the point at which marginal revenue equals marginal cost. And price is again $14—the point on the demand curve corresponding to 50,000 units of output (point A).

Now, let a charge of $5 per unit be put on the firm's polluting output, shifting the marginal cost curve up uniformly to the curve labeled "MC plus tax" in Figure 23–3(b). Then the profit-maximizing output falls to 37,000 units, for there MR = MC + tax charge. The new output, 37,000 units, is lower than the precharge output, 50,000 units. Thus, the charge will lead the monopolist to restrict his polluting output. The price of his product will rise to $15.50 (point B), the point on the demand curve corresponding to 37,000 units of output. But the rise in price from $14 to $15.50 is only a fraction of the $5 pollution charge per unit. Thus:

443

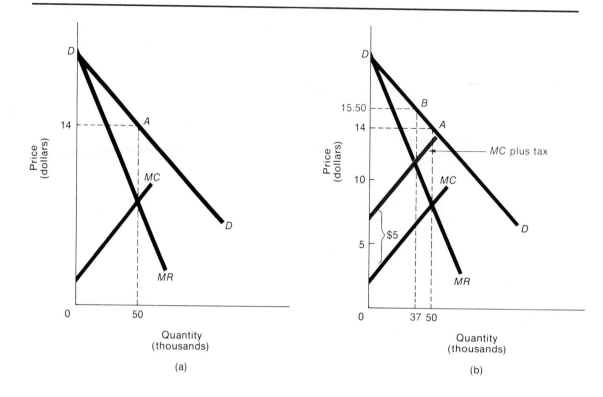

FIGURE 23–3

MONOPOLY PRICE AND OUTPUT WITH AND WITHOUT A POLLUTION TAX

Part (a) shows the monopoly equilibrium without a tax, with price equal to $14 and quantity equal to 50. In part (b) a $5 tax is levied on each unit of polluting output. This raises the marginal cost curve by the amount of the tax, from the black to the red line. As a result, the output at which $MC = MR$ falls from 50,000 to 37,000. Price rises from $14 to $15.50. Note that this $1.50 price rise is less than the $5 tax, so the monopolist will be stuck with the remaining $3.50 of the tax.

The pollution charge *does* hurt the polluter even if he is a profit-maximizing monopolist, and it *does* force him to cut his polluting outputs.

No wonder the polluter's lobbyists fight it so vehemently! Polluters realize that they often will be far better off with direct controls that cause them to suffer a financial penalty *only* if they are caught in a violation, prosecuted, and con-victed—and even then the fines are often negli-gible, as we will see in Chapter 34.

SUMMARY

1. While the demand curve of the competitive firm is horizontal, the demand curve of the competitive industry generally has a negative slope, meaning that a fall in price is needed to induce an increase in quantity demanded.
2. In the long run, the supply curve of the competitive industry is the same as the curve of average costs, including the cost of capital.
3. The equilibrium price and quantity sold within a competitive industry is given by the point of intersection between its supply and demand curves.
4. If the demand curve has a negative slope and the supply curve has a positive slope, a price above the equilibrium level will make quantity supplied greater than quantity demanded, and this will drive price back down toward its equilibrium level. The opposite will happen if price starts out below equilibrium level.
5. Under monopolistic competition, because products are differentiated, it is difficult to define the products that should be included in the industry.
6. A monopoly maximizes its profit by producing an output at which its marginal revenue equals its marginal cost. Its price is given by the point on its demand curve corresponding to that output.
7. In a monopolistic industry, if demand and cost curves are the same as those of a competitive industry, and if the demand curve has a negative slope and the supply curve a positive slope, output will be lower and monopoly price will be higher than those of the competitive industry.
8. Advertising may enable the monopolist to shift his demand curve above that of a comparable competitive industry's, and through economies such as large-scale input purchases, he may be able to shift his cost curves below those of a competitive industry.
9. If a tax per unit of output is imposed on the product of a profit-maximizing monopoly, that monopoly will raise its price, but normally not by the full amount of the tax. That is, the monopolist will end up paying part of the tax.

CONCEPTS FOR REVIEW

Industry
Supply–demand equilibrium
Pure monopoly

Natural monopoly
Shifting of pollution charges

QUESTIONS FOR DISCUSSION

1. Suppose *every* firm in a competitive industry doubles its output. Since each firm's demand curve is horizontal, price should remain unchanged. But because the industry's demand curve has a negative slope, price must fall when output doubles. Can you reconcile these two contradictory conclusions? (*Hint:* Which curves will shift and by how much?)
2. Suppose a monopoly industry produces less output than a similar competitive industry. Discuss why this may be considered "socially undesirable."
3. Which of the following industries are pure monopolies?
   a. the only supplier of water in an isolated desert town
   b. the only supplier of Exxon gas in town
   c. the only supplier of fuel oil in town
   Explain your answers.

4. Firm A produces pencils. Firm B produces pens. Firm C produces auto-
    mobiles. Firm D produces trucks. Firm E produces both cars and trucks.
    Would you say firms A and B should be considered as belonging to the
    same industry? Why or why not? (*Hint:* The products serve similar
    purposes but are produced by different firms.) Should firms C and D be
    considered as belonging to the same industry? Why or why not? (*Hint:* Do
    trucks and cars compete for the same customers?)
5. Suppose a tax of $5 is levied on each item sold by a monopolist, and as a
    result he decides to raise his price by exactly $5. Why may this decision
    be against his own best interest?

five

Big Business
and
Public Policy

24

The Corporation
and the Stock Market

Stocks and bonds provide millions of investors with the chance to earn generous returns on their savings, or, sometimes, to lose part or even all of the money they have put into "the market." From another perspective, stocks and bonds provide funds needed by the nation's business firms—funds that help finance much of their investment. In this chapter we describe the different types of firms that make up the U.S. economy and indicate how these businesses go about financing themselves. We then discuss the various types of securities that corporate firms offer to investors, the choices open to people who want to invest in corporate and other securities, the workings of the stock and bond markets, and, finally, the economic role of speculation.

The stock market is really something of an enigma. No other economic activity is reported in such detail in so many newspapers and followed with such concern by so many people; yet no activity seems to have been so successful in eluding those who devote themselves to predicting its future. There is no lack of people who are expert in analyzing individual stocks and who are prepared to evaluate the future of one stock versus that of another. And usually they are paid well for these labors. But there are very real questions about what they are able to deliver. For example, Burton G. Malkiel of Princeton University reported the following results from a study he conducted:

> We wrote to nineteen major Wall Street firms engaged in fundamental analysis. . . . They are among the most respected names in the investment business.
>
> We requested—and received—past earnings predictions on how these firms felt earnings for specific companies would behave over both a one-year and a five-year period. These estimates . . . were . . . compared with actual results to see how well the analysts forecast short-run and long-run earnings changes.
>
> Bluntly stated, the careful estimates of security analysts (based on industry studies, plant visits, etc.) do little, if any, better than those that would be obtained by simple extrapolation of past trends.
>
> For example . . . the analysts' estimates were compared [with] the assumption that every company in the economy would enjoy a growth in earnings of about 4 percent over the next year (approximately the long-run rate of growth of the national income). It turned out that . . . this naïve forecasting model . . . would make smaller errors in forecasting long-run earnings growth than . . . [did] the forecasts of the analysts.
>
> When confronted with the poor record of their five-year growth estimates, the security analysts honestly, if sheepishly, admitted that five years ahead is really too far in advance to make reliable projections. They protested that while long-term projections are admittedly important, they really ought to be judged on their ability to project earnings changes one year ahead.
>
> Believe it or not, it turned out that their one-year forecasts were even worse than their five-year projections.[1]

[1]Burton G. Malkiel, *A Random Walk Down Wall Street* (New York: W. W. Norton & Company, Inc., 1973), pages 140–41.

Later in this chapter we will be in a position to give the explanation many economists offer for this poor performance record.

FIRMS IN THE UNITED STATES

It is customary to divide firms into three groups: corporations, partnerships, and individual proprietorships (businesses having a single owner). To understand how important corporations are in the economy, consider that annual sales of corporations amount to more than 70 percent of GNP in the United States. Almost all large American firms are corporations. Exxon and General Motors each sold over $54 billion in 1977, and AT&T, Ford, Texaco, and Mobil each sold over $27 billion. The sales of these six firms alone amount to more than the GNP of any of the following countries: Australia, Austria, Belgium, Canada, the Netherlands, Sweden, Switzerland and many, many more.

But while economic power resides in the corporations, this form of business organization actually constitutes a *minority* of American business firms, measured in terms of the total number of enterprises. The reason is that most firms are small. Even a large proportion of the corporations are quite small—more than half of them have total assets (cash and physical property) worth less than $100,000. But by far the greatest number of firms (counting all firms large and small, and including the corner grocery store and shoe repair shop) are proprietorships. Similarly, many or most family farms are proprietorships.

Of the more than 11 million (!) business firms in the United States, nearly 9 million are proprietorships, somewhat more than a million are corporations, and somewhat fewer than a million are partnerships. Thus, just as is true of the income of individuals:

A very small proportion of American firms accounts for a very large share of U.S. business—

obviously, business is not distributed equally among firms.

This result is brought out strikingly by *Fortune* magazine's annual listing of the largest American firms, their assets, and their volume of business. Taken together, in 1977 the 500 largest industrial corporations—that is, a negligible proportion of America's more than 11 million firms—had over one trillion dollars in sales amounting to nearly 60 percent of the nation's GNP in that year.

At the other end of the spectrum, the nation's small business firms have a disproportionately small share of U.S. business. These small firms have earnings that are not only relatively low but that are also very risky, risky in the sense that the average new firm does not last very long—its average life is reported to be less than 7 years. When making economic decisions it is not only the buyer who has to beware!

PROPRIETORSHIPS

Just what are the three basic forms of organization of business firms, and what induces organizers of a firm to choose one of these forms rather than another?

DEFINITION
A *proprietorship* is a business firm owned by a single person.

The proprietorship is the form of business organization involving the fewest legal complications. A single individual simply decides to go into business and opens up a new firm or takes over an existing firm. Aside from special regulations, such as health requirements for a restaurant or zoning restrictions that limit business activity to particular geographical areas, the individual does not need anyone's permission or authorization to go into business.

This is one of the main advantages for many small business people of the proprietorship form of organization. But probably its main attraction is the fact that in the proprietorship the owner can be his or her own boss and the firm's sole decision maker. No partners or stockholders have to be consulted when the owner wants to expand or change the company's product line or modify the firm's advertising policy.

A proprietorship also has tax advantages, particularly compared with the corporation. The proprietor's income is only taxed once. If the firm were to incorporate, its income would be taxed twice—once as income of the firm (corporate income tax) and again as personal income of the owner. There are, on the other hand, two basic disadvantages of a proprietorship from the viewpoint of the firm's owners—difficulties that make it almost impossible to organize large-scale enterprises as proprietorships.

First, the owner has unlimited liability for the debts of the firm. If the company goes out of business leaving unpaid bills, the former owner can be forced to pay them out of personal savings. The owner can be made to sell the family home, private collections of stamps or paintings, or any other personal assets, no matter how unrelated to the business, so that the proceeds can be used to pay off the company's obligations. Often proprietors will guard themselves against this danger by signing away all their property to other members of their families or to others whom they feel they can trust. But such transfers are subject to federal and state gift taxes. In any event, there are many tales of tragedy that begin with the signing away of all of one's possessions—King Lear's betrayal by his daughters might well serve as the classic warning to those proprietors who are apt to be too trusting.

A second and equally basic shortcoming of the proprietorship is that it inhibits expansion of the firm by making it difficult to raise money. People are reluctant to put money into a firm over which they exercise no control. This means that the proprietorship's capital is usually no greater than the amount its owner is willing and able to put into it, plus the amount that banks or other commercial lenders are willing to provide.

SUMMARY
The three main advantages of the individual proprietorship are:

1. It leaves full control in the hands of the owner.
2. It involves little legal complication.
3. It generally subjects its owner to lower taxes.

Its two main disadvantages are:

1. The unlimited liability of the owner for the obligations of the company.
2. The difficulty of increasing the amount of funds that can be raised for the firm.

Most small retail firms, farms, and many small factories are run as proprietorships.

PARTNERSHIPS

DEFINITION
A *partnership* is a firm whose ownership is shared by a *fixed number* of proprietors.

Measured in terms of the amount of their capital, partnerships tend to be larger than proprietorships but smaller than corporations, though the largest partnerships greatly exceed the smallest corporations in terms of both their financing and their influence. The most prestigious of law firms and investment banks include partnerships among them. When you call a law firm and are greeted by "Smith, Jones, Brown, and Pfafufnik, Good Morning," you are almost certainly being treated to a listing of the company's senior partners (the partners who own the largest share of the firm or who founded the firm).

The advantage of the partnership over the proprietorship is that it brings together the funds and the expertise of a number of persons and permits them to be combined to form a company larger than any one of the owners could have financed or managed alone. If one cannot hope to run a particular type of firm with an inventory of less than $2,000,000, a person who is not rich may be unable to get into the business without the aid of a partner.

The partnership also offers the advantage of freedom from double taxation, a benefit it shares with the proprietorship. But the partnership has disadvantages, some of them substantial. Decision making in a partnership may be harder than in any other type of firm. The single proprietor need consult no one before acting; and the corporation appoints a set of officers who are authorized to decide things for the company. But in a partnership it may be necessary for every partner to agree before any steps are taken by the firm, and this is the primary bane of this form of enterprise. A partnership has been compared to two people in a horse costume, each supplying two of the legs, each prepared to go off in a different direction, and each unable to move without the other. Furthermore, in a partnership, the individual partners have unlimited liability, meaning that they can conceivably be in danger of losing their personal possessions to pay off company debts.

Finally, the partnership suffers from unique legal complications. A partnership agreement is like a marriage contract entered into solely for the financial advantage of the participants, and so there is likely to be considerable haggling about the terms. And under the law, if a partner dies, or decides to leave the firm, or the others decide to buy that person's share in the enterprise, the partnership may have to be dissolved and haggling about the contract may start all over again.

SUMMARY
The benefits of the partnership to the owners of the firm are:

1. Access to larger quantities of capital.
2. Protection from double taxation.

Its disadvantages are:

1. The need to obtain the agreement of many if not all partners to all major decisions.
2. Unlimited liability of the partners for the obligations of the company.
3. The legal complications, including automatic dissolution of the partnership when there is *any* change in ownership.

CORPORATIONS

DEFINITION

A *corporation* is a firm that has the legal status of a fictional individual. This fictional individual is owned by a number of persons, called its stockholders, and is run by a set of elected officers (usually headed by a president) and a board of directors, whose chairman is often also in a powerful position to influence the affairs of the firm.

Because the corporation is an individual in the eyes of the law, its earnings, like those of other individuals, are taxed. This leads to double taxation of the stockholders, who also pay tax on any dividends they receive from the firm. But this disadvantage is counterbalanced by an important advantage: Any debts of the corporation are regarded as an obligation of that fictitious individual, and not as liabilities of the firm's individual stockholders. This means that the stockholders benefit from the protection of limited liability—they can lose no more than the money they have put into the firm. Creditors cannot force them to sell their personal possessions to help repay any outstanding debts incurred by the firm.

Limited liability is the main secret of the success of the corporate form of organization. Thanks to that provision, individuals from every part of the world are willing to put money into firms whose operations they do not understand and whose managements they do not know. A giant firm may produce computers, locomotives, and electrical generators; it may have, as subsidiaries, publishing houses and shoe factories. Few of its stockholders will know (or care about) all of the activities in which it is engaged. Yet each investor knows that by providing money to the firm in return for a share of its ownership, no more is risked than the amount of money provided. This has permitted corporations to obtain financing from literally millions of shareholders, each of whom receives in return a claim on the firm's profits, and, at least in principle, a portion of the company's ownership.

As already indicated, the profits of a corporation are subject to income taxation. Smaller corporations get a tax break, but the larger firms, whose total profits are high, pay a federal tax rate of 46 percent on all *net* earnings over $100,000. In addition, most states levy corporate taxes of their own, pushing the total tax rate above 50 percent. This means that a corporate investor whose personal income tax also falls into the 50 percent bracket will be left with less than 25 percent of any portion of the earnings of the firm that are paid to her in dividends. Compare this with an investor in a partnership or a proprietorship who is in the same income bracket; she will get to keep twice as high a share of company earnings.

SUMMARY

The main advantage of the corporate form of organization is *limited liability,* which enables such a firm to raise vast amounts of money from many stockholders. Its main disadvantage is the tax that must be paid on its profits.

It is worth digressing briefly to consider the economic effects of the double taxation of corporate earnings. How does it affect the firm and the individual stockholder? Does the investor end up earning less by putting money in a corporation than by putting it in a security that is about equally risky but not subject to double taxation? Paradoxically, the answer is that investors, on the average, will *not* lose anything by choosing the corporate security. The tax will not and cannot put those who buy the one type of security at a disadvantage in comparison with those who buy the other.

How is this possible? How does the effect of the additional tax on corporate stocks disappear before it reaches the stockholder? There are two processes that achieve this act of magic. First, corporations are forced to avoid those less-profitable investment opportunities that partnerships and proprietorships can afford to take on. Suppose that in 1981 the market rate of return to people who provide money to firms is 6 percent, and a new product is invented that is expected to bring a 9 percent return to a firm that manufactures it. A proprietorship can afford to produce the new item—borrowing the necessary funds at 6 percent and keeping the 3 percent additional return on the new item for itself. But a large corporation *cannot* afford to produce the new item. For in order to compete for funds, it must also pay an investor 6 percent, but it will have to earn at least 12 percent on its investments since more than half of that money will be siphoned off into taxes. Thus, the effect of double taxation is to keep corporate business out of various economic activities that offer a real earnings potential, but one that is comparatively modest. This effect may be unfortunate from the viewpoint of the efficiency of the economy, because it means that many firms are induced to stay out of activities in which it would be useful for them to take part. For instance, corporations may find it too costly to open retail outlets in slum areas or to run trains to isolated rural areas even if it would be profitable in the absence of the tax.

Second, there is another fail-safe mechanism that protects new investors in corporate stocks from earning a lower return on the average than they would on other securities of equal risk. Suppose two otherwise identical securities, A and B, each offer a return of $60 per year but

A is subject to a 50 percent tax while B is not. *Question:* If the market price of security B is $1000, what will be the market price of A? *Answer:* The price of A will be only $500, exactly half the price of security B. Why? Because since it will bring in only $30 per year after taxes, exactly half of what security A returns, investors will be willing to pay only half as much for it as they are willing to pay for the untaxed security.

Double taxation of corporate earnings tends to restrict the activities of corporate firms, keeping them out of relatively low-profit operations. However, in general, double taxation does not mean that the individual investor earns less by putting money into a corporation than by putting it into other businesses.

FINANCING CORPORATE ACTIVITY

Our discussion of the earnings of an investor in corporate securities introduces a subject of interest to millions of Americans—stocks and bonds, the financial instruments that provide funds to the corporate sector of the economy. When a corporation needs money, it can get it by printing new stocks and new bonds and selling them to people who are looking for something in which to invest their money. What enables the firm to get money in exchange for printed paper? Doesn't the process seem a bit like counterfeiting? If done improperly, there are grounds for the suspicion. But carried out appropriately, it is a perfectly rational economic process.

As long as the funds derived from a new issue of stocks and bonds are used effectively to increase the firm's capacity to produce and earn a profit, then these funds will automatically yield the means for any required repayment and for the payment of appropriate amounts of interest and dividends to the purchasers of the new bonds and stocks. But there have been times when this did not happen. It is alleged that one of the favorite practices of the more notorious nineteenth century business barons was "watering" of company stocks—the issue of stocks with little or nothing to back them up. The term is derived from the practice of some cattle dealers who would force their animals to drink large quantities of water just before bringing them to be weighed for sale.

Another major source of funds is plowback.

DEFINITION

Plowback is the portion of the profits of a corporation that management decides to keep and invest back into the firm's operations rather than paying it out directly to stockholders in the form of dividends. If a company earns $30 million after taxes and pays out $10 million in dividends, the remaining $20 million is considered plowback.

A company can also obtain money by borrowing it from banks, insurance companies, or other private firms with money to lend out. It may also sometimes borrow from a U.S. government agency either directly or with the agency's help (the agency serves as guarantor in this instance, promising to make sure the loan is repaid). For example, loans may be arranged with the help of the national defense agencies if they want a private firm to undertake the design and production of an expensive new weapons system. Small business firms, too, are eligible for various forms of assistance in borrowing.

Figure 24–1 (a pie diagram) shows the relative importance of each of the different sources of funds to U.S. corporations. It indicates that plowback is by far the most important source of corporate financing, constituting some 79 percent of the total financing to the corporate sector of the economy in 1976. This is followed by issues of new bonds, which supply 15.5 percent of the total, while new stocks supply only 5.6 percent.

When business is profitable so that management has the funds to reinvest in the company, it will often prefer plowback to other

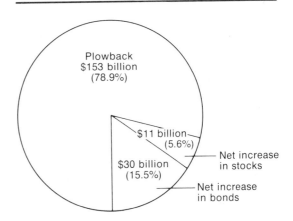

FIGURE 24–1

SOURCES OF NEW FUNDS, U.S. CORPORATIONS, 1976

Corporations in the United States get about 80 percent of their investment funds from plowback. A little over one-third of this consists of money earned by the firms as profits but not paid out to stockholders. The remaining two-thirds of plowback consists of depreciation—funds accumulated for replacement of plant, equipment, and so on, as it wears out or becomes obsolete. New stocks account for only a bit more than 5 percent of the total new funding of the corporation.

Source: *Federal Reserve Bulletin*, January 1978, pages 837–38.

sources of funding. One reason for this preference is that it is less risky to management. This source of funds does not require prior approval by the Securities and Exchange Commission (SEC), as do other sources. Moreover, plowback does not depend on the availability of eager customers for new company stocks and bonds, for an issue of such new securities turns into a disappointment if there is little demand for them when they are offered to the public. Above all, a plowback decision generally does not lead anyone to reexamine the efficiency of management's operation in the way that a new stock issue invariably does. In these instances, the SEC, potential buyers of the stock, and their professional advisers all scrutinize the company carefully.

The job of the Securities and Exchange Commission, established in 1934, is to protect the interests of people who buy securities. It requires firms that issue stocks and other securities to provide information about their financial condition, and it regulates the issue and trading of securities.

A second reason for the attractiveness of plowback is that issuing new stocks and bonds is usually an expensive and lengthy process. The company is required by the SEC to gather masses of data in its prospectus—a document describing the financial condition of the company—before the new issue is approved. Not only is this costly, but the many months of delay that are involved require the firm to wait for the funds when it needs them quickly, and also to subject the firm to the risk of a change in stock market conditions (during the period of delay a brisk demand for new stocks and bonds may conceivably dwindle or even evaporate).

Finally, plowback can offer a tax and brokerage fee advantage to stockholders. If profits are paid out in the form of dividends, many stockholders will simply reinvest the money in this company or some other. But in the process, they will pay income taxes on their dividend income, and they will also have to pay fees to their brokers when they buy stocks with the dividends. Plowback automatically reinvests (part of) the stockholders' money in the original firm, and does so without a round of income taxes and brokerage fees.

Of course, the stockholder gains from plowback of her funds only if the reinvestment is profitable—that is, only if the new investment permits a corresponding increase in company earnings. And in that case, the stockholder will ultimately have to pay taxes on those gains. But it is always a financial advantage to postpone tax payments so that the money can be employed gainfully in the meantime and, furthermore, the tax will be assessed at the lower tax paid on capital gains.

DEFINITION

A *capital gain* is an increase in the market value of a piece of property, such as a security or a house, that occurs during the period between when it is bought and when it is sold. For example, if you buy an old clock for $100, and two years later discover that it is a valuable antique and sell it for $5000, you have realized a capital gain of $4900.

A *real capital gain* is any increase in the price of a piece of property beyond the rate of increase in the average level of prices in the economy that has occurred since it was purchased. If the price of a house increases 30 percent during a period when the economy's price level has been inflated 20 percent, the real capital gain is 10 percent. The overall 30 percent rise in dollar price is called the *nominal capital gain*.

While incomes may be taxed at as high a rate as 70 percent, realized capital gains are taxed at less than half of normal income tax rates up to a maximum of 28 percent. This tax advantage has often been decried as a *loophole*—a provision that permits the wealthy to escape their share of taxes. However, at least three reasons have been offered to justify this relatively low tax rate. First, the capital gains tax applies to nominal not to real capital gains. This means that during an inflationary period one is required to pay capital gains taxes even on property whose value has not kept up with the price level—that is, on investments that have actually lost the owner purchasing power. Second, capital gains are sometimes earned over many years, so that even if the *total* increase in value over the lifetime of the investment is high, it will represent a much lower *annual* yield. If the real value of a house doubles over 25 years, the rate of return amounts to only about 3 percent a year—a rate of return that many think is low enough so that it should not be taxed very heavily. But under our system of progressive taxation, the percentage of income taxed away is higher for larger incomes. If such a long-term capital gain were taxed as ordinary income in the year the house was sold, it would therefore be taxed at a very high rate because it would add a great deal to the taxpayer's income during that year. If this is unfair, as many observers believe, then it is another argument supporting special lower rates on capital gains. Finally, it is often argued that our economy can only function effectively if people can be induced to risk their savings in new investments; and that capital gains are the rewards that induce people to take those risks.

THE FINANCING OF CORPORATE ACTIVITY: STOCKS AND BONDS

We come next to the other major sources of corporate financing besides plowback and borrowing—the corporate securities, like common stocks and bonds.

DEFINITION
A *common stock* of a corporation is a piece of paper that gives the holder of the stock a share of the ownership of the company.

For example, if a company issues 100,000 shares, then a person who owns 1000 shares actually owns 1 percent of the company and is entitled to 1 percent of the company's dividends, which are the corporation's annual payments to stockholders. The shareholder's vote counts for 1 percent of the total votes in an election of corporate officers or in a referendum on corporate policy, and he or she is entitled to 1 percent of the total number of opportunities to participate in running the corporation.

DEFINITION
A *bond* is simply an IOU by a corporation that promises to pay the holder of the piece of paper a fixed sum of money at the specified *maturity* date, and some other fixed amount of money (the *coupon* or the *interest payment*) every year up to the date of maturity.

The most obvious differences between stocks and bonds, then, are the following: (a) The purchaser of a bond *lends* money to the corporation. The purchaser of a stock *buys* a share of its ownership and receives some control over its affairs. (b) Bondholders know with a high degree of certainty how much money they will be paid if they hold on to their bonds to maturity. A bond with a face value of $1000, with an $80 coupon that matures in 1990, will provide to its owner $80 per year every year until 1990, and in addition it will repay the $1000 to the bondholder in 1990. Unless the company goes bankrupt, there is no doubt about this repayment schedule. By contrast, stockholders have no idea how much they will receive for their stocks when they sell them or how much they will receive in dividends each year in the meantime. (c) For this and other reasons, bonds are less risky than stocks. Legally, bondholders have *prior claim* on company earnings. Prior claim means that nothing is paid by the company to its stockholders until interest payments to the company's bondholders have been completed. The company must pay its interest obligations to bondholders every year if it is not to go into bankruptcy. Only after these interest payments are made can management make any dividend payments to stockholders.

Though many people accept these views, some of the differences between stocks and bonds are not as clear-cut as have just been described. Two such misconceptions are particularly worth noting. First, bonds *can* be quite risky to the bondholder. Persons who try to sell their bonds before maturity may find that the market price for bonds happens to be low, so that if they need to raise cash in a hurry, they may have to sell at a substantial loss. Also, bondholders may be exposed to losses from inflation. Whether the $1000 promised the bondholder at the 1990 maturity date represents substantial purchasing power or only a little depends on what happens to the general price level in the meantime. And no one can predict this far in advance with any accuracy.

Second, the ownership of the company represented by the holding of a few shares of its stock may be more apparent than real. A holder of 0.002 percent of the stocks of General Motors—which is a *very large* investment—exercises no real control over its operations. In fact, there are many economists who believe that in the large corporations stocks are diffused among so many holders that no stockholder or stockholder group has *any* effective control over management. In this view, the management of a corporation becomes a largely independent decision-making body. As long as it can keep enough cash flowing to stockholders to prevent discontent and rebellion, management can, according to this view, do anything it wants within the law. Looked at in another way, this last conclusion really says that stockholders are merely another class of persons who provide loans to the company. The only real difference between stockholders and bondholders, according to this interpretation, is that stockholders' loans are riskier and therefore entitled to higher payments.

BOND PRICES AND INTEREST RATES

Why is investment in bonds risky? That is, what makes their price go up and down? The main element in the answer is that changes in interest rates cause bond prices to change. There is a straightforward relationship between bond prices and interest rates. Whenever one goes up, the other must go down. For example, suppose that Sears Roebuck had issued some 15-year bonds when interest rates were comparatively low, so that the company had to offer to pay only 6 percent to find buyers for these bonds. People who invested $1000 in new Sears bonds received in return a contract that promised them $60 per year for 15 years, plus the return of their $1000 at the end of that period. Suppose further that 2 years later interest rates in the economy rise so that new 15-year bonds

of companies of similar quality pay 8 percent. Now for $1000 one can buy a contract that offers $80 per year. Obviously, no one will any longer pay as much as $1000 for a bond that promises only $60 per year. Consequently, the market price of the 2-year-old Sears bonds must fall.

When interest rates in the economy rise, there must be a fall in the prices of previously issued bonds with their lower interest earnings. For the same reason, when interest rates in the economy fall, the prices of previously issued bonds must rise.

It follows that as interest rates in the economy change because of changes in monetary policy or for other reasons, bond prices will also fluctuate. That is one reason investment in bonds can be risky.

TYPES OF STOCKS AND BONDS

Stocks and bonds come in many varieties, and the potential investor should be acquainted with the range of available choices. For example, we have described common stocks, but some companies also issue a type of security called a preferred stock.

DEFINITION
A *preferred stock* is a sort of hybrid between a stock and a bond. Payments to holders of preferred stocks are not guaranteed as are payments to bondholders. However, it is stipulated that a specified payment to preferred stockholders must be made before anything can be paid to holders of common stocks. In addition, holders of preferred stocks generally are not entitled to vote for company officers.

Preferred stocks are considered less risky than common stocks but riskier than bonds, because even the holders of preferred stock can be paid only *after* bondholders have received their interest payments. But in recent years, preferred stocks have become less popular and fewer firms offer them for sale. One primary reason for this decline is that from the company's point of view they are usually disadvantageous in their tax status compared with bonds. An interest payment to a bondholder is considered an *expense* to the corporation and so it is not subject to the corporate income tax. On the other hand, dividend payments to holders of preferred stocks are legally considered to be part of company *profit* and are therefore taxed at the full corporate income tax rate.

Bonds, too, come in different varieties. There are, for example, short-term bonds, long-term bonds, tax-exempt bonds, and convertible bonds.

DEFINITION
A bond is considered to be of *short* or *long term* depending on its maturity date. A bond that will be paid off 20 years in the future is a long-term bond, while a bond due to be paid off in 3 years is considered a fairly short-term bond. Such short-term bonds are often called *notes*. There are even shorter-term securities like bonds that are issued for periods as brief as 90 days. When issued by the U.S. Treasury, these are called *Treasury bills*.

The prices of long- and short-term bonds tend to go up and down together, but they will not always do so. When people expect interest rates to be higher in a few years than they are now, long-term bonds will generally fall in price compared with short-term bonds, and the reverse will often be true when the future is expected to bring a sharp reduction in interest rates. The reason is straightforward. Suppose you have $5000 to invest for 10 years and are offered your choice of a 5-year or a 10-year bond, each of which offers an interest rate of 6 percent a year until maturity. If you expect the interest rate to rise to 8 percent 5 years from now, you would pick the short-term bond, so that when you get your money back in 5 years

you can reinvest it in another 5-year bond, which at that time offers the higher 8 percent rate. But if, instead, you expect the interest rate to fall to 4 percent 5 years from now, you would buy the long-term bond and nail down the 6 percent interest rate it promises over its lifetime. These differences in demand will produce corresponding adjustments in the prices of the two types of bonds. So, in the first case, the short-term bond will rise in price in comparison with the longer-term bond. And, in the second case, the reverse must be true.

DEFINITION
Tax-exempt bonds are what their name suggests: bonds on whose interest earnings one pays no federal income tax, and, if their owner lives in the state in which they are issued, no state income tax either.

Tax-exempt bonds sound like a good deal— they pay interest that is not taxed. But there is a catch to the deal. Tax exempts usually pay much lower interest rates than do taxable bonds. When taxable bonds may be paying 9 percent, tax exempts are likely to return something in the neighborhood of 6 percent. Thus, if your income falls in a low tax bracket, tax exempts are not for you. They appeal only to high-income earners who make up in tax saving all that they lose in lower interest rates—and more.

Tax exemption is primarily a way for the federal government to subsidize borrowing by the state and local governments. For example, if a state wants to attract private industry, it may authorize the issue of tax-exempt bonds (called *industrial development bonds*) to help raise the capital. Because they are tax exempt, the money can be raised at a low interest cost, which makes them attractive to corporations. The companies and the state both reap gains. It is the federal government that loses out in terms of unpaid tax. Because only rich people can invest profitably in tax-exempt bonds, many reformers and economists have attacked tax exemption as an inequitable way to subsidize state and local government borrowing. It is also believed to be an inefficient way to provide such subsidies. Estimates suggest that the federal government's losses of income tax revenues *exceed* the interest saved by the states and localities.

DEFINITION

A *convertible bond* is a hybrid between a bond and a stock. It is a security that starts out as a bond, with a fixed annual coupon payment, a fixed maturity date, and a fixed value on that date. However, the owner of the convertible bond has the choice of exchanging the bond for a fixed number of (newly issued) common stocks at any date that person prefers within some specified time interval.

A convertible bond is always worth at least as much as an ordinary bond promising the same payments, and usually considerably more. That is, the company does not usually have to offer as high an interest rate on a convertible bond as it pays on an ordinary bond. The point is that the convertible bond gives its owner a choice—it permits that person to decide to hold either a bond *or* a fixed number of stocks, whichever happens to be more valuable. If the investor expects the company's stock to grow in market value, but prefers some protection in case that prediction turns out to be wrong, the convertible bond may prove ideal. The investor can hold on to the original bond so long as the company's stocks have not actually risen, but when the price of the stock goes up sufficiently, it is likely to pay the investor to exercise the right to convert the bond into stocks. Convertible bonds are often issued by new companies whose managements believe that their stocks will rise substantially in price but who feel that for the moment they can only hope to raise money by borrowing—that is, by selling bonds. In that way, if their forecast is right, the company's initial debt will eliminate itself when the bondholders decide to convert their bonds to stocks.

OTHER TYPES OF SECURITIES: OPTIONS

The list of available securities covers a vast array of investment possibilities in addition to those already described. One can, for example, invest in securities called *puts* and other securities called *calls*. Each of these is an example of the general class of securities called options.

DEFINITION

An *option* is a contract that permits (but does not require) its holder to purchase or to sell some specified piece of property at a price defined in the contract. If the owner of the option elects to "exercise the option," that is, to carry out the sale or the purchase permitted by the option, it can be done at whatever date the optionholder chooses within the period indicated in the contract.

A *call option* is a contract giving its owner the right to *purchase* a fixed number of shares of some stock at a given price (for example, 100 shares of General Electric stock at a price of $49.25) at any preferred date during the period specified.

A *put option* is a contract giving its owner the right to *sell* a fixed number of shares of some stock at a given price within a specified time period.

Option contracts are fairly expensive to purchase. They typically run between 5 and 10 percent of the value of the stocks to which they apply, depending on the duration of the option. That is, a call for $5000 worth of Chrysler Corporation stock may cost about $500. Why, then, do people purchase them? There are two reasons. First, they can be used as protection to the investor. Suppose an investor thinks the stock of a company, Shaky Futures, Inc., is likely to go up substantially, but recognizes that it is also possible that the bottom will drop out of its price. She buys a call option on 500 shares of Shaky Futures at its current price, $10 per share, paying $500 for the privilege. (Often options are more expensive for more speculative and volatile stocks.) Suppose Shaky Futures actually falls to $6 a share. Had she bought 500 shares of the stock outright, the value of her investment would have fallen from $5000 to $3000—a loss of $2000. But as the holder of an option she has the right *not* to buy it. She simply lets it lapse at the end of the option period and loses only the $500 paid for the option that was never used. The second and more frequent use of an option, paradoxically, is to transform a conservative investment into a more exciting gamble—one that is capable of bringing in larger gains than the investor could otherwise have gotten with a given amount of money, but that can, of course, also be capable of producing larger losses. An illustration will show how a call can be used for this purpose. Suppose our investor is interested in a fairly conservative stock whose price she expects to rise no more than 20 percent. But she also realizes that it may lose as much as 10 percent. If she has $10,000 to invest and uses the money to buy the stock outright, the most she can expect to gain is $2000, and she also will expect to lose no more than $1000. What if, instead of buying the stock, she puts all her $10,000 into call options upon that stock? At our illustrative 10 percent price for a call option, this gives her a contract for the delivery of $100,000 of the stock.

Now what happens if the price of the stock goes up 20 percent? The holder of the option gains 20 percent, not of the $10,000 she invested, but of the $100,000 in stock that her option controls. After a 20 percent price rise (if it occurs), the stock will be worth $120,000, so that she can ask the broker to buy it at the $100,000 price to which her option entitles her, and to then sell it immediately at its current market price. (She doesn't actually have to pay out any additional cash for this transaction.) The investor's gain will then be the $20,000 rise in the

value of the stock minus the $10,000 paid for the option—a net profit of $10,000—or about a 100 percent gain in 6 months.

However, what if the stock price goes down 10 percent? In that case, the holder of the call simply will not buy the stock; but she will lose her *entire* $10,000 investment instead of just the $1000 that would have been lost if the stock had been bought outright. Obviously, option trading of this variety is not for those who can't afford or who dislike taking risks.

BUYING STOCKS AND BONDS AND FOLLOWING THEIR PERFORMANCE

Although stocks and bonds can be purchased through any brokerage firm, not all brokers charge the same fees. Until recently, by industry agreement, the charges to small investors were absolutely fixed and did not vary from broker to broker. But in 1975, the SEC ruled this fixed price to be illegal. Since then, bargain brokerage houses have begun to appear. They usually advertise in the financial pages of newspapers, offering investors very little service—no advice, no research, no other frills—other than merely buying or selling what the customer wants them to, at lower fees than those charged by higher-service brokerage firms.

Many investors are not aware of the various ways in which stocks can be purchased (or sold). The following are some of the possibilities: (a) *Round lot* purchases: Purchases of 100 shares or 200 shares or any number of shares in multiples of 100. (b) *Odd lot* purchases: The purchase of some number of shares that is not a multiple of 100. The brokerage fee per dollar of investment is normally higher on an odd lot than on a round lot. (c) A *market order* purchase simply tells the broker to buy a specified quantity of stock (either a round lot or an odd lot) at the best price the market currently offers. (d) A *limit order* is an agreement to buy a given amount of a stock when its price falls to a specified level. If the investor offers to buy at $18, then shares will be purchased by the broker if and when the market price falls to $18 per share or less.

There are many investment information services that supply subscribers with a variety of information on performance of stocks, bonds, and other securities. These firms offer analyses of particular companies, forecasts, and advice. In addition, newspapers carry daily information on stock and bond prices. Figure 24–2 is an excerpt from a stock market report in *The Denver Post.* In the first two columns, before the name of the stock, the report gives the stock's highest and lowest price in the current year. In the colored example, the price of RCA stock is reported to have ranged between $32\frac{1}{2}$ and $25\frac{3}{8}$. Next, after the name of the stock, there appears the annual dividend per share ($1.20) and the *price earnings* (P/E) ratio (11 for RCA). This latter figure is the price per share divided by the company's net earnings per share in the previous year, and is usually taken as a basic measure indicating whether the current price of the stock overvalues or undervalues the company.

However, no simple rule enables us to interpret the P/E figures—for example, a very risky firm or a slowly growing firm with a low P/E may be considered overvalued, while a safe, rapidly growing firm with a high P/E may still be a bargain. The next column indicates the number of shares that were traded on the previous day (87,400), an indication of whether that stock is actively traded. Finally, the last four figures indicate yesterday's highest price ($29), its lowest price ($$28\frac{1}{4}$), the price at which the last transaction of the day took place ($29), and the change in that price from the previous day (up $\frac{1}{4}$).

Figure 24–3, taken from *The Chicago Tribune,* gives similar information about bonds. The first thing to notice here is that a given company may have several different bonds—differing in maturity date and coupon (annual interest payment). For example, Shell Oil offers

1977 High	1977 Low	Stocks	Div.	P-E Ratio	Sales in 100s	High	Low	Close	Net Chg.
		R							
32½	25⅜	RCA	1.20	11	874	29	28¼	29	+ ¼
15⅜	9⅛	RTE	.40	11	21	15	14¾	14⅞	— ⅛
17⅝	14	RalsPur	.40	13	275	16⅛	16	16⅛	+ ⅛
4½	3¼	Ramad	.09e	16	.83	3¾	3½	3⅝	......
24	13¼	RancoIn	.80	7	68	18	17⅝	17⅝	— ½
8⅞	4⅝	RapidAm		3	65	7⅛	7	7	— ⅛
33⅞	29⅛	Raybt	1.50b	6	8	30½	30¼	30½	......
28⅜	19	Raymnd	1	7	145	26½	25½	26⅛	+ ⅝
32	28¾	Raythn	1	9	238	28¾	d28½	28¾	— ⅛
24	16⅞	ReadBat	.80	8	89	21½	21	21½	+ ⅛
3⅝	2⅜	Redman		5	29	2⅝	2⅝	2⅝	......
12¾	8⅜	ReeceCp	.60	8	4	8⅞	8⅞	8⅞	+ ⅛
22¾	20¼	ReevsB	1.44	6	3	22¼	22⅛	22¼	+ ⅛
20⅛	16⅛	ReichCh	.74	9	19	16¾	16⅜	16½	— ⅛
14⅜	8⅞	ReliabSt	.68	8	20	14⅛	14⅛	14⅛	......
35¼	29¼	RelnEl	1.20	10	31	31½	31	31	— ⅜
26¾	18½	RelianGp		5	90	24¾	24¼	24¾	+ ⅛
43¼	34½	RelG pf	2.20	..	12	41	40⅝	40⅞	— ⅜
30	24	RelG pf	2.60	..	23	25⅛	24⅞	25	......
29¼	26⅝	RelIn pf	2.68	..	10	29¼	29	29	......
11	7⅝	RpubCp		7	11	9⅜	9	9⅛	— ¼
24¼	15¼	RepFinS	1	5	19	23⅞	23⅞	23⅞	+ ⅛
2	1½	RepMtg			8	1¾	1¾	1¾	......
34⅞	22	RepStl	1.60	8	426	23¼	22¾	22⅞	— ¼
34⅜	28⅜	RepTex	1.20	7	3	29¼	29¼	29¼	+ ⅛
21⅜	15⅛	ResrvOil	.20	15	198	18⅛	17⅝	18	+ ⅜
26¾	15¼	RevcoDS	.40	12	83	18⅛	18	18	......
21¾	9¾	Revere		10	56	13⅝	13¼	13⅜	......
44½	36⅛	Revlon	1	14	177	41⅜	40⅞	41⅜	+ ¼
13	9¾	Rexham	.50	8	139	12	11¾	12	+ ⅛
39½	32	Rexnrd	1.44	6	16	32¾	32½	32½	......
58	48	Rexn pf	2.36	..	2	50⅜	50⅜	50⅜	— ⅛
70⅝	63¼	ReynIn	3.28	9	130	67⅝	67⅜	67½	+ ¼
83¾	73	ReyIn pf	2.25	..	1	79	79	79	......
44⅞	33	ReyMet	1.20	7	366	33¾	d32½	32⅝	— 1
11⅞	8	ReynSe	.40a	8	52	8¼	8	8⅛	+ ⅛
16⅝	12¾	RichCo	1	6	x7	14	13⅞	13⅞	+ ⅛
26¼	18¾	RichMer	.90	10	791	24½	24	24½	+ ⅜
21⅝	17½	RiegelT	1.30	5	9	19¼	18⅞	18⅞	— ½
30⅜	20½	RioGran	.70	7	12	23½	23¼	23⅜	— ¼
17¾	12½	RioGr pf	.80	..	12	14	13⅞	14	+ ⅛
17⅛	13⅞	RiteAid	.32	10	91	16⅛	16	16⅛	+ ⅛
25¾	18⅞	Robshw	1.10	10	25	22¾	22½	22¾	+ ¼
25¾	21⅞	Robrtsn	1.50	8	11	22½	22	22½	+ ½
14¼	9⅜	Robins	.32	9	x67	9½	d 9¼	9⅜	+ ⅛
21¼	17¾	RochG	1.40	8	45	20⅝	20⅜	20⅜	— ⅛
17⅛	14¼	RochTl	1	9	42	16⅞	16¾	16¾	— ⅛
13¼	10¾	Rockowr	.76	5	15	11½	11⅜	11½	......
37¼	30⅞	Rockwl	2.20	8	103	32	31⅝	31⅞	......
32¾	28	RkInt pf	1.35	..	6	28⅜	28⅜	28⅜	— ⅝
51½	34¼	RohmH	1.28	11	46	34⅝	34½	34⅝	......
6⅞	5½	RohrInd		..	21	6	5¾	5⅞	+ ⅛
24¼	16½	Rollins	.50	10	38	18¾	18⅝	18¾	......
4⅛	3⅜	Ronson		70	7	3⅝	3½	3½	......
26¾	20⅝	Roper	1.40	5	22	24½	24	24⅛	— ⅜
14½	9¾	Rorer	.60	10	62	12⅜	12⅛	12¼	— ⅛
29⅜	20½	Rosario	.40b	13	31	22⅝	21½	21½	— ⅝
28½	14¼	Rowan	.12	12	294	25¼	25	25¼	+ ⅛
19¼	14⅝	RoyCCol	1	8	49	18⅝	18⅜	18½	......
61	51¼	RoylD	4.01e	5	698	57⅝	57⅜	57½	— ⅜
27½	21½	Rubbrm	.60	12	7	23¼	23⅛	23⅛	— ⅜
11⅞	10⅛	RussTog	.76	8	25	60⅞	10¾	10¾	......
18	12⅝	RyderS	.15r	7	184	17⅛	16⅞	17	......
		S							
4⅝	2¾	SCASv		10	127	3¾	3⅝	3¾	......
25⅛	19⅜	SCMCp	1	6	104	22⅛	21⅝	21⅝	— ⅝
15½	12¾	SOSCon	.50	5	11	12⅞	12⅞	12⅞	— ⅛

FIGURE 24–2

EXCERPT FROM A STOCK MARKET PAGE

This table from *The Denver Post* gives the highest and lowest price in the current year, the current dividend rate, the ratio of stock price to company earnings (P/E ratio), the number of shares sold, the highest, lowest, and final price on the previous day, and the change in price from the day before.

Source: *The Denver Post*, August 15, 1977, page 12F.

	Yld	Sales ($1000)	High	Low	Close	Net chg.
Searl 8s81	7.8	29	102	101⅝	101⅝	− ⅜
Sears 8⅝95	8.1	5	105½	105	105½	+ ½
Sears 7¾85	7.6	47	101⅞	101½	101⅞	+ ⅜
SearA 5s82	5.5	5	90⅛	90⅛	90⅛	− ⅜
Seatrin 6s94	cv	18	69⅜	68⅝	69⅜	+ ⅞
ShellO 8½00	8.2	10	103⅛	103⅛	103⅛	......
ShellO 7¼02	7.6	55	95	94⅞	94⅞	+ 1⅜
Signl 8.85s94	8.6	11	102	101½	102	......
Singer 8s99	8.9	1	89	89	89	− ⅝
Smith 10¼95	9.7	1	105	105	105	+ ¼
SoCBl 8¼04	8.2	5	101	100¼	100¼	− 1
SoCBl 8¼13	8.2	17	100¾	100⅛	100⅛	− ¾
SoBlT 6½79	6.5	30	99⅝	99⅝	99⅝	......
SoBlT 7⅜10	7.9	15	93¼	93⅛	93¼	+ ¾
SoBlT 7⅝13	8.0	52	94⅞	94⅞	94⅞	+ ⅛
SoBlT 8s14	8.0	12	99½	99½	99½	+ ⅜
SoBlT 8¼16	8.1	33	100⅞	100⅝	100⅞	− ½
SoBlT 8⅛17	8.1	60	100	99⅞	100	− ¼
SoCG 8.85s95	8.7	9	102	101½	101½	......
SoCG 10¼81	9.4	10	108¼	108¼	108¼	+ ¼
SCouG 9½95	9.0	4	105	105	105	− ⅛
SoNG 8¼86	8.0	20	102⅜	102⅜	102⅜	......
SPac 4½s81	5.0	17	90¼	89½	89½	− ¾
SouRy 5s94	6.9	13	72	72	72	− 2½
SoutF 10⅛86	9.4	2	107¼	107¼	107¼	......
SwBT 8¾07	8.3	13	105⅜	105⅜	105⅜	+ ⅝
SwBT 6⅞11	7.9	50	86½	86⅛	86½	+ ⅛
SwBT 7s78	7.0	4	99⅞	99⅞	99⅞	......
SwBT 7¾09	8.0	31	96⅛	96	96	− ¼
SwBT 7⅝13	8.0	36	95	94⅞	95	− ¼
SwBT 8¼14	8.1	38	101⅜	100¾	101⅜	+ 1
SwBT 8.2s82	7.9	10	102⅞	102⅞	102⅞	− ⅝
SwBT 8¼17	8.1	5	101	101	101	......
Spery 6s00	cv	9	101	101	101	+ ⅛
Squibb 8s85	7.7	5	102⅞	102⅞	102⅞	− ⅝
SOCal 5¾92	6.7	35	85⅜	84⅞	84⅞	− 1
StOln 4½83	5.1	35	88	87½	87½	......
StOln 6.1s89	6.0	87	100¾	100⅝	100⅝	− ⅛
StdOh 7.1s77	7.1	50	100	100	100	......
StdOh 7½86	7.5	20	99	99	99	− ½
StPkg 5¼90	cv	32	56¼	56¼	56¼	+ ¼
Stokly 8s98	8.4	3	95	95	95	+ 2
SunOil 8½00	8.2	20	103	103	103	+ ⅝
Sundstr 5s93	cv	50	78¾	78¾	78¾	+ ⅛
Sunsh 6½89	cv	3	98¾	98¾	98¾	......
Sybrn 7½94	7.9	5	94¾	94¾	94¾	+ 1½
TRE 9¾02	cv	12	100½	100½	100½	+ ⅛
TalcNtl 6s94	cv	10	55	55	55	− ½
Tandy 10s91	9.9	14	101½	101	101	− ¼
Teledy 7s99	8.6	4	80½	80⅛	80½	......

FIGURE 24–3

EXCERPT FROM A BOND PRICE TABLE

This report from *The Chicago Tribune* shows annual payment, the year in which the bond will be redeemed (that is, the year in which the company will repay that debt), the yield (that is, the annual payment per dollar of current market price), and the previous day's highest, lowest, and closing price of the bond, as well as the change in price from the day before that.

Source: Reprinted courtesy of *The Chicago Tribune*.

two different bonds. The one that is colored is labeled Shell Oil $7\frac{1}{4}$ 02, meaning that these are bonds that pay an annual interest of $7\frac{1}{4}$ percent on their face value (this is called their "coupon"), and that their maturity (redemption) date is 2002. Next, the current yield is reported as 7.6 percent. This is simply the coupon divided by the price. Since that yield, 7.6 percent, is higher than the coupon, it means that the bond must be selling at a price below its face value, so that the return per dollar is correspondingly high. The remaining information in the table means the same as that reported for stock prices.

STOCK EXCHANGES AND THEIR FUNCTIONS

The *New York Stock Exchange*—the "Big Board"—is the most prestigious of the stock markets. Located just at the beginning of Wall Street in New York City, it is "*the* establishment" of the securities industry. Only the best known and most heavily traded of securities are dealt with by the New York Stock Exchange, which handles some 2000 stocks altogether. The leading brokerage firms hold "seats" on the Stock Exchange, which enable them to trade directly on the floor of the Exchange. Altogether, the Exchange has about 1350 members. Seats are traded on the open market, and today a seat can be purchased for approximately $65,000. Some years ago a seat on the New York Stock Exchange was worth more than $500,000, but various regulatory actions that served to increase competition among brokers have since reduced the value of a seat.

Suppose you want to order 200 shares of General Motors from a broker. The broker you approach may be employed by a firm that holds a seat on the Exchange, or he may work through another firm that holds one. The broker who is to fill your order contacts a person called a "specialist," who works on the floor of the Exchange and who handles GM stock. The specialist will usually own some GM stock of his own that he will offer for sale to you if no other sellers are available at the moment. Usually, in addition, a number of investors will previously have given to the specialist limit orders offering to sell specified quantities of GM stock at specified prices. There may, for example, be one offer to sell 5000 shares at any price above $30\frac{5}{8}$ and another offer to sell 1200 shares at any price above $30\frac{7}{8}$. Similarly, the specialist is likely to have in his hands a number of limit orders to buy at various specified prices. Your order is brought by the floor broker to the specialist who determines a price that, in his judgment, more or less balances supply and demand as indicated by his recent sales and purchases and the limit orders in his possession. At this price the specialist will fill your order either from one of the limit orders to sell (he must do so whenever that is possible) or he will fill it from his personal inventory of General Motors stock. The price determination process that has just been described is sometimes called "the auction market" process.

The New York Stock Exchange is not the only exchange on which stocks are traded. While more than 80 percent of stock transactions (measured in dollars) are handled by the Big Board, the *American Stock Exchange,* located a few blocks away, trades many stocks that are heavily demanded but that are not exchanged in quite as large a volume as those handled by the Big Board. About 4 percent of the dollar volume of stock trades occurs on the American Stock Exchange.

There are also *regional exchanges*—the largest of which are the Midwest, Detroit, Cincinnati, Pacific Coast, Philadelphia, Boston, and Pittsburgh exchanges, which deal in many of the same stocks that are handled on the New York Stock Exchange. A good portion of the business of regional exchanges is serving large "institutional" customers, such as banks, insurance companies, and mutual funds. Their volume amounts to about 10 percent of the total stock traded.

In addition to these organized exchanges,

about another 4 percent is traded on the so-called third market. The third market is not a public market at all. It is not a place where many buyers and sellers meet to make their exchanges simultaneously. Rather, the third market is run by a number of firms, each operating more or less independently of the others. When a buyer brings an order to such a firm, the broker will simply shop around by telephone seeking to find someone to match the purchase demand with a corresponding supply offer, or the broker may buy or sell for his own account the stocks supplied or demanded by the order. Thus, in dealing on the third market, each broker does the job that is done by a specialist on one of the exchanges. Obviously, trading on the third market is a much less structured and less organized affair than it is on the exchanges.

With the advent of computers and improved electronic means of communication, there is now talk of arranging what is, in effect, a single national market. It would consist of an electronic network through which every buy or sell order would be announced from coast to coast, as would the price and quantity of every completed transaction. In this way, the market would, indeed, have the opportunity to match all supplies and demands and to produce an equilibrium reflecting the demands of every market participant. There are those who predict that such a national market will be in operation within a few years.

STOCK EXCHANGES AND CORPORATE CAPITAL NEEDS

While corporations often raise the funds they need by selling stocks, they do not normally do so through any of the stock exchanges. A new issue of stocks is usually handled by a special type of bank called an *investment bank.*

In contrast, the stock markets trade almost exclusively in "secondhand securities"—stocks in the hands of individuals and others who had bought them earlier and who now wish to sell them. Thus the stock market does not provide funds to corporations that need the financing to expand their productive activities. The markets only provide money to persons who already hold the stocks that the corporations had issued previously.

Yet the stock exchanges have two functions that are of critical importance for the financing of corporations: (a) By providing a secondhand market for stocks, they make it much less risky for an individual to invest in a company. Investors know that their money is not locked in—if they need the money, they can always sell their stocks to other investors or to the "specialist" at the price the market currently offers. This reduction in risk makes it far easier for corporations to sell their stocks when they decide to market a new issue. (b) The stock market also determines the current price of the company's stocks. That, in turn, determines whether it will be hard or easy for a corporation to raise money by selling new stocks. If the price of its stock is high, the corporation will not have to issue many shares in order to raise a given amount of money, while if the price of its stock is low it can raise the money only by selling many new stocks, thus forcing its current stockholders to share a larger proportion of their ownership and the profits of the company. Thus, suppose a company initially has 1 million shares and wants to raise $10 million. If the price is $40 per share, an issue of 250,000 shares can bring in the required funds, leaving the original stockholders with four-fifths of the company's ownership. But if the price of the stock is only $20, then 500,000 new shares will have to be issued, cutting the original stockholders back to two-thirds of the ownership of the company.

It is generally believed that the price of a company's stock is closely tied to the efficiency with which its productive activities are conducted, the effectiveness with which it matches its product to consumer demands, and the diligence with which it goes after profitable innovation. In this view, those firms that can make effective use of funds because of their efficiency are precisely the corporations whose stock prices will usually be comparatively high. In other words, the stock market serves as a means to channel the economy's investment funds to those firms that can make best use of the money. In sum:

If a firm has a promising future, its stock will tend to command a high price on the stock exchanges. At the same time, the high price of its stock will make it easier for it to raise capital by permitting it to amass a large amount of money through the sale of a comparatively small number of new stocks. Thus, *the stock market helps to allocate the economy's resources to those firms that can make the best use of those resources.*

THE ISSUE OF SPECULATION

Dealings in securities are often viewed with hostility and suspicion because it is felt that they are an instrument of speculation. When something goes wrong in the market, say, when there is a sudden fall in prices, speculators are often blamed. The word "speculators" is used by editorial writers as a term of strong disapproval, implying that those who engage in the activity are parasites who produce no benefits for society and often do it considerable harm.

Economists disagree vehemently with this judgment. They say that speculators perform two vital economic functions: (a) They sell *protection from risk* to other people, much as a fire insurance policy sells protection from risk to the owner of a home. (b) Speculators help to smooth out price fluctuations (and consumption patterns), buying items when they are abundant (and cheap) and holding them and reselling them when they are scarce (and expensive). In that way, they play a vital economic role in helping to alleviate and even prevent shortages.

DEFINITION

Speculators are individuals who deliberately invest in risky assets, hoping to obtain a profit from the changes in the prices in these assets that they expect to occur.

Some examples from outside the securities markets will make the role of speculators clear. A ticket broker attends a preview of a new musical comedy and suspects that it is likely to be a hit. He decides to speculate by buying a large block of tickets for future performances. In that way he takes over some of the producer's risk, for the producer now has some hard cash and has reduced his inventory of risky tickets. If when the show opens it is a flop, the broker is stuck with the tickets. If it is a hit, he can sell them at a premium, if the law allows (and be denounced as a speculator or a "scalper"). Similarly, speculators enable farmers or producers of metals and other commodities whose future price is uncertain to get rid of their risk. A farmer who has planted a large crop but who fears its price may fall before harvest time can protect himself by signing a *contract for future delivery* at an agreed upon price at which the speculator will purchase the crop when it comes in. In that case, if the price happens to fall, it is the speculator and not the farmer who will suffer the loss. Of course, if the price happens to rise, the speculator will reap the gain—that is the nature of risk bearing. As an alternative, our farmer may purchase a contract called an *option,* which gives him the choice of selling either at a price specified in the contract or at the price that then prevails on the market, whichever is higher. In either case, it is the speculator who has agreed to buy the crop at the preset price, regardless of market conditions at the time the sale takes place. The speculator has, in effect, sold an insurance policy to the farmer, surely a useful function.

The second role of the speculator is perhaps even more important; in effect, it is arranging for the accumulation and storage of goods in periods of abundance and making them available in periods of scarcity. Suppose the speculator has reason to suspect that next year's crop of a storable commodity will not be nearly as abundant as this year's. He will buy up some now, when it is cheap, for resale when it becomes scarce and expensive.

In the process, he will smooth out the swing in prices by adding his purchases to the total market demand in the period of low prices (which tends to bring the price up), and bringing in his supplies during the period of high prices (which tends to push the price down).

Thus, the successful speculator will help to relieve matters during periods of extreme shortage. There are cases in which he literally helps to relieve famine by releasing the supplies he has deliberately hoarded for such an occasion. Of course, he is cursed for the high prices he charges on such occasions. But those who curse him do not recognize how much higher prices are likely to have been if the speculator's foresight and avid pursuit of profit had not provided for the emergency.

On the securities market, of course, famine and severe shortages are not an issue, but the fact remains that successful speculators will tend to reduce price fluctuations by increasing demand for stocks when prices are low and contributing to supply when prices are high. Far from aggravating instability and fluctuations, speculators work as hard as they can to iron out fluctuations, for that is how they make their profits.

The role of speculation is one of the 12 Ideas for Beyond the Final Exam in our study of economics. Even among government officials, journalists, and other thoughtful individuals, it is widely believed that speculators perform no real service for the economy; that their activity generally aggravates high prices and increases scarcity in times of shortages; and that they add to the instability of the economy in other ways. These impressions are virtually the reverse of the truth. Whether or not speculators are personally virtuous people is not the point. The fact is that in earning their profits they make several vital contributions to the workings of the economy: (a) They take over risks from individuals seeking protection from risk; (b) They tend to add to supplies in periods of shortages; and (c) They work to depress prices when they are unusually high and to raise prices when they are unusually low—*for that is how they earn profits—by buying things when they are cheap in anticipation of their resale when they become expensive.*

STOCK PRICES AS RANDOM WALKS

The beginning of this chapter cited evidence indicating that the best of professional securities analysts have a forecasting record so miserable that investors may do as well by picking stocks by hunch, superstition, or any purely random process, as they would by following the advice of the professional. It has been said that the investor is well advised to pick stocks by throwing darts at the stock market page—since it is far cheaper to buy a set of darts than to obtain the apparently useless advice of a professional analyst. Indeed, there have been at least two experiments, one by a U.S. Senator and one by *Forbes* magazine, in which stocks picked by dart throwing actually outperformed the mutual funds, whose stocks are selected by the experts.

Does this mean that the analysts are incompetent people who do not know what they are doing? Not at all. Rather, there is overwhelming evidence that their poor forecasting performance is attributable to the fact that the task they have undertaken is basically impossible.

How can this be so? The answer is that to make a good forecast of any variable—GNP, population, or fuel usage—there must be something in the past whose behavior is closely related to the future behavior of the variable whose path it is desired to predict. If a 10 percent rise in this year's consumption always produces a 5 percent rise in next year's GNP, this fact provides us with an obvious procedure that can help us predict future GNP on the basis of current observations.

But if we want to forecast the future of a variable whose behavior is completely unrelated to the behavior of *any* current variable, then there is no objective evidence that can help us make that forecast. Throwing darts or gazing into a crystal ball is no less effective than the analysts' calculations.

There is by now a mass of statistical evidence that the behavior of stock prices is in fact unpredictable. In other words, the behavior of stock prices is essentially random, and the paths they follow are what statisticians call random walks.

DEFINITION
The time path of a variable, such as the price of a stock, is said to constitute a *random walk* if its magnitude in one period (say, February 2, 1980) is equal to its value in the preceding period (February 1, 1980) plus a completely random number. That is:

Price on Feb. 2, 1980 = Price on Feb. 1, 1980
+ Random number

where the random number (positive or negative) might be obtained by a roll of dice or some such procedure.

A random walk is like the path followed by a drunk. All we know about his position after his next step is that it will be given by his current position plus whatever random direction his next haphazard step will carry him.

The relevant feature of randomness, for our

purposes, is that it is by nature unpredictable, which is just what the word "random" means.

If the evidence that stock prices follow a random walk stands up to research in the future as it has so far, it is easy enough to understand why the forecasting record of security analysts is as poor as it is. They are trying to forecast behavior that is basically random or, in effect, trying to predict the unpredictable.

Two questions remain. First, does the evidence that stock prices follow a random walk mean that investment in stocks is a pure gamble and never worthwhile? And, second, how does one explain the random behavior of stock prices?

To answer the first question, it is false to conclude that investment in stocks is generally not worthwhile. The statistical evidence is that, taken over the long run, stock prices *as a whole* have had a marked upward trend, perhaps reflecting the long-term growth of the economy. The evidence of the past *does* indicate that stock prices are likely to rise if one waits long enough for them to do so. Thus the random walk does not proceed in just any direction—rather, it represents a set of erratic movements *around the basic trend in stock prices.* Moreover, it is not in the *overall* level of stock prices that the most pertinent random walk occurs, but in the performance of one company's stock compared with another's. For this reason professional advice may be able to predict that investment in the stock market is likely to be a good thing over the long haul. But, if the random walk evidence is valid, there is no way professionals can tell us *which* of the available stocks is most likely to go up—that is, which combination of stocks is best for the investor to buy.

The only appropriate answer to the second question is that no one is sure of the explanation. There are two widely offered hypotheses—each virtually the opposite of the other. The first asserts that stock prices are random because

clever professional speculators are able to foresee almost perfectly every influence that is *not* random. For example, suppose a change occurs that makes the probable earnings of some company higher than had previously been expected. Then, according to this view, the professionals will instantly become aware of this change and immediately drive up the price of the company's stock accordingly. Then, the only thing for that stock price to do between this year and next is wander randomly, because the professionals cannot predict random movements, and hence cannot force current stock prices to anticipate them.

The other explanation of random behavior of stock prices is at the opposite pole from the view that all nonrandom movements are wiped out by supersmart professionals. And that view is that buyers and sellers of stock prices have learned that they cannot predict the future of stock prices. As a result they latch on to any signal they can get, however irrational and irrelevant it appears. If the president catches cold, stock prices fall. If an astronaut's venture is successful, prices go up. For, according to this view, investors are, in the last analysis, trying to predict, not the prospects of the economy or of the company whose shares they buy, but the supply and demand behavior of other investors, which will ultimately determine the course of stock prices. Since all investors are equally in the dark, their groping can only result in the randomness that we observe.

The classic statement of this view of stock market behavior was provided by Lord Keynes, a successful professional speculator himself:

Professional investment may be likened to those newspaper competitions in which the competitors have to pick out the six prettiest faces from a hundred photographs, the prize being awarded to the competitor whose choice most nearly corresponds to the average preferences of the competitors as a whole; so that each competitor has to pick not those faces which he himself finds prettiest, but those which he thinks likeliest to catch the fancy of the other competitors, all of whom are looking at the problem from the same point of view. It is not a case of choosing those which, to the best of one's judgment, are really the prettiest, nor even those which average opinion genuinely thinks the prettiest. We have reached the third degree where we devote our intelligences to anticipating what average opinion expects the average opinion to be. And there are some, I believe, who practice the fourth, fifth and higher degrees.[2]

[2]John Maynard Keynes, *The General Theory of Employment, Interest, and Money* (New York: Harcourt Brace Jovanovich, 1936), page 156.

SUMMARY

1. The three basic types of firms are corporations, partnerships, and individual proprietorships.
2. Most U. S. firms are individual proprietorships, but most U.S. manufactured goods are produced by corporations.
3. Individual proprietorships and partnerships have tax advantages over corporations. But corporate investors have greater protection from risk because they have *limited liability*—they cannot be asked to pay more than they have invested in the firm.
4. Higher taxation of corporate earnings tends to limit the things in which corporations can invest and may lead to inefficiency in resource allocation.
5. Corporations finance their activities mostly by plowback (that is, by retaining part of their earnings and putting it back into the company) or by the sale of stocks and bonds.
6. A bond is an IOU by a company for money lent to it by the bondholder. A stock is a share in the ownership of the company.
7. Many observers argue that the purchase of a stock also really amounts to a loan to the company—a loan that is riskier than the purchase of a bond.
8. There are many different types of stocks, bonds, and other sorts of securities.
9. If interest rates rise, bond prices will fall. In other words, if some bond amounts to a contract to pay 8 percent and the market interest rate goes up to 10 percent, people will no longer be willing to pay the old price for that bond.
10. Stocks and bonds can be bought and sold with the help of professional brokers who usually obtain them through one of the organized stock exchanges.
11. If stock prices correctly reflect the future prospects of different companies, promising firms are helped to raise money because they are able to sell each stock they issue at favorable prices.
12. Speculation affects stock market prices, but (contrary to what is widely assumed) there is reason to believe that speculation actually *reduces* the frequency and size of price fluctuations.
13. Speculators are also useful to the economy because they undertake risks that others wish to avoid, thereby, in effect, providing others with insurance against risk. This is one of the 12 Ideas for Beyond the Final Exam.
14. Statistical evidence indicates that individual stock prices behave randomly.

CONCEPTS FOR REVIEW

Individual proprietorship
Partnership
Corporation
Limited liability
Unlimited liability
Plowback
Capital gain
Preferred stock
Bond

Convertible bond
Option
Price/earnings ratio
Yield
Coupon
Stock exchange
Third market
Speculation
Random walk

QUESTIONS FOR DISCUSSION

1. Why would it be difficult to run General Motors as a partnership or an individual proprietorship?
2. Do you think it is fair to tax a corporation more than a partnership doing the same amount of business? Why or why not?
3. If you hold shares in a corporation and management decides to plow back the company's earnings some year instead of paying dividends, what are the advantages and disadvantages to you?
4. Suppose interest rates are 6 percent in the economy and a safe bond promises to pay $6 a year in interest forever. What do you think the price of the bond will be? Why?
5. Suppose in the economy in the previous example, interest rates suddenly double, rising to 12 percent. What will happen to the price of the bond that pays $6 per year?
6. If you want to buy a stock, when might it be to your advantage to buy it using a market order? When will it pay to use a limit order?
7. Show that if a speculator were to buy when price is high and sell when price is low he would increase price fluctuations. Why would it be in his best interest *not* to do so?
8. If stock prices really are a random walk, can you nevertheless think of good reasons for getting professional advice before investing?

25

Limiting Market Power: Antitrust Policy

Antitrust policy is the term used to describe U.S. government programs that are designed to control the growth of monopoly and to prevent powerful firms from engaging in practices that are considered "undesirable." Such "undesirable practices" are vaguely defined by a number of federal laws and by a large number of court decisions. When a firm is accused of violation of the antitrust laws, the federal government is likely to sue it in the courts, seeking a ruling that both prevents the practice in the future and punishes the offender by fines or even a prison term.

By their nature, antitrust suits are likely to be big affairs because the accused firms are often the giants of industry. The more spectacular cases in the history of the antitrust programs involve such names as the Standard Oil Company, U.S. Steel, the Aluminum Company of America (Alcoa), and the General Electric Company. More recently, International Business Machines (IBM) and the American Telephone and Telegraph Company (AT&T) have been sued by the Department of Justice for alleged violations of the antitrust laws.

To anyone who has not been involved in an antitrust suit, its magnitude is difficult to envision. After the charges have been filed, it is not unusual for more than 5 years to elapse before the case even comes up for trial. The parties spend this period preparing their cases: assembling witnesses, gathering evidence, and drawing up documents, of which some are to be presented to the courts while others are only for the instruction of the lawyers. With the permission of the courts, the parties may undertake massive searches of one another's files. Dozens of lawyers, scores of witnesses, and hundreds of researchers are likely to participate in the process of preparation. The trial itself is likely to run for years, with each day's proceedings producing a fat volume of transcript. An antitrust case can literally pour forth several thousand *volumes* of material. The total cost to the defendant can easily run to *several hundred million* dollars, not to mention the cost to the government.

What all this means is that when the Department of Justice or the Federal Trade Commission decides to bring suit against a company, it automatically imposes a huge financial penalty upon that company *whether or not* that firm is subsequently found to have violated the law—or even if the case is thrown out of court before it ever comes to trial.

That is an awesome power and a great responsibility. What justifies the investment of so much power in a government agency? What is the purpose of the antitrust laws and how well has the program succeeded? In this chapter we will provide the materials that can help readers arrive at their own conclusions. Starting with a little history, we describe how the antitrust program has fared over the nine decades since its inception. We will also outline the activities that are currently prohibited by the law, and then ex-

amine the role of monopoly in the economy and the pros and cons of the antitrust program from the viewpoint of economic analysis.

THE PUBLIC IMAGE OF BUSINESS WHEN ANTITRUST LAWS WERE BORN

The Sherman Antitrust Act, the forerunner of all modern antitrust legislation, was passed in 1890. To understand what had brought Congress to attempt to interfere with freedom of business enterprise, we must glance briefly at the character of the most publicized business practices in the United States during the half century following the Civil War.

There were, no doubt, many businessmen at that time whose mode of operation was beyond serious criticism. But these were not the businessmen who made the headlines and who amassed the most spectacular fortunes. The adventures of the more daring breed of entrepreneurs, who have been described as "the robber barons," compete in lurid detail with the tales of their contemporaries in the Wild West. There was for example, the scandal of the Erie Railroad, during the decade after the Civil War, in which Jay Gould, Jim Fisk, and Daniel Drew extracted a fortune from "Commodore" Cornelius Vanderbilt. Vanderbilt, determined to eliminate Erie's competition to his New York Central Railroad on its route from New York to Buffalo, sought to buy enough stock to obtain control of the rival line. But Drew was in control of Erie and, in connivance with Fisk and Gould, purchased another small railroad line for a mere $250,000 and arranged for Erie to buy this valuable asset from them for $2 million in Erie bonds. They gained not only directly from this "appreciation" in their assets but also in a more subtle way by arranging (without publicity) for these new bonds to be made convertible into stock at the will of the holders. Thus, each time Vanderbilt thought he had bought enough Erie shares to gain control of the railroad, he suddenly found that the market offered still more stocks whose existence he had not suspected.[1] This was only an early round in a protracted affair. Later, Vanderbilt bribed a New York City judge to issue an injunction against his rivals, who staged a dramatic escape to New Jersey from where they continued to flood the market with new Erie stock. Jim Fisk announced publicly, "If this printing press don't break down, I'll be damned if I don't give the old hog [Vanderbilt] all he wants of Erie." Then the exiles, fearing reprisals, surrounded themselves with a force armed with Springfield rifles and three cannons, while Gould went off to Albany, passed out a million dollars in bribes (much of it in cash) to the legislature, and arranged for passage of a bill that legalized his stock manipulations and confirmed his control of the railroad.

There is much more to the story, most of it just as lurid. But there are also many other such tales: how Gould emptied the treasury of the Union Pacific Railroad, which was under his control, by buying up bankrupt parallel railroad lines and selling them to Union Pacific at many times what he had paid for them; how Gould and Fisk, in what may have been history's most spectacular market manipulation, tried to gain complete control of the entire gold market in the United States by bribing President Grant's brother-in-law to persuade the president to stand by as their stupendous manipulation progressed, forcing the price of gold to spectacular heights, and then (when the president found out what was really going on and moved to intervene) selling out in haste before the market collapsed on "Black Friday," ruining thousands, including the slower of Gould's confederates; how J. P. Morgan hired an army of toughs to engage literally in pitched battle for a contested section of railroad outside Binghamton, New York; how Philip Armour and his confederates obtained control of meat processing by an un-

derstanding with their rivals that each day a different one of them would offer a low bid for the morning shipment of cattle and no one else would ever enter a higher bid; how John D. Rockefeller gained control of the oil refining industry by forming a combination of refiners sufficiently strong to persuade the railroad people to raise their shipping rates for oil to ruinous levels, from which Rockefeller and his allies were protected by large rebates.

It is easy to go on and on with such stories. But the point is clear.

There was good reason in 1890 for popular distrust of free-swinging business activity. Business practices in the preceding decades had been ridden by scandal.

Business leaders repeatedly indicated their contempt for the public interest. J. P. Morgan announced, "I owe the public nothing," and people remembered W. H. Vanderbilt's phrase "the public be damned." The public was warned by advocates of control measures that it faced a country "in which the citizen was born to drink the milk furnished by the milk trust, eat the beef of the beef trust, illuminate his home by grace of the oil trust and die and be carried off by the coffin trust."[2] The circumstances were clearly propitious for some legislative action.

THE ANTITRUST LAWS

There are five acts of Congress that constitute the basis of the federal government's antitrust policy. Major provisions of these acts are summarized in Table 25–1 on the next page.

The Sherman Act is brief and very general, containing two main provisions: a prohibition of all contracts, combinations, and conspiracies in restraint of trade, and a prohibition of any acts of or attempts at monopolization of trade.

[1]Matthew Josephson, *The Robber Barons, The Great American Capitalists 1861–1901* (New York: Harcourt Brace Jovanovich, 1934), Chapter 6.

[2]Josephson, *The Robber Barons,* page 358

However, the Sherman Act provided for no special agency to oversee its enforcement, and 13 years elapsed after its passage before the establishment of the antitrust division of the Department of Justice under the energetic antitrust proclivities of Theodore Roosevelt. But another 8 years passed before the first major antitrust cases were decided by the Supreme Court. In 1911 the Supreme Court required the American Tobacco Company and John D. Rockefeller's Standard Oil Company to give up a substantial share of their holdings in other companies. Many of today's leading petroleum suppliers—Standard of California, Exxon, Sohio, and so on—are the offspring of the original Standard Oil Company and were spawned by those Court decisions.

At the same time, however, the Court also formulated the troublesome rule of reason,

which declared that combinations and trusts were not necessarily illegal per se—that they were against the law only if they were *unreasonable*. On that basis, in 1920 U.S. Steel was exonerated in a finding that mere size does not constitute an offense—that a firm must commit objectionable overt acts if it is to be found guilty of violating the law.

Despite the rulings against Standard Oil and American Tobacco, it was felt by many during Woodrow Wilson's administration that the Sherman Act did not provide adequate protection to the public against restrictive business practices. Consequently, in 1914 Congress passed two supplemental laws, the Clayton Act and the Federal Trade Commission Act.

The Clayton Act took two steps designed to protect smaller firms from what was considered unfair competition by larger rivals. First, it pro-

TABLE 25-1

BASIC ANTITRUST LAWS

NAME	DATE	MAJOR PROVISIONS
Sherman Act	1890	Prohibits restraint of trade and monopolization in interstate and foreign trade.
Clayton Act	1914	Prohibits price discrimination, contracts in which the seller prevents buyers from purchasing goods from the seller's competitors (tying contracts), and acquisition by one corporation of another's shares if these acts are likely to reduce competition or tend to create monopoly; also prohibits directors of one company from sitting on the board of a competitor's company.
Federal Trade Commission Act	1914	Establishes the FTC as an independent agency with authority to prosecute unfair competition and to prevent false and misleading advertising.
Robinson–Patman Act	1936	Prohibits special discounts and other discriminatory concessions to large purchasers unless based on differences in cost or "offered in good faith to meet an equally low price of a competitor."
Celler–Kefauver Antimerger Act	1950	Prohibits any corporation from acquiring the assets of another where the effect is to reduce competition substantially or to tend to create a monopoly.

hibited price discrimination, which is the act, by a seller, of charging different prices to different buyers of the same product. This provision would, for example, have prohibited the railroad rebates that John D. Rockefeller had used to squeeze out his rivals. The Clayton Act also prohibited tying contracts—contracts under which a customer who wants to buy some product, A, from a given seller is required as part of the price to agree to buy some other product, B, *exclusively* from that same seller.

To prevent a firm from simply buying out its rivals, the Clayton Act prohibited one firm from purchasing the stock of another if that acquisition tended to reduce competition. But businesses found it possible to circumvent this provision by buying a rival's plant and equipment rather than its stocks. When this practice was recognized, a new law—the Celler—Kefauver Antimerger Act of 1950—was enacted to prohibit it. Finally, the Clayton Act prohibited interlocking directorates between competitors, an arrangement under which two companies have in common some of the members of their boards of directors.

The Federal Trade Commission (FTC) Act created a commission to investigate "unfair" and "predatory" competitive practices and declared illegal all "unfair methods of competition in commerce." But since no definition of *unfairness* was provided by the law, and since, in any event, the Commission's powers were substantially restricted by the courts, the FTC was a rather ineffective agency for the first quarter century of its existence. In 1938, however, it was given the task of preventing false and deceptive advertising, a task to which it has subsequently devoted a substantial portion of its energies.

During the 15 years just after World War I, the vigor of antitrust activity declined substantially. The courts tended to interpret the laws in ways that weakened their constraint on business activities. Giants like U.S. Steel, Eastman Kodak, and International Harvester were exonerated from antitrust charges on the grounds that the very large share of the markets they controlled were not considered violations of the law under the rule of reason because they had not used predatory or coercive means to obtain their dominance of the markets.

DEVELOPMENTS SINCE THE 1930s

It was not until 1936, when Congress passed the Robinson—Patman Act, that antitrust activity regained its vigor. The Robinson—Patman Act was designed to protect independent sellers—both wholesalers and retailers (primarily in groceries and drugs)—from "unfair competition" between the chain stores and the mass distributors. But it is somewhat misleading to describe the Robinson—Patman Act as a natural step in the succession of antitrust laws, since it sought to *restrain* competition by protecting small firms from the competition of larger ones. It was felt that large firms were powerful enough to wrest special financial terms from their suppliers, which gave them an unfair competitive edge over their rivals. Accordingly, the Act prohibited several types of discriminatory arrangements, such as:

1. Special concessions, like promotional allowances by sellers to any favored set of buyers; any such allowances being legal only if available to all buyers on essentially equal terms.
2. Special discounts to favored buyers who purchase the same goods in the same quantities as other buyers who do not get the discount.
3. Lower prices in one geographic area than are charged in another, or prices that are "unreasonably low," if the objective is to eliminate competition.
4. Payment of brokerage fees to a buyer who doesn't actually use a middleman broker.
5. Discounts for larger purchases, or any other form of discrimination, that tends to *reduce* competition or encourage monopoly. This was perhaps the most important provision of the Act, although it did continue to permit

price discrimination if it could be justified either by differences in costs or by the necessity of meeting the price charged by a competitor.

In 1937, one year after the passage of the Robinson—Patman Act, the Department of Justice launched one of the landmark antitrust cases—against Alcoa (the Aluminum Company

A Citing of Precedent in Antitrust Decisions

The following excerpt is from Judge Wyzanski's noted 1954 decision, which represents a review of the change in judicial attitude toward monopolization before and after the Alcoa decision. It begins with Justice White's rule of reason, which implied that a monopoly is legal if it has not engaged in any illegal practices. Then it turns to the aluminum company decision, which held that a firm may violate the law simply by being too large, even if it has done nothing illegal. Only a monopoly that is "thrust upon" the firm is legal; that is, if the firm, in effect, cannot help being a monopoly.

UNITED STATES v. UNITED SHOE MACHINERY CORP.

Early Supreme Court decisions went in different directions, until Mr. Justice White announced "the 'rule of reason'" in 1911. . . . His opinions encouraged the view that there was no monopolization unless defendant had resorted to predatory practices. And this was unquestionably the view to which Mr. Justice McKenna led the Court in United States v. United Shoe Machinery Company of N.J., 247 U.S. 32, and United States v. United States Steel Corp., 251 U.S. 417. But a reversal of trend was effectuated through the landmark opinion of Judge Learned Hand in United States v. Aluminum Co. of American, 2 Cir., 148 F.2d 416.

In Aluminum Judge Hand . . . did not rest his judgment on the corporation's coercive or immoral practices. Instead, adopting an economic approach, he defined the appropriate market, found that Alcoa supplied 90% of it, determined that this control constituted a monopoly, and ruled that since Alcoa established this monopoly by its voluntary actions, such as building new plants, though, it was assumed, not by moral derelictions, it had "monopolized" in violation of §2. Judge Hand reserved the issue as to whether an enterprise could be said to "monopolize" if its control was purely the result of technological, production, distribution, or like objective factors, not dictated by the enterprise, but thrust upon it by the economic character of the industry; and he also reserved the question as to control achieved solely "by virtue of . . . superior skill, foresight and industry." At the same time, he emphasized that an enterprise had "monopolized" if, regardless of its intent, it had achieved a monopoly by manoeuvres which, though "honestly industrial," were not economically inevitable, but were rather the result of the firm's free choice of business policies. . . .

Source: *Federal Reporter*, Vol. 347, Washington, D.C., 1954, pages 521ff.

of America). The case was settled only 8 years later, in 1945. The relevant court ruled that Alcoa was guilty *because it controlled some 90 percent of the market,* even though it had not used means to gain this control that would previously have been declared "unreasonable." Thus, the Court's decision took the position that a firm's monopoly power, if sufficiently great, was illegal when *consciously maintained,* even if the firm had done nothing illegal to acquire that power. In other words, the Court decided that the legality of the organization of an industry could be determined at least in part from its observable structure (for example, from the market share of the largest firm) as well as from the conduct of any firm in that industry. This feature of the Alcoa decision has so far not been used widely as a precedent for other cases. But many observers felt that the conclusion about the illegality of monopoly, however acquired, heralded a new phase in the history of antitrust policy (see the boxed insert, opposite, in which another landmark Court decision describes these developments).

In 1961 the conspiracy clause of the Sherman Act came into its own. The General Electric Company and Westinghouse, along with several dozen other producers of electrical equipment, were found guilty of (literal) conspiracy to fix prices and divide the market among themselves. Several million dollars in fines were imposed, and, more remarkable, for the first time officials in the companies were sentenced to (brief) prison terms.

Finally the Court had begun to take a strong position against price fixing, which represented a reaffirmation of the basic doctrines of the Sherman Act. That position also received added force from a provision of the Clayton Act that *authorizes persons or firms whose interests are damaged by violations of the antitrust laws to sue for triple damages.* That is, the violators can be forced to compensate their victims three times the amount of actual damage their illegal actions caused.

Another landmark decision of the postwar period was the Brown Shoe Company case of 1962 in which the Brown Shoe Company, by no means the nation's largest manufacturer of shoes, was ordered to divest itself of the Kinney retail firm with which it had merged several years earlier. The decision was based on the Court's finding that the merger established both vertical and horizontal relationships between the two firms.

DEFINITION

A *vertical merger* is the union of two companies, one of which supplies products that the other uses as inputs. For example, an automobile manufacturer who acquires a tire producer or a film maker who acquires a chain of movie houses is engaging in vertical mergers.

A *horizontal merger* is the union of two companies, both of which carry out the same or similar economic activities; for example, the merger of two bread bakeries.

Since Brown was a producer of shoes and Kinney was a shoe retailer, their union was a vertical merger. On the other hand, since Brown itself had retail outlets, the acquisition also involved a horizontal merger. The Supreme Court objected to both these elements of the merger on the grounds that they involved the likelihood of substantial reduction in competition. Consequently, Brown was ordered to divest itself of Kinney. This decision set the precedent that asserts that while merger per se is not illegal, it does violate the law if the result may be a significant reduction in competition. In effect, this decision put teeth into the relevant portions of both the Clayton and the Celler—Kefauver Acts.

ISSUES IN CONCENTRATION OF INDUSTRY

Having reviewed the antitrust acts and their interpretation by the courts, we may next logically want to ask whether they work. One very rough way to measure the success of antitrust legislation is to look at what has happened to the share of American business in the hands of the largest firms. First, we can compare the degree of domination by large firms in the U.S. economy with that in other countries. American programs designed to limit monopoly power go back further and involve more powerful government machinery than do comparable programs in virtually any other major free-market economy. Indeed, in some European countries, monopoly is not really discouraged. Thus, one way to evaluate the effectiveness of an antitrust program is to compare the status of the larger firms in the United States and abroad.

A second evaluation involves observations of firms over a long period of time. Some observers, particularly the Marxists, have predicted that one of the basic tendencies of capitalism is concentration of industry, which means that small firms are increasingly driven out of business, especially during economic crises, and that large firms acquire ever larger shares of the market. One can therefore investigate whether such a tendency has been observed in the United States. If, in fact, concentration has not increased, someone who holds these views might be led to surmise that the antitrust program has had a hand in preventing the growth of monopoly. But first we should consider what might have been expected to happen to concentration in the United States in the absence of any countermeasures by government. Is there good reason to expect an inexorable trend toward bigness as the Marxists suggest?

There are two basic reasons why the larger firms in an industry may triumph over the small. First, larger firms may obtain monopoly power, which they can use to their advantage. They can force sellers of equipment, raw materials, and other inputs to give them better terms than are available to small competitors, and they can also force retailers to give preferences to their products. These are, of course, the sorts of advantages to bigness that the antitrust laws are designed to eliminate.

The second reason why an industry's output may tend to be divided among fewer and larger firms with the passage of time has to do

Judicial Humor

In a case involving a firm providing fire and burglar alarm service accused of monopolization, the judge who wrote the decision inserted the following to lighten the discussion:

When all the rest can see a typical American national business enterprise flourishing in an interstate market, federal courts too get the signal and can hear the alarm sounded when such a market is subject to restraint of trade or monopolization. . . .

From the decision in *United States* v. *Grinnell Corporation* (1966), *Federal Reporter,* Vol. 384, Washington, D.C., 1966, pages 563ff.

with technology. In some industries, fairly small firms can produce as cheaply or more cheaply than large ones, while in other industries only rather large firms can achieve maximal economy. By and large, the difference in number of firms from one industry to another has tended to correspond to the size of firm that is least costly. Automobile, steel, and airplane manufacturing are all industries in which tiny companies cannot hope to produce economically and, indeed, these are all industries made up of a relatively few large firms. In clothing production and farming, matters go quite the other way.

Frequently, innovation seems to have increased the size of plant needed to minimize cost. The examples of automated processes or of assembly lines suggest that new techniques always call for more gigantic equipment, but that is not always true. For example, the invention of the internal combustion engine and the consequent rise of trucking gave much of freight shipment to smaller firms, taking it away from the giant railroads. Technological change seems also to have favored the establishment of small electronics firms. Similarly, the continued development of cheaper and smaller computers is likely to provide a competitive advantage to smaller firms in many other industries.

If innovation provides increased cost advantages to larger firms, the growth of firms will be stimulated. But a fall in the number of firms in the industry need not inevitably result. If demand for the industry's output grows faster than optimal size of firm, we may end up with a larger number of firms, each of them bigger than before, but each having a smaller share of an expanded market.

For example, suppose in some industry a new process is invented that requires a far larger scale of operation than currently is typical. Specifically, suppose that the most efficient (that is, least costly) size of plant becomes twice as large. If demand for the industry's product increases only a little, we can expect a decrease in the number of firms. But if demand for the industry's product happens to triple at the same time, then the optimal number of firms will in fact increase to one and a half times the original number—each firm will be twice as big as before, so that together they serve three times the volume. In such a case, each firm's share of industry output will in fact have declined.

The upshot of this argument is that in the twentieth century, technological developments do, for the most part, seem to call for larger firms, which are best adapted to take advantage of the resulting economies. Probably this has somewhat outstripped even the rate of growth in output—that is, the growth of GNP. Thus, we should expect some fall in the number of firms in a typical industry, somewhat as many Marxists expect. However, not all technological change has worked in this direction, and in the absence of definitive empirical studies, this conclusion can be treated as little more than conjecture.

EVIDENCE ON CONCENTRATION OF INDUSTRY

There have been many statistical studies of concentration in American industry. One way of calculating concentration is via the concentration ratio.

DEFINITION

The *concentration ratio* for a particular industry is the percentage of that industry's output produced by its *four* largest firms. It is intended to measure the degree to which the industry is dominated by large firms—how closely it approximates a monopoly.

Of course, there is no reason why the three or five or ten largest firms should not be used for the purpose, but conventionally four firms are used as the standard.

Table 25–2 shows concentration ratios in a number of industries in the United States. We see that concentration varies greatly from industry to industry, with automobiles, electric lights, aluminum, chewing gum, and cigarettes produced by highly concentrated industries, while newspapers, clothing, soft drinks, and furniture show very little concentration.

But only comparisons over time and by geographic area can reveal the most significant implications of these figures. Here, the available evidence suggests that (perhaps simply because the American market is larger) concentration in U.S. industry is somewhat lower than it is in most other industrialized countries, with the possible exception of Great Britain and Japan. But the differences are not substantial, and because of other differences that make comparison difficult, the significance of these differences has been questioned.

TABLE 25–2

1972 CONCENTRATION RATIOS FOR REPRESENTATIVE INDUSTRIES

INDUSTRY	4-FIRM RATIO	NUMBER OF FIRMS	INDUSTRY	4-FIRM RATIO	NUMBER OF FIRMS
Motor vehicles and car bodies	93	165	Motors and generators	47	325
Electric lamps	90	103	Blast furnaces and steel mills	45	241
Chewing gum	87	15	Toilet preparations	38	593
Cigarettes	84	13	Flour and other grain mill products	33	340
Household laundry equipment	83	20	Petroleum refining	31	152
Primary aluminum	79	12	Footwear, except rubber	30	153
Aircraft engines and engine parts	77	189	Bread, cake and related products	29	2800
Photographic equipment and supplies	74	555	Pharmaceutical preparations	26	680
Tires and inner tubes	73	136	Cement	26	75
Calculating and accounting machines	73	74	Meatpacking	22	2293
Primary copper	72	11	Paints and allied products	22	1318
Aircraft	66	141	Men's and boys' suits and coats	19	721
Metal cans	66	134	Fluid milk	18	2024
Motorcycles, bicycles and parts	65	219	Newspapers.	17	7461
Soaps and other detergents	62	577	Bottled and canned soft drinks	14	2271
Environmental controls	57	117	Wood household furniture (not upholstered)	14	2160
Railroad equipment and locomotives	56	128	Women's and Misses' suits and coats	9	5294
Watches and clocks	55	183	Signs and advertising displays	6	3221
Radio and TV receiving sets	49	343			
Farm machinery and equipment	47	1465			

Source: "Concentration Ratios in Manufacturing," Bureau of the Census MC72(SR)-2, issued October 1975. Table 5 (selected items).

In the United States there seems to have been little trend in the concentration ratio, at least since the beginning of this century. The evidence is that, on the average during this period, concentration ratios remained remarkably constant. It has been estimated that at the turn of the century 32.9 percent of national income in manufactured goods was produced by "concentrated industries"—industries in which the concentration ratio was 50 percent or more (at least 50 percent of industry output was produced by the four largest firms). By 1963 the figure had risen only to 33.1 percent. And by 1970 it actually fell to 26.3 percent. These figures and those for other years are shown in Table 25–3. In a frequently quoted statement, M. A. Adelman, a noted authority on the subject, concluded, "Any tendency either way, if it does exist, must be at the pace of a glacial drift."[3] Or, as a more recent report puts it, "Almost all observers of the industrial scene . . . agree that . . . the evidence fails to support a claim that competition has declined. While concentration has increased in some areas, decreases have occurred elsewhere, leaving the overall structure unaffected."[4]

[3]M. A. Adelman, "The Measurement of Industrial Concentration," *Review of Economics and Statistics,* Vol. 33 (Nov. 1951), pages 295–96.
[4]P. W. McCracken and T. G. Moore, "Competition and Market Concentration in the American Economy," Subcommittee on Antitrust and Monopoly, U.S. Senate, March 29, 1973.

Concentration in the United States seems to be somewhat lower than it is in most other industrialized economies. Over the course of the twentieth century, concentration in the United States has shown no tendency to increase.

Since concentration is intended as a measure of the "bigness" of the firms in an industry, from such information one can perhaps surmise that the antitrust program has been effective to some degree in inhibiting whatever trend toward bigness may in fact exist. But even this very cautious conclusion has been questioned strongly. In fact, some economists and other observers have expressed the view that these laws have made virtually no difference in the size and the behavior of American business.

Whether it is desirable for the antitrust program or for some other program to inhibit concentration is an issue we turn to next.

THE PROS AND CONS OF BIGNESS

Why has antitrust become so accepted a part of government policy? Are the effects of bigness or monopoly always undesirable?

We *do* know that monopoly power can be abused; the history of the Rockefellers, the

TABLE 25–3
THE TREND IN CONCENTRATION IN MANUFACTURING INDUSTRIES (SELECTED YEARS)

	AROUND 1901	1947	1954	1958	1963	1966	1970
Percent of value added in industries with 4-firm concentration ratios over 50 percent	32.9	24.4	29.9	30.2	33.1	28.6	26.3

Source: P. W. McCracken and T. G. Moore, "Competition and Market Concentration in the American Economy," Subcommittee on Antitrust and Monopoly, U.S. Senate, March 29, 1973.

Goulds, and the Morgans described at the beginning of this chapter confirms that adequately. But even when the giants of business are not so swashbuckling in their operations, unrestrained monopoly and bigness give rise to a number of problems:

1. Distribution. A flow of wealth to firms with market power—and thus to those who are able to influence prices in their favor—is widely considered to be unfair and socially unacceptable.

2. Restriction of output. If an unrestrained monopoly is to maximize its profits, it must restrict its output to below the amount that would be provided by an equivalent competitive industry. We saw this analytically in Chapter 23, where the equilibrium output of the monopoly industry was shown to be lower than that of an industry operating under pure competition. What this means is that unregulated monopolized industries are likely to produce smaller outputs than the quantities that serve the interests of the community. This issue will be analyzed further in Chapter 31.

3. Lack of inducement for innovation. It is sometimes argued that firms in industries in which competitors are few, or in which competition is altogether absent, may be under less pressure to introduce new production methods and new products than are firms in industries in which each is constantly trying to beat out the others. Without competition, the management of a firm may choose the quiet life, taking no chances on risky investments in research and development. But a firm that operates in constant fear that its rivals will come up with a better idea, and come up with it first, can afford no such luxury.

So far we have presented only one side of the picture. In fact, bigness in industry need not be advantageous only to the firm. It can also, at least sometimes, work to the advantage of the general public. Again, there are several reasons:

1. Required scale for innovation. A number of noted economists have taken a position on firm size and innovation that is virtually the opposite of the view just summarized. These scholars argue that only large firms have the resources and the motivation for really significant innovation. Technological change these days is no longer a matter for backyard inventors using clothespins and bits of electric wire. It is an expensive, complex venture that can only be carried out on a large scale, and only large firms can afford the funds and bear the risks that such change demands. In addition, according to this view, only the large firm has the motivation to lay out the funds required for the innovation process, because it is the large firm that will get to keep a considerable share of the benefits. A small company, on the other hand, will find that its innovative idea is soon likely to be followed by close imitations, which enable competitors to profit from its research outlays.

2. Economies of large size. Probably a far more important advantage of bigness is to be found in those industries in which technology dictates that small scale is inefficient. One can hardly imagine the costs if automobiles were produced in little workshops rather than giant factories. The notion of a small firm operating a long-distance railroad does not even make sense, and a multiplicity of firms replicating the same railroad service would clearly be incredibly wasteful. On these grounds, most policymakers have never even considered an attempt to eliminate bigness. Their objective, rather, is to curb its potential abuses and to try at the same time to help the public benefit from its advantages.

Before turning to a discussion of the policy issues to which all this gives rise, we may note briefly some facts that cast additional light on the innovation issue. There have been many studies of the relationship between firm size, competitiveness of the industry, and the level of expenditure on research and development (R and D). While the evidence is far from conclusive, it does indicate that an industry in which firms are very small and highly competitive is *not* highly conducive to innovation. Up to a point, R and D outlays and innovation seem to increase with size of firm and concentration of industry. There are exceptions, however. After some point, greater concentration appears to provide no further stimulus to innovation and, in some cases, may even act as a deterrent.

OTHER GOVERNMENT PROGRAMS RELATED TO BIGNESS

Because the issues raised by bigness and concentration are complex, they would appear to call for a variety of policy measures. Certainly, antitrust programs alone cannot do everything that the public interest requires.

For example, because in some cases very large firms appear to be far more efficient than small ones, it does not seem reasonable to break up these giants of industry. In fact it is sometimes even considered most desirable, on grounds of economy, to permit a market to be served by only a single firm—such as a supplier of electricity, local transportation, or telecommunications services.

Where one firm offers considerable savings in comparison to a multiplicity of suppliers, we say that the industry is a *natural monopoly*, and it is usually agreed that it would not serve the social interest to subdivide the supplying firm into a number of rival companies.

Instead, one of two policies is usually adopted. Either (as is often done in Europe) the monopoly firm is nationalized and run as a government enterprise (telephone service in England and electricity generation in France are publicly owned and operated). Or, as in the United States, the natural monopoly is (usually) left as a private firm, but its operations are regulated by a federal or state agency designed to offer the public the economies of large-scale operation without the abuses of unrestricted

monopoly. This is true of AT&T, of the nation's airlines, and of its electric companies. Prices are regulated in a manner designed to prevent the earning of monopoly profits, and other industry practices are also subjected to regulatory control.[5] This will all be discussed in detail in the following chapter.

The inhibition of innovation by competition is another important issue, which, as we have seen, affects policy toward bigness and concentration. The main instrument government has employed in this area is the patent system, which rewards the innovator in even a small firm in a highly competitive industry by the grant of a temporary monopoly. The patent restricts imitation and is designed to offer small-firm innovators the same advantages from their research activities as are enjoyed by innovators in industries that contain no competitors ready to erode profits by imitation. Thus, somewhat ironically, the same government system that prohibits monopolies also guarantees monopoly power to protect small firms in competitive industries. Of course, sometimes the protected firms themselves grow big with the help of this protection. Once-small firms like Polaroid and Xerox grew into industry giants with the help of government protection through the patent laws.

Some questions have been raised about the effectiveness of patents in inducing expenditure on R and D, and the evidence certainly does not provide overwhelming support for the view that patents constitute a strong stimulus for innovation. Questions have also been raised about the desirability of granting an innovator an unrestricted monopoly for 17 years as the patent program now does in the United States. Similar issues have been raised about copyright laws, which restrict reproduction of written works.

[5]A critical issue in this area is raised by the AT&T case. AT&T has never denied that in some of its markets it is a monopoly, one whose activities are regulated by the Federal Communications Commission and state regulatory agencies. It has been permitted to continue as a monopoly because of the economies of scale it is believed to offer. The question to be settled by the courts is whether such a regulated monopoly is nevertheless vulnerable to antitrust prosecution.

Government policy has also sought to provide special help to small business in a variety of ways. For example, there have been programs designed to make it easier for small firms to raise capital, and special government agencies, such as the Small Business Administration, have been set up for the purpose. There is also some degree of *progressivity* in business taxation, meaning that smaller firms are subject to lower taxes than larger firms pay. And special legislation, such as the "fair trade" laws—which, though since repealed, permitted manufacturers to designate and enforce "fair" retail prices for products—is intended, in part, to protect small retailers from the competition of larger rivals whose scale economies might permit them to undercut smaller competitors.

ISSUES IN ANTITRUST POLICY

In recent years there has been great interest in reexamining government policy toward business. For example, there have been calls for a reevaluation of the work of the regulatory agencies, and the antitrust program is unlikely to be ignored in such a review. There are a few who would call for an abolition of the antitrust program altogether, while others advocate its strengthening and expansion. Whether or not it has been effective as an inhibitor of concentration, observers conclude that it has helped to change the rules of the game under which business is conducted.

Particularly in overseas operations of American firms one still finds examples of free-swinging, uninhibited business operations of the sort made notorious by the "robber barons" after the Civil War. But in domestic industry they are now comparatively rare. It takes discoveries such as the bribery scandals of 1975–1976, in which U.S. business firms operating abroad were shown to be involved in large illegal payments to foreign governments, to remind us that

there are some firms still apparently ready to revert to earlier practices if they feel they can get away with them.

But, even if one grants the desirability of an antitrust program with "teeth" in it, there still remain questions about whom or what to "bite"!

A major issue is the relative weight that should be assigned to *structure* and *conduct* in deciding which firms it is in the social interest to prosecute. Not many people object to the basic notion that socially damaging conduct, such as price fixing or threats of physical violence, should be discouraged, though there is not always complete agreement on what types of conduct are undesirable. But many more questions are raised about the use of structural criteria in antitrust policy. Is bigness always undesirable per se? What if the large firm is more efficient and has engaged in no practices that can reasonably be considered to constitute predatory competition?

Many economists have reservations about the prosecution of such a firm, fearing that it will only serve to grant protection to inefficient competitors and do so at the expense of consumers. Similarly, they point out the danger that successful firms will tend to be singled out for attention under the antitrust laws, simply because their success makes them noticeable and their efficiency enables them to outstrip their competitors. The fear is that such an orientation will discourage efficiency and entrepreneurship.

It is now widely recognized that policy in this area can in fact prove anticompetitive and an inhibition to efficiency, despite its contrary intentions. For example, the "fair trade" laws were repealed because it was finally recognized that they effectively prevented price competition by drug, appliance, and liquor retailers, among many others. The primary victims of the "fair trade" laws were the consumers, who were forced by law to pay higher prices while the primary beneficiaries were the least-efficient retailers who, without the protection of those laws, would have been forced out of business.

Another example of the lack of agreement

between economists and lawmakers about the sorts of conduct that the law should proscribe concerns the issue of *price discrimination*, which the law describes as the sale of the same item to two different customers at different prices. To economists, this legal definition is misleading. Suppose, for instance, that one person lives on a mountaintop far from the place where a good is produced, and another consumer is located in an area that enjoys easy access to the good in question. Economists would say that it is not discriminatory to charge each a different price. *On the contrary, economists hold that in such cases it is discriminatory to charge both customers the same price, which does not account for the substantial difference in the two delivery costs.*

Even more important than this definitional argument, though, is the issue of the desirability or undesirability of discrimination. The word *discrimination* is what has been called a "persuasive term"—in this case, a word that automatically implies gross misconduct. But, in fact, *price discrimination can sometimes be beneficial to all parties to a transaction.* Suppose a commodity is available to the poor only if it is sold at a relatively low price, though that price

more than covers its marginal cost (the cost incurred in expanding into the lower-income market). In this case, the contribution from the lower-income market may permit *some* reduction in price to the rich, though the firm may not be able to cover its total cost if it charges the rich the *same* low price that is necessary for entry into the low-income market. The result is that the poor, the wealthy, and the selling firm will all benefit from the discriminatory pricing. A good example is pricing by doctors, who often charge higher fees to their wealthy patients than they do to their poor ones. If the reduced fees permit more poor patients to visit a doctor, the doctor may be able to earn a comfortable living without charging the rich as high a fee as would be necessary without the low-income patients. Regulated firms, whose overall earnings are restrained by a regulatory profit ceiling, have often argued that lower fees to some classes of buyers can bring in a profit, for without the reduced price these potential customers would not purchase at all. In such cases, it is asserted, the regulatory profit ceiling forces the firm to charge lower fees than it would have otherwise—to all its customers. Are such acts of discrimination so unjust?

SUMMARY

1. The Sherman Act is the oldest U.S. antitrust law. It prohibits contracts, combinations, and conspiracies in restraint of trade and also prohibits monopolization.
2. The Clayton Act prohibits price discrimination that tends to reduce competition or create monopoly; it also prohibits competing firms from sharing directors.
3. There are several other important antitrust laws, including the Federal Trade Commission Act, which set the commission up as an independent antitrust agency, and the Robinson–Patman Act, which generally prohibits discriminatory price discounts.
4. In its earlier history, the courts generally held that a large share of market by a single firm was only illegal if the firm had acquired its relatively large share by illegal means; but in the early postwar period the courts seemed to take the view that bigness per se was presumed to be illegal unless such bigness was "thrust upon the firm" by economies of scale, unusual efficiency, or other similar influences.
5. The evidence indicates that there has been no significant increase in the

concentration of individual American industries into larger firms during the twentieth century.

6. The evidence as to whether antitrust laws have been effective in preventing monopoly is inconclusive, and observers disagree on the subject.

7. The arguments *against* unregulated monopoly are that it is likely to exploit consumers financially, produce undesirably small quantities of output, and have inadequate motive for innovation.

8. Defenders of big business argue that only large firms have funds sufficient for effective research, development, and innovation; and that where economies of scale are available, large firms can serve customers more cheaply than can small ones.

9. In industries in which economies of scale make competition impractical, monopolies are usually permitted by law. In the United States these monopolies are normally regulated by government. In European countries these firms are usually nationalized, that is, government owned and operated.

CONCEPTS FOR REVIEW

Sherman Act	Vertical merger
Clayton Act	Structure versus conduct
Rule of reason	Horizontal merger
Price discrimination	Concentration of industry
Tying contracts	Concentration ratio
Interlocking directorates	Patent system
	Natural monopoly

QUESTIONS FOR DISCUSSION

1. Suppose Sam lives in the central city while Fran's home is far away so that it requires much more gas to deliver newspapers to Fran than to Sam. Yet the newspaper charges them exactly the same amount. Would the courts consider this to be price discrimination? Would an economist? Would you? Why?

2. A shopkeeper sells his store and signs a contract that restrains him from opening another store in competition with the new owner. The courts have decided that this contract is a *reasonable* restraint of trade. Can you think of any other types of restraint of trade that seem reasonable? Any that seem unreasonable?

3. Which of the following industries do you expect to have high concentration ratios: meatpacking, production of farm machinery, production of men's clothing, production of automobiles, production of TV sets? Compare your answers with Table 25–2.

4. Why do you think the industries you selected in Question 3 are highly concentrated?

5. Do you think structure or conduct is the more reasonable basis for antitrust regulation? Give reasons for your answer.

6. Do you think it is in the public interest to launch an antitrust suit that costs a billion dollars (as may well be true of the IBM and the AT&T cases now under way)? What leads you to your conclusion?

26

Limiting Market Power: Regulation of Industry

We have seen why some industries in the United States are subject to regulation. In this chapter we will examine those industries more closely and describe the functioning of some of the principal regulatory agencies. We then will offer a more detailed account of the reasons for regulation; discuss the evidence on the effects and the effectiveness of regulation; consider the reasons why regulatory agencies have devoted a great deal of attention to limitation of price cuts; and then examine some of the criticisms of the regulatory process and some of the suggestions that have been made to improve it. Finally, we will conclude the chapter with a few comments on nationalization of industries.

MONOPOLY, REGULATION, AND NATIONALIZATION

Throughout the Western economies a number of industries are traditionally run as monopolies.

These include postal services, telephone services, and electricity generation; transportation and gas supply also are frequently accorded monopoly status.

Since there are no competitive pressures to protect the interests of consumers from monopolistic exploitation in these cases, it is generally agreed that some substitute form of protection for consumers should be found. Most of Western Europe has adopted nationalization as its solution, which means that the state owns and operates certain monopolistic industries. In the United States, we are more reluctant to have government involved in the running of businesses. Yet even here it has happened to some degree. Most cities now run their own public transport systems; the post office and much of the passenger railroad system in the United States are run by public corporations; and the Tennessee Valley Authority is one of this country's major experiments in electricity supply by a public agency.

In the United States, however, the main instrument of control of public utility industries has been the regulatory agency. Both the federal and the state governments have created a large number of agencies that regulate prices, standards of service, provisions for safety, and a variety of other aspects of the operations of telephone companies, radio and television stations, electric utilities, airlines, trucking companies, and firms in many other industries. Many of these industries are not pure monopolies, but include firms that nevertheless possess so much market power that their regulation is considered to be in the public interest.

PRACTICAL PROBLEM: PRICE FLOORS VERSUS PRICE CEILINGS

In a famous passage in the *Wealth of Nations*, Adam Smith tells us

It always is and must be the interest of the great body of the people to buy whatever they want of those who sell it cheapest. The proposition is so very manifest, that it seems ridiculous to take any pains to prove it; nor could it ever have been called into question had not the interested sophistry of merchants and manufacturers confounded the common sense of mankind.[1]

Since regulation of industry has presumably been instituted to protect "the interest of the great body of the people," it is quite natural to surmise that the bulk of the work of the regulatory agencies, so far as it is concerned with prices, would have been devoted to the imposition of price reductions. Thus, one would think that the typical case before a regulatory agency would be based on the complaint that a firm with monopoly power was charging prices that were excessively high, and that a typical decision of the regulatory agency would require such prices to be reduced.

In fact, this seems to be virtually the reverse of what has happened. Although in some cases, notably in the supply of natural gas, regulation *has* kept prices below the levels they might have reached in a free market, the bulk of cases devoted to price regulation has been in response to complaints that prices charged by the regulated firm are *too low!* Often the outcome in such cases has been a requirement on the part of regulators that the firms raise their prices higher than they wanted to. Where buyers have had a choice among several suppliers—for example, shippers of freight who have had a choice between trucks, railroads, and barges— the regulatory agency has effectively prevented the consumer from purchasing from "those who [are willing to] sell cheapest." Because the cost of additional shipments via railroad is sometimes lower than the cost of shipping via barges, regulators have, at least in some such cases, required the low-priced suppliers (railroads) to

[1]Adam Smith, *The Wealth of Nations* (New York: Modern Library, Random House, Inc., 1937), page 461.

raise their fees to match the prices charged by their high-cost competitors (barges).

How did regulation get itself into this curious pattern? What just reason is there for a regulatory agency to devote itself primarily to the imposition of price floors rather than price ceilings? Later in this chapter, through our analysis of the regulatory process, we will be able to indicate just how and why this has happened.

WHO IS REGULATED BY WHICH AGENCIES?

The regulatory agencies in the United States can be divided, roughly, into two classes: those devoted to limiting the market power of regulated firms, and those devoted to consumer protection and safety in the noneconomic sense. A primary example of an agency working toward the latter goal is the Food and Drug Administration (FDA) of the Department of Health, Education, and Welfare, which is assigned the task of protecting the public from the sale of harmful, spoiled or impure, infected, or adulterated foods, drugs, and cosmetics. It also has the task of preventing the mislabeling or bad packaging of any of these products. Similarly, the U.S. Department of Agriculture supervises the packing and grading of meats and poultry, tasks it has had since 1906.

The federal government also has become involved in regulating the safety of automobiles, mines, and emissions of such poisonous substances as dangerous pesticides. The Environmental Protection Agency (EPA), whose tasks include the protection of the health and welfare of the general public, has more recently taken its place among the other regulatory bodies.

An enormous proportion of the nation's economic activity is affected by these sorts of regulations. For instance, the drug industry, agriculture, auto manufacturing, and the chemical and power industries are just some of the businesses affected in one way or another by regulations designed to protect public health and safety, and virtually every manufacturing industry is affected by environmental regulations.

Equally pervasive are regulations designed to limit market power. At the federal level alone the number of agencies charged with this sort of task is substantial. Table 26–1 lists the main industries in the United States whose *rates* (prices) are subject to regulation and it also indicates their share of total GNP. The figures indicate that these industries play an important role in the economy. Together, they provide well over 10 percent of the GNP of the United States. Note that this table does not include those industries regulated just for the safety of their products or for protection of the environment.

TABLE 26–1

SHARE IN GNP OF SOME PRINCIPAL REGULATED U.S. INDUSTRIES

INDUSTRY	PERCENT OF 1976 GNP	
Railroad transportation	0.79	
Local interurban passenger transit	0.22	
Trucking and warehousing	1.50	
Water transportation	0.26	
Air transportation	0.61	
Other	0.23	
Total transportation		3.61
Telephone and telegraph	1.97	
Other	0.23	
Total communications		2.20
Electric, gas, and sanitary services		1.85
Banking		1.68
Insurance carriers		1.10
Total		10.44

This table shows that more than 10 percent of GNP in the United States is produced by regulated industries. Our economy is far from being controlled entirely by the free market!

Source: U.S. Bureau of Economic Analysis, *The National Income and Product Accounts of the U.S. 1929–74* and *Survey of Current Business,* July 1977.

The principal regulatory agencies of the federal government that control prices include the Interstate Commerce Commission (ICC), which regulates railroads, barges, pipelines, and some categories of trucking; the Federal Communications Commission (FCC), which regulates broadcasting and telecommunications; the Federal Energy Regulatory Commission (FERC), which regulates interstate transmission of electric power and sales of natural gas; the Civil Aeronautics Board (CAB), which supervises the operation of the airlines; the Securities and Exchange Commission (SEC), which regulates the sale of securities (stocks); and several agencies led by the Federal Reserve System, which control banking operations. The work of these agencies is complemented by a variety of state agencies, which regulate those of the firms' activities that do not enter into interstate commerce.

Regulation of industry in the United States first began when indignation over abuse of market power by the nation's railroads led to the establishment of the ICC in 1887. In particular, there was a public outcry over the support the railroads gave John D. Rockefeller, Sr. in the battle that his Standard Oil Company fought to suppress its rivals. This, along with other abuses by the railroads, invited government intervention. But for several decades afterward there was little attempt to expand regulation to other industries. Then the Federal Power Commission (FPC) was established in 1920 and the Federal Communications Commission in 1934; a substantial proportion of the remaining regulatory agencies were also formed during the 1930s as part of Roosevelt's New Deal.

Economists have long questioned the effectiveness of the regulatory process and the desirability of some of its consequences, but not until the mid-1970s did such questions begin to be raised seriously outside of academic discussions. Recently, several bills have gone before Congress proposing to limit the powers of the regulatory agencies and also proposing to require an explicit renewal by Congress of the charter of each agency every 5 years. The agency would automatically expire in the absence of such renewal legislation. The executive branch under both Presidents Ford and Carter also undertook studies to examine the desirability and the nature of substantial regulatory reform.

WHY REGULATION?

As we learned in the preceding chapter, the main reason for regulation of industry is the phenomenon of natural monopoly. In some industries it is apparently far cheaper to have production carried out by one firm rather than by a large number of firms or even only a few different firms. This will occur either because of economies of large-scale production or because it is sometimes cheaper to produce *a number of different commodities together* rather than turning them out separately, each by a different firm. The savings made possible by simultaneous production of many different products is called economies of scope.

Economies of scale, on the other hand, are savings that are acquired through large-scale production of the same product. An example might be a milk-processing plant to which individual farmers send their product daily to be pasteurized in giant machinery rather than performing that crucial process at home. Use of the more elaborate equipment, which only becomes possible economically when it is employed by many farmers, reduces significantly the cost of pasteurization of each gallon of milk. Here is a case in which savings are made possible by expanding the volume of an activity—a case of economies of scale.

An example of economies of scope is the manufacture of both cars and trucks by the same producer. The techniques employed in producing both commodities are sufficiently similar to make specialized production by different firms impractical.

Why Regulation?

Where there are great economies of scale *and* scope, society will obviously incur a significant cost penalty if it insists on maintaining competition. Supply by a number of smaller competing firms will be far more costly and use up far larger quantities of the community's resources in the production process than it would if the good were supplied by a monopoly. Moreover, in the presence of strong economies of scale and economies of scope, society *will not be able to preserve free competition, even if it wants to.* The large, multiproduct firm will have so great an advantage over its rivals that the small firms simply will be unable to survive. We say in such a case that free competition is *not sustainable.*

Where monopoly production is cheapest, and where free competition is not sustainable, the industry is a natural monopoly. Because monopoly is cheaper, society may not want to have competition; and if free competition is not sustainable, it will not even have a choice in the matter.

But even if society reconciles itself to monopoly, it will generally not want to let the monopoly firm do whatever it wants to with its market power. Therefore, it will consider either regulation or nationalization of these firms.

A second reason for regulation is the desire for "universal service," that is, the availability of service at "reasonable prices" even to small communities where the small scale of operation makes costs extremely high. In such cases, regulators have sometimes encouraged a public utility to supply services to some consumers at a financial loss. But a loss on some sales is financially feasible only when the firm is permitted to make up for it by obtaining higher profits on its other sales. This "averaging" of gains and losses is made possible when the firm is protected from price competition and free entry of new competitors in its more profitable markets. If no such protection is provided by a regulatory agency, potential competitors will sniff out the profit opportunities in the markets where service is supplied at a price well above cost. Many new firms will enter the business and cause prices to be driven down in those markets. This practice is referred to as "cream skimming." The entrants choose to enter only into the profitable markets and skim away the cream of the profits for themselves, leaving the unprofitable markets (the skimmed milk) to the supplier who had attempted to provide universal service.

Airlines and telecommunications are two industries in which these issues have arisen. In both cases, fears have been expressed that without regulation of entry and rates, or the granting of special subsidies, sparsely populated rural areas would effectively be isolated, losing their airline services and obtaining telephone service only at cripplingly high rates. Many economists question the validity of this argument for regulation, which, they say, calls for hidden subsidy of rural consumers by all other consumers.

A third reason for regulation is the danger of self-destructive competition, which, for example, economies of scale make possible. In an industry such as railroading, equipment—including roadbeds, tracks, switching facilities, locomotives, and cars—is extremely expensive. Suppose that two railroads, having been built and equipped, are competing for some limited business that happens to be insufficient to use their total facilities to anything near capacity. That is, to meet this level of consumer demand, each railroad may only have to run 80 percent as many trains over the track as can conveniently be scheduled over that route. The management of each road will feel that, with its unused capacity, any business will be worthwhile, provided that it covers more than its short-run marginal cost—fuel, labor, and expenses other than plant and equipment. If the short-run marginal cost of shipping an additional ton of, say, coal is $5, then either railroad will be happy to lure coal-shipping customers away from the other at a price of, say, $7 per ton, even though that price does not begin to cover the cost of track and equipment.

Each ton of business that pays $7 when short-run marginal cost is $5 will put the railroad $2 ahead of where it would have been without the business. The new business does not add to the cost of the tracks or locomotives or other equipment, which must be paid for whether that business is acquired or not. Thus, even if the business only pays for its own short-run marginal cost and a little more, it seems financially desirable. But the temptation to accept business on such terms will drive both firms' prices down toward their short-run marginal costs, and in the process, both railroads are likely to go broke. If no customer pays for the track, the roadbed, and the equipment, the railroad simply will be unable to go on.

Thus there are those who believe that regulation of rates can be sensible, even in industries subject to competitive pressures, simply to protect the industries from themselves. Without this regulation, self-destructive competition could end up sinking those industries financially, and the public would thereby be deprived of vital services.

A fourth reason often given for public regulation is that some industries base their operations on a public resource of limited capacity, so that a public agency must intervene to ration out that resource "fairly."

The most notable example of the need for this type of rationing is the field of radio and television broadcasting. The frequency spectrum that is available for broadcasting is rather limited, and so it must be divided up among the users. In any event, if it were not divided up in this way and entry were not limited, the airwaves might soon become crowded and interference of broadcasters with one another's transmissions would undermine the quality of reception and perhaps even make the airwaves totally useless.

Many economists have argued that government has no business allocating scarce resources like the radio and TV spectrum among commercial users who employ such public resources for a profit. These economists argue that government rationing of the airwaves is a giveaway of public resources to favored individuals who then grow rich at the public's expense—even though the FCC, in return, does retain some right to regulate the content of broadcasts. Rather, it is proposed that firms be required to bid against one another for licenses to run radio and TV stations. In that way the licenses would go to those who can make the best use of them—an ability that would be determined by their bids. The profits would then go into the public treasury rather than private pockets, and they could be used to finance non-profit public-interest activities, such as public broadcasting. In the same way, the airlines' access to crowded airfields can also be rationed, with airlines required to bid for the right to use a particular airport or serve a particular city.

A final reason for regulation is the danger that consumers will be misinformed, cheated, or subjected to health hazards by unscrupulous sellers or even conscientious sellers forced to keep up with the questionable practices of less scrupulous rivals. This sort of protection is the province of the second type of regulatory agency described earlier, and because economists have less to say about this category of regulation than about regulation of rates, the subject will not be discussed further in this chapter.

SUMMARY

There are five basic reasons for the activities of the regulatory agencies:

1. Prevention of excess profits and other undesirable practices in an industry that is considered to be a natural monopoly, because in such cases economies of scale and scope make monopoly production cheaper than competitive production.
2. The desire for universal service—that is, the desire to provide service at relatively low

rates to customers whom it is particularly expensive to serve, and to do so without government subsidy.

3. The desire to prevent self-destructive price competition in multifirm industries with large capital costs and low costs of fuel, labor, and raw materials (low short-run marginal costs).

4. The desire to allocate fairly public facilities of limited capacity.

5. The desire to protect customers from being cheated or endangered by unscrupulous suppliers.

HAS RATE REGULATION MADE A DIFFERENCE?

An obvious question is whether rate regulation has worked. In particular, has it made any difference in the rates paid by consumers? Would, for example, unregulated public utilities end up charging prices significantly higher than they are permitted to charge under regulation? The answer is by no means obvious. As a matter of fact, some analysts suggest that regulation may indeed make little or no difference in prices. In one careful study comparing rates charged for electric power by regulated and unregulated utility firms over the period 1912 to 1937, a period when there were a substantial number of firms in both categories, the authors concluded that there was no significant difference between the average rates charged in the two categories.[2] The interpretation of the figures found in the study has been disputed, and the factual issue is by no means settled. But if further research should support the conclusion that regulation has not had any significant effects on *average* prices, it would severely undercut the case of those who advocate the regulatory approach.

Several explanations are possible for a con-

---

[2]See George Stigler and Clair Friedland, "What Can Regulation Regulate?—The Case of Electricity." *Journal of Law and Economics*, October 1962, pages 1–16.

clusion that regulation has indeed not affected average prices. The first is that the regulatory procedure is simply a sloppy process that is inherently incapable of making much difference, one way or another. A second explanation that is often proposed is that the regulatory agencies are simply captives of the firms they are intended to regulate. Owing to the great political clout of these big firms (so the argument goes), and because of the powerful lawyers and consultants they are able to afford, the regulated firm can overwhelm the regulatory agency, which itself has only a small staff and a limited budget. In this way the firm can get virtually anything it wants out of the agency. But the evidence against this conclusion is substantial. One need only look at the frequency with which regulated firms lose crucial cases before the regulatory agencies to see the weakness of this argument. The railroads time and again have lost vital chunks of business when the ICC ruled against the price arrangements under which some new business was obtained. And AT&T is faced with more and more competition, plus the requirement by the FCC that it permit customers to attach equipment produced by firms other than Bell System suppliers to their telephone lines. Many other such examples can easily be cited.

A third explanation for the conjecture that regulation does not significantly affect *average* prices is the fact, noted before, that regulators, for reasons we will discuss later, often impose on the regulated firms prices *higher* than they would like to charge. That is precisely what the ICC did in the railroad regulation cases just mentioned. If regulators sometimes impose price increases, and sometimes impose price decreases, it is at least conceivable that *on the average* regulation will not affect the price level very much.

Whatever the overall effect of regulation on average prices, there is no doubt that in many individual cases it has significant effects on *particular* prices charged by regulated firms. One of the most widely publicized examples is the differences in airplane fares between San Francisco and Los Angeles and those between Washington, D.C., and New York City. The former fare is not regulated by the CAB (since the flight is entirely within the state of California), whereas the CAB does control the interstate flight between New York and Washington, D.C. The distance of the California trip is nearly twice as great as the East Coast trip, and neither is sparsely traveled nor beset by any other noteworthy features that would make for substantial differences in cost per passenger mile. Yet fares are a little over $30 for the long California trip and a little over $40 for the short Washington to New York City trip.

WHY SHOULD REGULATORS RAISE PRICES?

Why should regulators ever want to push for higher prices? The answer is that typically they do so when they want to introduce or preserve competition in an industry. We saw earlier that where there are strong economies of scale and scope it may simply be impossible for a number of firms to survive. The largest of the firms in the industry will have such cost advantages over their competitors that it will be able to drive them out of the market while still operating at prices that are profitable.

In addition, a firm that wants the market for itself may conceivably engage in price cutting even when such cuts are not justifiable in terms of cost. Low prices then are merely temporary bargains that, once they succeed in driving out the competition, will promptly be withdrawn. This sort of practice, sometimes referred to as predatory pricing, is considered undesirable by most persons who have analyzed regulatory issues.

But regulation sometimes goes beyond the prevention of predatory pricing. Firms that feel they are hurt by competitive pressures will complain to regulatory commissions that the prices charged by their rivals are unfairly low. (See the boxed insert, which shows how the bus companies complained that reduced standby air fares for young people were unfair.) The commission, afraid that unrestrained pricing will reduce the number of firms in the industry, then attempts to "equalize" matters by imposing price floors that permit all the firms in the industry to operate profitably. The ICC once described itself as a "giant handicapper" whose task was presumably to make sure that no firm within its jurisdiction got too far ahead of the others. It did not seem to show a similar concern with whether consumers were winning or losing.

This attitude has produced many strange patterns of resource utilization. For example, there is evidence that for distances of more than, say, 200 miles, railroads have a clear-cut cost advantage over trucks. Yet ICC influence over railroad rates has forced those rates upward sufficiently to make it possible for trucks to "compete" from coast to coast. The resulting waste of resources is probably enormous.

Many observers, notably economists, maintain that this approach to pricing is a perversion of the idea of competition. The virtue of competition is that where it occurs firms force one another to supply consumers with products of high quality at *low* prices. If competition does not do this, it loses its purpose because to the economist it is a means to an end, not an end in itself. An arrangement under which firms are enabled to coexist only by *preventing* them from competing with one another preserves the appearance of competition but destroys its substance.

MARGINAL VERSUS FULL-COST RATE FLOORS

The issue of rate floors has raged over hundreds of thousands of pages of hearing records

The Case for Regulatory Rate Increases

The following excerpts are from the Court of Appeals decision issued July 24, 1967, leading to the abolition of a youth standby program of fare reductions to persons under 22 years of age. The complaint was not by other categories of passengers who were allegedly discriminated against, but was made by the bus companies, which were demanding higher air fares. It is almost always the competitors who demand the regulatory rate increases.

IN THE

United States Court of Appeals

FOR THE FIFTH CIRCUIT

TRANSCONTINENTAL BUS SYSTEM, INC., ET AL; TRAILWAYS OF NEW ENGLAND, INC.; CAPITOL BUS COMPANY, INC., ET AL; VIRGINIA STAGE LINES, INC., ET AL; CONTINENTAL TENNESSEE LINES, ET AL; DELUXE TRAILWAYS, INC., ET AL; AMERICAN BUSLINES, INC., ET AL; CONTINENTAL PACIFIC LINES, ET AL; D.C.S.P. MOTOR WAY, INC., ET AL; ADIRONDACK TRANSIT LINES, INC., ET AL; NATIONAL TRAILWAYS BUS SYSTEM,

Petitioners,

versus

CIVIL AERONAUTICS BOARD,
Respondent.

GEWIN, Circuit Judge: These are consolidated petitions for review of several orders of the Civil Aeronautics Board (Board) dismissing without a hearing the petitioners consolidated complaints which sought the suspension and investigation of tariffs filed by numerous air carriers providing for reduced rates for military standby, youth standby, and young adult passengers . . .

The petitioners alleged before the Board and assert here on review that the tariffs are unreasonable and unjustly discriminatory in violation of the Federal Aviation Act of 1958 (FAA) . . .

The order of the Board in Docket No. 22,791, et al, refusing to investigate or suspend the military standby tariff is affirmed. The orders of the Board in Docket Nos. 23,410 and 23,411 refusing to investigate or suspend the youth and young adult fare tariffs are set aside and reversed and the cases are remanded to the Civil Aeronautics Board.

and has involved literally hundreds of millions of dollars of expenditures in fees for lawyers, expert witnesses, and research in preparation of the cases. But the question here has been not whether all floors on the prices of regulated utilities are improper, for virtually everyone seems to agree that some sort of lower boundary on prices is required in order to prevent predatory pricing practices, but rather what constitutes the proper *nature* of the rate floors.

The use of prices as a means to induce an efficient allocation of resources, the function of prices that usually concerns the economist most (see Chapter 30), is not the main concern of the regulatory hearings. Rather, the two primary concerns of regulation in relation to prices are: (1) Whether the prices under dispute are in some sense *unfair to competitors;* and (2) Whether the prices are *unfair to customers of other products* produced by the same firm. In other words, is that supplier overcharging for products for which he has little competition in order to be able to undercut his rivals in the supply of products for which competition is substantial?

If a firm charges such low prices for product Y that it is forced to raise the price of another of its products, X, in order to break even on the two, then the firm is said to be cross-subsidizing the sale of product Y at the expense of customers of product X. The issues of both cross-subsidy and fairness in competition are questions of equity and justice rather than efficiency in the use of resources.

Two alternative criteria have been proposed to determine appropriate floors for prices. Prices that fall below these levels are said to be unfair to competitors; that is, they involve the issue of cross-subsidy.

Criterion 1. The price of a commodity should never be less than its *long-run marginal cost.*

Criterion 2. The price should not be less than that commodity's *fully distributed cost*—that is,

its "fair share" of the firm's total cost as determined by some accounting calculation.

To calculate the fully distributed costs of the various products of the firm, one simply takes the firm's total costs and divides them up in some way among its various products. First, one allocates to each product the costs for which it is obviously directly responsible. For example, a railroad allocates to coal transportation the cost of hauling all cars that were devoted exclusively to carrying coal, plus the cost of operating locomotives on runs in which they carried only coal cars, and so on. Then, one takes all costs (such as the cost of constructing the roadbed and tracks) that are incurred *in common* for several or all of the outputs of the company and divides them on the basis of some rule of thumb (generally conceded to be arbitrary) among the firm's various products. Usually, the basis of this allocation is some measure of the relative use of the common facilities by the different products. But even "relative use" is an ambiguous term. How does one divide up the cost of the track of a railroad among its shipments of lead, lumber, and gold? If relative use is defined by the weight of the shipments, then the accountants will assign a high proportion of the cost to lead shipments. If prices are then required to exceed full cost, under this definition of "relative use" the railroad will be placed at a disadvantage in competing for lead traffic. If, instead, relative use is defined in terms of bulk, the railroad's lumber business will be harmed; if relative use is defined in terms of market value, it will lose out in competing for gold shipments.

Those who advocate the use of marginal cost rather than fully distributed cost as the appropriate basis for any floor on prices argue that long-run marginal cost is the relevant measure of the cost that any shipment actually causes. For, by definition, marginal cost is the difference that an additional shipment makes to the firm's total cost—it is the difference between the cost to the firm if that shipment takes place and its cost to the firm if the shipment is carried by some other means of transportation.

DEFINITION

The long-run marginal cost of an output is the *addition* to the supplier's total cost resulting from the supply of that output *including whatever additional plant and equipment* is needed in the long run to provide that output. The inclusion of this marginal capital cost (the cost of the necessary additions to plant and equipment) is the crucial feature that distinguishes *long-run* marginal cost from short-run marginal cost.

The advocates of marginal cost criteria argue that customers of *every* product of the supplier may benefit if the company is permitted to charge a price based on long-run marginal cost, particularly if, as is usual under regulation, there is a legal ceiling on the firm's total profits. For suppose that a railroad considers taking on some new business whose marginal cost is $7 and whose fully distributed cost is figured at $12. Suppose also that at any price over $10 the railroad will lose the business to the truckers. If the railroad charges $10 and gets the business, the price does not cover the fully distributed cost, but it still adds $3 to the company's net earnings for every unit it sells to the new customers. If it was already earning as much profit as the law allows, the company would normally be made to reduce its prices on its other products. Thus every group of customers can gain— the new customers because they get the product more cheaply than it can be supplied by competitors, and the old customers because the prices on their products must be cut in order to satisfy the firm's profit ceiling. Everyone gains except the company's competitors, who will, of course, complain that the price is unfair because it does not cover fully distributed cost. (For an example of an opinion by a regulator defending the use of marginal cost analysis

against fully distributed cost, see the boxed insert on page 498.)

PROBLEMS OF THE REGULATORY PROCESS

There are several features of the regulatory process that give rise to problems for which there is no clear-cut solution. Indeed, for some problems, *none* of the solutions that have so far been proposed may be very satisfactory. Three of these problems are:

1. The tendency of regulation to push prices upward.
2. The difficulty of simultaneously preventing profits from growing to levels that regulators consider excessive while at the same time preserving some financial incentive for efficiency of operation by the firm.
3. The adversary method of settling such technical issues as proper methods for accounting, demand forecasting, and cost calculation. Currently, the only way these issues are settled is through trial by combat— lawyers battling over the issues as though they were matters for crime and punishment rather than reasoned analysis.

We have already considered the first of these issues, and the third is self-explanatory. It is only the second that requires further discussion. We have seen that one of the primary tasks of regulation is to prevent the monopoly firm from earning excessive profits, while at the same time permitting it to earn enough to pay for the capital it needs to expand when growing markets justify such expansion. From this point of view, it would be ideal if the regulator would just permit the firm to take in that amount of revenue that covers its costs, including the cost of its capital. That is, the firm should earn exactly enough to pay for its ordinary costs plus the normal profit that potential investors can get elsewhere for the same money. If the prevailing rate of return is 10 percent, the regulated firm should recover its expenditures plus 10 percent on its investment and not a penny more or less.

The trouble with such an arrangement is that it removes all incentive for efficiency, responsiveness to consumer demand, and innovation. For under such an arrangement the firm is in effect *guaranteed* just *one standard rate* of profit, no more and no less. This is so whether its management is totally incompetent or ex-

tremely talented and hard working.

Competitive markets do *not* work in this way. While under pure competition the *average* firm generally will earn just the opportunity cost of capital, a firm with a specially ingenious and efficient management will do better, and a firm with an incompetent management is likely to go broke. It is the possibility of great rewards and harsh punishments that gives the market mechanism its power to cause firms to strive for high efficiency.

Marginal Versus Fully Distributed Cost in Rate Regulation

In the following dissenting opinion of Commissioner Hooks of the FCC (FCC Docket 18128, October 1, 1976, FCC Reports, second series), the commissioner argues that a fully distributed cost floor is illogical. He states that a marginal cost test has the blessing of Congress and other regulatory agencies. He says that a marginal cost test may cause more work for the regulator, but it is the public interest and not an easy job for regulators that is important. The rest of the commission disagreed, and voted for a fully distributed cost criterion.

The Commission here, over all dictates of common sense, views of Congressional experts,* the practices of other regulatory agencies,† and the protestations of state regulatory agencies, has adopted a Fully Distributed Cost accounting method that is all but unyielding and defies every proven rule of economic logic. Virtually every economist-observer cited in this proceeding concedes that incremental costs methods are the closest approximation to a free market environment and the courts have ratified the use of marginal cost pricing in the utility field.

I concede that there are imperfections inherent in monitoring marginal costing structures in terms of regulatory administration not present with a simplistic, Fully Distributed Cost basis. However, governmental decisions should not be predicated disproportionately on convenience to the government, but on the broader public interest. What was clearly called for out of this Docket was a system which allows flexibility. . . . Instead we have ordered *rigor mortis*.

*For a clear, concise attack on the FCC's notions about using Fully Distributed Costs as a basis for rate making, the dangers of higher prices from such a system, the anticompetitive outcome sure to follow, and some intelligent alternatives, see *Agenda For Oversight: Domestic Common Carrier Regulation, Prepared by the Staff for the Use of the Subcommittee on Communications of the House Committee on Interstate and Foreign Commerce*, 94th Cong., 2d Sess. at pp. 19–23, April 26, 1976.

†The Department of Justice contends:
Since firms in a competitive market may find it more efficient to engage in marginal cost pricing, especially where they have substantial fixed costs, enactment of the bill could result in higher consumer prices and inefficient resource allocation. Moreover, enactment of a "fully distributed cost" criterion would limit firm pricing flexibility thereby fostering undesirable price rigidity. . . .

We have strong evidence that where firms are guaranteed a fixed return, no matter how well or poorly they perform, gross inefficiencies are likely to result. For example, many contracts for purchases of military equipment have offered prices calculated on a cost-plus basis, meaning that the supplier was guaranteed that his costs would be covered and that, in addition, he would receive some prespecified amount as a contribution to profit. Studies of the resulting performance of cost-plus arrangements have confirmed that the suppliers' inefficiencies have been enormous.

A regulatory arrangement that in effect guarantees a firm its costs plus a "fair rate of return" on its investment is virtually the same as a cost-plus contract. Fortunately, under regulation, matters do not work out in exactly the same way.

For one thing, when a regulated industry is in financial trouble, as is true of the railroads, there is nothing the regulator can do to guarantee a "fair rate of return." If the current return on capital is 10 percent, but market demand for railroading is only sufficient to give it 3 percent at most, the regulatory agency cannot help matters by any act of magic. Even if it grants higher prices to the railroad (or forces the railroad to raise its prices) the result would be to drive even more business away and therefore cause the firm to earn still lower profits.

There is a second reason why profit regulation does not work in the same way as does a cost-plus arrangement. Curiously, this is a result of the much-criticized delays that characterize many regulatory procedures. In a number of regulated industries, a proposed change in rates is likely to take a minimum of several months before it gets through the regulatory machinery. Where it is bitterly contested, the resulting hearings before the regulatory commission, the appeals to the courts, and so on, are likely to last for years. Rate cases lasting 10 years are not unknown. This was true, for example, in the case before the FCC referred to in the boxed insert on the opposite page. This phenomenon,

known as regulatory lag, is perhaps the main reason that profit regulation has not eliminated all rewards for efficiency and all penalties for inefficiency.

Suppose, for example, the regulatory commission approves a set of prices calculated to yield exactly the "fair rate of return" to the company, say 10 percent. If management then invests successfully in new processes, which reduce its costs sharply, the rate of return under the prices may rise to, say, 12 percent. If it takes 2 years for the regulators to review the prices it had approved previously and adjust them to the new cost levels, the company will earn a 2 percent bonus reward for its efficiency during the 2 years of regulatory lag.

Similarly, if management makes a series of bad decisions, which reduces the company's return to 7 percent, the firm may well apply to the regulator for some adjustments in prices to permit it to recoup its losses. If the regulator takes 18 months to act, the firm suffers a penalty for its inefficiency. It may be added that where mismanagement is *clearly* the cause of losses, regulators will be reluctant to permit the regulated firm to make up for such losses by rate adjustments. But in most cases it is difficult to pinpoint responsibility for a firm's losses.

All in all, those who have studied regulated industries have come away deeply concerned about the effects of regulation upon economic efficiency. Although some regulated firms seem to operate very efficiently, others seem to behave in quite the opposite way.

While regulatory lag does permit some penalty for inefficiency and some reward for superior performance by the regulated firm, the arrangement only works in a rough and ready manner. It still leaves incentives for efficiency as one of the fundamental dilemmas of regulation. How can one prevent regulated firms from earning excessive profits, but also permit them to earn enough to attract the capital they need while still allowing rewards for superior performance and penalties for poor performance?

MODIFICATIONS IN REGULATORY ARRANGEMENTS: PRESERVING PRODUCTIVE EFFICIENCY

The problems of regulation just mentioned, along with some other criticisms, have in recent years produced a number of proposals for changes in the regulatory process.

Deregulation Plus Increased Competition

One of the most widely advocated proposals is that, at least in certain areas, regulators should largely get out of the business of regulating, leaving much more (if not all) of the task of looking after consumer interests to the natural forces of competition.

This approach appears to be promising in areas of the economy in which competition can be expected to survive without government intervention—for example, in freight transportation, airlines, and pipelines. As a consequence, a number of economists representing a broad range of political views have been advocating at least some deregulation in these fields. Accordingly, the CAB has recently made it much easier for an airline to lower fares or to serve new routes. Of course, deregulation will not work in industries where competitors can survive only if government protects them from real competition.

Performance Criteria for Permitted Rate of Return

The argument for deregulation addresses itself to all of the problems discussed in the previous section, but there are other proposals that are concerned with only one or another of these problems. We turn now to proposals designed to prevent profit controls from discouraging efficiency.

Some observers have advocated that the legally permitted rate of return not be set at a fixed number, say 10 percent, but that it be varied from firm to firm depending on the firm's record of efficiency and performance. That is, if some measure of quality of performance can be agreed upon (a measure that should take account of cost efficiency as well as product and service quality), then the better the performance score of the regulated firm the more it would be permitted to earn. A firm that performed well in a given year might be permitted 12 percent profits for that year, whereas a firm that did badly might be allowed only 8 percent, and a firm that performed abominably might be permitted only 4 percent.

Such incentives sometimes can be successfully built into the rules that control the operations of the firm. For example, such a program was designed for Amtrak, the public corporation that, in effect, rents passenger transportation services from U.S. railroads. Under this contract, accepted by a number of railroads in 1974, the amount Amtrak pays them depends upon such features as promptness of arrival of trains, infrequency of breakdowns of locomotives, and so on. Thus, the more frequently its trains are on time, the more Amtrak pays to that railroad. The results seem fairly clear. While over the period 1973 to 1975 the percentage of trains arriving on time increased for railroads as a whole by about 17.5 percentage points from its miserable 60 percent figure in 1973, the railroads that signed incentive contracts increased their on-time arrivals by about 29.5 percentage points from their initial (1973) average of 61 percent.

However, financial incentives cannot easily be built into rate of return formulas that contain no good objective criteria of performance (such as number of minutes behind schedule for a railroad train). Moreover, it is difficult to balance incentives for different aspects of performance. For example, if the formula assigns too high a weight to product quality and too low a weight to economy, the firm will be encouraged to incur costs that are unjustifiably high from the point of view of public welfare in order to turn out products whose slightly higher quality is not worth their extra cost. And of course the reverse will be true if it is economy rather than efficiency that is assigned too much weight.

Institutionalized Regulatory Lag

It has been proposed that instead of regulatory lag working haphazardly as it does now, regulation should consciously take advantage of the incentive for efficiency made possible by the lag. Under such a program, the regulator would assign product prices to the firms they oversee, decreeing that, *aside from automatic adjustments for inflation,* these prices are unchangeable until the next regulatory review, to occur *at a time selected by the agency.* The regulated firm would be told that the next review will occur, say, sometime between 2 and 6 years in the future, depending on what events occur in the economy. But in the meantime, any firm that can manage cost savings by economy or innovation, or that can attract more customers by improving its product without increasing its costs, will be permitted to keep the higher profits that this superior performance elicits. Of course, for the regulated firm there is a catch. If the firm proves able to reduce costs by, say, 30 percent during a period between regulatory reviews, it can, at the next review, expect to have its prices reduced correspondingly. Thus, in order to earn profits, management would constantly be forced to look for ever more improved and more economical ways of doing things.

This approach, too, has its problems. For one thing, in a period of inflation, when costs go up no matter how efficient management is, it is not clear how regulated prices should be adjusted to make up for inflation *between* review periods because it is not clear what part of the cost change should be attributed to inflation and what part to mismanagement.

MODIFICATIONS OF REGULATORY ARRANGEMENTS: PRICE FLOORS

Other proposals have been designed to deal with the problems created by regulatory agencies when they set floors on prices. That is, how can the regulator prevent unfair or predatory pricing without forcing consumers to pay unnecessarily high prices? Or, how can regulation be turned into a force that works for lower rather than higher prices? Two proposals that have been offered are summarized here.

Long-Run Marginal Cost Floors

As already noted, many economists have proposed that the firm should *never* be forced to raise the price of any product if revenue from the product is at least as large as its long-run marginal cost. The argument is that if the price passes this test, then that price is not being subsidized, meaning that the revenue from a sale the product brings in to the firm *more than covers the costs incurred to supply it.*

Advocates of this rule say that it would undercut most regulatory pressures to raise prices. But opponents of the proposal argue that it is difficult, in practice, for regulators to calculate marginal costs, and that even if the price of a product is above its marginal cost by some unspecified amount, this does not guarantee that buyers of the product contribute their "fair share" of the costs that are incurred in common for various company products (the cost of the railroad's tracks).

Irreversibility of Price Decreases

As a supplement or an alternative to the preceding suggestion, economists have advocated a rule that firms be permitted to reduce prices, if they wish to do so, for products that are under competitive pressure. However, once firms have made such a reduction, they will not be permitted to raise the product price again except as a consequence of inflation or any other increase in cost that is demonstrably beyond the control of the firm. The burden of proof that such a cost increase has occurred will fall on the regulated firm.

The purpose of this proposal is to prevent the regulated firm from lowering prices temporarily to drive out competitors and then promptly raising them again once competitors have indeed been driven out. The regulated firm would suffer a penalty if it misbehaved by pricing below cost by having to bear the resulting losses for the indefinite future.

The main weakness of this proposal is, again, the nature of the adjustment that would be permitted under inflation. There are also those who suspect that such a rule is not sufficiently strong for the job. But if enforced strictly, it is hard to see why this is so. Why should a firm voluntarily commit itself to prices that will incur losses for an indefinite period of time? There is now such a provision in the legislation regulating the railroads, but there is no evidence that the ICC has put it to use in its regulation of railroad rates, perhaps because that would be inconsistent with the ICC's traditional role as a "giant handicapper" protecting each competitor from "excessive" pressure from its rivals.

REVAMPING THE LEGAL PROCEDURES

We turn now to the final issue that was raised about the desirability of regulatory processes as now organized—the adversary procedure. As indicated before, the problem is that highly technical issues, such as the best methods of statistical evaluation of marginal costs, are settled largely by the arguments of lawyers who frequently admit they do not understand the issues involved. This is aggravated by the fact that in a set of regulatory hearings some of the parties will hire as advisers the leading specialists in the pertinent fields, while other parties often either choose not to have such advisers or are not able to afford them. The regulatory commissions themselves sometimes complain that they do not have the funds for the technical expertise they need.

To deal with this problem, it has been suggested that such technical matters be settled by what is, in effect, binding arbitration by an appointed panel of impartial experts. The hearing examiner (judge) in each case would have the power to determine when the matter at issue was sufficiently technical in character to require expert appointees. Furthermore, the list of experts submitted by the regulatory commission can be made subject to challenge by the parties in much the same way that potential jurors in a trial may be challenged. Some preliminary attempts at experimentation in this direction have been undertaken, but they have not yet gone far enough to permit any reliable evaluation.

SOME FINAL COMMENTS ON THE REGULATORY PROCESS

The problems we have described here and the proposals that have been made to deal with them are by no means all of the criticisms that have been raised or all of the proposals that have been offered. We have attempted only to provide here some feeling for the complexity of the regulatory process and to show the difficulty in finding workable alternatives.

It is too easy simply to seek villains and lay blame on them for all that has gone wrong—as many observers of regulation tend to do. For instance, it is often argued that what is wrong with the regulatory process is that the commissions have become captives of the firms they are supposed to regulate, doing whatever those companies want them to do. And perhaps there are some cases where the charge has some validity. But most of the time, matters are much more complicated. The regulated firms are often just as convinced that the regulators are "out to get them" and that the best they can hope for from a set of hearings is to delay a decision for as long as possible.

In truth, under the current process of regulation, virtually everyone may be dissatisfied by the decisions that are likely to emerge. The tendency of regulatory agencies to emphasize the prevention of low rather than high prices may be in part the source of this general dissatisfaction. The regulator does not enjoy the role of defender of high prices; the regulated firm that is prevented from charging proposed lower prices feels deprived of vital business; and customers certainly are not pleased by being forced to pay prices higher than the company wants to offer. On all these counts it is clear that the regulation of prices is not working as one might wish. But the solutions to these problems must be worked out by thoughtful deliberation; they will not disappear simply by willing them away.

A WORD ON NATIONALIZATION

As we indicated at the beginning of the chapter, in industries in which monopoly or near monopoly offers clear advantages to society over competition, there is an alternative to regulation. This alternative is government ownership and operation of the firms in that industry, or nationalization. In the United States, tradition does not favor such government operation, but the exceptions are growing in number. For example, we have government supply of electricity by the TVA; the U.S. Postal Service; and, more re-

cently, the operation of railroads by two new agencies, Amtrak and Conrail, which may be regarded as an intermediate step in the direction of nationalization. A number of cities operate their own public transport facilities, collect their own garbage, and offer other services that elsewhere are provided by private enterprise.

It is almost an instinctive reaction by people in the United States to consider such public enterprises as being prone to extreme mismanagement and waste. And the near-legendary problems of the Post Office do seem to support this supposition. However, here too, one should be careful not to jump to conclusions. In recent decades, when railroading was entirely in private hands, that industry had difficulties no less serious than those of the Post Office. It is true that visitors find the nationalized French telephone system a model of chaos and mismanagement. But at the same time, the Swedish telephone system, which is also nationalized, is smooth working and efficient. And the French government-supplied electricity system has set world standards in its use of the most modern analytic techniques of economics and engineering, which have helped them set innovative prices that promote efficiency.

Despite these accomplishments, no one has yet found a systematic incentive mechanism for efficiency that can do for nationalized industries what the profit motive does for private enterprise. Where the market is unsparing in its rewards for accomplishments and in its penalties for poor performance, one can be quite sure that a firm's inefficiency will not readily be tolerated. But nationalized industries have no such automatic mechanism handing out rewards and penalties dependably and impartially. We have seen, however, that there are analogous problems under regulation; where profits are controlled by the regulator, the rewards for efficiency are also far from automatic. (The two boxed inserts on the next page offer further evidence in support of these conclusions.)

Evidence of Efficiency in Public Enterprise

A recent study conducted by European producers and distributors of electricity yielded the following average figures for *annual rate of growth in productivity.*

A. Countries in which electricity is supplied largely by government-owned firms:

England and Wales	2.4%
France	4.5
Ireland	4.5
Netherlands	8.5
Spain	3.5
Sweden	7.5
Unweighted average	5.2%

B. Countries in which electricity is supplied largely by private firms:

Germany	2.1%
Switzerland	3.5
Unweighted average	2.8%

Source: The Group of Experts on Overall Productivity, "The Overall Productivity of the Electricity Supply Industry." The Hague Congress, Tariffs Study Committee, Aug. 27–31, 1973.

Evidence of Inefficiency in Public Enterprise

Since residential garbage collection is a relatively homogeneous task and is carried out both by government and private firms, this service is particularly well suited to comparing the costs of competition, private monopoly, and government monopoly. A recent study of the relative costs of private and public collection of garbage investigated the collection systems of about 300 municipalities in the United States.

The study found that collection costs were about the same whether the job was done by government or by a group of competing firms. Competition was expensive because each firm served only scattered customers, and there was much duplication of routes. On the other hand, the costs of both government collection and competitive private collection were some 34 percent higher than the costs of service by a private monopoly collector working under contract to the municipal government. The government services typically had significantly larger crews, higher rates of employee absenteeism, smaller trucks, and less frequent use of incentive systems than did the private collectors.

Source: E. S. Savas, "Evaluating the Organization of Service Delivery: Solid Waste Collection and Disposal; A Summary." Center for Government Studies, Graduate School of Business, Columbia University, April 1976.

SUMMARY

1. Regulation has two primary purposes: to put brakes on the decisions of industries with monopoly power, and to contribute to public health and safety.

2. Railroads, trucks, airlines, telecommunications, and gas and electricity supply are among the industries that are regulated in the United States. In Europe the firms that provide these services are usually owned by the government (they are nationalized).

3. Among the major reasons given for regulation are (a) economies of scale and scope, which make industries into natural monopolies; (b) the danger of self-destructive competition in industries with low (short-run) marginal costs; (c) the desire to provide service to isolated areas where supply is expensive and unprofitable; (d) the desire for fair allocation of scarce resources (such as radio and television air space); and (e) the protection of consumers from unscrupulous suppliers.

4. Some economists believe that regulation has had very little effect on regulated industries, but this conclusion is not accepted by everyone.

5. Regulators often reject proposals by regulated firms to cut their prices, and sometimes the regulators even force firms to raise their prices. The purpose of such action is to prevent "unfair competition," and to protect customers of some of the firm's products from being forced to subsidize customers of other products. Many economists disagree with such actions and argue that the result is usually to stifle competition and make all customers pay more than they otherwise would.

6. Economists generally argue that a firm should be permitted to cut its price as long as it covers its long-run marginal cost. However, others (usually noneconomists) argue that fully distributed cost is a better criterion. A fully distributed cost criterion, in this sense, usually means that price will be higher than it will be if marginal cost is used as the standard.

7. Regulation is often criticized for providing little or no incentive for efficiency, for tending to push prices upward, and for forcing the regulated parties to engage in an expensive and time-consuming adversary process.

8. Among the proposals that have been offered to improve regulation are (a) increased freedom of competition and reduction or elimination of regulatory power; (b) the use of built-in rewards for good performance by the regulated firm; and (c) freedom of regulated firms to cut prices but not to raise them.

9. Nationalized (government-run) industries are frequently suspected of being wasteful and inefficient, but the evidence is not uniform and there are exceptions.

CONCEPTS FOR REVIEW

Nationalization
Price floor
Price ceiling
Economies of scale
Economies of scope
Self-destructive competition
Predatory pricing

Short- and long-run marginal cost
Fully distributed cost
Cross-subsidy
Cost-plus arrangements
Regulatory lag
Deregulation

QUESTIONS FOR DISCUSSION

1. Why is an electric company in a city usually considered to be a natural monopoly? What would happen if two competing electric companies were established? How about telephone companies?

2. Suppose a 20 percent cut in the price of freight transportation brings in so much new business that it permits a railroad to cut its passenger fares by 2 percent. In your opinion, is this equitable? Is it a good idea or a bad one?

3. In some regulated industries, prices are prevented from falling by the regulatory agency and as a result many firms open up business in that industry. Is this competitive or anticompetitive? Is it a good idea or a bad one?

4. What industries in the United States can be considered nationalized or partly nationalized? What do you think of the quality of their services? Why might this criterion be inadequate as evidence on which to base a judgment of the idea of nationalization?

5. List some industries with regulated rates whose services you have bought. What do you think of the quality of their service?

6. In which if any of the regulated industries mentioned in your previous answer is there competition? Why, when there is competition, is it appropriate to regulate them? (Or is it inappropriate in your opinion, and if so, why?)

7. Regulators are much concerned about the prevention of "predatory pricing"—pricing policies designed to destroy competition. The U.S. Court of Appeals has, however, noted that "the term probably does not have a well-defined meaning, but it certainly bears a sinister connotation." How might one go about distinguishing "predatory" from "nonpredatory" pricing? What would you do about it? (Note that no one has yet come up with a final answer to this problem.)

8. A regulated industry is prohibited from earning profits higher than it now is getting. It begins to sell a new product at a price above its long-run marginal cost. Explain why the prices of other company products will, very likely, have to be reduced.

six

Factor Markets
and the Distribution of Income

27

The Labor Market and Wages

The chapters in Parts Four and Five were concerned with the markets for *goods*. Now, in Part Six, we turn our attention to the markets for factors of production, such as labor, capital, and land. The levels of the *prices* of these factors—the wage of labor, the profit on capital, and the rent of land—are often highly charged emotional and political issues. Outcries are frequently heard that unskilled workers are exploited by their employers and that their wages are too low. Many left-of-center social reformers view profits as too high, while manu- facturers' associations seem always to be complaining that profits are too low. Seemingly everyone except landlords thinks that rents are exorbitant. In this chapter and the next we will explain how these factor prices are determined by the interaction of supply and demand.

Our focus in this chapter is on the market for labor and the determination of wages. We begin with a review of a concept that was intro- duced in Chapter 21, the marginal product of a factor, and then show how the marginal produc- tivity of labor determines the demand curve for labor. Next we investigate how the supply of labor is governed by individual choice. By putting supply and demand together, we obtain an explanation of the determination of wages and employment in a competitive labor market.

But not all labor markets are competitive; so in the rest of the chapter we turn to two principal interferences with the operation of free labor markets: minimum wage laws and labor unions. An appendix takes up yet a third interference with free markets: monopoly power on the buying side of the labor market.

ARE WAGES TOO LOW? MINIMUM WAGE LAWS AND UNEMPLOYMENT

Unemployment among teen-agers is always higher than it is in the labor force as a whole, and among black teen-agers it is significantly higher still.

Figure 27–1 shows the record. It indicates that unemployment rates for all three groups have gone up and down together. Whenever unemployment went down in the economy as a whole, it almost always decreased for black teen-agers and for teen-agers generally. However, it will not surprise you that young workers, and especially young black workers, always have more severe employment problems than the average worker. When things are generally good, they are not quite as good for the young and the black; and when things are generally bad, things are much, much worse for them. What is somewhat surprising is that despite social and legislative pressures against race discrimination, efforts to improve the quality of education available to children in the ghettos, and many related programs, the data from recent years do not indicate any great improvement in the relative standing of young blacks. In fact, during the recovery from the depths of the most recent recession, while the unemployment rates of virtually every other demographic group declined, unem-

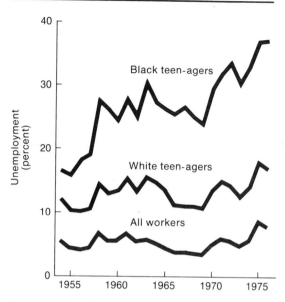

FIGURE 27–1

THE TEEN-AGE UNEMPLOYMENT PROBLEM
Teen-age unemployment rates have consistently been much higher than the overall unemployment rate, and black teen-agers have fared worse than white teen-agers. For the most part, the three unemployment rates have moved up and down together, as can be seen in this chart. But the unemployment of black teen-agers increased somewhat as the economy recovered from the 1974–1975 recession.

Source: U.S. Department of Labor, Bureau of Labor Statistics.

ployment among black teen-agers actually increased slightly.

Economists are less surprised than other concerned persons about the intractability of the problem. They maintain that despite all the legislation that has been adopted to improve the position of black people, there is a law on the books, which, though apparently designed to protect low-skilled workers, is in fact a crippling impediment to any attempt to improve job opportunities for blacks. As long as this law remains effective, the young, the inexperienced, and those with educational disadvantages will continue to find themselves handicapped on the job market, and attempts to eliminate their more serious unemployment problems will stand little chance of success.

What is this law? None other than the minimum wage law. In the first parts of this chapter we will explain why this law has such pernicious—and presumably unintended—effects.

MARGINAL PRODUCTIVITY AND THE DEMAND FOR LABOR

Minimum wage laws interfere with the operation of a free labor market. But to understand how, we must first understand how the labor market would operate in their absence. We approach this in three steps. First we consider the determinants of the *demand* for labor, then the determinants of *supply*, and finally the market *equilibrium*, in which both wages and employment levels are established.

The difference between a *firm's* demand for labor and a *consumer's* demand for a commodity is that firms want labor not for its own sake, but rather because the services of labor are useful in producing output. We say, therefore, that the demand for labor is a derived demand. Obviously, the more that labor contributes to the output of the employing firm—that is, the more productive it is—the more labor the firm will want. But just what is the relationship between the productivity of labor and the quantity of it that firms will want to buy at any given wage?

In Chapter 21, we defined the *marginal physical product* of any input that is used in a production process. We dealt there with the case of a farmer and his use of fertilizer, but the same analysis applies to labor. If an additional worker increases the firm's output by 150 back scratchers per week, we say that this amount is the worker's marginal physical product. We also defined the value of the marginal product as the amount of money the input's marginal product

is worth in the market. It is equal to the marginal physical product multiplied by the price of a unit of the product. Thus, if the price of a back scratcher is $2, then the value of the marginal product of the worker is $2 × 150, or $300 per week. Finally, and most important for our purpose, it was shown in Chapter 21 that:

A firm wishing to maximize its profits will purchase any input up to the point where diminishing returns reduce the value of that input's marginal product to the level of its price.

The reason is straightforward. If the market wage is $180 per week but the value of the marginal product of a worker is $300, then it will pay the firm to use *at least* one more worker, since that will bring the firm a net gain of $120—the excess of the value of the marginal product over the wage that the firm pays. Such possibilities for profit exist whenever the value of the marginal product of any input is greater than its price, and the opposite is true when the value of the marginal product is less than the price of the input.

The marginal productivity relationship gives us the information we need to construct the *demand curve for labor*. On the following page, Table 27–1 shows a value of marginal product schedule numerically, and Figure 27–2 portrays the same information in graphic form. With the help of this graph, we can demonstrate that:

A curve that shows how the value of an input's marginal product changes as the quantity of that input increases also shows the demand curve for that input. In other words, the demand curve for an input is its value-of-marginal-product curve.

How do we know this is true? The demand curve for labor, by definition, tells us how many workers the firm will want to hire at each possible wage rate. But if the firm wants to maximize profits, we can determine how many

TABLE 27–1

MARGINAL PRODUCT OF LABOR IN A BACK SCRATCHER PLANT

NUMBER OF WORKERS	MARGINAL PHYSICAL PRODUCT	VALUE OF MARGINAL PRODUCT AT PRICE $2 PER SCRATCHER
1	300	$600
2	290	580
3	270	540
4	250	500
5	200	400
6	150	300
7	90	180
8	25	50

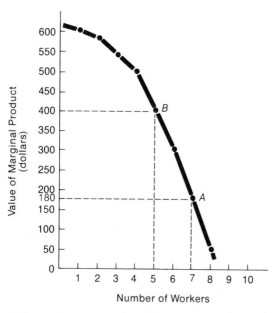

FIGURE 27–2

A VALUE-OF-MARGINAL-PRODUCT SCHEDULE

This graph displays the data in Table 27–1 for the marginal productivity of workers in a back scratcher plant. Its negative slope reflects the law of diminishing marginal returns: As more and more labor is applied to the same plant and equipment, the marginal product of an additional worker falls. As noted in the text, this curve is also the demand curve for labor.

workers it will want to hire with the aid of a graph such as shown in Figure 27–2. We know that it pays the firm to employ the number of laborers at which the wage is equal to the value of the marginal product. Suppose the wage is set by market forces at $180 a week. We see from the diagram that at this wage it pays the firm to hire 7 workers (point A) because only at that employment level is the value of the marginal product of labor equal to the prevailing wage. Thus, only this level of employment maximizes the firm's profits when the wage is $180. Similarly, if the wage is $400 per week, we see (point B) that it pays the firm to hire only 5 workers. In the same way, the graph tells us how many workers it will pay to employ at *any* wage that may happen to be set in the labor market and thus gives us the derived demand curve for the input, as was asserted before.

THE NEGATIVE SLOPE OF THE DERIVED DEMAND CURVE FOR LABOR

How do we know that the demand curve for labor slopes downward to the right, as depicted in the figure? As you will remember from Chapter 21, it is generally assumed that an expansion in the use of any one input, holding the quantities of every other input constant, will yield diminishing marginal returns, at least after a while. This *law of diminishing returns* tells us that the marginal physical product of an input will become smaller and smaller as its use is increased further and further compared with the quantities used of all other inputs. For this reason the value-of-marginal-product curve in Figure 27–2 normally will slope downward as employment increases. More generally, the derived demand curve for *any* input can be expected to have a negative slope.

The derived demand curve for an input can be expected to have a negative slope because of the law of diminishing marginal returns to increased use of any input, holding all other input quantities fixed. This means that if a higher price is charged for an input, then firms normally will employ less of it.

This conclusion is certainly not very startling. We would all expect higher steel prices to encourage the use of substitute metals and higher wages to encourage the use of labor-saving equipment, so that common sense alone indicates that an increase in the price of an input will reduce the quantity of it that is demanded. What the analysis has taught us is precisely how the demand curve is related to marginal productivity. We will see later that this knowledge leads to some specific policy conclusions.

THE SUPPLY OF LABOR

We turn now to the supply side of the labor market, and here, once again, our previous analysis of the goods market finds an immediate application. Given the fixed amount of time in a week, an individual's decision to *supply labor* to firms is simultaneously a decision to *demand leisure* time for herself. If, after necessary time

for eating and sleeping is deducted, a worker has 90 usable hours in a week, her decision to spend 40 of them working is simultaneously a decision to demand 50 of them for her own use.

In Chapter 19 on consumer choice we observed that the demand for leisure could be treated just like the demand for any other commodity: A consumer "buys" her own leisure time, just as she buys bananas, or back scratchers, or pizzas. To review the analysis, we noted there that a rise in the wage rate would have two conflicting effects on the amount of leisure time that a consumer demands:

1. Income effect. Higher wages make consumers richer. We would expect this increased wealth to increase their demand for most goods, leisure included. We can conclude, then, that:

The income effect of higher wages probably leads most workers to want to work less.

2. Substitution effect. Consumers "purchase" their own leisure time by giving up their hourly wages, so the wage rate is the "price" of leisure. When the wage rate rises, leisure becomes more expensive relative to other commodities that consumers might buy. Thus, we expect a wage increase to induce them to change their consumption habits toward buying *less* leisure time and *more* goods. Therefore:

The substitution effect of higher wages probably leads most workers to want to work more.

Putting these two effects together, we are forced to conclude that some workers may react to an increase in their wage rate by working more, while others may react by working less. In terms of the market as a whole, therefore, higher wages could lead to either a larger or smaller labor supply. (See the boxed insert on page 514.) Statistical studies of this question in the United States have reached the conclusions that (a) the response of labor supply to wage changes is not very strong for most workers; (b) for low-wage workers the substitution effect seems to dominate, so they work more when wages rise; (c) for high-wage workers the income effect seems to dominate, so they work less when wages rise. Figure 27–3 depicts these approximate "facts." It shows labor supply rising (slightly) as wages rise up to point A. Thereafter, labor supply falls (slightly) as wages rise.

Does the theory of labor supply apply to college students? A 1975 study of the hours of work performed by students at Princeton University found that it does.[1] About half the student body was found to work an average of about 9 hours per week. Estimated substitution effects of higher wages on labor supply were positive and income effects were negative, just as the theory predicts. Apparently, substitution

[1] Mary P. Hurley, "An Investigation of Employment Among Princeton Undergraduates During the Academic Year." Senior thesis submitted to the Department of Economics, May 1975.

Labor Supply Analysis and Welfare Reform

The economic analysis of labor supply has figured prominently in recent discussions of welfare reform—so prominently, in fact, that the U.S. government has spent millions of dollars conducting a series of social experiments to measure labor supply responses more precisely.

The issue arose in discussions about the negative income tax, an alternative type of income-support system that has been widely acclaimed by economists for years. Under a negative income tax (NIT) plan, as will be explained more fully in Chapter 29, families whose incomes fall short of some prescribed norm would be given cash grants, and these grants would shrink as the family's income expanded. Thus, in a sense, the NIT would change the breadwinner's effective wage rate. For example, if an employer paid a worker $3 per hour, but negative income tax payments were reduced by 50 cents for every additional dollar earned, then the effective wage that the individual earned would be only $1.50 per hour of work—$3 from the employer less a $1.50 reduction in payments from the government. As we know, such a reduction in the effective wage has substi-

tution effects that discourage work and income effects that encourage work.

But the NIT does not just mean lower effective wages. There is also a direct cash grant from the government, and this grant also has an income effect: Poor families are made better off, and thereby encouraged to buy more leisure time—that is, to work less. Critics of the plan have worried that the NIT, on balance, might create a strong disincentive to work.

Because it was seriously considering adoption of an NIT plan in the late 1960s, the government initiated a series of social experiments to estimate just how large these income and substitution effects would be. Experimental families were selected in a number of American cities and offered negative income tax payments in return for filling out questionnaires that enabled social scientists to monitor their behavior. A matched set of "control" families, who were not given NIT payments, was also observed. The idea was to measure how the behavior of the families receiving NIT payments differed from that of the families that did not receive them.

The last of the experiments was just recently concluded, and analysis of the data is still going on. But enough has been learned from the earlier experiments to indicate that the net effects of the NIT on labor supply were quite small. Apparently, the fears of those who claimed that NIT payments would induce people to stop working were unfounded.

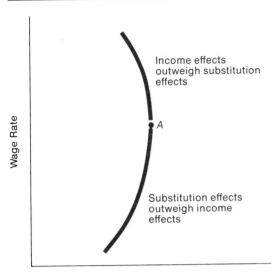

FIGURE 27–3

A TYPICAL LABOR SUPPLY SCHEDULE
The labor supply schedule depicted here has a positive
slope up to point A, as substitution effects outweigh
income effects. At higher wages, however, income
effects become the dominant factor, and the curve
acquires a negative slope. Economists call curves with
this shape "backward bending" supply curves.

effects outweighed income effects by a slim
margin, so that higher wages attracted a somewhat greater supply of labor. Specifically, a 10
percent rise in wages was estimated to increase
the hours of work of the Princeton student body
by about 3 percent.

THE COMPETITIVE DETERMINATION
OF WAGES

Now that we have the two building blocks—
demand and supply—we can consider the
market determination of wages and employment. To do so, we begin in a very simple

setting in which there is unfettered competition.
Specifically, there is no government interference in the form of minimum wages, nor are
there trade unions. We will take up these two
complications afterward.

The marginal productivity theory gives us
the demand curve for labor of each firm. By
summing the quantities of labor demanded at
each wage rate, we obtain the market demand
curve shown by DD in Figure 27–4. Notice
that while DD is not the marginal productivity
schedule of any particular firm, it is based on
the marginal productivity curves of all firms.

Figure 27–4 also includes a market labor
supply curve, labeled SS, much like the one
shown in Figure 27–3. As the figure is drawn,

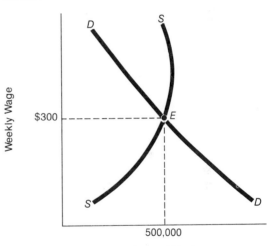

Number of Workers

FIGURE 27–4

EQUILIBRIUM IN A
COMPETITIVE LABOR MARKET
In a competitive labor market, equilibrium will be
established at the wage that equates the quantity
supplied with the quantity demanded. In this example,
equilibrium is at point E, where demand curve DD
crosses supply curve SS. The equilibrium wage is $300
per week and equilibrium employment is 500,000
workers.

there is one intersection point, *E*, of the supply and demand curves and this, as usual in supply–demand analysis, shows the equilibrium price and employment levels.[2] Specifically, it tells us that in equilibrium this market will employ 500,000 workers at a wage rate of $300 per week.

Together, these pieces of information tell us how much money will be earned by workers in the back scratcher industry, since the amount they earn is the wage times the number of workers employed. In exactly the same way, the marginal productivity theory accounts for the earnings of every other input—fuel, machinery, raw materials, land, and labor of every type of skill and training. Each of these inputs is sold on a market with its own supply and demand curve, and each has its own equilibrium point indicating the equilibrium price and the quantity of the input that will be sold. Together, these give us the total earnings of that input— and thus its share in the total income of the economy.

WHY WAGES DIFFER

So the market for each variety of labor has its own supply and demand curve, and the intersection of these curves determines the equilibrium wage rate for that particular type of worker. This at once tells us everything and nothing about why wage rates differ. Supply and demand analysis implies that wages will be relatively high in markets where demand is great and supply is small [see Figure 27–5(a)], and wages will be comparatively low in markets where demand is low and supply is high [see

Figure 27–5(b)]. We can use our preceding analyses of the demand for and supply of labor to breathe some life into these principles.

Starting with the supply of labor, it is clear that the *available working population* in a given area is of major importance. This helps explain why wages rose so high in Alaska when the Alaska pipeline created many new jobs, and why wages have been and remain so low in Appalachia. Second, it is clear that the *nonmonetary attractiveness* of any job will also influence the supply of workers to it. (The monetary attractiveness is the wage itself, which governs movements *along* the supply curve.) Jobs that many people find pleasant and satisfying—such as teaching school—will attract a larger supply of labor, and will consequently achieve a lower equilibrium wage, than jobs that are onerous and disagreeable. Finally, the *ease or difficulty of acquiring the skills* needed to enter a particular job or profession is relevant to its supply of labor. Brain surgeons and professional football quarterbacks earn generous incomes because there are few people as highly skilled as they.

Our analysis of the demand for labor has taught us that there are two types of influence to be considered on the demand side. Since the value of a worker's marginal product depends both on his *physical productivity* and on the *price of the product* that he produces, factors that influence either of these will influence his wage.

The factors influencing the prices of commodities were discussed at some length in earlier chapters, and there is no need to repeat them now. It is sufficient to remember that anything that raises or lowers the demand for a particular product will tend to raise or lower the wages of the workers that produce that product, because the demand for labor is a derived demand.

A worker's marginal physical product depends on several things, including of course his own *abilities* and *degree of effort* on the job. But sometimes these characteristics are less

[2]You may wonder how we can be sure that demand and supply intersect only once when the supply curve has the shape indicated in Figure 27–4. The answer is that we cannot. It is quite possible that there could be two equilibrium wage rates. In more advanced courses it is shown, however, that only one of these two equilibrium points can be expected to persist for very long.

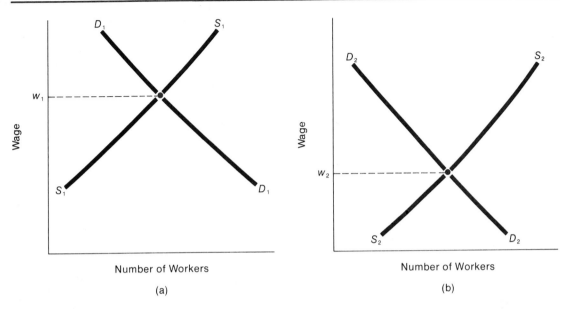

FIGURE 27–5

WAGE DIFFERENTIALS

(a) The market depicted here has a high equilibrium wage, w_1, because demand is high relative to supply. This can occur if qualified workers are scarce, or if productivity on the job is high, or if the demand for the product is great.
(b) By contrast, the equilibrium wage, w_2, is low here, where supply is high relative to demand. This can result from an abundant supply of qualified workers, or low productivity, or weak demand for the product.

important than the *other factors of production* that he has to work with. Workers in American industry are more productive than workers in many other countries because they have generous supplies of machinery, natural resources, and technical know-how to work with. As a consequence, they earn high wages.

LABOR AS CAPITAL: THE THEORY OF HUMAN CAPITAL

A worker's skill is of obvious relevance to his productivity, and thus to his wage. To some extent, and in some jobs, this skill is simply innate and unchangeable. But to a much greater extent, the skills necessary to earn high

wages can be *acquired* by individuals through *deliberate decisions*, such as going to school, taking other types of training, or relocating geographically.

One crucial aspect of these decisions is that they usually require some *current sacrifice* in order to reap *future benefits*. Education is perhaps the clearest example. You have made a conscious decision to go to college rather than to enter the labor market directly after high school. And you are probably acutely aware that this decision is now costing you money—lots of money. Your tuition payments may be only a minor part of the total cost of going to college. Think of a high school friend who chose not to go to college and is now working. The salary that he or she is earning could, perhaps, have been yours. You deliberately gave up this potential income in order to acquire more education.

In this sense, your education can be thought of as an *investment* in yourself, a *human investment*. Like a firm that devotes some of its money to building a plant that will yield profits at some future date, you are investing in your own future, hoping that your college education will help you earn more than your high-school-educated friend when you graduate. Economists call decisions like this investments in human capital, because they give the human being many of the attributes of a capital investment.

Will your investment pay off? Many generations of college students have supposed that it would, and, until recently, studies of the incomes earned by college students indicated that they were right. That is, the studies for many years showed that the income differentials earned by college graduates, when viewed as the "return" on the tuition payments and sacrificed earnings that they "invested" while in school, proved to be a far better investment than putting those same funds into a bank account. A recent book by Harvard economist Richard Freeman, however, found that this was much less true in the early 1970s. The reason for this deterioration in the financial return to going to college was the obvious one: Relative to high school graduates, the supply of college graduates expanded much more rapidly than the demand.[3]

This, of course, does not mean that only fools go to college: What it does mean is that the financial incentive *alone* is not as strong as it used do be. If you simply enjoy the experience, or want to acquire knowledge for its own sake rather than for the money it may subsequently help you earn, attending college can still be a perfectly rational decision. It may not, however, offer quite the financial bonanza you may have expected at the end.

[3]Richard B. Freeman, *The Over-educated American* (New York: Academic Press, 1976).

THE EFFECTS OF MINIMUM WAGE LEGISLATION

As we have just seen, the "labor market" is really composed of many submarkets for labor of different types, each with its own supply and demand curve. To consider the effects of minimum wages, it suffices to consider two such markets, which we call for convenience "skilled" and "unskilled" labor. These two markets are portrayed in the two parts of Figure 27–6. For obvious reasons, the marginal productivity of the unskilled and poorly educated workers will be far below that of the skilled workers, so we expect equilibrium wage rates for skilled workers to be much higher. Figure 27–6 reflects this supposition. The equilibrium point E in each diagram corresponds to an hourly wage of $6 for skilled labor and only $2 for unskilled labor.

Now suppose the government, finding $2 per hour to be intolerably low, imposes a legal minimum wage of $2.90 per hour. This increase is indicated by the heavy red line in both parts of Figure 27–6. Turning first to the skilled labor market, we see that the minimum wage has no effect on it. Since the market equilibrium wage was well above $2.90 per hour, a law prohibiting the payment of wage rates below $2.90 cannot possibly matter.

But the effects of the minimum wage are quite pronounced in the market for unskilled labor—and presumably quite different from those that Congress intended. Figure 27–6(b) indicates that at the $2.90 minimum wage, firms want to employ only 30 million unskilled workers (point A) while 45 million unskilled workers want jobs (point B). Although the 30 million unskilled workers lucky enough to retain their jobs do indeed earn a higher wage ($2.90 instead of $2 per hour), 10 million of their compatriots earn no wage at all because they have been laid off; and an additional 5 million workers, attracted into the market by prospective wages of $2.90

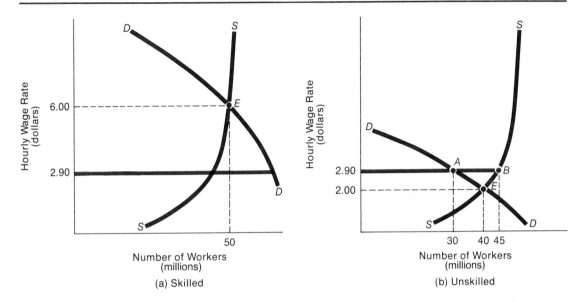

FIGURE 27–6
(a) Imposing a minimum wage of $2.90 per hour does not affect the market for skilled labor because the equilibrium wage there ($6 per hour) is well above the legal minimum. (b) However, the minimum-wage legislation does have important effects in the market for unskilled labor. There the equilibrium wage ($2 per hour) is below the minimum, so the minimum wage makes the quantity supplied (45 million workers) exceed the quantity demanded (30 million workers). So there is unemployment of unskilled labor.

rather than $2, have had their hopes disappointed. The job-losers will clearly be those workers with the lowest productivity, since the minimum wage effectively bans the employment of workers whose marginal product is less than $2.90 per hour.

The primary consequence of the minimum wage law is *not* an increase in the incomes of the least skilled workers but a restriction of their employment opportunities. In effect, the minimum wage law protects the skilled workers from the competition of the unskilled.

The high unemployment rate among black teen-agers, with all of its terrible social consequences, is, no doubt, partly a consequence of discrimination and other noneconomic factors. But as long as minimum wage laws continue to

hold, even an end to discrimination will not eliminate the handicap faced by all inexperienced workers, whether black or white, in their search for jobs (see the boxed insert on page 520).

UNIONISM IN AMERICA

Our analysis of a competitive labor market has ignored one rather important fact: The supply of labor is not at all competitive in many labor markets; instead it is controlled by a labor monopoly, a *union*.

While important, unions in America are not nearly so important as is popularly supposed. For example, most people who have not become acquainted with the data are astonished to learn that only about 22 percent of American workers belong to unions. This fraction is much higher than it was before the New Deal, when unions were quite unimportant in this country, but a bit lower than it was in the heyday of unionism in the mid-1950s and early 1960s—just over 25 percent (see Figure 27–7).

Unions seem much more prevalent than this to the public because they are such large, and therefore newsworthy, institutions. The giant Teamsters' union, for example, has about 2 million members; the United Auto Workers (UAW) and the United Steelworkers (USA) each have around 1½ million; and the largest labor federation, the American Federation of Labor and Congress of Industrial Organizations (AFL-CIO) has more than 17 million members. Because of their size, the actions of these unions are reported daily in the newspapers, on radio, and on television. By contrast, unless you are a student of labor statistics, you will hardly ever hear anything about the more than 75 million workers in America who do not belong to unions.

Unionization is also much less prevalent in America than it is in most other industrialized countries. For example, about 50 percent of British workers and about 80 percent of Swedish workers belong to unions. The differences are quite striking and doubtless have

Minimum Wages and the Fast-Food Industry

This report from *The Wall Street Journal* in 1978 exemplifies how higher minimum wages curtail employment opportunities in certain industries.

Rise in Minimum Wage Spurs Some Firms To Cut Work Hours and Hiring of Youths

LOMBARD, Ill. — Last summer Janet Straka started work at the Steak n Shake restaurant here in this Chicago suburb at 9 a.m. to get ready for the 10 o'clock opening.

But in January the federal minimum wage rose to $2.65 an hour from $2.30. Steak n Shake, seeking to blunt the impact, decided to open an hour later, since there were few early customers anyway. Steak n Shake also cut the opening waitress's preparation time to 30 minutes. So Miss Straka, a schoolteacher who works summers part-time at the hamburger chain, now starts work at 10:30 a.m., and her weekly earnings are down to about $36 from $40 last summer.

Her shortened workday shows one way in which the higher minimum wage is affecting employment in the U.S. There haven't been wholesale layoffs of low-wage workers, but some workers are putting in fewer hours on the job.

Another effect is that teen-agers, especially blacks, are having more trouble finding work as companies like Steak n Shake look for older, more-qualified workers likely to stay at a job longer. . . .

The $79-billion-a-year fast-food and restaurant industry has plenty of minimum-wage workers, and it's clear that as the minimum increases, so do companies' efforts to cut the number of workers at a restaurant. Employes aren't flying out of restaurants like hamburgers off a grill, but productivity efforts are beginning to show results.

At the Lombard Steak n Shake, for instance, total employe hours worked each week actually trail a year ago, even though business is up. The amount of the decline varies from week to week, but total hours are generally down 10%.

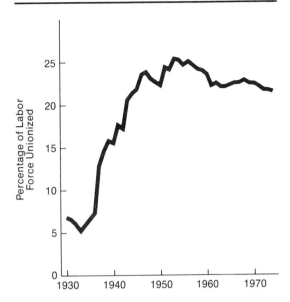

FIGURE 27–7

UNIONIZATION IN THE UNITED STATES,
1930–1974

In 1930, unions had enrolled just under 7 percent of
the U.S. labor force; and by 1933 this figure had
slipped to barely above 5 percent. Unionization took off
with the New Deal, reaching almost 16 percent of the
labor force by 1939. It then drifted irregularly upward
to a peak of about 25 to 26 percent of all workers in the
mid-1950s, and has since trailed off to about 22
percent.

Source: U.S. Department of Labor, Bureau of Labor Statistics,
Handbook of Labor Statistics, 1977 and 1975 Reference
Edition.

something to do with our tradition of "rugged
individualism."

While its roots can be traced back earlier,
serious unionism in America is only about 100
years old. Large-scale unions in this country
began with the Knights of Labor in the latter part
of the nineteenth century. But this very politically motivated workers' organization was quite
different from the unions of today. Indeed,
American unions are noteworthy for their
basically nonpolitical stance, in contrast

to the highly politicized unions of many
European countries.

The American labor movement as we know
it today began to take shape at the end of the
nineteenth century under the stewardship of
Samuel Gompers, who headed the AFL for
many years, and who did more to mold the
American labor movement than any other
person. Gompers strongly believed that unions
should be nonpolitical organizations concerned
with getting *more* for their members: more pay,
better working conditions, longer vacations, and
so on. He also believed that unions should be
organized along *craft* lines—carpenters in one
union, plumbers in another—rather than along
industrial lines, and he was a staunch advocate
of free collective bargaining without government interference.

The AFL grew rather steadily from about
1900 until the early 1920s, but then went into
decline during the Roaring Twenties, when
capitalism was riding high and every worker, it
seemed, dreamed of getting rich in the stock
market. The favorable attitudes and legislation
of the Roosevelt administration provided a great
stimulus to unionism in this country in the
1930s. The Norris—La Guardia Act of 1932
sharply limited the power of the federal courts
to interfere in labor disputes. Even more important, the Wagner Act in 1935 guaranteed
workers the right to form unions and to choose
the union that would represent them in collective bargaining. It also set up the National Labor
Relations Board (NLRB) to protect labor from
"unfair labor practices" by employers. By no
coincidence, that year also marked the foundation, by John L. Lewis, of the CIO, a federation
of many *industrial* unions that at first rivaled the
AFL for leadership of the U.S. labor movement.
The AFL, with its craft unions, and the CIO, with
its industrial unions, eventually merged in 1955.

The favorable public attitude toward unions
soured somewhat after World War II, perhaps
because of the rash of strikes that took place
in 1946 (see Figure 27–11 on page 526). One
result of these strikes was the Taft–Hartley Act

of 1947, which specified and outlawed certain "unfair labor practices" by unions; severely limited the extent of the so-called *closed shop*—an arrangement that specifies that only union members may be hired;[4] and provided for court injunctions to delay strikes that threaten the national interest for an 80-day "cooling off" period.

Today, the character of American unionism is still somewhat unsettled. Unions are struggling very hard to make inroads into labor markets that by tradition have not been unionized—such as agricultural workers and white-collar office workers. Notable successes have been achieved in organizing teachers and many government employees. But there remains a continuing public debate—resisted vehemently by union spokesmen—over whether unions have grown too powerful and need to be controlled in some way.

UNIONS AS A LABOR MONOPOLY

Unions require that we alter our economic analysis of the labor market in much the same way that monopolies required us to alter our analysis of the goods market (see Chapter 23). You will recall that in a monopolized product market, the firm selects the point on its demand curve that maximizes its profits.

Much the same idea applies to unions, which are, after all, monopoly sellers of labor. They too face a demand curve—derived this time from the marginal productivity schedules of firms—and can choose the point on it that suits them best. The problem for the economist trying to analyze union behavior—and perhaps also for the union leader trying to select a course of action—is how to decide which point on the demand curve is "best." There is no obvious

[4]Unions therefore generally press for a *union shop*, in which nonunion members may be hired but must join the union within a specified period of time. Employers often prefer an *open shop* in which employees are free not to join the union if they so choose.

goal analogous to profit maximization that clearly delineates what the union should do. Instead, there are a number of *alternative* goals that sound plausible.

Alternative Union Goals

These goals can be illustrated with the aid of Figure 27–8, which depicts a demand curve for labor, labeled *DD*. The union leadership must decide which point on the curve is best. One possibility is to treat the size of the union as fixed and force employers to pay the highest wage they will pay and still employ all the union members. If, for example, the union has 4000 members, this would be at point *A* in Figure 27–8, with a wage of $10 per hour.

Union leaders, however, may also be inter-

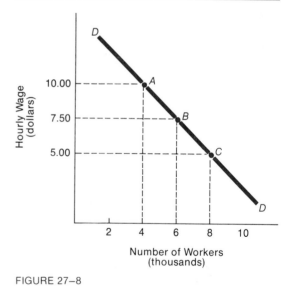

FIGURE 27–8

ALTERNATIVE GOALS FOR A UNION
DD is the demand curve for labor in a market that becomes unionized. Point C is the equilibrium point before the union, when wages were $5 per hour. If the union wants to push wages higher, it normally will have to sacrifice some jobs. Points A and B show two of its many alternatives.

ested in increasing the size of their unions. As an extreme case of this, they might try to make employment as large as possible without pushing the wage below the competitive level. If the competitive wage were $5 in the absence of the union, this strategy would correspond to selecting point C, with employment for 8000 workers. In this case the existence of the union makes no difference: Wages and employment are the same with or without a union.

An intermediate strategy that has often been suggested is that the union maximize the total income of all workers. This might dictate choosing some point like B, with a wage of $7.50 per hour and jobs for 6000 workers. Other possible strategies can also be dreamed up, but these suffice to make the basic point clear.

Unions, as monopoly sellers of labor, have the power to push wages above the competitive levels. However, since the demand curve for labor is downward sloping, such increases in wages normally can be accomplished only by reducing the number of jobs. Just as the monopolist must limit his output to push up his price, so the union must restrict employment to push up the wage.

This can be seen clearly by comparing points B and A with point C (the competitive solution). If it selects point B, the union raises wages by $2.50 per hour, but at the cost of 2000 jobs. If it goes all the way to point A, wages are raised to double the competitive level, but employment is cut in half.

What do unions actually do? There are probably as many different choices as there are unions. Some seem to pursue a maximum-employment goal much like point C, raising wages very little. Others seem to push for the highest possible wages, much like point A. Most probably select an intermediate route. This implies, of course, that the effects of unionization on wage rates and employment will differ markedly among industries. Many economists have sought to estimate the wage differential

attributable to unions—that is, how much does a union member earn compared with a nonmember of equal ability? The consensus that has emerged from this research would probably surprise most people. It seems that most union members earn wages 10 to 20 percent above their nonunion counterparts. While certainly not trivial, this can hardly be considered a cataclysmic effect. We should add, however, that there are unions that fall outside these limits. For example, it has been estimated that building trade unions have raised their members' wages by more than 40 percent.

Alternative Union Strategies

How would a union that has decided to push wages above the competitive level accomplish this task? There are two principal ways, and both are illustrated in Figure 27–9, where we suppose that point U on demand curve DD is the union's choice and point C is the competitive equilibrium.

In Figure 27–9(a), we suppose that the union pursues its goal by *restricting supply*. By keeping out some workers who would like to enter the industry or occupation, it shifts the supply curve of labor inward from $S_0 S_0$ to $S_1 S_1$. In Figure 27–9(b), instead of restricting supply, the union simply *fixes a high wage rate*, W in the example. In this case, it is the employers who will restrict entry into the job, because with wages so high they will not want to employ many workers. As the figure makes clear, the two strategies achieve the same result (point U in either case): Wages are raised by reducing employment.

Some unions, however, may be in a strong enough position to achieve wage gains without sacrificing unemployment. To do this, the union must be able to exercise effective control over the demand curve. Figure 27–10 illustrates such a possibility. Union actions push the demand curve outward from $D_0 D_0$ to $D_1 D_1$, simultaneously raising both wages and employment.

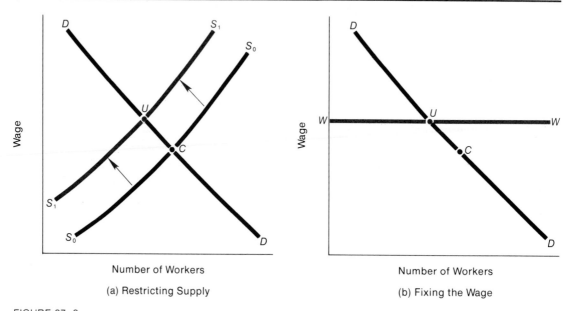

FIGURE 27–9

TWO UNION STRATEGIES

The two parts indicate two alternative ways for the union to move from point C to point U. In part (a), it keeps some workers out of the industry, thereby moving the supply curve to the left from S_0S_0 to S_1S_1. As a consequence, wages rise. In part (b), it fixes a high wage (W), and provides labor only at this wage. As a consequence, firms reduce employment. The effects are the same under both strategies.

FIGURE 27–10

UNION CONTROL OVER THE DEMAND CURVE
This diagram indicates yet a third way in which unions may affect the labor market—a pleasant alternative for workers in that wages can be raised while adding to employment. Strong unions may succeed in raising the demand curve from D_0D_0 to D_1D_1 by (a) feather-bedding, (b) raising worker productivity, or (c) using their political muscle to increase demand for the product. Equilibrium would then shift from point E to point A.

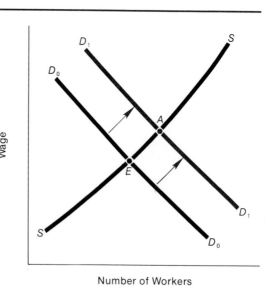

Typically, this will be difficult to accomplish. But some unions may be able to do this through the practice of featherbedding —forcing management to employ workers who are not really needed.[5] Alternatively, the union might institute a campaign to raise worker productivity or use its political influence to increase demand for the firm's product (for example, by keeping out foreign competition).

MONOPSONY AND BILATERAL MONOPOLY

While the analysis we have just presented has its applications, it is naïve in several important respects. For one thing, it envisions a market situation in which one powerful union is dealing with many powerless employers: The labor market is assumed to be monopolized on the selling side but competitive on the buying side. There are industries that more or less fit this model. The giant Teamsters' union negotiates with a trucking industry that comprises thousands of firms, most of them quite small. And most of the unions within the construction industry are much larger than the firms with which they bargain.

But there are many cases that simply do not fit the model. The "Big Four" automakers do not stand idly by while the UAW picks its favorite point on the demand curve for auto workers. Nor does the Steelworkers' union sit across the bargaining table from representatives of a perfectly competitive industry. In these and other industries, while the union certainly has a good deal of monopoly power over labor supply, the firms also have some monopsony power over labor demand.

DEFINITION
Monopsony refers to a market situation in which there is only one buyer.

Just as a monopoly union on the selling side of the labor market does not passively sell labor at the going wage, a monopsony firm on the buying side does not passively purchase labor at the going wage, nor at the wage suggested by the labor union.

DEFINITION
Economists use the term *bilateral monopoly* to refer to market situations in which there is both a monopoly on the selling side and a monopsony on the buying side.

Analysts find it very difficult to predict the wage and employment decisions that will emerge from a situation of bilateral monopoly. The difficulties here are quite similar to those we encountered in considering the behavior of oligopolistic industries in Chapter 22. Just as one oligopolist, in planning his strategy, is acutely aware that his rivals are likely to react to anything he does, a union dealing with a monopsony employer knows that any move it makes will elicit a countermove by the firm. And this knowledge makes the first decision that much more complicated. In our study of oligopoly, we mentioned that some economists view *game theory* as the most promising route to an understanding of oligopolistic behavior.[6] Similarly, some economists feel that this same mode of analysis may facilitate understanding of the bargaining process between monopoly unions and monopsony firms.

COLLECTIVE BARGAINING AND STRIKES

The process by which unions and management settle upon the terms of a labor contract is

[5]The best-known example of featherbedding involved the railroad unions, which for years forced management to keep firemen in the cabs of diesel engines, in which there were no burning fires. Similarly, the musicians' union in New York City forces producers of Broadway musicals to employ a minimum number of musicians—whether or not they actually play music.

[6]See Chapter 22, pages 430–431.

called collective bargaining. And the second respect in which our preceding analysis was naïve is that collective bargaining sessions range over many more issues than wages. For example, fringe benefits such as pensions, health and life insurance, paid holidays, and the like may be as important to both labor and management as are standard wage rates. Overtime premiums will also be negotiated, as will seniority privileges. Work conditions, such as the speed with which the assembly line should move, are often crucial issues. Many labor contracts specify in great detail the rights of labor and management to set work conditions— and also provide elaborate procedures for resolving grievances and disputes. This list could go on and on. The final contract that emerges from collective bargaining may well run to many pages of fine print.

With the issues so varied and complex, and with the stakes so high, it is no wonder that both labor and management employ skilled professionals who specialize in preparing for and carrying out these negotiations, and that each side enters a collective bargaining session armed with reams of evidence supporting its positions. The bargaining in these sessions is often heated, with outcomes riding as much on personalities and the skills of the negotiators as on cool-headed logic and economic facts. Each side may threaten the other with grave consequences if it does not accept its own terms. Unions, for their part, generally threaten with a strike or a work slow-down. Firms counter with the threats that they will take a strike rather than give in, or may even close the plant without a strike (a "lock-out").

Strikes

Most collective bargaining situations do not degenerate into strikes, but the right to strike, and to take a strike, remain fundamentally important for the bargaining process. Imagine, for example, a firm bargaining with a union that

had threatened to strike many times in the past, but had never actually carried through on this threat. It seems likely that the union's bargaining position would be quite weak. On the other hand, a firm that had always capitulated rather than suffer a strike would be virtually at the mercy of the union. So strikes, or more precisely, *the possibility of strikes,* serve an important economic purpose.

Fortunately, however, the incidence of strikes is not nearly so common as many people believe. Figure 27–11 reports the percentage of worker-days of labor lost as a result of strikes in the United States from 1939 to 1975. Despite the headline-grabbing nature of major national strikes, the total amount of work time lost to

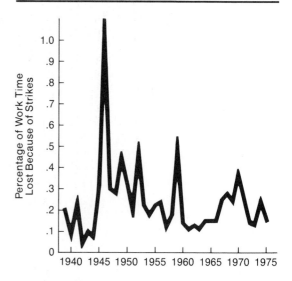

FIGURE 27–11

TIME LOST BECAUSE OF STRIKES, 1939–1975
The fraction of total work time lost to work stoppages varies greatly from year to year, but is never very large. In most years, it is between one-tenth and one-quarter of 1 percent. The worst year for strikes was 1946, and it is probably no coincidence that the Taft–Hartley Law was enacted in the following year.

Source: U.S. Department of Labor, Bureau of Labor Statistics, *Handbook of Labor Statistics,* 1977 and 1975 Reference Edition.

strikes is truly trivial—far less, for example, than the time lost to coffee breaks! Compared with other nations, America suffers more from strikes than say, Germany or Japan, but has many fewer strikes than such countries as Italy and Canada (see Figure 27–12).

Mediation and Arbitration

Since both workers and firms have much to lose from strikes, it is not surprising that several alternative ways of dealing with labor disputes have evolved. When the union and firm reach an apparent impasse, they may call in a professional mediator. This impartial observer will sit down with both sides separately to discuss their problems, and will try to persuade each side to yield a bit to the other. At some stage, when an agreement looks possible, he may call them back together for another bargaining session in his presence.

A mediator, however, has no power to force a settlement. His success hinges on his ability to smooth ruffled feathers and to find a common ground. This contrasts with an arbitrator. In cases where unions and firms simply cannot agree, and where neither wants a strike, they may decide to turn all the data over to an impartial, professional arbitrator, agreeing in advance to accept his decision. In fact, in some vital sectors where a strike is too injurious to the public interest, the labor contract or the law may stipulate that there must be *compulsory arbitration* if the two parties cannot agree. However, both labor and management are normally reluctant to accept this procedure.

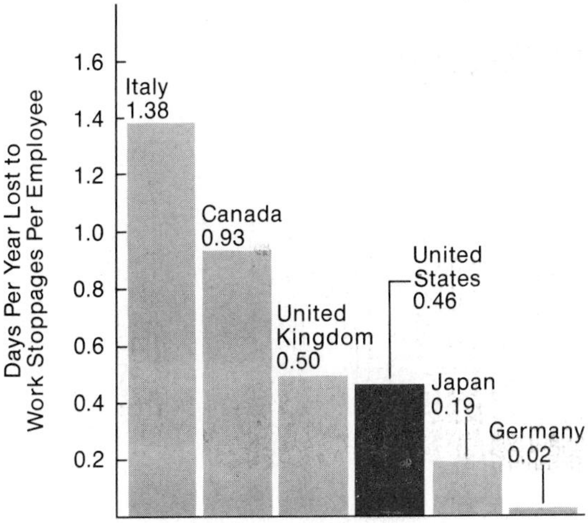

FIGURE 27–12

THE INCIDENCE OF STRIKES
IN INDUSTRIAL COUNTRIES

Contrary to popular impressions, the United States loses about as much work time to strikes as does the United Kingdom. Strikes here are much less common than they are in Italy or Canada, but much more common than they are in Japan or Germany. (*Note:* Data are averages for the 5-year period 1972–1976 or 1971–1975, depending on availability of data.)

Source: U.S. Department of Labor, Bureau of Labor Statistics.

COLLECTIVE BARGAINING IN THE PUBLIC SECTOR

We have argued that strikes serve an important function in private-sector bargaining, as a way of dividing the fruits of economic activity between big labor and big business. But does the same rationale for strikes apply to the public sector, where strikes or work stoppages seem increasingly common among mail carriers, police, fire fighters, air-traffic controllers, and so on?

It is not clear that it does. In most private-sector strikes, labor and management are inflicting harm upon one another in a kind of battle of "survival of the fittest." Consumers normally suffer only mild inconveniences. When General Motors is on strike, many potential car buyers will be disappointed, but they can turn to Ford, Chrysler, and American Motors, not to mention imports. Similarly, when other private products disappear from the shelves because of strikes, the consumer can easily replace them with close substitutes. Thus, with only minor exaggeration, we can think of consumers as being relatively innocent and unharmed spectators when large unions and large private firms slug it out.

But public-sector bargaining is different. Here, management does not represent the interests of capital against those of labor, but represents the public. And there is no pool of profits to be divided between the union and the stockholders. Instead, what management agrees to give to the union comes out of the pockets of the taxpayers. Finally, it is quite clear that the public is not just a spectator in such strikes, but is the primary victim. When police or fire-protection services are reduced, when mail delivery ceases, when public schools or airports shut down, consumers cannot find substitutes for these services. In a very real sense, then, strikes in the public sector are strikes against citizens, not strikes against management. They pit representatives of a particular group of workers against representatives of taxpayers as a whole.

For these reasons, the right of public employees to strike has traditionally been much more severely limited than the corresponding right of private-sector workers. In some states, public-sector strikes are simply outlawed, although this ban has proved hard to enforce. This system seemed logical and worked tolerably well when unionization in the public sector was rather rare. The public was protected, but the public-sector workers were not. As more and more government employees became organized, however, America's system of labor relations for public employees started showing signs of strain. Illegal strikes or "job actions," for example, became increasingly common. Lawyers, economists, politicians, and specialists in labor relations today are struggling to hammer out some more viable system of public collective bargaining that will protect the rights of both public-sector workers and citizens as a whole. Their task is, however, not an easy one.

SUMMARY

1. The demand for labor, like the demand for any factor of production, is a derived demand—derived from the demand for the output that labor produces.
2. Firms that seek to maximize profits will employ labor, or any other factor of production, up to the point where the value of the marginal product is equal to the prevailing wage. Thus, the value of the marginal product schedule is the demand schedule.
3. The demand curve for labor slopes downward because of the law of diminishing marginal returns.
4. In a free market, the supply of labor is determined by free choices made by individuals. Because of conflicting income and substitution effects, the quantity of labor supplied may rise or fall as a result of an increase in wages.
5. In a free market, the wage rate and the level of employment are determined by the interaction of supply and demand. Workers in great demand or short supply will command high wages and, conversely, low wages will be assigned to workers in abundant supply or with skills that are not in great demand.
6. Some skills can be acquired by "investments in human capital," such as education. The rate of return on college education is, however, not as high as it was in the 1960s.

7. One reason that teen-agers, and especially black teen-agers, suffer from such high unemployment rates is that minimum wage laws prevent the employment of low-productivity workers.

8. About 22 percent of all American workers belong to unions, which can be thought of as monopoly sellers of labor. Compared with many other industrialized countries, the union movement in America is younger, less widespread, and less political.

9. Analysis of union behavior is complicated by the fact that a union can have many goals. For the most part, unions probably force wages to be higher and employment to be lower than they would be in a competitive labor market. However, there are exceptions.

10. When a union bargains with a monopsony buyer of labor, we have a bilateral monopoly, and economic theory is unable to predict the outcome.

11. Collective bargaining agreements between labor and management are complex documents covering much more than employment and wage rates.

12. Strikes play an important role in collective bargaining as a way of dividing the fruits of economic activity between big business and big labor. Fortunately, strikes are not nearly so common as is often supposed.

13. Strikes in the public sector, however, take on a different character because the adversaries are no longer "labor" versus "capital" but rather "labor" versus the "public interest." For this reason, the rights of public employees to strike have been curtailed.

CONCEPTS FOR REVIEW

Factor of production
Marginal productivity
Minimum wage law
Derived demand
Value of marginal product
Income and substitution effects
Human capital
AFL-CIO
Wagner Act (1935)

Taft–Hartley Act (1947)
Featherbedding
Monopsony
Bilateral monopoly
Collective bargaining
Mediation
Arbitration
Public-sector bargaining

QUESTIONS FOR DISCUSSION

1. Colleges are known to pay rather low wages for student labor. Can this be explained by the operation of supply and demand in the local labor market? Is the concept of monopsony of any use? How might things differ if students formed a union?

2. College professors are highly skilled (or at least highly educated!) labor. Yet their wages are not very high. Is this a refutation of the theory of marginal productivity?

3. The following table shows the number of pizzas that can be produced by a large pizza parlor employing various numbers of pizza chefs.

NUMBER OF CHEFS	NUMBER OF PIZZAS PER DAY
1	80
2	150
3	205
4	240
5	250
6	230

   a. Find the marginal physical product schedule of chefs.

   b. Assuming a price of $3 per pizza, find the value of the marginal product schedule.

   c. If chefs are paid $30 per day, how many will this pizza parlor employ? How would your answer change if chefs' wages rose to $40 per day?

   d. Suppose the price of pizza rises from $3 to $4. Show what happens to the derived demand curve for chefs.

4. Discuss the concept of the financial rate of return to a college education. If this return is less than the return on a bank account, does that mean you should quit college? Why might you wish to stay in school anyway? Are there circumstances under which it might be rational not to go to college, even when the financial returns to college are very high?

5. Explain why many economists blame the minimum wage law for much of the employment problems of youth.

6. Approximately what fraction of the American labor force belongs to unions? (Try asking this question of a person who has never studied economics.) Why do you think this fraction is so low?

7. What are some reasonable goals for a union? Use the tools of supply and demand to explain how a union might pursue its goals, whatever they are. Consider a union that has been in the news recently. What was it trying to accomplish?

8. "Strikes are simply intolerable and should be outlawed." Comment.

9. "Public employees should have the same right to strike as private employees." Comment.

Appendix
The Effects of Minimum Wages
and Unions under Monopsony

We have argued in this chapter that in a competitive labor market a minimum wage that is set above the prevailing wage can only result in unemployment. In this appendix we show that:

When there is monopsony power on the buying side of the labor market, a minimum wage law or a union might succeed in raising wages without reducing employment. It might even be able to increase employment.

THE HIRING DECISIONS OF A MONOPSONIST

To establish these results, we begin by considering the hiring decision of a single firm

operating in a labor market that is competitive on the supply side. (Later we will bring unions back into the picture.) In such a market structure, there is a competitive *supply* curve for labor as usual, but there is a rather different sort of *demand* curve. In Figure 27–13, the supply curve is labeled *SS,* and the firm's value of marginal product schedule is labeled *VV.* In this context, however, the value of marginal product schedule is *not* the demand curve. The diagram has one additional curve, which will be explained presently.

How many workers will the monopsonist wish to hire? Table 27–2 helps us answer this question by displaying the monopsonist's cost–benefit calculation. What does he gain by hiring an additional worker? He gains the value of that worker's marginal product, which is given in column 5 of the table. What does he lose? Not

TABLE 27–2

LABOR COSTS AND VALUE OF MARGINAL PRODUCT OF A MONOPSONIST

(1) NUMBER OF WORKERS	(2) WAGE RATE	(3) TOTAL LABOR COST	(4) MARGINAL LABOR COST	(5) VALUE OF MARGINAL PRODUCT
1	$100	$ 100	$100	$475
2	125	250	150	450
3	150	450	200	425
4	175	700	250	400
5	200	1000	300	375
6	225	1350	350	350
7	250	1750	400	325
8	275	2200	450	275
9	300	2700	500	225
10	325	3250	550	150

just the wage he pays to the new worker. Because he is the only employer, and because the labor supply schedule is upward sloping, he can attract an additional worker only by *raising the wage rate*. And this higher wage must be paid to *all his employees*, not just the new one. For this reason, the cost of hiring an additional worker—what we call marginal labor costs— exceeds the wage rate. By how much? Table 27–2 provides the answer. The first two columns are just the labor supply schedule, curve *SS* of Figure 27–13. By multiplying the wage rate by the number of workers, we can compute the *total labor cost*, which is shown in column 3. For example, the total labor cost of hiring 5 workers is 5 times the weekly wage of

$200, or $1000. From these data, *marginal labor costs* are computed in the usual way—as the changes in successive total labor costs—and the results are displayed in column 4. This is the information the monopsonist wants, for it tells him that the first worker costs him $100, the next $150, and so on. The numbers in column 4 are dislayed on the graph by the schedule labeled *MLC* (marginal labor cost).

What employment level maximizes the monopsonist's profits? The usual marginal analysis applies. As he hires more workers, his profits rise if the value of the marginal product exceeds the marginal labor cost. For example, when he expands from 1 worker to 2, he receives $450 more in revenue and pays out only an additional $150 to labor; so profits rise by $300. This continues up to the point where marginal labor costs and the value of the marginal product are equal—at 6 workers in the example. Pushing beyond this point would reduce profits. For example, hiring the 7th worker would cost $400 and bring in only $325 in increased revenues—clearly a losing proposition. We therefore conclude:

A monopsonist maximizes profits by hiring workers up to the point where marginal labor costs are equal to the value of the marginal product.

In the example, it is optimal for the firm to hire 6 workers, and it does this by offering a wage of $225 per week. This solution is shown in Figure 27–13 by points *E* and *W*. Point *E* is the equilibrium of the firm, where marginal labor costs and value of marginal product are equal. To find the corresponding wage rate, we move vertically downward from *E* until we reach the supply curve at point *W*.

Let us compare this result with what would have emerged in a competitive labor market. As we know, equilibrium would be established where the supply curve of labor intersects the value-of-marginal-product curve because the value-of-marginal-product curve *is* the demand

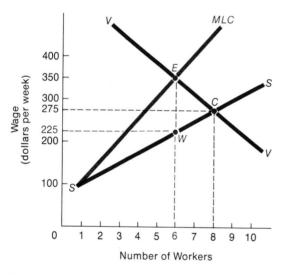

FIGURE 27–13

LABOR MARKET EQUILIBRIUM
UNDER MONOPSONY

Under monopsony, labor market equilibrium occurs at the employment level that equates marginal labor cost (curve *MLC* in the diagram) to the value of the marginal product (curve *VV*). In this case, equilibrium is at point *E*, where 6 workers are employed. The corresponding wage is $225 per week. By contrast, if this were a competitive market, equilibrium would be at point *C*, with a wage of $275 and employment of 8 workers.

curve of a competitive industry. Figure 27–13 shows that this competitive equilibrium (point C) would have been at a wage of $275 and employment of 8 workers.[7] In contrast, the monopsonist hires fewer workers (only 6) and pays each a lower wage (only $225 per week). This finding is quite a general result:

As long as the supply curve of labor is upward sloping and the value-of-marginal-product schedule is downward sloping, a monopsonist will hire fewer workers and pay lower wages than would a competitive industry.

MINIMUM WAGES UNDER MONOPSONY

Let us now consider what would happen if the government sought to protect workers by imposing a minimum wage of, say, $250 per

[7]This conclusion can also be seen in Table 27–2, where, in a competitive market, columns 1 and 2 give the supply curve, while columns 1 and 5 give the demand curve. Quantity supplied equals quantity demanded when the wage is $275.

week. This action would change the supply curve, and hence the MLC curve, that the monopsonist faces in a straightforward way. No labor could be hired at wages below $250 per week. At that wage, the monopsonist could attract up to 7 workers (see column 2 of Table 27–2). At higher wages, he could attract still more labor according to the supply curve. Thus his new effective supply curve would be *horizontal* at the wage of $250 up to the employment level of 7 workers, and then would follow the old supply curve. This is given numerically in column 2 of Table 27–3, and is shown graphically by the kinked curve SWS in Figure 27–14.

From this information, we can compute the revised marginal-labor-cost (MLC) schedule just as we did before. Column 3 in Table 27–3 gives us total labor costs at each employment level, and column 4 shows the corresponding marginal cost. The heavy red curve labeled MLC in Figure 27–14 depicts this information graphically. Notice that the marginal-labor-cost schedule has become *horizontal* up to the point where 7 workers are hired. This is a result of the government's minimum wage law, which means that the monopsonist must now pay the

TABLE 27–3

LABOR COSTS AND VALUE OF MARGINAL PRODUCT OF A MONOPSONIST AFTER ENACTMENT OF A MINIMUM WAGE LAW

(1) NUMBER OF WORKERS	(2) WAGE RATE	(3) TOTAL LABOR COST	(4) MARGINAL LABOR COST	(5) VALUE OF MARGINAL PRODUCT
1	$250	$ 250	$250	$475
2	250	500	250	450
3	250	750	250	425
4	250	1000	250	400
5	250	1250	250	375
6	250	1500	250	350
7	250	1750	250	325
8	275	2200	450	275
9	300	2700	500	225
10	325	3250	550	150

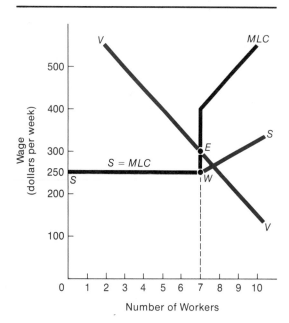

FIGURE 27–14

THE EFFECTS OF A MINIMUM WAGE
UNDER MONOPSONY

Minimum wage laws change the character of the *MLC* schedule facing a monopsonist. In this example, *MLC* is horizontal up to 7 workers, and then jumps as indicated by the heavy red line. Consequently, equilibrium employment is determined by point *E*, where 7 workers are employed at the minimum wage of $250. Comparing this with Figure 27–13, we see that the minimum wage can raise both wages and employment.

same wage per worker whether he hires 1 or 7 employees. Beyond 7 workers, the schedule returns to its previous level since the minimum wage is irrelevant.

The condition for profit maximization is unchanged, so the monopsonist seeks the employment level at which marginal labor costs and value of marginal product are equal. Since *MLC* jumps abruptly from $250 for the 7th worker to $450 for the 8th, this cannot be achieved exactly. But Table 27–3 makes it quite

clear that it is now profitable to employ the 7th worker (marginal labor cost equals $250, value of marginal product equals $325), but unprofitable to employ the 8th (marginal labor cost equals $450, value of marginal product equals $275). Points *E* and *W* in Figure 27–14 show, once again, the monopsonist's equilibrium point and the wage he must pay.

Comparing Figures 27–13 and 27–14 (or Tables 27–2 and 27–3), we see that the minimum wage law has raised wages from $225 to $250 per week, and at the same time *increased* employment from 6 to 7 workers. As was claimed, the minimum wage law can raise both wages and employment.

We caution you against reading strong policy conclusions into this finding. Examples of actual monopsony (one buyer) in labor markets are quite hard to find. Certainly the types of service establishments that tend to hire the lowest-paid workers—restaurants and snack bars, amusement parks, car washes, and so on—have no monopsony power whatever. While minimum wage laws *can* conceivably raise employment, few if any economists believe that they actually *do* have this pleasant effect.

UNIONS UNDER MONOPSONY

Virtually the same kind of result can be achieved by a union facing a monopsony firm, *if* the union selects a particular mode of behavior.[8]

Refer back to Figure 27–13, in which we depicted the equilibrium wage ($225 per week) and employment level (6 workers) in a monopsonized labor market with no union. As we mentioned earlier in the chapter, one option for a union is to fix a high wage rate, essentially

[8]Of course, as stressed earlier in the chapter, unions and firms in a situation of bilateral monopoly may do a wide variety of things. So the analysis here should be interpreted as one among many possible outcomes.

creating a horizontal supply curve at this wage. If the union does this, the effects will be much the same as the effects of the minimum wage law. In both cases, the differences between wages and marginal labor costs are eliminated. As an exercise, use Figure 27–13 to convince yourself that a union can succeed in raising *both* wages *and* employment by imposing a horizontal supply curve of labor at a wage between $225 and $350 per week. (*Hint*: What will be the monopsonist's *MLC* if the union makes the supply curve horizontal?)

SUMMARY

1. A profit-maximizing monopsonist hires labor up to the point where the value of the marginal product equals the marginal labor cost.
2. Because marginal labor cost exceeds the wage rate, this results in less employment and lower wages than those that would emerge from a competitive labor market.
3. By eliminating the difference between marginal labor costs and wages, it is possible that a minimum wage law could raise both wages and employment under monopsony.
4. For the same reason, a union can conceivably raise wages without sacrificing jobs if the employer is a monopsonist.

CONCEPT FOR REVIEW

Marginal labor costs

QUESTIONS FOR DISCUSSION

1. Consider the pizza chef example of Question 3 on pages 529–530 and suppose that pizzas sell for $3 each. Let the supply curve of chefs be as follows:

NUMBER OF CHEFS	WAGE PER DAY
1	$ 10
2	15
3	20
4	25
5	30
6	40

a. How many chefs will be employed, and at what wage, if the market is competitive?
b. How many chefs will be employed, and at what wage, if the market has a monopsony pizza parlor? (*Hint*: First figure out the schedule of marginal labor cost.)
c. Compare your answers to a and b. What do you conclude?
d. Now suppose that a union is organized to fight the monopsonist. If it insists on a wage of $30 per day, what will the monopsonist do?

2. Given what you have learned about minimum wage laws in the chapter and in the appendix, do you think they are a good or a bad idea?

28

Rent, Interest, and Profits

In this chapter we take up the determination of three factor prices: rent on land, interest on borrowed funds, and profit earned by capitalists. As with the determination of wages, controversies abound here too. Some we will examine now for the first time; others we have encountered in earlier chapters. At the end of the chapter we provide an overview of the theory of factor pricing, stressing the ways in which the markets for labor, land, funds, and capital are the same and the ways in which they differ. The analyses are then tied together with the aid of the marginal productivity model of distribution. By way of contrast, the appendix to this chapter describes the Ricardian distribution theory.

RENT: WHAT DETERMINES JOHNNY CARSON'S SALARY?

The high level of rents is a favorite topic of conversation, and people's strong feelings about this subject have led to the enactment of rent control statutes in many cities and towns, both in this country and elsewhere. A thorough discussion of this issue will be provided in Chapter 35 on urban problems, but we will have something to say about this pressing social problem in this chapter as well. First, though, it is important for the reader to understand economists' definition of the word *rent*: It is a much broader concept than the one in common usage. To economists, land and buildings are far from the only things that can bring in rent. And, as we shall see, it may be that a failure to understand this economic interpretation partly accounts for the popularity of rent controls.

Television personalities like Johnny Carson seem to have little in common with office space in the Sears, Roebuck Tower in Chicago. Yet, to an economist, the same analysis—the theory of rent—explains the incomes that these two factors of production earn. To understand this, we first need to understand the economist's general notion of rent.

DEFINITION

Economic rent is said to be earned whenever a factor of production receives a reward that exceeds the minimum amount necessary to induce the employed quantity of the factor to be supplied.

A moment's thought should explain why this definition applies to land. Land is an input that is not produced. Its supply is there whether rent is high, low, or zero. Thus payments to landlords are not necessary to induce land to be produced in the way car payments are necessary to get auto manufacturers to produce cars. Thus, by our definition, payment to landholders for their land is rent—it is not necessary to induce the provision of the land to the economy.

Extreme cases of economic rent are probably the easiest to grasp, and here Johnny Carson is (almost) a good example. Consider a factor of production, like Carson, that is completely unique and cannot be reproduced, except perhaps at unthinkable cost. What determines the income of such a factor? By now, you

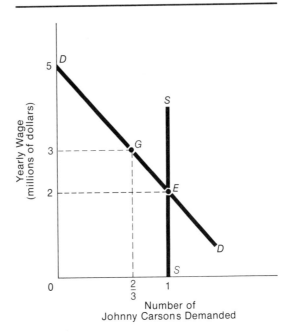

FIGURE 28–1

HYPOTHETICAL MARKET FOR JOHNNY CARSON'S SERVICES

At an annual wage of $5 million or more, no one is willing to bid for his time. At a somewhat lower wage, $3 million, two-thirds of his time will be demanded (point *G*). Only at an annual wage no higher than $2 million will all of Carson's available time be demanded (point *E*).

are probably responding automatically to any question like this by saying "the law of supply and demand." And this response is again correct but with an important amendment. For in the case of a unique, nonreproducible factor, the supply is absolutely fixed. Since supply is, therefore, unresponsive to price, demand plays a particularly crucial role in the pricing of such an item.

Figure 28–1 illustrates this analysis. Supply curve *SS* represents the fact that, no matter what wage he is paid, there is only one Johnny Carson. Demand curve *DD* is a marginal productivity curve of sorts but not the kind we encountered in the last chapter. Since the question,

What would be the value of a second unit of Johnny Carson? is nonsensical, the demand curve is constructed by considering alternative employers. The curve indicates that at an annual salary of $5 million, no employer can afford even a little bit of Johnny Carson. At a lower salary of, say, $3 million per year, however, there are enough profitable uses to absorb two-thirds of his time. At $2 million per year, Carson's full time is demanded by various employers; and at lower wage rates, the demand for Carson's time exceeds the amount of it that is for sale.[1]

Equilibrium in the "Johnny Carson market" is at point E in the diagram, where the supply of and demand for his time are equal. His annual salary here is $2 million. Notice that in this case of rigidly fixed supply, the price of the factor is totally determined by the demand side of the market. If NBC's advertising rates fall, so that the value of Carson's services to the network is reduced, the DD curve will shift down and Carson's salary will fall by the full amount of the decline in the demand curve. This is shown in Figure 28–2, where the equilibrium salary falls by the full $1 million by which the demand curve has declined (from point E to point K).

Now we can ask: How much of Johnny Carson's salary is economic rent? According to the economic definition of rent, his entire $2 million salary is rent. Since Carson would, according to the vertical supply schedule, work full time at any wage, every penny that he earns is rent. That is, his financial reward is unnecessary to get him to supply his services.

This is why we said that personalities like Carson were *almost* good examples of pure rent. For, in fact, at low enough salaries, Carson would probably prefer to stay home much of the time and watch someone else perform on TV. Suppose, for example, that $40,000 per year is the lowest salary at which Carson will offer even 1 minute of his services, and that his labor supply then increases with his wage up to an

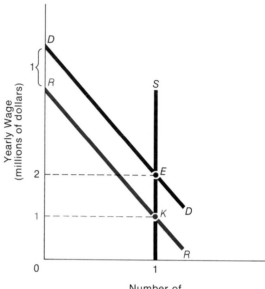

FIGURE 28–2

A SHIFT IN DEMAND WITH A VERTICAL SUPPLY CURVE

If the revenues of Carson's employer fall, the demand curve for Carson's services will shift downward (from DD to RR—a downward shift of $1 million). If the supply of Carson's services is absolutely fixed—if he does not supply less time when his wage falls—then his equilibrium wage will also fall $1 million. That is, his income will be reduced by the full amount of the downward shift in the demand curve for his services.

annual salary of $250,000, at which point he is willing to work full time. Then, while his equilibrium salary will still be $2 million per year, not all of it will be pure rent, because some of it, at least $40,000, is required to get him to supply his services.

This same analysis applies to *any* factor of production whose supply curve is not horizontal, that is, whose elasticity of supply is less than infinite. Any such factor earns some rent—or gets paid *more* than the minimum amount that would induce it to work. Almost all of us earn some rent.

[1]These numbers are not entirely hypothetical. According to newspaper reports, Carson earns nearly $3 million per year, working three to four nights a week.

What sorts of factors, then, earn no rent? Those that can be exactly reproduced by a number of producers at constant cost. No supplier of ball bearings will ever receive any rent on a ball bearing because, at least in the long run, any desired number of them can be produced at (roughly) constant costs. If one supplier tried to charge a price that included a rent for them, someone else would simply undercut him and take his customers away.

THE RENT OF LAND

The extreme case of pure rent does have some important applications. With some minor exceptions (such as landfill projects), the markets for undeveloped land and other fixed natural resources seem to fit the model of fixed supply. People may clear the land, drain its swamps, fertilize it, and build on it, but land itself cannot be created by human effort.

If all parcels of land were identical, the model of absolutely fixed supply in Figure 28–1 would be all there was to the theory of land rent. But this is obviously not the case. The available land varies considerably in potential usefulness to the production process. Because one piece of land is more fertile than another, or lies closer to where customers live, or needs less clearing, its marginal product will have a higher value than that of another piece of land.

The variability in the quality of land was taken into account by the classical economists in their analysis of rent determination. The analysis was formulated at the end of the eighteenth century and is still considered valid today.

The basic notion is that capital invested on any piece of available land must be expected to yield the same return as capital invested on any other available piece that actually finds a user. For if this is not so, capitalists will bid against each other for the more profitable pieces of land until the rents of these parcels are driven up to a point where their advantages over other pieces of land have been eliminated. Suppose that on one piece of land a given crop is produced for $160,000 per year in labor, fertilizer, fuel, and other nonland costs, while on a second piece of land the same crop is produced for $120,000. Our analysis tells us that the difference in rent on the two pieces of land must be exactly $40,000 per year, because otherwise production on one plot would be more profitable than on the other. We can see this by noting what would happen if the rent difference were, say, only $30,000 per year. Then it would clearly be $10,000 cheaper to produce on the second plot of land. No one would want to rent the first plot and every grower would instead bid for the second plot. Obviously, rent on the first plot would be forced down by lack of demand, and rent on the second would be driven up by high demand. These pressures would only come to an end when the rent difference reached $40,000, so that both plots became equally profitable.

At any given time, there will be some pieces of land whose productivity is so low that it does not pay to use them at all—remote deserts being a prime example. Any land that is exactly on the borderline of being used is called marginal land. By definition it will pay no rent because if any rent were charged for it, it would find no takers.

We now combine this observation with our previous conclusion that differences in the cost of producing on two pieces of land must equal the difference in their rent. Since zero rent is charged on marginal land, it follows that:

Rent on any piece of land will equal the difference between the cost of producing the output on that piece of land and the cost of producing it on marginal land.

That is, competition for the superior qualities of a piece of land will permit the landlord to charge a price that captures for him the full advantage of the use of his land over the use of inferior, marginal land.

A useful feature of this analysis is that it helps us to understand the effects of an increase in the demand for land. Suppose there is an increase in the demand for land because of a rise in population or because of a switch in consumer preferences toward commodities that need a great deal of land in their production or for some other reason. We would expect rents to rise, and the analysis confirms this. But it is important to see just how this comes about and what determines how high that rise will be.

In response to this upward shift in the demand curve, two things will happen:

1. It will now pay to employ some land whose use was formerly unprofitable. The land that was previously marginal will no longer be on the borderline, and some land that is so poor that it was formerly not even worth considering will now become marginal.
2. People will begin more intensive use of those pieces of land that were used before. Farmers will use more labor, machinery, and fertilizer to squeeze larger crops than before out of their acreage. In a city, on a piece of real estate on which a 10-story building previously made most sense, now a 12- or 15-story building will be more profitable. These are all ways to economize on the use of land—to get more out of the input whose demand has increased.

Rents will be increased in a predictable way by both these developments—the use of poorer lands than before and an increase in the intensity with which lands are used. Our rule about marginal land and the determination of rent tells us just how rent will be affected by the inclusion of inferior lands in the production process. The essence of the matter is that the land that is marginal *after* the change will be inferior to the land that was marginal previously. Simple arithmetic now tells us that rents must rise by the difference in yields of the lands that were previously marginal and the lands that are now on the margin.

Table 28–1 illustrates the relationship. We deal with three pieces of land: A, a very productive piece; B, a piece that was initially marginal; and C, a piece that is inferior to B but nevertheless becomes marginal when the upward shift in the demand curve for land occurs. The crop costs $80,000 more when produced on B than on A, and $12,000 more when produced on C than on B. Suppose, initially, that demand for the crop is low so that C is totally unused and B is just on the margin between being used and left idle. Since B is marginal, as we have seen, it will yield no rent. The rent on A then is simply equal to the cost saving it makes possible— $80,000. Now suppose demand for the product of the land shifts upward so that C must be brought into use and B is no longer marginal.

TABLE 28–1

NONRENT COSTS AND RENT ON THREE PIECES OF LAND

TYPE OF LAND	NONLAND COST OF PRODUCING A GIVEN CROP	TOTAL RENT	
		Before	After
A. A tract that was better than marginal before and after	$120,000	$80,000	$92,000
B. A tract that was marginal before but isn't anymore	200,000	0	12,000
C. A tract that was previously not worth using but is now marginal	212,000	—	0

C becomes marginal land and B acquires a rent of $12,000, the cost advantage of B over C.

This shows just how the increased land usage affects the rent payments. But we have seen that increased demand not only affects the amount of land that is used, it also affects the *intensity* with which the land is used, both before and after the change. As it turns out, this will affect rent payments in a way very similar to that described in Table 28–1. For the law of diminishing returns tells us that even on a given piece of land, more and more increases in output become successively harder to obtain, just as they become harder to obtain if one successively turns to poorer and poorer pieces of land; and in either case the landlord is able to capture in the form of rents the relative cost advantages of those units of output whose costs are not raised by diminishing returns. This, then, is the substance of the classical rent model:

As the use of land increases, landlords receive higher land payments from two sources because: (a) increased demand leads the community to employ land previously not good enough to use, the advantage of land previously used over the new marginal land increases, and rent will go up correspondingly; (b) as land is used more intensively the *marginal* cost of additional output will rise, and product price will rise correspondingly, thus increasing the ability of the producer who uses the land to pay rent.

As late as the end of the nineteenth century, this analysis still exerted a powerful influence beyond the technical economic writings. An American journalist, Henry George, was nearly elected mayor of New York in 1886, running on the platform that all government should be financed by "a single tax"—a tax on landlords who, he said, are the only ones who earn while contributing nothing to the productive process and who reap the fruits of economic growth as increased demand for land increases the amount of economic rent while, by the definition of rent, not expanding the supply.

RENT CONTROLS: THE MISPLACED ANALOGY

Somewhat similar reasoning seems to explain some of the popularity of rent controls. People may feel that the rent that they pay to their landlord is economic rent. After all, their apartments will still be there if they pay $500 per month, or $300, or $100. This view, while true in the short run, is quite myopic. For, unlike the raw land upon which they are built, *structures are not in inelastic supply except in the short run.* They can deteriorate and not be repaired or replaced, and this does happen when rents are held down too low.

In fact, far from being in perfectly *inelastic* supply, structures come rather close to being in perfectly *elastic* supply in the very long run. That is, the long-run supply curve for apartments and houses comes much closer to being horizontal than it does to being vertical. As we have learned from the theory of rent, builders and owners of buildings cannot collect economic rent in the long run. Only owners of land can do that. Since apartment owners collect very little economic rent, the payments that tenants make in a free market are just about enough to keep those apartments on the market. (This is the definition of zero economic rent.) If rent controls push these prices down, the apartments will start disappearing from the market.

We should note that none of this is meant to imply that *temporary* rent controls in certain locations cannot have salutory effects in the short run. In the short run, the supply of apartments and houses really is fixed, and large shifts in demand would hand windfall gains to landlords—gains that are true economic rents. Controls that eliminate such windfalls should not cause serious dislocations. But knowing when the "short run" fades into the "long run" can be a tricky matter. "Temporary" rent control laws, as we have seen, have a way of becoming rather permanent.

ARE INTEREST RATES TOO HIGH? THE ISSUE OF USURY LAWS

The rate of interest is the cost of obtaining (borrowing) money. And, like other factor prices, the rate of interest is determined by supply and demand. Here too, many people have been dissatisfied with the outcome of the supply—demand process.

Just as the vague feeling that somehow rents are often unjustifiably high has led to demands for rent control legislation, fears that interest rates, if left unregulated, would climb to exorbitant levels have made usury laws quite popular. Throughout the United States today, states have their own sets of usury laws prescribing maximum rates that can be charged on consumer loans, home mortgages, and the like. Like the minimum wage laws and rent controls, usury laws, when they are effective, interfere with the operation of supply and demand. As we learned in Chapter 6, they can cause particularly severe problems when there is rapid inflation, because interest rate ceilings generally are placed on *nominal* interest rates, not on *real* interest rates.

Whether a usury ceiling will or will not be effective depends on what the equilibrium rate of interest would have been in a free market. For example, a ceiling of 18 percent annual interest on consumer loans is quite irrelevant if the free-market equilibrium rate is 15 percent, but it can have important effects if the free-market rate is 25 percent. To see why this is so, we turn now to the market determination of interest rates through the forces of supply and demand.

THE DEMAND FOR FUNDS

There are many ways in which funds are rented: home mortgages, corporation or government bonds, consumer credit, and so on. On the demand side of these credit markets are *borrowers*—people or institutions that, for one reason or another, wish to spend more money than they currently have. Thus, as usual in factor markets, the demand for funds is a *derived demand*. The demand for home mortgages is derived from the demand for houses, the demand for corporate borrowing is derived from firms' desires to invest, and so on.

So the same basic marginal productivity principle governs the demand for funds as governs the demand for labor or for any other input (see Chapters 21 and 27).

Firms will demand borrowed funds up to the point where the marginal productivity of investment is reduced to the marginal cost of borrowing.

The new quirk is that, *in an investment activity, both the costs and the benefits accrue over a period of time, not all at once.* When Ford Motor Company borrows $10 million to finance an expansion in its productive capacity, it commits itself to a stream of interest payments of, say, $1 million per year (10 percent interest) for 20 years, and a final payment of $10 million at the end of 20 years. Thus, borrowing costs are incurred over a 20-year period. On the benefits side, though the company may see no revenue at all for, say, 2 years, after that time it will expect a certain revenue gain from the investment for many years to come. So the problem for rational decision making is being able to summarize in a single number the costs and benefits of an investment activity financed by borrowing, so that the potential borrower may decide which one is greater.

The difficulty of making such a determination is illustrated by the example given in Table 28–2. Here we have shown an investment in a machine that will add nothing to the firm's revenues this year (year 1) or next (year 2), but will generate $14,520 in additional revenues the year after that (year 3), after which time the machine will fall apart. The machine costs $11,000

TABLE 28–2
COSTS AND BENEFITS OF INVESTING IN A MACHINE

Benefits	Year 1	Year 2	Year 3
Value of the marginal product of the machine	0	0	$14,520
Costs			
Interest and principal on loan	$1100	$1100	$12,100

and can be financed by a 3-year loan bearing 10 percent interest. This means that the firm must pay $1100 in interest during each of the 3 years of the loan and also pay back the principal of the loan ($11,000) in year 3. By comparing the two lines, we see that the firm loses $1100 in years 1 and 2, and gains $2420 in year 3. Is the machine a good investment? The technique that economists and business people use to answer such a question is called discounting.

DISCOUNTING AND PRESENT VALUE

The most obvious approach, which turns out to be quite wrong in this case, is to simply add up all the costs and benefits. By this naïve calculation, the total benefits ($14,520) exceed the total costs ($1100 + $1100 + $12,100 = $14,300), so the machine appears to be a good idea. But the calculation is incorrect because a dollar received 1 or 2 years from now is not the same as a dollar received today. Adding them up is a bit like adding apples and oranges.

To see why this is so, consider what you could do with a dollar that you received today rather than a year from today. If the rate of interest were 10 percent, you could lend it out (for example, by putting it in a bank account), and receive $1.10 in a year's time—your original $1 plus 10 cents interest. If you kept the $1.10 in the bank for a 2nd year, you would accumulate $1.21 at the end of 2 years—your $1.10 plus 11 cents interest. Thus, because of compound interest:

At a rate of interest of 10 percent a year, $1 of today's money is equivalent to $1.10 one year from today, or $1.21 two years from today, and so on.

Let us now think of this question the other way around: How much is $1 received a year from today worth in terms of today's money? When we answer a question like this, we are discounting future flows of money, or computing their present value.

DEFINITION
The present value of a sum of money to be received in the future is the amount of current money that is equivalent to it. Discounting means computing the present value of a future sum of money.

To answer the question just posed, when the rate of interest is 10 percent, about 91 cents of today's money is the present value of $1 a year from now. This is because 91 cents of today's money will earn 9.1 cents in interest if the interest rate is 10 percent, giving a total accumulation of 91 cents + 9.1 cents = 100.1 cents. That is, we can be about equally wealthy a year from now if we get 91 cents now, or if instead we get $1 at the end of the year.

Similar considerations apply to any rate of interest. There is a general formula for present value at any specified interest rate for money paid at any specified future date:

The present value of $1 to be received (or paid) n years from today, when the interest rate is i, is:

$$\frac{\$1}{(1 + i)^n}$$

To see why this is so, suppose that the interest rate is some number i. Then $1 invested today will grow to $1 + i$ dollars in a year. Therefore, the present value of $1 to be received in a year is $\$1/(1 + i)$, because this amount will grow to $[\$1/(1 + i)] \times (1 + i) = \$1$ in a year's time. For the same reason, $1 invested today will, because of compounding, grow to $(1 + i) \times (1 + i) = (1 + i)^2$ after 2 years, so that the present value of $1 received in 2 years will be $\$1/(1 + i)^2$, and so on.

The present value formula highlights the two factors that determine the present value of any future flow of money: the rate of interest (i) and how long you have to wait before you get it (n).

Let us now apply this analysis to appraise the investment activity considered in Table 28–2. The present value of the benefits are easy to calculate since they all accrue 2 years from today. Thus:

$$\begin{aligned} \text{Present value} \\ \text{of benefits} \end{aligned} = \frac{\$14,520}{(1 + 0.1)^2}$$
$$= \frac{\$14,520}{(1.1)^2}$$
$$= \frac{\$14,520}{1.21}$$
$$= \$12,000$$

Why is $12,000 the present value of $14,520 two years in the future? Because if $12,000 were put in the bank for 2 years at a 10 percent rate of compound interest, at the end of the 2 years the account would amount to $14,520. That, in essence, is what the preceding calculation tells us. The present value of the costs is a bit trickier since it comes in three parts. The present value (in year 1 money) of the $1100 interest payment in year 1 is, of course, just $1100. The present value of the next interest payment is $\$1100/1.1 = \$1000$. And the present value of the final payment of interest plus principal is:

$$\frac{\$12,100}{(1.1)^2} = \frac{\$12,100}{1.21} = \$10,000$$

Now that we have expressed each sum in terms of its present value, it *is* valid to add them up. So the present value of all costs is:

Present value of costs = $1100 + $1000+ $10,000 = $12,100

Comparing this to the $12,000 present value of the benefits clearly shows that the machine is a poor investment after all. The firm will not want to buy the machine and therefore will not want to borrow the necessary $11,000.

The important procedure that has just been described is applicable to *all* investment decisions, both to decisions on the purchase of new plant and equipment (the economists' use of the term) and for financial decisions, such as the purchase of securities (the more common use of the term "investment"). In general:

To determine whether a loss or a gain will result from a decision whose costs and returns will come in at several different periods of time, the figures represented by these gains and losses must all be discounted to obtain their present value. One then adds together the present values of all the returns. Next, one adds together the present values of all the costs. If the sum of the present values of the returns is greater than the sum of the present values of the costs then the decision to invest will promise a net gain.

THE DOWNWARD-SLOPING DEMAND FOR FUNDS

Remembering now that the demand for funds is a demand derived from the demand for investment goods (which is, itself, a derived demand), we can see why the quantity of funds demanded is a decreasing function of the rate of interest.

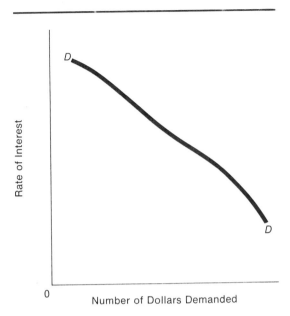

FIGURE 28–3

THE DERIVED DEMAND CURVE FOR LOANS
The rate of interest is the cost of a loan to the borrower. The lower the rate of interest, the more it will pay a business firm to borrow in order to finance new plant and equipment. That is why this demand curve has a negative slope.

The reason is fairly straightforward. We discount future earnings of an investment because we incur an opportunity cost when we get money later rather than immediately. If we had the money now we could begin to earn interest on it at once, but since the money will not come in until later we lose that interest. Naturally, the lower the interest rate, the lower those interest payments would be and so the lower is the opportunity cost of the investment. That is why a reduction in interest rate can turn an otherwise unprofitable investment into a profitable one.

As the rate of interest on borrowing falls, more and more investments that previously looked unprofitable start to look profitable. The demand for borrowing for investment purposes, therefore, is higher at lower rates of interest.

An example of a derived demand schedule for borrowing is given in Figure 28–3. Its negative slope conforms with the result at which we have just arrived—the lower the interest rate, the more money people and firms will want to borrow to finance their investments.

Suppose the interest rate falls. To keep the example as simple as possible, let it fall all the way to zero. Then the naïve calculation we made before would be valid. At a zero interest rate, our formula for present value shows that the present value of a dollar received in *any* year would be a dollar, so it would be correct simply to add up all the dollars.[2] When we did this earlier, we found that the benefits ($14,520) exceeded the costs ($14,300). The machine that is a poor investment at a 10 percent rate of interest becomes a fine investment at a zero rate of interest. While this example is quite contrived, the basic principle is generally true.

[2]If you do not see why, recall that the number 1 raised to any power is still 1, that is: $1 = 1^2 = 1^3 = \ldots$

SUPPLY OF FUNDS AND DETERMINATION OF INTEREST RATES

Discounting principles similar to those described earlier also apply on the supply side of the market for funds—where the *lenders* are consumers, banks, and other types of business firms. Money lent out returns to the owner (with interest) only over a period of time. Present value calculations must be made to determine how much the borrower is really promising to pay back *in terms of today's money.* Loans will look better to lenders when they bear higher interest rates, so it is natural to think of the supply schedule for loans as being upward sloping—at higher rates of interest, lenders supply more funds. Such a supply schedule is shown by the

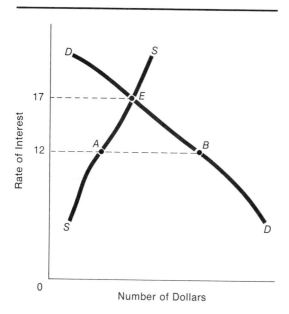

FIGURE 28–4

EQUILIBRIUM IN THE MARKET FOR LOANS
Here the free-market interest rate is 17 percent. At this interest rate, the supply of loans is equal to the demand. However, if an interest-rate ceiling is imposed, say, at 12 percent, the quantity of funds supplied (point A) will be smaller than the quantity demanded (point B).

though the banks consider them to be credit worthy.

Who gains and who loses from this usury law? The gainers are easiest to identify: those lucky consumers who are able to get loans at 12 percent even though they would have been willing to pay 17 percent. The law represents a windfall gain for them. The losers come on both the supply and the demand side. First, there are the consumers who would have been willing and able to get credit at 17 percent but who are not lucky enough to get it at 12 percent. Then there are the banks (or, rather, bank stockholders) who could have made profitable loans at rates of up to 17 percent if there were no interest-rate ceiling.

This analysis helps explain the political popularity of such usury laws. Few people sympathize with the bank stockholders; indeed, it is the feeling that banks are "gouging" their borrowers that provides much of the impetus for usury laws. The consumers who get loans at lower rates will, naturally, be quite pleased with the result of the law. The others, who would like to borrow at 12 percent but cannot because supply is less than demand, are quite likely to blame the bank for refusing to lend, rather than blame the government for outlawing mutually beneficial transactions.

This competitive analysis has little good to say about usury ceilings, and economists generally oppose them. However, as was the case with minimum wage laws (see the preceding chapter), interest-rate ceilings can play a constructive role when there is a monopoly over credit. If there is a monopoly lender, as we know, he will restrict his "output" (the volume of loans) by raising his "price" (the interest rate). Under such circumstances, an interest-rate ceiling could raise the volume of loans while lowering the interest rate. But, as in the case of minimum wages, *could* is not *would*. Most economists believe that, except for isolated instances, the credit market is far closer to the competitive model than it is to the monopoly model.

curve *SS* in Figure 28–4, where we also reproduce the demand curve, *DD*, from Figure 28–3.

The equilibrium rate of interest is, as always, at point *E*, where supply and demand are equal. If we suppose that the example refers to loans made by banks to consumers, then we can assume that the equilibrium interest rate is 17 percent.

Now what happens if there is a usury law that prohibits interest of more than 12 percent per annum on consumer loans? At this interest rate, the quantity supplied is indicated by point *A*, while the quantity demanded is indicated by point *B*. There is an excess of demand over supply, which means that many applicants for consumer loans are being turned down even

ARE PROFITS TOO HIGH?
THE ISSUE OF PROFITS TAXATION

America is an interesting country in that, with the exception of many economists, almost no one thinks that the rate of profit is at about the right level. Critics on the left point accusingly at the billion-dollar profits of some giant corporations and argue that they are unjustifiably high. They call for much stiffer profits taxation. On the other hand, the Chambers of Commerce, National Association of Manufacturers, and other business groups complain that regulations and "ruinous" competition keep profits too low, and they are constantly petitioning Congress for tax relief.

The public has many misconceptions about the nature of the U.S. economy, but probably none is more severe than the popular view of the amount of profit that American corporations earn. We suggest to you the following experiment. Ask five of your friends who have never had an economics course what fraction of the nation's income they imagine is accounted for by corporate profits. While the correct answer varies from year to year, data given in Table 17–3, page 322, showed that in 1977 only 9.5 percent of national income, or 7.6 percent of GNP, was corporate profits. The latter fraction has an intuitive interpretation that is quite easy to grasp. It says that 7.6 percent of the price of the average final good represents corporate profits. Most people think this figure is much, much higher. (See the boxed insert on page 548.)

As you have no doubt noticed by now, economists are reluctant to brand certain factor prices "too low" or "too high" in some moral or ethical sense. Rather, they are likely to ask, first, What is the free-market equilibrium price? And then they will ask whether there are any good reasons to interfere with the market solution. This, however, is not so easy to do with profits since it is hard to apply supply and demand analysis when you do not know what factor of

"Give him a nickel, sweetheart. After all, you made a couple of million on the war."

A radical view of profits . . . A cartoon by A. Redfield, published in the 1930s by *The Daily Worker*, the official Communist party newspaper in the United States.

production earns profit. In both a bookkeeping and an economic sense, *profits are the residual:* they are what remains from the selling price after all other factors have been paid. But what factor of production receives this reward? Which factor's marginal productivity constitutes the profit rate?

REASONS FOR PROFIT

The rate of interest is closely tied to the rate of profit; they tend to rise and fall together. To understand why, try to imagine a (rather uninteresting) world in which everything was certain and unchanging. There, capitalists who invested money in firms would simply earn as profit the equilibrium rate of interest on their funds. Profits beyond this level would be competed away. Profits below this level could not persist, because capitalists would withdraw their funds from the firms and deposit them in banks. Capitalists in such a world would be, in effect, no more than mere moneylenders.

But the real world is not at all like this; capitalists are much more than moneylenders, and the profits they earn often exceed the interest rate by a considerable margin. Those activist capitalists who seek out or even create earnings opportunities are called entrepreneurs.

DEFINITION
Entrepreneurs are people who use imagination and aggressiveness to turn business enterprises in new directions, who seek out and pounce upon new and profitable opportunities. They are the ones who are responsible for the constant change that characterizes business firms and who prevent the operations of the firms from stagnating.

There are three primary ways in which entrepreneurs drive profits above the level of interest rates:

1. Exercise of monopoly power. If the entrepreneur can establish a monopoly over some or all

What College Students Think about Profits

Even people as well informed as college students have a vastly exaggerated idea of the level of profits and other financial figures for business firms. The material reproduced here is taken from a Gallup opinion poll. Contrary to what the college students who were polled thought, the typical profit margin on sales is closer to 10 percent than to 45 percent, and the typical corporate tax on net earnings of $100,000 is about $42,000, not $15,000.

At the same time that a strong antibusiness mood prevails on campus, there is also widespread ignorance of the costs and rewards of doing business.

For example, the median average estimate by students of the profits made by a typical national corporation on its total business is 45 percent. The median average of what they feel would be a fair profit is 25 percent.

When students were asked how much federal income tax, in dollars, a corporation pays on net earnings of $100,000, the median estimate was $15,000.

The college population also has a distorted idea of the costs labor represents in the purchase price of such products as refrigerators and automobiles. The median average of college responses is 33 percent—less than half the true figure.

Source: *The Gallup Opinion Index*, Princeton, N.J., Report No. 123, September 1975.

of his products, he can use the monopoly power of his firm to earn monopoly profits. The nature of these monopoly earnings was analyzed in Chapter 23.

2. Risk bearing. The entrepreneur may engage in socially valuable activities whose payoff is more-or-less risky. For example, when a firm prospects for oil it will drill an exploratory shaft hoping to find a pool of petroleum at the bottom. But a high proportion of such attempts produce only dry holes, and the high cost of the operation is wasted. Of course, if the investor is lucky and does find oil, he may be rewarded handsomely. The income he obtains is a payment for risk.

Obviously, a few lucky individuals may make out well in this process, while many others lose heavily. How well can we expect risk takers to do on the average? If, on the average, one exploratory drilling out of ten pays off, do we expect its return to be exactly ten times as high as the interest rate, or more? The answer is that the payoff should be *more* than ten times the interest rate in a world in which investors do not love gambling; that is, if all other things are equal, they would prefer to avoid risk. For investors will be unwilling to put their money in this risky business without some sort of compensation for the financial peril to which they expose themselves. The scarcity of investment funds will drive up the price of the product until it yields a *risk premium* to the entrepreneur, that is, until the average return is sufficiently above the interest rate to make such projects attractive to investors despite their dangers.

In reality, however, there is no certainty that things will always work out this way. Some people do love to gamble, and they tend to be overoptimistic about their chances of coming out ahead. If so, they may plunge into projects to a degree unjustified by the odds. If there are enough such gamblers, the average payoff to risky undertakings may well turn out to be lower than the interest rate. The successful investor

will still make a good profit, just like the lucky winner in Las Vegas. But the average participant may well turn out to earn a *negative* risk premium.

3. Returns to innovation. A third major source of profits that exceed the interest rate is perhaps the most important of all from the point of view of social welfare. The entrepreneur who is first to market a desirable new product, or to employ a new cost-saving machine, or to *innovate* in some other way will receive a special profit as his reward. Innovation is defined as something different from *invention*. Invention is the act of generating a new idea; innovation is the next step, the act of putting the new idea into practical use. Business people are rarely inventors, but they are often innovators.

When an entrepreneur innovates, even if his new product or his new process is not protected by patents, he will be one step ahead of his competitors. He will be able to capture many of their customers either by offering them a better product or by supplying his product more cheaply than his rivals can. In either case he will temporarily find himself with some monopoly power left by the weakening of his competitors, and monopoly profit will be the reward for his initiative.

However, this monopoly profit, the reward for innovation, will only be temporary. As soon as the success of the idea has demonstrated itself to the world, other firms will find ways of imitating it. Even if they cannot turn out precisely the same product or use precisely the same process, they will find ways to supply close substitutes. They will have to do so in order to survive. In this way new ideas are spread through the economy, and the special profits of the innovator are brought to an end.

The innovator can only resume his earning of special profits by finding still another promising idea that is awaiting adoption. Entrepreneurs are forced to keep searching for new ideas, to keep instituting innovations, and to keep imitating those that they have not been the first to put into operation. This process is at the heart of the growth of the capitalist system: It is one of the secrets of its extraordinary dynamism.

PROFITS AND PROFITS TAXATION

So profits in excess of the market rate of interest can be considered as the return on entrepreneurial talent. But this is not really very helpful, since no one can accurately say what entrepreneurial talent is; certainly we cannot measure it. Nor can we tell how much of the observed profit rate is a pure economic rent and how much is the minimum necessary reward to attract this talent into the market.

The latter, rather unanswerable, question is crucial to the issue of profits taxation. For if profits are mostly economic rents, then entrepreneurs would remain entrepreneurs even at much higher rates of profit taxation. We could then raise taxes with impunity, without worrying about the harm that might be done to innovation and risk bearing. This, presumably, is the model of capitalist behavior that is believed in by many critics who call for high, if not confiscatory, profit taxes. But if they are quite wrong, if most of the observed profit rate is not rent but rather necessary payment to attract people into entrepreneurial roles, then raising the profits tax can be quite dangerous indeed. It can threaten the very lifeblood of the capitalist system. Business organizations seem quite convinced that this is the case. Economists, on the other hand, are much more willing to admit their ignorance on this important matter.

MARGINAL PRODUCTIVITY THEORY IN GENERAL

In studying this chapter and the previous one, you have probably noticed the similar treatments given the demand sides of the markets for labor, land, funds, and other factors of production. The reason is that the same marginal productivity principle, governs the demand for all factor inputs.

DEFINITION:
The *marginal productivity principle* states that, in a competitive factor market, it always pays for a profit-maximizing firm to expand its usage of any input up to the point where the value of the input's marginal product has been reduced to the price of the input.

There are several key words in this statement that our previous discussion has taught us to appreciate. First, note the restriction to *competitive* factor markets. As we have seen, a monopsonist (the only buyer of a factor) will equate the value of the marginal product *not* to the factor price but rather to the marginal factor cost. Second, the principle applies only to *profit-maximizing* firms, because it is really a rule that instructs the firm how to squeeze the last ounce of profit from its employment decisions. Firms with other goals may make different hiring decisions. Third, the notion that increasing usage of a factor *reduces* its marginal productivity reflects the assumption that the law of diminishing returns holds in most instances. There may, however, be exceptions to this, in which case the marginal productivity principle must be amended accordingly.

On balance, however, the theory of marginal productivity is of quite general applicability. Still, it tells us only half the story, for it helps to explain only the *demand* for a factor, not its *supply*.

It was on the supply side that we encountered substantial differences among factors. For example, there is an important distinction between factors that are and are not provided directly by human effort. Those that are--labor and that elusive factor, entrepreneurship—must be attracted away from alternative uses, such as leisure. Thus their supply curves normally will be neither vertical nor horizontal. The precise shapes of the curves will depend on the balancing of income and substitution effects that we have considered already, but as long as there is some positive slope, *most workers will collect some economic rent.* This explains why most people are not indifferent between having their jobs and not having them, which would be the case if there were no rents. Because their wages *exceed* the minimum payment that would coax them out of their easy chairs, people are quite unhappy when they lose their jobs.

The situation is quite different with inanimate factors of production. As mentioned above, ball bearings are produced at about constant cost. Their supply curve is horizontal, so there is no rent. The supplier of ball bearings *is* just on the margin of indifference between supplying and not supplying one more unit.

Thus if the long-run marginal cost of a particular size of ball bearing is 12 cents, no firm will be able to buy one at 11 cents. And no firm need pay 13 cents, for it can attract all of this factor that it wants at 12 cents each.

Fixed natural resources, like land of a given quality, are the other extreme. Since landowners have nothing to do with their land but to rent it out for use in some productive process, the supply curve is perfectly vertical, and every penny that the factor collects is rent in the economic sense. Land cannot stay home and watch TV if its factor payment gets too low. Of course, this does not necessarily mean that the price of land will be low. As always in economics, *scarcity* gives the commodity value and, as population growth continues on our finite globe, we can expect the price of land to rise higher and higher.

SUMMARY

1. Economic rent is any payment to the supplier of a factor of production that is greater than the minimum amount needed to induce the desired quantity of the factor to be supplied.
2. Factors of production that are unique in quality and difficult or impossible to reproduce will tend to be paid relatively high economic rents because of their scarcity.
3. Factors of production that are easy to produce without any increase in cost and that are provided by many suppliers will earn little or no economic rent.
4. Increased output of a good that needs land to produce it will encounter a rise in its cost either because it is grown on land inferior in quality to that which was used before the rise in output or because of diminishing returns to increased output on a given quantity of land.
5. When there is an increase in the output of a good whose production requires land, the landlord's rent will increase. This increase will equal the difference between the lower cost of production on the land already used before and the higher cost of production on the added land.
6. Rent controls do not significantly affect the supply of land, but they do tend to reduce the supply of buildings.
7. Interest rates are determined by the supply of and demand for funds. The demand for these funds is in part a derived demand, since they are used to finance business investment.
8. To determine whether it is worth putting funds into an investment, one must discount the expected costs and revenues and compare the sum of the discounted revenues with the sum of discounted costs.
9. Revenues and costs of an investment must be discounted to obtain their present values. This must be done because a dollar obtainable sooner is

worth more than a dollar obtainable later. Discounting translates the dollar values at different dates into comparable terms.

10. The present value of a dollar to be paid or received, say, 5 years in the future is $\$1/(1 + i)^5$, where i is the rate of interest.

11. Economic profits over and above the cost of capital are earned (a) by exercise of monopoly power, (b) as a payment for bearing risk, and (c) as the earnings of successful innovation.

12. The marginal product of any input together with its price (or its supply curve) determine how much of the input will be purchased by a profit-maximizing firm. That firm will purchase the quantity of the input at which the price of the input equals its marginal product.

CONCEPTS FOR REVIEW

Economic rent
Marginal land
Usury law
Discounting
Present value

Entrepreneurs
Risk bearing
Invention versus innovation
Marginal productivity principle

QUESTIONS FOR DISCUSSION

1. For which of the following inputs do you think rents constitute a high proportion of their earnings? (a) nails, (b) coal, (c) a champion racehorse. Explain your answer.

2. Three machines are available in an isolated area. They each produce 1000 units of output per month, the first requiring $17,000 in raw materials, the second $21,000, and the third $23,000. What would you expect to be the monthly charge for the first and second machines if the services of the third machine are available at a price of $9000 a month? What part of the charges for the first two machines is rent?

3. If the interest rate is 3 percent, what is the present value of $1 to be received 2 years from now?

4. A machine costs $2 million and lasts for 3 years earning $1 million in each year of its life. If the interest rate is 10 percent, what is the approximate present value of the machine's earnings? Is it a good investment?

5. Illustrate the difference between an invention and an innovation.

6. "Marginal productivity does not determine how much a worker will earn— it only determines how many workers will be hired at a given wage. Therefore, marginal productivity analysis is a theory of demand for labor, not a theory of distribution." What then do you think determines wages? Does marginal productivity affect their level? If so, how?

Appendix
David Ricardo's Theory of Income Distribution

Theories of the supply and demand for each factor of production enable us to determine both the price and employment of each factor, and thus that factor's income. Once this sort of analysis is applied to all factors of production, we have a complete *theory of income distribution,* because the entire national income will have been accounted for. That is, we are in a position to analyze the share of an economy's output that goes to workers, to capitalists, and to landlords.

The first such complete theory of income distribution was worked out in the early part of the nineteenth century by the British stockbroker-turned-economist David Ricardo. Ricardo's work, though much of it has been rendered obsolete by the passage of almost 200 years, is in many ways still a model of what an economic theory of income distribution should be. It shows clearly the role of landholders, capitalists, and workers, and seeks to bring out explicitly the extent to which their interests conflict or are held in common. It also attempts to account directly for the relative wealth or poverty of the different economic classes. But perhaps most important, it relates directly to issues of policy, suggesting measures that can be used to increase equality, stimulate economic growth, and so forth.

Ricardo's analysis rests on five major premises:

1. That land rents are determined in just the way we have described in this chapter (see pages 539–541).
2. That, after landlords are paid, the remainder of the product is divided between labor and capital, with the wage of labor determined by the law of supply and demand.
3. That an increase in wages above what constitutes the normal standard of living for workers in the economy ("the subsistence level of wages") simply enables workers to expand their families, thus leading to expansion of the population (the Malthusian population model).
4. That an increased population working with a fixed quantity of land will run into diminishing returns to increased quantities of labor input.
5. That the basic objective of capitalists is to accumulate wealth, and that they reinvest whatever profits they do not consume in order to expand their earning power.

These five assumptions lead to a simple scenario. Capitalists accumulate and invest their money. The resulting expansion of business activity increases the demand for labor and causes wages to be bid up. Workers respond by increasing the size of their families. Ultimately, the rise in population affects distribution in three ways:

1. It reduces the level of wages back toward subsistence as the supply of labor expands.
2. It increases the use of land and increases rents in the way described earlier in this chapter.
3. It ultimately must reduce profits because wages cannot be pushed below subsistence, because rents are increasing, and because (as a result of diminishing returns) production does not keep up with population size.

This last and crucial conclusion follows as a matter of simple arithmetic. When wages are at subsistence, wage payments will increase in proportion to the labor force, but diminishing returns cause production to expand less rapidly than does the labor force. With landlords increasing their share of the pie, less must be left over for profits.

Figure 28–5 summarizes the story. As we move from left to right, we see what happens as the population and the size of the labor force increase. The top curve represents total production of the economy. Because of diminishing returns it flattens out as the size of the labor force increases. The lower curve shows what remains of production after rent is deducted from it. Since rents increase as population grows, this curve must flatten out even faster than the total product curve. However, since the subsistence wage is a fixed amount per worker, total subsistence wages must increase *proportionately* with the size of the labor force. That is why *total* subsistence wages are represented by an upward-sloping straight line.

At a particular size of labor force, *L*, total wage payments are represented by *LW*, the distance to the subsistence wage line. Total profit is represented by *WP*, the distance between the subsistence wage line and the curve of total product minus rent. Total rent is therefore shown by *PR*, the amount of total product that has gone neither to wages nor to profits.

We see that as population increases—that is, as we move to the right in the graph—both rent and total wage payments increase, but total profits are squeezed lower and lower. That is, there is less and less distance between the subsistence wage line and the curve of production minus rent. The two finally meet at point *S* when population reaches *M*, and there profits are eliminated altogether. The classical economists called this point *the stationary state,* in which all growth ceases and stagnation is the normal state of affairs.

It would seem that only capitalists are hurt by this process. But, in fact, the workers suffer too. For, as we saw, it is only accumulation that can bring their wages above subsistence level. When profits are eliminated, there will be no further motivation to save and invest, so wages will be permanently limited to the subsistence level. This is in marked contrast with a period of growth and high profits when rapid accumulation will generally make the forces of supply and demand work more favorably for labor.

Ricardo drew several main conclusions from his analysis.

1. Landlords are the only ones who benefit from population growth. Capitalists are hurt by it directly, and workers suffer indirectly because it reduces the reward for investment, which decreases the demand for labor and drives wages toward subsistence.

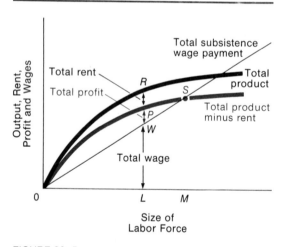

FIGURE 28–5

THE RICARDIAN DISTRIBUTION MODEL
This diagram illustrates the division of total product into wage, profit, and rent. Rent is determined by differences in quality of the lands that are in use and by diminishing returns to other inputs. If wages approximate subsistence, then profit is what is left over. As population increases, profits are squeezed by diminishing returns to labor and rising rents. When the labor force reaches *M*, profit vanishes (point *S*), and accumulation of capital ceases.

2. This process can be made less painful by unrestricted trade with foreign countries, which increases the supply of land used by the economy and counteracts diminishing returns. That is, by increasing the amount of land indirectly, it retards the speed with which diminishing returns set in.

3. There are two ways in which workers' standards of living can be raised. First, incentives for capital accumulation increase the demand for labor and lead wages to be bid up by the forces of supply and demand. Second, by getting workers to insist on higher living standards before they are ready to have children, the rate of population growth can be retarded and therefore the downward pressure on wages can be reduced. If people were unwilling to marry and begin having children until their earnings were high enough to support their families in a "decent" style of living, that, in Ricardo's judgment, would be the best thing that could happen from the point of view of workers' welfare. For that is the way to hold back the growth of population that subjects the economy to diminishing returns and the labor market to oversupply.

Nowadays, when workers' wages are bargained for by powerful unions, when continued innovations have held off the workings of diminishing returns for two centuries, and when population growth in the industrialized Western world has declined in some places almost to zero, the Ricardian model of income distribution seems more than a little out of date. But its relevance to the agricultural economies of its day was more immediate, as was its impact on policy. And there are many places in the Third World today where its message is all too relevant.

29

Poverty, Inequality, and Discrimination

In the last two chapters we studied the principles by which factor prices—wages, rentals, and interest rates—are determined in a market economy. One reason why we are so concerned with such questions is that these factor payments determine the *incomes* of the people who own them. The study of factor pricing is, therefore, an indirect way to learn about the distribution of income among individuals.

In this chapter we turn to the problem of income distribution more directly. Specifically, we seek answers to the following questions:

How much income inequality is there in the United States and why? How can society decide rationally on how much equality it will try to attain? And, once this decision is made, what policies are available to pursue this goal? In trying to answer these questions, we must necessarily consider the related problems of poverty and discrimination, and so these issues, too, receive attention in this chapter.

We will also offer a full explanation of one of the 12 Ideas for Beyond the Final Exam: *the fundamental trade-off between economic equality and economic efficiency.* Taking it for granted that equality and efficiency are both important social goals, we shall learn why policies that promote greater income equality (or less poverty or less discrimination) often threaten to interfere with economic efficiency. In this chapter we explain *why* this is so and *what* can be done about it.

THE POLITICS AND ECONOMICS OF INEQUALITY

That the trade-off between equality and efficiency is not widely understood is apparent from the political dialogue over questions like poverty, inequality, and discrimination. All too often social reformers will argue that society should adopt even the most outlandish programs to reduce discrimination or increase income equality or eradicate poverty, regardless of the potential side effects these policies might have. Economists feel that while the goals are certainly laudable, it is unduly myopic to ignore society's other goals. To cite just one example, a group of radical reformers during the early 1970s suggested that poverty could be eliminated by establishing a minimum wage of $3.50 per hour—a wage that at that time was close to the average hourly wage in the economy. This sounds great, but getting every worker up to the average wage or higher is surely beyond the realm of the possible. What would probably happen, for reasons explained at some length in Chapter 27, is that many people would end up with a wage of zero—that is, unemployed.

Defenders of the status quo, for their part, often seem so obsessed with these undesirable side effects—whether imagined or actual—that they ignore the benefits of redistribution or of antidiscrimination programs. For example, pointing with good reason to the likelihood that a negative income tax might induce *some* workers to work less, they draw the unwarranted conclusion that the program is therefore

not worth considering. In truth, the world is not so full of perfect social programs that we can afford to ignore every idea that falls short of perfection.

Economists, therefore, try not to paint these issues in black and white. They prefer to phrase things in terms of trade-offs—to reap gains on one front, you often must make sacrifices on another. A policy is not necessarily ill conceived simply because it has some undesirable side effects, *if* it makes an important enough contribution to one of society's basic goals. But, on the other hand, some policies have such severe side effects that they deserve to be rejected, even if they serve a laudable goal. Admitting that there is a trade-off between equality and efficiency may not be the best way to win votes, but it does face the facts. And in that way it helps us make the inherently political decisions about what should be done. If we are to understand these complex issues, a good place to start is, as always, with the facts.

THE FACTS: POVERTY

In 1962, Michael Harrington published a little book called *The Other America*, which was to have a profound impact on economics and on American society as a whole. The "other Americans" of whom Harrington wrote were the poor who lived in the land of plenty. Ill clothed in the richest country on earth, inadequately nourished in a nation where obesity was a problem, infirm in a country with some of the world's highest health standards, these people lived an almost unknown existence in their dilapidated hovels, according to Harrington. And, to make matters worse, their inadequate nutrition, lack of education, and generally demoralized state often condemned the children of the "other Americans" to repeat the lives of their parents. There was, Harrington argued, a "cycle of poverty"—a cycle that could be broken only by government action.

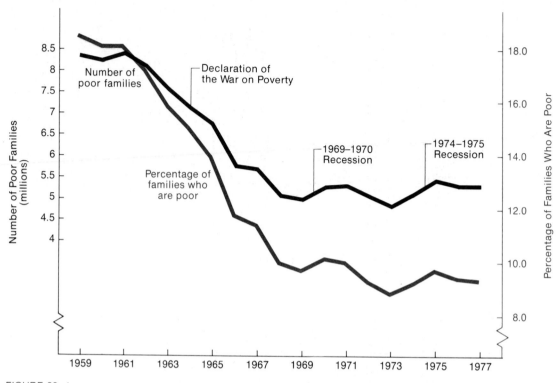

FIGURE 29–1

PROGRESS IN THE WAR ON POVERTY, 1959–1977

This figure charts the declines in the number and percentage of American families classified as "poor" by official definitions. While substantial progress has been made in the War on Poverty, more than 9 percent of American families remain below the poverty line.

Source: U.S. Bureau of the Census.

Harrington's work, and others like it, touched the hearts of many Americans who, it seemed, really had no idea of the abominable living conditions of some of their countrymen. Within a few years the growing outrage over the plight of the poor had crystallized into a "War on Poverty," which was declared by President Lyndon Johnson in 1964. An official definition of poverty was adopted: The poor were those families with an income below $3000 in 1964. This dividing line between the poor and the nonpoor was called the poverty line, and a goal was established: to get all Americans above the poverty line by the nation's bicentennial in 1976. The definition of the poverty line was subsequently modified to account for differences in family size and other considerations, and it is now also adjusted each year to reflect changes in the cost of living. In 1977 the poverty line for a typical family of four was about $6200.

Substantial progress toward this ambitious goal was made in the decade from 1964 to 1974 (see Figure 29–1). And, after a setback during the Great Recession of 1974–1975, the size of the poverty population resumed its downward trend. While the goal of eradicating poverty according to official definitions still had not been approached as the 1970s drew to a close, some journalists and economists were claiming that poverty could be considered a thing of the past if the official definition (based on cash income) were amended to include the many goods that the poor were being given in kind: public education, public housing, health care, food, and the like.

The steady downward drift in the poverty count vividly raises a fundamental question of definition: Just how do we tell who is poor? Continuing economic growth will eventually pull almost everyone above an arbitrarily established poverty line. Does this event mark the end of poverty? Some would say, "Yes." But others would insist that the biblical injunction was right: "The poor ye have always with you."

Life in a Slum and in a Castle

There can be little doubt that the unfortunate souls who inhabit America's worst urban slums are "poor" by any reasonable definition. Yet there are striking parallels between the standard of living of these people and that of the powerful but vermin-covered barons of the Middle Ages, as the following two passages show. Together these passages graphically point out the need for a relative concept of poverty.

A Twentieth Century Slum

We were living in deplorable conditions. We would cook a pot of oatmeal in the morning, then reheat it up on the radiator in the afternoon. . . . Whenever the sewer would back up, all that filth would come up under our floor and run around all over the floor . . . One time this went on for four days. My wife had to keep the kids up on the bed. All that stuff floating around through the apartment until they got the Roto-Rooter man there.

In the wintertime . . . we go to bed with all our clothes on. . . .

When it's real cold, we close off the two bedrooms completely and burn the oven and then we all sleep in here together. . . .

One of my babies has been in the hospital twice for lead poisoning. She'd pick plaster and paint and stuff off the walls. . . .*

*Herb Goro, *The Block* (New York: Random House, 1970), pages 82-86.

A Medieval Castle

The knight's castle was extremely simple and must have been most uncomfortable. There were usually two rooms: the hall and the chamber. In the hall the knight did his business. . . . The chamber was the private room of the lord and his family. There he entertained guests of high rank. At night the lord, his lady, and their children slept in beds, while their personal servants slept on the chamber floor. . . . The castles were cold and drafty. The windows were covered by boards, or open. If the castle was of wood—as most were before the thirteenth century—the knight could not have a fire. In a stone castle one could have fire, but as chimneys did not appear until the late twelfth century, the smoke must have been almost unbearable. It seems likely that if one of us were offered the choice between spending a winter night with the lord or his serf, he would choose the comparatively tight mud hut with the nice warm pigs on the floor.‡

‡Sydney Painter, *A History of the Middle Ages 284–1500* (New York: Alfred A. Knopf, 1953), page 122.

There are two ways to define poverty. The more optimistic definition uses an *absolute concept of poverty*: If you fall short of a certain minimum standard of living, you are poor; once you pass this standard, you are no longer poor. The second definition is based on a *relative concept of poverty*: The poor are those who fall too far behind the average income.

Each definition has its pros and cons. The basic problem with the absolute poverty concept is that it is arbitrary. Who sets the line? Most of the people of Bangladesh would be delighted to live a bit below the U.S. poverty line, and would consider themselves quite prosperous. Similarly, the standard of living that we now call "poor" would probably not have been considered so in America in 1780, and certainly not in Europe during the Middle Ages. (See the boxed insert on page 559.) Different times and different places apparently call for different poverty lines.

The fact that the concept of poverty is culturally, not physiologically, determined suggests that it must be a relative concept. But relative concepts can also run into trouble. For example, suppose we call the 20 percent of the population with the lowest incomes "the poor"—a definition that has been suggested by many. Then the War on Poverty becomes unwinnable, because the poverty population, *by definition*, grows at the same rate as the total population.

In fact, once we start moving away from an absolute concept of poverty toward a relative concept, the sharp distinction between the poor and the nonpoor starts to evaporate. Instead, we begin to think of a parade of people from the poorest soul to the richest millionaire. The "poverty problem," then, seems to be that the disparities in income are "too large" in some sense. The poor are so poor because the rich are so rich. If we follow this line of thought far enough, we are led away from the narrow problem of *poverty* toward the broader problem of *inequality of income*.

THE FACTS: INEQUALITY

There is nothing in the market mechanism that works to prevent large differences in income levels. On the contrary, it tends to breed inequality, for the basic source of the great efficiency of the market mechanism is its system of rewards and penalties. The market is generous to those who are successful in operating efficient enterprises that are responsive to consumer demands, and it is ruthless in penalizing those who are unable or unwilling to satisfy consumer demands efficiently. Its financial punishment of those who try and fail can be particularly severe. At times it even brings down the great and powerful. There is nothing especially unique about the case of Robert Morris, once perhaps the wealthiest resident of the American colonies, who ended up in debtors' prison. And newspaper accounts a few years ago told of an heir to the Du Pont fortune who is bankrupt and paying off his creditors over 10 years at 20 cents to the dollar.[1]

Most people have a pretty good idea that the income distribution is quite spread out—that the gulf between the rich and the poor is a wide one. But few have any concept of where they stand in the distribution. In the next paragraph, you will find some statistics on the 1977 income distribution in the United States. But before looking at these, try the following experiment. First, write down what you think your family's income before tax was in 1977. (If you do not know, take a guess.) Next, try to guess what percentage of American families had incomes *lower* than this. Finally, if we divide America into three broad income classes—rich, middle class, and poor—to which group do you think your family belongs?

Now that you have written down answers to these three questions, look at the income distribution data for 1977 in Table 29–1. If you are like most college students, these figures will

[1] *The New York Times*, July 4, 1976, page 20.

contain a few surprises for you. First, if we adopt the tentative definitions that the lowest 20 percent are the "poor," the highest 20 percent are the "rich," and the middle 60 percent are the "middle class," many fewer of you belong to the celebrated "middle class," than thought so. In fact, the cut-off point that defined membership in the "rich" class in 1977 was only about $26,000 before taxes, an income level exceeded by the parents of many college students. (Your parents may be shocked to learn that they are rich!)

Next, use Table 29–1 to estimate the fraction of U.S. families that have incomes lower

TABLE 29–2

INCOME SHARES IN SELECTED YEARS

INCOME GROUP	1977	1967	1957	1947
Lowest fifth	5.2%	5.5%	5.1%	5.0%
Second fifth	11.6	12.4	12.7	11.9
Middle fifth	17.5	17.9	18.1	17.0
Fourth fifth	24.2	23.9	23.8	23.1
Highest fifth	41.5	40.4	40.4	43.0

Source: U.S. Bureau of the Census.

than your own. (The caption to Table 29–1 has instructions to help you do this.) Most students who come from households of moderate prosperity have an instinctive feeling that they stand somewhere near the middle of the income distribution: So they estimate about half, or perhaps a little more. In fact, if your parents earn $40,000 a year, more than 95 percent of American families are poorer than yours!

This exercise has perhaps brought us down to earth. America is not nearly so rich as Madison Avenue would like us to believe.

Let us now look past the average level of income and see how the pie is divided. Table 29–2 shows the shares of income accruing to each fifth of the population in 1977 and several earlier years. In a perfectly equal society, all the numbers in this table would be "20 percent" since each fifth of the population would receive one-fifth of the income. In fact, as the table shows, this is certainly not the case. In 1977, for example, the poorest fifth of all families had just above 5 percent of the total income, while the richest fifth had more than 41 percent—eight times as much.

TABLE 29–1

DISTRIBUTION OF FAMILY INCOME IN THE UNITED STATES IN 1977

INCOME RANGE (dollars)	PERCENTAGE OF ALL FAMILIES IN THIS RANGE	PERCENTAGE OF FAMILIES IN THIS AND LOWER RANGES
Under 3000	3.6	3.6
3000 to 4999	5.8	9.4
5000 to 6999	7.2	16.6
7000 to 9999	10.9	27.5
10,000 to 11,999	7.1	34.6
12,000 to 14,999	11.3	45.9
15,000 to 19,999	17.7	63.6
20,000 to 24,999	13.9	77.5
25,000 to 49,999	19.8	97.3
50,000 and over	2.6	100.0

Source: U.S. Bureau of the Census.
If your family's income falls close to one of the end points of the ranges indicated here, you can approximate the fraction of families with income *lower* than yours just by looking at the last column.

If your family's income falls within one of the ranges, you can interpolate the answer. *Example:* Your family's income was $22,000. This is two-fifths of the way from $20,000 to $25,000, so your family was richer than roughly (²/₅) × 13.9 percent = 5.6 percent of the families in this class. Adding this to the percentage of families in lower income classes (63.6 percent in this case) gives the answer—about 69.2 percent of all families earned less than yours.

DEPICTING INCOME DISTRIBUTIONS: THE LORENZ CURVE

Statisticians and economists use a convenient tool to portray data like these graphically. The device, called a Lorenz curve, is shown in

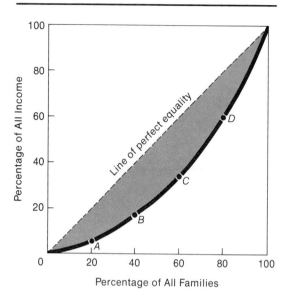

FIGURE 29–2

A LORENZ CURVE FOR THE UNITED STATES
This Lorenz curve for the United States is based on the 1977 distribution of income given in Table 29–2. The percentage of families is measured along the horizontal axis, and the percentage of income that these families receive is measured along the vertical axis. Thus, for example, point C indicates that the bottom 60 percent of American families received 34.3 percent of the total income in 1977.

Figure 29–2. To construct a Lorenz curve, we first draw a square whose vertical and horizontal dimensions both represent 100 percent. Then we record the percentage of families (or persons) on the horizontal axis and the percentage of income that these families (or persons) receive on the vertical axis, using all the data that we have. For example, point B in Figure 29–2 depicts the fact (known from Table 29–2) that the bottom 40 percent (the two lowest fifths) of American families in 1977 received 16.8 percent of the total income. Similarly, points A, C, and D represent the other information contained in Table 29–2.

We can list four important properties of a Lorenz curve.

1. It begins at the origin, where zero families of course have zero income.
2. It always ends at the upper-right corner of the square, since 100 percent of the nation's families must necessarily receive all of the nation's income.
3. If income were distributed equally, the Lorenz curve would be a straight line connecting these two points (the dashed line in Figure 29–2). This is because, with everybody equal, the bottom 20 percent of the families would receive 20 percent of the income, the bottom 40 percent would receive 40 percent, and so on.
4. In a real economy, with significant income differences, the Lorenz curve will "sag" downward from this line of perfect equality. It is easy to see why this is so. If there is any income inequality at all, the poorest 20 percent of families must get less than 20 percent of all the income. This corresponds to a point below the equality line, such as point A. Similarly, the bottom 40 percent of families must receive less than 40 percent of the income (point B), and so on.

In fact, the size of the area between the line of perfect equality and the Lorenz curve (the shaded area in Figure 29–2) is often used as a handy indicator of the nation's *degree of inequality*. The larger the gap is, the more unequal is the income distribution. For U.S. family incomes, this so-called area of inequality usually fills up about 40 percent of the total area underneath the equality line.

Standing by itself, the Lorenz curve tells us rather little. To interpret it, we must know what it looked like in earlier years or what it looks like in other countries.

The first fact is easier to obtain. The historical data in Table 29–2 show that *the U.S. Lorenz curve has not moved much in the last 30 years*. To some, this remarkable stability in the income distribution is deplorable. To others, it suggests some immutable law of the capitalist system.

Comparing the United States with other countries is much harder, since no two countries use precisely the same definition of income distribution. In 1976, the Organization for Economic Cooperation and Development (OECD) made a heroic effort to standardize the income distribution data of its member countries so they could be compared.[2] In this analysis, Japan stood out as the industrialized country with the most equal income distribution, with Australia, West Germany, the Netherlands, and Sweden bunched rather closely in second place. France and the United States seemed to have the most inequality. Interestingly, when the OECD study was published, these findings caused a furor in France, but not in America.

Before extrapolating from these findings, it should be pointed out that only 12 industrial countries were compared. Israel, which is often thought to have the most equal income distribution in the noncommunist world, is not in the OECD. Nor are any of the less developed countries, which are generally found to have much more inequality than the developed ones. The conclusion seems to be that:

The United States has rather more income inequality than most other developed countries.

THE FACTS: DISCRIMINATION

The facts about discrimination—often cited as a major cause of inequality in general and of poverty in particular—are not easy to come by. First we need a precise definition of economic discrimination.

[2] Malcolm Sawyer, "Income Distribution in OECD Countries," *OECD Occasional Studies*, July 1976, pages 3–36.

DEFINITION

Economic discrimination occurs when equivalent factors of production receive different payments for equal contributions to output.

Notice that discrimination is something quite different from *prejudice*. Though the latter is often a reason for the former, one can occur without the other. Prejudice is an attitude, whereas discrimination is a pattern of behavior. For example, an employer might discriminate against blacks even if he harbors no ill feelings against them because he believes that *on average* blacks have lower productivity. Conversely, another employer might be prejudiced against female workers but hire women because often they will work for lower wages than men.

When we try to apply this definition in practice, a difficulty arises in telling when two factors of production are "equivalent." Probably no one would call it "discrimination" if a woman with only a high school diploma receives a lower salary than a man with a college degree (though one might legitimately ask whether discrimination helps to explain the difference in their educational attainments). Even if they have the same education, the man may have 10 more years of work experience than the woman. If they receive different wages for this reason, are we to call that "discrimination"? Ideally, we would compare men and women whose *productivities* are equal. In this case, if women receive lower wages than men, we would clearly call it discrimination. But, very often, discrimination takes much more subtle forms than paying unequal wages for equal work. For instance, employers can simply keep women relegated to inferior jobs, thus justifying the lower salaries they pay them.

One clearly *incorrect* way to measure discrimination is to compare the typical incomes of different groups. Table 29–3 displays such data for white men, white women, black men, and black women in 1977. Virtually everyone

TABLE 29-3

MEDIAN INCOMES IN 1977

POPULATION GROUP*	MEDIAN INCOME	PERCENTAGE OF WHITE MALE INCOME
White males	$10,603	100
Black males	6292	59
White females	4001	38
Black females	3455	33

*Persons 14 years old and over.

Source: Bureau of the Census.

agrees that the amount of discrimination is less than these differentials suggest, but far greater than zero. Precisely how much is a topic of continuing economic research. One study several years ago concluded that about 40 percent of the observed wage differential between black and white men, and about two-thirds of the differential between white women and white men, was caused by discrimination in the labor market (though more might have been due to discrimination in education, and so on). Other studies have reached somewhat different conclusions. While no one denies the existence of discrimination, its quantitative importance is a matter of ongoing controversy and research.

SOME REASONS FOR UNEQUAL INCOMES

Let us now formulate a list of the causes of income inequality. Discrimination is already on this list. What are some others?

Differences in ability. Everyone knows that people have different capabilities. Some can run faster, jump higher, ski better, do calculations more quickly, type more accurately, and so on. Hence it should not be surprising that some people are more adept at earning income. Precisely what sort of ability is relevant to

earning income is a matter of intense debate among economists, sociologists, and psychologists. The kind of talents that make for success in school seem to have some effect, but hardly an overwhelming one. The same is true of innate intelligence ("IQ"). It is clear that some types of inventiveness are richly rewarded by the market, and the same is true of that elusive characteristic called "entrepreneurial ability."

Differences in intensity of work. Some people work longer hours than others, or labor more intensely when they are on the job. This results in certain income differences that are largely voluntary.

Risk taking. Most people who have acquired large sums of money have done so by taking risks—by investing their money in some uncertain venture. Those who gamble and succeed become wealthy. Those who try and fail go broke. Most others, of course, prefer not to take such chances and wind up somewhere in between. This is another way in which income differences arise through voluntary means.

Compensating wage differentials. Some jobs are more arduous than others, or more dangerous, or more unpleasant for other reasons. To induce people to take these jobs, some sort of financial incentive normally must be offered. For example, factory workers who work the night shift normally receive higher wages than those who work during the day.

Schooling and other types of training. In Chapter 27 we spoke of schooling and other types of training as "investments in human capital." We meant by this that workers can sacrifice *current* income in order to improve their skills so that their *future* incomes will be higher. When this is done, income differentials naturally rise. Consider a high school friend who did not go on to college. Even if you are working at a part-time job, your earnings are probably much below his or hers. Once you graduate from college, however, the statistics suggest that your earnings will rise and soon overtake your friend's earnings.

It is generally agreed that differences in schooling are an important cause of income differentials. But this particular cause has both voluntary and involuntary aspects. Young men or young women who *choose* not to go to college have made voluntary decisions that affect their incomes. But many never get the choice: Their parents simply cannot afford to send them. For them, the resulting income differential is not voluntary.

Inherited wealth. Not all income is derived from work. Some is the return on invested wealth, and part of this wealth is inherited. While this cause of inequality does not apply to very many people, a great number of America's super-rich got that way through inheritance.

Financial wealth is not the only type of capital that can be inherited; human capital also can be inherited. In part this happens naturally through genetics: Parents of high ability tend to have children of high ability, although the link is an imperfect one. But it also happens partly for economic reasons: Well-to-do parents send their children to the best schools, thereby transforming their own *financial* wealth into *human* wealth for their children. This type of inheritance may be much more important than the financial type.

Luck. We should not close our list without mentioning the role of chance. Some of the rich and some of the poor got there largely by good or bad fortune. A farmer digging for water discovers oil instead. An investor strikes it rich on the stock market. A student trains herself for a high-paying occupation only to find that the opportunity has disappeared while she was in college. A construction worker is unemployed for a whole year because of a recession that he had no part in creating. The list could go on and on. Many of the large income differentials among people arise purely by chance.

THE OPTIMAL AMOUNT OF INEQUALITY

We have seen that substantial income inequality exists in America and have noted some reasons for it. Let us now ask a question that is loaded with value judgments, but to which economic analysis has something to contribute nonetheless: *How much inequality is the ideal amount?* We shall not, of course, be able to give a precise answer to this question. Nobody can do that. Our objective is rather to see the type of analysis that is relevant to answering the question. We begin our analysis in a simple setting in which the answer is easily obtained. Then we shall see how the real world differs from this simple model.

Consider a world in which there are two people, Smith and Jones, and suppose that we want to divide $100 between them. Suppose further that Smith and Jones are alike in their ability to enjoy money, and we wish to divide the $100 in a way that yields the most *total utility*. Technically, we say that their *marginal utility* schedules are identical.[3] This identical marginal utility schedule is depicted in Figure 29–3.

We can now prove the following result: *The optimal distribution of income is to give $50 to Smith and $50 to Jones*, which is point E in Figure 29–3. To prove it, we show that if the income distribution is unequal, we can improve things by moving closer to equality. So suppose that Smith has $75 (point S in the figure) and Jones has $25 (point J). Then, as we can see, because of the law of diminishing marginal utility, Smith's *marginal* utility (which is s) must be *less* than Jones's (which is j). If we take $1 away from Smith, Smith *loses* the low marginal utility, s, of a dollar to him. Then, when we give it to Jones, Jones *gains* the high marginal utility, j, that a dollar gives him. On balance, then, society's total utility must rise by $j - s$ because

---

[3]If you need to refresh your memory about marginal utility, see Chapter 19, especially pages 350–354.

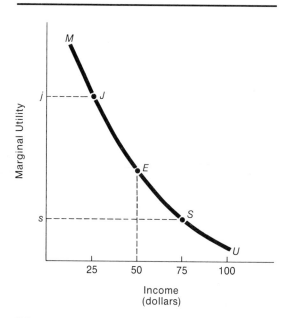

FIGURE 29–3

THE OPTIMAL DISTRIBUTION OF INCOME
If Smith and Jones have the identical marginal utility schedule (the curve *MU*) then the optimal way to distribute $100 between them is to give $50 to each (point *E*). If income is not distributed this way, then their marginal utilities will be unequal, so that a redistribution of income can make society better off. This is illustrated by points *J* and *S*, representing an income distribution in which Jones gets $25 (and hence has marginal utility *j*), while Smith gets $75 (and hence has marginal utility *s*).

Jones's gain exceeds Smith's loss. Therefore, a distribution with Smith getting only $74 is better than one in which he gets $75. Since the same argument can be used to show that a $73-$27 distribution is better than $74-$26, and so on, we have established our result that a $50-$50 distribution—point *E*—is best.

Now in this argument there is nothing special about the fact that we assumed only two people or that exactly $100 was available. Any number of people and dollars would do as well. What really *is* crucial is our assumption that the same amount of money would be available no matter how we chose to distribute it. Thus we have proved the following general result:

The optimal way to distribute any fixed amount of money among people with identical marginal utility schedules is to divide it equally.

THE TRADE-OFF BETWEEN EQUALITY AND EFFICIENCY

If we seek to apply this analysis to the real world, two major difficulties arise. First, people are different and have different marginal utility schedules. Thus *some* equality probably is optimal.[4]

The second problem is much more formidable.

The total amount of income in society is *not* independent of how we try to distribute it.

To see this in an extreme form, ask yourself the following question: What would happen if we tried to achieve perfect equality by putting a 100 percent income tax on all workers and then dividing the tax receipts equally among the population? No one would have any incentive to work, to invest, to take risks, or to do anything else to earn money, because the rewards for all such activities would disappear. The gross national product (GNP) would fall drastically, perhaps even disappear.

While the example is extreme, the same principle applies to more moderate policies to equalize incomes: Any such policy lessens the rewards for income-producing activities. It reduces the rewards of high-income earners while raising the rewards of low-income earners, and hence reduces the incentive to earn high income.

---

[4]It can be shown that if we know that people differ, but cannot tell who has the higher marginal utility schedule, then the best way to distribute income is still in equal shares.

This gives rise to a trade-off that is one of the most fundamental in all of economics, and one of our 12 Ideas for Beyond the Final Exam.

THE TRADE-OFF BETWEEN EQUALITY AND EFFICIENCY

Measures taken to increase the amount of economic equality will often reduce economic efficiency—that is, lower the gross national product. In trying to divide the pie more equally, we may inadvertently reduce its size.

Because of this trade-off, the result that equal incomes are always optimal cannot be applied to the real world. Instead:

The optimal distribution of income will always involve *some* inequality.

But this does not mean that attempts to reduce inequality are always misguided. What we should learn from this analysis are two things:

Lesson 1. There are better and worse ways to promote equality. In pursuing further income equality (or in fighting poverty), we should seek policies that do the least possible harm to the nation's productivity.

Lesson 2. Equality is bought at a price. Thus, like any commodity, we must decide rationally how much to purchase. We will probably want to spend some of our potential income on equality, but not all of it.

Figure 29–4 illustrates both these lessons. Point C indicates the present position of the U.S. economy, corresponding to a certain output (GNP) and a certain level of equality. The curves ABCDE and abCde represent two different policies for changing the degree of income equality. In both cases, as we move toward greater equality, the GNP falls (see, for example, points D and d). And, as we have

drawn them, there is also some room to raise the GNP by causing still more inequality (see points B and b).

The first lesson is that we should stick to the higher of the two curves. Any point chosen on curve abCde can be improved by moving to a point on curve ABCDE. In the rest of this chapter, we discuss alternative policies and try to indicate which ones are more efficient.

The second lesson is that neither point B nor point E would normally be society's optimal choice. At point B we are seeking the highest possible GNP, with utter disregard for whatever

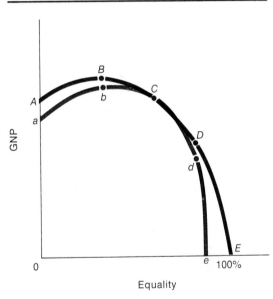

FIGURE 29–4

THE TRADE-OFF BETWEEN EQUALITY AND EFFICIENCY

This diagram represents the fundamental trade-off between equality and efficiency. If the economy is initially at point C, then movements toward greater equality (to the right) normally can be achieved only by reducing economic efficiency, and thus reducing the gross national product. The movements toward points D and d represent two alternative policies for equalizing the income distribution. The policy that leads to D is preferred since it is more efficient.

inequality might accompany it. At point E we are forcing complete equality, even if a minuscule GNP is the result.

It is astonishing how much confusion is caused by a failure to understand these two lessons. Proponents of measures that further economic equality often feel obligated to deny that their programs will have any harmful effects on economic efficiency. At times these vehement denials are so obviously unrealistic that they undermine the very case that the egalitarians are trying to defend. Conservatives who oppose these policies also undercut the strength of their case by making outlandish claims about the efficiency losses that are likely to arise from greater equality. Neither side, it seems, is willing or able to acknowledge the basic trade-off between equality and efficiency, as depicted in Figure 29–4. And hence the debate generates more heat than light. Since these debates are sure to continue for the next 10 or 20 years, and probably for the rest of your lives, we hope that some understanding of this trade-off stays with you well beyond the final exam.

But just understanding the terms of the trade-off will not tell you what the right answer is. By looking at Figure 29–4, we know that the optimal amount of equality lies between points B and E, but we do not know what it actually is. Is it something like point D, with more equality and less GNP than we now have? Or is it a movement back toward point B? Or is it point C, right where we are now? Everyone will have a different answer to this question, because it is basically one of value judgment. Just how much is more equality worth to you?

Economist Arthur Okun, a former chairman of the Council of Economic Advisers, put the issue graphically. Imagine that money is liquid, and that you have a bucket that you can use to transport some money from the rich to the poor. The problem, however, is that the bucket is leaky. As you move the money, some gets lost. Will you use the bucket if only 1 cent is lost for each $1 you move? Probably everyone would

say yes. But what if each $1 taken from the rich results in only 10 cents for the poor? Only the most extreme egalitarians will still say yes. Now try the hard questions. What if 20 to 40 cents is lost for each $1 that you move? If you can answer questions like these, you can decide how far down the hill from point C you think society should travel, for you will have expressed your value judgments in quantitative terms.

POLICIES TO COMBAT POVERTY

Let us take it for granted that the nation has a commitment to reduce the amount of poverty. What are some policies that can promote this goal? Which of these is most efficient?

The traditional approach to poverty fighting in the United States has utilized a variety of programs collectively known as *public assistance*. The best known, and most controversial, of these is Aid to Families with Dependent Children (AFDC). This program gives money to families in which there are children but no breadwinner, perhaps because there is no father and the children are too young to permit the mother to work. In 1977, about 11 million people received benefits from AFDC, and the average grant was about $875 per person. In total, some $10 billion was spent.

AFDC has been attacked as a classic example of an inefficient redistribution program. Why? One reason is that it provides little incentive for the mother to earn income; welfare payments are reduced by 67 cents for each $1 that the family earns as wages. Thus, if a member of the family gets a job, the family is subjected to a 67 percent tax rate. It is little wonder that many welfare recipients do not look very hard for work.

A second criticism is that AFDC provides an incentive for families to break up. As originally conceived, welfare was not to be paid to a family with a father who could work, even if he was unemployed. So if this father earned very little, or if he had no job, the children would get more income if he left them. Some fathers did. About half the states have now started a special AFDC-UF program (the "UF" stands for unemployed father) so that benefits can be paid to families with an unemployed father.

A third problem is geographical disparities in benefits. It is widely thought (though not conclusively proven) that many black families migrated from the South to northern cities because of the more generous welfare benefits available there. This placed an enormous financial burden on these cities.

Finally, the tedious case-by-case approach of AFDC, with its cumbersome bureaucracy and mountains of detailed regulations, seems to frustrate all parties concerned.

Another welfare program that has burgeoned in recent years is food stamps, under which poor families are sold stamps, which they can exchange for food. The dollar amount of the stamps they receive, and how much they pay for them, depends on the family's income. The more income the family earns, the more it must pay for the stamps. More than 17 million people now receive food stamps.

Other programs, such as public housing and Medicaid (as opposed to Medicare),[5] also offer benefits that decline as family income rises. Taken as a whole, all of these antipoverty programs may actually put a poor family in a position where it is *worse* off if its earnings *rise*—an effective tax rate of more than 100 percent. When this occurs, there is a powerful incentive not to work.

THE NEGATIVE INCOME TAX

These problems, and others like them, have contributed to the "welfare mess," and they

[5]The *Medicaid* program pays for the health care of low-income people, whereas *Medicare* is available to all elderly people, regardless of income.

have led to frequent calls to scrap the whole system and replace it with a simple structure designed to get income into the hands of the poor without providing such adverse incentives. The solution suggested most frequently, at least by economists, is the so-called negative income tax (NIT).

The name "negative income tax" derives from its similarity to the regular (positive) income tax. Let us illustrate how NIT would work. To describe a particular NIT plan we require two numbers: a minimum income level below which no family is allowed to fall (the "guarantee") and a rate at which benefits are "taxed away" as income rises. Consider a plan with a $4000 guaranteed income (for a family of four) and a 50 percent tax rate. A family with zero income would then receive a $4000 negative tax payment from the government. A family earning $1000 would have this basic benefit reduced by the 50 percent tax rate. Since half its earnings is $500, it would receive $3500 from the government plus the $1000 from its own earnings for a total income of $4500 (see Table 29–4).

Notice in Table 29–4 that the increase in total income as earnings rise is always half of the increase in earnings. With a 50 percent tax rate, there is always *some* incentive to work under an NIT system. Notice also that there is a "break-even" level of income at which benefits cease. In this case, the break-even level is $8000. This is not another number that policy-makers can arbitrarily select in the way they select the guarantee level and the tax rate. Rather, it is dictated by the choice of the guarantee level and the tax rate. This is easy to explain. In our example, since $4000 is the maximum possible benefit, and since benefits are reduced by 50 cents for each $1 of earnings, then benefits must cease when 50 percent of the earnings (the benefit reduction) is equal to $4000 (the maximum benefit). This occurs when earnings are $8000.

Other NIT plans can be devised that are either more or less generous than this. But the

TABLE 29–4

ILLUSTRATION OF A NEGATIVE INCOME
TAX PLAN

EARNINGS	BENEFITS PAID	TOTAL INCOME
0	$4000	$4000
$1000	3500	4500
2000	3000	5000
3000	2500	5500
4000	2000	6000
5000	1500	6500
6000	1000	7000
7000	500	7500
8000	0	8000
Above 8000	0	Same as earnings

fact that the break-even level is completely
determined by the guarantee and the tax rate
creates an annoying problem. In general, the
relation is:

$$\text{Guarantee} = \text{Tax rate} \times \text{Break-even level}$$

If we are truly to make a dent in the poverty
population through an NIT system, the guarantee will have to come fairly close to the
poverty line. But then, if we are to keep the tax
rate moderate, the break-even level will have to
be much above the poverty line. This means
that families who are not considered "poor"
(though they are certainly not very rich) will also
receive benefits. For example, a low tax rate of
$33\frac{1}{3}$ percent means that some benefits are paid
to families whose income is as high as three
times the guarantee level.

How can we avoid this problem? Only by
raising the tax rate (which brings the guarantee
and the break-even level closer together). But
as this tax rate rises, the incentive to work
shrinks, and with it the principal rationale for the
NIT in the first place. So the NIT is no magic
cure-all. Difficult choices must be made. As

summarized by the preceding formula, we must
be willing to sacrifice one of the following three
objectives (or some combination of them):

1. Preserving strong incentives to work,
   which we get by keeping the tax rate low.
2. Keeping people out of poverty, which we
   accomplish through a generous guarantee.
3. Concentrating benefits on the poverty population, which requires that the break-even
   level be kept low.

THE NEGATIVE INCOME TAX AND WORK INCENTIVES

We have just been discussing the NIT as a way
to get money into the hands of the poor while at
the same time preserving their *incentives* to
work. Yet in Chapter 27 we looked at the negative income tax experiments that the U.S.
government sponsored in order to appraise the
disincentive effects of such a program (see
page 514). These two discussions seem to
contradict each other, but they do not.

The reason is that two different comparisons are being made. When we applaud the
NIT's positive work incentives, we are
comparing it with the present welfare system,
which actually may penalize poor people for
working. When we worry about possible disincentive effects, we are thinking about those
poor and near-poor families who are not now on
welfare but who would be eligible for NIT
benefits. Since the NIT would both reduce their
rewards for working (by taking away benefits as
earnings rose) and give these families more
money (thus encouraging them to "buy" some
leisure), the concern is a very sensible one. To
summarize:

Replacing the current welfare system with a
comprehensive negative income tax would
provide *positive* work incentives for those fami-

lies now eligible for welfare but *negative* work incentives for some families who are now too well-off to collect welfare. The negative income tax experiments sought to measure the latter effect and found it to be quite small.

In terms of Figure 29–4, we are suggesting that it is more efficient to redistribute income through an NIT system than through the existing welfare system. The NIT is curve *ABCDE*, while the present system is curve *abCde*. But this does not mean that we can accomplish equalization without cost by using the NIT. The curve *ABCDE* still slopes downward—by increasing equality, we still diminish the GNP.

Economists have been advocating the NIT for years, at least since Milton Friedman's influential book *Capitalism and Freedom* (1962). And in 1970, after it was known that the initial results from the negative income tax experiment looked quite favorable, the United States almost got a negative income tax. Proposed by President Nixon under the title "Family Assistance Plan" as a major welfare reform, this program was greeted enthusiastically in some quarters. Unfortunately, it was killed in the Senate by an alliance of liberals who thought its benefit levels were insultingly low and conservatives who opposed the NIT on principle. In the 1972 presidential campaign, Democratic candidate George McGovern strongly endorsed a rather generous NIT, but the idea was packaged in a politically unattractive form that probably cost him more votes than it won. After that the idea remained politically dormant for a while until President Ford approved a small-scale version of it as an "earned income credit" in 1975. Then, as part of his multifaceted welfare reform proposal in 1977, President Carter proposed (without using the name) an NIT plan that looks very much like the one illustrated in Table 29–4. At this writing, however, it seems unlikely to be enacted.

THE PERSONAL INCOME TAX

If we take the broader viewpoint that society's objective is to reduce income disparities, not just to eliminate poverty, then the fact that many nonpoor families would receive benefits from the NIT is perhaps not a serious drawback. After all, unless the plan is outlandishly generous, these families will still be well below the average income. Still, in popular discussions the NIT is largely thought of as an antipoverty program, not as a tool for general income equalization.

By contrast, the federal personal income tax *is* thought to be a means of promoting equality. Indeed, it is probably given more credit for this than it actually deserves. The reason is that the income tax is widely known to be progressive.

DEFINITION
A *progressive tax* is one in which the fraction of income paid in tax goes up as a person's income increases.

Since the fraction of income paid in taxes is called the average tax rate, this definition can be restated as follows:

DEFINITION
A *progressive tax* is one in which the average tax rate paid by an individual rises as his income rises.

The fraction of each *additional* dollar of income that must be paid to the tax collector is called the marginal tax rate. The relation between the marginal tax rate and the average tax rate is just the same as the relation between marginal anything and average anything:[6] The average rises when the marginal is above it and falls when the marginal is below it. Thus, for

[6]If you need to review this, see Chapter 20, pages 384–387.

example, a progressive tax need not have rising marginal tax rates.

Taxes that are not progressive can be either proportional or regressive.

DEFINITION

A *proportional* tax is one in which the fraction of income paid as tax (the average tax rate) is the same at all income levels. A *regressive* tax is one in which the average tax rate declines as income rises.

The fact that the income tax is progressive means that incomes *after tax* are distributed more equally than incomes *before* tax because the rich turn over a larger share of their incomes to the tax collector. This is illustrated by the two Lorenz curves in Figure 29–5. These curves, however, are not drawn accurately to scale. If they were, they would lie almost on top of each other because the degree of equalization that can be attributed to the tax is rather modest.

Why such modest equalizing effects from a tax whose marginal rates escalate upward from zero to a maximum of 70 percent? One principal reason for the modest equalizing effect of the progressive income tax is that firms and individuals, acting in their own best interests, often take steps that frustrate the equalizing intent of the tax. An example from each end of the income distribution will illustrate how this might work.

Looking first at the rich, it is clear that a steeply progressive tax tries to place a heavy tax burden on a corporate executive. In order to preserve his incentive to work, his company may react by raising his before-tax salary. Or, better yet, it might give him fringe benefits (such as a company car, use of a yacht, expense accounts, and so on) which often escape taxation. At the other end of the income scale, welfare programs that give payments to the poor may lead the beneficiaries to "spend" some of their newly found income on "leisure," that is, to work less, and therefore to earn less.

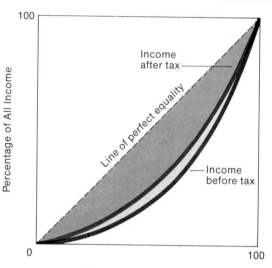

FIGURE 29–5

THE EFFECT OF PROGRESSIVE INCOME TAXATION ON THE LORENZ CURVE
Since a progressive income tax takes proportionately more income from the rich than it does from the poor, it has the effect of reducing income inequality. Graphically, this means that society's Lorenz curve shifts in the manner shown here. The magnitude of the shift, however, is exaggerated to make the graph more readable. In reality, the income tax has only a very small effect on the Lorenz curve.

Thus, we find that a redistributive tax system might induce the *before-tax* incomes of the rich to rise, and those of the poor to fall. Ironically, our efforts to *equalize* the *after-tax* distribution of income lead to more *inequality* in the *before-tax* distribution. In terms of Figure 29–5, this means that even the small distance between the two Lorenz curves *overstates* the equalizing effects of the income tax. The income distribution that we would have *if there were no income tax* is probably somewhere in between these two curves.

SOME TAX LOOPHOLES

The other principal reason why the personal income tax does not redistribute income as much as many people think is that the wealthy have learned, with the aid of expensive legal and financial advisers, about a variety of tax loopholes, and have managed to pare their tax payments significantly. There is nothing sinister about this tax avoidance; it is all perfectly legal and aboveboard. The simple truth is that Congress has provided so many loopholes that the tax system has been compared to a sieve. Let us see what some of them are.

Lenient taxation of capital gains. Our laws tax a capital gain—which is the profit made by selling an asset for a higher price than was paid for it—at less than half the rates at which other sources of income are taxed. Since such gains accrue almost exclusively to upper-income groups, this loophole is the reserve of the rich. Why did Congress do such a thing? Presumably because of the extremely high taxes that would have to be paid on large capital gains if they were treated like ordinary income.

For example, Jane Doe earns $30,000 a year and owns $100,000 worth of stock that she bought 10 years ago for $20,000. If she sells her stock this year, she will enjoy an $80,000 capital gain, which will push her income for the year up to $110,000. The tax bill on such an income is quite substantial. In particular, because of progressive rates, it is much larger than the tax she would have paid if the $80,000 capital gain had been earned evenly at the rate of $8000 a year over 10 years. To reduce this burden, Congress decided to exempt 60 percent of all capital gains, so that Jane's taxable income is only $30,000 + $32,000 = $62,000. But, tax reformers point out, there are many other ways to ease the tax burden on such gains. The simplest way perhaps is to charge individuals the tax they would have paid if the gain really

had occurred gradually; that is, to tax Jane Doe as if her income had been $30,000 + $8000 = $38,000 a year for 10 years.

Tax exempt status of municipal bonds. As a way of helping state and local governments and certain public authorities raise funds, Congress has made their bonds exempt from federal income tax. Whether or not this was the intent of Congress, this provision has turned out to be one of the biggest loopholes for the very rich, who invest much of their wealth in municipal bonds. In fact, this tax exemption is the principal reason why many millionaires pay no tax at all.

Tax benefits for homeowners. Among the sacred cows of our income tax system is the deductability of payments that homeowners make for mortgage interest and property taxes. These deductions substantially reduce the taxes

"I'm sorry, Mr. Jones . . . You're not rich enough to pay no taxes."

they pay and give them preferential treatment compared with renters. Since, on the average, homeowners are richer than people who rent, this too erodes the progressivity of the income tax.

But why do we call this a "loophole" at all? Are not other interest expenses and taxes (such as those paid by shopkeepers, for example) considered to be legitimate deductions? The answer is that it is a loophole because—unlike shopkeepers—homeowners do *not* have to declare the income they earn by incurring these expenses. This is because the "income" from owning a home accrues not in cash, but in the form of living without paying rent.

Once again, an example will make things clear. Mutt and Jeff are neighbors. Each earns $20,000 a year and lives in a $60,000 house. The difference is that Mutt owns his home while Jeff rents. Most observers would agree that Mutt and Jeff *should* pay the same income tax. Ignoring other deductions and exemptions, let us compare the taxable income of the two men.

Mutt has a $50,000 mortgage at an 8 percent interest rate, so he pays about $4000 a year in interest. Suppose he pays an additional $2000 a year in local property taxes. Since both these payments are tax deductible, he pays income tax on only $20,000 − $4000 − $2000 = $14,000 (see Table 29–5). Now consider Jeff, who, we may assume, pays $6000 in annual rent. (This just covers the bills that his landlord has to pay.) He pays tax on his entire

TABLE 29–5

OWNING VERSUS RENTING A HOME

ITEM	MUTT (owner)	JEFF (renter)
Income	$20,000	$20,000
Mortgage interest	4,000	—
Property tax	2,000	—
Rent	—	6,000
Taxable income	$14,000	$20,000

$20,000 income and thus pays far more tax than Mutt.

How could this situation be rectified? One way is to allow renters to deduct their rent bills. Another way would be to disallow the interest and tax deductions of homeowners. Still a third alternative would be to force homeowners to add their "imputed rent" ($6000 a year in this example) to their income. All of these would give Mutt and Jeff the same taxable income.

We could go on and on listing more tax loopholes, but enough has been said to illustrate the point:

Since loopholes are mainly beneficial to rich people, they erode the progressivity of the income tax.

DEATH DUTIES AND OTHER TAXES

Taxes on inheritances and estates levied both by the state and federal governments are another equalizing feature of our tax system. And in this case they seem clearly aimed at limiting the incomes of the rich, or at least at limiting their ability to transfer this largesse from one generation to the next. But the amount of money involved is too small to make much difference to the overall distribution of income. In 1976, for example, total receipts from estate and gift taxes by all levels of government were only about $7 billion—just over 1 percent of total tax revenues.

There are many other taxes in the U.S. system, and most experts agree that the remaining taxes as a group—including sales taxes, payroll taxes, and property taxes—are decidedly regressive. On balance, the evidence seems to suggest that:

The tax system as a whole is only slightly progressive.

POLICIES TO COMBAT DISCRIMINATION

The policies that we have considered so far for combating poverty or reducing income inequality are all based on taxes and transfer payments—on moving dollar bills from one set of hands to another. For reasons that are perhaps obvious, this has not been the approach used to fight discrimination. Instead, governments have decided to make it *illegal* to discriminate.

Perhaps the major milestone in the war against discrimination was the Civil Rights Act of 1964, which outlawed many forms of discrimination and established the Equal Employment Opportunities Commission (EEOC). When you read a want ad in which a company asserts it is "an equal opportunity employer," the firm is proclaiming its compliance with this and related legislation.

Originally, it was thought that the problem could best be attacked by outlawing discrimination in rates of pay and in hiring standards—and by devoting resources to enforcement of these provisions. While progress toward the elimination of discrimination according to race and sex undoubtedly was made between 1964 and the early 1970s, the pace was too slow for some. One reason was that discrimination in the labor market proved to be more subtle than was first thought.

Officials rarely could find proof that unequal pay was being given for equal work because determining when work was "equal" turned out to be a formidable task. And, as noted early in this chapter, discrimination often took the form of paying the *same* wages to blacks and whites (or men and women) who performed the same job, but relegating the less privileged groups to the inferior jobs.

So, in the early 1970s, a new wrinkle was added. Firms and other organizations with suspiciously small representation of blacks or women in their work forces were required not just to end discriminatory practices, but also to demonstrate that they were taking affirmative action to remedy this imbalance. That is, they had to *prove* that they were making efforts to locate members of minority groups and females and to hire them if they proved to be qualified.

This new approach to fighting discrimination was highly controversial and remains so to this day. (See the boxed insert on page 576.) Critics claim that affirmative action really means hiring quotas and compulsory hiring of unqualified workers simply because they are black or female. Proponents counter that without affirmative action discriminatory employers would simply claim they could not find qualified minority or female employees. The difficulty revolves around the impossibility of deciding *on purely objective criteria* who is "qualified" and who is not. What one person sees as government coercion to hire an unqualified applicant to fill a quota, another sees as a discriminatory employer being forced to mend his ways. Nothing in this book—or anywhere else—will teach you which view is correct in any particular instance.

In a way, this controversy provides yet another example of the trade-off between equality and efficiency. Without a doubt, giving more high-paying jobs to members of minority groups and to women would move society's Lorenz curve in the direction of greater equality. Supporters of affirmative action seek this result. But if it is done by disrupting industry and requiring firms to replace "qualified" white males by other "less qualified" workers, economic efficiency may suffer. Opponents of affirmative action are greatly troubled by these potential losses. How far should affirmative action be pushed? A good question, but one without a good answer.

The Supreme Court on Affirmative Action: The Bakke Case

The legal issues surrounding affirmative action programs are many and complex. Among the charges raised by opponents to such programs is that the "reverse discrimination" inherent in school admissions or hiring programs that favor disadvantaged groups constitutes a form of discrimination against white males. And this, they argue, violates the Fourteenth Amendment to the Constitution and the Civil Rights Act of 1964. In the case of the *Regents of the University of California v. Allan Bakke*, the U.S. Supreme Court ruled on this issue in a landmark case, which took four years to litigate and which will be discussed and interpreted for years to come.

Allan Bakke, then a 32-year-old white engineer from Los Altos, California, sought admission to the medical school of the University of California at Davis in 1973 and again in 1974. Both times he was rejected, while minority applicants with substantially inferior grades and test scores were accepted under the school's affirmative action admissions program—a program that reserved 16 out of 100 places in each entering class for minority students. After his second

rejection, Bakke filed suit, charging that the Davis medical school had violated both the Civil Rights Act and the Fourteenth Amendment by denying him admission solely because of his race. The California Supreme Court agreed with Bakke, and the University of California appealed the ruling to the U.S. Supreme Court.

The Court's decision, handed down in July 1978, was a momentous one for affirmative action, and for civil rights in general, because the California Supreme Court had ruled that race could not be considered a factor in making admissions decisions. If upheld, this ruling could have sounded the death knell for affirmative action. As it turned out, the Court's split decision (5 votes to 4) had something for everyone.

Allan Bakke was ordered admitted to the Davis medical school on the grounds that the rigid quota system used by the school illegally deprived him of his civil rights. But, at the same time, the Court reversed the opinion of the California Court, which held that race could not be a factor in admissions decisions. Justice Lewis F. Powell, Jr., writing for the majority, explicitly cited as legal and valid the admissions program at Harvard University, which uses race as one among many criteria but does not attempt to enforce rigid quotas. Thus both detractors and supporters of affirmative action could find solace in the Bakke decision. It apparently outlawed the quota system, but it left the door wide open for more moderate and less rigid forms of reverse discrimination.

As is so often the case with landmark decisions, the Bakke case raised as many questions as it answered. For one thing, the justices based their ruling on the Civil Rights Act, not on the Constitution; so the *constitutionality* of affirmative action was left an open question. Also, the legal issues in *hiring and employment programs* are not exactly the same as in school admissions, so more cases must be heard before the Bakke decision can be applied confidently to the labor market. And finally, the Bakke case dealt only with affirmative action based on *race*. The corresponding decision on affirmative action programs that favor women was left for another day.

SUMMARY

1. The War on Poverty was declared in 1964; by 1978 it had still not been won, though the fraction of families considered poor by official definitions had dropped substantially.

2. The difficulty in agreeing on a sharp dividing line between the poor and the nonpoor leads one to broaden the problem of poverty into the problem of inequality in incomes.

3. In the United States today, the richest 20 percent of families receive over 41 percent of the income, while the poorest 20 percent of families receive just above 5 percent. These numbers have changed little over the past 30 years and represent somewhat more inequality here than in many other advanced industrial nations.

4. Individual incomes differ for many reasons. Discrimination—that is, unequal pay for equal work—is obviously a reason, although it is hard to measure. Differences in native ability, in the desire to work hard and to take risks, in schooling, and in inherited wealth also account for income disparities. All of these factors, however, explain only part of the inequality that we observe. A portion of the rest is due simply to good or bad luck, and the balance is unexplained.

5. There is a trade-off between the goals of reducing inequality and enhancing economic efficiency: Policies that help on the equality front normally harm efficiency, and vice versa. This is one of the 12 Ideas for Beyond the Final Exam.

6. Because of this trade-off, there is an optimal degree of inequality for any society. Society finds this optimum in the same way that a consumer decides how much to buy of different commodities: The trade-off tells us how costly it is to "purchase" more equality, and preferences then determine how much should be "bought." However, since people differ in their value judgments about the importance of equality, there will inevitably be disagreement over the ideal amount of equality.

7. There may, however, be some hope of reaching agreement over the policies to use in pursuit of whatever goal for equality is selected. This is because the more efficient redistributive policies let us buy any amount of equality at a lower price in terms of lost output. Economists claim, for example, that a negative income tax is preferable to our current welfare system on these grounds.

8. Even the negative income tax, though, is no magical cure. Its primary virtue lies in the way it preserves incentives to work. But if this is done by keeping the tax rate low, then either the minimum guaranteed level of income will have to be very low or many nonpoor families will remain eligible for benefits.

9. The goal of income equality is also pursued through the tax system, especially through the progressive federal income tax. However, the equalization achieved by this tax is much less than is commonly believed because of tax loopholes and because people who are heavily burdened by the tax often can take steps to relieve themselves of these burdens. In addition, taxes other than income taxes are typically regressive, so that the tax system as a whole is only slightly progressive.

10. The problem of economic discrimination has been attacked by making it illegal, not through the tax and transfer system. But simply declaring discrimination to be illegal is much easier than actually ending discrimi-

nation. The trade-off between equality and efficiency applies once again: Strict enforcement of affirmative action will certainly reduce discrimination and increase income equality, but it may do so at a serious cost in terms of economic efficiency.

CONCEPTS FOR REVIEW

Poverty line
Absolute concept of poverty
Relative concept of poverty
Lorenz curve
Economic discrimination
Optimal amount of inequality
Trade-off between equality and efficiency
Aid to Families with Dependent Children (AFDC)

Food stamps
Negative income tax (NIT)
Progressive, proportional, and regressive taxes
Tax loopholes
Capital gains
Equal Employment Opportunities Commission (EEOC)
Affirmative action

QUESTIONS FOR DISCUSSION

1. Discuss the "leaky bucket" analogy (page 568) with your classmates. What maximum amount of income would you personally allow to leak from the bucket in transferring money from the rich to the poor? Explain why people differ in their answers to this question.

2. Continuing the leaky bucket example, explain why economists believe that replacing the present welfare system with a negative income tax would help reduce the leak.

3. Suppose you were to design a negative income tax system for the United States. Pick a guaranteed income level and a tax rate that seem reasonable to you. What break-even level of income is implied by these choices? For the plan you have just devised, construct a corresponding version of Table 29–4 (page 570).

4. Following is a complete list of the distribution of income in Disneyland. From these data, construct a Lorenz curve for Disneyland.

NAME	INCOME
Donald Duck	$ 50,000
Mickey Mouse	100,000
Minnie Mouse	25,000
Pluto	10,000
Ticket taker	15,000

How different is this from the Lorenz curve for the United States (Figure 29–2 on page 562)?

5. Suppose the War on Poverty were starting anew and you were part of a presidential commission assigned the task of defining the poor. Would you choose an absolute or relative concept of poverty? Why? What would be your specific definition of poverty?

6. Do you think that going to school will increase your earnings? For most people it does. Discuss some of the reasons for your belief.

7. Discuss the concept of the "optimal amount of inequality." What are some of the practical problems in determining how much inequality really is optimal?

seven

Resource Allocation: The Invisible Hand and Visible Interferences

30

The Price System
and the Case for Laissez Faire

Competition, by bringing into operation the law of value . . . brings
about the only organisation and arrangement of social production
which is possible in the circumstances. Only through the under-valua-
tion or over-valuation of products is it forcibly brought home to the individual commodity producers what things and what quantity of them
society requires or does not require. . . . [Otherwise] what guarantee
[do] we have that the necessary quantity and not more of each product
will be produced, that we shall not go hungry in regard to corn and
meat while we are choked in beet sugar and drowned in potato spirit,
that we shall not lack trousers to cover our nakedness while trouser
buttons flood us in millions.

Frederich Engels, Preface to *The Poverty of Philosophy*,
1st German edition (London: Martin Lawrence, Ltd., 1884), page 17.

This chapter and the next are, in a sense,
the culminating point of our microeconomic discussion. To show what tasks
the free-market economy is capable of carrying out well, we must bring together our
analysis of consumer demand and our analysis
of both the output and input decisions of
the firm. Only by examining the *interactions*
of consumers and producers can we see how
the market mechanism really works.

In this chapter we will show, first, that price,
in addition to determining the amounts of

money that change hands when something is
sold, also affects the efficiency with which the
economy uses its resources in serving the wants
of consumers. Second, we will show that, as a
result of their influence on efficiency in the use
of resources, price reductions do not always
serve the best interests of consumers, and that
sometimes consumers' interests would be better
served by price *increases*. Next, we will examine
the issue of efficiency in the use of resources by
dividing the discussion into three main question
areas: (1) What amounts of different goods

should be produced to match consumer demands most effectively? (2) Which consumers should get what combinations of the different goods? and (3) How should inputs be assigned among different industries to achieve efficiency in production? Following this, we will discuss the price mechanism and show how it is capable of dealing effectively with each of the problems posed by these questions. And finally, we will see that while the market mechanism can promote efficiency, its workings are still subject to reservations about its fairness—that is, its greater responsiveness to the desires of the wealthy than to those of the poor.

In the next chapter of this unit we will catalogue many other things that the free market will *not* do at all well if left to operate entirely on its own.

SCARCITY AND THE NEED TO COORDINATE ECONOMIC DECISIONS

Scarcity forces many difficult decisions upon an economy. In our free-market system the bulk of these decisions are made by individuals or by individual organizations, without any apparent coordination. A housewife in Peoria decides to purchase two dozen eggs, and on the same day a similar decision is made by many thousands of shoppers throughout the country. No one of the purchasers knows or cares about the purchase decisions of the others. Yet, scarcity requires that these demands *must* somehow all be coordinated with the production process so that total demand does not exceed the number of eggs that are available. The supermarkets, the wholesalers, the shippers, and the chicken farmers must somehow arrive at consistent decisions, for otherwise the supply–demand process will deteriorate into chaos.

As we will see, there are a good many other apparently independent decisions that must be coordinated. It is not simply a matter of choosing the most desirable alternative. One cannot run machines that are completed except for a few parts that have not been delivered. Refrigerators and cars cannot be used unless there is an adequate supply of fuel.

In an economy that is planned and centrally directed, it is easy to imagine how such coordination takes place—though the implementation turns out to be far more difficult than the idea. Radical critics have argued that in an unplanned economy we must expect chaos. Yet it does not seem to occur. Somehow, the activities in the economy are brought into harmony. Furthermore, the required coordination is provided by an invisible mechanism, which is not the product of any conscious design and which was never deliberately instituted.

Economies that are unplanned and unfettered by government regulations are called laissez-faire economies.

DEFINITION
Laissez faire is a term coined by eighteenth-century French economists to refer to a program of minimal government interference with the workings of the market system. Under such a program, government should prevent crime, enforce contracts, and build roads and other types of public works; but it should not set prices or grant monopolies to private firms or interfere in any other way with the workings of the market. In effect, the term means people should be left alone to carry out their economic tasks.

In such free-market economies, the price mechanism has an astonishing capacity to handle a calculation and coordination task of truly enormous proportions—one that will remain beyond the capabilities of electronic computers at least for the foreseeable future. It is true that like any mechanism, this one has its imperfections, some of them rather serious. But without understanding the nature of the overall task performed by the market system, it is all too easy to lose sight of the enormously demanding task that it constantly accomplishes, unnoticed, undirected, and at least in some respects, astonishingly well.

PRICING AND RESOURCE ALLOCATION

Prices play two basic roles in a market economy. First, and most noticeably, they affect the distribution of wealth between buyers and sellers. High rents make tenants poorer and often (but not always) make landlords richer. This distinctive role is the most obvious function of prices—the one that draws the attention of the public, of politicians, and of regulators.

But prices have a second role of comparable importance, one that is the primary focus of economic analysis. Prices, in effect, direct demands to products that are abundant and steer them away from items that are scarce. If supplies of one fuel begin to run out while enormous reserves of another remain, the price of the first can be expected to rise in comparison with the other. This will induce firms and consumers to switch from the fuel in short supply to the one that is comparatively abundant. Business firms will transform their equipment, and new homes will be built with heating that uses the cheaper fuel.

This allocative role of prices is referred to as the achievement of *efficiency in resource utilization.* Prices channel scarce resources into those tasks that most require them.

As the price of a scarce resource rises, only those for whom its use offers the greatest benefits will continue to buy it. Firms or individuals that can get along almost equally well with a cheaper alternative will switch when the scarce commodity gets too expensive. But others who find the alternative to be a poor or unacceptable substitute will continue to use the scarcer resource despite its higher price.

AN ILLUSTRATION: PRICING OF BRIDGES NEAR SAN FRANCISCO

The relationship between pricing and efficiency in the use (allocation) of resources can be clearly illustrated through a real-life example—in this case, the bridges in the San Francisco Bay Area.

Figure 30–1 on the next page is a map of the San Francisco Bay Area. It shows clearly the five bridges that serve the bulk of the traffic in and around the city. Now, a traveler going from north of Berkeley (point A) to Palo Alto (point B) has a choice of at least three routes:

1. He can go over the Richmond–San Rafael Bridge and then over the Golden Gate Bridge, through San Francisco and on southward.
2. He can stick to the eastern side of the Bay, cross at the San Francisco–Oakland Bay Bridge, and continue on southward as before.
3. He can stay on the eastern side of the Bay and cross the San Mateo–Hayward Bridge or the Dumbarton Bridge, then head on to Palo Alto.

Let's consider which of these three choices is most in the social interest. The most crowded of the bridges in question is the San Francisco–Oakland Bay Bridge, followed closely by the Golden Gate Bridge. The first carries nearly 19,000 cars per lane per day, and the second nearly 16,000. During rush hours, delays are frequent and traffic barely crawls across these bridges. In other words, space on these bridges is scarce, and every car that uses them makes it that much harder for others to get across. On the other hand, the San Mateo and Dumbarton Bridges carry approximately 4000 and 6000 cars per lane per day, respectively, and are obviously much less crowded.

From the point of view of the general public, it is best if any driver who has a choice of

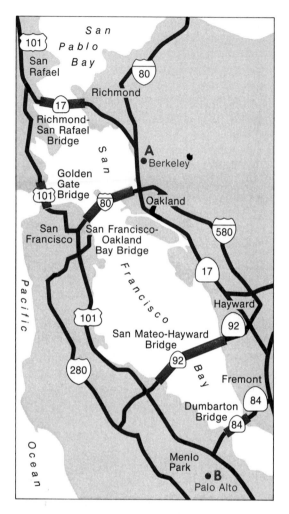

FIGURE 30–1

TOLL BRIDGES OF THE SAN FRANCISCO
BAY AREA

routes takes the one using the least crowded
bridges. This will help reduce the amount of
time wasted by the population as a whole in getting where they are going. Specifically, in our
illustration, Route 1, using the Golden Gate
Bridge, is not a socially desirable way for our
driver to get to Palo Alto. Route 2, with its use of
the San Francisco–Oakland Bay Bridge, is, if
anything, even worse because of the added
delays it contributes to everyone else. Route 3 is

the best choice from the viewpoint of the public
interest.

The pattern of prices that would promote
the most efficient utilization of bridges would involve a higher price (very likely a substantially
higher price) for the use of the most crowded
bridges, on which space is such a scarce resource, balanced off by lower prices on the uncrowded bridges. *That is what economists mean
by pricing to achieve efficiency in resource utilization.* For the same reason, economists favor
low prices for abundant minerals and high
prices for scarce ones, and advocate low prices
on trains during hours when space is abundant,
and higher prices during rush hours when
space is scarce.

Since these principles seem so clear and
rational, the reader may be interested to see at
what levels the actual bridge tolls were set until
recently. Travel on the crowded Golden Gate
Bridge required a 50-cent toll. But the other two
routes seem to have had an inverse relation between tolls and crowding, with a 25-cent toll on
the San Francisco–Oakland Bay Bridge and a
35-cent toll on both of the other two less-used
bridges. Even stranger, the Richmond–San
Rafael Bridge, which is about as sparsely used
as any, charged a 50-cent toll.

The pattern of tolls obviously seems quite
irrational. The most crowded bridges have the
lowest tolls! Similar pricing anomalies can be
shown to exist in a wide variety of other instances. Later in this chapter we will see why
this occurs, and you will be able to judge for
yourself whether the officials who set the tolls
for the four bridges in the Bay Area were,
indeed, irrational.

CAN PRICE INCREASES EVER SERVE THE PUBLIC INTEREST?

The preceding discussion suggests that increases in some prices can sometimes promote
the general welfare, and this is just the sort of

proposition one frequently runs across in public policy discussions. When shortages of natural gas threaten the nation, many observers suggest that a rise in price would help alleviate the problem. And when Congress and the president are concerned about how much oil we are importing from abroad, people often advocate a rise in price as a solution.

This is not an easy notion to accept. How can a higher price possibly benefit the general public? The politician who advocates an increase in fuel prices or in rents courts great unpopularity, and his argument is unlikely to carry much more conviction than the cliché announcement by the father who is about to spank his child that "This is going to hurt me much more than it hurts you!" Yet it is important to realize that *sometimes* rises in the prices of certain items are beneficial. Indeed, they may in some cases be essential.

A historic illustration is perhaps the most striking way to bring out the point. In 1834, some ten years before the great potato famine that brought so many persons from Ireland to the United States, a professor of economics named Mountifort Longfield lectured at the University of Dublin about the price system. And he offered the following remarkable illustration of his point:

> Suppose the crop of the ordinary food used in any country, as potatoes in Ireland, was to fall short in some year one-sixth of the usual consumption. If [there were no] increase of price, the whole stock of provisions destined for the supply of the year would be exhausted in ten months, and for the remaining two months a scene of misery and famine beyond description would ensue . . . But when prices [increase it is often believed by] the sufferers that it is not caused by a scarcity. . . . They suppose that there are provisions enough, but that the distress is caused by the insatiable rapacity of the possessors . . . [and] they have generally succeeded in obtaining laws against [the

price increases] . . . which alone can prevent the provisions from being entirely consumed long before a new supply can be obtained.[1]

Prevention of a rise in prices where a rise is appropriate can have serious consequences indeed. We have seen from Longfield's example that it can cause famine. We know that it has contributed to the surrender of cities under military siege when effective price ceilings discouraged the efforts of those who were taking the risk of smuggling food supplies through enemy lines. We know that it has discouraged the construction of housing in cities that employ rent controls by making building construction a losing proposition. We know that it has caused factories to shut down and schools to go unheated when fuels were in short supply. And, we know that it caused nationwide chaos in gasoline distribution during the petroleum embargo of 1973–1974.

Recall from Chapter 4 that one of the 12 Ideas for Beyond the Final Exam states that prevention of price increases can sometimes serve the public very badly. In extreme cases it can even produce havoc—undermining production and causing extreme shortages of vitally needed products.

Of course there are cases in which it is appropriate to resist price increases—where artificial combinations in restraint of trade would otherwise succeed in gouging the public; where taxes are imposed on products capriciously and inappropriately; and where rising prices threaten such injustice that rationing becomes the more acceptable option. But it is important to distinguish such unusual cases from the more numerous cases in which artificial restrictions on prices produce serious and even tragic consequences, a danger increased by the grad-

[1] Mountifort Longfield, *Lectures on Political Economy* (Dublin, 1834), pages 53–56.

ual and hence imperceptible way that these consequences creep up on us.

THREE COORDINATION TASKS IN THE ECONOMY

Because resources are limited, some of the economy's most critical decisions are those that determine the ways in which they are used. It is convenient to group the relevant decisions into three broad categories: (1) How much of each commodity should be produced (output selection)? (2) How shall the available input supplies be divided among individual producers (production planning)? and (3) How shall these products be divided among consumers (distribution among consumers)? This chapter analyzes these three questions.

While a planned economy must address itself explicitly to these issues, an unregulated economy must also provide some answers. At the end of any given week, every producer will have acquired some inputs, some specified quantities of output will have been produced, and every consumer will have received some quantity of a variety of commodities. Since no one has overseen the process and undertaken the task of preventing injustice and inefficiency in its workings, one may well wonder whether the end result is not likely to prove a caricature of a desirable resource allocation. Predictably, some extreme critics of the free-market system have assumed that no reasonable results can be expected from such an unsupervised system. "Unplanned chaos" is a term they have used more than once.

"Unplanned" the market economy certainly may be. But we will see that in appropriate circumstances it is capable of producing results far from chaotic. We will find that it can even yield an approximation of what has been called an "efficient allocation of resources." Indeed, this fact accounts for the great respect that economists pay to the price mechanism.

Under a free-enterprise system, it is the price mechanism that moves products to the consumers who want them when they want them, that apportions fuels and other raw materials among the different industries in accord with those industries' requirements, and that eliminates shortages (by means of rising prices that stimulate supplies and curtail demands) and gets rid of surpluses (through lower prices that increase demand and cut supplies).

It is the price mechanism that, in Engels' words, prevents us from going "hungry in regard to corn and meat while we are choked in beet sugar and drowned in potato spirit."

To make clear just what is achieved by the price mechanism we consider first what has to be done by the system that has sometimes been offered as a substitute—central planning. It is easier to begin that way because, by its nature, goals must be laid out specifically under central planning, and one thinks naturally in terms of a set of tasks to be accomplished. Let us consider the three coordination tasks in turn.

Output Selection

Because supplies of raw materials and other resources are limited, the economy has a very limited range of choices open to it. There simply is not enough petroleum on the planet to permit every family in the world to drive a Cadillac, and resource limitations rule out many other such choices. But even within the available set of options a tremendous number of choices remain. One may decide to produce more cheese and less milk, more goods and fewer services, more housing and fewer weapons—or any of these decisions can go the other way.

Since any nation's resources are limited, every decision to produce more of one good means that less of another will be available. If a central planner is to run the economy in a way that serves the desires of consumers as effectively as available resources allow, he has a complex calculation to undertake in deciding on the composition of outputs. He must continuously balance off the desirability of an increase in any one product against the losses incurred from curtailing the supplies of some other goods.

Production Planning

Having decided on the composition of output, the planner must determine just how those goods are going to be produced. As a matter of fact, these two decisions are interdependent—they cannot be decided one at a time. The method chosen for production determines what combinations of, say, coffee and bananas can be obtained, though it is simpler to think of these decisions as if they occurred one at a time.

The production planning problem includes, among other things, the assignment of inputs to enterprises—that is, which farm will get how much of which fertilizer or which factory will get how much of which materials. These decisions can be crucial. If a factory runs short of an essential input, the entire production plan may be undermined.

Shortly, we will study the immense difficulty of this particular portion of the planning problem. It need only be noted here that the allocation of inputs is one of the problems on which efforts have been focused in centrally planned economies. Not only is it a crucial component of the planning process, because if production breaks down the entire economy is in trouble, but it seems also to give planners their most serious difficulties. Some production units have found themselves short of critical inputs, and breakdowns of significant magnitude are reported to have resulted. Perhaps more serious are the natural reactions of factory managers who have responded by accumulating inventories of inputs as large as they can get away with. A large inventory of transistors provides a cush-

ion against the possibility that, at the next go-round, the planning authority will not assign enough of these items. But, for the economy as a whole, large inventories mean that many thousands or millions of transistors are held idle rather than used to expand production.

Distribution of Products among Consumers

The third task of the central planner is the critical decision as to which consumer gets which item of the goods that have been produced. The objective is to divide up the available supplies so as to match the differing preferences of consumers as well as possible.

In some respects the decisions about distribution are very similar to the task of production planning. In the latter, the central authority must coordinate the input demands of individual managers so that they do not exceed the resource quantities available to the economy. In distribution planning, the analogous objective is

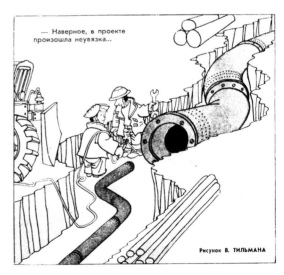

In this cartoon from a Soviet humor magazine, one construction worker comments to the other, "A slight mistake in the plans, perhaps."

to apportion final outputs among consumers in a way that corresponds with consumers' needs and preferences. Coffee lovers must not be flooded with tea while tea drinkers are showered with coffee.

INPUT–OUTPUT ANALYSIS: THE ARITHMETIC OF PRODUCTION PLANNING

So far, the three components of the coordination of the economy have been discussed fairly loosely. To show the *very complicated* character of the problems that must be solved both by the central planners and by the price system, it is useful to examine one of these calculations —production planning—somewhat more carefully. Though the discussion will refer to a few simple algebraic equations, there is no need for you to master those equations. They are given only to help describe the character of the problem and the methods that are required to deal with its complexities. There is really only one important message this section is intended to convey—that the task of allocation of resources is amazingly complicated. To bring out this point, we will describe the main tool that has been developed by economists for use in production planning: input–output analysis.

Input–output analysis, which was invented by U.S. economist Wassily Leontief, a Nobel-prize winner in 1973, is a method designed to take account of the interdependence of the various industries in the economy. In planning production, input–output analysis recognizes that an increase in the output of any good will require other goods as inputs, a fact that is important in calculating the net effect of the increased production of the good on the supplies of all commodities available to consumers.

Many industries in an economy produce not only consumer goods but also inputs for the productive processes of other industries. Gasoline, for example, is used not only by consumers to run cars, but also by truckers and manufacturers. The same is true of electrical equipment, steel, and so forth.

But the fact that the inputs of many industries constitute parts of the outputs of other industries causes serious problems for production planners. Without special calculation that takes explicit account of the resulting interdependencies among industries, the planners cannot be sure that the amounts of the various outputs turned out will be sufficient to meet both consumer and industrial demands. The trouble is that the output required from any industry depends on the output desired from every other industry. If we change the output target for one industry, every other industry's output target also must be adjusted. For instance, if we decide to increase the generation of electricity in order to meet a rise in consumers' electricity demands, then more steel will have to be produced for more electric generators. But the increase in steel output will require more coal to be mined. More mining in turn means that still more electricity is needed to light the mines, to run the elevators, and perhaps even to run some of the trains that carry the coal, and so on and on. Any single change in planned output, like the illustrative rise in electricity production, sets off a chain of adjustments throughout the economy that require even further adjustments in the planned output changes that led to the problem in the first place.

To decide how much of each output an economy must produce, the planner is forced to use statistics to form a set of equations, one equation for each product, and then solve those equations simultaneously. The nature of such equations is illustrated in the accompanying boxed insert. These input–output equations describe precisely how each industry's required output depends on every other industry's output target. Only by solving these equations *simultaneously* for the required outputs of electricity, steel, coal, and so on, can we be sure of a consistent solution that produces the required amounts of these products.

However complicated it may seem, the fact is that the small scale of the example described in the box makes the calculation seem far more simple than it is in practice. In a real economy, the number of commodities is obviously far greater than the three outputs in that example. In the United States, some large manufacturing companies individually deal in hundreds of thousands of items, and the armed forces keep several *million* different items in inventory. In planning, it is ultimately necessary to make calculations for each such item. It is not enough to plan the right number of bolts *in total;* we must make sure that the required number *of each size* is produced. Try to put 5 million large bolts

into 5 million small nuts. So, to be sure our plans will really work, we need a separate equation for every size of bolt (and one for every size and type of nut).

But then, to replicate the analysis described in the boxed insert, we will have to solve simultaneously several million equations! Unfortunately, there is as yet no electronic computer capable of doing this. Worse still is the data problem. *Each* of our *three* equations requires *three* pieces of statistical information, making 3×3, or 9, numbers in total. This is so because the equation for electricity must indicate on the basis of statistical information how much electricity is needed in steel production and how much in coal production. That is, the demand equation for each product must contain infor-

Input—Output Equations: An Example

For simplicity let us think of an economy in which there are only three outputs: electricity, steel, and coal; and let E, S, and C represent the dollar value of their respective outputs. Suppose that for every dollar's worth of steel, 20 cents' worth of electricity is used up, so that the total electricity demand of steel manufacturers is $0.2S$. Similarly, assume the coal manufacturers use up 30 cents of electricity in producing 1 dollar's worth of coal, or a total of $0.3C$ units of electricity. Since E dollars of electricity are produced in total, the amount left over for consumers, after subtraction of industrial demands for fuel, will be

$$E \quad - \quad 0.2S \quad - \quad 0.3C$$

E	$0.2S$	$0.3C$
(available electricity)	(use in steel production)	(use in coal production)

Suppose further that the central planners have decided to supply 15 million dollars' worth of

electricity to consumers. We end up with the electricity output equation

$$E - 0.2S - 0.3C = 15$$

The planner will also need one such equation for each of the two other industries, specifying for each of them the net supplies intended to be left for consumers after the industrial uses of these products. The full set of equations might then be:

$$E - 0.2S - 0.3C = 15$$
$$S - 0.1E - 0.06C = 7$$
$$C - 0.15E - 0.4S = 10$$

These are typical equations in an input—output analysis. Only, in practice, a typical analysis has dozens and sometimes hundreds of equations with similar numbers of unknowns. This, then, is the logic of the production planning process.

mation on the demand for that product by each of the other industries. And there will be one such equation for each product in the economy. Therefore, in a 5-industry analysis, 5×5, or 25, pieces of data are needed, a 100-industry analysis requires 100^2, or 10,000, statistical numbers, and a million-item input—output study might need 1,000,000,000,000 pieces of information. The data-gathering problems are therefore no easy task, to put it mildly.

There are other, somewhat more technical, complications that need not be gone into here. We have seen enough to conclude that:

A full, rigorous central planning calculation is a tremendous task, requiring an overwhelming quantity of information and some incredibly difficult calculations. The allocation of resources through central planning is an extremely complex task. It is this very difficult job that the price mechanism automatically carries out in a free-market economy.

SUPPLY, DEMAND, AND PRICES

Having seen how difficult a task is assigned to the market mechanism, let us now consider in general terms how it does its job—that is, how it deals with each of its three basic tasks: the distribution of goods among consumers, the allocation of inputs among different producers, and the allocation of resources among different commodities (output selection).

Consider first the distribution of commodities among consumers. Suppose the number of eggs demanded by the nation's families exceeds the available supply. For a very brief period consumers may be unable to find eggs in their markets. But soon enough there will be a price response. That is, prices will rise to a point where demand is discouraged sufficiently to bring the total quantity demanded down to the quantity supplied. Here the price acts as a rationing device, which apportions

commodities among the consumers who wish to purchase them most.

However, unlike most rationing devices, the price system is able to pay attention to consumer preferences. If eggs are rationed by the most obvious and usual means (say, two to a person), each individual will end up with the same quantity—whether he thinks eggs the more unpleasant component of his breakfast or the ingredients of his evening's soufflé, for which he pangs all day long. The price system, on the other hand, permits each consumer to set up his own priorities. If you just barely tolerate eggs, a rise in their price will readily induce you to get your protein from some other source. But the egg lover will not be induced to switch so readily. Thus:

The price system operates the distribution process by rationing goods on the basis of preferences *and relative incomes*.

Notice the last three words. This rationing process *is* rigged in favor of the rich. However, if that makes us unhappy, we may still want to think twice before declaring ourselves opposed to the price system. If equality is our goal, might not a more reasonable solution be to use the tax system to equalize incomes, and *then* let the market mechanism distribute goods in accord with preferences?

Prices are also helpful in achieving efficiency in production planning. Prices allocate inputs among producers in the same way that they distribute goods among consumers— in accord with preferences and income. The firm that needs a piece of equipment most urgently will be the last to drop out of the market when prices rise. If more grain is demanded by millers than is currently available, the price will rise and bring demand back into line with the available supply, always giving priority to those users who need the input most urgently, because they are the ones most willing to pay for it.

Here again there are some flies in the ointment. Monopolistic elements may reduce the price responsiveness of the market—firms may simply be reluctant to adjust prices rapidly when supply and demand are out of balance. Yet, the general notion just described is correct—the price system does get inputs to those producers that need them most, and it manages to do so with rather remarkable effectiveness.

Having gotten some inkling of the manner in which the price system deals with distribution and production, we may note briefly how it handles the third of the major tasks of planning—the allocation of resources, or output selection. This is just an extension of our discussion of the distribution process. When our shortage of eggs occurred and prices rose, consumer demands were cut down to the available supply. But this is not the end of the story. The increased prices presumably will serve to stimulate the production of eggs. In the first instance, it will get more eggs to market simply by getting them out of storage. Farmers will also find it more profitable than before to invest in expensive feeds that stimulate egg production, and to cut down on their sale of chickens for meat. Finally, if the excess demand is sufficient in magnitude and duration, flocks will be expanded in size by encouraging the birth of more chicks. Thus we conclude that:

The relative magnitudes of the different outputs—the allocation of society's resources among different products—will depend on two basic influences: consumer preferences and the relative difficulty of producing the goods, that is, their production costs.

A shift in consumer tastes that creates an increased demand for a product will stimulate its output, as we have just seen. But the same sort of result will follow when a technological discovery reduces the input quantities needed to produce some item, thus permitting the same consumer preferences to be served with a smaller amount of resources. The cost and thus the price of that item will fall, more will be demanded, and so more will be produced.

The mechanism whereby outputs are adjusted to consumer demands and to relative production costs as part and parcel of the business person's pursuit of profits is what Adam Smith in The Wealth of Nations (1776) referred to as the "invisible hand." It is that unseen force that plans and coordinates production, eliminates shortages, responds to consumer desires, and proscribes waste in the use of resources. And it does all this with no conscious regard for the public interest, guided only by the pursuit of profit. Economists have devoted much study to the invisible hand and how it promotes efficiency. Detailed proof that a perfectly competitive economy will be efficient is more technical than is appropriate for this discussion, and so for the next two sections we will describe only how such an economy deals with output selection—the first of the three tasks that constitute the allocation of resources. How it deals with production planning and with the distribution of products among consumers—the other two resource-allocation issues—is described in the appendix to this chapter.

The behavior of prices and the manner in which they ration inputs and outputs may at first glance seem obvious and perhaps even banal. Where are the marvels of the market mechanism that have been implied? To see them more clearly, the reader need only recall the input–output analysis of the preceding section. Notice that the market mechanism—designed by no inventor, controlled by no planning agency—automatically and effectively solves all the millions of simultaneous equations required by a full input–output analysis. It makes sure that the relative outputs of all industries are coordinated so that each can supply the input quantities demanded by the others and still leave enough to meet the requirements of consumers. The market mechanism has been described as a giant computer in which prices, output quantities, and demands all affect one another and adjust themselves in the manner that the input–output analysis requires.

THE CONCEPT OF EFFICIENT RESOURCE ALLOCATION

Before we can show what the price mechanism can do to promote efficiency, we must define more precisely the term efficiency. To economists, the concept of efficiency refers to the *absence of waste*. If resources are being utilized inefficiently, it will be possible to rearrange things so that people get more of the things they want; in a sense, it will be possible to get something for nothing.

One important caution. The concept of an "efficient" allocation of resources should not be confused with what is the "best" allocation of resources according to any particular person's value judgments. An economy can be just as efficient producing many mink coats and little bread as it can producing few mink coats and plentiful quantities of bread. Economic analysis offers little guidance on how to deal with such issues. What it can do, and do with some effectiveness, is to steer us away from situations where, because of inappropriate decisions, we could have had more bread *and* more coats.

Biographical Note: Adam Smith   (1723–1790)

Although Adam Smith is remembered as a leading advocate of freedom of international trade, he was born the son of a customs official, and his own last job was the well-paid post of collector of customs for Scotland. He was born in Scotland in 1723, and his youth coincided with the attempt of "Bonnie Prince Charlie" and his Scottish supporters to regain the British throne—a maneuver that fanned English prejudices against the Scots, prejudices that Smith would encounter at various times throughout his life.

Smith received an excellent education at Glasgow College, where, for the first time, some lectures were being given in English rather than Latin. He received a fellowship to Oxford University, where he studied for 6 years, mostly by himself since, at that time, teaching at Oxford was virtually nonexistent. After completing his studies, he was appointed professor of logic at Glasgow College and, later, professor of moral philosophy, a field which then included economics as one of its branches. Fortunately, Smith was a popular lecturer because, in those days, a professor's pay in Glasgow depended on the number of students who chose to attend his lectures. At Glasgow he was responsible for helping James Watt find a job

The Concept of Efficient Resource Allocation

Specifically, the concept of economic efficiency has to do with using society's resources most effectively to serve consumers' tastes *whatever those tastes happen to be.*

DEFINITION

Any reallocation of resources that makes some individuals in the economy better off in their own estimation while not worsening the lot of anyone else is an improvement in the functioning of the economy. Any allocation of resources that takes advantage of every such opportunity is called an *efficient* allocation.

This criterion undoubtedly appears at first to be trite. It is a principle that asserts, in effect, that anything agreed to unanimously is desirable. If some people are made better off and none are harmed, things must be "better" by anyone's definition. It is hard to argue with this as an ethical postulate. The miracle is that such a simple principle can get us anywhere. Where *does* it get us?

Let us see how this apparently trivial definition of efficiency enables us to get some concrete results on problems of resource allocation.

---

as an instrument maker. It was Watt who would later go on to invent the steam engine, so in this and many other respects, Smith was present virtually at the birth of the Industrial Revolution, whose prophet he was destined to become.

After 13 years at Glasgow, Smith accepted a highly paid post as tutor to a young Scottish nobleman with whom he spent several years in France, a customary way of educating nobles in the eighteenth century. Primarily because he was bored during these years in France, Smith began working on *The Wealth of Nations.* Several years after his return to England, in 1776, the book was published and rapidly achieved popularity.

The Wealth of Nations contains many brilliantly written passages. It was one of the first systematic treatises in economics, contributing both to theoretical and factual knowledge about the subject. Among the main points made in the book are the importance for a nation's prosperity of freedom of trade and the division of labor permitted by more widespread markets; the dangers of governmental protection of monopolies and imposition of tariffs; and the superiority of self-interest—the instrument of the "invisible hand"—over altruism as a means of improving the econ-

omy's service to the general public.

The British government was grateful for the ideas for new tax legislation Smith proposed, and to show its appreciation appointed him to the lucrative sinecure of collector of customs, which, together with the lifetime pension awarded him by his former pupil, left him very well off financially, although he eventually gave away most of his money to charitable causes.

In the eighteenth century the intellectual world was small, and among the many people with whom Smith was acquainted were David Hume, the philosopher; Samuel Johnson; James Boswell; Benjamin Franklin; and Jean Jacques Rousseau. Smith got along well with everyone except Samuel Johnson, who was noted for his dislike of Scots. Smith was absent-minded and apparently timid with women, being visibly embarrassed by the public attention of the eminent ladies of Paris during his visits there. He never married, and lived with his mother most of his life. When he died, the Edinburgh newspapers recalled only that when Smith was 4 years old he was kidnapped by gypsies. But thanks to his writings, he is remembered for a good deal more than that.

EFFICIENT OUTPUT SELECTION: WHAT TO PRODUCE

We consider now the first of the three allocative issues that must be handled by the price system: How much of each good should the economy produce? Is it better to produce more beef and less lamb, or to do the reverse? The economists' analysis of this issue is founded entirely upon one basic rule that must be satisfied for efficiency:

Efficiency in the choice of output quantities of the different products of the economy requires that for each product, such as beef,

Marginal cost (MC) of a pound of beef = Marginal utility (MU) of a pound of beef to each consumer

and a similar relationship must hold for each other product, such as lamb.

Let us see why this rule *must* be satisfied for an allocation to be efficient. If the marginal utility of a pound of beef to consumers is greater than its marginal cost of production, the value of the resources that would be used up to produce one more pound of beef (its MC) is less than the value of that additional pound to consumers (its MU).[2] Then an increase in output must be an improvement for society—the initial output cannot be optimal.

The opposite will be true if the MC of beef exceeds the MU of beef. In that case, the last pound of beef will have used up more value (MC) than it produced (MU). It would therefore be better to have less beef and more of something else.

What we have shown, then, is that if there is *any* product for which MU is not equal to MC, the economy must be wasting an opportunity to produce a net improvement in consumers' wel-

[2]Remember that marginal utility is measured in terms of money. See Chapter 19.

fare. This is just what we mean by using resources *inefficiently*. It follows that the mix of outputs in the economy can be efficient only if MU = MC for every good.

The case for a free-market economy begins by showing that under pure competition the price system *automatically* leads buyers and sellers to behave in a way that makes MU and MC equal.

To see this, recall from Chapter 22 that under pure competition it will be most profitable for each beef-producing firm to produce the quantity of beef at which

$$MC \text{ of beef} = \text{Price } (P) \text{ of beef}$$

We know this must be so because if the marginal cost of beef is less than the price, the farmer can add to his profits by increasing the size of his herd (or the amount of grain that he feeds his animals); and the reverse will be true if the marginal cost of beef is greater than its price.

We also learned, in Chapter 19, that it pays each consumer to buy the quantity of beef at which

$$MU \text{ of beef (in terms of money)} = P \text{ of beef}$$

since otherwise either an increase or a decrease in quantity purchased will obviously leave that consumer better off.

Comparing these last two equations, we see at once that if both the MC of beef and the MU of beef are equal to the same price, P, then they must be equal to each other. That is, it must be true that the quantity of beef produced and purchased will be such that

$$MC = P = MU$$

just as our optimality condition requires. The same will be true for lamb and every other product supplied by competitive industries. Thus:

Under pure competition, the uncoordinated decisions of producers and consumers can be expected *automatically* to produce a quantity of each product that satisfies the $MC = MU$ rule for efficiency in the quantities to be produced of the different goods.

This may all seem like sleight of hand. True enough, the equations all worked out the right way. But how can the price mechanism automatically satisfy all the exacting requirements for efficiency—requirements that no central planner could hope to handle because of the masses of statistics and the enormous calculations it would require? The conclusion seems analogous to the rabbit suddenly pulled from the magician's hat. But, as always, rabbits come out of hats only if they were hidden there in the first place. What really is the machinery by which our act of magic works?

The answer starts with the fact that the price system lets consumers and producers pursue their own best interests—something they may be very good at doing. Prices are the dollar costs of commodities to consumers. So, in pursuing their own best interests, consumers will buy the commodities that give them the most satisfaction *per dollar.*

Turning now to the firms, we know that competition equates prices with marginal costs. This means that the dollar cost of a good to the consumer is the same as the value of the resources used up in producing it. That is, *the cost of the good to consumers accurately reflects its resource cost to society.* Therefore, if consumers succeed in minimizing the *dollar cost to themselves* of achieving a given level of satisfaction, then they also automatically minimize the *resource costs to the community.* For this reason we say:

When prices are set equal to marginal costs, the price system is giving the correct cost signals to consumers. It has set prices at levels that induce consumers to husband the resources of society with the same care they devote to watching their own money.

So far, this discussion may seem theoretical. Its full significance will become clear in the next chapter, where we discuss what may go wrong with the workings of the price system. There we will see that the present discussion enables us to understand the significance of such real problems as the effects of unregulated monopoly and the sources of environmental damage.

FAIRNESS VERSUS EFFICIENCY: THE SAN FRANCISCO BRIDGE PRICES

Although we will discuss shortcomings of the price mechanism in the next chapter, there is one related issue that must be raised here: that is, income distribution and other matters relating to the equitability and justice of pricing decisions.

The analysis of this chapter pays a great deal of attention to the efficiency with which the economy does or does not serve consumer demands. But markets only serve demands that are backed up by consumers' desire *and ability* to pay. Though the market system may do well in serving a family below the poverty line, giving that family more food and clothing than a less efficient economy would provide, it offers far more to the family of a multimillionaire. Many observers object that an arrangement such as this represents a great *injustice,* however efficient it may be.[3]

Often, recommendations made by economists for improving the efficiency of the market system are opposed on the grounds that they are unfair. For example, for precisely the same reason that economists frequently suggest higher tolls on more crowded bridges, they advocate higher prices for facilities at the times of the day when they are most heavily used. They propose a pricing arrangement called peak, off-peak pricing by which prices for public trans-

[3]It may be interesting to note that Marx and Engels treated this view with contempt, as we will see in Chapter 39 on Marxian economics.

portation are higher during rush hours than they are during other hours. The objective of such price arrangements is to induce consumers to use facilities at times when they are less crowded in order to increase the efficiency with which those facilities can serve the public. Under such a plan, relatively low fares would be offered on commuter trains between 10:30 A.M. and 3:30 P.M., when the trains run fairly empty. The same notion applies to other services. Charges for nighttime long-distance telephone calls are much lower than those in the daytime and, in some places, electricity is sold more cheaply at night when demand does not strain the suppliers' generating capacity.

Yet the proposal that higher fares should be charged for public transportation in central cities during peak hours—say 8:00 A.M. to 9:30 A.M. and 4:30 P.M. to 6 P.M.—has often run into stiff opposition on the grounds that most of the burden will fall on lower-income working people who have no choice about the timing of their trips.

A survey in Great Britain of the views both of members of Parliament and of economists on the subject of peak, off-peak fares found that they were favored by 88 percent of the economists surveyed, but by only 35 percent of the Conservative Party M.P.'s and just 19 percent of the Labor Party M.P.'s! (See Table 30–1.) We may be sure that the M.P.'s reflected the views of the body politic more accurately than did the economists.

Somewhat different notions of fairness explain the apparently anomalous pricing of the San Francisco Bay Area bridges that was described at the beginning of the chapter. Why should it be considered fair to charge high prices on bridges with little traffic and low prices on crowded bridges? Many people feel that it is fair for those who travel on a bridge to pay for its costs—it would be unjust for those who use

TABLE 30–1

REPLIES TO A QUESTIONNAIRE

	ECONOMISTS (102) %	CONSERVATIVE M.P.'s (39) %	LABOR M.P.'s (52) %
In order to make the most efficient use of a city's resources, how should subway and bus fares vary during the day?			
(a) They should be relatively low during rush hour to transport as many people as possible at that time.	—	—	21
(b) They should be relatively low during rush hour to reduce costs for the maximum number of people (including those answering both [a] and [b]).	1	—	19
(c) They should be the same at all times to avoid making travelers alter their schedules because of high price differences.	4	60	39
(d) They should be relatively high during rush hour to minimize the amount of equipment needed to transport the daily travelers.	88	35	19
(e) Impossible to answer on the data and alternatives given.	7	5	2

Source: Samuel Brittan, *Is There an Economic Consensus?* (Atlantic Highlands, N.J.: Humanities Press, Inc., 1973), page 93. The figures in parentheses indicate the total number of respondents in each category.

the crowded San Francisco—Oakland Bay Bridge to pay for the less-crowded Richmond—San Rafael Bridge. By definition, a bridge that is traveled heavily will more quickly take in the revenue necessary to recoup the cost of building, maintaining, and running it. That is why fairness is widely believed to dictate low tolls on crowded bridges. On the other hand, the relatively few users of a less crowded bridge must pay higher tolls in order to make a fair contribution toward its costs.

Of course, such a pattern of tolls slows traffic, and it lures to the overcrowded bridges even more drivers than would otherwise use them. In other words, prices that offer a bonus for the use of overcrowded facilities almost certainly contribute to inefficiency and impose losses of time and other costs upon many people.

But one cannot legitimately conclude that advocates of such prices are "evil" or "stupid." Whether the pattern of prices illustrated by the tolls in the San Francisco Bay Area is or is not desirable must be decided, ultimately, on the basis of the public's sense of what constitutes unfairness and injustice in pricing and the amount it is willing to pay in terms of delays, inconvenience, and other inefficiencies in order to avoid such apparent injustices.[4]

Economics alone cannot decide the appropriate trade-off between fairness and efficiency. It cannot even pretend to judge what pricing arrangements are fair and what are unfair. But it can and should provide analyses indicating whether a particular pricing decision, proposed

[4]Recently these tolls have been adjusted to come much closer to what economists recommend. Tolls on the more crowded bridges have been raised while the others have been left unchanged.

because it is considered fair, will impose heavy inefficiency costs upon the community. Economic analysis can and should also indicate how these costs can be evaluated, so that the issues can be decided on the basis of an understanding of the facts.

TOWARD ASSESSMENT OF THE PRICE MECHANISM

Our analysis of the case for laissez faire is not a piece of propaganda intended to convince the reader that the price mechanism is an ideal of perfection, without flaw or room for improvement. In the next chapter, we will explore some of its shortcomings in considerable detail, and some have already been raised in earlier chapters. Yet recognition of the imperfections should not be allowed to conceal its enormous accomplishments. We have shown that, given the proper circumstances, it is capable of meeting the most exacting requirements of allocative efficiency, requirements that go well beyond the capacity of any central planning mechanism. The price mechanism has directed economies whose productive efficiency has provided an abundance of goods unprecedented in human history. Even economies in which central planning is practiced use the price mechanism to carry out considerable portions of the task of allocation, most notably the distribution of goods among consumers. No one has invented any instrument for the direction of the economy that can replace the price system—a mechanism that no one ever designed or planned for, but that grew by itself, a child of the processes of history.

SUMMARY

1. Prices determine how much money changes hands when a commodity is sold. But prices also determine the allocation of resources.
2. Resource allocation involves three issues: (a) What amounts of different goods should be produced? (b) How should these goods be divided among different consumers? and (c) How should inputs be divided among the producers of the different goods?

3. An allocation of resources is considered *inefficient* if it wastes opportunities to change the use of the economy's inputs in any way that makes consumers better off. Resource allocation is called *efficient* if there are no such wasted opportunities.

4. Under competition, the free-market mechanism adjusts prices so that the resulting resource allocation is efficient. It induces firms to buy and use inputs in ways that yield the most valuable outputs per unit of input; it divides products among consumers in ways that match the preferences of the consumers; and it produces commodities whose value to consumers exceeds the cost of producing them.

5. Sometimes improvements in efficiency will require some prices to be increased in order to stimulate their supply or to prevent waste in their use. In that way price increases can sometimes be beneficial to consumers.

6. The workings of the price mechanism can be criticized on the grounds that they are unfair because of the preferential treatment they accord to wealthy consumers.

CONCEPTS FOR REVIEW	Laissez faire Economic efficiency Resource allocation Peak, off-peak pricing Input–output analysis

QUESTIONS FOR DISCUSSION

1. What are the possible social advantages of price rises in each of the two following cases?
   a. Charging higher prices for electrical power on very hot days when many people use air conditioners
   b. Raising water prices in drought-stricken areas
2. Discuss the fairness of the two preceding proposals.
3. Discuss the nature of the inefficiency in each of the following cases:
   a. An arrangement whereby relatively little coffee and much tea is made available to people who prefer coffee and that accomplishes the reverse for tea lovers
   b. An arrangement in which watchmakers are assigned to ditch digging and unskilled laborers to watch repairing
   c. An arrangement that produces a large quantity of trucks and few cars, assuming both cost about the same to produce and to run but that most people in the community prefer cars to trucks
4. In reality, which of the following circumstances might give rise to each of the preceding problem situations?
   a. Regulation of output quantities by a government
   b. Rationing of commodities
   c. Assignment of soldiers to different jobs in an army
5. In a free market, how will the price mechanism deal with each of the inefficiencies described in Question 3?

Appendix
The Invisible Hand in the Distribution of Goods and in Production Planning

On pages 594–595 of this chapter we offered a glimpse of economists' technical analysis of the workings of the invisible hand. We showed how the market automatically handles the problem of efficiency in the first of the three tasks of resource allocation: the selection of outputs (for example, how much of the economy's inputs should be used to produce beef rather than lamb or some other commodities). We described the rule that must be followed for a set of outputs to be efficient, and showed also how a free market can induce people to act in a way that satisfies that rule, which in turn leads to efficiency in output selection.

In this appendix we complete the story, examining how the price mechanism handles the two other tasks of resource allocation: the distribution of goods among consumers and the planning of production.

EFFICIENT DISTRIBUTION OF COMMODITIES: WHO GETS WHAT?

We turn first to the way in which the price system deals with the second of its allocative tasks: the distribution of the economy's different products among its many consumers. The analysis turns out to be quite similar to our previous analysis of efficient output selection.

While issues of distribution among consumers often hinge entirely on value judgments, there is much that can be said purely on grounds of efficiency. For example, consumers'

desires are not being served efficiently if large quantities of buttermilk are given to someone whose preference is whiskey, while gallons of whiskey are assigned to a teetotaler. Deciding how much of which commodity goes to whom is a matter that requires delicate calculation. It is one that causes very great difficulties for planners who must ration goods during wartime. They generally end up utilizing a crude egalitarianism: the same amount of butter to everyone, the same amount of coffee to everyone, and so on. This may be justified, to paraphrase the statement of a high official in another country, by an "unwillingness to pander to acquired tastes," but it is easy to see that such fixed rations are unlikely to produce an efficient result.

Suppose the official ration is 1 pound of lamb and 1 pound of beef per week; and consider two individuals, Mr. Steaker and Ms. Chop. Steaker loves lots of beef and very little lamb, and the opposite is true of Chop. Obviously, without increasing their total ration of 2 pounds of beef and 2 pounds of lamb, it is possible to make both people better off if Mr. Steaker trades some of his lamb ration to Ms. Chop in return for some beef. The initial rations were not optimal because they left room for trades that yield *mutual* gains.

It is easy enough to think of allocations of commodities among consumers that are *inefficient*—simply assign to each person only what he does not like. But how does one define an allocation that *is* efficient? After all, there are many of us whose preferences have much in common. If two individuals both like beef and lamb, how shall the available amounts of the two commodities be divided between them?

We will now show that, as in the analysis of efficient output quantities, there is a simple rule that must be satisfied by *any* efficient distribution of products among consumers. Consider any two commodities in the economy, such as beef and lamb, and any two consumers, Mr. Steaker and Ms. Chop, each of whom likes to eat some of each type of meat (though Steaker wants most of his diet to be made up of beef and the reverse is true of Chop). Then:

The basic rule for the efficient distribution of beef between Steaker and Chop is that

$$\frac{\text{Steaker's } MU \text{ of beef}}{\text{Steaker's } MU \text{ of lamb}} = \frac{\text{Chop's } MU \text{ of beef}}{\text{Chop's } MU \text{ of lamb}}$$

Exactly the same sort of equation must be satisfied for every other pair of individuals, and for every other pair of products.

Why is this equation of the ratios of the marginal utilities of the two people required for efficiency? Recall that a distribution of commodities among consumers can be efficient only if it has taken advantage of every potential gain from trade. That is, if two people can trade in a way that makes them *both* better off, then the distribution cannot be efficient.

Suppose that Mr. Steaker's ratio of the marginal utility (*MU*) of beef to the *MU* of lamb is 2 to 1. This means that 1 additional pound of beef is worth as much to him as 2 additional pounds of lamb. Therefore, he is willing to give up as much as 2 pounds of lamb in order to acquire an additional pound of beef. Next, suppose that Ms. Chop's ratio of the *MU* of beef to the *MU* of lamb is different from this. Perhaps it is 1, that is, she is willing to trade only 1 pound of beef for an additional pound of lamb.

In such a case a mutually profitable exchange can be arranged. For example, let

Steaker give Chop $1\frac{1}{2}$ pounds of lamb in exchange for a pound of beef. Then both will come out ahead. Mr. Steaker is happy because he has paid $\frac{1}{2}$ pound less in lamb than the beef is worth to him. And Chop is delighted to get $\frac{1}{2}$ pound more lamb than, in her estimation, the beef she gave up is worth. The initial position in which the two ratios were unequal was therefore not optimal because *without any increase in the total amounts of beef and lamb available to them, both could be made better off.*

The lesson of this example is quite general:

Any time that two persons have unequal *MU* ratios for any two commodities, their welfare can always be increased by a simple exchange of commodities. Efficiency requires any two individuals to have the same *MU* ratios for any pair of goods, such as beef and lamb.

Unfortunately, without the price system, many opportunities for such profitable swaps might never take place. Steaker and Chop may not know each other (or they might not have been formally introduced), but as we will see, the price system does the job for them.

It will again be remembered from our discussion of consumer choice in Chapter 19 that it pays any consumer to buy any commodity up to the point where the good's money marginal utility is just equal to its price. In other words, in equilibrium

$$\begin{aligned}
\text{Mr. Steaker's } MU \text{ of beef} \\
= \text{Price of beef} \\
= \text{Ms. Chop's } MU \text{ of beef}
\end{aligned}$$

Recall that this is so because, if, say, Mr. Steaker's *MU* of beef is greater than the price of beef, he can improve his lot by exchanging more of his money for beef. And the reverse will be true if Steaker's *MU* of beef falls short of the price of beef.

For the same reason, since the price of lamb is the same to both individuals, each will choose voluntarily to buy quantities of lamb at which

> Mr. Steaker's *MU* of lamb
> = Price of lamb
> = Ms. Chop's *MU* of lamb

If we divide this equation into the similar equation for beef, we see that their independent decisions *must* satisfy our test equation for efficient distribution of beef and lamb between them:

$$\frac{\text{Steaker's } MU \text{ of beef}}{\text{Steaker's } MU \text{ of lamb}} = \frac{\text{Chop's } MU \text{ of beef}}{\text{Chop's } MU \text{ of lamb}}$$

as long as both consumers face the same prices for lamb and beef.

Given any prices for the two commodities, each purchaser, acting only in accord with his own preferences and with no necessary consideration of the effects on the other person, will automatically carry out the purchase behavior that efficiently serves the mutual interests of both purchasers.

This time, where have we sneaked the rabbit into our price system argument? The answer is that the market acts as a middleman between any pair of consumers. Given the prices offered by the market, each consumer will use his or her dollars in such a way as to use up all opportunities for gains from trade *with the market* at the prices at which the goods are offered. Mr. Steaker and Ms. Chop each take advantage of every such opportunity for gains from trade with the market, and in the process they automatically take advantage of every opportunity for advantageous trades between themselves.

Notice that all that is required for the process to work is that the market offer the same prices, *whatever those prices may be*, to *all* consumers. For only then does each consumer trade with the market middleman on equal

terms, and so each ends up in the appropriate relationship to every other consumer.

EFFICIENT PRODUCTION PLANNING: ALLOCATION OF INPUTS

Finally, we note briefly that exactly the same analysis can be used to show how the price system can lead to an efficient allocation of inputs among the different production processes—the third of our allocative issues. For precisely the same reasons as in the case of the distribution of products among consumers:

Efficient use of two inputs (say, labor and fertilizer) between the production of two goods (say, wheat and corn) requires that

$$\frac{\begin{array}{c}\text{Marginal product } (MP)\\ \text{of fertilizer in wheat}\\ \text{production}\end{array}}{\begin{array}{c}MP \text{ of labor in wheat}\\ \text{production}\end{array}} = \frac{\begin{array}{c}MP \text{ of fertilizer in corn}\\ \text{production}\end{array}}{\begin{array}{c}MP \text{ of labor in corn}\\ \text{production}\end{array}}$$

By the same logic as before, it can be shown that if this equation does not hold, it is possible to produce more corn and more wheat using no more labor and fertilizer than before but merely by redistributing the quantities of the two inputs between the two crops.

Similarly, since maximum profits require each farmer to hire each input until the value of the input's marginal product equals its price, and since the price of a ton of a given type of fertilizer is the same for both wheat farmers and corn growers, it follows that we must have

> *MP* of fertilizer in wheat production
> = Price of fertilizer
> = *MP* of fertilizer in corn production

The same relationship must be true for labor inputs:

MP of labor in wheat production
= Price of labor
= *MP* of labor in corn production

Since prices of labor and fertilizer are assumed the same to both types of farmers, dividing the fertilizer equation by the labor equation we obtain

$$\frac{MP \text{ of fertilizer in wheat production}}{MP \text{ of labor in wheat production}} = \frac{\text{Price of fertilizer}}{\text{Price of labor}}$$

$$= \frac{MP \text{ of fertilizer in corn production}}{MP \text{ of labor in corn production}}$$

which is the optimality condition we are dealing with. Thus, we conclude that by making the independent choices that maximize their own profits, and without necessarily considering the effects on anyone else, each farmer (firm) will *automatically* act in a way that satisfies the efficiency condition for the allocation of inputs among different products.

CONCLUSION

Efficiency in the choice of output of goods (output selection) requires that *MU* = *MC* for each good and each individual in the economy. There are similar rules that must be satisfied for efficiency in the distribution of goods among different individuals and for the distribution of inputs among different production processes (production planning). With the aid of the analysis of consumer and producer choice in earlier chapters, this appendix and the discussion in the chapter have shown how competition and the market mechanism can lead to the satisfaction of all three of these efficiency conditions.

All of this suggests why competition has served as a norm for efficiency in resource allocation. Under a universal regime of competition, all sellers will charge the same price for a given good and all purchasers will pay the same price; no buyer or seller will be powerful enough to affect those prices, which are set by the forces of supply and demand; and prices will be equal to marginal costs. The economy will therefore be efficient.

31

Shortcomings of the Market Mechanism and Government Attempts to Remedy Them

Observation confirms both the accomplishments and the weaknesses of the free-market economy. We have achieved levels of output, productive efficiency, variety in available consumer goods, and general overall prosperity that is unprecedented in history. Yet, amid the outpouring of goods and services, we find areas of depressing poverty, cities choked with traffic and pollution, and educational institutions and artistic organizations in serious financial trouble. Our economy, although capable of yielding an overwhelming abundance of material wealth, seems far less capable of eradicating social ills and controlling environmental damage.

In this chapter, we will examine the reasons for its failings in these areas and indicate specifically why the price system *by itself* may be incapable of dealing with them. Some of the issues that arise here are of such importance that they will be treated separately and in some detail in subsequent chapters.

While it may not be possible to construct an exhaustive list, we can identify seven major shortcomings of which the market system has been accused:

1. Inequality in income distribution
2. Instability in the economy as a whole and within particular sectors
3. Rising cost of public services
4. Monopolistic elements
5. Economic activities that incidentally harm (or benefit) others (these are called externalities)
6. Inadequate provision of public goods
7. Poor allocation between present and future

The first two items in this list have already been discussed in Chapter 29 and in Chapters 6 to 16. And in Chapter 35, on the problems of the cities, we will examine in detail the third item—the rising cost of public services. Therefore, in this chapter we need only mention these three problems in passing, to reemphasize their importance. We will, however, discuss in some detail the other four issues—monopolies, externalities, inadequate provision of public goods, and poor allocation between present and future—because they relate so directly to prices and resource allocation. In each case, we will see how the efficiency of the price mechanism is compromised.

THREE MAJOR PROBLEMS THAT BESET THE MARKET MECHANISM

Let us begin by mentioning briefly the problems of instability, inequality, and the cost disease of public services.

To appreciate the significance of the problem of instability, we remind the reader that almost a third of this book is devoted to this topic. With the market economy's propensity, from time to time, to bring inflations, recessions, and unemployment, one need hardly be reminded how serious this problem can be, both in terms of its devastating effects upon the individuals most heavily affected and the resulting losses in output and well-being to the community as a

whole. The point to be reemphasized is that while many people believe that the market mechanism can take care of these problems by itself in the *long run,* it certainly is not able to do so in the *short run.* It is true that recessions have rarely lasted longer than a few years, even when governments have done nothing about them; but the free market has shown an inability to avoid these periods of widespread misery.

A second thing the free market has not done is to eliminate the gap that separates the rich and the poor. By providing plentiful rewards to those who are successful and offering little to those who are not, it has, in fact, actually contributed to differences in wealth. Moreover, the market responds to the desires of the wealthy more effectively than it does to the demands of the poor, because the wealthy have more money with which to back up their desires. In other words, to those who have a strong desire to reduce inequality in wealth, in income, and in the enjoyment of goods and services, the workings of the market system in this area are likely to seem less than ideal.

A third problem that characterizes the workings of the market is the progressive deterioration in the quality of certain services, despite the persistent and substantial rise in their costs compared with the costs of everything else in the economy. City dwellers do not have to be told that standards of cleanliness and sanitation have been deteriorating even where services are provided by private firms. Analogous problems beset such related services as the repair of automobiles and the education system. Yet the costs of these services, both public and private, have been rising far faster than have the prices of other products of the economy. In fact, about every 15 years their prices have doubled compared with the prices of other commodities. That is, for these items the market system seems to give less and less, while charging more and more. This disturbing phenomenon has been called the cost disease of the public services. Its causes and its implications for the future welfare of society will be discussed in

Chapter 35 on the problems of the city and again in the final chapter of the book on the economic problems of the future.

To understand the remaining problems more clearly, we offer next a brief review of the issue of efficient resource allocation, the subject of the previous chapter. This review is formulated in a way that will make it easier to apply this analysis to the topics discussed in the rest of the chapter.

THE BASIC PROBLEM OF RESOURCE ALLOCATION: AN ALTERNATIVE INTERPRETATION

On first thought, it may seem that more is always better. That is, if we double the production of handkerchiefs or pinball machines or shoes, society will be better off. But careful thinking tells us that this is not necessarily true. Outputs are not created by magic—out of thin air. They are produced from the available supply of labor, fuel, raw materials, and machinery. And if we use those inputs to produce more handkerchiefs, we must take them away from the production of shirts or of linen or of some other products. We cannot have more of everything, because there simply are not enough resources to go around. So, to decide whether the increased production of handkerchiefs is really a good thing, we must compare the utility of that increase with the loss in utility caused by having to produce, for instance, less hospital linen. The increased output will be a good thing if society considers the increased handkerchief supply to be more valuable than the forgone hospital linen. But the increased handkerchief output will be a bad thing for society if the opposite is true.

Here it is worth repeating the definition of the concept of opportunity cost, which, you will recall, is another of the 12 Ideas for Beyond the Final Exam. The *opportunity cost* of an increase in the output of some product is the value of the other goods and services that must be forgone when inputs (resources) are taken away from their production in order to increase the output of the product in question.

In our example, the opportunity cost of the increased handkerchief output is the value of the decrease in output of hospital linen that results when resources are reallocated from the latter to the former. Our discussion then leads us to the following principle:

An increase in some output involves a *misallocation* of resources if the utility of that increased output is less than its opportunity cost.

This, in sum, is the meaning of the concept of misallocation of resources. To emphasize this concept further, we repeat here the graph that appeared in Chapter 3, where this topic was first discussed Curve *ABC* in Figure 31–1, called the production opportunity frontier, shows the different combinations of handkerchiefs and hospital linens the economy can produce by reallocating a given set of resources between the production of the two goods. We can produce lots of handkerchiefs and little linen, or we can do the reverse, or we can select something in between—a moderate output of both goods. For example, in Figure 31–1, point *A* amounts to an allocation of all the resources to handkerchief production so that 100 million of these items are produced and no hospital linens are produced. Point *C* represents the reverse situation, with all resources allocated to hospital linens and none to handkerchiefs. Point *B* represents an intermediate allocation, resulting in the production of 8 million yards of linen and 60 million handkerchiefs.

Suppose now that point *B* represents the optimal resource allocation—that combination of outputs that best satisfies the wants of society among all the points on curve *ABC*—that is, among all the output combinations the economy is capable of producing with its available resources. Two questions are pertinent to our discussion of the price system:

1. What prices will get the economy to produce this most-preferred output combination? Or, what prices will yield an *efficient* allocation of resources?
2. How can the wrong set of prices lead to a misallocation of resources?

The first of these questions was discussed in the previous chapter. There we saw that:

In general, an efficient allocation of resources requires each product's price to equal its marginal cost.

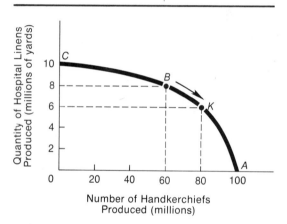

FIGURE 31–1

THE ECONOMY'S PRODUCTION OPPORTUNITY FRONTIER FOR THE PRODUCTION OF TWO GOODS
This graph shows all combinations of outputs of the two goods that the resources available to the economy enable it to produce. If B is the most desired (efficient) output combination among those that are possible, it will correspond to a market equilibrium in which each good's price is equal to its marginal cost. If the price of linen is above its marginal cost and the price of a handkerchief below its marginal cost, then linen output will be inefficiently small and handkerchief output inefficiently large (point K).

The reasoning in brief is that marginal cost measures the value (opportunity cost) of the resources needed to meet an additional unit of demand by a consumer. Thus, if the consumer buys one more handkerchief, that handkerchief's marginal cost is the value of the increased use of resources in handkerchief production needed to supply that item. If price equals marginal cost, it follows that the amount the consumer must pay for the item is equal to the value of the resources needed to meet her demand. Suppose the consumer buys the good if and only if it is worth the *money* she must pay for it. Then, if price equals marginal cost it must also be worth the *resources* required to produce it. In other words, if prices are determined by the marginal cost of the resources, the consumer who uses her money to maximize the utility she derives from her purchases also, automatically and without being aware of it, maximizes the utility she derives from the use of society's resources. That, roughly speaking, is the connection between marginal-cost pricing and efficient resource allocation. In principle, setting prices equal to marginal costs will induce consumers to demand the quantities of linens and handkerchiefs that move the economy to point B in Figure 31–1, which we assumed to be the point of efficient resource allocation.

This chapter is devoted mainly to the second question: How can the "wrong" prices cause a misallocation of resources? The answer to this question is not too difficult. The law of demand tells us that a rise in the price of a commodity normally will reduce the quantity demanded, and the opposite is true of a fall in price. Suppose then, for illustration, that the price of a handkerchief is below its marginal cost. This will increase the demand for handkerchiefs above the 60 million that would be purchased at point B on the curve. Similarly, suppose the price of linen is above its marginal cost. This would reduce its demand from the 8 million yards demanded at point B. Thus, the economy would be moved from point B to a point such as K, which provides more handkerchiefs and fewer linens than those most preferred by the community. By setting the "wrong" prices, the market would be inducing consumers to behave in a way that reduces the efficiency of the use of the economy's resources, for those resources would yield less than the maximum amount of consumer satisfaction. In sum:

If the price of a commodity is above its marginal cost, the economy will tend to produce less of that item than maximizes consumer benefits. The opposite will occur if an item's price is below its marginal cost.

MONOPOLY AND RESOURCE ALLOCATION

When we compared the price and output of a monopoly with a competitive industry in Chapter 23, we concluded, with some reservations, that there is a tendency for a monopoly industry to produce less output and to charge higher prices than its competitive counterpart. This is, of course, consistent with the widely held view that monopolies, if not regulated by government, tend to restrict output in order to force buyers to pay higher prices for their products.

This already suggests that unregulated monopoly has some tendency to cause a misallocation of resources. One way of looking at the matter, as suggested by the previous chapter, is that if there is some tendency for competitive industries to produce the outputs required for an efficient resource allocation, then a monopoly must produce less than the efficient amount. Thus, we should suspect that an undesirably small proportion of society's resources will end up being used in the production of the goods sold by monopolists and, consequently, too large a share of those resources will go to the rest of the economy.

We can now see more precisely why this is so. We know from our analysis of the monopoly

firm that a monopoly product's price will be above its marginal cost. This is so because at equilibrium the product's marginal revenue will equal its marginal cost, and its price will be higher than its marginal revenue, as shown in Figure 31–2. (These concepts were described in Chapter 20.)

But we saw in the previous section that if a product's price is greater than its marginal cost, an inefficiently small quantity of that product will be bought relative to other outputs. Therefore, since monopoly price is above marginal cost, the result will indeed be a misallocation of resources. From the point of view of economic efficiency, too small an amount of the economy's inputs will be used in turning out products of the monopoly industry, and hence too much will go to other products.

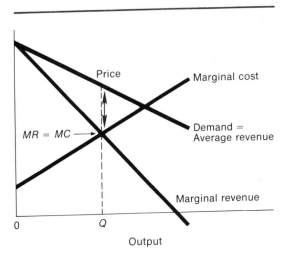

FIGURE 31–2

EQUILIBRIUM OF THE MONOPOLY FIRM, WITH PRICE GENERALLY ABOVE MARGINAL COST

Since the firm's demand curve has a negative slope, price must be above marginal revenue. Therefore, at equilibrium, where marginal revenue equals marginal cost, price must be above marginal cost.

In terms of the production opportunity frontier shown in Figure 31–1, suppose point *B* represents the optimal allocation of resources between handkerchiefs and hospital linens. Then, if linens are produced by a monopoly but handkerchiefs are not, the economy will tend to end up with an output combination like that represented by point *K*. Too few linens and too many handkerchiefs will be produced for maximal consumer satisfaction. This is all because the monopolist charges too high a price—a price greater than marginal cost—which is why monopolies can cause a misallocation of resources.

Because prices in an unregulated monopoly will generally be above marginal cost, the monopoly will tend to produce an inefficiently small output. Resources generally will be misallocated, with too small a proportion of society's inputs going to the monopoly industry and too high a proportion going elsewhere.

This is one of the reasons why many economists advocate government control of monopoly, either by direct regulation (as described in Chapter 26) or through antitrust policy (Chapter 25).

EXTERNALITIES

We come now to the second source of resource misallocation under the market system: one of the least obvious yet one of the most consequential imperfections in the workings of the price system.

Many economic activities provide incidental benefits to others for whom they are not specifically intended. Similarly, there are activities that indiscriminately impose costs on others. A homeowner who plants a beautiful garden in front of her house, incidentally and perhaps unintentionally provides pleasure to her neighbors and to those who pass by, from whom she receives no payment. We say then that her activity generates a beneficial externality. In the same way, the operator of a motorcycle repair garage, from which all sorts of noise besieges the neighborhood and for which he pays no compensation to others, is said to produce a detrimental externality. Pollution constitutes the classic illustration of a detrimental externality.

DEFINITION
An activity is said to generate beneficial or detrimental *externalities* if that activity causes incidental benefits or damages to others, and no corresponding compensation is provided to or paid by those who generate the externality.

To see why the presence of externalities creates difficulties for the price system's allocation of resources, we need only recall the argument that the system achieves efficiency by rewarding producers who serve consumers well—that is, at as low a cost as possible. This argument breaks down, however, as soon as some of the costs and benefits of their activities are left out of the profit calculation. When a firm pollutes a river, it uses up some of society's resources as effectively as when it burns some coal. However, if it pays for coal but not for the use of water, it is natural for management to be economical in its use of the former and wasteful in its use of the latter. Similarly, the firm that provides benefits to others for which it receives no payment is unlikely to be generous in allocating resources to the activity, no matter how socially desirable it may be.

In an important sense, the source of the difficulty is to be found in the definition of "property rights." Coal mines are *private property*, and so the owners will not let anyone take away coal from them without paying for it. Thus, because coal is valuable, it will not be used wastefully. But waterways are not private property. Since they belong to everyone in general, they belong to no one in particular. They therefore can be used at no money cost as dumping grounds for wastes by anyone who chooses to do so. No one is charged for the use of the oxygen in a public waterway; and since its price is zero, that oxygen will be used heavily and wastefully. That is the problem to which detrimental externalities lead. Later in this chapter we will analyze the nature of this problem more carefully, but first we pause to evaluate its special significance.

The Universality of Externalities

Externalities occur throughout the economy. Many of the economy's widespread externalities are beneficial. A factory that hires unskilled or semiskilled laborers gives them on-the-job training and provides the external benefit of better workers to future employers. Benefits to others are also generated by firms whose research produces useful but unpatentable results, or even patentable results that can be imitated by others to some degree. In some less developed countries there is a difficulty in getting growth processes started. And many observers attribute this difficulty, at least in part, to the countries' lack of beneficial externalities, which enable each firm in the economy to operate more efficiently because of the presence of other firms.

Detrimental externalities are at least as widespread. The emission of air and water pollutants by factories, cars, and airplanes is the source of some of our most pressing environmental problems. The abandonment of a building that causes the quality of its neighborhood to deteriorate is the source of serious externalities for the urban environment.

Externalities lie at the heart of some of society's most pressing problems: the problems of the cities, the environment, research policy, and a variety of other critical issues. For this reason, the concept of externalities is one of our 12 Ideas for Beyond the Final Exam, and you will find that the subject recurs again and again in this book as we discuss some of these problems in greater detail.

Externalities and Inefficient Choice of Output Levels

In discussing externalities and their relationship to marginal cost, it is helpful to distinguish between social and private marginal cost. We define marginal social cost (MSC) as the sum of two components: (1) the marginal private cost (MPC), that is, the share of the marginal cost caused by an activity that is paid for by the persons who are carrying out that activity; and (2) the *incidental cost* that is borne by others. If increased output by a firm increases the smoke it emits, then, in addition to its direct private costs as recorded in the company accounts, expansion of its production imposes added costs on others in the form of increased laundry bills, medical expenditures, outlays for air conditioning and electricity, as well as the unpleasantness of living in a cloud of noxious fumes. These must all be included in the firm's marginal *social* cost.

Using these concepts, we can now see precisely why an externality has socially undesirable effects on the allocation of resources. Where the firm's activities generate detrimental externalities, its marginal social cost, by definition, will be greater than its marginal private cost. In symbols, $MSC > MPC$. Since, in equilibrium, that firm will choose an output for which its marginal benefits are equal to its marginal private cost ($MB = MPC$), it follows that $MB = MPC < MSC$. That is, marginal benefits are smaller than marginal social costs. The economy would then necessarily benefit if output of that product were reduced. For example, if marginal benefits were $57 while marginal social costs were $67, a unit reduction of output would yield a *net* gain to society of $10. We conclude that:

Where the firm's activity causes detrimental externalities, free markets will leave us in a situation where marginal benefits are less than marginal social costs. Smaller outputs than those that maximize profits will be socially desirable.

We have already indicated why this is so. Private enterprise has no motivation to take into account costs that it causes to others but for which it does not have to pay. So goods that cause such externalities will be produced in undesirably large amounts by private firms.

For precisely analogous reasons:

Where the firm's activity generates beneficial externalities, free markets will produce too little output. Society would be better off with larger output levels.

These principles can be illustrated with the aid of Figure 31–3. This diagram repeats the two basic curves needed for the analysis of the

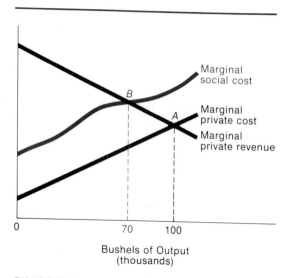

Marginal
social cost

B

A

Marginal
private cost

Marginal
private revenue

0   70   100

Bushels of Output
(thousands)

FIGURE 31–3

EQUILIBRIUM OF A FIRM WHOSE OUTPUT
PRODUCES DETRIMENTAL EXTERNALITIES
(POLLUTION)

The firm's profit-maximizing output, at which its private marginal cost and its private marginal revenue are equal, is 100,000 bushels. But if the firm paid all the social costs of its output instead of shifting some of them to others, its marginal cost curve would be the curve labeled "marginal social cost." Then it would pay the firm to reduce its output to 70,00 bushels, thereby reducing the pollution it causes.

equilibrium of the firm: a marginal revenue curve and a marginal cost curve (see Chapter 20). These represent *private* costs and revenues, that is, the costs and revenues actually accruing to a particular firm (in this case, a particular farmer). The farm's maximum profit is attained with 100,000 bushels of output corresponding to the intersection between marginal cost and marginal revenue (point A).

Now suppose that the farmer's runoff of fertilizer pollutes a nearby waterway, so that his production creates a detrimental externality whose cost the farmer does not himself pay. Then marginal social cost must be higher than marginal private cost. That is, the marginal social cost curve will lie above the marginal private cost curve, as in the diagram.

Notice that if instead of being able to impose the external costs on others the farmer were forced to pay them himself, his own private marginal cost curve would correspond to the higher of the two curves shown. His output of the polluting commodity would then fall to 70,000 bushels, corresponding to point B, the intersection between the marginal revenue curve and the marginal *social* cost curve. But because the farmer does not in fact pay for the pollution damage his output causes, he produces an output (100,000 bushels) that is larger than the output he would produce if the cost he imposed on the community were all borne by himself (70,000 bushels).

The same sort of diagram can be used to show that the opposite relationship will hold when the firm's activity produces beneficial externalities. The firm will produce less of its beneficial output than it would if it were rewarded fully for the benefits that its activities yield. But these results can perhaps be seen more clearly with the help of the production opportunity frontier diagram similar to that in Figure 31–1. In Figure 31–4 we see the opportunity locus for two industries: electricity generation, which causes air pollution (a detrimental externality), and tulip growing, which makes the area more attractive (a beneficial externality).

We have just seen that detrimental externalities make marginal social cost greater than marginal private cost. Hence, if the electric company charges a price equal to its own marginal (private) cost, that price will be less than the true marginal (social) cost. Similarly, in tulip growing, a price equal to marginal private cost will be above the true marginal cost to society.

We saw earlier in the chapter that an industry that charges a price above marginal cost will cut down demand through this high price, and so it will produce an output too small for an efficient allocation of resources. The opposite will be true for an industry whose price is below marginal social cost.

In terms of Figure 31–4, suppose point B

again represents the efficient allocation of resources, involving the production of E kilowatt hours of electricity and T dozen tulips. Because the electric company charges a price below marginal social cost, it will produce more than E kilowatt hours of electricity. Similarly, because tulip growers charge a price above marginal social cost, they will produce less than T dozen tulips. The economy will end up with the resource allocation represented by point K rather than that represented by point B. We will have too much smoky electricity production and too little attractive tulip growing.

An industry that generates detrimental externalities will have a marginal social cost higher than its marginal private cost. If its price is equal to its own marginal private cost, it will therefore be below the true marginal cost to society. The market mechanism thereby tends to encourage inefficiently large outputs of products that cause detrimental externalities. The opposite is true of products that cause beneficial externalities—private industry will provide inefficiently small quantities of these benefits.

In Chapters 34 and 35 we will see what an important influence externalities have on the environment and on the quality of life in our society.

Government Policy and Externalities

Because of this flaw in the market system, governments have found it appropriate to support activities that are felt to generate external benefits and to restrict those that bring external costs. Education is subsidized not only because it helps increase equal opportunity for all citizens but also because it is felt to generate beneficial externalities. For example, educated people, on the average, commit fewer crimes than uneducated people, so the more we educate people, the less we will need to spend on crime prevention. Also, academic research that has been provided partly as a byproduct of the

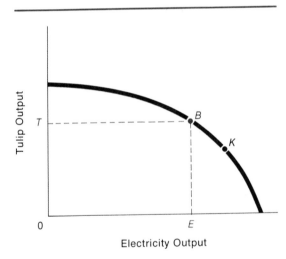

FIGURE 31–4

EXTERNALITIES, MARKET EQUILIBRIUM, AND EFFICIENT RESOURCE ALLOCATION
Because electricity producers emit smoke (a detrimental externality), they do not bear the true marginal social cost of their output. So electricity price will be below marginal social cost, and electricity output will be inefficiently large (point K, not point B). The opposite is true of tulip production. Because they generate beneficial externalities, tulips will be priced above social marginal cost, and in the market equilibrium, tulip output will be inefficiently small.

educational system often benefits the entire population. We have consequently come to believe that if education were offered only by profit-making institutions, the output of these beneficial services would be provided at less than the optimal level.

Similarly, governments have recently begun to impose fines on companies that contribute heavily to air and water pollution as a means of reducing the volume of smoke-producing activity. This approach to policy is in fact suggested by the economists' standard analysis of the effects of externalities upon resource allocation.

The basic problem, as we have seen, is that in the presence of externalities, the price system fails in its role as an allocator of resources. Resources are used for which no price is charged, and benefits are offered without financial compensation. As a result, with detrimental externalities, for example, the price does not cover the entire social marginal cost. It has therefore been suggested that:

One effective way to deal with externalities is through the use of taxes and subsidies.

For example, firms that generate beneficial externalities should be given a subsidy per unit of their output equal to the difference between their marginal social costs and their marginal private costs. Similarly, those that generate detrimental externalities should be taxed on analogous terms, so that the firm that creates them will have to pay the entire marginal cost it imposes on society. In terms of Figure 31–3, after paying the tax, the firm's marginal private cost curve will be shifted up until it coincides with its marginal social cost curve, and price can once again be set in a manner consistent with an efficient resource allocation.

While there is much to be said for this approach in principle, it often is not easy to implement in practice. Social costs are rarely easy to estimate, partly because they are so widely diffused through the community (everyone in the city is affected by pollution) and partly because

many of the costs and benefits (effects on health, unpleasantness of living in smog) are not readily assessed in monetary terms. As noted, the pros and cons of this approach and the alternative policies available for the control of externalities will be discussed in greater detail in Chapter 34 on environmental problems.

PUBLIC GOODS

Another area in which the market may fail to perform adequately is in the provision of public goods. It is easiest to explain what is meant by a public good by contrasting it with the sort of commodity called a private good, which is at the opposite end of the spectrum.

Private goods are characterized by two important attributes. One is called excludability, meaning that anyone who does not pay for the good can be excluded from enjoying its benefits. If you do not buy a ticket, you are excluded from the ball game. If you do not pay for an electric guitar, the storekeeper will not give it to you. But some goods or services are such that, if they are provided to anyone, they automatically become available to many other persons, whom it is difficult, if not impossible, to exclude from the benefits. If a street is cleared of snow, everyone who uses the street benefits, regardless of who paid for the snowplow. If a country provides a strong military establishment, everyone receives its protection, even persons who do not happen to want it. Or, compare two services: the cleaning of an office and the cleaning of the atmosphere in a city. Obviously, people who do not pay can be excluded from the first service but not from the second.

The other property that characterizes private goods but not public goods is depletability. If you eat a steak or use up a gallon of gasoline, there is so much less beef or fuel in the world available for others to use. Your consumption depletes the supply available for other people, either temporarily or permanently. But a pure public good is like the legendary widow's jar of oil, which always remains full no matter how many people use it. Once the snow has been removed from a street, the improved driving conditions are available to every driver who uses that street, whether 10 or 1000 cars pass that way. One passing car does not make the road less snow-free for another. The same is true of the spraying of swamps near a town to kill disease-bearing mosquitoes. The cost of the spraying is the same whether the town contains 10,000 or 20,000 persons. A resident of the town who benefits from this service does not deplete its advantages to others.

DEFINITION

A *public good* is defined as any commodity or service whose benefits are not *depleted* by an additional user and for which it is generally difficult or impossible to *exclude* people from its benefits, even if they are unwilling to pay for it.

Notice two important implications of this definition. First, since nonpaying users cannot be excluded from enjoying a public good, suppliers of such goods will find it *difficult or impossible to collect fees* proportionate to the benefits they provide. This is the so-called "free-rider" problem. How many people, for example, will *voluntarily* cough up $2000 a year to support our national defense establishment? Yet this is roughly what it costs, per American family. Services like national defense and public health, where excludability is simply impossible, *cannot* be provided by private enterprise because no one will pay for what he can get free. Since private firms are not in the business of giving services away, the supply of nonexcludable public goods must be left to government authorities and nonprofit institutions.

The second thing we notice is that, since the supply of a public good is not depleted by an additional user, *the marginal cost of serving an additional user is zero*. With zero marginal cost, the basic principles of optimal resource allocation call for provision of public goods and

services to anyone who wants them *at no charge*. In a word, not only is it often *impossible* to charge a market price for a public good, it is often *undesirable* as well. Any nonzero price would discourage some users from enjoying the public good; but this would be inefficient since one more person's enjoyment of the good costs society nothing. To summarize:

It is usually *not possible* to charge a price for a pure public good because people cannot be excluded from enjoying its benefits. It may also be *undesirable* to charge any price for it because that would discourage people from using it even though using it does *not deplete* its supply. For both these reasons we find government supplying many public goods.

Because no price can be charged for nonexcludable public goods, free enterprise, left to its own devices, will not be able to supply them, even if they are considered vital for the functioning of society. Without government intervention, these services simply would not be provided. Referring back to our example in Figure 31–1, if hospital linens were a public good and their production were left to private enterprise, the economy would end up at point A on the graph, with zero production of hospital linens and far more output of handkerchiefs than is called for by efficient allocation (point B).

Usually, communities have not been content to let that happen, and today a quite substantial proportion of government expenditure, indeed the bulk of municipal budgets, is devoted to the financing of public goods or, more generally, to services believed to generate substantial external benefits. National defense, public health, police and fire protection, and research are among the services provided by governments because they offer beneficial externalities or because they have characteristics of public goods.

The latest available (1975) figures show 7.0 percent of state and local expenditures going to health and hospitals and 33 percent, by far the largest single item on the budget, going to education. In 1977, the federal government spent $100.1 billion on defense; $21.1 billion on education, training, employment, and social services; $39.3 billion on health programs; and $138.1 billion on social security, together making up more than half the total federal budget. (See Figure 31–5.)

There are, however, many services financed

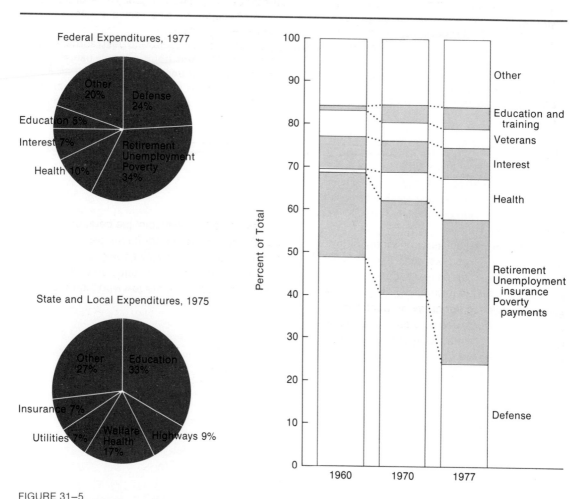

FIGURE 31–5

THE ALLOCATION OF GOVERNMENT EXPENDITURES

This chapter discusses *why* government spends money. These graphs show how that money is spent. We see that the federal government spends mostly on assistance to retirees, the poor, and the unemployed (34 percent), and national defense (24 percent). Many people will be surprised to learn how steadily and sharply the *share* of national defense has been falling—from about 50 percent of the total federal budget in 1960 to about 25 percent in 1977. State and local governments devoted half their expenditure to education (33 percent) and welfare and health (17 percent).

out of public budgets in the United States (and elsewhere) that are not *public goods,* as the economist uses the term. Many government-provided goods and services are both deplet-able and excludable. Yet, for reasons other than those we have just discussed, their provision is delegated to the public sector. Postal service is a good example; transportation services of all kinds (including highways) are probably another.

ALLOCATION OF RESOURCES BETWEEN PRESENT AND FUTURE

In principle, the market mechanism should be as efficient in allocating resources between present and future uses as it is in allocating resources among different outputs at any one time. If future demands for a particular commodity, say computers for the home, are expected to be higher than they are today, it will pay manufacturers to plan now to build the necessary plant and equipment so they will be ready to turn out the computers when the expanded market materializes. More resources are thereby allocated to future consumption, because more of today's resources will have to be devoted to the creation of producers' goods.

The allocation of resources between different time periods can be analyzed with the aid of an opportunity cost diagram just like Figure 31–1. Suppose the issue is how much labor and capital to devote to producing goods that will be consumed almost at once and how much will be devoted to construction of facto-ries that will produce output in the future. Then, instead of handkerchiefs and linens, the graph will show consumer goods and number of facto-ries on its axes, but otherwise it will be exactly the same as Figure 31–1, and the analyses of resource allocation on the two graphs will be identical. Such a graph appears here as Figure 31–6.

The profit motive directs the flow of

resources between one time period and another in the same way that it handles their allocation among different industries in a given period. The profit motive directs resources to those products *and those time periods* in which an abundance of demand promises to make output most profitable. Yet, despite what has just been said, a number of observers have questioned whether the market mechanism does a very effective job in allocating resources among different time periods.

There is one feature of the process of allo-cation of resources among different time periods that does distinguish it from the process of allocation among industries. This is the

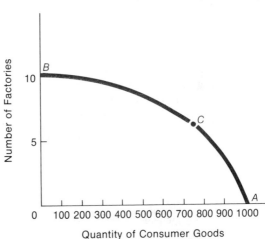

FIGURE 31–6

PRODUCTION OPPORTUNITY FRONTIER BETWEEN PRESENT AND FUTURE
With a given quantity of resources, the economy can produce 1 million cars for immediate use and build no factories for the future (point A). Alternatively, at the opposite extreme (point B), it can build 10 factories where products will become available in the future, while no cars are produced for current consumption. At points in between on the frontier, such as C, the economy will produce a combination of some cars for present consumption and some factories for future use.

special role that the *interest rate* plays in allocation among the periods. If the receipt of a given amount of money is delayed until some time in the future, the recipient suffers an *opportunity cost*—the interest that the money could have earned if it had been received earlier and invested. For example, if the rate of interest is 5 percent and you can persuade someone who owes you money to make a $100 payment one year earlier than originally planned, you come out $5 ahead. Put the other way, if the rate of interest is 5 percent and the payment of $100 is postponed one year, you lose the opportunity to earn $5. Thus, the rate of interest determines the size of the opportunity cost to the recipient who gets money at some date in the future instead of obtaining it at once.

As we learned in Chapter 8, when there is a reduction in interest rates, investment in plant and equipment will become more profitable because there will be a reduction in the opportunity cost of the time the investor must wait before that plant and equipment begins to turn out products and to bring in money.

Low interest rates will persuade people to invest more now, since the investments yield their benefits at some date in the future. Thus more resources will be devoted to the future if interest rates are low. Similarly, high interest rates make investment, with its yields in the future, less attractive. And so high interest rates will tend to increase the use of resources for current output at the expense of reduced future outputs.

Can the price system allocate resources among different time periods in the way consumers prefer? On the surface, it seems that the price system can perform this role. For the supply of and demand for loans, which determine the interest rate, reflects the public's preferences between present and future. Suppose, for example, that the public were suddenly to become more interested in future consumption (say, people were to want to save more for their old age). The supply of funds available for borrowing would increase, and interest rates would tend to fall, thus stimulating investment. This must add to the future output of goods at the expense of current consumption. Consequently, if consumers decide they want a higher proportion of the goods they consume during their lifetimes saved for the future, the market mechanism, acting through the interest rate, will tend automatically to adjust the flow of output in the same direction.

But many questions have been raised about the effectiveness, in practice, with which the market mechanism serves consumer welfare in the allocation of resources among different time periods. One reason economists are uneasy about this type of allocation process is that the rate of interest, besides serving as the price that controls that allocation, has also proved an extremely useful instrument for a variety of purposes in government policy. As we saw in Chapter 13, the interest rate can be helpful in dealing with such stabilization problems as inflationary pressure and unemployment. And in Chapter 37 we shall see that it plays an analogous role in responding to problems in international monetary relations. As a result, governments manipulate interest rates deliberately: They raise them when they fear an inflation or a balance of payments deficit, and reduce them when they fear a recession. In these decisions, policymakers do not seem to give much thought to the effects on the allocation of resources between present and future, and so one may well suspect that the resulting interest rates will not always be ideal from this point of view.

Second, it has been suggested that, even in the absence of government manipulation of the interest rate, the price system may still misallocate resources between present and future. In particular, some observers believe the market may devote too much to immediate consumption. One British economist, the late A. C. Pigou, argued simply that people suffer from "a defective telescopic faculty"—that they are too shortsighted to give adequate weight to the future. A "bird in hand" point of view leads people to care so much about the present that they sacrifice the legitimate interests of the future. As a result, too much goes into today's consumption and too little into investment for tomorrow. The most notorious exponent of the view that government should see to it that less is consumed and more is invested for the future was Joseph Stalin, who for many years kept consumption in the Soviet Union to the minimum level he could manage, devoting a correspondingly large proportion of his country's resources to investment (and to military uses).[1]

A third reason why the free market may not invest enough for the future is that an investment project, such as the construction of a new factory, is a much greater risk to the investor than to the community. Even if a factory falls into someone else's hands through bankruptcy, the factory will probably go on turning out goods, although the profits will not go to the investor or his heirs. Therefore, the loss to the community, if any, will be far less than the private loss to the individual investor. On such grounds, it is asserted, one may expect individual investment for the future to fall short of the amounts that are socially optimal, because investments too risky to be worthwhile to any group of private individuals may nevertheless be advantageous to society as a whole.

Fourth, our economy shortchanges the future when it despoils irreplaceable natural resources, exterminating whole species of plants and animals, flooding canyons, "developing" attractive areas into acres of potential slums, leaving mountains of slag near mines and quarries, and turning miles of land into foul wasteland. Worst of all, industry, military agencies, and individuals bequeath a ticking time bomb to the future when they leave behind lethal and slow-acting residues, such as nuclear wastes, which may remain dangerous for

[1]Soviet planning under Stalin is discussed in Chapter 40.

hundreds or even thousands of years and whose disposal containers are likely to fall apart long before their contents lose their lethal qualities. Such actions are essentially *irreversible.* If a factory or a school is not built this year, the deficiency in facilities provided for the future can be remedied by building them next year. But a canyon, once destroyed, can never be replaced. For this reason:

Many economists believe that irreversible decisions have a very special significance and must *not* be left entirely in the hands of private firms and individuals.

Fifth, and finally, governments in less developed countries often take the attitude that the free market will not allocate a sufficiently large quantity of resources to the future. As we will see in Chapter 38, these governments often adopt programs intended to increase the amounts their economies invest in productive facilities that will help produce goods and services for future generations. In the industrialized countries, it is not usually assumed that investment as a whole is systematically too low or too high, except during periods of recession or inflation. But, as we have just noted, particular types of investment do threaten the future by destroying irreplaceable natural resources. Consequently, environmental policy, which will be discussed in Chapter 34, seeks to control this type of investment to protect the future from harmful consequences of today's decisions.

Recently, however, several writers have questioned the general conclusion that the free market will not tend to invest enough for the future. They have pointed out that the prosperity of our economy has grown fairly steadily, from one decade to the next, and that there is every reason to expect future generations to have real incomes and an abundance of consumer goods far greater than our own. Pressures to increase investment for the future then may be like taking from the poor to give to the rich—a sort of backward Robin Hood redistribution of income.

EVALUATIVE COMMENTS

This chapter and the one preceding it have attempted together to offer a balanced evaluation of the price system. We come out, as in the nursery rhyme, concluding that where it is good, it is very, very good, but where it is bad, it is horrid. There seems to be nothing moderate about its performance. As a means of achieving efficiency in the production of ordinary consumer goods and of responding to changes in consumer preferences, it is unparalleled. It is, in fact, difficult to overstate the accomplishments of the market system in these areas. On the other hand, it has not proved able by itself to cope with income inequality, business fluctuations, or the consequences of monopoly. It has proved to be a very poor allocator of resources among outputs that generate external costs and external benefits, and it has shown itself completely incapable of arranging for the provision of public goods. Some of the most urgent problems that plague our society—the deterioration of services in the cities, the despoliation of our atmosphere, the social unrest attributable to poverty—can be ascribed in part to one or another of these shortcomings of the market system.

Most economists conclude from these observations that while the market mechanism is virtually irreplaceable, the public interest nevertheless requires considerable modifications in the way it works. Proposals designed to deal directly with the problems of poverty, monopoly, and intertemporal resource allocation abound in the economic literature. All of them call for the government to intervene in the economy, either by supplying directly those goods and services that, it is believed, private enterprise does not supply in adequate amounts, or by seeking to influence the workings of the economy more indirectly through regulation. Many of these programs have been discussed in earlier chapters; others will be encountered in chapters yet to come.

SUMMARY

1. There are at least seven major imperfections in the workings of the market mechanism: instability of economic activity (inflation and unemployment), inequality in income distribution, deteriorating quality and rising costs of services, monopolistic output restrictions, beneficial and detrimental externalities, inadequate provision of public goods, and finally, misallocation of resources between present and future.
2. Efficient resource allocation is basically a matter of balancing the benefits of producing more of one good against the benefits of devoting the required inputs to the production of some other good.
3. According to the law of demand, if the price of some good is above its marginal cost, less of it will tend to be demanded and produced than is socially efficient. The opposite will occur for a product whose price is below its marginal cost.
4. In an unregulated monopoly, producers generally will set prices above marginal cost. As a result, monopolies can cause a misallocation of resources, with too little of the community's inputs going to the manufacture of monopoly products, and too large an amount going elsewhere.
5. A detrimental externality occurs when an economic activity incidentally does harm to others; a beneficial externality occurs when an economic activity incidentally creates benefits for others.

6. When an activity causes a detrimental externality, the marginal social cost of the activity (including the harm it does to others) must be greater than the marginal private cost to those who carry on the activity. The opposite will be true when a beneficial externality occurs.

7. If manufacture of a product causes detrimental externalities, its price will generally not include all the marginal social cost it causes, since part of the cost will be borne by others. The opposite is true for beneficial externalities.

8. The market will therefore tend to overallocate resources to the production of goods that cause detrimental externalities and underallocate resources to the production of goods that create beneficial externalities. This is one of the 12 Ideas for Beyond the Final Exam.

9. A public good is defined by economists as a commodity that (like clean air) is not depleted by additional users and from whose use it is difficult to exclude anyone, even those who refuse to pay for it.

10. Free-enterprise firms generally will not produce a public good even if it is extremely useful to the community, because they cannot charge money for the use of the good.

11. Many observers feel that the market often shortchanges the future, particularly when it makes irreversible decisions that destroy natural resources.

CONCEPTS FOR REVIEW

Cost disease of the public services
Opportunity cost
Resource misallocation
Production opportunity frontier
Price above or below marginal cost
Externalities (detrimental and beneficial)

Marginal private cost and marginal social cost
Public goods
Private goods
Excludability
Depletability
Irreversible decisions

QUESTIONS FOR DISCUSSION

1. Specifically, what is the opportunity cost to society of a pair of shoes? Why may not the price of those shoes adequately represent that opportunity cost?

2. Suppose that because of a new disease that attacks coffee plants, far more labor and other inputs are required to raise a pound of coffee than before. How might that affect the efficient allocation of resources between tea and coffee? Why? How would the prices of coffee and tea react in a free market?

3. If you were given the job of regulating monopoly firms in the United States, what would you do to reduce the probability of misallocation of resources?

4. Give some examples of goods whose production causes detrimental externalities and some examples of goods that create beneficial externalities.

5. Give some examples of public goods, and discuss in each case why additional users do not deplete them and why it is difficult to exclude people from using them.
6. Think about the goods and services that your local government provides. Which of these are "public goods" as economists use the term?

32

Taxation and Resource Allocation

There is an old saying that nothing is certain but death and taxes. And it does indeed seem that the tax collector is everywhere. We have income and payroll taxes withheld from our paychecks, sales taxes added to our purchases, property taxes levied on our homes; we pay gasoline taxes, liquor taxes, and on and on. If there is one area of agreement among American consumers, it is that there are too many taxes and that they are too high.

Yet, by international standards, Americans are among the most lightly taxed people in the industrialized world. Figure 32–1 compares the fraction of income paid in taxes in the United States with that paid by residents of other industrialized nations. The tax collector clearly is much gentler here than in Sweden and Holland, although Americans do pay substantially more taxes than do the Japanese.

The relatively low level of taxation in the United States does not, however, mean that taxes are unimportant in our economy. On the contrary, taxation influences almost every aspect of our economic life. This chapter

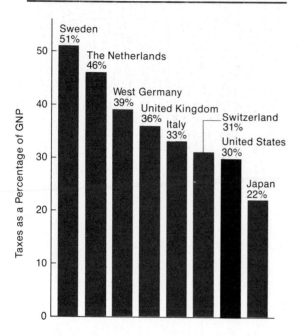

FIGURE 32–1

THE BURDEN OF TAXATION IN SELECTED COUNTRIES, 1976

Americans are not heavily taxed in comparison with the citizens of other advanced industrial countries. The Swedes and the Dutch, for example, pay far higher taxes than we do. The Japanese, however, pay much lower taxes.

Source: *National Accounts of OECD Countries,* 1976, vol. II.

discusses the kinds of taxes we have in the United States, the effects these taxes have on the distribution of income and on the allocation of resources, and the principles that distinguish "good" from "bad" taxes. In conjunction with the discussions in earlier chapters of government expenditure programs and regulations of various sorts, this chapter completes our study of how the government alters the distribution of income and the allocation of resources that is generated by market forces.

TAXES IN AMERICA: AN OVERVIEW

Figure 32–2 portrays the broad sweep of tax collections in the United States since 1929. Looked at in this way, the growth appears quite impressive. But a more revealing way to look at these data is to express taxes as a fraction of gross national product (GNP). We do this in Figure 32–3, which discloses some fascinating facts.[1]

The figure shows that the share of federal government taxes in GNP has been quite steady for about 30 years. It climbed from less than 4 percent in 1929 to more than 20 percent during World War II, fell back to 15 percent in the postwar period, and has been fluctuating in the 18 to 20 percent range ever since. It simply is not true that the federal government has been thrusting its hand deeper and deeper into our pockets each year. But the same cannot be said of state and local governments.

The share of GNP taken in taxes by the federal government has not increased since World War II. There has, however, been an unmistakable upward trend in the fraction of GNP taken in state and local taxes during the same time period.

This fraction climbed from 5.9 percent in 1947 to 7.7 percent in 1957, to 9.8 percent in 1967, and to 12 percent in 1977. This trend worries many tax reformers who, for reasons to be explained later in this chapter, view the federal tax system as far superior to that of the states and localities.

The main reason for the faster growth of state and local taxes than of federal taxes seems to be the differing expenditure patterns of the various levels of government. Apart from national defense, the federal government

[1]Refer to the discussion in Chapter 2 on interpreting growth trends. See pages 27–29.

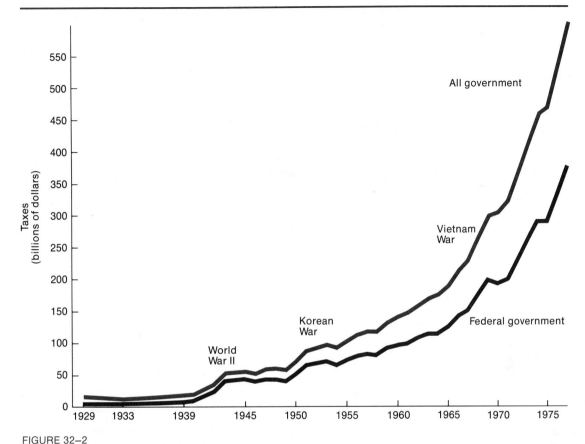

FIGURE 32–2

TAXES IN THE UNITED STATES SINCE 1929

Taxes have been growing steadily in the United States, as this diagram shows. The widening gap between all taxes and federal taxes illustrates the rapid growth of state and local taxes.

Source: Economic Report of the President, 1978.

spends very little on purchases of goods and services; but direct provision of public services accounts for the preponderant share of state and local budgets. It seems that citizens demand more and better schools, hospitals, parks, and other public services as the economy gets richer and that these services become ever more expensive.[2] The resulting strain on state

[2]Some reasons for the rising cost of public services are considered in Chapter 35, pages 696–697.

and local budgets has forced these units of government into tax increases that the federal government has, by and large, managed to avoid. And these tax increases, in turn, have helped bring on a taxpayers' revolt (see the boxed insert on pages 630–631).

Economists like to divide taxes into two broad categories: direct taxes and indirect taxes. Direct taxes are levied directly on *people*. Primary examples are *income taxes* and *inheritance taxes*, though the notoriously regressive

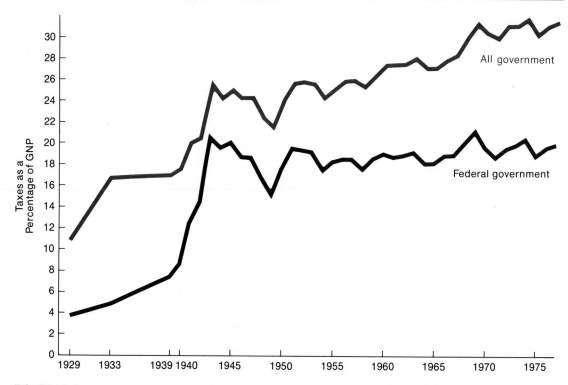

FIGURE 32–3

TAXES AS A PERCENTAGE OF GROSS NATIONAL PRODUCT
When we divide the numbers in Figure 32–2 by the gross national product of each year, the rapid growth disappears. Federal taxes have accounted for a fairly constant fraction of GNP. However, state and local taxes have absorbed an ever-increasing portion in recent years.

Source: Economic Report of the President, 1978.

head tax—which charges every person the same amount—is also a direct tax.[3] In contrast, indirect taxes are levied on goods and services, such as buying gasoline, using the telephone, owning a home, and so on. *Sales taxes* and *property taxes* are the most important indirect taxes in the United States, although many other countries rely heavily on the *value-added tax,* a tax that has never been adopted in the United

States.[4] In fact, as a broad generalization, the U.S. government relies more heavily on direct taxation than do the governments of most other countries. It is only a slight distortion of the facts to say that the federal government raises revenues by direct taxes, while the states and localities raise funds via indirect taxes. Just what are these direct and indirect taxes?

[3]"Progressive," "proportional," and "regressive" taxes were defined in Chapter 29, pages 571–572.

[4]The concept of value added was defined and explained in Chapter 17, pages 322–324. The value-added tax simply taxes each firm on the basis of its value added.

THE FEDERAL TAX SYSTEM

The personal income tax is the biggest single source of revenue to the federal government. Most people do not realize that the payroll tax—a tax levied on wages and salaries up to a certain limit—is the next biggest source. Furthermore, payroll taxes are growing much more rapidly than income taxes. In 1957, payroll tax collections were less than one-third as large as personal income tax collections; by 1967, this fraction had risen to over one-half; and by 1977, payroll taxes amounted to about 70 percent of personal income tax collections. Recent legisla-

tion will push this ratio still higher by 1987. The rest of the federal government's revenues come mostly from the corporate income tax and from various excise (sales) taxes. Figure 32–4 shows the breakdown of federal revenues anticipated for the fiscal year 1979 budget. Let us look at these taxes in more detail.

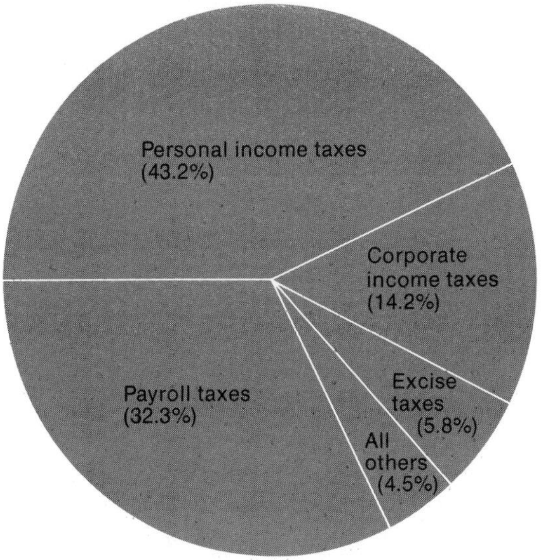

The Federal Personal Income Tax

The tax on individual incomes began with the Sixteenth Amendment to the Constitution in 1913, but was inconsequential until the beginning of World War II. Then, the tax was raised substantially to finance the war and has been the major source of federal revenue ever since.

It is well known that the tax is progressive, that is, it takes a larger share of higher incomes than of lower incomes. Table 32–1 is an abbreviated version of the 1979 tax table that applied to U.S. taxpayers during 1979. The progressivity is shown quite clearly by the way average tax rates (the ratio of taxes to income) rise as income rises. However, until very high

FIGURE 32–4
SOURCES OF FEDERAL GOVERNMENT
REVENUE, FISCAL YEAR 1979 (PROJECTION)
This pie diagram gives the projected shares of each of the major sources of federal revenues for fiscal year 1979 (October 1978 through September 1979). Personal income taxes and payroll taxes clearly account for the majority of federal revenues.
Source: Congressional Budget Office.

TABLE 32–1

FEDERAL PERSONAL INCOME TAX RATES
IN 1979*

TAXABLE INCOME	TAX	AVERAGE TAX RATE (percent)	MARGINAL TAX RATE (percent)
$ 3,000	$ 0	—	—
5,000	224	4.5	14
10,000	1,062	10.6	18
15,000	2,055	13.7	21
25,000	4,633	18.5	32
50,000	14,778	29.6	49
100,000	41,998	42.0	59
250,000	141,724	56.7	70
1,000,000	666,724	66.7	70

*For a married couple filing jointly.

income levels are reached, average tax rates are well below marginal tax rates, the rate of tax applied to the last dollar of taxable income.

In fact, the federal personal income tax is not nearly so progressive as Table 32–1 suggests. The major reason for this gap between appearance and reality is the existence of a bewildering variety of tax loopholes, some of which were discussed in Chapter 29. These loopholes enable large amounts of income to escape taxation, and, since they are beneficial mainly to high-income taxpayers, they erode the progressivity of the tax quite seriously.

Many taxpayers actually have very little tax to pay when the annual April 15th day of reckoning comes around, because income taxes are *withheld* from payrolls by employers and forwarded to the U.S. Treasury. In fact, many taxpayers are "overwithheld" during the year and receive a refund check from Uncle Sam in the spring.

The Payroll Tax

The second most important tax in the United States is the payroll tax, whose proceeds are earmarked to be paid into various "trust funds." These funds, in turn, are used to pay social security benefits, unemployment compensation, and other social insurance dividends.

The payroll tax is levied at a fixed percentage rate (now about 12¼ percent) that is divided between employees and employers, each paying roughly half the amount. This means that a firm paying an employee a gross monthly wage of, say, $1000 will deduct $61.25 (6.125 percent of $1000) from that worker's check, add an additional $61.25 of its own funds, and send the $122.50 to the government. On the face of it, this seems like a proportional tax, but it is actually highly regressive for two reasons. First, only wages and salaries are subject to the tax. People whose incomes come from interest and dividends do not pay. Second, because there are upper limits on social security

benefits, earnings above a certain level (which changes each year) are exempted from the tax. In 1979, this level is $22,900 per year, though it is scheduled to rise to $34,800 by 1983. Above this limit, the *marginal tax rate* on earnings is zero.

The Corporate Income Tax

The tax on corporate profits is also considered to be a "direct" tax, because corporations are considered to be fictitious "people" in the eyes of the law.[5] The basic marginal tax rate is now 46 percent, and this rate is paid by all large corporations (firms with smaller profits pay a lower rate). Since the tax applies to *profits,* not to income, all wages, rents, and interest paid by the corporation are deducted before the tax is applied.

Excise Taxes

An excise tax is what is more commonly called a sales tax—a tax on the purchase of some goods or services. While sales taxation is traditionally the preserve of the state and local governments in the United States, the federal government does levy excise taxes on a hodgepodge of miscellaneous goods and services, including cigarettes, gasoline, and tires. These taxes constitute a minor source of federal government revenue, but raising revenue is not their only goal. In some cases, these taxes are designed to discourage consumption of a commodity by raising its price.

THE PAYROLL TAX AND THE SOCIAL SECURITY SYSTEM

In government statistical documents, the payroll tax is euphemistically referred to as "contribu-

[5]For a full discussion of corporations and other forms of business organization, see Chapter 24.

tions for social insurance," though these "contributions" are far from voluntary. The term signifies the fact that, unlike other taxes, the proceeds from this particular tax are set aside in a "trust fund" for use in paying benefits to social security recipients and others.

But the standard notion of a trust fund really does not apply in this case. A private pension plan *is* a trust fund: You pay in money while you are working, it accumulates at compound interest, and then you withdraw it bit by bit in your retirement years. But the social security system does not operate in this way. Since its early years, the system simply has taken the payroll tax payments of the current working generations and handed them over to the current retired generation. The benefit checks that your grandparents receive each month are not, in any real sense, the dividends on the investments they made while they were working. Instead they are the payroll taxes that you and your parents pay each month.

So far this "pay as you go" system has managed to give every retired generation more in benefits than it contributed in payroll taxes. Social security "contributions" have indeed been a good investment! How has this miracle been achieved? It has relied very heavily on growth: both population growth and economic growth. As long as there is continued population growth, there always will be more and more young people to tax in order to pay the retirement benefits of senior citizens. Similarly, as long as wages keep increasing, the same payroll tax *rates* will permit the government to pay benefits to each generation that exceed that generation's contributions, without endangering the solvency of the system. Ten percent of today's average wage is clearly a lot more money than 10 percent of the wage your grandfather earned 50 years ago.

Yet the social security trust fund was in grave danger of running out of money until payroll taxes for the balance of the century were raised in 1977. Up to that point, the trust fund had been shrinking at an alarming rate. There were two principal reasons why benefits had been exceeding payroll tax receipts, and at least one of them is likely to be with us for some time.

The first was, perhaps, transitory; but it lasted long enough to become quite worrisome. Steady growth in real wages, one of the cornerstones of the solvency of the pay-as-you-go system, temporarily ceased in the early 1970s. Real wages at the end of 1977 were barely above what they were in 1972. But during this time social security benefits continued to grow rapidly and in 1975 became fully protected from inflation by *indexing*, whereas wages are not.[6]

The second reason poses a much longer-run problem: Population growth has slowed significantly in the United States. Birthrates in this country were very high from the close of World War II (the "postwar baby boom") until about 1958 and have generally been falling since then. As a result, the fraction of the U.S. population that is over 65 has climbed from only 7.5 percent in 1945 to 10.8 percent in 1977, and is certain to go much higher. Projections clearly show that by the time the people born between 1945 and 1958 reach retirement age, it will be impossible to have a social security system as generous as we have now if the current method of financing is maintained, and perhaps impossible under any method of financing. Long before that time, the projections show, something will have to be done either to increase the inflow of money into the social security trust fund or to decrease the outflow. Thus far Congress has relied exclusively on the first remedy, and current legislation makes provisions for continued increases in payroll taxes right through to the year 2011.

Since nobody seems very eager to try the second remedy—cutting social security benefits—many economists have suggested that we change the method of financing. In particular, a reform advocated by many would have the system drop the "trust fund" idea and rely instead on the great revenue-raising powers of

---

[6]For a full discussion of indexing, see Chapter 16.

the federal government to guarantee to senior citizens that they will indeed receive their promised benefits. If social security benefits were financed out of general tax revenues—which, aside from payroll taxes, come mainly from income taxes—there would no longer be any danger of insolvency for the trust fund. When higher benefits need to be paid, Congress would simply raise income taxes. Of course, the resulting tax burdens might become quite high during the first half of the the twenty-first century, when the ratio of retired people to working people is sure to be much higher than it is today. It seems a reasonable prediction that by the year 2020, say, either the retirement age will be pushed back beyond 65, or retirement benefits will be lower relative to wages than they are today, or both.

THE STATE AND LOCAL TAX SYSTEM

Indirect taxes are the backbone of state and local government revenues, though income taxes are becoming increasingly popular. Sales taxes are the principal source of revenue to the states, while cities and towns rely heavily on property taxes. Figure 32–5 shows the breakdown of state and local government receipts for fiscal year 1975–1976.

Sales and Excise Taxes

These days, the majority of states and large cities levy a broad-based sales tax on the purchase of most goods and services, with certain specific exemptions. For example, food is exempted from sales tax in many states. Overall sales tax rates are typically in the 5 to 7 percent range. In addition, there are special excise taxes in most states on such things as tobacco products, liquor, gasoline, and luxury items.

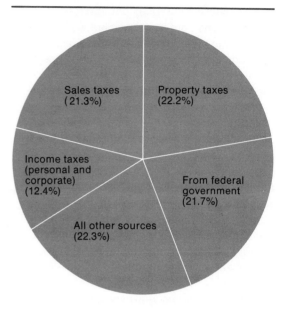

FIGURE 32–5

SOURCES OF STATE AND LOCAL REVENUE, FISCAL YEAR 1975–1976
As this pie diagram shows, sales taxes, property taxes, and grants-in-aid from the federal government are about equally important as sources of revenue to state and local governments. Income taxes are far less important, though they are growing rapidly.
Source: Economic Report of the President, 1978.

Property Taxes

Municipalities raise revenue by taxing the values of properties, such as houses and office buildings, again with certain exemptions (educational institutions, church property, and so on). The procedure is generally to assign to each taxable property an *assessed value,* which is an estimate of its market value, and then to place a tax rate on the community's total assessed value that yields enough revenue to cover expenditures on local services. Because properties are *reassessed* much less frequently than market values change, certain inequities arise. For example, one person's house may be assessed at almost 100 percent of its true market value while another's may be assessed at little more than 50 percent of its value. Property taxes generally run about 2 to 4 percent of true market value, though some communities deviate markedly from this norm. For example, property tax rates in older cities tend to be much higher than they are in wealthy suburbs.

At present, the property tax is perhaps the most controversial in the entire U.S. tax system. Some economists view it as a *proportional* tax on one particular type of wealth—real estate. In this view, since families with higher incomes generally own much more real estate than do families with low incomes, the property tax is *progressive* relative to income; that is, the ratio of property tax to income rises as we move up the income scale. However, other economists view the property tax as an excise tax on rents, and since expenditures on rent generally account for a larger fraction of the incomes of the poor than of the rich, this makes it seem *regressive* relative to income.

There is also intense political controversy over the property tax. Because local property tax revenues have been the traditional source of financing for public schools, wealthy communities with a lot of expensive real estate have been able to afford higher-quality schools than have poor communities. The reason is made clear with a simple arithmetical example. Suppose that real estate holdings in a wealthy school district average $100,000 per family, while in a poor district real estate holdings average only $40,000 per family. If both districts levy a 2 percent property tax to pay for their schools, the wealthy community will generate $2000 per family in tax receipts, while the poor one will generate only $800. To match the spending power of the wealthy district, the poor district would have to set its property tax rate at 5 percent—a rate these poorer families can ill afford.

In recent years, glaring inequalities like this have led the supreme courts of many states to declare that the financing of public schools by local property tax revenues is unconstitutional because it deprives children in poorer districts of an equal opportunity to receive a good education. For this and other reasons, many states are now grappling with the problem of how to revise their property tax system. One suggestion is uniform statewide property tax rates. Whatever emerges, it is clear that there will be great changes in the property tax in the next few years.

Local Income Taxes

Although some states and localities have been taxing individual and corporate incomes for many years, only recently have taxes on individual incomes begun to account for a substantial share of state and local revenue. Between 1938 and 1960, only one state enacted a personal income tax. Since 1961, however, 10 additional states have joined the club, with New Jersey being the latest (in 1976). It seems safe to predict that personal income taxes will be an increasingly important source of state and local revenues in years to come. Experts in public finance generally applaud this trend because, for reasons we will explain at the end of this chapter, they view the personal income tax as perhaps the best way to raise revenue.

FISCAL FEDERALISM

Figure 32–5 pointed out that grants from the federal government are a major source of revenue to state and local governments. In addition, grants from the states are vital to local governments. This system of transfers from one level of government to the next is referred to as fiscal federalism, and has a long history.

Aid from this source has come traditionally in the form of *restricted grants*, that is, money given from one level of government to the next on the condition that it be spent for a specific purpose. For example, the U.S. government may grant funds to a state *if* that state will use it to build highways. Or a state government may give money to a school district for expenditure on a specified program or facility. A more recent innovation is revenue sharing by the federal government, which now gives state and local governments substantial sums of money in the form of *unrestricted grants*, to be spent as the states and localities see fit. Such grants represented an inconsequential amount of revenue

until the early 1970s, but by fiscal year 1978 the federal government was giving away about $8 billion in unrestricted grants.

FIRST CONCEPT OF EQUITY IN TAXATION: HORIZONTAL EQUITY

Taxes are judged on two criteria: *equity* (Is the tax fair?) and *efficiency* (Does the tax inter-

A Taxpayer's Revolt in California

According to tradition, taxes are like the weather: everybody complains about them, but nobody ever does anything about them. In June 1978, disgruntled taxpayers in California "did something" about high taxes—something that stunned the nation and may have precipitated a nation-wide taxpayers' revolt.

The action concerned was an overwhelming vote in favor of an amendment to the California state constitution that drastically reduced property taxes. Variously called *Proposition 13* (for its place on the ballot) or the *Jarvis–Gann amendment* (for its sponsors, retired businessmen Howard Jarvis and Paul Gann), this citizens' initiative limited local property taxes to 1 percent of 1975–1976 market value instead of the usual 2.7 percent of *current* market value; placed severe limitations on any increases in a property's tax unless it was sold; and placed other restrictions on the ability of localities to raise taxes. In total, the amendment reduced property tax revenues by about 60 percent (approximately $7 billion), with about two-thirds of the reductions going to businesses and landlords and one-third going to homeowners.

Why did two out of every three Californians vote for this initiative, despite dire warnings from public officials, unions, and even large corporations that passage might mean drastic curtailments of such public services as police and fire

fere unduly with the workings of the market economy?). It is curious that economists have been mostly concerned with the latter, while public discussions about tax proposals almost always focus on the former. Let us, therefore, begin our discussion by investigating the concept of equitable taxation.

There are three distinct concepts of tax equity. The first is horizontal equity.

DEFINITION

Horizontal equality is the notion that equally situated individuals should be taxed equally.

Stated as such, there are few who would quarrel with the principle. But it is often quite difficult to apply in practice, and violations of horizontal equity can be found throughout the tax code.

Consider, for example, the personal income

---

protection, schools, health facilities, and so on? Several factors, only some of which were unique to California, help explain the vote. First, and perhaps foremost, property values in California had soared spectacularly during the 1970s; and with these higher property values came drastically higher taxes. Families whose houses had doubled or tripled in value found that their tax bills had doubled or tripled while their incomes had grown rather little. Second, due in part to a high state income tax and two tight-fisted governors in succession, the state had accumulated a whopping unspent surplus of about $5 billion—a tempting target for tax cutters. Third, voters were irritated by waste in government, and many apparently believed there was so much "fat" in local government budgets that the reduced tax revenues would not require any substantial cuts in public services. Finally, polls showed that many voters supported Jarvis–Gann because they were angry over generous welfare payments—a misguided action since welfare is financed mainly by state and federal govenments, not by local property taxes.

Whatever the reasons, Proposition 13 passed overwhelmingly, and local governments in California had to adjust quickly to a new, more frugal, way of life. Meeting in a crisis atmosphere, the California legislature cushioned the blow, or rather postponed it for a year, by enacting an emergency plan for distributing the state's huge budget surplus to the needy localities. Nonetheless, some of the necessary budget cutting was so substantial, and done in such haste, that it "amounted to doing hurry-up heart surgery with a meat ax—in the dark."[*]

Proposition 13 also raised a host of legal questions, including whether some of its provisions might violate the constitutions of California or of the United States. But the California Supreme Court upheld its constitutionality later in the year.

The message from California was heard throughout the country, and public opinion polls found citizens of many other states prepared to vote for similar measures. The California vote gave impetus to campaigns for tax reduction or limits on government spending in Arizona, Colorado, Idaho, Massachusetts, Oregon, Utah, and elsewhere. (Tennessee had acted earlier.) At the national level, support began to grow for the proposed Kemp–Roth bill to cut federal income taxes by about one-third over a three-year period. As with so many national trends, the taxpayers' revolt that started in California seemed to be spreading eastward, and no one knew quite where or when it might stop.

[*] *The Wall Street Journal,* June 28, 1978, page 28.

tax. It appears that horizontal equity calls for two families with the same income to pay the same tax. But what if one family has eight children and the other has one? Well, you answer, we must define "equally situated" to include equal family sizes, so only families with the same number of children can be compared on the grounds of horizontal equity. But what if one family has unusually high medical expenses, while the other has none? Are they still "equally situated"? By now the point should be clear: Determining when two families are "equally situated" is no simple task. In fact, the U.S. tax code lists scores, and perhaps even hundreds, of requirements that must be met before two families are construed to be "equal."

Property tax is another instance in which it is reasonably clear how to apply the concept of horizontal equity *in principle* but quite impossible to do it *in practice*. Since the value of a house (including land) is the base of the property tax, it is clear that two families may be considered "equal" for purposes of property taxation when their houses are of equal market value. But unless a house has recently been sold, which is usually not the case, tax authorities can only *estimate* its market value, and certain horizontal inequities inevitably arise from such estimates.

SECOND CONCEPT OF EQUITY IN TAXATION: VERTICAL EQUITY

The second concept of fair taxation seems to flow naturally from the first. If equals are to be treated equally, it appears that unequals should be treated unequally. This precept is known as vertical equity.

DEFINITION
Vertical equity refers to the notion that differently situated individuals should be taxed differently in a way that society deems to be fair.

This, of course, does not get us very far. For the most part, it has been translated into the ability-to-pay principle.

DEFINITION
The *ability-to-pay principle* refers to the idea that people with greater ability to pay taxes should pay higher taxes.

This still leaves a definitional problem similar to the problem of defining "equally situated": How are we to measure ability to pay? The nature of each tax often provides a straightforward answer. In income taxation, we measure ability to pay by income; in property taxation, we measure it by property value; and so on.

A thornier problem arises when we try to translate the notion into concrete terms. Consider the three alternative income-tax plans listed in Table 32–2. Under all three plans, families with higher incomes pay higher income taxes. So all three plans could be said to operate on the ability-to-pay concept of vertical equity. Yet the three are quite different in their distributive consequences. Plan 1 is a progressive tax, something like the individual income tax in the United States: The average tax rate is higher for richer families. Plan 2 is a proportional tax: Every family pays 10 percent of its income. Plan 3 is quite regressive: Since tax payments rise more slowly than income, the tax rate for richer families is lower than that for poorer families.

Which plan comes closest to the ideal notion of vertical equity? Many people find that Plan 3 offends their sense of "fairness," but there is much less agreement over the relative merits of Plan 1 (progressive taxation) and Plan 2 (proportional taxation). Very often, in fact, the notion of vertical equity is taken to be synonymous with progressivity. Other things being equal, progressive taxes are seen as "good" taxes in some ethical sense while regressive taxes are seen as "bad." On these grounds, advocates of greater equality of incomes

TABLE 32-2

THREE ALTERNATIVE INCOME-TAX PLANS

| | TAX PAYMENTS | | | AVERAGE TAX RATES | | |
INCOME	PLAN 1	PLAN 2	PLAN 3	PLAN 1	PLAN 2 (percent)	PLAN 3
$ 1,000	$ 100	$ 100	$ 100	10	10	10
10,000	2,000	1,000	500	20	10	5
100,000	40,000	10,000	2,500	40	10	$2\frac{1}{2}$

support progressive income taxes and oppose sales taxes.

THIRD CONCEPT OF EQUITY IN TAXATION: THE BENEFITS PRINCIPLE

Whereas the principles of horizontal and vertical equity, for all their ambiguities and practical problems, at least do not conflict with one another, the third principle of fair taxation may often violate commonly accepted notions of vertical equity.

DEFINITION
The *benefits principle of taxation*, which is often applied when the proceeds from certain taxes are earmarked for specific public services, holds that people who derive the benefits from the service should pay the taxes that finance it.

One clear example is gasoline taxes. Receipts from gasoline taxes typically are earmarked for maintenance and construction of roads. Thus, those who use the roads pay the tax roughly in proportion to the amount they use them. Most people seem to find this system fair, even if they grumble that gasoline taxes are exorbitant.[7]

[7]In fact, gasoline taxes in the United States are much lower than they are almost anywhere else in the world.

THE CONCEPT OF EFFICIENCY IN TAXATION

The concept of economic *efficiency* is the central notion of Part Seven of this text. The economy is said to be efficient if it has used every available opportunity to make someone better off without making someone else worse off. In this sense, taxes are almost always *inefficient*. In other words, for reasons we will discuss next, if the tax were removed, some people could be made better off without anyone being harmed. However, comparing a world with taxes to a world without taxes is not terribly meaningful. The government does, after all, need to raise revenues to pay for the goods and services it provides. For this reason, when economists discuss notions of "efficient" taxation, they are usually looking for the taxes that cause the least amount of inefficiency.

Because most taxes lead to some inefficiencies, the total burden of a tax generally exceeds the amount of money that the tax raises.

DEFINITION
The *burden* of a particular tax to an individual is the amount of money he would have to be given to make him just as well off with the tax as he was without it.

An example will clarify this notion and also make clear why the burden of a tax normally exceeds the revenues raised by the tax. Suppose the government, in the interest of energy conservation, levies a high tax on the biggest gas-guzzling cars, with progressively lower taxes on smaller cars.[8] For example, a simple tax schedule might be the following:

CAR TYPE	TAX
Cadillac	$500
Dodge	250
Gremlin	0

Harry has a taste for big cars, and has always bought Cadillacs. (Harry is clearly no pauper.) Once the new tax takes effect, he has three options. He can still buy a Cadillac and pay $500 in tax, he can switch to a Dodge and avoid half the tax, or he can switch to a Gremlin and avoid the entire tax.

If Harry chooses the first option, we have a case in which the burden of the tax is exactly equal to the amount of tax the person pays. Why? Because if Harry's rich uncle gives him $500, Harry clearly is in exactly the same position that he was before the tax was enacted. Hence, he must be just as happy as before. In general:

When a tax induces no change in economic behavior, the burden of the tax can be measured accurately by the revenue collected.

However, this is not what we normally expect to happen. And it is certainly not what the government intends by levying a tax on big cars. Normally, we expect taxes to induce some people to alter their behavior in ways that reduce or avoid tax payments. So let us look into Harry's other two options.

If he decides to purchase a Dodge, Harry pays only $250 in tax. But this is an inadequate

[8]President Carter actually proposed such a tax in 1977 as part of his energy program.

measure of the burden of the new tax because Harry is greatly chagrined by the fact that he no longer drives a Cadillac. How much money would it take to make Harry just as well off as he was before the tax? Only Harry knows for sure. But we do know that it is more than the $250 tax that he pays. Why? Because, even if someone were to give Harry $250, he would still be less happy than he was before the tax was introduced, owing to his switch from a Cadillac to a Dodge.

Whatever this unknown sum is, the amount by which it exceeds the $250 tax bill is called the excess burden of the tax.

DEFINITION
The *excess burden* of a tax to an individual is the amount by which the burden of the tax exceeds the tax that is paid.

Harry's final option makes the importance of understanding excess burden even more clear. If he switches to buying a Gremlin, Harry will pay no tax. Are we therefore to say he has suffered no burden? Clearly not; he longs for the Cadillac that he doesn't have. The general principle is:

Whenever a tax induces some people to change their behavior—that is, whenever it "distorts" their choices—the tax has an excess burden. This means that the revenue collected by the tax systematically understates the true burden of the tax.

The excess burdens that arise from tax-induced changes in economic behavior are precisely the inefficiencies we referred to at the outset of this discussion. And the basic precept of efficient taxation is to try to devise a tax system that minimizes these inefficiencies. In particular:

In comparing two taxes that raise the same total revenue, the one that produces less excess burden is the more efficient.

Excess Burden and Mr. Figg

Humorist Russell Baker discusses the problems of excess burden in the newspaper column reproduced below. It seems that every time his mythical Mr. Figg took a step to avoid paying taxes and to satisfy the tax man, he became progressively less happy.

Observer

American Way of Tax
By Russell Baker

New York—The tax man was very cross about Figg. Figg's way of life did not conform to the way of life several governments wanted Figg to pursue. Nothing inflamed the tax man more than insolent and capricious disdain for governmental desires. He summoned Figg to the temple of taxation.

"What's the idea of living in a rental apartment over a delicatessen in the city, Figg?" he inquired. Figg explained that he liked urban life. In that case, said the tax man, he was raising Figg's city sales and income taxes. "If you want them cut, you'll have to move out to the suburbs," he said.

To satisfy his local government, Figg gave up the city and rented a suburban house. The tax man summoned him back to the temple.

"Figg" he said, "you have made me sore wroth with your way of life. Therefore, I am going to soak you for more federal income taxes." And he squeezed Figg until beads of blood popped out along the seams of Figg's wallet.

"Mercy, good tax man" Figg gasped. "Tell me how to live so that I may please my government, and I shall obey."

The tax man told Figg to quit renting and buy a house. The government wanted everyone to accept large mortgage loans from bankers. If Figg complied, it would cut his taxes.

Figg bought a house, which he did not want, in a suburb where he did not want to live, and he invited his friends and relatives to attend a party celebrating his surrender to a way of life that pleased his government.

The tax man was so furious that he showed up at the party with blood-shot eyes. "I have had enough of this, Figg" he declared. "Your government doesn't want you entertaining friends and relatives. This will cost you plenty."

Figg immediately threw out all his friends and relatives, then asked the tax man what sort of people his government wished him to entertain. "Business associates," said the tax man. "Entertain plenty of business associates, and I shall cut your taxes."

To make the tax man and his government happy, Figg began entertaining people he didn't like in the house he didn't want in the suburb where he didn't want to live.

Then was the tax man enraged indeed. "Figg," he thundered, "I will not cut your taxes for entertaining straw bosses, truck drivers and pothole fillers."

"Why not?" said Figg. "These are the people I associate with in my business."

"Which is what?" asked the tax man.

"Earning my pay by the sweat of my brow," said Figg.

"Your government is not going to bribe you for performing salaried labor," said the tax man. "Don't you know, you imbecile, that tax rates on salaried income are higher than on any other kind?"

And he taxed the sweat of Figg's brow at a rate that drew exquisite shrieks of agony from Figg and little cries of joy from Washington, which already had more sweated brows than it needed to sustain the federally approved way of life.

"Get into business, or minerals, or international oil," warned the tax man, "or I shall make your taxes as the taxes of 10."

Figg went into business, which he hated, and entertained people he didn't like in the house he didn't want in the suburb where he did not want to live.

At length the tax man summoned Figg for an angry lecture. He demanded to know why Figg had not bought a new plastic factory to replace his old metal and wooden plant. "I hate plastic," said Figg. "Your government is sick and tired of metal, wood and everything else that smacks of the real stuff, Figg," roared the tax man, seizing Figg's purse. "Your depreciation is all used up."

There was nothing for Figg to do but go to plastic, and the tax man rewarded him with a brand new depreciation schedule plus an investment credit deduction from the bottom line.

Source: *International Herald Tribune,* April 13, 1977, page 14. ©1977 by The New York Times Company. Reprinted by permission.

Notice the proviso that the two taxes being compared must yield the *same* revenue. We are really interested in the *total* burden of each tax. Since:

$$\text{Total burden} = \text{Tax collections} + \text{Excess burden}$$

only when tax collections are equal can we unambiguously state that the tax with less excess burden is more efficient.

Since excess burdens arise when consumers and firms alter their behavior on account of taxation, this precept of sound tax policy can be restated loosely as follows:

In devising a tax system to raise revenue, try to raise any given amount of revenue through taxes that induce the least important changes in behavior.[9]

SHIFTING THE BURDEN OF TAXATION: TAX INCIDENCE

When economists speak of the incidence of a tax, they are referring to a hypothetical list of all the people who bear the burden of the tax, indicating how much of the burden each person bears. Of course, in practice, economists never have enough information to derive such a detailed description for any tax, but instead consider incidence by broad groups such as "consumers," or "workers," or "capitalists."

In discussing the tax on gas-guzzling autos, we have adhered so far to what has been called the flypaper theory of tax incidence: that the burden of any tax sticks where the government puts it. In this case, the theory holds that the burden stays on Harry. But often things do not work out this way. Consider, for example, what

[9]Sometimes, however, a tax is levied not primarily as a revenue-raiser, but as a way of inducing individuals or firms to alter their behavior. This possibility will be discussed in a later section.

will happen if thousands of Harrys all over America decide to stop buying luxury cars like Cadillacs. The demand schedule for luxury cars will shift downward sharply, as depicted in Figure 32–6 by the movement from D_0D_0 to D_1D_1. Assuming that the supply schedule of luxury cars is unchanged, we see that the price falls from \$12,000 to \$11,750 in the example—a drop of \$250. This means that those consumers who continue to buy luxury cars will now be paying \$11,750 to the dealer plus \$500 to the U.S. Treasury for a total of \$12,250. This is only \$250 more than what they were paying before

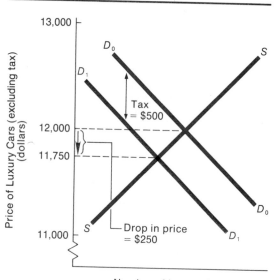

FIGURE 32–6

THE INCIDENCE OF AN EXCISE TAX
When the government imposes a \$500 tax on luxury cars, the demand curve relating quantity demanded to price *exclusive of tax* shifts downward from D_0D_0 to D_1D_1. The equilibrium price in this example falls from \$12,000 to \$11,750, so the burden of the tax is shared equally between car sellers (who receive \$250 less) and car buyers (who pay \$250 more, including the tax). In general, how the burden is shared depends on the elasticities of demand and supply.

the tax, so the burden that they bear is only $250—just half the tax that they pay!

Does this mean that the tax imposes a *negative* excess burden? Certainly not. What it means is that consumers who refrain from buying the taxed commodity have managed to *shift* much of the burden of the tax away from consumers as a whole, including those who continue to buy luxury cars.

DEFINITION
Tax shifting occurs when the economic reactions to a tax cause prices and outputs in the economy to change.

To whom has the tax been shifted? In our example, there are two main candidates. First are the automakers, or, more precisely, their stockholders. Stockholders bear the burden to the extent that the tax, by reducing auto sales, cuts into their profits. The other principal candidates are auto workers. To the extent that reduced production leads to layoffs, or to lower wages, the automobile workers bear part of the burden of the tax.

People who have never studied economics almost always believe in the flypaper theory of incidence, which holds that sales taxes are borne by consumers, property taxes are borne by homeowners, and taxes on corporations are borne by stockholders. Perhaps the most important lesson of this chapter is that:

The flypaper theory of incidence is often wrong.

Another illustration will drive the point home. Consider a big increase in the price of gasoline. Will car owners pay all of it? Of course not. It will hit airline profits. It will result in higher food prices because the shipment of food requires the use of fuel. It may even affect the wages of lawn mower mechanics. In short, the cost of almost every economic activity will be *indirectly* affected by a tax on gasoline.

Failure to grasp this basic point has led to all sorts of misguided tax legislation in which Congress, or state legislatures, *thinking* they were placing a tax burden on one group of people inadvertently placed it squarely on another. Of course, there are cases where the flypaper theory of incidence comes very close to being correct. So let us consider some specific examples of tax incidence.

THE INCIDENCE OF EXCISE TAXES

Excise taxes have already been covered by our automobile example, because Figure 32–6 could represent any commodity that is taxed. The basic finding is that *part* of the burden will fall on consumers of the taxed commodity (including those who stop buying it because of the tax), and part will be shifted to the firms and the workers who produce the commodity.

The amount that is shifted depends on the sensitivity of the demand curve to the tax and on the slope of the supply curve. We can see intuitively how this works. If consumers are very loyal to the taxed commodity so that they will continue to buy almost the same quantity no matter what the price, then it is clear that they will be stuck with most of the tax bill because they have left themselves vulnerable to it. Thus we would expect that the more inelastic the consumers' demand for the product is, the larger the share of the tax they will pay. Similarly, if suppliers are determined to supply the same amount of the product no matter how low the price (that is, if supply is very inelastic), then more of the tax will be borne by suppliers. This is in fact what will happen.

One extreme case arises when no one stops buying luxury cars when their prices rise. The demand curve becomes vertical, like the demand curve *DD* in Figure 32–7, and does not move at all when the tax is enacted. Then there can be no tax shifting. The price of a luxury car (exclusive of tax) remains at $12,000. So consumers bear the entire burden.

The other extreme case arises when the

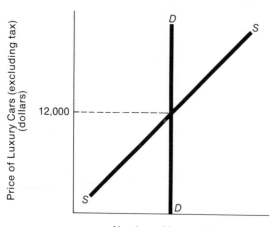

FIGURE 32–7

AN EXTREME CASE OF TAX INCIDENCE

If the quantity demanded is totally insensitive to price (completely *inelastic*), then the demand curve will be vertical and it will not shift when a tax is imposed. As the diagram shows, the price *exclusive of tax* remains at $12,000 so suppliers bear none of the burden. Since price *inclusive of tax* rises to $12,500, the entire burden falls on the buyers.

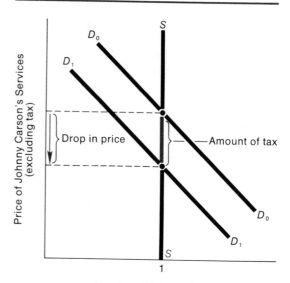

Number of Johnny Carsons

FIGURE 32–8

ANOTHER EXTREME CASE OF TAX INCIDENCE

If the quantity supplied is totally insensitive to price, then the supply curve *SS* will be vertical. When the demand curve shifts vertically downward from D_0D_0 to D_1D_1 on account of an excise tax, the seller will bear the entire burden, because the price that he receives will fall by the full amount of the tax.

supply curve is vertical, that is, when the commodity or service is in absolutely fixed supply. In Chapter 28, we used the services of Johnny Carson as an example of such a case, and this example is repeated here and illustrated in Figure 32–8. Since the supply of Johnny Carsons is 1.0 at any price (except prices that are so low that he stops working), Carson must bear the full burden of any tax that is placed on his services.[10] Figure 32–8 shows that the before-tax price falls by the full amount of the tax, which, of course, means that the after-tax price (the price that NBC pays) cannot be changed by the tax.

[10]We ignore here the possibility that Carson might reduce his hours of work. This circumstance was dealt with in Chapter 28.

Demand and supply schedules for most goods and services are not as extreme as those depicted in Figures 32–7 and 32–8, so the burden is shared. Precisely how it is shared depends on the elasticities of supply and demand curves.

When demand for a commodity or service is very inelastic, consumers will bear much of the burden of any tax that is placed on it. On the other hand, market forces will shift most of the burden away from consumers and onto firms when supply is quite inelastic.

THE INCIDENCE OF THE PAYROLL TAX

The payroll tax may be thought of as an excise tax on the employment of labor. As we mentioned earlier, the U.S. payroll tax comes in two parts: Half is levied on employees (payroll deductions) and half on employers. A fundamental point, which people who have never studied economics often fail to grasp, is that:

The incidence of a payroll tax is the same whether it is levied on employers or employees.

A simple numerical example can illustrate how this works. Consider an employee earning $100 a week with a 12 percent payroll tax that is "shared" equally between the employer and the employee, as under our present law. How much does it cost the firm to hire this worker? It costs $100 in wages paid to the worker plus $6 in taxes paid to the government, for a total of $106 a week. How much does the worker receive? He gets $100 in wages paid by the employer less $6 deducted and sent to the government, or $94 a week. The difference between wages paid and wages received is $106 − $94 = $12.

Now suppose Congress tries to "shift" the burden of the tax entirely onto firms, by raising the employer's tax to 12 percent while lowering the employee's tax to zero. Firms would still demand the same amount of labor at a cost of $106 a week, and workers would still supply the same amount at $94 a week. The necessary $12 difference between the wage that the firm pays and the wage that the worker receives can be restored by lowering the stated wage to $94 a week. Since firms still pay $106, and workers still receive $94, nothing has really changed. Nor would things be any different if the worker were forced to "pay" the full 12 percent payroll tax. It would still be true that the wage paid by the firms would exceed the wage received by the workers by $12.

This is one of those cases where Congress, misled by the flypaper theory of incidence, thinks it is "taxing firms" when it raises the employer's share and that it is "taxing workers" when it raises the employee's share. In truth, who it is really taxing depends on the incidence of the tax. But no difference results from a change in the employee's and the employer's shares. To think that there can be a difference is like thinking that the tax on cigarettes would have a different incidence if the government made the buyers, rather than the sellers, collect the revenues. Apart from the dubious enforceability of the tax if the buyers had to collect it, the two situations are identical.

Who, then, really bears the burden of the payroll tax? Like an excise tax, the incidence of the payroll tax depends on the elasticities of the supply and demand schedules. In the case of labor supply, there is a large body of empirical evidence pointing to the conclusion that the quantity of labor supplied is not very responsive to price for most population groups. The supply curve is almost vertical, like that shown in Figure 32–8. The result is that workers as a group are in much the same boat as Johnny Carson—they are able to shift very little of the burden of the payroll tax.

But employers *can* shift it in most cases. Even though the tax is collected by the firm, it is really borne by workers and consumers. Firms view their share of the payroll tax as an additional cost of using labor. So when payroll taxes go up, firms try to substitute cheaper factors of production (capital) for labor wherever they can. This reduces the demand for labor, lowering the wage received by workers (see Figure 32–8). And this is how market forces shift part of the tax burden from firms to workers.

To the extent that the supply curve of labor has some positive slope, the quantity of labor supplied will fall when the wage goes down, and in this way workers can shift some of the burden back onto firms. But the firms, in turn, can shift that burden onto consumers by raising their prices. As we know from Part Four, prices in competitive markets generally rise when costs (like labor costs) increase. It is doubtful, therefore, that firms bear any of the burden of the payroll tax. The flypaper theory of incidence could not be further from the truth.

THE INCIDENCE OF THE CORPORATE INCOME TAX

Such definite conclusions cannot be reached with respect to the incidence of the tax on corporate profits. Economists who have studied the question have reached no consensus because no one has been able to pin down definitively just what the supply curve of corporate capital looks like. Since the theory of incidence rests squarely on elasticities of supply and demand curves, the incidence of the corporate profits tax remains an unresolved issue.

WHEN TAXATION CAN IMPROVE EFFICIENCY

We have spent much of this chapter discussing the kinds of inefficiencies and excess burdens that arise from taxation. But, before we finish this discussion, two things must be pointed out.

First, economic efficiency is not society's only goal. For example, the hypothetical tax on gas-guzzling cars causes inefficiencies if it changes people's behavior patterns. But this, presumably, was exactly what the government sought to accomplish. The government wanted to reduce the number of big cars on the road to conserve energy, and it was willing to tolerate some economic inefficiency to accomplish this end. We can, of course, argue whether this was a good idea—whether the conservation achieved was worth the efficiency loss. But the general point is that:

Some taxes are a good idea because even when they introduce economic inefficiencies, they help achieve some other goal.

The equality—efficiency trade-off, which we discussed at length in Chapter 29, is another example. As we noted there, taxation aimed at equalizing incomes normally leads to losses in efficiency, but, even so, *some* redistributive taxation is probably optimal.

A second, and more fundamental, point is that:

Some taxes that change economic behavior may lead to efficiency *gains*, rather than to efficiency *losses*.

As you might guess, this can only happen when there is an inefficiency in the system prior to the tax. Then an appropriate tax may help set things right. A very clear-cut example of this will occupy much of Chapter 34 on the environment. We will see there that because firms and individuals who despoil clean air and clean water often do so without paying any price, these precious resources are used inefficiently. A corrective tax on pollution can remedy this.

EQUITY, EFFICIENCY, AND THE OPTIMAL TAX

In a perfect world, the ideal tax would reflect society's views on the optimal distribution of income (see Chapter 29), and it would induce no changes in economic behavior and so would have no excess burden. Unfortunately, there is no such tax.

Sometimes, in fact, the taxes with the smallest excess burdens are the most regressive. For instance, a head tax, which charges every person the same number of dollars, is very regressive. But it is also quite efficient. Since there is no change in economic behavior that will enable anyone to avoid it, there is no reason for anyone to change her behavior. As we have noted, the regressive payroll tax also seems to have small excess burdens.

Fortunately, however, there is a tax that, while not ideal, still scores very high on both the equity and efficiency criteria: the personal income tax.

While it is true that income taxes can be avoided by earning less income, we have already observed that in reality the supply of labor is changed little by taxation. So income from work responds very little. Investing in relatively safe assets (like government bonds) rather than risky ones (like common stocks) is another possible reaction that would reduce tax bills, since less risky assets pay lower rates of return. But it is not clear that the income tax actually induces such behavior because, while it takes away some of the profits when investments turn out well, it also offers a tax deduction when investments turn sour. Because the tax reduces the return on saving, many economists have worried that it would discourage saving, and thus retard economic growth. But the empirical evidence does not suggest that this has happened to any great extent. On balance then, while there are still unresolved questions and research is continuing:

The evidence collected to date suggests that the personal income tax induces few of the behavioral reactions that would reduce consumer well-being, and thus has a rather small excess burden.

On the equity criterion, we know that personal income taxes can be made as progressive as society deems desirable, though if marginal tax rates on rich people get extremely high, some of the potential efficiency losses might get more serious than they now seem to be. On both grounds, then, many economists—including both liberals and conservatives—view the personal income tax as the best way for a government to raise revenue.

SUMMARY

1. Taxes in the United States are generally lower than they are in most other industrial countries. While federal taxes as a percentage of gross national product have been quite constant, state and local taxes have been increasing.
2. The federal government raises most of its revenue by direct taxes, such as the personal and corporate income taxes and the payroll tax. Of these, the payroll tax is increasing the most rapidly.
3. While the personal income tax is not as progressive as it might be because of its many loopholes, it undoubtedly is a progressive tax. The payroll tax, by contrast, is a regressive tax.
4. Keeping the social security system solvent has been a serious problem during the 1970s, and is likely to remain a serious problem because of the decrease in population growth. Changes in the method of financing, or reductions in retirement benefits, may be necessary to keep the system afloat.
5. State and local governments raise most of their tax revenues by indirect taxes. States rely mainly on sales taxes, while localities are dependent upon property taxes.
6. There is controversy over whether the property tax is progressive or regressive, and even more controversy over whether local property taxes are an equitable way to finance public education. Courts in several states have decided that they are not.

7. In our multilevel system of government, the federal government makes various sorts of grants to state and local governments, and states in turn make grants to municipalities and school districts. This system of inter-governmental transfers is called fiscal federalism.

8. There are three concepts of fair, or "equitable," taxation that occasionally conflict. Horizontal equity simply calls for equals to be treated equally. Vertical equity, which calls for unequals to be treated unequally, has often been translated into the ability-to-pay principle—that people who are more able to pay taxes should be taxed more heavily. The benefits principle of tax equity ignores ability to pay and calls for taxing people according to the benefits they receive.

9. The burden of a tax is the amount of money an individual would have to be given to make her as well off with the tax as she was without it. This burden normally exceeds the taxes that are paid; and the difference between the two is called the excess burden of the tax.

10. Excess burden arises when a tax induces some people or firms to change their behavior. Excess burdens represent a loss of economic efficiency, so the basic principle of efficient taxation is to utilize taxes that have small excess burdens.

11. When people change their behavior on account of a tax, they often shift the burden of the tax onto someone else. This is why the "flypaper theory of incidence"—the belief that the burden of any tax always stays where Congress puts it—is often incorrect.

12. The burden of a sales or excise tax normally is shared between the suppliers and the demanders. The manner in which it is shared depends on the elasticities of supply and demand.

13. The payroll tax is like an excise tax on labor services. Since the supply of labor is much less elastic than the demand for labor, workers bear most of the burden of the payroll tax. This includes both the employer's and the employee's share of the tax.

14. Sometimes, "inefficient" taxes—that is, taxes that cause a good deal of excess burden—are nonetheless desirable because the changes in behavior they induce further some other social goal.

15. When there are inefficiencies in the system due to factors other than the tax system (for example, externalities), taxation can conceivably improve efficiency.

16. When both equity and efficiency are considered, most economists feel that the personal income tax is the best way to raise revenue.

CONCEPTS FOR REVIEW

Direct versus indirect taxes
Personal income tax
Payroll tax
Corporate income tax
Average and marginal tax rates
Loopholes
Progressive, proportional, and regressive taxes
Social security system
Property tax
Fiscal federalism

Revenue sharing
Horizontal equity
Vertical equity
Ability-to-pay principle
Benefits principle
Burden of a tax
Excess burden
Incidence of a tax
Flypaper theory of incidence
Tax shifting

QUESTIONS FOR DISCUSSION

1. "If the federal government continues to raise taxes as it has been doing, it will ruin the country." Comment.
2. Why have state and local taxes been increasing so much faster than federal taxes? Is this trend likely to continue?
3. Based on the following hypothetical income tax table, compute the marginal and average rates of tax. Is the tax progressive, proportional, or regressive?

INCOME	TAX
$100	$10
200	12
300	15
400	16

4. Explain why local property taxes are thought by many to be an unfair way of financing the public schools. What do you think would be a better way? What is your own state doing about this problem?
5. Which concept of tax equity, if any, seems to be served by each of the following:
   a. The progressive income tax
   b. The federal tax on gasoline
   c. The property tax
6. Use the example of Mr. Figg (see the boxed insert on page 635) to explain the concepts of efficient taxes and excess burden.
7. Think of some tax that you personally pay. What steps have you taken or could you take to reduce your tax payments? Is there an excess burden on you? Why or why not?
8. The country of Taxmania produces only two commodities: bread and mink coats. The poor spend all their income on bread, while the rich purchase both goods. Both demand for and supply of bread are quite inelastic. In the mink coat market, both supply and demand are quite elastic. Which good would be heavily taxed if Taxmanians cared mostly about efficiency? What if they cared mostly about vertical equity?
9. Suppose the supply and demand schedules for cigarettes are as follows:

PRICE PER CARTON	QUANTITY DEMANDED (millions of cartons per year)	QUANTITY SUPPLIED (millions of cartons per year)
$3.00	240	120
3.25	230	140
3.50	220	160
3.75	210	180
4.00	200	200
4.25	190	220
4.50	180	240
4.75	170	260
5.00	160	280

Now the government levies a 75 cents per carton excise tax on cigarettes.
   a. What is the equilibrium price paid by consumers before and after the tax?

b. What is the equilibrium price received by producers before and after the tax?

c. Explain why it makes no difference whether Congress levies the 75 cent tax on the consumer or the producer. (Relate your answer to the discussion of the payroll tax on page 639 of the text.)

d. Suppose the tax is levied on the producers. How much of the tax are producers able to shift onto consumers? Explain how they manage to do this.

e. Will there be any excess burden from this tax? Why? Who bears this excess burden?

f. By how much has cigarette consumption declined on account of the tax? Why might the government be happy about this outcome, despite the excess burden?

eight

Economic Growth and the
Quality of Life

33

Economic Growth: Causes, Virtues, and Vices

The development of capitalist production makes it constantly necessary
to keep increasing the amount of capital laid out. . . . It compels
[the individual capitalist] to keep constantly extending his capital
. . . by means of progressive accumulation. . . . Fanatically bent on
making value expand itself, he ruthlessly forces the human race to
produce for production's sake; he thus forces the development of the
productive powers of society, and creates those material conditions,
which alone can form the real basis of a higher form of society.

Karl Marx, *Capital*, vol. 1 (Chicago: Charles H. Kerr Publishing Co., 1906),
page 649 (ordering of passages inverted).

In this chapter we discuss the factors that determine the rate at which an economy grows and examine the desirability of rapid growth. While our primary focus is the free-market economy, like the one in which we live, much of the discussion is applicable to any growing economy. We begin by pointing out some of the controversies that have arisen over this subject and then consider several of the ways that growth can be measured. We go on to examine the effects of population growth on prospects for rising incomes per capita, and then take a look at some problems in forecasting growth and some pessimistic predictions that can be ascribed, in part, to these forecasting problems. Next, we examine the views of those who have argued that economic growth is a mixed blessing that may do more harm than good; and finally, we describe several of the conditions necessary for achieving growth.

SOME ISSUES IN THE ANALYSIS OF GROWTH

Capital accumulation and economic expansion have been subjects of controversy ever since economics became a specialized discipline. One of the main topics for discussion has been the effect of saving on economic growth. It seems more than a little curious that some eminent economists have emphasized the vital role saving plays in the process of economic growth, arguing that economic expansion without saving is all but impossible, while other, equally prominent, economists have warned that saving tends to undermine the growth process and, in practice, is often the most dangerous enemy of growth. Even more curious, though, as we will see, is that *both* viewpoints are essentially right. If you object that two contradictory positions *cannot* be right, we can assure you that you are also right!

The resolution of this important controversy hinges on the fact that the two positions are each correct *in different circumstances*, and each is of considerable importance for issues in economic policy. Later in this chapter we will see how a more comprehensive view of this matter enables economists to assign proper places to the two positions in the accumulation process. We will see that each interpretation of the role of saving has valid and important implications for policy issues. One of them will help us to understand the requisites for growth in an underdeveloped area or in a nation seeking to expand its output rapidly. The other will make clearer the source of the problem of an economy whose expansion is threatened by recession and unemployment. In short, the explanation of the enigma that saving is an absolute requirement of growth, and yet its most dangerous enemy, will help us analyze some of the most significant of the world's economic issues.

There are, however, other controversies surrounding the subject of growth. For instance, there is a heated debate over the desirability of growth itself. Here again, knowledgeable people hold positions that are almost diametrically opposed. Some see in growth the only possible cure to many of the world's most serious economic ills. Others see growth as the *cause* of these problems. In this dispute, while it is not quite possible to conclude that both positions are right, there is a considerable and important element of truth in each of them. The trick, from the point of view of the welfare of humanity, will be to use growth in a way that extracts its benefits and yet avoids, or at least minimizes its dangers. Though this may seem easier to suggest than to carry out, we will find that the problem is by no means beyond us—economics offers methods that appear able to deal effectively with these issues.

HOW TO MEASURE GROWTH: TOTAL OUTPUT OR OUTPUT PER CAPITA?

Preoccupation with economic growth and with the ability of an economy to produce an outpouring of goods and services goes back at least to Adam Smith, who in 1776 published the book that was to become the root of modern economics. One of the primary messages of Smith's book was that the free-market economy is an efficient instrument for the production of an abundance of outputs, as long as it is unhampered by artificial monopoly or arbitrary government restrictions. The abbreviated title of the book, *The Wealth of Nations,* indicates clearly Smith's main concern in the volume—the material prosperity of the society.

Not only did Smith, like many of his successors, take it for granted that expansion of productive capacity is inherently desirable, he also took it for granted, apparently without examining the matter very closely, that growth in the size of population is to be wished for. Thus, he spoke of "the sober and industrious poor who generally bring up the most numerous families, and who principally supply the demand for useful labor,'' and he indicated that one of the virtues of a tax upon luxuries consumed by the poor is that the ability of the poor "to bring up families . . . instead of being diminished, is frequently, perhaps, increased by the tax."[1]

The reason for Smith's approval of population growth seems to have been that a larger population provides a larger work force, and a larger work force makes possible a larger national output.

Few economists since Smith's time have argued in this way. Nowadays we usually measure a nation's prosperity not in terms of its total output but in terms of its output *per person*. India has a GNP more than 40 percent larger than Sweden's. But with a population more than 75 times as large as Sweden's, India remains a poor country while Sweden is highly prosperous. The point is that:

If the objective of growth is the material welfare *of the individuals* who make up a country, then the proper measure of the success of a program of economic development is how much its adds to output per person. The relevant index is not total output. It is total output *divided by total population; that is, output per capita.*

From this point of view, the appropriate objective of growth is not, as the old cliché puts it, "the greatest good for the *greatest number*"—it is the greatest good *per person* in the economy. Per capita figures tell this story well. To make the appropriate comparison of well-being in Sweden and India, we note that per capita GNP in Sweden is over $8000 a year, whereas in India, even after a generous adjustment to correct for lower prices in that country, the figure is under $400 a year.

Only where the objective of the government is grandeur or military strength may the number of inhabitants alone seem an appropriate part

of its goal. A small country like Finland, for instance, cannot hope to overwhelm a giant neighbor like the Soviet Union, even if Finland has a much higher per capita GNP than the Soviet Union.[2] But where the goal of the government is not national power but the elimination of poverty, illiteracy, and inadequate medical care, sheer increase in population becomes a questionable pursuit.

ON GROWTH IN POPULATION: IS LESS REALLY MORE?

That law of Nature which makes food necessary to the life of man . . . implies a strong and constantly operating check on population. . . . Through the animal and vegetable kingdoms, nature has been comparatively sparing in the room and the nourishment necessary to rear them. . . . Among plants and animals its effects are waste of seed, sickness, and premature death. Among mankind, misery and vice.[3]

Just before the beginning of the nineteenth century, in 1798, the Reverend Thomas R. Malthus (who was to become England's first professor of political economy) published *An Essay on the Principle of Population*. This book was to have a profound effect on people's attitudes toward population growth. Malthus argued that sexual drives and other influences induce people to reproduce themselves as rapidly as their means permit. Unfortunately, he said, when the number of humans increases, the production of food and other consumption goods generally cannot keep up. As the earth

---

[2]Even where military power is the primary objective, a large but impoverished population may not be a very effective means to that end. China has long had an enormous population, but in the modern era its military presence is certainly quite recent.

[3]T. R. Malthus, *An Essay on the Principle of Population,* 1798 (Totawa, N.J.: Rowman & Littlefield, 1973), Chapter 1.

[1]Adam Smith, *The Wealth of Nations*, Edwin Cannan, ed. (New York: Modern Library, Random House, Inc.), page 823.

becomes more crowded, people are forced to farm land more intensively, using more labor, fertilizer, and equipment to extract larger outputs from the same acreage. Besides working each farmed piece of land much more intensively than before, people will also have to look for new lands to farm. But neither of these ways to increase the product will help enough to meet the increased need. There are limits to what a given piece of land can produce. Moreover, as people put soil under cultivation, they will naturally tend to pick the best lots first. Thus, as they extend the area that is cultivated, people will be forced to make use of increasingly inferior farmland.

Together, these two phenomena lead to the noted *law of diminishing returns* to additional labor used with a fixed supply of land, a relationship we encountered before (in Chapter 21). This hypothesis states if we use more and more labor to cultivate a fixed stock of land, ultimately we will reach a point at which each additional laborer will contribute less additional output than the previous laborer. Ultimately, as the labor force increases, output per worker will decline.

Based on these observations, Malthus and his followers concluded that the tendency of humankind to reproduce itself must constantly also be exerting pressure on the economy to keep living standards from rising. There will be a tendency for wages to approximate some minimal subsistence level—the lowest income on which people are willing to marry and raise a family. If wages are above subsistence level, the population can and will grow. But, as we have seen, rising population without any rise in available land must reduce output per worker because of the law of diminishing returns. Thus, a wage that is above subsistence will set forces into motion that will force the wage level down toward subsistence.

Sometimes, according to Malthus, the population will grow beyond the capability of the economy to support it. Then the number of people will be brought back into line by means

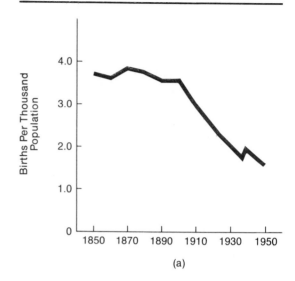

(a)

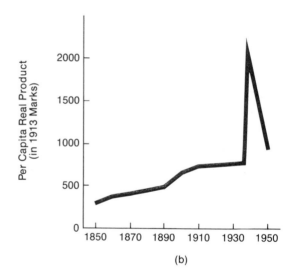

(b)

FIGURE 33–1

GERMAN BIRTHRATES AND REAL NET PRODUCT PER CAPITA, 1850–1950
(a) German birthrate (births per thousand population); (b) German product per capita (net real social product, in marks of 1913 purchasing power per capita). Note the steady fall in birthrate and the rise in product per capita.

Source: Walter G. Hoffman, *Das Wachstum der Deutschen Wirtschaft Seit der Mitte des 19 Jahrhunderts* (Berlin: Springer-Verlag, 1965), pages 172–74 and 827–28.

that are far more unpleasant than a decrease in wages—it can happen by starvation and disease or by military involvements that produce the required number of casualties.

Later in the nineteenth century and during the first half of the twentieth century, the gloomy Malthusian vision seemed to lose credibility. New technology and improved agricultural practices generally enabled the output of food and other agricultural products to increase faster than the population (at least in the wealthier industrialized nations). In addition, it turned out that as living standards rose, people became less anxious to reproduce, and so the expansion of population slowed substantially. Figures 33–1(a) and 33–1(b) illustrate this trend in Germany over a 100-year period. All in all, it began to look as though population growth constituted no significant threat—it was something with which human technological skills and ingenuity could cope.

More recently, however, there has been a renewed concern over the population problem. With improvements in medicine—notably improved hospital sanitation, the use of such public health measures as swamp drainage, and the discovery of antibiotics—death rates have plunged in the developing countries, especially for infants. At the same time, birth control programs in most of these countries have, at least until quite recently, not been very successful. As a result, the populations of developing countries have continued to expand dramatically, eating up a good proportion of any output increases obtained through their governments' economic development programs.

Currently, the populations of North America and Europe are growing so slowly that if present rates continue it will take well over a century for them to double. But in Latin America and Africa populations double about every 25 years, and in Asia every 35 years.

A Population Crisis in Africa

The following report shows that the Malthusian spectre still haunts part of the globe:

Population pressure on the fragile desert ecosystem has been steadily gathering force in the African countries that border the Sahara. On the southern fringe in the Sahelian zone, a prolonged drought beginning in the late sixties and continuing into the seventies brought the deteriorating situation into painfully sharp focus. . . .

There is no record of how many lives were claimed as food systems collapsed all across Africa. In an appearance before a Congressional committee after a tour of the Sahelian zone, Michael Latham, Professor of International Nutrition at Cornell University and a Member of the Committee on International Nutrition Programs of the National Academy of Sciences, testified that the number of lives lost was probably somewhere between 100,000 and a quarter of a million; no one will ever know for sure, he said.

Source: Lester R. Brown, *World Population Trends: Signs of Hope, Signs of Stress*, Worldwatch Paper 8, October 1976, pages 23–24.

From these observations, it has been widely concluded that significant improvement in living standards in the developing areas is impossible without a substantial reduction in the population growth rates of those areas. But the neo-Malthusians, as one dedicated group is sometimes called, go further than this, arguing that a rapid approach to birthrates so low that populations cease expanding—that is, to *zero population growth*—is virtually a matter of life and death even for the most prosperous nations. It is illuminating to consider the logic of their argument.

THE CROWDED PLANET: EXPONENTIAL POPULATION GROWTH

In advocating his position, Malthus adopted a line of argument that has caught the imagination of students of Malthusian theory ever since.

> Population, when unchecked, increases in a geometrical ratio. Subsistence increases only in an arithmetical ratio. A slight acquaintance with numbers will shew the immensity of the first power in comparison of the second.[4]

Population growth in what Malthus called a "geometric ratio" has a simple structure. In modern discussions, such a growth pattern is referred to as exponential growth, or "compounded growth" or "snowballing."

Exponential growth is growth at a constant *percentage* rate. For example, at a 10 percent growth rate, a population of 100 persons will increase by 10 persons a year; but a population of a million persons will increase by 100,000 persons a year. Thus, although the *rate* of growth is the same for large and small popula-

tions, the *numbers* are dramatically different. So, the bigger the population, the more it will add annually. And each year's growth implies still faster growth in the following year. It is like a snowball rolling downhill, accumulating more snow the bigger it gets and so expanding faster and faster all the time.

If population doubles (grows 100 percent) in 35 years, it will quadruple (grow another 100 percent) in 70 years, increase 8-fold in 105 years, 16-fold in 140 years, and so on indefinitely. The doubling sequence 2, 4, 8, 16, 32, 64, and so on is the basic pattern of exponential growth. Figure 33–2 shows how astronomical such a growth sequence can be. By projecting the world's population 175 years into the future

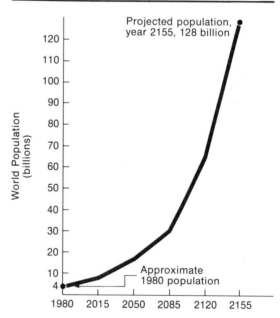

FIGURE 33–2

PROJECTED GROWTH OF THE WORLD'S POPULATION IN 175 YEARS AT A CONSTANT 2 PERCENT RATE OF GROWTH

This figure shows the sensational acceleration of population growth *if* population expands exponentially.

[4]Malthus, *An Essay on the Principle of Population* (New York: W. W. Norton and Co., 1976), page 20.

on the assumption that population will grow exponentially at about its current rate, it shows that by the year 2155 the population will have grown to about 128 billion, with more than 30 times as many inhabitants on the earth as there are today.

It turns out that in his assumptions about exponential growth, Malthus was being conservative. He did not begin to spell out the wonders and the horrors that his premise implied. Consider some calculations of one leading authority on population (who has derived his conclusions simply by carrying through the arithmetic of exponential growth rates):

- If population were to grow at today's rates for another 600–700 years, every square foot of the surface of the earth would contain a human being;

- If it were to expand at the same rate for 1200 years, the combined weight of the human population would exceed that of the earth itself;

- If that growth rate were to go on for 6000 years (a very short period of time in terms of biological history), the globe would constitute a sphere whose diameter was growing with the speed of light.[5]

And none of this is conjecture. It is *sure* to come about *if* the present (exponential) rate of growth of the earth's population (about 2 percent a year) continues unabated.

Of course, none of this can really happen. Our finite earth just does not have room for that sort of expansion. The fate of humanity is not determined by the rules of arithmetic—it depends on the course of nature and on the behavior of the human race. It is true that if the number of humans continues to swell until it presses upon the earth's capacity, the process will ultimately be brought to a halt in a Malthusian apocalypse. Disease, famine, and war must

finally put a stop to the expansion process. But there is a better alternative. People can choose to stop raising large families. There is no inevitability about the family of six or ten children. As we have just noted, there has in fact been a decline in the rate of expansion in the wealthier societies—so much so that in the United States in the last few years the rate of reproduction has reached what can ultimately give us zero population growth (see Figure 33–3). Even in the developing nations, as we will see in Chapter 38, the birthrate has recently been decelerating.

A more balanced view of the matter recognizes the serious difficulties that rapid population growth can lead to, and suggests that its encouragement will not serve the interests of society. Yet, it does *not* imply that a great catastrophe is at hand or that the appropriate reaction is panic.

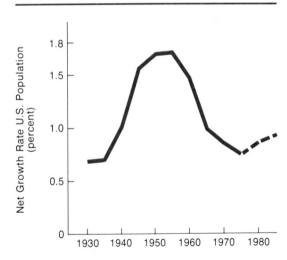

FIGURE 33–3

ANNUAL PERCENTAGE GROWTH RATE OF THE U.S. POPULATION
Note how rapidly the rate has fallen in recent years. It has just about returned to the low level it was at during the Great Depression.

Source: U.S. Bureau of the Census, *Current Population Reports*, Series P-25.

[5]Ansley J. Coale, "Man and His Environment," *Science*, vol. 179 (October 9, 1970), pages 132–36. Copyright 1970 by the American Association for the Advancement of Science.

EXPONENTIAL RESOURCE DEPLETION AND POLLUTION

The exponential doubling sequence 2, 4, 8, 16, 32, 64 . . . , with its explosive growth pattern, seems to have a strong fascination for those who want to forecast the long-run future. If we assume that the use of copper and coal, for instance, follows this sequence, we can more-or-less predict the date at which such finite resources will run out. If we assume that emissions of carbon monoxide or lead into the atmosphere will also follow the same sequence, we can predict when the human race will expire from strangulation or poisoning. The computer has permitted the design of some rather complex predictive models that build elaborate forecasts on the assumption that growth will be exponential. Some of the resulting reports have made headlines because of their sensational prophesies of major catastrophies within the next 50 or 100 years. These reports talk of exhaustion of some of our most critical resources, massive environmental deterioration, and widespread starvation within the next century.[6]

There is no doubt that these conclusions do follow from the assumption of exponential growth. But the question remains whether that assumption is valid. In fact, the workings of the economy are far more complex than those analyses admit. And a market economy has powerful safety features that protect it from sudden and catastrophic exhaustion of any critical resource.

Let us see how the price system itself provides a safety valve that lets the economy down gently when signs appear that a valuable resource is growing scarce. When once easily accessible supplies begin to run out, the price of the item rises. While no one really welcomes a price rise, it serves several useful functions:

[6]For the most noteworthy example, see the Club of Rome Report, Donella H. Meadows, et al., *The Limits to Growth* (New York: Universe Books, 1972). This book created a minor sensation when it was published.

1. A rapidly rising price will hold back demand by inducing those who have been making inessential uses of the scarce item to give up those marginal uses. For example, a rise in the price of oil may lead people to use paper for wrapping where they had formerly used plastic (which is made from petroleum) and may induce industry to substitute copper pipes for plastic ones. Higher prices are the most effective conservation technique that anyone has yet discovered.

2. The rising price makes it profitable to find and exploit sources of the scarce item that formerly were not worth the cost. Currently it is profitable to pump oil from the forbidding North Sea—an activity that, while technically possible 10 years ago, was not then economically feasible. Higher oil prices have also led drillers to reopen wells in the United States that had been shut down, even though more expensive methods must be used to extract the remaining petroleum (often a very high percentage of the original contents of the wells).

3. The high price of the scarce resource encourages the search for substitutes. Coal, solar energy, geothermal energy, and nuclear fission and fusion are all substitutes for petroleum as an energy source.

On all of these counts, the economy will find that the letdown resulting from the depletion of a valuable resource will not be abrupt and chaotic. Rising prices will help to make it smooth and gradual, with plenty of time for and encouragement of the reorganization of the productive system to adapt to the changing circumstances.

To all this we must add the evidence that there are, in fact, few important resources that are likely to run out in the near future. For example, a study of changes in proven reserves—that is, reserves that have already been explored and tested—of eight leading mineral products—copper, lead, zinc, tin, nickel, bauxite (aluminum), iron, and oil—showed that the quantity available for use of four of these eight minerals was actually increasing faster than the demands for them during the 1960s. In one case (tin), the reserve/demand ratio had remained constant, and while the known reserves of oil fell slightly behind demand during the 1960s, they had in fact risen compared with their position in 1950. Only in the case of nickel did proven reserves fall significantly behind demand.[7] (See Table 33–1.)

More recent figures provided by the U.S. government (Table 33–2)[8] show the same thing—a growing ratio of reserves to demand. Even in the case of petroleum, while the available reserve in 1970 was sufficient to cover about 18 years' projected consumption, by 1974, reserves had risen to 26 years' projected consumption.

These figures are not really as surprising as they may seem. Exploring for minerals is expensive, and firms do not find it profitable to search for new reserves of a mineral when a 20-, 30-, or even a 100-year supply is already on hand. Only as some of the known reserves are used up does it pay to go out and find replacements, and that is why proven reserves of most minerals have, over the years, more or less kept abreast of demand.

In a free-market economy, the ultimate test of growing scarcity is the behavior of prices. If the price of an item is not rising, it is safe to guess that it is not scarce relative to the demand for it.

Accordingly, there has been a study of the prices of 15 major mineral products over the first seven decades of the twentieth century. This study showed that from 1900 to 1975 the prices of seven of the minerals, including oil, had actually failed to keep up with the general price level. Among those whose prices rose,

[7]See Roy W. Wright, "Ferrous and Non-Ferrous Metal Resources," *Centennial Volume, American Institute of Mining, Metallurgical and Petroleum Engineers* (Dallas: Storm, 1971), page 18.

[8]Unfortunately, the two tables are not comparable so that the figures cannot be related.

TABLE 33–1

RESERVE/DEMAND INDICES FOR NONCOMMUNIST COUNTRIES

	1950	1960	1969
Copper	63	49	59
Lead	18	16	26
Zinc	26	26	22
Tin*	25	25	25
Bauxite	—	252	279
Nickel*	140	195	135
Iron*	527	686	over 1000?
Oil	25	39	32

The figures represent the number of years known reserves will last at current consumption rates. Note that this table shows that known reserves of many minerals have been growing faster than demand during the postwar period. In 1969, the ratio of reserves to current annual demand was at least as high as it was in 1950 for lead, tin, iron, and oil. Supply of bauxite also had probably grown. And the supply of copper had also recently been increasing relative to demand.
*Possible as well as probable reserves.
Source: Roy W. Wright, "Ferrous and Non-Ferrous Metal Resources," *Centennial Volume, American Institute of Mining, Metallurgical and Petroleum Engineers* (Dallas: Storm, 1971), page 18.

TABLE 33–2

WORLD RESERVE/DEMAND RATIOS FOR VARIOUS MINERALS (Number of years' demand that can be met from available reserves)

	1970	1976
Copper	26.1	38.4
Lead	14.1	26.4
Zinc	15.9	19.2
Tin	14.4	36
Aluminum	76.2	139.1
Nickel	53.1	52.8
Iron ore	144.6	122.4
Petroleum	17.7	26*

The reserves here are calculated on the basis of prices prevailing at the dates indicated. This is relevant since a rise in price increases the quantity of usable reserves. That is why, according to this table, reserves for all but two major minerals have been growing more quickly than demand.
*1974 figure—last available figure in series before transfer of petroleum from Bureau of Mines to Department of Energy.
Source: Personal communications, U.S. Bureau of Mines.

none had gone up substantially faster than the overall price level.

In other words, there is little evidence that "we are about to run out of practically everything," as one popular magazine put it a few years ago. True, artificial shortages have been created by the petroleum cartel and the actions of a number of other agencies that have tried to restrict production and sales in order to keep prices high. But several of the items that seemed hard to obtain in 1972–1973 experienced a sharp cut in prices during the 1974–1975 recession. Paper product prices fell sharply and forced many recycling centers to close down, and the price of copper also collapsed and caused severe dislocations in the industry, which continued well after the recession.

None of this is meant to deny the necessity of being careful in our use of resources, of encouraging a decline in population growth, and of containing pollution. But recognizing that these are issues for concern is not tantamount to saying that the end of the world as we know it is just around the corner.

IS MORE GROWTH REALLY BETTER?

Writings such as the Club of Rome Report (see footnote on page 654) raise questions about the desirability of faster economic growth as an end in itself. Yet faster growth means more wealth, and to most people the desirability of wealth is beyond question. "I've been rich and I've been poor—and I can tell you, rich is better," a noted stage personality is said to have told an interviewer, and most people seem to have the same attitude about the economy as a whole. To those who hold this belief, a healthy economy is one that is capable of turning out vast quantities of shoes, food, cars, and TV sets. An economy whose capacity to provide all these things is not expanding is said to have succumbed to the disease of *stagnation*.

Economists from Adam Smith to Karl Marx saw great virtue in economic growth. Marx argued that capitalism, at least in its earlier historical stages, was a vital form of economic organization by which society got out of the rut in which the medieval stage of history had trapped it. As we saw in the opening quotation of this chapter, Marx believed that "the development of the productive powers of society . . . alone can form the real basis of a higher form of society. . . . " Marx went on to tell us that only where such great productive powers have been unleashed can one have "a society in which the full and free development of every individual forms the ruling principle."[9] In other words, only a wealthy economy can afford to give all individuals the opportunity for full personal satisfaction through the use of their special abilities in their jobs and through increased leisure activities.

Yet the desirability of economic growth has been questioned on grounds that undoubtedly have a good deal of validity. It is pointed out that the sheer increase in quantity of products has imposed an enormous cost on society in the form of pollution, crowding, proliferation of wastes that need disposal, and debilitating psychological and social effects. It is said that industry has transformed the satisfying and creative tasks of the artisan into the mechanical and dehumanizing routine of the assembly line. It has dotted our roadsides with junkyards, filled our air with smoke, and poisoned our food with dangerous chemicals. The question is whether the outpouring of frozen foods, talking dolls, CB radios, and headache remedies is worth its high cost to society. As one well-known British economist put it:

> The continued pursuit of economic growth by Western Societies is more likely on balance to reduce rather than increase social welfare. . . . Technological innova-

[9] Marx, *Capital*, page 649.

tions may offer to add to men's material opportunities. But by increasing the risks of their obsolescence it adds also to their anxiety. Swifter means of communications have the paradoxical effect of isolating people; increased mobility has led to more hours commuting; increased automobilization to increased separation; more television to less communication. In consequence, people know less of their neighbors than ever before in history.[10]

Virtually every economist agrees that these concerns are valid, though many question whether economic growth is their major cause. Nevertheless, they all emphasize that pollution of air and water, noise and congestion, and the mechanization of the work process are very real and very serious problems. There is every reason for society to undertake programs that grapple with these problems. In the next chapter, which deals with problems of the environment, we will examine these issues more closely and describe some policies that can deal with them.

Economists agree also that growth in human well-being is measured very poorly by statistics such as GNP, which indicates only the growth rate of the production of *material* goods and services and takes no account of the effects of growth on the quality of life. Two economists at Yale University, William Nordhaus and James Tobin, have attempted to calculate a better set of figures for the purpose. Their index, the *measure of economic welfare* (MEW), attempts to take into account such items as pollution and congestion as well as the more tangible products of the economy.[11]

Despite the costs of growth in terms of human and environmental damage, there is

strong evidence that if the economy's total output were kept at its present level, the community would pay a high price over and above the loss of additional goods and services.

First, it is not easy to carry out a decision to prevent further economic growth. Mandatory controls are abhorrent to most Americans. We cannot *order* people to stop inventing means to expand productivity. Nor does it make any sense to order every firm and industry to freeze its output level, since changing tastes and needs require some industries to expand their outputs at the same time that others are contracting. But who is to decide which should grow and which should contract, and how shall such decisions be made? *The achievement of zero economic growth may very well require government intervention on a scale that becomes expensive and even repressive.*

Second, zero economic growth may seriously hamper efforts to eliminate poverty both within our economy and throughout the world. Much of the earth's population today lives in a state of extreme want. And though wealthier nations have been reluctant to provide more than token amounts of help to the underdeveloped countries, less wealth means there would be even less to share. So perhaps the only hope for improved living standards in the impoverished countries of Africa, Asia, and Latin America lies in continued increases in output.

Finally, without continued growth, it will be no easy matter to finance effective programs of environmental protection. To improve the purity of our air and water and to clean up urban neighborhoods, tens of billions of dollars must be made available every year. Continued growth would enable the required resources to be provided without any reduction in the availability of consumer goods. But without such growth, we may actually be forced to cut back on our programs to protect the environment. Society could thus end up with fewer goods and a worse environment.

[10]From *The Costs of Economic Growth*, by Ezra J. Mishan, pages 171, 175. Copyright © 1967 by E. J. Mishan. Reprinted by permission of Holt, Rinehart and Winston and E. J. Mishan.

[11]W. Nordhaus and J. Tobin, "Is Growth Obsolete?" *Fiftieth Anniversary Colloquium*, V, National Bureau of Economic Research (New York: Columbia University Press, 1972).

REQUIREMENTS FOR INCREASED GROWTH

Assuming that we do want to increase the growth rate of the economy—as most countries do—the next question is, What can be done about it? Unfortunately, no one has a handy list of recipes for the stimulation of economic growth. If there were such a list, much of the world's hunger and disease could be eliminated.

Growth can only be attributed to a number of factors that no one knows how to explain: (1) *inventiveness,* which produces the new technology and other innovations that have contributed so much to economic expansion; (2) *entrepreneurship*, the leadership that recognizes no obstacles and undertakes the daring industrial ventures needed to move the economy ahead; and (3) *the work ethic* that leads a work force to high levels of productivity. No one really knows what features of economic organization and social psychology actually lead a community to adopt these goals, as Great Britain is said to have done at the beginning of the nineteenth century, as the United States is reputed to have done in the first half of the twentieth century, and as Japan is apparently doing today. We do know, however, that:

Growth requires two things that people can directly influence:

1. A large expenditure on *capital equipment:* factories, machinery, transportation, and telecommunications equipment.
2. The devotion of considerable effort to research and development from which innovations are derived.

Both of these types of expenditures help to increase the economy's ability to *supply* goods. But additional supplies will not be produced unless the *demand* is there to provide a market for these outputs.

This observation brings us back to the analysis of Part Three of this book, where it was stressed that the level (and, consequently, the growth) of national income is determined by the interaction of aggregate supply and aggregate demand. Much attention was devoted to the monetary and fiscal techniques by which aggregate demand can be managed and to the consequences of a failure to perform this task skillfully. There the focus was on unemployment and inflation. But we said relatively little about the determinants of supply and its rate of growth.

The need for capital equipment in any growth process provides a vital link between aggregate demand and aggregate supply. How does an economy acquire a larger capital stock? By investing. Recall that aggregate demand (in the Keynesian approach) is the sum of consumption, investment, and government spending, $Y = C + I + G$. But I is the only part of Y that creates more capital for the future.

The composition of aggregate demand is a major determinant of the rate of economic growth. If a larger fraction of total spending goes toward investment rather than toward consumption or government purchases, the capital stock will grow faster and the aggregate supply schedule will shift more quickly to the right.

ACCUMULATING CAPITAL BY SACRIFICING CONSUMPTION: THE CASE OF SOVIET RUSSIA

The importance of the *composition* of demand stands out in sharp relief if we turn away from the United States and consider a *centrally planned* economy, such as the Soviet Union.

When the Soviet Union undertook to expand its industrial output very rapidly, it was clear from the earliest stage of planning that a tremendous amount of capital equipment would be required to carry out the expansion. Not only did the Russians have to build modern factories and acquire sophisticated machinery, they also needed a social infrastructure—a transportation network to bring raw materials to the factories and take finished products to the markets, an efficient telecommunications system, and schools in which to train the population sufficiently to be an effective labor force. All this and much more was needed, and all of it required raw material and fuel for its construction.

Obviously, such a use of resources has its *opportunity cost.* Fuel and steel that are employed to build a train become unavailable for the production of refrigerators and washing machines. The real price of accumulating plant, equipment, and infrastructure is paid in the form of consumer goods that must be given up in order to build that capital equipment. In other words:

Through saving, the public gives up some consumption, which is the price it must pay for the accumulation of plant, equipment, and infrastructure. Without this sacrifice, growth generally cannot occur.

This is the hard lesson that the inhabitants of the Soviet Union have been living with for over half a century. Ever since the Russian Revolution in 1917, the Soviet leadership has been determined to promote rapid economic growth and has imposed on the general public whatever sacrifices of current consumption were deemed necessary for the purpose. Only in the most recent decades has an increase in the supply of consumer goods been assigned any priority. Yet, even now, investment in the U.S.S.R. is still 25 percent of GNP, while in the United States the figure stands at about 12 percent. As a result, Soviet living standards have been rising very slowly, particularly because the demands of the military forces have joined those of the growth planners in competing for the resources that might otherwise go into consumption.

The reason for this harsh trade-off is clear enough. If the economy is producing at its full potential—and the Russian economy generally has been—then real output Y cannot be increased further. Since $Y = C + I + G$, a decision to devote more resources to the production of heavy machinery (which is in I) or armaments (which are in G) is simultaneously a decision to forgo some consumption. Where resources are already fully employed, it is simply not possible to have both more guns and more butter.

This is precisely the sense in which saving is an absolute prerequisite for growth. If the economy is to grow, consumers must be coaxed, cajoled, or forced into saving. Every planner who adopts growth as his goal must decide just how he is going to generate the necessary saving.

THE PAYOFF TO GROWTH: HIGHER CONSUMPTION IN THE FUTURE

We may seem to be painting a rather grim picture of growth, and indeed, the process has often been harsh in the U.S.S.R. and in other nations that have enforced a high rate of economic growth. But it is also true that if the growth process is successful, the sacrifice of consumption that it requires is only a temporary loss. Consumers give up goods and services now in order to make possible the construction of a productive capacity that will permit them to consume even more goods and services at a later date. After all, from the consumers' point of view, that is what growth is all about. It is not an end in itself, but a means to an end—a standard of living higher than they could have attained without the process of economic expansion.

At least in a consumer-oriented economy, the decision to save in order to promote economic growth is simply an exchange between present and future consumption. Consumers sacrifice consumption now in order to be able to increase consumption in the future by more than they gave up in the past.

Of course, the payoff may never come if something goes wrong. An earthquake may destroy factories and roads, or a government with military ambitions may divert the increased productive capacity into the manufacture of armaments. So there is a risk in the decision to give up consumption now for increased consumption later. The growth process is a gamble—it means trading in a relatively sure thing (present consumption) for a risky future return (increased future consumption).

But betting on the future is not necessarily foolhardy. Economies would remain stagnant if people were unwilling to take chances. And some of the risk of investment plans can be reduced if decision makers understand fully the terms of the trade-off.

GROWTH WITHOUT SACRIFICING CONSUMPTION: SOMETHING FOR NOTHING?

Of course, some growth can be achieved without much sacrifice of present consumption. For at least one of the main engines of growth can be powered with relatively small increases in the nation's stock of factories, equipment, and infrastructure. Research and development can teach society new and more efficient ways of using the nation's productive resources. Thus, *innovation*—the process of putting inventions into operation—can permit an economy to get more output from the same input rather than by *expansion* of capital stock.

Everyone knows that this has in fact occurred. From the invention of the steam engine to that of the modern computer, our economy has benefited from a stream of inventions, some sensational, some more routine, which together have increased enormously the productivity of the nation's resources. Estimates of the relative contributions of innovation and accumulation to the growth process differ. A number of analysts attribute considerably more than half of the economic growth of the United States to research and invention. But whatever the correct figure, it is certainly large.

Another way of describing this conclusion is to say that while a substantial proportion of growth is *embodied* in increased quantities of plant, equipment, and infrastructure, a very large proportion of the economy's growth is *disembodied.* That is, it is attributable to better ideas—to improved methods of finding and using the same quantities of resources.

Typically, though, growth involves a combination of the two: the new ideas and the commitment of capital to put them into effect. The widespread use of computers could not have happened without the electronic gear from which they are composed and the flow of electricity by which they are operated. Computers are worthwhile because they reduce the quantities of resources necessary to do a given job, but originally some accumulation of resources was required in order to make possible the resulting savings.

For the long run, society has a considerable stake in the relative role of embodied and disembodied growth. Embodied growth has two serious costs that disembodied growth avoids. First, embodied growth necessarily speeds up the use of society's depletable resources: its iron ore, its petroleum supplies, and its stocks of other minerals and fuels. This means that smaller quantities of those resources will be available to future generations.

The second cost of embodied growth is of comparable importance. The resources that are used up in a process of embodied growth must ultimately end up on society's garbage heap. The physical laws of conservation of matter and energy tell us that no raw material can ever disappear. It can be transformed into smoke or solid waste, but unless it is recycled *entirely* (something that is both beyond the capability of our technology and impractical for other reasons), the greater the quantity of resources used in the productive process, the greater the quantity of wastes that must ultimately result.

Economist Kenneth Boulding has likened our planet to a spaceship hurtling through the solar system but constrained by terrestrial littering laws to keep its garbage on board. In spaceship Earth, we can transform waste materials into other forms—as by melting old bottles for reuse or converting them into energy, or by burning combustible garbage for heat—but we cannot simply toss them overboard.

Both of these environmental concerns—resource depletion and waste disposal—lead us to favor disembodied over embodied growth. To the extent that we can succeed in increasing the productivity of our resources, we can reduce both the rate at which they are depleted and the severity of the community's waste-disposal problems.

So far, we have enjoyed substantial success in trying to achieve growth in output without commensurate increase in our use of resources. One statistical analysis, for example, has provided evidence that attributes only about half of the growth in the United States during the period 1929–1969 to increased use of physical inputs. The remainder must be ascribed to improvements in technology as well as to increased education and skill of the labor force.[12]

One final remark on disembodied growth is in order. Economists are fond of pointing out that there is no such thing as a free lunch. Except in rare instances, improvements in technology are not "manna from heaven." They result, instead, from the work of scientists and technicians in government and industrial laboratories, from the labor of inventors in their basements or garages, and from the effort of management specialists studying the organiza-

tion of factories and assembly lines. This means that labor (along with other resources) is diverted from other activities into the production of knowledge. *In a fully employed economy, the opportunity costs of investing in the discovery of new knowledge are the consumption of or physical investment in goods that would otherwise have been produced.* So even here, we cannot get something for nothing.

SAVING AS THE ENEMY OF GROWTH: THE PARADOX OF THRIFT

[If] the capitalists themselves, together with the landlords and other rich persons . . . have . . . agreed . . . by depriving themselves of their usual conveniences and luxuries to save from their revenue and add to their capital . . . how is it possible to suppose that [an] increased quantity of commodities . . . should find purchasers [?][13]

We have now explained how saving works as the handmaiden of growth. But at the start of this chapter we mentioned an alternative view: that saving can be an impediment to growth. How can this be?

We can find the answer by worrying less about the *composition* of aggregate demand and more about its total *volume*. As we learned in Part Three, an unplanned economy—where saving and investing are typically done by different people—often has trouble keeping aggregate demand in line with aggregate supply. Keynesian national income analysis shows how *an effort to save more can actually result in everyone saving less.*

This so-called paradox of thrift is a phenomenon we have encountered earlier (in Chapter

---

[12]Edward F. Denison, *Accounting for United States Economic Growth 1929–1969* (Washington: The Brookings Institution, 1974).

[13]T. R. Malthus, quoted by Piero Sraffa in *The Works and Correspondence of David Ricardo*, vol. 2 (Cambridge: Cambridge University Press, 1951), pages 302–303.

9). Let us recall the analysis used there. With no government, aggregate demand is the sum $C + I$. Figure 33–4 is a diagram showing a typical 45° line diagram: curve C is the consumption function and curve $C + I$ is the total expenditure schedule, that is, the sum of consumption and investment demand. National income, as we know, is determined by the intersection of the $C + I$ curve with the 45° line (point A in the figure). The GNP is $1200 billion, of which $1000 billion is consumed and $200 billion is invested. Since saving is the gap between income ($1200 billion) and consumption ($1000 billion), it is shown by the vertical distance AB from the 45° line to the consumption schedule.

Now suppose that, due to a government campaign to reduce consumption, people agree to save a higher proportion of their income. The result, of course, is a drop in the consumption function. Figure 33–5, which repeats the C and $C + I$ curves from Figure 33–4 (in black), shows the new consumption function as the red line C' and the new aggregate demand schedule as the red line $C' + I$. National income will spiral down to point D, where GNP is only $900 billion, because aggregate demand is insufficient to support the previous production level. *Because saving depends on income,* saving—which is now the distance DE between the 45° line and the C' consumption function—drops to $175 billion. Thus the *attempt* to save more (the fall in the consumption function) is frustrated by the drop in GNP.

The explanation of the paradox of thrift is quite straightforward. If people are set on saving a large proportion of their income, then only a low quantity of output will find a market. Output will have to be low because there will be no demand for larger quantities of production. But because the public's income will consequently be low, it will not be able to save very much—it simply will not be able to afford to put large quantities of resources into saving. In this way, a strong desire to save may actually *reduce* the amount the community can ultimately manage

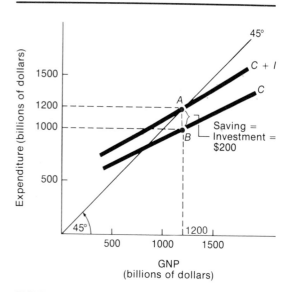

FIGURE 33–4

DETERMINATION OF NATIONAL INCOME IN KEYNESIAN ANALYSIS

This figure reviews the Keynesian national income analysis that was first introduced in Chapter 8. The equilibrium level of GNP is determined by the intersection of the $C + I$ schedule and the 45° line—point A in the diagram. At this level of income, both saving and investment are $200 billion, as indicated by the distance AB.

to save, and that is the paradox of thrift.

More important for our purposes, this mechanism shows how a strong desire to save can spell trouble for growth. Every increase in desired saving constitutes, other things being equal, an identical *reduction* in the demand to purchase goods for consumption. For saving, by definition, implies abstinence from consumption. And as we know, lack of demand for goods naturally leads the nation's businesses to reduce their production levels.

To engineer a successful acceleration in the rate of economic growth, any increase in the propensity to save must be matched by an increase in the willingness of firms

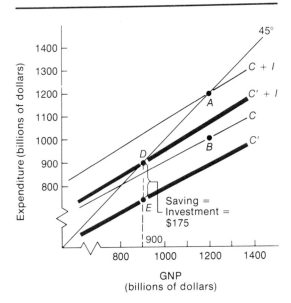

FIGURE 33–5

THE PARADOX OF THRIFT

This diagram indicates how a successful campaign to persuade consumers to save more might actually result in less total saving—the so-called *paradox of thrift*. The increased desire to save shifts the $C + I$ schedule downward to the position indicated by schedule $C' + I$, because saving more out of any given income means spending less. Equilibrium drops from point *A* to point *D*—from a GNP of $1200 billion to one of only $900 billion. In this example, total saving at this lower equilibrium point—distance *DE*—is only $175 billion, whereas it was formerly $200 billion.

to invest. That is, an increased demand for output by business firms must compensate for the reduction in consumers' demand for goods, which is a consequence of their increased saving.

RESOLUTION OF THE SAVING ENIGMA

Now that we have examined the arguments on both sides, we are in a position to resolve the

enigma with which this chapter began: How can saving be both a blessing and a curse for economic growth?

When an economy is producing as much as it can with its available resources, faster growth can only be achieved by shifting resources away from C (or G) and into I. *Saving is a way to release resources from consumption so that they may be used to produce investment goods.* Without enough saving, growth will be retarded by sluggish movement in the economy's aggregate supply curve. We may term this phenomenon supply-constrained growth, because output expansion is limited by the capability of firms to produce.

On the other hand, if firms cannot sell as much as their productive capacity enables them to manufacture, greater saving can only hinder the growth process. More saving will not call forth correspondingly more investment but will instead lower GNP. We may call such circumstances a case of demand-constrained growth, because expansion of output is limited by what customers will buy.

Which type of growth process prevails in the real world? Both—at different places and at different times.

We have already considered the case of a centrally planned economy as an example of supply-constrained growth. Since the managers of the Russian economy set aggregate demand wherever they please, they need never worry about insufficient demand. They do, however, have to cajole or coerce Russian consumers into abstaining from consumption so that more factories can be built.

The growth problem is rather similar in most of the developing nations of the world. While these poor countries desperately need to build the factories, machinery, and infrastructure necessary to support a modern economy, their inhabitants barely have enough income to survive. Such poor people can be expected to consume almost entirely the little incomes they do have, so they will be unable to provide the saving that can be used to build roads and factories. In such an economy, saving and accumulation will represent a very great sacrifice. Policymakers in this situation rarely, if ever, will have to deal with the problem of what to do with an embarrassing surplus of savings. Their task will be to know just how far they can go in inducing accumulation without causing unbearable hardships for the population.

A final example of a supply-constrained growth process is provided by a *developed economy operating at or near capacity levels*. When aggregate demand is sufficient to employ all the available capital and labor, the only way to speed up growth (apart from accelerating the pace of innovation) is to divert resources away from consumption or government spending and toward investment. As we learned in Part Three,

one way to do this is to pursue a national economic policy predicated on a combination of "easy money" to hold interest rates down (to stimulate investment) and government budget surpluses either through high taxes (to hold consumption down) or low government spending.

However, as we stressed in Part Three, the situation in the rich, industrialized capitalist economies—especially the United States—is often one of inadequate aggregate demand, so that economic expansion becomes demand-constrained. Under these circumstances, a kind of "free lunch" becomes possible, since *both* consumption *and* investment can be increased through an increase in aggregate demand. Here, more saving can only make a bad situation worse.

SUMMARY

1. If growth is evaluated in terms of its affect upon the well-being of individuals, a country's economic growth should be measured in terms of *per capita* income, not in terms of GNP or some other index of total output of the economy.
2. A rapidly rising population poses a threat to growth of per capita incomes.
3. On our finite planet, exponential growth (growth at a constant percentage rate) is, in general, impossible except for relatively brief periods.
4. Predictions are often based on the assumption that exponential growth rates will continue for a long period of time. This usually leads to frightening forecasts, but such prophesies of doom rest on an indefensible foundation.
5. Many observers argue that even if continued growth does not lead to catastrophes in terms of rapid depletion of resources, famine, and so forth (as some have predicted), its desirability is nevertheless questionable because it produces pollution, overcrowding, and many other undesirable consequences.
6. Those who favor growth argue that without it there is no chance of ridding the world of poverty.
7. Increases in growth depend heavily on entrepreneurship, accumulation of capital equipment, and research and development.
8. Saving is necessary for the accumulation of resources with which to produce factories, machinery, and other capital equipment. Thus, saving is a critical requisite for growth, particularly in less developed countries.
9. In some circumstances, particularly in industrialized countries, substantial saving by consumers can impede growth by reducing consumption

demand and therefore cutting down the amount it pays business firms to produce.

10. A strong desire to save may actually reduce the economy's saving by cutting consumer demand and thereby reducing income, which is the source of saving. This is called the paradox of thrift.

11. Saving and investment involve a sacrifice of current consumption in exchange for more output in the future. It is a trade-off between current and future consumption.

CONCEPTS FOR REVIEW

Output per capita
Exponential growth
Proven reserves
Social infrastructure
Exchange between present and
    future consumption

Embodied growth
Disembodied growth
Paradox of thrift
Supply-constrained growth
Demand-constrained growth

QUESTIONS FOR DISCUSSION

1. Which do you think has the higher total GNP, Pakistan or Luxembourg? Which has the higher per capita GNP? In which do you think people are better off economically?

2. Suppose output of product X grows at a constant exponential rate and doubles every 10 years. How many times will it have grown in 30 years? How many years does it require to expand to 16 times its initial level?

3. Can you think of any innovations that permit growth without proportionate increases in use of inputs?

4. What do you think is likely to happen to the availability of fuel in the twenty-first century? Describe some alternative scenarios, and discuss the likelihood of each.

5. Name as many undesirable consequences of growth as you can think of.

6. Are the undesirable consequences of growth more likely to be considered serious in a less developed country or in an industrialized country? Why?

7. During a period of inflation, is increased saving likely to be a stimulus or a hindrance to growth? Explain.

34

The Economics
of Environmental Protection

The problems of environmental deterioration are by no means new. What *is* new and different is the amount of attention the community is now prepared to give to environmental problems. Perhaps much of this increased interest can be attributed to rising income levels, which have freed people from the more urgent concerns about food, clothing, and shelter, allowing them to concentrate on the next priority level of needs—the *quality* of their lives.

Economic thought on these issues preceded the outburst of public concern with the subject by nearly half a century. Just after the first decade of the twentieth century, a noted British economist, A. C. Pigou, wrote a groundbreaking book, *The Economics of Welfare*, in which he offered an explanation of the market economy's poor environmental performance, an explanation that is still generally accepted by economists today. What is more, that same book outlined an approach to environmental policy that is still favored by most economists, though among lawmakers and bureaucrats this approach has so far attracted relatively little support. Pigou's analysis will be explained here in some detail.

This chapter is really an application of our earlier analysis of the imperfections of the price mechanism. In Chapter 31 we saw that major problems for the economy arise when one type of activity unintentionally has damaging or beneficial effects upon persons not directly involved in the activity—upon persons *external* to that activity. These incidental effects, called externalities, play a crucial role in the problems that beset our environment. We will see also that an understanding of the economic analysis of externalities helps to indicate policies that are appropriate for their control.

In particular, this chapter will show first that environmental problems have beset society long before the modern industrial era and that they affect planned as well as market economies. Second, we will see that individuals and government agencies contribute to environmental damage, and that private industry is not the only source of environmental problems. Third, we will show that emission of pollutants is considered an externality because of the harm it does to people not directly involved in the activities that generate the pollution. And finally, we will demonstrate, on the basis of the externalities analysis, that a system of charges or taxes on pollution emissions may be an appropriate and effective means of controlling them. Ironically, this amounts to using the price mechanism to remedy one of its own shortcomings.

THE DELAWARE: HOW *NOT* TO CLEAN UP A RIVER

Some of the measures that have been taken to clean up the Delaware River illustrate well the nature of the standard government approach to environmental policy and some of the ways that economists believe this approach can be improved.[1] A major rehabilitation program has been planned for this river, which flows through four states and past a number of industrial cities. After a 4-year period of extensive study and planning in the early 1960s, a committee composed of the Secretary of the Interior and the governors of the four states decided on a program.

The primary objective of any such program can be to protect human life and health, or it can be the improvement of recreational facilities, or it can be mainly aesthetic—the removal of unpleasant odors or unsightly scum or coloring matter. Which of these objectives is in fact pursued will determine the particular pollutants that the program will be designed to reduce. The plan that actually was chosen in the Delaware River project aimed primarily to decrease the amount of organic wastes in the river. This choice has since been criticized on the grounds that (1) it gave no priority to the removal of toxic chemicals, whose presence in the river is suspected of being a serious danger to human health; and (2) a reduction of wastes by the amounts contemplated almost certainly would not yield significant health benefits, or make the river suitable for swimming, or reduce its unsightliness and odor. At best, the plan can slightly reduce the time it takes some sportsmen to reach good fishing areas.

More important for our purpose was the *method* chosen to carry out the program. The Delaware River Basin Commission decided in June 1968 that the best way to improve the quality of the river was to require everyone who had been discharging wastes into it to reduce the amount of discharge (measured in terms of its expected oxygen use) by approximately the same percentage—a reduction of between 85 and 90 percent.

While this approach may seem both fair and effective, it turned out to have neither of these virtues. In fact, when a team of economists compared the cost of achieving the stated goals in this way with the more efficient method discussed later in this chapter, they estimated that the technique proposed by the Commission

[1] The following discussion is based primarily on Bruce A. Ackerman, Susan Rose Ackerman, James W. Sawyer, Jr., and Dale W. Henderson, *The Uncertain Search for Environmental Quality* (New York: The Free Press, 1974).

would be between 100 and 150 percent more expensive.[2] The total cost of the initial few years of the program has been estimated at nearly $750 million, so the amount that could have been saved is not insignificant.

In addition, after the haggling and negotiations had been completed, it turned out that the required reductions in emissions were (predictably) far from uniform. For example, petroleum refineries of rather similar output capacity were assigned quotas for reductions in emissions of oxygen-demanding wastes ranging from 2900 to 14,400 pounds per day.

The analysis presented in this chapter will enable us to see why assignment of equal percentage reductions, the method often favored by environmental authorities, is, in general, both inefficient and grossly inequitable. Worse yet, these problems can make the selected assignment of reductions politically unenforceable, as actually happened in the Delaware case.

THE ENVIRONMENT IN PERSPECTIVE: IS EVERYTHING GETTING STEADILY WORSE?

Much of the discussion of environmental problems in the popular press leaves the reader with the impression that matters have been growing steadily worse, and that pollution is largely a product of the profit system and modern industrialization. Neither of these conclusions is correct.

Medieval cities were pestholes—the streets and rivers were littered with garbage and the air stank of rotting wastes. At the beginning of the eighteenth century, a German traveler reported that to get a view of London from the tower of St. Paul's, one had to get there very early in the morning "before the air was full of coal smoke." And early in the twentieth century the automobile was hailed as a source of major improvement in the cleanliness of city streets, which until then had fought a losing battle against the proliferation of horse dung.

Since World War II there has been marked progress in solving a number of pollution problems, much of it the result of concerted efforts to protect the environment. Progress in cleaning up New York City's dirty air has been remarkable. In Manhattan, the concentration of pollutant particles has dropped 66 percent from its level right after World War II; and in Brooklyn, the corresponding fall is more than 80 percent. The famous, or rather infamous, "fogs" of London are almost a thing of the past because of the improvement in air quality since 1950. The cleaner air in Britain's capital city has resulted in an astounding 50 percent increase in the number of hours of winter sunshine. There have been improvements in the cleanliness of the air in other cities as well as striking increases in the purity of a number of bodies of water. In short, pollution problems are not new, nor is every part of the environment deteriorating relentlessly.

There is also plenty of evidence that environmental problems do not occur exclusively in capitalist economies. The Soviet Union has all sorts of serious environmental troubles, to which it has given substantial publicity in its own newspapers and magazines.[3] For example, because of smoke in the air, the number of clear daylight hours is 40 percent lower in Leningrad than in Pavlovsk—a town only 20 miles away. The Iset and the Volga rivers are so filled with chemicals that they have actually caught fire! The number of dams, canals, and reservoirs along the waterways leading into the Aral and Caspian seas have caused so much evaporation that both seas have fallen rapidly. In fact, some claim that by the end of the

---

[2]For details see A. Kneese, S. Rolfe, and J. Harned, editors, *Managing the Environment: International Economic · Cooperation for Pollution Control* (New York: Praeger Publishers, 1971), Appendix C, pages 225–74.

[3]For an excellent nontechnical discussion see Marshall Goldman, *The Spoils of Progress* (Cambridge, Mass.: M.I.T. Press, 1972).

century, the Aral Sea may have deteriorated into a salt marsh.

None of the preceding discussion is meant to suggest that all is well in our economy as far as the environment is concerned, or that there is nothing we can or should do about it. Along with the improvements that have been described, our world has been subject to a number of new pollutants, some of which are more dangerous than those we have reduced, even though they are less visible and less malodorous. A variety of highly toxic substances—PCBs (polychlorinated biphenyls), chlorinated hydrocarbons, fluorocarbons, and radioactive materials—are prevalent in the environment and are suspected of causing cancer and of threatening life and health in other ways. Other substances break down so slowly that they are likely to constitute a threat for many thousands of years. The accumulation of these and other byproducts of recent technology may well cause damage that is all but irreversible.

While environmental problems are neither new nor confined only to capitalist, industrialized economies, these facts are not legitimate grounds for complacency. The potential damage that we may be inflicting on ourselves, as well as on our surroundings, is very real and very substantial.

THE LAW OF CONSERVATION OF MATTER AND ENERGY

It is impossible to describe completely all the ways in which we damage our environment. Our very existence creates pollution problems. We exhale ''used'' air and excrete food wastes; we cut down trees for housing and clear fields to plant crops; the explanations can go on and on. Nevertheless, we can point to three major sources of environmental damage that have continued to play a major role in these difficulties. They are: (1) the law of conservation of matter and energy, which tells us that all produced goods that are not recycled must ultimately constitute disposal problems; (2) the ''edifice complex,'' which is the notion that

A Case of Environmental Improvement

The story of the cleanup of the Willamette [River] is heartening. It shows that a major river, even if heavily polluted, can be restored to health. . . . Fifty years ago men refused to work on riverside construction because of the water's intolerable stench. Now thousands regularly swim, fish,

water ski, and boat on summer weekends and for the first time Chinook salmon ascend the Willamette to spawn in the fall. . . . Without doubt the single major factor behind the cleanup of the Willamette was the strong commitment and concern of the people of Oregon. . . . Oregon's experience demonstrates how a major river can be restored if the people are determined, the government committed, and the legal tools available. . . . The Willamette is a practical demonstration that treatment technology . . . can remove sufficient wastes so that a large population, extensive industry, and a clean river can coexist in harmony.

Source: *Environmental Quality, The Fourth Annual Report of the Council on Environmental Quality* (Washington, D.C.: U.S. Government Printing Office, September 1973), pages 43–71.

anything that can be done by the bulldozer and the crane necessarily constitutes progress—and the bigger the project the better; and (3) the problem of externalities, the fact that under current economic arrangements the harm done by the polluter predominantly affects people other than himself, so that he has no economic motivation to bring under control the damage he does to the environment. We will discuss each of these issues in turn.

The physical law of conservation of matter and energy tells us there is no way that objects can be made to disappear—at most they can be changed into something else. Oil, for instance, can be transformed into heat (and smoke) or into plastic—but it will never vanish. This means that after a raw material has been used, either it must be used again (recycled) or it becomes a waste product that must somehow be disposed of.

Environmental Causes of Disease

Insidious health hazards have been introduced by people into their environment for centuries. The superbly engineered aqueducts of Rome brought the populace not only water but poisonous lead, which leaked from the lead pipes into the drinking supply. Documented cases of sterility and permanent mental impairment have been traced to lead poisoning; some historians even believe that lead poisoning may have contributed to the fall of the Empire. Similarly, coal-fired smog hanging above the sunless, Dickensian factory towns and big city slums of the 19th century has been linked to a hormone deficiency among children. Insufficient exposure to the sun's ultraviolet radiation, which activates the formation of the Vitamin D essential to healthy growth, is thought to have caused a widespread incidence of crippling rickets. The "mad hatters" of the 19th century suffered from neurological disorders caused by inhalation of mercury used in treating furs and felts.

Thus disease caused by or associated with chemicals introduced into the environment is nothing new. In our own day, various lung diseases such as emphysema have been linked with air pollution. Oxygen transport by the blood can be impaired by nitrite—sometimes found in well water or used as a preservative in many meat products—and it can also be impaired by carbon monoxide. Chemicals are believed to affect the incidence of heart disease (carbon monoxide), cause permanent nerve disorders (mercury), and induce bone abnormalities (vinyl chloride). A disconcerting, growing body of evidence indicates that subtle, manmade hazards are supplanting famine and infectious disease as significant determinants of life expectancy in 20th century developed nations.

Discovering links between chemicals and health problems is a slow process, usually succeeding only after a relatively long history of use or exposure. In the meantime, however, chemical development proceeds at a rapid pace. About 2 million chemical compounds are known, and each year thousands more are discovered by the U.S. chemical industry and hundreds are introduced commercially. We know very little about the possible health consequences of these new compounds. Many are not toxic, but the sheer number of chemical compounds, the diversity of their use, and the adverse effects already encountered from some make it increasingly probable that chemical contaminants in our environment have become a significant determinant of human health and life expectancy.

Source: *Environmental Quality, The Sixth Annual Report of the Council of Environmental Quality* (Washington, D.C.: U.S. Government Printing Office, December, 1975, pages 11–12.

In the preceding chapter we indicated that the expansion of economic activity and its resulting products usually requires an ever-increasing use of minerals, fuels, and other raw materials. After their initial use, it may be profitable to employ some of them again. Recycled copper constitutes a substantial portion of our copper supply, and when steel prices are sufficiently high, used automobiles are profitably turned into scrap metals.

Still, only a small proportion of the economy's inputs are made up of recycled materials, and recycling activities have in many cases been declining despite the large amount of volunteer effort and publicity that has been devoted to them in recent years.

The number of firms in the United States that reprocess used oil (the "re-refineries") has fallen by two-thirds since 1965. The recycling of waste paper declined relative to the use of raw-material paper during the 1960s. And during the recession of 1974–1975, many voluntary collection centers were forced to close their doors because they simply could find no takers for the products that had previously enabled them to meet their expenses.

If it is not recycled, any input used in the production process *must* ultimately become a waste product. It may end up on the garbage heap of some municipal dump. It may literally go up in smoke, contributing its bit to the pollution of the atmosphere. Or it may even be transformed into heat, warming up adjacent waterways and killing aquatic life in the process. The laws of physics tell us there is nothing we can do to make used inputs disappear altogether from the earth.

The upshot is that in an economy whose output is growing and whose input use is consequently increasing, waste disposal or pollution or both is virtually certain to be a growing problem. There are only three ways to ameliorate these difficulties: (1) increased recycling, (2) increased durability or reuse of the products (that is, the use of returnable bottles instead of throwaway containers), and (3) increased efficiency in the use of raw materials so that smaller quantities are utilized in a given quantity of output. In fact, this last remedy has already been used to some extent in our economy, in which nearly two-thirds of our output growth has been achieved without an increased use of raw materials.

THE EDIFICE COMPLEX

One tends to think of industry as the primary villain in environmental damage. But:

While private firms have done their share in harming the environment, private individuals and government have also been prime contributors.

In the United Kingdom the open fireplace in the private home may well have been the largest single source of air pollution, and the emissions of private passenger cars play an important role in the air pollution problems of most major cities. Wastes from flush toilets and residential washing machines also cause significant harm.

Governments, too, add to the problem in many ways. The wastes of municipal treatment plants are a major source of water pollution. Military aircraft leave a long trail of exhaust and make a lot of noise. Obsolete atomic materials and byproducts associated with chemical and nuclear weapons are among the most dangerous of all types of wastes, and the problem of their disposal is far from solved. The Tennessee Valley Authority, the one generator of electricity that is owned and operated by the federal government, is far behind the rest of the industry in complying with federal emissions regulations.

There is at least one type of environmental damage that, in particular, has been closely associated with government activity.

Government agencies, presumably in an attempt to maximize their influence, have undertaken the construction of giant dams and reservoirs that flood farmlands and destroy canyons, that render other soil unusable because of seepage of salts into the earth, and that change the water table (the level of water under the ground) by evaporation and seepage. Often, the drainage of swamps has subsequently altered local ecology irrevocably; the building of canals has diverted the flow of rivers; and the construction of dams has flooded and destroyed irreplaceable areas of natural beauty.

The automatic association of progress with the large-scale products of the bulldozer is an attitude that is encountered in many economies, including the United States. The U.S. Army Corps of Engineers has often been accused of acting on the basis of this "edifice complex," although it seems recently to have modified its behavior in the direction of environmental preservation, at least in a few cases.

But the edifice complex (also referred to as the "beaver complex") has reached its heights in the communist states, where government control of the economy is so much greater than it is in the United States. Perhaps the leading advocate of giant earth-moving projects was Joseph Stalin himself, and his pride in enormous hydroelectric installations and huge canals was well publicized in the Soviet press. There is evidence that the environmental effects of the edifice complex are far more severe in the centrally planned economies than they are in free-enterprise societies.

THE ENVIRONMENT AS A PUBLIC GOOD

We have already indicated that our very existence means that some environmental damage is inevitable. Products of the earth must be used up, and wastes must be generated in the process of creating the means of subsistence.

There is no question of reducing environmental damage to zero. As long as the human race survives and produces its livelihood, complete elimination of such damage is literally impossible. *It is not even desirable to get as close as possible to zero damage.* Some pollutants in small quantities are quickly dispersed and rendered harmless by natural processes, and it is not worth the opportunity cost to eliminate others whose damage is slight. Use of a large quantity of resources for this purpose may so limit their supply that there will not be materials available for the construction of hospitals, schools, and other things more important to society than the elimination of some pollutants.

The real issue then is not that pollution exists at all, but that in an unregulated market economy environmental damage tends to be more serious and widespread than the public interest can tolerate. This assertion immediately raises three key questions. First, why do economists believe that environmental damage is unacceptably severe *in terms of the public interest?* And how do they measure "the public interest"? Second, why does a market economy generate too much pollution when it is so good at providing about the right number of toasters and trucks? What has gone wrong with the economic system? And, third, what can we do about it?

Economists normally are unwilling to claim any special ability to judge what is good for the public interest. Instead, they prefer to accept as adequate indicators of "the public interest" the wishes of the members of the public. When the economy reflects these wishes as closely as it can, given the resources and technology available, economists conclude that it is working effectively. When it operates in a way that frustrates the desires of the people who make up society, they conclude that the economy is functioning improperly. From this point of view, we can gather why the free-enterprise economy is better at following the public's wishes when it produces and supplies consumer goods than when it affects the state of the environment.

Any consumer can go into the marketplace (the nearest shop) and, by offering the required amount of money, order the quantity of shirts, cigars, or loaves of bread he desires. But that person has no effective way of ordering a better environment. While he can sometimes "place his order" through the ballot box, the consumer cannot obtain the environment he wishes via the market.

The problem here is one we have encountered earlier, in Chapter 31.

A better environment is a *public good*. Once it is supplied to any one individual, it must automatically be available to a great many others.

If the Czar of all the Russias had ordered the purification of the air of St. Petersburg to avoid offense to the royal noses of his family, purer air would automatically have also been provided to the humblest nearby residents. You can buy a shirt for yourself without providing one to your neighbor in the process. But you *alone* cannot breathe cleaner air, despite the help you can get from an air conditioner or a gas mask (both of which are private goods). That, of course, is why no one person can afford to pay for purer air. Since it must be "bought" for the entire community or not at all, it is just too expensive for one person acting alone.

Because no single individual or small group can afford to pay the full cost of such public goods, they normally are supplied by governments. By using the coercive powers of taxation, the state can force all those who benefit from cleaner air to pay an appropriate share of its cost. In the absence of such action by government, the free-enterprise economy will not supply as much environmental quality *as the public wants* because business firms that might provide clean air and water for a fee cannot effectively *exclude* nonpayers from enjoying their output. Thus *no one* can be charged a price for breathing the cleaner air, and no private firm will undertake the work of air cleaning without being paid for doing so. It is for this reason that environmental damage tends to be more serious and widespread in a market economy than public interest justifies.

POLLUTION AS AN EXTERNALITY

There is a closely related aspect of this matter that indicates not only why environmental damage tends to be excessive but also how large that excess is likely to be. Here we deal with the fundamental 1911 analysis of A. C. Pigou that we referred to at the beginning of this chapter. In Chapter 31 we discussed some of the general failures of the market mechanism and singled out externalities as a primary cause of such imperfections. An *externality,* it will be recalled, is an incidental consequence of some economic activity that can be either beneficial or detrimental to someone who neither controls the activity nor is intentionally served by it. The smoke from a plant that produces some specialized chemical affects persons other than the management of the plant or its customers. The emission of pollutants constitutes one of the most clear-cut and standard examples of a detrimental externality.

These examples illustrate the importance of externalities for public policy and indicate why their analysis is one of the 12 Ideas for Beyond the Final Exam.

Because the damage done by the smoke to incidentally involved parties does not enter the financial accounts of the firm whose plant produces the emissions, the owners of the firm have no financial motivation to restrain those emissions, particularly since emission control costs money. Instead, they will find it profitable to produce their chemical product and to emit their smoke as though it caused no damage to the community.

One way to look at the matter is as a failure of the pricing system.

Through the smoke externality, the business firm is able to use up some of the community's clean air without paying anything for the privilege of doing so. Just as the firm would undoubtedly use oil and electricity wastefully if they were obtainable at zero charge, the firm will also use the community's air wastefully, despoiling it with smoke far beyond any level that the public interest can justify. Rather than being at the (low) socially desirable level, the quantity of smoke will be at whatever amount is necessary (usually high) to save as much money as possible for the firm that emits it.

SUPPLY–DEMAND ANALYSIS OF ENVIRONMENTAL PROBLEMS

The basic supply–demand model can help to explain the externalities analysis of environmental problems and its implication for public policy. As an illustration, let us deal with the problem of solid wastes—and the damage that the massive generation of garbage is doing to our environment.

In Figure 34–1 we see a demand curve, DE, for waste disposal. As usual, this curve has a negative slope, meaning that if the price of garbage removal is set sufficiently high, people will become more careful about the amount of garbage they produce—they will more often bring papers, bottles, and cans to recycling centers; they will begin to demand less elaborate packaging on the goods they buy; they will repair broken items rather than throwing them

out; and so on. In short, a higher price of garbage removal can in the long run be expected to reduce the amount of garbage generated, as our basic demand analysis usually leads us to expect.

The graph also shows the supply curve, SS, which we can expect to prevail in an ideal market for garbage removal. Garbage disposal is expensive to society—it requires people and trucks to haul it away; garbage dumps occupy valuable land; and the use of fire or other means to get rid of the garbage creates pollution which, as we have seen, has a high real cost to the community. As we saw in our analysis of competitive industries (Chapter 23), the position of the market's supply curve depends on costs.

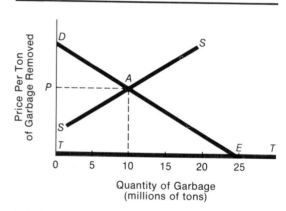

FIGURE 34–1

FREE DUMPING OF POLLUTANTS AS AN INDUCEMENT TO DAMAGE THE ENVIRONMENT

Whether wastes are solid, liquid, or gaseous, they impose costs upon the community. If the emitter is not charged for the damage, it is as though the resulting wastes were removed with zero charges to the polluter (red removal supply curve TT). The polluter is then induced to emit a great deal (25 million tons in the figure). If the charges to him reflected the true cost to the community (supply curve SS of waste removal), it would pay to emit a much smaller amount (10 million tons in the figure).

Thus, if suppliers had to pay the full costs of garbage removal, the supply curve would be comparably high (as drawn in the graph) and with a positive slope, meaning that the unit cost of garbage disposal rises as the quantity rises.

We see that in a free market, for the community depicted in the graph, the price of garbage removal will be P dollars per ton, and at that price 10 million tons will be generated (point A).

But what if the community's government decides to remove garbage "free"? Of course, that means the government is really charging the consumer for the service in the form of taxes but not in a way that makes each consumer pay an amount that reflects the quantity of garbage that consumer produces. The result is that the supply curve is no longer SS; rather, it becomes the red line TT, which lies along the horizontal axis. What this says is that any one household can increase the garbage it throws away as much as it wishes and still pay a zero price for the additional amount.

Now the intersection of the supply and demand curve is no longer point A. Rather it is point E, at which the price is zero and the quantity of garbage generated is 25 million tons—an amount substantially greater than would be produced if those who make the garbage had to pay the cost of getting rid of it.

Similar problems occur if the community offers the oxygen of its waterways and the purity of its atmosphere at a zero price to all who choose to utilize them, however wastefully and however great the quantities they decide to use up. The amount that will be wasted and otherwise used up is likely to be enormously greater than it would be if users had to pay for the cost of their actions to society. And that, in the view of economists, is the major reason for the severity of our environmental problems.

Several conclusions follow:

1. The magnitude of our pollution problems is attributable in large part to the fact that the community lets individuals, firms, and government agencies deplete without financial charge such resources as oxygen in the water and pure air.
2. One way of dealing with pollution problems is to charge those who emit pollution, and who cause other sorts of environmental damage, a price commensurate with the costs they impose on the community.
3. This is another instance in which higher prices—on environmentally damaging activities— can be beneficial to the community.

BASIC APPROACHES TO ENVIRONMENTAL POLICY

In broad terms, three general methods have been proposed for the control of activities that damage the environment.

1. Voluntary programs, such as nonmandatory investment in pollution control equipment by firms that decide to act in a manner that meets their social responsibilities, or voluntary separation of solid wastes by consumers who deliver them to collection centers for recycling.
2. Direct controls, which either (a) impose legal ceilings on the amount any polluter is permitted to emit (as in the Delaware River program); or (b) specify how particular activities must be carried on—for example, they may prohibit backyard incinerators, or the use of high-sulfur coal, or require smokestack "scrubbers" to capture some of the emissions of electric-generating installations.
3. Taxes on emissions, or the use of other monetary incentives or penalties to make it unattractive financially for emitters of pollutants to continue to pollute as usual.

Each of these methods has its place. If used appropriately, together they can constitute an effective and efficient environmental program. Let us consider each of them in turn.

VOLUNTARISM

We can deal very briefly with voluntary programs. As one might surmise, the voluntary control of pollution has usually proved to be weak and unreliable. Voluntary programs for the collection and separation of garbage into different and easily recyclable materials have rarely managed to reroute more than a small fraction of a community's wastes from the garbage dump to the recycling plants. Some business people with strong consciences have manifested good intentions and made sincere attempts to improve the practices of their companies. Yet competition has usually prevented them from spending more than token amounts for this purpose. No business, whatever its virtues, can long afford to have the prices of its products undercut by rival suppliers. As a result, voluntary business programs have usually been more helpful to the companies' public relations activities than to the environment, and those with a real interest in environmental protection have called for legislation that *requires* all firms, including competitors, to undertake the same measures, thereby subjecting all firms in the industry to similar handicaps. (See the boxed insert on the next page.)

Yet voluntary measures do have their place. They are appropriate where alternative measures are not readily available. Where surveillance and, consequently, enforcement is impractical, as in the prevention of littering by campers in isolated areas, there is no choice but an appeal to people's consciences. And in brief but serious emergencies, in which there is no time to plan and enact a systematic program, there may also be no good substitute for voluntary compliance. Several major cities have, for example, experienced episodes in which dangerous concentrations of pollutants resulted from unfavorable atmospheric conditions, such as absence of wind to scatter pollutants and a peculiar pattern of atmospheric temperature that prevented the pollutants from rising. In such cases where there had been no advance preparation, the authorities were forced to appeal to the public to avoid activities that would have aggravated the problem.

One can easily cite cases in which experience shows that public response to appeals requiring cooperation for short periods has been enthusiastic and gratifying. To summarize:

Voluntary programs are not dependable ways to protect the environment. However, in brief, unexpected emergencies or where effective surveillance is impossible, the policymaker may have no other choice. Sometimes in these cases voluntary programs even work.

DIRECT CONTROLS VERSUS POLLUTION CHARGES

Direct controls have been the chief instrument of environmental policy in the United States. The federal government, through the Environmental Protection Agency, formulates standards for air and water quality and requires state and local governments to adopt rules that will assure achievement of those goals. Probably the best known of these are the standards for automobile emissions. Since 1968, new automobiles have been required to pass tests showing that their emissions of a number of pollutants do not exceed specified amounts. Table 34–1 lists these emissions standards. In addition, several states have required that used cars also adhere to certain limits on emissions. As another example, localities may prohibit the use of particularly "dirty" fuels by industry or may require the adoption of certain processes to "cleanse" those fuels or their emissions. Typical of these programs are local ordinances regulating the type and sulfur content of the fuels used by power plants, factories, and other stationary sources of sulfur dioxide pollution. Relocation of such pollution sources outside

Pollution: Puffery or Progress?

"It cost us a bundle but the Clearwater River still runs clear," read the headline beneath the picture. And sure enough, it was a scene of breath-taking natural beauty—hills, shaggy with evergreens, framing a stretch of clear, blue water flecked with white foam where it raced over hidden rocks. But what Potlatch Forests, Inc., neglected to mention in its national ad campaign was that the picture had been snapped some 50 miles upstream from the company's pulp and paper plant in Lewiston, Idaho. What is more, Potlatch pumps its fresh water from the Clearwater—but dumps up to 40 tons of suspended organic wastes back into the Clearwater and the nearby Snake River every day.

Aside from the filth that spews into the river, Potlatch concedes, some 2.5 million tons of sulphur gases and 1.8 million pounds of particulates billowed from the plant stacks last year; in fact, the Lewiston plant enjoys the dubious distinction of being the only industrial mill in the U.S. to have been the subject of separate air- and water-pollution abatement hearings before Federal authorities. Each day, on leaving the plant's parking lot, employees sluice down their autos with a company-installed car wash to protect the cars' paint from the corrosive sodium sulphate that sifts from the air. When an enterprising local college newspaper editor pointed out the discrepancy between ad copy and reality, the company responded by canceling all corporate advertising. As Potlatch president Benton R. Cancell explained it: "We tried our best. You just can't say anything right any more—so to hell with it."

FISHING: The Potlatch incident is certainly not the whole story of industry's role in pollution. U.S. companies will have spent some $1 billion in 1970 alone to clean up the nation's fouled air and water, according to the President's Council on Environmental Quality (CEQ). Indeed, under pressure from Federal agencies, Potlatch itself has announced plans to spend $9.6 million on pollution-abatement equipment for the Lewiston plant. And some companies have gone all-out to prove their good intentions. Armco Steel won the highest award of the American Society of Civil Engineers this year for its virtually pollution-free steel mill in Middletown, Ohio, where even the pickling pond, usually a cauldron of acid and water, is so pure that it has been stocked for fishing. Campbell Soup Co. solved a tough problem in Paris, Texas, by using water laced with food scraps to irrigate 500 acres of pastureland.

Still, there is growing concern among Washington officials, conservationists and even some industrialists that too many companies are declaring war on pollution mainly with TV commercials, lavish brochures, press releases and ads in newspapers and magazines—without doing enough actual spending to wage the war effectively. "I think there has been widespread acceptance by industry of the reality of the environmental problem but at this point, I don't feel they have a now-or-never attitude," CEQ chairman Russell E. Train told Newsweek's James Bishop, Jr.

Drawing by Stevenson © 1970 The New Yorker Magazine, Inc.

'So *that's* where it goes! Well, I'd like to thank you fellows for bringing this to my attention'

populated areas, and the required installation of smokestack emissions controls, have also contributed to better air quality.

Taxes

Most economists agree that a nearly exclusive reliance on direct controls is a mistake and that, in most cases, financial penalties on polluters can do the same job more dependably, more effectively, and more economically. The most common suggestion is that firms be permitted to pollute all they want but be forced to pay a tax for the privilege to make them *want* to pollute less. A tax on emissions simply requires the polluter to install a meter that records his emissions in the same way his electric meter records his use of electricity. At the end of the month the government automatically sends him a bill charging him a stipulated amount for each gallon of wastes (the amount must also vary with the quality of the wastes—a higher tax rate being imposed on wastes that are more dangerous or unpleasant). Thus, the more

damage the polluter does (the more he emits) the more he must pay. This tax is deliberately designed to *encourage* the use of its glaring loophole—the polluter *can* reduce the tax he pays by decreasing the amount he emits. In terms of Figure 34–1, if the tax is used to increase the payment for waste emissions from zero (red supply line *TT*) and instead forces the polluter to pay its true cost to society, emissions will automatically be reduced from 25 down to 10 million tons.

It is important to see why this approach may prove more effective and reliable than direct controls. Direct controls essentially rely on the enforcement mechanism of the criminal justice system. Rules are set up that the polluter must obey. If the polluter violates those rules, he must first be caught. Then the regulatory agency must decide whether it has enough evidence to prosecute. Next, it must win its case before the courts. And, finally, the courts must impose a penalty that is more than just a token gesture. If any one of these steps does not occur, then the polluter gets away with his damaging activities.

TABLE 34–1

U.S. AUTOMOBILE EMISSIONS STANDARDS (grams per mile)

	HYDROCARBONS	CARBON MONOXIDE	NITROGEN OXIDES
1. Uncontrolled car	8.7	87.0	4.0
2. Interim federal standards for 1975 and 1976	1.5	15.0	3.1
3. Interim California standards for 1975 and 1976	0.9	9.0	2.0
4. Ultimate target federal standards (as defined in the 1970 amendments to the Clean Air Act)	0.41	3.4	0.4

This table shows emissions of three pollutants by unregulated automobiles (row 1) and under three different regulatory targets. The lower the number in a column, the smaller the amount of pollution permitted. The second row shows the transition standards under federal law, and the third row shows the tougher transition standards enacted in California. The last row reports the controversial targets enacted in 1970, which were supposed to go into effect in 1975 but have been postponed several times.

Source: *Environmental Quality, The Fifth Annual Report of the Council on Environmental Quality* (Washington, D.C.: U.S. Government Printing Office, December 1974), pages 125–29; National Academy of Sciences and National Academy of Engineering, "Air Quality and Automobile Emission Control," Prepared for the Committee on Public Works, U.S. Senate, September 1974, Volume 4 (The Costs and Benefits of Automobile Emission Control), page 57.

Enforcing Direct Controls

The enforcement of direct controls requires vigilance and enthusiasm by the regulatory agency, which must assign the resources and persons needed to carry out the task of enforcement. Yet experience indicates that regulatory vigor is far from universal and often evaporates as time passes and public concern recedes. There are many cases in which the resources devoted to enforcement are pitifully small.

The effectiveness of direct controls also depends upon the speed and rigor of the courts. Yet the courts are often slow and lenient. An example is the notorious case of the Reserve Mining Company. Several Minnesota communities, including Duluth, have been trying to stop this company from pouring its wastes (which contain certain asbestos-like fibers, believed to cause cancer) into Lake Superior, which is the source of the communities' drinking water. After nearly a decade of litigation and no less than 16 judicial decisions, the courts still have failed to curb this discharge.

Finally, direct controls can work only if the legislation imposes sizable penalties for violators. One can cite many cases in which large firms have been convicted of polluting and fined less than $5000—an amount beneath the notice of even a relatively small corporation. The following examples are not atypical of the sorts of fines to which polluters may be subjected:

> Ten Philadelphia firms were fined a total of $2,900 Friday in the seventh week of the City's accelerated drive for violation of the air-pollution code.[4]

> Seven companies, six from the Chicago area, have been charged with pollution of area rivers and waterways . . . the corporations could be fined up to $2,500 on each count if convicted.[5]

[4]Joseph H. Trachtman, "10 Firms Fined a Total of $2,900 in Phila.'s Pollution Crackdown." Reprinted by permission of *The Philadelphia Inquirer*, October 30, 1970.

[5]Robert Davis, "7 Firms Charged with Water Pollution." *Chicago Tribune*, September 21, 1971, page 8, Section 1A. Reprinted courtesy of the *Chicago Tribune*.

> [New York City] has collected $800,000 in fines against [all] air and noise polluters over the last three years. . . .[6]

Where more drastic penalties are available, their very magnitude may make the authorities reluctant to impose them. In an extreme case, in which the only legal remedy is to force the closing of an offending plant, the government agency is likely to back down under local pressure to preserve the community's source of jobs and income.

Enforcing Taxes

In contrast, pollution taxes are automatic and certain. No one need be caught, prosecuted, convicted, and punished. The tax bills are just sent out automatically by the untiring tax collector.

The only sure way for the polluter to work his way out of paying pollution charges is to cut down his emissions.

A second difference between direct controls and taxes is worth noting. Suppose there is a ruling under a program of direct controls that Filth, Inc., must cut its emissions by 50 percent. Then that firm has absolutely no motivation to go one drop further. Why should it cut its emissions by 55 or even 52 percent when the law offers it neither reward nor encouragement for going beyond the selected quota? Under a system of emission taxes, however, the more the firm cuts back on its pollution, the more it saves in tax payments.

A third important difference between direct controls and taxes on emissions—one that is emphasized heavily by economists—is the greater efficiency of the latter in the use of resources. It is claimed that the tax approach can do the job far more cheaply, saving labor, fuel, and raw materials, which can instead

[6]"Pollution Fines $800,000 in 3 Years." *The New York Times*, June 25, 1974, page 37. © 1974 by The New York Times Company. Reprinted by permission.

be used to build schools, hospitals, and housing for low-income groups. Statistical estimates for several pollution control programs suggest that the cost of doing the job through direct controls can easily be twice as high as under the tax alternative.

Why should there be such a difference? The answer is that under direct controls the job of cutting back emissions is apportioned among the various polluters on some principle (usually intended to approximate some standard of equality) that is selected by the regulators. This rarely assigns the task in accord with ability to carry it out cheaply and efficiently. Suppose it costs firm A only 3 cents a gallon to reduce emissions while firm B must spend 20 cents a gallon to do the same job. If both firms spew out 2000 gallons of pollution a day, a 50 percent reduction in pollution can be achieved by ordering both firms to limit emissions to 1000 gallons a day. This may or may not be just, but it is certainly not efficient. The social cost will be 1000 times 3 cents, or $30, to firm A and 1000 times 20 cents, or $200, to firm B, a total of $230.

If, instead, a tax of 10 cents a gallon has been imposed, all the work would have been done by firm A—which can do it more cheaply. Firm A would have cut its emissions out altogether, paying the 3 cents a gallon this requires, to avoid the 10 cents a gallon tax. Firm B would go on polluting as before, because it is cheaper to pay the tax than the 20 cents a gallon it costs to control its pollution. In this way, under the tax, *total daily emissions will still be cut by 2000 gallons a day.* But the entire job will be done by the polluter who can do it more cheaply, and the total daily cost of the program will therefore be $60 (3 cents $\times$ 2000 gallons) instead of the $230 it would cost under direct controls.

The secret of the efficiency induced by a tax on pollution is straightforward. Only polluters who can reduce emissions cheaply and efficiently can afford to take advantage of the built-in loophole— the opportunity to save on taxes by

reducing emissions. The tax approach simply assigns the job to those who can do it most effectively.

Advantages and Disadvantages

Given all these advantages of the tax approach, why would anyone want to use direct controls?

There are three general and important situations in which direct controls have a clear advantage:

1. *Where an emission is so dangerous that it is decided to prohibit it altogether.* Here there is obviously nothing to be gained by installing complicated procedures for the collection of taxes that will never be paid because there will be no emissions for which payment is required.
2. *Where a sudden change in circumstances— for example, a dangerous air quality crisis— calls for prompt and substantial changes in conduct,* such as temporary reductions in use of cars, incinerators, and so on. It is difficult and clumsy to change tax rules, and direct controls will usually do a better job here. The mayor of the threatened city can, for example, forbid the use of private passenger cars until the crisis passes.
3. *Where effective and dependable metering devices have not been invented or are prohibitively costly to install and operate.* In such cases there is no way to operate an effective tax program because the amount of wastes the polluter has emitted cannot be determined and so his tax bill cannot be calculated. In that case the only effective option may be to *require* him to use "clean" fuel, or install emissions-purification equipment.

In reality there is often no device analogous to a gas or water meter that can be used to measure pollution emissions cheaply and effectively. For example, to evaluate emissions in waterways, the standard procedure is to take samples, bring them to a laboratory, and subject them to a series of complicated tests that often take weeks to carry out, to determine the chemical contents of the emissions. For a polluter whose emissions are very large, this may be worth doing. But for the emitter who only spews out a few gallons of pollutants a day, the cost of such a complex process is likely to exceed the benefits. Whatever their other inefficiencies, direct controls are still likely to do the job of controlling such sources of pollution more cheaply. On the other side of the argument, however, the widespread adoption of emissions charges and the resulting rise in demand for metering devices may lead to research and development that produces cheaper and more effective meters.

OTHER FINANCIAL DEVICES TO PROTECT THE ENVIRONMENT

The basic idea underlying the emissions-tax approach to environmental protection is that it provides financial incentives that will induce the polluter to reduce the damage he does to the environment. But emissions taxes are not the only form of financial inducement that have been proposed. There are at least two others that deserve consideration: subsidies for reduced emissions and the requirement of emissions permits for polluters, each permit authorizing the emission of a specified quantity of pollutant. Such permits would be offered for sale in limited quantities fixed by the authorities at prices determined by the forces of demand and supply.

Subsidies

Subsidies are already in use. Their advocates say that financial inducements can be just as effective when they take the form of a reward for good behavior as when they are composed of penalties (taxes) on behavior that is considered

harmful. A donkey can be induced to move forward just as surely (and with much less unpleasantness) by dangling a carrot in front of his nose as by applying a stick to his rump.

Environmental subsidies usually take one of two forms:

1. Partial payment of the cost of installation of some sort of pollution control equipment.
2. The offer of a fixed reward for every reduction in emissions from some base level, usually some amount that the polluter used to emit in the past.

Subsidies for the purchase of equipment sometimes take the form of outright grants— for example, for the construction and operation of experimental recycling facilities. And often the subsidies offered to private firms for the installation of pollution control equipment take the form of tax incentives rather than direct government payments.

A subsidy to help defray the cost of control equipment can be effective when the purchaser of the equipment was considering doing it anyhow but did not because of the high cost. This may be the case for a municipality that wants to treat its wastes more thoroughly but has not found a way to afford the cost. It may also be the case in private industry, where collection of the wastes that would otherwise be emitted can yield products that are valuable and reusable but where the equipment required for the process is too costly. In these cases, a subsidy may be just what is needed to enable the polluter to afford to control his emissions. But where the polluter gains nothing from such control, a partial subsidy for the purchase of control equipment is not likely to be very effective. It simply reduces the cost of something he does not want to do in any event. Even if that cost is cut down substantially, it is still a cost; and so it still provides no net incentive for him to plunge enthusiastically into pollution control.

The second type of subsidy—a reward based on quantity of reduced emissions—does indeed have the same sort of incentive effects as a tax for the *individual* polluter. In both cases the more he emits, the worse off he is financially, either because he receives a smaller subsidy payment or because his tax bill is higher.

But as far as the *industry* is concerned, there is a world of difference between the effect of a tax and the effect of a subsidy. A *tax discourages the output of commodities whose production causes pollution, whereas a subsidy encourages such outputs to expand.* Consider the difference between the tax and subsidy approaches in the case of automotive emissions. A tax will increase the cost of operating cars, thereby encouraging the use of public transportation (which produces far lower quantities of emissions than does the automobile per passenger-mile traveled). On the other hand, a subsidy for the installation of emissions-control devices will tend to encourage the use of autos at the expense of public transportation by keeping down the price of cars.

It is a paradox that a subsidy intended to induce an industry to reduce its emissions can actually *increase* the size of the industry's output and consequently *increase* its total emissions.

This paradox is readily illustrated with the help of a standard supply–demand diagram for a competitive industry. We see in Figure 34–2 that a tax on polluting output will raise the costs of the industry and hence raise the price of whatever quantity it supplies. Thus, the supply curve will be shifted upward by a tax to the curve labeled "supply after tax." Similarly, the subsidy will reduce dollar costs to the industry and so will shift the supply curve downward to the curve labeled "supply after subsidy." So, under a tax on emissions, the equilibrium point will move from point *E* to point *T*, reducing the output of the polluting product from *e* to *t*. But the subsidy, which moves the supply–demand equilibrium point from *E* to *S*, will actually

increase the output of the polluting industry from *e* to *s*! How does this happen? While the pollution-reduction subsidy will induce firms to decrease their emissions somewhat, it will attract new polluting firms into the industry, and as the graph shows, the net result may be that the subsidy will backfire, and instead of reducing pollution, as it is intended to do, it will actually increase it!

The main advantage of subsidies over taxes as a financial inducement to decrease pollution is that subsidies attract less opposition and are therefore more easily adopted through the political process. Obviously, industry always prefers a subsidy to a tax. But the rest of the community may well be worse off if a subsidy is selected instead of an emissions tax.

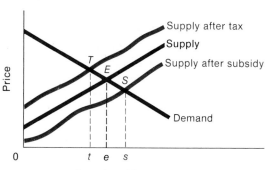

FIGURE 34–2

SUPPLY–DEMAND EQUILIBRIUM IN A POLLUTING COMPETITIVE INDUSTRY
A tax on pollution raises costs and so shifts the supply curve upward; that is, a higher price is needed to elicit a given supply. This causes equilibrium output to fall from *e* to *t* and succeeds in its purpose—reducing pollution. But a subsidy to those who decrease polluting output reduces costs and shifts the supply curve downward. By reducing costs, it attracts more firms into the industry. Paradoxically, output of the polluting product actually must increase from *e* to *s*.

Emissions Permits

A third type of financial inducement strongly advocated by some economists, but so far not adopted by any government, is the sale of emissions permits. Under this arrangement, the environmental agency decides what quantity of emissions per unit of time (say, per month) is tolerable and then issues a batch of permits authorizing (altogether) just that amount of pollution. The permits are offered for sale to the highest bidders. Their price is therefore determined by demand and supply. It will be high if the number of permits offered for sale is small and there is a large amount of industrial activity that must use the permits. Similarly, the price of a permit will be low if many permits are issued but the quantity of pollution for which they are demanded is small.

The emissions permit in many ways works like a tax—it simply makes it too expensive for the polluter to continue emitting as much as he would have without it. In addition, the permit offers two clear advantages over the tax approach. First, it reduces uncertainty about the quantity that will be emitted into the community. Under a tax we cannot be sure about this in advance, since that depends on the extent to which polluters respond to the tax rate that is selected. In the case of permits, the ceiling on emissions is decided in advance by the environmental authorities, who enforce the ceiling simply by issuing permits authorizing a specific total quantity of emissions. Second, a given tax on emissions can be made ineffective by inflation or by a growth in industrial activity. For example, a tax of X dollars may become insignificant as inflation erodes the value of the dollar, even though it may have been effective when it was first enacted and the price level was much lower. However, as long as there is no change in quantity of emissions authorized by license, inflation will obviously have no effect on the amount of pollution. It will simply raise the price of a license along with the prices of other commodities.

A major failing of the pollution license idea is its apparent political unattractiveness. Many people react indignantly to the notion of "licenses to pollute." A second weakness is that the program may break down altogether if it imposes an unrealistic and inflexible ceiling upon emissions. Its cost may simply be too great in terms of the amount of industrial activity needed to sustain economic growth and adequate levels of employment.

ON THE EQUITY AND COST OF SOME CURRENT PROGRAMS

This chapter began with a discussion of some shortcomings in the plans for the protection of the Delaware River. We are now in a position to identify the sources of those shortcomings and to note why the same difficulties are likely to be encountered in other environmental programs. It will be recalled that the two issues that were raised were the unnecessarily high costs of the plans for the Delaware, and the inequities that appear to beset the emissions quotas assigned under the program.

The source of the inefficiencies should be clear from the discussion of the last section. The Delaware program is one of direct controls, and consequently it does not have any procedures to apportion the task of emissions reduction in accord with the relative efficiency with which different emitters can carry it out. Because much of the job is assigned to those for whom the cost of controlling discharges is high, the entire program becomes unnecessarily costly. This is just a particular example of the cost of using direct controls rather than a tax on emissions, a cost to which, economists believe, policymakers have given inadequate attention.

Under direct controls the authorities usually aim at an *equitable* assignment of emissions quotas. For example, they may require all polluters to reduce their discharges by the same percentage. How, then, did it happen that one large firm was assigned a quota five times as large as another similar enterprise? The answer is that equal percentage reductions turn out to be far less equitable than they sound at first. As a result, any attempt to put them into practice almost always results in complaints, political pressures, renegotiation of quotas and a consequent set of assignments that seem to have been designed with the aid of a roulette wheel rather than a deliberate decision-making process.

Why are equal percentage reductions in emissions not generally equitable? We have already seen one reason: Costs of reductions are not the same for all industries or all plants in an industry. For example, the cost for a typical beet sugar plant to reduce its emissions (as measured in terms of the oxygen these wastes use up) is only about one-sixth as large as an equivalent reduction for a petroleum refinery. A modern paper plant can usually decrease its discharges at much less cost than can an anti-

quated plant in the same industry. Is it really *fair* to require all these firms to cut back their emissions by the same amounts when, through no fault of their own, the resulting financial burden is so different?

There are even clearer examples of the potential inequity in equal percentage reductions. Consider two companies, one run by a conscientious environmentalist who has voluntarily installed substantial amounts of equipment to cleanse and reduce his emissions, and the other run by an irresponsible management, which has continued to allow as much garbage to pour into public waterways as maximum profitability requires. Is it really fair for both these firms to be told to cut back equally?

Once such problems and others like them are recognized, and an attempt made to reassign emissions quotas accordingly, it will become clear that each emitter is a special case requiring special treatment. The regulator is almost forced to proceed case by case, and the resulting quotas end up following complex patterns that are at best difficult to defend in terms of equity or any other criterion.

SUMMARY

1. Pollution is as old as human history; and contrary to some popular notions, some forms of pollution were actually decreasing even before recent programs were initiated to protect the environment.

2. Both socialist and capitalist economies suffer from substantial environmental problems.

3. Economic activity *must* cause waste disposal problems unless everything is recycled, but even recycling processes cause pollution (and use up energy).

4. Industrial activity causes environmental damage, but so does the activity of private individuals (as when they drive cars that emit pollutants). Government agencies also damage the environment (as when military airplanes emit noise and exhaust, or a hydroelectric project floods large areas).

5. A clean environment is a public good, and hence environmental protection is a proper function of government. It cannot be left to the free market.

6. Pollution is an externality—when a factory emits smoke, it dirties laundry and may damage the health of persons who neither work for the smoking factory nor buy its products.

7. Pollution can be controlled by voluntary programs, direct controls, or taxes on emissions or other monetary incentives for the reduction of emissions.
8. Most economists believe that the tax approach is the one that is best suited for the control of externalities. They suggest it will often be the most efficient and effective way to cut pollution.
9. Subsidies for reduced pollution by the individual firm may actually backfire by making it profitable for more polluting firms to go into business.

CONCEPTS FOR REVIEW

Externality
Public good
Direct controls

Pollution charges (taxes)
Subsidies for reduced emissions
Emissions permits

QUESTIONS FOR DISCUSSION

1. What sorts of pollution problems would you expect in a small African village? In a city in India? In communist China?
2. Some scientists fear that the use of solar heating may constitute a net *loss* of energy for the economy. How can that be? (*Hint:* What sorts of inputs would you guess are required to produce the equipment that collects solar energy?)
3. Give some examples of externalities other than pollution. Can you think of externalities that do people good rather than harm?
4. Economists maintain that while some *reduction* in pollution is usually desirable, it is not desirable to reduce most pollutants to zero. Why may this be a reasonable view?
5. Suppose you are assigned the task of drafting a law to impose a tax on the emission of smoke. What provisions would you put into the law?
   a. How would you decide the size of the tax?
   b. What would you do about smoke emitted by a municipal electricity plant?
   c. Would you use the same tax rate on densely and sparsely settled areas? What information will you need to collect before determining what you would do about each of the preceding provisions?

35

Economic Problems
of the Cities

Our environment does not consist only of trees and rivers. It is also congested streets and attractive boulevards, innovative public buildings and dilapidated slum dwellings. An enormous proportion of the nation's population lives in "urbanized areas," the cities and their suburbs. In fact, the 1970 census figures indicate that 73 percent of the population lives in such places, which helps explain the increasing amount of public attention recently given to the problems of the cities.

Since World War II, many of the cities of the United States have been in a process of catastrophic decline. Land values in their centers have in many cases plunged dramatically. Once-busy shopping areas have assumed the appearance of old battlegrounds; many shops are now boarded up and buildings burnt out or simply abandoned. More affluent residents have emigrated to the suburbs, and industrial activity has also moved out. Along with this exodus, the cities have faced financial crises that have threatened to undermine normal municipal activities.

In this chapter, we offer some explanations that help account for part of the problem and suggest which policy measures offer some promise and which are no more than temporary palliatives that accomplish little more than painting over the underlying difficulties.

We begin by reviewing the economic functions of a city and the recent technological changes that have eroded its advantages for industry. Next we discuss the difference between cities and suburbs in the quality of services, such as education and sanitation, as part of the explanation for the exodus of middle- and upper-income groups from the cities. And then we examine some of the recent court decisions that were intended to reduce these inequalities in public services. We will describe and explain the rapidly rising cost of urban services; show that some of the cities' problems are analogous to the externalities that play so important a role in our environmental problems; discuss rent controls and their consequences for the supply of housing; and, finally, describe briefly a number of policy proposals.

A Picture of a Slum

There is a part of Detroit called the Lower East Side which visitors, in awed voices, compare with the bombed-out cities of Europe after World War II and, later, of Vietnam. Half and more of the houses on any given block are boarded up with plywood squares. The gutters hang, rain washes in through the holes in the roofs. Ruined by the elements and gutted by thieves, the houses seem to be disintegrating like the stumps of rotted trees. Fires at night cremate the remains. The next day the family moves out of the house next door and another house is abandoned and eventually destroyed.

One equivalent of this area in New York City is known as the South Bronx; another is Brooklyn; a third, Harlem. The weary miles of abandoned houses in Chicago are in Woodlawn on the South Side, and in Austin on the West Side, next to Oak Park. Then, . . . the ruin is repeated in North Philadelphia, St. Louis, Seattle, Los Angeles and Lubbock, Texas.

Source: Brian D. Boyer, *Cities Destroyed for Cash* (Chicago: Follett Publishing Company, 1973), page 1.

The corner of Jacob and Ferry Streets, where this photograph of an urban renewal project was taken, is no longer in existence. The site—about a block from the Brooklyn Bridge in New York City, and once the heart of the leather-tanning industry—is now covered over by a large, modern office building.

SOME SOURCES OF URBAN PROBLEMS

Some of the fundamental troubles of the cities clearly go beyond economics. These include a variety of social issues—crime, racial discrimi-nation, and the like—topics that are more frequently discussed by sociologists and social psychologists than by economists. There are, however, a number of crucial problems for the cities that are primarily economic in nature, and these can usefully be examined here.

Some of the contributing factors to the

World Urbanization: 1950, 1975, 2000

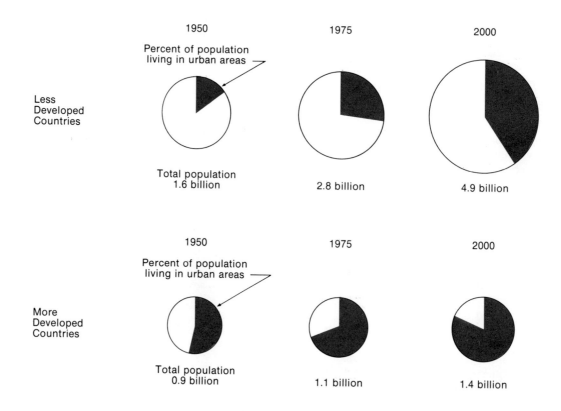

The world is growing increasingly urban. By the year 2000 half the population of the earth is expected to live in urban areas. While it is true that in the older U.S. cities, people are leaving the center of the cities for the surrounding suburbs, most of the suburbs are also urban in character.

Source: *Population Bulletin,* Population Reference Bureau, vol. 31, no. 4, Dec. 1976, page 2.

crisis of the cities are discussed elsewhere in this book, and we will mention them here only briefly. The most immediate difficulty was the unfortunate combination of inflation and recession that hit the country toward the end of the Vietnam War. With inflation increasing the cost of operation of local governments and recession reducing their tax revenues, municipalities were caught in the resulting squeeze. This, more than any other factor, was immediately responsible for the rapid deterioration in the financial position of a number of cities in the early 1970s, which as we will see, had contributed to their physical decline.

A second contributing cause was the welfare burden resulting from earlier migration patterns. During the early postwar period there was a large-scale exodus from the South, particularly by rural black residents who had been displaced by mechanized farming techniques. Many of them made their way North to the nation's large industrial cities, looking for jobs and inexpensive housing. They were joined in many cities by an influx of poor migrants and refugees from the Caribbean, Mexico, China, and so on. Those who could not find jobs turned to local welfare programs for support. The result was another major drain upon the finances of the cities. Since the issues of poverty and welfare are examined in detail in Chapter 29, no more will be said about them here. Instead, we turn to a number of other important issues, several of which are not widely understood. These topics include the exodus of businesses and of middle- and upper-class inhabitants from the cities; the consequent reduction in sources of taxes; and the extraordinarily rapid rise in the cost of municipal services.

POLICY PROBLEM: URBAN RENEWAL

Public policy has not ignored the problems of the cities. Particularly after the riots of the late 1960s, the federal government was led to devote substantial amounts of money to programs designed to rescue and revive the nation's cities. In 1974, the profusion of federal programs was replaced by a single program, which provided $8.6 billion to cities over a period of 6 years. There have been programs to stimulate jobs, to help ghetto businesses, to improve urban housing, and to help in a variety of other ways.

Despite all this activity, the results have been largely disappointing. With a few possible exceptions, there has been no turnabout in the fortunes of the nation's cities. Businesses and white and middle-class families continue to flee the city, and venerable downtown department stores and hotels continue to close. There is no evidence of any significant fall in crime rates; and unemployment, particularly among minority teen-agers, is still spectacularly high.

A good example of the programs whose results have proved so disenchanting is the massive urban renewal projects heavily supported by federal funds, which attempted to improve housing conditions and the quality of neighborhoods generally. The approach widely adopted since the passage of the 1949 Housing Act utilized the bulldozer to level entire slum neighborhoods, replacing them with high-rise apartment houses and eye-catching public buildings. It was hoped that in this way the slum dweller would be offered a new life style and a chance to participate in the benefits of the great society.

Unfortunately, things did not work out quite the way the planners envisioned. There were loud complaints arguing that, along with the slums, the bulldozer had wiped out the cultural character of the neighborhood. People were dispersed during the period of reconstruction, allegedly temporarily, but often never to return. Instead they found themselves living in conditions less satisfactory than before, forcibly separated from lifetime friends, neighborhood stores where they had always shopped, and other familiar and reassuring landmarks.

Above all, the high-rise apartment building that was typical of public housing projects became the symbol upon which former slum dwellers focused their anger. They felt their new living quarters "dehumanized" their homes and forced them to adapt to a life style better suited to the factory than to family life. In many cases the new buildings rapidly fell victim to vandalism, arson, the accumulation of trash, and general rapid deterioration. In the opinion of its critics, which is certainly not without basis, the urban renewal program, after the expenditure of billions of dollars and years of effort and planning, succeeded in exacerbating the anger of those it was designed to benefit. It destroyed neighborhood institutions that made life tolerable and replaced century-old slums with a new set of slums, which, while they were perhaps only 5 or 10 years old, were slums nonetheless.

According to one observer, under these programs:

- More than a million people were forced out of their homes.
- More homes were destroyed than were built.
- Those destroyed were predominantly low-rent homes.
- Those built were predominantly high-rent homes.
- Housing conditions were made worse for those whose housing conditions were least good.
- Housing conditions were improved for those whose housing conditions were best.[1]

We cannot pretend that anyone knows precisely what went wrong or how foolproof programs can be designed for the future. We will, however, show later in this chapter that economics offers some significant insights into the matter and that there is good reason to

[1]Quotation from an article by Martin Anderson, "The Federal Bulldozer," reprinted in James Q. Wilson, ed., *Urban Renewal: The Record and the Controversy* (Cambridge, Mass.: M.I.T. Press, 1966), page 495.

believe that some of the mistakes of urban renewal might have been avoided had the planners given adequate weight to these considerations.

ECONOMIC FUNCTIONS OF A CITY

In order to understand the roots of the decline of the cities in the postwar period, we must first consider the economic functions of such large, densely populated areas and the reasons the cities have become less effective in their economic role in recent years.

The close proximity of the people and business activities that distinguish a city has in the past offered at least three critical advantages.

1. Low transportation costs. If the people or firms that trade with one another are close together, transporation costs will be quite low. This is also true of the labor force. A factory that can draw its employees from nearby will be under no pressure to cover commuting costs in its wage settlements.

Aside from this obvious advantage of proximity, the age of the railroad brought another transportation advantage to the city. Because the route of a train is inflexibly tied to a layout of tracks, railroad transportation is not at its best in deliveries to many widely dispersed customers. Rather, it operates most efficiently if it can deliver large quantities to a single destination. The central railroad depot in a city is ideally suited to the purpose, and so, in the late nineteenth and early twentieth century, firms whose activities involved a great deal of shipment of raw materials from suppliers and finished products to customers gained a great economic advantage by locating in cities, preferably not far from the railroad terminal.

2. Ease and speed of communication. For similar reasons, the cities offered great advantages to groups of persons, firms, and public

agencies whose activities required them to communicate quickly and frequently. That is why, for example, stock exchanges have until now always operated in cities, since in buying and selling securities so much depends on quick receipt of information and on the ability to receive orders quickly from customers and to carry out the requested purchases and sales without delay.

3. Availability of large-scale personal services. Some products by their very nature are difficult or impossible to transport, because they must be provided to the recipient on a face-to-face basis. This is true of the services of a doctor, a teacher, a retail clerk, or a musician at a live performance. For services that need not be offered on a large scale, a small town is as well off as a large city. The country doctor and the local schoolteacher may always have served their community as well as their urban counterparts. Large hospitals, however, with all sorts of specialized facilities, which are economical only if they are used by hundreds of patients daily, can be found only in a large city. An opera house that needs 3000 customers a night to survive can only be found in a city, and it is only a city that can support giant department stores that stock a vast variety of items, giving their customers an enormous choice—and, usually, better prices.

TECHNOLOGICAL CHANGE AND THE CITY'S LOST ADVANTAGES

The middle of the twentieth century brought with it a series of technological changes that robbed the city of the bulk of each of these advantages.

Two of the most critical of these changes were the gradual takeover of the automobile as a primary mode of passenger transportation and the development of the truck as a major carrier of freight. The characteristic of both these vehicles that distinguishes them sharply from the railroad is their ability to transport from door to door—their flexibility in adapting their routes to the origin and destination of a particular item to be transported. With this change, and particularly with the completion of much of the interstate highway network in the 1960s, the advantage of proximity to a central railway depot all but evaporated.

Indeed, an urban location is a liability for an industry that requires a great deal of transportation. Truck deliveries are slowed down by congested city streets, and expenses are increased correspondingly. The result is that many industries have been more or less pushed out of the cities.

Other technological developments have had the same effect. For example, modern factory methods, which automatically carry goods in process from one production stage to another, are most efficient in a single-story plant that does not require items to be carried from one story to another. The high-rise factory has been replaced by low buildings that extend over many acres. In the city, it is too expensive to use the large quantities of land required for this purpose. Moreover, even if affordable, it is often very difficult to acquire enough contiguous lots to provide a piece of land sufficiently large for this type of production.

Communication also does not require the degree of proximity it used to. The telephone has made it quick and easy to talk to persons who are very far away. Computers, linked by the telecommunications network, permit many business transactions to be carried out quickly over great distances so that firms that formerly had to be close to one another need no longer be so. A national stock exchange system operated entirely by computer is now on the drawing boards, and work is under way to arrange electronic clearing of bank transactions, with interbank debts, payment of checks, and other such operations carried out virtually instantaneously through a computer terminal. All of this means a considerable reduction in the advantage of

691

closeness for businesses that depend on a great deal of communication.

Finally, at least some of the personal services have become increasingly available to those who live outside the city. The availability of the mass media means that one does not always have to come to the center of the city for one's entertainment. And suburban shopping centers, while they do not offer the variety of products obtainable in a great city, have begun to provide what to many people is a tolerable approximation. This decentralization of shopping, too, was made possible by technological change, for the family car and the new road network permitted the stores in such shopping centers to attract people from considerable distances, so that even in a sparsely settled area they could draw enough customers to enable them to operate at a profit.

The automobile, the telephone, and modern factory design have taken away many of the city's former advantages of transportation, communication, and the supply of services.

This does not mean that every city has completely lost every one of its special attractions. On the contrary, the cities continue to be the preferred locations of most financial and cultural activities. In no small town can one find the variety of ethnic cultures, of shops, and restaurants that a major metropolis contains. But each one of the technological changes that has been described has certainly eroded the special advantages offered by the city. Cosmopolitan cities have become a little or even a great deal less attractive than they once were. Marginal cities have become communities that are largely without a purpose, aside from the relatively cheap residential facilities they offer out of their stock of decaying housing. They are no longer cities in the sense of an interconnected and viable social organism. Rather they have become warehouses in which society stores its impecunious humans who cannot afford to live anywhere but the crowded neigh-

borhoods that have been abandoned by their former residents.

SUBURBAN HOMES FOR UPPER INCOME GROUPS AND QUALITY OF SERVICES

Not only industry, but many families that can afford to do so have chosen to leave the cities for the suburbs. There are many reasons for this relocation, but undoubtedly an important influence is the difference in quality of services between the inner city and the wealthy suburbs.

A community that spends large amounts on its schools, its libraries, and its museums offers its inhabitants services that are not readily available to those who live in a municipality with tighter budgets. However, people in communities with more abundant services must pay for them and for their availability through higher taxes. Since many people do not attend museums or use libraries, and others have no children of school age, they may prefer communities that offer fewer services and that collect correspondingly lower taxes.

The availability of a wide range of municipal expenditure patterns offers a variety of choices to the family that is deciding where it wants to live. Those who prefer high-quality service and are willing to pay the bill can live in one community, and those who want to avoid high taxes can live in another. In this way, people can select the quality of public services they want in exactly the same way they can choose between a Volkswagen and a Cadillac. One might expect that the community in which a family decides to locate will depend very much on its income, with the wealthy living in towns with Cadillac-quality services and the poor living in communities whose quality of services and tax rates are tailored to their pocketbooks. Thus, the exodus from the cities by the upper-income groups has been interpreted as a deliberate decision by those who can and are willing to pay for very good schools and for an abundance of other public services.

But in practice, this is not quite the way things work.

The wealthy communities in the suburbs have, as expected, ended up with better schools—classes are smaller and teachers are better paid. Nevertheless, despite the cost of this and other services these communities enjoy, the high-income cities and towns have ended up with far *lower* tax rates than have the cities the poor inhabit.

New Jersey is a striking illustration of this curious situation. The property tax is by far the largest single source of income for most local governments. Princeton township, one of the wealthiest towns in the state, pays a tax rate of some 3.49 percent of the assessed value of a piece of real estate in property taxes, and the tax rates in other high-income towns lie at the same end of the spectrum. Meanwhile, Newark, Jersey City, Hoboken, Trenton, and Bayonne—communities with huge slum areas, large minority populations, and widespread poverty—pay tax rates ranging from 7.36 to 10.85 percent. In other words, in these central cities, large groups of poor residents pay tax rates on property running two and three times higher than in wealthier communities.

In an era in which astronomical figures have become commonplace, a tax rate of 8 or 9 percent may not seem very high, but it is really enormous. To see why this is so, it is crucial to recognize that this tax rate is expressed in terms of *total property values,* not in terms of *annual rental.* Consider the effects on a business firm whose operations involve a good deal of real estate—say a renter of warehouse space whose property is worth a million dollars. We can expect him to rent out his warehouse at an annual rent charge of about 10 percent of the market value of his property, or about $100,000 a year. Now, an 8 percent annual tax on the million-dollar property is $80,000 dollars—which

is 80 percent of the landlord's annual rental income.

Because property values run about 10 times as high as rentals, the seemingly low tax *on property* amounts to an enormous sales tax *on rental* of apartments, warehouses, factories, and other business properties. An equivalent sales tax would have a devastating effect on sales of any goods or services. It is an enormous handicap to job-providing industries in the cities.

WHY DO THE WEALTHY HAVE BOTH LOWER TAX RATES AND BETTER SERVICES?

It is natural to ask how the suburbs were able to achieve their economic miracle—both better services *and* lower tax rates. The answer has three major elements:

1. Higher property values. Wealthy suburbs simply contain a great deal more that can be taxed. Where the typical family lives in a home worth $100,000, a given property-tax rate brings in a lot more money than a community in which the typical residence is worth $15,000. Even if the former has a tax rate of 4 percent and the latter has a tax rate of 8 percent, the first town will still get $4000 (4 percent of $100,000) in public revenues from each resident family, which it can spend for schooling and other public services, while the poorer community, despite its much higher tax rate, will get only $1200 from each family.

2. High public costs generated by poverty. For many reasons, poor communities just cost more to run—they have high welfare costs, high costs of supporting public hospitals and clinics, high costs of crime control and fire fighting. While the services typically are of poorer quality than they are in a wealthy town, the very presence of poverty means that it is difficult for the local

government to avoid spending a great deal on the items just mentioned.

3. Suburban burdens shifted to the cities. There is a third and less obvious reason why taxes tend to be higher in the poor cities than in the affluent suburbs. Over the years the suburbs have partially—and without conscious planning—shifted to the cities part of the costs generated directly or indirectly by suburban residents. For instance, commuters use subsidized urban facilities, such as public transportation, and they require police and fire protection during their working day in the city. Often they hire poor urban residents to clean their suburban homes and tend their gardens, but the children of these lower-income groups go to school in the city and receive medical care in city clinics.

It is true that commuters pay some urban taxes—sales taxes on purchases they make while in the city and, in many cases, a special *commuter tax* on their earnings in the city. Yet the evidence is that the taxes paid by the commuter cover only a fraction of the cost of the services they obtain from the city directly and indirectly.

THE COURTS AND EQUAL OPPORTUNITY

The double economic advantage of the wealthy suburbs that we have just considered—their better services and their lower tax rates—has given rise to some troublesome issues of equity, issues that recently have led to intervention by the courts.

The most obvious problem of injustice is the systematic difference in school quality between poor and rich communities. Despite some rhetoric to the contrary, our national goals have in practice not generally included a clear commitment to equalization of incomes. It is true that income tax rates are higher in higher income

brackets, but there are also large loopholes that are particularly advantageous to the very rich. For a long time Americans have proclaimed their dedication to *equality of opportunity*. Children of poor families should not be deprived of the *chance* to make their way up the economic ladder if their dedication and their abilities make that possible.

But if the children of the poor almost always receive an inferior education, at least insofar as money is able to purchase educational quality, is this not a direct denial of educational opportunity? In the last few years, courts throughout the nation have answered that it *is* a deprivation of equal opportunity. The most important decisions were those of the courts of California and New Jersey, which have held that great inequalities in outlays per pupil are illegal, and these decisions have required the state legislatures to undertake remedial measures.

A second source of inequity also has recently led to judicial intervention, with the landmark decision, curiously, being handed down once more by the courts of New Jersey. The issue this time was the attempt by the wealthy suburbs to erect barriers to prevent, or at least to discourage, the poor from moving into them. With their better services and their lower tax rates, it is naturally to be expected that many people will want to relocate in such communities, bringing with them all the economic problems from which those suburbs were previously immune.

To protect their position as idyllic enclaves, these privileged suburbs have made systematic use of zoning ordinances for the purpose.

DEFINITION
A *zoning ordinance* is a set of regulations specifying what sort of construction is permitted in a particular neighborhood. It may specify what types of buildings are permitted—there are residential zones, commercial zones, industrial zones, and agricultural zones. It may require fireproof construction materials or particular methods of disposal of waste liquids; and it may

specify how much floor space and how much ground area is required per family.

By prohibiting multifamily housing—apartment houses or even attached "row houses"—and by requiring each house to occupy at least one-third or one-half acre of land, zoning ordinances have effectively made it too expensive for poor families to buy or rent homes in many suburban areas. While such regulations have always ostensibly been adopted to protect the environment of the community, in many cases their exclusionary purpose was quite clear.

In the Mount Laurel decision of March 24, 1975, the New Jersey Supreme Court ruled that the zoning code for this New Jersey township was exclusionary and ordered the community to devise a plan that would enable a fair share of the region's poor to live there, urging Mount Laurel to seek state and federal subsidies for public housing.

EXODUS OF TAXPAYERS AS A CUMULATIVE PROCESS

Whatever the reasons that started the exodus to the suburbs by more affluent families and by industry, the important thing to recognize is that this migration activity is a process that feeds itself. Each departure makes it less attractive for others to stay behind.

Specifically, for reasons we have already considered, when people in higher-income brackets leave the city, a higher tax burden must be borne by the remaining residents of the city who are capable of paying. One reason for this is that persons in upper-income brackets usually pay higher taxes than poorer persons. Although a rich family that has, say, 10 times the average income level may well pay less than 10 times the average in taxes, it certainly does normally pay *more tax dollars* than a lower-income family. Moreover, the rich family is not likely to draw heavily on municipal services.

Poorer people ordinarily are the biggest users of municipal services. Besides welfare payments, they require a variety of other social services: care at public hospitals, more police and fire protection, and so on. Thus, as well-to-do residents leave the city and are replaced by poorer families arriving from elsewhere, municipal costs tend to rise and the number of persons able to pay taxes decreases. The higher taxes that result tend, in turn, to drive away some of the remaining taxpayers, and so each exodus paves the way for the next.

The process is aggravated by the equally cumulative character of urban deterioration. As the upper- and middle-income classes are replaced by the poor, the condition of neighborhoods tends to worsen. Poverty often brings with it crime, dirt, and reduced upkeep of housing, public buildings, and other neighborhood facilities. These characteristic phenomena of urban deterioration may do even more than rising taxes to hasten the exit of upper- and middle-income groups. And here too, each step brings on the next—deterioration encourages the exodus, the exodus leads to further deterioration, and so it proceeds, on and on.

Each wave of affluent families moving out of the city makes the city a less pleasant and more costly place for those who remain behind. As a result, some of those who otherwise would have preferred to stay in the city will no longer find the city to be the place for them, and they, in turn, will follow their predecessors into the suburbs. Their exit, in turn, will lead to further deterioration and further increases in costs and taxes, thus leading still others to leave, and so on, one round leading to the next in a cumulative process of urban decline.

Industry too, is drawn into the stream as its most valued employees leave the city and its taxes rise along with everyone else's; firms find it increasingly attractive to move out of the city. But their exit also means a decrease in the number of taxpayers who remain in the central city, which leads to rises in the tax rates that force still other firms to follow. The exodus of firms proves as contagious as the departure of families, and both together are likely to turn into an epidemic that leaves the center of the city an economic wasteland with property values collapsed, shops and movie houses closed down, and blight enveloping previously attractive and affluent neighborhoods.

Such cumulative processes hit the city elsewhere as well. Its public transportation is the victim of an analogous chain of events. As ridership falls, fares are increased and frequency of service is reduced. But that leads the remaining ridership to decline still more, which sets off still further rounds of fare increases and service cuts. And so the process goes on, until the transportation system, which was once cheap and efficient, is reduced to a shambles.

The reversal of such cumulative processes is not easy, and no one has produced a set of foolproof remedies. But the analysis does show that a number of simplistic measures, many of which have already been tried, are foredoomed to failure.

The most obvious approach is to pour money into the process—to seek federal subsidies for improved equipment for the transportation network, or funds to help provide social services for the poor. But if these are "once-and-for-all" measures, rather than permanent changes in the cities' financial arrangements, any improvements achieved in the process must prove temporary. In a process of *cumulative* deterioration, what matters is not the point from which one starts but the direction in which one is going. A good subway system undergoing a process of cumulative deterioration can stay close behind one that was initially inferior to it, as they both go downhill. Replacements for old slum buildings are soon transformed into little more than newer slums. The trick is to find a procedure that can *reverse* the process of deterioration, not something that contributes a few once-and-for-all improvements.

At the end of this chapter we will discuss some policy proposals for the city that seem more promising; but first we must deal with several other problems that are not widely recognized by noneconomists.

THE COST DISEASE OF MUNICIPAL SERVICES

Another long-term problem affecting the cities is the behavior of the costs of their services. During the inflationary period of the 1970s virtually all costs in the economy rose, but the cost of municipal public services rose even faster than most. During earlier periods, when the nation's price level was nearly stationary, municipal service costs nevertheless rose at a significant rate. One typical observation will illustrate the point. Education is one of the largest components of a municipal budget, typically constituting about 40 percent of the total. During the two decades immediately following World War II in the United States, the cost of elementary and high school education per pupil day rose, on the average, 3.9 percent a year *more rapidly* than the general price level. This means that every year—even when other prices in the economy were not increasing—the cost of education was rising, and rising faster than costs elsewhere in the economy. These cost differentials were cumulative and compounded so that over the two decades as a whole, the cost of education per pupil had risen by more than 200 percent in comparison with the cost of manufactured goods. That is, as much as manufactured goods had risen in price, at the end of the period the cost of an education was equivalent to twice as many cars or refrigerators as it was at the beginning. There is evidence that a similar pattern is followed by the costs of other municipal services, such as health care and libraries.

What explains this terrible financial burden for the municipalities? Is it to be attributed to inefficiencies in government activities or to political mismanagement and corruption? Perhaps, in part. But there is another source of the problem, one that could not be avoided by any municipal administration no matter what its integrity and administrative efficiency. The problem stems from the nature of the services provided by a city and the peculiarity of the technology used in their production. Many of the municipal services, by their very nature, require direct contact between those who consume the service and those who are employed in providing it. Doctors, teachers, and librarians are all engaged in activities that require direct person-to-person contact. Moreover, the quality of the service deteriorates if less time is provided by doctors, teachers, and librarians to each user of their services. In contrast, the buyer of an automobile usually has no idea who worked on it, and could not care less how much labor time went into its production. There need be no reduction in product quality just because of a labor-saving innovation in auto production.

As a result, it has proved far easier for technological change to save labor in producing manufactured goods than in providing municipal services. While the number of teacher hours per pupil actually increased during the postwar period because classes became smaller, output per hour of labor in manufacturing went up year after year, at an average rate of something like 3 or 4 percent *per year*. These disparate performances in productivity have grave consequences for prices.

When wages in manufacturing rise 3 or 4 percent, the cost of manufactured products need not be affected because increased productivity just about exactly makes up for the rise in wages. But the nature of their technology makes it very difficult to introduce labor-saving devices in the municipal services. So a 4 percent rise in the wages of teachers or police is not offset by higher productivity and must lead to an equivalent rise in municipal budgets.

In the long run, wages and salaries throughout the economy tend to go up and down together, for otherwise the activity whose wage rate falls seriously behind will tend to lose its labor force. Auto workers and police officers will see their wages rise at roughly the same rate in the long run.

This phenomenon is another of our 12 Ideas for Beyond the Final Exam. Because productivity improvements are very difficult for most municipal services, their cost can be expected to rise faster, year in, year out, than the cost of manufactured goods. Over a period of several decades, this difference in the growth rate in costs of the two sectors can add up, making services enormously more expensive, compared with manufactured goods, than they were at the beginning of the period. This is the *cost disease of the municipal public services* and one of the chronic financial problems of city governments.

EXTERNALITIES AND THE AILMENTS OF THE CITY

We have just seen that the city suffers from several special problems of its own—the cumulative character of its economic decline and the cost disease of its services. But in addition to these special difficulties, the city also suffers from problems that are similar to those that beset the environment outside the urban areas.

We examined earlier the important role played by externalities in the process of environmental deterioration. We saw that pollution is encouraged by the fact that its effects fall on persons other than those who cause it. In the absence of legal penalties, polluters do not pay the full social cost of their emissions, and therefore they have little economic motive to spend any money or effort to keep their emissions in check.

Deterioration of neighborhoods has much in common with the pollution of air or rivers. The landlord who permits his building to turn into a slum or who abandons it altogether surely affects his own fortunes. But, in the process, he incidentally affects the quality of the neighborhood. His building becomes an eyesore to neighbors. Worse than that, it becomes a fire hazard and, perhaps, a breeding ground for crime and disease. Just as the public is made to bear the costs of the abandoned chemicals that a firm spews into a waterway, the inhabitants of the neighborhood are forced to bear the social costs of the landlord's method of waste disposal when he decides that the cheapest way to get rid of his building is to abandon it.

Externalities, one of the most important defects of the market mechanism, must bear a significant share of the blame for the deterioration of the nation's cities, as well as for the problems of our natural environment. And in both cases, because of the presence of externalities, the free-enterprise system is incapable of dealing with the problem without some help from the government, either in the form of direct controls (the enforcement of rules about upgrading and maintaining buildings) or financial inducements to increase the profitability of improving buildings in slum neighborhoods.

For example, financial inducements can be provided by a change in the laws on real-estate taxation. One possible reform is a change in the tax schedules that would impose upon a landlord whose properties are found to be substandard taxes much higher than those paid by an average owner of property of equal value, while substantially reducing taxes on buildings that have been significantly upgraded. With a little ingenuity, such a tax schedule can be designed so that the total amount collected from all landlords together will be the same as under the present system. Yet, while in some cases it may stimulate abandonment of highly deteriorated property, one can be quite confident that such a

change in the tax laws will induce landlords to try much harder to improve their property, just as a sizable tax on pollution emissions can be expected to induce polluters to try much harder to keep their emissions under control.

RENT CONTROL IN NEW YORK CITY[2]

Most economists are united in their belief that rent control is a measure that does *not* help the cities or their inhabitants and that, in the long run, makes almost everyone worse off as a result. The main example of rent control in the United States will illustrate the problems. By the mid-1960s New York was the only major city in the United States that still controlled rents; although with the inflation of the 1970s other cities that had abandoned this measure during the 1950s began to reinstitute rent controls. The objective of such a law is, of course, to protect the consumer from the skyrocketing increases in rents that accompany a housing shortage. A supply–demand diagram tells us what in fact happens.

In Figure 35–1, which is a supply–demand diagram for housing units (apartments and private homes), we see that in order to produce some effect, rent ceilings must be set below the equilibrium level, point *P*, because otherwise one would simply be permitting the rent level to settle at the point determined by market forces. But with any lower rent ceiling, say point *R* in the figure, we can expect the quantity supplied to fall short of the quantity demanded. With rents forced down to *R*, we see that the quantity of housing demanded will be *B* while the quantity supplied will only be *C*.

In fact that is precisely what happened. Between 1950 and 1960, rental vacancies in New York City hovered around 1.3 percent of

[2]The information in this section is based mainly on L. N. Bloomberg and H. H. Lamale, *The Rental Housing Situation in New York City* (City of New York, Housing and Development Administration, 1976).

the total number of apartments, while in the remainder of the country, as controls were abandoned, the stock of vacant houses and apartments rose from 2 percent to nearly 5 percent of the total. In 1970, the vacancy rate in New York (2 percent) was less than one-third the rate for all other central cities in the United States (6.3 percent). In 1975, despite the imposition of controls in several other cities and considerable construction of uncontrolled luxury apartments in New York, the New York City figure was still only about half that for all U.S. central cities.

As is shown by the positive slope of the supply curve in our diagram, rent controls can be expected to decrease supplies; that is, they will discourage the construction of rental apartments. In this way, in the long run, rent controls aggravate the problem they are intended to solve. In New York, since it is still possible to build uncontrolled luxury apartments, private construction did not come to a halt, but it was nevertheless discouraged. In the decade from

1960 to 1970, the net housing stock in New York City rose about 22 percent less rapidly than that in central cities of the United States as a whole, though other northeastern cities did still more poorly.

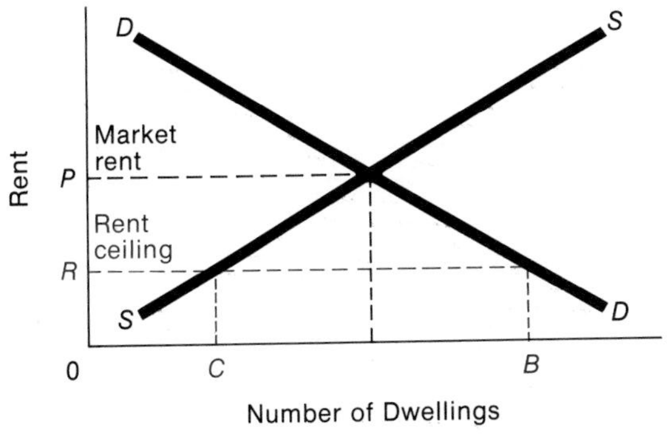

More immediate was the effect of rent control on the supply of housing already in existence. When rents are forced below their equilibrium level, landlords find that they have no trouble renting apartments even if little or no money is invested in maintenance. With rising costs and relatively fixed rents, landlords may also feel that they simply cannot afford the cost of normal upkeep.

While in the past decade the quality of urban housing generally has improved to a surprising degree (housing classed as "dilapidated" by the census fell steadily from 16 percent in 1950 to only 6 percent in 1975), the improvement in New York City was significantly lower than that in the other central cities of the Northeast, which, in turn, lagged behind the rest of the country. Two noteworthy exceptions were New York's government-subsidized housing and housing that was exempt from rent controls. At the same time, the city experienced an enormous rate of abandonment—houses simply left to their fate by landlords seeking to escape deteriorating neighborhoods, taxes, and maintenance costs. It is estimated that during the past decade New York lost in this way as many as 200,000 housing units—about 7 percent of its total supply.[3] Indeed, between 1970 and 1975, despite an unprecedented addition to the supply through construction and renovation, there was actually a net loss in the number of available housing units. It has been estimated that housing units are being abandoned now at the rate of 21,000 per year in New York City by landlords seeking to avoid expensive repairs. In addition, landlords who have been able to get away with it have completely removed good property in good condition from the housing market. Many apartment buildings have been

FIGURE 35–1

SUPPLY—DEMAND DIAGRAM FOR HOUSING
When market forces are permitted to set rents, the supply of dwellings will equal the number demanded. But when a rent ceiling forces rent below the market level, the number of dwellings supplied (point C) will be less than the number demanded (point B). Thus, rent ceilings always induce housing shortages.

[3]City Almanac, vol. 10, February 1976.

converted, illegally, into office space in order to escape controls.

All of this suggests that the underlying problem—the shortage in supply—becomes more serious the longer controls remain in force. As usually occurs when there is an attempt to interfere with the market, rent controls have been accompanied by a variety of repricing devices designed to circumvent the law. The black market in housing operates in a variety of ways: through bribes, "key money" paid to put the prospective tenant higher on the waiting list, or by the purchase of worthless furniture at inflated prices as a side deal involved in acquiring the apartment. Often, controls are escaped altogether by reselling the apartments to their tenants (at free-market prices or higher) so that the apartments become owner-occupied dwellings totally exempt from controls. It has been estimated that in New York City this process removed more than 160,000 dwelling units from the rental market between 1940 and 1960.

RENT CONTROLS: GENERAL CONCLUSIONS

Several observations sum up the consequences of rent controls:

1. Rent controls are likely to have a disastrous effect upon the supply of housing—leading to deterioration, abandonment, and other forms of removal from the market.

One economist (who is, incidentally, considered quite left of center) remarked that rent controls are probably not as effective as wartime bombing in destroying a city but that he would not be surprised if the facts showed things to be the other way around.

2. Once adopted, rent controls, like other price controls, are very difficult to eliminate.

A tenant who has paid thousands of dollars in "key money" for the right to move into a rent-controlled apartment will, with some justice, feel cheated if the controls for which he paid so dearly are suddenly lifted. The reason is that price controls, by their very nature, increase the market value of the properties that benefit from them—a rent-controlled apartment is worth more to a prospective tenant than one that is not controlled. Anyone who purchases such an apartment at its high market price acquires a vested interest in preserving those controls, whether or not they are socially desirable.

3. Paradoxically, rent controls may in the long run actually increase rents—even those paid on controlled apartments.

When the controls cause the supply of housing to decrease, the equilibrium price will rise, as a supply—demand diagram will readily confirm. Thus, even if controlled rents are kept, say, at a steady 80 percent of their equilibrium level, if the equilibrium level of rents rises enough, tenants will end up paying more than they would have in the absence of the controls. For example, if as a result of controls, rents on an apartment that initially had an equilibrium level of $150 a month now rise to an equilibrium value of $200, controls that reduce rents by 20 percent below their equilibrium value will cut the latter figure to 80 percent of $200, or $160—$10 higher than the initial $150 monthly rental.

The reason controlled rentals do (and must) rise with equilibrium rentals is that the further the two spread apart, the greater may be the rate of deterioration and abandonment, and certainly the greater the temptation to circumvent the law. To prevent a system of controls from breaking down altogether, controlled prices must keep pace with equilibrium prices; and so, as is probably the case in New York, the controls may in fact have effects that are the very opposite from those they are intended to produce—they may result in higher costs to those whose financial interest the laws are intended to protect. We can conclude that rent controls have not really been able to suppress the underlying market forces. They have only succeeded in deflecting these forces, leading to results far from the intentions of the authorities who introduced the regulations. The market mechanism is obviously a tough bird, which is able to impose suitable retribution on those who seek to circumvent it by legislative decree!

It is in fact possible, and may sometimes be desirable, for a government authority to act to reduce particular prices effectively. It may, for example, be desirable to provide inexpensive housing or inexpensive education to those who otherwise could not afford it. But this requires the painful decision to provide the requisite subsidy funds out of taxes, for there is no act of magic that will reduce prices without reducing supplies, unless someone is willing to pay the costs out of some other source of funds.

Our supply–demand analysis (Figure 35–2)

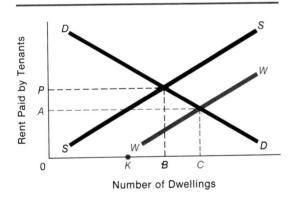

FIGURE 35–2

SUPPLY–DEMAND ANALYSIS OF RENT SUBSIDY
A rent subsidy means that suppliers of dwellings receive more money than tenants pay. This means that more dwellings will be supplied at any level of rent to tenants. That is, the supply curve shifts rightward from black line SS to red line WW. The market-determined level of rent falls from P to A, and the number of dwellings supplied increases from B to C.

shows that a subsidy provided to people who supply apartment houses will reduce their money cost and so will shift the supply curve to the right, from SS to WW. That is, given any rent paid by the tenant (A, for example), more money will be received by the landlord, so he will be willing to supply more housing units (C housing units rather than the K units he would supply without the subsidy). With the new supply curve, WW, equilibrium rent will be lower (A rather than P) and the quantity supplied will be greater (C rather than B) than they would be without a subsidy. This should be compared with Figure 35–1, the rent-control diagram, in which supplies are cut rather than raised, as they will be by a subsidy. Supporters of price controls might do well to study the supply–demand analysis to determine the likely effects of the measures they advocate.

SOME POLICY PROPOSALS: POVERTY AND UNEMPLOYMENT

It is possible to formulate a number of policy programs, which seem, on the basis of the logic of the underlying economic issues, to be more promising than some of the obvious and standard methods that have usually been employed up to now. Yet it must be emphasized that, at least so far, no one has come up with a miracle policy that can confidently be expected to dispose of the many difficult problems of our cities. In part, this is to be attributed to the recent precipitate decline in the cities' special economic advantages—an issue that was discussed earlier in this chapter. Partially it is also because cumulative processes, such as those involved in the decline of the city, are inherently very difficult to reverse—the problem is to turn about a powerful set of forces whose tendency is to make things worse, and that is no easy matter.

Yet there is a great deal that can be done, as we will see. It must be remembered, however, that given the very difficult nature of the under-lying problems, any one of these by itself is likely to have very little impact, and that only by a comprehensive set of measures can one hope to get the urban economies moving upward again.

Jobs for urban residents must be the keystone in any effective program to revive the cities. With higher incomes, the tax base will be increased and services will be improved. More-over, there will be a reduction in the need for special services dealing with the problems of the poor. As incomes rise, they will inevitably be accompanied by a demand for better housing, which is very likely the most effective and most durable means of dealing with the problem of slums and deteriorating neighborhoods.

There is no magic formula that will provide the desired employment rate, but we will describe three measures that can undoubtedly make a difference:

1. Creation of an urban job corps program of substantial magnitude. During the Great Depression, the U.S. government undertook large-scale programs to provide jobs for the unemployed. The victims of the Depression, whose labor power would otherwise have been wasted, were enrolled in programs that planted forests, built post offices, painted murals in public buildings, and performed hundreds of other useful tasks. We still make good use of many of the facilities that were provided under these programs. Whatever reservations one may have about the efficiency of this sort of activity, whatever doubts one may have about the desir-ability of public works projects relative to private activity, they are certainly preferable to the waste of complete and widespread idleness. An enormous amount of work is crying to be done in our cities. And in the course of such work the unskilled can learn useful skills on the job. Until a more effective way to provide jobs in the city

can be found, this may well be the priority item in any budget devoted to urban problems.

2. Rescinding of minimum-wage legislation for urban teen-agers. One of the reasons ghetto teen-agers cannot find jobs is that with their lack of skill and experience, it is not worth the potential employer's while to hire them at the wage level required by the minimum wage laws. Employers can use inexperienced workers but not at that price. The result is a Catch-22 under which young people cannot acquire experience because they have no jobs, and they cannot get jobs because they lack experience.

Minimum wage laws are another example of an attempt to interfere with the price mechanism of which we have spoken so many times in this book. In this case the legislation does benefit one group—the semiskilled workers who have jobs and who are protected from the competi-tion of the inexperienced. But minimum wage regulation also has its victims—the young and inexperienced—who are forced into the ranks of the unemployed.[4]

3. Reduction or elimination of differentials in property tax rates. We saw earlier in the chapter that it is not unusual for cities to find themselves forced to charge a property tax rate in the range of 70 to 90 percent on rental properties, which is a rate between two and three times higher than that paid in the wealthy suburbs. When one thinks about it, this difference is an incredible handicap imposed on the business activity that is needed to provide jobs in the central cities. It is not only an extremely high tax upon the urban firm's rental costs, but it is a tax rate that is largely escaped by its suburban competitors.

To remove this persistent handicap, it has been proposed that local property taxes be replaced, at least in part, either by uniform property taxes that apply statewide or by some other revenue source, such as the income tax,

[4]A full discussion of minimum wage laws appears in Chapter 27.

that does not discriminate against the cities. In fact, some legislatures, prodded by the courts, are already moving in this direction. Curiously, they have been motivated not by a desire to revive the urban economies but by the issue of equality of educational opportunities between rich and poor communities, which was discussed before. As such changes begin to take effect, they will remove one powerful force inhibiting business activities in the central city.

The proposals we have just examined are by no means *all* of the measures that can be used to stimulate industry in the city. A variety of acts, including government insurance of business loans to firms in ghetto areas, training programs for unskilled workers, and transportation improvements, have all been proposed. We have deliberately not emphasized these relatively obvious measures in order to focus attention on those that are more likely to be overlooked.

SOME PROPOSALS ON HOUSING

While it has been emphasized that employment and the resulting increases in income may well be the most effective way to deal with the urban housing problem, there are several other useful things that can be done and that are worth our notice.

One of the critical elements required for a durable solution to housing problems is freedom of choice by the tenants and an increased ownership interest in the property in which they reside.

As long as poor people are forced to live in buildings whose specifications have been judged by some architect to be ''good for the poor,'' we are likely to find a serious mismatch between tenant preferences and the type of housing they are supplied with. Residents frequently detest the sorts of buildings they are forced to inhabit and are likely to give vent to their anger by vandalizing those buildings. Moreover, since the buildings are not their property, they have no financial interest in keeping them in good condition. One may well suspect that only when people have a stake in the houses they inhabit will there be a significant decrease in the destructiveness that characterizes so many of the public housing projects.

We turn next to one way of moving toward the goal of tenants having real financial interests in their residences: a plan that has recently been gaining favor and that can also help the cities to cope with two other problems: unemployment and owner abandonment of unprofitable buildings.

1. Extended homesteading and abandoned buildings. In a number of major cities, homes that have been abandoned have been made available to poor people for a token payment ($1 in at least one case) in return for an agreement to rehabilitate the house and to live in it for at least three years. This program, which is called urban homesteading has several obvious advantages. It puts to good use properties that would otherwise be left to rot; it puts people to work who might otherwise have no outlet for their labor; it may teach them some skills; and it offers them a financial stake in the condition of the house and its neighborhood.

It has recently been proposed that this program might usefully be extended by organizing such potential homeowners into construction teams who would work under the instruction and supervision of skilled workers—carpenters, electricians, plumbers, and so on. By encouraging rehabilitation of large numbers of abandoned buildings, some proportion of which would be sold on the real estate market, the program would become self-financing, providing raw materials and some income to the workers who in the process would be learning valuable skills and whose own rehabilitated homes would increase in value.

Such a program offers real incentives and some promise for the future. Moreover, it may well make the externalities and the cumulative processes begin to work *in favor* of the city. Each house that is rehabilitated improves the neighborhood and makes adjacent properties more valuable. Each rehabilitated home makes it more profitable to rehabilitate the next one. This, then, is one case in which contagion can, for a change, favor the neighborhood and the general welfare.

2. Elimination of rent controls. As the matter was put by the Senate Banking Committee, rent control programs are "a major cause of the decline of [the cities'] housing stock and the erosion of its real estate tax base."[5] As we saw earlier in this chapter, rent controls discourage both new construction and expenditures to maintain and improve existing buildings. They aggravate the abandonment problem. It is ironic that by producing artificial shortages they actually raise rents in the long run. Rent controls make the destruction of a city's housing supply a virtual certainty, and any effective program to improve housing requires their elimination.

3. Abandonment deposits. As we have seen, abandonment is serious not only because it reduces the number of available housing units but also because abandoned buildings contribute to deterioration of the neighborhood. They pose problems of fire, sanitation, and disease and frequently become a haven for petty crime.

After the building is abandoned, usually with substantial unpaid taxes, the erstwhile landlord is often impossible to track down, should the city want to try to force him either to repair it or pull it down. Such landlords cannot be found because they often hide behind dummy corporations or other devices that effectively conceal their identities.

[5] *The New York Times*, May 17, 1976, page 1.

One way that has been proposed to deal with the problem is to require every landlord to deposit with the city an amount sufficient to pay for restoration or removal of the building in the event it is abandoned. The landlord would be paid full interest on the deposit by the city, which would use the funds as part of its normal borrowing. In that way the landlord would be compensated financially for the burden of making the deposit, and the deposit would be returned to him either after he sells the building to someone else (who would in turn be required to provide his own deposit) or tears it down in an acceptable manner. A deposit would also make it cheaper and easier to replace the building with something newer and better, which would constitute an asset rather than a liability to the neighborhood.

4. Land versus property taxes. Usually taxes are based on an estimate of the market value of taxed properties. Consequently, slum dwellings with their low market value are taxed less heavily than are properties in good condition. The result is a perverse incentive—a tax benefit to those who let their buildings deteriorate.

To avoid this and to provide a strong financial incentive for building improvements, it has been proposed that real estate taxes in the cities be based not on the market value of the buildings but on the market value of the *land* on which the buildings stand.

How would this improve matters? The answer is that it would make it unprofitable for a landlord to keep valuable and highly taxed land tied up in slum properties or other buildings whose income potential is low. Profits could be made only by upgrading the buildings or replacing them with more valuable structures that bring an income commensurate with the taxes. Since the increased value of the buildings would not lead to a higher tax bill (tax would not be based on building value), this move would constitute a substantial and continuing stimulus to improve urban real estate, as any long-term improvement of cities requires.

The housing programs that have just been summarized are meant to remind you that unemployment is not the only problem that besets the cities. And there are still others. For example, there is the cost of welfare programs—direct financial support for the impoverished, which now runs to some 20 percent of urban budgets. It is often argued that these welfare programs have attracted poor people from the entire nation to the major northern and western cities, which are then left with the problem of providing money to the poor of the entire country. Consequently, it has been proposed that the federal government should take over welfare programs from the cities, because the problem is national, not local, and because the federal government can manage the funding while the cities cannot.

Yet, it is concluded by many careful observers that unemployment is still the key urban issue, and that until it is alleviated substantially, all other urban problems will remain secondary.

As a final comment, it should be noted that the illustrative programs that have been discussed are not calculated to appeal particularly either to the right or to the left. Conservatives may well take issue with the idea that government should provide jobs for the unemployed. Those at the other end of the political spectrum may be put off by the extent to which the proposals rely on financial incentives and call for an end to destructive regulations such as rent controls. That may help explain why it has been so difficult to launch effective programs for the cities, for such programs require difficult decisions and an abandonment of cherished positions by virtually everyone concerned.

SUMMARY

1. The city derives its economic advantages from the density of its population and from its production activities, both of which make cities easier to serve by railroad, reduce the cost of communication, and make it possible to provide services that require large numbers of users.
2. The increased use of automobiles and trucks and the growth of the nation's road and telecommunications networks have tended to erode the economic advantages of the city.
3. Despite the fact that their schools and other municipal services are better, the wealthy suburbs end up with far lower tax rates than exist in the cities. This is because even a low tax rate applied to a valuable piece of real estate can bring in substantial tax revenues, and poverty imposes high costs on city governments.
4. Exodus of middle- and higher-income families and of industry from the cities is a cumulative process. Each time there is a wave of relocation out of the city, tax rates in the city are subjected to upward pressure and deterioration is hastened, thus inducing still others to leave the city.
5. Municipal services suffer from a cost disease, which results from the fact that the *quality* of many of these services (such as teaching, health care, and police protection) depends on the *quantity* of labor that goes into them. As a result, labor productivity in these services is difficult to increase, and so their costs rise steadily at a faster rate than do costs elsewhere in the economy. This is one of the 12 Ideas for Beyond the Final Exam.
6. Each time a building is permitted by its owner to deteriorate, it damages the quality of the neighborhood and makes it less profitable to maintain other nearby buildings. This is a detrimental *externalities* problem similar to that which underlies environmental deterioration.

7. Rent controls make it unprofitable to build or maintain housing. By reducing housing supplies, rent controls may actually raise rents in the long run. Certainly they have a devastating effect on the quality of housing in a city.

8. Jobs are probably the key element in any effective program to help the cities. Without more jobs and increased incomes, one cannot hope to improve housing, reduce crime, or eliminate the other ills of the city.

CONCEPTS FOR REVIEW

Urban renewal
Property tax rates
Zoning ordinance
Exodus as a cumulative process
Cost disease of municipal services

Externalities and neighborhood decay
Rent control
Urban job corps
Urban homesteading

QUESTIONS FOR DISCUSSION

1. Forty years ago anyone who wanted to shop in a big department store had to go to the city. Why is this no longer true? What technological developments underlie the change?

2. Name some municipal services that are better in wealthy suburbs than in the cities. Can you think of any exceptions?

3. List some costs that result for a community when many poor families move into it.

4. If deterioration and exodus from the city by people who are not poor are cumulative processes, why is the expenditure of a lot of money on rebuilding neighborhoods only temporarily helpful, at best?

5. There are many economic activities, in addition to the municipal services, that are affected by cost disease. In light of the reason for the problem, which of the following economic activities would you expect to suffer from cost disease? (a) auto manufacturing, (b) auto repair, (c) auto insurance. Explain your answers.

6. Why do most people understand that cars or TV sets will not be manufactured by private industry if their price is too low to permit any profit, when so few people feel the same way about rent controls and housing? (No one really has an answer to this question, but it *is* worth discussing!)

7. Explain the difference between a tax on land value and a tax on property value. Why does the latter inhibit construction while the former may actually stimulate it?

nine

The
World
Economy

36

International Trade
and Comparative Advantage

W hile the United States can supply much of its own fuel, it is almost *entirely* dependent on the rest of the world for a number of other products, such as rubber and coffee. For these and many other vital inputs, such as oil and copper, the United States must depend on trade with other countries. Still, in numerical terms, imports and exports are not nearly as important for the United States as they are for smaller nations, such as Great Britain, Israel, and the Netherlands. For instance, in 1976 exports constituted only 8 percent of the GNP in the United States, whereas corresponding figures for the Israelis and the Dutch were 32 and 51 percent, respectively.

In this chapter, we will examine the purposes of foreign trade and the ways in which governments have sought to influence or limit it. First, we will examine why countries engage in trade. Second, we will see why the populations of both countries may benefit from an exchange even though they are, in effect, merely "swapping goods." Third, we will study the crucial law of comparative advantage, which determines what commodities a country finds advantageous to export and what commodities it finds advantageous to import. Fourth, we will see how the prices of goods traded between countries are determined by supply and demand. And, finally, we will examine the pros and cons of tariffs and other devices designed to protect a country's industries from foreign competition.

ISSUE: THE COMPETITION OF "CHEAP FOREIGN LABOR"

In analyzing the issues of international trade, common sense can be extremely valuable; indeed, there is no substitute for it. Yet sometimes conclusions based on common sense without factual confirmation and careful analysis can be very misleading.

One example of a foreign trade issue that has been misunderstood for lack of factual analysis is the argument that buying products made by cheap foreign labor is unfair and destructive to domestic interests. Some U.S. business people and union leaders argue that such purchases take bread out of the mouths of American workers and depress standards of living in this country. According to this view, cheap imports cause job losses and put pressure on U.S. businesses to lower wages. Moreover, they encourage the continued exploitation of workers in the countries from which we obtain our imports by providing rewards to sweatshop proprietors abroad and by making clear to them that low prices and, consequently, low wages are the only basis on which they can compete.

Yet the facts do not seem entirely consistent with this scenario. First, wages have risen spectacularly among the industrialized suppliers of products bought by Americans, where earnings rates were indeed relatively low only a few years ago. As Table 36–1 shows, a dramatic change occurred during the first half of the 1970s. Note that in 1970, hourly wages in manu-

facturing in eight countries of Western Europe and in Japan averaged about 45 percent of those in the United States. Yet by mid-1975, the average hourly compensation in these countries had risen to more than 80 percent of the U.S. level; and two of the countries had exceeded the U.S. level and two others had almost equaled it. International comparisons like those in the table do run into some problems because of the different currencies. American workers are paid in dollars and Japanese workers are paid in yen, and during the period in question the value of the yen increased substantially relative to the dollar. Yet the basic pattern that emerges from the table correctly indicates the underlying reality: American imports of Volkswagens from Germany, Volvos from Sweden, and electronic products from Japan have continued, despite the fact that wages have risen in those countries.

More important, the rise in these foreign wages, compared with those in the United States, has not brought with them an increasing strength in the American position in the international marketplace. In the 1950s, when Euro-

TABLE 36–1

HOURLY COMPENSATION RATES
IN NINE INDUSTRIALIZED COUNTRIES

	1970	MIDYEAR 1975
Belgium	$2.08	$6.46
Britain	1.48	3.20
France	1.74	4.57
Germany	2.32	6.19
Italy	1.75	4.52
Japan	0.99	3.10
Netherlands	1.99	5.98
Sweden	2.93	7.12
United States	4.20	6.22

Data are compensation estimates per hour worked and relate essentially to all employees in the manufacturing sector. Sources: U.S. Bureau of Labor Statistics and Citibank estimates.

pean and Japanese wages were far below those in the United States, we had no trouble marketing our products abroad. It was far easier then than now to sell the amount of exports needed to pay for the amount of goods that were imported. In fact, the main problem then was to bring imports up to the level at which they roughly balanced our exports. Then, in the decade of the 1960s, as wages in Europe and Japan began to rise closer to those in the United States, America ran into serious trouble in its ability to sell goods abroad. We were, and still are, often unable to export enough to pay for our imports. Clearly, cheap foreign labor does not always serve as a crucial obstacle to U.S. sales abroad as a "common sense" view of the matter suggests. In this chapter we will see what has gone wrong with that view.

WHY TRADE?

The main reason that countries trade with one another rather than try to run completely independent economies is that the earth's resources are not equally distributed across its surface. The United States has an abundant supply of coal, an energy source that is quite scarce in most of the rest of the world. Saudi Arabia has very little land that is suitable for farming, but it sits atop a huge pool of oil. By contrast, Israel, despite its proximity to the world's richest petroleum deposits, has virtually no oil of its own. Because of this seemingly whimsical distribution of vital resources, every nation must trade with others to acquire what it lacks. In general, the more varied the endowment of a particular country, the less it will have to depend on others to make up for its deficiencies.

Furthermore, even if a country had all the resources it would like to use, other reasons would lead it to engage in trade. We have seen that countries differ in their natural conditions and resource endowments. Americans *could,* with great difficulty, grow their own banana trees and coffee shrubs in hothouses; but these items are much more efficiently grown in such places as Honduras and Brazil, where the climate is appropriate. On the other hand, wheat grows in the United States with little difficulty. And aluminum is produced most efficiently in areas with abundant supplies of hydroelectric power.

The skills of a country's labor force also play a role. If Argentina has a large group of efficient farmers and few workers with industrial experience while the opposite is true in Great Britain, it will generally pay Argentina to specialize in agriculture and let Great Britain concentrate on manufacturing.

This last point suggests one other important reason why countries trade—the advantage of specialization. If one country were to try to produce everything, it would end up with a number of industries whose scale of operation was too small to permit the use of mass-production techniques, specialized training facilities, and the other arrangements that can give a cost advantage to large-volume operations. Even now, despite the considerable volume of trade in the world economy, this problem seems to arise for some countries whose operation of their own international airlines or their own steel mills, for example, seems explainable only in political rather than economic terms. Inevitably, nations with small markets find that enterprises that are economical only when their scale of operation is large can only survive with the aid of large government subsidies.

To summarize: International trade is essential for the prosperity of the trading nations for at least three reasons: (1) every country lacks some vital resources that it can get only by trading with others; (2) each country's climate and other natural endowments make it a relatively efficient producer of some goods and an inefficient producer of other goods; and (3) specialization permits larger outputs and can therefore offer economies of large-scale production.

INTERNATIONAL VERSUS INTRANATIONAL TRADE: MOBILITY OF INPUTS

Trading takes place not only among countries but also among regions of a country. Florida and California "export" oranges to states in the East and the Middle West, which in turn produce automobiles and grain for other regions of the country. The logic of such domestic exchange is basically no different from that underlying trade among different countries; the three primary reasons for international trade just listed are equally applicable to trade *within* countries.

If one can learn about trade from strictly domestic exchanges why study international trade as a special subject? There are at least three basic reasons: (1) domestic trade takes place under a single government, while foreign trade must involve at least two governments; (2) domestic trade involves only one currency, while foreign trade must involve the monies of different countries; and (3) in domestic trading it is usually easier for labor and capital to move to the jobs where they are most needed, whereas in international trading labor and capital must move from one country to another—a much more difficult task. Let us look a bit more closely at these differences between domestic and international trade.

Political Factors in International Trade

At least in theory, the government of a nation is concerned with the welfare of all its citizens. But governments are not necessarily concerned with the welfare of the countries with which they trade. Thus, in accord with the provisions of the Constitution of the United States, domestic trade is not subject to overt tariffs and other trade barriers designed to increase the gains from trade of one group of its inhabitants at the expense of another. In contrast, a major issue in

the economic analysis of international trade is the use and misuse of political impediments to free international trade. Later in the chapter, these impediments and other policy issues related to international trade will be discussed in some detail.

The Many Currencies Involved in International Trade

All trade within the borders of the United States is carried out in dollars. But the trade of American grain for British woolens involves two different monetary units—dollars and pounds. Rates of exchange between different currencies can and do change. Thirty years ago the pound was worth more than $4; since then it has been as low in value as $1.55. This variability in exchange rates brings with it a host of complications and policy problems that are discussed in the next chapter.

Impediments to Mobility of Labor and Capital among Countries

If there are jobs in California but none in Michigan, workers can move freely to follow the job opportunities. Of course, there are personal costs—not only the dollar cost of moving, but also the psychological cost of giving up friends and familiar surroundings. But such moves are not inhibited by immigration quotas, by laws restricting the employment of foreigners, or by the need to learn a new language, as are moves from one country to another.

There are also greater impediments to the transfer of capital from one country to another than to its movement within a country. The shipment of plant and equipment between countries can be expensive, and the international shipment of capital in the form of money to be invested in foreign firms is likely to encounter many restrictions (for example, in many countries there are rules limiting the share of foreign ownership in a company). Such investment abroad is also subject to special risks, such as the danger of outright expropriation if, say, after a political revolution the new government decides to take over all foreign properties without compensation. But even if nothing so extreme occurs, capital invested abroad faces risks from possible variations in exchange rates. An investment yielding a million pounds a year will be worth $2 million to American investors if the pound is worth $2 but only $1.5 million if the pound should fall to $1.50.

While labor, capital, and other factors of production do move from country to country when offered an opportunity to increase their earnings abroad, they are less likely to do so than to move from one region of a country to another to gain similar increases.

MUTUAL GAINS FROM TRADE

In some of the very early writings on international trade, it was implied that one nation could gain from an exchange only at the expense of another. It was argued (fallaciously) that since nothing is produced in the act of trading, the total collection of goods in the hands of the two parties at the end of the exchange could not be greater than it was before the exchange took place. Therefore, if one country gets more out of a swap than it put in, the other country must necessarily end up with less than it started with.

One of the consequences of this view was the policy prescription calling for each country, in the interests of its citizens, to do its very best to act to the disadvantage of its trading partners—in Adam Smith's terms, to "beggar its neighbors." The idea that one nation's gain must be another's loss means that a country can promote its own welfare only by harming others.

Yet, as Adam Smith and others after him emphasized, in any *voluntary exchange,* unless there is misunderstanding of the facts, both parties *must* gain (or at least expect to gain) something from the transaction. Otherwise why would both parties agree to the exchange?

But how can mere exchange, in which no net production takes place, actually leave both parties better off? The answer is that while there can of course be no gain in the physical quantity of the products exchanged, the holdings of both parties can end up much better suited to the needs of each. Suppose individual A has four sandwiches and nothing to drink, while B has four bottles of Coke and nothing to eat. A trade of two sandwiches for two bottles of Coke does not increase the total supply of either food or beverages, but it clearly produces a net increase in the welfare of both parties.

Any *voluntary exchange* must promise to make *both* parties better off. Trade can bring about mutual gains by redistributing products in such a way that each participant ends up holding a combination of goods that is better adapted to his preferences than the goods he held before.

And this, as we shall now see, is precisely what trade among nations accomplishes.

COMPARATIVE ADVANTAGE: THE FUNDAMENTAL PRINCIPLE OF SPECIALIZATION

We know that coffee can be produced in Colombia using less labor and smaller quantities of other inputs than would be needed to grow it in the United States. And we know that the United States can produce large passenger aircraft at a lower resource cost than can Colombia. We say then that Colombia has an absolute advantage over the United States in coffee production, and the United States has an absolute advantage over Colombia in aircraft production.

DEFINITION

One country is said to have an *absolute advantage* over another in the production of a particular good if it can produce that good at a lower resource cost than can the other country.

Obviously, if the United States wants coffee and Colombia wants airplanes, both can save resources by trading—each exporting to the other the good in which it has an absolute advantage.

Suppose, however, that one country is more efficient than another in producing *every* item. Can they still gain by trading? The surprising answer is *definitely yes.*

How is this possible? A simple parable will help make the reason clear. The work of a highly paid business consultant frequently requires computer analysis. Now suppose the consultant herself began her career as a computer operator, doing her own key punching and programming and had been extremely good at it. Consequently, in her current position it is likely that she may grow impatient with the slow, sloppy work of some of the low-paid key punchers who work for her, and at times she is tempted to do all the work herself. Good judgment, however, tells her that though she is better both at giving business advice and at key punching than are her employees, it is foolish to devote any of her valuable time to the low-skilled punching job.

Here is an example of *comparative advantage* at work. The consultant specializes in business advice despite her absolute advantage in computer work, because she has a *still greater* absolute advantage in her role as a business consultant. Every hour she decides not to devote to key punching causes her some direct loss because it puts the work into hands less competent than hers. But that loss is more than compensated for by the earnings she makes selling her services to clients during that hour.

This example brings out the fundamental principle that underlies the bulk of economic analysis of patterns of specialization and exchange among different nations, and that is one of our 12 Ideas for Beyond the Final Exam. The principle, called the *law of comparative advantage,* was discovered by David Ricardo, one of the giants in the history of economic analysis.

Even if one country is at an absolute *disad*vantage relative to another country in the production of *every* good, it is said to have a *comparative advantage* in making the good in whose production it is *least inefficient* in comparison with the other country.

Ricardo's basic finding was that even if one country is more efficient than another in the production of every commodity (that is, it has an absolute advantage in every commodity), both countries can still gain by trading.

Let's see how this works by using Ricardo's own example. Suppose it takes less labor in Portugal than in England to produce either a yard of cloth or a barrel of wine, so that Portugal has an absolute advantage in both cloth and wine production. If Portugal's advantage in wine production is proportionately greater than its advantage in cloth production, for the reasons specified in our consultant—keypuncher example, it may nevertheless pay Portugal to specialize in the production of wine and to get cloth from England.

Ricardo found that:

In determining the most efficient patterns of production, what matters is *comparative* advantage not *absolute* advantage. Thus it will often pay a country to import a certain good even if that good can be produced at home more efficiently than it can in the country from which it is imported. Such imports will be profitable if the country produces *even more* efficiently the goods that it exports in exchange.

THE ARITHMETIC OF COMPARATIVE ADVANTAGE

A numerical illustration will help us to grasp the logic of the principle of comparative advantage. Table 36–2 gives some hypothetical figures indicating how much labor is required to produce a yard of cloth and a barrel of wine in England and Portugal. We see from the figures that Portugal produces cloth twice as efficiently as England, taking only 1 hour of labor to produce a yard of cloth, while 2 hours are required for the purpose in England. However, Portugal is four times as efficient as England in wine production, where it takes 40 hours to supply a barrel of wine.

Figure 36–1 depicts the two countries' production opportunity frontiers corresponding to the numbers in the table and a given quantity of labor.[1] Given, say, 80 million hours of labor, the line EF tells us what combinations of wine and cloth England can produce. For example, since it takes England 40 labor hours to produce 1 barrel, if it used those 80 million hours to produce only wine, it would end up at point E, with 2 million barrels of wine and zero cloth. Similarly, if it devoted all 80 million hours to cloth production at 2 hours per yard, it would obtain 40 million yards of cloth and no wine (point F). Or it could devote some labor to wine and some labor to cloth. For example, with a 50/50 division of its labor between the two outputs, it is easy to see that it would obtain

[1]To review the concept of the production opportunity frontier, see Chapter 3, pages 42–43.

TABLE 36–2

HYPOTHETICAL LABOR REQUIREMENTS TO ILLUSTRATE COMPARATIVE ADVANTAGE

	IN ENGLAND (hours)	IN PORTUGAL (hours)
One yard of cloth	2	1
One barrel of wine	40	10

1 million barrels of wine and 20 million yards of cloth (point G). In short, line EF shows all the options in terms of wine and cloth output that its 80 million labor hours make available to England.

Using precisely the same reasoning, we deduce that line PQ shows all the wine and cloth output options available to Portugal if it had exactly the same amount of labor time avail-

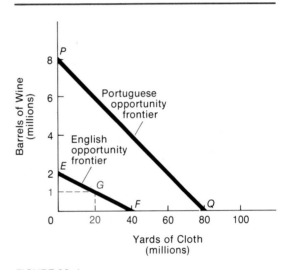

FIGURE 36–1

ABSOLUTE AND COMPARATIVE ADVANTAGE SHOWN BY TWO COUNTRIES' PRODUCTION OPPORTUNITY FRONTIERS
Portugal's absolute advantage is shown by its ability to produce more of every commodity using the same quantity of labor as does England. Therefore, Portugal's opportunity frontier, PQ, is higher than England's, EF. But England has a comparative advantage in cloth production in which it is only half as productive as Portugal (it can produce 40 million yards, point F, compared with Portugal's 80 million, point Q). On the other hand, England is one-quarter as productive in wine production (point E) as is Portugal (point P). Thus, England is least inefficient in producing cloth, where it consequently has a comparative advantage.

Biographical Note:
David Ricardo (1772–1823)

David Ricardo was born four years before publication of Adam Smith's *Wealth of Nations.* Descended from a family of well-to-do stock-brokers of the Jewish faith who migrated to London from Amsterdam and were, in turn, descended from Portuguese Jews, he had about twenty brothers and sisters. In accord with Jewish tradition, Ricardo's formal education ended at the age of 13, and so he was largely self-educated. He began his career by working in his father's brokerage firm. At age 21, Ricardo married a Quaker woman and decided to become a Unitarian, a sect then considered "little better than atheist." By Jewish custom, Ricardo's father broke with him, though apparently they never actually became enemies. Ricardo then decided to go into the brokerage business on his own and was enormously successful. During the Napoleonic Wars he regularly scored business coups over leading British and foreign financiers, including the Rothschilds. After gaining a huge profit on government securities that he had bought just before the Battle of Waterloo, Ricardo decided to retire from business when he was just over 40 years old.

He purchased a country estate, Gatcomb (now owned by the royal family), where a brilliant group of intellectuals met regularly. Particularly remarkable for the period was the number of women included in the circle, among them Maria Edgeworth, the novelist (who wrote extravagant praise of Ricardo's mind), and Jane Marcet, an author of textbooks including what was probably the first text in economics. Ricardo's close friends included the economists T. R. Malthus and James Mill, father of John Stuart Mill the noted philosopher–economist. Malthus remained close friends with Ricardo even though they disagreed on many subjects and continued their arguments in personal correspondence and in their published works.

James Mill persuaded Ricardo to go into Parliament. As was then customary, Ricardo purchased his seat by buying a piece of land that entitled its owner to a seat in Parliament. There he proved to be a noteworthy liberal, strongly supporting many causes that were against his personal interests.

James Mill also helped persuade Ricardo to write his masterpiece, *The Principles of Political Economy and Taxation,* which may have been the first book of pure economic theory. It was noteworthy that Ricardo, the most practical of practical men, had little patience with empirical economics and preferred instead to rest his analysis explicitly and exclusively on theory.

His book made considerable contributions to the analysis of pricing, wage determination, and the effects of various types of taxes, among many other subjects. It also gave us the law of comparative advantage. In addition, the book described what has come to be called the Ricardian rent theory—even though Ricardo did not discover the analysis and explicitly denied having done so.

Ricardo died in 1823 at the age of 51. He seems to have been a wholly admirable person—honest, charming, witty, conscientious, brilliant—altogether too good to be true.

able as England does—80 million hours. For example, point P is obtained because if Portugal produces nothing but wine, at 10 labor hours per barrel, it will be able to produce 8 million barrels and no cloth.

Note that Portugal's opportunity frontier lies above England's throughout the diagram. That is because Portugal is the more efficient producer of both commodities. With the same amount of labor, it can obtain more wine and more cloth than England. Thus, the higher position of Portugal's opportunity frontier is the graph's way of showing Portugal's *absolute* advantgage.

Portugal's *comparative* advantage in wine production and England's comparative advantage in cloth production is shown in a different way—by the relative slopes of the two opportunity frontiers. Portugal's opportunity frontier is not only higher than England's, it is also steeper. What does this mean economically? One way of looking at the difference is to remember that while Portugal can produce four times as much wine as England (compare points P and E), it can produce only twice as much cloth as England (points Q and F). England is, relatively speaking, only half as bad at cloth production as at wine production. That is what is meant when we say it has a comparative advantage in the former.

We may express this difference more directly in terms of the slopes of the two lines. The slope of Portugal's opportunity frontier is $OP/OQ = 8/80 = 1/10$. This means that if Portugal switches from pure wine production (point P) to pure cloth production (point Q), it must give up 1 barrel of wine for every 10 yards of cloth it obtains. That is, the opportunity cost of cloth to Portugal is 1/10 of a barrel of wine for each yard of cloth it produces.

In the case of England, the slope of the opportunity frontier is $OE/OF = 2/40 = 1/20$. That is, to get an additional yard of cloth, it must give up only half as much wine production as is required in Portugal. Why? Because, in the example, English workers are such bad wine

producers that by transferring them out of such work, the resulting loss in wine production is so much smaller than Portugal's.

A country's absolute advantage in production over another country is shown by its having a higher production opportunity frontier. The difference in the comparative advantages of the two countries is shown by the difference in the slopes of their opportunity frontiers.

Arithmetic of the Gains from Comparative Advantage

Comparative advantage now shows us directly how it is possible for both countries to gain from trade, despite England's inferiority in both types of labor.

Suppose, in Figure 36–2, that without trade Portugal would end up at point R (60 million yards of cloth and 2 million barrels of wine), and that without trade England would end up at point J. After negotiation, England agrees to reduce its wine output by 1 million barrels (moving from J to H), with Portugal just replacing this output by the move from R to S. But Portugal cannot simply expand its wine production—it must get the necessary labor by transferring it out of cloth production. That is, it must remain on its opportunity frontier. Thus it will end up at point T, with 3 million barrels of wine and only 50 million yards of cloth. It will have had to give up 10 million yards of cloth output, represented by ST, to obtain the wine, RS, which it promised England.

Similarly, England, having given up 1 million barrels of wine production (JH), can use the labor time thereby released to increase its ouput of cloth and so bring it back to its opportunity frontier (point E), where cloth output is now increased by 20 million yards.

The net outcome of this process is clear. The two countries together end up with the same amount of wine as before—3.5 million barrels between them. Here things balance out.

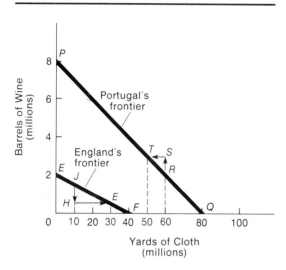

FIGURE 36–2

THE GAINS FROM TRADE AS A RESULT OF COMPARATIVE ADVANTAGE

In the absence of trade, say, England ends up at point J and Portugal at point R. Then, if England reduces its wine production (JH) and Portugal increases its wine production by the same amount (RS), Portugal's cloth output must fall (ST) but England's can rise (HE). However, since England is such a bad wine producer, its resulting increase in cloth production (from 10 million to 30 million yards of cloth) is much greater than the fall in Portugal's cloth output. In sum, wine output remains constant, while cloth output increases as a result of the beginning of trade. Portugal produces wine for England, and England produces cloth for Portugal.

But in cloth output things do not balance out—they do much better than that. True, Portugal reduced its cloth output by 10 million yards (ST). But England, by getting its workers out of wine production, in which they have no competence, either absolute or relative, is enabled to increase its cloth output by 20 million yards. Obviously, the two countries together have gained 10 million yards of cloth, which they can share between them and both be better off.

Just how much each will gain in the process depends on the price that will be set for wine and cloth. The process by which that price is determined by supply and demand will be seen in a later section. For now we need merely note that the higher the price of wine (Portugal's export), the greater the share of the gain that will go to Portugal; and the higher the price of cloth, the greater the share that will go to England.

To see what each country may gain from an exchange in our example, let us suppose that the price settles at 15 yards of cloth per barrel of wine when Portugal and England decide to begin trading. By ceasing to produce 10 yards of cloth for itself, Portugal saves 10 hours of labor (see Table 36–2), which it can use instead to produce 1 additional barrel of wine (again see Table 36–2) to export to England. Since it gets 15 yards of cloth in exchange, it is 5 yards of cloth ahead in the process; that is, it ends up with 15 yards of cloth instead of 10.

What about England? It expands its output of cloth by 20 yards, using for this purpose the labor time released by reducing its wine output by 1 barrel. But at the prices in our example, England can replace this barrel of wine by offering Portugal 15 yards of cloth in exchange. Thus through trade, England has gained 5 yards of cloth.

There certainly seems to be some sleight of hand here! All that has taken place is an exchange. Yet, in the process, Portugal and England each gained 5 yards of cloth without losing any wine. How can such gains in physical output be possible for both parties?

The explanation is that the trade process we have just described involves more than just a swap of a fixed bundle of commodities. It is also a change in the *production* arrangements, with some of England's wine production taken over by the more efficient producers of Portuguese wine, and with some of Portugal's cloth production taken over by English weavers who are *less* *in*efficient at producing cloth than English vintners are at producing wine.

With every country doing what it can do best, more of every commodity can be turned out with any given amount of world labor; and everyone benefits in the process. Efficiency in international trade requires each country to produce the goods at which it is least inefficient—in which it has a comparative advantage.

COMPARATIVE ADVANTAGE AND COMPETITION OF CHEAP FOREIGN LABOR

The principle of comparative advantage takes us a good part of the way toward an explanation of the fallacy in the "cheap foreign labor" argument described earlier in the chapter. Given the assumed productive efficiency of Portuguese labor and the inefficiency of British labor in Ricardo's example, we would expect wages to be much higher in Portugal than in England. Indeed, if workers receive all of the nation's output, and wine and cloth are produced in the same proportions in both countries, then this *must* be so, because output per person in Portugal is so much higher.

In these circumstances, one can expect some Portuguese workers to be apprehensive about an agreement to permit trade between the countries—"How can we hope to meet the unfair competition of those underpaid British workers?" And British laborers are also likely to be concerned—"How can we hope to meet the competition of those Portuguese, who are so efficient in producing everything?"

The principle of comparative advantage shows us that both fears are unjustified. As we have just seen, when trade is opened up between Portugal and England *workers in both countries will be able to earn higher real wages than before* because of the increased productivity that comes about through specialization.

The numerical example shows this fact quite directly. We have seen that at our illustra-

tive price of 15 yards of cloth per barrel of wine, every barrel of wine Portugal sends to England gives Portugal 5 yards of cloth more than its own labor could have produced; and it gives England a quarter barrel more wine than British labor could have produced. England ends up with the same quantity of cloth and more wine than it had before, and so the living standards of its workers can rise even though they have been left vulnerable to the competition of the superefficient Portuguese. Portugal ends up with the same amount of wine as before and with more cloth, so the living standards of its workers can rise even though they have been exposed to the competition of cheap British labor.

The lesson to be learned here is that nothing helps raise standards of living more than does a greater abundance of goods.

SUPPLY—DEMAND EQUILIBRIUM AND PRICING IN FOREIGN TRADE

In our discussion of comparative advantage we obtained an initial idea of how countries determine the prices at which they will trade their goods. In this section we will go further in analyzing price determination. As is true elsewhere, prices in international trade are affected by a variety of influences acting through many different mechanisms. The Organization of Petroleum Exporting Countries (OPEC) simply sets prices of oil unilaterally, by decision of its members. Grain deals have been arranged between Soviet and American exporters based on terms arrived at in secret negotiations. But though such acts of pricing partially circumvent the normal market process and are greatly influenced by political considerations, they are also heavily affected by supply and demand. OPEC's deliberations are influenced by new oil discoveries and by estimates of the response of future world demand to their pricing decisions.

While negotiated prices of wheat deviate from the prices found in the competitive marketplace, prices on the free market clearly set limits on the price range open to the negotiators. In short, in international exchange, as elsewhere in the economy, supply and demand are at the center of the price-determination mechanism.

In the context of international trade, the supply–demand model runs into several complications we have not encountered before. First, it involves at least two demand curves: that of the exporting country and that of the importing country. Second, it may also involve two supply curves, since the importing country may produce some part of its own domestic needs. The third and final complication is that equilibrium does not take place at the intersection point of *either* pair of supply–demand curves. Why? Because if there is any trade, the

exporting country's quantity supplied must be *greater* than its quantity demanded, while the quantity supplied by the importing country must be *less* than the quantity demanded by its inhabitants at the equilibrium price.

These complications are illustrated in Figure 36–3, where we show the supply and demand curves of a country that exports wine, (a), and the supply and demand curves of a country that imports wine, (b). For simplicity, we assume that these countries do not deal in wine with anyone else. The equilibrium price of wine is shown as $100 per barrel. At that price, the horizontal distance AB between the exporting country's supply and demand curves shows the difference between what that country produces (point B) and what residents of the exporting country want to consume themselves (point A). Similarly, the distance CD is the gap between

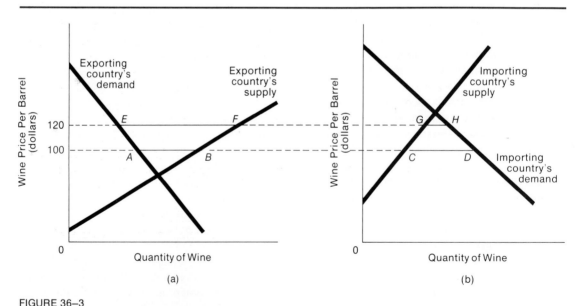

FIGURE 36–3

SUPPLY–DEMAND EQUILIBRIUM IN THE INTERNATIONAL WINE TRADE

Equilibrium requires that the net export supply, *AB* (which is the exporting nation's quantity supplied, *B*, minus the exporter's quantity demanded, *A*), exactly balances *net* demand, *CD*, by the importing country. At $100 per barrel of wine, there is equilibrium. But at a higher price, say $120, there is disequilibrium because net export supply, *EF*, exceeds net import demand, *GH*.

the quantity demanded by residents of the importing country (point *D*) and the quantity supplied by its own producers (point *C*). Where these two horizontal distances are equal, the amount the exporting country has available to sell abroad is exactly equal to the amount the importer wants to buy, and matters are in balance. In the example, the distance *AB* is equal to distance *CD,* so $100 per barrel is the market price.

At a price higher than $100, we can expect producers in both countries to want to sell more and consumers in both countries to want to buy less. For example, if the price rises to $120 per barrel, the exporter's quantity supplied will rise from *B* to *F,* and the exporter's quantity demanded will fall from *A* to *E,* as shown in Figure 36–3(a). As a result, there will be a rise in the amount available for export, from *AB* to *EF.* For exactly the same reason, the price rise will cause higher production and lower sales in the importing country, leading to a shrinkage in the amount the importing country wants to import—from *CD* to *GH* in part (b). This means that the new price, $120 per barrel, cannot be sustained if the international market is free and competitive. With export supply *EF* far greater than import demand *GH,* there must be downward pressure on price and a move back toward the $100 equilibrium price. Similar reasoning shows that prices below $100 also cannot be sustained.

We can now see the straightforward role of supply–demand equilibrium in international trade:

In international trade, the equilibrium price must be at a level at which the excess of the exporter's quantity supplied over his domestic quantity demanded is exactly equal to the excess of the importer's quantity demanded over his quantity supplied. Equilibrium will occur at a price at which the horizontal distance *AB* in Figure 36–3(a) (the excess of the exporter's supply over his demand) is equal to the horizontal distance *CD* in Figure 36–3(b)

(the excess of the importer's demand over his supply). At this price, the *world's* quantity demanded is equal to the *world's* quantity supplied.

TARIFFS, QUOTAS, AND OTHER INTERFERENCES WITH TRADE

Despite the mutual gains obtained, international trade has historically been subjected to unrelenting pressure for government interference. In fact, until the rise of a free-trade movement in England at the end of the eighteenth and the beginning of the nineteenth centuries (with such economists as Adam Smith and David Ricardo at its vanguard), it was taken for granted that one of the essential tasks of government was the imposition and administration of regulations to impede trade, presumably in the national interest.

There were many who argued then (and some who still argue today) that a nation's wealth consists of the amount of gold or other monies at its command. Consequently, the proper aim of government policy is to do everything it can to promote exports (in order to increase the amount foreigners owe to it) and to discourage imports (in order to decrease the amount the country owes to foreigners).

Obviously, there are limits to which this policy can be carried out. A country *must* import vital foodstuffs or critical raw materials that it cannot supply for itself, for if it does not, it must suffer a severe fall in living standards as well as a deterioration in its military strength. Moreover, it is mathematically impossible for *every* country to sell more than it buys—one country's exports *must* be some other country's imports. If everyone competes in this game and cuts imports to the bone, then obviously exports must go the same way. The result must be that everyone is deprived of most of the mutual gains that trade can provide.

In more recent times, notably in the United

States during the first three decades of the twentieth century, there was a return to an active policy designed to reduce the competition of foreign imports. Since then, the United States has gradually assumed a leading role in attempts to promote freedom of trade, and barriers have gradually been reduced, though, very recently, there have been pressures to move back the other way.

Three main devices have been used by modern governments to control trade: tariffs, import quotas, and export subsidies.

DEFINITION

A *tariff* is a tax on imports. For example, the importer may be charged 10 cents per dollar of wine or $2 per barrel of wine.

A *quota* specifies the maximum amount of a good that is permitted into the country from abroad per unit of time. For example, no more than 2 million barrels of wine per year may be permitted to enter the country.

An *export subsidy* is a payment by the government to exporters to permit them to reduce the selling price of their goods so they can compete more effectively in foreign markets. For example, they may be given 5 cents per dollar of wine or $1 per barrel of wine they export.

Both tariffs and quotas will restrict supplies coming from abroad into the country that imposes them, and they will also drive up prices. The tariff works by raising prices and hence cutting down the demand for imports, while the sequence associated with a quota goes the other way—the restriction in supply forces prices up.

There are two more important distinctions between the workings of quotas and tariffs. First, profits from the price increases produced by a quota usually go into the pockets of the foreign and domestic sellers of the product. Because supplies are limited by quotas, customers in the importing country must pay more for the product. So the suppliers, be they foreign or domestic, receive more for every unit they sell. On the other hand, when trade is restricted by a tariff, the profits go as tax revenues to the *government* of the importing country. In effect, the government increases its tax revenues partially at the expense of its citizens and partly at the expense of foreign exporters, who will lose customers in the country that imposes the tariff. (Domestic producers again benefit, because they are exempt from the tariff.) In this respect, a tariff is certainly a better proposition than a quota from the viewpoint of the country that enacts it.

Another important distinction between the two measures is the difference in their implications for productive efficiency and long-run prices. A tariff handicaps all exporters equally. It simply awards the sales to the importers who are most efficient and can therefore supply the goods most cheaply.

A quota, on the other hand, necessarily awards its import licenses more or less capriciously—such as on a first come, first served basis or in proportion to past sales or by some other arbitrary standard or perhaps some political criteria. There is not the slightest reason to expect the most efficient and least costly suppliers to get the import permits. In the long run, the population of the importing country is likely to end up with significantly higher prices, poorer products, or both.

We conclude that if a country must inhibit imports, there are two important reasons for it to give preference to tariffs over quotas: (1) some of the resulting financial gains from tariffs go to the government of the importing country rather than to foreign and domestic producers; and (2) unlike quotas, tariffs offer no special benefits to inefficient exports.

WHY INHIBIT TRADE?

To state that tariffs are a better way to inhibit international trade than quotas leaves open a

Why Inhibit Trade?

far more basic question: Why limit trade in the first place? There are two primary reasons for the adoption of measures that restrict trade: First, they may help the importing country get more advantageous prices for its goods, and second, they protect particular industries from foreign competition.

How can a tariff make prices more advantageous for the importing country if it raises consumer prices there? The answer is that it forces foreign exporters to sell more cheaply. Because their market is restricted by the tariff, they will be left with unsold goods unless they cut their prices. Suppose, as in Figure 36–4(b), that a tariff on wine raises the price of wine in the importing country from $100 to $120 per barrel. This rise in price, in turn, is likely to drive down the demand for imports, from an amount represented by the length of black line *EF* to the smaller amount represented by red line *AB*. And to the exporting country, this must mean an

equal reduction in demand for its exports [see the change from *EF* to *AB* in Figure 36–4(a)]. What this means is that the price at which the exporting country can sell its wine will be driven down (from $100 to $90 in the example), while at the same time, producers in the importing country—being exempt from the tariff—can charge $120 per barrel.

In effect, such a tariff amounts to government intervention to rig import prices in favor of domestic producers and to exploit foreign sellers by forcing them to sell more cheaply than they otherwise would. However, this technique works only as long as foreigners accept tariff exploitation passively. And they rarely do. Instead, they retaliate, usually by imposing tariffs of their own on their imports from the country that first began the tariff game. This can easily lead to a tariff war in which no one gains in terms of more favorable prices and everyone loses in terms of the resulting reductions in

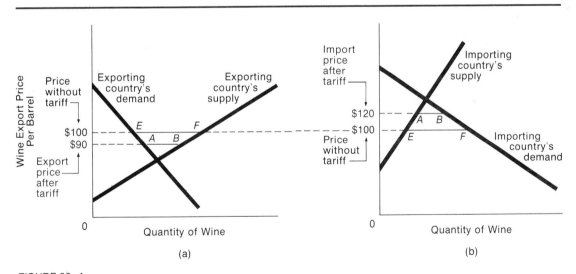

(a)

(b)

FIGURE 36–4

EXPORT AND IMPORT PRICES UNDER A TARIFF

The tariff raises the import price from $100 to $120 so it cuts (net) import demand from *EF* to *AB* in part (b). Equilibrium requires net export supply to fall by the same amount, so the export price *falls* from $100 to $90 in part (a). Note that when there is no tariff, export and import prices are the same; a tariff separates them.

overall trade. Something like this happened to the world economy in the 1930s and helped prolong the worldwide depression.

Tariffs can benefit a country that is able to impose them without fear of retaliation. But when every country uses them, everyone is likely to lose in the long run.

RESTRICTING TRADE TO PROTECT PARTICULAR INDUSTRIES

The second and probably more frequent reason why countries undertake programs to restrict trade is to protect particular industries that are vulnerable to foreign competition. If foreigners can produce steel or watches or shoes more cheaply, domestic businesses and unions in these industries are quick to demand protection; and their government is often reluctant to deny it to them. It is here that the cheap foreign labor argument is most likely to be invoked.

But the fact is that in a free market, the industries that are unable to compete will be those whose relative inefficiency does not permit them to beat foreign exporters at their own game. Protective tariffs and quotas are designed to undercut the harsh competition that gives consumers the benefits of international specialization. In Ricardo's example of comparative advantage, one can well imagine the complaints from Portuguese cloth makers as the opening of trade with England led to increased Portuguese importation of cloth. At the same time, the English grape growers would, very likely, have expressed equal concern over the flood of imported wine from Portugal.

Indeed, the complaints of these merchants are well justified unless something is done to ease the cost to the individual workers of switching to those lines of production that trade has now made profitable. The rationale for free trade between countries cannot be considered airtight if there is no adequate program to assist the minority of citizens in each country who will be harmed whenever patterns of production change drastically, as would happen, for example, if tariff and quota barriers were suddenly brought down. Owners of wineries in Britain and of textile mills in Portugal may see heavy investments suddenly rendered unprofitable as would workers in these vineyards and factories whose investments in acquiring special skills and training are no longer marketable. Nor are the costs to displaced workers only monetary. Often they will have to move to new locations as well as to new industries, uprooting their families, losing old friends and neighbors, and so on. That the *majority* of citizens undoubtedly will gain from free trade will be no consolation to those who are its victims.

To help alleviate this problem, the United States (and other countries) has set up programs to assist workers who have lost jobs because of the changing patterns of world trade. In the United States such "adjustment assistance" is supplied to firms or workers who, as a result of a government agreement to ease international trade, suffer idle facilities, unprofitability, and unemployment because of sharp increases in imports. Firms may be eligible for technical assistance designed to improve their efficiency, financial assistance in the form of government loans or government guarantees of private loans, and tax assistance in the form of permission to delay tax payments. Workers are eligible for retraining programs, lengthened periods of eligibility for unemployment compensation, and allowances to help pay for the cost of moving to other jobs. In sum, the United States and other countries recognize how important it is to help those who suffer when trade barriers come down.

Two other protectionist arguments warrant mention: the national defense argument and the infant-industry argument. Each has some merit in special circumstances.

National Defense and Other Noneconomic Considerations

There are times when a tariff or some other measure to interfere with trade may be justified on noneconomic grounds. If a country considers itself vulnerable to military attack, it may be perfectly rational to keep alive industries whose outputs can be obtained more cheaply abroad but whose supplies may dry up during an emergency. For example, airplane production by small countries makes sense only in

Unfair Foreign Competition

Satire and ridicule are often more persuasive than logic and statistics. Exasperated by the spread of protectionism to so many industries under the prevailing Mercantilist philosophy, French economist Frédéric Bastiat decided to take the protectionist argument to its illogical conclusion. The fictitious petition of the French candlemakers to the Chamber of Deputies, written in 1845 and excerpted below, has become a classic in the battle for free trade.

We are subject to the intolerable competition of a foreign rival, who enjoys, it would seem, such superior facilities for the production of light, that he is enabled to *inundate* our *national market* at so exceedingly reduced a price, that, the moment he makes his appearance, he draws off all custom for us; and thus an important branch of French industry, with all its innumerable ramifications, is suddenly reduced to a state of complete stagnation. This rival is no other than the sun.

Our petition is, that it would please your honorable body to pass a law whereby shall be directed the shutting up of all windows, dormers, skylights, shutters, curtains, in a word, all openings, holes, chinks, and fissures through which the light of the sun is used to penetrate our dwellings, to the prejudice of the profitable manufactures which we flatter ourselves we have been enabled to bestow upon the country . . .

We foresee your objections, gentlemen; but there is not one that you can oppose to us . . . which is not equally opposed to your own practice and the principle which guides your policy. . . .

Labor and nature concur in different proportions, according to country and climate, in every article of production . . . If a Lisbon orange can be sold at half the price of a Parisian one, it is because a natural and gratuitous heat does for the one what the other only obtains from an artificial and consequently expensive one . . .

Does it not argue the greatest inconsistency to check as you do the importation of coal, iron, cheese, and goods of foreign manufacture, merely because and even in proportion as their price approaches *zero,* while at the same time you freely admit, and without limitation, the light of the sun, whose price is during the whole day at *zero?*

Source: F. Bastiat, *Economic Sophisms* (New York: G. P. Putnam's Sons, 1922).

such circumstances. The danger is that every industry, even those with the most peripheral defense relationship, is likely to invoke this argument on its behalf. For instance, the U.S. watch-making industry claimed protection for itself for many years on the grounds that it trained skilled workers whose craftsmanship would be invaluable in wartime. Perhaps so, but a technicians' training program probably could have done the job more cheaply and even more effectively by teaching exactly the skills needed for military purposes.

Noneconomic reasons also explain quotas on importation of whaling products and total prohibition of imports of alligator skins and the furs of other endangered species. These quotas may be a competitive boon to the domestic leather and fur industries, but protection of endangered species rather than protection of industries is their justification.

The Infant-Industry Argument

It is often suggested that temporary protection of a newly established industry can serve the national interest. Until that industry can expand to a point at which it is able to compete unaided with established foreign firms, it may be essential to prevent its strangulation by foreign competition.

The argument, while valid in certain instances, is less defensible than it may at first appear. It makes sense only if the industry's prospective future gains are sufficient to pay the social losses incurred by protection during its establishment. But if it really is likely to be so profitable in the future, why doesn't private capital rush in to take advantage of the prospective net profits? The annals of business are full of cases in which a new product or a new firm lost money at first but profited handsomely later. Only where funds are not available to a particular industry for some reason, despite its glowing profit prospects, does the infant-industry argument for protection stand up fully.

It is hard to think of examples, but even if such a case were found one would have to be careful that the industry would not remain in diapers forever. There are too many cases in which new industries were awarded protection when they were being established and, somehow, the time to withdraw that protection never arrived. One must beware of infant-industries that never grow up.

WHAT IMPORT PRICE LEVELS BENEFIT A COUNTRY?

One of the most curious features of the protectionist position is the fear of low prices charged by foreign sellers. Earlier we mentioned export subsidies, a practice that always elicits great indignation, for countries that make such payments are accused of "dumping"—of getting rid of their goods at unconscionably low prices. For example, in the last few years Japan has frequently been accused of dumping various goods on the United States market because the Japanese government exempts exports from taxes that are levied on goods sold within Japan.

A moment's thought should indicate why this complaint must be considered curious. As a nation of consumers, we should be indignant when the prices of our imports are very *high*, not when they are *low*. That is the common-sense rule that guides every consumer, and the consumers of imported commodities should be no exception. Only from the topsy-turvy viewpoint of an industry seeking protection from competition are high prices seen as being in the public interest.

Ultimately, it is always in the interest of a country to get its imports as cheaply as possible. It would be ideal for the United States if the rest of the world were willing to provide its exports to us free or virtually so. We could then live in luxury at the expense of the rest of the world.

The notion that low import prices are bad for a country is a fitting companion to the idea—so often heard—that it is good for the country to export much more than it imports. True, this means that foreigners will end up owing us a good deal of money. But it also means that we will have given them large quantities of our products and have gotten relatively little value in foreign products in exchange. That surely is not an ideal way for a country to benefit from its foreign transactions!

Our gains from trade do not consist of accumulations of gold or of heavy debts owed us by foreigners. Rather, our gains are composed of the goods and services that others provide minus the goods and services we must provide them in return.

CONCLUSION: A LAST LOOK AT THE "CHEAP FOREIGN LABOR" ARGUMENT

The preceding discussion should indicate the fundamental fallacy in the argument that American workers have to fear cheap foreign labor. If workers in other countries are willing to supply their products to us with little compensation, this must ultimately *raise* the standard of living of the average American worker. As long as the government's monetary and fiscal policies succeed in maintaining high levels of employment at home, how can we possibly lose out by getting the products of the world at little cost to ourselves?

It must be admitted that there are two dangers to this prognosis. First, our employment policy may not be effective. If workers who are displaced by foreign competition cannot find jobs in other industries, then American workers will indeed suffer from international trade. But that is a shortcoming of the government's employment program, not of its international trade policies.

Second, we have noted that an abrupt stiffening of foreign competition resulting from a major innovation in another country, or from a discovery of a new and better source of raw materials, or from a sharp increase in export subsidies by a foreign country, *can* hurt U.S. workers by not giving them an adequate chance to adapt gradually to the new conditions. The more rapid the change, the more painful it will be. If it occurs fairly gradually, workers can retrain and move on to those industries that now require their services. If the change is even more gradual, no one may have to move. People who retire or leave the threatened industry for other reasons simply need not be replaced. But competition that inflicts its damage overnight is certain to impose very real costs upon the affected workers, costs that are no less painful for being temporary.

But these are, after all, minor qualifications to an overwhelming argument. They call for intelligent monetary and fiscal policies and for transitional assistance to unemployed workers, not for abandonment of free trade.

In the long run, labor will be "cheap" only where it is not very productive. Wages will tend to be highest in those countries in which high labor productivity keeps costs down and permits exporters to compete effectively despite high wages. It is thus misleading to say that the United States has held its own in the international marketplace over the years despite the high wages of its workers. Rather it is much more illuminating to point out that the high wages of American workers were a result of high worker productivity, which gave the United States a heavy competitive edge in the international marketplace.

We note that in this matter it is absolute advantage, not comparative advantage, that counts. The country that is most efficient in every output can pay its workers more in every industry.

SUMMARY

1. Countries trade because differences in their natural resources and other inputs create discrepancies in the efficiency with which they can produce different goods, and because specialization may offer them greater economies of large-scale production.

2. Voluntary trade will generally be advantageous to both parties in an exchange.

3. Both countries will gain from trade with one another if each exports goods in whose production it has a comparative advantage. That is, even a country that is generally inefficient will benefit by exporting the goods in whose production it is least inefficient. This is one of the 12 Ideas for Beyond the Final Exam.

4. Even trade with countries whose wages are low can be beneficial to high-wage countries. The high wages in those countries are at least partly attributable to the high productivity of their labor force, which enables them to compete with workers in other countries whose wages and productivity are both low.

5. In the long run, foreign trade permits workers in all countries to attain higher living standards. In the short run, however, assistance may be required for workers (and business firms) who are displaced by certain international trade agreements.

6. The prices of goods traded between countries are determined by supply and demand, but the analysis is more complicated than the usual one since in international trade one must consider explicitly the demand curve and the supply curve of *each* country involved.

7. Tariffs and quotas are designed to protect a country's industries from foreign competition. Such protection may sometimes be advantageous to that country, but not if foreign countries adopt tariffs and quotas of their own as a means of retaliation.

CONCEPTS FOR REVIEW

Imports
Exports
Specialization
Mutual gains from trade
Absolute advantage
Law of comparative advantage

Tariff
Quota
Export subsidy
Adjustment assistance
Infant-industry argument

QUESTIONS FOR DISCUSSION

1. You have a dozen eggs worth 80 cents and your neighbor has a pound of bacon worth about the same. You decide to swap six eggs for a half pound of bacon. In financial terms, neither of you gains anything. Explain why you are nevertheless both likely to be better off.

2. In the eighteenth century, some writers argued that one person in a trade could be made better off only by gaining at the expense of the other. Explain the fallacy in the argument.

3. A brilliant chemist is also a master glass blower. In what circumstances does it pay him to hire a glass blower for his lab? When does it make sense for him to do some glass blowing for himself?

4. Country A has lots of hydroelectric power, a cold climate, and a highly skilled labor force. What sorts of products do you think it is likely to produce? What are the characteristics of the countries with which you would expect it to trade?

5. Upon removal of a tariff on watches, a U.S. watch-making firm goes bankrupt. Discuss the pros and cons of the tariff removal in the short run and in the long run.

6. Country A's government believes that it is best always to export more (in money terms) than the value of its imports. As a consequence, it exports more to country B every year than it imports from country B. After 100 years of this arrangement, both countries are destroyed in an earthquake. What were the advantages and disadvantages of the surplus to country A? To country B?

37

The International Monetary System:
Order or Disorder?

In the last chapter, we discussed the reasons for international trade and the benefits that accrue to all nations when countries specialize in producing those goods in which they have a comparative advantage. But the movement of goods across national borders generally requires the movement of money in the opposite direction. For example, when the United States buys coffee from Brazil, we must send money to the Brazilians. When Japan purchases petroleum from Saudi Arabia, it must send money to

the Saudis, and so on. This chapter takes a look at the system that has been set up to handle these international movements of money—the international monetary system.

In the first parts of this chapter, we investigate two polar forms of the international monetary system. The first is a system in which rates of exchange among national currencies are determined in free markets by the laws of supply and demand. Here the key concept to be studied is the *exchange rate:* what it is and what determines its value. The other polar system is one in which exchange rates are rigidly fixed by government authority. Here the key concept is the *balance of payments,* and, as we shall see, even the simple question "What is it?" turns out to be quite difficult to answer.

These two systems are studied to illustrate the important principles, *not* to describe the actual international monetary system as it is now or as it was at any time in the past. Therefore, in the remainder of the chapter we turn to more realistic intermediate systems that have elements of both pure forms, including the old *gold standard,* the so-called *gold-exchange system* that prevailed from 1944 until 1971, and the current *mixed* system—a system that defies any short description because each country, it seems, handles its international monetary relations somewhat differently.

WHAT ARE EXCHANGE RATES?

The 50 states of the United States may be the most eloquent testimony to the power of comparative advantage and free trade. Florida specializes in growing oranges, Iowa in growing corn, Pennsylvania makes steel, and Michigan builds cars. All these states trade freely with one another and enjoy great material prosperity. Try to imagine how much lower living standards would be if your own state had to make all of these goods, plus the thousands of other things you consume each year.

But the states of the United States have an important advantage that facilitates trade: there are no national borders to be crossed when, say, California lettuce is shipped to Massachusetts. The consumer in Boston pays with *dollars,* just the currency that the farmer in Salinas wants. But if that same farmer ships his lettuce to Japan, consumers there will have only Japanese *yen* with which to pay, rather than the dollars the farmer in California wants. Thus, if international trade is to take place, there must

be a way to transform one currency (yen) into another (dollars). The rates at which such transformations are made are called exchange rates.

DEFINITION
The *exchange rate* states the price, in terms of one currency, at which another currency can be bought. Thus there is an exchange rate between every pair of currencies.

For example, $1 is currently the equivalent of about 5 French francs. The exchange rate between the franc and the dollar, then, may be expressed as "5 francs to the dollar" (meaning that it costs 5 francs to buy a dollar) or "20 cents to the franc" (meaning that it costs 20 cents to buy a franc). Similarly, there is an exchange rate between the U.S. dollar and every other currency. Although these rates change all the time, Table 37–1 gives an indication of exchange rates prevailing in January 1979, showing how many dollars or cents it cost at that time to buy each unit of foreign currency.

Under our present system, currency rates change frequently. When other currencies get more expensive in terms of dollars, we say that they have appreciated relative to the dollar. Alternatively, we can look at this same event in terms of the dollar buying less foreign currency, meaning that the dollar has depreciated relative to another currency.

DEFINITION
A nation's currency is said to *appreciate* when exchange rates change so that a unit of its own currency can buy more units of foreign currency. The currency is said to *depreciate* when exchange rates change so that a unit of its currency can buy fewer units of foreign currency.

Notice that *what is a depreciation to one country must be an appreciation to the other.* For example, if the dollar cost of a German mark rises from 40 cents to 50 cents, the cost of a U.S. dollar in terms of marks simultaneously

TABLE 37–1

EXCHANGE RATES WITH THE U.S. DOLLAR, JANUARY 1979
(dollars per unit of foreign currency)

COUNTRY	CURRENCY UNIT	SYMBOL	COST IN DOLLARS
Australia	dollar	$	$1.15
Canada	dollar	$	0.84
France	franc	FF	0.24
Germany	mark	DM	0.55
Italy	lira	L	0.0012
Japan	yen	¥	0.0051
Mexico	peso	$	0.044
Sweden	krona	Kr	0.23
Switzerland	franc	S. Fr.	0.62
United Kingdom	pound	£	2.03

Source: *The Wall Street Journal.*

falls from $2\frac{1}{2}$ marks to 2 marks. The Germans have had a currency *appreciation* while we have had a currency *depreciation.*

Notice also that, when many currencies are changing in value, the dollar may be appreciating with respect to one currency but depreciating with respect to another. Consider, for example, this set of hypothetical exchange rates in two years:

	HYPOTHETICAL EXCHANGE RATES	
	1984	1985
British pound	1 pound = $1.80	1 pound = $1.70
German mark	1 mark = $0.48	1 mark = $0.50

According to this example, between 1984 and 1985 the dollar would have *depreciated* relative to the mark and *appreciated* relative to the pound.

While this is the terminology used to describe movements of exchange rates in free markets, another set of terms is used to describe changes in currency values when these values are set by government decree.

DEFINITION
When an officially set exchange rate is altered so that a unit of a nation's currency can buy *fewer* units of foreign currency, we say that there has been a *devaluation* of that currency. When an officially set exchange rate is altered so that the currency can buy *more* units of foreign currency, we say that there has been a *revaluation.*

EXCHANGE RATE DETERMINATION IN A FREE MARKET

Why is it that a German mark costs 50 cents and not 40 cents or 60 cents? If exchange rates were floating freely, with no government interferences, the answer would be fairly straightforward. In such a world, exchange rates would be determined by the forces of supply and demand, just like the prices of apples, or typewriters, or haircuts.

DEFINITION
Floating exchange rates are rates determined in free markets by the law of supply and demand.

In a leap of abstraction, imagine that the United States and West Germany were the only countries on earth, so there was only one exchange rate to be determined. Figure 37–1 depicts the determination of this exchange rate at the point (denoted *E* in the figure) where demand curve *DD* crosses supply curve *SS*. At this price (50 cents per mark), we know that the number of marks demanded is equal to the number of marks supplied.

In a free market, exchange rates are determined by the law of supply and demand. If the rate were below the equilibrium level, the demand for marks would exceed the supply, and the price of a mark would be bid up. If the rate were above the equilibrium level, supply would exceed demand, and the price of a mark would fall. Only at the equilibrium exchange rate is there no tendency for the rate to change.

As usual, supply and demand determine price. What we must ask in this case is, Where do the supply and demand come from? Why does anyone demand a German mark?

First, there is international trade in goods and services—the subject of the last chapter. For example, if Jane Doe, an American, wants to buy a German automobile, she will first have to buy marks with which to pay the dealer in Munich.[1] So Jane's demand for a German *car* leads to a demand for German *marks*. In general, *demand for a country's export goods and services leads to a demand for its currency.*

Second, there is international trading in financial instruments like stocks and bonds. For example, if American investors want to purchase German stocks, they will first have to acquire the marks that the sellers will insist on. In this way, demand for German financial assets leads to demand for German marks. Thus,

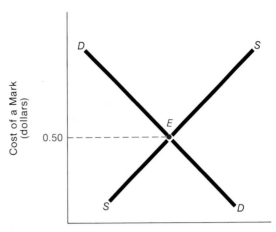

FIGURE 37–1

DETERMINATION OF EXCHANGE RATES IN A FREE MARKET

Like any price, an exchange rate will be determined by the intersection of the demand and supply curves in a free market. Point *E* depicts this point for the exchange rate between the U.S. dollar and the German mark, which settles at 50 cents per mark in this example.

demand for a country's financial assets leads to a demand for its currency.

Finally, we must consider purchases of factories and machinery. If IBM wants to buy out a small German computer manufacturer, the owners will no doubt want to receive marks. So IBM will first have to acquire German currency. In general, *direct foreign investment leads to a demand for a country's currency.*

Now, where does the supply come from? To answer this, we need only turn all of these transactions around. Germans wanting to buy U.S. goods and services, or to invest in U.S. financial markets, or to make direct investments in America will have to offer their marks for sale in the foreign-exchange market (which is similar to the stock market) to acquire the needed dollars.

[1] Actually she will not do this because banks generally handle foreign exchange transactions for consumers. An American bank probably will buy the marks for her. But the effect is exactly the same as if Jane had done it herself.

To summarize: The *demand* for a country's currency is derived from the demands of foreigners for its export goods and services and for its assets, including financial assets, factories, and machinery. The *supply* of a country's foreign currency arises from its imports, and from foreign investment by its own citizens.

To appreciate the usefulness of even this simple supply and demand analysis, let us consider how the exchange rate between the dollar and the mark would change if there were an economic boom in the United States. One important effect of such a boom would be to stimulate American demand for German products, such as automobiles, cameras, and wines. In terms of the supply–demand diagram shown in Figure 37–2, the increased desires of Americans for German products would lead to an increased demand for German marks, thus shifting the demand curve out from D_1D_1 (the black line in the figure) to D_2D_2 (the red line). Equilibrium would shift from point E to point A, and the exchange rate would rise from 50 cents per mark to 55 cents per mark. In a word, the increased demand for marks by U.S. citizens causes the mark to appreciate relative to the dollar.

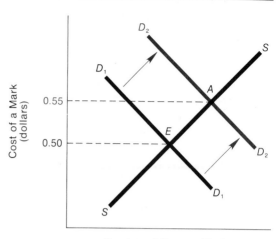

FIGURE 37–2
THE EFFECT OF AN ECONOMIC BOOM ON THE EXCHANGE RATE
If the U.S. economy suddenly booms, Americans will spend more on imports from Germany. Thus the demand curve for German marks will rise from D_1D_1 to D_2D_2 as Americans seek to acquire the marks they need. The diagram shows that this will cause the mark to appreciate, from 50 cents to 55 cents, as equilibrium shifts from point E to point A. Looked at from the American perspective, the dollar will depreciate.

EXERCISE

Test your understanding of the supply and demand analysis of exchange rates by showing why each of the following events also would lead to an appreciation of the mark (depreciation of the dollar) in a free market:

1. A recession in Germany cuts German purchases of American goods.
2. American investors are attracted by prospects for profit in the German stock market.
3. Interest rates on government bonds fall in the United States but are stable in Germany. (*Hint:* Which country's citizens will be attracted by high interest rates in the other country?)

To say that supply and demand determine exchange rates in a free market is at once to say everything and to say nothing. If we are to gain some understanding of why, for example, the German mark seems always to be appreciating while the Italian lira is so often depreciating, we must look into the factors that move the supply and demand curves.

Economists believe that the principal determinants of exchange rate movements are rather different in the long, medium, and short runs. So we turn in the next three sections to the analysis of exchange rate movements over these three "runs." We begin with the long run.

THE PURCHASING-POWER PARITY THEORY: THE LONG RUN

As long as there is free trade across national borders, exchange rates eventually will adjust so that the same product costs the same number of dollars (or the same amount of any other currency) in every country, except for differences attributable to transportation costs and the like. This simple statement forms the basis of the major theory of exchange-rate determination in the long run.

DEFINITION
The *purchasing-power parity theory of exchange rate determination* holds that the exchange rate between any two national currencies adjusts to reflect differences in the price levels in the two countries.

An example will bring out the basic truth in this theory and also suggest some of its limitations.

Suppose that Swedish and American steel is identical and that these two nations are the only producers of steel for the world market. Suppose further that steel is the only tradable good that either country produces.

Question: If American steel costs $75 per ton and Swedish steel costs 300 kronor per ton, what must be the exchange rate between the dollar and the krona?

Answer: Since 300 kronor must be the equivalent of $75, each krona must be worth 25 cents. Why? Because if a krona costs 30 cents, then Swedish steel would cost $90 per ton (300 kronor at 30 cents each) while American steel would cost $75 per ton, and all foreign customers would shop for their steel in the United States. The exchange rate of 30 cents per krona would be too high.

EXERCISE
Show why an exchange rate of 20 cents per krona is too low.

The purchasing-power parity theory is used to make long-run predictions about the effects of inflation on exchange rates. To continue our example, suppose that over a 5-year period, prices in the United States rise by one-third while prices in Sweden rise by two-thirds. The purchasing-power parity theory predicts that the krona would depreciate relative to the dollar. It also predicts the amount of the currency depreciation. Say that after the inflation, American steel costs $100 per ton (one-third more than $75) while Swedish steel costs 500 kronor per ton (two-thirds more than 300 kronor). For these two prices to be equivalent, 500 kronor must be worth $100, or 1 krona must be worth 20 cents. The krona, therefore, must have fallen from 25 cents to 20 cents.

According to the purchasing-power parity theory, differences in domestic inflation rates are a major cause of adjustments in exchange rates. For instance, if one country has a faster rate of inflation than another, then its exchange rate must be depreciating.

Unfortunately, the purchasing-power parity theory may not always be applicable because it ignores a number of complications. First, changes in any of the interferences with free trade, such as tariffs and quotas, can upset simple calculations based on purchasing-power parity. For example, if Swedish prices rise faster than American prices but, at the same time, foreign countries erect tariff barriers to keep American (but not Swedish) steel out, then the krona might not have to depreciate. Second, some goods and services cannot be traded across national frontiers. Land and buildings are only the most obvious examples; most services can be traded only to a limited extent (as when tourists from one country have their hair cut in another). Inflation rates for goods and services that are *not tradable* have little bearing on exchange rates.

For these and other reasons:

Most economists believe that other factors are much more important than relative price levels for exchange rate determination in the short run. But in the long run, purchasing-power parity plays the decisive role.

ECONOMIC ACTIVITY AND EXCHANGE RATES: THE MEDIUM RUN

Since consumer spending grows quite regularly when income expands, and contracts when income contracts, the same is likely to happen to spending on imported goods. For this reason:

A country's imports will rise quickly when its economy is booming and slowly when its economy is stagnating.

We have already illustrated this point with Figure 37–2. There we saw that a boom in the United States would add to the demand for marks and therefore lead to a depreciation of the dollar (appreciation of the mark) as American imports from Germany surge. However, if Germany were booming at the same time, German citizens would be buying more American exports, which would add to the supply of marks. On balance, the value of the dollar might or might not fall. What matters is whether exports are growing faster than imports.

The general lesson is that:

Holding other things equal, a country that grows faster than the rest of the world normally finds its currency depreciating because its imports grow faster than its exports, so that its demand for foreign currency grows faster than the amount of foreign currency that is supplied to it.

While this factor is very important for exchange rate determination in the medium run, "other things" often are not equal in the very short run.

INTEREST RATES AND EXCHANGE RATES: THE SHORT RUN

Specifically, one factor that often seems to call the tune in determining exchange rates in the short run is *interest rate differentials*. There is an enormous fund of so-called "hot money"— owned by banks, multinational corporations, and wealthy individuals of all nations, which amounts to perhaps $100 to $200 billion—that travels around the globe in search of the highest interest rates.

Thus suppose that U.S. government bonds are paying a 6 percent rate of interest when yields on equally safe British government securities rise to 8 percent. American investors will be attracted by the high interest rates in the United Kingdom and will offer dollars for sale in order to buy pounds, planning to use those pounds to buy British securities. At the same time, British investors will no longer find investing in the United States attractive, so fewer pounds will be supplied to this country.

When the demand schedule rises and the supply curve falls, the effect on price is quite predictable: the pound will appreciate, as Figure 37–3 shows. In the figure, the demand curve for pounds rises from D_1D_1 to D_2D_2 when American investors seek to acquire the pounds needed to purchase British securities. At the same time, British investors offer fewer pounds for sale because they no longer wish to invest in American securities. Thus the supply curve shifts inward from S_1S_1 to S_2S_2. The result, in our example, is an appreciation of the pound from $1.80 to $1.90. In general:

Holding other things equal, countries with high interest rates are able to attract more capital

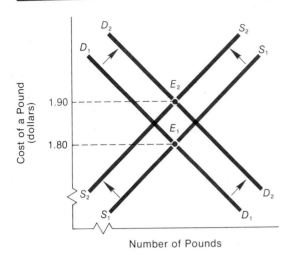

FIGURE 37–3

THE EFFECT OF A RISE IN BRITISH INTEREST RATES

When Britain raises its interest rates, more Americans will want to buy British bonds, and so the demand curve for pounds will shift upward from D_1D_1 to D_2D_2. At the same time, fewer Britons will seek to buy American bonds, so the supply curve of pounds will shift inward from S_1S_1 to S_2S_2. The combined effect of these two shifts is to move the market equilibrium from point E_1 to point E_2. The British pound appreciates, and the dollar depreciates.

than are countries with low interest rates. Thus a rise in interest rates often will lead to an appreciation of the currency, and a drop in interest rates will lead to a depreciation.

Most experts in international finance agree that this fund of hot money is so big, and so volatile, that interest rate movements are the chief determinant of exchange rate fluctuations in the short run. So, when a country finds its currency depreciating, a typical reaction is to attempt to jack up its interest rates. Chapter 12 detailed how this can be done by using any of the tools of central banking.

MARKET DETERMINATION OF EXCHANGE RATES: SUMMARY

To summarize this discussion of exchange rate determination in free markets, currencies generally will be *appreciating* in countries whose inflation rates are lower than the rest of the world, for otherwise it would be increasingly difficult for the other countries to market their goods. Exchange rates would also be expected to rise in countries whose levels of economic activity are lower than average, because these countries will be importing rather little. Finally, we expect to find appreciating currencies in countries whose interest rates are relatively high because these countries will attract capital from all over the world. Conversely, currencies will be *depreciating* in countries with relatively high inflation rates, or high levels of economic activity, or low interest rates.

FIXED EXCHANGE RATES AND THE DEFINITION OF "THE BALANCE OF PAYMENTS"

History records rather few instances of truly free exchange rates, determined by supply and demand without government interference. Much more typical are cases where governments have stubbornly resisted market forces and kept their exchange rates either above or below the equilibrium price for long periods of time. For this reason, we turn our attention next to the opposite of free (or floating) exchange rates, a system of fixed exchange rates, or rates that are set by governments. Naturally, under such a system the exchange rate (being fixed) is not closely watched. Instead, international financial specialists focus on a country's balance of payments—a term we are now ready to define.

To understand what the balance of payments is, look at Figure 37–4, which depicts

737

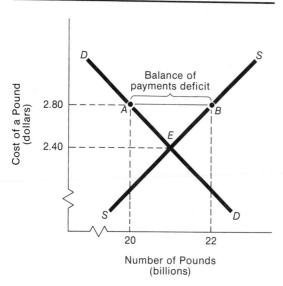

FIGURE 37–4

A BALANCE OF PAYMENTS DEFICIT
At a fixed exchange rate of $2.80 per pound, which is
well above the equilibrium level of $2.40 per pound,
England's currency is overvalued in this example. As
a consequence, more pounds will be supplied (point B)
than are demanded (point A). The difference—distance
AB, or £2 billion per year—represents Britain's
balance of payments deficit.

a situation that might represent, say, Great
Britain before its major devaluation in 1967—an
overvalued currency. While the supply and
demand curve for British pounds indicates an
equilibrium exchange rate of $2.40 to the pound
(point E) the British government is keeping the
rate at $2.80. Notice that at $2.80 more people
are supplying pounds than are demanding
them. In the example, suppliers are selling £22
billion per year, but demanders are purchasing
only £20 billion.

This gap between the £22 billion that some
people sell and the £20 billion that other people
buy is what we mean by Britain's balance of
payments deficit—£2 billion per year in this
case. It is shown by the horizontal distance
between points A and B in Figure 37–4.

DEFINITION
The *balance of payments deficit* is the amount
by which the supply of a country's currency (per
year) exceeds the demand for it. Balance of
payments deficits arise whenever the exchange
rate is pegged at an artificially high level.

How can market forces be flouted in this
way? Since sales and purchases on any market
must be equal, as a simple piece of arithmetic,
the excess of supply over demand for currency
(£2 billion per year in this example) must be
bought by the Bank of England, Britain's central
bank. In buying these pounds, it must give up
some of the gold and foreign currencies that it
keeps as *reserves*. Thus the Bank of England
would be losing £2 billion in reserves per year
as the cost of keeping the pound at $2.80.

Naturally, this cannot go on forever; the
reserves eventually will run out. And this is the
fatal flaw in the system of fixed exchange rates.
Once speculators become convinced that the
exchange rate can be held only a short while
longer, they will sell pounds in massive amounts
rather than hold on to a currency whose value
they soon expect to fall sharply. The supply
curve of pounds will shift outward drastically, as
shown in Figure 37–5, causing an astronomical
rise in the balance of payments deficit (from £22
billion to £25 billion in the example). This is
called a "run" on the currency. Lacking sufficient reserves, the central bank will have to
permit the exchange rate to fall to its equilibrium
level, and this might amount to an even larger
devalution than would have been required
before the speculative run on the pound began.

For an example of the reverse case, a
severely *undervalued* currency, let us consider
Germany in 1971. Figure 37–6 depicts a
demand and supply curve for marks that intersect at an equilibrium price of 42 cents per mark
(point E in the diagram). Yet, in the example, we
suppose that the German authorities are
holding the rate at 35 cents. At this rate, the
demand for marks (50 billion) greatly exceeds
the supply of marks (40 billion). The difference

is Germany's balance of payments surplus, and is shown by the horizontal distance *AB*.

DEFINITION
The *balance of payments surplus* is the amount by which the demand for a country's currency (per year) exceeds its supply. Balance of payments surpluses arise whenever the exchange rate is pegged at an artificially low level.

Germany can keep the rate at 35 cents only by providing the marks that foreigners want to buy: 10 billion marks per year in this example. In return, it receives U.S. dollars, British pounds, French francs, gold, and so on. All of this serves to increase Germany's reserves of foreign currencies. But notice the important difference between this case and Britain's overvalued pound.

The accumulation of reserves rarely will *force* a central bank to revalue in the way that depletion of reserves can force a devaluation.

This was another weakness of the old system of fixed exchange rates. In principle, imbalances in exchange rates could be cured either by a devaluation by the country with a balance of payments deficit or by an upward revaluation by the country with a balance of payments surplus. In practice, though, it was almost always the deficit countries that were forced to act.

Why did the surplus countries refuse to revalue? One reason was a simple misunderstanding of basic economics. They viewed the disequilibrium as the problem of the deficit

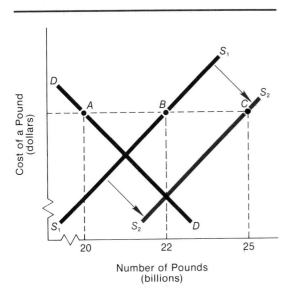

FIGURE 37–5

A SPECULATIVE RUN ON THE POUND
When speculators become convinced that a devaluation of the pound is in the offing, they will rush to sell all their pounds. Their actions shift the supply curve outward from S_1S_1 to S_2S_2 and, in the process, widen England's balance of payments deficit from *AB* to *AC*.

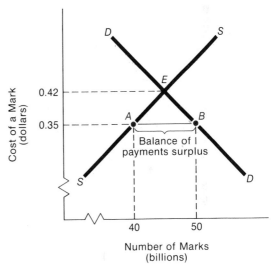

FIGURE 37–6

A BALANCE OF PAYMENTS SURPLUS
In this example, Germany's currency is undervalued at 35 cents per mark, since the equilibrium exchange rate is 42 cents per mark. Consequently, more marks are being demanded (point *B*) than are being supplied (point *A*). The gap between demand and supply—distance *AB*, or 10 billion marks per year—measures Germany's balance of payments surplus.

countries and believed that the deficit countries, therefore, should take the corrective steps. This, of course, is nonsense. Some currencies are overvalued *because* some other currencies are undervalued. In fact, the two statements mean exactly the same thing.

The other reason is that exporters in Germany, Japan, and other surplus countries resisted upward revaluations because they knew that such actions would make their products more expensive to foreigners and thus cut into their sales. And these exporters had the political clout to make that view stick. Meanwhile, German and Japanese consumers were put in the unenviable position of having to pay more for imported goods than they need have paid, while they watched domestically produced goods go overseas in return for pieces of paper (dollars, francs, pounds, and so on).

DEFINING THE BALANCE OF PAYMENTS IN PRACTICE

From the preceding discussion it may seem that measuring a nation's balance of payments position is a simple task: we simply count up the private demand for and supply of its currency, and subtract supply from demand. Conceptually, this is all there is to it. But in practice, the difficulties are great because we never have statistics on the number of dollars demanded and supplied. There is no way to observe these directly.

If we look at actual market transactions, we will see that the number of U.S. dollars actually *purchased* and the number of U.S. dollars actually *sold* are identical. Unless someone has made a bookkeeping error, this must always be so. How, then, can we recognize a balance of payments surplus or deficit? Easy, you say. Just look at the transactions of the central bank, whose purchases or sales must make up the difference between private demand and private supply. If the Federal Reserve is buying dollars,

its purchases measure our balance of payments deficit. If it is selling, its sales represent our balance of payments surplus.

Thus the suggestion is to measure the balance of payments by *excluding official transactions among governments.* This is roughly how the balance of payments surplus or deficit is defined today, though, for a variety of complicated reasons, the U.S. government decided in the mid-1970s to stop publishing any official statistic called "the balance of payments deficit." Instead, all foreign transactions are listed and readers are invited to define the balance of payments in any way they wish. Let us now see just what data are published in these official accounts.

THE U.S. BALANCE OF PAYMENTS ACCOUNTS

Using 1977 as an example, Table 37–2 shows the official U.S. balance of payments accounts. There is nothing that purports to measure America's overall balance of payments surplus or deficit. The top section of the table summarizes America's trade in currently produced goods and services—the so-called *current account.* The positive or negative sign attached to each entry indicates whether the transaction represented a *gain* (+) or a *loss* (−) of foreign currency. Looking first at the top of the table, we see that in merchandise transactions Americans imported about $31 billion more than they exported, leading to a whopping deficit in what is called the *balance of trade* (see lines 1–3).

The small entry in line 4 indicates the net effect of a large number of dollars spent by U.S. military installations abroad (transactions that cost us foreign currency), and a large amount of foreign currency earned by selling armaments. On balance, these gained about $1.3 billion in foreign currency for the United States.

Line 5 shows that in 1977 American tourists

The U.S. Balance of Payments Accounts

TABLE 37–2

U.S. BALANCE OF PAYMENTS ACCOUNTS, 1977 (billions of dollars)

Current Account

(1)	Balance of trade		− $31.0
(2)	Merchandise exports	+ 120.6	
(3)	Merchandise imports	− 151.6	
(4)	Net military transactions		+ 1.3
(5)	Travel and transportation (net)		− 3.0
(6)	Net income from investments and other services		+ 22.2
(7)	Balance on goods and services (Lines 1 plus 4 plus 5 plus 6)		− 10.5
(8)	Unilateral transfers		− 4.7
(9)	Private	1.0	
(10)	U.S. government (nonmilitary)	− 3.7	
(11)	Balance on current account (Lines 7 plus 8)		− 15.2

Capital Account

(12)	Net private capital flows		− 17.0
(13)	Change in U.S. assets abroad	− 30.7	
(14)	Change in foreign assets in the U.S.	+ 13.7	
(15)	Net governmental capital flows		+ 33.2
(16)	Change in U.S. government assets	− 3.9	
(17)	Change in foreign official assets in the U.S.	+ 37.1	
(18)	Balance on capital account (Lines 12 plus 15)		+ 16.2

Addendum

(19)	Sum of lines (11) and (18)	+ 1.0
(20)	Statistical discrepancy	+ 1.0

Source: *Federal Reserve Bulletin,* and *Survey of Current Business.* Organization of tables changed by authors.

and shippers spent about $3 billion more on foreign services than foreign tourists and shippers spent here. Line 6 displays our major source of foreign currency earnings in the services category: We earned about $22 billion more on our investments overseas (and on some other miscellaneous services) than foreign investors earned here.

Line 7 gives the net result of all trading in goods and services—the balance on goods and services. The entry in line 7 means that the United States spent about $10.5 billion more than it received during 1977. Lines 8–10 indicate the so-called "unilateral transfers," including both private gifts to foreigners and official foreign aid. Together these cost us just under $5 billion in foreign currency, and when these unilateral transfers are added to the deficit on goods and services, we find (in line 11) a tremendous $15 billion deficit in America's *current account.* This deficit, which continued into 1978, caused quite a bit of discussion and public concern.

But this hardly represents our "balance of payments," as it leaves out all purchases and sales of assets. This group of transactions is shown in the *capital account* (lines 12–18). Line 12 shows that, on balance, American individuals and businesses bought $17 billion more in assets abroad than private foreign investors bought here. The net entry is *minus* $17 billion because $30.7 billion dollars flowed *out of* the United States to buy foreign assets (line 13), while only $13.7 billion in foreign money flowed *into* the United States to buy American assets (line 14).

This deficit on private capital flows added to the deficit on current account. How was it all financed? Line 15 shows the answer. The large outflow of *private* dollars was more than canceled out by official government capital transactions, mostly in the form of foreign governments increasing their holdings of U.S. financial assets ($37.1 billion, line 17). As a result, the capital account wound up with a surplus of $16.2 billion.

You may have noticed, and line 19 shows, that the current account deficit ($15.2 billion) and the capital account surplus ($16.2 billion) do not balance. Since, as a matter of simple arithmetic, they must balance (dollars purchased = dollars sold), the difference is considered a *statistical discrepancy* (line 20). While part of this discrepancy simply comes from errors in data collection and computation, the lion's share reflects the U.S. government's inability to monitor all the flows of money, goods, and services across its borders.

Lest the recent situation be seen as normal, it should be mentioned that the accounts for 1977 are quite unrepresentative of postwar U.S. history. In more typical years, we have run a large surplus in the balance of trade, given some of this away in gifts, and run a large deficit in capital transactions, meaning that Americans were buying more factories and securities abroad than foreigners were buying here.

A BIT OF HISTORY: THE GOLD STANDARD

Just as in the case of pure floating rates, it is hard to find examples of strictly fixed exchange rates in the historical record. About the only time that exchange rates were truly fixed was under the old gold standard, at least when it was practiced in its ideal form.[2]

Under the gold standard, fixed exchange rates were maintained by an automatic equilibrating mechanism that went something like this: All currencies were defined in terms of gold; indeed, some were actually made of gold. When a nation had a deficit in its balance of

payments, this meant, essentially, that more gold was flowing *out* than was flowing *in.* Since the domestic money supply was based on gold, losing gold to foreigners meant that the quantity of money automatically fell. Thus, "monetary policy" *automatically* turned restrictive, and interest rates rose, bringing in foreign capital. At the same time, the restrictive monetary policy pulled down national output and prices, discouraging imports and encouraging exports. The balance of payments problem quickly rectified itself. This meant, of course, that:

Under the gold standard, no nation had control of its domestic monetary policy, and therefore no country could control its domestic economy very well.

At least in principle, the effects on surplus countries were perfectly symmetrical under the gold standard. A balance of payments surplus led, via gold inflows, to an increase in the domestic money supply whether the surplus country liked the idea or not. This raised prices and output, thereby increasing imports and decreasing exports, and also lowered interest rates, thereby encouraging outflows of capital. Because of these automatic adjustments, nations rarely reached the point at which devaluations or revaluations were necessary. Exchange rates were fixed as long as countries abided by the rules of the gold standard game.

In addition to the complete loss of control over domestic monetary conditions, the gold standard posed one other serious difficulty.

A fundamental problem with the gold standard was that the world's commerce was at the mercy of gold discoveries.

Discoveries of gold meant higher prices in the long run and higher real economic activity in the short run, through the standard monetary-policy mechanisms that we studied in Part Three. And when the supply of gold did not keep pace with growth of the world economy,

---

[2]As a matter of fact, while the gold standard lasted (on and off) for hundreds of years, it was rarely practiced in its ideal form. Except for a brief period of fixed exchange rates in the late nineteenth and early twentieth centuries, there were periodic adjustments of exchange rates even under the gold standard.

prices had to fall in the long run and employment had to fall in the short run.

THE BRETTON WOODS SYSTEM AND THE INTERNATIONAL MONETARY FUND

The gold standard, which had faltered many
times before, finally collapsed amid the financial
chaos of the Great Depression of the 1930s.
Without it, the world struggled through nearly
15 years of almost complete breakdown in international trade.

Then, as World War II drew to a close, with
much of Europe in ruins and with the United
States holding the lion's share of the free
world's reserves, officials of the industrial
nations met at Bretton Woods, New Hampshire,
in 1944 to try to establish a new international
economic order. Their goal was to provide a
stable monetary environment that would facilitate world trade. And since the dollar was
almost the only "strong" currency at that time, it
was natural that the nations of the world would
turn to the dollar as the basis of the new international monetary system.

This is just what they did. The Bretton
Woods agreements reestablished a system of
fixed exchange rates based not on the old gold
standard but on the free convertibility of the
U.S. dollar into gold. The United States agreed
to buy or sell gold so as to maintain the $35 per
ounce price that had been established by President Franklin Roosevelt in 1933. And the other
signatory nations, which had almost no gold in
any case, agreed to buy and sell dollars to
maintain their exchange rates at agreed-upon
levels. Thus all currencies were indirectly on a
modified "gold standard." A holder of French
francs, for example, could exchange these for
dollars at (roughly) 5 francs per dollar and then
exchange these into gold at $35 per ounce. In
this way, the value of the franc was fixed at 175
francs per ounce of gold (5 francs per dollar

times 35 dollars per ounce). The new system
was dubbed the gold-exchange system, and
often referred to as the Bretton Woods system.

The International Monetary Fund (IMF) was
set up to police and manage this new system.
Using funds that had been contributed by
member countries, the IMF was empowered to
make loans to countries that were running low
on reserves. Only in the case of a "fundamental
disequilibrium" in a nation's balance of
payments was a change in exchange rates to be
permitted. For it was believed that only relatively
fixed exchange rates could provide the stable
climate needed to restore world trade.

Of course, the Bretton Woods conferees
did not define clearly what a "fundamental disequilibrium" was, nor could they have. As the
system evolved, it came to mean a chronic
deficit in the balance of payments of sizable
proportions. Such nations would then *devalue*
relative to the dollar; that is, they would reduce
the value of their currencies in terms of dollars.
So the system was not really one of fixed exchange rates but rather one where rates were
"fixed until further notice."

Several flaws in the Bretton Woods system
have already been mentioned in our discussion
of the pure system of fixed exchange rates.

Drawing by Lorenz; © 1973 The New Yorker Magazine, Inc.

"Damn it! How *can* I relax, knowing that out
there, somewhere, somehow, someone's
attacking the dollar?"

First, since devaluations were permitted only after a long run of balance of payments deficits, these devaluations (a) could be clearly foreseen, and (b) normally had to be quite large. Speculators then saw opportunities for profit and would "attack" weak currencies with a wave of selling. This led many economists to question whether the system of fixed exchange rates was really providing the stable climate for world trade that had been intended. Was a system where rates were constant for long periods and then altered by very large amounts really more conducive to international trade than one where overvalued currencies would gradually depreciate, as they would under a system of floating rates?

The second problem arose from the custom that deficit nations were expected to devalue when forced to, while surplus nations (mainly Germany and Japan) could resist upward revaluations. Since the U.S. dollar defined the monetary value of gold (at $35 per ounce), America was the one nation in the world that had no way to devalue its currency relative to gold, no matter how "fundamental" the disequilibrium became. The only way exchange rates between the dollar and foreign currencies could change was if the surplus nations revalued their currencies upward relative to the dollar. They did not do this frequently enough, so the United States, with its chronically overvalued currency, ran persistent balance of payments deficits. Between 1957 and 1968, for example, this country had to sell more than half its gold stock in an effort to keep the dollar pegged at the artificially high rate of $35 per ounce of gold.

ADJUSTMENT MECHANISMS UNDER THE BRETTON WOODS SYSTEM

Under the Bretton Woods system, devaluation was viewed as a last resort, to be used only after other methods of adjusting to payments imbalances had failed. What were these other methods?

We have already encountered most of them in our discussion of exchange rate determination in free markets (see pages 732–37 above). Any factor that increases the demand for, say, British pounds or that reduces the supply will push the exchange rate upward if it is free to adjust. If, however, the exchange rate is pegged, it is the balance of payments deficit rather than the exchange rate that will adjust when supply of or demand for a nation's money changes. Specifically, the British balance of payments deficit will shrink if either the demand for pounds increases or the supply decreases.

The two panels of Figure 37—7 illustrate this adjustment. In each case, the United Kingdom has a payments deficit, since the official exchange rate ($2.80) exceeds the equilibrium rate ($2.40). The deficit starts at AB in each diagram. Then either the demand curve moves outward as in part (a), or the supply curve moves inward as in part (b). With the exchange rate held at $2.80, the balance of payments deficit shrinks—to CB in (a) or AC in (b).

Referring back to our earlier discussions, then, we see that a deficit nation can improve its balance of payments picture by *reducing its aggregate demand,* thus discouraging imports and cutting down its demand for foreign currency. Or it can *slow its rate of inflation,* thus encouraging exports and discouraging imports. Finally, it can *raise its interest rates* in order to attract more foreign capital. In a word, deficit nations were expected to follow restrictive monetary and fiscal policies *voluntarily* just as they would *automatically* have done under the old gold standard. However, just as under the gold standard, this medicine was often unpalatable, so deficit nations frequently resorted to a bewildering variety of exchange controls—laws and regulations that made it very difficult for its nationals to sell their own currency to get foreign exchange. Many countries still have such controls.

Surplus nations could, of course, have taken the opposite measures: pursuing expansive monetary and fiscal policies to increase economic growth and lower interest rates. But they often did not relish the inflation that would come with such actions, and, once again, left the burden of adjustment to the deficit nations.

The general point about fixed exchange rates is that:

Under a system of fixed exchange rates, the government of a country loses some control over its domestic economy. There may be times when balance of payments considerations force it to contract its economy in order to cut down its demand for foreign currency, even though domestic needs are calling for expansion. Conversely, there may be times when the domestic economy needs to be reined in, but balance of payments considerations call for expansion.

For these and other reasons, the gold-exchange standard that prevailed from 1944 to 1971 was not really one of fixed exchange rates but of rates that were fixed until they were changed.

The system worked fairly well for a number of years, but it finally broke down over its inability to "devalue" the U.S. dollar. In August 1971, President Richard M. Nixon began the dismantling of the Bretton Woods system by announcing that the United States would no longer peg the value of the dollar by buying and selling gold. Most observers today agree that the gold-exchange system could not have

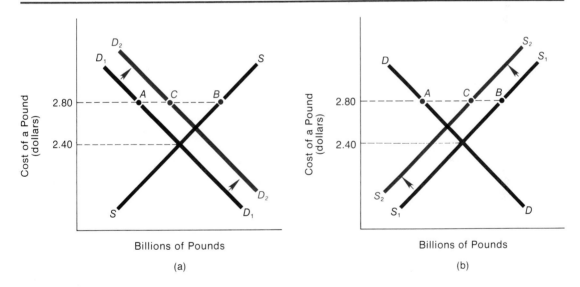

FIGURE 37–7

ADJUSTING TO BALANCE OF PAYMENTS DEFICITS

The two parts of this diagram illustrate alternative ways to cut England's balance of payments deficit while maintaining the exchange rate at $2.80 per pound. Part (a) might represent a reduction in British inflation, which would increase world demand for her export products. Or it could represent a rise in British interest rates, which would attract foreign capital. Part (b) might represent a reduction in British incomes, which would diminish English appetites for foreign goods. In either case, whether demand rises or supply falls, the balance of payments deficit is reduced: from AB to CB in part (a) and from AB to AC in part (b).

survived the incredible events of the 1970s in any case. The worldwide inflationary boom of 1972, the poor food harvests in 1972–1974, the quadrupling of the price of oil in 1973–1974, and the great worldwide recession of 1974–1976 all called for *major* changes in currency values, changes that the Bretton Woods system was ill-suited to handle.

WHY TRY TO FIX EXCHANGE RATES?

In view of these and other severe problems with the Bretton Woods system, why did the international financial community work so hard to maintain fixed rates for so many years? The answer is that floating exchange rates, determined in free markets by supply and demand, also pose problems.

Chief among these is the worry that freely floating rates would be highly variable rates, which would add an unwanted element of riski-

"Then it's agreed. Until the dollar firms up, we let the clamshell float."

ness to foreign trade. For example, if the exchange rate is 20 cents to the French franc, then a 1000-franc Parisian dress will cost $200. But should the franc appreciate to 25 cents, this same dress would cost $250. An American department store thinking of buying this dress may need to place its order far in advance and will want to know the cost *in dollars*. It may be worried about the possibility that the value of the franc will rise, so that the dress will cost more than $200. And such worries might inhibit trade.

There are two answers to this worry, though neither eliminates it entirely. First, rates that are free to float need not be very volatile. Prices of most domestic consumer goods, for example, are determined by supply and demand in free markets and yet do not fluctuate unduly. Similarly, the volatility in international exchange rates, since exchange rates began to float in the early 1970s, has proved to be of manageable proportions.

Second, speculators may relieve business firms of exchange rate risks—for a fee, of course. Consider the department store example. If French francs cost 20 cents today, the department store manager can assure herself of paying exactly $200 for the dress several months from now by arranging for a speculator to deliver francs to her at 20 cents on the day she needs them. If the franc appreciates in the interim, it is the speculator, not the department store, that will take the financial beating. (And, of course, if the franc depreciates, the speculator will pocket the profits.)

This role of speculation, which is one of our 12 Ideas for Beyond the Final Exam, has been described earlier in the text—first in Chapter 1 and later in our discussion of the stock market in Chapter 24. We learned also that the widespread fears that speculative activity in free markets will lead to wild gyrations, while occasionally valid, are more often unfounded. For speculators, if they are to make profits, must buy a currency when its value is low (thus helping to support the currency by pushing up its demand curve) and sell it when its value is high (thus holding down the price by adding to the supply curve). In this sense, speculators will only destabilize prices if they are willing systematically to lose money. This stands in marked contrast to the system of fixed exchange rates in which speculation often led to wild "runs" on currencies that were on the verge of devaluation.

We do not mean to imply here that there are no difficulties at all under floating exchange rates; we only suggest that life is liable to be more placid than is commonly supposed. Indeed, it may prove impossible to eliminate all exchange rate risks through speculation and, even if that were possible, speculators would demand a fee for this service—a fee that would add to the costs of trading across national borders.

THE CURRENT MIXED SYSTEM

Our current international financial system—where some currencies are still pegged in the old Bretton Woods manner, others are floating freely, and many more are floating subject to government interferences—has evolved gradually since Nixon severed the dollar's link to gold. Though it continues to change and adapt, two trends are evident.

The first is the decline in the notion that exchange rates should be fixed for relatively long periods of time. The demand by many countries in the early 1970s that the world quickly return to fixed exchange rates had largely subsided by the mid-1970s. Even where rates are still pegged to the dollar, devaluations and revaluations are now much more frequent—and smaller—than they were in the 1944–1971 period. Most free-world currency rates change very slightly on a day-to-day basis. Market forces determine the basic trends, up or down, in exchange rates. But central banks intervene to moderate these changes whenever they feel

that such actions are appropriate. Deficit nations like Italy and Spain are often in the market buying their own currencies to slow down the rates of depreciation. Germany, Japan, and other surplus nations are in the market selling their currencies. But they do not have to buy or sell as much as they did under the old fixed-rates system.

The second unmistakable trend is the declining role of gold in the international monetary system. This trend actually began *before* Nixon's dramatic announcement in 1971, and by now it is only a minor exaggeration so that gold plays no role in the world's financial system.

The decline of gold in international monetary affairs began much as it did in the history of domestic monies—with the introduction of a paper substitute. In 1970, the IMF began to issue bookkeeping entries called Special Drawing Rights (SDRs). SDRs serve as a form of international reserves, supplanting gold to some extent, because member nations can exchange SDRs for currency among themselves. They were quickly dubbed "paper gold" by the news media. The advantage of SDRs over gold, of course, is that they can be created whenever the world's commerce seems to need them, rather than when South African gold mines are in high gear. Just as central banking gave nations control over their money supplies, SDRs have given the world control over its supply of reserves.

The next stage in the decline of gold came when the link between the dollar and gold was severed in August 1971. The overvalued dollar immediately depreciated relative to many other currencies, and the price of gold skyrocketed. Nowadays there is a *free market,* which enables those who wish to invest in gold—dentists, jewelers, industrial users, speculators, and ordinary citizens who think of gold as a good store of value—to buy or sell as they wish. The price of gold, determined each day by the law of supply and demand, has proved to be quite volatile. Fortunes have been made and lost by investors in gold.

RECENT DEVELOPMENTS IN INTERNATIONAL FINANCIAL MARKETS

The Smithsonian Agreement

President Nixon was forced to end fixed exchange rates because of the rapid depletion of America's reserves and the accumulation of foreign debts resulting from America's balance of payment deficits. The industrial nations attempted to restore fixed rates at a meeting held at the Smithsonian Institution in late 1971, but their success was short-lived. In early 1973, the United States was forced to devalue once again, and this sounded the death knell for the Bretton Woods system.

Oil Prices and "Petrodollars"

The next big jolt to the international monetary system came in late 1973 and early 1974, when the Organization of Petroleum Exporting Countries (OPEC) quadrupled the price of oil. This naturally led to huge surpluses in the balance of payments of the OPEC nations: Their combined current account surplus in 1974, for example, was a colossal $70 billion. Because the sum of the current-account balances of all nations must necessarily be zero (since one country's exports are another's imports), this meant that the rest of the world had a combined deficit of $70 billion. And this $70 billion total deficit was distributed quite unevenly across the nations of the world. The United States, with its large supplies of domestic energy resources, suffered a deficit in the current account of only about $3.5 billion in 1974, while the much smaller economy of the United Kingdom (which did not yet have oil from the North Sea) had a deficit of about $8.5 billion. It is hard to imagine fixed exchange rates being maintained under such circumstances.

The fact that OPEC's oil exports exceeded its imports by such large amounts led to a financial problem that journalists dubbed "recycling petrodollars." The OPEC nations could not or would not spend all of their enormous receipts from oil sales. Instead, they invested their unspendable revenues in the securities of several of the advanced industrial nations. While America, Switzerland, and other industrial nations were paying much more for oil, Arab funds were flowing back into New York, Zurich, and other financial centers. Thus the balance of payments problems were manageable for these countries. But virtually none of this capital flowed to the less developed countries that did not export oil. This left these poor countries in an almost impossible position: They needed foreign exchange to pay for oil, but they did not receive any through capital flows.

To deal with this problem, the IMF set up a *recycling facility* through which the foreign capital flowing into some developed countries could be funneled to the countries most in need of foreign exchange. This facility, which lasted only until 1976, helped alleviate the short-run crisis in some nations. But as it turned out, much of the financial assistance went from the advanced nations who were in good shape to the advanced nations who were in distress. This left the developing nations to solve their foreign currency problems by borrowing in the private market, and several years of this practice left them heavily in debt. No one yet knows how they will deal with the long-run problem of earning enough foreign currency to pay their oil bills and redeem their IOUs.

The Further Decline of Gold

The drift away from gold picked up steam in 1975 and 1976 through a series of important events. First, the U.S. Treasury auctioned off a small part of its gold stock in 1975 and indicated that it was prepared to sell more in an effort to "demonetize" gold. Then, the IMF abolished the official price of gold in 1975, and subsequently followed the lead of the U.S. Treasury by initiating a program of periodic gold sales that continues to this day. During 1978 there was much discussion in the United States of the possibility that the Treasury might sell off much of its remaining holdings of gold.

The European "Snake"

As already noted, floating exchange rates are no magical cure-all. One particular problem beset the members of the European Economic Community (EEC). These Common Market countries seek a unified market like the United States and have a long-range goal of establishing a single currency for all member countries. Floating rates would make this goal impossible. So the member countries entered into an agreement whereby exchange rates *within* the Common Market would remain relatively *fixed* while Common Market currencies as a group would rise or fall *relative to the rest of the world.* International financial institutions seem always to acquire colorful nicknames, and this one was dubbed "the snake."

Within a short time, however, both Britain and Italy found themselves unable to maintain a parity with the strong currencies of Germany and the Netherlands. Britain was the first to break the snake and let the pound float. But soon Italy and France also had to devalue relative to the mark. Since then, several countries have dropped in and out of the snake. In 1976, all the exchange rates in the snake were adjusted, with the mark appreciating and the others depreciating to varying degrees. But with inflation running at only about 4 percent in Germany, 16 percent in England, and over 20 percent in Italy, the rates within the snake could not remain stable for very long. By early 1978, only Belgium, Denmark, Germany, the Netherlands, and Norway remained in the snake. And during that year several European nations began to talk of replacing the snake with a new system for stabilizing exchange rates.

CONCLUDING REMARK: WHERE DO WE GO FROM HERE?

The 1970s saw drastic changes in the international monetary system, and no one can be sure that the changes during the 1980s will not be equally dramatic. Just where is the international monetary system headed? No one really knows. The system is still in a state of flux, as each nation decides to what extent it wants to influence its exchange rate, and how.

In such an environment, predictions are no doubt foolhardy. Yet it seems unlikely that the world will move back to a system of fixed exchange rates as under the Bretton Woods agreements. For better or for worse, floating rates are here to stay—at least in some form. And most economists feel that the change has been for the better.

SUMMARY

1. Exchange rates state the value of one currency in terms of another, and thus influence the patterns of world trade in important ways.
2. If governments do not interfere, exchange rates will be determined in free markets by the usual laws of supply and demand. Such a system is called floating exchange rates.
3. Demand for a nation's currency is derived from foreigners' desires to purchase that country's goods and services or to invest in its assets. Any change that increases the demand for a nation's currency will cause its exchange rate to appreciate under floating rates.
4. Supply of a nation's currency is derived from the desire of that country's citizens to purchase foreign goods and services or to invest in foreign assets. Any change that increases the supply of a nation's

currency will cause its exchange rate to depreciate under floating rates.

5. In the long run, the purchasing-power parity theory governs exchange rate movements. This theory states that relative price levels in any two countries determine the exchange rate between their currencies. Therefore, countries with relatively low inflation rates normally will have appreciating currencies.

6. Over shorter periods, the pace of economic activity and the level of interest rates exert a greater influence on the exchange rate.

7. Exchange rates can be fixed at nonequilibrium levels by goverments that are willing and able to mop up any excess of supply over demand or provide any excess of demand over supply. In the first case, the country is suffering from a balance of payments deficit because of its overvalued currency. In the second, an undervalued currency has given it a balance of payments surplus.

8. This conceptual definition of the balance of payments is often hard to apply in practice, so the actual U.S. balance of payments statistics are rather complicated and are sometimes difficult to interpret.

9. In the early part of this century, the world was on a particular system of fixed exchange rates called the gold standard, in which the value of every nation's currency was fixed in terms of gold. But this created problems because nations could not control their own money supplies and because the world could not control its total supply of gold.

10. After World War II, the gold standard was replaced by the gold-exchange (or Bretton Woods) system where rates were again fixed, or rather, fixed until further notice. In this system, the U.S. dollar was the basis of international currency values.

11. The gold-exchange system served the world well and helped restore world trade, but it got into trouble when the dollar became chronically overvalued since the system provided no way to remedy this situation.

12. Since 1971, the world has gradually been moving toward a system of relatively free exchange rates, though there are plenty of exceptions. We now have a thoroughly mixed system, which continues to evolve and adapt.

13. Floating rates are not without their problems; importers and exporters justifiably worry about fluctions in exchange rates. But these problems seem manageable, if not completely solvable, and few people think that a return to fixed exchange rates is likely.

CONCEPTS FOR REVIEW

International monetary system	Current account
Exchange rate	Capital account
Appreciation	Balance of trade
Depreciation	Gold standard
Devaluation	Gold-exchange system (Bretton Woods system)
Revaluation	
Floating exchange rates	International Monetary Fund (IMF)
Purchasing-power parity theory	Exchange controls
Fixed exchange rates	Special Drawing Rights (SDRs)
Balance of payments deficit and surplus	The European "snake"

QUESTIONS FOR DISCUSSION

1. What items do you own, or routinely consume, that are produced abroad? What countries do these come from? How have your purchases affected the exchange rates between the dollar and these currencies?

2. If the dollar appreciates relative to the Japanese yen, will the Sony TV you have longed for become more or less expensive? What effect do you imagine this will have on American demands for Sonys? Does the American demand curve for yen, therefore, slope upward or downward? Explain.

3. Inflation in West Germany has been steadily below that in the United States. What, then, does the purchasing-power parity theory predict should be happening to the exchange rate between the mark and the dollar? Ask your instructor what actually has happened.

4. Use supply and demand diagrams to analyze the effect on the exchange rate between the dollar and the British pound if:
   a. Britain's flow of North Sea oil becomes so large that England starts exporting oil to America.
   b. British dockworkers refuse to unload ships that arrive with cargo from America but continue to load ships that sail from Britain.
   c. The Federal Reserve raises interest rates in America.
   d. The U.S. government, to help settle the problems of the Middle East, gives huge amounts of foreign aid to Israel and her Arab neighbors.

5. How are the problems of a country faced with a balance of payments deficit similar to those posed by a government regulation that holds the price of peanuts above the equilibrium level? (*Hint:* Think of each in terms of a supply–demand diagram.)

6. Look at the U.S. balance of payments accounts table in the text (Table 37–2 on page 741). Figure out where each of the following actions you could have taken in 1977 would have been recorded in these accounts:
   a. You spent the summer traveling in Europe.
   b. You sent $25 to your uncle in Canada as a birthday present.
   c. You bought a new Volkswagen.
   d. You sold stock on the Japanese stock market.
   e. You drove over the Canadian border carrying American records in your trunk and sold them to a friend in Canada. (*Hint:* Would your sale have been recorded anywhere?)

7. Under the old gold standard, what would have happened to world prices if there was a huge gold strike in California in 1849? What would have happened if the world went without any important new gold strikes for 20 years or so?

8. Explain why the members of the Bretton Woods conference in 1944 wanted to establish a system of fixed exchange rates. What was the flaw that led to the ultimate breakdown of the system in 1971?

9. Suppose you want to reserve hotel rooms in London for the coming summer but are worried that the value of the pound may rise between now and then, making the rooms too expensive for your budget. Explain how a speculator could relieve you of this worry (Don't actually try it. Speculators deal only in very large sums!)

38

Problems of the
Less Developed Countries

In this chapter we will describe some of the special problems of the less developed countries (LDCs) and look at the measures that have been proposed to increase their rate of growth. We will show that although in recent years standards of living in the LDCs have begun to rise significantly, their rapid population growth and their vulnerability to such external shocks as the rise in oil prices and other similar perils mean that many problems still threaten their economies. Next, we will examine the problems that impede growth in the LDCs, including scarcity of capital, poor natural resources, lack of

education, and unemployment. Then we consider what the LDCs can do to help themselves and what the rest of the world can do to help them. Finally, we describe some specific forms of aid industrialized countries can and do provide to the developing nations.

LIVING IN THE LDCs

Just about two-thirds of the world's population lives in countries whose per capita GNP is less than $400 per year, evaluated (as well as it is possible to do) in terms of today's prices in the United States. Table 38–1 shows that there are a number of countries in which annual per capita income is under $200. Even after adjustment for differences in measurement of GNP in the United States and the poorer countries, this probably comes to an annual income figure under $600. To us, residents of an economy that offers an average income more than 10 times as high, such a figure is not only likely to seem incredible, it is all but incomprehensible. Few of us can *really* imagine what life would be like if our family income were reduced, to, say, $2000 per year. It is even hard to envision survival on such amounts. It must be emphasized that these figures do *not* represent the living standards of a small group of outcasts from their own societies. Rather, they are *typical* of perhaps a majority of those who live in Asia, Africa, and much of Latin America.

What can life be like in such circumstances? No brief description can really bridge the gulf between our range of experience and theirs. Yet it can offer us a glimpse into a way of life that few of us will want to share.

Inhabitants of many of the less developed countries live with their large families in one-room shanties or apartments, their water supplies are scanty, polluted, and often miles from the home, their only source of energy is that of man and beast, and their sparse harvests are wrung from miserable soil in good years, with starvation threatened perhaps every 5 years when the rains do not come and the crops fail.[1] With no surplus in production, no food can be put into reserves, and the old, the infirm, and the very young are likely to perish.

The life of a man in an LDC is hard enough, with its low nutritional level, its lack of equipment to help him in his work, and its frequency

TABLE 38–1

PER CAPITA GNP IN DEVELOPED AND LESS DEVELOPED COUNTRIES, 1976 (measured in U.S. dollars)

Developed Countries	
United States	$7890
West Germany	7380
Sweden	8670

Less Developed Countries	
Bolivia	$390
Burma	120
Egypt	280
Ethiopia	100
Haiti	200
India	150

Source: World Bank.

of debilitating diseases. But his life is luxurious compared with that of his wife. She is usually married by the age of 14, bears 8 or 10 children, and by 35 is often a toothless old crone. If (as is true of some 80 percent of the population) she inhabits a rural area, she may have to trudge miles every day to fetch water for the family. She sews all the family's clothes by hand and cooks its meals. There is not enough money for preground flour, so part of the woman's daily work is to pound the grain by hand for food for the family—perhaps an additional 2 hours of hard labor. She also tends the gardens that produce food for the family, although, except in Moslem countries where women are sequestered, she is also expected to put in a full day in the fields during the 6 months of the agricultural season.

Another duty of the woman in an LDC is to bring produce, wood, or whatever she has to trade to market a couple of times a week, and she must often walk as many as 10 miles each way with bundles as heavy as she can carry on her back or on her head. She has no respite in the raising of her children, since they are likely

[1] It has been estimated that in some famine years in the 1970s, half a million people died as a result in Bangladesh; 200,000 in Ethiopia; 100,000–250,000 in the Sahelian zone of Africa; and more than 800,000 in just three of the states of India (*The New York Times,* October 27, 1976).

not to have a school to attend when they are well or a hospital to go to when they are sick. It is no wonder that she ages so much faster than a woman in our society.

Table 38–2 gives the percentage of infant deaths for each 1000 live births and the average life expectancy of a newborn child in some countries ranging from the most underdeveloped to the most affluent. The contrasts are dramatic. In Bolivia, 157 babies die of every 1000 that are born, while the comparable figure in Sweden is only 9. In many countries people survive only until their late forties, while in Scandinavia they live to be 75.

There is little question about the quality of life in less developed lands.

Most of the inhabitants of many LDCs are shockingly poor. Malnutrition and disease are widespread. The sheer process of living and surviving taxes the people to the utmost and makes them old before their time.

RECENT TRENDS

Do recent trends offer hope of improvement? Here there is both good news and bad. The good news is perhaps the most remarkable. In the last decade, real GNP in the LDCs has been estimated to have grown as rapidly as 5 percent a year (see Table 38–3). Even more important, income per capita has been growing at an annual rate greater than $2\frac{1}{2}$ percent. This means that:

Despite population increases, some LDCs have succeeded in breaking out of the stagnation trap. If growth continues as it has recently, an average family in an underdeveloped area can look forward to a doubling of its living standards in less than 30 years. Or put another way, standards of living will be increasing faster than they did in the United States in the nineteenth century!

TABLE 38–2

INFANT MORTALITY AND LIFE EXPECTANCY IN DEVELOPED AND LESS DEVELOPED COUNTRIES, 1975–1976

	INFANT MORTALITY (deaths per 1000 births)	LIFE EXPECTANCY AT BIRTH (years)
Developed Countries		
United States	15	73
West Germany	17	71
Sweden	9	75
Less Developed Countries		
Bolivia	157	48
Burma	140	50
Egypt	108	53
Ethiopia	162	42
Haiti	115	50
India	129	49

Source: World Bank.

TABLE 38–3

AVERAGE ANNUAL GROWTH RATES OF REAL GROSS DOMESTIC PRODUCT IN DEVELOPED
AND LESS DEVELOPED COUNTRIES, APPROXIMATELY 1965–1975

	APPROXIMATELY 1965–1970 (percent)	APPROXIMATELY 1970–1975 (percent)
Developed Countries		
United States	4.3	2.5
West Germany	4.6	2.2
Sweden	4.4	2.6
Less Developed Countries		
Colombia	5.1	6.5
Egypt	3.4	3.9
Haiti	0.7	4.2
Iran	9.6	20.2
Pakistan	5.4	3.3
Panama	7.8	5.2
Zaire	9.0	4.9

Source: United Nations.

Clearly, for the first time there is hope for a major reduction in absolute poverty in the LDCs.

Thus, the good news is very good indeed. The bad news is not so straightforward, and its seriousness is partially a matter of interpretation. There are several developments that can be considered either as merely unfortunate or as thoroughly ominous.

First, while the percentage rates of growth of per capita incomes in the LDCs have been very impressive, the industrialized countries, with their initially high incomes, have not exactly been standing still. Indeed, largely because their population growth has been slower, the percentage growth rate in per capita incomes has been higher in the developed countries. But even if the *percentage* increases in their per capita incomes had been very similar, *absolute* incomes would have continued to rise more quickly in the richer lands. Where per capita income is $100 a year, a $2\frac{1}{2}$ percent growth rate

translates into a $2.50 annual improvement; however, where per capita income is $5000 a year, the same $2\frac{1}{2}$ percent rate of growth adds $125 a year to the income of the average person. As a result:

The purchasing power of the average family in an LDC is falling further behind that of a typical family in a wealthy economy. That is, relative poverty (the difference between the purchasing power of families in the two types of economies) continues to grow worse, despite the noteworthy postwar improvement in the LDCs.

Second, many critics, notably those on the left, believe that the $2\frac{1}{2}$ percent growth rate has been accompanied by a worsening distribution of income in the LDCs. The rise in population has worsened the living standards of people on marginal lands with inadequate rain (about 40 percent of Indian farmers and a large proportion of Africans). Add the massive explosion of urban unemployment, and one gets several hundred million people who are no better off and possibly worse off.

Third, a continuing problem within the LDCs is the relatively high growth rate of their populations.

While in the United States and some countries of Western Europe, net population growth has fallen almost to zero, the population explosion continues in many of the LDCs.

Table 38–4 tells the story. For the sample of LDCs shown, the annual growth rate of population continues perhaps ten times as high as it is in the industrialized countries. Clearly, the more closely the growth in population approximates the growth in national income, the more slowly standards of living will rise, since there will be that many more persons among whom the additional product must be divided. If population growth is exactly equal to the growth rate of national income, obviously the average standard of living must be at an absolute standstill. A recent estimate indicates that the rise in population in LDCs is in fact consuming nearly half the increase in their GNP.

Fourth, the relatively high growth rate in per capita incomes has not been uniform throughout the LDCs. In some countries, such as Sri Lanka, Malaysia, and Cuba, growth rates have been extremely slow.

Finally, the LDCs have shown themselves highly vulnerable to such shocks as the oil crisis of 1973–1974. Much as the oil embargo and the rise in oil prices affected the industrialized economies, there is reason to believe that it damaged the LDCs even more. In other words, the new growth trends in the LDCs may be quite fragile, and their continuation cannot simply be taken for granted.

Before leaving the issue of recent growth in the LDCs, it may be helpful to offer a little perspective on the entire matter. First, it should be recognized that sustained growth is a very

TABLE 38–4

BIRTHRATE MINUS DEATH RATE IN DEVELOPED AND LESS DEVELOPED COUNTRIES, 1978 (ESTIMATED)
(births minus deaths per 1000 population)

Developed Countries	
United States	6
West Germany	−2
Sweden	1
Less Developed Countries	
Bolivia	29
Burma	24
Egypt	25
Ethiopia	24
Haiti	22
India	20

Source: United Nations.

recent invention, dating from the Industrial Revolution—the beginning of the eighteenth century. It has been estimated that per capita income in England in 1800 was no higher than in third-century Rome. Before the Industrial Revolution, real wages in England may have reached their peak in the fifteenth century—the end of the Middle Ages—from which they fell to their lowest level ever reached after the Middle Ages in the reign of Queen Elizabeth, more than a century later.

On the other hand, growth in the LDCs is not an innovation of recent decades. In the three decades before World War I, exports from the tropical countries grew faster than national income in the wealthier countries, and, no doubt, in these LDCs output per capita was also growing. Since income data for that period are not available, we do not know by how much, but we do know that the earlier growth was vulnerable to disruption—World War I, the Great Depression, and other catastrophic events all but ended growth in the LDCs for nearly 40 years! Thus, today's high growth rates cannot just be taken for granted and extrapolated into the future.

IMPEDIMENTS TO PROSPERITY IN THE LDCs

No one has produced a definitive list of causes of the poverty of the LDCs, just as no one can pretend to have produced a foolproof prescription for its cure. Yet there is a general agreement on the main conditions contributing to the economic problems of LDCs. These include lack of physical capital, scarcity of valuable natural resources, rapid growth of populations, lack of education, unemployment, and social and political impediments to business activity. Let us examine each of these in turn.

Scarcity of Physical Capital

The LDCs are obviously handicapped by their lack of modern factories and machinery. In addition, they lack infrastructure—good roads, railroads, port facilities, and so on. But capital is not easy to acquire. If it is to be provided by the populations of the LDCs themselves, they must save the required resources—that is, as we saw in Chapter 33, they must give up consumption in order to free the resources needed to build plants, equipment, and roads. That is fairly easy in a rich community, where substantial saving still leaves the public well off in terms of current consumption. But in an LDC, where malnutrition is a constant threat, the bulk of the inhabitants cannot save except at enormous sacrifice to their families. Moreover, in many of the LDCs, tradition imputes little virtue to investment in business, so that even the wealthy are not terribly anxious to put their savings into productive equipment. Thus:

Because of poverty, which makes saving diffi-

cult, if not impossible, and because of traditions that do not encourage investment, the LDCs have rates of growth of capital lower than those in the developed countries, at least as financed out of domestic resources. In an industrialized country, some 15 percent of its own GNP typically goes into capital formation, while for the LDCs the figure is closer to 10 percent.

One way to help matters is to obtain the funds for investment from abroad. There is a long tradition of foreign investment in developing countries. For example, throughout the first half of the nineteenth century the United States almost constantly drew capital from abroad, though the amounts involved were only a small proportion of U.S. GNP. In recent decades a considerable share of the resources going to the LDCs from abroad has come from foreign governments as part of their aid programs. While some of the resources provided in this way have been used wastefully, informed observers generally agree that the waste incurred under these programs has not been spectacularly great, and they conclude that these capital transfers from the rich countries to the poor have at least worked in the right direction.

Capital can also be transferred to an LDC when a private firm chooses to invest money in such a country to build a factory or to explore for oil in order to increase its own profits. This too seems to have been helpful to the LDCs. In earlier days, it sometimes gave an unacceptable degree of political influence to the foreign firms, particularly when the LDC was a colony of an industrial country. In recent years this difficulty may have become rarer. Nowadays, it is more often the outside firm that is afraid of the government of the LDC rather than vice versa, with foreign proprietors frequently fearful of rigid control by the government of the LDC in which it invests. Sometimes it even fears outright expropriation—that the government will simply take over its property in the LDC with, or even without, compensation.

It is true that foreign firms hope to make more money out of an LDC than they put into it, but that is only natural, since otherwise their investment would not have been expected to be profitable, and the funds would therefore not have been invested in the first place. But there are usually *mutual* gains from trade. Investment will be useful to the LDCs if in the process of earning these profits foreign firms build factories, infrastructure, and provide jobs that leave the community wealthier than it would otherwise have been. The evidence is that this is in fact what foreign private investment has typically accomplished in recent decades.

A problem with foreign business investment that is more serious is the danger that foreign firms will fail to train native personnel in the skills necessary to run the factories built by those companies. Often the foreigner will bring with him his own managers, engineers, and technicians, and the work force from the LDCs is kept in menial jobs in which on-the-job training is minimal. In recent years the LDCs have begun to deal with this problem by restricting immigration of foreign personnel, giving them work permits only for limited periods and requiring at least some minimum employment of native personnel in key positions.

Another danger posed by foreign investment is that it may prevent future financial independence. Profits are a major source of the funds used for investment. If foreign investment takes over the LDCs' most profitable industries, then newly formed capital—new plants and equipment—will also be owned predominantly by foreigners.

Scarcity of Valuable Natural Resources

Many of the LDCs suffer from poor natural resources—shortages of minerals, large desert areas, and climates that are not conducive to productivity because they are too dry or too hot. Obviously, a country in which natural resources are poor in quality suffers a serious handicap. Of those LDCs whose incomes have grown most rapidly in the postwar period, a high proportion have been rich in mineral products, which they were able to export—copper, iron ore, bauxite, and especially oil.

Yet abundant natural resources are not absolutely essential for economic growth. Nearly half the LDCs whose national incomes have grown more than 5 percent a year in recent decades have *not* been major exporters of raw materials. And several industrial countries, notably Switzerland and Japan, have achieved high and rapidly rising living standards despite their very limited endowments of natural resources.

The importance of a country's raw material endowment depends very heavily on the cost of transportation. When transport is expensive and risky, the economy that must get its raw materials from abroad suffers a serious handicap. But as the cost of transportation declines, this problem is correspondingly diminished. The invention of railroads and of steamships with metal hulls has made a tremendous difference in the cost of transportation of bulky inputs from abroad, as has the substitution of oil and electricity for coal—a fuel that is extremely bulky and costly to transport. Improved methods of iron and steel processing, which have sharply reduced the amount of coal needed per ton of metal, have also helped a good deal.

Thus, while natural resources are important for economic development, they are less critical than they once were, and they have never been an absolute precondition for economic growth. In any event, the scarcity or abundance of raw materials is not a promising instrument for development policy, since a country can do little about the quantity of natural resources with which it is endowed (though it *can* influence the rate of exploration for them and the rate at which they are depleted).

Population Growth

Population growth is often described as the primary villain in the LDCs. We have already noted that, on the average, their populations grow far more rapidly than those in the wealthier countries. And though the growth rate has recently been declining in many of the less developed countries, overall the population of the LDCs is expanding at a rate that will double in less than 30 years, requiring a doubling of housing, schools, hospitals, and so on—a heavy real cost for an LDC.

The growth in population has perhaps been stimulated by improvements in medical care, which have reduced death rates spectacularly. Today, in some areas, death rates (ratio of deaths to population) are only one-quarter or one-fifth as high as birthrates. While formerly it was not unusual for half a nation's children to die before the age of 20, today in many countries this is true of only some 4 percent of those populations. This dramatic decline can be attributed primarily to inexpensive public health measures—reduction in stomach diseases through purer water supplies, reduction in the incidence of malaria by the draining of swamps, insecticide spraying of the breeding grounds of infectious mosquitoes, eradication of smallpox by vaccination, and so forth. The more expensive treatment of illness, using modern medical techniques and miracle drugs, seems to have contributed far less to population growth than have public health measures.

But not all LDCs suffer from serious population problems. India, Indonesia, and Egypt are frequently cited examples of population pressures. On the other hand, many African countries and parts of Latin America still have populations so small that they are denied economies of larger scale communication and transportation. The economy of a sparsely settled country whose electric power and telecommunication lines must traverse great unpopulated areas is under a costly handicap.

Even most countries with rapidly growing populations have somehow been able to increase their per capita outputs. New technology, particularly in agriculture, has played a critical role. The *green revolution*—breeding new species of grain whose yields per acre are spectacularly greater than their predecessors'—has contributed enormously. Of course, no one can guess how long food production can stay ahead of population growth in this vital race.

Experience has shown also that there is no iron law of population growth such as that envisioned by Malthus. Higher incomes do not inevitably lead to a corresponding rise in population. On the contrary, as countries have grown wealthier, more urbanized, and their people better educated, population growth has often declined significantly, perhaps because consumers had other things to occupy them, or perhaps because they needed to depend less on a large family for security in old age or for a labor force on the family farm.

There is also evidence that campaigns for family planning can significantly decrease birthrates in LDCs if these programs are adequately organized, planned, and financed.

In sum: Population growth is a crucial problem for economic growth in the LDCs, whose governments have begun to realize what a large capital drain it represents. Yet not all LDCs suffer from overpopulation; and while there have been some failures, birth control programs appear to be promising.

Educational and Technical Training

Everyone knows that educational levels in the LDCs are much lower than they are in the wealthier countries. There are fewer graduates of elementary schools, far fewer graduates of high schools, and enormously fewer college graduates. The percentage of the population that is literate is much lower than in industrialized nations. The issue is how much of a handicap this constitutes for economic growth.

If, by "education," we refer to general learning rather than technical (trade) schooling, the evidence is that it makes considerably less difference for economic growth than is often believed. For example, the number of jobs that clearly require secondary (high school) education rarely seems to exceed 10 percent of the labor force. Various studies that have investigated whether there is a statistical relationship between the economic growth of an economy and its typical educational level have so far failed to turn up any significant correlation between the two. Other suggestive evidence can easily be cited. For example, in 1840 when Great Britain ruled the markets of the world, only 59 percent of the British adult population was literate, while in the United States, Scandinavia, and Germany the figure was about 80 percent.

All of this is not meant to imply that education is worthless. On the contrary, it obviously offers many benefits in and of itself, which need not be discussed here. But it does suggest that if a government invests in education *purely as a means to stimulate economic growth,* only a very limited outlay is justifiable on these grounds.

Matters are quite different when we turn to technical training. There is clearly a high payoff to the training of electricians, machinists, draftsmen, construction workers, and the like. While the number of persons involved need not be very high in proportion to the population, the role played by such specialists is crucial. However, the LDCs would find it a very heavy drain upon their scarce foreign currency to send young people abroad to learn these skills in the numbers called for by the needs of the economy. One of the main inhibitions to adequate training in these areas is that in many countries such skills are held in low esteem and considered inferior to training in the liberal arts. Consequently, technical education is often

handicapped by low budgets, low teacher salaries—which discourage good people from entering the field—and the prejudice of potential students against such fields.

Training in improved farming methods also has a great deal to contribute. In many of the LDCs, agricultural methods produce yields far lower than the best of the known techniques can offer. As one leading observer has remarked:

> If this gap could be closed, the economies of these countries would be unrecognizable. Indeed . . . no impact can be made on mass living standards without revolutionizing agricultural performance.[2]

There seem to be no easy ways to provide the necessary education to the farmers who cannot spare the time to attend schools; and training their children also involves a number of critical obstacles. Religious beliefs often lead parents to object to schooling of their children, particularly of girls; in areas where literacy is low (where the problem is generally most serious), truly literate and knowledgeable teachers are almost impossible to find in any substantial numbers; and children who do complete schooling have a tendency to leave the farms and move to the cities. Programs to provide help to the peasants on their own farms have had only limited success. Indeed, lack of training is only part of the problem. Many other things are needed to make modern farming methods possible—farms larger than the 5 acres that are typical in a number of countries are required to permit the use of modern machinery where it is appropriate. Roads and storage facilities must be built. Credit must be made available to farmers. Financial arrangements must be changed so the farmer need no longer give up half his crop to landlords and tax collectors

[2]W. A. Lewis, *Development Economics, An Outline* (Morristown, N.J.: General Learning Press, 1974), page 25.

whom he can surely regard as little more than parasites and who undermine his incentives for improved productivity.

Unemployment

One of the most noteworthy features of the growth of the LDCs has been an increase in unemployment as population shifted out of agriculture into the cities. Increased schooling has stimulated the migration out of the rural areas, as has unionization, which has often produced a huge gap between urban and rural wages. Government investment policies have also favored construction of schools, hospitals, and other facilities in the cities, and as a result, large numbers of migrants have entered the cities to swell the ranks of the unemployed. The unemployment rate among young urban workers has been particularly high; indeed, rates as high as 50 percent are not unheard of.

These figures are compounded by the phenomenon of disguised unemployment. For example, ten persons may do a job for which only six are needed. The statistics would show no unemployment among the ten workers, even though four of them really contribute nothing to output. Some observers believe that this is such a widespread problem in rural areas that even a substantial reverse migration of the urban unemployed back to the farms would add very little to production, at least in some of the LDCs.

An important consequence of all this is that in many LDCs unemployment may not be accompanied by any substantial reduction in output, in contrast to the situation in industrialized economies. But this does not mean that unemployment in the LDCs is not a serious problem. What it does mean is that it may sometimes be desirable for those economies to avoid the use of labor-saving equipment, partly because it will result in better use of an abundant resource, and partly because it will contribute to the solution of a serious social

problem. Thus, increased output is desirable perhaps primarily because it helps to sop up unemployed labor. This is in contrast to the usual situation in the developed countries in which increased employment is desirable perhaps primarily because it increases income and output.

Entrepreneurship and Social Impediments to Business Activity

One of the magic ingredients of economic growth is entrepreneurship. As discussed in Chapter 28, entrepreneurship is a combination of attributes: imagination, daring, willingness to take risks, a sense of timing, and an ability to recognize profitable opportunities, all driven by a love of money, power, or some other such goal, which together combine to make up the quality of business leadership. There are many persons who believe that the main source of the decline of the British economy is the disappearance of entrepreneurship, and others suggest that in the United States the drive for achievement, which is needed to produce effective entrepreneurs, is not what it once was. Countries with remarkable growth records, such as Japan, are said to be today's centers of entrepreneurial drive.

Whatever the truth of these diagnoses, it is clear that the LDCs need entrepreneurs if their economies are to grow rapidly. But in many of these economies, there are serious inhibitions to entrepreneurship. Traditional social values often accord relatively low status to business activity. Indeed, those traditional values even prevent businesses from seeking ways to attract and please their customers and their work force. In addition, high positions in business, as elsewhere in many LDCs, are often determined by family connections and inheritance, not by ability.

In the LDCs growth will be inhibited until customs can be modified to increase the social status of economic activity, to make it respectable for private business people and managers of public enterprises to do their best to attract business and increase productivity, and to assign responsibility on the basis of ability rather than family connections.

Government Inhibition of Business Activity

In addition to social impediments to business, the political situation in the LDCs often is detrimental to business success. Business is not helped by unstable governments or by the uncertainty that accompanies such an environment, especially if there is a high likelihood of revolution. Foreign investment will be discouraged where there is fear of expropriation or of unstable currencies that may fall in value and wipe out hard-earned profits. And native business people may live in fear of nationalization or even imprisonment—possibilities that are not likely to encourage investment.

In addition, in the normal course of events, governments in the LDCs are often inclined to interfere with business activity in a variety of ways that seem relatively innocuous—but whose effects can be deadly. Price controls are often imposed at levels that make the controlled activity totally unprofitable and cause it to wither. Licenses and other direct controls are frequently administered by incompetent bureaucrats, who tie up business activity in red tape. As a matter of prestige of the currency, exchange rates are often set so high that exports from the LDC cannot compete on the world market. The governments sometimes expropriate and seek to operate foreign firms before they have trained native personnel to run them. In short:

Poorly conceived economic policies can impede business activity and hence economic growth in the LDCs. But, then, it must be admitted that the LDCs have no monopoly on foolish economic policies!

WHAT LDCs CAN DO TO HELP THEMSELVES

This completes our list of some of the main problems that limit growth in the LDCs. Of course, no such list can really be complete, but it can indicate the sorts of issues that have occupied the attention of development economists.

The list also indicates directly some of the things that can be usefully done by governments in the LDCs to stimulate the development of their economies. We will go backward through the list since the last item (government inhibition of business activity) is obviously the most directly amenable to improved government policies.

In brief list form we suggest here some of the things the LDCs can do for themselves.[3]

1. The government of an LDC should go as far as possible to eliminate red tape in the administration of any regulations that control business activity.
2. Any price controls, if they cannot be avoided altogether, must establish levels of prices that do not destroy the economic activities to which they apply.
3. Exchange rates must not be set so high as to discourage exports of the products of the LDC. Foreign trade is of critical importance to the developing countries, and it is essential that the country's monetary and exchange rate policies not prevent its exports from competing on the world market.
4. The government should do what it can to encourage mobility of people and resources to where they are needed most. It must do what it can to remove impediments to innovation and entrepreneurial initiative. One type of measure that can help in this respect

[3]This list is based on W. A. Lewis, *Development Economics, An Outline,* especially pages 46-47.

is a change in agricultural ownership arrangements, which now effectively subjugate small farmers, keep them in poverty, and discourage or prevent the use of modern agricultural techniques. Another important step is the encouragement of equal opportunity by vigorous opposition to discrimination by race or creed, which has all too frequently repressed entrepreneurial activity by unpopular minority groups in the LDCs.

5. Priority must be given to the training of skilled artisans and technicians, as well as to the preparation of persons for administrative positions in government and business.

6. Investment and saving must be provided. The experience of the Soviet Union has confirmed how important it is for rapid economic growth to encourage the nation to save until it hurts. Of course in the LDCs a good part of the new capital will have to come from abroad in the form of grants and loans, but they will not be able to rely exclusively on foreign resources.

These last two requirements are by far the most critical. In the words of W. A. Lewis, a world-reknowned authority on LDCs, "any economy with underdeveloped natural resources that can raise 30 percent of national income in savings, borrowings and taxes, and that also has a well-trained cadre, is capable of removing all other obstacles to rapid economic growth."[4]

HOW THE INDUSTRIALIZED ECONOMIES CAN HELP THE LDCs

We have just seen that the two primary needs of the LDCs are technical skills and capital resources. Happily, these are precisely the things that the more prosperous nations are in

[4]W. A. Lewis, *Development Economics, An Outline*, page 47.

a position to offer. Educational facilities in the industrial world have grown to a magnitude unprecedented in human history. Never before has such a high proportion of the population of the developed countries received a college education. This means that we now have the trained teachers, classrooms, laboratories, and equipment necessary to provide an education of the highest quality to students from the LDCs. Thus, one of the main things that the United States and other advanced countries can offer is encouragement and financing to students from less developed lands, particularly to graduate students receiving professional training.

However, there are several dangers here. One that has received a great deal of attention is the so-called brain drain—the temptation of students from LDCs to try to stay in the countries where they have studied and enjoy the higher living standard it offers, rather than returning home where their abilities are needed so badly. There are several ways to deal with this issue. For example, one can use arrangements requiring students to return to their homelands for at least some given number of years after completion of the educational program, or offer higher wages for trained persons in the LDCs to make returning more attractive. Yet the problem is there, and the large number of doctors, teachers, and other skilled personnel from LDCs who are seeking jobs in the developed countries suggests that the issue is not negligible.

Another danger in the training offered by the wealthier countries stems from the fact that, as in the LDCs, the developed countries have tended to give higher prestige to training in the liberal arts than to technical training. This may well be the right choice from our own point of view. In our abundant economies, emphasis on the contribution of education to production is less urgent than it is in a country whose people live on the edge of survival. But the tendency to accord higher prestige to nontechnical training may also discourage students from abroad from entering those fields in which trained personnel are needed most urgently in their homelands.

A second major contribution that the wealthier countries can make to the LDCs is to offer them trained technicians and technical advice from their own populations. Such counseling and personnel can be very helpful as a temporary measure, but in the long run they can prove detrimental if provision for the training of local personnel for the ultimate replacement of the foreign technicians and advisers is not built in to the program.

A third, and very important, type of assistance from the developed to the less developed countries takes the form of money or physical resources provided either as loans made on favorable terms or as outright grants (gifts). In a moment we will consider some of the contributions that the industrial world has recently made in this area.

Fourth, the world can help the LDCs through research. One of the hardest problems for the developing world is what to do in the rural areas that suffer from inadequate rainfall, where several hundred million people live in both Asia and Africa. These people are badly in need of a new dry-farming technology. Until one is discovered, their poverty will increase as their numbers grow. An international research organization devoted to food production in problem areas in the LDCs would have much to contribute.

Finally, and perhaps most important, the developed countries can help by encouraging freedom of trade and investment. This will help those LDCs whose exports are readily expanded but that are now being held back by barriers to trade. Exports of sugar, meat, cotton, and other agricultural products are inhibited by tariffs and other restrictions. There are many discriminatory duties against processed, as distinct from crude, materials. A significant number of LDCs would also benefit substantially from a lifting of quotas and other restrictions upon the export of manufactured goods. Increased freedom of trade will also help those LDCs whose economies offer business prospects sufficiently bright to attract significant quantities of private capital from abroad. All in all, increased freedom of trade is a matter of highest priority for the LDCs.[5]

LOANS AND GRANTS BY THE UNITED STATES AND OTHERS

In the postwar period a number of countries have provided capital resources to the LDCs. Indeed, soon after World War II an international organization was set up with aid to LDCs as one of its major tasks. This organization, the International Bank for Reconstruction and Development, commonly referred to as the World Bank, has 122 member countries. Each member provides an amount of capital to the bank that is related to the member country's wealth; for instance, the United States has contributed approximately one-third of the total. The Bank makes loans that are financed by bonds that it issues and sells, and has acted as guarantor of repayment to encourage some private lending. The World Bank has established two affiliated agencies, the International Development Association and the International Finance Corporation, that have played major roles in providing funds to the LDCs.

The Bank has loaned more than $20 billion to LDCs and to countries that can be consid-

[5]However, not everyone agrees with this conclusion. There are those who have argued that participation of LDCs in international trade is bad for them because it weakens their capacity to develop as self-reliant, mature economies. It is held that new manufacturing industries in the LDCs will not take off without protection from foreign competition. Development of primary product exports creates a rich and politically powerful vested interest that inhibits measures that would favor manufacturing. The extent to which foreign trade and production of exports are in foreign hands inhibits domestic saving and the development of local entrepreneurship.

In this view, LDCs are therefore held back by international trade and would do better to integrate regionally and develop their own home markets without foreigners, who also bring unsuitable habits, unsuitable tastes, and unsuitable technology, and impart a crippling inferiority complex to the natives.

ered on the borderline. It has tended to emphasize loans for infrastructure, dams, communications and transportation, and, in addition, has provided technical assistance and planning advice. Some economists have criticized the Bank's conservatism in its lending policies and its unwillingness to take risks. Recently, however, it and its affiliates have become more adventuresome in their lending practices.

The United States itself has been a major source of funds to the LDCs. Indeed, its loans and grants have exceeded the total given by all other countries and international agencies. U.S. interest rates and its allowed length of time for repayment of loans have generally been far more generous than the terms offered by other governments. During the 1960s, our expenditures on aid ran to more than $3 billion per year, with about half this amount consisting of loans and the remainder made up of grants. In the past few years, expenditures on foreign aid have become less popular politically, and the amounts provided consequently have gone down significantly. The bulk of the assistance provided by the United States has gone to a small number of countries—India, Pakistan,

South Korea, and Turkey have been among the primary recipients.

In addition to the United States, aid has come from other industrialized countries, notably France, Great Britain, and West Germany. The Soviet Union has also become a major source of assistance to the LDCs, now providing, along with its associated countries, about $1 billion a year. While the Soviet funds have obviously been distributed in a way intended to maximize its political advantage, it can hardly be claimed that the U.S. foreign aid program has been entirely free of political considerations.

Many economists have advocated greater generosity in our assistance to LDCs and have deplored the recent cuts in our aid programs. Aside from any moral responsibility to help the impoverished countries, it is argued that an effective aid program that really helps the growth of LDCs will also serve our own interests. By making those countries more stable economically and politically, we can contribute to our own economic tranquility. By increasing the LDCs' power to buy and sell, we are in effect contributing to the prosperity of the entire world.

SUMMARY

1. Standards of living in many LDCs are extremely low; per capita incomes that are equivalent to $600 a year are not uncommon. Life expectancy is low and daily living is very difficult, particularly for women.
2. GNP and per capita incomes in the LDCs have grown considerably in recent years.
3. Nevertheless, the gap between family incomes in the less developed and the industrialized countries has continued to widen.
4. In many LDCs population continues to grow much faster than that in the industrialized countries.
5. Growth in the LDCs is impeded by shortages of capital caused by poverty and by traditions that do not encourage investment; by poor natural resources; rapid population growth; poor education; unemployment; lack of entrepreneurship; and government impediments to business activity.
6. The LDCs can encourage their own growth by cutting government red tape, by minimizing those interferences with prices and exchange rates that discourage economic activity, by encouraging mobility of people and resources to where they are needed, by encouraging technical training and education, and by encouraging saving and investment.

7. Industrialized countries can help the LDCs by providing capital through loans and grants, by offering training and education to people from those lands, and by encouraging freedom of trade with the LDCs.
8. In the postwar period many countries, including the United States and the Soviet Union, have provided large amounts of money to the LDCs in the form of loans and grants. At its peak, the United States provided about $3 billion per year, and the Soviet Union and its allies have been providing about $1 billion annually.
9. Several international organizations, most notably the World Bank, have been organized to provide economic assistance to the LDCs.

CONCEPTS FOR REVIEW

Less developed countries (LDCs) Entrepreneurship
Growth rate in GNP Brain drain
Growth rate in per capita income World Bank
Disguised unemployment

QUESTIONS FOR DISCUSSION

1. To many families living in less developed countries, an income equivalent to $2000 per year is considered a high standard of living. Can you make up a budget for a U.S. family of four earning $2000 a year?
2. Explain how it is possible for the per capita income of an LDC to grow at a faster rate than that in the United States and yet for the difference between the incomes of average families in the two countries to increase. Can you give a numerical example showing how this happens?
3. Discuss the advantages and disadvantages to an LDC of a U. S. manufacturing company investing in that country.
4. If you were economic adviser to the president of an LDC, how would you suggest that he or she might encourage increases in saving and investment?
5. No one knows what encourages or discourages the supply of entrepreneurs. Do you have any ideas about policies that may be capable of stimulating entrepreneurship?
6. Name some countries in which entrepreneurship seems to be abundant these days; some countries in which it seems to be scarce. What is your impression about what is happening to the supply of entrepreneurs in the United States?

ten

Alternative
Economic Systems

39

Marxian Economics

For more than a century radical and reformist groups throughout the world have drawn inspiration from the writings of Karl Marx. Nations with governments claiming to be run on Marxist principles include the Soviet Union, the People's Republic of China, Cuba, and at least a dozen other countries in Eastern Europe, Asia, Africa, and Latin America, containing among them more than one-third of the world's population.

In this chapter we summarize the major ideas in Marx's economic theories. And one of the main conclusions we draw is that his work contains very little that is helpful to a communist economy. This judgment is made not because the Marxian analysis is poor in quality or short of ideas. On the contrary, even some very conservative economists have acknowledged the originality and importance of at least some of Marx's analyses. Rather, we find that his ideas are not particularly helpful to a central planner because Marx chose to devote almost all of his attention to the *capitalist* economy, seeking to explain the principles of its evolution, its strengths, and its weaknesses. Hence, he left wide open the questions about how a communist economy should be run.

It is a mistake to think that Marx despised every feature of capitalism. It is true that he believed its accomplishments exacted a very high cost in human misery and exploitation. And he believed also that it was rapidly outliving its usefulness and its historical role. But he was a profound admirer of its early vigor and enormous accomplishments, which, in his phrase, rescued humanity from the "universal mediocrity" that feudalism had imposed upon the economy.

Except for Marx's use of the word *bourgeoisie*, the following passage from the *Communist Manifesto* (1848) might have been penned by a publicist for the Chamber of Commerce:

The bourgeoisie . . . has accomplished wonders far surpassing Egyptian pyramids, Roman aqueducts, and Gothic

Biographical Note: Karl Marx (1818–1883)

Karl Marx was born in Trier, Germany, the son of a successful Jewish lawyer who later converted to Christianity. Marx's acquaintances considered him brilliant, but he was also stubborn and quarrelsome. Throughout his life he broke with one associate after another, with the only exception being Friedrich Engels, his lifelong friend, collaborator, and benefactor.

Marx studied at the universities of Bonn and Berlin, hoping first to become a poet. After a resounding failure at poetry, he entered a circle of young philosophers in Berlin, all devoted followers of Hegel, whose ideas about the crucial role of history in understanding current events, art, and science had recently swept German universities. The young Hegelians, however, were radical in their opposition to Hegel's religious views, and this attitude may have influenced Marx's later attacks against religion. Marx received his doctorate of philosophy at the age of 23, meanwhile having married ("above his station") Jenny von Westphalen, the daughter of his father's closest friend. Jenny's family opposed the marriage, and, as it turned out, their

cathedrals. . . . The bourgeoisie cannot exist without constantly revolutionizing the instruments of production. . . . The bourgeoisie, during its rule of scarce one hundred years, has created more massive and more collosal productive forces than have all preceding generations together.''[1]

Because Marx wrote about capitalist rather than communist societies, it is much easier to find applications of his ideas to a free-enterprise economy than to one that is centrally planned.

[1]Karl Marx, *Communist Manifesto, Collected Works,* vol. 6 (New York: International Publishers, 1976), pages 487–89.

And since Marx was particularly interested in the vitality of capitalism—that is, with the forces that helped determine its dynamism at various stages in its history—we can perhaps use his writings to learn something about this subject.

APPLICATION: RESCUING FIRMS FROM BANKRUPTCY

The vitality of our economy and its firms is stimulated by both the carrot and the stick. It rewards those firms that serve the market effi-

---

reasons were justified since Marx was never able to support her. Much of their lives was spent in great poverty, and the deaths of three of their six children were probably the result of privation.

After a brief stint as a newspaper editor, Marx's troubles with the authorities propelled him first out of Germany and then Paris and Belgium. It was in Paris that Marx first met Engels, and in Brussels they together wrote the *Communist Manifesto,* a revolutionary pamphlet that was the only writing of Marx's to achieve wide circulation during his lifetime. After the demise of the revolutions that shook all of Europe in 1848, but in which Marx played little part, he fled finally to London where he spent the rest of his life. There Marx helped form revolutionary groups, and otherwise spent most of his time cloistered in the British Museum studying the history of economic thought and writing *Das Kapital.* Aside from some meager earnings as correspondent for *The New York Tribune,* a job he held for about ten years, Marx lived entirely on money given to him by Engels (who, although an anticapitalist, never-

theless owned factories in Manchester and Germany) and by other admirers.

Although Marx was devoted to his family, he quarreled with all his associates but Engels, and finally engineered the breakup of The First International, the revolutionary organization that he had helped found and develop but which seemed about to fall into the hands of opponent radicals. Marx finished writing volume I of *Capital* and saw it published in 1867. He had previously written most of volumes II and III, but never completed them in the 15 years that remained to him. It was left to Engels to edit and publish these volumes after Marx's death. Marx died in 1883, two years after the death of his wife, Jenny, and only several months after the unexpected death of his eldest daughter, Jenny Longuet.

Throughout his life Marx attracted and fascinated many people by his brilliance and through the force of his personality and ideas. And though most of his associates eventually became estranged from Marx the man, almost all retained their allegiance to his theories.

ciently and effectively, and bankrupts those enterprises that fail to do so. But a number of times in recent years, governments of free-enterprise economies have given financial aid in one form or another to companies that were experiencing financial difficulties. The assistance given to Lockheed Corporation by the U.S. government (1971) and the help provided to Rolls Royce by the government of the United Kingdom (1970) are two instances of such help that received a great deal of publicity. In each case the threat of bankruptcy was interpreted as a serious threat to the entire economy, with unemployment, cessation of production, loss of exports, and other dire consequences the likely results.

To avoid these potential disasters, the British government stepped in with a grant of up to $100 million to save Rolls Royce, and the U.S. government voted loan guarantees of up to $250 million to Lockheed, inspiring demands for similar treatment by other troubled firms, such as Grumman Aircraft and Litton Industries.

As we will see, Marx's view of the role of bankruptcy in a capitalist society suggests that a very different approach would have been appropriate in both these cases. We will also see why Marxian analysis suggests that the prevention of bankruptcy, where circumstances warrant it, can impair the vigor and efficiency of a free-market economy. It is interesting that today many non-Marxist economists, including some who are quite conservative politically, agree with this judgment.

THE MARXIAN FRAMEWORK— HISTORICAL MATERIALISM

To Marx, a historical perspective was essential to understand the capitalist system, or any other form of economic organization. All economic systems evolve from ones that are very different, and they can each be expected to be replaced by some other form of economic organization.

Thus, to understand how a particular economy works we must keep in mind the predecessor from which it evolved and the process by which it grew. Marx frequently criticized the classical economists for their nonhistorical viewpoint, their treatment of all other economic forms as more or less mini-capitalist systems, and their tacit assumption that capitalism will prevail throughout all time. He said, with some scorn, that to these economists "there has been history, but there is no longer any."

What determines the evolutionary direction of a society? According to Marx the primary influence is economic—the current state of technology and the method of organizing production. At each stage of history, these factors determine which group will be in charge of the economy and which groups will be subjugated. In the feudal economy, for instance, the manor lords were in control of the economy while the serfs were under their domination. Under the free-enterprise economy, the medieval lord has been replaced by the modern capitalist and the serf by the free laborer—in reality a propertyless proletarian who "has nothing to sell but his hands." But the relationship between the serf and his lord was, of course, very different from that between the free laborer and the capitalist. Technology, which is primarily responsible for this difference, affected the productivity of the two economies, which in turn changed the course of the economy's growth and the character of the struggle between the dominant and dominated groups.

By saying that economic conditions determine the direction of the evolutionary process, Marx did *not* mean that people care only about their financial well-being. Unlike a number of later historians and modern (non-Marxist) economists who have analyzed everything in human activity—from crime and marriage to the provisions of the U.S. Constitution—in terms of the narrow economic interests of those involved, Marxian analysts have always recognized that history is affected by altruism, passion, prejudice, social pressures, and a wide variety of other *non*economic influences. Nevertheless, these Marxists are quick to point out that such influences are themselves strongly affected by the nature of the economic system.

To underline the distinction between the Marxian view of the process of change and the view that people are motivated only by their own economic interests, one need only look at the fact that revolutionary fervor among lower income groups often accelerates rather than wanes when their economic conditions improve. The reason, according to some Marxian economists, is that increased income and leisure finally afford the poorest members of the economy the time to think about their miserable condition and the material strength and means to do something about it. Thus, economic conditions are indeed an important determinant of the timing of revolutionary unrest, but unrest does not necessarily peak at the moment in history when the lowest classes have the most to gain from it.

Marx's historical materialism asserts that we cannot understand any economy without recognizing its place in history. It asserts also that while historical events are influenced primarily (though not exclusively) by economic conditions, the form of this influence is often very indirect and subtle—filtering through current social customs, political organizations, and so forth. Historical materialism does *not* assert that people follow only their monetary self-interest.

ON THE NATURE OF COMMUNIST SOCIETY

Of the many thousands of pages published by Marx, and of those published by others after his death, there are scarcely a dozen dealing with the nature of the economy under socialism (which Marx never distinguished clearly from communism). Marx did tell us that socialism must come, and that it must begin with "the dictatorship of the proletariat," though this concept, too, is left somewhat fuzzy. There is no doubt, however, about his ideology. He clearly and repeatedly stated that this "higher form of society" will be dedicated to "the full and free development of every individual," with work transformed into a stimulating and pleasant activity and the deadening effects of extreme specialization brought to an end.

Perhaps Marx's most famous passage on the nature of socialism appears in his last economic writing, in which he envisions the post-capitalist society passing through two stages. In the first, there is already "common ownership of production." But this early socialist society is "still stamped with the birth marks of the old society from whose womb it emerges." In this stage, the income of the individual is exactly equivalent to the amount of labor he contributes. "He receives a certificate from society that he has furnished such and such an amount of labour . . . and with this certificate he draws from the social stock of means of consumption as much as costs the same amount of labour. The same amount of labour which he has given to society in one form he receives back in another." However:

> In a higher phase of communist society, after the enslaving subordination of the individual to the division of labour, and with it also the antithesis between mental and physical labour, has vanished; after labour has become not only a means of life but itself life's prime want; after the productive forces have also increased with the all-round development of the individual, and all the springs of co-operative wealth flow more abundantly—only then can the narrow horizon of bourgeois right be crossed in its entirety and society inscribe on its banners: From each according to his ability, to each according to his needs![2]

[2]Karl Marx, *Critique of the Gotha Programme* (Moscow: Progress Publishers, 1971), pages 17–18.

About the only other concrete attribute of a communist society described in Marx's writings is the abolition of the division of labor, which, claimed Marx, transforms workers from creative, satisfied humans into discontented, alienated near-machines (a concept that will be discussed later in this chapter). According to Marx and Engels:

> In communist society, where nobody has one exclusive sphere of activity but each can become accomplished in any branch he wishes, society regulates the general production and thus makes it possible for me to do one thing today and another tomorrow, to hunt in the morning, fish in the afternoon, rear cattle in the evening, criticise after dinner, just as I have a mind, without ever becoming hunter, fisherman, cowboy or critic.[3]

Certainly these are fascinating notions, but they tell us nothing about the coordination of production, the planning of new plant and equipment, the arrangements for industrial research, the devising of a monetary policy (if money is to be used), and the many other issues that must be settled in designing any (even a communist) economy.

It seems clear that Marx did not intend to provide detailed guidance to the leaders of communist societies. Rather, his work was devoted to a meticulous analysis and critique of capitalism.

COMMODITIES, PRODUCTIVE LABOR, AND CAPITAL

One of the reasons it is hard to understand Marx is that he often employed words to mean things other than what they mean in ordinary usage. (Marx was, after all, an economist!) Since Marx considered it so important to distinguish capitalism from all other economic systems, he defined his basic economic terms and concepts in a way intended to emphasize their role in a free-enterprise economy.

A *commodity* for Marx is therefore not simply any good or service that consumers consider useful—which is how modern economists would define the term. Thus, when a primitive stoneworker trades some of his handiwork (say, arrowheads) for the meat that has been brought in by a hunter, neither the meat nor the arrowheads are "commodities" in Marxian terminology. Meat and arrowheads become commodities only when they are processed or produced by commercial firms. And not because they are any more useful than the meat and arrowheads traded by the stoneworker and the hunter, but because they are produced as means to earn *profits*.

Commodity production is therefore just another element serving the one central purpose of the capitalist system—the accumulation of wealth, which in turn is the engine for the continuing expansion of the economy.

Analogously, Marx called labor under capitalism "productive" only when it turns out commodities, that is, when its outputs are offered for sale as part of the normal process of profit making and accumulation. Two pieces of work may appear perfectly identical, yet one can be productive and the other unproductive in Marx's view. Thus, a baker on the staff of the White House who makes a cake for a diplomatic dinner is engaged in "unproductive activity" (as are the diplomats!). The cake has no part in the capitalistic economy and does not differ in any way from the work of a baker in the court of a medieval prince. But another baker who makes an identical cake for a commercial bakery is "productive" because, to his employer, he is producing not cake but profit.

Capital also was defined by Marx in a way that differs from the modern economists' use of

[3]K. Marx and F. Engels *The German Ideology, Collected Works*, vol. 5 (New York: International Publishers, 1976), page 47.

the term, who employ it to mean plant, equipment, and other produced means of production. To Marx, capital meant a social process rather than a set of physical objects. The term can include the hiring of labor power, the construction of machinery, the production of commodities, the exchange of products for money, and the reinvestment of that money into another round of the profit-generating process. *Capitalism* is the all-embracing term that includes every one of the steps of this mechanism. With such a broad definition, it is no wonder that Marx chose the word "capital" as the title of his most important book.

MARX'S VALUE THEORY: SURPLUS AS THE SOURCE OF ACCUMULATION

Perhaps the single most confusing thing about Marx's book *Capital* is its use of the term *exchange value*. To classical economists, this term was a synonym for *price*, and much of their work was intended to explain how market prices are determined—why a particular pair of shoes sells for a price twice as high as a certain hat, for example. But to Marx, the revolutionary, this was not an important issue. Rather, his central purpose, as we have said, was to explain the accumulation process. And for this it was convenient to use a totally different concept of value.

Central to Marx's value analysis is something he regarded as a puzzle of fundamental importance—one whose solution had escaped his predecessors. Accumulation, the engine of economic growth, is financed out of profits, and profits appear to come from the sale of commodities. But how, he asked, can that possibly be? If two people exchange two goods of equal value, they may both be better off, for each may prefer the goods he gets to the goods he gives up. But in such a process neither party can gain *financially* since each has given as much value as he has received. It is true that

one party in the exchange can profit at the expense of the other if he delivers less value than he receives, but the other party must then lose as much as the first one gains. The mystery, then, is this: How can the economy as a whole pour forth the profits needed for accumulation if the exchange process on which accumulation is based is fundamentally incapable of yielding net gains to the group of parties involved?

Marx's proposed solution starts off with a definition: The *value* of a commodity is precisely equal to the labor time necessary for its production. Note that Marx clearly stated that this is a *definition*, not a deduction: "[A good] which is not the product of labour cannot have a value; in other words, it cannot be *defined* . . . as the social expression of a certain quantity of labour."[4]

Ricardo and other predecessors of Marx had already proposed something that *sounded* very similar but really was not. They had argued that, in certain circumstances, pure competition tends to drive relative market prices of different goods very close to the relative amounts of labor needed to produce them. Notice that this can be *deduced* from economic theory if most production costs are labor costs, since under pure competition, as we saw in Chapter 22, price tends to equal marginal cost. But Marx spurned this theory and criticized Ricardo severely for it, saying that in fact prices usually differ substantially from each good's labor content. Though Ricardo considered such deviations to be exceptions to a generally accurate rule, Marx said they happen so often that Ricardo's "rule becomes the exception and the exception the rule."

By divorcing the concepts of price and value, Marx freed himself to play with the word *value*. He could now define value and labor time to be the same thing, even though he believed that prices differ systematically from the labor time required in the production process.

[4]Karl Marx, *Theories of Surplus Value*, vol. III (Moscow: Progress Publishers, 1963), page 520. Italics added.

Why did he adopt this apparently curious definition? Because, in his view, it helps to explain where profits really come from and, concurrently, how wealth is accumulated. For this purpose he formulated one more concept, the value of labor power, about which he wrote:

> The value of labour-power is determined, as in the case of every other commodity, by the labour-time necessary for the production, and consequently also the reproduction, of this special article. . . . The value of labour-power is the value of the means of subsistence necessary for the maintenance of the labourer.[5]

In defining the *value of labor power* as a *minimum* subsistence level for the worker, Marx did not mean that *wages* are in fact always set at that subsistence level. Just as the price of a commodity is not generally equal to its (Marxian) value, the wage for an hour of labor need not be equal to the value of that much labor power. In fact, Marx argued vigorously that the level of wages is determined by the outcome of a constant struggle between workers and capitalists, and that one of the main purposes of union activity is to force wages above bare subsistence.

The value analysis gave Marx his solution to his puzzle about the origin of profits. Suppose that the average worker needs to labor for five hours to produce a day's subsistence but that the standard workday is eight hours. Then, in one workday, labor power, which has a value of five hours, is transformed into a product that carries a value of eight hours. The difference, which Marx called surplus value, is the portion of output that does not have to be consumed by the worker for his survival and that instead can be accumulated and used by the capitalist to expand his property and to make the economy grow.

According to Marx, profits and accumulation are possible only because the value of labor power—the amount of labor needed to produce a worker's daily subsistence—is no more than a fraction of a workday. The remainder of the worker's day goes into the production of surplus value, which can be accumulated by the capitalist.

THE ETHICS OF SURPLUS VALUE

Over the years, many people have concluded that Marx's aim was to establish that capitalism is immoral and that profits amount to robbery of the worker who really deserves the surplus he earns. Marx explicitly and repeatedly denied that this was his opinion; in fact, his anger was aroused by others who did hold such views. Marx made clear, right at the point in *Capital* where he defined the value of labor power, that:

> It is a very cheap sort of sentimentality which declares this method of determining the value of labour-power, a method prescribed by the very nature of the case, to be a brutal method.[6]

But if it was not Marx's goal to show that surplus value is robbery, then what was the purpose of the value theory? Engels stated that the purpose of Marx's analysis, the very analysis on which he based his revolutionary demands, was to demonstrate "the inevitable collapse of the capitalist mode of production." Later in this chapter we will see how the value theory could, in Marx's view, help explain the "laws of motion of capitalism." It was these laws that he interpreted as calling for precisely the sort of revolutionary change he was advocating—the replacement of capitalism by a communist society.

There is also a second issue that the value theory was intended to deal with. In providing

---

[5]Karl Marx, *Capital*, vol. I (Chicago: Charles H. Kerr Publishing Company, 1906), pages 189–96.

[6]Marx, *Capital*, vol. I, page 192.

himself the answer to the question of how profits can be produced by an exchange economy, Marx believed he had also shown that profits (as well as rents and interest payments) are *produced by workers.* Put the other way, Marx believed he had shown that profit is *not* produced by the capitalist, that interest is *not* produced by the moneylender, and that rent is *not* produced by the landlord.

In saying this, Marx never denied that land and produced means of production contribute to the output of the economy. Nor did he ever argue that labor is the only useful means of production:

> [When he does his work, the laborer] is constantly helped by natural forces. We see, then, that labour is not the only source of material wealth, of use-values produced by labour. . . . labour is its father and the earth its mother.[7]

But while *land* (or natural resources generally) contributes to production, it does not necessarily follow that the *landlord*, the person who happens to own the land, contributes anything. A given output can be produced just as well if the land is publicly owned and there is no landlord to collect income from the production process. It was Marx's contention, therefore, that labor is the only *human* (he called it "social") input that contributes to production. True, a capitalist may sometimes help in the production process by organizing and planning it, but then, according to Marx, he is merely serving as a (part-time) laborer.

Marx emphasized that labor is not the only useful factor of production. However he did argue that it is the only useful factor of production contributed by *human society.* In this sense he considered it necessary to define all value and, therefore, all surplus value (profit, interest, and rent) as something that is produced by labor.

[7]Marx, *Capital*, vol. I, page 50.

THE MARXIAN ANALYSIS OF PRICING AND PROFIT

If in Marxian economics, price and value are generally *unequal,* then how are prices determined? The answer is that they are determined in exactly the same way as proposed by the classical economists, such as Adam Smith and David Ricardo. Marx repeatedly stated that he had no new analysis of pricing to offer. But he did maintain that he had an important new insight into the relationship between price and value, which underlies the relationship between surplus values and profits.

Having asserted that only labor is capable of producing surplus value, Marx concluded that the surplus value produced by any industry will be roughly proportional to the amount of labor time it uses. This means that such service industries as restaurants and theaters—whose inputs contain a very high proportion of labor—can be expected to yield a great deal of surplus value while other sorts of industries, such as public utilities—which use enormous amounts of equipment but relatively little labor—will end up producing comparatively small amounts of surplus value. If each industry kept all the surplus value it generated, it would follow that a theater would be far more profitable than an electric utility company. But the competitive mechanism permits no such imbalance in the *profitability* of different industries.

Where differences in profitability do occur, investors rush to withdraw their funds from the less profitable businesses and transfer them to those industries whose earnings are high. This means that the industries that are initially more profitable expand, and that their increased production then forces down their prices and hence their profits. This is the law of supply and demand in action. At the same time, the industries that are initially *less* profitable will have to reduce production levels as their capital exits, which will then raise the prices of their products and hence their profit rates. Competition will always tend to eliminate differences in profit rates among industries in this way. For as long as one industry is significantly more profitable than another, funds will flow into the more profitable industry and out of the industry in which profits are low. This mechanism, which had already been described in detail by Smith and Ricardo, was adopted by Marx without reservation.

Thus, regardless of how much surplus value is produced by any one industry, competition will force prices and outputs to adjust in ways that redistribute the goods and services that make up this surplus value and every capitalist will end up with an equal share of the wealth. He called this type of sharing "capitalist communism."

According to Marx, then, prices under capitalism are set so as to redistribute the *surplus value* produced by the entire economy. All capitalists end up receiving an equal rate of return on their investments. And in order for this to happen, the price of each commodity must be equal to its cost of production, including the opportunity cost of capital (the standard rate of profit on each capitalist's investment). Price must cover the wages of labor, the cost of raw materials, and the opportunity cost of capital.

As we learned in Chapter 22, this analysis of the way prices will be set under pure competition is precisely the view taken by modern economists. It is also exactly the same as the one Adam Smith outlined nearly a century before Marx. Marx knew this very well, and said so repeatedly:

> The price of production includes the average profit. . . . It is, as a matter of fact, the same thing which Adam Smith calls *natural price*, Ricardo *price of production*, or *cost of production*.[8]

In Marxian theory, commodity prices are equal to average costs of production, including

a competitive return to capital. This is the pricing rule that appears both in classical and modern competitive analyses. Marx recognized that there was nothing new in this pricing result.

In the next section we will see the novel insights to which Marx was led by his restatement of the analyses of his predecessors.

THE PURPOSE OF THE MARXIAN PRICE–VALUE ANALYSIS

If Marx knew that his pricing analysis got him to exactly the same point at which the classical economists had all arrived much earlier, why did he make so much of his discussion of price? Why did he get back to Smith's pricing principle in such a roundabout manner, that is, by starting with the *unequal production* of surplus value by different industries and its *redistribution* through the price mechanism? Marx explains that prices and the resulting distribution of profits are merely an "outward disguise," that they show simply how the economy *appears* to work, whereas through his value analysis, "the actual state of things is here revealed for the first time."

The fact that profits are paid to capitalists in proportion to the amount they invest, and that landlords are paid rent in proportion to the amount of land they provide, makes it *appear* as though two inanimate things, money and land, had actually produced the surplus value received by owners.

> It is an enchanted, perverted, topsy-turvy world, in which Mister Capital and Mistress Land carry on their goblin tricks as social characters and at the same time as mere things. . . . these are the forms of the illusion . . . *proclaiming the natural necessity and eternal justification of* [the ruling classes'] *sources of revenue.*[9]

[8] Karl Marx, *Capital,* vol. III (Chicago: Charles H. Kerr Publishing Company, 1909), page 233.

[9] Marx, *Capital,* vol. III, pages 966–67.

Marx said that value analysis taught us that labor time, not inanimate land and equipment, produces surplus value. Land and equipment do, of course, play a role in the production of goods, but labor is the only factor that human society contributes to the production of surplus value. And it is surplus value that constitutes the resources that enable both the economy's production and the capitalists' wealth to grow.

While Marx's value analysis does *not* claim to give us any new model of price determination, it does claim to give us a new insight into the source of surplus value by stripping away "the forms of illusion" created by the manner in which prices redistribute labor's products.

ALIENATION

From the time Marx began to write about economics in 1843 until about 1858 (roughly a decade before *Capital* was published), he devoted a significant portion of his writing to a phenomenon he called alienation. Yet hardly a word on the subject was published during his lifetime. Thus we do not know whether Marx really considered it important and would have included it in the portions of *Capital* published after his death, or whether he purposely did not publish it because he changed his mind and decided it was a false direction.

It was not until the middle of the twentieth century, when the Soviet Union began to publish some of Marx's accumulated notes and manuscripts, that the materials on alienation became available to the public. But once the idea was made public, it attracted a great deal of attention among Marxist scholars, particularly among those who specialized in political science and sociology. And while the concept of alienation seems to hold less appeal for economists, it is useful for helping us reconstruct some of what Marx was after.

Actually, alienation seems to refer to at least two different concepts. The first, which has most intrigued noneconomists, describes the psychological state of workers in relation to the capitalist production process. According to Marx, capitalism, by replacing artisanship with mass-production techniques, by putting workers on assembly lines where their functions are reduced to repetitive detail rather than concern with the quality of the whole product, and by treating workers (or, rather, their labor power) as mere commodities that are bought and sold as part of the profit-making process, causes workers to lose any sense of satisfaction from their labor and any means for identifying with their output. In short, modern workers are *alienated* from the production process in ways that the medieval artisans were not.

> What . . . constitutes the alienation of labour? First . . . that in his work . . . he does not . . . feel content but unhappy, does not develop freely his physical and mental energy but mortifies his body and ruins his mind. . . . Lastly, the external [alien] character of labour for the worker appears in the fact that it is not his own, but someone else's . . . that in it he belongs, not to himself, but to another.[10]

The second concept of alienation, which has more relevance to our present discussion, describes the connection between the accumulation process and the produced means of production that are made available to the economy. According to Marx, such items as plant and equipment are as much the product of labor as are any other commodities. However, in industrial economies, the worker's job depends on the availability of factories and machinery. Thus, after he has labored to make these particular products, the worker must confront them again, this time as domineering, alien objects that hold the power to determine whether he will remain employed. The very items that the

[10]Marx, *Economic and Philosophical Manuscripts of 1844, Collected Works,* vol. 3, pages 273–74.

worker has made with his own hands become the means by which capitalists can control him.

Aside from the domination to which the worker is subjected by the alienated products of his own making, this form of alienation is significant because it has an inherent tendency to escalate. Accumulation, by its very nature, builds up the economy's stock of productive equipment. As this happens, workers become increasingly dependent on more and more equipment in order to remain employed. And as time passes, their dependence on the alienated products of their labor continues to grow proportionally with the economy.

In the early stages of capitalism, workers could easily find employment on their own in industries that utilized relatively few machines. But as capitalism matures, workers more and more are forced into automated factories with all the frustration and alienation that attends such work places. Here we have the seeds of the class antagonism that Marx predicted would contribute to the demise of capitalism. In other words, here we have a law of motion of capitalism.

If this interpretation of alienation is valid (and it is not entirely clear from Marx's unfinished writing on the subject), it is a problem that lies at the heart of the dynamics of capitalism as Marx saw them. The very mechanism that produces surplus value and capital accumulation must aggravate alienation, and through it, we are told, capitalism does indeed sow the seeds of its own destruction.

Thus, Marx felt that a revolution spurred by worker alienation might be one way that capitalism would die. Another would be through a spasmodic business cycle.

MARXIAN CRISIS THEORY

Marx wrote at a time when most leading economists believed that general overproduction is impossible because "supply creates its own demand." This view, dating back to Adam Smith, is now called *Say's Law* after the French economist J. B. Say, who publicized it early in the nineteenth century. The argument states that anybody who earns income from the production process must be doing so in order either to spend it on consumer goods or to invest it in a way that earns more money. In the latter case, there is an implicit or explicit demand for more production goods, such as plant and equipment. Thus, in either case, every penny earned in the production process is quickly spent so that the effective demand for any economy's output is always exactly equal to the amount it costs to produce the output. In this way, argued the classical predecessors of Marx, there can never be a general insufficiency of the demand needed to sell an economy's output. True, there can be overproduction of individual items. Industry may miscalculate and produce too many yo-yos at a time when the public would rather buy Frisbees, but such errors are quickly corrected when toy manufacturers notice unsold yo-yo inventories beginning to pile up.

However, not every economist in the early nineteenth century believed that general overproduction was impossible. There were some, including the conservative Thomas Robert Malthus and a number of early socialists, who believed that the threat of depression was very real; and the harsh facts of economic reality certainly supported them. Unfortunately, though, their analysis was confused and unsystematic, and no match for the powerful logic of the followers of Adam Smith and J. B. Say. Among those who argued that economic crises were a real danger, a recurrent theme was that the economy tends not to give consumers enough purchasing power to buy all the available output. This idea provided the basis for the underconsumption models set forth by writers at both ends of the political spectrum. Malthus implied that the remedy is to provide more money to the idle rich. He felt that if those who demand goods without producing them had more money to spend, they would increase the demand without adding to the supply. The early socialists, on the other hand, argued that the proper way to deal with the problem is to pay more money to workers because their poverty forces them to spend everything they earn, whereas large portions of capitalists' profits, because they are not spent on consumption, reduce the effective demand.

Marx rejected both arguments—those that claimed overproduction is impossible as well as those that have been called the "naïve underconsumption" theories. Marx's grounds for rejection were remarkably compatible with modern ideas on the subject. He believed that general overproduction would result if those who sell inputs and receive income from the production of products decided not to use their money *at once* to demand goods or if they decided to hold on to the money itself instead of spending it. But even the capitalists' savings is *not* a deduction from demand if they use their money to buy new factories and machines instead of consumer goods.

Having established that business fluctuations can be a real problem for a profit economy and that the reasons are more complex than those offered by the naïve underconsumption model, Marx went on to propose a variety of crisis analyses of his own. Implicit in his argument was the view that there is not necessarily only one model to explain all business fluctuations. Accordingly, his analyses varied widely.

For example, one of his models emphasized the delay between the time the building of a large project, such as a railroad, produces income for construction workers (thus creating demand) and the later time when the products of such projects begin to be available (thus creating supply). At this later time, the former construction workers of a completed railroad no longer are earning the income with which to demand the goods the railroad carries.

Another of Marx's cycle models stressed the way accumulation leads to competition for workers, which in turn bids up wages and cuts into profits, causing trouble for business firms. A third model indicated that problems can arise when the timing of outputs by industries that make producers' goods does not match the needs of the industries that make consumers' goods. And still another model was a more plausible version of the underconsumption analysis.

In fact, the Marxian models covered such a wide range of cyclical relationships that there is hardly a modern theory of the business cycle that cannot find some antecedent in Marx's writings. And for this reason Marx must be considered the father of all modern cycle analyses. Yet the Marxian models were never fully worked out. Marx discussed them only briefly and unsystematically, and none ever went beyond a mere outline or hint of the full mechanism underlying the analysis.

WILL THE BUSINESS CYCLE KILL CAPITALISM?

One issue in particular that has given rise to considerable speculation is Marx's views about the future of business cycles. Did he see them as growing increasingly more severe? Did he predict that capitalism would inevitably collapse in one gigantic crisis? The answers are unclear because Marx never thoroughly discussed the specific ways in which capitalism would collapse. To be sure, there are several colorful passages that paint a dramatic picture of its ruin, but these can hardly have been meant to constitute serious analysis. Here is an example from the first volume of *Capital*:

> Along with the constantly diminishing number of magnates of capital, who usurp and monopolise all advantages . . . grows the mass of misery, oppression, slavery, degradation, exploitation; but with

this too grows the revolt of the working class, a class always increasing in numbers, and disciplined, united, organized by the very mechanism of capitalist production itself. The monopoly of capital becomes a fetter upon the mode of production, which has sprung up and flourished along with, and under it. Centralisation of means of the production and socialisation of labour at last reach a point where they become incompatible with their capitalist integument. This integument is burst asunder. The knell of capitalist private property sounds. The expropriators are expropriated.[11]

In the *Communist Manifesto* (1848) Marx and Engels mention "the commercial crises that by their periodic return put on its trial, each time more threateningly, the existence of the entire bourgeois society." And they do say that the process of recovery paves "the way for more extensive and destructive crises."

However, the *Communist Manifesto* appeared two decades before *Capital,* Marx's mature work, and we are not told how he felt about the subject at this later time. There is, though, one place in which a much older Engels specifically states that crises of increasing severity are *not* inevitable under capitalism. In 1884, writing about trends he had recently been observing (this was one year after the death of Marx and nearly 40 years after the *Communist Manifesto*), Engels said, "The period of general prosperity preceding the crisis still fails to appear. If it should fail altogether, then chronic stagnation would necessarily become the normal condition of modern industry, with only insignificant fluctuations."[12] In short, Marx was convinced that capitalism must fall. But just how that fall will occur, from what causes and in what stages, is never made clear in his writings.

[11]Marx, *Capital*, vol. I, pages 836–37.
[12]Preface to the First German Edition (1884) of *Poverty of the Philosophy* (London: Martin Lawrence, Ltd., N.D.), page 18fn.

BANKRUPTCY AND THE VIGOR OF CAPITALIST SOCIETY

According to Marx, it is no accident that the capitalist mechanism runs into periodic problems—crises that turn the growth process into a disconnected series of "fits and starts." But it is precisely such crises that are in part responsible for the growth of capitalist economies. The accumulation of capital tends to push wages up temporarily and to reduce profits, meaning that investment can no longer earn the same rate of return as before. In this sense capital becomes "overvalued"—its new rate of return does not justify the prices of the factories and equipment necessary to earn it. Financial difficulties are encountered by firms faced with debts they had acquired on the basis of the earnings they had originally expected.

The principal means used by the economy to rectify this situation is "a slaughtering of the *values* of capitals." This reduction in the value of firms and their assets occurs through bankruptcy or through less drastic forms of revaluation, such as a fall in the price of stocks. This not only makes possible the survival of firms that would otherwise have failed, but actually serves as a stimulus to future economic growth.

Marx pointed out that the process of bankruptcy need not and often does not lead to the cessation of activities by the affected firm. When capitalists are ruined, their capital can "pass into the hands of their conquerors." This observation leads directly toward the modern analysis of bankruptcy, which views it not as something that destroys productive capacity and economic activity but as a means by which the disabled enterprise is transferred into other, more competent hands. In this view, bankruptcy is simply a resale of overpriced or badly run facilities to those whom the market mechanism shows to be most capable of running them. The new owners then readjust prices to a competitively viable level, and the business reenters the economy with new vigor. When unhampered, the institution of bankruptcy serves several useful functions.

1. It stands as a warning to managers of business firms to keep on their toes and to operate as efficiently as possible.
2. It causes overpriced assets to decrease in price. An office building or factory that is losing money on its original investment cost may well be able to function profitably if the cost of the investment is decreased.
3. It takes productive facilities away from business people whose records show them to be inefficient and ineffective, and makes them available to those whom the competitive struggle for survival selects as their superiors.
4. It may prevent unemployment by permitting a dying firm to be rescued under new management.

In short, in the spirit, if not the letter, of the Marxian analysis one can conclude that government attempts to prevent bankruptcies—as in the cases of Lockheed or Rolls Royce described earlier in the chapter—can only undermine the vigor of the market mechanism and increase its vulnerability to rival economic systems.

CONCLUSION

The writings of Marx are stamped by brilliance and originality. Parts of the writings are long-winded and dull (in fact Marx told Engels he did this deliberately to make his work "weightier"), but they contain many sparkling and powerful passages. Many of Marx's ideas are still highly illuminating, even to non-Marxists, and in areas such as business-cycle analysis, almost all modern thinking stems from his, either directly or indirectly. In short, he contributed enormously to current thought within the discipline of economics as well as in politics throughout the world.

SUMMARY

1. Marx agreed that capitalism had been extraordinarily productive and had contributed to general economic advancement, but he also believed that it had outlived its usefulness and had become a drag upon further progress.
2. Marx deliberately offered almost no guidance for the running of socialist economies.
3. Historical materialism, Marx's basic philosophy, asserts that one can only understand a society from a study of its history, and that this history is determined primarily by economic conditions.
4. To Marx, the central task of the capitalist is accumulation of profits, which are then invested in ways that expand the output of the economy.
5. The purpose of Marx's value theory was to show that labor is the source of the profits accumulated by capitalists.
6. Marx denied that the objective of his value analysis was to show that capitalism robs the workers and that they deserve all the economy's output. Rather, he wished to show how the process of accumulation increases the unhappiness of workers and undermines the capitalist economy.
7. Marx is considered the father of modern analyses of business cycles because most of today's theories have their roots in Marx's writings.

**CONCEPTS
FOR
REVIEW**

Historical materialism
Accumulation
Surplus value
Underconsumption theory

Value of labor power
Alienation
Marxian "commodity"
Marxian value versus market price

**QUESTIONS
FOR
DISCUSSION**

1. Given how little Marx said about the actual running of a socialist (or communist) society, do you think that the economies of the Soviet Union and China are consistent or inconsistent with Marx's views, or that the two have nothing to do with each other or with Marx's intentions?

2. Do you think that, if Marxian theory is valid, labor deserves 100 percent of the national output? Why do you think Marx and Engels disagreed with this conclusion?

3. In the Middle Ages, according to Marx, the nobility were the exploiters while the serfs were the exploited. What did the medieval nobles "do for a living," and how, in Marx's view, does the answer to this question explain why GNP did not grow during the Middle Ages as it does under capitalism?

4. Can you make some guesses about what Marx might have thought would most likely cause the end of capitalism?

5. Some economists have suggested that many human decisions, including marriage, family size, and even suicide, can be explained to a considerable extent by the narrow economic self-interest of the decision maker. Would Marx have agreed?

40

Comparative Economic Systems:
What Are the Choices?

Every generation regards as natural the institutions
to which it is accustomed.

Reprinted courtesy of Barnes & Noble Books (Div.
Harper & Row Publishers, Inc.), page 91 of *Equality*
by R. H. Tawney © George Allen & Unwin, Ltd., 1964.

These words of the British historian and economist R. H. Tawney are worth heeding as we near the end of this book, which has been geared very closely to the particular circumstances of the contemporary United States. Our current economic institutions are not eternal, because no economic system is static. Instead, economic systems are constantly growing, adapting, and evolving. Even in the relatively stable environment of the United States, the economy of the 1970s was far different from the economy of the 1870s; and by the year 2070 our economy will have changed even more.

Tawney's remark can be applied across geographical space as well as through time. The world today has a great diversity of economic systems, and this diversity seems likely to prevail in the future. There are, in fact, many ways to organize an economy other than the mixed capitalistic structure that we have focused on in this book. And no one form of economic organization is likely to be the right one for all countries for all time.

In this chapter we examine some of these *alternative economic systems* and consider the question of how a society might choose an appropriate form of economic organization. The first parts of the chapter sketch out the elements of the two major choices that must be made by every society: Should economic activity be organized through *markets,* or by government *plan*? and Should industry be *privately* or *publicly* owned? As we shall see, there are arguments on both sides of each question; and, as you might expect, different countries in different times have made different choices. In the last sections of the chapter, we therefore turn to some of the actual choices that have been made in the contemporary world. We examine, in turn, the economic structures of Sweden, France, Yugoslavia, the Soviet Union, and the People's Republic of China, looking in each case for similarities and differences among countries, and for areas in which one system has either succeeded admirably or failed miserably. Does the United States have much to learn from the experiences of these other countries? Read this chapter, and then decide.

THE CHALLENGE TO MODERN CAPITALISM

The question of choosing among economic systems is far from academic. Indeed, it has been of vital concern to people throughout the world for centuries; and it remains a live issue today.

For example, about 20 years ago former Russian leader Nikita Khrushchev made his famous promise to Americans that "we will bury you." This was not a military threat, nor a prediction that capitalism would perish under the weight of its own garbage; rather it was a pledge that the great productivity and growth of the Soviet economy would enable it to surpass the productive capacity of the U.S. economy. So far, the Russians have not redeemed this pledge. (See the boxed insert on pages 788–789.) But the economic competition between these two giant nations has captured the attention of the world for decades.

Many of the observers of this competition have a keen interest in its outcome. Nations of the Third World have watched attentively, wondering which economic system might be best for them. During the years since Khrushchev's declaration, a number of these nations seem to have made a choice. But many others are still teetering on the brink of indecision. Should they try to emulate the U.S. system of free markets, as, to a degree, Taiwan and Brazil have done? Should they follow the route of "democratic socialism" that is favored by many Western European nations, a route approximately traveled by Israel and India? Should they enter the Soviet sphere, and opt for a communist system with rigid state planning, as North Korea and Vietnam seem to have done? Or, finally, should they choose a more revolutionary brand of communism, following the model of Cuba and the People's Republic of China?

The choices are many. And they are of the utmost importance because a nation's economic structure has a profound influence not only over its material well-being, but also over its political system, the individual rights of its citizens, its relations with other countries, and so on.

And the Third World is not the only place where the contest among alternative economic systems is going on. At this writing, several countries in Western Europe—including France, Spain, and especially Italy—are flirting with communism in a serious way, making it a distinct possibility that Europe might see its first freely elected communist government sometime during the 1980s. Most observers agree that the miserable failure of the capitalist world to perform satisfactorily during the 1970s gave Eurocommunism, as it is called, much of its momentum. Conversely, several nations on the other side of the Iron Curtain are flirting with capitalism. Yugoslavia and Hungary, in particular, rely very heavily on markets and the price system to guide their "communist" economies.

Even in the United States, where modern, mixed capitalism reigns supreme, and where only a few fanatics believe that capitalism should be abandoned in favor of the Russian model, there has been a vocal debate in recent years over the question of national economic planning.

Naturally, noneconomic factors play major roles in any debate over the future of a nation's economic system. Internal political considerations, for example, are probably far more important than economic analysis. Yet, to a considerable extent, the proof of the pudding will be in the eating. Demonstrated success of either free markets or state planning in solving economic problems probably will do more to sway the undecided nations than all the ideological incantations in the world.

ECONOMIC SYSTEMS: TWO IMPORTANT DISTINCTIONS

Economic systems can be distinguished along many lines, but two seem most important.

The first is, *How is economic activity coordinated—by the market or by the plan*? The question does not, of course, demand an "either, or" answer. Rather the choice extends over an entire range, running from laissez faire to rigid central planning, with many, many gradations in between. Society must decide to what extent it wants decisions made by individual businesses and consumers, each acting in their own self-interest, to determine its economic destiny, and to what extent it wants to persuade these businesses and consumers to act more "in the national interest." It is worth noting that most types of planning involve some degree of *coercion,* a term that is not necessarily pejorative. All societies, for example,

coerce people into not stealing from their neighbors.

The second crucial distinction among economic systems concerns the question, *Who owns the means of production*; specifically, are they privately owned by individuals or publicly owned by the state?

DEFINITION
Capitalism refers to a method of economic organization in which private individuals own the means of production, either directly or indirectly through corporations.

Socialism refers to a method of economic organization in which the state owns the means of production.

Again, there is a wide range of choice and, to our knowledge, there are no examples of nations at either the capitalist extreme where all property is privately owned or at the socialist extreme where no private property whatever is permitted. For example, in the U.S. economy, most industries are privately owned, but the owners face restrictions on what they can do with their capital. Owners of automobile companies must comply with environmental and safety regulations. Owners of communication and transportation companies, where these are privately owned, often have both their prices and the conditions of their services regulated by the government. And in communist Russia, where no one can own a factory, anyone who can afford it can own a car or hold a bank account. There is also a small "capitalist" sector in which, for example, peasant farmers can sell what they have grown on their small private plots of land.

There is a tendency to merge the two distinctions between economic systems and think of capitalist economies as those that have both a great deal of privately owned property *and* rely heavily on free markets. By the same token, socialist economies typically are thought of as heavily planned. However:

Will They Bury Us?

Nikita S. Khrushchev

In 1958, Soviet Premier Nikita Khrushchev made his boastful pledge about "burying" the United States economically. His optimistic mood was probably colored both by Russia's recent success in launching the first earth satellite that worked and by the outstanding performance of the Soviet economy that year: real growth of almost 11 percent over 1957. With the United States simultaneously slipping into a severe recession, the ratio of soviet GNP to American GNP jumped from 39 percent in 1957 to 44 percent in 1958 (see the accompanying chart).

No sensible statistician would extrapolate the performance of one year very far into the future. But Khrushchev was a flamboyant political leader, not a sensible statistician. By 1965, the ratio was still stalled at 44 percent and, perhaps by coincidence, Khrushchev had been ousted and was living the quiet life. As the chart shows, the Soviet/U.S. GNP ratio resumed its upward climb in the late 1960s, and by 1975 had reached 53 percent—owing in part to another serious recession in the United States.

It may be helpful to put these figures into historical perspective. According to one recent estimate, Russian and American GNPs were about equal on the eve of the Civil War (*our* Civil War). With Russia's population more than double ours, however, this put its per capita GNP at about 40 percent of the American level. Czarist Russia did not do well compared with capitalist America. Thus, by 1913 Russian GNP had dwindled to only 39 percent of American GNP. With the enormous human and economic losses of World War I, the Russian Revolution, and the ensuing civil war, Soviet GNP fell still further—to only about 27 percent of U.S. GNP at the start of the First Five-Year Plan (1928).

Then came the beginnings of rapid economic growth in the U.S.S.R. and the Great Depression in the United States. Soviet GNP climbed swiftly to 42 percent of the U.S. level at the start of World War II, only to fall back to 29 percent after the wartime devastation. From that point, it climbed rather steadily and was still rising when Khrushchev made his famous boast.

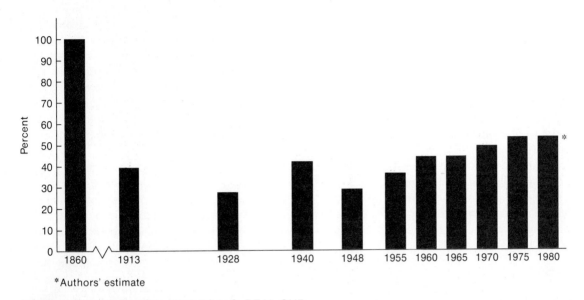

*Authors' estimate

RATIO OF RUSSIAN REAL GNP TO U.S. REAL GNP

Source: Herbert Block, "Soviet Economic Power Growth—Achievements under Handicaps," *Soviet Economy in a New Perspective, A Compendium of Papers Submitted to the Joint Economic Committee*, Congress of the United States, 94th Congress, 2nd Session, October 1976.

What of the future? It is anyone's guess. A prudent long-run estimate for the U.S. growth rate might be $3\frac{1}{2}$ percent a year, the current growth rate for potential GNP as estimated by the Council of Economic Advisers. As for the Soviet Union, a 5 to $5\frac{1}{2}$ percent a year growth rate might be a reasonable guess, but only a guess. If the United States grows at $3\frac{1}{2}$ percent a year while the Soviet Union grows at $5\frac{1}{2}$ percent a year, Russia will indeed "bury" us with a larger GNP in the year 2013. (Remember, though, that Russia's population is about 20 percent larger than ours.) This estimate, however, could easily err by several decades. For example, if we achieve 4 percent growth while the U.S.S.R. achieves only 5 percent, the "burial" will be delayed until the year 2046. And it is always possible that as the Soviet economy expands, its growth will decelerate, and that it will therefore never catch up.

Source for data: Herbert Block, "Soviet Economic Power Growth—Achievements under Handicaps," *The Soviet Economy in a New Perspective, A Compendium of Papers Submitted to the Joint Economic Committee*, 94th Congress, 2nd Session, October 1976, page 246.

While there is an undeniable association between the degree of socialism in a country and the degree to which it plans its economy, it would be a mistake to regard these two features as equivalent.

Modern Yugoslavia, for example, provides an important instance of a country in which the means of production are socially owned but economic activity is organized mainly by markets. Closer to home, there is a great deal of state ownership in the United Kingdom, which is most assuredly a market economy. On the other hand, Germany under Hitler provided an example of a capitalist economy with rigid central planning.

Our point is not that socialist economies are no more heavily planned than capitalist ones. *In practice,* they normally are. But, *in principle,* when thinking about a society's *choice* among economic systems, it is best to keep the two distinctions separate.

THE MARKET OR THE PLAN? SOME ISSUES

The choice between planning and relying on free markets requires an understanding of just what the market accomplishes and where its strengths and weaknesses lie. Since these are issues that have been treated at length in earlier chapters, our review can be rather concise here.

What goods to produce and how much of each. In a market economy, consumers, by registering their dollar votes, determine which goods and services shall be provided and in what quantities. Items that are not wanted, or that are overproduced, will suffer a fall in price, while items that are in short supply will rise in price. These price movements act as *signals* to profit-seeking firms, which then produce larger

amounts of the goods whose prices rise and less of the goods whose prices fall. This mechanism is what we call consumer sovereignty.

Of course, the doctrine of consumer sovereignty must be modified in several ways when we consider real-world (as opposed to ideal) market systems. For one thing, governments interfere with the price mechanism in many ways—taxing some goods and services while subsidizing others. These interferences certainly alter the bill of goods that the economy produces. For another, we have learned that in the presence of *externalities* the price system may send out false signals, leading to inappropriate levels of output for certain commodities.

How to produce each good. In a market economy, firms decide on the production technique, guided once again by the price system. Inputs that have high productivity or that are in short supply will be assigned high prices by the market. This will encourage producers to use them sparingly. Other inputs whose supply is more abundant or whose productivity is lower will be priced lower, which will encourage firms to use them.

Once again, the same two qualifications apply: Government taxes and subsidies alter relative prices, and externalities may make the price system malfunction. But on the whole, the market system has yet to meet its match as an engine of productive efficiency.

How income is distributed. The same price system that determines the levels of wages, interest rates, and profits also determines the distribution of income among individuals in a market economy. As we have stressed (especially in Chapter 29), there is no reason to expect the resulting income distribution to be "good" from an ethical point of view. And, in fact, the evidence shows that capitalist market economies produce a considerable degree of inequality. This is certainly one of capitalism's weak points, though there are many ways for the government to alter the distribution of income without destroying either free markets or private property (for example, through progressive income taxation or a negative income tax, both of which were discussed in Chapter 29).

Economic growth. The rate of economic growth depends fundamentally upon how much society decides to save and invest. In a free-market economy, these decisions are left to private firms and individuals who determine how much of their current income they will consume today and how much they will invest for the future. Once again, however, government policies can influence these choices by, for example, making investment more or less attractive through tax policy.

Business fluctuations. As we explained in Part Three, a market economy is subject to business fluctuations—periods of boom and bust, inflation and unemployment. This holds not only in capitalist market economies like the United States, but also in socialist market economies like Yugoslavia. Interestingly, the highly planned but mostly capitalist economy of France showed very little evidence of business cycle problems from 1958 until the Great Recession of the 1970s. Thus it seems that the business cycle, which Marx dubbed one of the fundamental flaws of *capitalism,* is really a problem for *market* economies, be they capitalist or socialist.

Let us now go over this list again, seeing how each question is resolved in a planned economy, and comparing this with a market economy.

What to produce and how much. Under central planning, the bill of goods that society will produce normally is not selected by consumer sovereignty. Instead, the planners decide. Depending on their particular beliefs and on the political structure of the country, their decisions may or may not be strongly influenced by consumers' desires.

Whether this is a strength or weakness of central planning depends upon your point of view. On the one hand, there is the danger that society's resources will be devoted to producing items that nobody wants. In Soviet Russia, for example, there are clearly fewer cars and more copies of Marx's *Capital* than consumers want to buy. On the other hand, consumer sovereignty can lead to some bizarre products, the kinds of things that social reformers find offensive: pet rocks, chrome plating on automobiles, fast-food chains, low-quality television programming, and so on. But, on balance, most adherents to traditional Western values will find more to like than to dislike under consumer sovereignty. After all, who knows what is good for consumers better than consumers themselves?

How to produce. Planned economies can allow plant managers to choose a production technique, or they can let central planners do it instead. Under Soviet-style planning, plant managers have rather little discretion, and this has led to such monumental inefficiencies as production curtailments due to lack of materials, poor quality, and high production costs. No incentive system has yet been designed that can match the profit motive of competitive firms for keeping costs down.

How income is distributed. The distribution of income is always planned to some extent. Even in basically market economies like ours, the government taxes different people at different rates and pays transfer payments to others, seeking thereby to mitigate the degree of income inequality that capitalism and free markets tend to generate. Planned economies do the same thing, only more so. For instance, they may try to tamper directly with the income distribution by having the planners, rather than the market, set relative wage rates. This, however, leads to troubles similar to those mentioned in the previous paragraph. Thus, even in the Soviet Union (though not in China) relative wages are established more or less by the laws of supply and demand.

Economic growth. In general, planned ecnomies have much better control over their growth rates than do unplanned ones, simply because the state can determine the volume of investment. They therefore can, if they choose to, engineer very high growth rates—an option they often have exercised. Whether such rapid growth is a good idea, however, is another question. In the Soviet Union and China, for example, this goal has been achieved at enormous cost—some of it paid for by sacrificing current consumption, some by sacrificing personal freedom, and some by bloodshed. Furthermore, rapid growth can be achieved without planning: Some of the fastest growth rates in the postwar world have been achieved by two market economies, Japan and West Germany.

Business fluctuations. We explained in Chapter 8 that business fluctuations are not much of a problem for highly planned economies. This is because total spending in such economies is conrolled tightly by the planners, and it is not permitted to get far out of line with the economy's capacity to produce. As we shall see later in this chapter, the U.S.S.R. has many serious economic problems, but the business cycle is not one of them.

THE MARKET OR THE PLAN?
THE SCOREBOARD

As we look back over this list, what do we find?

Concerning *what to produce,* an adherent to Western values probably would give a clear edge to the market, though conceding the need to curb some of its more flagrant abuses. But, of course, much of the world does not prize individualism as dearly as we in the West do.

As to *productive efficiency,* the market mechanism is clearly superior. But when we consider the *distribution of income,* we find that all societies have decided to plan; they differ only in degree.

High growth, it seems, can be achieved with or without planning, though planned systems have an easier time of it. Here an advanced nation will pause to question whether faster is always better, and often will conclude that it is not. But among the less developed countries, the goal of rapid development is typically of paramount importance. Many of these countries also lack the savings and the financial markets needed to channel funds into their most productive uses. If so, they may have little choice but to plan.

Finally, in managing *business fluctuations,* there is no question that planned economies can do much better.

The results on our scoreboard are clearly mixed. Do we, therefore, score the contest a tie? Certainly not. What we do conclude is that:

Different countries—with their different political systems, value judgments, traditions, and aspirations—will score the contest differently. Some will find the market more attractive, while others will opt for the plan. Most will divide their economies into two sectors—leaving some decisions to the market mechanism and others to conscious planning.

Thus, in the United States, for example, income distribution and macroeconomic activity are substantially "planned," while other decisions are left mainly to the market.

CAPITALISM OR SOCIALISM?

Although the choice between capitalism and socialism seems to excite more ideological fervor, it may be much less important than the choice between the market and the plan.

If it could design an appropriate incentive structure, a socialist market economy could do just as well as a capitalist market economy in terms of producing the right set of goods in the most efficient way. However, we have emphasized the word "if" to underscore the fact that designing such an incentive system may be quite difficult under socialism, while it is quite easy under capitalism. Lacking the profit motive, a socialist society must provide incentives, either material or otherwise, for its plant managers to behave in the optimal way. This has proved difficult enough. But a still deeper problem caused by the absence of the profit motive is the need to maintain inventiveness, innovation, and risk-taking in a system in which large accumulations of personal wealth are impossible. Socialist systems are noticeably low on "high rollers."

Income distribution under socialism is naturally more equal than under capitalism simply because the profits of industry do not go to a small group of stockholders but instead are dispersed among the workers or among the populace as a whole. However, if supply and demand rules the labor market, a socialist nation may have just as much inequality in the distribution of labor income as a capitalist economy does—and for the very same reasons: to attract workers into risky, or highly skilled, or difficult occupations. Indeed, students of the Soviet economy have concluded that labor incomes in the U.S.S.R. are distributed with roughly the same degree of inequality as those in the United States. Yugoslavia also seems to have a rather unequal income distribution, though for rather special reasons (which will be discussed in a later section).

The capitalist—socialist cleavage is much more important in regard to the issue of economic growth. To oversimplify, under capitalism it is the capitalists who determine the growth rate, while under socialism it is the state. Still, government incentives can prod capitalists to invest more; and instances of both fast and slow growth can be found under both systems.

Finally, the persistence of business fluctuations in a country depends much more on whether its economy is planned or unplanned than on whether its industries are publicly or privately owned.

SOCIALISM, PLANNING, AND FREEDOM

There is, however, a *noneconomic* criterion that is of the utmost importance in choosing between capitalism and socialism, or between the market and the plan: that is, *individual freedom*.

Planning must by necessity involve some degree of coercion; if it does not, then the plan may degenerate into wishful thinking. In the extreme case of a command economy (Soviet Russia, Nazi Germany), the abridgement of personal freedom is painfully obvious. Less rigid forms of planning involve commensurately smaller infringements of individual rights, infringements that most people find quite tolerable. Even within a basic framework of free markets, some activities may be banned—such as prostitution and selling liquor to minors. Other economic activities may be compelled by law—safety devices in automobiles and labeling requirements on foods and drugs are just two examples. Each of these can be considered a type of planning, and each limits the freedom of some people. Yet most of these restrictions command broad public support in the United States. The doctrines of consumer sovereignty and freedom of enterprise are not absolutes.

Taxation is a still more subtle form of coercion. Most people do not view taxes as seriously impairing their personal freedom because, even though tax laws may make them pay for the privilege, they remain free to choose the courses of action that suit them best. Indeed, this is one major reason why most economists favor taxes over quotas and outright prohibitions in many instances. It is true, however, that taxation can be a very potent tool for changing individual behavior. As Chief Justice John Marshall pointed out with characteristic perspicacity, "The power to tax involves the power to destroy."

Individual freedom is also involved in the choice between capitalism and socialism. After all, under socialism there are many more restrictions on what a person can do with his or her wealth than there are under capitalism. On the other hand, the poorest people in a capitalist society may find little solace in their "freedom" if they are homeless and hungry.

Once again, it would be a mistake to paint the issue in black and white. Under extremely rigid authoritarian planning, the restrictions on individual liberties are so severe that they are probably intolerable to most people with Western values. But more moderate and relaxed forms of planning—for example, the French system discussed later in this chapter—seem quite compatible with personal freedoms. Similarly, a doctrinaire brand of socialism that bans all private property (even the clothes on your back?) would entail a major loss of liberty; but a country with a large socialized sector can be basically free. The English, for example, do not feel any less free than do Americans. So:

The real question is not *whether* we want to allow elements of socialism or planning to abridge our personal freedoms, but by *how much*.

Just as your freedom to extend your arm is limited by the proximity of your neighbor's chin, the freedom to build a factory need not extend to building it in the midst of a residential neighborhood. Just as freedom of speech does not justify yelling "Fire!" in a crowded movie theater when there is no fire, freedom of enterprise does not imply the right to monopolize trade.

A CATALOG OF BLUEPRINTS

Different societies have struck the balance between the market and the plan and between socialism and capitalism in different places. What follows in the rest of this chapter are rather brief descriptions of some of the alternative economic systems actually in existence today.

The catalog is ordered from the least socialized economy to the most. Thus we start with Sweden, where public ownership of the means of production is only slightly more common than it is in the United States, and work our way toward the "revolutionary socialist" economy of the People's Republic of China, where capitalism has been virtually stamped out.

This sampling of countries brings home the point that socialism and planning are not iden-

TABLE 40–1

ECONOMIC SYSTEMS OF SELECTED COUNTRIES

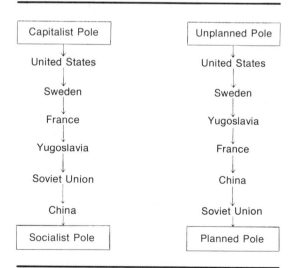

Capitalist Pole		Unplanned Pole
United States		United States
Sweden		Sweden
France		Yugoslavia
Yugoslavia		France
Soviet Union		China
China		Soviet Union
Socialist Pole		Planned Pole

Economic systems may be ranked according to the extent of socialism or the extent of central planning. As this table shows, the rankings do not always correspond. The United States, however, stands out as among the least socialistic and least planned economies in the world.

tical. Had we ordered the countries from the least highly planned to the most, Yugoslavia would have come before France (perhaps even before Sweden), and China would have come before Russia (see Table 40–1).

SWEDEN'S WELFARE STATE

The Swedish economy has been characterized as a happy marriage between capitalism and socialism. But in fact, at least as we have defined the terms, Sweden is almost as capitalistic as the United States: More than 90 percent of Swedish industry is privately owned. A more accurate statement is that:

Sweden has a capitalist market economy very much like our own, but with much more extensive government interference to ensure that the system serves two social goals of overriding importance: full employment and an equal distribution of income.

Full Employment Policy

Sweden has one of the longest and most active traditions of Keynesian macroeconomic management in the world—a tradition that even predates Keynes's *General Theory of Employment, Interest, and Money* (1936). In addition to using the standard tools of monetary and fiscal policy more frequently and more vigorously than we do in the United States, the Swedes have invented a few novel tools of their own. The most important of these is the investment reserve system.

This system, which has been in effect since the 1950s, is based on tax incentives that induce firms to do most of their investing at times when the government thinks more spending is desirable. Specifically, firms can exempt a large portion of their profits from taxation by depositing them in special accounts at the central bank. When private demand looks weak, the government "releases" these funds and offers substantial tax advantages to firms who then use them for investment. In this way, investment spending is "planned" by the government though conducted through free markets.

Judging by the results, the Swedish stabilization policy efforts seem to have borne fruit. Figure 40–1 compares the unemployment rates in Sweden and in the United States from 1956 to 1977. It is clear not only that the average rate of unemployment has been kept quite low (less than 2 percent), but also that the fluctuations have been quite restrained. However, as our discussion of the trade-off between inflation and unemployment suggests, the Swedes have paid the price for this good performance by making sacrifices on the inflation front (see Figure 40–2). Their inflation rate has been consistently higher than that of many other Western countries, and has been alarmingly high in the late 1970s.

Income Distribution Policy

Sweden, as is well known, has one of the world's most comprehensive welfare states, with social programs that extend, quite literally, from the cradle to the grave. There are financial allowances for children, free education at all levels, a national health service, extensive benefits for the unemployed, a state retirement pension far more generous than our own social security system, and many more social welfare programs. Naturally, the heavy burden of financing these programs leads to commensurately high taxes, and in recent years more and more Swedes have objected to the oppressiveness of the tax system. These critics argue, for example, that the steeply progressive Swedish income tax is destroying incentives to work.

Swedish social welfare programs seem to be quite successful. It is really difficult to find the telltale signs of poverty, such as slums and shabby clothing, in Sweden. And it is widely agreed that Sweden has one of the most equal income distributions anywhere—a feat it has managed to accomplish while also becoming one of the richest nations in the world. Yet, here too there are problems. Absenteeism has been rising, demands for greater worker control over industry are being heard, and class antagonisms have arisen in this "classless" society.

Sweden and the United States

In many ways, the Swedish and American economic systems seem quite similar, and the apparent success of Swedish economic policy has raised the question of whether their principles can be applied here. Yet some fundamental differences exist, differences that may make it

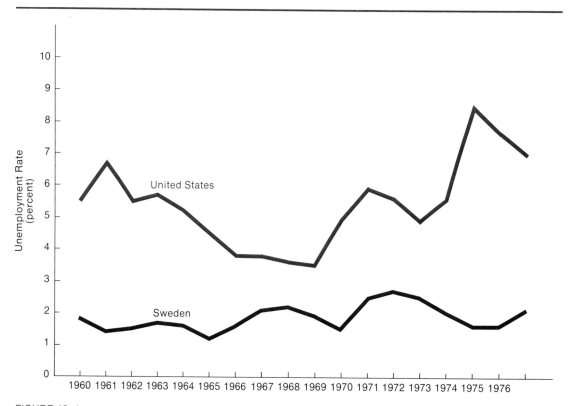

FIGURE 40–1

UNEMPLOYMENT IN SWEDEN AND THE UNITED STATES

As this figure indicates, Sweden's unemployment rate has been consistently lower than our own, and its fluctuations have also been less severe. Notice in particular the absence of high unemployment in Sweden during 1975 and 1976. While Swedish and American unemployment statistics are not exactly comparable, most experts agree that the superior Swedish performance is real, not a statistical illusion.

Source: Organization for Economic Cooperation and Development, U.S. Bureau of Labor Statistics, and *Statistical Abstract of Sweden*.

impossible to import Swedish economic policy to America. First, Sweden is a very small country whose labor unions and industries are both highly concentrated. This facilitates "consensus building" and also makes coordination easy to accomplish without formal planning. Second, Sweden is an ethnically homogeneous country. So the racial and ethnic antagonisms that underlie some of America's worst social problems are absent. Third, the Swedes care much more about full employment and much less about inflation than Americans do. They are proud of their strong record on employment and less concerned with their inability to maintain price stability. Americans might react differently to this same record.

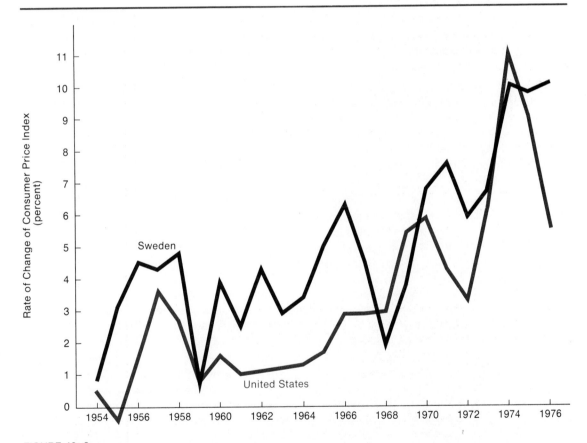

FIGURE 40–2

INFLATION IN SWEDEN AND THE UNITED STATES

As might be expected, Sweden has paid the price for lower unemployment by having more inflation than the United States. This figure shows that, except for 1974 and a few years during the Vietnam War, inflation in Sweden has been consistently higher than inflation in the United States.

Source: *Statistical Abstract of Sweden*, 1977.

FRANCE: PLANNING BY CONSENSUS

The basically capitalist economy of France has developed a unique method of organizing economic activity that one expert has called "the most elaborate and detailed planning system among the advanced Western nations."[1] The system is called *indicative planning*, a name meant to suggest planning by voluntary compliance and agreement rather than by government coercion.

Under the French system, a national economic plan is hammered out and agreed upon by representatives of government, industry, and labor, along with other technical experts. By passing both information and ideas back and forth among all the parties, it is hoped that a good degree of *coordination* of economic activity can be achieved without the need for coercion. For example, if it turned out that the production plan of the automobile industry required the use of more steel than the steel industry was expecting to sell, the participants in the plan could sit down and reconcile the differences. Was one forecast too optimistic or one too pessimistic? Would government actions (such as tariffs and import quotas) render these two forecasts consistent or inconsistent?

Through negotiations like these, French planners hope that individual industries can discover potential shortages and surpluses before they arise, and thereby adjust their own plans to conform with a broad overall plan for the nation. They further hope that *participation* in the plan will lead to *voluntary compliance*. Often this is so. But when it fails, the French government does not hesitate to use a wide variety of tools—including taxes, subsidies, and price controls—to persuade businesses to abide by the plan. It has been said that "French plan-

ning may be indicative, but it is not permissive or passive."[2]

The government exercises particularly strong control over both the volume and direction of investment spending: It directly controls about half of national investment and strongly influences the rest by regulating access to the credit market.

How well has the system performed? Apparently, very well indeed. The French record from 1958 until the Great Recession of the mid-1970s was one of full employment and rapid growth, unbroken by recessions (see Figure 40–3). Of course, this does not prove that indicative planning has been the key to France's success. West Germany, for example, grew even faster without planning. But it does suggest that something has gone right.

Indicative Planning for the United States?

Many countries have envied the French growth record, and some have tried to emulate it. Could indicative planning be practiced successfully in the United States? There are several reasons to think that it would not work as well here. First, the U.S. government controls a much smaller fraction of total investment (perhaps 20 percent) than does the French government, and the comprehensive controls that the French government exercises over the credit market run counter to American financial practice. A second difference is that the United States does not have the French tradition of a close marriage between government and industry. The "old boy" network is particularly strong in France, and many of the government officials and industrialists who work together on the plan are old friends from their days as students at France's elite *écoles*. State intervention in business has long been the norm in France; here it would be a major departure. Third, planning

[1]Gregory Grossman, *Economic Systems*, Second Edition (Englewood Cliffs, N.J.: Prentice-Hall, 1974), page 87.

[2]Egon Neuberger and William Duffy, *Comparative Economic Systems* (Boston: Allyn and Bacon, 1976), page 235.

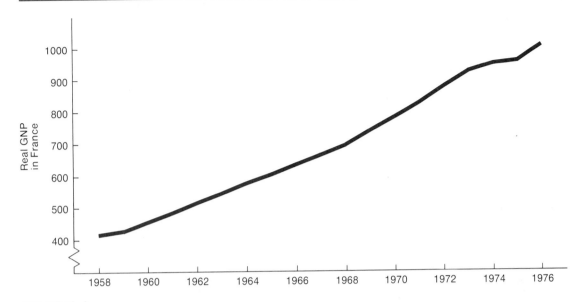

FIGURE 40–3

FRENCH ECONOMIC GROWTH SINCE 1958

This chart of real gross national product in France shows a remarkable absence of business fluctuations. Only the severe worldwide recession of 1974–1975 broke the upward march of real GNP in France.

Source: Organization for Economic Cooperation and Development.

along French lines would run afoul of America's antitrust laws. With firms sharing common forecasts and production plans, and with the government parceling out investment allotments to industries that then divide them among their constituent firms, collusion among firms is almost inevitable. This sort of cozy arrangement is widely accepted in France, where government tolerance of and even support for monopolies and cartels is traditional. But it runs counter to deeply held beliefs about American capitalism.

WORKERS' MANAGEMENT IN YUGOSLAVIA

Yugoslavia was forced by events to become the clearest illustration in the contemporary world of the fact that "socialism" need not be synonymous with "planning." A serious political rift between Tito and Stalin in the late 1940s led to the ouster of Yugoslavia from the Soviet economic sphere. Up to that point, the Yugoslav economy had been built on the Soviet model, and relied very heavily on trade with the U.S.S.R.

Searching for a way out of their economic plight, the Yugoslavs embarked on a great economic experiment by passing the *Law on Worker Management of Enterprises* in 1950. This law and subsequent legislation gave to the workers of each firm the authority to make most of the decisions that are normally reserved for management. The world has watched this experiment with great interest. Nowadays there is even talk that nations as far apart ideologically as Great Britain and China may want to emulate the Yugoslav system, and experiments with workers' management have been made in the United States and Canada.

While Yugoslav industry is almost wholly socialistic, enterprises are *not* run by state-appointed managers following a national plan. Instead, Yugoslav managers are chosen by the workers and are expected to seek after high profits.

Subject only to the usual sorts of regulations that are found even in the United States, each firm can decide for itself *what* to produce, *how much* to produce, and by *what technique* to produce. Though there are a number of price controls, taxes, and subsidies, most commodity prices are established in free markets, and consumer sovereignty calls the tune. Firms flourish if they produce what consumers want and produce it efficiently. After paying for its nonlabor inputs, each enterprise can decide how much of its net income to invest in expansion and how much to pay out in wages to its workers.

Under workers' management, Yugoslavia has achieved a record of very good growth in total output, but a number of problems have surfaced.

For one, like other market economies, Yugoslavia is subject to the ups and downs that we call the *business cycle*. This country has had periodic bouts with stagnation, and seems plagued with both chronically high inflation and unemployment. Lately, the persistent inflation has led to greater and greater reliance on price controls—a movement away from free markets that has been motivated not by ideology, but by desperation.

Income distribution has posed another problem. Since what is called *wages* in Yugoslavia include a share of what is called *profits* in a capitalist system, equal work in different firms is not rewarded equally. Instead, workers in the

most efficient enterprises earn a bonus, and the resulting wage disparities among different firms and different regions in the country have caused social frictions.

Related to this are the twin problems of inadequate labor mobility and sluggish employment growth. In a capitalist system, the most efficient firms would expand, hiring more workers, and thus driving down their marginal productivity. Under Yugoslavia's system of worker control, this may not happen because workers in a highly profitable firm may care more about maximizing *profits per worker* than about *total* profits. Since profits per worker may well *fall* if more labor is allowed to join the enterprise, new employment opportunities may not arise very often.

While there is virtually no central planning of the Soviet variety, we would not want to leave the impression that the Yugoslav economy is totally unmanaged. This is not the case. But what planning there is, is of the French *indicative* style. As in France, the government exercises its control, often quite rigorously, through the credit market. There it influences both the overall volume of credit for investment purposes and the allocation of these funds among regions and industries.

THE SOVIET ECONOMY: HISTORICAL BACKGROUND

In November 1917, a determined group of Bolsheviks led by V. I. Lenin overthrew the democratic provisional government that Kerensky had established after the fall of the Czar just eight months earlier, and Russia became the first country in the world to establish a communist government.[3] There is a great irony here in that this first triumph of communism contradicted one of the tenets of Marxian

[3] By the old calendar then in use, the month was October. Hence Russians refer to the Great October Socialist Revolution.

theory. Marx had prophesied that socialism would be the inevitable outgrowth of a decaying, advanced capitalist system. Instead, it came first to a land that had barely emerged from feudalism.

The Russian Revolution both surprised and dismayed the Western world, the more so since Lenin was an outspoken apostle of worldwide communist revolution. Thus, outside support for the anticommunists helped prolong a bloody civil war between "Red" and "White" Russians, a war that Lenin's army finally won. It was out of the dire circumstances of a wartime economy that the Soviet system of state planning as we know it today emerged.

When the war was won, a pragmatic Lenin reacted to the many apparent problems besetting detailed central planning by permitting the temporary reintroduction of substantial amounts of both capitalist ownership and market organization under his New Economic Policy (NEP). The NEP was a great success, especially among the peasants who were very hostile to the Communist regime, and it helped rebuild the badly battered Russian economy. After Lenin's death, there was both a fierce struggle for power within the Communist party and a vigorous policy debate over basic economic strategy. Joseph Stalin won both contests and ruthlessly set the Soviet Union on a course that it has followed, more or less, to this day.

Stalin's strategy called for single-minded application of Soviet resources to the goal of rapid *industrial* development with emphasis on *heavy* industry, particularly *armaments*.

To achieve such rapid growth and industrialization, it was necessary to limit consumption severely; so the Russian consumer was asked—or rather forced—to make sacrifices. To feed the urban laborers needed for industrial expansion, Russia's backward agricultural peasants were forced onto collective farms—at an extremely high human and economic cost. Furthermore, the starving peasants were forced

to sell their food at very low prices and to work for pitifully low wages.

The events of the early Stalinist years left their mark on Soviet economic life. To this day, the Russian economy is characterized by:

- A high degree of centralization, with basic economic goals set by planners, particularly by the leaders of the Communist party. Lower levels of the hierarchy are expected to follow orders, though the methods for guaranteeing compliance are far less Draconian than in Stalin's day.
- A stress on growth, industrialization, and military power, with corresponding downgrading of consumption. While the Soviet GNP has grown quite rapidly since 1928, the Russian consumer shared little of the fruits of this growth until quite recently.
- Continuing problems in the agricultural sector, where productivity is very low and the rural peasants remain quite poor.
- A planning system based on quantity targets and quotas, which makes very little use of the price system.

In surveying almost fifty years of Soviet economic development, one expert commented that "the surprising thing about the Soviet planning system is not how much it changed since its inception, but how little."[4]

CENTRAL PLANNING IN THE COMMAND ECONOMY

The structure of the Russian economic system is in many ways similar to the hierarchy of a giant corporation.

At the top may be a single strongman (like Stalin) or a ruling clique (like Brezhnev–Kosygin–Podgorny). This person or group plays

[4]Neuberger and Duffy, *Comparative Economic Systems,* page 168.

the role of chairman of the board, setting overall policy objectives, but has much more absolute authority than that of the chairman of any corporation.

Given the overall goals and priorities established by the top echelons of the Communist party, the State Planning Commission (*Gosplan*, in Russian) has responsibility for the preparation of the national economic plans (discussed below). Beneath the Gosplan are a number of ministries, which direct each industrial sector, and the various regional authorities. These bureaus oversee the day-to-day management of the individual industries or regions within their purview. Several other layers of the hierarchy intervene as we move down the organizational pyramid. Finally, we reach the level of the enterprise. Enterprise managers in the U.S.S.R. have far less authority than do their counterparts in the United States. They are expected to carry out directives handed down from above, fill their quotas, and send information back up the hierarchical ladder. They have more in common with bureaucrats than with innovative entrepreneurs.

Communications within the hierarchy are almost exclusively vertical. Orders flow down from top to bottom, while data flow up from bottom to top. Since the data requirements are so immense, and the number of layers within the bureaucracy so large, the problems of accurate data transmission and processing are monumental.[5] A detailed study of the operation of a large Soviet enterprise in the 1960s found that compliance with the plan required that 44 *million* characters of information be passed up to the next highest level in a single year, and that this was only about 12 to 15 percent of the total information gathered by the enterprise. This situation led one Soviet cyberneticist, in one of those wild extrapolations, to observe that preservation of the same planning apparatus

until 1980 would require the employment of every Russian adult.[6] As far as we know, the prophecy has not been fulfilled.

MARKETS AND PRICES IN SOVIET ECONOMIC LIFE

Although central planning is certainly dominant in Soviet economic life, the Russians do rely on the market mechanism for some purposes and in some spheres.

For instance, *given* the production target for each consumer good as set down in the plan, Soviet planners try to set prices to ration demand down to the available supply. The result is that consumer prices often are set far above production costs, with the difference made up by the so-called *turnover tax*, the main source of government revenue. But the planners often do not succeed in equating supply and demand, and any visitor to the Soviet Union is struck by the frequency with which long lines appear in front of many stores. Conversely, large stocks of unwanted goods sit waiting for customers at other establishments. Thus, while consumers do exercise free choice among the available goods, they are certainly not sovereign.

The price system is used even more extensively in the labor market. Given the plan for industrial output, Soviet planners try to set wages to attract workers to the right industries and the right regions. With some exceptions (for instance, peasants who must stay on collective farms), Soviet workers now have considerable freedom to work where they please—a far cry from the situation in Stalin's day. To provide material incentives for high productivity, many Soviet workers are paid *piece rates* rather than straight hourly wages. (Ironically, this is precisely the form of compensation that American

---

[5]Giant corporations have a similar problem of handling and transmitting data. However, not even the largest corporation approaches the size and scope of the Soviet economy.

[6]Neuberger and Duffy, *Comparative Economic Systems*, pages 179–80.

labor unions find most objectionable and inhumane.) Partly as a result of the piece-rate system, but also because of the strong desire to direct labor to the areas assigned top priority by the plan, wage differentials in the Soviet Union are quite large. According to most observers, they are at least as large as those in the United States, and they lead to considerable inequality in the distribution of labor income. Of course, income from property is negligible in the U.S.S.R., so the overall distribution of income is more equal than ours.

THE FIVE-YEAR AND ONE-YEAR PLANS

Russia's celebrated Five-Year Plans lay down the basic strategies and growth targets for Soviet economic development, but in many ways they are not as important as the less well known One-Year Plans.

Both of these documents are the responsibility of the Gosplan.

The Five-Year Plans set the nation's basic strategy for resource allocation: How much for investment? How much for consumption? How much for military procurement and for scientific research? They also provide guidelines for the distribution of these totals among the various industries (Will there be more cars or more refrigerators?), and they may include specific large construction projects, such as hydroelectric power plants. Much attention is paid, both in the West and in the U.S.S.R., to the numerical goals posted by these plans. Table 40–2 lists a few of the goals of the Tenth Five-Year Plan (1976–1980), comparing each to the stated goals and actual achievements of the Ninth Five-Year Plan (1971–1975).

But the Five-Year Plans are not detailed enough to serve as blueprints for action. This job is left to the One-Year Plans — enormous sets of documents covering almost every facet of Soviet economic life. In fact, One-Year Plans are so detailed and complex that any one of them is normally not completed until well into the year to which it applies. Sometimes these plans are never completed at all.

The planning procedure starts with a set of broad national goals (and some rather specific ones) handed down from the political leadership to the Gosplan. The planners then attempt to translate these goals — which are partly reflections of the current Five-Year Plan — into a set of specific directives for subordinate ministries and

TABLE 40–2

THE NINTH AND TENTH SOVIET FIVE-YEAR PLANS

ITEM	TENTH FIVE-YEAR PLAN (1976–1980) TARGET GROWTH (percent)	NINTH FIVE-YEAR PLAN (1971–1975) TARGET GROWTH (percent)	ACTUAL GROWTH (percent)
National income	24–28	38.6	28
Real per capita income	20–22	31	24
Industrial output	35–39	47	43
Agricultural output	14–17	21.7	13
Investment	24–26	41.6	41.3
Retail trade	27–29	40	36

Source: *The Soviet Economy in a New Perspective, A Compendium of Papers Submitted to the Joint Economic Committee*, 94th Congress, 2nd Session, October 1976, page 305.

agencies. As the plan is passed down from one level of the hierarchy to the next, the lower level is constantly supplying the higher level with both data and suggestions for changes—changes in specific tactics, not in basic goals (which are never questioned). One perennial problem of Soviet planning is that enterprises strive to obtain low production quotas that they will find easy to meet and surpass, because their success is measured by their ability to meet the quotas. To this end, they may deliberately mislead their superiors and understate their productive capacity.

The process of give-and-take up and down the hierarchy eventually leads to a complete One-Year Plan that, the planners hope, is *internally consistent*. Consistency, however, is not often achieved. To see why, let us briefly consider one of the major problems of Soviet planning—achieving what they call material balance. This phrase means nothing more than equating the supply and demand for each type of input—a relatively easy task for a market economy, but an impossibly difficult one for Soviet planners.

To take a simple example, suppose three industries (called A, B, and C) use ball bearings. The output targets for industries A, B, and C will then imply a need for corresponding inputs of ball bearings. This quantity (the demand for ball bearings) must, then, be equal to the output target of the ball-bearing industry (the supply of ball bearings). This seems simple enough. But the complications become apparent once it is realized that the ball-bearing industry needs inputs, too, and that some of these inputs may be the outputs of industries A, B, and C. So if, for example, the supply of ball bearings is to be increased, more steel and machinery may be required; and these additional outputs will require more ball bearings as inputs; and so on and so on.

To gain an appreciation of the complexity of the task facing Soviet planners, try your hand at the following simple problem. Suppose there are only three goods—ball bearings, steel, and automobiles—and that the national plan calls for individual consumers to get no ball bearings, $\frac{1}{2}$ unit of steel, and 1 unit of automobiles. How much must each of the three industries produce to achieve material balance?

To try to answer this, you must know the input requirements of each industry. Suppose the inputs required *per unit of output* of each industry are as follows:

OUTPUT	NECESSARY INPUTS
Ball bearings (one unit)	$\frac{1}{2}$ unit of steel *plus* $\frac{1}{4}$ unit of automobiles
Steel (one unit)	$\frac{1}{4}$ unit of ball bearings *plus* $\frac{1}{4}$ unit of steel *plus* $\frac{1}{4}$ unit of automobiles
Automobiles (one unit)	$\frac{1}{3}$ unit of ball bearings *plus* $\frac{1}{2}$ unit of steel *plus* $\frac{1}{6}$ unit of automobiles

Use trial and error to figure out the necessary production levels for each industry. It will not take long to convince yourself that the problem is quite difficult.[7]

The mathematical technique devised to cope with problems like this is called *input–output analysis*,[8] and the preceding little problem is easily solved using this method. But the Russian planners face a problem of this character with, literally, tens of thousands of commodities. Not even the most sophisticated high-speed computer is capable of carrying out the necessary calculations—even if all the data were available. In short, a perfectly correct

[7]The answer is: 2 units of ball bearings, 4 units of steel, and 3 units of automobiles.
[8]Input–output analysis was discussed in Chapter 30. pages 588–590.

solution to the problem of material balance is impossible.

What, then, do the Russians do? In practice, input—output analysis is of little use in formulating One-Year Plans. Trial and error is the only viable approach, and planners seek to avoid as many material imbalances as they can in the time allotted to them. They concentrate particularly on avoiding bottlenecks in those industries that are accorded highest priority by the political leadership. If necessary, Soviet planners will redirect scarce inputs to the high-priority sectors to make sure that production there is not interrupted. Thus Soviet spacecraft factories are unlikely to close down for lack of steel, but factories producing toasters are quite likely to.

PERFORMANCE AND PROBLEMS OF SOVIET PLANNING

Most observers rate the Soviet performance as quite good on growth but quite poor on economic efficiency.

Rigorous economic planning brought the backward Soviet economy of the 1920s into the modern age very quickly. Postwar economic growth averaged about 7 percent in the 1950s and somewhat more than 5 percent in the 1960s. For comparison, typical annual growth rates for the U.S. economy were $3\frac{1}{2}$ to 4 percent. If we extrapolate these trends, the Soviets—whose per capita GNP is now about half of ours—will indeed "bury us" in Khrushchev's sense.

But it is not clear that mechanical extrapolation is appropriate. For one thing, part of the rapid growth was achieved by borrowing advanced technology from the West; and it is not clear how much longer the Soviets can rely on this important source of growth. For another, the Soviet Union (like the United States) achieved part of its industrial growth through the migration of peasants to the cities. Given the poor performance of Soviet agriculture, it is not clear how much further the Russian government can push this migration and still be able to feed its citizens. So growth in the industrial labor force may not be as rapid as it was in earlier years. A third factor is the increasing outcry of the Soviet citizenry for more and better consumer goods. There is now some indication that the regime is willing to accommodate these demands, and this can only be done by cutting back on investment.

When we turn to questions of efficiency, most Western experts find little to envy in the Soviet record. The problems are many, often leading to ludicrous situations.

- We have already mentioned the tremendous *burden of information transmission*. The result is that planners are often misinformed and make correspondingly incorrect decisions. Compounding this problem, firms seeking easy quotas have an incentive to falsify information deliberately.

- The system of production targets based on physical quantities rather than on profits or sales often leads to *huge stockpiles of unwanted and inferior goods and equally huge waiting lines for other goods*. For example, since automobile factories generally have quotas stated in terms of cars, there is an almost legendary shortage of spare parts in the Soviet Union. Manufacturers simply do not want to produce things that do not help fulfill their quotas. Similarly, a manufacturer ordered to produce 10,000 pairs of shoes, but faced with a shortage of leather, may produce 10,000 pairs of children's shoes. Selling them is not his concern.

- Because government policy has generally led to shortages of most consumer goods, managers of enterprises producing these goods have been able to turn out *low-quality merchandise*, knowing that eager consumers will buy up almost anything. (See the boxed insert on pages 806–807.)

- Concern with quotas and targets also *stifles innovation*, despite rewards for plant managers who innovate. Innovation carries risks, and Russian managers worry about not fulfilling their plan. They also realize that a brilliant production performance this year will bring with it a much tougher quota next year.
- Worries about the future unavailability of materials have led some Soviet enterprises to maintain *inventories of crucial materials at levels that would be considered ludicrous in the United States*, and sometimes even to hide this fact from the authorities.

Widely publicized reforms in 1965, following suggestions made by the Soviet economist E.

The Visible Absence of the Invisible Hand

Since we live in such a consumer-oriented society, it is sometimes hard to imagine what everyday life is like in a society where the consumer is not king. No one disputes the fact that the consumer has not yet ascended to the throne in the Soviet Union. In the following excerpt from a 1976 article in *Time* magazine, we get a glimpse of the typical problems that plague the Russian consumer.

The workingman, and particularly the working woman (85% of all working-age women have jobs), spends an inordinate amount of time tracking down scarce consumer goods. The ubiquitous mesh shopping bag is familiarly called an *avoska,* "perhaps" bag, meaning, "Perhaps I'll find something to buy today, perhaps not." Although the capital is by far the best-supplied city in the Soviet Union, TIME Moscow Bureau Chief Marsh Clark reports that "soap, toothpaste, perfumes, detergents, toilet paper, hairpins and matches are either of inferior quality or not available at all. The soaps don't clean, the mint-flavored toothpaste is harsh and repugnant, and the perfumes smell like overripe raspberries." The shortages are so common that people join any queue they see, then ask what it is for. In Moscow recently, Clark spotted a crowd jostling about a man selling something at a table. As the eager buyers got nearer, they saw that the choice item on sale was an English-language textbook entitled *Animal Physiology.*

Liberman (and hence dubbed "Libermanism"), attempted to deal with some of these problems by introducing the profit motive into Soviet enterprise. With managerial bonuses based on *sales* or *profits,* it was hoped that some of the adverse incentives of the quantity-oriented planning system could be avoided. The reforms have scored some measure of success, but most observers feel that they were too limited to change the basic character of Soviet industry. For many enterprises, the quantity of output is still the most important indicator of success. Furthermore, the profit motive may not produce desirable results when market prices indicate neither production costs nor values to consumers.

Items imported from East bloc countries are nearly always made better than their Soviet counterparts and can precipitate near riots when placed on sale in department stores. Even foreknowledge of their availability is worth money. Clark tells about a Muscovite who recently visited the flea market in Odessa. Hearing a man calling, "I'll sell one sentence for a ruble," the intrigued visitor inquired what the sentence could be. "For a ruble, I'll give you some valuable information," replied the hawker, who got his ruble and then whispered: "Imported pantyhose will be sold at 10 A.M. tomorrow on the second floor of the Central Department Store."

Along with shortages, there are bizarre examples of superabundance. Because of poorly coordinated planning and lack of inventory control, goods may suddenly appear in disproportionate profusion. Tiny commissaries on collective farms that carry only the barest necessities may suddenly receive shipments of silk neckties or Italian vermouth. A decade ago there was a glut of condoms, which Russians casually used as bottle caps and garters; today, there is a rubber shortage, and prophylactics can scarcely be found in Moscow. Consumer demand for goods may also be met too enthusiastically or too late. State factories, for example, are producing millions of women's platform shoes and stretch boots. Three years ago, they were in great demand; now, few buyers can be found.

Letters and editorials in the Soviet press often complain about the inferior quality of Soviet-made merchandise. The worst are footwear and clothing. According to Moscow's *Literary Gazette,* the seal of quality, which indicates that an item conforms to international standards, was awarded in 1974 to only .6% of all Soviet footwear and less than 1% of clothes. *Krokodil* [a Soviet humor magazine] recently published a satirical sketch about a couple seeking to buy furniture. The sofas were all big, clumsy and "of a shade combining the colors of a country backroad in autumn and of a World War I dreadnought destroyer." The author recommended against buying these dreadnought sofas because "one mustn't scare the children with furniture."

Source: "Inside Russia: A Nation of Parallel Lives," *Time,* March 8, 1976, pages 7–8. Reprinted by permission from *Time, The Weekly Newsmagazine;* copyright Time Inc., 1976.

REVOLUTIONARY COMMUNISM: CHINA

The People's Republic of China is still a bit of a mystery to Western economists, although it has opened up considerably since President Nixon's visit in 1972. One problem is that most scholars find Chinese economic data even scarcer and less reliable than Russian data.

Immediately after the communist takeover in 1949, the Chinese economy was patterned on the Russian model and developed with Russian economic aid and technical expertise.

Despite the subsequent tremendous political rift between the two giants of the communist world, their economic structures remain quite similar today.

In particular, China's is very much a command economy, perhaps even more so than the Soviet economy. (Russians, for example, have more freedom of occupational choice.) Also, the Chinese emphasis on rapid economic growth, particularly industrial growth, is quite similar to Russia's. Finally China, like Russia, has accorded high priority to the goal of economic self-sufficiency. Until the mid-1970s, China's foreign trade was negligible.

But there are also important differences. Probably the most important of these derive from the conscious decision by Mao Tse-tung *not* to rely on material incentives to motivate the work force. Mao and the Chinese leadership looked with disdain at this "bourgeois" practice, and preferred to motivate Chinese workers by exhortation, patriotism, and, where necessary, force. Whereas Russian communism bent its socialist doctrine somewhat in order to accommodate human nature, Chinese communism for many years seemed determined to bend human nature to accommodate Maoist doctrine—to create "the new man in the new China."

A second, less important, difference is that Chinese planning is rather less centralized than Russian planning. Local and industrial authorities have more power and discretion than they do in the U.S.S.R. In part, some decentralization probably was dictated by China's immense size and economic backwardness in 1949. Without modern communications equipment (and perhaps even *with* it), there was no way for planners in Peking to hope to control economic activity in the outlying provinces.

Chinese economic growth under the communist regime has proceeded in fits and starts.

The immediate problem after the Maoist takeover was to lift China from the devastation of World World II, and to establish communist institutions and values in a vast and semiliterate country. With Soviet assistance, the plan was apparently quite successful.

China's next step, however, was the Great Leap Forward (1958–1960), which turned out to be a giant step backward. No one seems to know why Mao abandoned the apparently successful attempt to transplant Soviet economic planning to China, but everyone seems to agree that the results were disastrous. Why did the Great Leap Forward fail so miserably? First, the Great Leap's production goals were unrealistically ambitious from the start. Second, because the ideologically pure "Reds" were in Mao's favor while the technocratic "experts" were not, the means selected for carrying out the Great Leap were more romantic than rational. China's vast economic structure was supposed to be decentralized, though tightly controlled by the Communist party; massive applications of brute labor were supposed to make up for China's shortages of machinery and advanced technology; and material incentives were deemphasized. In retrospect, the Great Leap Forward seems to have achieved several things—most of them not very good for China. First, China's gross national product fell substantially (see Figure 40–4), particularly in the agricultural

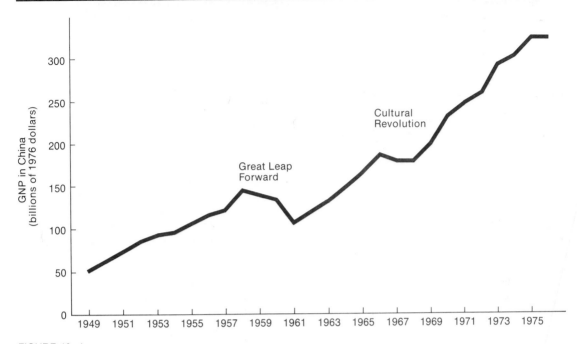

FIGURE 40–4

REAL GNP IN THE PEOPLE'S REPUBLIC OF CHINA

While Chinese economic statistics are notoriously inaccurate, one attempt to piece together a series on real GNP for China resulted in the data portrayed here. Other observers of China have reached rather different conclusions. But all agree that the Great Leap Forward and the Cultural Revolution stand out as major blemishes on the record of Chinese economic growth.

Source: Central Intelligence Agency.

sector. It took years to make up for the losses of 1958–1960. Second, the ideological excesses of the period accelerated the growing schism between Russia and China. Third, it persuaded the Chinese leadership to throw out the "Reds" and bring back the "experts," signaling a return to rational economic calculation.

In large measure, China's Five-Year Plan covering 1961 to 1965 moved this giant nation back toward the Soviet model, though some elements of decentralization from the Great Leap were retained. One departure both from Soviet practice and from China's first Five-Year Plan (1953–1957), however, was the greater emphasis on agricultural development—no

doubt a wise decision given China's resources. As a result, economic growth resumed.

Then, inexplicably, Mao changed China's course once again with the Great Proletarian Cultural Revolution (1966–1969). The "Reds" were in and the "experts" were out as never before. The infamous Red Guards (later assisted by the army) were sent out to purge rightist elements from Chinese society, organize revolutionary cadres, and spread the teachings of Chairman Mao. If anyone worried about economic productivity in this environment, it did not show. By the summer of 1967, both the Chinese economy and other elements of Chinese society were in utter disarray. Output fell again, but recovered much more quickly than it had from the Great Leap (see Figure 40—4).

The period from 1970 until Mao's death in 1976 was again one of consolidation and economic growth. The Chinese revolutionary fever receded and, once again, the "experts" were rehabilitated. There was a restoration of material incentives and of rational economic calculation—both of which had been considered reactionary during the Cultural Revolution. In general, there was less politics and ideology and more economic growth.

What will China do next? The power vacuum left by Mao seems to have been filled by a ruling clique, with no single strongman. No fundamental upheavals in Chinese economic life occurred during the 1970s, and the new leadership seems to want to follow—and even accelerate—the more moderate path set down in the last years of Chairman Mao's rule. Newspaper reports in 1977 and 1978 suggested that technicians who had been put into disgrace by the Cultural Revolution were being rehabilitated, material incentives were being reintroduced, and the Chinese leadership was even studying the Yugoslav system of workers' management as a possible way to improve the motivation of China's discontented work force. Furthermore, the opening of full diplomatic relations between the United States and China in 1979 seems likely to lead to much more extensive economic interactions with the West. But what all these developments portend for China's economic future is anybody's guess.

SUMMARY

1. Economic systems differ in the amount of planning they do and in the extent to which they permit private ownership of property. However, socialism (state ownership of the means of production) need not go hand in hand with central planning, and capitalism need not rely on free markets. The two choices are distinct, at least conceptually.
2. Free markets seem to do a good job of selecting the bill of goods and services to be produced and at choosing the most efficient techniques for producing these goods and services. Planned systems have difficulties with both these choices.
3. Market economies, however, do not guarantee an equitable distribution of income and are often plagued by business fluctuations. In these two areas, planning seems to have clear advantages.
4. A major problem for socialism is how to motivate management to achieve maximal efficiency and to maintain inventiveness in the absence of the profit motive.
5. Individual freedom is a noneconomic goal that is of major importance in the choice among economic systems. Any elements of planning or of socialism will infringe upon the personal freedoms of some individuals. Yet complete freedom does not exist anywhere, and certain limitations on individual freedom command wide popular support.
6. The Swedish economy is almost entirely capitalistic, and there is little planning. The chief departures from the economic structure of the United States are in the comprehensive ways in which the Swedish government intervenes to maintain full employment and in Sweden's extensive "welfare state."
7. Much more planning is done in France, which also has a rather larger socialist sector than does Sweden. But French planning differs from coercive Soviet-style planning in that it is "indicative," that is, it relies on consensus-building and on voluntary compliance.

Questions for Discussion

8. Yugoslavia has a unique type of economic system called workers' management in which the managers of a firm are actually employed by the workers, who make all major decisions for themselves. While it is almost entirely socialist, the Yugoslav economy relies mainly on free markets and does very little planning.

9. Since the days of Stalin, the Soviet Union has followed a rather rigid system of central planning in which heavy industry and armaments are emphasized and consumer needs are deemphasized.

10. Russia's planning system is very bureaucratic and hierarchical; it has encountered monumental difficulties in transmitting accurate information. Goals and methods are set forth in Five-Year Plans and in even more detailed One-Year Plans.

11. While Soviet consumers are free to spend their money on what they please, there is no consumer sovereignty. Instead, it is the planners, not the consumers, who decide what will be produced. The labor market, however, operates much like it does in America—using wage rates to equate supply and demand.

12. With central planning replacing the price system, even tasks that are rather simple for a market economy can become inordinately complex. The Soviet Union's difficulties in achieving material balance—that is, in equating supply and demand for the various inputs—illustrate this complexity.

13. The Chinese economic system has changed several times since the Communist takeover in 1949. After passing through several periods of intense revolutionary fervor and little economic progress, things seem to have normalized in China, where planning appears now to be similar to that in Russia, although somewhat less centralized. In addition, the Chinese traditionally have relied less on material incentives to motivate their workers than have the Russians.

CONCEPTS FOR REVIEW

Capitalism
Socialism
Planning
Free markets
Consumer sovereignty
Sweden's investment reserve system
Welfare state
Indicative planning
Workers' management
Soviet Five-Year and One-Year Plans
Material balance
Material incentives
Great Leap Forward
Great Proletarian Cultural Revolution

QUESTIONS FOR DISCUSSION

1. Explain why the choice between capitalism and socialism is not the same as the choice between markets and central planning. Cite an example of a socialist market economy and of a planned capitalist economy.

2. If you were the leader of a small, developing country, what are some of the factors that would weigh heavily in your choice of an economic system?

3. Which type of economic system generally has the most trouble achieving each of the following goals? In each case, explain why.
   a. An equal distribution of income
   b. Adequate incentives for industrial managers
   c. Eliminating business fluctuations
   d. Balancing supply and demand for inputs
4. What are some of the advantages and disadvantages of the system of workers' management of industry as it is practiced in Yugoslavia?
5. "Both the goals and the techniques of Soviet economic planning have changed dramatically since Stalin's day." Comment.
6. If you were a Russian plant manager, what are some of the things you might do to make your life easier and more successful? (Use your imagination. Russian plant managers do!)
7. At the beginning of the chapter, we posed the question, "Does America have much to learn from the experiences of these other countries?" Given what you now know about Sweden, France, Yugoslavia, the U.S.S.R., and the Peoples' Republic of China, what do you think?

41

Dissenting Opinions:
Conservative, Moderate, and Radical

The principles that have been expounded in this book represent the mainstream view of modern economics. While they command the assent of a very large majority of American economists, there are dissenters. And these dissenters are not all fanatics and polemicists. Many of them are serious thinkers who are disturbed in one way or another by some aspects either of the modern American economy or the state of economic science, or both.

The dissent comes both from the left and the right of the mainstream of economics. On the right are the *libertarians,* who, while they agree with the portrayal of the virtues of the capitalist market economy given in this book, would no doubt insist that we have vastly overstated its vices and that we have limited the realm of the market much too severely. To libertarians, the market rather than the state is the ultimate guarantor of freedom, and, consequently, they argue that the realm of the market should be expanded at the expense of the state. These are economic Jeffersonians who believe "that government is best that governs least."

They want the government to keep its hands off the market.

Toward the left, the celebrated liberal economist and author John Kenneth Galbraith has been arguing for more than 25 years that most of the economics profession has been using the wrong model of the economy and, as a predictable result, has been generating policy prescriptions that look more and more absurd. Still farther to the left, a new group of *radical economists,* claiming to be the intellectual heirs of Marx, has attracted increasing numbers of adherents since its beginnings in the late 1960s. These mostly younger economists claim that mainstream economists not only are asking all the wrong questions and seeking answers in all the wrong ways, but are little more than apologists for the interests of the capitalist ruling class.

The reader who has come this far will no doubt realize that the authors of this book generally ascribe to the mainstream view. But since that perspective has had a sufficiently long airing in this book, we believe it is useful now to take a brief look at the views of the dissenters. For one thing, history may yet prove that at least some of the dissenters have it right after all. In any event, it is likely that each of the critiques carries a valuable lesson for mainstream economic analysis. Indeed, as we shall see, parts of each dissenting view have already been integrated into the body of standard economic analysis.

THE LIBERTARIAN CREDO

Libertarianism is really a philosophy rather than a system of economic thought. Libertarians are people who prize individual freedom above all other social goals—way above them. They are willing to tolerate restrictions on individual freedom in only a very few cases; so few, in fact, that most observers find the more extreme variants of libertarian doctrine totally outlandish.

Would you, for example, permit unhappy 10-year-olds to run away from home *legally,* provided only that they could support themselves? Would you sell city streets and highways to private businesses to operate for a profit? Would you permit drug companies to sell anything they want, without labeling requirements (but with legal liability for any harm done by their products)? There are libertarians who would advocate all of these measures, and many, many more.[1]

On economic matters, libertarians are usually associated with the political right wing as staunch defenders of laissez faire. But in issues concerning civil rights, legislation of morality, and protection of citizens against government coercion, their views coincide more with the political left wing. There can be no question that they fervently support civil liberties. As one outspoken libertarian put it:

> The central idea of libertarianism is that people should be permitted to run their own lives as they wish. We totally reject the idea that people must be forcibly protected from themselves. A libertarian society would have no laws against drugs, gambling, pornography—and no compulsory seat belts in cars. We also reject the idea that people have an enforceable claim on others, for anything more than being left alone.[2]

THE LIBERTARIAN ECONOMICS OF MILTON FRIEDMAN

The hallmark of libertarian economics is a belief—we might call it a *devout* belief—in the ability of free markets not only to do the tasks

---

[1]See, for example, David Friedman, *The Machinery of Freedom* (New York: Harper & Row, 1973), where each of these is advocated. David Friedman is the son of Nobel laureate Milton Friedman, the most famous of all libertarian economists.

[2]David Friedman, *The Machinery of Freedom,* page xiii.

The Libertarian Economics of Milton Friedman

Milton Friedman

that Friedman has received the most notice, or notoriety. We might as well treat Friedman as the spokesman for all libertarian economists, for that is more or less what he is.

According to Friedman:

> The kind of economic organization that provides economic freedom directly, namely, competitive capitalism, also promotes political freedom because it separates economic power from political power and in this way enables the one to offset the other.
>
> Historical evidence speaks with one voice on the relation between political freedom and a free market. I know of no example in time or place of a society that has been marked by a large measure of political freedom, and that has not also used something comparable to a free market to organize the bulk of economic activity.[4]

We have spent many pages in this book detailing the appropriate role of government in a modern mixed capitalist society (see especially Chapters 30 and 31). Friedman would make this role much smaller, limiting it essentially to the following three tasks.

1. The government as umpire. Friedman is surely no anarchist, although some libertarians are. He recognizes that any society needs laws, and that legislation and enforcement of the law are proper roles for government in a free society. The government must, for example, enforce private contracts and adjudicate disputes.[5]

2. Control of natural monopoly. As we have noted in earlier chapters (see especially Chapters 25 and 26), some industries have such

normally assigned to them by economists (efficient production of goods, utilization of scarce resources, and so on), but to do *almost everything*.

There is no question that the leading apostle of libertarian economics is Milton Friedman. So unquestioned is his preeminence that the libertarian school is often referred to by economists as the "Chicago School," a name acquired during the many years that Friedman taught at the University of Chicago.[3] While he is a sufficiently brilliant technical economist to have earned the Nobel Prize, he is also an irrepressible public advocate of his libertarian views. In fact, it is in this latter role (often voiced through his columns in *Newsweek* magazine)

---

[3]He is now retired and a resident scholar at the Hoover Institution in Stanford, California. In fairness, we should note that the University of Chicago has had several other great libertarian economists on its faculty.

[4]Reprinted from *Capitalism and Freedom* by Milton Friedman by permission of the University of Chicago Press (Chicago: University of Chicago Press, 1962), page 9.

[5]More extreme libertarians will suggest that even police protection could be a private enterprise. See, for example, Robert Nozick, *Anarchy, State, and Utopia* (New York: Basic Books, 1974), in which the state *arises from* a private system of police protection.

strong economies of large-scale production that it is inevitable, for technical reasons, that only one firm can survive. Telephone service, for example, probably comes close to fitting this model. Some have suggested (though others have disputed the claim) that the postal service also is a good example. In such cases, *competi-* *tive* capitalism is simply impossible, so society has only three choices:

- Allow an unregulated monopoly to exist.
- Make the industry a public monopoly (as in the case of the U.S. Postal Service).
- Allow private monopoly to exist, but regulate it

An Application of Libertarian Economics: The Licensing of Doctors

Your family doctor has a license to practice medicine in your state. He probably displays it prominently on the wall of his office. You probably would be worried if he did not have one. Yet libertarians like Professor Friedman think that licensing of doctors is a bad idea. He explains why in this excerpt from his celebrated book *Capitalism and Freedom.* *

*For further discussion of this issue, see Discussion Question 3 at the end of this chapter (page 831).

Offhand, the question, "Ought we to let incompetent physicians practice?" seems to admit of only a negative answer. But I want to urge that second thought may give pause.

Licensure is the key to the control that the medical profession can exercise over the number of physicians. . . . The American Medical Association is perhaps the strongest trade union in the United States. The essence of the power of a trade union is its power to restrict the number who may engage in a particular occupation.

How can it do this? The essential control is at the stage of admission to medical school. The Council on Medical Education and Hospitals of the American Medical Association approves medical schools.

In almost every state in the United States, a person must be licensed to practice medicine, and to get the license, he must be a graduate of an approved school.

Control over admission to medical school and later licensure enables the profession to limit entry in two ways. The obvious one is simply by turning down many applicants. The less obvious, but probably far more important one, is by establishing standards for admission and licensure that make entry so difficult as to discourage young people from ever trying to get admission.

To avoid misunderstanding, let me emphasize that I am not saying that individual members of the medical profession . . . deliberately go out of their way to limit entry in order to raise their own incomes.

In ordinary times, the rationalization for restriction is that the members of the medical profession want to raise what they regard as the standards of "quality" of the profession. The defect in this rationalization is a common one; . . . the failure to distinguish between technical efficiency and economic efficiency.

carefully "in the public interest" (as we do, for example, with the telephone company).

To Friedman, "all three are bad, so we must choose among evils." While Friedman is willing to decide which of the three alternatives is least bad on a case-by-case basis, he is skeptical that the choice typically made in America (regulated monopoly) is the best one.

3. Externalities. For reasons we have elaborated at some length in this book (see especially Chapters 31 and 34), the government must intervene to promote or protect the public

It is easy to demonstrate that quality is only a rationalization and not the underlying reason for restriction. The power of the Council on Medical Education and Hospitals of the American Medical Association has been used to limit numbers in ways that cannot possibly have any connection whatsoever with quality. The simplest example is their recommendation to various states that citizenship be made a requirement for the practice of medicine. I find it inconceivable to see how this is relevant to medical performance.

It is clear that licensure has been at the core of the restriction of entry and that this involves a heavy social cost. . . . Does licensure have the good effects that it is said to have?

It is by no means clear that it does raise the standards of competence in the actual practice of the profession. . . . The rise of the professions of osteopathy and of chiropractic is not unrelated to the restriction of entry into medicine. . . . These alternatives may well be of lower quality than medical practice would have been without the restrictions on entry into medicine.

More generally, if the number of physicians is less than it otherwise would be, and if they are all fully occupied, as they generally are, this means that there is a smaller total of medical practice by trained physicians.

When these effects are taken into account, I am myself persuaded that licensure has reduced both the quantity and quality of medical practice. . . . I conclude that licensure should be eliminated as a requirement for the practice of medicine.

Suppose that anyone had been free to practice medicine without restriction except for legal and financial responsibility for any harm done to others through fraud and negligence. I conjecture that the whole development of medicine would have been different. . . . Instead of individual practice plus large . . . hospitals, . . . there might have developed medical partnerships or corporations.

These medical teams—department stores of medicine, if you will—would be intermediaries between the patients and the physician. Being long lived and immobile, they would have a great interest in establishing a reputation for reliability and quality. For the same reason, consumers would get to know their reputation.

I would not want to maintain that the medical teams would dominate the field. My aim is only to show that there are many alternatives to the present organization of practice.

Reprinted from *Capitalism and Freedom* by Milton Friedman by permission of the University of Chicago Press (Chicago: University of Chicago Press, 1962), pages 149–59.

welfare wherever there are beneficial or detrimental externalities. If it does not, the competitive price system will send out false signals and, as a result, will misallocate resources. Friedman accepts this analysis, adding only the caution that we should not apply it too freely. The externalities argument, he notes, often is just an excuse for allocating to the public sector something that could be done better by the private sector.

> Parks are an interesting example because they illustrate the difference between cases that can and cases that cannot be justified by neighborhood effects,[6] and because almost everyone at first sight regards the conduct of National Parks as obviously a valid function of government. In fact, however, neighborhood effects may justify a city park, they do not justify a national park, like Yellowstone. . . . What is the fundamental difference between the two? . . . If there is a park in the middle of the city, the houses on all sides get the benefit of the open space, and people who walk through it or by it also benefit. To maintain toll collectors at the gates or to impose annual charges per window overlooking the park would be very expensive and difficult. The entrances to a national park like Yellowstone, on the other hand, are few; most of the people who come stay for a considerable period of time and it is perfectly feasible to set up toll gates and collect admission charges. . . . If the public wants this kind of an activity enough to pay for it, private enterprises will have every incentive to provide such parks.[7]

Beyond this short list, Friedman believes, there is little else for government to do in a free society.

6["Neighborhood effects" is Friedman's term for what we have been calling "externalities."

7M. Friedman, *Capitalism and Freedom,* page 31.

LIBERTARIAN ECONOMICS AND PUBLIC POLICY

We began this discussion of libertarianism by giving some examples of rather extreme policy proposals made by some libertarians (though not necessarily by Milton Friedman). Yet some of Friedman's suggestions, which many people considered absurd when they were first made, have since either been incorporated into the mainstream of economic thought or have become the law of the land, or both.

For example, Friedman's was one of the first voices arguing that the system of fixed exchange rates among currencies was potentially dangerous and should be replaced by a system of floating rates, set not by governments but by supply and demand. We now have such a system. Friedman was also among the earliest advocates of the all-volunteer army. This piece of "insanity" became fact in 1973. His proposal for a negative income tax as a means to help poor people is now supported by almost all economists—be they of the left, the center, or the right—as well as by our last three presidents (though often in disguised form). The hostility toward the many government regulatory agencies that is now so much in vogue was present in Friedman's speeches and writings long before it became fashionable.

Yet there are many, many other issues about which the majority of economists and society as a whole continue to believe that Friedman is wrong. (See the boxed insert on pages 816–817.) His voice continues to be one of dissent, and one that is every bit as radical as those on the far left.

JOHN KENNETH GALBRAITH: THE ECONOMIST AS ICONOCLAST

Milton Friedman is barely over 5 feet tall; John Kenneth Galbraith is about 6½ feet tall. There the similarity ends. Friedman's reverence for the market is countered by Galbraith's irreverance about almost everything. Friedman's proposals for laissez faire are opposed by Galbraith's proposals to control almost everything.

John Kenneth Galbraith is a phenomenon in modern economics. This perpetual maverick, who has been blasting (often in ascerbic tones) what he calls "the conventional wisdom" for more than 25 years now, was a member of the Department of Economics at Harvard University—the bastion of the "establishment"—until his retirement in 1975. Without a doubt the most widely read economist in the world, he is perhaps more highly regarded outside the profession than within it. Yet his fellow economists elected him president of the prestigious American Economic Association in 1972. In addition to his achievements in economics, he has been an adviser to presidents, the U.S. ambassador to India, leader of the Americans for Democratic Action, novelist, and TV personality. As one prominent economist put it:

John Kenneth Galbraith

> Galbraith is, after all, something special. His books are not only widely read, but actually enjoyed. He is a public figure of some significance; he shares . . . the power to shake stock prices by simply uttering nonsense. He is known and attended to all over the world. He mingles with the Beautiful People; for all I know, he may actually be a Beautiful Person himself.[8]

Galbraith began to move away from his successful career as a mainstream economist— which included a stint as a price-controller during World War II—with the publication of his book *American Capitalism* in 1952. There he argued that economists, in focusing on the interplay between supply and demand in impersonal markets, ignored the pervasiveness of economic power, and thereby blinded themselves to some of the most important things that were going on in the economy. He added further wrinkles to his developing view of the modern capitalist economy in his best-selling book *The Affluent Society* (1958) in which he argued that modern corporations, far from being the servants of consumer sovereignty they are supposed to be, actually *create* demand for their products through advertising.

These and other strands of Galbraithean thought were brought together in *The New Industrial State* (1967), which remains perhaps the most comprehensive statement of his views on modern capitalist enterprise. The book was, and is, quite controversial.

THE GALBRAITHEAN CRITIQUE OF CONVENTIONAL ECONOMIC THEORY

Galbraith maintains that conventional economists have squirreled themselves away in a

---

[8]Robert M. Solow, "The New Industrial State or Son of Affluence," *The Public Interest*, no. 9 (Fall 1967), page 100. Copyright © 1967 by National Affairs, Inc.

dream world of their own creation, a world that has less and less to do with the real modern economy. In this hypothetical framework:

> The best society is the one that best serves the economic needs of the individual. Wants are original with the individual; the more of these that are supplied the greater the general good. Generally speaking, the wants to be supplied are effectively translated by the market to firms maximizing profits therein. If firms maximize profits they respond to the market and ultimately to the sovereign choices of the consumer.[9]

The crucial omission from this picture, in Galbraith's view, is *power*, especially the power of the giant corporation, but also the power of big labor, government bureaucracies, and so on. Rather than being controlled by the market, he believes, the modern corporation controls, or even supplants, the market.

Ignoring these "facts," Galbraith claims, has led economists into increasingly ridiculous policy positions. For example, the theory of monopoly (outlined in Chapters 23 and 31) stresses the *inefficiency* caused by its *restriction of output* in order to raise prices. Yet, as Galbraith sees the world, it is precisely the giant corporations that are *most efficient* and who produce *excessive amounts* of output. They do this by advertising campaigns that create the demand for the goods they are so adept at supplying. As another example, the focus on markets has led the vast majority of economists to oppose wage and price controls and therefore to accept the disagreeable trade-off between inflation and unemployment (see Chapter 15). Galbraith's is one of the few voices that refuses to accept this trade-off, putting his faith instead in a *permanent* system of wage–price controls.

What does the Galbraithean model of our economy look like? In the first place, Galbraith sees an economy with a great deal of *planning*.

> In place of the market system, we must now assume that for approximately half of all economic output, there is a power or planning system . . . I cannot think that the power of the modern corporation, the purposes for which it is used or the associated power of the modern union would seem implausible or even very novel were they not in conflict with the vested doctrine.[10]

This planning system is run by *technocrats*: managers, engineers, accountants, lawyers, cyberneticists, even economists! The kinds of work they do, and the kinds of hierarchical structures they create, are more or less similar in corporations, nonprofit institutions, government bureaus, and even (to a limited extent) labor unions. The nature of their work is also basically the same under capitalism as it is under socialism, in market economies, or in planned economies. It is dictated not by ideology, but by the overwhelming complexity of modern technology. "The enemy of the market is not ideology but the engineer."[11]

These technocrats, whom Galbraith calls the technostructure, manipulate consumer demand through advertising. They also manipulate costs to a considerable degree, or else render them quite predictable through long-term contracts with labor unions and suppliers of other inputs (which are also giant corporations). Thus, the market is basically supplanted. And since these industrial giants can finance their own investment through retained earnings, even the capital market is bypassed.

The firm must take every feasible step to see that what it decides to produce is

---

[9]J. K. Galbraith, "A Review of a Review," *The Public Interest,* Fall 1967, page 117.

[10]J. K. Galbraith, "Power and the Useful Economist," *American Economic Review,* March 1973, page 4.
[11]J. K. Galbraith, *The New Industrial State* (Boston: Houghton Mifflin, 1967, and London: André Deutsch, Ltd., 1967), page 33.

wanted by the consumer at a remunerative price. And it must see that the labor, materials, and equipment that it needs will be available at a cost consistent with the price it will receive. It must exercise control over what is sold. It must exercise control over what is supplied. It must replace the market with planning.[12]

The technocrats are guided by their own self-interest, not by the interests of their stockholders. In particular, they are certainly *not* interested in maximizing profits.

Instead, their primary interest is growth and expansion.

If the technostructure . . . maximizes profits, it maximizes them . . . for the owners. If it maximizes growth, it maximizes opportunity for . . . advancement, promotion and pecuniary return for itself. That people should so pursue their own interest is not implausible.[13]

Apart from rapid growth, the technostructure cares about perpetuating the hierarchy of which it is a part, achieving technological triumphs, and earning enough profits both to keep stockholders satisfied and to allow it to finance its investments without borrowing.

THE GALBRAITHEAN CRITIQUE OF THE AMERICAN ECONOMY

What are the results of this system for organizing economic activity? Not very good, according to Galbraith.

First, American society is deluged with a dazzling array of private consumption goods of dubious merit:

What is called a high standard of living consists, in considerable measure, in

arrangements for avoiding muscular energy, increasing sensual pleasure and for enhancing caloric intake above any conceivable nutritional requirement.[14]

Second, the nature of the system of want-creation effected by the planning system dictates that the outputs of the giant corporations will be produced in abundance while the outputs of what might be considered "competitive" industries (home building, for example) will remain puny:

That the present system should lead to an excessive output of automobiles, an improbable effort to cover the economically developed sections of the planet with asphalt, a lunar preoccupation with moon exploration, a fantastically expensive and potentially suicidal investment in missiles, submarines, bombers, and aircraft carriers, is as one would expect. These are the industries with power.[15]

Third, there is a shocking disparity between the abundant supplies of private consumption goods and the pitiful supplies of public consumption goods. The reason? Madison Avenue does not whet consumers' appetites for public goods. "The engines of mass communication, in their highest state of development, assail the eyes and ears of the community on behalf of more beer but not of more schools.[16]

Fourth, and finally, the system shows a shocking disregard for the environment, or what may be termed more generally "the quality of life":

The family which takes its mauve and cerise, air-conditioned, power-steered, and power-braked automobile out for a tour passes through cities that are badly

---

[12]Galbraith, *The New Industrial State*, page 24.
[13]Galbraith, "A Review of a Review," page 113.

[14]J. K. Galbraith, as quoted by R. M. Solow, "The New Industrial State or Son of Affluence," page 107.
[15]J. K. Galbraith, "Power and the Useful Economist," page 7.
[16]Galbraith, *The Affluent Society* (Boston: Houghton Mifflin Company, 1958, and London: André Deutsch, Ltd., 1958), page 205.

paved, made hideous by litter, blighted buildings, billboards, and posts for wires that should long since have been put underground. They pass on to a countryside that has been rendered largely invisible by commercial art. . . . They picnic on exquisitely packaged food from a portable icebox by a polluted stream and go on to spend the night at a park which is a menace to the public health and morals. Just before dozing off on an air mattress, beneath a nylon tent, amid the stench of decaying refuse, they may reflect vaguely on the curious unevenness of their blessings. Is this, indeed, the American genius?[17]

A CRITIQUE OF THE CRITIQUE

The typical mainstream economist's reaction to Galbraith is to ignore him. However, on occasion, the Galbraithean challenge has been met head-on.

Undoubtedly, the best of these occasions was when a prominent mainstream economist, Professor Robert Solow of M.I.T., published a scathing review of *The New Industrial State* in 1967. Solow's basic contentions were, first, that while the Galbraithean view of the economy no doubt contains some important insights (for example, modern economics pays too little attention to the giant corporation), the things that Galbraith appeals to as "facts" are really not facts at all; and second, that the Galbraithean model as a whole lacks structure and coherence. Our guess is that Solow's review of Galbraith represents the views of many economists. And since Solow is one of the few economists who can match Galbraith's wit and verbal dexterity, their debate is both lively and informative.

Has the modern corporation really

[17]Galbraith, *The Affluent Society*, pages 199–200.

preempted the market mechanism? Solow thinks not:

> It is unlikely that the economic system can usefully be described either as General Motors writ larger or as the family farm writ everywhere . . . it will behave like neither extreme. . . . Galbraith's story that the industrial firm has "planned" itself into complete insulation from the vagaries of the market is an exaggeration, so much an exaggeration that it smacks of the put-on.[18]

Has advertising really robbed the consumer of his sovereignty and made him a puppet of the corporation? Solow finds the claim vaguely implausible, and wants to see evidence:

> Professor Galbraith offers none; perhaps that is why he states his conclusion so confidently and so often. . . . I should think a case could be made that much advertising serves only to cancel other advertising.
> If Hertz and Avis were each to reduce their advertising expenditures by half . . . what would happen to the total car rental business? Galbraith presumably believes it would shrink. People would walk more, and spend their money instead on the still-advertised deodorants. But suppose . . . that all advertising were reduced . . . Galbraith believes that in the absence of persuasion . . . total consumer spending would fall. Pending some evidence, I am not inclined to take this popular doctrine very seriously.[19]

Is the model of profit maximization, so beloved by mainstream economists, really irrelevant to modern forms of business organization? While recognizing that profit maximization

[18]R. M. Solow, "The New Industrial State or Son of Affluence," pages 103–104.
[19]Solow, "The New Industrial State or Son of Affluence," page 105.

cannot be a *literal* description of corporate behavior ("Most large corporations are free enough from competitive pressure to afford a donation to the Community Chest"), Solow suggests that it is still a workable *approximation*. There is, for example, an *opportunity cost* of funds even when those funds are generated by internal financing. Furthermore, managements that stray too far from profit maximization in the pursuit of other goals, thereby depressing the value of their common stock, may find their jobs threatened by a takeover bid.

Are the outputs of the system really that bad? As Solow notes, it is hard to disagree with Galbraith's disparaging remarks about chrome-plated automobiles, pungent deodorants, and ostentatiously useless gadgets "without appearing boorish." Yet these are not the wasteful expenditures of the idle rich. It must be remembered that the median family income in the United States is not excessively high—it is currently about $17,500 per year. And by definition, fully *half* of American families earn less than this. Are they squandering their money on frivolities, or are these the things that the American people really want?

> His [Galbraith's] attitudes toward ordinary consumption remind one of the Duchess who, upon acquiring a full appreciation of sex, asked the Duke if it were perhaps too good for the common people.[20]

In sum, Solow views *The New Industrial State* as strong on style and wit, but weak on substance: "A book for the dinner table not for the desk."

Not surprisingly, Galbraith was unmoved by this and other attacks, viewing them as the predictable reactions of conventional economists who see their vested interests threatened:

[20]Solow, "The New Industrial State or Son of Affluence," page 108.

Neoclassical economics is not without its instinct for survival. It rightly sees the unmanaged consumer, the ultimate sovereignty of the citizen and the maximization of profits and resulting subordination of the firm to the market as the three legs of a tripod on which it stands. These are what exclude the role of power in the system. All three propositions tax the capacity for belief.[21]

THE RADICAL ECONOMICS OF THE NEW LEFT

The newest of the three major challenges to mainstream economics comes from the far left. Spawned by the radical student movement of the 1960s, the "New Left" is highly critical both of contemporary capitalism as practiced in America (and elsewhere) and of contemporary economic analysis as practiced by most economists. Radical economists' numbers have grown rapidly in the past decade, and their views have moved from leaflets handed out on street corners to the most prestigious scholarly journals and even into testimony before Congress. While the movement is still too young to have clearly defined itself, it behooves us to take a close look at what the New Left is saying.[22]

[21]J. K. Galbraith, "Power and the Useful Economist," page 5.

[22]There are now two introductory textbooks offering a radical alternative to the type of economics presented in this and most other texts. *Economics: An Introduction to Traditional and Radical Views*, Second Edition (New York: Harper & Row, 1975) by E. K. Hunt and Howard J. Sherman of the University of California at Riverside is the older of the two and offers both viewpoints side by side (with no question left as to where the authors stand). *Anti-Samuelson* (New York: Urizen Books, 1977) by Marc Linder is, as the title suggests, a pointed rebuttal to the best-selling economics text of all time, Paul A. Samuelson's *Economics* (New York: McGraw-Hill, 1976), now in its tenth edition.

New Left economists view themselves as the inheritors of Marxism, both of its intellectual traditions and its political activism.

Like Marx, they stress the pervasive importance of the *mode of production,* including not only its influence on economic activity, but also its effects on personal attitudes and social institutions. They write much about the *class struggle,* and leave no doubt about where they line up. Like Marx, they seek to uncover the inner *contradictions* in modern capitalism, contradictions that, they believe, will contribute to its ultimate demise. And, also like Marx, their writings are replete with stinging criticisms of both contemporary economic analysis and contemporary economic institutions, but they tell us very little about the type of system they would like to see take its place.

There is also much of Galbraith in the writings of the New Left: They share his emphasis on power rather than on markets, his critique of the giant corporation, his belief that consumers are manipulated by producers, and his dismay over the outputs of the industrial system. But Galbraith is surely no radical economist, and the radical economists are not Galbraithean. They find his propensity to turn to the government to solve problems hopelessly naïve. In their view, the government is part and parcel of the corporate state—a contributor to the problem, not an instrument toward a solution.

THE PROBLEM WITH MAINSTREAM ECONOMICS: POINT AND COUNTERPOINT

In brief, New Left economists hold that mainstream economists are asking all the wrong questions and using the wrong set of tools (economic models) to provide the answers:

It is our contention that [a neoclassical economist] . . . holds in his hand a flash-light . . . that is shining in the wrong direction. Hence, he must either change the questions or point his flashlight in another direction.[23]

Let us examine their complaints one by one.[24]

Narrowness of Focus

Radicals argue that economists typically narrow their field of inquiry so much that they are incapable of addressing the important questions.

For one thing, in contrast to Marx's teachings, modern economics is *ahistorical.* It is very much based on the here and now, with scant attention paid to the origins of the current system or the directions in which it may be headed. Perhaps as a consequence of this narrow scope, mainstream economics *accepts institutions as given and (tacitly) as immutable.* Little attention is paid to how institutions change.

Orthodox economics takes the existing social system for granted, much as though it were part of the natural order of things.[25]

Amplifying the attack, the New Left chides conventional economists for their preoccupation with analysis of *marginal* changes, using the celebrated tools of marginal analysis that we have described in earlier chapters. This, they argue, makes economics incapable of dealing with the really big issues: the institution of private property, poverty and discrimination,

[23]S. Hymer and F. Roosevelt, "Comment," *Quarterly Journal of Economics,* November 1972, page 645.

[24]Another attempt to draw up a list of key tenets of the New Left, similar in spirit to what we do here, appears in Assar Lindbeck's *The Political Economy of the New Left: An Outsider's View,* Second Edition (New York: Harper & Row, 1977).

[25]Paul Sweezy, "Toward a Critique of Economics," *Monthly Review,* vol. 21, no. 8 (January 1970), page 1. Copyright © 1970 by Monthly Review, Inc. Reprinted by permission of Monthly Review Press.

unemployment, and alienation. For example, Professor John Gurley of Stanford University, who converted from conventional to radical economics many years ago, scoffed at a prominent economist who expressed the belief that reducing unemployment would do more good things for the distribution of income than any measure he could imagine.

> Well, any radical economist can imagine a direct measure that would do even better things—expropriation of the capitalist class and turning over of ownership of capital goods and land to all the people. That, of course, sounds wild—unimaginable—to anyone who does not question the existing system.[26]

The consequence of this disciplinary narrowness, radicals contend, is that economists become, whether deliberately or unwittingly, apologists for the present system, supporters of the propertied class, and defenders of the status quo.

Most economists are prepared to plead guilty to the charge of disciplinary narrowness. As Yale's James Tobin put it:

> Most contemporary economists feel ill at ease with respect to big topics—national economic organization, interpretation of economic history, relations of economic and political power, origins and functions of economic institutions. The terrain is unsuitable for our tools. We find it hard even to frame meaningful questions, much less to answer them.[27]

But mainstream economists tend to view their inadequacy in this area as a misdemeanor, not a felony. They point out, in their defense, that a narrow focus is imperative if progress in analysis is to be made. And they are quite proud

[26]J. G. Gurley, "The State of Political Economics," *American Economic Review*, May 1971, page 59.

[27]J. Tobin, book review of Lindbeck's *The Political Economy of the New Left, Journal of Economic Literature*, December 1972, page 1216.

of the achievements of economic science compared with those of the more diffuse social sciences, such as sociology and political science. They counter that radicals try to paint with such broad strokes that everything becomes necessarily superficial and imprecise. And they argue that the radicals, with their very clear political biases, are hardly in a position to question the objectivity of other economists.

Acceptance of Tastes and Motivation as Given

Just as they do with institutions, conventional economists accept the tastes of consumers and the motivations of workers and managers as given and unchangeable: "just human nature."

Radicals, on the other hand, agree with Galbraith that the consumer is manipulated; and they go on to widen the charge. Not only is the consumer bombarded by Madison Avenue, he is brainwashed in the school system, influenced by politicians, and subtly molded by other social institutions.

These institutions, furthermore, are set up for the convenience of the ruling (capitalist) class.

> Economics . . . takes preferences as being exogenously determined and then shifts the burden of studying their formation and change onto "other disciplines." The New Left rejects this compartmentalization and takes the Marxian view . . . that new needs are created by the same process by which their means of satisfaction are produced.[28]

This argument is broadened further by the assertion that the need for material incentives to motivate both workers and managers is culturally acquired rather than innate, a product of capitalism rather than a cause of it. They admire the efforts in Cuba and China to create "the new man." In Che Guevara's words:

[28]Hymer and Roosevelt, "Comment," page 649.

825

We are doing everything possible to give work this new category of social duty and to join it to the development of technology, on the one hand, and to voluntary work on the other, based on the Marxian concept that man truly achieves his full human condition when he produces without being compelled by the physical necessity of selling himself as a commodity. . . . We will make the twenty-first-century man.[29]

Naturally, mainstream economists do not really believe that tastes are God-given. Everyone realizes that they are acquired, and influenced by many things. The question is: What are we to do about this? Lacking a theory of taste formation, basic economic analysis proceeds on the assumption that consumer tastes are to be respected *regardless* of how they got to be what they are. If we were to forsake this principle we would find ourselves on some dangerous ground: If consumers do not know what's good for them, who does? Still, most economists would willingly concede that more research into taste formation would be desirable; and some are working on this right now. The radicals have no doubt pushed the profession in a healthy direction.

Obsession with Efficiency Rather Than Equality

Earlier in this book we described in some detail the fundamental trade-off between efficiency and equality. All modern economists appreciate and understand this principle, and a great many—in their role as private citizens—advocate greater equality. However, the New Left is quite right to complain that:

The preponderant majority of economic analysis and research is concerned with efficiency, not with equality.

Many conventional economists agree with this criticism. Such "establishment" figures as Alice M. Rivlin, head of the Congressional Budget Office, and the late Robert Aaron Gordon, a past president of the American Economic Association, have echoed these sentiments.[30]

But New Left economists do not ask simply for a change in emphasis; they also want a change in the economist's tool kit. The marginal productivity theory of income distribution, they argue, is irrelevant. They maintain that to understand the distribution of income in contemporary America, we must first understand the distribution of *power*, which is largely determined by who controls the means of production.

According to marginal-productivity theory, workers receive the marginal product of labor and capitalists receive the marginal product of capital. This conservative theory tries to justify the present distribution of income. Critics . . . claim that it explains nothing, is unrealistic and refers to nothing measurable, and confuses the product of capital with the product of the capitalist.

According to radical theory, workers produce the whole product but capitalists expropriate part of it in profits (by means of their control of all the resources and productive facilities).[31]

As a radical economist sees it, the shares of national income going to workers and to property owners are largely determined by the relative power of the two groups.[32]

[29]John Gerassi, ed., *Venceremos: The Speeches and Writings of Che Guevara* (New York: Simon and Schuster, 1968), pages 394 and 400. (Copyright © 1968 by John Gerassi.)

[30]Alice M. Rivlin, "Income Distribution—Can Economists Help?" *American Economic Review*, May 1975, pages 1–15; R. A. Gordon, "Rigor and Relevance in a Changing Institutional Setting," *American Economic Review*, March 1976, pages 1–14.

[31]Hunt and Sherman, *Economics*, pages 249–50.

[32]Gurley, "The State of Political Economics," page 59.

Here the conventional and the radical economists part company. The conventional economist wants to know just how this "power" is measured. Are there statistical studies showing that "power" influences the distribution of income? In short, mainstream economics treats this approach to distribution theory as rhetoric, not as science.

Myopic Concentration on Quantity Rather Than Quality

Much like Galbraith, the New Left is critical of mainstream economists' preoccupation with policies designed to increase the gross national product. They argue that a great deal of this output is no more than junk, and using society's resources to produce such things is patently irrational. They also point to the spoliation of the environment caused by modern industrial production, though at least some radicals concede that conventional economics has some solutions to these problems (see Chapter 34). And they echo Galbraith's dismay that a system that is so good at producing private consumer goods should be so pathetically bad at feeding the hungry, housing and clothing the poor, and providing public services of all kinds.

The New Left adds one further element to Galbraith's indictment. In addition to ruining the quality of the environment, capitalist production ruins human beings.

It makes them aggressive, competitive, even dehumanized, by forcing them into a rat race for material gain. In Marxian terms, workers have little voice in determining the nature of their productive activities and so become *alienated* from their work rather than being proud of their accomplishments. (See Chapter 39, especially pages 779–780.)

The answers that conventional economists have to most of these charges have already been noted in connection with our discussion of Galbraith (see pages 822–823 above). The new charges are those of alienation and the dehumanizing effects of capitalism. We think it is safe to say that conventional economists have never known what to make of the notion of alienation. They scratch their heads about it, but that is about all. If this is an important way in which capitalism has damaged the quality of life, then conventional economics surely has been blind to it. Like "power," however, no one has yet figured out a way to measure alienation. As to the alleged dehumanization of the labor force, this seems to be a side effect of modern industrial activity—whether that activity is conducted under capitalism or under socialism.

Naïve Conception of the State

New Left economists maintain that both mainstream economists and Galbraith hold a naïve and sentimental view of the state. In this view, government is available to set things right when the market system fails (as in the case of externalities, for example), and in so doing, government decisions are dictated by the broad public interest. By contrast:

> The State, in the radical view, operates ultimately to serve the interest of the controlling class in a class society. Since the "capitalist" class fundamentally controls capitalist societies, the state functions in capitalist societies to serve that class. It does so either directly, by providing services only to members of that class, or indirectly, and probably more frequently, by helping preserve and support the system of basic institutions which support and maintain the power of that class.[33]

This *subservience of the state to the capitalists* manifests itself in several ways. First,

[33]D. M. Gordon, *Theories of Poverty and Underemployment* (Lexington, Mass.: D. C. Heath & Company, 1972), page 61.

Mainstream economists are willing to admit to a certain political naïvete. Yet most economists are unimpressed by the radicals' view of the state. Without denying that corporations often curry political favor, and often succeed, mainstream economists wonder how the radical model can explain progressive income taxation, inheritance taxes, antitrust legislation, equal opportunity laws, affirmative action regulations, and many, many more acts that the preponderance of the wealthy opposed bitterly at the time they were enacted. Furthermore, they point out, the policy prescriptions that conventional economists offer to improve the functioning of markets are intended as just that—as prescriptions for improvement, not as predictions about what government will actually do. Economists are not *that* naïve.

THE RADICAL CRITIQUE OF THE AMERICAN ECONOMY

The economics profession is by no means the only element in contemporary American society that the New Left finds objectionable. Much of its criticism of modern industrial capitalism has already been mentioned in connection with its criticism of modern economics. Radicals dislike the great disparities in income and wealth that the system produces; they despise the discrimination against blacks and women that, they argue, capitalism promotes; they blame the system for alienating its labor force and dehumanizing people in other ways (as in the schools); they cite the irrational use of resources to produce too much private junk and too few public services; they abhor what they see as its imperialist and militaristic tendencies; and they claim that the system is unable to cope with the problem of macroeconomic instability.

Taken as a whole, this is a powerful indictment. But almost all these problems have been raised many times before by nonradical economists.

since capitalists are driven by competition to accumulate capital continually and to expand production, more and bigger markets are necessary on which to sell this bountiful output. As a result, capitalist nations turn to *imperialist ventures* to secure new markets. Second, in order to maintain domestic demand at high levels, the military-industrial complex promotes a *war economy*, which, if not actually at war, is continually spending inordinate sums on armaments. Third, even reforms that appear to be pro-labor, such as social welfare programs, unemployment insurance, and the like, are really intended to *"buy off" the working class* so that they will not rise up in revolt, as they imply Marx had predicted. In this view, for example, Franklin Roosevelt's New Deal policies were not motivated by a desire to help the working class, but rather by a desire to forestall the coming revolution.

What distinguishes the radical attack from the attitudes of liberal reformers is that the radicals have a unified view of it all.

> Liberals see each of these . . . problems as separate and distinct. The problems, they believe, are the results of past mistakes, inabilities, and ineptitudes or the results of random cases of individual perversity . . . liberals generally favor government-sponsored reforms designed to mitigate the many evils of capitalism. These reforms never threaten the two most important features of capitalism: private ownership of the means of production, and the free market.
>
> Radicals, however, see each of the . . . problems . . . as the *direct consequence* of private ownership of capital and the process of social decision making within the impersonal cash nexus of the market. The problems cannot be solved until their underlying causes are eliminated, but this means a fundamental, radical economic reorganization.[34]

WHAT IS THE RADICAL ALTERNATIVE?

What would the radicals put in place of our system of market capitalism? There are many answers, but none commands anything like universal support among members of the New Left.

Some prefer a system of rigid state planning along Soviet lines, but they are a minority. For the most part, radicals see oppression by bureaucrats of the Soviet type as little better than (and little different from) oppression by capitalists. And radicals disdain the losses of human rights that accompany totalitarianism. Another group advocates a system of market socialism, along Yugoslav lines. But this runs counter to the argument that the institution of

markets is one of the root causes of America's difficulties.

Indeed, these hostile attitudes both toward markets *and* central planning put most radicals in an awkward position. As one thoughtful critic of the New Left put it:

> It may be possible to make a strong case against either markets or administrative systems, but if we are against *both* we are in trouble; there is hardly a third method for allocating resources and coordinating economic decisions, if we eliminate physical force.
>
> I think it is fair to say that most followers of the New Left have never faced up to the fact that we must have *some* mechanism for (1) obtaining *information* about preferences; (2) *allocating* resources . . . in accordance with these preferences; (3) deciding which *production* techniques to use; (4) creating *incentives* to economize on the use of resources, to invest, and to develop new technologies; and finally, (5) *coordinating* the decisions of millions of individual firms and households to make them consistent.[35]

If both the market and the plan are discarded, how are these problems to be solved? Even the "new man," though he may not need to be motivated, will not be able to accomplish the rest. Only two characteristics of the New Left's blueprint for the future seem clear: It wants a *decentralized* system, not one in which orders flow from the top down; and it wants a *participatory* system, in which workers have control over their own jobs and also, we might add, over their political leaders. Beyond this, the blueprint is vague, and many mainstream economists find it more romantic than practical. Consider this evaluation by Paul Samuelson, America's first Nobel laureate in economics:

---

[34]Hunt and Sherman, *Economics*, page 186.

[35]Assar Lindbeck, *The Political Economy of the New Left: An Outsider's View*, pages 32–33.

How can students be both against bureaucracy and against the market, the objective stranger asks. The only alternative is utopian self-sufficient kibbutzim. Yes, indeed it is. Students are not out to make the university like life; they wish to make life like the university, the nearest thing to the kibbutz one will ever know. Read *Walden* and you will realize that Thoreau was able to lead the good life there precisely because the rest of the world provided him with the library books and sustenance that could not be grown on the shores of Walden Pond. Read Fred Skinner's *Walden Two,* and try to draw up the balance sheet and income statement of his utopian colony. I defy you to show that it can continue to exist as a viable economic entity without monthly allowance checks from parents outside the community.[36]

[36]P. A. Samuelson, foreword to Lindbeck, *The Political Economy of the New Left,* page xxi.

SUMMARY

1. Mainstream economic analysis is not without its dissenters—conservative, moderate, and radical.
2. The libertarian philosophy translates, in economic matters, to a defense of laissez faire and to a devout belief in the workings of markets. This is because libertarians see free markets as the best guarantor of individual freedom.
3. Libertarian economists like Milton Friedman would limit government to three basic roles: enforcement of the law, regulation of natural monopolies, and control of externalities. Some libertarians would give government even less scope than this.
4. John Kenneth Galbraith has argued for years that conventional economic analysis has accorded insufficient attention to large and powerful organizations like the modern corporation. In his view, this omission has made modern economics largely irrelevant to modern society.
5. According to Galbraith, large corporations have the power to control, or even supplant, market forces by creating the demand for their products through advertising, and by manipulating their own costs. This "planning system" is run by technocrats, who are more interested in growth and expansion than in maximizing profits.
6. Because the modern corporation controls the market, rather than vice versa, the U.S. economy, according to Galbraith, turns out tons of consumer baubles of dubious merit but underproduces crucial goods like housing, keeps the public sector starved, and despoils the environment.
7. Mainstream economists feel that Galbraith overstates his case and substitutes assertion for fact. They doubt that the corporation can avoid the discipline of the market entirely, and are skeptical of the view that the consumer is a puppet of Madison Avenue.
8. Radical economists are the economic and political heirs of Marx, though their analysis of twentieth century capitalism bears the unmistakable stamp of Galbraith. However, they disdain Galbraith's "liberal" view of the state and view the government as an instrument of the capitalist class.

9. Radicals criticize mainstream economists for having an unduly narrow focus; for accepting consumer tastes and human nature as "givens" rather than treating them as the results of the economic system; for stressing efficiency rather than equality as an economic goal; and for concentrating on increasing the quantity of output rather than the quality of life.
10. While their critique of both economic theory and the modern economy is quite clear and forceful, radicals are much less clear about what type of system should be put in its place.

CONCEPTS FOR REVIEW

Libertarianism
Economic power
Planning system
Technostructure
New Left economics

Manipulation of the consumer
Alienation
Liberal versus radical views of the state

QUESTIONS FOR DISCUSSION

1. What might a libertarian think of:
   a. laws prohibiting smoking cigarettes in public places?
   b. laws prohibiting smoking marijuana in private?
   c. compulsory seat belts in cars?
   d. speed limits on highways?
   e. censorship?
2. Explain why a libertarian would support the all-volunteer army. Explain why many who are not libertarians also support it. How are the concepts of *supply and demand* and *opportunity cost* relevant?
3. Friedman believes that the medical profession has kept doctors' fees high by making it difficult to get into medical school (see pages 816–817). Explain his argument with a supply and demand diagram. What are the costs and benefits to society of licensing doctors? How would you go about deciding whether the benefits exceed the costs, or vice versa?
4. Galbraith says that about 50 percent of the American economy is in the "planning system" rather than in the competitive market. What are some industries that seem to fall under both headings?
5. Some years ago, sharp limitations were placed on cigarette advertising— including the banning of such ads from TV. Yet smoking has not fallen noticeably. How does this experience bear on Galbraith's claim that the modern corporation creates demand through advertising?
6. According to Galbraith, modern economic analysis rests on three assumptions: consumer sovereignty, profit maximization, and the subordination of the firm to the market. Explain what he means.
7. Discuss the divergent views of the role of the state in the economy held by (a) libertarians, (b) Galbraith, and (c) radical economists. Which do you find most appealing?

8. Discuss the radical critique of conventional economics, point by point. Where do you find room for improvement in mainstream economics?
9. Radicals blame the American economic system for inequality, alienation and dehumanization, irrational use of resources, militarism, and macroeconomic instability. In your view, which of these are valid criticisms? Do you think these criticisms are indictments of private ownership of capital, of a market system, or of industrial systems in general?

eleven

The Future

42

Economic Problems
of the Next Century

The future is like everything else,
it isn't what it used to be.

Crystal balls are notoriously cloudy. As events come to pass they all too often confirm the forecasters' fallibility.

Why, then, do we turn in this last chapter to suppositions about economic problems in the year 2000 and beyond? The answer is partly that long-run problems have a way of creeping up on us. If we deal with issues only on a day-by-day basis, we are likely to be lured, in imperceptible steps, into situations that we deplore but from which it is extremely difficult to extricate ourselves. For example, during the past half century, urban streets have become so clogged that traffic is often all but immobilized. Measures are occasionally taken to relieve the congestion—one-way traffic is decreed along major arteries, the timing of signal lights is coordinated, and, sometimes, the city obtains a new freeway. But these short-run measures do not address themselves to the underlying long-run problem; and so the process of strangulation of urban transportation continues.

Economists have always tended to preoccupy themselves with long-run problems, so much so that John Maynard Keynes once had to remind us that short-run problems can also be important. While his remark that "in the long run we are all dead" is both valid and important, it does not mean that long-run problems should be ignored. For if they are permitted to get out of hand, even if we manage to escape the consequences in our own lifetime, our children will surely bear the cost.

No one can claim to know all the long-term problems that will arise from seeds being planted today. Yet we can identify a few primary candidates, because their bitter fruits are already starting to emerge. Environmental deterioration is clearly not a short-term issue, nor is there any reason to consider the declining quality and higher costs of urban services only a temporary illness of the cities. Huge income differentials among people in the various countries of the world are also unlikely to vanish in the near future. And the trade-off between inflation and unemployment is likely to plague us for years to come. In this chapter we will deal only briefly with some of these matters because we have already discussed them earlier in the book. But there are a few other prospective problems of the next century's economy that we have not yet discussed. We begin the chapter with these.

THE FUTURE OF ENTREPRENEURSHIP

We know that much of the credit for the astonishing record of productivity in capitalist economies can be attributed to entrepreneurship. It has been this willingness to take risks, combined with a degree of ruthlessness, that has made possible the building of mighty empires. And this same adventurous spirit, which sought out and exploited every opportunity for self-enrichment, has also been intolerant of waste and inefficiency in the means of production. It has sought constantly after larger

factories, more efficient equipment, and more powerful processes, and while doing so it has contributed to the growth of the economy and the material well-being of the population.

As we mentioned in Chapter 38, the eclipse of the British economy has often been ascribed in large part to the disappearance of entrepreneurship in that country. There are those who warn that entrepreneurial drive is also weakening in the United States, and that our preeminence is consequently threatened by the Japanese, the Germans, and other societies in which this attribute is still in ample supply.

Since we do not know precisely how to define entrepreneurship, no one has in fact been able to measure the trends in its supply or to verify any of the conjectures about its role in the economic history of the different countries. Nor do we know what accounts for changes in these trends. Some writers hold that the major determinant lies in cultural and social development. Max Weber's classic work *The Protestant Ethic and the Spirit of Capitalism* (1930) attributes the emergence of modern capitalism to the triumph of "the Protestant ethic"—the principles of the Lutheran and Calvinist churches that encourage hard work, saving, and economic accomplishment. These attributes clearly help produce successful business people. In this view, social changes that include the weakening of the sway of religion may help explain the (alleged) decline in business initiative.

Others have maintained that sharply progressive taxation is a more tangible and serious threat to entrepreneurship. Why should people struggle to increase their incomes if the main result is an increased tax bill? It is hardly surprising that this view has been espoused by those who stand to gain from a reduction in tax progressivity—the earners of the highest incomes. But there are also neutral observers who believe there is something in this view, and who argue that the West is already beginning to pay a heavy price for its attempts to increase the equality of incomes. It is suggested that equal slices of a very much smaller pie will only prove equally disappointing to everyone.

Still others argue that entrepreneurship is discouraged by changes in philosophical outlook that pervade our society and are drilled into us by the schools. The self-made person who battles for financial success is no longer the hero of popular fiction as he was in the nineteenth century. Rather, it is widely felt today that such an individual's obsession with success needs looking into by competent psychiatric personnel. Vigorous competition, once extolled as a primary virtue, is now often looked upon as antisocial behavior.

Whether any or all of these conjectures about entrepreneurship have any basis in fact, there is good reason to be concerned about the future of vigorous competition in our economy and its implications for the workings of the market economy. This is a crucial issue, which we turn to next.

PROTECTION OF THE FIRM AND EMASCULATION OF THE MARKET

As was indicated in Chapter 25, there certainly has been no spectacular growth in the concentration of industry in the United States. Since the share of output in the hands of the biggest firms is not substantially larger today than it was at the beginning of our century, there seems to be no serious threat to competition from this quarter.

Yet there is very real cause for concern— not over the number of firms, but rather over the vigor with which they compete with one another.

As concern with human welfare has grown in importance, modern societies have founded a series of institutions designed to protect individuals from a variety of misfortunes. For example, social security has been adopted to protect us from inadequate savings in our old age, and unemployment insurance has been provided to

protect us when we cannot find jobs. These measures are easy to defend. But it is not easy to explain systematic attempts to offer analogous protective measures to business firms— measures like protective tariffs and financial aid to companies whose managements have led them to the brink of bankruptcy.

The public may question the value judgments that treat a business firm as a deserving recipient of public charity. But, to an economist, the likely consequences of such aid for the functioning of the market mechanism are far more disturbing.

To see the nature of the threat, we must understand the role of competition in the workings of the invisible hand. Our economy is propelled to efficiency by its intolerance of incompetent business firms. The company whose performance is second best will lose its markets to its competitors. The firm whose operations do not change with the times, and that does not keep up with the front ranks in the race for innovation, will fall by the wayside; its place will be taken by those who can run more rapidly. Managers who cannot bring a company to its full potential will find their firm taken from them by bankruptcy, by a stockholder revolt, or by a successful takeover bid by a rival group.

The process depends for its success on its mercilessness. While capitalism may continue to function effectively as we take humane measures to protect the welfare of individual *human beings,* it is difficult to see how it can survive measures to protect *business firms* from their own inefficiency. The law of the jungle must govern the market economy's treatment of business firms. It cannot tolerate failure and inefficiency, for in doing so it undermines its prime virtue: its unparalleled productivity and the efficiency with which it serves the wishes of consumers.

Naturally, business people cannot be relied upon to encourage this principle. Instead, they often will seek measures that protect them from the dangers of the competitive jungle; under the banner of "fair competition" they seek to stifle *effective* competition. Examples abound in contemporary America.

- Tariffs are sought to protect firms from the "ungentlemanly conduct" of foreigners who are willing to offer goods to consumers at lower prices, or to provide better goods at the same prices.
- Firms in danger of bankruptcy turn to the government for help to save them from the consequences of their own mismanagement.
- Regulatory agencies are petitioned to adopt more restrictive rules prohibiting "predatory pricing." Often this means that more efficient firms are prevented from offering prices as low as their costs permit, for by doing so they threaten the welfare of the less efficient enterprises. That regulatory agencies often protect the industry rather than the consumer is revealed all too clearly by the reaction of many regulated firms to proposals for deregulation. Instead of celebrating the opportunity for an increase in their freedom of action, the managements of, say, bus transportation and trucking firms bemoan the "chaos" that is likely to result; meaning, of course, that they are unhappy about the prospect of being thrown upon their own resources in a world of unrestricted competition.

SUMMARY

The market mechanism relies for its efficiency on the ruthlessness with which it treats firms that have not measured up to standards. By weeding out the inefficient and forcing the efficient to strive to their utmost capabilities, it exacts from the economy a degree of productivity unparalleled in previous history. But business people are naturally inclined to seek protection from the severities of the market mechanism through legal mechanisms. If they succeed, the vitality of the capitalist economy is endangered. Such protective measures as tariffs, regulations that force prices upward, or aid to firms threatened with bankruptcy, can emasculate the market mechanism.

Thus, one of the long-run problems that threatens our economy is a tendency toward an increase in protection for business, which by impeding the process of survival of the fittest, can undermine our prosperity. A joke that made the rounds when automotive emissions standards were first enacted claimed that when the news reached the Japanese auto manufacturers they immediately called an emergency conference of their engineers. But when the news reached Detroit, the U.S. auto manufacturers immediately called an emergency conference of their lawyers. If the story is not far from the mark, it does not bode well for the state of our economy in the next century.

PATTERNS OF LAND USE

In recent years, the public increasingly has come to recognize that there is more to good living than material possessions alone. Two cars and a ranch house on a quarter-acre lot may not be very satisfying if the family members must simultaneously breathe air that is malodorous and unhealthy; if the roar of overhead aircraft leaves them no peace; and if the formerly charming countryside where they vacation is "developed" into unattractive shopping centers. In measuring the quality of life, we must at least take into account the state of the natural environment—the purity of the community's air and waters and the beauty of its natural resources.

As we saw in Chapter 34, the 1960s and 1970s ushered in a new degree of concern with environmental issues, not only among the general public but also among politicians. Stronger legislation was enacted, particularly at the federal level, and it seems to have proved effective in many cases. The quality of the air and of our waterways has improved dramatically. Fish have returned to rivers from which they had long been absent, dirty fogs have become less frequent, and other such improvements are reported from many quarters.

While there is reason to hope that pollution problems will be much improved by the end of the century, there remains another long-term issue affecting the quality of life arising from land-use patterns. By and large, land usage is regulated by state and local agencies rather than by the federal government. For a variety of reasons, local governments that have concerned themselves with the issue have tended to emphasize the uses made of *individual* pieces of property—the construction specifications of the individual home and the amount of land it must occupy—rather than with the condition of the *region as a whole*. For example, one frequently encounters regulations specifying some minimum quantity of land that an individual dwelling must occupy so that one may not be permitted to build a home on any lot smaller than, say, a quarter acre.

The objective of such a rule, of course, is to prevent the construction of shabby, crowded dwellings. The cost of the required piece of land means that it will not pay the homeowner to build an inexpensive house in an area where such a regulation holds. The land requirement also means that there will be room for trees and shrubs. But the end result may be a form of homogenized suburban sprawl in which no empty land and unspoiled nature is left to be enjoyed, in which the individual can expect mile after mile of sameness with neither impressive buildings nor magnificent bits of nature to relieve the monotony.

Of course, some people may disagree with this evaluation and equate suburbanization of the country with the ideal way of life. If most people feel this way, it will be both difficult and inadvisable to prevent these developments. The danger is that even if most people do *not* want suburban sprawl everywhere, we may end up with it anyway as rising wealth and rising population increase the demand for individual homes. So there is reason to be concerned with the prospect that great regions will be

"Take it from me and come back. The future is definitely on land."

transformed into vast suburbias through the attempts by individual localities to protect the quality of their neighborhoods.

This is an example of what has been referred to as "the tyranny of the small decision," in which a series of minor actions, each intended to produce limited consequences, in fact, when taken together produce a significant, unanticipated, and, perhaps, unwanted result.

QUALITY OF LIFE AND THE PERSONAL SERVICES

The quality of life has also been threatened by another set of significant developments. While private standards of living have increased, and material possessions have grown, the community has simultaneously been forced to cope with deterioration in a variety of services, both public and private. Throughout the world, streets and subways have grown increasingly dirty. Public safety has declined as crimes of violence have become more commonplace in almost every major city. Bus and train schedules have been cut so that service has grown ever less frequent. In the middle of the nineteenth century in suburban London, there were 12 mail deliveries per day on weekdays, and one on Sundays. We all know what has happened to postal services since then.

In the private sector, there have been parallel cutbacks in the quality of service. Doctors have become increasingly reluctant to visit patients at home; in many areas the house call, which fifty years ago had been a commonplace event, has now become something that occurs only in a life and death emergency, if even then. Another example, though undoubtedly a matter for less general concern, is what has happened to restaurants. Although they are reluctant to publicize the fact, a great number of restaurants, including some of the most elegant and expensive, serve preprepared, frozen, and reheated meals. They charge high prices for what amounts to little more than TV dinners.

There is no single explanation for all these matters. It would be naïve to offer any cut-and-dried hypothesis purporting to account for the rise in crimes and violence throughout Western society in recent decades. Undoubtedly, the Vietnam War, racial tensions, political frustrations, and a variety of other influences all played their role. Moreover, it is possible that many of these influences will prove transitory—a peculiar feature of the decades of the 1960s and 1970s—so that there is no special reason to expect *those* particular influences to grow more significant in the twenty-first century.

However, there is one common influence that, at least in part, underlies all these problems of deterioration in service quality—an influence that is economic in character and that may be expected to grow more serious with the passage of time. This influence has already been discussed in some detail in Chapter 35, so it is appropriate to sum it up briefly here, with emphasis on its profound implications for the future. The issue is what we have called the cost disease of the personal services.

The quality of personal services, such as police and fire protection, medical care, and teaching, depends much more on the amount of attention the tasks receive from the individuals performing them than does assembly-line manufacturing. So shortcuts in performance usually mean that the consumer is shortchanged in quality. You know and care how much time your doctor spends with you when you are ill but probably have no idea how much time went into producing your car. Consequently, it is difficult to increase productivity of labor in service industries at anything near the rate that innovation has permitted productivity to grow in manufacturing industries.

The result is that the relative cost of services must grow disproportionately to the cost of manufactured goods. If labor productivity in manufacturing grows 2 percent a year faster than it does in the services (and the difference is probably greater than this), then the rules of compounding tell us that the relative cost of services will double every 35 years, quadruple every 70 years, and rise eightfold in little more than a century (see Chapter 33, pages 652–653). It is no wonder that, with the passage of time, the services grow ever more expensive and more difficult to obtain.

The implications for life in the future are profound indeed. This analysis portends a world in which the typical home contains luxuries and furnishings that we can hardly imagine; but it is a home surrounded by garbage and perhaps by violence. It portends a future in which the services of doctors, teachers, and police officers are increasingly mass-produced and impersonal, and in which the arts and crafts are increasingly supplied only by amateurs because the relative cost of professional work in these fields will be far greater than anyone can afford.

If this is the shape of the economy a hundred years from now, it will be significantly different from our own, and some persons will undoubtedly question whether the quality of life will have increased commensurately with the increased material prosperity. Some may even ask whether it has increased at all.

Is this future inevitable? If we wish to escape it, is there anything that can be done? The answer is that it is by no means inevitable. To see why, we must first recognize that the source of the problem, paradoxically, is the growth in productivity of our economy—or rather, the *unevenness* of that growth. Trash removal costs go up not because garbage collectors become less efficient but because labor in car manufacturing becomes *more* efficient, thus enhancing the sanitation worker's value as a potential employee on the automotive assembly line. His wages must go up to keep him at his job of garbage removal.

But increasing productivity, by definition, can never make a nation poorer. It can never make it unable to afford things it was able to afford in the past. Increasing productivity means that we can afford more of *all* things—medical care and education as well as TV sets and electric toothbrushes. The role of services in our future depends on how we order our priorities.

If we value services sufficiently, we can have more and better services—at *some* sacrifice in the rate of growth of manufactured goods. Whether that is a good choice for the community is not for the authors of this book to say. But it is important for the community to recognize that it *does* have a choice, and that if it fails to exercise it, matters are very likely to proceed relentlessly in the direction they are now headed—toward a society in which there is an enormous abundance of material goods and a great scarcity of many of the things that most people now consider primary requisites for a high quality of life.

ARE WE RUNNING OUT OF EVERYTHING?

Thus far we have concerned ourselves with issues that are likely to increase in importance

and that are not generally recognized by the public. In this section, we consider a problem that is likely to prove *less* serious in the long run than is widely supposed.

Just as the natural workings of the market economy lead to rising costs of services, so do they also lead to ever increasing prices of natural resources, such as oil and coal. And these price adjustments will have similarly profound effects on our lives. We have already seen some of these effects in the area of energy. Higher gasoline prices have led to smaller and more efficient cars (and to a larger share of imports in our car market); builders are spending more money on insulation; and homes are a bit chillier in the winter and a bit warmer in the summer than they used to be.

While economists tend to view "the energy crisis" and related issues as problems of adjustment to higher relative prices for some goods, the public, helped along by politicians, see these things quite differently. The media bombard us with frightening projections that suggest we will soon "run out" of oil, or natural gas, or potassium, or titanium—almost everything, it seems. It does not take much imagination to foresee the dire consequences of actually running out of, say, energy resources; and projections of impending disaster make for exciting headlines and stirring speeches.

Yet economists are not impressed by predictions that doomsday is near. For such projections (which have been heard many times before) are generally based on the most naïve sort of extrapolation of current trends. We may be told, for example, that *at current rates of usage* the *existing* oil supply will be exhausted by the year 2000. What these projections ignore is the role of prices in a market economy. As explained in Chapter 33:

As a natural resource becomes more and more scarce, the operation of markets will give it a higher and higher price unless governments intervene to keep this from happening. And it is precisely this higher price that will keep us from suddenly running out of the scarce resource.

Let us consider the case of fossil fuels (oil, natural gas, and coal), for these have grabbed most of the headlines in recent years, and President Carter has branded the battle to cope with the impending shortage of energy resources "the moral equivalent of war." How will rising prices help us avert an energy crisis?

First, there is the usual effect of higher prices on the quantity demanded: Consumers normally buy less of things that carry high price tags. There is evidence that higher energy prices have led to reduced gasoline consumption, reduced use of fuel for home heating, and reduced energy inputs by industry. We may thus anticipate that extrapolations of energy usage based on historical patterns will exaggerate future demands. Indeed, there are striking examples of this in the context of other resources. In 1951, President Harry Truman established a Materials Policy Commission to study the long-range prospects for supply and demand for basic minerals. Then, as now, there was widespread concern about impending shortages. The Commission first projected the growth of the economy to 1975, and used this as the basis for projecting the consumption of 24 basic minerals. But the projections were not very accurate; despite a drastic *underestimate* of gross national product, the Commission *overestimated* the demand for 17 of the 24 minerals. While many factors led the predictions astray, most economists feel that rising prices for relatively scarce materials played a major role.[1]

Effects on the supply side may be even more dramatic. For one thing, when oil, gas, and coal fetch higher prices on the market, we may be sure that there will be more exploration, and more effective utilization of the resources that have already been discovered (using more expensive methods of resource recovery).

For another thing, new and expensive tech-

nologies may become economically viable as the cost of oil rises. For example, the western United States has enormous supplies of shale from which oil can be extracted, although only at high cost. To date, it has not paid to use this resource very much. But, as the price of energy continues to rise, its day will come. In addition, the eastern United States has huge stores of coal, which are expensive to mine (except by unsightly strip mining) and expensive to burn cleanly. However, when oil and natural gas get costly enough, these alternative sources will be tapped.

It should also be remembered that the impending shortage involves primarily the *fossil fuels*, not energy sources in general. In recent years, the burning of fossil fuels has been the most economical way of producing usable energy. But a little historical perspective shows that this was not always so. A hundred years ago, oil and natural gas were almost untapped energy resources; coal was in use, but so were wind and water power; burning wood provided much of our energy. At higher oil prices, it is conceivable that we could go back to some of these older techniques.

Even more important are potential new techniques for the production of energy without reliance on fossil fuels. Already solar heating has become economically viable in certain cases (especially for private homes in the Sun Belt states) and can be expected to spread. Scientists are studying the use of geothermal energy, and, probably most important, nuclear fusion promises a virtually unlimited supply of energy if we can learn to harness it.

In all these ways, then, higher prices will lead to lower demand for and greater supply of energy, thus helping to avert an "energy crisis." Calculations that show when *current* demand will exhaust the *current* supply are simply beside the point.

Yet we do not want to paint too rosy a picture. Adjustment to higher relative prices can be painful, as owners of gas-guzzling cars and fuel-inefficient homes have already found out. In

---

[1] See Richard N. Cooper, "Resource Needs Revisited," *Brookings Papers on Economic Activity* (1975:1), pages 238–45. Professor Cooper, a Yale economist, is now Undersecretary of State.

peering into the crystal ball, we can only see more of this in store. Goods and services that rely either directly or indirectly on fossil fuels are destined to become ever more expensive, leaving less money for other things. This can hardly be considered good news.

But the point to emphasize is that we can see an end to this process, albeit perhaps far in the future. And this end is not a cataclysmic one where we run out of energy, industrial activity ceases, and we all freeze. Instead, it is one where new technologies based on *nondepletable* energy resources like the sun and the atom take over the business of powering vehicles, heating homes, and turning the wheels of industry. Energy then will probably be more expensive than it is today, but it will be available.

THE STUBBORN TRADE-OFF BETWEEN INFLATION AND UNEMPLOYMENT

We have devoted many pages in this book to exploration of the trade-off between inflation and unemployment. We return to it briefly here because it seems unlikely that the trade-off will be repealed any time soon. Given our inheritance of a relatively high rate of inflation (by U.S. standards), the devising of ways to cope with the trade-off will remain one of the major challenges for economists during the balance of this century, and maybe during the next century as well.

What, precisely, are the choices for the future? There are two major approaches that economists can pursue. They can try to devise ways of robbing inflation and unemployment of some of their terrors, and they can try to devise ways of easing the trade-off itself; that is, of increasing the amount of employment the economy can produce without accelerating inflation.

In Chapter 6, we discussed the American

system of unemployment insurance, which surely takes much of the sting out of unemployment. We also noted the likelihood that the system itself contributes to the level of unemployment by reducing the incentive to take available jobs. This is an instance of a general problem: Measures that take some of the sting out of unemployment or inflation are likely to reduce the economy's resistance to them. As a result, future Americans may find it necessary to overhaul some of our basic economic institutions, adopting in the future ideas that no one has yet thought of, or that today have been dismissed as crackpot schemes. The Japanese tradition, for example, virtually eliminates unemployment by obligating firms to retain their workers even when they are not producing output. Recently, Sweden has experimented with a system under which production is maintained even when demand drops; the surplus inventories are simply stored away until demand recovers. We do not mean to suggest that either of these plans would work well in the United States. We mention them only to point out that there are many methods of "coping with unemployment" that we have not yet tried, and perhaps others that have not yet occurred to us.

Similarly, there may be new approaches for living with inflation. In Chapter 16, we discussed *indexing*, and observed that inflation would carry very little sting in an appropriately indexed economy, in which the purchasing power of savings, pensions, and wages was protected from inflation. However, we also observed that many people worry that an indexed economy would have less resistance to inflation than a conventional economy, in which contracts are not indexed. Whether the future economy will offer more indexing than our own is anyone's guess.

If we cannot successfully devise policies that eliminate the social costs of inflation and unemployment, we must try very hard to work out methods of improving the trade-off itself. *Incomes policies* were also discussed in Chapter 16, where we observed that their record is mostly one of dismal failure. Some economists interpret this as evidence that we should give up on incomes policy. Others, however, conclude that we should be more imaginative and try to think up new and more effective ways to hold down wages and prices without interfering unduly with the market mechanism. This has been the motive, for example, behind recent proposals for a "tax-based incomes policy" (TIP) that would give labor and management tax incentives to hold down wages and prices. Since no specific TIP plan has ever been tried in this country, no one really knows whether it would work. But such a plan may be in the offing in the not-too-distant future. The twenty-first century may see innovative versions of income policies that no one has dreamed of yet.

THE STRUGGLE FOR EQUALITY

Economists are no better at predicting the future than anyone else. It is with some trepidation, therefore, that we have tried in this closing chapter to anticipate some of the major economic problems of the next hundred years. However, since early warnings of all these maladies are visible already, the predictions may not be all that bold.

We have saved what may prove to be the most serious and stubborn problem for last. It is not a new problem; in fact it has been with us since time immemorial. Historian Arnold Toynbee put it this way:

> However high the minimum standard of his material living may be raised, that will not cure his soul of demanding social justice; and the unequal distribution of the world's goods between a privileged minority and an underprivileged majority has been transformed from an unavoidable evil into an intolerable injustice by the technological inventions of western man.[2]

[2]A. J. Toynbee, *Civilization on Trial* (Oxford: Oxford University Press, 1948), page 25.

Within the United States, we seem destined to see a muted version of the struggle for greater equality of incomes in the years to come, just as we have in the past. Examples abound in the arena of public policy. Welfare reform has now been high on the political agenda for more than a decade. The Congress rejected President Nixon's proposal for a version of the negative income tax in 1970; and President Carter's sweeping welfare-reform package is under consideration by Congress at the time of this writing. It is sure to arouse a vigorous, and partisan, debate. Tax reform is another area in which the struggle over income shares is simmering. Whenever the tax code is changed, the burden of taxation is shifted from some shoulders to others. Who shall pay more and who shall pay less? In January 1978, President Carter proposed that we take a few small steps toward closing tax loopholes and making the tax system more progressive. But his tax reform proposals were for the most part rejected by Congress. These issues are bound to crop up again and again in future years.

As these public-policy debates rage, nothing in this book will enable you to "prove" that one side or the other is "right." The unavoidable trade-off between equality and efficiency precludes that, and guarantees us that people with different value judgments will reach different opinions. Yet the tools provided in this book should help you see that there are many ways to achieve any desired redistribution of income, and that some may carry high price tags in terms of efficiency losses while others carry low ones. Obviously, the egalitarian policies that are least harmful to efficiency are to be preferred *regardless* of how much equality you think is morally correct.

In the international sphere, however, the struggle over income shares is likely to be pressed far harder. The large—and growing—disparities between the rich and poor nations of the world is a festering sore that may well threaten world peace during the next hundred years. It is really hard to emphasize sufficiently the importance of this problem. And it is also hard to see a way out.

One key is population growth. Many less developed countries are plagued by populations that stubbornly grow much faster than their economies' ability to feed, clothe, and shelter all the new citizens. The projections of what will happen if population growth is not curbed are almost too awful to contemplate: mass starvation, civil strife, wars among nations, and so on. Malthus warned us years ago that these are nature's ways of controlling the world's population if we do not design more humane methods for ourselves.

There is perhaps some reason for optimism on this score: Many poor nations are trying very hard to limit population growth, and technological advances in birth control techniques have been and probably will continue to make this task easier. But in some respects it is already too late. There are now so many young people in the less developed countries that, even if they married and had only the number of children that is consistent with "zero population growth," the combined population of these countries would increase by about two-thirds— *about 2 billion more people*—before population growth ceased!

Another problem that we have mentioned (see Chapter 38) is the huge international indebtedness that many less developed countries have incurred. Part of this debt was acquired to finance ambitious development plans; but where the plans have not been successful, the additional output needed to pay interest and principal on the loans simply is not forthcoming. Another part of the enormous debt was acquired because these countries could not pay their oil bills; and this debt continues to pile up. Already we are seeing signs of countries reaching the limits of their borrowing ability and suggestions that some of them will default on their loans. The implications of this are also rather frightening. Without credit from abroad— and who will lend to a country that has already

defaulted on past loans?—many less developed countries will find it impossible to acquire the capital needed for their development plans. And a failure of these development plans will mean that a rapidly growing population will be struggling over a slowly growing national income.

It may seem as if these problems, serious as they may be, are restricted to the poor nations. Indians and Pakistanis may starve, but not Americans and Canadians. This is a myopic view. The poor nations are resentful of the prosperity of the rich nations and believe that the rich nations have been niggardly with foreign aid. What has been called the "revolution of rising expectations" means that as people learn more and more about how much better life could be, their own miserable state seems less and less tolerable. As we gaze into that unreliable crystal ball, we can see a scenario in which the demands of the less developed countries for "social justice" escalate well beyond rhetoric to produce social upheavals, revolutions, and wars. There is, after all, only one planet Earth, and no nation can insulate itself fully from what is going on elsewhere on the globe.

IN CLOSING

As we look back over this list of potential problems for the future, we are struck by how much they have in common with the problems of the past: the creation and maintenance of incentives, the efficient use of markets, congestion and environmental decay caused by externalities, adjustments to the rising prices of services and exhaustible resources, and the troublesome trade-offs between inflation and unemployment and between efficiency and equality.

All of these will look different in the future than they do today; but there are unmistakable similarities. Fortunately, our knowledge and ability to cope with these problems are greater than they were 25 or 50 years ago. Furthermore, despite all these problems, the record of world history during the past two centuries is predominantly one of growth, progress, and increases in material well-being, not one of increasing misery. In this respect, we believe, the future will also be much like the past. So there is room for cautious optimism. We are a long way from paradise, but neither are we on the verge of the apocalypse.

SUMMARY

1. People are concerned that the supply of that elusive, but all-important, quality—entrepreneurship—will dwindle. Although entrepreneurial ability is impossible to measure and difficult even to define precisely, there can be no question that it is one of the mainsprings of the success of the capitalist system. Should it start to disappear in America, and many think it already is, the consequences could be grave indeed.

2. The threat to entrepreneurship is related to the attacks on the rigors of competitive capitalism that come from within the business establishment itself. The increasing tendency for businesses to turn to government for protection, either from other firms or from their own mistakes, threatens to undermine the ruthless process of survival of the fittest upon which the entire capitalist market system is based.

3. Regulations and ordinances governing the use of land are made in a piecemeal fashion, without regard for their possible effects on a region as a whole. As a result, zoning ordinances for specific parcels of land that look sensible when viewed one at a time may lead to a uniform suburban sprawl that pleases no one.

4. The wages paid to manufacturing and service workers must rise more or less in line with each other, but the productivity improvements in manufacturing industries cannot be matched by those in service industries. The result is that the costs of services can be expected to grow faster than the prices of goods. This phenomenon already has had profound effects on the budgets of state and local governments and, over the next hundred years, it may have even greater effects on the provision of private services. Unless steps are taken, U.S. citizens of the late twenty-first century may find themselves blessed with an abundance of luxury goods but unable to afford some of the most basic services.

5. The operations of markets are almost certain to lead to rapidly rising prices of natural resources. By definition, irreplaceable resources must become more scarce with the passage of time; and free markets will consequently assign them higher and higher prices. In one respect, this is all to the good, for it is precisely these gradually rising prices that will keep us from running out of, say, fossil fuels all of a sudden. But, on the other hand, no one can look with cheer at the prospect of heating and gasoline bills that may well grow faster than wages for many years to come.

6. The trade-off between inflation and unemployment will continue to make it difficult for government to attack both these macroeconomic problems at once. Future economists and public officials will continue to search either for ways to improve the trade-off or ways to lessen the severity of the two problems.

7. The struggle for greater income equality—both within and among nations—seems likely to assume more and more importance in future years. Given the rapid population growth that seems in store for the less developed countries in the next hundred years, there is a danger that the income gap between rich and poor nations will not be closed. And, if it is not, one can only speculate as to which of a number of rather horrible alternatives will result.

CONCEPTS FOR REVIEW

Entrepreneurship
Emasculation of the market economy
Cost disease of the personal services
Trade-off between inflation and unemployment
Trade-off between equality and efficiency

QUESTIONS FOR DISCUSSION

1. How do you look upon a career as a business manager or as a "capitalist?" Is your attitude different from those of your parents' generation? If so, what are the implications for the future of American capitalism?
2. Explain the important differences between providing social welfare measures to protect individuals and providing similar measures to protect firms. Can you cite a recent newspaper story about an actual or proposed measure to protect some firm or industry? What is your opinion on this matter?
3. What sort of zoning ordinances are there in the town or city where you live or where you go to college? Do they seem like good laws to you? To what extent, if any, do they contribute to the environment of the region as a whole?
4. What, in your opinion, should the president and Congress do about the "energy crisis?" Have the principles of economics that you have learned in this book changed your mind on this subject?
5. Discuss the future prospects for the citizens of the so-called Third World, that is, the poor nations in Asia, Africa, and South America. Of what relevance is this to you, as a citizen of a rich nation? What can the U.S. government do about this problem? What *should* it do?
6. Today an inexpensive 10-speed bicycle can be bought for about twice the price of the best seats at the opera, while a motorcycle costs, say, 16 times as much as an opera seat. At their present rates of growth, the cost of an opera seat will catch up with that of a bicycle in about 18 years. If motorcycle and bicycle prices increase at the same rate, how long will it take for opera tickets to catch up with the price of a motorcycle? What does this suggest about the long-term future of opera?
7. Costs of medical care have been rising at an alarming rate in recent decades. What, if anything, can be done about it? What does it suggest about the health of your future grandchildren?

CREDITS AND ACKNOWLEDGMENTS

p. 12, top: © Rand McNally & Company, R.L. 78-Y-98; bottom: © 1971, General Drafting Co., Inc.; p. 13: Gousha; p. 15: The London School of Economics and Political Science; p. 26: U.S. Geological Survey; p. 29: William J. Baumol and William G. Bowen, PERFORMING ARTS: THE ECONOMIC DILEMMA. Copyright © 1966 by the Twentieth Century Fund, Inc., New York, page 46, Figure III-1; p. 32 and 33, right: © by the New York Times Company. Reprinted by permission; p. 72: Brown Brothers; p. 103: Camera Press—PHOTO TRENDS; p. 152: Culver Pictures; p. 154: Brown Brothers; p. 200 and 201: B.C. by permission of Johnny Hart and Field Enterprises, Inc.; p. 307: Drawing by D. Reilly, © 1976 The New Yorker Magazine, Inc.; p. 462: UPI/Denver Post; p. 463: UPI/Chicago Tribune; p. 547: *Daily World,* successor to *The Daily Worker;* p. 573: © Taxation With Representation; p. 576: UPI; p. 587: Krokodil/Sovfoto; p. 592: Brown Brothers; p. 630: Marvin Lichtner/Lee Gross; p. 677: Drawing by Stevenson; © 1970 The New Yorker Magazine, Inc.; p. 687: © David Glaubinger/Jeroboam, Inc., 1977; p. 716: Culver Pictures; p. 743: Drawing by Lorenz; © 1973 The New Yorker Magazine, Inc.; p. 746: Drawing by Ed Fisher; © 1971 The New Yorker Magazine, Inc.; p. 770: The Bettmann Archive, Inc.; p. 788: UPI; p. 806: Sovfoto; p. 815: UPI; p. 819: UPI; p. 828: The Wizard of Id by permission of Johnny Hart and Field Enterprises, Inc.; p. 839: Sidney Harris.

Index

The **boldface** page numbers are a guide to where you will find definitions of key terms and concepts. Page numbers that appear in *italics* refer to figures and tables.

failures of, in United States, 1915–1975, 198, *199;* fractional reserve banking, 204; loans, investments, and caution, 205; management of, profits vs. safety, 205–206; profitability, 205; regulation of, 198, 206, 213–214; deposit insurance, 206, examinations and audits, 206, limits on investments, 206, minimum required reserves, 206; reserve levels, 205; runs on banks, 198

Barter, **198,** 198

Base-period weight index, **108**

Benefits principle of taxation, 633

Ben-Porath, Yoram, 306, *305*

Big business, oligopoly, 427–428

Big business and public policy, 447–470; bond prices and interest rates, 458; buying stocks and bonds, 461–463, *462;* corporate activities, sources of funds, 454–456, *455,* corporations, **453,** 453–454; financing corporate activities, stocks and bonds, 457–458; firms in United States, 450–451; options, 460–461; partnerships, **452,** 452–453; proprietorships, **451,** 451–452; speculation, **466,** 465–467; stock exchanges and corporate capital needs, 464–465; stock exchanges and their function, 463–464; stock prices as random walks, 467–469; types of stocks and bonds, 458–460

Bilateral monopoly, **525**

Blacks, discrimination, 563–564, *564;* discrimination, affirmative action, and, 575–576; geographical disparity of welfare benefits and, 569; migration to cities, 689; unemployment, minimum wage, and, 510–522, *510*

Blough, Robert M., 296

Board of Governors, Federal Reserve System, 219

Bond(s) **457,** 457–458; convertible bond, **460'** excerpt from newspaper price table, 462; performance information, 463, *462;* prices of, and interest, 458; purchasing, 461; short- or long-term, 459; stocks and, 457–458; tax-exempt, *459;* stocks vs., 457

Bosworth, Barry, 296

Boulding, Kenneth, 661

Brain drain, **763**

Brazil, 711, 786

Brenner, Harvey, 88, *88*

Brezhnev, Leonid, Soviet hierarchy and, 801

Bretton Woods, New Hampshire, Conference, 155, 743

Bretton Woods System (gold-exchange system), **743,** 743–744, 747

Budget balancing, 191–192; monetarists and, 260

Budget cycle, lags in policymaking and, 257

Budget deficits, 9, 191–192

Budget, balancing, pro and con, 191–192; decisions, 178; for fiscal year 1979, 319–320, *319*

Budget line, **42–43, 361,** 360–361, *41,*

360; consumer choice and, 366–367, *366;* government and, 43–44, *43;* household and, 40–42; indifference curve and, slopes of, 364–366, *365;* point of tangency to indifference curve, 366–367, *366;* price changes, effect of, 362, *362;* production indifference curve and, 412, *412;* slope of, 364–366; shifts in and income, 361–362; *362*

Budget message, 178

Bundle of good, 363

Bundle of inputs, 412

Burden of a tax, **633,** 633–636; excess, **634**

Bureaucracy, as business impediment in less developed countries, 762; New Left and, 829–830

Bureau of Labor Statistics, 70, 108

Business cycle(s), 214; market system vs. planning, 791–792; Marxian analysis of, 781; politically induced, 302–306; typical, 258–259, *259*

Business decisions, input choices, 393–409; output choices, 371–391

Call option, **460,** 460–461

Cancell, Benton R., 678

Capital, advantage of partnerships and, 452; cost of, 423–424; international transfer of, impediments to, 712–713; labor as, 517–518; Marxian definition, 774–775; national debt, future generations, and, 310–311; needs of corporations and stock exchanges, 464–465; overinvestment by public utilities, 393–395; production indifference curves and, 411–412, *411;* proprietorships and, 451–452; public utilities, profit ceilings, and, 393–395; Ricardo's theory of income distribution and, 553–555; scarcity of, in less developed countries, 757; taxation of, 574

Capital account, 740–742, *741*

Capital gain(s), **456,** 456–457; tax exempt bonds and, 459

Capitalism, **787,** 790; competition with other systems, 786–787; individual freedom and, 793–794; Marx and, 772–773, 775

Capital–labor ratio, profit ceilings and, 393–394

Carter, Jimmy, 9, 58; budget balancing and, 191; deficiency of aggregate demand and, 189; energy shortages and, 842; Ford vs. 282–283; inflation and unemployment, policy toward, 274–275, 279; jawboning and, 296; negative income tax and, 571; proposed 1979 budget, 319, *319;* recessionary gap in 1977 and, 152; welfare-reform package, 844

Celler–Kefauver Antimerger Act of 1950, 475, *474*

Central banking, 217–234

Central planning, 586–590, 597, 658–659, 787, 790, see also: China; Soviet Union.

Chamberlain, Edward, 424

Checking deposits, **202;** money balances and, 227; reserve requirements for, *221;* velocity and, 240

Che Guevara, 825–826

China, cost of economic growth, 792; cultural revolution in, 809–810; income distribution in, 791–792; Marxian economics and, 769; population size and military power, 649; "Reds" and "experts," 808–810; revolutionary communism in, 808–810; socialism and planning, 794–795, *794;* workers' management and, 799–800

CIO (Congress of Industrial Organizations), 521

Circular flow diagram of expenditure and income, 114–116, *115, 140;* government spending and, 178–179, *178;* in relation to saving and investment, 154; simplified circular flow, 140–141, *140*

Cities, *see:* Urban problems; Urban services.

Civil Aeronautics Board (CAB), 384, 490, 494–495

Civil Rights Act of 1964, 575

Clayton Act, 474–475, *474*

Clemenceau, Georges, 155

Closed shop, **522**

Collective bargaining, **526;** history of, in United States, 521–522; in public sector, 527–528; strikes and, 525–527, *526, 527*

Command economy, 793; in China, 808; in Soviet Union, 801–802

Commodity money, 201–204

Commodity (commodities), budget line and trade-off between, 360–361, *360;* distribution of, 599–601; inferior goods, **355;** leisure time, 357; Marxian definition, **774;** price of, and effect on demand, 336

Common Market, 749

Common ratio, 167

Common stock(s), **457,** 457–458

Communism, 547, 672, 773–774, 801

Comparative advantage, 7–8; arithmetic of, 715–717, *725;* cheap foreign labor and, 719; gains from, 717–719, *718;* international trade and, **714,** 713–714; specialization in production and, 8

Comparative economic systems, 787, 790–795, *794*

Competition, concentration and, 481; deregulation and, 500; economies of scale and scope and, 491; efficiency in resource allocation and, 602; fairness in, 496; large vs. small firms, 478–479; monopolistic competition, **424,** 418; oligopoly, **427;** price regulation and, 494; pure competition, **418–419,** 417; self-destructive, and regulation, 491

Competitive firms, 419–422, *420*

Competitive industries, 419, 435–437, *436, 439*

Competitive market, for labor, wage determination in, 515–516, *515;* monopolistic competition, **424,** 424–426; oligopolistic competition,